HANDBOOK OF
Child and Adolescent Psychiatry

Volume Two

HANDBOOK OF
Child and
Adolescent
Psychiatry

Joseph D. Noshpitz / Editor-in-Chief

VOLUME TWO

The Grade-School Child:
Development and Syndromes

PAULINA F. KERNBERG

AND

JULES R. BEMPORAD

EDITORS

John Wiley & Sons, Inc.
New York • Chichester • Weinheim • Brisbane • Singapore • Toronto

This text is printed on acid-free paper.

This publication is designed to provide accurate and authoritative information in regard to the subject matter covered. It
is sold with the understanding that the publisher is not engaged in rendering professional services. If legal, accounting,
medical, psychological, or any other expert assistance is required, the services of a competent professional person
should be sought.

ISBN 0-471-55079-5 (vol. 1)
    0-471-55075-2 (vol. 2)
    0-471-55076-0 (vol. 3)
    0-471-55078-7 (vol. 4)
    0-471-17640-0 (set)

Printed in the United States of America

10 9 8 7 6 5 4 3 2 1

DEDICATION

This set of volumes grows out of an attitude that reflects the field itself. To put it succinctly, the basic theme of child and adolescent psychiatry is hope. Albeit formally a medical discipline, child and adolescent psychiatry is a field of growth, of unfolding, of progressive advance; like childhood itself, it is a realm of building toward a future and finding ways to better the outcome for the young. But within the field, an even greater theme inspires an even more dominant regard. For, beyond treating children, child and adolescent psychiatry is ultimately about rearing children. This is literally the first time in human history that we are on the verge of knowing *how* to rear a child. While people have reared children since we were arboreal, they did it by instinct, or by cultural practice, or in keeping with grandma's injunctions, or by reenacting the memories, conscious and unconscious, of their own childhood experiences. They did what they did for many reasons, but never because they really knew what their actions portended, what caused what, what was a precondition for what, or what meant what.

At this moment in history, however, things are different. The efforts of researchers, neuroscientists, child developmental specialists—in short, of the host of those who seek to understand, treat, and educate children and to work with parents—are beginning to converge and to produce a body of knowledge that tells us what children are, what they need, what hurts them, and what helps them. Hard science has begun to study the fetus, rating scales and in-depth therapeutic techniques have emerged for the mother with the infant in her arms, increasing precision is being achieved in assessing temperament, in measuring mother/infant

fit, and in detecting the forerunners of personality organization. Adolescence and the intricacies of pubertal transformation are being explored as never before. Indeed, a quiet revolution is coming into being: the gradual dissemination of knowledge about child rearing that, within a few generations, could well alter the quality of the human beings who fall under its aegis.

If children—all children—could be reared in a fashion that gave them a healthier organization of conscience, that preserved the buds of cognitive growth and helped these to flower (instead of pinching them off as so many current practices do), that could recognize from the outset any special needs a child might have in respect to impulse control or emotional stability—and could step in from the earliest moments in development with the appropriate tactics and strategies, anodynes and remedies, techniques of healing and practices of enabling to allow the youngster to better manage his or her inner life and interpersonal transactions—consider what fruit this would bear.

Today this is far more than a dream, far more than a wistful yearning for a better day to come. The beginnings are already accomplished, much of the initial work has been done, the directions of future research are becoming ever more evident. The heretofore cryptic equations of development are beginning to be found and some of their solutions to be discerned, the once-mystical runes are being read—and are here inscribed in page after page of research report and clinical observation.

Some of the initial changes are already well under way. As with all science first a process of demystification must occur. Bit by bit, we have had to unlearn a host of formulaic mythologies about children and about parenting that have been part of Western civilization for centuries.

We have indeed begun to do so. We have been able to admit to the realities of child abuse, first to the violence directed toward children and then to their sexual exploitation. And we have had to admit to children's sexuality. Simply to allow those things to appear in print, to become part of common parlance, has taken immense cultural energy, the overcoming of tremendous defensiveness; after all, such things had been known but not spoken of for generations. Right now the sanctity, the hallowed quality of family life, is the focus of enormous cultural upheaval. There is much to suggest that the nuclear family set in the bosom of a body of extended kin relationships that had for so long served as the basic site for human child rearing is no longer the most likely context within which future generations of our children will grow. The quest is on for new social arrangements, and it is within this milieu that the impact of scientific knowledge, the huge and ever-increasing array of insights into the nature of childhood, the chemistry of human relationships, the psychodynamics of parent-child interplay—in short, within the area of development that this work so carefully details—that we find the wellsprings of hope. As nursery schools, kindergartens, grade schools, and high schools become more sophisticated, as the psychiatric diagnostic manuals become more specific and more differentiated, as doctors become better trained and better prepared to address human issues with dynamic understanding, as what children need in order to grow well becomes ever more part of everyday cultural practice, the realization of this hope will slowly and quietly steal across the face of our civilization, and we will produce children who will be emotionally sounder, cognitively stronger, and mentally healthier than their parents. These volumes are dedicated to advancing this goal.

Joseph D. Noshpitz, M.D.
Editor-in-Chief

vi

PREFACE

Some 16 years ago the first two volumes of the *Basic Handbook of Child Psychiatry* were published, to be followed shortly by volumes III and IV, and then, in 1985, by the fifth volume. More than a decade has passed since that volume was released, during which time the field of child psychiatry has advanced at a remarkable pace. Indeed, it has even changed its name to be more inclusive of the teenage years. New advances in neuroscience, in genetics, in psychoanalytic theory, in psychopharmacology, in animal studies— new findings in a host of areas have poured out during these years. It is therefore necessary to revise the handbook, to reorganize it, to update many of the clinical accounts, and to bring it to the level where the active practitioner can use its encyclopedic format to explore the enormous variety of clinical possibilities he or she may encounter.

The focus of this work is on development. It is no exaggeration to look on child development as the basic science of child and adolescent psychiatry. Development is so vital a concern that in this revision, we have abandoned the classical way of presenting the material. Rather than following tradition, wherein development, diagnosis and assessment, syndromes, treatment, and so on are discussed for a variety of related topics, in these volumes the bulk of the material is presented developmentally. Thus, volumes I, II, and III focus on development and syndromes of infancy and preschool, of grade school, and of adolescence, respectively. Within each of these larger sections, the material on development comes first, followed by chapters on syndromes, conceptualized as disturbances of development. While syndromes are

described in depth, they are discussed only within the framework of the developmental level under study. Volume IV, entitled "Varieties of Development," explores a host of ecological niches within which children are reared.

Volumes V and VI will contain sections on consultation/liaison, emergencies in child and adolescent psychiatry, the prehistory of child and adolescent psychiatry, current cultural issues that impinge on young people, forensic issues involving children and youth, and professional challenges facing the child and adolescent psychiatrist. Volume VI will include a most unusually rich banquet of studies on the assessment and evaluation of children, adolescents, and their families, plus reports on the basic science issues of the field and the current status of the various treatment techniques.

The intention of the work is to be as comprehensive and as readable as possible. In an encyclopedic work of this sort, concerns always arise as to how much space to allot to each topic and to which topics should be covered. To deal with such questions, a number of readers reviewed each submission. One editor had primary responsibility for each section; a coeditor also reviewed submissions. Then the editor of another section reviewed the submissions, exchanging his or her chapters with the first colleague so that someone outside the section read each chapter. In addition, one editor reviewed all submissions with an eye to contradictions or excessive overlap. Finally, the editor-in-chief reviewed and commented on a large proportion of the materials submitted. In short, while the submission process was not juried, a number of readers reviewed each chapter. Each author was confronted with the in cumulative critiques and asked to make appropriate changes. Most did so cheerfully, although not always with alacrity.

The writing and review process lasted from about 1990 to 1996. For much of this time, a host of authors were busy writing, revising, and polishing their work. The editors worked unstintingly, suffering all the ups and downs that accompany large projects: many meetings, huge expenses, moments of despair, episodes of elation, professional growth on the part of practically all the participants (a couple of authors who never came through with their material may be presumed to have shrunk), profound disappointments and thrilling breakthroughs, lost causes that were snatched from the jaws of defeat and borne aloft to victory, and, ultimately, the final feeling that we did it!

I speak for all the editors when I say that it was our purpose and it is our earnest wish that these volumes make for better understanding of young people, greater access to knowledge about children and adolescents, a richer sense of what this field of human endeavor entails, and a better outcome for the growth, development, mental health, and happiness of all the young in our land and of those who would help them.

Joseph D. Noshpitz, M.D.
Editor-in-Chief

CONTENTS

Contents

CONTRIBUTORS

ALBERT JOHN ALLEN, M.D., PH.D.
Assistant Professor, Department of Psychiatry, Division of Child and Adolescent Psychiatry, University of Illinois, Chicago, Illinois.

MARK R. BANSCHICK, M.D.
Private Practice, Katonah, New York.

WILLIAM D. BECKER, M.D.
Clinical Instructor of Psychiatry, Cornell University Medical College, New York, New York.

JULES R. BEMPORAD, M.D.
Clinical Professor of Psychiatry, New York Medical College, Valhalla, New York.

EUGENE V. BERESIN, M.D.
Director of Child and Adolescent Psychiatry, Residency Training, Massachusetts General Hospital, Boston, Massachusetts and McLean Hospital, Belmont, Massachusetts; Assistant Professor of Psychiatry, Harvard Medical School, Boston, Massachusetts.

AUDREY J. CLARKIN, PH.D.
Clinical Assistant Professor of Psychiatry, Cornell Medical College, New York, New York; Director of Psychology, Scarsdale School System, Scarsdale, New York.

SUSAN COATES, PH.D.
Director, Childhood Gender Identity Center, St. Luke's-Roosevelt Hospital Center, New York, New York.

BARBARA J. COFFEY, M.D.
Director, Pediatric Psychopharmacology Clinic, McLean Hospital, Belmont, Massachusetts.

DAVID ELKIND, PH.D.
Professor of Child Study, Tufts University, Medford, Massachusetts.

CARL FEINSTEIN, M.D.
Associate Professor, Johns Hopkins University School of Medicine, Baltimore, Maryland; Director of

Psychiatry, Kennedy-Krieger Institute, Baltimore, Maryland.

GREGORY, K. FRITZ, M.D.
Professor of Psychiatry; Director, Division of Child and Adolescent Psychiatry, Department of Psychiatry and Human Behavior, Brown University School of Medicine, Providence, Rhode Island.

ERNA FURMAN, B.A. (HONORARY), LONDON
Faculty, Cleveland Center for Research in Child Development; Assistant Clinical Professor, Department of Psychiatry, Case Western Reserve School of Medicine, Cleveland, Ohio.

STEWART GABEL, M.D.
Chairman, Department of Psychiatry and Behavioral Science. The Children's Hospital; Associate Professor of Psychiatry, University of Colorado Health Sciences Center, Denver, Colorado.

ARTHUR H. GREEN, M.D.
Medical Director, Therapeutic Nursery, Columbia-Presbyterian Medical Center; Clinical Professor of Psychiatry, Columbia University College of Physicians and Surgeons, New York, New York.

EDWARD GREENBLATT, PH.D.
Assistant Professor of Psychiatry, The Mount Sinai School of Medicine, New York, New York.

RENA MATISON GREENBLATT, PH.D.
Adjunct Associate Professor, New York University School of Social Work, New York, New York.

ELISABETH GUTHRIE, M.D.
Chief, Department of Psychiatry-Psychology, Blythedale Children's Hospital, Valhalla, New York; Assistant Clinical Professor of Pediatrics and Psychiatry, Columbia Presbyterian Medical Center, New York, New York.

FADY HAJAL, M.D.
Medical Director, Stony Lodge Hospital, Ossining, New York; Clinical Associate Professor in Psychiatry,

Contributors

Cornell University Medical College, The New York Hospital-Cornell Medical Center, Westchester Division, White Plains, New York.

GRAEME HANSON, M.D.
Associate Clinical Professor in Psychiatry and Pediatrics, University of California at San Francisco; Director of Clinical Services in Child and Adolescent Program, Langley Porter Psychiatric Institute, San Francisco, California.

MARK H. HENIGAN, D.O.
Private Practice, Modesto, California; Medical Director, Child and Adolescent Inpatient Program, Stanislaus Behavioral Health Center, Modesto, California.

MARGARET E. HERTZIG, M.D.
Professor of Psychiatry, Cornell University Medical College; Director, Child and Adolescent Outpatient Department, The New York Hospital-Payne Whitney Clinic, New York, New York.

LAUREN HUMMEL, M.A., CCC-SLP
Clinical Department Supervisor, Communication Disorders Department, Emma Pendleton Bradley Hospital, East Providence, Rhode Island; Adjunct Faculty, Division of Communication Disorders, Emerson College, Boston, Massachusetts.

SANDRA KAPLAN, M.D.
Associate Professor of Clinical Psychiatry, Cornell University Medical College, New York, New York; Associate Chairman, Department of Psychiatry for Child and Adolescent Psychiatry, North Shore University Hospital, Manhasset, New York.

JAVAD H. KASHANI, M.D.
Professor of Psychiatry, Psychology and Pediatrics; Director, Children's Services, Mid-Missouri Mental Health Center, Columbia, Missouri.

PAULINA F. KERNBERG, M.D.
Professor of Psychiatry, Cornell University Medical College, New York, New York; Director, Child and Adolescent Psychiatry, Director, Child and Adolescent Psychiatry Training Program, The New York Hospital-Cornell Medical Center, Westchester Division, White Plains, New York.

MARY D. KLINNERT, PH.D.
Associate Professor of Psychiatry, University of Colorado Health Sciences Center; Chief, Pediatric Psychology, National Jewish Center for Immunology and Respiratory Medicine, Denver, Colorado.

ELEANOR B. KROLIAN, M.S.W.
Private Practice, White Plains, New York.

HENRIETTA L. LEONARD, M.D.
Professor of Psychiatry and Human Behavior, Brown University School of Medicine, Providence, Rhode Island.

DONNA LOFGREN, PH.D.
Assistant Professor, Department of Psychiatry, Harvard Medical School, Boston, Massachusetts; Associate Attending, McLean Hospital, Belmont, Massachusetts.

EDWIN J. MIKKELSEN, M.D.
Associate Professor of Psychiatry, Harvard Medical School; Medical Director, Mentor Clinical Care, Boston, Massachusetts; Consulting Child Psychiatrist, The Eunice Kennedy Shriver Center, Waltham, Massachusetts.

JOSEPH D. NOSHPITZ, M.D.
Clinical Professor of Psychiatry and Behavioral Science, George Washington University; Private Practice, Washington, D.C.

LAURETTE OLSON, M.A.
Coordinator, Child and Adolescent Curriculum in Occupational Therapy, Mercy College, Dobbs Ferry, New York; Occupational Therapy Consultant, Mamaroneck Union-Free School District, Mamaroneck, New York.

ANNA ORNSTEIN, M.D.
Professor, Child Psychiatry, University of Cincinnati College of Medicine, Cincinnati, Ohio.

DAVID PELCOVITZ, PH.D.
Chief Psychologist, Division of Child and Adolescent Psychiatry, North Shore University Hospital, Manhasset, New York.

CYNTHIA R. PFEFFER, M.D.
Professor of Psychiatry, Cornell University Medical College, New York, New York; Director, Children at Risk for Suicidal Behavior Research Program, The New York Hospital-Cornell Medical Center, Westchester Division, White Plains, New York.

CHARLES P. POLLAK, M.D.
Professor of Neurology, Division of Sleep Medicine, Department of Neurology, Ohio State University, Columbus, Ohio.

JUDITH L. RAPOPORT, M.D.
Chief, Child Psychiatry Branch, National Institute of Mental Health, Bethesda, Maryland.

PAULA K. RAUCH, M.D.
Associate Director, Child Psychiatry Consultation Service to Pediatrics, Massachusetts General Hospital; Clinical Instructor, Harvard Medical School, Boston, Massachusetts.

RANDY M. ROCKNEY, M.D.
Assistant Professor, Pediatrics and Family Medicine, Brown University School of Medicine, Hasbro Children's Hospital, Providence, Rhode Island.

Contributors

VIVIENNE ROSEBY, PH.D.
Teaching and Research Associate, Center for the Family in Transition, Corte Madera, California; Private Practice, Davis, California; Consulting Faculty, Child and Family Studies Program, University of California, Davis, California.

CLYDE L. ROUSEY, PH.D.
Private Practice, Topeka, Kansas.

CHARLES A. SARNOFF, M.D.
Lecturer, Child Development, The Psychoanalytic Center for Training and Research, The College of Physicians and Surgeons, Columbia University; Private Practice, New York, New York.

KLAUS SCHREIBER, M.D.
Assistant Professor of Psychiatry and Pediatrics, New York Medical College, Valhalla, New York.

THEODORE SHAPIRO, M.D.
Professor of Psychiatry, Professor of Psychiatry in Pediatrics, Cornell University Medical College; Director, Child and Adolescent Psychiatry, Payne Whitney Clinic, The New York Hospital-Cornell Medical Center, New York, New York.

JOYANNA L. SILBERG, PH.D.
Senior Psychologist, The Sheppard and Enoch Pratt Hospital, Baltimore, Maryland.

MARTIN A. SILVERMAN, M.D.
Clinical Professor of Psychiatry; Past Chairman, Child Analysis Section, New York University College of Medicine, New York, New York.

MAE S. SOKOL, M.D.
Staff Psychiatrist, Eating Disorders Program, C. F. Menninger Memorial Hospital, Topeka, Kansas.

GAIL E. SOLOMON, M.D.
Associate Professor of Clinical Neurology; Associate Professor of Clinical Neurology in Pediatrics and Psychiatry; Associate Attending in Neurology and Pediatrics; Director, EEG Laboratory, The New York Hospital-Cornell University Medical Center, New York, New York.

HANS STEINER, DR. MED. UNIV.
Professor of Psychiatry, Stanford University School of Medicine, Stanford, California.

JOHN J. STINE, M.D.
Clinical Associate Professor of Psychiatry, The New York Hospital-Cornell Medical Center, Westchester Division, White Plains, New York; Private Practice, Chappaqua, New York.

SUSAN E. SWEDO, M.D.
Acting Scientific Director, National Institute of Mental Health, Bethesda, Maryland.

PAUL V. TRAD, M.D.
Dr. Trad passed away in October of 1994. At that time he was an Associate Professor of Clinical Psychiatry, Cornell University Medical College, and Director of the Child Outpatient Services, The New York Hospital-Cornell Medical Center, Westchester Division. Dr. Trad was also Editor of the American Journal of Psychotherapy *and a recognized scholar in the areas of Infant Psychiatry and Parent-Infant Psychotherapy.*

JUDITH WALLERSTEIN, PH.D.
Senior Lecturer Emerita, School of Social Welfare, University of California, Berkeley, California; Founder, Center for the Family in Transition, Corte Madera, California.

ALAN S. WEINER, PH.D.
Clinical Assistant Attending Psychologist, The New York Hospital-Cornell Medical Center, Westchester Division, White Plains, New York; Clinical Assistant Professor of Psychology and Psychiatry, Cornell University Medical College, New York, New York.

DANIEL T. WILLIAMS, M.D.
Assistant Clinical Professor of Psychiatry, Columbia University College of Physicians and Surgeons, New York, New York.

SABRINA WOLFE, PH.D.
Part-time Instructor in Clinical Psychology, College of Physicians, Columbia University-St. Luke's-Roosevelt Hospital Center; Private practice, New York, New York.

SECTION I
Normal Development of the Grade-School Child

1 / The Early Grade-School Child: Introduction

Theodore Shapiro and William Becker

Our theoretical understanding of the behavior of the early grade-school child has been dominated by two 20th-century giants, Sigmund Freud and Jean Piaget. Freud called this period the latency stage. He believed that, with the resolution of the Oedipus complex, the surging phallic-stage instincts quieted, permitting learning and industry.

The child's behavior during latency may be described as one of "persistent denial of the struggle against the breakthrough of instinctual impulses" (Bornstein, 1951, p. 282). Behaviorally, the child turns from the family to peers, activities, and school when it is culturally prescribed. Other theorists have labeled this period in accord with their own theoretical perspectives. Erickson (1950) called this *the age of industry* to signify the persistence of these children at tasks. Sullivan (1940) referred to it as the *juvenile era,* and Piaget (1929) described in detail the concrete operations that bridge the earlier sensorimotor stage with the later stage of abstract operations. Thomas and Chess (1972) argued that we should simply call the period middle childhood because latency is too theory specific.

Even the span of the period is defined differently among researchers. It is generally viewed to begin in coordination with the entry to primary school, at 6 or 7 in most cultures, and to end with the onset of puberty. Perhaps the largest controversy about this period of life centers on whether it represents a maturational landmark that is beyond culture, and whether it has a uniform set of descriptors.

Gesell and Ilg (1946), working at the Yale Child Study Center and later the Gesell Institute, attempted to describe the behavioral characteristics of normal school-age children. Although their sample was drawn from middle-class America in the 1930s and 1940s, it is worthwhile to review their descriptions, as they are a cogent point of orientation and have relevance for American psychiatrists.

About 7-year-olds they write, "There is a kind of quieting down at seven. Six-year-olds tended to produce brash reactions and bursts of activities. The seven year old goes into lengthy periods of calmness and self absorption" (Gesell & Ilg, 1946, p. 131). Later they state:

At home as at school the child's personal-social behavior shows an increasing awareness of both self and of others. He's more companionable. . . . He is not a good loser. He tattletales. If a playground situation grows too complex and things go badly, the seven year old runs home with a more or less righteous declaration, "I'm quitting." Let us be duly grateful for his germinating righteousness. It is evident that the seven year old is developing an ethical sense. (pp. 134–135)

Gesell and Ilg continue about the 8-year-old: "Eight is more a person by adult standards and in terms of adult-child relationships. One converses with an eight year old with lessening condescension. . . . There are three traits which characterize the dynamics of his behavior: speediness, expansiveness, evaluativeness" (p. 160). And later they write, "The nine year old is no longer a mere child; nor is he yet a youth. Nine is an intermediate age in the middle zone which lies between the kindergarten and the junior high school teens" (p. 188).

Thus, even within a single time and culture, the early school years, are a period of rapid change and significant behavioral reorganizations. This leads toward a preoccupation not only with self but also an increased focus on peer relations, with the growing child showing a markedly expanded social orientation.

New Academic Demands/ Cognitive Advances

Shapiro and Perry (1976) have argued that part of the maturational design feature of the human

3

organism permits sequentially higher-level organizations and, therefore, latency. This occurs around the age of 7 and represents a stage of new capacities and new opportunities to be seized. They suggested that different societies and cultures seem to have empirically discovered that those aged 7 and older were significantly more capable than younger children and therefore open to new tasks and responsibilities.

In the past, children were first sent away from home to become pages at court at age 7. At the time of the guilds, children also were apprenticed at that age (Pitchbeck & Hewitt, 1969). In probably every postindustrial society, a child of 6 or 7 is considered ready to enter the equivalent of primary school. Preschools and kindergartens are designed essentially as early socialization and play experiences, with some preparation for the "real" schoolwork to come. Kohlberg and Gilligan (1971) note that almost all cultures recognize two great stages of transformations of development. The periods of 5 to 7 and of adolescence usher in and end periods of compulsory education. Moral conviction as reflected in church practices has led the Roman Catholic Church to consider 7 "the age of reason" and, therefore, the time when the first communion becomes possible because of new cognitive advances. English Common Law has directed our own legal practices to the idea that children under age 7 are incapable of criminal intent, and although the age of minority is variously construed, historically 7 has been a critical age. Thus past and current social **practice** provides ample evidence that this **period represents** a time of discontinuous change. **It is a time** of expansion and development when **the child** enters into and becomes an essential **participant in** many societal practices.

Jean Piaget, using a methodology based on sequential naturalistic observation, concluded that between the ages of 7 and 11 there emerges a distinct stage that he termed a period of concrete operations. Children below 7, in the "preoperational stage," are markedly less prepared for the vicissitudes of formal education. Younger children use egocentric speech—they do not show the ability to take the other person's point of view, a fundamental requisite for significant discussion. Young children often engage in simple repetitions or in monologues that do not permit true topic maintenance. When young children offer an explanation,

it often appears to be a juxtaposition of apparently unrelated items with little causal connection. These children use "because" idiosyncratically. Adult listeners must interpret the communication based on their knowledge of the child and of the situation. The concrete-operational child, on the other hand, can increasingly engage in logical dialogue, invoking some causal sequences. This ability is an essential prerequisite for formal education.

Prior to the age of about 7, children have a static, egocentric view of nonhuman objects. This view markedly inhibits their ability to manipulate and make predictions about relationships and sequences. On the other hand, concrete-operational children can envision and reproduce a chain of related circumstances. For example, they can bring the past into active memory and structure the future in a similar vein: "After we get to Grandma's we'll go to our room and unpack and then we will open presents and have dinner. It will be fun!" This represents the essence of reasoning. They also can understand that objects can be related and transformed in a number of different ways, even simultaneously, and that these transformations can be reproduced and reversed; for example, "When you put on the mask at Halloween I got scared. But I knew it was really you and that you only seemed scary and soon you'd be you again!" These children also now show the capacity to infer conservation—that the water in a shallow pitcher remains the same quantity when shifted to a tall one, for example. These fundamental shifts in ability enable children to assimilate the tasks of formal elementary education, for they have gained some capacity for true logical thought and communication.

The Piagetian growth from preoperational thought to concrete operational thought corresponds to a spurt in brain maturation, according to Rabinowicz (1986). This is a period of cortical "remodeling." Cortical thickness grows, and accelerated change occurs in pyramidal cell shape and size. Neurodevelopmental studies show that the brain attains about 90% of its total weight by age 7 (Shapiro & Perry, 1976). From the perspective of brain pathology, lesions to the left brain occurring after age 6 leave children with continuing dysphasic problems, whereas children who experience lesions prior to age 6 have a decreased percentage of dysphasic problems. The difference is due to brain plasticity in younger children. These changes represent some evidence that the discontinuities of latency (Lenneberg, 1975) are based on neural mechanisms and remain a built-in feature of human maturation that is independent of culture.

At a higher level of integration, there is ample evidence of significant perceptual and postural maturation at this age. A series of investigators (Bender, 1938; Belmont, 1965; Birch & Lefford, 1964; Koppitz, 1964, 1968; Goldfarb, 1957; Pollock & Gordon, 1960; Schilder, 1950); all record the increasing regularity with which children can perform on a variety of visual motor and neuroperceptual tests without error as they approach age 7. These include the informal and formal tests generally discussed under the heading of soft (or nonfocal) neurologic signs and of visual-motor integrations or intersensory integrations. The characteristic achievements of latency include right-left discrimination in self and others and the firm establishment of handedness, eyedness, and footedness. In addition, prior plasticity of function is superseded by newly established developmental structures. Children now can make new reliable intersensory integrations (e.g., auditory-visual), and they also can mediate motility more smoothly. Sequencing motor behaviors and time sense become better established. They master knowledge of the days of the week, monthly sequences, cardinality and ordinality of numbers. Early math relationships and reading with its associated comprehension of sequences are newly mastered as well.

Latency-age children may have undergone the neuronal and intellectual maturation necessary to begin formal education, but other fundamental shifts occur in the experience of children as they enter primary school. The children now attend school on a half- to full-time, daily basis. The experience is no longer focused on play, socialization, and readiness skills. This is the "real thing," replete with the need to learn and master basic skills in the 3Rs that can be applied later to larger and more complex tasks. To function in a classroom setting requires that children be able to modulate their behavior significantly. They must pay attention, not disrupt others, and wait to be called on. Egocentrism must give way in favor of group functioning and delayed reward. The specter of homework sorely tests children's organizational skills and perseverance. They must have the

wherewithal to leave home every day, resting relatively assured that their mother, father, and caregivers will be all right and waiting when they return. The pressures of keeping up with expectations and demands may lead children to manipulate situations to their presumed advantage by lying or cheating. If their competence and coping abilities are not up to the challenge, anxiety, anger, a lowering of self-esteem, and depression may result.

How children will respond to school depends on the integration of a number of inputs on many levels. How much emphasis does their culture and family place on education? How helpful and supportive is the family? How well does the structure of the particular school, classroom, and teacher meld with the needs of the particular child? Most important, how well are the children equipped emotionally and intellectually to manage without a parent and to attract and make peer friends? It is no surprise that the entry into primary school generates a plethora of referrals to child psychiatrists. Teachers are often the first to pick up learning disabilities, mental retardation, and even oppositional, anxious, depressive, and attentional disturbances. This is due to the new stresses and tasks placed on children at this time and to the expanding awareness of primary school educators of childhood psychopathology. School also represents a new stressor insofar as children cannot turn to the parent at will, have to accept another adult's authority, and also have to reorganize experience in terms of new constraints on motor and vocal expression.

Thomas and Chess (1972) admit to the changes of latency but counter Freud on the idea that anything, including sexual curiosity, quiets down. They prefer to look at middle childhood as a period of continued development and psychological change. They emphasize, as do Gesell and Ilg and even Freud, the industriousness, the increase in number and kinds of relationships, and the ability to appreciate belonging to a peer group. They recommend that the period be viewed as a time of gradual transition from action to ideation, which of course makes it ideally suited for school learning.

In their longitudinal study of middle-class children, they note that five types of course emerge. The first is characterized by steady developmental success. This group represents the majority of the children studied. The second, who had shown earlier behavioral difficulties, resolved their problems during this period. A third group with earlier behavior problems developed new problems in middle childhood in response to new stresses. A fourth group showed continuation of earlier behavioral problems well into middle childhood. The fifth group developed new problems in middle childhood that did not seem to reflect a repetition of problems from the earlier period.

Thomas and Chess then proffer the concept of the "difficult child" and provide a profile of behaviors to alert parents and clinicians. The temperamental constellation of such a child includes slow adaptability to new situations. Intense negative reaction to stimuli and irregularity of function round out the picture. This is the group from which a significantly higher percentage of problem children ($n = 47$) emerged in their small sample of 133 middle-class children. However, 34 of the group had the onset of their disorder before the age of 6. Only one new case developed and was referred between the ages of 9 and 12.

Thomas and Chess concur with data derived from earlier epidemiologic studies. LaPouse and Monk (1959) and McFarland, Allen, and Honzik (1954) showed that as age advances, there is a decreasing prevalence of behavior disorders in middle-class school-age children. These data are noted simply to suggest the discontinuities and ruptures with earlier behavior that may occur as new demands are placed on the latency-age child.

Latency-age children also show an increased capacity for small-group and club formation but are still full of ambition to be the boss, captain, or president. Thus cooperativeness is tentative and fragile. Yet they also can be hypermoral and self-righteous.

Freud's view of the period derives from his notion that these behaviors are the aftermath of the resolution of the Oedipus complex, to which we now turn.

The Closing Out of the Oedipus Complex

Although recent psychoanalytic theorists have sought to diminish its singular importance somewhat, Freud viewed the Oedipus complex as the cornerstone of psychoanalytic theory—the nuclear complex. He saw it as the necessary precursor of latency. His conceptualizations remain the theoretical underpinning of much of our current understanding of this time of life. We therefore briefly recapitulate the elements that comprise the Oedipus complex.

The oedipal period, for most children, is described as occurring between the ages of 3 and 5. Freud (1905/1953) understood and described the complex primarily as it affected the male child. (The limited scope of this chapter does not allow description of and commentary on the recent lively debate regarding the nature of the Oedipus complex and its resolution in the female.) Unlike the tragic protagonist of Sophocles' *Oedipus Rex*, who actually, though unwittingly, killed his father, Laius, and married Queen Jocasta, his mother, this is a story of impossible and hence unfulfilled desires. Nonetheless, it is a tale of the profoundest emotions, active in the rich fantasy life of the phallic stage child.

The male child's Oedipus complex centers around his love for his mother. At this stage the love involves the desire to marry and consummate the relationship sexually in whatever form the young child construes sexuality. The child, however, has a most imposing rival, his father. His emotions, in the manner of grand Italian opera, overwhelm him, and he seethes with desire to do away with his rival. In this stage of life, an internal struggle ensues. Reality intervenes, and tragedy is narrowly averted.

In fact, as Freud felt children are innately psychologically bisexual, he viewed what was just described as only the "positive" Oedipus complex. The "negative" complex, occurring simultaneously, involves a passion for the father, with concomitant hatred for the rivalrous mother.

Freud (1924/1961) argued that several aspects of the child's reality, in conjunction with "preordained" development, lead to a dissolution of the Oedipus complex, with profound ramifications on the internal and external lives of the child. Writing again in regard to the male child, he believed that it was the real or fantasied threat of castration that brought about the destruction of the child's phallic genital organization and, with this, the end of the Oedipus complex.

The observation which finally breaks down his unbelief is the sight of the female genitals. Sooner or later the

6

child, who is so proud of his possession of a penis, has a view of the genital region of a little girl, and cannot help being convinced of the absence of a penis in a creature who is so like himself. With this, the loss of his own penis becomes imaginable, and the threat of castration takes its deferred effect (pp. 175–176).

Thus castration anxiety, in league with the reality of an unavailable mother and a father whose size far outstrips his, creates an intense conflict with the child's desires. The boy solves this dilemma, in essence, by giving up the mother as an object of his sexual desires and by intensifying his identification with the father (Freud, 1923/1960).

Freud (1924/1961) believed that his understanding of the female's Oedipus complex was incomplete. His description was essentially analogous to what he described for the male. However, the girl child turns to the father only when she, in disappointment, abandons hope of getting a phallus from her mother. Thus, for the girl it is the realization of castration that initiates the oedipal triangle. Freud stated that "the essential difference thus comes about that the girl accepts castration as an accomplished fact, whereas the boy fears the possibility of its occurrence" (p. 178). He added that, in compensation for not receiving the wished-for penis, the female desires to receive a baby from the father. The dawning realization that this wish cannot be fulfilled necessitates the gradual abandonment of her desires and postponement of her wishes until puberty.

Freud (1914/1955), wrote that

psycho-analysis has taught us that the individual's emotional attitudes to other people, which are of such extreme importance to his later behavior, are already established at an unexpectedly early age. The nature and quality of the human child's relations to people of his own and the opposite sex have already been laid down in the first six years of his life. He may afterwards develop and transform them in certain directions, but he can no longer get rid of them (p. 243).

This controversial assertion underscores, in part, the lasting impact of the oedipal resolution. In more formulaic and less dramatic terms, the oedipal constellation consists of the positive and negative emotions directed toward and against the first love objects of both sexes and creates the paradigm for later relationships to be enacted after puberty. The particular constellation and resolution becomes the bases of later attitudes and distortions in intimacy and sexuality (Shapiro, 1977).

With the end of the Oedipus complex, the child's tumultuous world of oedipal fantasies is assertively repressed. His or her behavior begins to manifest a "persistent denial of the struggle against the breakthrough of instinctual impulses" (Bornstein, 1951, p. 282). The liberation of these formerly lively energies allows for a turning outward to the accomplishment of tasks. That is the hallmark of the latency-age child. "Latency" is, in point of fact, a psychoanalytic term referring to the presumed quieting down of the sexual and aggressive instincts. These instincts, of course, do not disappear altogether. Their striking resurgence later will toll the demise of latency and mark the advent of the next stage of adolescence, as the hormonal surge at puberty redirects the child's attention and drives toward sexuality and intimate companionship.

Regression to Anal Interests

In the early phase of latency, the genital impulses remain strong and the newly formed superego, the agency of inner control, is harsh and rigid. The ego defends itself via a partial regression to anal fantasy (Bornstein, 1951). This is manifested in many characteristic behaviors seen in latency.

With cognitive advancement to the stage of concrete operations, the child can now tell a joke with a clearly understandable punchline. What is striking is the frequent smutty content of this material and the titter it sets up in the latency age group. The wit typically centers around some aspect of the body's elimination functions. Children of this age take great pleasure in talking about or performing "farts," "burps," and other bodily functions that are frowned upon in "good society."

Another well-acknowledged anal-stage derivative is the remarkable zeal for collecting in latency-age children. Their pockets and schoolbags are filled with a potpourri of bric-a-brac: pinecones, pocketknives, combs, used tissues, toys, and pieces of things that might conceivably be useful someday. Their rooms are adorned with various piles. The less well sublimated child might have a disorganized pile of rocks, strikingly reminiscent of feces. At the other extreme are the well-ordered and extensively cataloged collections. Stamp and coin collections are typical. Baseball cards, bottle caps, matchbooks, and buttons round out the picture. These activities have spawned large and highly profitable archives and exchanges, as typified by the current fascination with baseball cards. This, as well as collections of comic books and other superhero paraphernalia, also demonstrates the latency child's intense early identifications with new heroes, heralding the later surge of crushes and idealizations of adolescence.

Children of this age also struggle with physical mastery of their bodies. Great pleasure and long hours are spent playing baseball or learning how to tap dance. These activities are performed with peer groups. Alliances are formed and disbanded. Their identity begins to be defined by their relationships to their peers. Children begin to select their friends and to be selected by others. Friendships are typically strictly unisex. There is tremendous internal and external pressure to conform, and the dangers of sexuality, flirted with during the prior oedipal period, are repressed and defended with a reaction formation that can induce violent nausea with the merest hint that a child should associate with a peer of the opposite sex. If this were not enough, the bitter shame of being linked to another in any conceivably romantic way is driven home with rhymed taunts such as "Billy and Nina sitting in a tree, k-i-s-s-i-n-g." The obvious anal derivatives of contamination by touch can result from even less eventful contact with the accusation "You've got cooties!" Such scandalous allegations mandate a response of assorted expletives. The need to "one-up" the other during this period is likely to result in a progression ending in fisticuffs, tears, and a bloody nose. To maintain the boundaries, traditions of isolation and contamination have been maintained, such as the use of "cootie shots" after a particularly dangerous contact. Perhaps the only other experience that is as provocative is any suggestive allegation about a child's mother. The fierce oedipal love resurfaces as a visceral requirement to defend the first object of children's desire. It is as if to say "How dare you in any way slander the object of my deepest love!" The oedipal yearnings are, to paraphrase a cliché, forgotten but not gone. They have become regressively represented and in any way possible disguised by compromise formation and idealization. The madonna image, pure, giving, and fiercely protective and loyal, is formulated and molded during this period.

This also is a time to separate and begin friendship and exploit prowess in forays into leadership and peer roles. The latency-age boy or girl makes clubs and draws up rules and decides on who is "in" or "out." Sometimes the clubs are all officers and the relationships are somewhat fickle, with abandonment and petulance as part of the hasty retreats that may accompany small incidents and pouts. Sports bring boys together just as dance and ballet bring latency-age girls together. The early adulation of sports and dance heroes and heroines may have a significant determining effect on existing talent and future roles. Moreover, success in these endeavors and the experience of being popular and accepted become the early groundwork for adequate self-esteem and sense of personal worth. Thus while academic success may be the way to some parents' hearts, the latency-age child also begins to exploit skills that attract peer admiration as well as parental approval.

Development of the Superego

In 1923 Freud delineated his structural theory of the mind, including the rules for the formation of the superego as a fundamental resultant of the resolution of the Oedipus complex. He believed there was a resolution both to the positive and to the negative Oedipus complexes because humans are intrinsically bisexual. The resolution required an identification with and an introjection of both parental figures. The relative strength of the masculine and feminine sexual dispositions determined the preponderance of one or the other of the two.

Freud (1923/1960) went on to state:

The broad general outcome of the sexual phase dominated by the Oedipus complex may, therefore, be taken to be the forming of a precipitate in the ego, consisting of these two identifications in some way united with each other. This modification of the ego retains its special position; it confronts the other contents of the ego as an ego ideal or superego. The super-ego is, however, not simply a residue of the earliest object-choices of the id; it also represents an energetic reaction-formation against those choices. Its relation to the ego is not exhausted by the precept: "You ought to be like this (like your father)." It also comprises the prohibition: "You

8

may not be like this (like your father)—that is, you may not do all that he does; some things are his prerogative." This double aspect of the ego ideal derives from the fact that the ego ideal had the task of repressing the Oedipus complex; indeed, it is to that revolutionary event that it owes its existence. (p. 30)

The identification with and incorporation of the parental figures and the responses to the drives permits post-oedipal children to modulate their behavior from within. They are no longer dependent primarily on external control of their impulses. There is an inner voice now, carrying with it the injunctions and prohibitions of the parents and more. It begins as a harsh and inflexible enforcer, in response to the dangerous oedipal impulses. "Good" and "bad" have absolutely no shades of gray. It functions on both the conscious and the unconscious mind. Transgressions invoke a sense of guilt. On an unconscious level, this can ultimately lead to significant psychopathology, for guilt invokes a need for punishment, which may take the form of unpleasant symptoms and curtailment of pleasure.

The attainment of a greater level of internal control interphases with the attainment of concrete operational thought and with the latency-age child's anal-regressive propensity toward obsessional, detail-oriented work to make him or her the ideal candidate for primary school education. Indeed, latency is the period where the child learns the rules of society. It is the time of socialization. The expression "He is a real boy scout" contains all the admiring and snickering irony of this period.

As children are no longer dependent on parents to monitor behavior, they are free and even eager to explore social dimensions beyond the boundaries of the family and even prescribe rules to others with sanctimony. Certainly extended exposure to peer groups during school further encourages this exploration. With exposure to an expanded group of children and adults, children also begin the process of reassessing their parents and their ideals. This reassessment, of course, reaches a crescendo in adolescence.

The superego contains another critical component, the ego ideal. Freud initially used this term as a synonym for the superego, and signified its derivation from the precepts and personae of the parents. It has come to mean something related but different. It is the ideal self that one strives to become and measures oneself against. (Psychoanalysts are uncertain as to whether Freud meant it to be another independent agency or one shared by ego and superego.) Although a little girl might be inclined to say that she'd like to grow up to be just like her mommy, it is unlikely and generally undesirable that this simple desire be maintained throughout her life. Furthermore, as portions of the ego ideal are also unconscious, there is much more than meets the eye. It incorporates the unconscious standards against which one judges oneself. It is therefore of fundamental significance in the maintenance of self-esteem, or lack thereof. Thus we can witness the contradiction of an individual who by all objective standards is beautiful, successful, and presumably to be envied yet who feels unsightly, insecure, and most unhappy.

The latency-age child readily touts and preaches to others these newly found values securing inner control and setting external ideals to measure performance. It is not unheard of for a 7-year-old to "turn his father in" inadvertently when he hears his dad tell a white lie. Similarly, latency-age children notice and criticize minor laxity regarding religious practice.

Jean Piaget (1948) studied the morality of latency-age children by assessing how they followed a system of rules. He observed a group of about 20 boys as they played the game of marbles. Feigning ignorance, he asked them to explain the workings of the game to him. He concluded from his interactions that there are a number of stages in the acquisition of morality. From the ages of about 4 to 7 children are egocentric—they are unable to take another's perspective, and follow an idiosyncratic and fluctuating set of their own rules. In essence, each child of this age made the game up as he went. From the ages of 7 to 11, there was a greater grasp of the rules, with an attempt to follow them, and by 11 or 12 there was a firm grasp of the rules and a need to follow them more or less scrupulously.

Piaget was also interested in children's attitudes toward these rules. He found that young children, from about 5 to 9, believe that the rules are inviolable and originated in some absolute authority. Later, at about 10 or 11, children begin to question this, viewing rules as the consequence of a mutable social contract.

Piaget went on to pose a series of ethical questions to children. He found that younger children tended to believe that if you did something bad, you should be punished, and that older children tended to take motivation into account. This has a parallel in the strictness of the superego in early latency. It is also representative of latency-age children's sense of fairness; that is, early latency-age children feel the need to "get even," whereas later on they begin to weigh the "fairness" of situations.

Kohlberg and his colleagues (Colby & Kohlberg, 1987; Colby, Kohlberg, Gibbs, & Lieberman, 1983; Kohlberg, 1964), using Piagetian techniques of posing standard moral dilemmas, explored the development of morality in children, studying primarily a group of boys 10 years or older. They formulated a series of 6 stages of moral development, which they believed was an invariable sequence—a child must first pass through prior stages to progress to the next stage.

Level 1 consists of two stages, and is described as the level of "preconventional" morality. The vast majority of 10-year-old boys were found to be at this level. In the first stage, the child has an egocentric point of view in which the rights of others are irrelevant, and action is deferred to avoid punishment. In the second stage, the child begins to acknowledge that other people have interests too, but the child's own interest prevails.

Level 2 involves "conventional" morality. In stage 3, the child experiences "being good" as living up to what people generally expect of you. At stage 4, the orientation is primarily toward maintaining societal norms. The "system" defines what is right.

Level 3 is characterized by "postconventional" morality. Stage 5 individuals consider both moral and legal points of view, recognizing that these can be in conflict. Decisions are borne on the principle of "the greatest good for the greatest number." At stage 6 one recognizes that there are universal moral principles of justice and equality that may override man-made law.

Gilligan (1982) has focused on females and has argued that there are fundamental sex differences in "orientation" toward moral issues, with men primarily interested in questions of justice and rights, while women focus on care and responsibility in relationships. Walker (1989) further explored both models in a longitudinal study, finding support for the sequence of Kohlberg's stages but not for the existence of significant differences between the sexes.

Buchsbaum and Emde (1990) have argued that considerable moral development occurs prior to the oedipal period. They examined 26 3-year-olds of both sexes. Their technique involved the introduction of simple narrative moral dilemmas called "story stems" that provided conflict between parental rules and personal desires in play. Then they asked the children to complete the stems. Three-year-olds could represent and narrate themes of empathy, reciprocity, adherence to rules, and could struggle with alternative prosocial choices in a moral dilemma. The authors concluded that there was evidence of variable but coherent organization in the area of moral development, even at this early age, and prior to structuralization of oedipal resolution.

The latency stage ends with a combination of biological and social events that impinge on psychology. The hormonal upsurge of puberty and the new roles that signify entry into adolescence lure latency-age children into the next step of the developmental process. The more they have learned about themselves and their roles as schoolchildren, companions, and loyal and moral buddies, the better they will weather what is ahead in adolescence.

REFERENCES

Bender, L. (1938). *A visual-motor Gestalt test and its clinical use.* Research Monograph No. 3. New York. American Ortho-psychiatric Association.

Birch, H., & Belmont, L. (1965). Auditory-visual integration. *Perceptual Motor Skills, 20,* 295.

Birch, H., & Lefford, A. (1964). Two strategies for studying perception in "brain damaged" children. In H. G. Birch (Ed.), *Brain damage in children* (pp. 46–60). Baltimore: Williams & Wilkins.

Bornstein, B. (1951). On latency. *Psychoanalytic Study of the Child, 6,* 279.

Buchsbaum, H., & Emde, R. (1990). Play narratives in 36-month-old children. (Early moral development and family relationships). *Psychoanalytic Study of the Child, 45,* 129–155.

Colby, A., & Kohlberg, L. (1987). *The measurement of moral judgment: Vol 1. Theoretical foundations and research validation.* Cambridge: Cambridge University Press.

Colby, A., Kohlberg, L., Gibbs, J., & Lieberman, M. (1983). A longitudinal study of moral judgment.

Monograph of the Society for Research in Child Development, 48, 1–2.

Erickson, E. H. (1950). *Childhood and society.* New York: W. W. Norton.

Freud, S. (1953). Three essays on the theory of sexuality. In J. Strachey (Ed. and Trans.), *The Standard Edition of the complete psychological works of Sigmund Freud* (hereafter *Standard edition*) (Vol. 7, pp. 125–243). London: Hogarth Press. (Originally published 1905.)

Freud, S. (1955). Some references on school boy psychology. In *Standard edition* (Vol. 13, pp. 239–244). (Originally published 1914.)

Freud, S. (1961). The ego and the id. In *Standard edition* (Vol. 19, pp. 3–66). (Originally published 1923.)

Freud, S. (1961). The dissolution of the Oedipus complex. In *Standard edition* (Vol. 19, pp. 173–179). (Originally published 1924.)

Gesell, A., & Ilg, F. L. (1946). *The child from five to ten.* New York: Harper & Brothers.

Gilligan, C. (1982). In a different voice: Psychological theory and women's Development. Cambridge, MA: Harvard University Press.

Kohlberg, L. (1964). Development of moral character and moral ideology. In M. L. Hoffman & L. W. E. Hoffman (Eds.), *Review of child development research* (pp. 383–432). New York: Russell Sage Foundation.

Kohlberg, L., & Gilligan, C. (1971). The adolescent as a philosopher. *Daedalus, 100,* 1051.

Koppitz, E. M. (1964). The Bender Gestalt test for young children. New York: Grune & Stratton.

Koppitz, E. M. (1968). *Psychological evaluation of children's human figure drawings.* New York: Grune & Stratton.

LaPouse, R., & Monk, M. A. (1959). Fears and worries in a representative sample of children. *American Journal of Orthopsychiatry, 29,* 803.

Lenneberg, E. H. (1975). In search of a dynamic theory of aphasia. In *Foundations of language development* (Vol. 2, pp. 3–20). New York: Academic Press.

McFarland, J., Allen, L., & Honzik, M. (1954). A developmental study of the behavior problems of normal children between 21 months and 14 years. Berkeley: University of California Press.

Piaget, J. (1929). *The child's conception of the world.* New York: Harcourt Brace.

Piaget, J. (1948). *The moral judgment of the child.* New York: Free Press.

Pitchbeck, I., & Hewitt, M. (1969). *Children in English society* (Vol. 1). London: Routledge & Kegan Paul.

Pollock, M., & Goldfarb, W. (1957). The face-hand test in schizophrenic children. *Archives of General Psychiatry, 77,* 635.

Pollock, M., & Gordon, E. (1960). The face-hand test in retarded and nonretarded emotionally disturbed children. *American Journal of Mental Deficiency, 64,* 758.

Rabinowicz, T. (1986). The differentiated maturation of the cerebral cortex. In F. Falkner & J. M. Tanner (Eds.), *Human growth: A comprehensive treatise* (Vol. 2, pp. 385–410). New York: Plenum Press.

Schilder, P. (1950). *The image and appearance of the human body.* New York: International Universities Press.

Shapiro, T. (1977). Varieties of Oedipal distortions in severe character pathology: Developmental and theoretical considerations. *Psychoanalytic Quarterly, 46,* 559–579.

Shapiro, T., & Perry, R. (1976). Latency revisited: The significance of age 7 plus or minus 1. *Psychoanalytic Study of the Child, 31,* 79.

Sullivan, H. S. (1940). Conceptions of modern psychiatry. *Psychiatry, 3,* 1.

Thomas, T., & Chess, S. (1972). Development in middle childhood. *Semin Psychiatry, 4,* 331.

Walker, L. J. (1989). A longitudinal study of moral reasoning. *Child Development, 60,* 157–166.

2 / **The Biology of the School-Age Child**

Elisabeth Guthrie

The concept of growth velocity, growth rate, or incremental growth is most important when understanding child development. The growth of the school-age child should be viewed along the continuum of childhood development. Rate of growth is not constant in any one child, nor are the changes in rate constant in all children.

When compared to the rapid rate of growth during infancy and later on in puberty, the school-age years are a period of relatively decreased growth velocity (Malina, 1975). The decrement in weight and height acceleration may cause the unsophisticated observer to wonder whether the child has "stopped growing." However, examination of the growth charts for children ages 6 through 11 illustrates that what we see during

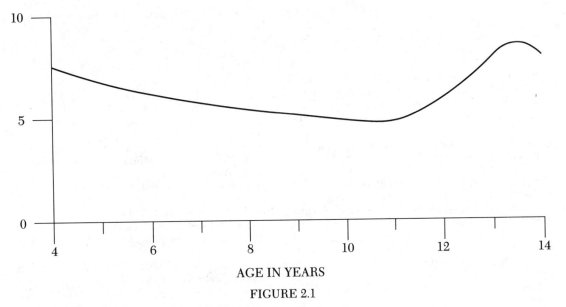

FIGURE 2.1

Change in height growth cm/year

NOTE: Adapted from *Growth and Development: The First 20 Years in Man* by R. M. Malina, 1975. Minneapolis: Burgess Publishing Co.

these years is a relative decrease in rate of growth. (See Figure 2.1.) Such an examination is most helpful when counseling parents who are preoccupied with their child's normal decrease in appetite at this stage of development.

Height velocity reaches its lowest point immediately prior to the pubertal growth spurt. While this is generally just an extension of the gradual decrease in growth velocity, a minority of children will experience a "midgrowth spurt" about the age of 6.

Histologically, growth involves increases in cell number as well as cell size. Cellular growth profoundly influences cell function and produces a variety of biological changes.

The two most influential biological factors affecting growth are nutrition and genetic endowment. Height, weight, endocrine, skeletal, and dental development all have been found to be a function of nutritional status and parental growth histories.

vitamins and minerals. Malnutrition does not occur in the average child who sustains short periods of relative or even extreme deprivation. The developing body is quite able to catch up on growth that has been interrupted by short-lived malnourishment, as may occur with acute deprivation or illness. On the other hand, sustained dietary restrictions over a prolonged period can significantly affect growth.

From the middle of the second year until approximately age 7, the percentage of body fat decreases. It is the norm for a child of this age to appear thin. Thereafter a slight increase in body fat occurs, distributed primarily over the torso and upper extremities. A child who continues to eat and gain weight at the same rate throughout childhood is at risk for obesity in adulthood. The obese 7-year-old has a 40% risk of being an obese adult, whereas obesity at age 12 increases that risk to approximately 70% (Epstein, Wing, & Valoshi, 1985).

Nutrition

Proper nutrition refers to the availability (and bio-availability) of a balanced diet and the appropriate

Genetics

Genetic endowment plays a major role in growth. A child's size and growth perinatally are most affected by the intrauterine environment. After the age of 3, genetic factors play an increasingly powerful role. Stature reflects genetic pooling, as evidenced by ethnic differences in height not attributable to nutritional variation. The height of a school-age child is a function of the average of both parental heights (Rudolf, Hoffman, & Rudolf, 1996). Genetic and behavioral factors play a significant role in weight determination. The rate of maturation is also under the influence of genetic and nutritional factors, a fact illustrated by the inheritance of menarche, whose time of occurrence is closely associated between mother and daughter, but can be delayed by a drastic drop in weight as seen in anorexia nervosa.

Body Changes in Proportions

Body appearance evolves during the school-age years. Gross musculoskeletal growth accounts for much of this evolution. Growth rate follows a cephalocaudal and proximal-distal orientation. The head and the torso mature in advance of the extremities, albeit at a slower rate. Truncal growth includes a gradual broadening and flattening of the chest and downward sloping of the ribs. The shoulders drop and give the neck an appearance of relative lengthening. Facial changes include vertical growth of the nose and a slow, variable maturation of ethmoid, maxillary, and frontal sinuses. The head-to-body ratio for a preschooler is in the range of 1:4; this drops down to 1:7.5 by adulthood.

The lengthening of the limbs occurs in a stepwise fashion, with the arms before the legs and the more distal extremity parts (hands and feet) before the more proximal ones (forearms and calves). Upright, straight-legged posture is assumed, and this stance leads to a weight shift and gradual remodeling of the pelvis. The femoral acetabulum deepens and the hip joints are stabilized.

The upper-to-lower body ratio refers to the body proportion factor, where the denominator (lower segment) equals the distance from the top of the symphysis pubis to the floor, and the numerator (upper segment) equals total body height minus the lower segment (Nelson, Behrman, Kliegman, & Arvin, 1996). The increased rate of limb growth during the school-age years accounts for the gradual change in upper body–to–lower body ratio. In early childhood this ratio is greater than 1. By age 10, upper body size is more or less equivalent to lower body size, and resembles adult proportions. During adolescence there is a brief period in which this ratio is less than 1, hence the appearance of "all arms and legs."

General Body Constituents

Muscle mass increases in size throughout most of the school-age years. At birth, both boys and girls have the adult complement of muscle fibers (Rudolf, Hoffman, & Rudolf, 1996). Girls experience a continued increment in fiber size until puberty, while in boys this muscle growth continues until adulthood.

Adipose tissue in girls increases during this time. At the beginning of the school-age years, fat makes up approximately 13% of total body weight in both sexes. By the age of 13, this reaches 24% for females and drops to 12% for males.

Body compartments shift, with a gradual decrease in intravascular water content and a corresponding increase in the extravascular space. Blood is composed of formed elements, colloid, and chemical components in solution. With a few exceptions, the blood chemistry values for the school-age child are remarkably similar to those for an adult. Higher alkaline phosphatase values are due to ongoing bone growth.

Bone growth consists primarily of ossification of the long bones and incremental growth at the epiphyseal plates. Bone age determination may be used to assess developmental maturity. The bones of the wrist are most commonly X-rayed for this purpose. Ossification occurs at an earlier age in females than males.

At age 6, seven out of eight wrist bones are calcified, including the capitate, hamate, lunare, triangularis, major and minor multangulum, and navicular. By age 12, 100% of girls and over 50% of boys demonstrate calcification of the eighth and final wrist bone, the pisiform. In all boys, calcification should be complete by the age of 15.

Dentition is another accepted way of assessing physical maturation. The eruption of permanent teeth begins about age 6. As illustrated in Figure

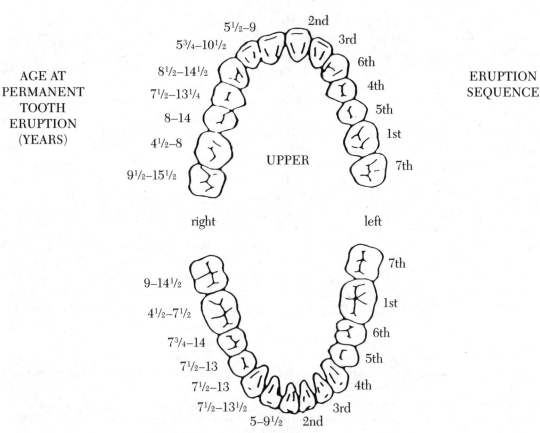

AGE AT PERMANENT TOOTH ERUPTION (YEARS)

5½–9
5¾–10½
8½–14½
7½–13¼
8–14
4½–8
9½–15½

2nd
3rd
6th
4th
5th
1st
7th

UPPER

ERUPTION SEQUENCE

right   left

7th
1st
6th
5th
4th
3rd
2nd

9–14½
4½–7½
7¾–14
7½–13
7½–13
7½–13½
5–9½

FIGURE 2.2

Age and timing of dentition

2.2, the lower central incisors are the first to appear, followed by the adjacent molars. Then the upper permanent teeth emerge with the central incisors followed by the lateral upper and then lower incisors. Bicuspids appear around age 10, and the second set of permanent molars are present from the age of 12.

Specific Organ System Growth

Internal organs grow at varying rates (Lowrey, 1986). Table 2.1 outlines the change in weight of vital organs during middle childhood.

It is interesting to note the differences in the amount of growth in the central nervous system as compared to the liver, heart, or lung. Absolute gross increment in size is not always synonymous with functional maturity.

The steady growth of the heart during the school years accounts for its more than doubling in size between the ages of 6 and 12. The relative increase in the size of the left ventricle and the descent of the diaphragm allow for a more vertical placement of the heart within the thoracic cavity. The axis of the electrocardiogram reflects this position and remains in the range of 60 degrees throughout childhood. Greater vagal input and increased elasticity of the cardiac muscle result in a decreasing heart rate and a quicker and more extensive relaxation of the myocardium in diastole. Ventricular depolarization and repolarization become more synchronous and sequential, respectively (Emmanouilides, Riemenschneider,

14

TABLE 2.1

Change in Organ Weight with Age

Age	1 year (gm)	6 years (gm)	15 years (gm)
Brain	910	1,200	1,300
Heart	45	95	220
Thymus	20	24	30
Kidneys	70	120	170
Liver	300	550	1,500
Lungs	130	260	410

NOTE. Adapted from *Growth and Development of Children* (8th ed., p. 482), by G. H. Lowrey, 1986, Chicago: Year Book Medical Publishers.

TABLE 2.2

Normal Blood Pressure and Heart Rate

Normal Blood Pressures for Age in Mm.HG				
Age (years)	Systolic	2 S.D.	Diastolic	2 S.D.
4	99	25	65	20
8	105	15	60	10
12	115	19	60	10

Average Resting Heart Rate for Age

Age (years)	Average heart rate	2 S.D.
6–10	95 beats/min	30
10–14	85 beats/min	30

NOTE. Adapted from *Growth and Development of Children* (8th ed., pp. 247, 479), by G. H. Lowrey, 1986, Chicago: Year Book Medical Publishers.

Allen, & Gutgessel, 1995). These phenomena are reflected in heart rate and T wave changes in the pediatric electrocardiogram. T waves should be upright in V6 through V4 by age 6, V3 by age 10, and V2 by age 12. As Table 2.2 indicates, heart rate slows and systolic blood pressure gradually rises over these years.

Congenital cardiac abnormalities occasionally become manifest in the school-age years. Such lesions as coarctation of the aorta or some degree of pulmonary stenosis are generally subclinical early on and result in gradual compromise of cardiac efficiency. Over 50% of all children will have a heart murmur noted at some point in their childhood, and the early school-age years are a common time for such a finding. The vast majority of these murmurs are innocent, resulting from the routine turbulence of blood flow across normal cardiac structures. Pathologic murmurs have their own distinct qualities and often are associated with other abnormalities (Rudolf et al., 1996).

Pulmonary growth is marked by enlargement of the thoracic cavity and elongation and widening of the trachea. By age 12, the bifurcation of the trachea shifts downward from the level of the fourth rib to the level of the fifth and sixth rib. Lung alveolar tissue increases through age 8, resulting in increased arborization of bronchioles. These changes increase the surface area available for gas exchange. The accessory and thoracic muscles play a greater role in respiratory effort as compared to early childhood, when the diaphragm assumed the bulk of this task. Respiratory rate decreases gradually from an average of 20 breaths per minute at 5 years of age to 15 breaths

per minute at 15 years. A corresponding increase in inspiratory capacity occurs such that tidal volume more than doubles in the same time period. Respiratory problems are common, and asthma often presents for the first time during the early school-age years. (Phelan, Olinsky, & Robertson, 1994).

Despite the fact that the gastrointestinal lining is constantly being replaced, the digestion, absorption, and assimilation of nutrients during the school-age years is similar to what occurs in adulthood. Liver size increases approximately threefold, but hepatic metabolism remains essentially equivalent to that of the adult. The increased incidence of diarrheal disease in childhood is a common transient cause of malabsorption (Kearns & Reed, 1989). Total protein variations in plasma and some minor differences in absorption may account for slight inconsistencies in drug bioavailability during these years (Reed & Besunder, 1989). Recurrent abdominal pain is a complaint among 10% of school-age children. The pain is typically periumbilical, episodic, and often results in school absence. Medical evaluation, while necessary, rarely reveals significant pathology (Roy, Silverman, & Alagille, 1995).

Genitourinary changes include movement of the bladder and ureters to a more pelvic and inferior location; but, like the gastrointestinal tract, the physiologic function of the kidneys remains essentially similar to that of an adult. There is a slight and gradual improvement in the efficacy of concentrating and diluting capacity within the glomeruli and renal tubules. Benign postural proteinuria is found in about 2.5% of school-age children—urinary protein is found in the absence of any renal pathology. Thought to be due to a relative impairment in the venous blood supply from the kidneys in children who maintain an upright position with pronounced lordosis, this condition generally resolves by puberty (Gonzales & Roth, 1991).

Hematopoiesis becomes restricted primarily to the skull, pelvis, sternum, and ribs at this age, and these flat bones remain the source of blood cell precursors into adulthood. White blood cell counts are slightly increased in childhood. There is a steady increase in blood volume with a parallel rise in hemoglobin concentrations and mean corpuscular volume (Dallman & Siimes 1979).

Mild iron-deficit anemia is common and may be difficult to diagnose. Nonspecific complaints of malaise, fatigue, and poor appetite are found in anemia and may mimic a psychiatric condition. Anemia may be discovered on routine blood test, and a trial of iron supplementation is not only therapeutic but also diagnostic.

Lymphatic tissue increases steadily throughout childhood. Prepubertal hypertrophy of lymphatic glands and nodes is a normal physiologic occurrence, followed by involution of these tissues in late adolescence. The thymus enlarges to three times its perinatal size by about age 7 and remains this size through puberty. Its role in maintaining cellular immunocompetence during childhood is well established. To some degree, humoral immunity depends on cellular immunity as well as on B cell response to antigenic challenges. Immunoglobulin production varies with age. Between the ages of 6 and 14, there is a modest decrease in the level of IgG and a somewhat smaller increase in the concentration of IgM.

Endocrine Development

Endocrine factors play a critical role in growth rate and outcome. The anterior pituitary releases growth hormone. Its secretion is stimulated by the hypothalamic production of growth hormone re-

leasing factor and inhibited by somatostatin. Growth hormone is released into the bloodstream in a pulsatile manner, with greater frequency and amplitude during the childhood years. Its biological half-life is approximately 15 to 20 minutes. Physiologic stimuli for the release of growth hormone include sleep, exercise, and insulin responses to food intake (DeGennaro Colonna et al., 1989).

In order to obtain a representative quantification of growth hormone, sequential measurements over a 12- to 24-hour period are needed. Growth hormone concentrations are greater during Stages 3 and 4 of the early phase of slow-wave sleep and lowest during the day. Disorders disrupting normal sleep physiology may interfere with normal growth hormone secretion.

The growth-promoting action of growth hormone on bone and tissues is thought to be mediated by somatomedins or insulinlike growth factors (IGF-1 and IGF-2). Upon stimulation by growth hormone, several different somatomedins are synthesized in the liver. They are thought to promote bone growth by attaching to cartilage receptors and promoting mitosis. A deficiency of growth hormone results in a delayed bone age and short stature, but body proportions remain essentially normal (Westphal, 1995).

Growth hormone increases blood glucose levels. Hypoglycemia is another serious complication of growth hormone deficiency in early childhood.

Thyrotropin (thyroid stimulating hormone [TSH]) is another anterior pituitary hormone released on stimulation by thyroid releasing factor (TRF) from the hypothalamus. TSH released by the pituitary, then promotes the synthesis of T3 and T4, which in turn provides a negative feedback mechanism at the level of the pituitary by blocking TRF stimulation. Normal values for thyroid hormone and thyroid binding globulin change subtly during the school-age years. Deficiency in thyroid hormone during these years will result in delayed bone age and an abnormal increase in the upper-to-lower body ratio due to the relative lack of limb growth. Severely hypothyroid children may not respond to growth hormone stimulation tests, which suggests that normal thyroid function is necessary for the proper secretion of growth hormone. Unlike congenital hypothyroidism, acquired hypothyroidism in the school-age child does not carry the risk of mental retardation. While it may give rise to slowed mentation and/or a deterioration in academic performance, these symptoms are reversible upon appropriate therapeutic intervention. The pubertal growth spurt generally is delayed in cases of hypothyroidism.

Excess thyroid hormone is rare, but when it occurs during childhood, it is most commonly due to Hashimoto's thyroiditis. It has been diagnosed increasingly in the pediatric population, where often a family history of thyroiditis is found, and the afflicted child is typically female. While uncommon, the diagnosis is of particular importance to the child psychiatrist, as the onset is often insidious and the symptoms include weakness, inattention, and emotional lability.

The parathyroid gland plays a central role in maintaining homeostatic calcium metabolism. Parathyroid hormone (PTH) is secreted in response to low serum ionized calcium concentrations and serves to increase the active absorption of calcium from the small intestine.

The pituitary secretes prolactin solely for the purposes of lactation. In pediatric endocrinology, a prolactin challenge test will elucidate aspects of hypothalamic or pituitary dysfunction.

Adrenal activity is under the influence of hypothalamic and pituitary hormones. Corticotropin releasing factor (CRF) originates in the median eminence of the hypothalamus and stimulates the anterior pituitary secretion of adrenocorticotrophic hormone (ACTH). ACTH in turn acts upon the adrenal cortex to stimulate the production of glucocorticoids and, to a lesser degree, mineralocorticoids. The adrenal cortex produces steroid compounds derived from cholesterol, including cortisol and aldosterone. The adrenal medulla, which is derived from ectodermal tissue, produces catecholamines. The adrenal circulation is such that blood flows from the cortex through the adrenal medulla where cortisol stimulates the conversion of norepinephrine to epinephrine.

Pituitary ACTH stimulates the conversion of cholesterol to pregnenolone, a precursor in the synthesis of cortisol and aldosterone. Unbound blood cortisol levels exert a negative feedback control on the secretion of pituitary ACTH. The interactions of the hypothalamic-pituitary-adrenal axis have a profound diurnal pattern. ACTH secretion rises dramatically around 4:00 A.M. followed by increasing cortisol levels that reach a maximum between 6:00 A.M. and 10:00 A.M. Urinary metabolites known as 17-OHCS may be measured to reflect adrenal steroid production. The dexamethasone suppression test assesses the integrity of the pituitary-adrenal axis. Administration of dexamethasone, a potent glucocorticosteriod, will normally suppress pituitary ACTH production, resulting in a decreased excretion of 17-OHCS. Aldosterone levels are controlled indirectly via the juxtaglomerular apparatus through changes in intravascular volume and serum sodium concentrations.

The incidence of adrenal dysfunction in the school-age population is relatively low. Addison's disease is the name for adrenal insufficiency; autoimmune phenomena are the most common etiological factors. Addison's disease manifests as a progressive incapacitating disorder with gastrointestinal signs and hyperpigmentation. Rarely, degenerative syndromes involving both the central nervous system and adrenal insufficiency (known as adrenoleukodystrophy) occur in afflicted males with progressive mental deterioration.

Increased cortisol production occurs in both Cushing disease and Cushing syndrome. In the disease, the pituitary secretes excess ACTH; in the syndrome, an adrenal tumor is generally responsible for the overproduction of the glucocorticoid. Cushing's syndrome is more common in early childhood; during the middle school-age years, Cushing's disease is more prevalent. The typical clinical findings include decreased muscle mass, characteristic deposition of adipose tissue (buffalo hump), striae, and edema. These children have abnormal dexamethasone suppression test results.

Virilizing syndromes are rare occurrences in the school-age population and result from the presence of a virilizing tumor. Their presentation is similar to that of the congenital adrenal hyperplasia seen perinatally; however, in the female with acquired adrenogenital syndrome, no labial fusion takes place.

The onset of puberty occurs between the ages of 8 and 13 for girls or 9 and 14 for boys. Hypothalamic centers control the pituitary gland, which secretes ACTH and gonadotropins targeted at regulating the production of sex steroids in the adrenal glands and gonads respectively. The anterior pituitary secretes luteinizing hormone (LH) and follicle stimulating hormone (FSH) in a pulsatile pattern during sleep. As puberty progresses,

LH and FSH are secreted continuously with no diurnal variations. In the school-age boy, LH stimulates testosterone production by the Leydig cells. In girls, FSH stimulates ovarian follicle formation and estrogen production. By age 11, most boys and almost all girls have completed Tanner Stage II Development (i.e., enlarged testes with scrotal rugae and reddening in boys; breast bud formation in girls).

Gender identity is a function of social, psychological, phenotypic, and genotypic factors. Its formation begins perinatally, and it is normally well established prior to the school-age years. Preference for same-sex play partners antedates the school-age period. During the ages 6 to 12, this playmate preference intensifies and is reflected in recreational choices as well. Boys appear to choose more contact and rough-and-tumble activities. Girls participate in rough-and-tumble play to varying degrees, but also display greater interest in dressing up, playing house, and grooming dolls. These differences reflect psychosocial as well as biological factors distinguishing the sexes during the school-age years (DiPietro, 1981). Children with disorders of gender identity often show sex-atypical play preferences, though this is not diagnostic of the disorder. The onset of secondary sexual characteristics usually serves to cement a child's gender identity. Where atypical pubertal development is in the offing, certain psychosexual issues may arise during the school-age years.

Clinical presentations suggestive of atypical pubertal development in late childhood include females with extremely short stature (gonadal dysgenesis) or clitoral enlargement (adrenogenital syndrome) and adolescent males with small testes, gynecomastia, or eunuchoidism (Klinefelter's syndrome). Gonadal dysgenesis (Turner's syndrome) may become evident in the prepubertal years, when young girls often fall off the growth curve. Additional anomalies seen in Turner's syndrome include webbing of the neck, coarctation of the aorta, broad chest, and cubitus valgus. Occasionally mild androgen supplementation or growth hormone treatment is administered to increase these patients' height growth prepubertally. Issues of gender identity are not a major factor in the psychosexual development of the school-age child with a 45 XO karyotype who has been phenotypically a female from the first day of life. Virilizing tumors causing acquired adrenogenital syndrome result in hirsutism and premature adrenarche. While the psychosexual impact of such symptoms is felt to be significant in terms of socialization and self-image, it is not felt to have a strong influence on core gender identity (Mazur & Clopper, 1991). Klinefelter's syndrome, or seminiferous tubule dysgenesis, occurs in about 0.9 per 1,000 males.

Precocious puberty is an aberration of development often defined as the inception of puberty before the age of 6 in girls and 8 in boys. It occurs twice as commonly in females as in males. Although a large proportion of cases are considered to be idiopathic, precocious puberty always warrants a full diagnostic workup.

About half of all boys develop gynecomastia during puberty, and over 10% will continue to have appreciable breast enlargement for most of their pubertal growth spurt (Mazur & Clopper, 1991). Gynecomastia of this sort may present problems for the adolescent male, including social anxiety and disturbances of body image, but usually does not precipitate a disturbance of gender identity.

Neurological Development

During the school-age years, brain growth is of proportionately less magnitude than other major organs, primarily because of the brain's massive in utero growth and the need for the body to catch up to head size during early childhood. Between the ages of 6 and 11, the central nervous system grows approximately 10%, due primarily to an increase in cell size and myelination. Myelination accounts for the pronounced thickening of the cortical mantle between the ages of 6 and 10. Thalamic and cortical structures are the last areas to be myelinated, and this process may occur throughout the first decade of life. Myelination of the spinal cord proceeds in a cephalocaudal direction and accounts for an approximate doubling in weight of the cord between the ages of 5 and 10.

Myelinization is needed for the refinement of the motor, sensory, and higher integrative capacities of the central nervous system. Clinically the growth of myelin is represented by the increase in fine motor coordination and balance of the school-age child. Refinement of vestibular reflexes improves equilibrium via proprioceptive and gaze stabilization.

Binocular vision and depth perception also are refined during these years. When asymmetric visual impairment or malalignment occurs, as in severe discrepancies in lens refraction or persistent strabismus, the child compensates by suppressing visual input from one eye. If therapeutic intervention is not undertaken promptly, the risk for incurable amblyopia is great (Greenwald, 1983).

Brain growth and maturation may be followed in the evolution of the electroencephalogram (EEG) (Holmes, 1987). Table 2.3. outlines the chronology of EEG changes between the ages of 4 and 14. Alpha rhythms emerge and become well defined, particularly in the anterior regions of the brain. The gradual increase in faster activity peaks between ages 13 to 15. The posterior regions continue to display predominately slower theta and delta activity. States of alertness correlate with increased alpha activity. Drowsiness represents a relative replacement of alpha activity by delta and theta waves.

The total time spent in sleep decreases during the school-age period, from about 12 hours per night in the preschool years to approximately 8 hours nightly (Sheldon, Spire, & Levy, 1992). As the child grows, rapid eye movement (REM) sleep accounts for proportionately less of total sleep time. Between the ages of 6 to 9 there is a qualitative as well as quantative change in REM sleep. About 20% of total sleep time is spent in REM sleep, and the rapid eye movements have become more distinctly organized into discrete periods of burst activity. Phasic inhibition to auditory stimuli during REM is generated in the parapontine reticular formation and relies on the vestibular nucleus for expression.

Throughout childhood the central nervous system's capacity to exert inhibitory responses to stimuli appears to increase. This reflects further development of higher central nervous system functions. Two developmental phases characterized the maturation of brainstem, auditory, and somatosensory evoked potentials. The steeper growth curve occurs in the first 2 years of life, to be followed by a second, more gradual phase. For the most part this second stage is completed by the school-age period, but occasionally it lasts until about age 8. At any age, brainstem

TABLE 2.3

Developmental Changes in EEG Ages 4 to 14 Years

	Age in years										
	4	5	6	7	8	9	10	11	12	13	14
Posterior slow wave of youth	–	–	–	–	–	o	o	o	o	o	o
MU	–	–	–	–	–	–	o	o	o	o	o
Anterior rhythmic 6–7Hz	–	–	o	o	o	o	o	o	o	–	–
Lambda waves	–	o	o	o	o	o	o	o	o	o	o
14/6 positive spikes	–	–	o	o	o	o	o	o	o	o	o
6 Hz spike & wave								–	–	o	o
Rolandic Spikes	–	o	o	o	o	o	o	o	o	o	o
Occipital Spikes	o	o	o	–	–	–	–	–	–	–	–

KEY: – – – variably present; o o o o o commonly present
NOTE. Adapted from *Diagnosis and Management of Seizures in Children* (p. 38), by G. L. Holmes, 1987, Philadelphia: W. B. Saunders.

evoked responses may vary with modality. Thus, auditory evoked responses display faster transmission time, visual evoked potentials demonstrate a decreased latency period in response to more subtle stimuli, and somatosensory evoked potentials register increased central conduction velocity.

Disorders in the integrative functions of the brain are relatively common during the school-age years. The incidence of epilepsy before the tenth birthday has been described as being 0.3 to 2 per 100. Partial complex seizures typically are identified during the school-age period (Menkes, 1995). Sleep disturbances most commonly seen in childhood include somnambulism and night terrors (Sheldon et al., 1992). Sleepwalkers tend to be boys, ages 5 to 12, and the condition often is associated with night terrors. Somnambulism occurs in non-REM sleep Stages 3 and 4, and EEG findings are not consistent with seizure activity. Night terrors also occur in Stages 3 and 4 of slow-wave sleep and involve an intense autonomic discharge. The children are unresponsive to arousal during the terror and amnestic for the event afterward.

While night terrors are more typically seen in toddlers, they may persist or develop de novo during the school-age period.

REFERENCES

Dallman, P. R., & Siimes, M. A. (1979). Percentile curve for hemoglobin and red cell volume in infancy and childhood. *Journal of Pediatrics, 94* (1), 26–31.

De Gennaro Colonna, V., Cella, S. G., Locatelli, V., Loche, S., Ghigo, E., Cocchi, D., & Muller, E. E. (1989). Neuroendocrine control of growth hormone secretion *Acta Pediatrica Scandinavica,* [Suppl.] *349,* 87–92.

DiPietro, J. A. (1981). Rough and tumble play: A function of gender. *Developmental Psychology, 17,* 50.

Emmanouilides, G. C., Riemenschneider, T. A., Allen, H. D., & Gutgesell, H. P. (1995). *Moss and Adams heart disease in infants, children and adolescents* (5th ed.), Vol. 1. Baltimore: Williams & Wilkins.

Epstein, L. H., Wing, R. R., & Valoshi, A. (1985). Childhood obesity. *Pediatric Clinics of North America, 32* (2), 363–379.

Gonzales, E. T., & Roth, D. (1991). *Common problems in pediatric urology.* St. Louis: Mosby Year Book.

Greenwald, M. J. (1983). Visual development in infancy and childhood. *Pediatric Clinics of North America, 30* (6), 977–992.

Holmes, G. L. (1987). *Diagnosis and management of seizures in children.* Philadelphia: W. B. Saunders.

Kearns, G. L., & Reed, M. D. (1989). Clinical pharmacokinetics in infants and children. A reappraisal. *Clinical Pharmacokinetics, 17* [Suppl 2], 29–67.

Lowrey, G. H. (1986). *Growth and development of children* (8th ed.). Chicago: Year Book Medical Publishers.

Malina, R. M. (1975). *Growth and development: The first 20 years in man.* Minneapolis: Burgess Publishing.

Mazur, T., & Clopper, R. R. (1991). Pubertal disorders: Psychology and clinical management. *Endocrinology and Metabolism Clinics of North America, 20* (1), 211–230.

Menkes, J. H. (1995). *Textbook of child neurology* (5th ed.). Baltimore: Williams & Wilkins.

Nelson, W. E., Behrman, R. E., Kliegman, R. M., & Arvin, A. M. (1996). *Nelson textbook of pediatrics* (15th ed.). Philadelphia: W. B. Saunders.

Phelan, D., Olinsky, A., & Robertson, C. (1994). *Respiratory illness in children* (4th ed.). Oxford: Blackwell Scientific Publications.

Reed, M. D., & Besunder, J. B. (1989). Developmental pharmacology: Ontogenic basis of drug deposition. *Pediatric Clinics of North America, 36* (5), 1053–1074.

Roy, C. C., Silverman, A., & Alagille, D. (1995). *Pediatric clinical gastroenterology* (4th ed.). St. Louis: Mosby Year Book.

Rudolf, A. B., Hoffman, J. I. E., & Rudolf, C. D. (1996). *Rudolf's pediatrics* (20th ed.). Stanford, CT: Appleton and Lange.

Sheldon, S. H., Spire, J. P., & Levy, H. B. (1992). *Pediatric sleep medicine.* Philadelphia: W. B. Saunders.

Westphal, O. (1995). Normal growth and growth disorders in children. *Acta Odontologica Scandinavica, 53,* 174–178.

3 / Cognitive Development in Children

Charles A. Sarnoff

The Fantasies of the Grade-School Years

Latency is a magic road that wends its way through a landscape of fantasies. In these fantasies, derivatives of the Oedipus complex loom like a mountain range running ever beside it. Tracing the same course, but as foothills, are anal-sadistic preoccupations. Scattered along the way, as the grade-school and junior-high-school years unfold, there is a march of fantasy responses to the challenges that accompany cognitive, physical, and social maturation. The challenges include humiliation, sibling rivalry, budding sexuality, and passivity.

THE AGE FRAMES OF FANTASY

Early Latency—Oedipality and Guilt: At the beginning of the latency period and before grade-school attendance begins (5 to 6 years of age), pleasing fantasy content is informed by the Oedipus complex. As the child reaches 6, the capacity to experience guilt develops. Then oedipal fantasies (taking the role of either of the parents) cease to be the source of pleasant musings. Associated with guilt, these latent oedipal fantasies generate fear. Guilt and expected retribution are transmuted into manifest fantasies of theft and imprisonment or into ones such as that of a peasant leader killing a king in a long ago and faraway land. These fantasies discharge tension and, in a part of the psyche, sequestered from reality, provide a sense of expiation or mastery for the feelings and situations involved. Such fantasies predominate through the latency period.

Should these fantasies fail to resolve the oedipal pressures, however, the ego responds with a regression that directs attention to anal-sadistic preoccupations, replacing the new and perilous Oedipus complex with an area that already has been dealt with in prior years—now to be confronted with a far more sophisticated and a mature set of defenses. In the healthiest possible response, the anal-sadistic impulses are defended against by the mobilization of the *mechanisms of restraint*—reaction formation, symbolization, isolation, doing and undoing, and obsessive-compulsive defenses—which defuses the strength of the drives that impel the child to fantasy. The mechanisms of restraint produce a *state of latency* in the child. To the casual observer, the child appears to have socially appropriate periods of calm, pliability, reasonableness, and educability during these states. These attributes underly readiness for the activities of the grade- and junior-high-school years. Should drives be stirred by maturation or accidents of fate (physical and sexual growth, seduction, humiliation, losses), there is a danger that the calm will be placed beyond the control of the mechanisms of restraint. This alternative is averted by the assertion of an organization of the ego with an unique association to latency—*the structure of latency* (Sarnoff, 1976, pp. 13–36), which serves as a safety valve to preserve the state of latency. This ego configuration provides alternative outlets for excess drive energies. By de-flecting drive energies and diminishing the pressure on the static and brittle mechanisms of restraint, it becomes a support for a successful defensive regression to anal-sadistic preoccupations. This regression erases the need for conscious attention to oedipal concerns. Through the action of the structure of latency, the offending stress is excluded from consciousness. Its content is fragmented, then displaced, and then represented by symbols that are organized into manifest fantasies which become the dream, play, and daydream fantasies of childhood. Often the child, unequipped to deal with the dragons of reality, turns to victories in these fantasies as recompense and resolution for the problems of the day. In this way the structure of latency defeats anal-sadistic preoccupations. However, they are never vanquished. Within cohorts of peers cloistered in the permissive zone found in the backseats of carpool vehicles, they sing of dooty and of a man with diarrhea.

With the passing of years, additional fantasy contents appear, resulting in a deemphasis of oedipal fantasy in the middle and late latency years. These contents are responses to the problems presented to the child during the stage of latency development at which they occur.

Middle Latency—Loneliness and Separation: A sense of independence from the parents at about 7 or 8 years of age projects children into a psychic reality in which they are all alone in the big world. Fear fantasies of being small and vulnerable follow. The impotence they feel may be symbolized by a dread of monsters, which represent both what they fear and serve as masking vehicles for projections of the children's own defensively mobilized aggression.

Late Middle Latency—Passivity: Beyond the age of 9 or 10, the problem of passivity becomes a major issue. A sense of independence has grown in these children to the point that they now wish to break free of parental control. They object to the passive role that they have to take in relation to the decision-making parent. This is in many ways a recapitulation of the 2-year-olds demand to know "Who's the boss of me?" These children would like to run their own lives. They object to parental control and interference on an ever-widening horizon of activities. Eventually this trend becomes so intense that they have little else on their minds. The child confronts the parent with "Don't treat me like a baby!" This is evidence of a child readying him- or herself to turn adaptive energies from inward-turning fantasies that solve problems through the manipulation of symbols to demands and actions that will intrude on the world. The children become especially sensitive to situations in which their decisions are challenged or their immaturity emphasized.

Late Latency—Ethical Individuation: Sensitivity to challenge to their social decisions leads to feelings of humiliation and inferiority, when faced with ethical conflicts that estrange them from their parents. This can include activities as simple as crossing the street alone and as major as peer pressure involving stealing, drugs, and sex. In defense, the children generate fantasies about being movie stars, championship athletes, owning motorbikes, and the like. Some children who are conflicted about such confrontations deflect the challenge into fantasies of defiance, which can take the form of fantasies of theft and crime that are at times acted out.

Late Latency—Sexual Identity Crises: Awakening concern about sexual identity intensifies when there is a growth spurt, which occurs at about 9 years of age. Body changes, though too slight to be detected by a casual observer, alert the child to pubertal changes. Children activate old concerns about sexual identity. They worry about what they will look like as adults. It is not uncommon for boys to mistake breast buds as evidence of a sex change. This stirs up other fantasies and castration fears.

If the conflicts of prelatency and of latency can be resolved through discharge and mastery involving the use of state-of-latency fantasy or interactions with parents, the stresses that distorting and sensitizing fantasies bring to adolescent and adult life can be defused. On the other hand, fantasy can deflect a child from confronting reality and lead to a persistence of neurosogenic factors. Latency is a time when a reshaping of the self becomes possible. If, as is said, "As the twig is bent, so grows the tree," latency can be seen as a time for unbending.

THE MECHANISMS OF FANTASY

Future Planning: When those whose fantasies are the product of an intact structure of latency reach adolescence, their capacity for future planning is strong. Early and middle-latency fantasies are plans that bypass problems through distraction, drive discharge, and diminution of affect and mood. This is done through displacement from affect-charged latent symbols to manifest symbols that do not carry or attract affect. The manifest symbols of early latency are selected from nonhuman unrealistic elements that exist in a context of timelessness. As cognition matures, bringing latency to its end, the symbolic forms from which manifest forms are selected shift. Late-latency manifest symbols come to include real people in real situations in a linear time frame; with this change in symbols, the structure of latency is converted into a tool that solves problems through fantasies that manipulate the world. As more reality-influenced symbols are used in fantasy, problem resolution evolves from fantasy formation to future planning.

Fantasy as Reparative Mastery: Daily events are interpreted in light of memories that the children call forth, which can result in distortion of reality and misunderstandings. Children can reduce such daily sources of tension by discharge through fantasy play. Rage released in a fantasy locale reduces tension in home, school, and play. Discomfort can be neutralized by displacement of activities to zones of calm where mastery can be assured. Not only do events evoke conflicts, conflicts can seek out events. The forces of mastery and repetition seek successful new experiences in fantasy to resolve past traumas. Drive pressures associated with the latent fantasy are reduced. Cognitive transformations can then progress, and pathological mechanisms, which if made manifest in latency years, adolescence, and adulthood, would have given rise to problems of adaptation and adjustment, can remain dormant.

Fantasy as a Manifestation of Compulsion to Repeat: Not all fantasy activity achieves resolution through manifest latency fantasy discharge. Typical of this is the persecutory fantasy, which in latency depicts a cruel monster attacking the child and which in later life, when real people are recruited to populate fantasies, takes the form of recurrent experiences of being treated cruelly by lovers and peers. In this situation repeated latency-age fantasies are a manifestation of the repetition compulsion. At the later ages, the manifest fantasy is expressed through the symbolic forms and level of cognitive maturation appropriate to the cognitive level of development.

Cognitive Transformations

The cognitive transformations of the latency years produce a capacity to deal with reality commensurate with changes in size and strength in the growing child. They also produce a shift in object relatedness necessary for the effectuation of reproductive potential commensurate with sexual maturation.

When there are immaturities in latency-age cognitive transformations and other cognitive defects, the drives that underlie fantasy contribute to psychopathology. Failure of the symbolizing function to mature impairs the search for an object in reality for the expression of drives. The evocative pole in symbol formation persists and, symbols fail to go from amorphous to human manifest forms, facts that underlie the androphobic nature of the manifest symbols that populate neurotic symptoms. During the parallel development of primary and secondary process thinking, the latter form may fail to outstrip the former in the rivalry for the attention of consciousness. This problem can be the result of a defect in the development of repression and a failure of symbols in their role as masquers that socialize the manifestations of drives. Failure in secondary process thinking results in impaired reality testing and an ascendance of the personalized sense of reality at the expense of socially shared reality testing (i.e., the reality one feels transcends the reality that all can touch). Disordered memory systems result in perceptual and interpretive distortions. Failure to effect a transition from preoperational to operational thinking results in action orientation and narcissistic (symbolic and intuitive) thinking, which undermines reality testing.

COGNITIVE DEVELOPMENT

The development of the way that reality is perceived, remembered, and understood is far from complete when a child reaches the age of 6. Piaget

(1951) has described the development of the capacity to interpret observed phenomena during the latency-age period, and Freud (1926/1959) has described the cognitive structures necessary for the acquisition of socially acceptable behavior during latency. Their contributions fit into a context of extensive cognitive changes that can be organized into three periods.

THE COGNITIVE ORGANIZING PERIODS

Each cognitive organizing period represents years during which specific cognitive skills mature and develop. The first such period occurs in prelatency, the period between 2 and 6 years of age. The effectiveness of latency during the latency-age period depends on the adequacy of prelatency development of the symbolizing function, repression, verbal-conceptual memory organization, and behavioral constancy (the ability to recognize clues to appropriate behavior).

The second cognitive organizing period encompasses the age period 7½ to 8½ years of age. The cognitive areas that mature during this period are concrete operational thinking, abstract conceptual memory organization, the shift in fantasy content from thoughts about fantasy objects to thoughts about reality objects, and reorganization of superego contents in the direction of ethical individuation of the child's own motivations from contents derived from parental demands. The maturation of these cognitive skills becomes manifest clinically at about 8½ years of age, approximately the age at which late latency begins.

The third cognitive organizing period encompasses the years between 10 and 13. The cognitive areas of development during these years are involved in achieving a shift from a mental life that focuses on personalized fantasy to reality knowledge of the world and an ability to find an object in reality to share the expression of drives. The developmental events related to cognition that appear during this period are the preadolescent vicissitudes of projection, changes in body image associated with pubertal body changes, object-oriented changes in the intensity and direction of object relatedness, intensification of narcissistic investment of the libido in fantasy structures (the content of the fantasies changes to reality objects, but the fantasy remains an important factor), and a shift from the evocative to the comunicative mode in the selection of symbolic forms. (See Sarnoff, 1987b.)

MEMORY ORGANIZATIONS

Vygotsky (Luria, 1976) said in the 1920s that "Although a young child thinks by remembering, an adolescent remembers by thinking" (p. 11). The cognitive organizations involved in this change are named, in order of increasing maturation, affecto-motor memory organization and conceptual memory, which consists of verbal conceptual memory organization and abstract conceptual memory organization. These are the primary conduits through which the world of experience is apprehended and carried forward in time by memory.

Affecto-Motor Memory Organization: The affecto-motor memory organization begins in the first years of life. It consists of two components, motor components and affective components. The motor component, the first one to be acquired, consists of purposefully modified patterns of motor activity. Essentially, motor syntaxes form the contents of memory of this component. Affect and sensory stimuli can activate the spontaneous recall of these syntaxes.

The affect component of the affecto-motor memory organization consists of the ability to evoke recall of learned patterns in the form of affects, perceptions, and bodily postures associated with the initial experience. It represents the ability to organize recall around sensory experiences. Usually these are recalled in their entirety.

The Conceptual Memory Organizations: Conceptual memory is defined as the ability to evoke recall of learned patterns in the form of verbal signifiers, such as words and related symbols. Conceptual memory can be divided into the earlier-appearing verbal conceptual memory and the relatively late-appearing abstract conceptual memory.

Verbal conceptual memory organization is present and able to be operative by the 3rd year of life at the latest. It is not the primary means of memory used until about 6 years of age, when latency begins. The extent to which it is used is strongly determined by environmental and social factors.

Abstract conceptual memory organization is a maturationally based modification of conceptual memory. It first appears between 7½ and 8½ years of age and consists of the skill of interpreting events in terms of their intrinsic substance and retaining this substance in memory through abstractions with or without words (Sarnoff, 1976, pp. 117–120; 1987a, p. 281ff.). The most common area in which such interpretation takes place is in "getting the main idea" during reading. By the age of 12 enough abstractions should have accumulated in memory so that they can be applied to interpret other abstractions.

SYMBOLIC FORMS

Symbols stand at the interface between cognitive functions and the world. Drive energies can be masked as they find acceptable form through symbolization. The strength of secondary process thinking depends on the ability of symbols to limit displacements to representations with low valance for attracting affect. Psychoanalytic symbols—called *secondary symbols* by Piaget (1951)—are symbols whose abstract link to that which they represent has succumbed to repression. This repression begins at about 26 months of age. The march of symbolic forms can best be studied in the objects chosen to express persecutory fantasies. At first there are states of being, such as loneliness and darkness, which are directly expressed. During the 3rd year of life, hostile wishes directed at loved ones are denied and displaced (projection) to plants and animals. With the onset of the latency years, amorphous forms such as ghosts and goblins predominate. At about 8 years of age, humanoid forms, such as witches, are created to represent persecutory figures. At 11, the small-size play figures (ludic symbols) that can be used in fantasy play give way to full-size objects for fear and play. These include peers and adults who are invested with protagonist membership in the child's world of inner fears. In late latency peers begin to be recruited in reality to play out roles in scenarios derived from the latency fantasies of the child.

Running parallel to these events is a shift in emphasis in the selection of symbols from those that merely evoke inner affects to those symbols that play a dual role. The latter serve both to evoke memory and trauma and to enable mastery of trauma through the communication of information in a context of comprehension of the needs of others (Sarnoff 1987b). When the march of symbols has reached the point that real figures can be selected to populate fantasies the communicative pole dominates selection of symbols, and situations are constructed and interpreted on the basis of reality testing derived from operational thinking, the cognitive underpinnings of the ability to fall in love have been achieved and the task of latency has been completed.

The Shift from Primary Process to Secondary Process Thinking

The shift from primary process to secondary process is syncretic with changes in latency-age cognition that enhance the ability to appreciate reality. The terms *primary process* and *secondary process* were first used in those contributions of Freud (1900, 1953, 1915) that describe these cognitive changes. The reality testing attained is oriented toward pragmatic imperatives placed in a child's path by objective reality. The devaluation of an immature sense of reality, informed by hopes and wishes, is an achievement that occurs at the expense of the pleasure principle.

PRIMARY PROCESS AND SECONDARY PROCESS

Freud introduced the term *two systems,* or primary and secondary process, in 1900/1953 (p. 603). The processes were an integral part of the topographic theory. In this early Freudian theory, the areas of mental functioning—the system unconscious (Ucs), the system preconscious (Pcs), and the system consciousness (Cs)—are organized according to their availability to self-reflexive awareness and illustrated as a topographic map. Freud recognized two types of psychic energies, unbound and bound, as fueling the topographic system. Unbound energies characterized unconscious processes (system Ucs). Bound energies characterized conscious processes (system Cs).

Freud (1900/1953) called the context of mechanisms that define unconscious mental life *primary process* (p. 603). It is characterized by free energy expressing uninhibited motivations. Freud (1.900/1953) called the context of mechanisms that po-

lice the passage of unconscious contents into consciousness *secondary process* (p. 603). It is characterized by a search for internal consistency in conscious thought and the formation of acceptable substitutes for primitive wishes. Of the substitute formations, the foremost are communicative symbols, which consist of passions of the mind clothed in the uniforms of culture.

The inhibitory nature of the secondary process was clearly stated by Freud (1900/1953) when he wrote "I propose to describe the psychical process of which the first system alone admits as the 'primary process', and the process which results from the inhibition imposed by the second system as the 'secondary process'" (p. 601). The role of substitute formations (e.g., symbols) in executing the inhibiting requirements of reality and the system consciousness appears in the phrase "loose connections are merely obligatory substitutes for others which are valid and significant" (p. 591).

Primary process refers to the characteristics of the area of the mind that Freud (1915/1957) called "the Unconscious." These characteristics include:

- Mobile cathexes (energized attentions), achieved through displacement and condensation. (These mechanisms sometimes are considered to be all that there is to the primary process.) Energy cathexes can be shifted from one idea or object to another. Cathexes associated with many ideas can be funneled into one idea. Drive energies can be shifted in the direction of a new idea or object in a way that results in repression of the original ideas or objects to which attention cathexes had been directed.
- Unconscious under the sway of the pleasure principle.
- Little influence from objective reality.
- Wish impulses "exist independently side by side, and are exempt from mutual contradiction" (Freud, 1915/1957, pp. 186–187).
- No negation, no varying degree of certainty.
- Timelessness.

Secondary process refers to the characteristics of the structure through which the preconscious guards the gates of consciousness. The activities of this structure are:

- Inhibition of drive discharge.
- Exclusion of displacement and condensation.
- Enablement of communication between ideas to permit them to modify and influence one another.

- Introduction of time constraints on the discharge of wish impulses.
- Establishment of a censorship that will effect both social and personal inhibitions of direct expression of wish impulses.
- Establishment of conscious memory.
- Organization of a testing of reality that is based on the influence of objectivity and socially organized ideation.

SYMBOLS

Drives, wishes, and passions are not ignored as the result of the strengthening of secondary process mechanisms that occurs during the latency years. Standing athwart the gulf between that which primary process proposes and that which secondary process can allow as final disposition are compromise formations. Free displacement and condensation in primary process permits the selection of substitute representations. The inhibition that guides secondary process function limits the choice to compromises. Of all the substitute formations produced by this interaction, symbols serve best as vehicles to bring wish fantasies within grasp of a world of actuality from which wishing can wrest gratification. Reality-oriented substitutes (symbols) represent drive derivatives at the same time that they protect the consciousness from unmodified incursions of the same drives that would challenge reality and create danger.

Though the formation of symbols requires mechanisms with the characteristics of the primary process, especially displacement and condensation, the final form of the symbol is influenced by the adaptations to reality needs that are the hallmark of secondary process. Symbols are a safe-conduct pass through which unconscious content can travel freely and unencumbered within the precincts of consciousness.

The shift from primary to secondary process is only apparent. In fact, both processes persist into adult life. Primary process persists in dreams, fantasies, and neurotic symptom formation, while secondary process persists in functions that free the ego to take part in the adaptive commerce of daily interactions. The apparent shift between processes represents a change in the level of maturity of the symbolic forms used, since symbols themselves undergo a maturation and development that color the communication between un-

conscious wishes and the world. In this regard, the maturation of symbols traces two developmental tracks. The first is the march of symbolic forms from distorted images to real people, which is most sharply detectable in persecutory fantasies. The second is a shift from the evocative pole to the communicative pole in the selection of symbols by the symbolizing function. (See Sarnoff 1987, chap. 3.) As symbolic representation comes more and more to be shaped by communicative needs and justice for partners in drive discharge, the more does it appear that a shift to secondary process has occurred.

Failure to achieve maturation of symbolic forms in secondary process functioning permits hegemony of the unconscious, which is a state congruent with psychosis. Freud (1915/1957) points out that primary process content normally can appear in waking fantasy in children since "a sharp and final division of the contents of the two systems does not . . . take place until puberty" (p. 195).

The Shift from Preoperational Thinking to Concrete Operational Thinking

The terms *preoperational thinking* and *concrete operational thinking* are used in those writings of Jean Piaget (1951) that relate to changes in latency-age cognition which enhance the role of reality in the interpretation of perception. Preoperational thinking (concrete interpretations of perceptions and experiences) requires sensorimotor intelligence. Operational thinking (abstract interpretations of perceptions and experiences) requires conceptual intelligence. The shift from primary emphasis in thinking from sensorimotor intelligence to conceptual intelligence takes place in early latency (from 6 to 7½ years of age).

PREOPERATIONAL THINKING

Preoperational thinking has two stages—sensorimotor thinking and symbolic intuitive thinking. The first is solely an expression of a sensorimotor intelligence based on a memory system that encodes sensation and motor schemata. The second, which begins after 26 months, adds unconscious personalized symbolic interpretation of occurrences to thinking.

At first preoperational thinking consists of isolated linkages of successive perceptions and movements. There is a failure to place the current experience in a whole context, consisting of a predisposing past and a sense of implications for the future of the event at hand. As Piaget (1951) describes it, "Sensory motor intelligence . . . functions like a slow motion film, representing one static image after another without achieving a fusion of the images" (p. 238). This is an intelligence that is "lived and not thought" (p. 238). Only motor and perceptual events inform this intelligence. Related signs, symbols, and concepts are excluded. Because such intelligence lacks verbal representations that would make possible the efficient storage of information, verbal communication of interpretations of perception and experience that are able to be validated consensually within a context of a time sense is not possible. The sensorimotor intellectual experience therefore is limited to the moment of experiencing and to the observer alone. It offers no potential for a social organization of shared knowledge.

Toward the end of the first year of life, a second stage edges into view. Verbal concepts induced by social interactions appear. At that point, words can be used to represent schemas of experience and action, and classifications and relationships between experiences begin to be established in the child's mind. The narcissism of the young child is expressed in a tendency to assimilate all new experience to previously experienced and established conceptions. Such personalized interpretations of events, when coupled with repression, become the basis for intuitive thinking and symbolic reasoning, which begins at about 26 months (Piaget, 1951; Sarnoff, 1970). Symbolic reasoning is dominated by personal influences that keep at bay those pragmatic reality pressures which would limit latitude in the free creation of concepts. Personalized symbols are used for recall. Perceptions and combinations of images are organized into exotic entities that correspond more to the child's desires than they do to the realities of form (Piaget, 1951, p. 230). This state dominates during the rest of early childhood and the first years of latency.

Percepts remembered through words become organized into a verbal memory system by 6 years of age (Sarnoff, 1976, p. 106). Constant reworking of concepts through verbal interaction in an interpersonal setting and through testing impressions against pragmatic imperatives spawned by reality diminishes the strength of symbols and intuition and creates definitions, classifications, and relationships that are shared in society. In this way individual thought is accommodated to the influence of ". . . a common, objective reality" (Piaget, 1951, p. 239). Thus, a verbal conceptual memory organization evolves that can support conceptual intelligence, which in turn supports the development of concrete operational thinking at about 7 years of age.

CONCRETE OPERATIONAL THINKING

Concrete operational thinking is characterized by interpretation of perceived concrete events in light of preconceived socially or observationally validated concepts. Such "concepts are either systems of classes, sets of objects grouped according to relations between wholes and parts, or systems of particular relations grouped according to their symetrical or assymetrical nature" (Piaget, 1951, p. 218). In establishing these clusters of concepts, assimilation to previously established conceptions gives way to accommodation to "the qualities of the objects composing the groups whether or not the child himself and his own activity are also involved" (p. 218). Concrete operations serve reality in areas where bound energies contribute to adaptation, such as academic work.

With the advance of primacy for concrete operations, the individual symbol in waking life gives way to the properly social sign. Secondary (psychoanalytic) symbols persist in dreams (oeniric symbols) and contribute an element that runs counter to the move toward reality accommodation in waking life. During the latency years the ludic symbol (e.g., a playtoy used to manifest an unconscious fantasy concept) survives until it is extinguished (ludic demise) at 10 to 12 years of age. (See Sarnoff, 1987a, p. 94.) Ludic symbols have a mobility of potential meaning that permits the expression of unconscious drive derivatives. The ludic symbol subverts the demand of concrete operations that social definition set the boundaries of meaning of verbalizations and signs.

For the latency-age child, the ludic symbol, manifested in fantasy play, provides for the persistence of intuitive and symbolic thinking during the latency years, enabling the discharge of unbound energies and the mastery of emotional stresses, both real and the result of intrusions from the unconscious.

A small but not inconsiderable percentage of children fail to develop a full capacity to use words and symbols, including ludic symbols. Such youngsters have little imagination. Their outlet takes the form of physical activity such as sports. Under stress, their decompensations take the form of somatic symptoms and behavior disorders (Kernberg, 1991).

The development of concrete operational thinking between the age of 7 and 8 is associated with "reversal." When reversal is operative, the "assimilation" of perceptions to idiosyncratic preconceptions is balanced by an "accommodation" of the child's understanding to a remembered socially defined concept of an object. The object itself comes to serve as an example of the concept rather than as the source of the definition.

When internalized definitions that were learned from others come to dominate the interpretation of perceptions, the phenomenon appears to be a form of assimilation that counters the reality strengthening provided by accommodation. The process perpetuates and supports the myths of culture producing socially influenced and consensually validated concepts that may distort interpretations of new experiences. These responses are socially shared and reflect previously injected influences of society. They may be considered to be a priori social accommodations to reality and a manifestation of reversal.

The ability to separate words from things and to organize them into concepts makes it possible to create categories that are independent of individual percepts. Once established, at about age 8, such thought and memory groupings, often shared by society, offer a medium for memory that permits the storage of abstract concepts (the abstract conceptual memory organization; Sarnoff, 1976, p. 117). At first interpretation of only those items that can be seen concretely contribute to these abstract conceptualizations (concrete operations). By the age of 12 this skill is sufficiently honed so that verbal abstractions and the intrinsic nature of events can be comprehended and the knowledge so gained applied to new situations (abstract operations).

CLINICAL CONSIDERATIONS

Failure of cognitive development to proceed beyond sensorimotor thinking is a symptom congruent with states of infantile autism. In healthy children of all cultures, cognition unfolds naturally up to the level of concrete operations. Development beyond that is a product of social customs. Concrete operations can support tribal living, while adaption to industrial society requires abstract operations (Nurcombe, 1976). Although failure to achieve the level of abstract operations has not yet been included under the rubric of pathology, such youngsters can easily be seen as potentially dysfunctional underachievers. The development of abstract operations is accompanied at the age of 11 by the ability to interpret proverbs: It is at that age that concrete thinking on proverb interpretation tests can indicate persistence of a predominance of concrete rather than abstract operations.

REFERENCES

Freud, S. (1953). The interpretation of dreams. In J. Strachey (Ed. and Trans.), *The standard edition of the complete psychological works of Sigmund Freud* (hereafter *Standard edition*) (Vol. 5). London: Hogarth Press. (Originally published 1900.)

Freud, S. (1957). The unconscious. In *Standard edition* (Vol. 14). London: Hogarth Press. (Originally published 1915).

Freud, S. (1959). Inhibitions, symptoms and anxiety. In *Standard edition* (Vol. 20, pp. 77–178). London: Hogarth Press. (Originally published 1926.)

Kernberg, P. (1991). *Children with conduct disorders.* New York: Basic Books.

Luria, A. R. (1976). *Cognitive development: Its cultural and social foundations.* Boston: Harvard University Press.

Nurcombe, B. (1976). *Children of the dispossessed.* Honolulu: University of Hawaii Press.

Piaget, J. (1951). *Play dreams and imitation in child-hood.* New York: W. W. Norton.

Sarnoff, C. A. (1970). Symbols and symptoms, phyto-phobia in a two-year-old girl. *Psychoanalytic Quar-terly, 39,* 550–562.

Sarnoff, C. A. (1976). *Latency.* Northvale, NJ: Jason Ar-onson.

Sarnoff, C. A. (1987a). *Psychotherapeutic strategies— The latency years.* Northvale, NJ: Jason Aronson.

Sarnoff, C. A. (1987b). The shifting symbolic forms of late latency, early adolescence. In *Psychotherapeutic strategies—The latency years* (pp. 47–68). North-vale, NJ: Jason Aronson.

---

4 / Sexual Development and Gender Identity

Martin A. Silverman

Masturbation During the Grade School Years

Autostimulation, which begins shortly after birth or perhaps even in utero, plays an important role in the developmental process of the child. In utero thumbsucking may provide valuable affer-entation to the central nervous system that is nec-essary to prepare the child for participation in the feeding experiences that constitute the baby's central waking activities after birth.

The baby's pleasurable exploration and manip-ulation of his or her own body parts plays a role in cognitive, psychosocial, and psychosexual devel-opment in a number of ways. Cognitive develop-ment at first is sensorimotor in nature. As Piaget and his coworkers have demonstrated, the child begins to learn about the world via the coordina-tion of sensory and motor activity. (See Silverman, 1971.) The body builds up cognitive schemata (i.e., recognizable, patterned, sensorimotor units of experience), through repetitive, sensory obser-vation of its own motor activities. These schemata enable developing children to identify and be-come familiar with details of their own self and of the external world with which they interact, as well as with the differences between the two.

Children use their mouth for sucking, gum-ming, and exploring the world, all the while feel-ing, smelling, seeing, and hearing what is taking place. When they suck on their own thumb, ba-bies experience a set of sensorimotor schemata that involves two parts of their own body. When they suck on a nipple presented to them from out-side and receive warm milk in their mouth, babies experience a very different set of schemata (Sar-noff, 1976, pp. 39–47). The contrast between the two sets of repeated experiences promotes ap-preciation of the differences between self and nonself as well as of the specific details of each. The same applies to use of the hands in grasping parts of a baby's own body versus taking hold of objects in the environment. It applies, too, to chil-dren's experience in their anal and genital zones of the sensations associated with their own excretory processes as opposed to those associated with being cleansed and diapered from the out-side.

The pleasurable nature of these experiences fa-cilitates cognitive advance. The child's growing ability to cognitively recognize and categorize the experiences in turn gives shape and form to the pleasure that is innately connected with them. In other words, throughout the developmental pro-cess there is a vital, intrinsic coordination between cognitive awareness on the one hand and gratify-ing, pleasurable bodily experience on the other. An equally vital interaction occurs between auto-erotic, self-stimulatory experience and exciting, pleasurable, interpersonal experience in shaping developing children's outlook on life and the op-portunities it offers to enjoy being alive in a world that includes other animate beings who are as wondrous and wonderful as one's own self.

Parents accept a certain amount of autoerotic activity on the part of young children. Thumb-sucking as a pleasurable form of self-stimulation generally is permitted up to a point. Other forms of autoerotic activity are less well tolerated. The pleasure children obtain from their excretory activities is not readily accepted, and sooner or later they are expected to accede to their parents' expectation that they forgo that pleasure and learn to urinate and defecate where and when it suits their parents.

Even in this enlightened age, parents restrict their children's masturbatory handling of their genitals for the pleasurable sensations it affords and they convey, either overtly or more subtly, an attitude that opposes it. This attitude probably derives from a variable combination of the impact of their own conflicted feelings about masturbation, unconscious envy of the freedom of action displayed by their children, the wish to socialize their children rather than permit an ease of self-gratification, the effects of their own training when they themselves were little, and current cultural pressures. There is an inherent, dialectical tension between the urge for unrestricted self-expression by the individual and a societal demand for self-denial and self-control.

By the time children have gone through the interpersonal and intrapsychic struggles of the preschool years, they have come to accept more or less the societal restraints that parents and other adults in authority have been imposing on them. Their physical and emotional immaturity, their own ambivalence conflicts, and their relative weakness vis-à-vis the adult world impel them to accept, at least temporarily, the preoedipal and oedipal defeats that have been thrust upon them. Since the urges and fantasies connected with their oedipal and preoedipal conflicts have become intimately connected with the act of masturbation as a central form of sensual and sexual gratification, they unite with their parents in (ambivalently and conflictedly) opposing their own masturbatory urges.

The urges, and the surges of sexual excitement that underlie them, do not disappear, however. Application of the term *latency period* to sexual development during the school-age years is misleading unless it refers only to obvious, overt behavior. What characterizes the school-age years is the variably successful *struggle* against masturbatory impulses rather than their total cessation. Children in this age group try very hard to resist masturbatory urges; to a large extent they are able to do so.

Girls tend to be more successful in this regard than boys for a number of reasons. More pressure has always and continues to be applied to them, especially by their mothers, to be contained and controlled, neat and clean, well behaved and socially conscious. In part this is related to their closeness to and union with their mothers in a dedication to order, control, and social consciousness in their current role in maintaining cohesion and control within the family and their future role in bearing and caring for children. In part it appears to be related to a greater expectation for girls to avoid touching their genitals, an expectation connected with a cloacal coalescence of the image of the female external genitalia with that of the urethral and anal excretory openings with which they are closely and complexly related anatomically.

The strong demands placed on girls to be neat, clean, and well controlled aids them in resisting masturbatory urges. Girls also appear to be more intrinsically capable of order and self-control than boys. In girls who have heightened self-esteem problems leading to intense penis envy, dissatisfaction with fantasied genital inferiority might add an additional impetus to avoid masturbation. Boys, furthermore, with their more protuberant and tumescent genitalia, are less protected against periodic, mechanical, external stimulation of their sexual organs. Together with the lesser external pressure placed on them from adults to control and contain themselves than is placed on girls, this contributes to the greater restlessness, fidgetiness, impulsivity, and repeated touching of the genitals observable in boys in the early elementary school grades compared to what is observed in girls of the same age.

To a significant extent, school-age children suppress overt masturbation and repress the exciting fantasies that accompany it. Other, more acceptable, substitute physical activities take their place. There is regression to nail biting, hair twirling, cracking knuckles, and the like. Boys and girls alike tend to emphasize large-muscle, total body activity, such as running, jumping, climbing, moving rapidly through space via the use of playground equipment, and so on. Organized games and sports, which are even more important to boys than to girls, offer necessary, substitutive, physical pleasure. Through the rules and regulations that pertain, however, they also provide assistance in maintaining order and self-control that is very welcome to the school-age child struggling to suppress and control masturbatory urges. The same applies to the jump roping, dance, and gymnastic activities favored by girls. At the same time, however, all these vigorous physical activities offer covert sexual satisfaction via the unobtrusive genital stimulation that is embedded in the overall experience but kept out of conscious awareness.

In fact, both school-age boys and girls do engage in a considerable amount of covered-up, disguised masturbation. Since the girl's vulva is more safely removed from sources of casual stimulation, and her clitoral, vulval, and deep pelvic sexual sensations are more diffusely distributed and less readily observable than are the boy's comparable genital sensations, it is easier for girls to stimulate their genitals indirectly and even without conscious awareness that they are doing so. They can manipulate their external genitalia via thigh pressure, bicycle riding, or perineal cleansing with a sponge or a shower spray without being consciously aware that they are masturbating. A woman in analysis, for example, did not recall ever having masturbated prior to adolescence. The thought occurred to her, however, that as a schoolgirl she always had been eager to sew for her mother even though she rebelled against all other forms of housework. When this was explored further, it became apparent that she had used an old-fashioned sewing machine with a curved, flat handle that "turned the machine on" when she pushed it with her upper thigh. The handle, she recalled further, pressed tightly against her genitals when she "didn't sit right."

The sexual fantasies that are associated with masturbatory activity are vigorously repressed out of consciousness, split off from the physical act of masturbation, and permitted reemergence in disguised form within the content of stories, activities, and fantasy play. School and devotion to learning offer an avenue for redirecting mental activity away from the exciting, rivalrous, competitive, sexual content of masturbatory, oedipal fantasies into more neutral intellectual activities. They also provide external restraint and constraint and training in self-discipline and self-control. Certain aspects of the fantasies are expressed in action in the form of academic competition, ri-

valry in games and sports activities, and the shifting alliances and exclusions of the social scene. The locus of the rivalrous, oedipal drama shifts from the family to the peer group and the school setting.

Sexual fantasy breaks through into consciousness periodically, but for the most part it is separated off from the physical act of masturbation and is regressively reworked into sadomasochistic form and content that more or less successfully disguise its sexual nature. Adding further impetus to their efforts to suppress their masturbatory excitement are the revulsion and anxiety experienced by children in response to their cruel fantasies and inclinations, to their fearful thoughts of being kidnapped and carried off by dangerous individuals, or to their families (or those of friends and neighbors) being attacked by robbers invading their homes or being consumed by fire. School-age children may go so far as to become totally anesthetic genitally (Freiberg, 1972), although some children are capable of masturbatory, genital crescendos of sensation that approach orgastic intensity (Bernstein, 1975; Clower, 1975; Kinsey, Pomeroy, & Martin, 1948; Kinsey, Pomeroy, Martin, & Gephard, 1953).

Normal Heterosexual and Homosexual Issues

School-age children in part renounce their excited, sexual oedipal interests, in accordance with the realization that defeat is inevitable. To a great extent, however, sexual interests are merely repressed out of consciousness. The repression is reinforced by displacement of sexual feelings onto siblings, teachers, and members of the peer group; by regression and reaction formation; by sublimation into academic and athletic competition and into interest in ready-made stories, books, cartoons, film, and television themes; and by characteristic phobic and obsessional mechanisms aimed at establishing a sense of control over excited and angry feelings that continually threaten to turn things topsy turvy and out of control.

Feelings toward parents are to a large extent

desexualized, in favor of a heightening of tender, affectionate feelings toward them. Excited feelings tend to be shifted to siblings, with whom sexual exploration, teasing, and physical horseplay tends to be common. Episodic seduction of sisters, brothers, and cousins into mutual masturbation and other forms of sexual play is relatively common.

Exemplifying the shift in sexual interest from parents to siblings that is common during the school-age years, a woman in psychoanalysis recalled detaching herself as an elementary school child from her father, whom she had loved and worshipped before then. Instead, she became very involved, albeit ambivalently, with her older brother. Although she fought with him repeatedly and complained about him regularly to her parents, she also loved and revered him. While she struggled against her masturbatory impulses, she periodically gave in to them, especially when she was alone in the house. Her favorite masturbatory activity involved stuffing her brother's pajamas or underclothes into her own pajamas so that she looked fat (i.e., unconsciously pregnant) and then masturbating with the fantasy that she was a slave to a powerful, strapping captain in the army of ancient Rome who would approach her in a frenzy of romantic, sexual excitement after he had successfully led his troops to victory in a heroic battle. At times, in the fantasy, she would do her best to struggle against his advances but eventually would have to succumb to the combined power of his ardor, his physical strength, and his authority over her. At other times, he would be killed in battle and she would be taken as a prize by a new master, or she would fight him off and, defending her honor, kill or cripple him with his own sword. Elements of a romanticized rape fantasy and of regression from the exciting oedipal daydreams of her earlier years to a new, sadomasochistic theme are clearly discernible. She traced the ideas contained in her masturbatory fantasies to a movie she had seen on television when she was in first or second grade that had so captivated her that she found herself thinking about it repeatedly afterward.

After each episode in which she gave in to her masturbatory urges as a school-age girl, she felt ashamed, guilty, and disgusted with herself, especially after a female baby-sitter caught her in bed with her hand to her genitals and told her that she was consigning herself to perdition for all eternity.

Her neurotic problems were reflected only in part in her masturbatory conflicts. Even more important was that in her effort to detach herself from her oedipal entanglement with her parents, she was not able to move beyond her brother into the peer relations that normally are the most important aspect of the interpersonal life of the school-age child. Although she was some what involved with other children, especially in the Girl Scouts, and even had the courage at one point to engage with a boy in mutual examination of each other's bodies, she withdrew into social isolation at age 7 when the family of her best friend moved far away. She rationalized this retreat in terms of reluctance to risk the possibility of investing once again in a valued friendship that might be lost. From then on she stayed close to her family, angrily resenting and shunning the rambunctious boys and resigning herself to the loneliness she felt as a shy, quiet "outsider" who could not insinuate herself into any of the in groups of "popular" girls.

Normally, peer relations assume an extremely important role in the life of children once they begin elementary school. The intensity of emotional ties to friends and schoolmates increases markedly. Other children's views and opinions become very important, as do the clothes they wear, the possessions they acquire, the hobbies and interests they undertake. Social relations become increasingly meaningful, and the insider-outsider dichotomy of the oedipal triangle is replaced by that of cliques and social groups in which membership is limited and exclusive.

The sexes at first, at least on the surface, tend to be carefully separated from one another. Boys express disdain for girls and girls look down on boys as wild, unruly, immature roughnecks. These attitudes are defensive against the interest in the opposite sex that needs to be disavowed in order to maintain a safe distance. The attraction boys and girls feel toward one another tends to be expressed via how much disdain they express toward one another. An underachieving, borderline 9-year-old boy in treatment because of social difficulties was puzzled by the ostracism he experienced at the hands of his classmates. After trying for some time to figure it out, he finally exclaimed: "I used to think I was different from other kids because I liked girls. But I'm beginning to see that I wasn't really so different from them as I thought. In second and third grade all the boys like girls and all the girls like boys, but they can't show that they like them. They have to hide that they like each other. They even hide it from themselves. That's why it bothered them when I showed I liked girls. *But I couldn't help myself*!"

The outward disinterest in the opposite sex that is typical of children in this age group is defensive, as this observant boy pointed out. Actually, there is a great deal of interest in the opposite sex. Boys know very well which girls are the prettiest, which are the kindest and most charming, which have the most winning personalities. Girls likewise are quite aware which boys are handsome, which are smart or athletically proficient, which are really nice.

Mothers and sisters are frequently called upon to apprise a daughter or younger sister that a boy is teasing or picking on her because he likes her. Boys and girls go through crushes on one another, but in the early grade-school years, they have to keep them hidden or risk being teased and publicly shamed for it by their contemporaries who, unless they are exceptionally popular and well liked, join together in taunting them about it. When they get to be a little older and more certain of themselves (with regard to the increasing reliability of their defenses and the development of their self-esteem), they can begin to dare to let it be known that they are attracted to a particular girl or boy. Restraints and safeguards tend to be established, however, by the group. Friends will act as brokers, conveying messages about who likes whom or even fomenting a liaison by asking on their own who likes whom.

School-age children's games not infrequently reflect the sexual currents that are active within them, although they usually do so in a disguised form. Playing house or school, for example, derives in part from an excited interest in learning about the mysteries of married life, the sexual secrets of the adult world. Playing doctor, which provides an avenue for examination and exploration of the human body, gives an opportunity to satisfy sexual curiosity. It often leads to or is related to mutual examination by boys and girls of each other's genitals. Competitive games in which the loser is required to kiss a boy or a girl or to expose his or her buttocks or genitals are carried out far from the eyes of disapproving adults.

Rules, which afford a measure of control, group sanction, and the illusion that the participants are *required* to do what they do not *really* want to do,

enable individual superego criticism to be overcome. Rules in general are extremely important during the school-age years. Boys, in their games, appear to be as preoccupied with arguing over the rules of the games they play as in playing the games themselves, as Gilligan (1982) has emphasized, while girls in this age group (especially in the early school-age years) tend to be very concerned that feelings not be excessively hurt and group cohesion is not excessively threatened by the results of competitive games.

The competitiveness is important as an outlet for the expression of the oedipal tensions and rivalries that are there beneath the surface; and the rules play an important role in the process of building up of the self-restraint and self-control that are necessary for the eventual return to open, triangular, sexual rivalry and competition as adolescence approaches. School does as much to train children in self-discipline as it does to educate them. Children who are not able to effect a relative moratorium (at least consciously) from the sexual (and aggressive) conflicts with which they entered the school years will not be prepared for the intense struggles that lie ahead of them as adolescents.

In the ancient Stone Age cultures exemplified by the Pacific Island groups and the Northwest Indian and Inuit (Eskimo) cultures, which all but succumbed to the incursion of "modernity" during the 19th and 20th centuries, boys and girls were by and large formally separated from one another from early childhood to adolescence. Boys associated with men, who taught them to hunt or to farm and who trained them to be warriors. Girls associated with women, who trained them to cook, sew, tend the garden, and raise children. (Exceptions did exist; in some cultures children were encouraged not only to associate with one another but even to engage in active sexual relationships.)

In modern society, the formal separation of the sexes in childhood (e.g., by educating them in separate schools) has tended to drop away. The cultural vehicle for maintaining separation between the sexes has been the same-sex peer group. Adults foster this by segregating children by sex in the Boy Scouts and Girl Scouts. Gym classes are separated (although this, too, is changing), and there are separate bathrooms for boys and girls in school. Boys and girls are sent to separate sleep-away camps or, if they are sent to coed camps, the girls' and boys' bunks tend to be placed on separate campuses.

School-age boys and girls tend to congregate in separate groups for play and for games. The emphasis, at least on the surface, is on activities that are nonsexual in nature. The very fact that boys are excluded from the girls' social groups and vice versa points up the defense against sexuality involved in this segregation of the sexes. Early in latency members of the opposite sex tend to be publicly shunned and derided. Girls devote themselves to "feminine" interests involving doll play, romantic fantasy, art projects, narcissistic-exhibitionistic dance, gymnastics, and swimming activities, and the "secrets" in which little girls delight. Boys join together in sports activities, "clubs," and such active competitive, individual, and team games as hide and seek, cops and robbers, ringolevio, and king of the hill.

The best friend is a very important aspect of the latency-age child's life. The best friend relationship is even more urgent for a girl to maintain than it is for a boy. For a girl, the loss of a best friend can be so painful that it can lead to longlasting depression or despair. Girls often jealously guard a relationship with a best friend against intrusion by a third girl. This is reminiscent of the oedipal, triangular relationship from which it in part evolves. In this age group the best friend relationship derives partly from displacement of oedipal yearnings toward the girl's father, with regressive reworking into a homosexual theme that provides relief from the painful narcissistic injury of his rejection of her as the love object she has wished to be for him. Through her special relationship with her best friend she can turn away not only from her father as her principal love object but from all males, and instead love and be loved by a girl like herself.

The best friend also is unconsciously connected with the girl's mother. Her mother was her very first love object, and she continues to have a very special, although ambivalent, relationship even after she has largely turned away from her to her father as an exciting new love object. The ambiva-

lence is expressed in the periodic fights, breakups, and subsequent makeups that are so common in the best friend relationships of school-age girls. The sexual and aggressive conflicts that power the relationship usually are intensely repressed and sublimated, so that the relationship appears strictly platonic and asexual. There is periodic hugging, kissing, and interest in each other's bodies, but it seems on the surface to be no more than friendly and playful in nature. Frank homosexual activity can erupt from time to time—for example, when one girl "teaches" her best friend to masturbate during a sleepover visit—but it is more often disguised or toned down into playfully urinating into a sink together up in the attic or taking turns playing the harem bride and the pasha whose slave she has become in a secret, repetitive, exciting, erotic game when they are alone together.

Boys' best friend relationships tend to be less important during the early school-age years than that of girls and tend to be more disguised in their sexual aspects. Usually they tend to be embedded to a greater extent than those of girls into the larger matrix of the group to which they both belong, although at times the relationships achieve greater prominence. The extent to which roughand-tumble sports and other physical activities present boys with considerable opportunity for body contact, including touching of each other's genitals and buttocks, allows them to express a great deal of subdued and disguised homosexual interest in one another. Especially toward the later school-age years, as puberty and adolescence approach, this will at times evolve into sexual discussions, episodes of mutual masturbation, joint investigation of the body of the sister or of a female cousin, and so on.

Sexuality, in other words, does not disappear during the school-age years. It is consciously denied, disguised, displaced to substitute activities and interests, hidden from adult eyes, defended against, sublimated into learning and into social activities, transformed, and restrained. But it is very much a central part of children's lives.

REFERENCES

Bernstein, I. (1975). Integrative aspects of masturbation. In I. Marcus & J. J. Francis (Eds.), *Masturba-* *tion From infancy to senescence.* New York: International Universities Press.

Clower, V. (1975). Significance of masturbation in female sexual development and function. In I. Marcus & J. J. Francis (Eds.), *Masturbation: From infancy to senescence* (pp. 107–143). New York: International Universities Press.

Freiberg, S. (1972). Some characteristics of genital arousal and discharge in latency girls. *Psychoanalalytic Study of the Child, 27,* 439–475.

Gilligan, C. (1982). *In a different voice: Women's conceptions of the self and morality.* Cambridge, MA: Harvard University Press.

Kinsey, A. C., Pomeroy, W. B., & Martin, C. E. (1948). *Sexual behavior in the human male.* Philadelphia: W. B. Saunders.

Kinsey, A. C., Pomeroy, W. B., Martin, C. E., & Gebhard, P. H. (1953). *Sexual behavior in the human female.* Philadelphia: W. B. Saunders.

Sarnoff, C. (1976). *Latency.* New York: Jason Aronson.

Silverman, M. (1971). The growth of logical thinking: Piaget's contribution to ego psychology. *Psychoanalytic Quarterly, 40,* 317–341.

5 / Infantile Narcissism in the Grade-School Years

Joseph D. Noshpitz

For the grade-school child, narcissism serves three major functions: regulation, resilience, and repair. Regulation arises from the yearning to live up to an ideal and to behave in accordance with some preconceived notion of perfection; for the normal child, this is a significant element in helping manage temptation, impulse, rage, the seduction of peers, and other such urges to engage in deviant behavior. Resilience implies the presence of an inner feeling of worth and self-love that buffers the child against the everyday experiences of teasing, confrontation, and correction that might otherwise result in feelings of sadness and personal devaluation. Repair consists of the ameliorative fantasies that follow experiences of humiliation or injury to one's sense of personal worth; the youngster so afflicted is likely to engage in a sequence of imaginary scenarios that allow him or her to escape the ravages of the pain and to emerge less wounded by injurious experience.

A number of authors have dealt with pathological narcissism in these early years (Bleiberg, 1984; Kernberg, 1989; Rinsley, 1988, to name a few). However, problems of normal narcissism during this epoch are relatively uncharted. It therefore seems reasonable to touch briefly on some of the inner structures of mind that give rise to the phenomena associated with narcissistic experience. To begin with, there is the realistic awareness of how one looks, how one comes across to others, what one's competencies are, and what form one's vulnerabilities take. All these together form a layered set of images of the self that are collectively called the self-concept. For the normal child, this tends to be both rather concrete and fairly accurate.

Formation of the Ego Ideal

In a different area of mind, where the superego is solidifying, there seems to be quite a distinct set of functions that collectively form a contrasting organization. This organization involves an inner core of specialness and grandiosity that almost everyone harbors to some extent; in the heart of hearts, everyone sees him- or herself as unique, meritorious, deserving of more recognition than has so far come his way, capable of yet greater attainments than have so far been her lot, and yearning for more praise and recognition then are normally forthcoming from the usually rather grudging environment. For most youngsters this comes down to an inner sense of a perfected self, an ideal of self that is enshrined as part of the conscience somewhere in the inner recesses of human awareness. What we deal with here is the residuum of all the unresolved yearnings and wishes of earlier years, all the specialness awarded by loving parents, all the wished-for recognitions and capacities created by a fertile childhood imagination. It is an image of the self that has been glorified and idealized; it makes sense then to designate it as the ego ideal.

The realistic self-concept stands in a kind of tense equilibrium with this ego ideal; the ideal component offers a prompting and a press toward achieving a level of competence, attainment, romantic attractiveness, interpersonal grace, social importance, and overall status that the self usually never attains but toward which it always strives.

The characteristic outcome of the tension between these two elements of mind makes for the state of affairs we call self-esteem, the subjective experience of feeling good about oneself (if self-esteem is high) or feeling bad (if it is low). The distance experienced between the ego ideal and the self-concept is the index that measures self-esteem; if the individual feels he or she is not anywhere near to living up to the ideal, self-esteem plummets. If, on the other hand, a person has come very close to behaving as the ego ideal postulates he or she should behave, then the inner feeling is the warm glow of meeting his or her ideals, a sense of satisfaction that, in its more extreme form, can become a feeling of elation. The maintenance of a good feeling about the self is thus very much a function of how the gap between one's self-representation and one's ego ideal is managed.

Idealized Object Representations

A somewhat similar set of factors holds true for our view of significant others in our social world. On the one hand, we can make realistic estimates and judgments about the people about us. We see them, we interact with them, and we form inner images of who they are and what they are like. This inner picture comprises the real object representation. Alongside this is the image we form of the significant others as we would wish them to be: beautiful, generous, giving, loving, supportive, exciting, romantic, and interested primarily in us. This view comprises the idealized object representation. (We can observe this idealized representation in particularly vivid form in the way we regard someone with whom we have just fallen in love, or in the adulation young people extend to cult figures, such as rock stars or other entertainers. The loved or venerated one is larger than life, by several orders of magnitude.)

By the same token, when we are hurt by others, we can form very negative images of what they are like. In effect, we devalue them, view them as mean, hostile, malicious, untrustworthy, perhaps even venomous. For us they become as thoroughly wicked and evil as their idealized counterparts are noble and rewarding. If we should happen to be more primitively organized, perhaps with a ready tendency toward paranoia, then the negative images of this kind become demonic in character, totally malign and implacably hostile.

Nor, alas, does the process of devaluation stop there. We can apply it with equal readiness to ourselves. Parallel with our realistic self-representation and our ego ideal, we can (and all too often do) maintain an inner image of the self as no good, filthy, worthless, and meriting only criticism, humiliation, and punishment.

Entry into the Grade-School Years

If we set this array of inner presences up against our model of development, we can study how these elements of mind elaborate during the grade-school years.

For the normal child, the oedipal period is a time when fantasy runs riot (Freud 1905/1953). The little 4- and 5-year-old thinks expansively of ousting one parent and taking over the other—an inherently grandiose notion. Moreover, all these thoughts are taking place at a developmental moment when wish and the magic of word and thought are at their highest pitch in the life cycle. For children of this age, wishing will make it so; it is merely a matter of wishing hard enough, getting the magic right, imagining with enough intensity, playing it out as if it were true—and poof, it will happen.

Part of the work of leaving this epoch behind and moving into the grade-school period is the transmutation from preoperational thinking to the level of concrete operations (Piaget, 1954). This period corresponds to the second of Freud's two principles of mental functioning (Freud, 1911/1958), with an accompanying shift from the pleasure principle to the reality principle. In making this transition, children renounce not only the bodies of the parents as objects of erotic and aggressive thinking, but the whole style of thinking that accompanies this oedipal stance. Now a new relationship to fantasy supervenes. Fantasy is no longer the means for coercing reality to do children's bidding; fantasy now serves as a refuge from reality, a retreat and safe haven, in effect, a means for repairing the damage encountered in the real world. It is a site where children may dream what they wish with no one the wiser. Many grade-school children are great daydreamers, but they are all too aware that such images are merely second-best alternatives to their true business, that of acquiring the skills and competencies requisite for their time of life. This is a complex, multifaceted business. At this moment in development, youngsters must learn to get along with peers, to deal appropriately with nonparental adults, to master the context of school lessons, and to become proficient at the games, sports, crafts, and skills of their age group. Moreover, within their homes, they must become familiar with extended family members, with the intricacies of the familial social hierarchy, and with the religious, cultural, and subcultural practices of their immediate milieu. In addition, both at home and away from home, there are important interpersonal issues to be addressed; they must learn to define and to defend a personal territory, they must encounter and come to terms with the social expectations for their gender-related behavior, and so on. As they begin to deal with these multiple demands, some areas will be more challenging than others, and some areas will all too likely be sites of failure. In the face of the ensuing frustrations, many youngsters cope by making up wished-for scenarios where they reverse their misfortunes. They drift into daydreamy states where fantasies of achievement and success take the place of the frustrations and disappointments. In the daydreams, they achieve startling scores on the same ball field where they recently struck out. The boy enchants the little girl to whom he was attracted but in whose presence he was tongue-tied. The failed scholar knows more than the teacher and dazzles her classmates, and the youngster who couldn't finish his piece at the student recital plays masterfully at the imagined keyboard. The grandiose fantasy serves in some measure as reparative: Instead of failure, the child achieves success; instead of depression, the child experiences an elevation of spirits, an elation.

Such flights are, as a rule, transient states, temporary respites before children pick up the burden and go on.

Despite their transience, however, these fantasies can be curiously intense. Youngsters may walk along the street, barely aware of what goes on about them, making odd noises as they dramatize the various situations they imagine, sometimes calling out sotto voce their defiance or triumph, sometimes changing facial expressions or posture, and all in all swept up to a remarkable degree in the living-out of these dreams. This is often called building castles in the air, since the foundation of the dream rests on nothing more substantial than the wish; but the proportions of what is dreamed—ah, there is a castle indeed, with all of its grandiose pretensions. Within the daydream, little boys think of strength, of daring rescues, of great escapes; little girls may well think of such adventures too, but they are also likely to have additional dreams either of alluring beauty or of motherhood and child care—or both. The degree of overlap and variation is considerable. It is not surprising that what is true of fantasy is also characteristic of play in general. Much of the play of childhood is an attempt to deal with narcissistic issues. It involves combat and trials and contests, wherein good guys and bad guys in one guise or another meet in some critical arena and battle to the death. For a previous generation it was cowboys and Indians on the Western plains; currently it may be intergalactic warfare with Darth Vader as the dreaded foe. Little girls may have similar play sequences and may, in addition, win oedipal battles, have their own babies, trade places with teacher and conduct school, or otherwise achieve triumphs and experience glory. The fact that it is all in play gives permission for the expression of themes of grandiosity that could not otherwise be accepted either by the people around the child or the child him- or herself. The outcome of some of this work is the creation of a set of idealized versions of the self that maintains a dynamic equilibrium with the real self. These versions emerge alongside the sense of self as children realistically know themselves to be. Under optimal circumstances there is not too great a gap between the images created by these two functions of mind. Under more unfortunate circumstances, there may be yet a third element present, a sense of self as troubled and troublesome, as unlovable and worthless, even as horrid and disgusting. This is a departure from the norm, and we note it only to include it among the potential factors that may be at work in a given child's inner organization.

In parallel fashion, children will have similar images of the important people in their social world. The parents may be idealized and often are: My pop can lick your pop; my mom is the most beautiful lady in the whole world; no one could be sweeter than Grandma. Alternatively, a child may fall in love with another child, and that object of first-grade love may then become transfigured in the lover's eyes. The mechanism for idealizing the other is already established; it now becomes a question of whom will be selected, under what conditions, and for how long. Sometimes the idealizations are fleeting businesses, ephemeral, transient, lasting a few days to a few weeks. In other cases, the process is deep-rooted and prolonged, especially in cases where a child has known a good deal of deprivation and where the idealized fantasy serves powerful ameliorative and defensive purposes.

The associated process of forming a negative inner image is less well understood, in part because the associated phenomena are typically unconscious. But the fact that debased and devalued images are formed, both of self and of significant others, has played a major role in various theoretical approaches. Kernberg's formulation, for example (1976), has amounted to saying that the demonized self and the demonized other are expelled from the self by means of projection and externalization; the child is thus left with only the vainglorious idealized self and object representations retained as parts of the self. Because of the warping effects of development, these components of self lose their discreteness and become inextricably fused with one another. The result is enormous self-centerdness and self-aggrandizement; in short, the formation of a grandiose self.

Idealization and Conscience Formation

In the normal child, however, these several elements retain their discreteness. The realistic awareness of self and the reality of others; the idealized self and the idealized other; each has its niche. The child's conscience functions in a normal way: The ego ideal is operational but does not place immoderate or impossible demands on the self, and a punitive conscience is present but is not so primitive and sadistic as to maintain a constant need for suffering and expiation. The primary issue for children then becomes a matter of living each day with some awareness of how close they have come to living up to their ideal or how far they have departed from that preferred state.

To be sure, healthy children may well suffer an occasional lapse in comportment, but conscience will take over, and often enough the children will confess their misdeed or act in some way to expiate the wrongdoing (apologize, ask for forgiveness, accept or even prescribe a suitable punishment, or agree to pay some sort of indemnity). Living up to their ideal means a great deal to such children, and maintaining their self-esteem depends on acting in acceptable fashion. This system functions as a major regulator of behavior, and it is further reinforced by the threat of a bad conscience if the children continue to misbehave. For normal children this is a potent set of inner controls. Hence, normal narcissism acts as a powerful regulating force in children's lives.

Beyond that, however, the ego ideal in particular shapes many of the children's aspirations, the choice of models, the setting of goals for the self, the kind and degree of dedication to work, and the efforts expended to win the positive regard of significant authority figures. The common phrase "My dad (or mom) would kill me if I did that" bespeaks less a fear of destruction than a sense of the boundary between the acceptable and the unacceptable and an awareness of the painful consequences of embarking on a dubious course of behavior. What children often mean by such a statement is that they would be in big trouble within themselves if they were to depart from their ideal to that extent. Even the anticipated unhappiness of their parent(s) might be felt more keenly in terms of the inner sense of having disappointed these idealized figures. In brief, it is the combination of guilt, shame, and the bite of anticipated low self-esteem that the children turn to in order to help resist temptation.

On the other hand, the dreams of glory that can figure so largely in the lives of all children are derived directly from the ego ideal and can act as remarkable motivators toward exemplary performance. In particular, where children manifest some talent, unusual IQ, innate grasp of mathematics, gift for performing on some musical instrument, unusual ability in athletics, precocious coordination in the enactment of gymnastic feats or the execution of demanding ballet routines, the dreams of mastery and achievement that then ensue (aided and abetted, one may be sure, by parental encouragement) can become powerful shaping forces in youngsters' lives. It is because of this narcissistic drivenness that these children can so dedicate themselves to long hours of grueling practice and, in effect, total life commitment. The ego ideal elements have received enormous reinforcement by the combination of the children's awareness of their ability and the environment's designation of the children as special. Where the narcissism is too great, children will become excessively demanding, will be unable to tolerate any frustration, and the effort will fall. But for essentially normal children, there is enough healthy ego ideal and functioning conscience to make for a pattern of great and serious effort, sometimes

with extraordinary results. Many great artists have begun their careers in just this fashion.

Conclusion

In brief, normal narcissism has many gifts to offer children. It is a major factor in behavioral self-regulation and helps maintain the everyday self-esteem (or, more simply, happiness) of children. It plays a role in helping children set goals and formulate aspirations for their lives and futures. And it acts as cushion and preserver of self-confidence in the face of adversity. There is a reparative quality to many of the daydreams of childhood; when life is stressful and depriving, they can be a refuge and preserve. Like so many elements of mind, these factors can be either helpful and rewarding or problematic and disruptive depending on context and quantity. When not excessive, and when set within a basically healthy personality organization, narcissism can be a source of major constructive potential for children's further development.

REFERENCES

Bleiberg, E. (1984). Narcissistic disorders in children. *Bulletin of the Menninger Clinic, 48* (6), 501–517.

Freud, S. (1958). Formulation on the two principles of mental functioning. In J. Strachey (Ed. and Trans.), *The standard edition of the complete psychological works of Sigmund Freud* (hereafter *Standard edition*) (Vol. 12, pp. 213–226). London: Hogarth Press. (Originally published 1911.)

Freud, S. (1953). Three essays on the theory of sexuality. In *Standard edition* (Vol. 7, pp. 3–122). (Originally published 1905).

Kernberg, O. (1976). *Borderline conditions and pathological narcissism.* New York: Jason Aronson.

Kernberg, P. (1989). Narcissistic personality disorders in childhood. *Psychiatric Clinics of North America, 12* (3), 671–694.

Piaget, J. (1954). *The construction of reality in the child.* New York: Basic Books.

Rinsley, D. B. (1988). A review of the pathogenesis of borderline and narcissistic personality disorders. *Adolescent Psychiatry, 15,* 387–406.

6 / Identity Issues in the Grade-School Years

Joseph D. Noshpitz

It was Erik Erikson who first called attention to the importance of identity as a factor in personality development. His seminal studies appeared in his landmark book, *Childhood and Society* (1950), in a chapter entitled "The Eight Ages of Man." The focus of the material was to give illustration and substance to the notion that identity elaborated in a characteristic way through the stages of psychosexual development. As the chapter proceeded, Erikson used the term *identity* in a number of different ways. (I studied the original article and came up with 16 different formulations that appear throughout the text.) Essentially, however, Erikson indicated that the term was a summation of all the work of the separate Freudian stages—oral, anal, phallic-oedipal, latency, and puberty—as these expressed themselves in relationship to children's interaction with their social world (Freud, 1905/1953).

Thus, basic trust vs. mistrust speaks of the infants' outlook on their human environment. This outlook is the final summation of a host of interactions among oral yearnings, needs for fusion, and early attempts at autonomy on the one hand, with caregiver availability, empathy, consistency, and responsiveness on the other. When all these have played their role and been lived out in interaction, children are left with a particular outlook, the final product of the interplay of these processes. The same holds true for all the succeeding stages. When we come to the grade-school years, the outcome is summarized as industry vs. inferiority. That is to say, Erikson conceived of this epoch as the time when children learn to cope with the immediacies of reality, to study, to learn, to work, to acquire technical know-how, to master the elements of the social graces, to participate in rites and rituals, and to emerge at the end with a feeling of competence and confidence. Or, contrariwise, they learn to experience themselves as failures and to take on a sense of inferiority as their identity position for that time in their lives.

It is important at the outset to recognize the composite nature of identity. There is first the matter of what it is composed and then the associated issue of how it functions. For our purposes, identity is not a static presence within the organization of human personality. It consists rather of a large number of elements, all pursuing their own developmental course and capable of adaptive change in the face of altered circumstances. Moreover, each serves a myriad of functions that require much adjustment and sometimes delicate attunement to the varying contexts of everyday life.

In terms of its composition, identity can be likened to a spiral staircase winding around a central pillar. Each tread of the staircase is unique and represents a different aspect of identity, but each also overlaps and interdigitates with all the others at the centerpost. It is this central realm of overlap that forms the core sense of self. Thus, a given child may belong to a family with a certain stated characteristic (all us Joneses have bad tempers, no Jones woman has ever had a stain on her honor, or all the men in our family enter law, or the military, or whatever), and this comprises one tread on the stair.

Children also may know themselves to be members of a certain race, ethnic group, religion, occupational determinant (army brat, minister's kid), socioeconomic class (wealthy or welfare), nation, culture, and subculture—each in turn a tread on the staircase, and each a vital part of the self. If some other children, or neighbor, or teacher, disparages one's family, one's nation, one's race, or one's faith, the sense of wounding and the reaction (whether experienced as internalized pain or expressed as externalized action) are likely to be intense.

Moreover, each of these elements of identity has a history. It has persisted through time, it has evolved, and it has taken on additional force and accrued additional meanings by the waves of successive experiences that have left their mark on the children. Thus, repeated Seders, or a confluence of memories about Christmases past, or suffusions with nostalgic familiarity arising from other ethnic observances, will serve over time to heighten and intensify this aspect of identity organization. The children see themselves as profoundly linked to the past and, at the same time, as part of a larger cultural (or professional, or political, or national, or intellectual, etc.) advance.

In many ways, identity serves as a prime source of group affiliation. It is the impress of group values as they are taken in by the individual, and it is the expression of group attachment in the way people think of themselves.

But these social dimensions do not exhaust the content of the layers of who-ness. Children have identity as children, babies, or junior adults (as we see all too often in parentified children). Within the family, a child is the oldest or the youngest, or the only or the middle child. They have identity as the member of a given gender, with all the variations that that implies (from sissy boy to macho jock, from prissy princess to hoyden tomboy). (Note that this is quite different from object choice. There is a subgroup of homosexual men who pride themselves on their masculinity. Indeed, they value it to such an extent that they can only love someone who is masculine. Thus, the object choice is homosexual, but the identity is strongly masculine.) Nor do these exhaust the list. Within the classroom or the playground there are subordinate images of self: teacher's favorite, class entertainer, troublemaker, outsider, regular boy or girl, oddball or weirdo, stupid, nerd. These are not merely social roles or assigned statuses; what concerns us here are inner images of self (evoked, to be sure, by specific social contexts) that interweave with the many other identity positions we have noted.

Thus anatomically, so to speak, children's identity is a composite of the many internalized designations that have emerged in the course of development and that together contribute to the formal quality of the sense of self. Much of what will constitute awareness of identity has to be discovered through social experience. The arrival of a new baby in the family will challenge the existing identity organization of all the children in that family, but particularly of the youngest (the current "baby"). Sometimes a crisis in identity will occur, and we have the familiar picture of regression with the coming of the newborn. Obviously far more is involved here than merely identity, yet, among the other dimensions of necessary reorga-

nization, this too will have to undergo radical transformation.

Each of these identity dimensions tends to persist over time. Each is an enduring structure, always in flux to be sure, but with a stable core of coherence that seeks to preserve its outlines in the face of stress. The flux is usually confined to the surface. For example, within a given schoolyard, under certain circumstances the domineering bully may become a cringing coward; shifts and changes in the face of perceived adaptive needs are almost constant. But that same bully/coward does not alter his or her particular ethnic, religious, familial, gender, or socioeconomic self-reference in the face of threat. And when circumstances permit, the bully will be there again in full force. In the course of a schoolyard confrontation, he or she may well undergo an identity crisis of sorts and may even stop much of the bullying. But most of his or her identity organization will remain intact.

The general principle that seems to hold is that each continuous or recurring significant context in children's lives will lead to the formation of an adaptive identity structure. (For any given child, riding up in an elevator with strangers may be a recurring context, but probably not a significant one.) Children are not merely in a situation or a part of one; within that setting and in response to its requirements, they become a particular someone. They feel a certain way about themselves (I am most at home in the library; I come into my own on the playing field; I feel unwanted at home), and they respond in keeping with the social expectations of the milieu (to oppose or challenge it, to seek to ingratiate oneself with it, to play innocent while seeking to subvert it, etc.). Clearly there is at once an inner and an outer face to identity; it is a consequence of work on both interfaces. Indeed, the most economic way of defining it is to regard it as the outcome of the work of an identity function, a superordinate part of the self that scans at once the inner templates, for how a boy or girl, an Irishman, a Jones, should act, and the outer ones—what the reality threats, requirements, and rewards of the environment may be—and finds a way to weave all this information together in order to be a certain kind of person. The outcome of such identity work is at once to shore up and further define who children are.

We may try to narrow down the likely environments of childhood to a few primary sites—home, school, and neighborhood—but, in fact, each of these has multiple aspects, and identity organization will dictate a differential response in the face of each specific context. Thus, a boy with strong oedipal yearnings directed toward mother may show a very different face—and feel a very different person—when he is alone in the house with her, or when his hated stepfather/rival is present. The girl who has been sexually abused may feel herself to be, and may actually behave, as a very different person when the abusive parent is present or absent. One of her inner templates, one of the treads on the great identity helix, may be the self-as-victim, and every time this is evoked, she becomes freighted with the old and all-too-familiar sense of shame, anger, and helplessness. Depending on her temperament and on the social nexus within which she is situated, she might then attack, dissociate, or withdraw.

Identity Work

With this as prelude, let us consider the identity work during the grade-school years. The same identity formations that give strength and definition to children's sense of self often are enough sites of vulnerability as well. Thus membership within a race, class, nationality, or religion can all expose youngsters to challenge. Indeed, any or several of these factors can be used as powerful instruments for teasing and humiliating given children. Gender issues are ready sources of attack. To begin with, generations of older sisters have sung to younger brothers the "What Are Little Boys Made Of?" song, much to the discomfiture of the boys. Nor are grade-school boys any kinder with their female peers. Beyond that, let a boy give any hint of effeminacy, and there are always some youngsters in the schoolyard who will shift into feeding frenzy. Any sort of physical impairment will evoke similar reactions from many peers. Even more provocative is the suggestion of intellectual or emotional difficulty; there are any number of derogatory terms for children who attend the "slow" class or the special ed program. Indeed, it is the very multiplicity of mosaic bits that make up identity which allows for the multi-

tude of points of possible attack. In brief, one of the great shaping forces that act on identity during the grade-school years is the inevitable assault that at least some identity elements will undergo as part of universal experience.

The interplay between syndromes and identity is inherently complex and occurs at many sites. Children with attention deficit hyperactivity disorder, for example, are constantly running after their sense of self, unable to keep up with it as their driven motoric patterns and constantly shifting attention draw them ever this way and that, from one beckoning, distracting element in the environment to another. For such children, the necessary scanning of the internal and external milieu that shape one another and must be woven together to develop a sense of who-ness is in itself uneven and disjointed. The ensuing sense of who one is is accordingly shifting and fragmented. This stands in contrast to the identity of depressed children whose inner sense of badness permeates all the other layers of their identity organization and makes them see the world in dismal, defeated terms. An eerie stability is likely to pervade the full roster of identity elements, and, as a result, such children can become frozen, immobilized, and static.

In contrast to these troubled states, for healthy children, their array of social roles is informed by the inner sense of worth and worthwhileness that arises from the cluster of historical experiences in the several domains of self. They may regard themselves better on the playing field than in class, or they may be more comfortable at home with dolls than out on field trips, but there is an adequate sense of fitting in in all these contexts, and things work.

Although many identity elements are conscious, some are unconscious. There are treads on the spiral that become repressed and are thus out of awareness, albeit nonetheless functional for all that. Thus, a sense of self as victim of some early abuse experience may not be available as conscious memory but may act to lend a quality of taint to the self-experience. A forgotten early rejection or abandonment may give rise to an enduring feeling of unloveability that clings to the sense of selfhood and identity. One of the well-documented techniques for adaptation in cases with a history of incestuous sexual abuse of a female child by her father is for the little girl to dissociate.

If the abuse persists over several years and is repeated a number of times a week, ultimately the child will have had to deal with literally hundreds of encounters. Some of these children find a way to split off a different, partial self from the person involved in the activity; they elaborate a fantasy that they have become someone else. Paradoxically, such a girl preserves herself by fragmenting herself. This mode of coping may then become her preferred adaptive style, and, depending on other developmental events, later she may appear as a borderline personality disorder with a shifting, unstable sense of self, or as a multiple personality disorder with a wide variety of independent selves.

In the more normal developmental sequence, group experience will have a great deal of influence on the emerging forms of self. Early in the grade-school years, the pretend style of play so characteristic of the oedipal period may still prevail. Thus, a common form of group play for first and second graders is for one child to assume the role of monster and then to make wide, lumbering strides in pursuit of the others, who flee in mock terror (Thorne, 1985). (This probably continues the theme of the encounter with the primitive superego that gave the 4-year-old nightmares.) As children grow, this kind of fantasy orientation tends to fade out and to be replaced by more realistic games, such as tag and formally structured sports. The identity roles of monster and victim then are replaced (although not necessarily erased) by the many varieties of peer-participant status. In more general terms, as identity forms over time, it is initially a series of discrete images evoked by transient but significant experiences. One carries the ring at the wedding; one has the best costume; one is Mommy's or Daddy's favorite; one is a big boy or a pretty girl. Gradually these floating islands of self-definition come together and form a continent, experienced in part as self-representation. And then, particularly in the face of challenges, an ever deeper awareness of who one is begins to form within the psyche, so that the initial collection of transient glimpses of different aspects of self gives way to an enduring and continuous state of fully formed identity. While this may allow for a great deal of flexible adaptability in children's management of everyday encounters, a firm core of self, rooted in the past and connected with an image of the future toward which they strive, is retained.

Summary

Each new developmental experience offers a spectrum of novel identity postures that may be experimented with and adopted or discarded as seems best. Entrance into school, into Boy Scouts, or Camp Fire girls, into church groups, into neighborhood gangs: Each offers its threats and its opportunities, and each will give rise to its own adaptive identity work. Ultimately children will not be any one of the images that comprise the elements of their helix; instead, they will be their summation, their composite, or, in a certain sense, their resultant. As these layerings of experience superimpose and intermingle, they add up to an organizational set that takes ever more specific form. Children feel this subjectively as knowing who they are; others perceived it as a person's "personality." This identity elaborates with advancing development and eventually plays a vital role in the organization of character, in human adjustment, and in human happiness.

REFERENCES

Erikson, E. (1950). *Childhood and society.* New York: W. W. Norton.

Freud, S. (1953). Three essays on the theory of sexuality. In J. Strachey (Ed. and Trans.), *The standard edition of the complete psychological works of Sigmund Freud* (Vol. 7, pp. 3–122). (Originally published 1905.)

Thorne, B. (1985). Boys and girls together . . . but mostly apart: Gender arrangements in elementary schools. In W. W. Hartup & Z. Rubin (Eds.), *Relationships and development* (pp. 167–184). Hillsdale, NJ: Erlbaum.

7 / Fantasy Heroes and Superheroes

Joseph D. Noshpitz

Our culture is rich in powerful figures to serve as models, inspirations, and objects of identification for youngsters. There are, to begin with, certain perennial favorites, classical images, that the culture carries forward. Specifically, parental recollections, the school system, the comic book publishers, the many authors, past and present, who write children's books, and the makers of movies and videos support one another and continue to keep these presences alive. Currently, for example, a Robin Hood series is appearing on TV. It comes in the wake of the new, recently released movie version of Robin Hood. There have been any number of Robin Hoods in the past, and there probably will be others in the future. This keen-eyed shooter of phallic arrows lives with his peer group in the woods and regularly confronts the parental authority of the Nottingham police force; he thus has a great many things going for him that obviously contribute to his continued appeal.

An earlier exemplar of nobility and chivalry, King Arthur and his Round Table is still in the running, although he does not seem to be doing as well. Yet another perennial favorite is Tarzan. He too lives in the woods, although his peer group consists largely of anthropoid apes. Notwithstanding, however, the peer group is present, and its function is preserved. There are evidently many such figures, some of them curious blends of fantasy and reality. For certain girls, the American Indian holds a peculiar fascination. The notion of living close to nature, making one's own habitat, riding horseback everywhere are inviting images and, where physical circumstances allowed, youngsters could live them out in some detail.

The superhero falls into quite a different category of fantasy. Here the conceptualization is less real and more infantile; accordingly it is at once more expansionary and capable of even greater distortion. The ensuing images are usually a picture of the primitive superego aborning. Here there is perennial battle, good fights forever against evil, and the story never ends; there is always another chapter. The figures involved are often quite inhuman: superrobots, cyborgs, or androids, all sorts of weddings of flesh and mechanism (as youngsters sense their capacity to think and feel changing within). The evil ones are an equally varied array of monsters. The characteristics of both sides are their extraordinary (magical) powers: forcefields, ray guns, tractor beams, heat rays, freezers, lasers, powers to change form or read minds, or hurl objects by mental force alone; the ability to transfix or to penetrate with a look; the capacity to fly through the air at will. All the fantasies of the pregenital and phallic child, now in more dressed-up versions to be sure, more sophisticated, better described, but filled with the same fiery malevolence of sadistic fantasy, the same transcendent sweep of phallic grandiosity, and the same primitive morality of early conscience structures, are in place and give their characters a powerful allure to the young mind. For the earlier grade-school group in particular, the role of emotion is a key agent in the invoking of magic. The yearning for a change to take place in response to one's feelings—does one's heart skip a beat when an exciting other passes by? Oh, to become something great, impressive, remarkable, at that very moment. In the actual situation, one stands riveted to earth, but within, ah, how fantasy soars! When the emotion is rage, how much one might wish to become a puissant, all-powerful figure who sweeps all before him or her. The culture was not slow in responding to these yearnings. Television, that most malleable and responsive of media, spawned a host of embodiments of this set of wishes. One of the most illustrative figures that was a longtime popular favorite with the younger set was the Hulk. The hero was a very average young man who carried within him a special germ of change. In the course of the stories he would encounter stresses that provoked fear and rage. At this point a change would come over him and, in a trice, he would grow a head taller, huge muscles would balloon out all over his body, bursting out of his clothes, his face would transform into a Gorgon mask of ferocity, and his

44

skin would turn green. He was now deus ex machina, a new entity, the Hulk, savage, uncontrollable, and irresistible—and he would proceed to undo the bad guys, thwart their evil designs, and make everything come right. The younger grade schoolers loved this; it matched their wishes exactly.

Parallel with this was the appearance of a set of toys called Transformers to which many of these grade-school children became very attached. These playthings would be innocent-looking cars, trucks, buses, or even articles of furniture, which, with the rotation and manipulation of their parts, turned into heavily armed futuristic robots with a host of superweapons to turn loose on enemy forces. Such a transformation had been adumbrated by Superman (who changed from bumbling Clark Kent to the soaring superbeing he was), by Captain Marvel (who had but to say "Shazam" to effect the necessary alterations), and by Wonder Woman (who spun around as the trigger for her transfiguration). Now, instead of merely watching the change from a plebeian figure to a heroic one, the child had a world of change at his or her fingertips; the little Transformer toy became an overt expression of the wish. It allowed for the sudden acquisition of enormous powers or, more exactly, for the sudden revelation of powers that had always been present but that had heretofore been concealed.

Thus far we have addressed the images of superstrength or superpowers. Both boys and girls play with these transforming toys. But there exist toys that are closer to the immediate realities of the child, and for these toys there often is a good deal of difference between the interests of the sexes. Thus that perennial favorite, the Barbie doll, is largely the plaything of younger girls. By and large, the boys who prefer such items as their playthings are likely to be regarded askance by their communities and to be considered effeminate. For little girls, however, Barbie becomes a site for the wreathing of considerable swaths of fantasy. Whether it be dress-up play or any sort of body ornament or adornment (hairdos, jewelry, sports outfits, or elaborate costumes), Barbie is there to allow one's dreams to come true. Through the figurine, an endless panoply of domestic and romantic issues get relived and reenacted. Glorious erotic fantasies can be realized, conquests achieved, sinners converted to virtue, and every manner of wish fulfillment attained. For several generations of American women, one Barbie doll or several (Barbie plus her male counterpart, Ken, and several girlfriends) have been an essential element in their growing up. For more maternal girls, the Cabbage Patch Doll has served to offer endless diversion and satisfaction of all manner of child-caring impulses. A great variety of these rather ugly infant replicas are available (including a preemie), and they have been tenderly nursed, fed, changed, pampered, spanked, sung to, and mused over by literally thousands of little girls. The closest correlate for boys, and for some girls, is probably G.I. Joe. This modern soldier, the archetypical American fighting man, has been armed with everything from standard combat gear to the most futuristic and elaborate laser emplacements. Brave, fearless, intrepid, aggressive, intrusive, powerful, and sweeping all before him, he allows for all kinds of grandiose, warlike play. Endless scenarios of combat and conquest are the child's for the asking. G.I. Joe remains a perennial favorite. For the older latency-age child, the naive fantasies of the prior years often no longer suffice. The nature of the developmental thrust of the time is to move from fantasy solutions to more concrete and practical ways to attain fame and glory. More and more individual proclivities find behavioral expression, and the youngsters begin to strive for achievement in many arenas. They learn athletic skills and seek to excel, and they then turn to the great athletes of the day as model and hero. These figures are evidently quite different from the strictly fantasy images just described. The sports hero may be a television idol, but more than that, he or she is real, human, current, an individual one might see in the ballpark and meet in person—even approach for an autograph. The role of such a figure in development is also rather different. The fantasy superhero is a flight from reality. Once the world is too painful, children take refuge in dreams of glory. It is an enclave of blissful make-believe that allows some respite from the less rewarding, often gritty context of the everyday. Real-life heroes or heroines are something else again. They are figures to emulate, people to be like, guides, poles of attraction for one's efforts. They are models for identification. It is out of recognition of this aspect of development that so much emphasis is placed on the probity of the public figure. The classic appeal addressed to a shamed baseball player by a disillusioned child:

"Say it isn't so!" bears witness to the intensity of the pain youngsters experience as their ideal is shattered. This theme reverberates with particular intensity in the black community, which is today struggling with powerful regressive forces that are affecting its children. Each fall from grace of a black athlete or civic leader is experienced as a blow against the ideals and self-respect of youngsters who are struggling to survive and to grow in the inner cities. The maelstrom of gangs, rackets, and escapist activity sucks down all too many of these vulnerable youngsters, and the powerful model of a respected and successful achiever is perceived as a material presence for the young person to hold onto, something to help him or her resist the tug of the troubled community life.

But it is not only athletes who serve as heroes. More bookish boys and girls might turn to intellectual giants such as Einstein, to master poets of their day or of bygone days, or to creative musicians or performers, as avatars of triumphant achievement. They may dream of meeting these famous people, knowing them, impressing them, or possibly transcending them. Depending on earlier fixations, many residua from earlier stages of development may color the fantasy life of a particular youngster. Thus some deprived children have extraordinary daydreams about food and eating. There is a terrible innocence to these powerful, primitive images. Not infrequently they will spin off thinly disguised stories about being themselves the victims of the oral gorging of some monstrous, hugely fanged entity. Some children fixated at a somewhat later level may be fascinated by torture and dream either of inflicting pain on helpless victims or of being the subject of some torturer's ministrations. Often the significant other is some figure from the movies or from the video images of the day. There is quite an array of such monstrous presences to choose from, including Freddy Krueger and Jason. More anxious children may be tormented by the fears such entities create, especially when a bout of TV watching or attendance at a horror movie has evoked their inner vulnerabilities and given form and immediacy to the imminent but heretofore contained terrors lying in wait in their minds. (Even *The Attack of the Killer Tomatoes*, which was intended as a spoof on horror films, was able to send one 6-year-old patient whom I treated into a year-long bout of anxiety attacks. Evidently the sense of a large soft body pressing down upon its victims and destroying them echoed enough of this child's own experience to evoke an enduring panicky reaction.) Then there are grade-school children who never enter latency at all. They are overstimulated either by seduction or by an unaware pattern of child rearing that exposes them repeatedly to adult nakedness and/or sexual activity. In any case, the majority of such children will not fantasize these events but will seek instead to enact them, much to the detriment of their psychological development as well as to the well-being of their playmates. However, some of these youngsters (probably those with a more internalizing constitutional endowment) maintain their fixations on a strictly fantasy level. Their inner life recapitulates the things that have happened to them as a kind of theme and variations; they are endlessly preoccupied by a sense of eroticism, and they imagine all sorts of adventures involving highly sexualized interactions.

Toward the end of the grade-school years, one of the inevitable emergents is a partial deidealization of the parents. Children now have lived long enough and matured sufficiently to see that the parents are all too human, with the faults and foibles of all human beings. The adults begin to lose some of the sheen that protected them from childhood critique; their several faults are perceived and beginning to be understood; and they are found wanting in a number of critical areas. Children then begin to dream of other parents, their true parents, not like these deficient people whom they live with at home but people of nobler, purer stuff, of more sterling qualities, of greater wealth or importance, people who know the children are theirs and who will someday come to claim them as their own. At that point in the fantasy, youngsters will see themselves driving off in a blaze of glory and leaving behind these pedestrian clods with whom they are now compelled to live.

This is the family romance fantasy made famous by Freud (Freud 1909/1959). Many people can recall this particular image in later years and remember it with a combination of humor and pathos.

In summary, then, early grade-school children are dominated largely by the struggle to finish consolidation of the superego and to shore up the means to contain the oedipal yearnings. Later in this epoch, the interest turns more toward the ego ideal, toward realizing what the ego can do, toward the setting of goals and the achievement of aspirations. Toward the end of the grade-school years, with the family romance, there is a begin- ning thought of separation from the parents, leaving them behind to find a better way of life. And with this foreshadowing of puberty, the grade-school era comes to an end.

REFERENCES

Freud, S. (1959). Family romances. In J. Strachey (Ed. and Trans.), *The Standard edition of the complete psychological works of Sigmund Freud* (Vol. 9, pp. 235–241). London: Hogarth Press. (Originally published 1909.)

8 / Moral Development

Alan S. Weiner

Introduction

OVERVIEW OF CHAPTER

This chapter focuses on moral development in the school-age child. This is an area of importance in its own right; it also serves as a window through which shifts in theoretical conceptualizations in developmental psychology, and social emotional development in particular, can be observed. There are important clinical implications associated with these theoretical perspectives.

Human functioning often has been compartmentalized into three domains: behavior, affect, and thought. Various developmental approaches to the child's moral functioning have taken each of these areas as their central focus. This chapter begins by reviewing the approaches that have emphasized each of these areas. It then considers emerging conceptualizations that seek to describe the interaction between these domains in order to explain moral development more effectively. Developmental change in components of moral functioning that are relevant to all theoretical perspectives also is discussed.

A multimodal approach to therapeutic intervention is proposed for children showing deficits in the various components of moral functioning. Throughout the chapter clinical vignettes are presented to illustrate intervention for moral phenomena best understood from a particular theoretical perspective. The concluding section summarizes and discusses the integration of the components of the multimodal approach.

OVERVIEW OF DEVELOPMENTAL PERSPECTIVES

Cognitive theories of moral development have focused on developmental changes in the child's conceptual understanding of the world. Such theories seek to explain how these conceptual changes serve as the driving force that motivates moral development. This cognitive approach leads to an emphasis on morality as justice, which is examined primarily through developmental change in the child's moral judgment. This area of research is most identified with the work of Piaget (1965) and Kohlberg (1976).

Information-processing approaches to moral development have also highlighted cognitive processes. These models do not focus on the constructionist qualities of the Piaget tradition. Instead, they emphasize the child's increasing awareness of the multiplicity of factors that contribute to a situation and that give it moral bearing. This, in turn, leads to an evaluation of the child's ability to weigh and integrate the relevant factors in the situation in reaching a decision.

Behavioral approaches to moral development had focused on observable aspects of moral behavior, such as conformity to rules and obedience to others. More recent social learning approaches have integrated findings from cognitive development and have increasingly included motivational aspects. The behavioral approach leads practitioners to look at factors that promote moral behavior, such as rewards, punishment, and modeling effects.

The role of affect in moral development has been primarily the focus of psychodynamic and behavioral approaches. The psychodynamic perspective has considered emotions such as shame and guilt arising from the development of superego functioning. Both the psychodynamic and behavioral approaches have carefully considered the role of anxiety in moral behavior. These approaches examine those factors that would enhance or reduce affects that promote or interfere with acceptable moral behavior in order to understand moral growth.

Trends in Theories of Moral Development

While several approaches to moral development have described orderly stage transitions, there has been a continual movement away from painting strict stage boundaries. The picture of moral development that is emerging is one of gradualness, with clear signs of moral functioning seen well before school age, "the age of reason," and with development proceeding through adolescence. Topics that illustrate this trend include the precursors of superego functioning in early childhood, findings that suggest gradual superego development during school age, and the appearance of key components of moral functioning, such as shame, empathy, and the development of standards, in the very young child.

Another trend may be a shifting emphasis from "negative" to "positive" aspects of moral development. That is, increasing research attention has been given to prosocial behaviors, empathy, and perspective taking, rather than negative, antisocial behaviors, or disobedience as exemplars of moral

development. Similarly, there is more of an emphasis on loving, idealizing aspects of the superego rather than punishing, anxiety-evoking components.

Affect has been given a central role in moral development. Increasingly, it is being seen as the essential component in normal moral development and a major component for fostering change in those who show deficits in moral functioning, such as delinquents.

Definitions of Moral Functioning

The concept of internalization is central to several theoretical approaches. Basically, this concept is derived from the observation that children progress from having their behavior controlled by external factors (e.g., the presence or absence of punishing or rewarding others) toward increasing autonomy in functioning. Thus, by school age, children are expected to function in a morally appropriate way (e.g., uphold standards, know right from wrong) in the absence of someone watching over them. That is, appropriate behavior is expected even in the absence of fear of detection. Paradigms to study internalization include assessing factors that promote or hinder children's resistance to deviation, obedience, and delay of gratification. Explanatory mechanisms ranging from self-reward, to modeling, to superego functioning have been posited to account for this internalization process.

More recently, approaches influenced by cognitive developmental and social interactional conceptualizations have taken a different tact. Morality, according to Damon (1988), is not something that had once been external and then becomes internal. Instead it is seen to be something that "arises naturally" out of the child's relationship with others. That is, just as children construct their conceptualization of the world from their actions upon the world, they also can be viewed as constructing a sense of morality derived from interactions with others. Damon expresses moral development as children's changing ideas about right and wrong as they get older, along with their emotional and behavioral responses to these evolving moral concerns. According to Maccoby

(1992), relationships are constructed over time, and socialization emerges from children being allowed to participate and actively interact in close relationships, to become part of a "system of reciprocity" (p. 1013).

Damon (1988, p. 5) has provided descriptions that illustrate the various ways in which moral functioning has been conceptualized. These descriptions can be grouped under three general headings.

MORALITY AS STANDARDS

1. Evaluation of actions and events that distinguish good from bad and outline behaviors that are considered good.
2. A sense of obligation toward shared standards.
3. A commitment to honesty as a norm in interactions with others.

MORALITY AS A CONCERN FOR OTHERS

4. A concern for others' welfare that is not restricted to or constrained by one's own desires.
5. A sense of responsibility for carrying out or implementing one's concern for others, which can include actions such as kindness.
6. A concern for the rights of others, which includes a sense of justice and a belief in fair resolution of conflicts.

MORALITY AS AN EMOTIONAL REACTION

7. Not upholding morality induces upsetting self-judgments and emotional responses. This can include shame, guilt, and contempt.

Morality and Convention

Turiel (1983) has distinguished between moral and conventional functioning. He describes moral behavior as that which is obligatory, generalizes across situations, and is not a function of any specific social rule or the presence of authority. Further, moral rules cannot be changed in any arbitrary way. Examples of the moral domain include physical harm and the welfare of others, the psychological harm of others (e.g., hurting their feelings or calling them names), and behaviors related to fairness and the rights of others (e.g., stealing, destroying other's property, and breaking a promise).

Conventions, unlike morality, are based on a particular social organization. Generally they are less important and have less severe consequences. Examples of convention would include school rules such as not chewing gum, not eating in class, not talking without raising one's hand, not calling the teacher by his or her first name, and customs such as not eating with one's hands.

Young children, certainly by 6 years of age, can distinguish between conventional and moral transgressions (Turiel, 1983). Older children—those well into school age—rate moral transgressions as more serious than conventional ones, while younger children—preschoolers—rate conventional transgressions (e.g., wearing pajamas to school) as more serious than moral transgressions of minor consequence (e.g., stealing a pencil). Further, older children distinguish between conventionality and morality more consistently than do younger children, and, by 10 years of age, they can extend this distinction to unfamiliar as well as familiar settings and employ it with novel as well as familiar issues. Helwig, Hildebrandt, and Turiel (1995) have illustrated how children's ratings of a moral act can be influenced by the context in which the moral act occurs.

The distinction Turiel is making indicates that adults and children may view certain events as being of differing import. Thus, the meaning an adult attaches to a particular convention may not match the degree of import attributed to it by a school-age child. This fact can leave adult and child working at cross-purposes, with the adult viewing the child as less moral, and with the child viewing the adult as arbitrary (i.e., unfair) or silly. As Frank, an extremely intelligent 12-year old, kept complaining, "Why does my father mess up every dinner by yelling at me about the proper way to use a knife and fork?" Frank's father wondered why his son showed such disrespect to elders, as reflected by his table manners, and was concerned that this portended later, more ominous problems that would threaten the social order.

Shweder and Much (1987) have looked at the convention-morality distinction in a variety of cultures. They point out that adults, like Frank's father, describe an objective moral universe and expect their children to uphold the moral order, to care about upholding that order, and to become autonomously functioning moral individuals. Shweder and Much found that culture-specific and universal moral exemplars show an equal rate of acquisition. Since they are learned at the same rate, the processes that account for the learning may be the same. Therefore, while the distinction outlined by Turiel between convention and morality is of theoretical import and of practical value in certain situations, it is significant that the acquisition of the contents of these classes of behaviors may be controlled by the same processes. Accordingly, the principles that are of clinical import will apply to both.

Perspectives on Moral Development

The goal in the following descriptions of several developmental perspectives on the acquisition of moral functioning is to depict the strategies that each has formulated concerning questions of conscience and internalization. First we examine the domains of moral functioning each perspective emphasizes, and then we develop approaches that can be useful for the clinician in evaluating and treating children.

SOCIAL LEARNING PERSPECTIVE

A social learning perspective derives from earlier behavioral theories. The emphasis has been not only on behavioral indices of conscience but also on the application of the principles of learning in order to explain the acquisition of moral functioning. Theoretical progress has involved an increasing recognition of the role of cognitive processes in learning along with the incorporation of this awareness in explaining the child's moral behavior. In addition, there has been an increasing emphasis on the role of affect as a major factor in motivating and reinforcing moral behavior. Topics studied within the social learning tradition follow.

Self-control and Punishment: Aronfreed (1976) has demonstrated the role that punishment can play in the child's resistance to transgression, in the internalization of moral rules, and in suppressing behaviors. Because punishment often is viewed as being ineffective for promoting proso-

cial or moral behaviors, Aronfreed's work is valuable in demonstrating conditions under which punishment is effective. In a typical paradigm studying resistance to transgression, a child might be shown two toys, one attractive, one unattractive. The child is instructed to talk about one of the toys. He or she is not told explicitly which to select but, at the same time, is informed that one of the toys—the more attractive one—is more appropriate for older children and therefore should be avoided. When the child picks the more attractive toy up and tries to talk about it, he or she is immediately told "no" by the experimenter, who repeats that it is "for older children." The examiner then tells the child not to touch the toys and leaves the room. The child's internalization of the expected behavior is then assessed, with his or her delay in touching the toys taken as an index of resistance to the transgression. Experimental control allows the examiner to vary when the punishment is introduced into the behavioral sequence. For example, the child could be told "no" while reaching for the toy, while touching the toy, or while picking it up and talking about it. The consistent finding is that the more immediate the punishment, the greater the suppression of the behavior and the longer the latency to touch the toys. Aronfreed's explanation is that punishment (being told "no") and the withdrawal of candy, which also occurs during the training phase, result in anxiety. This anxiety, in turn, can become associated to the cues that lead up to the punished behavior. Thus, the child can feel anxiety about reaching for the toys or even thinking about doing so. The latter anxiety will be more effective in suppressing the behavior than anxiety associated with behaviors much later in the sequence, such as touching the toy or playing with it. Street signs that state DON'T EVEN THINK OF DOUBLE PARKING HERE, demonstrate the application of these principles to adult behavior.

In addition, it is theorized that *not* receiving punishment is reinforcing because it reduces anxiety. Thus, picking up the less attractive toy will produce cues for the child that he or she is not going to be punished. The avoidance of that punishment becomes reinforcing and increases the likelihood of picking the unattractive toy.

Because it is impossible to punish the child immediately in a consistent fashion, and because of an increasing awareness of the role played by cognitive factors in learning, investigators turned toward an examination of the role of mediational processes, and in particular verbal mediation, in evaluating the effects of punishment on the suppression of behavior. Basically, the finding is that language (i.e., explanations) can be used to bridge the time gap between the child's enactment of the forbidden behavior and the delivery of punishment. That is, the disciplining agent can connect the anxiety of the punishment with the child's intention to do the act by providing reasons that make it clear to the child that this punishment is being delivered because of what was done awhile ago (Cheyne & Walters, 1969). Reasons emphasizing the physical consequences of what the child did are more effective for younger children. Reasons stressing less observable, more internal features, such as empathy and the property rights of others, are more effective with older, school-age children (Pressley, 1979).

Clinically, parents can be taught to incorporate these distinctions into their admonishments. Some parents realize that their guilt-inducing comments are counterproductive (e.g., the mother of a 9-year-old boy who told him that his suicidal comment following a minor problem at school suggested she was an unfit mother and perhaps she was the one who should kill herself); unfortunately, their own learning histories and psychopathology inhibit their formulating alternative responses. These parents can be provided with meaningful explanations of the learning principles that underlie psychological growth in children, which, in turn, can foster the parents to take a less egocentric position. In time, through modeling procedures with the clinician, they can be shown how to focus their response on the child's behavior, remain aware of his or her developmental level, and use reasoning to relate response consequences (e.g., reward, deprivation of privileges) to the child's action as it affects others (e.g., peers, sibling, parent). This helps parents to avoid labeling the child as "bad." It also allows them to develop procedures that naturally promote structure and limits in their child's daily life while maintaining appropriate intergenerational boundaries.

Delay of Gratification: Children's developing ability to employ mediational skills also enhances their ability to be less impulsive and to delay gratification. Mischel and Mischel (1983) have described developmental changes both in the strategies children use to enhance their self-control and in their awareness of these strategies. According

to the Mischels' work, children are able to delay gratification if they let themselves think of other things besides the gratification. While they may have to remind themselves, at times, of what the reward is that they are waiting for, they wait best when they can shift their attention to other things besides the reward itself. These studies point out that preschoolers choose ineffective strategies. For example, they will choose to look at the reward rather than covering it. By third grade, children recognize that covering the reward, not looking at it, and focusing their ideas on the task, rather than thinking about what they are going to do with the reward, makes the waiting easier. By the sixth grade, children know that some kind of abstract ideation is best for enhancing the delay. Some sixth graders also will come up with ideation that represents the reward in a negative way. For example, if they think of what they are waiting for as being disgusting, or if they tell themselves that they really do not want it, then they will find waiting easier. It may be that the preschoolers are not able to take a step back and separate what they want (the toy, the reward, the food) from what will work best to help them delay gratification and actually get what they want at the later time. Mischel and Mischel (1983) suggest that before age 8, the most effective strategies involve forms of self-distraction, for example, the child saying "I'm not going to think about this." It seems that after age 8, the more effective self-instructional strategy is to focus on the task to be done; this will take the child's mind off the hoped-for reward.

The use of these self-control strategies is consistent with the approach taken in cognitive/behavioral approaches to psychotherapy, such as that used for depression with adults as well as with children. The acquisition of self-instructional strategies and self-reward during the school years allows the children to perform socially acceptable behaviors in the absence of an external agent who is watching them, monitoring them, and rewarding or punishing them.

Parents can be taught to use these developmental findings as a basis for instructing their children. An example is a 10-year-old boy with an attention deficit disorder and a borderline level of personality organization. When he wanted something he was unbearably insistent, and he had an overwhelming need to spend immediately whatever money he had. He showed significant improvement in object relations in individual, psychodynamically oriented psychotherapy and was helped by stimulant medication. His parents were taught to replace comments such as "You have to wait; you can't have it now; the stores are closed" with instructions to the child about thinking what he would buy when he can go to the store, varying these self-instructions with others designed to have him think about other issues besides the money. Practice in delaying gratification, followed by praise or tangible rewards, were effectively employed as well.

Modeling: It would be difficult to account for the wide range of behaviors shown by school-children based solely on direct reward and punishment for their actions. Clearly they learn a great deal from observing others, both adults and children. In that connection, social learning theorists have delineated a number of factors that promote or interfere with socially acceptable behaviors derived from observational learning. There have been numerous demonstrations that a child will acquire the behaviors performed by a model. Moreover, the child's actual performance of those behaviors, or an approximation of them, will depend on whether reward or punishment will be forthcoming for copying the model.

A number of characteristics of the model will influence whether the child copies its behavior. For example, nurturant models and, most important, powerful models (those who control or dispense rewards for others) are likely to be imitated.

Regarding moral development, Wolf and Cheyne (1972) showed that children who were exposed to a model who resisted temptation were more likely to resist temptation. Children will acquire high standards for performance and self-reward from a model if they perceive that model as being powerful (Mischel & Grusec, 1966). The consistency between the standards espoused by a model and that model's own behavior is an important determinant of the child copying that model. When the model's standards and behavior are consistent, the child will adopt those standards, even if they are high, stringent ones (Mischel & Liebert, 1966).

THE PSYCHOANALYTIC PERSPECTIVE

The formation of the superego as the basis for conscience has already been described in Chapter 1. The psychoanalytic model focuses in part on the role of anxiety in conscience development.

Unlike the learning model, which ties anxiety to response consequences to the child's behavior, the psychoanalytic model describes how the superego and its attendant anxiety are tied to specific objects in the child's life.

The course of superego formation and the resolution of the oedipal situation lead to the development of a more impersonal, less object-tied superego. In school-age children, the movement away from the family toward peer groups will have a bearing on superego functioning and developing objects relations. However, as Holder (1982) notes, children do not renounce real relations in the formation of the superego. Instead, children are relinquishing a fantasy of being one parent's sexual object by taking the place of the other parent. This emphasis on fantasy distinguishes the psychodynamic approach as a theory that deals with the mental life of the individual. On a practical level, it can be useful to help some parents appreciate the distinction between their child's fantasy life and behavior, without describing the content of the child's fantasy. For example, parents who have some popular knowledge of psychodynamic theory may pridefully see their child enacting oedipal behavior and unconsciously encourage it (e.g., let their child sleep in or by their bed when frightened; act seductively while intellectualizing the mature way in which their child discusses sexuality) can be helped to appreciate the importance of letting the child's fantasy remain with the child while the parent's role is to focus on the child's overt behaviors and expressed feelings.

Ritvo and Solnit (1960) characterized superego formation as the end result of a developmental process in which externally imposed prohibitions come to be expressed by the internal representation of the individuals with whom those prohibitions had been associated. This transition may be expressed as a continuum going from initial perceptions, followed by subsequent imitations, followed by identifications in the older school-age child. Ritvo and Solnit indicate that if superego functioning remains at an imitative level, the child will behave as if he or she is still being watched by the mother when the mother is not present. At this level the child will be more likely to ask "Will Mother approve?" than "Do I approve?"

Ritvo and Solnit (1960) suggest that the identification with a nurturing and protective mother will lead to the development of an ego that is protective and a superego that is flexible and adaptive. It is the adaptive, flexible superego that allows the child to move toward the peer group during the school years and to function as someone who is open to new influences rather than being constrained by a rigid adherence to parental admonitions (Sarnoff, 1976). It is of interest that children with a strong moral orientation have parents who show flexibility in choice of disciplinary techniques (Grusec & Goodnow, 1994). Regardless of the explanatory mechanism that is invoked, there is reason to believe then that mature moral behavior, which includes a nonrigid conscience, may be best nurtured by parents who themselves are flexible, who tailor their intervention according to the nature of the child's misdeed.

Sarnoff (1976) emphasizes the advances in ego functioning that identify the well-adapted latency-age child. He describes the use of symbol formation and fantasy formation as being the hallmark of "the structure of latency" (p. 30). Other defenses sometimes seen in the early school years would include a regression to anal sadistic drive organization to defend against oedipal and genital issues. Also seen are obsessive-compulsive defenses (doing/undoing), reaction formation, and sublimation. These include the rituals, counting, and collections of the young schoolchild.

Several writers have distinguished among components of the superego. Holder (1982) distinguishes between the ideal self ("the self I would like to be," p. 251) and the ego ideal ("the self I ought to be," p. 251). The ego ideal develops later than the ideal self and is part of the superego. The ego tries to attain the standards of the ego ideal; there is a sense of fulfillment when this occurs (Milrod, 1990). The child's fantasy life begins to take precedence such that living up to the ego ideal and getting its approval can be more important than the actual praise or disapproval of parents.

The ego ideal provides the standards against which the child's wishes, fantasies, impulses, and behaviors are measured. Failure to live up to the standards of the ego ideal promote feelings of inferiority that are derived from the loss of love of the superego (Schafer, 1960). Failure also produces feelings of guilt and superego anxiety (Milrod, 1990), and the guilt corresponds to the superego's feelings of hatred (Schafer, 1960). Guilt may provide a signal anxiety, and in this way the superego can guide and protect the ego (Schafer, 1960).

Milrod (1990) suggests that shame is engendered by not measuring up to expectations of peers and is associated with social anxiety. Shame also reflects the individual's sense of him- or herself as being weak, defective, dirty (Gilman, 1990). There is also an empathic component to guilt in that it implies an action as part of a relationship in which the other person feels some distress or discomfort (Gilman, 1990).

The superego continues to develop during the school-age years. It is not a finished product when the child enters school nor when the oedipal process is resolved. Indeed, Holder (1982) describes children who experience guilt. They have shown the development of independent, internal standards, implying a well-developed superego, but they also show signs of neither having resolved the oedipal situation nor identifying with parents in a postoedipal style. The persistent oedipal wishes of these children provoke their guilt. Sam's functioning, to be described in the following case example, illustrates this description. Holder's finding may be consistent with Westen's (1986) suggestion that superego components related to conscience formation may have a different line of development than those components related to gender identification.

Sam was an extremely intelligent, verbally sophisticated 9-year-old boy with features of a narcissistic personality disorder. His professionally successful parents were very involved with him and took great pride in his verbal facility and athletic ability. He was precocious and ostensibly knowledgeable about a range of topics, from sexuality to family finances. He would inappropriately ask adults personal questions as if he were their peer. He had a close but different relationship with each parent.

The parents' rivalry for Sam's affection led them to do separate things with him. Thus, the father would fill Sam's weekends with athletic events, which the mother hated. In school, Sam generally did quite well academically, but he had some problems with peers and would act out in class. Sam felt terrible each time he got into trouble in school. His school problems centered around his grandiosity and reactions to others when he thought they were being favored or doing better than he was. His understanding of moral situations was excellent, and, after the fact, he would readily describe what was inappropriate about what he did and could state what he should have done.

A multimodal approach to treatment was employed. Individual psychotherapy for the mother helped the couple improve. Father was hesitant to and/or unavailable for individual or family meetings. Sam's parents were able to make some progress in utilizing behaviorally oriented techniques to establish limits. After initial protests that these parental actions made him feel excluded, Sam increasingly experienced these limits as protective. In once-weekly psychodynamically oriented psychotherapy, Sam tried to dominate the therapist, needing to win every contest. This, however, was not done with hostility. Once he could feel safe and reassured that there would be no retaliation, Sam was able to use fantasy and the symbolic functioning of latency effectively (Sarnoff, 1976). He created stories in which the child always returned from the brink of defeat and injury to defeat the adult. Sam eventually created an ongoing story in which Prince Sam vied with the king and others to see who would be the greatest knight. In one session, Sam inadvertently blurted out that the prince wanted to kill his father, the king. He withdrew from telling the story but later returned to it and included how the prince felt less frightened that the king would destroy him because of his jealousy. (Throughout the many weeks of this story, it was important that the king should not know Sam's intentions.) The prince eventually realized that his time would come to be king and, in the meantime, he and the king could have fun and hunt together. Sam's school behavior greatly improved, he no longer demanded to sit in the therapist's seat, and he began to be less involved in his mother's daily life. His behavior toward peers showed full understanding of their feelings.

THE COGNITIVE DEVELOPMENTAL PERSPECTIVE

The "rediscovery" of Piaget's (1965) work, originally published in 1932, on the moral judgment of the child and the subsequent extensions of this work by Kohlberg (1969) have stimulated a wealth of research and theorizing about the moral judgment of the child. This viewpoint regards moral functioning neither as the effect of external factors such as reward, praise, and punishment nor as the internalization of the agents of discipline and rule givers. Instead, moral development is viewed as an outgrowth of the child's construction of his or her world. It is not that the child is social-

ized by others, but rather, through interaction with others, he or she comes to construct a social order in which moral functioning is a natural and necessary outgrowth. In his work on the development of logic and thought, Piaget describes "conservation" as a necessity, as something that must be true; hence its violations "should not be." In a similar sense, violations of the moral necessity of justice should also not be.

Piaget used a "clinical interview" to study children. In his classic work on moral development, he studied children's play at games such as marbles and asked them about rules, their origins, and their malleability. He also presented children with hypothetical situations and had them make judgments about protagonists in the situation. For example, they were asked to judge who is more blameworthy, a child who breaks many cups while trying to help his or her mother, or one who breaks fewer cups while disobeying the mother?

Piaget (1965) classified the findings into two major phases. The various terms used to characterize these phases reflect a shift in the basis of the child's moral perspective from an objective to a subjective orientation. Thus, the preschool phase has been called "the morality of constraint," which is replaced by the "morality of cooperation" during the grade-school years. Also, the morality of the younger child has been referred to as heteronomous morality and moral realism; it is replaced by autonomous morality and moral relativism in the older child. The following are some of the transitions described by Piaget between the morality of constraint and the morality of cooperation.

1. The younger child views rules as universal and unchangeable, as if they were handed down by divine right or some other sacred authority. The older child views rules as being more flexible, understands that rules can be changed, and recognizes that people in different places may use different rules. Subsequent research (Lickona, 1976) raised the possibility that young children may not distinguish between breaking rules and changing rules. Thus, their beliefs may not be merely a function of a morality of constraint but, instead, reflect too global a conceptualization of rules. The practical implication is to help parents (and teachers) develop ways of involving children in discussions about the formation of rules without relinquishing control to them.

2. The change from objective to subjective responsibility. This may be the most intensely studied area that Piaget developed. Piaget asserts that by around seven years of age, the child begins to judge responsibility and blameworthiness based on an individual's intentions rather than on the objective outcome. For example, the older child would choose as being more blameworthy the child who broke one cup while secretly disobeying his or her mother than the child who broke seven cups while trying to help the mother. The younger child, however, would focus on external, perceptually dominated events and judge as more blameworthy the child who did the greater damage. We look at the research in this area in more detail later. The complexities of the experimental paradigm used to assess objective and subjective concepts of responsibility have attracted theorists with different perspectives.

3. Movement away from the belief in immanent justice. The younger child is more likely to believe that if a child did something wrong punishment is inevitable, and that if something bad happened to the child, it must be because he or she did something wrong and is therefore being punished for it. Certain adults who might be described as having superego pathology hold similar views.

Kohlberg (1984) described stages of moral development that were based on the person's reasoning or justifications for decisions in resolving moral dilemmas. An example would be a situation in which a man's wife is dying. A druggist is the only source of the one drug that might save her. However, the medicine is very expensive; the druggist charges ten times what it cost him to make it. The husband does not have enough money to purchase it. He tries to borrow money. He tells the druggist his wife is dying, asks if he could reduce the price or be paid later. The druggist refuses. The husband gets desperate and steals the drug for his wife. Should he have done that and why? (c.f. Kohlberg, 1976). In this exercise, Kohlberg was less concerned with an individual's particular decision than with the reasoning behind the decision.

Kohlberg classified the obtained responses into six stages grouped according to three major levels. There is support for the "universality" of the first three stages across cultures (Snarey, 1985), and few gender differences in judgment appear before adulthood. However, the final two stages are not applicable to the school-age child, and it would be

very rare indeed to find a school-age child even at the second level in Kohlberg's typology.

The first and second stages comprise Level 1 in Kohlberg's system. The first stage describes a concrete, physicalistic understanding of morality (e.g., you should keep a promise because the other person will beat you up; the father is the boss because he is the biggest; it is better to save many lives rather than a single life because many people have more goods that are more valuable; don't steal the drug because you can get into trouble). The second stage involves a very egoistic orientation; however, it reflects a transition from the emphasis on physical features to a more psychological perspective. The child is basically focused on a tit-for-tat reciprocity (e.g., one should keep a promise because the other person recently did you a favor; you follow a rule if it's in your own interest; it was right to steal the drug because his wife took care of him and cooked for him). The third stage, the first of Level 2 functioning in Kohlberg's system, reflects what he calls "conventional morality." In the third stage, the child actually begins to move beyond relationships based on obligation and shows a greater understanding of mutuality in mature relationships. At this stage, there is value in being good, in living up to expectations (e.g., if you steal [don't steal] the drug, people will think you are a bad [not a good] person). This stage of functioning is more likely to be found in adolescents than in late elementary school-age children.

The stages described by Kohlberg reflect successive forms of reciprocity (Gibbs, 1991) with each doing a more adequate job of integrating the self and other's needs and goals. Most people, child or adult, reason at a predominant stage, and they offer some reasons that are consistent with adjacent stages. Those individuals whose reasoning varies across a few stages, and who offer more reasons above rather than below the predominant stage, may be in transition to the next higher stage (Walker & Taylor, 1991b).

The principles of development described by Piaget that account for cognitive growth are also thought to contribute to the growth of moral reasoning. The Piagetian equilibration model and the concepts of assimilation and accommodation (Piaget, 1952) provide a conceptual underpinning for thinking about moral development. In general, successive cognitive stages are thought to provide more adequate modes of adaptation—more effective ways of handling information and interacting with the world. Similarly, the stages of moral development, especially within Kohlberg's system, are thought to provide increasingly more sophisticated ways of handling the information present in moral dilemmas. In particular, these stages reflect successive forms of reciprocity in which the rights of the self and other are more adequately managed. For example, Gibbs (1987) reports that delinquent children and adolescents are more likely than nondelinquent children to be at the two lowest stages of Kohlberg's system. These lower stages are more self-centered and allow for antisocial behavior. Gibbs (1987) has suggested that the harsh treatment delinquent children have experienced while growing up enhances the likelihood that they will not learn any perspective but their own. Astor (1994) offers another perspective. He presented violent and nonviolent boys and girls from grades 2, 4, and 6 with hypothetical situations that included aggressive and nonaggressive provocations. Astor suggested that both the violent and nonviolent children base their judgments on a reciprocal moral system. However, the violent children focus on the immorality of the provocations while the nonviolent children place greater weight on the immorality of the retribution of hitting back. Thus, nonviolent children distinguish between nonviolent provocations (e.g., stealing, name calling) and violent ones (e.g., hitting). However, the violent children seem to equate these two classes of provocations. Therefore, within this framework, hitting back even when nonviolently provoked represents reciprocal justice. Astor suggests that the violent children's socialization history may have included severe pain caused by both physical and nonphysical provocations. Because no one came to their defense, hitting back is their way of restoring reciprocal justice.

Within the cognitive developmental framework, morality is based on cooperation that expresses the rights and obligations of equals. Change in the child's role in the social order, from someone to whom rules are handed down to becoming someone who participates in the formation of rules, clearly can contribute to change in this area. For young children, rules are imposed by adults and older children. When children enter school, they are more likely to be in positions of increasing social equality where their perspective and that of others are given more equal standing. This is thought to create at least two important outcomes that can promote moral development. First, it will help the children to see that there can be multiple perspectives on a situation. Second, this, in turn, will contribute to a decline in the children's egocentricism; they will move away from focusing on their own position to becoming more cognizant of multiple points of view that will need to be coordinated. Preschool children often tend to confuse the subjective inner experience and objective outer experience. Because of this, moral rules are externalized and treated as immutable. This confusion of subjective and objective experience is seen in other areas of development as well. For example, physical events, such as clouds, can be given psychological features and a child may say that clouds move because they want to. Conversely, psychological events, such as dreams, may be given objective qualities and a young child will express beliefs indicating that dreams are tangible and not just internal creations.

The change from an egocentric position to a more decentered one is reminiscent of other cognitive changes seen during the grade-school years. For example, in the conservation task where the child is asked to judge the amount of liquid in different size containers, one sees a shift from a centration on a single feature (e.g., the height of the container) to a coordination of multiple features (e.g., the height and the width of the container); an understanding of the issues of reciprocity (the relationship between the height and the width of the container); and an understanding of issues such as compensation (how a change in the width of a container can be compensated for by the height of the container and thus the amount of liquid inside does not change). The implication is that procedures which are thought to promote general cognitive development could be modified to foster the development of moral reasoning.

School-age children do not show a consistent level of performance across the different Piagetian cognitive tasks (e.g., Berzonsky, Weiner, & Raphael, 1975). That is, young children cannot be assigned to "being in a stage" with the expectation that all their performance in different situations will reflect only that stage of cognitive development. This is true for the social world as well as for the logical world. Thus, the school-age child's understanding of rules may not be in exact correspondence with his or her understanding of lying or concepts of justice. Changes in the situation (e.g., in the type or amount of harm done by a character in a moral vignettes) will affect the child's level of moral reasoning.

A purely cognitive perspective may not be adequate for describing the factors that facilitate the shift to conventional morality in late childhood and adolescence. For example, Henry (1983) suggests that ego strength allows reasoning to be transferred into action. Thus, she feels an individual's moral stage is not the best predictor of action. Similarly, Haan (1985), studying college students, argues that it is the emotional component of moral social conflict that provides for moral growth. Haan suggests that it is young children's capacity to tolerate conflict with others, not their lack of reciprocity, that lets them manage their tension during an argument; as a result, the argument can be sustained long enough for them to come to recognize each other's perspective. Selman and Yeates (1987) also emphasize affect as being central to the development of the intimacy necessary for progress in the therapeutic dyads they used.

Tom, a highly verbal 9-year-old boy who was quite anxious, with many bodily concerns and grandiose, narcissistic qualities, could readily talk with his mother about the inappropriateness of his behavior, which disrupted and hurt his classmates. In psychotherapy, however, he spoke with great animation and satisfaction about the pleasure he felt when he did such things as hurt his tormentors with the spikes of his soccer shoes. When his friends teased him, his sense of being small and attacked left him feeling overwhelmed, and he attacked first. Ego strength, capacity to tolerate tension, the factors that allowed him to depict normal judgments in controlled settings, became lost in the heat of battle. For Tom, moral growth did not merely involve learning high-level cognitive responses. As he progressed from being somewhat isolated to eagerly seeking friends and being envious of the most popular boy, he first became aware of how his behavior differed from that boy's (e.g., the popular child was less aggressive), but he literally could not understand why his own ag-

gressive behavior would alienate his peers. The oedipal component, that he wishes to destroy his rival rather than emulate him, provided an emotional roadblock to further cognitive and moral growth. In addition, consistent with Astor's (1994) findings, Tom viewed the retribution he meted out as being just because no one was defending him from the unfair attacks of the other children.

SOCIAL CONSTRUCTION PERSPECTIVE

James Youniss (1981, 1987) has written extensively about the child's construction of the social order as a basis of moral development. Youniss describes a perspective that is quite different from the cognitive developmental, psychodynamic, and social learning views.

Youniss rejects the priority given to self-generated moral codes such as those found in Kohlberg's system. He does not believe that individuals deduce moral principles that they then rationally justify, or that moral development is the outcome of a self-reflective process that results in logically correct, elaborate, emotionless justifications. While a system based on reasoning allows the individual a range of choices that he or she can justify by rational discourse, Youniss asserts that a theory which gives a central role to affect, that includes commitment and caring for another, does not allow such choice.

Youniss rejects the psychoanalytic perspective because it represents moral maturity as involving greater distance from its original sources and as being more impersonal. For Youniss, the individual does not outgrow communicative relationships. These are not lower stages to be left behind. Nor does Youniss believe that children learn conformity to convention from adults who control power and who know the social systems that children have yet to learn about. Internalization alone cannot lead to creative, novel, sociomoral behaviors.

Instead, Youniss suggests that individuals in a real moral dilemma try to assess the other's needs and try to find a course of action that ensures their care and well-being. Cooperation, based on mutual respect, has both a cognitive and an affective component. The cognitive aspect includes joint reasoning where ideas can be combined, criticism can take place, and individuals struggle to resolve differences. The affective component involves the felt commitment to helping one another. Together, through reciprocity, which serves as the basis for cooperation, children can discover that they can produce mutually satisfying outcomes.

Consistent with Piaget's viewpoint, Youniss emphasizes that peer interactions in particular help children learn both about caring and commitment and about social systems that can be constructed with others and, therefore, also modified with others. These peer interactions, unlike unilateral adult-child interactions that try to impose an agreement, allow children to become aware of their subjective bias, and do not limit them as causal agents by minimizing their role in co-constructing moral rules.

As children construct their social world in relation to others, they come into contact with multiple viewpoints, which can pose a communications problem. Reciprocal interactions with peers can facilitate the discovery of procedures such as argumentation, discussion, debate, compromise, and negotiation. Utilizing these procedures of discourse can lead to growth in several ways. One way is to help children become more aware of their own view by seeing it reflected by others; another is to make it more apparent that the validity of children's views requires the endorsement of others; yet another is that youngsters must get the support and validation of others in order to attain consensus. This entire process highlights to children their interdependence with others and can provide the motivation to maintain friendships that will guard against developing grandiose, self-deceptive beliefs (Youniss, 1981, 1987).

This perspective can provide a useful way for speculating about the social, interpersonal difficulties of some children in social interactions, such as those with a language disorder or with a learning disability. It may be an error to attribute some children's noncooperation with peers merely to not having learned the rules. Instead, it may make more sense to think of their difficulty as involving identifying when discourse is needed, which aspects of discourse are called for at a particular time, recognizing cues from others (e.g., when to stop an argument and reach resolution), and the like. When viewed from this complex standpoint, the proper intervention by clinician and teachers is not just to tell the child the right

thing to do and reinforce the child, but rather to help the child to learn "the rules of the game" of cooperation, mutuality, and shared feelings.

Development of Discourse: Berkowitz, Oser, and Althof (1987) and Keller and Reuss (1985) have delineated stages or levels in the development of the child's capacity to engage in social discourse during the school years. Berkowitz et al. describe an initial "Pre-argument Level" during which young children do not recognize a need for discourse. They justify themselves only when asked to, and the reasons they offer can be idiosyncratic or irrelevant. Because they have a minimal capacity for perspective taking, they do not see the point in justifying to others what they did. They try to resolve conflict by manipulating others, either physically or verbally. In their arguments they will repeatedly restate their position and goal, and they may change the topic or argument abruptly, offer illogical justifications for what they want, or simply agree or disagree. They try to win by outlasting the other person. Similarly, Keller and Reuss describe the first level of interpersonal moral reasoning, which is seen in children 7 to 9 years of age, as reflecting little consideration of others. At this age the child's limitations include little awareness of the need to obtain everyone's consent in order for discourse to occur and little awareness of the need to justify one's decisions to others. Their own needs and interests predominate, and this suffices for the child as explanation and justification to others.

In the second stage described by Berkowitz et al. (1987), "Simple-Reason Argumentation," children recognize that they have to justify changing someone else's mind but find it difficult to come up with good reasons. Generally, they produce solutions or positions they have always held, and the purpose of their argument is to try to maintain that position. They may merely continue to repeat their argument, change the topic, or rely on their personal experience to show that their solution, which was based on an earlier conviction, is correct. In the third stage, "Maintaining Connections," children try to have some logical coherence among the different justifications they offer, and they try to seek shared solutions and enhance each others' understanding. The children now can provide several arguments for their position, anticipate counterarguments because they are more aware of the weaknesses in their own position, and identify similarities between themselves and others. They are more likely to try to avoid direct confrontation with others.

The second level in the Keller and Reuss system, beginning at about 12 years of age, describes the children feeling obligation toward others with whom they have a relationship. They will consult with others and discuss matters before taking action or making a decision. If they do not do this, they experience guilt. They recognize the need for reciprocity, but they may not be able clearly to balance their own claims and those of someone else. The third level, beginning at 14 years of age, allows for greater balance. These youngsters recognize that when there is a conflict, they must engage in discourse with the goal of reaching a shared agreement. The third and fourth stages in the Berkowitz et al. system, respectively, involve being able to deal with counterevidence and with mutuality in discourse where the goal is to find shared meaning.

In those children who seem to be lagging, the question for the clinician often involves how to facilitate movement through such phases. The clinician can involve him- or herself in working with the school and family, and in enhancing peer interaction. The Stevens family can serve as a case in point. Both parents were hardworking, extremely caring people, whose standards of perfection required that they intervene in many aspects of their children's lives. This included confronting teachers anytime they thought their child was being treated unjustly. They generally felt this way whenever the teacher made any critical comment about their children. They expected that their children would never argue with each other, yet they also recognized that they had difficulty controlling their own tempers when things were not going perfectly. Both of the Stevenses came from homes where their parents and siblings were alcoholic. Mrs. Stevens described how she would intervene when her parents fought, stop the fight, and somehow become the focus of the battle. It was possible to demonstrate to them how they assumed similar roles when their children argued and how they tried to impose solutions on the children in order to keep peace and "have things perfect." This tactic prevented the children from developing and consistently deploying discourse

procedures with each other and peers. Work with the family helped the parents to develop strategies and rules for getting the children to talk to each other and to develop solutions to problems that were mutually acceptable (e.g., how to work out a schedule for getting dressed in the morning in the bedroom they shared). It also helped free the parents from feeling that they had to come up with the "right" solution for the children and that they must be at fault if their children argued.

It is evident from the social construction position that the child's interaction with friends plays a crucial role in sociomoral development. Therefore, it is incumbent upon the clinician to do a careful assessment of the child's relationship with friends and to develop an understanding of factors that may be interfering with those interactions. Interventions can include helping the parents establish situations for the child to have ongoing contact with peers with varying degrees of adult supervision. In this way the child can become increasingly aware of the perspective of other children and his or her own perspective. In short, parents can help provide the settings that increase the likelihood of the development of appropriate discourse strategies.

Friendship and Moral Development: Youniss (1981) and Berndt (1987) have described developmental levels in the interchange between friends that contribute to the development of sociomoral functioning. These levels offer a framework for evaluating the peer interactional component of a child's moral development.

The first stage in friendship, below age 8, is characterized as "Symmetrical Reciprocity" (Youniss, 1981). Here the child tries to maintain a symmetry in the relationship—"I do for you what you do for me." The children may say such things as "Good friends share all the time" yet describe other situations in which they insult or do to their friends just what their friends said or did to them, thereby maintaining a symmetry. The next stage, "Reciprocity of Principle," occurs between ages 9 to 13 years. It is recognized that if they need help and, in fact, are helped by another child, they do not have to reciprocate at that moment. However, it is expected that at some other time they will help the other child in some way. At this level, cooperation involves an understanding that things do not need to be tit-for-tat but that friends are bound by some sort of voluntary cooperation. It is seen as unkind not to do something that would be expected by a friend. The third level described by Youniss (1981) involves mutual understanding. This includes taking turns (a friend is someone who is not always the boss, it is someone who also lets you decide); reversing roles (I'll do for my friend what he did for me if I can); concessions (giving in at alternate times); support (a friend is someone who doesn't tell if you did something wrong); explanation (a friend is someone who talks to you and gives you advice); discussion (a friend is someone who talks to you about problems); mutual reflection (a friend is someone who has had similar experiences so they can help you understand how you feel); mutual respect; and correcting hurt (a friend is someone who would be aware of acts of unkindness and potential threats to the friendship). There is an increasing awareness that verbal apology, ignoring the friends who offended you for a while, and making promises of doing the right thing in the future will remedy breaches in the friendship.

Voluntary cooperation by both children in a friendship working to keep the relationship going serves to enhance mutual respect; by definition, moral maturity is built into the friendship. Kurtines (1987) also suggests looking at the role of conflict, in addition to cooperation, as a factor that can enhance friendship. The conflict can produce new mutual understanding if it is dealt with constructively.

Berndt (1987) describes features of friendship, as contrasted with acquaintance, that can be expected to have a positive impact on sociomoral development. Friends are more connected with one another and become mutually involved in conversation, which also can include a greater degree of fantasy. Friends respond more to each other's request for clarification but less to commands or suggestions. Conversations between friends are more emotionally intense and include more positive and negative affect. Children tend to be less confrontational with nonfriends when trying to reach consensus; with friends, more negative comments can be made. The aroused affect is expected to promote sociomoral development, and these conflicts seem to generate discussion that enhances children's reasoning. Features of discourse that promote greater changes in moral reasoning, such as paraphrasing, clarification, and criticism of the other child's reasoning, are more likely to be present in conversation between friends. The content of the conversation, though, between friends and nonfriends can be quite similar (at least under certain observed conditions).

Parker and Gottman (1989) find that in middle childhood, three-child and large groups become more common, replacing the dyads that were more frequent with younger children. Now play becomes more focused on games with formal rules. In middle childhood there is increased concern about being hurt, rejected, or ridiculed, so children put more effort into sustaining social acceptance. Parker and Gottman also note that friends help children learn behavioral norms and the skills for self-presentation and impression management. This can be especially useful in helping children learn how to make appropriate, acceptable emotional displays.

Damon and Colby (1987) studied sharing and fairness in children. They found that children change more when interacting with peers than with adults. They suggest that with peers, new goals are jointly discovered, whereas with adults, goals are imposed. It is this joint discovery that enhances change.

Intervention by the clinician can include separately helping the child and parents to tolerate the lack of closure present in interaction with friends and demonstrating that there is pleasure for the child working on a process with another child or with a sibling and not having immediate resolution. As the parents can come to function as mediators who encourage and enhance discourse, they can be helped to allow for the discovery of goals and resolution of conflict. This type of intervention also prevents parents from acting as if they are taking sides and, therefore, becoming the joint target of their children's anger and frustration. Parents, especially those whose elementary schoolchild has been having difficulty with peers, also need to understand that it can be normative for their child to have conflict with a friend. Mr. and Mrs. Freed were distraught that their second-grade daughter, who had significant learning disabilities and emotional problems, fought with her friend after a sleepover and one-and-one-half days of positive play. Their child, who had formerly expressed no interest in friends, was recently showing social improvement; hence the parents took this argument to mean that all was lost. Understanding their daughter's argument in the context of what friends do was helpful to them.

The Role of Affect in Moral Development

Martin Hoffman (1983) has been instrumental in drawing attention to the role of affect in moral development. In an attempt to understand the internalization process, he has written extensively about the integration of cognition and affect, with a focus on empathy and guilt. Hoffman has tried to delineate cognitive processes that help the child to abstract affect-cognitive principles and to develop an internal structure in which the controlling adult becomes less salient and empathic distress and associated cognition become the primary motivators for prosocial behavior and moral behavior.

Hoffman (1977) has observed empathy in very young children. As innocent bystanders, children below 2 years of age can feel empathic distress or empathic sympathy for others who are in pain and can act to soothe them. It is this apparently inherent tendency that Hoffman feels is an essential part of moral growth.

Hoffman (1983) suggests a series of steps that incorporate findings from recent research on cognitive development. First, he assumes that the child's affect (guilt and/or empathy) is the most salient component of moral situations. The association of these feelings with the cognitive content of the parent's comments can lead to the development of emotionally charged cognitive structures that the child begins to feel are his or her own. This takes place because the emotion of the situation and perhaps what is said become more significant than the adult who said it, and the adult begins to fade into the background. The source of the comment (e.g., parent, teachers), when the comment was originally made, is superficial and, Hoffman assumes, according to current theorizing about memory, is not processed as deeply and therefore not remembered as well as the more semantically meaningful content and emotion of the moral situation. It is the assimilation over time of these meaningful moments that leads to the development of the affectively charged cognitive structures.

Roberts and Strayer (1996) illustrate the complex processes that may be basic to the development of empathy. They discuss how, with age, emotional expressiveness, insight, and role-taking contribute to the development of empathy, which, in turn, promotes prosocial behavior. They suggest that empathic responses are probably greatest at moderate levels of emotional expressiveness. If children are insightful, they accurately recognize their own emotions and do not deny feelings such as anger. This, in turn, promotes role-taking because self-understanding allows for understanding of others. Children's accurate identification of their feelings implies that others have responded in a positive fashion to their emotional expression. Roberts and Strayer studied children at ages 5, 9, and 13 years of age. Role-taking and empathy increased with age. Expressed anger and emotional insight did not. Increased empathy was associated with children's tendency to clearly experience and accept their emotions, such as sadness, happiness, and fear. These more empathic children also are able to moderate their anger.

Hoffman's attempt to explain internalization is valuable, because certain findings suggest that a simplistic internalization concept cannot work. For example, children who engage in helping behaviors are more likely to do so in subsequent situations if their prosocial responses are noncoerced. It seems that their self-attributions change if the responses are internally motivated, and the children are more likely to be helpful again (Eisenberg, 1987). Fabes, Fultz, Eisenberg, May-Plumlee, and Christopher (1989) studied second, third, fourth, and fifth graders, evaluating the effect of rewards and the parents' attitudes toward tangible rewards on their children's prosocial behaviors. It was found that when rewards were no longer forthcoming, the children engaged in less prosocial behavior. It seems that the children's helpful behavior toward others during a free-choice situation was undermined by previous rewards, especially from those mothers who had positive attitudes about reward. It is as if when the mother relies on rewards, their absence may mean to the child that that behavior is no longer required and, therefore, there is minimal internal motivation to engage in the behavior. The mothers who use rewards reported that their children showed less spontaneous prosocial behavior. Damon (1988) points out that the minimal sufficiency principle may apply to reinforcement effectiveness. That is, it may be necessary to induce enough force or to use enough reward merely to induce the new behavior in the child, but it is important not to make the reward the most salient part of the new behavior.

Cognition and Moral Development

Moral situations have considerable cognitive complexity. Yet the school-age child's cognitive sophistication is also impressive. Here we examine some of the cognitive processes needed for moral development at this epoch, illustrating additional ways in which moral development has been conceptualized and permitting an examination of some factors that can constrain a child's level of moral development.

INTENTIONALITY

The task designed by Piaget, referred to earlier, that evaluated the child's emphasis on outcome versus the intentionality of the story character has been studied in great detail. This task can be quite complex, allowing examiners to vary several factors and examine their impact on the child's judgment. For example, the effect of positive versus negative outcome, large versus small damage, and damage to person versus property can be examined, damage can be held constant and other variables varied.

Costanzo, Coie, Grumet, and Farnhill (1973) studied children in kindergarten and grades 2 and 4. When the stories that were read to the children had positive consequences, in all three grades the children focused on the intention of the story character when rating him or her. When the consequences were negative, the youngest children did not distinguish between story characters who had positive or negative intentions. Elkind and Dabak (1977) also studied children in kindergarten and second and fourth grades. At all ages, when the amount of damage in the story was held constant, the children focused more on intentional rather than unintentional acts when rating

the blameworthiness of the story character. McKechnie (1971) noted that school-age children gave more mature responses when the consequences in the story were small. They seem to learn to evaluate "bad" before "good."

The implication of these studies is that at all ages (i.e., kindergarten through elementary school), children are able to focus on the intentions of the one who acts, although the older children are more likely to do so. However, when intention of story character and the type of consequences covary, and when the children are forced to choose between them when making a judgment, then the younger children generally select damage as being the more salient attribute, with factors such as personal injury being given more weight than property damage. The older children are more likely to remain focused on intention (Elkind & Dabak, 1977). Elkind and Dabak (1977) also noted that when dealing with personal injury, there was a developmental shift, from a focus on pain and how hurt someone was at the kindergarten level, to attributes such as cost and then to abstract humanistic principles for the older children.

The origin of these developmental trends is not clear. It may be that the younger children, in general, focus on more observable, perceptually salient factors such as outcome, while older children are less perceptually dominated and are more able to focus on internal states. This would be true in general, not just in the area of moral growth. Thus, when observable consequences such as damage are minimized, even young children show their capacity to understand and make judgments about intention. When consequences are made more evident, younger children seem drawn to them; only the older children are able to step back and continue to exercise moral judgments based on more abstract, internal principles. Alternatively, we can speculate that these developmental trends in part reflect ways in which children are dealt with. To what extent do children receive negative feedback when they do something wrong, regardless of their intentions? Are parents generally more inconsistent in rewarding good behaviors but more clear and consistent about punishing bad behavior for fear of losing control of the child? If so, it may be harder for younger children to follow the parents' comments in a punishing situation, even if the parents do make some reference to intention. This would imply that learning about intentionality, or at least the exercise of the knowledge of intentionality in certain situations, would take place more slowly for negative events when the child is feeling more fearful and there is higher level of emotional arousal both in the child and the parents. High arousal generally affects attention and restricts the range of cues to which a child can attend. This would leave the child attending to the more dramatic, observable outcome and perhaps, at first, think that intention is less important.

More formal cognitive factors also can have an impact on the child's judgment both in these experimental situations and, probably, in naturally occurring situations. The stories used and the amount of information they contain can be quite complex. Austin, Ruble, and Trabasso (1977) studied children in grades kindergarten through 3. They suggested that developmental differences in memory could contribute to the developmental changes in moral judgment that have been described. To examine this, they had their subjects repeat the story before asking them for any judgments in order to ensure that the youngsters recalled all of its elements. Without such a procedure, children may be more likely to base their judgment on the last part of the story they heard. This would be consistent with general developmental trends in memory—younger children have more difficulty remembering earlier items in a sequence because to do so would require the use of memory strategies such as rehearsal, which become more prominent at mid and late elementary school age. Austin, Ruble, and Trabasso (1977) found that the rehearsal tends to reduce or eliminate the age effects in the use of intentionality.

Berg-Cross (1975) studied first graders. She presented the children stories in which there was either a single character to judge or pairs of characters were pitted against each other for judgment. With single-character stories, the children gave more punishment when damage was high than when it was low, and they were quite capable of using intention when determining punishment. Also with single-character stories, punishment was greater when the story character had malevolent intent. Punishment decreased as the outcome was clearly more accidental, even when the amount of damage was considerable. With paired-character stories, the children focused more on consequence than intention. The character pairs can be considered to be more cognitively complex than single-character stories, and as the situational complexity increases, again the younger child is less able to use the more mature—developmentally advanced—strategy of focusing on intention. Helwig et al. (1995) examined the effect of presenting the moral components (e.g., harmful intentions and consequences) of a situation within a particular social context (e.g., a game). They studied children in grades 1, 3, and 5. The younger children were able to focus on intention in some situations but emphasized consequences when the situation became more complex and required that they coordinate moral and social conventional features. In this study, the evaluative procedure also may have presented a context that constrained the role-taking of the younger children, thereby reducing their emphasis on intentionality.

These findings indicate that the younger children's limitation is not an ignorance of intentionality but rather that certain factors can minimize or mask their ability to use mature moral competencies. In turn, this implies that a function of adults, whether parent, therapist, or teacher, is to try both to minimize those factors that interfere with the child's optimal responses and to create situations that enhance the more mature responses. These responses then can be highlighted in some way. For example, doing so might involve a questioning approach that helps the child to break down a complex social situation into its constituents, which can then be reasoned about.

INFORMATION PROCESSING

Under the rubric of information processing, Darley and Shultz (1990) have reviewed a good deal of the work done in the Piagetian tradition and its extensions. They defined information processing as the information and inference rules that people use in making judgments to reason about case information. Their strategy contrasts with Kohlberg's approach, which asks the subject to rationalize past decisions and requires him or her to have an awareness of the rules being used. Kohlberg's strategy may underestimate the moral reasoning ability of the child, at least as described by the information processing approach.

When the focus is on the principles that school-age children use for making moral judgments (i.e., responsibility, blame, punishment) and the rules they use for reward distribution, a notable level of sophistication is found. Consistent with the conventional/moral distinction made earlier, Darley and Schultz (1990) define a moral rule as one to which adherence is obligatory and that applies to everyone regardless of their attitude.

The rules for making a decision about an action with moral implications can involve the following sequence (Darley & Shultz, 1990). A statement of causality is implicit if a decision is made that someone is to blame. That someone is to blame presupposes moral responsibility. Moral responsibility, in turn, presupposes punishment. Without a judgment of moral responsibility, there is no need to consider blame and, in turn, no need for punishment.

A child or an adult makes a decision about moral responsibility after the joint consideration of causation and excuses. Excuses can include that something was done accidentally (without intention, recklessness, or negligence), involuntarily (under pressure or duress), or without foresight of the resulting harm. Judgments of blame also involve the recognition that intentional harm is more blameworthy than harm caused by negligence, which, in turn, is more blameworthy than accidental harm. When people offer an excuse, they are admitting that they caused harm but are not accepting responsibility for it. When they offer justification, they are accepting moral responsibility for harm, but they deny that it was a bad thing to do (e.g., it was done in self-defense). There is also the recognition that mitigating circumstances reduce one's blameworthiness. The severity of harm generally determines the amount of punishment.

The following rule use is seen when children weigh the severity of harm versus the intentionality behind the action which produced the harm (Darley & Shultz, 1990; Shultz, Wright, & Schleifer, 1986). By 3 to 4 years of age, children rate foreseeable harm as being more punishable than harm that was unforeseen. Between 4 and 6 years of age, children can distinguish between intentional and unintentional harm, foreseeable and unforeseeable harm, and justified and unjustified harm. By 6 to 7 years of age, intentional harm is seen as clearly more blameworthy and punishable than accidental harm. By 7 years, in-

tentional harm is more punishable than unintentional, foreseeable harm. By age 6, children allow for the mitigation of punishment. Restitution mitigates punishment by 4 to 5 years of age, and apologies mitigate the punishment children mete out by 6 to 7 years of age. In the much younger child, the ubiquitous "I'm sorry," which is overgeneralized and expected to mitigate all punishment in all situations, precedes the development of an understanding of which specific, concrete, reparative actions can indeed mitigate punishment. Darley and Shultz note that retributive judgments follow similar rules in children and adults. However, in natural situations or in situations where there is missing information, children and adults will differ in how they interpret and fill in the missing information and therefore will arrive at different judgments about blame and punishment.

Shultz et al. (1986) report that above age 7, children first determine causation, then moral responsibility, and then affix blame. From age 5 onward, these investigators found that all children understood the issues and pursued the question of moral responsibility for someone who caused harm but not for someone who does not cause harm. Five-year-olds generally do not raise spontaneously questions about an individual's moral responsibility. Instead, they move directly to issues of punishment based on the outcome. Seven-year-olds focus on questions of punishment or restitution. Therefore, when compared to older school-age children, the 5-year-old's emphasis on retribution overwhelms the ability to deal with questions of causality and restitution.

Thus, with advancing development during the school years, children show both an increased sensitivity to issues such as negligence and a greater tolerance of blameworthy acts as measured by lower ratings of punishments. As children get older, they also put more emphasis on restitution and less on punishment. It is as if the restitution is taken as a form of self-punishment; it therefore reduces the amount of punishment that an individual is still due. An overly punishing parent who does not allow for parent-child discourse would be working against these trends.

ATTRIBUTION OF CAUSALITY

Attribution theory applied to the study of causality in adults and children has had clinical utility, especially with conceptualizations of depression and, in particular, with learned helplessness. For example, etiologic status can be attributed to global or specific causes, internal or external causes, enduring or short-lived causes. Developmental changes should be expected in the child's judgment of causality. For example, with age, and with the associated development of relevant cognitive operations, such as memory, children become better able to appreciate and utilize the serial order of events when making inferences about causality. Their attribution of causality is relevant to certain components of moral development.

Sedlack and Kurtz (1981) provided a comprehensive review of factors that can affect causal inferences in children. A developmental shift takes place during the school years in the child's determination of the sources of internal motivation. In a typical experimental paradigm, subjects are asked to make judgments about protagonists in stories. In one story type the motivation is clearly internal, such as the protagonist's interest in an activity, and also might be affected by an internal factor, such as ability. In the other story type, the character's actions are constrained in some way by an external factor, such as the delivery of a reward for an action; in addition, the reward might be noncontingent on the behavior. It would be expected that subjects hearing these stories would infer that the protagonist who was induced by reward to act in a particular way was less internally motivated. Paradoxically, younger children select someone as being more internally motivated who in fact had his or her actions constrained by some other person, such as through the use of rewards. Younger children may see the extrinsic cause (i.e., the reward) as an added incentive that increases internal motivation. This interpretation could account for an effect already described in which the removal of reinforcement sometimes results in the reduction of internal motivation. It is as if the external reinforcement or constraint adds to the younger child's sense of there being an internal cause and, if it is removed, then the internal cause is lessened. One implication is that reinforcements should not be applied in a global, mechanical manner across developmental phases. Instead, the way in which they are used, and the explanations that accompany their use (or lack of use), must vary with the age and developmental level of the child.

Thompson (1989) reports that school-age children feel proud when the locus of causality is internal and not external; moreover, this turn toward internality increases with age during the elementary school years. The gratitude children feel if they see the other person's action as being voluntary also increases with age. The developmental trend for anger seems to be more complex and somewhat different from that for guilt, pride, and gratitude. More developmentally advanced reasoning in the understanding of anger is manifested at a younger age when judging others than when judging the self. Younger children can appreciate that another person's anger may be due to his or her experience of failure that may be derived from a lack of effort before these children realize that their own guilt is a function of personal failure for a lack of effort.

Thompson (1989) reports that younger children are more likely to make emotional inferences based on outcome (i.e., success/failure—external, readily observable factors), while older children are more likely to look for causal elements that relate to the outcome. When younger children can attribute outcome to some clearly identifiable cause—for example, when they exert effort and achieve success—their causal reasoning is more like that seen with older children. However, when their failure is due to uncontrollable factors, such as chance or bad luck, younger children still seem to search for causes, even when none are apparent. They may then assume that they are personally responsible. It is as if each event must have a cause, and, if they cannot easily find it, they invent it. Moreover, those inventions often involve their taking personal responsibility. Within this framework, the readiness of some youngsters to blame others when they make mistakes becomes understandable. If they are convinced that blame must be fixed and if the cause is not apparent, then they may assume they are likely to be blamed. It makes sense to blame someone else before they get blamed. Between ages 7 and 9 children begin to make correct inferences about multiple causative factors that facilitate an event (Sedlack & Kurtz, 1981).

Helping parents and teachers to focus on causal factors such as effort, factors over which the child can have some degree of control, and not to focus only on outcome is useful in light of this information. Doing so would be consistent with the general shift in the child's developmental orientation, would be more readily assimilated, and, therefore, would be more likely to foster further growth. It is particularly useful to do this with children who show elements of a narcissistic personality disorder. In addition, focusing only on outcome also restricts the range of events about which the parents can feel pride in their child; anything that increases the range of a child's actions as sources of parental pride can enhance mutually satisfying interactions.

Developmental Trends in the Components of Moral Functioning

GUILT

Zahn-Waxler and associates (Zahn-Waxler & Kochanska, 1990; Zahn-Waxler, Kochanska, Krupnick, & McKnew, 1990) have studied the development of guilt in children between 4 and 12 years of age, observing both normally functioning families and those in which the mother had been depressed. The investigators assessed guilt by means of psychiatric interview, direct observation, and projective approaches, such as response to stories. Exemplars of guilt included conscious, action-oriented, and self-critical behavior, such as direct statements of remorse and reparative behaviors, as well as, from a psychodynamic perspective, painful experiences that followed real or imagined transgressions. The latter behavioral reactions could include nightmares, accidents, and unrealistic fears, such as of external punishment. Thus, Zahn-Waxler included behavior, verbal expressions, and unconscious defenses against guilt to indicate its presence.

The guilt reactions of children of depressed mothers are different from those of children whose mothers are not depressed. When the children were asked to comment on hypothetical situations of distress and conflict, the younger children of depressed mothers showed more involvement in these situations than did younger normal children. However, this pattern reversed with age, so that the older children with normal mothers showed more involvement than older children with depressed mothers. On the semi-projective measure, older children of normal

parents expressed more guilt than did younger children. Older children, especially older girls, expressed more empathy than did younger girls and older boys. In children of nondepressed mothers, guilt was associated with prosocial feelings and behavior. Zahn-Waxler et al. (1990) indicate that guilt increases with age in children of non-depressed mothers, and their guilt is very open and functional. In older children of depressed mothers, the guilt appears to be more arrested. These youngsters show high levels of responsibility but may get overly involved with their parents before they have the cognitive skills to deal with the situation.

Perhaps children who experience too much guilt pull back emotionally too soon as they get older. They then become less available to integrate the multiple feelings and information that arise in a charged situation or to do the deeper causal analysis that children generally become capable of as they move through the school years. Zahn-Waxler et al. point out that depressed mothers use guilt-inducing and anxiety-inducing parenting techniques to show their disapproval. At a young age, their children come to feel omnipotent when they make their parents feel better and helpless when they fail. Thus, although they cannot solve their parents' problems, they nonetheless accept a causal role for those problems. This leads to an internal, stable disposition that may result in less ego resiliency and, in the long run, reduced capacity for handling problems and becoming caregivers as adults.

SHAME AND PRIDE

Lewis, Alessandri, and Sullivan (1991) found that embarrassment and empathy precede shame and pride in 3-year-olds. Harris and Saarni (1989) report that by 6 to 7 years of age, children are able to judge that pride and shame are felt when someone does something in the presence of another person who approves or disapproves of the act. At a later age, consistent with the general theme of increased internalization with development, children come to understand the presence of an internal audience, and that shame and pride can be felt even when they are alone. Also during the school years, children are increasingly likely to conclude that pride is a function of the locus of success and is greater when the locus is internal rather than external. Consistent with their increasing developmental capacity to understand and integrate emotions, children realize that pride and shame each involve the appearance of two successive, causally linked emotions. That is, when another person expresses approval or happiness, the self feels pride. When another expresses disapproval or anger, the self feels sadness or shame. This can be viewed as a script between the self and the other. When this script becomes well rehearsed, the presence of the other person is unnecessary. The child can mentally assume the other's role as well, and pride and shame can then exist without the person's presence. Thus, whether we speak in terms of superego components, scripts, or internal standards, it is clear that the ability to feel and discuss pride and shame grows during the school years and that these feelings increasingly occur in the absence of others who are observing or commenting on the child.

FAIRNESS AND SHARING

Damon and Colby (1987) studied children at 4, 6, 8, and 10 years of age. The children were required to divide candy bars among themselves as a reward for making bracelets. The task was so arranged that the children could not get any rewards until they had reached consensus on how to divide the candy. Such a demand promotes equality solutions and, at each age, as the children's experience in working out the reward distribution continued, they were more likely to opt for a distribution based on equality, thus conforming to task demands. Older children recognized this more quickly, while also realizing that this solution might leave some children dissatisfied. Darley and Shultz (1990) report that younger children tend to divide equally, whereas older children tend to calibrate rewards so that they become a ratio of the amount or quality of the person's work. Damon and Colby (1987) found that the 6-year-olds prefer equality as the solution, while older children are more likely to use concepts such as merit (e.g., extra pay for extra work) and benevolence (inequality of rewards can exist if it acknowledges someone's special need or deprivation).

Children are more likely to change in their distribution of rewards following interaction with peers than with adults (Damon & Colby, 1987). Also, moderate degrees of conflict between pairs of children on distributive justice tasks are more likely to be related to greater change than small amounts of conflict between children (Damon & Phelps, 1989). Damon suggests that the interaction with peers can lead to the joint discovery of new goals and that this is less likely to occur when adults try to establish the goals (Damon & Colby, 1987). Thus, the construction of fairness standards is accomplished best by children in collaboration with other children.

Children will show a great deal of self-interest in these negotiations (Damon & Phelps, 1989). When they think they have the best claim for the rewards, they will propose standards such as merit. If their claims are less valid, they are more likely to suggest equal distribution of rewards. In general, at all ages, the children are less likely to demand the whole pie and are able to coordinate both merit and social desirability in making suggestions about distributive justice. By mid-elementary school, children can evaluate the implications of hard work and poverty, and by late elementary school they can simultaneously judge these claims. Berndt (1987) reported that children are more likely to share with friends when they believe they can achieve equality through sharing. If they believe that sharing will let the other one win and that they themselves will lose some important gain or contest, they are less likely to share and more likely to compete with their friends than with nonfriends. Adolescents, more so than younger children, prefer equal sharing over competition with friends.

GENDER

The gender differences in moral functioning that have been reported in school-age children do not conform to neat summary statements. For example, young girls are more likely to experience shame than are boys, especially when failing easy tasks. Boys tend to show a significant, negative correlation between pride and shame while girls show a positive, non-significant correlation between these affects (Lewis et al., 1992). Lewis et al. (1992) do not report any gender differences in guilt or pride. Zahn-Waxler and Kochanska (1990) note that girls may be more sensitive than boys to the emotional states of others and may be more vulnerable to experiencing guilt. Lewis et al. (1992) note that by 3 years of age, girls show a greater variety of emotions than boys. Thompson (1989) reports no gender differences in children's causal inferences about guilt, pride, anger, or gratitude. In a comprehensive review of gender differences within the cognitive developmental approach to morality, Walker (1984) concludes that gender differences in moral reasoning in childhood and early adolescence are rare, but, when they occur, they favor girls. A few studies show more mature moral reasoning in males in late adolescence and young adulthood. Baumrind (1986) questioned the latter conclusion and noted that educational level has a differential impact on moral reasoning in men and women. At middle levels of education there are no gender differences in moral reasoning.

The work of Carol Gilligan (e.g., Gilligan & Wiggins, 1987) is central to a discussion of gender differences in moral development. Gilligan points out that the psychoanalytic and cognitive perspectives draw heavily on the young child's position of inequality vis-à-vis older children and adults. These perspectives highlight the child's feeling of being small and powerless. Morality, in this context, becomes defined in terms of justice, which would provide rules and procedures for reducing inequality and/or protecting those who are small and powerless. By definition then, development constitutes a movement toward a position of greater equality and greater independence. The moral goal within the inequality model is not to treat the other unfairly. Inequality is remedied by justice, and the affect involved can be sympathy *for* another. Reactions such as shame or guilt imply inequality. That is, a person might feel lower than the other person and experience shame or feel guilty because of being more powerful and capable of doing harm.

Gilligan and Wiggins (1987) also describe a contrasting morality based on attachment. Within the attachment framework, morality can be conceived as love, and the moral goal would be not to turn from others who are in need. In this model, problems are remedied by care, and the emotion produced would be love. The distinction between the inequality and attachment models is captured by the various protestations young children can make that have a moral basis to them: "It's not fair," "You have no right . . ." contrasted with "You don't care," "I don't love you."

Gilligan and Wiggins (1987) speculate that the early closeness between mother and daughter may lead to an emphasis on forming interpersonal relations with others as a basic component of self-concept and self-esteem. While boys may feel quite close to their mother, they identify with their father, whose power and authority is salient for them. This situation may distance girls from problems that can arise from inequality, while boys may be distanced from problems that arise from emotional detachment. The gender difference then would be a conflict between standards of fairness and standards of helpfulness.

Gilligan and Wiggins (1987) asked 11- and 15-year-old children to solve Aesop's fables. They found that boys are more likely to frame a problem as one that involves justice (the solution would involve honoring contracts, respecting rights, or following principles of fairness). Girls are more likely to frame a problem in terms of care (the solution is to respond to everyone's needs). Of importance, they note that boys and girls can shift orientation and be aware of both justice and care. Hoffman (1977) notes that boys and girls are equally adept at identifying and understanding other's feelings, but girls also are more likely to experience the feelings of the other.

Gilligan and Wiggins (1987) distinguish between *empathy* and *cofeeling*. Empathy implies an identity of feelings with another. Cofeeling includes an emotional responsiveness toward another person, but the other person's feelings are experienced as separate, different, and distinguishable from one's own. Detachment, perhaps more prominent with boys, can create a sense of emotional safety and engender insight, but it also means a lessening of cofeeling, not knowing what the other is feeling, an "egocentric ignorance" (Gilligan & Wiggins, 1987, p. 291). They note that detachment can easily be confused with objectivity. A rule-based sympathy without true cofeeling can lead to intellectually justified inaction in which the other is not helped. As Gilligan and Wiggins also note, empathy and concern about feelings, an affect that seems increasingly to be viewed as the essence of morality, is no longer thought to be restricted to girls. Thus, emotions, which had once been seen as a major limitation in moral reasoning, are now seen as basic to moral growth.

68

THE ROLE OF PARENTING IN MORAL DEVELOPMENT

Walker and Taylor (1991a) report no significant correlation between the actual level of moral reasoning of parents and their children. They did find that discussions between parent and child of real-life moral dilemmas, rather than hypothetical dilemmas, predicted moral judgment two years later. They were able to identify parental techniques that were effective in inducing moral development and those that were less likely to enhance development. Effective techniques include eliciting the child's opinion, asking clarifying questions, paraphrasing, and checking for understanding. These techniques would reduce the sense of inequality between parent and child and also would foster the development of the communication and interactional skills that are basic elements of moral development. Walker and Taylor found that children show less developmentally advanced moral behavior when parents directly challenge them and when their position is criticized. The children may feel assailed by hostile criticism, which enhances defensiveness. Another ineffective modality is an approach in which parents present their opinions, as if lecturing the child. These parents also would be providing ineffective models of how to communicate and solve problems.

In thinking about children's moral development, two frameworks for characterizing parental behavior have been most useful. Hoffman and Saltzstein (1967), differentiated power assertive, inductive, and love withdrawal approaches to moral development. Baumrind (1971b) has distinguished among authoritarian, authoritative, and permissive approaches to parenting. She also has noted (Baumrind, 1971a) that there is a small group of harmonious parents who are not obviously controlling, yet who promote compliance and mature, independent behavior in their children.

Hoffman and Saltzstein (1967) have described three general disciplinary techniques that parents use when their child is blameworthy. *Induction* points out the consequences of the child's action on the victim; alternatively, *power assertion* and *love withdrawal* emphasize for the child him- or herself the consequence of the wrongdoing.

Power assertion can include threats or actual punishment, deprivation of privileges, and physical techniques, while love withdrawal includes some sort of threat that induces guilt and increases fearfulness about the loss of parental love. Hoffman (1983) notes that most parents use all techniques; it is the predominant technique that defines the parents' general approach.

Because each moral situation includes some response from the parent, verbal as well as emotional or physical, it is desirable that the disciplinary technique enhance the child's attention to the content of what the parent is telling him or her. Thus, if children are too anxious and fearful of the parent's response, they will not be able to pay sufficient attention to and process its content. If too little anxiety is aroused, children will not be sufficiently motivated to pay attention or adhere to what the parent is saying. It is thought that induction, besides focusing children's attention on the victim, thereby helping them to decenter from their own perspective, also produces an optimal level of arousal for the processing of the cognitive component in the moral situation, which then can be integrated more effectively with the emphatic, affective component.

Authoritarian parents exercise a high level of control over their children coupled with low clarity of communication and little warmth. Authoritative parents also exercise high control of their children, but it is coupled with both a high clarity of communication and warmth and nurturance (Damon, 1988). Although they can be quite warm with their children, permissive parents are more inconsistent in their control and clarity of communication. They may even be anxious about disciplining their children. Henry (1983) finds that liberal parents are most concerned about their children's expression of aggression, and their sons develop more anxiety about aggression. Authoritarian parents are most concerned about their child's direct expression of aggression or sexuality toward authority figures, and their children will show less anxiety about aggression than those of liberal parents.

Certain common features attributed to authoritarian control and power assertive control inhibit moral development. With power assertion, the parents' harshness may prevent the child from learning any perspective but their own. These parents do not direct their child's attention either to other people's feelings or to the consequences of their child's behavior for others. Furthermore, these parents tend to direct the child's attention away from what he or she did wrong, how he or she may have hurt the other child and, instead, bring attention to focus on the threatening parent. In this way, morality becomes at once externally imposed and arbitrary. Gibbs (1987) also notes that if parents become victimizers, then children who transgress come to see themselves as victims of the parents, and the other child's feelings are again lost sight of. Finally, power assertion creates such a high level of emotional arousal that children may be less able to attend to whatever reasoning the parents may provide. Maccoby (1983) has reported that younger children in particular do not search for intention when there is a salient external cause. Power-assertive parents, by creating an emphasis on external factors, may slow children's developing search for internal causal inferences as the basis for other's behavior. Thus, the authoritarian parents then may get compliance, but children may not feel that their behavior is voluntary and will therefore be less likely to do the right thing in the absence of external control. Permissive parents provide insufficient pressure on the child to promote compliance and are likely to strengthen the child's noncompliance (Maccoby, 1983).

With both inductive and authoritative parenting, the role of the parent is less prominent, which enhances the likelihood that children will believe that it was their own choice to behave in a prosocial manner. The parent, then, as the source for the moral norm gets relegated to the background, and children can take pride in this self-attributed moral behavior (Gibbs, 1987; Maccoby, 1983). Empathy and anticipatory empathy derived from guilt allow the induction-generated behaviors to overcome children's own egoistic motives and aggressive propensities. Gibbs (1987) notes that decreased empathy and increased egocentrism are basic to delinquency. Examples abound in which delinquents express no feelings about their victims or indicate that somehow the victims deserved what was done to them. Abusive parents primarily use power assertive techniques (Grusec & Goodnow, 1994).

A consensus seems to be developing about features of parental discipline that promote internal-

ized moral actions in children. These features highlight the interactive elements in the parent-child relationship, the importance of shared positive affect, and the development of reciprocity and mutual respect. Grusec and Goodnow (1994), while noting that so much of our knowledge is more valid for mothers than fathers and is based primarily on the study of middle-class families, highlight the importance of parental flexibility. Parental flexibility, which requires that parents match the discipline to the misdeed, allows the child to evaluate the appropriateness of the punishment. Children do not question the parent's right to intervene. Flexibility enhances the likelihood that children will be able to discern accurately the parent's message; it conveys that there is meaning to the parent's behavior and that it is not arbitrarily chosen. When children feel that the parent's message is appropriate, motivated compliance increases, and they can develop the sense that the message is self-generated, not imposed. Maccoby (1992) similarly argues that authoritative parents invite children to enter reciprocal relationships with them in which they promote their children's interests while theirs are allowed to fade into the background. This conveys the idea that the parent is trying to promote the best interests of the child. If the relationship between parent and child is coercive, they are not able to sustain on ongoing, joint activity. Kochanska and Aksan (1995) studied 3-year-old children and viewed the mother-child dyad as the unit of measurement. They distinguished between committed compliance and situational compliance. Situational compliance is maintained by maternal control, relates to the specific situation, and does not predict internalization. The essence of committed compliance by the child is that the mother and child share mutual positive affect. The child in such a relationship is eager to be socialized, complies eagerly, rarely resists parental demands, and responds by resisting temptation when left alone in an experimental situation.

Ratner and Steltner (1991) find that if the child's negative affect is ignored, it increases and begins to dominate the child's thinking and mood. The parents' behavior toward the child transmits a belief system about how emotions are to be expressed; indeed, affect often is socialized by the parents' affective expression and not by rewards or punishments. In effect, these authors suggest that emotional expression should not be viewed as a class of behaviors that are shaped and modeled by contingencies of reward and punishment, but that sympathetic responses to the child promote his or her ability to regulate its own emotional expression. The most effective parental approach for regulating the child's emotional responsiveness is reciprocal interactions between parent and child. These interactions become represented or internalized by the child and reenacted in internal dialogue when decisions need to be made. Thus, according to Ratner and Steltner, the child is simultaneously playing his or her and the other person's role. If the parents are unaccepting of the child's emotional expression, the child will have no recourse but to reject these feelings in the self and will not learn how to provide comfort to the self or to others.

Joshua, an 8-year-old child with multiple physical difficulties, was showing increasing argumentativeness with parents, peers, and teachers. His parents were also quite ill physically. He was able to acknowledge that he was fighting more with his parents because, as an adoptive child, he was told that his birth mother had loved him but could not take care of him. He became alarmed that his ill adoptive mother also could not take care of him and that he would be given away once again. He would then fight with her and disobey her to increase her responsiveness. The only way he could get her out of her lethargy and pain and have her seem emotionally connected to him was to be angry and get her angry and have a shared affective experience with her and his adoptive father. He was concerned that if he was good, meaning compliant with all the household rules, there would be no arguing, he would be forgotten about, and he would feel unconnected.

Just as Joshua expressed a concern about giving up a particular affective state that was familiar and formed the basis of important object relations, parents too may be reluctant to change their primary approach to disciplining their child and promoting moral behavior. It is important to make parents aware of techniques such as induction and authoritative approaches in contrast to either the more permissive or power-assertive or love-withdrawal techniques they may be using. However, it is also important for the clinician to be aware of the affect that parents are using in disciplining their child and to consider how that affect pro-

vides a connection for the parent both to the child and to their own parents. In order for the parents to take a step back from a particular emotion they use that dominates their connection to their child and to their own parents, they often need to understand better the meaning of that emotion to them. Only then will they be able to use effective parenting techniques that allow the child to feel greater ownership of his or her feelings and moral decision making.

Multimodal Intervention

EVALUATION

The child's level of moral functioning can be determined as part of the clinician's standard evaluation procedure using information typically provided by parents, teachers, and the child. The evaluation requires information about the child's functioning in various settings, parental intervention techniques, and the child's reaction to those interventions.

The focus is on moral criteria, including the child's behavioral compliance with rules, upholding standards, emotional reactions to other's distress, emotional (e.g., guilt) and behavioral (e.g., reparation, apology) reactions to his or her own wrongdoing, judgment of causality, and sense of responsibility. It is also necessary to consider the child's level of personality organization as a way of understanding oedipal organization and object relations. This provides additional insight into the child's potential for experiencing empathy and other affects in relations with others.

Child Functioning: Parent and teacher interviews, along with questionnaire responses provided by these sources, should allow for an initial determination if the child's behaviors that are of concern are primarily violations of convention or moral codes. Moral violations imply more serious socialization deficits and the greater likelihood of deficits in the emotional components of moral functioning such as empathy and guilt. It is also necessary to determine if the child has deficits in role-taking skills. In effect, a distinction is being drawn between the cognitive and affective components of the interpersonal behavioral act because they have different intervention implications. For example, a child may be capable of understanding how the other might have a deficit in empathic concern or distress. It is also possible that the child's empathic reaction is limited by a lack of appreciation of the other as a separate entity with feelings that are different from the self. The child who is exhibiting moral behavioral difficulties, with associated deficits in empathy, can be expected to have more serious psychopathology, with a greater likelihood of a personality disorder, than a child who presents primarily with conventional behavioral problems.

The child's role-taking competency and empathic skill can be assessed during the course of a semistructured clinical interview in which he or she is asked to recount, in detail, some events that prompted the evaluation. The child's relationship with the clinician will be an equally important source of information.

The child's relationship with peers also is an important area of inquiry. Child, parents, and teachers should be asked about this. The degree of detail that the child can provide about friends, and the associated affect, offers further information about the child's empathic skill, understanding of social causality, willingness to accept responsibility, and knowledge of the discourse procedures needed for maintaining friendships.

It is also important to determine if the child's acquisition of appropriate social behaviors and inhibitions has been affected by the presence of a learning disability or attention deficit disorder. The latter, in particular, may influence the development of inhibitory mechanisms that are necessary for pro-social behaviors. Temperament may also have an impact on early conscience development (Kochanska, DeVet, Goldman, Murray, & Putnam, 1994). An assessment of the child's dispositional style is valuable for thinking about the impact that the child has on those around him or her and aids in understanding how particular interventions need to be tailored to the particular child and family.

Parent Functioning: Parents willingly describe their child's behavioral problems. They can be helped to reflect on his or her emotional reactions to these events (e.g., whether the child is angry, sad; if the child shows guilt, remorse; does the child accept responsibility; will the child make reparations). Parents also will readily describe their response to their child's behavior ("what

happened next?"; "then what happened?"; "what did you do then?"); the child's reaction; and their own subsequent response. This is usually sufficient for determining the parents' primary disciplinary techniques, the content of their verbalization, and the accompanying emotional climate. It is also possible from this dialogue to assess the frustration tolerance of parent and child, the parents' ability to sustain a disciplinary approach, and the clarity of parent-child boundaries in the family.

INTERVENTION

Intervention involves procedures often used by the child clinician. The approach suggested here combines procedures derived from each of the theoretical perspectives described earlier. Each procedure focuses on a different but essential component of the child's moral functioning. The combined use of these procedures provides the clinician and the parents with a comprehensive strategy.

Parents: Work with parents is essential. Parents readily understand the moral/conventional distinction and can be helped to determine which conventional acts matter enough to them to do battle over. They also can be helped to appreciate the child's need for control over some areas in his or her life; this discussion can help foster appropriate steps in the separation process.

Behavioral techniques provide an important component in working with most parents. These are useful for moral and conventional violations and appropriate, as well, for children who have personality disorders requiring individual, psychodynamically oriented psychotherapy. These procedures can include "time out"; systematic use of reward, punishment, and extinction concepts; "point" systems; and "contracts." These procedures not only give parents potential environmental control of their child and reduce the parents' sense of helplessness, they also indirectly provide the child with a degree of control over parents. That is, if parents comply with behavioral interventions and find them to be effective, their behavior will become more predictable to the child, and the parents also will reduce their use of ineffective coercive techniques that have been more likely to produce mutual hostility. In addition, when these techniques are effective, parents and child argue less and have the potential to play more. The parents also may have to be taught how to play. These techniques help the child feel that he or she can be controlled and that the parents can do it without being harsh, coercive, or abusive. These interventions reflect an attempt to help parents move along a path from shared hostility and mutual coercion to a position marked by greater reciprocity and shared positive affect, as exemplified by playing together.

Although some families may not need elaborate behavioral systems, most families are helped by a discussion of behavioral principles. Assigned readings and "homework" can be a helpful adjunct with some families. The basic principles that need to be expressed to parents include the importance of the immediacy of discipline and the role of verbal mediation (reasoning). A movement away from the belief in harsh punishment is especially helpful and easier to accomplish when it is explained that harsh punishment is counterproductive—namely, it generates hostility in the child; makes the child try to avoid the parent, thereby reducing their potential effectiveness; and is less effective than mild, immediate punishment. A valuable distinction can be made between punishment and discipline. Punishment provides the parent with a vehicle for hurting the child, getting revenge, for whatever ego blow he or she may have suffered—be it public humiliation or feeling ineffectual for not being a good-enough parent who could control the child. Alternatively, discipline, in which the child becomes the disciple, provides a model in which the parent serves to teach the child a more acceptable way of behaving. The imagery associated with these two terms is meaningful to parents and allows them contrasting models with which they can think about their anger toward their child and how to modulate this anger.

Parents can be helped to replace noneffective verbalizations with those that emphasize induction and authoritative control. With all parents, the therapist should offer clear examples of verbal responses to concrete examples of the child's behavior that the parents provided. As they are provided with more examples to model, parents show a greater propensity spontaneously to generate appropriate comments in new situations. It is incorrect to assume that even parents who sound quite sophisticated in their understanding of their

child will use these approaches spontaneously. The clinician must explain that if the child is too aroused or not aroused, he or she will not take in and make use of the moral message implicit in inductive approaches.

The exploration of situations described by parents will help enumerate the many factors that can contribute to their child's moral decision making. When parents come to appreciate the cognitive complexity of the situation, they become less likely to oversimplify, causal connections become clearer for the child, and the salience of certain components (e.g., damage) become less likely to overshadow other important elements. Finally, the cognitive developmental perspective emphasizes the "problem of the match." That is, in order to be assimilated, new information must bear an optimal relation to established reasoning levels. Therefore, if a parent is expecting moral reasoning and functioning that is too discrepant from the child's predominant level and from developmentally expectable levels, the parent's comments will not be appreciated readily, and both parent and child will be frustrated. The "match" must be made to the situation and event as well as to the child's developmental level. That is, the conventional moral distinction also calls for a discrimination to be made by the parent so that the intervention is appropriate. Thinking in this manner helps promote the flexibility that characterizes parents who are effective in producing prosocial behaviors in their children.

Moral development, in this presentation, has been viewed as the joint outcome of cognitive and emotional development occurring in the context of family and peer interactions. The child's socialization and conscience development is seen to derive from parental intervention, extrafamilial contacts, and the ensuing development of skills that influence empathy, perception of others' intent, inhibitory control, and discourse and negotiation skills. Increasingly it seems to be found that more developmentally mature moral behavior is seen in the presence of clear demands and expectation by parents, in the context of parental flexibility, and in a setting that induces a positive affective climate between parent and child. In such a setting, the child is more likely to show voluntary and spontaneous compliance than when more coercive techniques are used habitually. The latter tends to promote situational compliance. More structured reinforcement programs include potentially powerful interventions that can shape the child's behavior. In a clinical setting, these techniques are turned to when the situation has already broken down. It is less clear if these techniques will induce internally motivated pro-social behavior, but they are necessary in many clinical situations to create or return to a point where a positive affective climate can become more frequent. The child seems more likely to develop internally motivated moral behaviors and self-regulatory systems that promote pro-social behaviors that are stable across person and situation when development occurs in settings marked by reciprocity, mutual respect, and the meaningfulness of the parents' intervention.

Parents may need to be encouraged to get their child more involved with peers. Some parents may be surprised by such a recommendation because they did not think it was so important ("they get to see their friends in school"; "he usually plays with a friend on the weekend"; "there's no time during the week for friends"). Activities can include attending after-school centers, Ys, cooking classes, and scouts. These out-of-home activities are valuable because they involve children in supervised activities and help them acquire new interpersonal skills and discourse strategies. Furthermore, these activities take place in settings in which the parents do not have to hover over their child, ready to intervene if all does not go well.

Child: Including children in some discussions of behavioral interventions with parents will give them a feeling of hopefulness that something is being done to help them. They also need to help work out certain point and contract systems. Children's negativism about these procedures is usually commensurate with their parents' cynicism. The family system's reluctance to change must be analyzed. In some instances, where the moral dysfunction is a shared difficulty, family therapy may prove to be the treatment of choice.

Individual psychodynamically oriented psychotherapy is aided when family functioning has been stabilized. In the examples given earlier (of Sam and Tom), time-out procedures, point systems, and modeling procedures with parents were important components. These helped calm daily life in the family, set limits on inappropriate behaviors, and established proper boundaries (e.g., not going into parents' bedrooms and bathrooms at certain times). After daily family life had become less disruptive to them, the children participated in individual therapy more effectively and daily problems were less likely to dominate a particular therapy session. It was then possible to treat more effectively the impact of the personality disorder, object relations, and associated deficits in moral functioning.

It was noted earlier that reliance on rewards can reduce the intrinsic motivation of an act and diminish the spontaneous occurrence of certain components of moral functioning. This likelihood can be minimized by fading specific rewards once the child begins to show consistent compliance with household rules. Increased reliance on parental verbalizations and praise for maintaining appropriate behavior can then occur.

REFERENCES

Aronfreed, J. (1976). Moral development from the standpoint of general psychological theory. In T. Lickona (Ed.), *Moral development and behavior* (pp. 54–69). New York: Holt, Rinehart & Winston.

Astor, R. (1994). Children's moral reasoning about family and peer violence: The role of provocation and retribution. *Child Development, 65,* 1054–1067.

Austin, V., Ruble, D., & Trabasso, T. (1977). Recall and order effects as factors in children's moral judgments. *Child Development, 48,* 470–474.

Baumrind, D. (1971a). Current patterns of parental authority. *Developmental Psychology Monograph, 4* (1), 1–103.

Baumrind, D. (1971b). Note: Harmonious parents and their preschool children. *Developmental Psychology, 4,* 99–102.

Baumrind, D. (1986). Sex differences in moral reasoning: Response to Walker's (1984) conclusion that there are none. *Child Development, 57,* 511–521.

Berg-Cross, L. (1975). Intentionality, degree of damage, and moral judgments. *Child Development, 46,* 970–974.

Berkowitz, M., Oser, F., & Althof, W. (1987). The development of sociomoral discourse. In W. Kurtines & J. Gewirtz (Eds.), *Moral development through social interaction* (pp. 322–352). New York: John Wiley & Sons.

Berndt, T. (1987). The distinctive features of conversations between friends: Theories, research and implications for sociomoral development. In W. Kurtines & J. Gewirtz (Eds.), *Moral development through social interaction* (pp. 281–300). New York: John Wiley & Sons.

Berzonsky, M., Weiner, A., & Raphael, D. (1975). Interdependence of formal reasoning. *Developmental Psychology, 11*, 258.

Cheyne, J. A., & Walters, R. (1969). Intensity of punishment, time of punishment, and cognitive structure as determinants of response inhibition. *Journal of Experimental Child Psychology, 7*, 231–244.

Costanzo, P., Coie, J., Grumet, J., & Farnhill, D. (1973). A reexamination of the effects of intent and consequence on children's moral judgments. *Child Development, 44* (1), 154–161.

Damon, W. (1988). *The moral child.* New York: The Free Press.

Damon, W., & Colby, A. (1987). Social influence and moral change. In W. Kurtines & J. Gewirtz (Eds.), *Moral development through social interaction* (pp. 3–19). New York: John Wiley & Sons.

Damon, W., & Phelps, E. (1989). Strategic use of peer learning in child education. In T. Berndt & G. Ladd (Eds.), *Peer relationships in child development* (pp. 135–157). New York: John Wiley & Sons.

Darley, J., & Shultz, T. (1990). Moral rules: Their content and acquisition. *Annual Review of Psychology, 41*, 525–552.

Eisenberg, N. (1987). Self attributions, social interaction, and moral development. In W. Kurtines & J. Gewirtz (Eds.), *Moral development through social interaction* (pp. 20–40). New York: John Wiley & Sons.

Elkind, D., & Dabak, R. (1977). Personal injury and property damage in the moral judgments of children. *Child Development, 48*, 518–522.

Fabes, R., Fultz, J., Eisenberg, N., May-Plumlee, T., & Christopher, F. (1989). Effects of rewards on children's prosocial motivation. *Developmental Psychology, 25*, 509–515.

Gibbs, J. (1987). Social processes in delinquency: The need to facilitate empathy as well as sociomoral reasoning. In W. Kurtines & J. Gewirtz (Eds.), *Moral development through social interaction* (pp. 301–321). New York: John Wiley & Sons.

Gibbs, J. (1991). Toward an integration of Kohlberg's and Hoffman's moral development theories. *Human Development, 34*, 88–104.

Gilligan, C., & Wiggins, G. (1987). The origins of morality in early childhood relationships. In J. Kagan & S. Lamb (Eds.), *The emergence of morality in young children* (pp. 277–305). Chicago: University of Chicago Press.

Gilman, R. (1990) Oedipal organization of shame. *Psychoanalytic Study of the Child, 45*, 357–375.

Grusec, J., & Goodnow, J. (1994). Impact of parental discipline methods on the child's internalization of values: A reconceptualization of current points of view. *Developmental Psychology, 30*, 4–19.

Haan, N. (1985). Processes of moral development: Cog-

nitive or social disequilibrium. *Developmental Psychology, 21*, 996–1006.

Harris, P., & Saarni, C. (1989). Children's understanding of emotion: An introduction. In C. Saarni & P. Harris (Eds.), *Children's understanding of emotions* (pp. 3–24). New York: Cambridge University Press.

Helwig, C., Hildebrandt, C., & Turiel, E. (1995). Children's judgments about psychological harm in social context. *Child Development, 66*, 1680–1693.

Henry, R. (1983). The cognitive vs. psychodynamic debate about morality. *Human Development, 26*, 173–179.

Hoffman, M. (1977). Empathy, its development and prosocial implications. In C. B. Keasey (Ed.), *Nebraska Symposium on Motivation, 25*, 169–218.

Hoffman, M. L. (1983). Affective and cognitive processes in moral internalization. In E. T. Higgins, D. Ruble & W. Hartup (Eds.), *Social cognition and social development* (pp. 236–274). London: Cambridge University Press.

Hoffman, M. L., & Saltzstein, H. D. (1967). Parent discipline and the child's moral development. *Journal of Personality and Social Psychology, 5* (1), 45–57.

Holder, A. (1982). Preoedipal contributions to the formation of the superego. *Psychoanalytic Study of the Child*, 245–272.

Keller, M., & Reuss, S. (1985). The process of moral decision-making: Normative and empirical conditions of participating in moral discourse. In M. Berkowitz and F. Oser (Eds.), *Moral education: Theory and application.* Hillsdale, NJ: Erlbaum.

Kochanska, G., & Absan, N. (1995). Mother-child mutually positive affect, the quality of child compliance to requests and prohibitions, and maternal control as correlates of early internalization. *Child Development, 66*, 236–254.

Kochanska, G., DeVet, K., Goldman, M., Murray, K., & Putnam, S. (1994). Maternal reports of conscience development and temperament in young children. *Child Development, 65*, 852–868.

Kohlberg, L. (1969). Stage and sequence: The cognitive-developmental approach to socialization. In D. Goslin (Ed.), *Handbook of socialization theory and research* (pp. 347–480). Chicago: Rand McNally.

Kohlberg, L. (1976). Moral stages and moralization: The cognitive-developmental approach. In T. Lickona (Ed.), *Moral development and behavior* (pp. 31–53). New York: Holt, Rinehart & Winston.

Kohlberg, L. (1984). *The psychology of moral development.* San Francisco: Harper & Row.

Kurtines, W. (1987). Sociomoral behavior and development from a rule-governed perspective: Psychosocial theory as a normative science. In W. Kurtines & J. Gewirtz (Eds.), *Moral development through social interaction* (pp. 149–194). New York: John Wiley & Sons.

Lewis, M., Alessandri, S., & Sullivan, M. (1992). Differences in shame and pride as a function of children's gender and task difficulty. *Child Development, 63*, 630–638.

Lickona, T. (1976). Research on Piaget's theory of moral development. In T. Lickona (Ed.), *Morality: Theory, research, and social issues.* New York: Holt, Rinehart & Winston.

Maccoby, E. (1983). Let's not overattribute to the attribution process. In E. T. Higgins, D. Ruble, & W. Hartup (Eds.), *Social cognition and social development* (pp. 213–217). Cambridge: Cambridge University Press.

Maccoby, E. (1992). The role of parents in the socialization of children: An historical overview. *Developmental Psychology, 28,* 1006–1017.

McKechnie, R. J. (1971). Between Piaget's stages: A study in moral development. *British Journal of Educational Psychology, 41,* 213–217.

Milrod, D. (1990). The ego ideal. *Psychoanalytic Study of the Child, 45,* 43–60.

Mischel, W., & Grusec, J. (1966). Determinants of the rehearsal and transmission of neutral and aversive behaviors. *Journal of Personality and Social Psychology, 3,* 197–205.

Mischel, W., & Liebert, R. (1966). Effects of discrepancies between observed and imposed reward criteria on their acquisition and transmission. *Journal of Personality and Social Psychology, 3,* 45–53.

Mischel, H. N., & Mischel, W. (1983). The development of children's knowledge of self-control strategies. *Child Development, 54,* 603–619.

Parker, J., & Gottman, J. (1989). Social and emotional development in a relational context. In T. Berndt & G. Ladd (Eds.), *Peer relations in child development* (pp. 95–131). New York: John Wiley & Sons.

Piaget, J. (1952). *The origins of intelligence in children.* New York: W. W. Norton.

Piaget, J. (1965). *The moral judgement of the child.* New York: Free Press.

Pressley, G. (1979). Increasing children's self-control through cognitive interventions. *Review of Educational Research.*

Ratner, W., & Steltner, L. (1991). Thinking and feeling: Putting Humpty Dumpty together again. *Merrill-Palmer Quarterly, 37,* 1–26.

Ritvo, S., & Solnit, A. (1960). The relationship of early ego identifications to superego formation. *International Journal of Psycho-Analysis, 41,* 295–300.

Roberts, W., & Strayer, J. (1996). Empathy, emotional expressiveness, and prosocial behavior. *Child Development, 67,* 449–470.

Sarnoff, C. (1976). *Latency.* New York: Jason Aronson.

Schafer, R. (1960). Loving and beloved superego in Freud's structural theory. *Psychoanalytic Study of the Child, 13,* 375–404.

Sedlack, A., & Kurtz, S. (1981). A review of children's use of causal inference principles. *Child Development, 52,* 759–784.

Selman, R., & Yeates, K. (1987). Childhood social regulation of intimacy and autonomy: A developmental-constructionist perspective. In W. Kurtines & J. Gewirtz (Eds.), *Moral development through social interaction* (pp. 43–101). New York: John Wiley & Sons.

Shultz, T., Wright, K., & Schleifer, M. (1986). Assignment of moral responsibility and punishment. *Child Development, 57,* 177–184.

Shweder, R., & Much, N. (1987). Determinants of meaning: Discourse and moral socialization. In W. Kurtines & J. Gewirtz (Eds.), *Moral development through social interaction* (pp. 197–244). New York: John Wiley & Sons.

Snarey, J. (1985). Cross-cultural universality of social-moral development: A critical review of Kohlbergian research. *Psychological Bulletin, 97,* 202–232.

Thompson, R. (1989). Causal attributions and children's emotional understanding. In C. Saarni & P. Harris (Eds.), *Children's understanding of emotions* (pp. 117–149). New York: Cambridge University Press.

Turiel, E. (1983). *The development of social knowledge.* Cambridge: Cambridge University Press.

Turiel, E., Killen, M., & Helwig, C. (1987). Morality: Its structure, functions and vagaries. In J. Kagan & M. Lamb (Eds.), *The emergence of morality in young children* (pp. 155–244). Chicago: University of Chicago Press.

Walker, L. (1984). Sex differences in the development of moral reasoning: A critical review. *Child Development, 55,* 677–691.

Walker, L., & Taylor, J. (1991a). Family interactions and the development of moral reasoning. *Child Development, 62,* 264–283.

Walker, L., & Taylor, J. (1991b). Stage transitions in moral reasoning: A longitudinal study of developmental process. *Developmental Psychology, 27,* 330–337.

Westen, D. (1986). The superego: A revised developmental model. *Journal of the American Academy of Psychoanalysis, 14,* 181–202.

Wolf, T., & Cheyne, J. A. (1972). Persistence of effects of live behavioral, televised behavioral, and live verbal models on resistance to deviation. *Child Development, 43,* 1429–1436.

Youniss, J. (1981). Moral development through a theory of social construction: An analysis. *Merrill-Palmer Quarterly, 27,* 385–403.

Youniss, J. (1987). Social construction and moral development: Update and expansion of an idea. In W. Kurtines & J. Gewirtz (Eds.), *Moral development through social interaction.* New York: John Wiley & Sons.

Zahn-Waxler, C., & Kochanska, G. (1990). The origins of guilt. In R. Dienstier & R. Thompson (Eds.), *Nebraska symposium on motivation 1988: Socioemotional development* (pp. 183–258). Lincoln: University of Nebraska Press.

Zahn-Waxler, C., Kochanska, G., Krupnick, J., & McKnew, D. (1990). Patterns of guilt in children of depressed and well mothers. *Developmental Psychology, 26,* 51–59.

9 / Religious Development of the School-Age Child

Mark R. Banschick

History

In 20th-century psychiatric thought, there is a long history of contentious debate about the nature and legitimacy of religious life. From William James in *The Varieties of the Religious Experience* (1902) to Robert Coles's recent work entitled *The Spiritual Life of Children* (1990), the argument about the nature and quality of a person's religious life remains an open question.

For much of the past century, Sigmund Freud's enormous impact on psychiatric thought has profoundly influenced how we think about religion. Freud essentially argued for a delegitimization of religion as a healthy part of development. His four books on the subject, *Totem and Taboo* (1913/1955), *Future of an Illusion* (1927/1961), *Civilization and Its Discontents* (1930/1961), and *Moses and Monotheism* (1939/1964), all find religion a highly suspect method of defensive functioning, a product of helpless human beings attempting to struggle with the difficult nature of life. God became for Freud, and others after him, a variety of wish fulfillment and illusion. While there is evidence that Freud himself may have longed for a personal religious experience, his theoretical formulations nevertheless provided little place for healthy religious belief. In recent years other writers, such as Eric Fromm (1955), Paul Pruyser (1968), Mortimer Ostow (Ostow & Scharfstein, 1966), William Meissner (1984), Anna Marie Rizzuto (1979), and, as mentioned, Robert Coles have all attempted to reformulate the psychoanalytic view of God, arriving at a more neutral and open approach to the assessment of a person's religious life.

Today's clinician has a number of theoretical constructs available to aid in the assessment of religious ideation. Indeed, Freud's suspicion of religion has enormous value, particularly in understanding religion in its more nonadaptive and pathological forms. D. W. Winnicott's notion (1953) of transitional objects recently has been argued as providing a more developmentally appropriate model for appreciating religious development. Object relations theory provides yet another method of clinically organizing the religious thought of a patient. In addition, clinicians who work in the field of substance abuse have been incorporating religious thinking into their treatment programs for decades (Walant, 1995).

Overall, it is fair to say that there is probably both healthy and unhealthy religious life. The clinician needs to use all of his or her tools to assess properly the adaptive quality of any one person's belief.

PSYCHOLOGY AND THEOLOGY

In the assessment of any patient's religious life, a number of variables can be pointed to in formulating a working model of that patient's belief system. Clearly, no one can know whether God truly exists. These matters are theological and not psychiatric. Yet the person experiencing the religious moment maintains this special experience through the substrate of the human mind. Therefore, cognitive development, religious training, family dynamics, and ultimately the world of object relations all may provide useful insights about an individual patient's religious life.

The Religious Life of the School-Age Child

GOD: AN IMPORTANT RELATIONSHIP

For the school-age child, the relationship with God can be very real and living. Both concrete operations and magical thinking are generally operative in this age group. This cognitive mix creates a potent opportunity for imaginary friends, pretend play, and belief in a real God. The powerful nature of this relationship should never be underestimated.

In the active mind of the young child, a spiritual experience can be as normative as monsters under the bed or the tooth fairy. Religious life can play a small or large role in the emotional world of the child. When religious imagery is important to a child, the clinician is obligated to be aware of it.

Prayer, for instance, can be particularly meaningful as a means to evoke a soothing sense of other (Banschickr, 1992). This writer once examined a 6-year-old girl who had recently been pinned under an automobile in a car accident. In a matter-of-fact tone she explained what happened to her while under the car: "I prayed to God that I would be okay. I did it because that is what he is there for. I thought I'd be okay." This prayer was answered in that this little girl was able to maintain hope under the most horrific of circumstances. Similar imagery is common in this age group under substantially less fearsome conditions. Rituals around sleep, including prayers, often are helpful as a means to process separation anxiety by evoking an internalized soothing object.

A MORAL UNIVERSE

While the authority of God and religious tradition can vary widely for the developing child, it generally remains a powerful reinforcer of social rules, even in our relatively secular culture. For many children (and adults), God exists as the final arbiter of moral behavior—of good and evil. In most Western traditions, there is an interesting and mutually reinforcing relationship between parental authority and divine authority. Each supports the other, and the school-age child generally does not make the distinction between the two. What one's parents want and what God wants are essentially one and the same.

As the child develops through latency toward early adolescence, God and parents become subject to more autonomous critical review. An increased awareness of social differences among people, the development of higher-level cognitive functioning, and natural autonomous striving all lead to reformulating the locus of moral authority as the adolescent matures.

Adult religious development may get stymied at the adolescent struggle for autonomy and moral independence. Many adults stop their religious/spiritual development right here. In my clinical experience, the religious resolutions of adolescence sadly appear to be of an enduring nature.

RELIGIOUS EDUCATION AND RELIGIOUS BELIEF

The school-age child's religious education, both in the home and in the place of worship, dominates that particular child's construction of the image of God. School-age children usually believe what they are taught. Generally not until the development of abstract thinking in early adolescence does the developmental moment bring about a reformulation of religious experience and a more unique and personal theology. While adolescents may generate theologies of their own, school-age children usually work with existing theologies, which they may reinterpret in ways consistent with what is meaningful in their lives.

Bible stories can be of great significance to children. The basic dynamics of development, oedipal struggles, separation anxiety, and fear of punishment are all abundantly found both in the Old and New Testaments. In assessing the school-age child, it is useful to ask about favorite Bible stories. The story of Cain and Abel, for example, addresses sibling rivalry in a powerful way. Heroes are abundant in biblical literature. Moses, David, Jesus, and Mary are all evocative heroes who may rival even those of secular culture.

When negative, satanic, or demonic imagery exists within a tradition, some children can become frightened by the possibility of a punitive God in the world. Most children do not experience a severe God, but for those who live with an abusive situation in the home, such imagery can be painfully toxic. I am reminded of a boy who talked about "demons coming to visit at night." It was difficult for this child to find the good, soothing object in prayer. His family history included abuse and neglect.

FAMILY LIFE AND RELIGIOUS BELIEF

The quality of a child's religious life is profoundly influenced by the nature of the child's experience of his or her own family. God can serve as a powerful object of displacement for fears and longing as the child attempts to manage these feelings with respect to parental figures. A benign God may well reflect a child's sense of a benign family. Alternatively, a benign God may indicate a hoped-for family member created by the child in an attempt to appreciate an unhappy world in a more stable way. A negative God experience can involve punitive superego elements, anxiety about separation, or displaced realistic fears. The clinician can better understand the nature of any particular God representation by getting a full history of the family and the child's place in it.

A good family assessment is critical to understanding the milieu within which a child grows up. Each family has a matrix of meaning, a set of values, which provides direction to family members. More often than not, this matrix is religious in nature. Even in our secular culture, religious life is alive and well. In observant homes, religious imagery carries an immediate and real quality to it. God and/or Jesus can be active characters (participants?) in the lives of such families and their children.

Cults, of course, play a role at the pathological end of the religious spectrum. Children from these homes require a careful assessment of functioning because of the risk of psychiatric disturbance in their immediate environment.

The Clinical Relevance of a Child's Religious Life

A child's religious life can provide insight about the object relations and personality organization of that particular child. Understanding his or her religious life can help the clinician better assess the child's cognitive functioning, the capacity to self-soothe, recall "good objects," and experience basic trust.

An understanding of a child's religious life also can be helpful in assessing charged family dynam-
ics. Discussion of stories and the God a particular child experiences can be helpful in this regard. Like any other form of imaginative life, religious life can serve as a means to understand the way the child organizes his or her own world. The language of religious life is a good one for us all to learn.

Summary

Clinicians should be aware that children do have religious lives that are dependent on their cognitive abilities, quality of family life, and defensive functioning.

Clinicians also must be aware that, ultimately, the religious life of a person is nonreduceable; the God experience is ultimately beyond description. Nevertheless, human beings perceive God, and, therefore, the human functions of development and defense formation give us insight into the kind of God a person creates (co-creates?) in religious imagery.

When assessing a school-age child, clinicians may find certain techniques helpful in bringing out religious material. These techniques include having the child draw a picture of a religious scene appropriate to his or her spiritual tradition. A drawing of a deceased person or pet may tap into important issues of loss, trust, and meaning. Often asking whether he or she prays and, if so, what feelings are evoked can bring about an appreciation of the child's capacity to soothe and feel secure. This line of inquiry can yield powerful insights into the religious life of children and provides helpful data in assessing overall functioning.

REFERENCES

Banschick, M. R. (1992). God-representations in adolescence. In M. Finn & J. Gartner, *Object relations theory and religion: Clinical applications* (pp. 73–76). Westport, CT: Praeger.

Coles, R. (1990). *The spiritual life of children.* Boston: Houghton Mifflin.

Freud, S. (1961). Civilization and its discontents. In J. Strachey (Ed. and Trans.), *The standard edition of the complete psychological works of Sigmund Freud* (vol. 21, pp. 59–145) (hereafter *Standard edition*)
(London: Hogarth Press). (Originally published 1930.)

Freud, S. (1961). Future of an illusion. In *Standard edition* (vol. 21, pp. 5–56). (Originally published 1927.)

Freud, S. (1964). Moses and monotheism. In *Standard edition* (vol. 23, pp. 7–137). (Originally published 1939).

Freud, S. (1955). Totem and taboo. In *Standard edition* (vol. 13, pp. 1–161). (Originally published 1913).

Fromm, E. (1955). *The sane society.* Greenwich, CT: Fawcett.

James, W. (1983). *The varieties of the religious experience.* New York: Penguin. (Originally published 1902.)

Jones, J. W. (1995). *In the middle of this road we call our life: The courage to search for something more.* San Francisco: HarperSanFrancisco.

Lovinger, R. (1984). *Working with religious issues in therapy.* New York: Jason Aronson.

Meissner, W. W. (1984). *Psychoanalysis and religious experience.* New Haven, CT: Yale University Press.

Ostow, M., & Scharfstein, D. (1966). *The need to be-* *lieve: The psychology of religion.* New York: International Universities Press.

Pruyser, P. (1968). *A dynamic psychology of religion.* New York: Harper & Row.

Rizzuto, A. M. (1979). *The birth of a living God.* Chicago: University of Chicago Press.

Walant, K. B. (1995). *Creating the capacity for attachment: Treating addictions and the alienated self.* Northvale, NJ: Jason Aronson.

Winnicott, D. W. (1953). Transitional objects in traditional phenomena. *International Journal of Psychoanalysis,* 34 (2), 89–97.

10 / Late Latency: New Levels of Authority Relationships

Fady Hajal

Contrary to the traditional belief that latency is a quiescent time, the years of middle childhood are a time of continuous change and growth. Yet growth takes place in such a slow and steady fashion that "The end of latency flows over into the early precursors of puberty without sharp or set markers" (Noshpitz & King, 1991, p. 360).

Latency is a period of significant change and development in the cognitive, neuropsychological, social, and moral areas. Children show a greater capacity for thinking, memory, speech, and conceptualizing, and for learning and following social rules (Lewis & Volkmar, 1990; Shapiro & Perry, 1976). These acquisitions are crucial not only for children's behavioral adjustment and scholastic learning in school but also for their integration into an ever widening network of social relations. They make children more pliable and adaptable to external demands, more "educable" about the social world beyond their family.

Latency-age children's shift in psychological organization from action to ideation facilitates the emergence of capacities and competencies that help them develop a new sense of self, a "latency identity" based on the experience of an emerging social self (Noshpitz & King, 1991). Children are increasingly capable of interacting and of being influenced by peers and adults other than the parents. Children "acquire a contextual sense of self across multiple settings—family, school and peer groups" (Reid, Landesman, Treder, & Jaccard,

1989, p. 896). Thanks to their "emergent capacities for formal thought, . . . ability to think about thinking and to reason things out in a logical way," preadolescent children are able to become freer from their dependence on authority (especially their parents) and to find solutions to problems by themselves (Gilligan, 1982). By late latency, children become increasingly concerned with as well as more realistic about how others perceive them.

Entry into School

A striking feature of development in middle childhood is the widening social horizon of the child. One hallmark of latency is the move of the child from a family-centered world to a multifaceted one. A child's entry into school inaugurates a new phase in the life of the child and the family. It is as if the family is "handing the child over" to the world, stepping back and letting go. The child's focus of activity shifts outward from home to school and to play areas away from home. School and home become dual headquarters of the child's social operations (Benson & Harrison, 1980). In each of these environments, the child will encounter new expectations and values, and will stake out different roles for him- or herself.

Whereas parents had been the only important people in the preschool child's life, now they have to share the stage with a diverse group including teachers, coaches, other adults, and most important, peers. All of these now provide guidance, reassurance, and comfort to the child. The parents' authority, although still present and operative, is somewhat diluted by the emergence of these additional poles of attraction.

Relationship with Parents

During latency, children remain firmly attached to their parents, even as they accelerate the process of separation from them, both as external objects and as idealized internal representations. Typically, children loosen their intense relationship with their mothers while drawing closer to their fathers. It is not unusual for children to spend more time with their fathers and come to appreciate and enjoy them more. They express curiosity—and at times pride—in their father's work or, in dual-career families, in both parents' occupations (Ames & Haber, 1991).

While children become more self-motivated, pulling free from parental dominance, they are nonetheless firmly imbedded in their family environment. Parents describe fluctuations in their children's behavior toward them during these years. Children often switch from being affectionate, looking for closeness, and confiding in their mothers, to withdrawing, complaining, sulking, and fault finding at the slightest excuse. They fluctuate from being respectful and obedient to acting in rude and rebellious ways. They swing back and forth between the wish to pull away from a close relationship with their mothers (and their dependency on them) on the one hand and yearnings to be involved in family life on the other. They may complain about many of their family's attributes, but they still want to be in the middle of the action. They may challenge and argue with their parents, especially their mothers, but unlike adolescents, they still care about what their parents think and do (Ames, Ilg, & Baker, 1988).

As the sphere of their social activities expands and their observational powers increase, children begin comparing their parents to other adults and their family to other families. Out of these experiences and comparative "studies," children develop a growing awareness of their parents' idiosyncrasies and faults. They reevaluate their idealized notion of their parents, even of adults in general, as they see them having fights, being cruel, looking or acting silly, lying or being dishonest. Their former belief in their parents' perfection is shattered—if not dramatically and at once, then slowly and bit by bit. Through this process, children begin to see parents as real people, far from perfect. This process leads to inevitable transformations in the parent-child relationship.

Because of this process of disillusionment and the gradual detachment from the parents that accompanies it, strains appear in their relationship in late latency. Latency-age children begin to look to new sources of authority and information. At first they look to other adults. Later they turn to peers as primary source of support and validation. By age 9 or 10, children become more and more critical of their parents, questioning their wisdom, authority, and the fairness of their rules, at times loudly, at other times quietly or sullenly.

Latency-age children become increasingly interested in fairness, particularly in the way their parents treat them when it comes to assigning blame and meting out punishments for misbehavior. Through middle childhood, children become more capable cognitively (better concrete operational thinkers) and morally, with the development of a morality of cooperation (involving a sharing of perspectives in the context of reciprocal relationships with peers in particular). As a result, their response to parental demands shifts from being an automatic response based on absolute acceptance of higher law and authority, characteristic of an earlier age's morality of restraint, to a more reasoned response that involves mental processing. Decisions are then reached through a process of mental trial-action in which the children strive to integrate internalized parental expectations and newly acquired societal values and prescriptions.

Latency-age children resent being bossed around by their parents. They are exquisitely sensitive to their parental criticism and admonitions. They resent most of all being patronized or "treated like a baby." Parents sometimes interpret their children's indifference toward them as a threat to their authority and react in a negative and controlling manner. In return, children may respond negatively by talking back or using angry sarcasm as a way of delineating their separateness (their identity). Some become rude or sulky. In this process of distancing from the parents, preadolescents may look to an older sibling as a source of support and authority. Often this move turns out to be a successful compromise, allowing the younger children to maintain affectionate ties and loyalties within the family group.

The disenchantment with parents (and other adults) is accelerated and intensified when there is severe marital conflict, separation, or divorce during this stage of a child's life. Such events may shatter children's trust in their parents' ability to protect and care for them. Parents may push children into a prematurely independent position or into taking on a spousal or parental role, further confusing the lines of authority and caregiving. This situation may persist for a substantial period of time in single-parent families.

The issue of authority in the parent-child relationship in middle childhood is complicated by recent trends in child rearing in the United States that further blur the dividing line between adults and children (Franks, 1993). Traditionally, adults were uniformly perceived as authoritative and protective, while children were perceived as dependent on adults, cared for and free of adult-type burdens and concerns. The new zeitgeist favors involving children prematurely with adult-type concerns and information, and has resulted in the establishment of a sort of psychological parity between children and adults. For instance, children in divorcing families are led to play a mediator role between their feuding parents. In single-parent families, children often are involved in parenting their younger siblings; they may be enlisted in the role of confidant by their lonely, single parent who uses them as sounding boards at times, as sources of consoling, of advice on a range of adult issues (household budget, family finances, job-related problems). Latch-key children in dual-career families generally are left to fend for themselves, to prepare dinner for themselves or even for the whole family, and to be alone without adult supervision for extended periods of time. This parity does not generally work to benefit a smooth unfolding of children's development, as they are thrust prematurely into social and psychological arenas for which they are unprepared (Winn, 1984).

The increased place occupied by secrets in the lives of latency-age children is one aspect of the withdrawal away from total dependence on parents and family. Secrets between children, excluding not only adults but also at times other children, draw boundaries between the child and others. The prevalence of clubs with secret passwords is a sign of the child's capacity to invest in extrafamilial relationships not just as an addition to, but to the exclusion of, the family. The growing importance of modesty and of privacy in the child's life at home work in this direction too.

Developmental researchers have analyzed four categories of social support: emotional, informational, instrumental, and companionship. Parents compete with friends and siblings as sources of companionship and emotional support, and teachers become alternative sources of information. While intimacy with friends increases with age, and with it reliance on them for emotional support, the level of support and intimacy with parents seem to remain relatively constant through the years of middle childhood. Through latency, parental appraisals of their children also become more complex. Both sides report more instances of conflict as children approach adolescence. Parents and teachers are perceived as less conflict-generating than siblings but more than friends (Reid, Ramey, & Burchinal, 1990).

Relationships with Teachers and Other Adults

Disillusioned with their parents, latency-age children turn admiringly toward other adults. Teachers, coaches, scout leaders, ministers, priests, and other adults with whom the children come in close contact gain in stature in the eyes of the children. Their authority further erodes that of the children's parents. This process of shifting allegiance from parents to other adults is accompanied by a willingness to accept social rules and conventions, to shift (albeit gradually) from morality and values imbedded in the family environment to a group morality (or moralities, as the children move in and out of several social spheres).

A similar challenge to parental authority stems from the access to information afforded children by the extensive presence of mass media, most notably television in its ever-pervasive presence. Television penetrates into the deepest recesses of the lives of families and children.

Even though latency-age children remain essentially respectful of parents and adults, patterns of compliance to parental or other adult authority are interspersed during these years with patterns of defiance and challenge of adult rules and norms. Teachers who, for a while, are counterpoints to the parents now themselves begin to be subjected to critical revisions; they, too, are lowered from their pedestals: "No more pencils, no more books, no more teacher's dirty looks!"

Children's relationships with their teachers are constantly evolving. In the early school years, teachers are idealized. Children want their teachers to like them; they perceive them as mother surrogates or as friends. With time, teachers' significance to children as sources of emotional and companionship support diminishes. By preadolescence, teachers are still perceived as a good source of information support but a poor source of fun companionship and emotional support. Children at that point perceive their relationships with teachers as significantly more conflictual than they did at a younger age (Reid et al., 1990). Prepubertal children turn increasingly to their peers as alternative sources of support, advice, and emotional well-being. Group standards gradually become more important than and may even supplant parental standards. The influence of the peer group reinforces oppositional, counterdependent trends in children. They establish a personal and social identity separate from the one developed earlier when wholly imbedded and dependent on the family. They gradually cease to be predictably compliant and eager to please adults.

Parents experience themselves as excluded from significant arenas of their child's life. Some react with sadness, nostalgia, and a sense of loss. Others feel anger and disappointment. Yet others react to the challenge to their authority in a controlling and punitive manner, with feelings of rejection or fears of being abandoned by their child. Negative consequences can follow if these feelings lead parents to interfere with their children's socialization and individuation, for example, blocking their access to peers and friends, or discouraging them from establishing ties with extrafamilial adults.

Crushes

Competing with the parents' prominent position and authority in the life of their latency-age child are two features in the child's fantasy life: the family romance and the phenomenon of crushes. The family romance is considered most typical of fantasy life of latency-age children. Most children at this age flirt in one way or another with such a fantasy.

Latency is characterized by the important role played by fantasy as a preferred means of impulse discharge (Sarnoff, 1976). A corollary of this function of fantasy in latency is the role played by the intense idealization of objects, some proximal to the child, others distant and unattainable. For example, such idealization may form the basis of a chumship, an exclusive peer relationship where the best friend is strongly idealized. At other times, a peer, more often an older adolescent (or even an adult sometimes), comes to embody all the traits and achievements the child wishes for. He or she becomes a concrete ego ideal (Goldings, 1979). This process becomes more widespread among adolescents and has given rise to several literary depictions, most notably those of Thomas Mann in *Tonio Kroger* (1964) and John Knowles in *A Separate Peace* (1959).

These intense idealizations form the basis of crushes and infatuations. Latency infatuations are seldom stable. Their objects change, sometimes at a breakneck speed, as processes of disillusionment and deidealization alternate with reorientations toward, and idealizations of, new objects that promise to fulfill the current interests and leanings of the child. The plasticity of idealizations is most evident in children's infatuation with distant figures: their hero worship.

These crushes and infatuations constitute an important stage in children's development. Boys and girls target their adoration and passion toward teens or young adults in the public eye, be they stars in show business, sports, or science. Rock stars, television and movie stars, and athletes are particularly favored by latency-age boys and girls who are attracted to glamour, physical prowess, and wealth. Both boys and girls are equally likely to develop infatuations. Yet because girls are more verbal and expressive about them, they are generally considered more prone to suffer from these bursts of passion.

Girls tend to be attracted to both male and female figures. For them, passionate attachments to distant, unattainable figures play a dual function: an identificatory self-aggrandizing function as well as a trying out of the girl's "capacity for loving and attachment in a safe, protected way with an unattainable and securely distant object" (Noshpitz & King, 1991, p. 365). Falling in love with somebody at a distance ensures them against the possibility of rejection. It also may have a group function; it is not unusual for a group of female (or male) friends to adore and ache for the same star, strengthening their group bonding by allowing them to live through a shared experience.

Boys, on the other hand, typically direct their admiration and glorification at male figures only, with a predominance of action figures among the icons of latency-age boys. This hero worship may help in the crystallization of special interests in the boy or girl, forming the basis for later career orientation.

At times, the object selected for admiration and love is a counterculture star (e.g., a heavy metal rock star) notorious for his or her bizarre or violent behavior. Adults become concerned about the meaning of such a choice. They worry whether the children are expressing thus a morbid, psychopathological tendency, whether they will be at risk for suicidal or antisocial-delinquent activities in their desire to emulate the "antihero." Yet this choice is often a sign of children's budding individuation, with a touch of rebellion mixed in. Unless this infatuation develops into a destructive obsession, invading other parts of children's lives, such a passion should be considered a part of growing up.

It is tempting for some parents to join in their children's crushes either as a way of protecting them or, more perniciously, as a way of blurring generational boundaries in an attempt to keep them close and family-bound. In either case, the parents feel threatened by the intrusion of this "worshipped other" who has such a powerful claim on their child's heart and mind. It may be reassuring for these parents to remember that for the large majority of preadolescent children, their parents remain the "real" heroes to be emulated.

REFERENCES

Ames, L. B., Ilg, F. L., & Baker, S. M. (1988). *Your ten-to-fourteen-year-old.* New York: Dell Publishing.

Ames, L. B., & Haber, C. C. (1991). *Your nine-year-old.* New York: Dell Publishing.

Benson, R., & Harrison, S. (1980). The eye of the hurricane: From seven to ten. In S. I. Greenspan and G. H. Pollock (Eds.), *The course of life* (pp. 137–144). Adelphi, MD: NIMH.

Franks, L. (1993, October 10). Little big people. *New York Times Magazine,* 28–34.

Gilligan, C. (1982). New maps of development: New visions of maturity. *American Journal of Orthopsychiatry, 52,* 199–212.

Goldings, H. (1979). Development from ten to thirteen years. In J. Noshpitz (Ed.), *Basic handbook of child psychiatry: Vol. 1 Development* (pp. 199–204). New York: Basic Books.

Knowles, J. (1959). *A separate peace.* New York: Bantam Books.

Lewis, M., & Volkmar, F. (1990). *Clinical aspects of child and adolescent development* (3rd ed.). Philadelphia: Lea & Febiger.

Mann, T. (1964). *Tonio Kroger in death in Venice and seven other stories.* New York: Vintage Books.

Noshpitz, J., & King, R. (1991). *Pathways of growth* (Vol. 1). New York: John Wiley & Sons.

Reid, M., Landesman, S., Treder, R., & Jaccard, J. (1989). My family and friends: Six- to twelve-year-old children's perceptions of social support. *Child Development, 60,* 896–910.

Reid, M., Ramey, S. L., & Burchinal, M. (1990). Dialogues with children about their families. *New Directions for Child Development, 48,* 5–27.

Sarnoff, C. (1976). *Latency.* New York: Jason Aronson.

Shapiro, T., & Perry, R. (1976). Latency revisited. *Psychoanalytic Study of the Child, 31,* 79–105.

Winn, M. (1984). *Children without childhood.* New York: Penguin Books.

11 / Transformation of Interpersonal Relationships

Audrey J. Clarkin

An 8-year-old boy who is always welcome in playground games, a newcomer who plays by the rules and knows how to be on a team, a third-grade girl who whines when she doesn't get her way and seems to find fault with playmates, a youngster who runs to an adult for help when there is a disagreement, a boy bigger than his agemates who gets his way by bullying. These are some of the children found in a typical school setting, where group activities are the norm and getting along with others is an important skill.

The latency-age child presents as attentive, reasonably behaved, and actively involved outside of home and family. Cognitively at Piaget's concrete-operational level, the child's developmental task is to gain a sense of competency in the world outside of home. School provides opportunity for intellectual achievement and for expanded social contacts. Responsibilities increase as do accomplishments in academics, rule-governed games, hobbies, and group and team activities. With mastery comes a positive self-image. With doubts and failure, the child experiences frustration and a sense of inadequacy.

We can ask about a latency-age child, "What has happened up to now to explain this youngster's positive or negative social behavior?" While the answer is complicated, we can begin with the premise that a child's social competence comes from experience in multiple and close relationships.

Initially, attachments are vertical, starting with parents and then with other significant adults who protect the infant and expect submission. Horizontal attachments arise later with other children and provide lessons in cooperation and competition. Within every relationship, two individuals are responding and adapting. Thus, the latency-age child needs to be understood from the context of earlier social experiences.

MATERNAL ATTACHMENT — A PREREQUISITE FOR SOCIALIZATION

Adequate mothering is critical for bonding. Besides safety and nurturance, the mother shares her attitude toward the environment. She facilitates exploration of the larger world, allays fears, and encourages initial contact with peers. The mother teaches the child how to begin and maintain personal interactions. Without this contribution, deprivation studies show long-term negative effects with children displaying inappropriate avoidance or aggression. Secure attachment to the mother is followed by bonding to both parents. Early protection and affection provide a sense of "basic trust" that enables the child to take the next developmental step.

PARENT IDEALIZATION

Initial emotional support, physical care, and learning come to the child from parents. The young child regards parents as all-powerful, all-knowing, all-caring, and all-controlling. At early developmental levels, a child's physical and psychological needs dictate parental idealization, whether it is of physical strength, skills, and capabilities, or of power to direct or change the sequence of events that impact on the child on a day-to-day basis. Others are seen and experienced in relation to parents.

The role of parents in early socialization cannot be emphasized enough. They serve as models for the child to imitate. Their social attitudes, skills, and predispositions are communicated both verbally and nonverbally and serve as a baseline for how the child will respond socially. If parents are strict and punitive at home, they tend to have children who are either too submissive or too aggressive. In contrast, parents who talk about their own feelings and the feelings of others tend to have children who are more sensitive and interact more successfully. Examinations of interpersonal characteristics of parents, parenting styles, parental discipline, and infant-parent attachment have shown predictable links between parent-child interactions and child-peer relationships (Maccoby, 1993; Putallaz & Heflin, 1990).

Two specific aspects of parental social influence—power and warmth—have been suggested as necessary linkage for social experiences (Maccoby & Martin, 1983). (See Table 11.1.)

Parents who make reasonable and developmentally appropriate demands on their children and communicate expectations with affection promote social and emotional maturity. When parents are undemanding yet accepting, children exhibit immaturity, dependence, and low impulse control. When parents are rejecting and demanding, children display aggression and/or withdrawal with peers. Children most negatively affected are those who have rejecting and undemanding parents. These children, lacking both inner and outer support, are drawn toward antisocial peer groups.

Parents serve many functions in encouraging peer relations: providing security, direct coaching of how to get along with peers, acting as role models, selecting a favorable environment (neighborhood and school), and arranging peer activities (Rubin & Sloman, 1984). While parental supervision diminishes as the child becomes more independent, the quality of affective bonding still remains important.

INFLUENCE OF SIBLINGS

Because the family is a child's initial social group, the impact of siblings, not just of parents, is salient: Although sibling relationships are "a given," not under the child's control, the growth-promoting aspects of sibling contacts include perspective taking, understanding of social consequences, handling of aggression, and learning ways to resolve conflict (Dunn, 1988).

Four types of early sibling relationships have been studied: supportive, cooperative, ambivalent, and hostile (Dunn, 1983). Age and sex differences, parental attitudes, the temperament of the child and of the sibling, and the quality of the environment are factors that promote cooperative and supportive exchanges or, if aversive, can result in hostile and ambivalent sibling relationships. Jealousy, sibling rivalry for the attention of parents, and regression and aggression toward the

TABLE 11.1

Parental Influences on Social Development

Dimension	Type
Power	Demanding vs. undemanding
Warmth	Accepting vs. rejecting

new family member are all familiar negative reactions. When these responses are not resolved, the sibling relationship can become disturbed and disturbing.

Generally, an older, more mature sibling exerts more influence than a younger one. Most children have at least one sibling and because they are usually close in age, a sibling is the first peer the child experiences. Not only are sibling relationships long-standing, but siblings between the ages of 4 to 6 spend more than twice as much time together as they spend with their parents. Siblings enjoy the first child-child relationship with the opportunity for bilaterality and mutuality. Age differences (except with twins) as well as sharing parents and parent-planned activities differentiate sibling from peer interactions.

Sibling relationships, although sometimes conflictual, enable a child to practice social exchanges without worry of rejection and with increased proficiency, mutual support, and comradeship. The result is that a child experiences increased self-esteem and confidence and reaches out to age mates who are not related. Siblings are not selected freely the same way as friends, and sometimes they can be a constant source of friction, having negative impact on a child. This is particularly true when a child serves a consistent role vis-à-vis the sibling, as the scapegoat, the gofer, the lowly one. Unfortunately, the child often expects and fulfills the same role in the peer group.

The Process of Socialization

As the child's world enlarges and begins to include people other than parents and siblings, social expectations change. The child can no longer depend on unconditional love but now must begin to relate to different individuals, both adult and age mates, and handle appropriate developmental tasks.

CONTRIBUTING FACTORS

Temperament, categorized according to 9 variables in terms of "easy," "slow to warm-up," and "difficult" (Chess & Thomas, 1984) provides a set that enables some children to develop socially more easily than others. From early on, children with "easy" temperaments move toward others, appreciate them, and learn from them without great effort. Time is the important ingredient for "slow to warm-up" children. New situations, new people, new surroundings cause them discomfort, and they require an adjustment period and much reassurance. Children with "difficult" temperaments are inconsistent, unpredictable, and overreactive. Their negative behaviors often satisfy immediate needs, get reinforced, and are repeated, but peers perceive these children as annoying and unlikeable (Eisenberg et al., 1995; Rothart, Ahadi, & Hershey, 1994).

Certain traits are pervasive. The social progress of shy children depends very much on parenting strategies (Kagan, 1982). Mothers who are calm and consistent in their expectations encourage their shy children to deal with social anxiety. They help them to adapt to both the setting and the people in it. Although the child's personality does not change, the mother teaches him or her to cope and adjust to social demands.

Environment as a contributing factor to a child's development can promote social awareness and facilitate adjustment by appearing safe and comfortable or raise fears and anxiety if it is threatening or noxious. Careful selection of where children live, play, and attend school can provide positive social opportunities but is not an available option for many families.

Family communication patterns can impact either positively or negatively on how children view themselves and how effective they can be with others. Parents who engage in direct, honest interchange on issues, problems, and expectations encourage the same in their children. Aggressive, demeaning comments serve to lower self-confidence. Avoiding talk about feelings and reactions is a strong message from parents to children that such dialogue is unimportant and irrelevant.

As children mature, they naturally move from the confines of the nuclear family to the extended family, to the neighborhood, and to the bigger world of school and community. As a result, parents and siblings remain important but become less dominant.

PRESCHOOL PEERS

Latest statistics indicate that in the United States, more than half of the mothers with preschool children are working full time. Consequently, child-care arrangements and parent surrogates become important ingredients in the socialization of young children even before they are old enough to attend preschool programs. Many nursery schools accept young children; it is no longer an exception for 2-year-olds who have not yet achieved independence in toilet training, eating, and dressing to be in a setting with other children. Numerous young children are spending most of their waking hours, and some of their sleeping hours, in the company of age mates in day-care centers. Children outnumber adults in these programs so that there is constant opportunity for peer communication, imitation, and interaction. Toddlers soon learn to connect to each other and refer to individual peers as "friends" because of daily contact.

Many children spend 3 to 4 years in a preschool setting where play has provided opportunities for socialization (Furman & Bierman, 1984). They begin kindergarten having had numerous and diverse prior social experiences that shape their current and future behavior. The establishment of peer relationships can be considered a stage-salient developmental issue starting with preschoolers and continuing throughout the life span (Cicchetti, Toth, & Bush, 1988). Because of these frequent, early interactions, peer relationships become more intense and adult influence is diminished.

PLAYMATES

What is the effect on the child as parents, siblings, and home become less prominent? The impact of new activities, relationships, and settings offers the child data for new perspectives. Peers are more available—in day care, in the neighborhood, on the playground—and occupy the child's thoughts, wishes, and free time. Enjoyment and satisfaction come from fantasy and coordinated play that involves agreement and excitement. When play activity escalates, children need to accommodate to each other, thus learning the give and take of sharing and cooperating with equals.

ROLE OF ADULTS

Early latency children tend to idealize parents, especially the same-sex parent with whom they identify. They gradually come to realize that parents are fallible. Normally, latency-age youngsters do not overtly oppose or reject their parents' norms and are generally acquiesent. Children show opposition only indirectly as they become more verbal, more eager to debate issues using their new cognitive skills to challenge parents. Other adults—teachers, coaches, scout leaders—assume supportive roles or exert pressures on the child to perform, to measure up, to succeed. The child's horizons expand with the recognition that other grown-ups are important and can provide nurturance, direction, and instruction as well as criticism and frustration.

Peer Relationships

An observation of a school playground affords an immediate view of the continuum of social interactions. A child sitting or wandering alone who does not initiate contact and is unnoticed by peers probably has spent many recesses this way. Pairs of children playing and talking suggests mutual enjoyment and satisfaction. Group games that depend on cooperation, following rules, and a certain skill level appeal to older youngsters.

The role of peers becomes increasingly important for the school-age child. Family relationships (Putallaz, 1983), a child's early socialization (Ladd and Price, 1986), as well as temperamental (Olweus, 1980) and environmental factors already have been cited as contributing to the quality of peer interactions. Contact with peers leads to closer relationships, and some become friends. Friends offer companionship and recreation, opportunities to share thoughts and possessions, to serve as confidant and critic, to learn loyalty and tolerance, and to support and be supported in

times of stress and transition (Asher & Parker, 1989).

Some children find enjoyment within structured groups where there is adult direction and supervision, such as scouts, sports teams, music and art groups. Conflict is minimized in such settings because of the organized nature of the activity, and the child completes constructive, enjoyable activities with satisfaction. When an immature or socially inappropriate child has the opportunity to make a special friend within such a group, the next step can be more spontaneous play dates with selected peers and finally increased social acceptance in a peer group.

As peer interactions become a major influence in the lives of most children, children become more adept at resolving conflict. They tune in to the needs and wants of their age mates and work out goals with mutual satisfaction. During this period of childhood, behavioral norms are learned through the many interactions, positive and negative, within the peer group and reinforced by a powerful sense of belonging.

Peers and play represent the two important foci of this developmental period that provide learning experiences not available in parent-child interactions. To relate as an equal establishes comradeship and companionship and can set up friction with the demands or expectations of adults just because they are older, more experienced, and able to inflict consequences or bestow rewards. More important, age mates are usually at the same developmental level and can enjoy the commonalities of imagination, of ideas, and of feelings in spontaneous play that promote good feelings.

The Neighborhood Peer Group

Historically, the neighborhood peer group was a cross-age, informal, available interpersonal opportunity that allowed children to go from their homes to the street or nearby play area where they could spend all or most of their free time. Older children were given the chance to become role models and teachers. Immature children had an opportunity to play with younger ones without being criticized or ridiculed. Siblings were included in the same activity. Neighborhood play did not require much structure, organization, or equipment as it involved spontaneous games such as tag, hide and seek, or two children playing catch.

In the neighborhood context, it was easier to enter or leave the group without accusations or banishment so that an individual's tolerance for interaction and conflict could be accomodated without consequence. At the same time, the neighborhood was viewed as a comfortable way to have friends and to enjoy leisure time. Close emotional bonds were formed and maintained. Many youngsters learned informal lessons of how to deal with others, how to resolve differences, and how to negotiate what they wanted.

In contrast to structured activities or scheduled play dates, the neighborhood peer group did not involve an adult who monitored, supervised, influenced, or judged. "Neighborhood" is a relative concept in different areas, for example, an 8-year-old boy whose closest neighbor lives on a farm 5 miles away is quite different from the suburban child whose friend is a car ride away or the urban child whose friend is in the next apartment.

Current societal changes—two working parents, single-parent and blended families, staggered work schedules, and safety issues—often do not permit children to be supervised at home. As child-care arrangements overrule other considerations, opportunities for neighborhood friends do not exist as readily as they have in the past. Some children are overprogrammed into daily after-school activities and do not develop the social skills that emerge from spontaneous play. Some use their busy schedules as an excuse not to develop close friendships. Other children view every play date as an issue of acceptance or rejection, reacting so personally to refusal that it lowers their self-esteem. When play dates do occur but the activity is TV watching or video game playing, there is minimal communication of thoughts and feelings and children do not get to know each other as separate and different.

Peer Interactions

SCHOOL INFLUENCES

School-related activities provide the greatest opportunity for socialization and tend to promote similarities among age mates rather than differ-

ences. In their efforts to be accepted, children adopt the looks, the actions, and the perspectives of their peers. Attitudes and reactions of peers rival those of parents in importance as youngsters pursue self-definition and social acceptance. Achievement contributes to self-image. For most children, school is the setting not only for academic success but for social and athletic recognition. It is in school that children interact with classmates, acquaintances, teammates, and friends. Children from different ethnic and socioeconomic backgrounds who exhibit varying skills and abilities come to school where they must meet common expectations for academic performance and group behavior. The bond that results makes children aware of each other, prompting them to imitate and conform to group norms as they seek social acceptance.

For many children, school is the most reliable, most secure part of their growing-up years, 6 hours per day, 5 days per week with a teacher assigned for a whole year, special teachers in art and music who teach them year after year, classmates with whom the child connects daily. Studies dealing with positive peer influences (Berndt, 1989), negative peer consequences (Asher & Wheeler, 1985), and ongoing peer rejection within the school setting (Coie & Dodge, 1983) emphasize that as children develop, peer companionship and support become even greater determinants of social adjustment or maladjustment.

Especially when the family at home is dysfunctional, age mates are needed to sustain and support the child. Peers replace parents in affection and affiliation. Home neglect or abuse is repressed and the child invests emotionally in the activities and interactions of the learning environment. For children who are too inhibited or disinterested or antagonistic toward age mates and achievement, school experiences can be negative and aversive. The more these children feel isolated from schoolmates, the more they can become deviant and disliked as other children ignore or actively reject them.

Responsibility for nurturing and providing social and emotional support to children from troubled backgrounds and families is taxing for teachers. From a teacher's perspective, support systems other than school are minimal and the number of troubled children has increased dramatically as has the seriousness of the problems, which include poverty, physical violence, and sexual abuse.

Some teachers feel they have not received sufficient training to deal with such extremes of social or emotional crises, others are personally unavailable, and still others are heroic in their dedication of time and personal effort.

Peers on the Playground

When children interact positively, they can learn effective communication, control of aggression and of sexual impulses, and develop loyalty and a sense of identity, both personal and sexual (Hartup, 1989). The academic skills required in a classroom are quite different from the skills that are necessary on the playground. Children who are physically well coordinated, who play fairly, and who know how to follow game rules often are sought after. Athletic ability and persistence are highly regarded, so these youngsters can achieve high social status. As children mature, group play becomes more common and more important. It is not only physical dexterity but social skills that determine playground success.

When age mixing is an option on a playground, all children play predominantly with same-grade peers, but popular children have more older, upper-grade friends while rejected children feel more comfortable with younger playmates (Ladd, 1983). Sometimes troubled children attach to older kids for protection or submit to their influence for acceptance or to avoid contact with age mates.

Friendships

There is a special quality about a friend that does not apply to peers. Friendships develop over time and in relation to age and capacity. Because friendship involves closeness and reciprocity as children mature, selection tends to those with similar attitudes and behaviors. This tendency strengthens personal identity but also excludes age mates who are different in culture, in language, in background. Developmental changes in friendship proceed from a focus on concrete, ex-

ternal attributes and move to more abstract levels of loyalty and intimacy. Selman (1980) has provided a model to describe stages that occur in children's conceptions of friendship, offering a continuum that begins with minimal interaction, then one-way assistance, cooperation, mutual sharing, and can develop, finally, into autonomous interdependence.

Initially, friendship is defined as the interaction of two individuals who come together to play. Two young boys play with a truck by racing it to each other. Quickly, one boy takes the truck and wants it for himself. The other boy grabs the truck and runs away with it. The physical battle that follows is both cause and justification for separation. The next stage involves a beginning awareness of the thoughts and feelings of the other, but the conflict and decision is one-sided. Two children are playing soccer. The ball is kicked back and forth with enjoyment until the better player decides to show up her friend. Anger and jealousy are feelings prompted by this action, and the game ends with one child going home. Reciprocity describes Stage 2, not only in maintaining the relationship but also in dissolving it.

Two 7-year-old girls have been playing chess and decide to stop after three games as they have had enough. Mutual support in Stage 3 provides complementarity and conflicts often are resolved by talking things out in order to continue the relationship. Two friends who are working on a joint science project agree to divide the work according to their strengths; one will do the writing, the other will do the artwork. What is evident is their recognition of each other's skills and feelings, the need for a plan to get the project completed and wish to remain friends. In the fourth stage, commitment is based on trust, toleration for the other, and acceptance of differences and is atypical of the latency child, both cognitively and emotionally.

Interactions that occur between children on a regular basis increase the quantity, complexity, and degree of their social interactions. Children begin to use the word "friend" during the early preschool years, and the development of children's understandings about friendships has been studied at different ages (Berndt & Perry, 1986; Selman, 1980). Friendships become more stable as children grow older. Children's social success not only promotes relationships but improves as a result of making and keeping friends. When children perceive each other as friends, they interact more by laughing, by sharing, by cooperating, and by working out differences (Newcomb & Brady, 1982).

Developmental changes in friendship parallel advances in the way children think about the world (Berndt, 1987), moving from the practical, concrete level to the more abstract and conceptual. What is unique about friendships in contrast to peer interactions is the two-way commitment. As children move through the latency phase, contact with age mates and special friendships consume more of their time, thought, and energy and provide much social satisfaction or dissatisfaction.

GENDER DIFFERENCES

Young children seem not to attend to gender and are quite content to have a playmate. By third grade, girls prefer to socialize with other girls while boys enjoy physical games with other boys. This tendency for same-sex friends continues until middle school (Sullivan, 1953), except for individual friendships that have a special basis, such as two children whose families are friends, a girl who is an outstanding athlete and welcome on the boys' team, a common interest such as chess or art. During the elementary years, girls choose smaller groups of friends and spend time sharing experiences and opinions. Boys are more involved in physical activities and tend to have a wider circle of friends without doing much disclosure.

When boys argue, their exchange is immediate and intense but usually gets resolved on the spot. Girls tend to react emotionally when conflict reflects on their self-image. They experience hurt feelings and retreat from the other person.

FRIENDSHIP FORMATION AND MAINTENANCE

Making friends is a different skill from keeping friends. Often children who are outer-directed, who have a high energy level, and who are ready and willing to initiate activities are successful in their contacts with new age mates. The same characteristics that help them to engage also can prompt them to become quickly demanding or disinterested and ready for other social experiences. In contrast is the child who takes time to connect with a peer, who waits, often longer than

the other person wants, but slowly and carefully approaches and transforms an acquaintance into a friend. These children may be described as cautious and shy, but when they have established themselves with age mates, they do bond. They have no need to collect many friends but prove themselves loyal and dependable to those they select.

Children learn about friendships in early childhood via play and in dyads. Interest is based on another child's toy or activity and can be of short duration as there is minimal attachment. In middle childhood, inclusion and peer group acceptance often is achieved by verbal exchange (gossip), which establishes rapport and solidarity. Social contacts become complex, not just in number but in variability. Time spent with peers provides a framework for understanding cooperation and competition so that friendships are maintained despite conflict. Groups of friends emerge on numerous bases—interests, athletics, classes—and usually include commonalities of age, sex, and sometimes race. Peers represent co-equals who promote prosocial skills of communication, control of aggression, sexual impulses, and formation of inner values. Generally same-sex peers who become friends provide mutual support and security, exchange genuine affection, and instill mutual confidence.

The perceptions of friends and peers have been studied by interviewing latency-age children (Kernberg, Clarkin, Greenblatt, & Cohen, 1992). Progressive levels of social development present a wide continuum, ranging from isolation to highly positive interactions, as seen in Table 11.2.

An observable sequential developmental pattern of peer selection begins with young children focusing on concrete, external attributes. A friend is someone who is fun to play with and has toys. In preschool interactions, age mates associate physically with each other in play and progress to a level at age 5 or 6 where physical characteristics—"Bobby is bigger"—or special possessions—"Joey has a Nintendo or a super car"—become the norm. By age 7, selection is based on similarities—"Jessica and I are friends because we both like . . ." Between the ages of 8 and 10, the need and desire for a special friend includes secrets and sharing. Older children appreciate more abstract aspects of friendships such as trusting or caring, but in late childhood or adolescence

TABLE 11.2

Cornell Subscale on Developmental Appropriateness

0 Does not show any social awareness of peers; makes no attempt to interact.

1 Not able to initiate friendships with peers, although may relate to adults as "friends." Observes other kids from a distance.

2 Participates with peers only with adult support and direction. Does not have friends even in structured situations.

3 Interacts with a few peers in structured settings (e.g., school, camp) but does not initiate new peer contacts easily; physical aggression or other alienating behaviors interfere with making friends.

4 Frequent peer interactions, at times disrupted, but can maintain one or two friends seen outside structured settings. Does not initiate new friendships easily.

5 Well liked by peers, included easily. No difficulty in making friends and has two or three close friends.

6 Has close friends with whom there is frequent contact and reciprocal sharing of experiences. May have relationships with older, younger, and opposite-gender peers. Has friends for a long time, is popular, can be a leader, and can initiate new friendships with ease.

qualities such as loyalty and intimacy become central. The range of appropriate, age-related social interactions is wide and includes variability related to temperament, previous experiences, and current opportunities. There is a common developmental progression even though not all children of the same age will be at the same level.

LOSING FRIENDS

Losing friends can be distressful regardless of the reason. Many children are devastated when a friend moves away. Their first thought is "I wish I hadn't become friends." That response can be momentary but often is replaced by loneliness. Sometimes friends are mismatched, because of temperament or goals or actual behavior, and they are relieved when the friendship ends. Other times friendships start out mutually satisfying but stop being so. Dyads become one-sided, with the abandoned friend wondering why and how it happened. In some instances, friends initially connect but develop socially and emotionally at different rates. They then distance from each other as they no longer share common interests.

Social Success and Failure

What are the ingredients that help children to be socially successful? Many social interactions become reciprocal at an early age so when a child enters a classroom and says "hello" to a peer, that age mate generally will respond. Moreover, the probability that both children will repeat the greeting has been reinforced.

For children who spend most of their waking time in school and for whom traditional support systems, such as extended family or neighbors, are unavailable, school becomes the critical environment for social learning. Statistics indicate that anywhere from 30 to 75% of the children referred to clinics (depending on age) experience peer difficulties (Achenbach & Edelbrock, 1981).

Teachers appreciate the social skills that children need in a group, such as cooperation, concern for others, and acceptance of different opinions. However, pressures of time to cover academic curriculum can prompt teachers to see socialization as an interruption. When student interactions are negative and interfere with learning, they can affect classroom climate in a disruptive way that becomes contagious.

Some schools have introduced sequential social skills training programs integrated with literature or social studies with the goal of improving students' interpersonal skills. Based on the premise that well-adjusted students can serve as models for their classmates and that brainstorming within a classroom can provide many more alternatives for problem solving, this model has proven especially helpful to three clusters of children: impulsive children who are smart but who act too quickly; shy, inhibited children who know the right answer but are too timid to act; and multicultural students who have learned different behavioral norms.

As thinking skills develop, children become more aware of others' actions and responses and the different feelings that prompt behaviors. By about the age 8, children can recognize how they think and feel in a given situation and can predict how other age mates will handle themselves. They understand that responses can be the same or different from their own. It is at this developmental point that peer interactions take on even greater significance (Smollar & Youniss, 1982). Knowing oneself is enriched by comparing and contrasting with the perceived status or skills of age mates. New social behaviors are tested out with peers doing different actions for the same reasons or the same actions for different reasons. Usually children seek out peers at their same level so friendships develop gradually in a mutual context or in some cases move quickly from enjoyable play to reciprocal sharing and personal concern. Specific behaviors such as peer conversations (Gottman, 1983), actions that bring peers toward each other (Coie & Kupersmidt, 1983), peer quarrels (Shantz, 1986) and how peers perceive peer responses (Ladd & Mars, 1986) help us to understand the social process.

The requisite social skills to begin interactions so that a friendship can develop involve initiation, a level of social ease, and an ability to engage. They can be described and recorded to determine success or failure. Five critical areas of interaction have been suggested as determining school social success: how to enter a group, how to deal with success, how to manage failure, awareness of social expectations, and awareness of teacher expectations (Putallaz & Gottman, 1981).

GROUP ENTRY

Let us illustrate the first task of entering a group. The socially attuned child approaches a group that is playing a game, first stands and watches, becoming a participant observer. The child then makes a gesture or comment, a smile or notice of success—a clap for a soccer goal or a shout "Great kick!"—then moves in closer to the group. These subtle maneuvers provide a message to other children not only that the child wishes to join in their play but can do it in an agreeable way. Often there is a waiting time. The child, although eager to participate, does not impulsively rush up to demand but delays until an invitation is offered. Sometimes the child suggests an acceptable plan: "I'll get another player so the teams can be even."

Contrast this behavior with the too-rapid insistence of another child who ends up puzzled by the group's refusal. Unaware of the social process and propelled by what he wants, he ends up disappointed by the rejection he receives. Externalizers move too quickly without appreciating the group's perspective and often brag about success without considering other children's feelings. They are puzzled when they meet resentment. Anger, temper tantrums, and physical aggression can be products of the youngster who doesn't know how to handle failure, and these behaviors alienate peers.

Another cluster characterized as internalizers are anxious, withdrawn, and insecure. They also wish to be included in peer activities but are unsuccessful because they do not translate their wishes into actions. Internalizers, although inwardly pleased about their achievements, tend to inhibit what they have accomplished. They go unnoticed and unappreciated. Internalizers get caught up in worry so they do not take a realistic view of situations. They remain immobilized and friendless. Internalizers endure failure and disappointment without comment and end up with lowered self-esteem. The degree of their loneliness can depend on the degree of rejection, differences in behavioral style, and self-perceptions (Strauss, 1988). Some find satisfaction in personal interests or creative solitary pursuits.

ISOLATION AND REJECTION

While children who are ignored by peers can experience unhappiness, those who are rejected by peers feel unwanted and isolated. Rejection can bring negative self-image, intense loneliness, and long-term maladjustment (Parker & Asher, 1977). Children whose serious social problems result in rejection are most often described as aggressive and disruptive. It should be emphasized that not all aggressive children are rejected. Some aggressive children have other appealing qualities, such as a sense of humor or athletic ability, that redeem them to their peers. It is when a youngster prevents other children from achieving their goals and does so in a provocative, aggravating way that behavior is labeled as disruptive and noxious.

Rejected children have difficulty interpreting specific social situations, controlling their reactions, and thinking of effective ways to get along with peers. Between 5 and 10% of children have fairly serious chronic problems with being rejected (Asher, 1990). Rejected internalizers experience more loneliness than aggressive-rejected children (Asher, Parkhurst, Hymel, & Williams,

1990), because they have fewer outlets for their unhappiness.

Rejection starts with a particular child's social ineptness (Coie, 1990). Because of how the child thinks and feels, negative reactions from the peer group are anticipated. The youngsters in the peer group respond with intense dislike. The cycle gets perpetuated with the recurring actions of the rejected child and the reactions of others.

Externalizing forms of dysfunction, such as delinquency, can be predicted by rejection based on aggression and disruptive behavior. Internalizing forms of disorder, such as depression, are better predicted by rejection based on anxious, withdrawn behavior (Hymel & Rubin, 1985). Aggression, disruptiveness, and withdrawal account for only two thirds of the rejected population; the critical factor seems connected with the aversive impact on others.

Children who experience continuous rejection are subject to greater stress, more aggression, more loneliness, less support, and have lower self-esteem than their age mates (Coie & Dodge, 1983).

Self-Esteem

The critical dimension for social success is understanding the concerns and goals of others. Sensitivity to the other child and empathy for the present experience seems most valued. When a child can answer affirmatively the question "Does this other child make me feel good about myself?" a positive, mutual relationship can develop. This capacity to appreciate others implies a positive sense of self, an ability to understand another's viewpoint, and an acceptance of self and other. Positive self-esteem and interpersonal sensitivity result from successful social relationships.

Friendship and Popularity

A distinction can be made between friendship, defined as interpersonal closeness, and popularity, defined as group reputation (Bukowski & Hoza, 1989). Measures of self-worth are more strongly predicted by friendships whereas popularity relates to perceived self-confidence. Children's reputations in a group can enhance (Ladd & Price, 1987) or inhibit (Asher & Wheeler, 1985) their sense of peer belongingness and acceptance. Social isolation and low popularity correlate highly with poor academic achievement and low self-esteem. Unsatisfactory interpersonal behaviors involving aggression and withdrawal can result in significant unhappiness and long-term maladjustment (Coie, Belding, & Underwood, 1988).

Conflict Resolution

Time spent together in cooperative interaction (Hartup, 1989) is a requisite for friendship. Childhood friends provide emotional support as well as opportunities for learning new skills, for companionship, and for having fun. Disagreements among friends occur more often than with nonfriends, but there is a greater effort made to resolve the conflict and arrive at a mutual solution. During middle childhood, both cooperation and conflict resolution are necessary to maintain friendship. Regardless of gender, conflict between friends differ qualitatively as well as quantitatively from that between nonfriends.

An interaction exists between friendship and age in relation to conflict resolution (Furman & Bierman, 1984; Selman, 1980). Research suggests that the resolution strategies adopted by school-age children and their friends are what make the difference in maintaining friendships, not the number of interpersonal problems. Recent school programs that teach resolution techniques emphasize alternative solutions: take turns, give your reasons, team up with someone who agrees with you, give in, find another group that thinks your way, distract from the problem, do something agreeable, compromise, and so on. Youngsters successful in settling disagreements not only understand the position of their opponent but also utilize a variety of strategies to work things out and are not restricted to one approach. Besides compromise, children can relinquish their position for the sake of harmony or agree to disagree. The critical aspect is how two people feel toward each other after the response.

Selman (1980) describes conflict resolution as

contributing to two most important tasks of childhood: *individuation,* or gaining a sense of self, and *differentiation,* or recognizing one's uniqueness in contrast to others. Shantz (1986) sees conflict management as the process that helps children develop appreciation of others, empathy, and problem-solving skills. He views working out differences as a critical determinant for social acceptance or rejection. Referred children in contrast to nonreferred children do not recognize the reciprocity in conflict resolution.

Learning as a Critical Factor in Socialization

PEER LEARNING

Schools remain traditional in their organization, structure, and expectations. Despite studies that show peer learning promotes communication skills, creative and critical thinking, empathy, and other positive behaviors, schools have not changed.

Three approaches to socialized learning can promote students' academic and social progress within a classroom: peer tutoring, cooperative learning, and peer collaboration (Damon & Phelps, 1989). Tutoring can be educationally valuable by offering personal benefit to the tutor by increasing self-worth. Cooperative learning involves students working in small heterogeneous groups where each member contributes and profits from the efforts of others. Sometimes the task is divided into parts or according to abilities, so that readers, writers, and artists contribute their special skill to complete a finished product. Through discovery learning, peer collaboration offers classmates the opportunity to think aloud and to share ideas.

In all three learning contexts, teachers continue to play a critical role in directing instruction. If their attitude is supportive, the peer process that motivates, sensitizes, and strengthens student social and academic achievement can be realized.

SCHOOL ATTENDANCE

Although some students view school as a haven from the day-to-day storms of the world around them, other youngsters who face neglect and abuse from irresponsible parents avoid school. Frequent absences provide relief from assignments and from daily routines, and a pattern of chronic absenteeism develops. The child has neither home nor school as a base and tends to connect with other "drifting" children who bond with each other as truants and engage in inappropriate, often antisocial behavior. For these children, loyalty to the group surpasses all other commitments, and members fulfill the need for affiliation and support.

Individual needs steming from problems such as substance abuse, physical and sexual abuse, homelessness, and neglect produce children who are unable to contribute to group cohesiveness in a classroom. These students are burdened by family secrets that prevent them from making friends, having play dates, participating in school activities, and sharing feelings and thoughts with peers. Reluctance to return home, early school arrival, torn or soiled clothing, bruise marks, and refusal to share personal information are cues to alert teachers to home problems that can require legal and medical intervention. A team approach including teacher, nurse, psychologist, social worker, and principal is needed to deal with such crises.

Children who derive little pleasure from learning and do not interact with age mates view school as meaningless and irrelevant. Withdrawn and anxious, they do not relate easily with peers and have neither academic nor social connections. These children become truant, not making the effort to attend class, remaining at home to watch TV or sleep. They establish dysfunctional patterns at a young age and continue to be nonfunctioning and isolated as they get older, often depending on public assistance.

Children who are threatened, verbally or physically, by a peer or older student view staying away from school as a relief, and they regress socially. In persistent cases of bullying, where children are intimidated and frightened, the help of parents, school staff, and outside professionals is required to set firm limits to deter the bully, to protect the victim, and to provide counseling for both.

Children with separation anxiety and those who are school phobic are two distinct populations. Historically, the term *separation anxiety* described the fear of leaving mother or home. Often the child fantasizes the pleasures of remaining with the favored parent because of intense attachment and need for security. Sometimes the child anticipates the parent's destruction if the child were to leave, and this fear prompts the child to remain close to the parent to prevent trauma. In both cases, the child's anxiety increases and is exhibited when leaving the parent and when the parent is expected to return. Emotions escalate and the child becomes visibly distressed. Some children are not conscious of the etiology but seek excuses to remain at home, often citing felt physical complaints, such as stomachaches or headaches. If such excuses are permitted, the child becomes increasingly preoccupied and less available for social contacts.

School phobia represents a type of school avoidance that is considered in another chapter. Phobic reactions to school can start with an unpleasant social experience, such as exclusion from playground games, that becomes exaggerated and causes distress to the child so that a pattern of avoidance develops. Teachers often are unaware of the child's discomfort and fail to appreciate the seriousness of the situation. The child feels isolated and different from other children; if teacher and parent do not intervene quickly, the situation worsens.

CHILDREN WITH SPECIAL NEEDS

Learning is more than a cognitive function. It is conditioned by biological heritage and early environment and influenced by social/emotional factors. Much learning has occurred before the child leaves the family to enter school. If children have been encouraged to explore, to listen, to interact, they come to school eager, unafraid of challenges, and able to connect with ideas and with classmates. Children who feel good about themselves, who demonstrate social skills, and who are liked by their peers, tend to learn well.

For inhibited children, new surroundings and expectations can be frightening and unsettling. Their wish is to flee from them and retreat to previous securities. Impulsive, distractable children who attend to all stimuli indiscriminately appear more difficult to manage and less capable than they actually are. For children who need individualized instruction, such as those who are physically or learning disabled, the number of classmates, the routine of the classroom, and the sensitivity of the teacher are critical factors.

Mental efficiency often determines classroom proficiency. If the child exhibits readiness skills of listening, organizing, understanding language, and verbal responding, success usually follows. Youngsters with disabilities in one or more of the sense modalities—visual, auditory, motoric, kinesthetic—experience difficulties acquiring new information and connecting it with old knowledge. If their learning difficulties are compounded by distractability, hyperactivity, impulsivity, and accumulated failures, negative peer reactions occur. Children who experience serious social problems usually perform below their ability level.

Authority Issues

At first in children's lives, only the parent sets limits on behavior, provides for needs, and offers self as a model. In time, other adults—housekeepers, teachers, principals, nurses, coaches, baby-sitters—become parent substitutes. Because parents are children's first teachers and the family their first group, many of the early learned behaviors determine subsequent actions. Parental style, whether it is authoritative or permissive, conditions children to expect the same from other adults. In this context, adult authority can be challenged, ignored, or defied. It is up to the parent surrogate to work out authority issues.

Essential to normal development and positive adjustment is the child's sense of self, capacity to form relationships, and ability to make favorable choices as independence increases. Parents often can explain the child's past patterns. Although adults serve a critical role for children in teaching and modeling appropriate behaviors toward authority, peers can reinforce or change those attitudes.

As children get older, their behavior toward adults does change and is more influenced by peers. Results will follow a continuum. At one end will be the blind obedience of the excessively dependent or needy child, who replaces the tyranny of a parent with a powerful peer. At midpoint will be age-appropriate testing of limits that are expected from normal children as they cite what their friends can do and hope to do the same. At the other extreme are the maladaptive responses of conduct-disordered children who seek peers like themselves to display more deviant acts (Stroufe & Rutter, 1984).

Summary

Although physical height or weight can be an indicator of generalized maturity, it is the child who is aware of others' feelings, who can empathize, interact, and engage others who wins positive regard. Children successful with peers have been described as sensitive to other people's feelings and responsive to other people's needs (Asher, 1983). They have good ideas for activities and a good sense of humor. In return, friendships bring positive feelings about self, comfort, enjoyment, a sense of security, mutual trust, and loyalty.

REFERENCES

Achenbach, T. M., & Edelbrock, C. S. (1981). Behavioral problems and competencies reported by parents of normal and disturbed children aged 4 through 16. *Monographs of the Society for Research in Child Development, 46* (1, Serial No. 188), 1–82.

Asher, S. R. (1983). Social competence and peer status: Recent advances, future directions. *Child Development, 54,* 1427–1434.

Asher, S. R. (1990). Recent advances in the study of peer-rejected children. In S. R. Asher & J. D. Coie (Eds.), *Peer rejection in childhood* (pp. 3–16). New York: Cambridge University Press.

Asher, S. R., & Parker, J. G. (1989). The significance of peer relationship problems in childhood. In B. H. Schneider, G. Attil, J. Nadel, & R. P. Weissberg (Eds.), *Social competence in developmental perspective* (pp. 5–23). Amsterdam: Kluwer Academic Publishing.

Asher, S. R., Parkhurst, J. T., Hymel, S., & Williams, G. A. (1990). Peer rejection and loneliness in childhood. In S. R. Asher & J. D. Coie (Eds.), *Peer rejection in childhood* (pp. 253–273). New York: Cambridge University Press.

Asher, S. R., & Wheeler, V. A. (1985). Children's loneliness: A comparison of rejected and neglected peer status. *Journal of Consulting and Clinical Psychology, 53,* 500–505.

Berndt, T. J. (1987). Conversations between friends: Theories, research and implications for sociomoral development. In W. M. Kurtines & J. L. Gerwitz (Eds.), *Moral development through social interaction* (pp. 281–300). New York: John Wiley & Sons.

Berndt, T. J. (1989). Contributions of peer relationships to children's development. In T. J. Berndt & G. W. Ladd (Eds.), *Peer relationships in child development* (pp. 407–416). New York: John Wiley & Sons.

Berndt, T. J., & Perry, T. B. (1986). Children's perceptions of friendships as supportive relationships. *Developmental Psychology, 22,* 640–648.

Bukowski, W. M., & Hoza, W. M. (1989). Popularity and friendship: Issues in theory, measurement and outcome. In T. J. Berndt & G. W. Ladd (Eds.), *Peer relationships in child development* (pp. 15–45). New York: John Wiley & Sons.

Chess, S., & Thomas, A. (1984). *Origins and evolution of behavior disorders: From infancy to early adult life.* New York: Brunner/Mazel.

Cicchetti, D., Toth, S., & Bush, M. (1988). Developmental psychopathology and incompetence in childhood: suggestions for intervention. In B. B. Lahey & A. E. Kazdin (Eds.), *Advances in clinical child psychology: Vol. 12* (pp. 1–59). New York: Plenum.

Coie, J. D. (1990). Toward a theory of peer rejection. In S. R. Asher & J. D. Coie (Eds.), *Peer rejection in childhood* (pp. 365–402). New York: Cambridge University Press.

Coie, J. D., Belding, M., & Underwood, M. (1988). Aggression and peer rejection in childhood. In B. B. Lahey & A. E. Kazdin (Eds.), *Advances in clinical psychology* (pp. 125–154). New York: Plenum.

Coie, J. D., & Dodge, K. A. (1983). Continuities and changes in children's social status: A five-year longitudinal study. *Merrill-Palmer Quarterly, 29,* 261–282.

Coie, J. D., & Kupersmidt, J. B. (1983). A behavioral analysis of emerging social status in boys' groups. *Child Development, 54,* 1400–1416.

Damon, W., & Phelps, E. (1989). Strategic uses of peer learning in children's education. In T. J. Berndt & G. W. Ladd (Eds.), *Peer relationships in child development* (pp. 135–157). New York: John Wiley & Sons.

Dunn, J. (1983). Sibling relationships in early childhood. *Child Development, 54,* 787–811.

Dunn, J. (1988). Sibling influences on childhood development. *Journal of Child and Adolescent Psychiatry, 29,* 119–127.

Eisenberg, N., Fabes, R. A., Murphy, B., Maszk, P., Smith, M., & Karbon, M. (1995). The role of emotionality and regulation in children's social functioning. A longitudinal study. *Child Development, 66,* 1360–1384.

Furman, W., & Bierman, K. L. (1983). Developmental changes in young children's conceptions of friendship. *Child Development, 54,* 549–556.

Furman, W., & Bierman, K. L. (1984). Children's conceptions of friendships: A multimethod study of developmental changes. *Developmental Psychology, 20,* 925–931.

Gottman, J. M. (1983). How children become friends. *Monographs of the Society for Research in Child Development, 48* (3, Serial No. 201).

Hartup, W. M. (1989). Behavioral manifestations of children's friendships (1989). In T. J. Berndt & G. W. Ladd (Eds.), *Peer relationships in child development* (pp. 46–70). New York: John Wiley & Sons.

Hymel, C., & Rubin, K. H. (1985). Children with peer relationship and social skills problems: Conceptual, methodological and developmental issues. In G. J. Whitehurst (Ed.), *Annals of Child Development: Vol. 2,* (pp. 251–297). Greenwich, CT: JAI Press.

Kagan, J. (1982). *Psychological research on the human infant: An evaluative summary.* New York: William T. Grant Foundation.

Kernberg, P. F., Clarkin, A. J., Greenblatt, E., & Cohen, J. (1992). The Cornell interview of peers and friends: Development and validation. *Journal of American Academy of Child and Adolescent Psychiatry, 31,* 483–489.

Ladd, G. W. (1983). Social networks of popular, average and rejected children in school settings. *Merrill Palmer Quarterly, 29,* 282–307.

Ladd, G. W., & Mars, K. T. (1986). Reliability and validity of preschoolers perceptions of peer behavior. *Journal of Clinical Child Psychiatry, 15,* 16–25.

Ladd, G. W., & Price, J. P. (1987). Predicting children's social and school adjustment following the transition from preschool to kindergarten. *Child Development, 58,* 1168–1189.

Maccoby, E. E. (1993). The role of parents in the socialization of children: A historical overview. *Developmental Psychology, 28* (6), 1006–1017.

Maccoby, E. E., & Martin, J. A. (1983). Socialization in the context of the family: Parent-child interaction. In E. M. Hetherington (Ed.) & P. H. Mussen (Series Ed.), *Handbook of child psychology: Vol. 4. Socialization, personality and development* (pp. 1–101). New York: John Wiley & Sons.

Newcomb, A. F., & Brady, J. E. (1982). Mutuality in boys' friendship relations. *Child Development, 53,* 393–395.

Olweus, D. (1980). Familial and temperamental detriments of aggressive behavior in adolescent boys: A causal analysis. *Developmental Psychology 16,* 644–660.

Parker, J., & Asher, S. R. (1977). Peer acceptance and later personal adjustment: Are low-accepted children at risk? *Psychological Bulletin, 102,* 357–389.

Putallaz, M. (1983). Predicting children's sociometric status from their behavior. *Child Development, 54,* 1417–1426.

Putallaz, M. (1987). Maternal behavior and children's sociometric status. *Child Development, 58,* 324–340.

Putallaz, M., & Gottman, J. M. (1981). An interactional model of children's entry into peer groups. *Child Development, 52,* 986–994.

Putallaz, M., & Heflin, A. H. (1990). Parent-child relations and peer rejection. In S. R. Asher & J. D. Coie (Eds.), *Peer rejection in childhood* (pp. 189–216). New York: Cambridge University Press.

Rothbart, M. K., Ahadi, S. A., & Hershey, K. L. (1994). Temperament and social behavior in childhood. *Merrill-Palmer Quarterly, 40,* 21–39.

Rubin, Z., & Sloman, J. (1984). How parents influence their children's friendships. In M. Lewis (Ed.), *Beyond the dyad* (pp. 223–250). New York: Plenum.

Selman, R. L. (1980). *The growth of interpersonal understanding: Developmental and clinical analyses.* New York: Academic Press.

Shantz, D. W. (1986). Conflict, aggression and peer status: An observational study. *Child Development, 57,* 1322–1332.

Smollar, J., & Youniss, J. (1982). Social development through friendship. In K. H. Rubin & H. S. Ross (Eds.), *Peer relationships and social skills in childhood* (pp. 279–298). New York: Springer-Verlag.

Strauss, C. C. (1988). Social deficits of children with internalizing disorders. In B. B. Lahey & A. E. Kazdin (Eds.), *Advances in clinical psychology* (pp. 159–185). New York: Plenum.

Stroufe, L. A., & Rutter, M. (1984). The domain of developmental psychopathology. *Child Development, 55,* 17–29.

Sullivan, H. S. (1953). *The interpersonal theory of psychiatry.* New York: W. W. Norton.

12 / Prepuberty (Late Latency): Personal Changes

Audrey J. Clarkin

The period of later childhood—from about 9 to 12 or 13 years of age—has a dual aspect: It marks the end of childhood and the beginning of adolescence. The transition to puberty usually comes earlier for girls than for boys.

Physically, obvious bodily changes in height and

shape and secondary sex characteristics accompany fluctuating moods of delight and despair. Psychologically, it is a time of anticipation accompanied by uncertainty. Emotionally, preadolescents still are connected to parents but are struggling to separate from them and to establish a unique identity. Mentally, they can appreciate concepts and have learned to apply themselves to academics, hobbies, and special interests. Energy level is high and directed toward organized activities, such as scouts, athletic teams, dramatics. Competency and conformity characterize this stage of development.

Many children at this age have a beginning sense of their own individuality. They are conscious of their uniqueness and recognize many variables—genetic, ethnic, and cultural—that have contributed to their self-image. They are able to defend themselves both verbally and physically from intrusion by siblings and peers. For some children, oversensitivity and mood swings can be indicators of the many changes that they are experiencing.

Peers

A school visit during the change of classes provides a capsulated view of late-latency-age youngsters. Noise level is high, not only from conversations, but from squeals and sounds that these students make to express immediate responses to their peers. Clothes appear to be uniforms, very similar in style and brand. Some students are moving in pairs, usually of the same sex and engrossed in what the other is saying or doing. Others are proceeding in larger groups, and it seems that several are vying for leadership by the loud wisecrack or rush of words. Intense energy is felt as the students enjoy some moments of socialization before they must settle down again to the routine of class. Lunch partners are sought as a "social" security and after-school plans are organized with friends.

Children learn different skills from peers than from adults (Erwin, 1993). In a social context, learning how to inhibit some impulses, accept influences, maintain behavior, and achieve goals despite one's emotions is indicative of social learn-

ing. As children develop, peer relationships become more interactive, reciprocal, and complicated, demanding more varied and complex skills (Brown & Lohr, 1987).

For 9- to 12-year-olds, to be happy is to be busy with friends. Clubs, groups, and teams provide those opportunities. The wish for a special friend is very strong. Communication (including talking at recess, sending notes in class, calling friends on the phone) becomes the focus and presupposes that children already have mastered the prerequisite social skills (listening, taking turns, sharing) to engage positively with family and age mates. In order to strengthen gender identity, sex roles, and appropriate responses to the opposite sex, preadolescents have a developmental need to attach initially to same-sex friends.

FORMS OF HETEROSEXUAL OBJECT SEEKING

As children advance in school, boys are less exclusive than girls and have a wider circle of companions. Boys engage in team sports and physical activity with same-sex companions. Competition and concern with rules is evident not only in their play but in their avid interest in favorite teams, rankings, and athletic heroes.

Socially, girls choose smaller groups of same-sex friends and do more verbal sharing. Secrets among girls help to bond friendships, allay their anxiety about physical changes that are occurring, and support their increasing independence from parents. Much conversation reveals their preoccupation with self—that is, with their changing body and new feelings. Girls are interested in the opposite sex, although this interest often is couched in terms of complaints regarding particular boys or revealed in secret fantasies.

Advances in sexual development and sexual awareness become evident. Games are interrupted by charges or attacks from a group of the opposite sex. Annoyance, flattery, and uncertainty are the usual responses, but there is a sense of shared excitement and daring. Usually incidents of attention-getting between girls and boys—chasing, taking a personal object, and verbal teasing—camouflage their interest in each other.

It is not unusual for boys and girls in grades 4, 5, and 6 to spend time talking in groups or on the phone, passing notes to each other in class, or inviting each other to the movies or for pizza. Beginning contacts involve groups of boys and girls without pairing off. Sometimes early heterosexual activity is prompted by a more mature youngster or originates from the imitation of older siblings so that gifts are exchanged or the other is referred to as "my steady." The media has contributed to early heterosexual interest where "boy" friend and "girl" friend are viewed differently from mere friendships and encouraged by movies, songs, and parents, who think the behavior is cute. Sexual curiosity for both boys and girls shifts from anatomy to function; there is much talking, joking, and teasing with sexual innuendoes.

GENDER DIFFERENCES

Boys tend to find social enjoyment from group activities that are physical. A high energy level characterizes the age, and they are happiest when "doing." Boys who mature physically early have an advantage and are admired for their size and strength. Peer acceptance often depends on being a player. Boys describe physical aggression, verbal aggression, and property damage as reasons for disliking peers.

Girls are more selective than boys in their relationships at this age. They spend much time talking and sharing. Much of their conversation compares what each knows and notices about bodily changes, having been told "the facts" by parent or friend. Closeness is important, thus their circle of friends is smaller and some are excluded. Secrets are shared, best friendships promised, and fantasies about themselves and others preoccupies them with excited anticipation. Sometimes girls of this age develop a "crush" on a particular boy or older female adolescent who becomes the target for idealized expectations.

Girls exhibit increasing sharing of confidences as they get older, indicating the importance of intimacy with same-sex friends. Verbal aggression, rule violation, and bothersome behavior are considered negative behaviors by girls.

Feminist perspectives on gender equality and skill competence have encouraged girls to engage in athletics and to be competitive. The result has been to strengthen independence and to promote a more egalitarian role with boys on the athletic field. Whether this confidence extends to the classroom and to other social arenas has been questioned. Gillingan (1992) suggests that young women, ages 10 and above, encounter gender ex-

pectations of what is socially acceptable that impede their autonomy.

Although girls may perform some prosocial behaviors more frequently than boys, there is no clear and consistent evidence of gender differences (Eisenberg & Mussen, 1989). Child-rearing techniques—such as mothers' demonstrated affection for girls—and more cultural reinforcement of helpful behavior for girls can explain gender differences.

CONNECTIONS WITH PARENTS AND OTHER ADULTS

Developmentally, horizontal relationships take on priority so that peers rival parents in establishing children's self-image and confidence. Verbal debates, challenges, and arguments between child and parent attest to new cognitive skills. Increased physical strength and endurance prompt preadolescents to enjoy some shared leisure activities with adults. Socially there can be moments of humor and enjoyment.

Peer values that coincide with parental values help the preadolescent to feel secure in relations with family and age mates. When peer values conflict with parental values, the result will depend on past history. Youniss (1980) suggests that positive attachment to parents and their acceptance of their child's increasing independence in making decisions will predict positive resolution. However, if parents are authoritative or punitive, peer values can be viewed as freedom or revenge.

Preadolescents no longer inform parents about all their activities. The thoughts and wishes of preadolescents become more private. Their attitudes toward adults are more critical; reality has taught the late-latency child that grown-ups are neither perfect nor all the same. There are still chosen heroes, whether it is a special teacher, a rock star, or a superathlete.

OTHER ISSUES

Few studies have investigated peer relationships or friendships with lower socioeconomic, minority, or diverse culture groups. Research needs to be undertaken on children living in an environment with limited adult supervision where basic needs are not consistently met or where there are different rules for interacting.

Friends

Friendship provides social skill learning, facilitates social comparisons, and fosters a sense of group belonging. Communication involves listening and appreciating another's perspective, stating opinions, and resolving disagreements verbally. Awareness of physical, cognitive, and social similarities and differences helps preadolescents to accept their unique identity. Shared time and activities promotes strong attachment and a common bond.

PERCEIVED COMMONALITIES STRENGTHEN SPECIAL FRIENDSHIPS

The period of preadolescence encourages youngsters to expand their previous boundaries. As they develop physically and socially, they engage in both formal and informal activities with age mates that take them out of their immediate neighborhood and broaden their contact with peers (Rowe, Woulbroun, & Gulley, 1994).

Developmentally, children move from external characteristics, such as size and possessions, to awareness and appreciation of less obvious qualities. The ability to understand themselves and what others are thinking and feeling builds social connections. Because of similar abilities, interests, and mutual liking, some age mates choose to become friends. Likewise, preadolescents also can decide that they do not want to be close with some age mates, deliberately ignoring or being mean to them.

Friendship is based on reciprocity and commitment. Mutual understanding, loyalty, and willingness to disclose one's secrets are common markers of friendship (Hartup, 1989). Friends become a sounding board, secrets are told, and feelings shared. Self-identity solidifies as individuals measure thoughts, feelings, and actions against those of others. This affiliation based on age, proximity, and perceived similarity is an essential aspect of social experience and contributes to self-identity and self-esteem.

BEST-FRIEND ISSUES

Early friendships of school-age children are followed in middle childhood by a special "chum" period with a same-sex friend before heterosexual relations begin. The chum relationship is based on mutual sensitivity that is a prototype for later romantic, marital, and parental relationships (Sullivan, 1953). During the chum period, best friends emerge. Ninety percent of the children of this age are nominated by at least one person as a best friend (Hartup, 1989). Best friends help each other with challenging situations, whether they are starting a new grade or joining a club. They borrow and lend clothing and objects freely as indications of how close they are.

The exclusive quality of a best friend can be a threat and a security. Children feel anxious about having revealed too much. They worry that the friend might stop being so close and could leave to be best friends with someone else. Awareness exists that the other person is so familiar that he or she is often a self-reflection. Loyalty and trust are qualities implicit with best friends that allow them to share secrets and self-disclosures. Close friendships consume the moment, are intense, and can be possessive. Entitlement characterizes best friends and can become extreme when best friends become too exclusive. Reactions of anger and jealousy occur when a partner is not totally available to the other.

GROUP FORMATIONS

Many social activities represent open groups, and children move in and out of them by choice. Some are more selective and require an invitation. They can be described as closed groups—such as a special music club. Another distinction is whether the group is goal-directed with a common focus acknowledged by the participants, as a swim team is, for example, or interpersonal, such as classmates who get together every recess to gossip.

The peer group becomes more homogenous during later childhood, and games having many formal rules become more organized. It has been estimated that children spend 50% of their time with peers during this period and get satisfaction from belonging to a group. Important changes in attitude and motivation occur. Peer acceptance increases self-confidence and self-identity and validates one's worth (self-esteem) Brown & Lohr (1995).

Perceptions of friends and peers have been studied (Kernberg, Clarkin, Greenblatt, & Cohen,

TABLE 12.1

Cornell Subscale of Self-Esteem

Level 0: Feels like a nobody, unnoticed by others, not taken into account and feels that nobody cares.

Level 1: Mostly feels rejected, excluded or looked down upon. Sense of self-worth is based primarily on what he does for friends or gives to peers.

Level 2: Thinks of himself as a fall-back guy when there is no one better around.

Level 3: Does not take for granted that he will be well received by his peers. Insecure when not in his friends' company.

Level 4: Is one of the group but never number 1 or 2 or the leader. He feels good and expects to be included.

Level 5: Feels he is a necessary member of the group, can occasionally be a leader and considers himself a regular guy.

Level 6: Feels good about himself, is self-confident, feels consistently appreciated by others and values his friends. He is comfortable with being both a leader and a follower.

1992). Table 12.1 provide's a scale to evaluate increasing levels of self-esteem associated with positive peer relationships.

PEER PRESSURE

Peer pressure can be both positive and negative. Although children can serve as negative role models for each other and influence friends to follow their deviant actions, many incidents can be cited where the example and encouragement of age mates permit youngsters to achieve more than they expected of themselves, whether in the classroom or on the athletic field. Parents and teachers often underestimate the positive aspects of peer relationships. Criticism and nonacceptance of children's friends can stem from parental resentment of their own diminished influence or failure to recognize that normal social development is based on peer relationships. As the child builds a unique identity, the process of comparing and contrasting with age mates promotes the working out of loyalties, aggression, and inner values and contributes to emotional security.

CLUBS AND CLIQUES

The formation of clubs and cliques offers inclusion and acceptance as well as reassurance at this age. Members of a group perceive themselves as similar and experience higher self-esteem than those students who wish to belong but are not accepted (Brown & Lohr, 1987). Issues of control and conformity often arise in terms of "Who's the leader?" and "If you're going to be one of us, you have to . . . dress, act . . . a certain way." Fear of disagreeing with group members results in repression of contrary opinions. Eagerness to win group approval can prompt participation even though it violates one's personal norms. Allegiance to a group can become so unconditional because of the perceived advantages, such as popularity or protection, that members surrender individual identity and judgment.

In most groups a hierarchical order can be identified, starting with the leader or boss, an assistant or second-in-command, and including others such as the compromiser, the helper, the fighter. At the bottom of the pecking order would be the scapegoat and the tag-along. Marginal children are willing to be members but their acceptance is dependent on the convenience or whim of the members. In-group and out-group membership is fluid and a continual source of stress and anxiety. During this period children's social status derives mainly from peer awareness and acceptance.

GANGS

Gangs imply cohesive groups that achieve their goals by negative means, including harassment and intimidation. It is estimated that gang membership in the United States has more than doubled in the past decade and has risen dramatically in middle-class communities. Some gangs are territorial, fighting over turf. Others do not care about geography; money is the prime force that keeps them together. Youth gangs result from poverty, discrimination, family disorganization, cultural differences, social class resentments, and dislocations. Gang behavior can result in physical harm, violence, misuse of power, and breaking the law. The sense of belonging and of identification and, in some instances, the protection and security provided by the gang explains its existence and loyalty of its members. The gang can serve as a substitute family, providing attention, support, and acceptance that children have never received or now reject from their family of origin.

Some individuals who are bigger and stronger derive pleasure from harassing those who are weak or unprotected. Often bullies join together with a common goal of provoking and frightening others. Bullying can be prompted by a wish for power, a desire for money or goods, or the delight of tormenting. Adult intervention is usually required, especially in cases of group bullying.

Role of the School

Schools play an important role in facilitating or impeding new and diverse friendships by how children are grouped for instruction and activities. Homogeneous grouping often involves academic, cultural, and socioeconomic similarities and does not encourage more expansive socialization. A comparative study of fourth and eight graders (Berndt, Hawkins, & Hoyle, 1986) found that the older students made fewer new friends but that both groups reported the same number of friends. Two explanations are the departmental structure of the school and the reduced involvement of the teacher in fostering social interactions.

Much has been written about the potential role of the school in promoting prosocial behavior. Peer relations are an important part of the climate of classrooms and schools. Individual and group counseling, affective classroom programs, social skills curriculum, cross-age groupings, behavior management strategies, and parent education are just a few interventions that can be utilized.

In reality, school systems often do not encourage children's social development, using curriculum demands, teachers' lack of training, and/or parental expectations as reasons for avoiding this critical aspect of education. Some teachers tend to perceive student social interactions as interfering with learning. Friendships are discouraged by seating arrangements and yearly redistribution of classes so that there is no continuity of friendships. These procedures can be especially negative for those children whose family supports are problematic; such children view their peer con-

nections as even more essential than other children of this age. Studies show that when teachers do intervene with direct, confidential, and personal instruction with children whose behavior is inappropriate, about 50% of children with social problems improve (Asher, 1983).

Social Status

Friendship can be distinguished from popularity. Friendship implies a mutuality of regard and affection between two individuals while popularity refers to being known and liked by others. Relationships that are dyadic versus those that are group-oriented seem to develop differently, provide different experiences, and contribute differently to self-concept (Bukowski & Hoza, 1989). Judgment by a group of significant peers can be based on a variety of factors, including skills, status, clothes, and ability.

Peer evaluation can be either positive or negative. Preadolescents are positive about peers who are helpful, friendly, cooperative, cheerful, and prosocial. They regard negatively those who display aggression, disruption, and off-task behavior. Some preadolescents who are not perceived positively are ignored. Others whose behavior is seen as negative are rejected. Rejection and isolation increase vulnerability to anxiety and depression.

When a number of peers actively dislike a child, group dynamics become important and influence the thoughts, feelings, and behavior toward the targeted child. If he or she has not learned adequate coping skills, the child misses out on peer social support and experiences low self-esteem. While group acceptance contributes to social adjustment and to self-confidence, friendship is essential for social development.

SOCIAL NETWORKING

Social networking in school settings has been studied (Coie & Dodge, 1988; Ladd, 1983). Children can be categorized as popular, average, controversial, ignored, and rejected on the basis of two dimensions: social preference and social impact. (See Table 12.2.)

Popular children are sought after by peers; re-

TABLE 12.2

Children's Social Status

Category	Social Preference	Social Impact
Popular	High	High
Rejected	Low	High
Controversial	Both High/Low	High
Neglected	Neither High/Low	Low
Average	Moderate	Moderate

jected children are not. Controversial children have high social impact and neglected children have low social impact. This second dimension, social impact, differentiates two groups of children who vary on aggressive behavior: Controversial children are highly aggressive, neglected children are very unaggressive. In a study of new peer group contacts (Coie & Benenson, 1983), aggression led to rejection. When status is measured with both positive and negative nominations as assessed by behavioral observations, rejected boys were more aggressive. Dominance-oriented aggression is more commonly cause for rejection with boys who sacrifice relationships for immediate gratification (first in line, last blow).

Peer Rejection

Childhood peer rejection (active dislike) is a critical predictor for later social-emotional maladaption. Rejected children are heterogeneous and manifest multiple areas of maladjustment. Bierman (1989) urges clinicians to utilize an integrated intervention approach based on the developmental level and the needs of the individual rejected child.

Studies show that peer perceptions of the rejected child do not change even when there is significant improvement in behavior; group members continue to hold on to the same negative opinion of the child. Peer-rejected children are actively disliked by peers; 45% remain rejected after 1 year and 30% are still rejected after 4 years (Coie & Kupersmidt, 1983). With intervention, rejected children can become neglected or at best average, but seldom popular. Because rejected

children can be perceived by their age mates as disruptive, aggressive, dependent, noncompliant, and uncooperative, they are not sought as work partners or playmates.

Rejected children exhibit inappropriate and provocative behavior, especially in unstructured situations. Shoving, pushing, hitting, calling names, mean teasing, and insulting others characterize their interactions on the playground. Even though this aversive behavior can be in retaliation for perceived offenses, peers consider it antagonistic so that it increases the alienation of the rejected child.

Cross-situational investigation across family and school settings (French & Waas, 1985) found that academic difficulties as well as conduct problems are greater for rejected children. Bierman (1986) found that one third of aggressive boys are not rejected by peers and suggests that aggressive behavior contributes to rejection when it is extensive and accompanied by inappropriate, immature behaviors or academic problems but aggression is not the total explanation.

Intervention Strategies

Models for intervention with children experiencing social difficulties derive from three distinct causes: social skill deficits, coercive behavior, and negative group dynamics. (See Table 12.3.) For those who lack social skills, peer instruction and modeling improve self-control and interpersonal problem solving. Behavioral contingency management addresses the aggressive and negative behavior of coercive interactions learned at home that generalize to school with antagonism toward and from peers. Cooperative peer involvement with closely supervised specific interactional goals represents the third intervention.

An intervention model that integrates all three interventions is recommended as most effective (Hartup, 1983). A specific program for helping aggressive children (Coie & Koeppl, 1990) includes modeling positive play skills, teaching social cues to permit group entry, learning to problem-solve social situations, and developing greater tolerance for negative emotions.

TABLE 12.3

Interventions for Social Problems

Problem	Intervention
Social deficits	Peer instruction/Modeling
Coercive behavior	Contingency management
Negative group dynamics	Cooperative peer involvement and specific interpersonal goals

Dysfunctional Children and Those with Dysfunctional Parents

Children with specific psychiatric disorders are considered in greater detail in other chapters. The relationship between childhood social functioning and future academic, psychological, and behavioral adjustment has been researched and documented (Michelson & DiLorenzo, 1981). Children whose social history is atypical or who have parents with a psychiatric disorder can be "at risk" for psychological problems. These children tend to form sporadic and incosistent friendships in contrast with normal youngsters (Howes, 1983).

Narcissistic children perceive others in terms of their own wishes, needs, and impulses. They lack the ability to appreciate another's feelings or situation and attribute to others their own reactions. They resent the capacity of others to have fun, and their best friendships are with children they can control or coerce or who reflect well on their image. Socially, they fail to relate successfully to acquaintances because they are preoccupied with self. Their interactions lack the reciprocity and commitment needed to bond with an age mate.

Depressed youngsters are depleted in energy and caught up in their own problems or in self-pity. They find it too burdensome to be aware of peers and to seek them out for enjoyment. Seclusion and isolation characterize depressed children. They tend to avoid social situations where the positive affect of their peers could intensify their own distress.

Aggressive youngsters act without regard for consequences, and their approach is often intrusive and intimidating. Whether verbally or physically, they make demands, expect acquiescence, and do not regard the other person's feelings and reactions.

Children with specific learning disabilities and attention deficit disorders can have difficulty appreciating cause-effect relationships and not recognize the subtle cues that are part of social interactions (Whalen & Henker, 1985). They can stand too close, say the wrong thing, miss the obvious, and be unaware of how their actions are received by peers. Often they are lonely and uphappy. Their social attempts are unsuccessful as they are too impulsive in initiating contact or lack sensitivity to the other child's feelings and wants.

Children with physical handicaps see themselves negatively or have been affected by the reactions of age mates who perceive them as different or damaged. Self-doubts and experiences of past rejection prevent them from reaching out to nonhandicapped peers. Their reaction to frequent teasing and ridicule is a conviction that they will never have "regular" friends.

Children who have a parent with a serious mental disorder, such as schizophrenia, depression, or chemical dependency, have not received needed emotional support. Sporadic attention, inconsistent nurturing, and faulty communication have contributed to their sense of insecurity and inadequacy. Some children become caregivers for the parent and surrender their childhood needs to assume a pseudoadult role in the family. These children are not age appropriate with peers and may remove themselves from social situations. Others may seek to have their many social/emotional needs met outside of the family; instead of a reciprocal relationship, they may expect or use others to compensate for familial deprivation.

Prediction of Later Maladjustment

Longitudinal studies (Cowen, Pederson, Babigian, Izzo & Troust, 1973) suggest that the early peer relationships of a child can serve as the best single predictor for later adjustment. Unsatisfactory peer relations have diagnostic significance for emotionally and behaviorally disturbed children. Impaired peer relations differentiate problematic from nonproblematic children (Achenbach & Edelbrock, 1981).

Follow-forward and follow-backward studies (Kupersmidt, Coie, & Dodge, 1990) offer valuable information linking childhood peer relationship problems to disorders in adolescence and early adulthood. Developmental pathways have been tracked and validated. Preschizophrenic females were consistently withdrawn during childhood and adolescence. Preschizophrenic males showed adolescent antisocial behavior. Low peer status in childhood was predictive of nonspecific later mental health problems. Delinquent and adult criminals revealed past histories of childhood aggression and antisocial behavior.

Summary

Positive social relationships during childhood and preadolescence with family and peers contribute uniquely to later adjustment. A developmental progression of social learning begins with early childhood coordinated play, moves to the desire for belonging and social acceptance of middle childhood, and progresses to the adolescent task of self-exploration and self-definition. Reinforcement of prosocial behavior and early intervention with children experiencing social difficulties is strongly recommended.

REFERENCES

Achenbach, T. M., & Edelbrock, C. S. (1981). Behavioral problems and competencies reported by parents of normal and disturbed children aged four through sixteen. *Monographs of the Society for Research in Child Development, 46* (1, Serial No. 188), 1–82.

Asher, S. (1983). Social competence and peer status: Recent advances and future directions. *Child Development, 54,* 1427–1434.

Berndt, T. J., Hawkins, J. A., & Hoyle, S. G. (1986). Changes in friendships during a school year: Effects of children's and adolescents' impressions of friendship and sharing with friends. *Child Development, 57,* 1284–1297.

Bierman, K. L. (1986). Process of change during social skills training with preadolescents and its relationship to treatment outcome. *Child Development, 57,* 230–240.

Bierman, K. L. (1989). Peer rejection in children. In B. B. Lahey & A. E. Kazdin (Eds.), *Advances in clinical child psychology* (pp. 100–124). New York: Plenum.

Brown, B., & Lohr, M. (1995). Peers. In J. E. Hall & A. E. Case (Eds.), *Advances in clinical psychology* (pp. 100–124). New York: John Wiley & Sons.

Brown, B., & Lohr, M. (1987). Peer group affiliation and adolescent self-esteem. An integration of ego-identity and symbolic interaction theories. *Journal of Personality and Social Psychology, 52,* 47–54.

Bukowski, W. M., & Hoza, B. (1989). Popularity and friendship: issues in theory, measurement and outcome. In T. S. Berndt & G. W. Ladd (Eds.), *Peer relations in child development* (pp. 15–45). New York: John Wiley & Sons.

Coie, J. D., & Benenson, J. F. (1983). *A qualitative analysis of the relationship between peer rejection and physically aggressive behavior.* Unpublished manuscript, Duke University, Durham, NC.

Coie, J. D., & Dodge, K. (1988). Multiple sources of data on social behavior and social status in the school: A cross-age comparison. *Child Development, 59,* 815–829.

Coie, J. D., & Koeppl, G. K. (1990). Adapting intervention to the problems of aggressive and disruptive rejected children. In S. R. Asher & J. D. Coie (Eds.), *Peer rejection in childhood.* (pp. 309–337). New York: Cambridge University Press.

Coie, J. D., & Kupersmidt, J. (1983). A behavioral analysis of emerging social status in boys' groups. *Child Development 54,* 1400–1416.

Cowen, E. L., Pederson, A., Babigian, H., Izzo, L. D., & Troust, M. A. (1973). Long-term follow-up of early detected vulnerable children. *Journal of Consulting and Clinical Psychology, 41,* 438–446.

Eisenberg, N., & Mussen, P. (1989). *The Roots of Prosocial Behavior in Children.* New York: Cambridge University Press.

Erwin, P. (1993). *Friendship and peer relations in children.* New York: John Wiley & Sons.

French, D. C., & Waas, G. A. (1985). Behavior problems of peer-neglected and peer-rejected elementary age children: Parents' and teacher's perspectives. *Child Development, 56,* 246–252.

Gillingan, C. (1992). *Making connections: The relational world of adolescent girls.* Boston: Harvard University Press.

Hartup, W. W. (1983). Peer relations. In E. M. Hetherington (Ed.) & P. H. Mussen (Series Ed.), *Handbook of child psychology. Vol. 4, Socialization, personality and social development* (pp. 103–196). New York: John Wiley & Sons.

Hartup, W. W. (1989). Social relationships and their developmental significance. *American Psychologist, 44,* 120–126.

Howes, C. (1983). Patterns of friendship. *Child Development, 54,* 1041–1053.

Kernberg, P. F., Clarkin, A. J., Greenblatt, E., & Cohen, J. (1992). The Cornell Interview of Peers and Friends: Development and validation. *Journal of*

American Academy of Child and Adolescent Psychiatry, 31, 483–489.

Kupersmidt, J. B., Coie, J. D., & Dodge, K. A. (1990). The role of poor peer relationships in the development of disorder. In S. A. Asher & J. D. Coie (Eds.), *Peer rejection in childhood* (pp. 274–305). New York: Cambridge University Press.

Ladd, G. (1983). Social networks of popular, average, and rejected children in school settings. *Merrill-Palmer Quarterly, 29,* 283–308.

Michelson, L., & DiLorenzo, T. M. (1981). Behavioral assessment of peer interactions and social functioning in institutional and structured settings. *Journal of Clinical Psychology, 87,* 499–504.

Rowe, D. C., Woulbroun, J., & Gulley, B. L. (1994). Peers and friends as non-shared environmental influences. In E. M. Hetherington, D. Reiss, & R. Plomin, (Eds.), *Separate worlds of siblings* (pp. 159–173). Hillsdale, NJ: Lawrence Erlbaum.

Sullivan, H. S. (1953). *The interpersonal theory of psychiatry.* New York: Norton.

Whalen, C. K., & Henker, B. (1985). The social worlds of hyperactive (ADHD) children. *Clinical Psychology Review, 5,* 447–478.

Youniss, J. (1980). *Parents and peers in social development: A Sullivan-Piaget perspective.* Chicago: University Press.

13 / The Sublimations of the Grade-School Child

Laurette Olson

According to Loewald (1988), sublimation is an unconscious process through which the aims, energies, and passions of primitive instinctual impulses are redirected, channeled, and organized into culturally acceptable and pleasurable activity. It creates an intermediate level of nonconflictual experience between an individual's primitive libidinal and aggressive impulses and the constraints of his or her external world including family, community, and the world at large. At this level, activities simultaneously meet psychic needs and facilitate a person's integration into his or her culture.

In the process leading to sublimation, attention is first attracted to and then held in an activity that absorbs instinctual urges and offers opportunities for their disguised expression in productive social, physical, and/or cognitive interchange. Activity skills are developed and refined that enhance self-esteem, engagement, and status in one's community as well as promote the investment of time and physical and psychic energy in the activity beyond the need for discharge of instinctual drives. People achieve sublimation when their engagement in an activity evolves into an important part of their identity within their social group. They are scientists, dancers, athletes, or collectors, for example. Instinctual passion shines through sublimatory activity without conflict or ambivalence

that direct discharge of primitive impulses can engender. At times, the intensity and depth of feelings that people display in such tasks surprise the people as well as others in their life who were unaware of the powerful energies hidden inside of the people.

Sandler and Joffe (1966) described sublimation as an achievement, not a specific ego function. They identified some "preconditions for the attainment of sublimation," including "frustration tolerance, capacity for obtaining substitute gratifications, inborn talents, the capacity for postponement and delay of discharge" (p. 345). In order to truly work, an individual must have these capacities. A child ideally develops these capacities by growing along the lines from play to work (A. Freud, 1965).

As defined by Csikszentmihalyi (1990), flow is likely an important part of the physical and mental processes that occur in sublimatory activities. It is the way people describe their state of mind when "consciousness is harmoniously ordered and they want to pursue what they are doing for its own sake" (p. 6). Other internal and external stimuli are irrelevant and ignored for the time being. Awareness of self and action in the activity merge, which results in greater psychic organization and smooth, focused external behavior. Csikszentmihalyi theorizes that the imposed order defends against entropy, the natural state of all objects (including the mind). With order, anxieties and fears are neutralized; exhilaration and joy are achieved. Children begin to experience this as they invest in and concentrate on activity.

Flow occurs within sequences of activities that are goal-directed, bound by rules, and require investment of psychic energy and a particular level of skill. These reality-oriented principles are important elements of potential sublimatory activities. Goals give direction and allow for external feedback. Rules constrain behavior but also help an individual concentrate on perfecting certain skills. Committing to something aids in focusing attention and directing energies as opposed to scattering attention and energies on endless possibility. Individuals who are skilled in an activity are free to seek out greater complexity and challenge, which will continually sustain their attention and push them toward higher levels of performance. Through increasing knowledge and ability to act on and react to objects effectively, people's emotional security grows. Individuals can exert power and influence or warmly engage with others in activity as they desire or need. In addition, they likely receive positive feedback on such behaviors from significant others. Their self-esteem and sense of self-efficacy are supported.

Sublimatory capacities develop through childhood play. Play serves as a mode of expression through which anxiety and aggression can be displaced. This limits their direct expression in interaction with caregivers, which can be disorganizing for children, because authority figures often firmly censor uncontrolled emotional expression. Play not only displaces feelings but transforms them for greater adaptation. Through passionately enacting and identifying with the roles and emotions of others, children develop mastery of their environment through greater social understanding and increased emotional control. In the process, children also may attract positive regard from their caregivers who may observe the play. Ideally, caregivers foster children's investment in developing imaginative play into a sublimatory channel.

In early childhood group play activities, such as singing rounds or playing jumprope, children experience the pleasure of synchronous human activity, which provides substitute gratifications for primitive impulses. By attending to and getting in step with the direction, rhythm, and order of movement and sounds, children lose their self-consciousness. They become "one" with their peers and continuous with the activity. The exhilaration that is experienced supports and fosters interest in developing the necessary discipline to participate in more complex synergistic activities, such as a choir, band, or team sport.

When children are unable effectively to displace and transform primitive impulses in activity, free-floating anxiety and instinctual tension grow as impulses must be actively and consciously inhibited instead of being absorbed, redirected, and transformed. Impulses burst through as stressors build and conscious emotional control weakens. Although their internal tension is relieved momentarily through direct discharge of impulses, new stressors develop as children's society sanction their primitive behavior. Without intervention that includes helping children to develop the ego strength to successfully focus, invest, and meet the challenges in particular activities that are meaningful to them, as well as to their society, emotional discontrol will hamper their integration and acceptance in their community.

Games, Hobbies, Sports, Puzzles, Jokes, and Karate

In the process of moving toward healthy psychosocial adaptation, which includes the achievement of sublimatory outlets, young children use a range of activities to channel and organize their energies and urges. Different activities provide different outlets for expression. They are satisfying at different times, related to children's momentary psychic state and environmental opportunities. Concurrently, the children also are building concrete cognitive and physical skills in those activities that support their capacities to use them to meet their psychic needs.

Learning activities, in general, are primary pathways through which children gain ego strength and are introduced to sublimatory opportunities. Ingesting cognitive and physical knowledge sharpens children's awareness of their interests and innate abilities. Children learn about opportunities for reality-based engagement in the world through self-directed, family, and peer activities; formalized learning opportunities in school; at community clubs and camps; and by reading books and watching television and movies. Erikson (1959, p. 82) called latency a time when the self is defined as "I am what I learn." With information, children gain confidence in their ability to explore and understand their environment, to fit into it, and then to manipulate and control parts of it.

Games serve to displace, channel, and reorganize aggressive impulses. Children match their powers against one or more peers and attempt to triumph. Instead of physically beating up a peer, pleasure is gotten by outwitting another or exhibiting superior physical skill within the confines of the ritualized interaction of a game. The descriptions of street games by Opie and Opie (1984) well exemplify this point. Chasing, catching, seeking, hunting, racing, dueling, exerting, and daring are typical foci of games. In the security of a game, children confront their uncertainty and fears, accept not getting their way, dominate and are dominated briefly by others, and act heroically without real danger. According to Redl and Wineman (1952, p. 112), most games have "special impulse encouraging promises" in them but also have automatic limitations and taboos "built in to guarantee impulse control." This is important so that games remain organized and pleasurable to all of the players. For example, in kickball, a player may throw a ball with some force at another, but only to "make an out"; the child stops the attack once an out is made.

Some games develop over time from particular features of a culture—a neighborhood, city, or country. They are based on what is particularly important in a culture or to what materials are available for game use. Objects used by adults for functional purposes are given new values in games. Computers are an integral part of adult life in Western culture; pop culture activities such as Nintendo use the technology for play. Fire hydrants, windowless walls, and manholes are part of an inner-city landscape; they have also been staples of city games. Due to the availability of these features and games' ability to organize and incorporate members of varying skill levels with each other at any time, these activities become an important part of the fabric of a community. They engender strong positive feelings for the activity and, by extension, to the people with whom the activity is shared. Some children invest much time and energy in these mass culture or specific culture-based activities because there is community support and status for skill development. Cultural activities make commonalities evident, provide a sense of identity within a group, are a pleasurable and harmonious way to connect to others, and offer opportunities for recognition of individual talents or skills.

During middle childhood, interest in hobbies emerge. Many youngsters begin collecting stamps, baseball cards, comic books, dolls, or memorabilia. The goal of collecting is to find and possess objects that are perceived as rare, beautiful, or representative of an ego ideal or a favorite activity. Children then spend many hours organizing these valued objects so that they are attractively, meaningfully, and safely exhibited. Giving order and meaning to objects randomly found in the world is a source of pride. Children enjoy showing off and talking about their collections to peers or family members who can share their love of the objects. Anna Freud (1965) described hobbies as activities that were midway between work and play. Though hobbies are approached with preconceived plans in a reality-oriented manner and aims of instinctual impulses are displaced, the aims are not far removed from direct gratifications of aggressive or libidinal drives.

The desire to master certain activities becomes urgent to grade-school children. They have developed capacities to withstand some frustration in the learning process and to delay immediate gratification for a different type of pleasure and satisfaction that comes from mastery. Mastery brings a reality-oriented joy of power and control over one's body or part of the environment. Children begin to understand that skills are developed primarily through disciplined repetition. For example, there is a right way and a wrong way to swing a tennis racket, to hold a bat, to build a model ship, or to solve a puzzle. This is in sharp contrast to the carefree running and exploration of young children.

Activities such as model building, jewelry making, and arts and crafts facilitate children's development of manipulative skills, impulse control, planning, and organizational skills, which are foundations for adult work. Primitive impulses to destroy need to be inhibited, channeled, and transformed in the interest of creating something of value. Raw materials are reorganized into something beautiful or functional. Children toil for hours on what can appear to an adult to be repetitive and tedious tasks in order to gain mastery over materials by carrying out their plans and achieving their desired outcomes. In the process of building, they also handle materials robustly and wield tools to hammer, carve, and shape materials to force their vision on inanimate objects. In other activities, children learn to manipulate gently or mold delicate materials that are likely to break with rough handling.

Puzzles draw latency-age youngsters to use their cognitive skills and wits to figure out the unknown. Puzzle pieces are rearranged concretely or abstractly to find an object, uncover an answer, or unravel a mystery. Success supports children's self-efficacy and confidence to manage in an ever-changing world of larger and more powerful people than them.

As children's view of their world continues to become more reality-based and they more readily accept inflexible group rules, sports such a football, baseball, or basketball may attract their interest. Through these sports, children's aggressive impulses are channeled and organized into potentially more complex sublimatory levels than early childhood games. The greater number of rules and formalized checks or penalties in sports as opposed to games helps to contain impulses and increases concentration on specific skill development. Effective blocking and tackling in football require an understanding of very specific rules and developed strategies. Often in sports, individuals must react swiftly and decisively to another. In tennis, players control by the speed and placement of their shots and also are controlled by their opponent's similar abilities. If the challenger is an equal or slightly more skilled, a player is driven to maximum effort in the use of physical and mental potential. Reaching this optimal balance of opportunity and personal capacities within such an activity with clear goals and feedback on performance results in an experience of flow. This gratification leads to increased investment in the activity beyond drive discharge and toward value cathexis. The activity may develop into a lifelong interest and an important sublimatory channel for the individual.

Within the confines of a group sport, members play as a synchronized unit. Basketball players often say they get more satisfaction out of passing for an assist than making a basket themselves. Team members achieve a perception of greater power and strength and share intense joy in victory through pooling and coordinating their talents.

When children do not have the opportunity to use or develop skills in interesting prosocial activities, they may seek out or successfully be sought out by gangs or other youths who find opportunities, challenges, and a sense of identity through delinquency. Instead of using objects to achieve greater meaning and organization, intentional chaos or destruction is the goal. Synergy and harmony with others also can be achieved in crimes (Csikszentmihalyi, 1990).

Fantasies and daydreaming support a child's development of sublimatory capacities as children strive toward achievement and triumph. Sarnoff (1976, p. 130) stated that "Dreams of great achievement produce a willingness to undertake truly difficult tasks. . . . Narcisstic invasion of reality situation with fantasies can serve useful purposes; for they give reality a chance to impress and win frightened fledglings on the brink of life." These fantasies inhibit fears. They bolster children's confidence so that they can remain composed in the presence of a formidable opponent or when confronted with temporary defeat. The children believe in and work toward their ideal, temporarily tolerating discrepancies between goals and performance along the way. Books and movies can be important supports in this regard. Latency-age children often become absorbed in stories about famous historical or sports figures who rose up from ordinary childhoods or harsh circumstances to become heroic or mythical. Tales of adventure allow children to taste the possibilities and face the challenges of the world through characters. Children share the experiences, they become frightened, excited, brave, daring, and clever along with the characters.

Wolfenstein (1954) well described children's developing abilities to use jokes and humor as a sublimatory vehicle. Jokes are in direct contrast to fantasies and are a way for an individual to reconcile reality. In fairy tales, the protagonist's frustrated wishes are finally fulfilled after a struggle;

in jokes, wish fulfillment leads to absurdity. The large size of adults is incapacitating; the demands of adults are ridiculous. Adults, in jest, are chopped down to a more manageable size. Ineptitude or inappropriate behaviors of children in a humorous story lead to laughing with the storyteller as opposed to laughing at him or her. Wolfenstein stated that humor is an adaptive way to ease frustration inherent in the everyday life of children and the disappointment and disillusionment with the reality of less-than-ideal parental figures. Painful experiences are transformed into something that is pleasurable. Though children are experiencing great strides in mastering the physical world around them, they also are becoming increasingly cognizant of their limitations. Their relative powerlessness as opposed to adults is evident. The omnipotent fantasies of early childhood are given up in favor of reality. *Mad* and *Cracked* magazines, which parody the adult world and media idols, are frequently favorites of 11- and 12-year-old children. The situations or characteristics of powerful or idealistic beings are exaggerated to absurdity, and these adults are metaphorically "crushed" through the power of the child's parody.

Jokes also serve as another way to manage libidinal impulses. The forbidden is not directly stated; word play is used to couch themes of exhibition, aggression, and sexual play. It is not the joke teller who is responsible for the content, but the characters in the joke or the listener who interprets the joke in a particular way. Aggression against authority figures is taboo, and healthy children can inhibit such impulses; accidental aggression, though, is very funny. Depending on the setup of the situation, children may not only laugh heartily during such an occurrence but also may enjoy repeating the story many times afterward.

Karate and other forms of self-defense training consciously focus children on controlling impulses as well as their state of mind. Before they can use this method of self-defense, children must learn to concentrate so intensely that they control their movements precisely. During a competitive tournament, the contestants move as if they were really fighting, but kicks and punches stop within one inch of the opponent's face. To achieve karate's noble end goal of controlling consciousness, one's body and mind must move in harmony. This requires the development of greater ego strengths

for the achievement of sublimation than most sports.

Through the process of exploring, participating, and developing skills over time and over a continuum of childhood activities such as those discussed, children develop the ego capacities critical for achieving sublimation.

Early Career Directions

All children discover that some activities offer them more gratification than others; their innate talents, interests, and level of development of ego strength are determining factors in this process. As they seek out frequent and varied opportunities to participate in gratifying activities, ideally their skills develop and broaden in support of these activities evolving into sublimatory vehicles. For example, children who have special interests in science may read voraciously about it. They may also seek out school clubs and community activities that offer opportunities to become more expert as well as involved with others who share their interest. Over time, although they may approach their scientific pursuits with a creative and playful attitude, they mature along the developmental lines of play to work (A. Freud, 1965). Their engagement is increasingly like that of adult work. They are reality-oriented, carrying out their planned activities with minimum regard for immediate gratification or the frustration that occurs and maximum regard for the pleasure of achieving their goals. Their love of science may become the central focus of their identity with other life activities organized around it. As they approach adulthood, this affinity will play an important role in the children's search for a satisfying career.

EARLY EVIDENCES OF TALENT

Innate talent fosters children's ability to develop specific sublimatory channels. When children display early signs of talent in a particular activity, their development of perseverance, attention, organization, problem solving, and work habits occurs rapidly in that activity. Adult structure and limits are not required in order for children to effectively face some difficult challenges. This occurs because children do not question any expense of energy in pursuit of perfection; it is natural and they feel compelled to do it. They are unusually intense about the particular activity and can concentrate on it for long periods of time. Their practice of the activity appears effortless; they are not self-conscious and do not exhibit the degree of frustration in the process of learning as other children often do. This allows children to use the activity fully to meet their intrapsychic needs.

BALLET, GYMNASTICS, AND MUSIC

To participate successfully in activities such as ballet, gymnastics, and music, children must have developed a significant level of ego strength, including impulse control and the ability to delay immediate gratification. To participate competently in these activities, they must perfect specific motor skills and patterns. Movements must be precise in time and space. Though the barre in a ballet studio might appear to invite physically pleasureable childhood activities such as hanging upside down, the little ballerina inhibits this wish. The barre is used only to maintain balance while performing very controlled exercises. To perfect meaningful combinations of sound, young musicians practice motor patterns and rhythms on their particular instrument for hours. The end result for which children inhibit immediate gratification and strive for is the physical, sensual, and mental sense of organization and harmony in performance of the art; this is part of task mastery.

Grade-school children embrace the reality that "practice makes perfect." They accept structure, routine, and lessons from teachers or activity leaders as the way to achieve excellence. As skill develops, so does passion and a work ethic. Practice leads to skill, then to joy and self-esteem in accomplishment.

Young performing artists or serious athletes experience a different type of relationship with their coach or teacher from that experienced with other adults in their life. It is often a singular, intense, very goal-focused relationship. Its objective is to pass specific expertise from the teacher to the child; that is why the relationship exists; it is similar to the relationships adults have with mentors. Therefore, libidinal and aggressive impulses that children might express toward parental figures must be inhibited and transformed in this relationship if the children are to remain focused on approaching their ego ideal in reality. They accept greater criticism in the context of this relationship than they can tolerate from a parent. As a result, children's ego development is strengthened and their further development of sublimatory capacities is supported.

Role of Pets

Caring for pets is not far removed from direct gratification of libidinal impulses and is therefore a very enticing activity for grade-school children. Pets help children develop an awareness and appreciation of the needs of another and skill in providing for those needs. This evolves in an environment that is not as conflictual as the human one is. As children teach a pet, they become very sensitive to the unique responses and cues of the pet and learn to respond empathically. They learn to play gently so as not to injure the animal. They need to provide for the pet's basic needs, even when they do not want to. They must learn to be a "good enough" parent. Children can freely project their needs and impulses onto the pet, identify with the animal, and transform their own regressive longings into a desire to parent the pet as they unconsciously wish to be cared for. The unconditional love, physical closeness, play, and protectiveness shared are fruits of this relationship. Children frequently develop a love and concern for a pet that rivals their concerns for people in their life.

The characteristics and instinctual behavior of certain pets or the context in which children care for them foster the development of different facets of their caregiving skills. For example, dogs allow a child a more directive caregiving and teaching role. They are concerned with pleasing their masters, and they give in to demands more easily than other animals. Puppies have boundless energy; unless they are trained, their play knows no control or boundaries. Just as children's own parents train them, children must train the dog to contain destructive and aggressive impulses, gain control of bodily functions, and acclimate to routine.

When children find injured or orphaned wildlife, they are drawn to nurse the babies back to health. Turning a scared and hurt animal into a calm, happy, and affectionate one is a joyful accomplishment. Children experience the roles of empathic and resourceful therapist, nurse, or doctor. In addition, children metaphorically learn about separation by learning how gradually to push the animal back toward freedom, back to its natural habitat.

Summary

Anna Freud (1965, p. 135) well summarized the value of sublimation when she wrote that if children can find relief of tension and frustration through "healthy displacement and neutralization of drive energy" in activities that inhibit and redirect original aims, they will likely safeguard their mental health.

REFERENCES

Csikszentmihalyi, M. (1990). *Flow, The psychology of optimal experience.* New York: HarperCollins.

Csikszentmihalyi, M., & Larson, R. (1978). Intrinsic rewards of school crime. *Crime and Delinquency, 24,* 322–335.

Erikson, E. (1959). *Identity and the life cycle.* New York: International Universities Press.

Erikson, E. (1963). *Childhood and society.* New York: W. W. Norton.

Freud, A. (1965). *Normality and pathology in childhood.* New York: International Universities Press.

Loewald, H. (1988). *Sublimation, inquiries into theoretical psychoanalysis.* New Haven, CT: Yale University Press.

Opie, I. & P. (1984). *Children's games in street and playground.* Oxford: Oxford University Press.

Redl, F., & Wineman, D. (1952). *Controls from within: Techniques for the treatment of the aggressive child.* New York: Free Press.

Sandler, J., & Joffe, W. G. (1966). On skill and sublimation. *Journal of the American Psychoanalytic Association, 14,* 335–355.

Sarnoff, C. (1976). *Latency.* New York: Jason Aronson.

Wolfenstein, M. (1954). *Children's humor: A psychological analysis,* Glencoe, IL: The Free Press.

14 / **Effects of Pop Culture on Children**

David Elkind

Pop (popular) culture generally is understood as including all of those artifacts of public communication that are, or are capable of being, mass produced and available to the public at large. Television commercials are a form of pop art; TV soap operas are an example of pop drama. Sports superstar Michael Jordan and astronaut Neil Armstrong, both of whose fame rests in part on the media, are pop culture heroes. Madonna and Elvis Presley are icons of pop culture. Hula hoops, Cabbage Patch dolls, Superman, Batman, and Mickey Mouse are as well. Unlike folk art and music, which are limited to particular places and times, what is most noteworthy about pop culture is its availability to vast audiences. It is that aspect of culture that involves mass production and mass communication.

Pop culture usually is regarded as having emerged in the 1960s with pop artists such as Andy Warhol leading the revolt against (nonpopular) abstract and impressionistic art. But pop culture really began with the invention of the printing press. Its growth was accelerated when, in the 19th century, free public education for all citizens became a mandate of democratic societies. That is to say, universal literacy is a necessary precondition for the existence of pop culture. The progressive availability to the general public of inexpensive printed magazines and books, of radio, of films, and of television have marked the successive stages of the evolution of pop culture.

Theories of Pop Culture and Its Effects on Children

There have been several conflicting theories as to the effects of pop culture on children and adolescents. Perhaps the most widespread and intuitive theory might be called *media determinism.* From this point of view, pop culture is regarded as both a causal and a negative influence. Dime novels, comic books, radio, movies, and television have, in turn, been accused of corrupting the young. Such claims never were substantiated. Nonetheless, recently Neil Postman (1982) has argued that television is bringing about the "disappearance" of childhood. Likewise, in her two books, Marie Winn has described television as a *plug-in drug* (1977) that is creating, *children without childhood* (1983). Perhaps the major exponent of media determinism, however, was Marshall McCluhan (McCluhan, 1964), who argued that the media available in any given society was the "message" that largely determined the character of that society.

Like economic determinism, however, media determinism is much too limited to account for the diversity of social forces impinging upon a child's life. An alternative interpretation is that of what might be called *media reflectionism.* From this point of view, rather than determine the nature of a social life, pop culture is more likely to mirror the perceptions and attitudes toward children that are already in play within the larger society. That is to say, from this standpoint, pop culture is not the cause but rather an effect of the social changes that are corrupting the young. This view of pop culture is most ardently advocated by some of its practitioners (Gross, 1989). When a "heavy metal" rock group such as Motley Crew is accused of being obscene and too lurid for young people, band members argue that they are merely reflecting what is "out there," not creating it. It is not their music and lyrics, but society itself, that corrupts youth.

A third interpretation, widely held among social scientists, is that of *media-society interactionism* (Comstock, 1972). According to this view, pop culture is indeed a reflection of what is happening in society. But it is also more than that. Pop culture not only reflects but also reinforces, and thus strengthens, preexisting attitudes and perceptions. From this interactionism perspective, pop culture is *both* a reflection of society and a determinant of it. In the same way, society is *both* a determinant of pop culture and also is reinforced by it. From an interactionist position, it is difficult, if not impossible, to tease out the extent to which pop culture affects society or society affects pop culture. It is an ongoing dynamic process, and the causal relations will vary for different individuals, with the type of pop culture, and with the social forces operative at any given time.

In this chapter I approach the question of the effects of pop culture on children from the interactionist perspective. In particular I illustrate how changes in our perceptions of children over the last century have been both reflected and reinforced by pop culture. Our changed perception of children, however, is part of a larger change in our perception of the family and of parenting. It is necessary, therefore, first to present the larger changes that have occurred within the society and family before turning to the alterations that have occurred in our perceptions of children. Only in the context of these larger transformations can the relation between children and pop culture be meaningfully understood.

From the Modern to the Postmodern Family

THE ASSUMPTIONS OF MODERNITY AND THE NUCLEAR FAMILY

Late modernism, which has been said to have ended around the middle of this century was founded on three fundamental assumptions about the nature of the world: progress, universality, and regularity. With respect to society, the idea of progress assumed that social life progressed from primitive "savage" societies to "civilized" cultured societies. This social progress also was supposed to be a universal one that was occurring, albeit at different rates, in all parts of the world. Finally, social progress was assumed to follow a regular, predictable, lawful course. Darwin's theory of biological evolution provided a general paradigm for this conception of progressive, universal, and regular social progress.

These fundamental assumptions were embodied in the modern *nuclear* family. It was assumed that the nuclear family was the ideal end product of a long evolutionary process:

Social Science developed only one comprehensive theory of family change, one based on nineteenth century evolutionary ideas . . . the theory asserted that in the course of man's development the family had "progressed" from the primitive sexual promiscuity of a semi-animal horde through group marriage, matriarchy, and patriarchy in some polygynous form, to culminate in the highest spiritual expression of the family, Victorian Monogamy. (Goode, 1977, p. 76)

The nuclear family—two parents, one working and one staying home to rear the children—which was relatively isolated from the larger society, also was regarded as an ideal kinship pattern that should be universally aspired to. In addition, it was seen as the most "regular" kinship pattern against which all other patterns had to be measured. Single-parent families, two-parent working families, blended families, and adoptive families were all seen as irregular and, therefore, inferior in kinship structure to the nuclear family. In short, in the modern era, the nuclear family took on moral dimensions and was regarded as the only "good" family structure for healthy child rearing.

THE ASSUMPTIONS OF POSTMODERNITY AND THE PERMEABLE FAMILY

Events of the first half of the 20th century, however, challenged the basic tenets of late modernism on every score. The assumption that societies, as they became progressively more civilized, educated, and cultured, also became more humanitarian and less savage was challenged by two world wars, the holocaust, and the atomic bomb. In the same way, the assumption that the course of social progress was universal has been undermined by the growing economic power of Asia. While in the West democracy preceded the industrial and now the information revolutions, in Asia the industrial

and information revolutions have occurred before the establishment of true democracy. Likewise, the regularity and lawfulness of social progress is contradicted by the different fates of communism in Russia and China. The idea of a single course of social progress that is both universal and regular is simply no longer tenable.

As a consequence, a new set of assumptions have come into play regarding the social world. Instead of progress we now have the notion of connectedness. Nations are progressively connected to one another in various ways, and this connectedness can take many different forms. Connectedness is perhaps most evident in commerce, where "multinational" companies manufacture and distribute their products in many different countries. Pop culture is another form of connectedness as evidenced by the international appeal of rock music, jeans, cigarettes, and Coca-Cola. If progress occurs, it is in the connectedness among nations, not within a single nation. The Common Market treaty and the North American Free Trade Agreement are other manifestations of postmodern international connectedness.

The assumption of universality also has been displaced. In its stead we now have the assumption of particularity. A good illustration of this change is the modern belief in the United States as a kind of "melting pot," a mixing bowl into which peoples from all parts of the world would be placed and from which would emerge a common, assimilated product. Today we recognize that the United States was never a melting pot and that people from different countries retain some of their cultural traditions. Rather than try to erase these traditions, we now value them as part of our national diversity. We are fortunate to be able to accept this diversity. In other parts of the world, the new emphasis on particularity has led to religious, ethnic, and racial partisanship and, all too often, to armed conflict.

Finally, the assumption of regularity has been modified by the recognition that much in society is irregular and that irregularity is not the same as abnormal. This change is perhaps most evident in science, where irregular phenomena were once regarded as "errors of measurement" or "noise" in the system. Einstein was assuming regularity when he wrote that "God does not play dice with the universe," and Freud was assuming regularity when he argued that even the slightest psychological "errors," such as slips of the tongue or pen and forgetting, were determined by unconscious motivations. Today, however, we recognize that there are many "chaotic" phenomena, such as the weather, that are not regular in the traditional sense but that are nonetheless genuine phenomena that are capable of mathematical description. In social life, too, we now recognize that there is tremendous variation among social systems and many different systems can function well and effectively.

These changed assumptions about the nature of our world have been incorporated into a new conception of the family, the postmodern *permeable* family (Elkind, 1994). The progressively more solid boundaries of the nuclear family ensured a clear distinction between public and private, between homeplace and workplace, and between children and adults. In contrast, the boundaries of the postmodern family are highly permeable and connect it to, rather than isolate it from, the larger society. For example, the public\private distinction has dissolved now that television programs such as *Donahue, The Oprah Winfrey Show, Geraldo,* and *Sally Jessy Raphael* probe the most intimate facets of family life. Likewise, private issues, such as abortion, have become public issues addressed in national debate.

In the same way, the distinctions between homeplace and workplace have been all but obliterated. The introduction of personal computers, modems, desktop publishing, and fax machines have made it possible for many people to conduct their business from workplaces in their homes. Half of the small businesses begun by women over the past 20 years have been initiated by women working where they live. At the same time, more than 4,000 companies now have child care centers located in or near their buildings. In a very real sense the workplace has moved into the homeplace much as the homeplace has moved into the workplace. Finally, the tradition of wise, mentoring adults imparting their knowledge, skills, and values to the innocent, naive, next generation has become blurred now that the pace of social change is such that the young are often more knowledgeable and skilled than their parents (e.g., playing computer games). Accordingly, progressive connection with, rather than isolation from, the larger society characterizes the postmodern, permeable family.

In a like manner, the universality of the nuclear family also has been deconstructed. We now acknowledge, if not fully accept, a variety of different kinship structures that serve to rear children. Single-parent families, two-parent working families, blended families, adoptive families, surrogate-mother families, and test-tube baby families now far outnumber the traditional nuclear families in our society. The nuclear family is not now, and perhaps never was, the universal family form. In the same way, we now recognize that the nuclear family can conceal much demeaning pain and abuse just as "nonregular" families can be deeply loving and caring. It is the maturity of the people involved and the emotional climate of the family, not its "regular" kinship structure, that are critical to successful child rearing.

Modern and Postmodern Family Ties

Family ties include the sentiments, values, and perceptions that bind family members one with the other. As we have moved from the nuclear to the permeable family, the corresponding family ties have changed as well. Moreover, this change in family ties has been mirrored and reinforced by pop culture. It is through this reflection and strengthening of the current family ties (and by the derision of previous ones) that pop culture exerts its most powerful influence on families and children.

MODERN FAMILY TIES

Sentimental Ties: The modern nuclear family was characterized by the sentimental ties of *romantic love, maternal love, and domesticity* (Shorter, 1977). Romantic love was the idea that there is one person in the world for whom you are destined and that once you meet that "stranger across a crowded room," you will wed and live "happily ever after." The idea of maternal love emerged in the 19th century coincident with the drop in infant mortality. It was the idea that women had a "maternal instinct" that necessitated their staying home to love and care for infants and young children. Any woman who did not show this instinct was somehow "abnormal." Finally, the notion of domesticity was the idea that family members were more tightly bound to one another than to relationships in the outside world.

These ties were mirrored and idealized in much of pop culture of the 19th century and the first half of the 20th century. Romantic novels of the 19th century, such as those of Jane Austen (Austen, 1811/1960), often were centered on the sentiments of romantic love, maternal love, and domesticity. In this century, not only novels but radio programs, movies, and television dramas all provide stories that echo the sentiments of the nuclear family.

Perhaps the best example of the pop culture portrayal of these sentiments is provided by the motion picture *It's a Wonderful Life*, directed by Frank Capra and starring James Stewart and Donna Reed. It is now shown on national TV every year at Christmastime. Stewart is an ambitious young man who forgoes his ambitions to take over the family business, a savings and loan firm. He marries his childhood sweetheart, Donna Reed, and they soon have two children. His wife stays home to rear the children and to provide support and nurturance for him. It is a touching portrayal of romantic love, maternal love, and domesticity. When money is lost and Stewart is about to lose everything, his friends in the community contribute their savings so that the savings and loan does not have to fold. In this way, the values of the nuclear family are not merely mirrored but rewarded and reinforced as well.

Perceptual Ties: Perceptual ties have to do with the perceptions of parents, children, and teenagers that mediate interactions between family members as well as those with the larger society. These perceptions derive from the character of the family's sentimental ties. Romantic love, maternal love, and domesticity were all thought to be "natural" inborn sentiments that are part of our human endowment. It follows, therefore, that parenting also would be seen as an unlearned, *intuitive* set of skills. The child-rearing literature reflected this perception. Benjamin Spock, for example, wrote:

Don't take too seriously all that the neighbors say. Don't be overawed by what experts say. Don't be afraid to trust your own common sense. Bringing up your child won't be a complicated job if you take it easy, trust your instincts, and follow the directions that your doctor gives you. We know for a fact that the natural loving

care that kindly parents give their children is a hundred times more valuable than their knowing how to pin a diaper on just right or how to make a formula expertly. (1968, p. 8)

In short, given knowledge about child development, well-meaning parents would intuitively do the right thing.

Modern family sentiments also dictated the perception of children. Romantic love presupposed a lifelong commitment to the young, and maternal love presupposed an innocent, helpless child in need of maternal nurturance and care. Domesticity ensured a warm, safe, and protected haven for innocent and relatively defenseless children. Indeed, the nuclear family was seen (and still is in some circles) as the ideal family system for the rearing of children. The perception of childhood innocence was both reflected and reinforced by the pop culture, particularly the literature for and about children:

Caring and even sentimental attitudes to children gathered strength through the nineteenth century. This movement of opinion was gradual but, on evidence of books written for children, a new spirit emerged in the 1880's. After a long period of moral seriousness, the plain but virtuous child fell out of favor. Instead, ringleted heroines, dainty and innocent, gave the upstairs nursery its tone. Among older children, playfulness and mischief became acceptable, and their reading (bought by relative) positively urged them to be madcaps and tomboys. With the dawning recognition that it is possible for children to be too good, we have crossed into the modern world. (Roberts, 1980, p. 26)

This perception of childhood as a period during which children should be expected only to be playful was mirrored by the books and stories for the young written during the early decades of this century:

Nowhere is this [the sense of difference and distance between childhood and adulthood] more charmingly expressed than in Kenneth Grahame's account of his own childhood, *The Golden Age*. Wherein children see themselves as the fortunate ones, and adults the Olympians, powerful but misguided. When adults have the power to do otherwise, how can they possibly wish to spend a lovely Sunday going to Church and drinking tea on the lawn instead of climbing trees and digging for buried treasure. Childhood is the ideal estate. The assumption is also made in other books of the period such as *The Wind in the Willows* (in which the animals are really children), the Nesbit books and, most of all, in

Barrie's *Peter Pan* (produced first as a play in 1904). It was not that the children in these books wanted to evade maturity and responsibility; it was rather that childhood had its own special character and flavor, one that could not be given up without a sense of loss. Childhood was to be prolonged as long as possible. (Egoff, 1981, p. 7)

If children were seen as innocent, then adolescents were regarded as immature, and this perception was again reflected in the pop culture. In movies such as the Andy Hardy series, teenagers were presented as immature and getting into adolescent scrapes from which they had to be extricated by adults. In books such as *The Hardy Boys* and *The Nancy Drew Mysteries,* there was much modeling of adult roles, skills, and attitudes. Always in the background, however, was a protective adult world ready to provide help, guidance, and direction when it was needed. Late modern television series such as *Ozzie and Harriet* and *My Three Sons* further reflected and reinforced the perception of adolescent immaturity.

The pop culture of books and television, thus both reflected and reinforced the modern perceptions of parents' intuitive child-rearing competence, of childhood innocence, and of adolescent immaturity.

POSTMODERN FAMILY TIES

Sentimental Ties: In contrast to the sentiments of the nuclear family, those of the permeable family are *consensual love, shared parenting, and urbanity.* Romantic love was severely damaged by the sexual revolution of the 1960s, when premarital sex became commonplace. Romantic love assumed that one (particularly the woman) "saved" oneself for one's destined mate. Once premarital sex became the rule, this aspect of romantic love dissipated. Likewise, the ease and availability, and postmodern social acceptability, of divorce made the lifelong commitment of romantic love less binding upon unhappy couples. In place of romantic love we now have what might be called consensual love. Couples have a relationship by mutual consent and without necessarily any binding commitments. Notions of "safe sex" and of prenuptial agreements are reflective of consensual, not romantic, love.

With the movement of large numbers of mothers into the workforce, the sentiment of maternal love has changed as well. It is now recognized that women can love their children and still want to work and pursue a career. As a result a new sentiment regarding child rearing has emerged: the sentiment of shared parenting. According to this sentiment, rearing the children is not the sole responsibility of the mother. The father and nonparental caregivers also may be involved. The recent passage by the federal government of the ABC (Action for Better Childcare) bill, which provides support for out-of-home child care, is public recognition of this new sentiment of shared parenting.

Finally, the nuclear sentiment of domesticity has given way to the postmodern sentiment of urbanity. Thanks to the permeable membranes of the postmodern family, even young children are exposed to all facets of society. Television graphically depicts events occurring in all parts of the world and brings famine, war, and terror into our living rooms. At the same time we are able to visit museums, attend concerts, and explore the oceans, deserts, and mountains, all without leaving the comfort of our living room. Moreover, modern jet travel has made it fast and cheap to visit other countries and experience other cultures. The postmodern, permeable family is necessarily more urbane than the modern nuclear family.

This change in family sentiments has been both mirrored and reinforced by pop culture. Contemporary TV programs and films convey the sentiments and values of the permeable family in much the same way that the programs of the 1950s and 1960s brought forth the sentiments and values of the nuclear family. Both the long-running *Love Boat* and *Hotel* were paeans to consensual love and "recreational sex." Shared parenting is also a common theme in contemporary TV dramas. In the long-running sitcom *Who's the Boss,* for example, a male is both the housekeeper and nanny. Likewise, single-mother Murphy Brown's son Avery is cared for mostly by a male friend. The urbanity of the permeable family is echoed in the frequency with which these shows deal with topics such as AIDS, drugs, abuse, and deviant behavior. All of these pop culture portrayals both reflect and reinforce the sentiments of the permeable family.

At the same time, other pop cultural vehicles are devoted to ridiculing the sentiments and values of the modern nuclear family. Families such as the cartoon Simpsons, the Connors of *Rose-*

anne, and the Bundys of *Married with Children* are parodies of nuclear family life.

Seemingly overnight, Fox Broadcasting's "The Simpsons" has emerged as a breakaway ratings hit, an industry trend setter, a merchandising phenomena, a cultural template and among its most fanatical followers, a viewing experience verging on the religious. Of course there are others who find this video brood eminently obnoxious, if not downright nasty. In any case the whole thing's totally improbable: We're talking about a half hour *cartoon.*

Perhaps the weirdest part is that these five rather crudely drawn characters—basically bug eyed squiggles with hideous overbites—embody a genuine Sociological Force. If you buy the argument that television mirrors us more than it molds us, then suddenly its sending out an intriguing message about ourselves. We're beginning to revolt against the tube's idealized images of domestic life—and at the same time, lovingly embracing messed up families with collars of blue.

"'The Simpsons' is a joke on traditional sitcoms because its characters are so far removed from what is depicted as the norm," says Jack Nachbar, professor of popular culture at Bowling Green State University, "But in actuality, they're closer to the real thing than anything we have ever seen." (Waters, 1990, p. 59)

Shows like *The Simpsons* and *Married with Children* are thus humorous postmodern parodies of the ideal modern nuclear family. They satirize the nuclear family sentiments of romantic love, maternal love, and domesticity as well as the modern family value of togetherness. In their own way, therefore, these programs make shows that offer positive depictions of the permeable family sentiments such as *Who's the Boss?* and *Murphy Brown* more acceptable. In other words, pop culture can not only mirror and reinforce the prevailing values but also serve to reinforce the negative attitudes toward those that are out of favor.

Perceptual Ties: The perceptual ties of the permeable family have changed in accord with the alteration in family sentiments. Consensual love, shared parenting, and urbanity are learned rather than inborn sentiments. In accord with these sentiments, the perception of parenting has changed from one of unlearned intuition to what Jacques Ellul (Ellul, 1964) has called acquired *technique.* According to Ellul, technique refers to "the totality of methods rationally arrived at and having absolute efficiency [for a given stage of development] in every field of human activity" (p. xxv). Although technique became prominent in indus-

try during the modern era, it is only in the postmodern era that it has been applied to parenting.

This new perception of parenting as technique can be illustrated by the pop literature for parents that began to appear after midcentury. What characterizes this literature is not only the specificity of the advice given but also the idea that there is a "right" and a "wrong" way to parent—quite a different position from that of Spock. In the following illustration, the advice giver not only directs parents in the "right" direction but also, by inference, tells them what they have not been doing or have been doing wrong:

To do a good job, all people need to know the rules. Like any employee [*sic!*] children too need to know what's expected of them and what they can expect when they follow the rules and what will happen to them if they don't. Limit setting will give your children these guidelines. . . . When you finish reading this book, you will be able to set and enforce limits like the following which includes all three components [limit, reason, consequence].
Limit: "Johnny, you can play outside in the backyard but you cannot go in the front yard, or on the sidewalk, or out into the street."
Reason: "In the backyard you are safe from being hit by a car."
Consequence: "If you go out of the backyard, you will have to come into the house and stay for the rest of the day." (Schaefer, 1991, pp. 60–61)

In this example, the focus on technique excludes the issue of development. Indeed the child is likened to an employee. The postmodern enthrallment with parenting as technique even has led some writers to advocate that parents use techniques not only to teach infants to read (Doman, 1964) but to train fetuses in utero:
"*Stroke* your fetus and say, 'Stroke, I'm stroking you.'
"*Pat* your fetus and say, 'Pat, I'm patting you.'
"*Gently squeeze* your fetus and say, 'Squeeze, I'm squeezing you.'
"*Rub* your fetus and say, 'Rub, I'm rubbing you'" (Ludington-Hoe, 1985, p. 24).

In both of these examples, the emphasis is not only on technique but also takes for granted the child's ability to profit from these techniques. This reflects not only a changed perception of parenting but also a changed perception of the child. In contrast to the modern perception of childhood innocence, the postmodern view is that of childhood *competence*. In the permeable family, where children can no longer be protected from the barrage of information coming into the home via television, with the need for out-of-home care from an early age, and with the frequency of divorce and remarriage, children have to be seen as competent to deal with all of these vicissitudes. And while children are competent, they often are less so than we would like to believe.

Again, we can evidence this new perception of children not only by the advice given to parents but by the pop literature for and about children.

On the top shelf at the local bookstore, the Sesame Street gang stars in a volume about coping with daycare. One shelf below, a happy-go-lucky family of bears offers to teach our four-year-old a cautionary tale about meeting strangers.

Afraid of the dark, moving? Pet died? There's a slim, gaily colored book exploring each of these subjects.

Welcome to the neurotic new world of children's literature. The benign land of cats in the hat and Mother Goose is being elbowed aside by self-help volumes for the preschool set. The children's sections of most stores are crammed with a startling array of books aimed at child sized anxieties. A chain outlet we visited recently had little books dealing with the fear of flying, bedwetting, security blankets, making friends, eating junk food, cleaning up messy rooms, going home when asked, waiting turns, telling the truth and many others. (Farhi & Farhi, 1989, p. C6)

The pop literature for older children also is geared to teaching them about topics from which, at an earlier time, adults thought they should be shielded:

Daniel is a little boy who adored his Uncle Tim. He remembered him as "more funny than any other grown-up I knew." They used to go for long walks in the woods, and tried to outwit each other in hard fought battles of checkers. Then one winter Uncle Tim began to stay home and sleep a lot, and Daniel's mother told him the awful truth: Uncle Tim had AIDS.

Daniel's sad and fearful reaction to Uncle Tim's worsening condition and his eventual acceptance of his death are the story of "Losing Uncle Tim," a book that was written for an audience of six-year-old readers. With it vivid and poignant treatment of AIDS, "Losing Uncle Tim" by Mary Kate Jordan, is but one example of the stark new realism of children's books. (Lawson, 1990, p. C1)

In these books as in the other pop media, the child is portrayed, or assumed to be, competent to deal with any all of life's necessary losses. Pop culture thus mirrored and reinforced the modern image of childhood innocence and now mirrors and reinforces the postmodern perception of childhood competence. In fact, pop culture always distorts the reality of childhood. Children were more competent than the pop culture portrayal of innocence suggested, but they also are less competent than the postmodern pop culture would have them be. Because children are doing less well than they did in the modern era, the perception of childhood competence and its reflection and reinforcement by pop culture has to be regarded as less beneficial than the pop cultural portrayal of the modern innocent child.

The same is true for the postmodern perception of adolescence and its mirroring by pop culture. Once children were seen as competent, immaturity was no longer a fitting sequel. Instead, and in keeping with the postmodern family sentiments of consensual love, shared parenting, and urbanity, the postmodern perception of adolescents is that of young people who are sophisticated, ready and able to cope with sex, drugs, and the consumer economy. Again, pop culture portrayals of adolescence reflect this new perception. In shows such as *Married with Children* and *Roseanne*, the teenage daughters are sexually active.

Perhaps nowhere is the pop portrayal of teenage sophistication more explicit than in the music written for and played to this age group. Whereas in the modern era young people listened to music meant for adults, the emergence of "rock" in the 1960s was directed toward youth and alienated adults. The sexually explicit lyrics and sexually suggestive antics of some rock performers presuppose a sophisticated teenage audience. Many computer Nintendo games also have violent themes, repeat sexual stereotypes, and presuppose young people who are sophisticated and who will not be affected by the messages of the games. As in the case of children, while modern adolescents may have been more sophisticated than they were given credit for, postmodern adolescents are probably less sophisticated than is assumed by pop culture.

In conclusion, pop culture both mirrors and reinforces the prevailing family sentiments, values, and perceptions. In the modern era, the perceptions of childhood innocence and adolescent immaturity encouraged adults to provide protection and security for the young and the pop culture gave adults support in this endeavor. In general, young people benefited from this type of adult intervention. In the postmodern world, the perception of childhood competence and adolescent sophistication has encouraged adults to abrogate many of their modern responsibilities to children and youth. And the pop culture, to the extent that

it mirrors these perceptions, contributes to that abrogation of adult responsibility.

On every measure that we have—health, education, or welfare—children and youth are doing more poorly than they did in the modern era. While popular culture is certainly not the cause of this deterioration in the well-being of children and youth, it certainly is a major contributor.

REFERENCES

Austen, J. (1960). *The complete novels of Jane Austen.* New York: Modern Library. (Originally published 1811).

Comstock, G. A., & Rubinstein, D. (1972). *Television and social behavior* (DHEW Publication No. HSM 72-9060). Washington, DC:

Doman, G. (1964). *Teach your baby to read.* London: Jonathan Cape.

Egoff, S. A. (1981). *Thursday's child.* Chicago: American Library Association.

Elkind, D. (1994). *Ties that Stress: The new imbalance.* Cambridge, MA: Harvard University Press.

Ellul, J. (1964). *The technological society.* New York: Alfred A. Knopf.

Farhi, S. P., & Farhi, L. K. (1989). The new children's books, grimmer than Grimm. *Washington Post,* September 3, p. C5.

Goode, W. J. (1977). *World revolution and family patterns.* New York: Free Press.

Gross, R. L. (1989). Heavy metal music. *Journal of Pop Culture,* 119–130.

Lawson, C. (1990, November 8). Once upon a time in the land of bibliotherapy. *New York Times,* p. C1.

Ludington-Hoe, S. (1985). *How to have a smarter baby.* New York: Rawson Associates.

McCluhan, M. (1964). *Understanding media.* New York: Mentor.

Postman, N. (1982). *The disappearance of childhood.* New York: Laurel.

Roberts, A. (1980). *Out to Play.* Aberdeen: Aberdeen University Press.

Schaefer, C., & Digeronimo, R. (1991). *Teach your child to behave.* New York: Plume.

Shorter, E. (1977). *The making of the modern family.* New York: Basic Books.

Spock, B. (1968). *Baby and child care.* New York: Hawthorne Books.

Waters, H. F. (1990, April 23). Family feuds. *Newsweek,* p. 58.

Winn, M. (1977). *The plug in drug.* New York: Viking Press.

Winn, M. (1983). *Children without childhood.* New York: Penguin Books.

15 / School-Age Development from a Self Psychological Perspective

Anna Ornstein

The term *latency* has been interpreted in various ways in the course of the history of psychoanalysis. For Freud, latency designated a period in development during which repression was established as a principal mental mechanism, a period during which "the influx of sexuality does not stop . . . but its energy is deflected either wholly or partially from sexual utilization and conducted to other

aims" (Freud, 1905/1953, p. 178). Central to the traditional conceptualization of latency has been the resolution of the Oedipus complex, the consolidation of superego functioning, and the reorganization of the defensive structures of the ego. Within this theoretical frame of reference, the developmental task was considered to be the child's ability to maintain a positive equilibrium between defenses and drives. The division between early and late latency (Bornstein, 1951) arose from the observation that in the early part of latency, the child still has to struggle against incestuous impulses and be responsive to a harsh and ineffective superego. However, in the second half of latency, between the ages of 8 and 12, the superego was supposed to have achieved greater stability. More recently Kaplan (1965) considered this division to be related to maturation of the motor-perceptual system.

Since psychoanalytic self psychology represents a new model of psychological organization and functioning, concepts that explain the developmental changes in this age period differ from those used in traditional psychoanalysis. In psychoanalytic self psychology, development during the elementary school years is viewed as involving (1) an increase in the consolidation of the nuclear self, specifically in the sense of mastery and competence, (2) a consolidation of the self-esteem regulatory system, and (3) advances in moral development.

Because the psychology of the school-age child has been associated with the resolution of the Oedipus complex, I shall first offer a self psychological perspective on the oedipal stage of development.

A Self Psychological Perspective on the Oedipus Complex

It was a reexamination of the Oedipus complex that permitted Kohut to formulate the bipolar self as a supraordinate structure within the psyche (Kohut, 1977). In this new psychoanalytic paradigm, all three subphases of the oedipal period—the child's readiness to enter the phase, the actual experiencing of the oedipal passions, and the resolution of the "conflict"—had to undergo reexamination (Ornstein, 1992).

Like other analysts, Kohut considered "the presence of a firm self . . . to be a precondition for the experience of the Oedipus complex" (1977, p. 227). However, in relation to the actual experiencing of the related affects—the desire sexually to possess the parent of the opposite sex, competi-

tion, jealousy, and, most important, castration anxiety—there is considerable difference between the traditional view and that of self psychology. In traditional psychoanalytic theory, the inherently conflictual nature of the experience and the inevitability of castration anxiety make repression, the walling off of the conflict with its incestuous and murderous content, mandatory. Since the walled-off conflict is laden with guilt, it becomes forever a potential source of neurosis. This formulation lends an essentially pathological content to a normal developmental phase that can be explained by the fact that Freud conceptualizied *normal* oedipal phase on the basis of reconstructions from the analyses of adults who suffered from various forms of neurotic disorder. Kohut too depended on such data for his hypothesis regarding normal development. However, his observations led him to a very different conclusion from that of Freud. In analyzing patients with primary self disorders, Kohut found that at the end of such analyses, once self cohesion became established, some patients developed an oedipal constellation. This "brief oedipal phase," he said, "was accompanied by a warm glow of joy, a joy that has all the earmarks of an emotionality that accompanies a maturational or developmental achievement" (1977, p. 228). From such clinical observations, Kohut has drawn the conclusion that in normal development, where parents experience joy and pride in the child's developmental achievements, the oedipal phase, rather than being fraught with guilt and anxiety, is experienced joyfully. Kohut distinguished a relatively silent and joyful normal developmental *phase* from an Oedipus *complex* when, in the absence of empathic parental responsiveness, normal development becomes derailed. Under these circumstances, infantile sexuality fragments into compulsive seeking of sexual stimulation and healthy assertiveness fragments into destructive aggression.

During the oedipal phase, the early childhood idealization of the caregivers' strength and omnipotence shifts to an idealization of their values and ideals. In this regard, the transition from earlier developmental periods into latency is imperceptible; the idealization of the primary caregivers overlaps with and transitions into the idealization of teachers, scout leaders, sport and other national heroes. According to the theory of self psychology, internalization of values and standards for behavior occurs by the gradual, nontraumatic deidealization of caregivers. As values and standards become gradually, and in an increasingly more complex manner, integrated into the growing psyche, they lay the foundation for moral development.

Self-Cohesion and the Consolidation of Self-Esteem During Latency

The increase in self-cohesion and the consolidation of the self-esteem regulatory system are intimately related to the changes in the neuromuscular-perceptual systems and the changes that the school-age child experiences in his or her social environment. Most impressive among the *maturational changes* is the fact that the brain attains 90% of its total weight around age 7 and that the myelinization of the corticopyramidal system is completed around age 8. In discussing the various changes in neurobiology during latency, Shapiro and Perry (1976) were careful to point out that we do not know how these various systems interact. All that can be said is that there is a *simultaneity* here, one that would indicate interdependence among changes in brain anatomy, physiology, and chemistry that correspond with changes in perceptual and cognitive development. While careful not to be "reductionistic," Shapiro and Perry do consider the biological maturation "as a most important variable determining the changes we call latency" (p. 81).

The exploratory-assertive motivational system facilitates the integration of maturational changes in the physical realm into the child's emotional life (Lichtenberg, 1989). Together, these changes result in an increase in the sense of mastery, efficacy, and competence that are ingredients of a cohesive nuclear self. To postulate an exploratory-motivational system is in keeping with Robert White's (1959) assertion that when human beings are not motivated by hunger, by sexual desire, or by fear, they are motivated to exercise their neuromuscular apparatus and to acquire knowledge. This provides them with a map of the environment with which they must interact and that has to be mastered.

Growth in the perceptual-motor system plus the development of laterality and directionality are fundamental to the formation of body image. Freud's assertion that the ego is first and foremost a body ego (1923/1961) is also applicable to the self psychological perspective on development. However, there is a difference: For Freud, it was the sexual and aggressive drives that anchored the psyche in biology; for self psychology, it is the relatively seamless integration of body changes into the child's emotional life that firms up the self by increasing its sense of efficacy, mastery, and competence. On the other hand, whether a sense of competence will or will not develop depends on the environment's responsiveness to the child's newly developing capacities and the achievements related to them. In traditional theory, the consolidation of the superego is supposed to create a relatively closed, autonomous system; in contrast, psychoanalytic self psychology conceptualizes the psyche as a relatively open system. Within such an organization, the affirming and validating responses of the child's emotional environment continue to have structure-building significance. Such environmental responses become particularly important in relation to newly acquired skills and capacities: It is through the affirmation by significant adults that such skills and capacities will be experienced as *real* and as constituting aspects of the child's *own* (expanding) self. The significance of this can best be appreciated when disturbances arise in the motor and perceptual areas in various forms of symptomatic behavior, such as tics, stuttering, or reading and writing difficulties.

Among the psychological changes, the most impressive one occurs in cognitive development. This is the age at which the child is able to construct stable concepts of numerical relationships, time, and space. It is thus a transitional period between sensorimotor intelligence and formal operations. However, these capacities are still limited in scope; they only can be applied to actual, concrete situations (Piaget & Inhelder, 1969). As the advances in neuromuscular-perceptual systems, cognition, and language development become progressively integrated, there occurs a further increase in self-cohesion, indicated by the latency age child's ability both to take initiative in relation to increasingly more complex physical and intellectual tasks and to pursue these tasks aggressively and assertively.

However, if the activities that the child now can perform were not accompanied by feelings of pride and pleasure, the increased consolidation of the nuclear self could be considered only an improved machine. Pride in one's self and in one's activities is heir to the modification and transformation of infantile narcissistic structures (grandiosity, exhibitionism, and omnipotence) into an internal structure—transformation that occurs in response to the environment's enthusiastic responses to the child's accomplishments. Pride and pleasure in one's self and in one's activities represent self-esteem—a subjective experience of vigor, vitality, pride, and pleasure in what one does and in who one is.

In traditional psychoanalytic theory, the fate of the infantile narcissistic structures has been linked to self and object differentiation. Specifically, the theory maintained that infantile grandiosity and omnipotence have to be given up once self and object become differentiated; all that remains is a strand of narcissism that becomes part of the ego ideal. According to this theory, in the process of separating and individuating out of a symbiotic fusion with their mothers, toddlers experience a "phase-specific conflict" that is accompanied by a traumatic deflation of their infantile omnipotence (Mahler, Pine, & Bergman, 1975).

This view of development has been challenged by modern infant researchers (Sander, 1975; Stechler & Kaplan, 1980; Stern, 1985), who maintain that infants do not "emerge" from an autistic shell but are, from birth on, endowed with the capacity to elicit social responses. Rather than experiencing a traumatic deflation in toddler years, infantile omnipotence gives way to the sense of reality, and infantile grandiosity gradually becomes transformed into mature self-esteem (Kohut, 1971). By school years, a relatively complex self-esteem regulatory system appears to be in place (Cotton, 1983). Accordingly, school-age children are increasingly better able to *maintain* internalized values and standards in the face of expectable failures, criticism, and disappointments. However, this internal regulatory system is *relative,* since there is an expectable reciprocity between resiliency (provided by stable internal structures) and the need for reassurance by an empathically responsive environment. The question is not whether a child can maintain self-esteem under stress, but how quickly and effectively

he or she is able to restore it after expectable failures and humiliations. In cases where transformation of infantile grandiosity has not taken place or is incomplete, grandiose fantasies will be driven into repression, and the child will vacillate between irrational overestimation of the self and feelings of inferiority. These children are shy and withdraw from challenging academic tasks and from interactions with their peers; they are prone to shame experiences, are irritable, and are unable to develop and maintain satisfactory work habits. This is what Erikson (1963) meant when he described the latency age child as being either capable of industry or prone to painful experiences of inferiority.

Group Formation and Advances in the Theory of Moral Development

In school-age children a dialectic continues between striving for independence on the one hand and a need for attachment on the other. The resolution of this dialectic is facilitated by group affiliations when children begin to look to their peers for acceptance and praise and are no longer dependent for these responses only on their primary caregivers. However, it is also in group settings that a child's competence is first challenged in a major way. The solution children find to their need for affiliation on the one hand and their desire to assert their competence and individuality on the other significantly advances their moral development. This solution takes place primarily in the context of competitive games.

There is an ongoing debate in psychoanalysis whether moral development is a function of cognitive or affective development. However, since affective and cognitive functioning are aspects of mental development that form a unity (Nass, 1966), this is a moot question. Team games and various play activities provide unique opportunities to learn to respect rules and to consider another person's perspective when it conflicts with one's own. There is an obvious difference in the way girls and boys negotiate moral issues at this age. Traditional psychoanalytic theory related this to the difference in superego development between boys and girls. Since the formation of the superego is tied to castration anxiety, women were supposed to have been deprived of this clear-cut impetus for the resolution of the Oedipus complex and therefore of a reliable sense of morality. Gilligan (1982) conducted research with latency age girls by giving them problems that involved moral decisions. Based on her findings, she came to the conclusion that this difference is not the function of superego development. It is, rather, related to girl's greater concern with the maintenance of relationships than with an abstract notion of what constitutes morality: "In this conception, the moral problem arises from conflicting responsibilities rather than from competing rights and requires for its resolution a mode of thinking that is contextual and narrative rather than formal and abstract" (p. 19).

In the elementary school years, boys and girls exercise their gender-related capacities within predominantly gender-specific groups. Within this context, play activities are not only ideal opportunities for enhancing moral values, they also consolidate gender identity. In self psychology, identification is not considered a response to the threat of castration. Instead, a sense of "maleness" in the male child is expected to develop in response to the (idealized) caregivers' unambivalent mirroring of those features of the male child's personality that, in our Western culture, are considered to be "masculine." Similarly, the enthusiastic validation of the female child's "femininity" is expected to consolidate a female child's femininity. Group activities in predominantly same-gender groups further enhance the consolidation of gender identities.

REFERENCES

Bornstein, B. (1951). On latency. *Psychoanalytic Study of the Child, 6,* 279–285.

Cotton, N. (1983). The development of self-esteem and self-esteem regulation. In J. Mack & S. Ablon (Eds.), *The development and sustaining of self-esteem in childhood.* New York: International Universities Press.

Erikson, E. H. (1963). *Childhood and society.* New York: W. W. Norton.

Freud S. (1953). Three essays on the theory of sexuality. In J. Strachey (Ed. & Trans.), *The Standard edition of the complete psychological works of Sigmund Freud* (hereafter *Standard edition*) (Vol. 7, pp. 135–243). London: Hogarth Press. (Original work published 1905.)

Freud, S. (1961). The ego and the id. In *Standard edition* (vol. 19, pp. 3–66). London: Hogarth Press. (Original work published 1923.)

Gilligan, C. (1982). *In a different voice: Psychological theory and women's development.* Cambridge, MA: Harvard University Press.

Kaplan, E. B. (1965). Reflections regarding psychomotor activities during latency period. *Psychoanalytic Study of the Child, 20,* 220–237.

Kohut, H. (1971). *The analysis of the self.* New York: International Universities Press.

Kohut, H. (1977). *The restoration of the self.* New York: International Universities Press.

Lichtenberg, J. D. (1989). *Psychoanalysis and motivation.* Hillsdale, NJ: Analytic Press.

Mahler, M., Pine, F., & Bergman, A. (1975). *The psychological birth of the human infant.* New York: Basic Books.

Nass, M. L. (1966). The superego and moral development in the theories of Freud and Piaget. *Psychoanalytic Study of the Child,* 51–68.

Ornstein, A. (1992). Little Hans: His phobia and his Oedipus complex. *Freud's case studies: Self psychological perspectives.* Hillsdale, NJ: Analytic Press.

Piaget, J., & Inhelder, B. (1969). *The psychology of the child.* New York: Basic Books.

Sander, L. (1975). Infant and caretaking environment: Investigation and conceptualization of adaptive behavior of increasing complexity. In J. Anthony (Ed.), *Exploration in child psychiatry* (pp. 129–166). New York: Plenum Press.

Shapiro, T., & Perry, R. (1976). Latency revisited: The age 7 plus or minus 1. *Psychoanalytic Study of the Child, 31,* 79–105.

Stern, D. (1985). *The interpersonal world of the child.* New York: Basic Books.

White, R. (1959). Motivation reconsidered: The concept of competence. *Psychology Review, 66,* 297–333.

16 / The Psychological Structure of the Grade-School Child

Jules R. Bemporad

Some Ethological Considerations

Since the time of Greek philosophers, it has been observed that as species progress in phylogenesis, they manifest an ever more prolonged childhood period of helpless and dependency. Relatively primitive animals, such as reptiles, appear to require no parental supervision and seem to function adequately on the basis of innate programs from birth. However, among more highly evolved species, such as birds or mammals, the young require care and instruction from adults before they can begin to show even the rudiments of adult behavior. This prolonged period of dependency and learning, which characterizes childhood, reaches its most developed forms in primates, when an individual may spend up to one fourth of his or her life in preparation for maturity. This period of early life can itself be subdivided into a sequence of particular phases, usually attachment, separation, and procreation. In simple primates, each of these phases follow rapidly upon one another. The lemur, for example, has a life span of about 25 years, yet it is suckled for only a few days, joins a group of other juveniles after a few weeks, and is sexually mature at 1 year of age. If these developmental milestones were extrapolated to humans, a child would be weaned at 2 or 3 weeks, be socially independent before 2 months of age, and become a parent before his or her third birthday. Therefore, as primates increase their social and behavioral complexity as adults, they also increase the amount of time (relative to their life span) that they spend in childhood, ostensibly in order to learn the more complicated requirements of adult life. The chimpanzee, which is possibly the closest primate to humans in the phylogenetic scale, lives to about 40 years, is dependent on the mother for about 6 months, and may not reach sexual maturity until 8 years of age.

Therefore, as animals have evolved, the sequence of attachment, separation, and procreation has become more protracted; however, the time between separation and procreation in particular has lengthened. The human child may be able to separate at age 3 or 4 but will not reach sexual maturity for another 9 or 10 years. It is during this postseparation phase, which is fairly specific to more evolved species, that a new developmental phase emerges; in apes it has been called the juvenile stage, in humans, latency by psychoanalysts and middle to late childhood by developmental psychologists. The purpose of this emergent stage is manifold, embracing cognitive, social, emotional, moral, and physiological lines of development. However, when viewed from an ethological perspective, it becomes clear that the more complex the society of adults, the longer this period of life, with procreative capacity postponed until the child has had time to master the myriad tasks necessary for membership in adult society. Therefore, childhood proper may be considered a phylogenetically recent development during which the individual is acculturated to his or her particular society. Given the extensive requirements of human culture with its mastery of spoken and written language, complex relational structures, moral codes, and societal ranking, it is no surprise that the juvenile stage of adult development is relatively so lengthy. Yet despite this striking elongation in comparison to other species, it is remarkable how much is learned and achieved in so short a period of time.

PSYCHOANALYTIC INTERPRETATIONS OF LATENCY

The fact that there is a prolonged phase between separation and procreation in humans did not escape the notice of so acute an observer of the human condition as Sigmund Freud. Throughout his works, Freud constantly returns to his interpretation of this phase of childhood as dividing the two major eras of childhood sexuality. In his three *Essays on Sexuality,* Freud (1905/ 1953) proposed a system of development in which the child manifests sexual desires toward the opposite-sex parent as early as 3 or 4 years of age. This peak of oedipal excitement is not continued but soon becomes dormant until it is revived by the hormonal stimuli of puberty. Freud called this period of sexual quiescence the latency stage, to emphasize that sexual drives have not disappeared but have become hidden, either behind repression and its defensive derivatives or diverted into nonsexual behaviors (sublimation) observed during childhood. These latent instincts may still become manifest if provoked excessively by the environment or by the failure of repression. During the latency period the child was observed to become more compliant and pliable (due to the repression of instinctual forces) and to demonstrate a heightened interest in nonsexual areas (due to the diversion of sexual energy into nonerotic pursuits). This placid interlude was brought to end when the defensive forces of the ego were challenged once more by the forces of the id, reinforced by the biological transformation of puberty. Freud therefore agreed with previous nonpsychoanalytic observers that middle childhood was a time of cooperation, cognitive growth, and moral and social maturation, but ascribed these phenomena to the repression or diversion of instinctual drives. The reasons given by psychoanalysis for the emergence of latency were a preprogrammed, genetic diminution of sexual energy at this time, an increased ability of the ego to create better defenses against instinctual forces due to cognitive maturation, and as a resolution to the oedipal complex, in which boys give up erotic desires for the mother for fear of rivalrous injury by the father and girls turn away from active sexuality in angry disappointment for having been created without a male genital. At times Freud seemed to favor an almost purely biological cause of latency, conceiving of it as a genetically determined period when the strength of the instincts are physiologically weakened: In 1905 he stated

But in reality, this development (i.e., latency) is organically determined and fixed by heredity, and it can occasionally occur without any help at all from education. Education will not be trespassing beyond its appropriate domain if it limits itself to following the lines which have already been laid down organically and to impressing them somewhat more clearly and deeply. (pp. 43–44).

At other times Freud seemed to value environmental factors, such as the fear of retaliatory cas-

tration, or noninstinctual forces, such as the development of the ability to create defenses, as major factors in producing latency. In a footnote added to text toward the end of his life, Freud seemed to take both factors into consideration, writing: "The period of latency is a physiological phenomenon. It can, however, only give rise to a complete interruption of sexual life in cultural organizations which have made suppression of infantile sexuality a part of their system" (1925/1959, p. 37). Whatever its ultimate causes, latency remained to Freud, and for later orthodox psychoanalysts, an interval of instinctual quiescence between two stages of sexual arousal (the oedipal phase and adolescence) during which occurs remarkable growth and maturation.

Subsequent psychoanalysts continued to view middle childhood as a precarious balancing act between the striving of the instincts for release and the repressive, defensive forces of the ego. The prevailing psychoanalytic view of latency has been described in detail by Bornstein (1951), who divides this developmental stage into two substages. The first, which lasts from age 5½ to 8, is characterized by (1) the replacement of incestuous attachment to the parent by an identification with him or her; (2) the formation of the superego as a result of these identifications; (3) the internal regulation of inner drives as manifested by guilt and a rudimentary morality; and (4) the creation of defenses against inner drives or external frustrations, demonstrating the beginning of character formation and sublimatory interests. The second phase of latency, extending from about age 8 to age 10, is described by Bornstein as a still more quiescent time during which children are content with themselves and their environment. At this time, the defenses against inner threats evolved in the early latency phase are more dependable and consolidated so that the children can turn their attention to the real world and derive gratifications from new interests or activities. The superego becomes less strict as the children devalue their parents and view them more realistically so that their inner representations also become less severe. Finally, Bornstein believes that there is an actual diminution in the strengths of the instincts themselves. The major tasks of both subphases, for Bornstein, are for children to develop adequate defenses against incestuous and other drives and to resist the regressive pull of the drives that would force the children to adopt more immature modes of functioning, sabotaging the progressive forces of development.

The major psychoanalytic proposition that the impressive cognitive and social maturation seen during latency is the result of an innate lessened pressure from the id or as a manifestation of pre-determined defenses against these drives has been criticized almost from the time this theory was first promulgated. Malinowski (1927/1961) reported that among the Trobriand Islanders, who make no effort to suppress the expression of sexuality in children, youngsters in middle childhood appear to demonstrate the same cognitive and social development as in Western culture despite their lack of repression. More recently, Aries (1960) suggested that prior to the 17th century, open sexual behavior was accepted in most European countries and that even under these circumstances, children continued to learn the necessary rules and regulations of adult society. Therefore, there is some doubt over whether the impressive intellectual advances of the grade-school child are fueled by diverted sexual energy or are simply an autonomous unfolding of developmental abilities, independent of other forces. Certainly, some particular skills may become the vehicle for sublimation, but that skill, so utilized, must have been present before it could be used in such a fashion (Sandler & Joffee, 1966).[1]

Despite this, and other, controversies, the psychoanalytic view of middle childhood has done much to enhance our knowledge of this particular developmental epoch. At this stage, children do begin to regulate their demonstration of instinctual behavior. They may suddenly show a sense of modesty over nudity or bathroom functions, exhibiting an indoctrination in the social standards of their families or their culture. This emergence of an internal regulating moral aging (the superego) also may be evidenced by the delight that the grade-school child takes in defying internalized cultural sanctions by giggling over scatological jokes or limericks. This rebellious pleasure would have been unintelligible to a younger child who has not yet integrated those prohibitions that are secretly flaunted among comrades by the older child.

Another major contribution of psychoanalytic theory is its indicating the tendency of the post-oedipal-age child to initiate a strong identification with adults of his or her own gender. Boys begin to congregate together and share idealized heros who are supermasculine, exhibiting highly desired qualities such as athletic prowess, great strength or courage, and a highly muscular appearance. Girls also form unigender groups and idealize highly feminine popular figures. Grade-school boys are found most often playing contact sports or other games that mimic their idealized heros. Grade-school girls begin to study ballet or other more feminine pursuits, likewise copying esteemed heroines. The dedication shown for these activities can be demonstrated by the fact that many star athletes, dancers, entertainers, and even chess champions trace the beginning of their careers to this stage of life. Therefore, whether the Freudian concept is or is not accepted, there is little doubt that the grade-school child exercises, with utmost seriousness and stamina, a host of new activities and interests leading to social recognition and personal pride in achievements.

Psychoanalysts point out another aspect of sublimatory activity that blossoms during the grade-school years: the importance of fantasy in the psychic life of the child. This developmental step is of extreme pertinence for it allows the child to exercise, in imagination, behaviors that would be not only impossible but also dangerous in real life both to the child and to the immediate culture. Older children can compensate for their relative developmentally inferior status by daydreams of themselves as supercompetent or successful. This compensatory fantasizing helps to salvage the self-esteem of the children and also to act as a safety valve against the realization of retaliatory or rebelliousness action in actual behavior. These fantasied scenarios also help in consolidating a social identity for children as they adopt firsthand experiences from life or vicarious experiences from television or comic books to suit their own personal purposes. By this transformation into fantasy, the effects of culture (particularly the media) are internalized and shape the values of the children in terms of codes of conduct and future aspirations, which are modeled after influential figures that are commonly admired.

Finally, the restraint of impulses and the gradual devaluation of the parents, as described by psychoanalysts, allows the latency-age child to participate in group activities with nonfamilial adults or peers. Middle childhood is the first time that children spend more of their waking hours with individuals other than parents. School, athletic teams, clubs, a variety of lessons, or simply play with peers occupy more and more of the children's time and interest. This psychological weaning permits children to depend less on the immediate family and to become comfortable in a larger social framework, paving the way for a more profound separation at adolescence. This exposure to external influences also ensures the uniform acculturation of children to social mores in which the family may not have conformed totally. Aside from the relevance of its basic metapsychology, classical psychoanalytic theory has done much to document the myriad changes that occur during latency.

The enormous developmental strides of middle childhood become apparent immediately if the status of a child entering and completing this maturational phase is compared. The former could be imagined as a youngster on his or her first day of school, darting around in excitement or shyly clinging to a parent. This prototypical child has yet to consolidate a workable system of ethics, an ability to consider reality beyond what is perceptually available, or a social estimation of self beyond the family orbit. Throughout the next 6 or 7 years, he or she will master an incredible amount of knowledge and form a lasting sense of self, emerging as a individual on the brink of assuming an independent role in society as an adolescent. Contrast the image of a gangly junior-high-school student who is acutely aware of his or her appearance and its effect on the opposite sex, who tries to effect a pose of confidence while seeking the security of a clique of close friends, and who is ready to tackle abstract thought, with the prior image of a kindergarten pupil and the remarkable developmental achievements of latency become apparent. In the following sections, various developmental paths of latency are considered separately for convenience in exposition. However, it must be recognized that these progressions occur simultaneously and affect one another constantly.

Cognitive Development

Perhaps the most impressive development to transpire during middle childhood is in the area of cognition. While most children who enter latency have already mastered the ability to substitute symbols, such as spoken or sometimes written words, for actual things, they still rely on memory and appearance rather than logic or reason in their apprehending or interpreting reality. The Swiss psychologist Jean Piaget has proposed and experimentally documented that children utilize a progression of cognitive principles during development to organize and make sense of their experiences. Piaget proposes that the organizing principles, which he calls schemata, are the core feature of cognitive development, underlying the various problem-solving behaviors of children at different ages. These schemata are innately created and environmentally reinforced processes that become more complex and sophisticated as children develop. According to Piaget, young latency-age children use mainly schemata based on perception in order to make sense of reality. At this early age, things are taken as pretty much what they appear to be and the belief in how things work is not based on a rational analysis but on intuition. The world is the way it is simply because it looks that way; no other reasons are deemed necessary. This mode of knowing the environment may be illustrated by one of Piaget's classic experiments in which he presented children with two beakers of equal size, each containing an identical amount of liquid. The young latency age child could agree that the liquid contained in each was the same since both volumes were perceptually equal. Then, in front of each child, Piaget poured the liquid from one beaker into a thinner, taller columnar beaker and asked the child if there was more, less, or the same amount of liquid in the new beaker as in the other one of two original beakers, which still contained the unpoured liquid. Children at this stage rapidly answered that there was more liquid in the columnar beaker since the level of liquid was now higher than in the comparison beaker. In this case, children were making a judgment based on a perceptual clue, the relative height of the level of liquid over the two beakers.

As children passed the age of about 7, they correctly assessed that the amount of liquid remained the same since, only a few seconds previously, it had been equal in both identical beakers. Piaget asserts that children have now formed new cognitive schemata, such as conservation or reversibility, that allow them to separate thought from appearance and to use these schemata to interpret or construct reality more correctly. The use of these newer cognitive strategies to understand the environment, rather that simply reacting to what is experientially presented, comprises "operational" thinking, emphasizing the use of mental operations to assess reality. In everyday terms, this transformation in thought means that children are less prone to magical thinking or snap judgments and are more interested in finding out how things work and in puzzling out problems that confront them. In a larger sense, the new schemata of the operational period can be seen as imposing a greater sense of order and logic between the immediate world of perceptions and the conclusions drawn from experience. Behavior is increasingly guided by judgments that are conceptually removed from experience and is less reactive to the current situation. Personal beliefs are now based on expectations of the self and others as the reasons behind surface events sought out and considered. It is as if a cognitive filter has been inserted between the individual and his or her surroundings, and this filter influences the manner by which experiences are evaluated and judged. At this time children's adaptive or aberrant behavior ceases to be a direct reaction to their environment and becomes crystallized into enduring personality patterns founded on idiosyncratic beliefs. Changes in immediate circumstances no longer have a profound effect on children's behavior, which has become increasingly determined by internal convictions.

The development of operational thinking represents a tremendous advance as children rely on logical concepts rather than pure appearance. However, during this early stage, the nascent logical structures are limited to the manipulation of actual objects that are palpably present to children. The contents of the materials presented to children in a problem-solving situation are directly linked with the stated task. For example, a child may correctly solve a conservation task with beads (a discontinuous medium) but not with a liquid (a continuous medium). Therefore, Piaget called this stage *concrete operations,* stressing the utilization of tangible objects in the applications of strategies. It is not until the end of latency (age 11 or 12) that children reach what Piaget has termed *formal operations,* which is more indicative of true abstract thought. At this final stage, children can separate their cognitive actions from the restrictions of concrete reality and arrive at

logical principles that are laws in themselves and are not limited to the content of the immediate situation. Therefore, adolescents and adults utilize everyday experiences to generate universal laws that transcend the concrete situation and may be applied to different, including imaginary, problems. Individuals now formulate hypotheses about the possible as well as the actual.

It is at this later stage, when individuals are on the threshold of adolescence, that thought truly takes on wings and flies beyond the confines of what is concretely possible. Youngsters can now project themselves into the future, can visualize a whole range of possibilities, or think about thinking. The more prosaic and reality-grounded intellectual life of grade-school children reflects this more pragmatic and factual orientation, utilizing the possibilities of thought to focus on concrete reality. This limited advancement may be reflected in the children's everyday preoccupation with collecting a vast array of objects and arranging these into a particular order, of building concrete objects such as models, or of seeking to find the inner mechanical reasons for the way familiar objects operate. These activities may be seen as exercises that reinforce and consolidate the newly formed operational schemata.

Another area of cognitive advance in middle childhood that has been described at greater length by clinicians than academic psychologists concerns the ability to utilize fantasy more creatively and to model the self after fantasied (as well as real) characters. Therefore, children may imagine an entire script in which they play the lead role according to an idealized view of the self and then attempt to act in accordance with the characteristics of their fantasied alter-ego. Latency-age children may "replay" movies, novels, or television programs, substituting themselves as the portrayed hero or heroine, and also modify actual behavior to conform to this image. Writers of fiction aimed at children have long been aware of this tendency and purposely created figures of amazing ability (adult heros) who keep their special prowess secret behind shy, meek persona (child characters). Mild-mannered Clark Kent really hides the all-powerful Superman, just as a myriad of other ordinary fictional characters harbor a superhero. These fictional characters allow children to sense a secret power even though, like Clark Kent and the rest of his ilk, they are weaker and less assertive than the people they encounter in everyday life. These fantasies serve compensatory functions for children's realistic position of little power over their own life, allow for the fantasied, rather than actual, retaliation for the hurts and slights that are part of everyday life, and shape children's values toward admired (if not always admirable) characteristics. Finally, the enlarged use of the imagination aids in the formation of friendships as some of these fantasies are shared among friends and not only discussed but even acted out in groups, as when children reenact a scene from a movie, often alternating roles. Therefore, the widening of the representational abilities are part of the development of children's self-identity, moral structure, and social role.

Moral Development

Another area of tremendous advancement during middle childhood concerns the individual's evolving sense of morality, of justice and of crime and punishment. As previously mentioned, Freud suggested that latency was contemporaneous with the creation of a superego as the child increasingly identifies with the parent and, in so doing, takes on the latter's sense of values and ethics. Freud was correct in observing that, during latency, the child begins to develop a conscience or a code of morality.

Clinicians working with children had noted that during middle childhood, the individual begins to modify behavior to conform to societal mores and not simply to escape punishment or win praise of authority figures. Children at this age will "behave themselves" even if the parents are not around and will experience guilt over the breaking of social rules. Moral standards are said to be "internalized" and increasingly less dependent on the concrete presence of external enforcers. This internal moral agent, which Freud called the *superego*, becomes responsible for the conformity to familial or cultural standards. As antisocial temptations challenge this new agency, a conflict arises within children whereas previously the prohibiting factor had been the environment rather than a part of the self. This intrapsychic conflict may manifest itself in normal developmental symptoms or, in

some cases, the initiation of a true neurotic disorder. Children may create magical rituals to "undo" perceived transgressions or may express forbidden thoughts or wishes in symbolic guise. Therefore, most children may be observed to go through a transient period of marked inhibition, some symptom formation, and, eventually, sublimation of wishes that go against the newly formed standards of ethics.

Although clinicians had documented these changes in the morality of the child, the basic objective studies in this area, however, awaited the interest of Piaget, who investigated the growth of moral judgment as well as general cognition. Piaget approached this aspect of development by asking children of different ages how they played the game of marbles and by listening to them describe the rules of conduct. He also asked children to comment on various situations involving instances such as disobedience, causing damage, or lying. Through these interviews with children, Piaget found that the latency age child goes from an ethics of constraint or moral realism to an ethics of cooperation or moral relativism. The earlier stage of moral realism gets its name from its similarity to cognitive realism, where the world is accepted, unquestioning, as it appears. Therefore, younger children believed the rules for a game of marbles to be imminent and unchangeable (although they broke the rules regularly in their play), while older children understood these rules as merely conventions that represented only previous agreements between individuals (although once the rules were accepted, the children adhered strictly to them). Children only gradually understand that moral judgments are man-made codes of behavior rather than eternal dictates inherent in nature. Similarly, younger children base the seriousness of an offense on the magnitude of its consequences rather than the perpetrator's intentions. Therefore, a child who accidentally breaks 10 dishes is naughtier than the child who breaks only 1 intentionally. The younger child ascribes to what Piaget calls *objective responsibility* based on how much or how little an act conforms to a set law of conduct rather than a malicious intent to willfully break the law. Piaget found that young children, early in latency, believed that veracity is external to the individual so that a lie is serious to the extent that it differs from objective truth rather than the intent to deceive. For example, children believed that telling their family that they received a good grade in school when no such event occurred was a lesser infraction than telling their family that they were frightened by a dog as big as a cow after actually being frightened by a normal-size dog. The children reasoned that the first lie was not so bad because it could have happened and would be believed, while the latter exaggeration was more serious because dogs are never as big as cows and so could never be believed. Later children begin to appreciate the importance of motives in their burgeoning system of ethics, eventually considering the intent as equal, if not of more significance, than the possibility or consequences of an act.

Piaget found similar results when he investigated the child's concept of justice and punishment. In early latency (up to ages 7 or 8), children regard as fair whatever punishment parents (or nature) dispense. Later (age 8 to 11 or 12) children strive for an egalitarian system in which all children must be treated equally despite mitigating circumstances. Finally, adolescents ascribe to a flexible punitive regime taking all factors into consideration.

It is apparent from Piaget's studies that morality develops gradually during middle childhood. Ethical judgments, during this developmental stage, mirror the overall cognitive development of the child, starting with intuitive, nonreflective, strong beliefs in a system of rules and codes of behavior that are imposed from without and relate to real consequences of behavior. This black-or-white "realism" is transformed into a more reasonable and flexible model that is based on a rational inquiry into internal and psychological aspects of each situation. In the last stages of moral development, abstract principles become more pronounced, paralleling the growth of logical thought into formal operations. As adolescents, individuals can formulate universal ideas of justice or morality that transcend any particular instance and may be applied to a variety of situations.

Social Development

The expansion of social interests during middle childhood may be the characteristic that is most obvious to parents and other adults. While most children have had experience with peers prior to latency, much of this contact has been characterized as parallel play or activity centered, rather than a true relationship between similar-age individuals. Prior to latency, children are still bonded emotionally to the parent, not only for protection and nurturance but also for social stimulation and approval as well. As latency progresses, children shift their idealization and loyalty to extrafamilial figures—both to esteemed nonfamilial adults, such as teachers or coaches, as well as to peers either on an individual basis, as a best pal, or to a group, as a gang or clique. Anna Freud (1965) has traced the developmental line of peer relationships (from egocentricity to companionship), differentiating the "task-determined" nature of the young preschooler's interaction with peers from the "person-oriented" companionship of the school-age child. In the former, the relationship is secondary to the execution of some mutual task, while in the latter, children are sought out in their own right and become the recipients of love, hate, fear, admiration, and a host of other feelings. Perhaps the most significant change is that children can identify and empathize with others, putting themselves in their particular situation.

The formation of these latency-age groups appears to parallel the similar grouping of juveniles into separate bands in nonhuman social primates. Goodall (1965), for example, has noted that chimpanzees go through a gradual separation from the mother with increasing amounts of time spent with age mates until the young chimpanzee separates totally to join a group of juvenile monkeys. This transference of interest from parents to peers and the formation of a less dependent, more mutual relationship has raised the possibility that a preprogrammed affiliative bond exists, corresponding to the earlier anaclitic infantile bonding of infant and mother or the later heterosexual bonding of adult life. Harry Stack Sullivan (1953) placed a great deal of importance in terms of future adjustment of the individual on the development of chumships during latency. He wrote that a close friendship during this time of life can be "rather fantastically valuable in salvaging one from the effects of unfortunate accidents up to then" (p. 227). Among psychoanalysts Sullivan was the most insistent in calling attention to the spontaneous emergence of affiliative needs and abilities during latency and the significance of the fulfillment of these needs at an age-appropriate stage for normal social functioning in adult life.

A major differentiation in the middle childhood of humans, as in the juvenile stage of primates, is the separation of the sexes. At this time of life boys and girls truly follow divergent paths, with separate activities, preferences, idealized heros, and fantasy lives. This apparently self-selected segregation allows for the consolidation of a gender model as expressed by the particular culture and prepares the individual for an appropriate adult role in society. Organizations such as Girl Scouts or Boy Scouts allow the child to evolve a sense of self as male or female in social terms and to pursue talents or interests in the context of a group of the same sex. Current cultural norms have relaxed considerably the rigid and narrow gender roles that traditionally were considered as masculine or feminine. Girls now can compete in some body-contact sports or take part in science or math clubs. Similarly, boys may study dance or cooking without sanction. However, there is still a difference between the development of boys and girls in terms of cultural identity at this time and in their tendency to form groups of their own gender. As mentioned, these groups assist in the consolidation of a social sense but also are important in initiating the child to issues of cooperation, working together toward a mutual goal, and adhering to hierarchical relational structures such as competitiveness and dominance.

It is also in middle childhood that the individual begins to spend most of his or her waking hours in social settings such as the classroom and after-school group activities. During this time, children shift from enjoying a particular status within the family system to the assumption of a social role in which they are treated as the equal of others. Children are exposed to value structures that may differ from those within the family and are subject to new systems of reward and punishment. The classroom setting has a social structure of its own based on specific hierarchical status, rules of conduct, and explicit reinforcement techniques to promote adherence and conformity to institutional regulations. The sociologist Durkheim (1922/1961) strongly advocated that the school should be the proper setting for moral education and wrote an influential manual describing how this could be achieved. He believed the family to be far too influenced by kinship ties and feelings of intimacy to instill a sense of duty. He also discounted the church as founded on revelation rather than reason and other agencies as too demanding for the capacities of the child. More contemporary sociologists, such as Parsons (1969), also have envisioned the classroom as a miniature social system with its organization of roles and system of expectations and rewards. The teacher is the agent of society who influences children's social status by evaluating them solely in terms of performance and conformity to community norms. Once again, most school systems take developmental differences into account, so that kindergarten teachers are more parental and more lenient in their expectations. As children progress through ascending years, there is greater emphasis on objective assessment of competence and motivation, introducing children to Western cultural beliefs of results through effort and of self-reliance. In addition to teachers and other adults in the school setting, classmates also confer status on each other, ushering in a new system for estimating self-regard and social acceptance according to standards that may contrast with the immediate family. In most cases, the school setting is an equalizing experience, judging each child on his or her own merits independent of the often irrationally positive or negative status that the family has assigned. Within the overall grouping of children into a large social institution such as school, further subgroups develop as latency progresses. One of the most prominent is the segregation of the sexes into exclusively male and female subgroups, each with their own activities and interests, which may mimic the behavior of the adult of each respective gender. This large bifurcation of social activities by gender may be further divided into cliques or gangs of the same sex and into chumships within each of these. Therefore, a child who had been accustomed to an assigned role within a constant family unit has to negotiate a myriad of new relational systems, each with its own complex code of conduct. That this transition usually is accomplished with relatively few problems is an amazing achievement that illustrates the burgeoning intellectual capacity during middle childhood.[2]

While multiple new loyalties outside the home arise, the family still has an important influence during latency. The parents as well as other relatives in the household continue to be major players in the child's psychological world. Their opinions, behaviors, and interactions continue to shape greatly the child's view of self and others. However, the family loses its prior position as the sole source of knowledge about the ways of the world and shares its educative role with other institutions and individuals. In our own culture, it is expected that as children progress through latency, they become less reliant on the family and more able to create a comfortable role in society so as to prepare for the eventual break with family and assumption of autonomy at adolescence.

The Initiation of a Stable Self-Image

The psychological world of the prelatency child, as indicated by Piaget's studies, is characterized by a nonreflective, intuitive style in which judgments about the self and others may vary markedly with each new situation. Children may believe they are bad if they are punished or good if they are praised, even for the same action. Reality and fantasy may be indistinguishable at times so that memory cannot readily be separated from imagination nor dreams from perceptions.

Young children, in fact, believe that dreams are external to the dreamer and the same as waking life perceptions of reality. Piaget cites his subjects as commenting that certain rooms were "full of dreams," as if these internally generated experiences had an objective existence of their own. In such a transient world that appears to vary from situation to situation, children display a fluid sense of self based on superficial attributes and changing with external circumstances.

With the advent of reflective thought, comparable to Piaget's notion of concrete operations, children look beyond the immediate appearance of things and attempt to order their world by more logical principles. Children create interpretive concepts that help in making sense of reality and serve as guides in making judgments. These concepts may be conceived of, in a loose fashion, as filters that shape the apprehension of the environment. Just as these serve to supply explanations of impersonal events, other filters crystallize to affect the children's estimation of themselves and oth-

ers. Children now search for reasons for the behavior of others as well as for their own actions. As such, children create a self-image that persists across time and across varying situations. These elaborations and justifications of experience become more complex and more penetrating with increasing maturation although they may be quite erroneous due to children's immaturity and lack of experience. A relevant illustration of this maturational progression can be found in a study of childhood depression by McConville, Boag, and Purohit (1973). They describe three age-related types of depressive phenomena in 75 latency-age children. The youngest children (ages 6 to 8) manifested an almost pure affective state of sadness without giving reasons for their plight. The middle group (ages 8 to 10) were able to verbalize low self-esteem as part of their depression. The oldest group (ages 10 to 13) added a sense of guilt to their depressive symptoms, intimating that they were wicked and should be punished. This study beautifully shows how the latency-age child goes from a state of almost pure nonreflective reactivity to the environment that still can elicit a dysphoric response, to a state that encompasses a cognitive, self-evaluative component, to a further elaboration of the self including guilt and self-blame in the experience of depression. Therefore, as children progress through latency, an increasingly differentiated sense of self and others is subjected to evaluation and judgment. Children formulate internal standards for conduct as well as the ability to compare their performance to that of others. Rosenberg's (1979) study of the formation of self-concept in normal children also suggests a developmental transformation of how the self is conceived of at different ages. The younger latency child forms a self-concept based on social and exterior items that can be observed, such as physical characteristics, social identity (i.e., boy or girl, child or adult, native or foreign) and relatively specific actions, abilities, or interests. Other researchers (Guardo & Bohan, 1971; Selman, 1980) also have documented an evolution of self-understanding and self-conception during middle childhood. They describe children before age 8 as considering themselves in terms of material and active qualities, such as physical attributes, usual activities or possessions. Beyond the age of 8, children introduce psychological characteristics in their self-descriptions and begin to realize that they are different from other children in terms of psychological qualities. The self-concept at this early stage is relatively unreflective, mainly because children are not overly interested in self-discovery at the expense of interesting and enjoyable activities. As children progress toward adolescence, they continue to utilize physical characteristics, social identity, and habits or interests in formulating a self-concept but, in addition, consider psychologically interior concepts, such as the awareness of an inner world of thought, feeling, and experience. Youngsters also begin to characterize the self in terms of abstract traits and from the point of view of others. According to Rosenberg, early latency is generally a time of a satisfactory self-concept, which begins to waver as children's cognitive abilities force them to question former certain and absolute truths as they approaches adolescence.

These evaluative capacities can enhance, thwart, or exploit children's budding drive toward mastery and affiliation. Latency-age children naturally apply their newly formed cognitive skills in their everyday behavior, both during school and in leisure time, which becomes taken up with games of skill, building things, or participating in clubs. Environmental authorities, such as teachers, parents, and also peers can manipulate this inherent sense of industry, transforming it in an appreciation of effort for its own sake or in a competitive struggle to win acclaim or special status. Erikson (1950) has focused on this theme in his discussion of latency, calling this Stage 1 of "Industry versus Inferiority." For Erikson, the work principle emerges in latency when children can utilize tools and skills and have the needed diligence to complete tasks. Children seek for a meaningful place in their circumscribed world that is preparatory for a later role in society at large. If children are led to conclude that their efforts are without social value, they may develop a sense of inferiority, which inhibits later creativity or productivity.

This conflict implies the children's ability to evaluate their performance and to create a longer-lasting image of the self as capable or inferior. Similar self-evaluations arise from relationships with family members, peers, or other adults. This crystallization of a self-evaluative agency may be responsible for the appearance of true personality disorders and neuroses at this stage of life, as enduring patterns of behavior and cognition

are instituted. The children's mode of interaction is no longer rapidly responsive to environmental changes, since it is based on a system of ideas rather than a passing reaction to the stimuli of the moment.

Summary

As we have separated these lines of development through latency for reasons of exposition, we therefore have presented a somewhat artificial portrait of a real-life child in whom these various aspects work together simultaneously. The interplay and synthesis of developmental lines may be appreciated by considering actual phenomena in middle and late childhood as they appear in everyday life. The formation of gangs might serve as an example that has practical as well as theoretical relevance. Bronfenbrenner (1975) has noted that changes in social structures, such as urbanization, maternal employment, and father absence in lower socioeconomic homes, have resulted in a major lessening of adult influences on the latency-age child. Many youngsters now grow up with fewer siblings, without an extended family, and with parents who are both employed and away from home for long periods of each day. As latency-age children develop in these circumstances, their readiness for moral development may be met not by traditional carriers of society, such as parents or other family members, but by the standards of television programs and the often counterculture mores of peer groups. Since the usual reinforcement for response to other nascent developments such as academic achievement, individual mastery of some activity or hobby, or feeling part of a family unit are missing, loyalty to the peer group may assume inflated importance as it replaces or substitutes for other avenues of growth. The normal pressure for mastery, for example, which appears at this age may thus be diverted into agility in delinquent behavior, if sanctioned or encouraged by the group, rather than being satisfied through the learning of more long-range effective tasks at home, in school, or in the community.

Finally, the self-evaluative tendencies that also crystallize at this time use social categories such as

135

peer approval and status in the group rather than rewards from institutions or individual accomplishment. Therefore, new abilities such as mastery, morality, sociability, self-evaluation, and cognitive advancement are all met by an often antisocial peer society that takes the place of parents, social institutions, and self-initiated learning. The convergence of all of these new abilities at the same time and the ease by which a peer group may absorb and utilize them may help explain the stability and attractiveness of gangs among the urban poor. These structures supply a sense of self to the child and allow the consolidation of latency development into an adolescent self-image that is impervious to modification toward more traditional social roles.

Another not uncommon example of the interplay of the variety of developmental lines through latency is the child with a cognitive disability. Children who are hampered in school performance secondary to difficulties in processing or integrating information may react to this failure in mastery by distorting the manner through which their other emergent abilities are fulfilled. Such children may retreat from peer contact out of shame and perpetuate their dependent relationship with adults, thereby missing an optimal period for the formation of affiliative bonds. Such children also may perceive the school situation as

a source of humiliation, rejecting its nonacademic training in social skills and acculturation together with scholastic focus. Finally, the failure to master schoolwork may result in a generalized sense of low self-regard or may cause children to seek esteem-building activities through antisocial behavior, with a concomitant deviation in moral development. Therefore, a blockage in only one thread in the fabric of latency development may have severe repercussions for the manner by which the overall passage through latency is achieved.

A child enters middle childhood as a recent toddler and leaves it as a soon-to-be adult. Within the confines of this developmental epoch, the individual truly becomes a member of society, meeting his or her cultural environment with the abilities and the desire to participate in, internalize, and master the intricacies of an organized communal existence. It is a time of enormous growth and change in almost every area of psychological experience. Each area may greatly affect others so that it may be best to conceive of the disparate developmental lines as closely interrelated and interdependent. If the inherent abilities of the latency-age child are allowed to be developed to their fullest, the child should be ready to face the subsequent challenges of adolescence in a relatively harmonious and gratifying fashion.

NOTES

1. Taken in its historical context, the psychoanalytic theory of middle to late childhood appears based on larger biological and phylogenetic formulations that imply an almost Lamarkian view of evolution, suggesting that the repression of sexuality seen in latency is the recapitulation, in the individual, of an era in the history of humankind when sexual frustration was enforced by realistic hardships, such as during the Ice Age. A "lost" manuscript of Freud's, dating to 1915, that was recently discovered (Freud 1915/1987) clearly demonstrates his suggested proposal that the alleged realistic privations of primitive humans are inherited and recapitulated during development in later generations without an environmental impetus.

2. Humphrey (cited in Oakley, 1985) has argued that the neocortex has evolved in primates to meet social demands rather than simply to solve problems in isolation. He noted that most primates are far too intelligent for the requirements of their environments if social relationships are excluded and only life-preserving aspects are considered.

REFERENCES

Aries, P. (1960). *Centuries of childhood.* New York: Vintage Press.

Bornstein, B. (1951). On latency. *Psychoanalytic Study of the Child, 6,* 279–285.

Bornstein, B. (1953). Masturbation in the latency period. *Psychoanalytic Study of the Child, 8,* 65–78.

Bronfenbrenner, V. (1975). The split-level American family. In W. C. Sze (Ed.), *Human life cycle* (pp. 179–192). New York: Jason Aronson.

Durkheim, E. (1961). *Moral education.* New York: Free Press. (Original work published 1922.)

Erikson, E. (1950). *Childhood and society.* New York: W. W. Norton.

Freud, A. (1965). *Normality and pathology in child-*

hood: Assessments of development. New York: International Universities Press.

Freud, S. (1953). Three essays on the theory of sexuality. In J. Strachey (Ed. and Trans.), *The Standard edition of the complete psychological works of Sigmund Freud* (hereafter *Standard edition*) (vol. 7, pp. 123–243). London: Hogarth Press. (Original work published 1905.)

Freud, S. (1959). An autobiographical study. In *Standard edition* (vol. 20, pp. 7–76). London: Hogarth Press. (Original work published 1925; footnote added in 1935.)

Freud, S. (1987). *A phylogenetic fantasy.* Cambridge, MA: Harvard University Press. (Original work published 1915.)

Goodall, J. (1965). Chimpanzees of the Gombe stream reserve. In J. DeVore (Ed.), *Primate behavior* (pp. 425–473). New York: Holt, Rinehart & Winston.

Guardo, C. J., & Bohan, J. B. (1971). Development of a sense of self identity in children. *Child Development, 42,* 1909–1921.

Hendrick, I. (1943). Work and the pleasure principle. *Psychoanalytic Quarterly, 12,* 311–329.

Malinowski, B. (1955). *Sex and repression in savage so-ciety.* New York: Meridian Books. (Originally published 1927.)

McConville, B. J., Boag, L. C., & Purohit, A. P. (1973). Three types of childhood depression. *Canadian Psychiatric Association Journal, 18,* 133–138.

Mead, M. (1963) *Coming of age in Samoa.* New York: Mentor Books. (Original work published 1928.)

Oakley, D. A. (1985). *Brain and mind.* New York: Methuen.

Piaget, J. (1932). *The moral judgement of the child.* London: Kegan Paul.

Piaget, J., & Inhelder, B. (1967). *The psychology of the child.* New York: Basic Books.

Rosenberg, M. (1979). *Concerning the self.* New York: Basic Books.

Sandler, J., & Joffe, W. G. (1966). On skill and sublimation. *Journal of the American Psychoanalytic Association, 14,* 335–355.

Sarnoff, C. (1976). *Latency.* New York: Jason Aronson.

Selman, R. (1980). *The growth of interpersonal understanding.* New York: Academic Press.

Sullivan, H. S. (1953). *The interpersonal theory of psychiatry.* New York: W. W. Norton.

SECTION II
Assessment and Evaluation of the Grade-School Child

17 / Syndromes of the Grade-School Years

Paul V. Trad

Introduction

According to the orthodox definition, a syndrome is a constellation of symptoms that together characterizes a specific condition or disease. Syndromes are distinctive in the sense that they tend to be both pervasive and proliferative. That is, a syndrome has a repercussive effect on a variety of different areas of developmental functioning simultaneously. The child's cognitive and affective skills as well as prosocial behavior, representational abilities, psychomotor functioning, and sense of self may all be affected, in one way or another, by the syndrome. Because syndromes are capable of exerting such a dramatic impact on different areas of developmental skill, they tend to become more prevalent during the years of grade school. After all, it is only at this juncture of development that the child has sufficiently differentiated areas of maturational functioning into segregated domains.

The infiltrating and pervasive presence of a syndrome can be distressing, since multiple areas of functioning may be impaired or damaged. Yet the fact that syndromes pervade several areas of development also facilitates their diagnosis. Most syndromes have a unique profile that makes them fairly easy to recognize. Clinicians should be familiar with the most frequent syndromes encountered among grade-school children. This knowledge will ease the diagnostic process.

This chapter describes some of the major psychiatric syndromes commonly found in children of grade-school age. In addition to enumerating the characteristic features of these syndromes, guidelines for performing a differential diagnosis are provided.

Major Syndromes Affecting Grade-School Children

The syndromes to be described are those most commonly encountered in the population of grade-school children. During the administration of the mental status examination, clinicians should be alert to the symptoms that signify the presence of these syndromes.

PERVASIVE DEVELOPMENTAL DISORDERS INCLUDING AUTISTIC DISORDER

Pervasive developmental disorders have several characteristic features that first appear in infancy or early childhood and become more pronounced as the child ages. The disorder is typified by qualitative impairment of verbal and nonverbal communication skills and impairment in imaginative ability. Frequently the child displays a markedly restricted repertoire of activities and interests. The exhibition of stereotypical and repetitive behavior is also common. The extent of these deficits may vary dramatically from child to child (Kanner, 1943; Rutter, 1978). Differential diagnosis includes: other pervasive developmental disorders; Rett's disorder; schizophrenia; specific developmental disorders; schizotypal personality disorder; and hearing or visual impairments.

MENTAL RETARDATION

The syndrome of mental retardation is characterized by intellectual functioning that is significantly below normal. In addition, significant lags in most major areas of development are present—although conscience development and gender identity usually are not affected. Age of onset is ordinarily prior to 18 (Grossman, 1973). The differential diagnosis includes: learning disorders; communication disorders; borderline intellectual functioning; pervasive developmental disorders; and developmental disorders.

ATTENTION DEFICIT HYPERACTIVITY DISORDER

Attention deficit hyperactivity disorder is characterized by a developmentally inappropriate degree of inattention, impulsiveness, and hyperactivity. Children with the disorder generally exhibit marked disturbance in each of these areas. These children also have difficulty regulating their attention and engaging in appropriate forms of social interaction. The differential diagnosis includes: pervasive developmental disorder; mental retardation; psychotic disorders; mood disorders; undifferentiated attention deficit; age-appropriate overactivity in children from disorganized environments; other substance-related disorder not otherwise specified.

SEPARATION ANXIETY DISORDER

Separation anxiety disorder is characterized by excessive anxiety, enduring for a minimum of 2 weeks, that customarily involves separation from an individual to whom the child is attached. When separation from this significant other occurs, the child may experience anxiety to the point of becoming panicked. Onset is prior to age 18. The differential diagnosis includes: generalized anxiety disorder; overanxious disorder; pervasive developmental disorder; schizophrenia; panic disorder with agoraphobia; conduct disorder; psychotic disorders; and major depression.

CONDUCT DISORDER

Conduct disorder is characterized by a persistent pattern of conduct in which the basic rights of others, as well as major age-appropriate social norms and rules, are violated. The behavior pattern is typically present in the home, at school, with peers, and in the community. There is no age limit before which the diagnosis cannot be made and the upper age limit remains unclear. The differential diagnosis includes: oppositional defiant disorder; attention deficit hyperactivity disorder; adjustment disorder; antisocial personality disorder; and specific developmental disorders.

ANOREXIA NERVOSA

Anorexia nervosa is characterized by the child's refusal to maintain normal body weight (for age/height); extreme fear of gaining weight or becoming fat, distorted body image, and amenorrhea are among the common symptoms. The syndrome is significantly more prevalent in girls than in boys (Bryant-Waugh, 1988; Halmi, 1988). The differential diagnosis includes: major depressive disorder; social phobia; obsessive-compulsive disorder; body dysmorphic disorder; affective disorders and certain physical disorders; schizophrenia; and bulimia nervosa.

BULIMIA NERVOSA

Bulimia nervosa is characterized by recurrent episodes of binge eating, feelings of lack of control, gorging oneself during binges, self-induced vomiting, use of diuretics and laxatives, strict dieting or fasting, or vigorous exercise to prevent weight gain; and persistent concern almost to the point of obsession with body shape and weight. For an accurate diagnosis, the child must have had an average of 2 binge-eating episodes per week for the last 3 months (Hsu, 1990). The differential diagnosis includes: anorexia nervosa; binge-eating/purging type; schizophrenia; and borderline personality disorder.

GENDER IDENTITY DISORDER OF CHILDHOOD

Gender identity disorder of childhood is characterized by persistent distress arising from a sense that one's assigned sex is incorrect; the child desires to be, or asserts that he or she will grow up to be or is of the other sex. There is an aversion to assigned sex activities (or preoccupation with activities stereotypical of the other sex) as well as repudiation of one's own anatomical characteristics. In effect, these children lack a "core gender identity," a phrase coined by Stoller (1964) to describe a fundamental sense of belonging to one sex. The differential diagnosis includes: physical abnormalities of the sex organs and children whose behavior does not fit stereotypes of masculinity or femininity; and transvestic fetishism.

SCHIZOPHRENIA

During its active phase, schizophrenia is characterized by psychotic symptoms with the child functioning in a fashion below the highest developmental level previously achieved; in addition, this pathological state must have persisted for at least 6 months and may include characteristic prodromal or residual symptoms. Delusions, hallucinations, or characteristic disturbances in affect are present during some phase of the disturbance. The differential diagnosis includes: organic mental disorder; mood disorder due to a medical condition; depressive disorder; psychotic disorder; substance-induced delirium; substance-induced persisting dementia; delusional disorder; pervasive developmental disorders; obsessive-compulsive disorder; and mental retardation.

MAJOR DEPRESSION

Major depression is characterized by a depressed or irritable mood and loss of interest or pleasure in all or almost all activities for 2 weeks or longer, occurring for most of the day, nearly every day. Symptoms include appetite disturbance, change in weight, sleep disturbance, psychomotor disturbance, decreased energy, feelings of worthlessness or excessive guilt, difficulty in thinking or concentrating, and recurrent thoughts of death, or suicidal ideation or attempts. The differential diagnosis includes: organic mood disorder; substance-induced mood disorder; dysthymic disorder; schizophrenia; degenerative dementia; and bereavement reaction.

DYSTHYMIA

Dysthymia is characterized by chronic disturbance of mood involving a depressed or irritable mood for most of the day, for a majority of the week, for at least 1 year. The condition may include poor appetite or overeating, insomnia or hypersomnia, low energy or fatigue, low self-esteem, poor concentration or difficulty making decisions, and feelings of hopelessness. The differential diagnosis includes: major depressive disorder; psychotic disorder; mood disorder due to a medical condition; substance-induced mood disorder; and personality disorders.

SLEEP DISORDERS

Sleep disorders are manifested in several forms. For example, the child may display insomnia, characterized by difficulty initiating or maintaining sleep or by an unrested feeling after an adequate amount of sleep; hypersomnia, characterized by excessive daytime sleepiness or sleep attacks; sleep-wake schedule disorder, characterized by a mismatch between a normal sleep-wake schedule and circadian sleep-wake patterns; sleep terror disorder, characterized by repeated sudden awakenings, usually with a panicky scream and autonomic arousal; and sleepwalking disorder, characterized by repeated episodes that involve getting out of bed and walking around while the person is asleep. The differential diagnosis for sleeping disorders includes: organic disturbance; primary hypersomnia; circadian rhythm sleep disorder; personality disorder; and seizure disorder.

ANTISOCIAL PERSONALITY DISORDER

Antisocial personality disorder is characterized by irresponsible and antisocial behavior, including lying, stealing, truancy, vandalism, initiated fights, running away from home, and physical cruelty, all beginning before age 15. The differential diagnosis includes: conduct disorder; substance abuse; mental retardation; and manic episodes. Clinicians also should be sensitive to patients from poverty stricken backgrounds who often present at ages 6 or 7. These children may manifest a hyperactive frenetic state and set about systematically to provoke people to reject them. The combined clinical signs of attention deficit hyperactivity disorder, affective disorder, substance-related disorder, learning disorder, and borderline personality disorder that may be encountered in these children warrants assessment. Such patients are appropriately placed in this category and should receive treatment.

BORDERLINE PERSONALITY DISORDER

Borderline personality disorder is characterized by a pervasive pattern of instability of self-image, interpersonal relationships, and mood (Pine, 1974). The differential diagnosis includes: identity disorder; histrionic personality disorder; schizotypal personality disorder; paranoid personality disorder; antisocial personality disorder; and cyclothymia.

Conclusion

This chapter has described some of the major syndromes that may affect latency-age children. As noted, a two-pronged diagnostic protocol should be adhered to in these cases. First, the clinician is challenged to arrive at an accurate diagnosis that conforms to the presenting problem, to parental and teacher reports, and to material gathered from the mental status examination. In addition, the diagnosis should, whenever possible, explain all of the child's clinical signs and subjective symp-

toms. Subsequently, the clinician should review the major differential diagnoses associated with the suspected condition. The clinician also should investigate the degree to which the child's condition has affected various domains of functioning. A syndrome may interfere with an already attained developmental skill, causing regressed behavior, or, in some instances, the syndrome's effects may be so pervasive that a particular developmental skill has failed to develop adaptively altogether.

Moreover, monitoring of the child's developmental functioning is strongly recommended during the treatment period. If certain areas of functioning do not resume adaptive development, the clinician is advised to investigate further. The process of correctly identifying these syndromes is complex, requiring continual review, monitoring, and observation by the clinician.

REFERENCES

Bryant-Waugh, R. (1988). Dealing with children and young adolescents: Special considerations. In D. Scott (Ed.), *Anorexia and bulimia nervosa. Practical approaches* (pp. 192–203). New York: New York University Press.

Grossman, H. J. (1973). *Manual on terminology and classification in mental retardation*. Washington, DC: American Association on Mental Deficiency.

Halmi, A. K. (1988). Appetite regulation in anorexia nervosa. In M. Winick (Ed.), *Control of appetite.* (pp. 125–135). New York: John Wiley & Sons.

Hsu, L. K. G. (1990). *Eating disorders*. New York: Guilford Press.

Kanner, L. (1943). Autistic disturbances of affective contact. *Nervous Child, 2*, 217–250.

Pine, F. (1974). On the concept "borderline". *Psychoanalytic Study Child, 29*, 341–368.

Robson, K. S. (Ed.) (1982). *The borderline child*. New York: McGraw-Hill.

Rutter, M. (1978). Diagnosis and definition. In M. Rutter & E. Schopler (Eds.), *Autism: A reappraisal of concepts and treatment.* (pp. 1–25). New York: Plenum Press.

Stoller, R. J. (1964). The hermaphroditic identity of hermaphrodites. *Journal of Nervous and Mental Disease, 139*, 453–457.

18 / The Young Grade-School Child: Assessment, Evaluation, and Diagnosis

Paul V. Trad

Introduction

The evaluation of an early grade-school child is a challenging task for the clinician. Children of this age already have mastered the developmental

skills of infancy. They possess a coherent sense of self, they can control bodily functions, and they are capable of engaging in representational thought. Despite these accomplishments, however, at this age children lack sophisticated linguistic skills and will tend to use symbols in a rudimentary manner with which the clinician may be unfamiliar.

Because of their unique developmental status, these children require an evaluation that is appropriate to their level of maturational attainment. To obtain information on the background of the child, as well as an objective profile of the child's functioning, two criteria should be kept in mind. First, it is necessary to rely on third-party reports, including parent and teacher reports. Although children of this age are verbally competent, they lack information about their own developmental histories and are not yet adept at describing themselves in objective terms. Second, children of this age frequently divulge their subjective perceptions through pretend play rather than direct verbal disclosure. As a result, the evaluation of an early grade-school child should include a diagnostic play session during which the clinician may discern the child's ability to regulate his or her emotional state.

In addition, the family and medical history of the child, a description of developmental milestone attainment, and a history of the presenting problem also should be addressed. Various standardized psychological examinations may add useful insights. Finally, the record should include comments relating to how the clinician arrived at a differential diagnosis and should identify the diagnosis on the five axes of the fourth edition of the *Diagnostic and Statistical Manual of Mental Disorders.*

Case Example

The following case may serve as an illustration of the process of the assessment of a young grade-school child.

The patient is a 5½-year-old Caucasian female brought to the clinic by the mother because of possible suicidal ideation. The mother reported that she was concerned because of an ongoing investigation for alleged sexual abuse between the patient and her father.

HISTORY OF PRESENTING PROBLEM

The patient, Lisa, is the product of the mother's second marriage. When Lisa was 3 years old, her parents were divorced. After the divorce, Lisa's father did not see her for 1 year. When the child was 4 years old, however, the father's visitation rights were reinstated and Lisa was sent for a 2-week stay with him. The mother reports that after this visit Lisa began to display contradictory behaviors. At times she was withdrawn and quiet; then, without warning, she would have temper tantrums during which she cursed and hit her peers. The child's symptoms worsened after a subsequent visit with the father. The mother reports that Lisa said her father had touched her genitals.

The mother reported additional signs of disorder in the child as well. For example, she noted nocturnal enuresis approximately twice a week and said the child often awakened with nightmares. The mother also described the child's behavior as being "self-destructive," commenting that Lisa expresses a desire to be with a recently deceased cousin and that she has made sexual motions during her sleep.

The child was brought to a pediatrician who performed a physical examination and filed a child abuse report. The child was also brought for psychiatric treatment; a court evaluation regarding the charges of sexual abuse was initiated simultaneously. In the interim, the court has ordered that visits continue between the child and her father. However, the mother reports that Lisa does not want to visit her father and becomes anxious at the time of her visits.

The mother reports that Lisa's self-destructive behavior has increased in the past few months. The mother denies any psychiatric history in the family but says that her former husband, Lisa's father, had a tendency to drink to excess and "smack" her.

DEVELOPMENTAL AND MEDICAL HISTORIES

The patient was the result of a planned pregnancy and was born after 35 weeks of gestation. At the time, the mother was 37 and the father 36. Lisa weighed 5 pounds 3 ounces at birth. There were no postpartum complications and the child was begun on breastfeeding with supplemental formula.

Lisa developed normally throughout infancy and toddlerhood. She achieved motoric and cognitive milestones appropriately and has been in good health for all of her life. The pediatric examination for sexual abuse revealed a normal intact hymen. No other physical evidence of sexual abuse was disclosed upon examination.

FAMILY ASSESSMENT

The child's maternal grandparents were prosperous businesspeople, and Lisa's mother had grown up in wealthy surroundings. The mother observed that she was an obedient daughter who adhered to "traditional values." She decided to become an elementary school teacher because it was a profession that would not interfere with her ability to raise a family.

At the age of 20, Lisa's mother married for the first time. The marriage lasted for 8 years and produced no children. Lisa's mother was saddened by this marriage. "I began to believe that I was unable to have a baby and I became desperate," she said. In her mid-30s, she married Lisa's father, a computer programmer. Shortly after the marriage, the father began working for a major corporation. The couple purchased an expensive home that, according to Lisa's mother, was "beyond our means financially."

This marriage lasted for 8 years. Lisa's mother attributed the breakup to the fact that her husband was a "very controlling person who often flew into a rage." After the divorce, Lisa and her mother moved back to the home of the maternal grandparents. The family is now beset with financial problems. Lisa's mother has worked only sporadically in the past 2 years, and the grandparents have become the main economic providers. Lisa's mother is bitter about her former husband who has a live-in girlfriend and has attained a prominent position at work.

MENTAL STATUS EXAMINATION — STRUCTURED INTERVIEW

The child's mother was present only during the first half of the interview. Lisa was observed to be a well-groomed and well-developed child. The clinician noted that the child's clothing was unusually expensive and excessively feminized. Her posture was normal and she displayed no unusual movements, although occasionally she would rearrange her skirt. Her mother chided her gently, saying "stop fussing." Lisa's psychomotor behavior was optimal. She could perform a variety of fine

and gross motor tasks appropriate to an early grade-school child, including tying shoelaces, fastening buttons, copying figures, writing her name and address, assembling puzzles, and hopping on one foot.

The child was friendly and cooperative. However, when her mother was present Lisa would glance in her direction as if waiting for a cue. The child's affect was normal. She displayed a range of emotions—happiness, surprise, excitement, sadness—and the transitions between emotional states were well regulated. Her thought processes were logical and goal-oriented with no evidence of psychosis or suicidal ideation. Language skills were appropriate. The child had a rich vocabulary and enunciated her words clearly. In addition, she could distinguish between external events and inner perceptual experience. No evidence of perceptual aberrations was present. Her level of social relatedness was also appropriate. While initially shy with the clinician, she gradually became more verbal and seemed eager to establish a bond. Lisa stated that her father had once touched her "private parts" while she was sleeping and that she did not awaken. When the clinician asked how Lisa knew what had happened even though she was asleep, she appeared confused and glanced at her mother.

MENTAL STATUS EXAMINATION — PLAY INTERVIEW

One week after the structured interview, Lisa returned for a play interview. The child was brought into a large playroom and told she could play with any of the toys. Initially Lisa gravitated to a table with paper and crayons. She seemed fascinated by the variety of colors in the crayon box. At one point, she commented that a magenta-colored crayon matched her hair ribbon, a discovery that seemed to please her.

The clinician asked if there were any other toys that Lisa liked. Gazing around the room, the child suddenly noticed a large doll house. She approached the doll house and seemed fascinated by the intricate furnishings in each room. When the clinician suggested that Lisa make up a story about a family living in the house, she complied. She selected an adult female doll, a little girl doll, and an adult male doll to live in the house. She gave the clinician the adult male doll and said, "You're the daddy." She then placed the little girl doll in her bed and commented, "The little girl is sick with a cold upstairs. Daddy just came home from work and Mommy is preparing dinner." Lisa then described a "12-course dinner with all kinds of food."

The clinician simulated that the father doll had just arrived home. Lisa, acting the role of the mother doll, said, "Where were you? You didn't make enough money today." She used the mommy doll to tap the daddy doll on the head. This bantering continued until Lisa said, "Now we have to fight." When the clinician asked Lisa how the little girl doll felt when her parents were fighting, Lisa said, "She is sleeping and doesn't know."

To elicit material relating to the allegations of sexual abuse in this case, the clinician used anatomically correct dolls. Lisa made no reference to this fact, however. To further evoke material in the child, the clinician said, "Let's pretend it's the next day and the little girl wakes up to go to school." Lisa complied. "The little girl knows she has to go to school, so she wakes up." Lisa has the doll go to the little girl's closet and made an elaborate showing of how many "nice dresses" the little girl had. Lisa then proceeded to undress the little girl doll and provide her with a new outfit. She did not exhibit any strong emotions when she saw the doll naked with genitalia depicted.

The clinician then suggested a scene at the breakfast table. The dialogue was standard, until Lisa suddenly had the mother doll "crying." Asked what had caused the mother doll to cry, Lisa said, "She says Daddy doesn't love her anymore. If he loved her, he would buy her nice clothes." Playing the role of the daddy doll, the clinician apologized to the mommy doll. "That's not good enough," Lisa had the mommy doll say. When the clinician asked why the mommy doll was so angry, Lisa said that she didn't want to play with the dolls anymore. She wandered back to the table with the crayons and began drawing several ornate flowers until the session ended.

The child's play behavior was developmentally appropriate and adaptive. She displayed the capacity for interactive play, collaborating readily with the clinician in a cooperative manner that revealed the capacity for turn-taking and reciprocity. Moreover, Lisa's ability to partake in a fantasy sequence appeared intact. She followed the clinician's cues and easily adapted to role playing. Finally, her capacity to move back and forth between a fantasy scenario and reality was also adaptive. At no time did she carry over affective responses from the fantasy to reality. Significantly, the child displayed no symbolic behavior indicative of abuse, despite the fact that the clinician had provided her with ample opportunity to express this behavior metaphorically.

DIAGNOSTIC PEER GROUP

Lisa also was evaluated in a diagnostic peer group. Upon entering the evaluation room, she focused on another little girl wearing a dress similar to her own. This little girl was playing with crayons. Lisa approached the little girl and began playing with a nearby doll house. Within several more minutes, Lisa moved into the other little girl's space and began narrating a pretend story using dolls. The other little girl followed Lisa's lead. For the duration of the play session they continued collaborating on their pretend scenario. The dialogue and content of the fantasy was adaptive, and Lisa displayed no aberrant sexual behavior.

It was recommended that Lisa continue in individual psychotherapy, preferably with a female therapist. Parental counseling for the mother was also recommended.

Axis I:	Adjustment Disorder with Emotional Features
	Disturbed Family Circumstances
Axis II:	None
Axis III:	Diseases of the Genitourinary System—Enuresis
Axis IV:	Custody Dispute; Alleged Sexual Abuse
Axis V:	60

A course of family therapy involving both Lisa and her parents was clearly warranted in this case. In addition, it was advised that the parents enter a program of marital counseling to better understand how their conflict was spilling over to influence the relationship with their child in a negative fashion.

The Diagnostic Profile of the Early Grade-School Child

During the early grade-school years in particular, children undergo continual developmental change and growth. As a result, rapid alterations in skill occasionally are misinterpreted as being symptomatic, when these changes are actually signs of adaptive maturation. It is therefore important to incorporate several assessments and evaluations into the diagnostic process.

The mental status examination remains the primary vehicle for evaluating the child's psychological status. Moreover, to accommodate the dramatic developmental changes the early grade-school-age child is experiencing, it is recommended that this pivotal examination be divided into two phases. First, a traditional examination may be conducted, covering such areas as presenting problem, family history, and the child's current level of functioning. The second phase of the mental status examination should focus on play behavior. Children of early grade school age may lack facility with verbal expression; even when language abilities are advanced, a child may not be comfortable expressing emotions verbally. As a consequence, clinicians should seek a domain of competence that is appropriate to the child's developmental level. For the early grade-school child, this domain may be found in the world of fantasy play. Indeed, in recent years the play session involving just the child and the clinician has come to represent the centerpiece of the early grade-school child's evaluation. In addition, a diagnostic play group involving the child and age-matched peers is also an outstanding assessment tool for a child in this age group because this format encourages the child to demonstrate developmental skills. During the play portions of the examination, the clinician should assess the child's use of symbols, ability to engage in pretend play and to interact with peers in an adaptive fashion. The assessment of the early grade-school child also should include standardized tests designed to evaluate developmental functioning, educational attainment, intelligence, personality profile and neuropsychological behavior. Depending on the symptoms the child exhibits, a neuroendocrine assessment may be warranted as well.

THE MULTIAXIAL APPROACH TO DIAGNOSIS

The *DSM-IV* (1994) adopts a multiaxial evaluation format requiring that each case be assessed on five different axes. Each axis classifies a different type of functioning. Each child should thus be evaluated based on the following axes:

Axis I:	Clinical Syndromes and Other Conditions That May Be a Focus of Clinical Attention
Axis II:	Personality Disorders, Mental Retardation
Axis III:	General Medical Conditions
Axis IV:	Psychosocial and Environmental Problems
Axis V:	Global Assessment of Functioning Scale

Axes I and II comprise the entire classification of mental disorders. On Axis III, the clinician may note any current physical disorder or condition relevant to the case. Axis IV codes the overall severity of a psychosocial stressor, while Axis V permits the clinician to present a general judgment of the person's psychological, social, and occupational functioning.

MENTAL STATUS EXAMINATION — STRUCTURED INTERVIEW

The mental status examination is the instrument used to explore the child's emotional and cognitive states through behavior manifestations. During the mental status examination signs and symptoms should be distinguished. Signs are aspects of the patient's presentation that the clinician notes objectively. For example, a clinician may notice that the child does not respond to certain questions. In contrast, symptoms refer to subjective perceptions experienced only by the patient and reported to the clinician. Symptoms include complaints, explanations, or comments patients make about themselves. Clinicians should indicate in writing whether information is gathered from clinical observation, patient reports, or parental history.

The mental status examination enables the clinician to formulate a preliminary diagnosis and treatment plan for the child. Shapiro (1979) recommends that certain strategies be followed during the conduct of the examination. Specifically, the clinician should focus on the assessment rather than strive to establish an alliance with the child. Ambiguous or contradictory statements made by the child should be clarified. Finally, the record should clearly differentiate between inferred and observed information.

The mental status examination contains 8 primary elements: physical appearance, abnormalities of posture, psychomotor activity, affect, mood, speech and language, social relatedness, and perception.

Physical Appearance: The clinician should record the child's general physical characteristics, noting any abnormalities. In particular, the child's apparent age, appropriateness of dress, and general demeanor should be described.

Abnormalities of Posture: The physical positioning of the child during the interview is of significance. Abnormalities may include muscular rigidity or inflexibility, and the repetition of gestures.

Psychomotor Activity: Psychomotor activity encompasses both the child's fine and gross motor movements. Such activities may range from psychomotor agitation, manifested through overactivity, restlessness, and the inability to sit still, to psychomotor retardation, manifested by a pervasive slowness of motor movements. The determination of these states may be made by clinical observation and questioning. In addition, the child should be asked to perform the following activities: fasten shirt buttons, tie shoelaces, assemble puzzles, copy letters on paper, bounce and catch a ball, and hop on one foot.

Affect: Affect refers to the child's emotional state during the interview. The child's affect may be apprehensive, joyous, aggressive, angry, sad, anxious, flat, or situationally inappropriate. Affect may be evaluated through observation of facial expression and through questions such as: What makes you happy? What makes you sad?

Mood: In contrast to affect, which is externally displayed, the child's mood reflects the inner emotional state. Abnormal moods include feelings of depression and hopelessness, feelings of elation, and labile feelings that change rapidly regardless of the situation. While mood may be detected through observation, the clinician should supplement observations with reports from others and inquiries concerning the child's overall outlook.

Speech and Language: The child of this age should use language skills with relative ease and fluidity. Deficits in the child's verbal abilities include voluntary abstinence from speaking in certain situations, a continuous flow of unrelated sentences, abnormalities in articulation or rate of speech, and limitations in expressive skills. Speech and language abnormalities may be detected by listening during the interview and by questioning the child. The clinician also should attempt to discern whether the child understands questions and can follow directions, combine words, name objects, use pronouns and plurals, and build sentences.

Social Relatedness: The child's ability to func-

tion adaptively in a social setting needs to be evaluated. Skills that enable the child to develop friendships, to empathize with others, and to display attachments are significant in this regard. Abnormalities may be detected by observing the child's interactive skills during the interview as well as by the reports of others. Information obtained from a play session with peers will offer further insights about the child's social relatedness.

Perception: Perception refers to the child's integration of external stimuli. Abnormalities of perception include misinterpretations or misrepresentations of environmental stimuli as well as hallucinations, which are perceptions that occur in the absence of external stimuli. Hallucinations in young children tend to be associated with anxious states, such as separation. The clinician may deduce the child's perceptual state through inquiry, observation, and the reports of parents.

The clinician also should investigate the child's locus of control, the degree to which the child perceives events to be contingent on his or her own actions rather than on external forces. Children with an internal locus of control tend to be goal-oriented. The presence of suicidal ideation and the degree of impulsivity should be assessed as well. Impulsivity, in this context, refers to the child's tendency to make quick decisions in uncertain circumstances.

Other areas that should be evaluated during the mental status examination include the child's sense of self, body image, somatic complaints, appetite and sleep disturbances, attention and concentration spans. It is also important to investigate memory capacity and resistance to the process of memory. Scripts are believed to be the earliest vehicles through which the young child represents early life memories (Nelson, 1986). Hudson (1986) and Nelson and Gruendel (1981) have argued that an event that deviates from a script with which the child is familiar is more likely to be retained in memory. Other reports have found that young children have trouble establishing autobiographical memories because they have difficulty dealing with novel aspects of routine events (Fivush & Hamond, 1990). One study found that younger children organize memories into general and specific events, particularly when they are learning about an event for the first time (Farrar & Goodman, 1992). For example, 4-year-olds tended to merge events and become confused easily, while 7-year-olds were more adept at distinguishing between events. The clinician therefore should be patient when evaluating the memory of the early grade-school child. Memory impairments in such children may be aspects of normative developmental trends rather than signs of actual psychopathology.

Finally, the clinician should assess the child's reliance on defense mechanisms, unconscious processes that help the child deal with inner conflicts or anxieties. Some of the more common defense mechanisms used by early grade-school children are repression, denial, displacement, somatization, idealization, passive/aggressive behavior, projection, and splitting.

Beyond these traditional areas of assessment, some additional developmental proclivities are encountered among children of early grade school age. For example, beginning at approximately age 4, children become aware of group identity (Clark & Clark, 1965). According to Aboud (1988), intense group favoritism is demonstrated by 5- to 7-year-olds. Emotions associated with a fear of the unknown also surface at this age. Moreover, the child is in the preoperational period of thought (Piaget, 1954), a time when perceptual cues—in contrast to abstract perceptions—dominate.

Yee and Brown (1994) have reported that self-esteem and group identification are especially positive by age 5. Thus, clinicians evaluating children in this age group should determine the child's attitude toward various social groups as a sign of adaptation. Acceptance and rejection by peers are also prominent issues among children during the early grade school years. Studies have found that rejected children interact with peers differently from other children. Ladd (1983) noted that such children do not remain engaged with other children for long periods but instead shift from interaction to interaction. Rejected children also tend to elicit fewer expressions of interest and receive more negative treatment from peers (Dodge, 1983; Gottman, Gonso, & Rasmussen, 1975). Cassidy and Asher (1992), who studied 5- to 7-year-olds, determined that even children of this age possessed a basic understanding of their loneliness and knew they were being rejected by peers. These children displayed impaired patterns of prosocial interaction, suggesting that diagnostic peer group sessions may be useful for clarifying their diagnoses.

In the case under discussion, the child's functioning on the mental status examination was highly pertinent. In particular, her normal range of affect and age-appropriate behaviors suggested optimal development and appeared to contradict reports of child sexual abuse. Moreover, her comments about being touched by her father while she remained asleep were inconsistent with evidence of abuse.

MENTAL STATUS EXAMINATION — PLAY INTERVIEW

One useful technique for assessing the mental status of the prelatency-age child is through the observation of play behavior. Indeed, play serves as a primary vehicle for assessing the child's adaptive functioning or maladaptive behavior patterns. Play activities provide the early grade-school child who has not yet mastered the nuances of language with an effective tool for communicating thoughts and emotions. Moore (1964) notes that play opens up the world of pretend and make-believe, a domain in which the child is enthralled with forging a balance between external and internal reality. Woltmann (1964) comments that the unstructured play environment permits the child to project internal struggles onto an external panorama. Thus, by observing play situations, the clinician may characterize the child's behavior according to diagnostic categories (Crowell, Feldman, & Ginsberg, 1988).

An all-encompassing definition of play does not exist. However, Piaget (1962) viewed play as an activity that allows the child to ascribe meaning to key people and objects. Vygotsky (1967) posited that play exists whenever the child creates an imaginary universe in which symbols assume prominence. Significantly, both language and symbolic play first emerge during the second year of life. Pretend activities proliferate during the next several years and then begin to decline (Fein, 1981). Interactive pretend play is most prominent between 3 and 6 years (Corsaro, 1979). During pretend play, the child distinguishes between the "signifier" and the "object" or its signified role, a skill termed *metacommunication* (Bateson, 1956). The child who identifies the symbol and separates it from its referent can play adaptively. In contrast, the child whose metacommunication skills are deficient may engage in maladaptive play.

Fairy tales are one means by which prelatency-age children master metacommunication skills. By analyzing fairy tales, the clinician obtains clues about the child's functioning. Schwartz (1964) has identified several characteristics in the fairy tale that offer insight about the child's perceptions. Specifically, fairy tales contain hidden meanings; they are structured around opposites (such as good vs. evil); they may involve a distortion of reality; they tend to contain dramatic elements; they express wishes; and they utilize condensation, substitution, and displacement. Scarlett and Wolf (1979) have noted that children enter the fairy-tale frame yet simultaneously maintain the boundaries of real-life situations. In this fashion, children may enact and work through internal conflicts symbolically.

Fantasy is a domain in which the constraints of real life may be relinquished. As a result, the child becomes able to express aggressive behavior. In turn, the violent tendencies that emerge during play may arouse fear, causing the child to retreat back to a real-life situation or to curtail the fantasy altogether.

Clinicians may diagnose a variety of developmental deficits from observing the child's pretend play. For example, a child who fails to limit aggressive fantasy play may have trouble distinguishing between pretend and real-life situations. The aggressive play enacted by the child may be a prelude to self-destructive behavior, unless the child can be brought back to reality rapidly. Clinicians also should evaluate the cognitive material contained in the child's fantasy play. All of this information helps the clinician define the child's risk for engaging in maladaptive behavior. Moreover, as Irwin (1983) advises, the clinician may use symbolic play to observe the child's emotional life from the following 4 perspectives: (1) the child's self-representations, including the roles he or she assumes; (2) the child's representations of others; (3) the child's wishes, conflicts, and defense mechanisms; and (4) the child's perception of the world and thinking patterns (including intellectual capacities) and problem-solving skills. Play further enables the clinician to diagnose the status of the child's attachment behaviors.

During the prelatency years, play behavior becomes more sophisticated. Iwanaga (1973) reports the following progression in the structure of interpersonal play:

1. Independent structure: Play lacks the involvement of others; 3 years old.
2. Parallel structure: Two or more children engage in play. Although each child plays independently, the children remain in close physical proximity; 3, 4 years old.
3. Complementary structure: Play occurs between 2 or more children. Although there is some cooperation, the roles of the children are enacted independently of each other; 4 years old.
4. Interactive structure: Play occurs between 2 or more children. Roles are intertwined during the exchange. Each child focuses on how the other behaves and is cognizant of shifts in the other child's behavior; 5 years old.

Iwanaga (1973) reports that the shift to interactive structure marks a transition from an egocentric position to a reciprocal position. The child's ability to play in a developmentally appropriate manner correlates with the ability to relate to the environment adaptively. For example, a 5-year-old who persists in remaining isolated from peers during play may lack the social skills necessary for further development.

Observation of play behavior offers the clinician the opportunity to assess a broad array of skills implicating the child's psychological status. For example, according to Singer (1973, 1979), the degree to which 3- to 6-year-olds display pretend behavior is contingent on the encouragement of the caregiver. Peller (1952) determined that children's role-playing choices are based on their feelings toward people in real life. Some researchers have posited that language skill and symbolic play mirror the child's representational abilities (Bates, Camaioni, & Volterra, 1975; Casby & Della Corte, 1986). That is, children who are able to produce complex language combinations tend to have greater representational abilities than those who cannot (Casby & Della Corte, 1986).

Aside from the variations in play behaviors noted above, five types of childhood psychopathology are associated with aberrant play patterns, including: separation anxiety, autism, suicidal behaviors, conduct disordered behaviors, and depression (Trad, 1989; Willock, 1983; Wulff, 1985). Children who manifest signs of separation anxiety, for example, prefer to play with toys relevant to their anxiety (Gilmore, 1966), while autistic children are notable for a lack of symbolic play and verbal language systems (Wulff, 1985). Suicidal children tend to misuse toys and engage in reckless behaviors (Trad, 1989). In contrast, conduct-disordered children act out against the environment in destructive ways (Willock, 1983). Depressed children frequently are indifferent to pretend situations and may lack the appetite for fantasy play (Trad, 1989).

The clinician observing the child's play behavior should be cognizant of the child's developmental status. Changes in play behaviors may be used to chart the child's mental level. Moreover, allowing the child to enact symbolic behaviors during play provides access to internal perceptions that may be indicative of disorder and helpful in arriving at a diagnosis.

In the case discussed earlier, the pretend scenario of a family scene enacted by the child with the dolls provided key information that contributed to the diagnosis. Specifically, the child's enactment of marital conflict strongly hinted that her parents—particularly her mother—were using her as the scapegoat to resolve their own emotional disputes.

THE DIAGNOSTIC PEER GROUP

One diagnostic tool that may be of special assistance in the evaluation of the early grade-school child is the diagnostic peer group. Although children of this age often are acutely aware of their external environment as well as internal developmental changes, they tend to lack sophisticated linguistic skills for expressing their emotions verbally. Instead, emotional responses frequently are acted out in a forum in which the child feels most comfortable—the arena of play. During play the child uses make-believe and pretend activities to convey the emotional issues that are troubling him or her.

A problem may arise because young children may be reticent about engaging in fantasy play with an unfamiliar adult, such as the clinician. In an environment of peers, however, such children often reveal their emotions in a candid manner. The peer group concept is highly effective in this regard. During a peer group, the child is placed in an unstructured play setting with peers of approximately his or her own developmental status. The play area is amply equipped with toys and other play activities, and there is sufficient space for the child to engage in interactive play or to withdraw. Children are told that they may play in the room while their parents are being interviewed.

The diagnostic peer group is an especially valuable tool with early grade-school children because it fosters their developmental proclivities to engage in fantasy behavior. In addition, the peer group may be used to evaluate the child's response to separation from and reunion with the primary caregiver, the child's prosocial skills, the child's ability to traverse from fantasy to reality adaptively, and the child's developmental competence in relation to other children of comparable maturational level. Moreover, the peer group may confirm or clarify a diagnosis when the results of the mental status examination are uncertain.

The diagnostic peer group provided salient information in the case under discussion. In effect, the child spontaneously gravitated to a peer of her age and initiated an appropriate play sequence that was devoid of conflict. This behavior further reinforced the hypothesis that this child was being used as a pawn in a custody dispute and that the likelihood of sexual abuse was minimal.

THE FAMILIAL ENVIRONMENT OF THE CHILD

Understanding the familial environment is a key component of the child's assessment. In this regard, the parents' function as the primary interpreters of the child's perceptual world should be noted. Clinicians should remember that when parents' reports are used, there may be a danger that the child's disturbance will either be overestimated or underestimated (Weissman et al., 1986). To clarify the scope of parental influence, an interview focusing on the dynamics of family functioning should be conducted.

For the early grade-school child, the family plays a crucial role in the evolution of many disorders. It is thus imperative for the clinician to assess the child's family of origin.

One risk factor associated with childhood psychiatric disorder is disrupted marital status (i.e., separated, divorced, or remarried). Brady, Bray, and Zeeb (1986) found that children from separated families displayed a host of psychiatric disturbances, ranging from immature behavior, to sleep disorders, to hyperactivity. Parental psychopathology is another risk factor that has been associated with psychiatric disorder in early grade-school children. Specifically, maternal depression has a deleterious influence on the child's psychological well-being. Fergusson, Horwood, and Shannon (1984), for example, found striking correlations between maternal depression and child-rearing problems in young children. This finding was attributed to two mechanisms. First, it is posited that children with depressed mothers react to depression by exhibiting an increased number of behavior problems. Alternatively, the mother's depression may affect her perceptions of her child. That is, depressed women may evaluate their children as being more problematic. A study by Orvaschel, Weissmann, and Kidd (1980) strongly suggests, however, that it is not merely maternal perception of the child's behavior; rather, children with depressed parents are significantly more likely to exhibit psychopathology than children with normal parents.

Other forms of parental psychopathology also have been found to heighten the likelihood of childhood disorder. Rutter and Shaffer (1980) and Rutter (1981) listed such family stressors as the father's employment status, overcrowding in the home, parental conviction of a crime, and marital discord. Considered alone, none of these factors is significant. When two or more factors are present, however, the risk of emotional problems in the child doubles. Substantiating the theory that family stressors contribute to childhood disorder, Lahey et al. (1988) found that parents with a history of aggression, arrest, imprisonment, or substance abuse were more likely to have a child with attention deficit hyperactivity disorder.

These studies provide ample support for the notion that the child's family environment is a strong factor in psychiatric illness. As such, a thorough investigation of the family's structure, parental psychopathology, and family history is essential in the formulation of an accurate diagnosis.

In the case under discussion, the marital history of the family was pertinent. The mother's description of two stormy marriages, her bout with depression, her diminished socioeconomic circumstances, and her acknowledged bitterness toward her husband suggested that problems within the marriage were being enacted by the child. Lending further credence to this hypothesis was the child's tendency to look to the mother for visual "cues" or signs of approval during the mental status examination. However, it was essential for

the clinician to verify this diagnostic hypothesis through the other components of the assessment.

EPIDEMIOLOGICAL CONSIDERATIONS

One problematic task in assessing the early grade-school child is distinguishing between problems that are likely to persist and problems that represent temporary perturbations in the developmental course. It is not difficult to understand why this dilemma occurs. First, the child is in the throes of the developmental process, meaning that new skills may emerge precipitously and then recede. In this atmosphere of continual and rapid change, identifying which phenomena are due to adaptive maturational trends and which are due to genuine deviation can be a challenge. Second, tremendous variability exists among observations of behavior. That is, the parent is likely to possess biases stemming from his or her own expectations of the child. These are among the factors that make it difficult to define symptomatic behavior in this population. Nonetheless, even conservative estimates hold that approximately 12% of early grade-school children have some diagnosable psychiatric disorder (Garrison and Earls, 1986). As a result, it is important to outline the basic epidemiology of this age group.

Before approaching symptoms from a nosological point of view, the frequency of certain symptoms reported by children of this age will be noted. Specifically, bedwetting, sleep problems, poor concentration, and volatile tempers are the most common signs of a psychiatric disturbance in early grade-school children (Richman, Stevenson, & Graham, 1975). Among children of this age in a psychiatric hospital setting, Bentovim and Boston (1973) determined that 30% had management problems, 10% were anxious, 15% had primary retardation, 13% were autistic, and 11% had speech and language problems.

Finally, the clinician should weigh the stability of symptomatology. Researchers have demonstrated that certain behaviors persist from preschool to school age and beyond (Coleman, Wolkind, & Ashley, 1977). For example, Coleman et al. found that separation difficulties in preschool girls predicted later school difficulties, while in boys hyperactivity at home predicted conduct disorders at school. Campbell et al. (1986) followed 3-year-olds with behavior problems; at age 6 fully half of a sample of 54 children manifested clinically significant problems. The dominant symptoms of these children were inattention, impulsivity, or aggressive behavior, and one third of the group met *DSM-III* criteria for attention deficit disorder.

In sum, although each child is unique, certain epidemiological considerations should be evaluated. By weighing the child's developmental status, age, gender, presence of organic mental disease, and the known stability of certain symptoms, a more accurate diagnosis may be achieved.

PSYCHOLOGICAL TEST ASSESSMENT

Psychological testing is an important adjunct to the mental status examination (Akiskal, 1986). Plenk and Hinchey (1985) recommend that a complete evaluation include standardized testing geared to the age and developmental status of the child; any known deficits or disabilities should be considered when selecting and interpreting a test.

The following tests may be used in the psychological assessment of the prelatency-age child:

- *Gesell Developmental Schedule:* Used in children ages 4 weeks to 6 years, these empirically derived standardized measures reflect infant and early childhood skill in motor, adaptive, language, and personal-social functioning. The schedules rely on observations of the child's activities as compared to established norms.
- *Kaufman Assessment Battery for Children (K-ABC):* Recommended for children between the ages of 2½ and 12½ years, this test evaluates neuropsychological development using the Mental Processing Scales and the Achievement Scale. The former assesses the child's ability to solve problems and mental functioning that does not depend on formal training, the latter assesses the child's current academic knowledge.
- *Weschler Preschool Primary Scale of Intelligence (WPPSI):* The WPPSI assesses the intelligence of children ages 4 to 6 and is a structured test divided into verbal and performance sections. Children who have been raised in a different culture, speak a different primary language, or have grown up in poverty may score low on the verbal section of the test and their combined IQ score may not represent their intellectual capacity accurately.
- *Rorschach Test:* The Rorschach is an unstructured projective technique in which 10 ink blots are presented and the child conveys the visual picture he or she sees. The unstructured quality of the Rorschach elucidates the prelatency child's inner

world, since children of this age may not be able to communicate the complexities of their inner psychological state without an external stimulus. Diagnostically, the Rorschach can confirm a current thought disorder and alert the therapist to the existence of impaired perception by the child.
- *Child's Apperception Test (CAT):* The CAT is a projective test used for children ages 3 to 10 years. The test consists of a series of pictures that depict a story. The child is asked to relate a story about the events that are happening, including what led up to the current portrait, and to describe what the future will be like.
- *Vineland Adaptive Behavior Scales:* This scale may be used on subjects from birth through 18 years to assess the child's personal and social sufficiency and capacity for self-care in terms of communication, daily living skills, socialization, and motor skills.
- *Projective Drawings:* These tests request that the child draw a person, a house, or a tree. Deviations from normal drawing are noted. Of diagnostic significance are graphomotor factors such as erasing, placement, pressure, shading, and size as well as factors such as detailing, distortions, and omissions, symmetry, and transparencies (Odgon, 1982).
- *Bender-Gestalt:* This test consists of 9 geometric figures the child is asked to draw. During the first part of the test, the child is shown several cards and asked to draw each geometrical figure. During the second part of the test the child is asked to draw as many figures as he or she can from memory. The perceptual-motor activities inherent in the test are posited to help delineate facets of the child's neuromotor organization and functioning.

Psychological testing is a useful adjunct to other diagnostic tools. These tests may significantly affect the course of clinical treatment by enhancing differential diagnosis and by aiding in the monitoring and evaluation of interventions.

NEUROENDOCRINE FACTORS IN CHILDHOOD PSYCHOPATHOLOGY

Psychiatric disorders in children have been subjected to biological scrutiny for more than a quarter of a century. In recent years, investigators have identified some aberrant physiological phenomena that appear to underlie specific psychiatric conditions, including mood disorders, pervasive developmental disorder, schizophrenia, and anxiety disorders.

In particular, the neuroendocrine profile of a child who manifests severe depression or self-destructive behavior deviates dramatically from that of a child with normal behavioral signs. For example, elevated cortisol levels, low levels of serotonin metabolite in the cerebrospinal fluid, low monoamine oxidase platelet activity, and a blunted response of thyroid stimulating hormone to thyrotropin releasing hormone have been correlated with suicidal behavior in adults (Banki & Arato, 1983). It is unclear, however, whether this profile of neuroendocrine dysregulation is the cause or the result of the condition. Abnormalities in cortisol levels and a blunted thyroid stimulating hormone response may indicate dysregulation within the hypothalamic-pituitary-adrenal axis, the site of emotional mediation. Finally, researchers posit that if a single neurophysiologic mechanism underlies self-destructive behavior in adults, a likely candidate appears to be hypoactivity of serotonergic functioning. Moreover, it is posited that a similar mechanism may operate in children (Banki, 1985).

Evidence also suggests that dopamine levels are implicated in the etiology of schizophrenia. Neuroleptics almost universally inhibit the action of dopamine in the central nervous system (Freedman, Adler, Waldo, Pachtman, & Franks, 1983). Investigations have implicated serotonergic hyperfunctioning in the etiology of obsessive-compulsive disorder (Thoren, Asberg, Cronholm, Jornestedt, & Traskman, 1980), as well as a hyperserotonergic mechanism underlying autism (August, Ray, & Baird, 1987). Given these findings, use of the dexamethasone suppression and thyrotropin releasing hormone tests can clearly help identify abnormal neuroendocrine patterns in adults and also may be of benefit in revealing these abnormalities in children (Chabrol, Claverie, & Moron, 1983).

Conclusion

This chapter has focused on the diagnostic profile of the early grade-school child. As was noted,

a wide variety of areas should be assessed with such children in order to arrive at an accurate diagnosis. Such a formulation takes full account of the child's developmental status and proclivities.

The assessment of the prelatency-age child should begin with a review of several key areas. For example, a thorough mental status examination should be conducted. During the first phase of the mental status examination, all areas of psychological functioning must be reviewed. The presenting problem and a developmental analysis of the child's level of functioning are components of this phase of the examination. Subsequently, during the second phase of the mental status examination, the clinician should focus on the child's play behavior, including the use of symbols, ability to engage in pretend scenarios, ability to role-play and to interact with others adaptively. The play evaluation is a significant component of the evaluation of children in this age group, since they often are unable to express their internal emotional state except through pretend behaviors. Moreover, a diagnostic play group can provide further insights about the child's fantasy behavior and socialization skills as well as offering an opportunity to compare the child with others of his or her developmental level.

The family environment of the child also should be evaluated, and the epidemiology of the child's presenting problem should be assessed. In addition, standardized tests that evaluate developmental achievement, intelligence, and personality profile may provide further information. With some disorders, including depression, self-destructive behavior, schizophrenia, obsessive-compulsive behavior, and anxiety, a neuroendocrine evaluation may further confirm initial diagnostic impressions. Finally, the clinician should adopt a multiaxial approach, which yields the most comprehensive assessment of the child's functioning.

REFERENCES

Aboud, F. (1988). *Children and prejudice.* Oxford: Blackwell.

Akiskal, H. S. (1986). A developmental perspective on recurrent mood disorders: A review of studies in man. *Psychopharmacology Bulletin, 22,* 579–586.

American Psychiatric Association. (1994). *Diagnostic*

and statistical manual of mental disorders (4th ed.). Washington, DC: Author.

August, G. J., Ray, N., & Baird, T. D. (1987). Fenfluramine response in high and low functioning autistic children. *Journal of the American Academy of Child and Adolescent Psychiatry, 26,* 342–346.

Banki, C. M. (1985). Biochemical markers for suicidal behavior. *American Journal of Psychiatry, 142,* 147–148.

Banki, C. M., & Arato, M. (1983). Amine metabolites, neuroendocrine findings, and personality dimensions as correlated of suicidal behavior. *Psychiatry Research, 10,* 253–261.

Bates, E., Camaioni, L., & Volterra, V. (1975). The acquisition of performances prior to speech. *Merrill Palmer Quarterly, 21,* 205–226.

Bateson, G. (1956). The message "This is play." In B. Schanner (Ed.), *Group processes.* New York: Macy Foundation.

Bentovim, A., & Boston, M. (1973). A day-centre for disturbed young children and their parents. *Journal of Child Psychotherapy, 3,* 46–60.

Brady, C. P., Bray, J. H., & and Zeeb, L. (1986). Behavior problems of clinic children; Relation to parental marital status, age and sex of child. *American Journal of Orthopsychiatry, 56,* 388–412.

Campbell, S. B., Ewing, L. J., Breaux, A. M., & Szumowski, E. K. (1986). Parent-referred problem three-year-olds: Follow-up at school entry. *Journal of Child Psychology and Psychiatry and Allied Disciplines, 27* (4), 473–488.

Casby, M. W., & Della Corte, M. (1986). Symbolic play performance and early language development. *Journal of Psycholinguistic Research, 16,* 31–42.

Cassidy, J., & Asher, S. R. (1992). Loneliness and peer relations in young children. *Child Development, 63,* 350–365.

Chabrol, H., Claverie, J., & Moron, P. (1983). TI DST, TRH test, and adolescent suicide attempts. *American Journal of Psychiatry, 140,* 265.

Clark, K. B., & Clark, M. P. (1965). Racial identification and preference in Negro children. In H. Proshanshky & H. Seidenberg (Eds.), *Basic studies in social psychology* (pp. 308–317). New York: Holt, Rinehart & Winston.

Coleman, L., Wolkind, S., & Ashley, L. (1977). Symptoms of behaviour disturbance and adjustment to school. *Journal of Child Psychology and Psychiatry, 18,* 201–209.

Corsaro, W. (1979). Young children's conception of status and role. *Sociology of Education, 52,* 46–59.

Crowell, J. A., Feldman, S. S., & Ginsberg, N. (1988). Assessment of mother-child interaction in preschoolers with behavior problems. *Journal of the American Academy of Child and Adolescent Psychiatry, 27,* 303–311.

Dodge, K. A. (1983). Behavioral antecedents of peer social status. *Child Development, 54,* 1386–1399.

Farrar, M. J., & Goodman, G. S. (1992). Developmental changes in event Memory. *Child Development, 63,* 173–187.

Fein, G. (1981). Pretend play in childhood: An integrative review. *Child Development, 52,* 1095–1118.

Fergusson, D. M., Horwood, L. J., & Shannon, F. T. (1984). Relationship of family life events, maternal depression, and child-rearing problems. *Pediatrics, 73,* 773–776.

Fivush, R., & Hamond, N. (1990). Autobiographical memory across the preschool years: Toward reconceptualizing childhood amnesia. In R. Fivush & J. Hudson (Eds.), *Knowing and remembering in young children* (pp. 223–248). New York: Cambridge University Press.

Freedman, R., Adler, L. E., Waldo, M. C., Pachtman, E., & Franks, R. D. (1983). Neurophysical evidence for a defect in inhibitory pathways in schizophrenia: Comparison of medicated and drug-free patients. *Biological Psychiatry, 18,* 537–551.

Garrison, W., & Earls, F. (1986). Epidemiological perspectives on maternal depression and the young child. *New Directions for Child Development, 34,* 13–30.

Gilmore, J. B. (1966). The role of anxiety and cognitive factors in children's play behavior. *Child Development, 37,* 397–416.

Gottman, J. M., Gonso, J., & Rasmussen, R. (1975). Social interaction, social competence, and friendship in children. *Child Development, 46,* 709–718.

Hudson, J., & Nelson, K. (1986). Repeated encounters of a similar kind: Effects of familiarity on children's autobiographic memory. *Cognitive Development, 1* (3), 253–271.

Irwin, E. (1983). The diagnostic and therapeutic use of pretend play. In C. Schaefer & K. O'Connor (Eds.), *Handbook of play therapy* (pp. 148–173). New York: John Wiley & Sons.

Iwanaga, M. (1973). Development of interpersonal play structure in three-, four- and five-year-old children. *Journal of Research and Development in Education, 6,* 71–82.

Ladd, G. W. (1983). Social networks of popular, average, and rejected children in school settings. *Merrill-Palmer Quarterly, 29,* 283–307.

Lahey, B. B., Piacentini, J. C., McBurnett, K., Stone, P., Hartdagen, S., & Hynd, G. (1988). Psychopathology in the parents of children with conduct disorder and hyperactivity. *Journal of the American Academy of Child and Adolescent Psychiatry, 27,* 163–170.

Moore, T. (1964). Realism and fantasy in children's play. *Journal of Child Psychology and Psychiatry, 5,* 15–36.

Nelson, K. (Ed.) (1986). *Event knowledge: Structure and function and development.* Hillsdale, NJ: Erlbaum.

Nelson, K., & Gruendel, J. (1981). Generalized event representations: Basic building blocks of cognitive development. In M. E. Lamb & A. L. Brown (Eds.), *Advances in developmental psychology* (Vol. 1, pp. 131–158). Hillsdale, NJ: Erlbaum.

Odgon, D. P. (1982). *Psychodiagnostics and personality assessment: A handbook.* Los Angeles: Western Psychological Services.

Orvaschel, H., Weissman, M. M., & and Kidd, K. K. (1980). Children and depression. The children of depressed parents; the childhood of depressed patients; depression in children. *Journal of Affective Disorders, 2*(1), 1–16.

Peller, L. (1952). Models of children's play. *Mental Hygiene, 36,* 66–83.

Pfeffer, C. (1996). *The suicidal child.* New York: Guilford Press.

Piaget, J. (1954). *The construction of reality in the child.* New York: Basic Books.

Piaget, J. (1962). *Play, dreams and imitation in childhood.* New York: W. W. Norton.

Plenk, A. M., & Hinchey, F. S. (1985). Clinical assessment of maladjusted preschool children. *Child Welfare, 64*(2), 127–134.

Richman, N., Stevenson, J. E., & Graham, P. J. (1975). Prevalence of behaviour problems in 3-year-old children: An epidemiological study in a London borough. *Journal of Child Psychology and Psychiatry, 16,* 277–287.

Rutter, M., & Shaffer, D. (1980). A step forward or back in terms of the classification of child psychiatric disorders? *Journal of the American Academy of Child Psychiatry, 19,* 371–394.

Rutter, M. (1981). Psychological sequelae of brain damage in children. *American Journal of Psychiatry, 138,* 1533–1544.

Scarlett, W. G., & Wolf, D. (1979). When it's only make-believe: The construction of a boundary between fantasy and reality storytelling. *New Directions for Child Development, 6,* 29–40.

Schwartz, E. K. (1964). A psychoanalytic study of the fairy tale. In M. R. Haworth (Ed.), *Child psychotherapy: Practice and theory* (pp. 383–395). New York: Basic Books.

Shapiro, T. (1979). *Clinical psycholinguistics.* New York: Plenum Press.

Singer, J. L. (1973). *The child's world of make believe.* New York: Academic Press.

Singer, J. L. (1979). Affect and imagination in play and fantasy. In C. Izard (Ed.), *Emotions in personality and psychopathology* (pp. 13–34). New York: Plenum Press.

Thoren, P., Asberg, M., Cronholm, B., Jornestedt, L., & Traskman, L. (1980). Clomipramine treatment of obsessive-compulsive disorder: I. A controlled clinical trial. *Archives of General Psychiatry, 37,* 1281–1285.

Trad, P. V. (1989). *Treating suicidelike behavior in a Preschooler.* Madison, CT: International Universities Press.

Vygotsky, L. (1967). Play and its role in the mental development of the child. *Soviet Psychology, 5,* 6–18.

Weissman, M. M., Merikangas, K. R., Wickramaratne, P., Kidd, K. K., Prusoff, B. A., Lechman, J. F., & Pauls, D. L. (1986). Understanding the clinical heterogenity of major depression using family data. *Archives of General Psychiatry, 43,* 430–434.

Willock, B. (1983). Play therapy with the aggressive, acting-out child. In C. E. Schaefer & K. J. O'Connor (Eds.), *Handbook of play therapy* (pp. 386–411). New York: John Wiley & Sons.

Woltmann, A. G. (1964). Concepts of play therapy techniques. In M. R. Haworth (Ed.), *Child psychotherapy* (pp. 35–51). New York: Basic Books.

Wulff, S. B. (1985). The symbolic and object play of children with autism: A review. *Journal of Autism and Development Disorders, 15*(2), 139–148.

Yee, M., & Brown, R. J. (1994). The development of gender differentiation in young children. *British Journal of Social Psychology, 33*(2), 183–196.

---

19 / The Grade-School Child: Assessment, Evaluation, and Diagnosis

Paul V. Trad

Introduction

The grade-school years are a time of stability for the child. In general, as the egocentrism of the prelatency years is relinquished, several major developmental changes occur. First, mastery of motor skills now allows the child to perform a wide variety of functions, from drawing a human figure to playing complex games with peers. Children of this age also become aware of gender. In general, boys may become immersed in sports, while girls tend to pursue behaviors designed more for cooperation and mutual endeavors. However, it should be noted that changes in social mores have modified the activities associated with a particular gender.

Notable changes in the child's cognitive abilities

also may be observed. Piaget has referred to this period as the era of concrete operations. Egocentric thought patterns are relinquished, as the child masters the principles that function in objective reality. Rules are viewed as the vehicle through which goals are accomplished, and the child becomes acutely aware of the significance of rules. Perhaps the most dramatic cognitive accomplishment of this period concerns the child's ability to distinguish between objective and subjective reality. The child is now fully aware that he or she possesses internal perceptions that emanate from inner consciousness and has a point of view that differs from that of others. Moreover, the child becomes sensitive to the reality of the external world and is concerned about reconciling internal and external perceptions.

Finally, the child's social maturation assumes preeminence. For the first time, status at school becomes more important than status within the family. Thus, it is important for the clinician to consider whether the child has been integrated into the school environment and has made friends.

With these developmental observations in mind, the clinician may embark upon the assessment of the latency-age child. Clinical interviews conducted alone with the child or in the presence of parents will provide the main source of information. The information required by the mental status examination may be obtained from such an interview. In addition, peer group sessions may be used to supplement clinical interviews.

Case Example

Performing a comprehensive assessment of the child is a mandatory first step in achieving a correct diagnosis. The assessment process may be divided into two main parts. First, an objective version of the child's case history should be obtained. In keeping with the developmental status of a latency-age child, parental information often is extremely helpful for resolving inconsistencies and clarifying material provided by the child. It is important to keep in mind that this is an age when symbiosis with the parents and the emergence of a coherent personality structure are important themes. As a result, the parent should be interviewed separately to acquire a thorough case history. The second feature of the assessment process is the performance of a mental status examination. The clinician should interview the latency-age child alone during both an unstructured and a structured play session. When properly conducted, these examinations enable the clinician to evaluate the child's capacities and deficits. Beyond these assessments, clinicians also may rely on tertiary diagnostic aids, including teacher reports and diagnostic peer group sessions, to help verify a working diagnosis. Nevertheless, the mental status examination remains the centerpiece of the diagnostic assessment.

The following case example may serve as an illustration of the process of assessment of a grade-school child. It details the assessment of an 8-year-old boy. Descriptions of background material obtained during a parental interview and observational material gathered during the mental status examination are provided.

HISTORY OF PRESENTING PROBLEM

Sam R. is an 8-year-old boy from an intact family. He has recently exhibited temper tantrums and learning difficulties. Both his teacher and mother confirm these problems.

Sam's family requested an evaluation for their son because of alleged "uncontrollable attacks of rage." According to the parents, Sam becomes easily angered and, when angry, damages property. The parents fear that if these "episodes" persist, Sam's schoolwork will suffer. In addition, the parents are afraid that the child may injure himself. The parents also voiced concern about a recurring urinary problem.

Three years prior to presentation, when Sam was 5 years old, he was diagnosed with a learning disability involving visual perception and short-term memory. To correct the situation, Sam received private tutoring. At the beginning of first grade, Sam was unable to read; now, however, he has attained his grade level. His parents report that he continues to require support when doing homework and that he becomes easily frustrated. Sam's parents are convinced that the child is not achieving his potential.

The most problematic issue for the parents is Sam's "violent temper." His "tantrums" are described as being out of proportion to the events that precipitate them—for example, being told to finish homework before watching television. The tantrums usually begin with verbal aggression. The child then throws objects and flails his arms and legs. Occasionally he runs out of the house and sulks in the backyard until he calms down. In the course of his temper tantrums, Sam has destroyed furniture and other objects but has not injured himself or anyone else. The parents often have attempted to restrain Sam. Sam says that he does not remember his "rages" entirely but that he sometimes feels like "killing his parents."

While the parents do not specifically mention low self-esteem as a problem, they report that Sam is "sensitive." As an example, they say that Sam repeatedly loses the music book used for his guitar lessons. He does not like taking guitar lessons and several days earlier refused to attend a session, claiming that his teacher would do something to punish him for "being bad."

DEVELOPMENTAL AND MEDICAL HISTORIES

Sam is the product of a planned pregnancy followed by an uncomplicated cesarean section. He weighed 6 pounds 7 ounces at birth. At the time of Sam's birth, his father had been sober from alcohol abuse for approximately 3 months. Sam's parents describe him as a quiet infant who was easily engaged and rarely cried.

The child achieved most major developmental milestones at appropriate ages, although the achievement of speech was slower and more problematic. He sat up at 5 months, walked at 12 months, and was talking in phrases by 16 months. He could use longer phrases by the age of 2 years. Upon entrance into kindergarten at age 5, however, the teacher noticed that Sam was not pronouncing words clearly. At that time, he was evaluated by a speech pathologist, who reported that the child had a pattern of articulation errors. The speech pathologist recommended that Sam be monitored, since it was believed that the problem would resolve spontaneously. Sam's mother also describes him as being a "negotiator" from about the age of 2 years. She notes that he has always been adept at having rules changed to his advantage.

During the first grade, Sam performed satisfactorily in all areas, with the exception of written expression. His teacher noted that Sam preferred to perform orally but rated his ability to organize thoughts in writing, including capitalization and punctuation, as below average. Nonetheless, Sam achieved overall progress. His teacher reported that he was an eager participant in activities and discussions, that he persisted with an assigned task until it was completed, and that he had congenial relationships with classmates.

Sam is currently in good physical health. He has had numerous ear infections during his childhood. In addition, he was diagnosed with Lyme disease at age 4. He was treated with antibiotics until the condition was eradicated. On several occasions during the preceding year Sam complained of pain after urinating, but a urine culture was negative.

FAMILY ASSESSMENT

Sam is the second of three children. One sister is 2 years older and the other 2 years younger. Sam's mother was pregnant a fourth time when Sam was 6 years old. Both Sam and his older sister were informed of this pregnancy. Shortly thereafter, however, his mother had a miscarriage. According to his mother's report, Sam was very upset when she spent several days in the hospital and subsequently told him that he would not have a new sibling.

When Sam was 7 years old, illness became a prevalent theme for this family. His maternal grandmother had cardiac difficulties and was hospitalized. Sam's mother also was hospitalized for 1 month because of pneumonia. In addition, the patient's uncle was diagnosed with AIDS believed to be contracted by intravenous drug abuse. This uncle visited with the family during the Christmas holidays. Sam was aware of his uncle's imminent death. When the uncle died several months later, Sam was taken to the funeral but, his mother reported, he did not verbalize his feelings.

The patient's mother says she comes from a dysfunctional family. Her mother abused prescription medications yet denied using these substances. The mother's stepfather, a physician, apparently provided these medications. The stepfather is described as a "tyrant" who did not tolerate imperfection.

Sam's father is an alcoholic currently in recovery. He has been involved with self-help groups since Sam's birth. Sam apparently has seen his father have "temper tantrums" and break furniture. These episodes were a common occurrence during the first few years of the father's sobriety. Prior to attaining sobriety, Sam's father had been drinking "around the clock" for a number of years. According to Sam's father, he eventually "hit rock bottom" and sought treatment.

MENTAL STATUS EXAMINATION

Sam, a well-groomed child, is the proper size for his age. He displays no abnormalities of posture or motor activity. He exhibits a full spectrum of affective expressions. During the session, he played cooperatively and displayed numerous positive emotions. Nonetheless, several times Sam became oppositional and defiant. On other occasions, he presented a grandiose facade.

During the mental status examination, it became evident that the child's inappropriate behavior and grandiosity were linked to feelings of inadequacy. He was hypersensitive to any indications that he had not performed a task perfectly or answered a question correctly. Receptive and expressive language skills were intact. Sam's verbal abilities were in the superior range and his vocabulary was excellent. As a result, he sometimes seemed older than his age.

Sam readily engaged in the evaluation process. Although he described his mood as being "happy most of the time," during the examination he displayed several abrupt emotional changes. For example, he appeared dysphoric when the therapist questioned him about one of the tasks he had been asked to complete. But he was unable to confirm why he felt that way. His mood alterations appeared to be linked to social interactions. In particular, when Sam believed that others were judging him, he became glum.

No difficulties in reality testing emerged. The child denied having any hallucinations, delusions, or boundary blurring. Thought processes were coherent, although it was evident that Sam harbored unrealistic worries about how others viewed him and interpreted his behaviors. There was no evidence of suicidal ideation, and Sam's parents said that he had never mentioned any suicidal thoughts. He has no history of self-injurious behavior, although when he is angry and flails his arms, his parents fear that he may hurt himself.

Sam was noted to be impulsive and to have a low frustration tolerance. For instance, he responded to the request to help with the clean-up chores by muttering and tossing items into inappropriate places. His memory was assessed to be intact with recall of three words after 1 and 5 minutes. However, he displayed some difficulty with left/right discrimination as well as with number reversal. Attention and concentration were deemed to be within normal limits. On the neurobiological exam, he evidenced "soft signs," which included difficulty with finger tapping, dysdiadochokinesia, and the inability to follow a three-part motor command.

DIAGNOSTIC PEER GROUP

To further clarify the diagnostic impressions obtained from the mental status examination, Sam was placed in a diagnostic group with 6 other children (4 boys, 2 girls) of approximately his age. When Sam entered the room, an immediate change was noted in his demeanor. He assumed a strut. Approaching another little boy playing with blocks, he knocked all the blocks off the table with a swipe of his arm and stuck his tongue out at the child. The clinician controlled Sam and moved him away from the other child. For several minutes Sam played quietly with another boy, but soon his antisocial behavior was repeated. This time he began hitting the other child. When the clinician was unable to control him, Sam was removed from the evaluation room.

DIAGNOSTIC IMPRESSION

Axis I: Adjustment Disorder: Oppositional Defiant Disorder
            Rule Out Major Depression
            Rule Out Dysthymic Disorder
Axis II: Antisocial Personality Disorder
            Narcissistic Personality Disorder
Axis III: Disease of the Genitourinary System: Intermittent Spasmodic Urethral Pain
            Rule Out Psychogenic Etiology
            Rule Out Recurrent Otitis Media
            Rule Out Lyme Disease
            Soft Signs on Neurological Examination
Axis IV: Moderate Financial Difficulties
            Recent Deaths in the Family
Axis V: 50

Perhaps the most dramatic clues as to the source of dysfunction with this child emerged from the family assessment, the mental status examination, and the peer group assessment. As the family attitude toward Sam became apparent, the reasons for his acting-out behavior both at home and at school became more evident. A course of treatment involving the entire family was recommended so that the underlying causes of Sam's oppositional behavior could be worked through and resolved.

Developmental Factors Affecting the Latency-Age Child

Familiarity with the major issues confronting children of this age group is essential for conducting an assessment. In particular, three main issues attain prominence with these children, including changes in the child's body from the prelatency years, advances in cognitive development, and social maturation, including acclimation to the school environment and formulation of a sense of self in society. In addition, a more entrenched sense of gender identity and of one's sex role surfaces at this time.

PHYSIOLOGICAL CHANGES

As the child leaves the prelatency years and embarks upon the years of middle childhood, several physiologic changes may be noted. For example, the child's sophistication in fine motor skills will now permit him or her to copy shapes as well as to draw a human figure with substantial detail. During this period the strivings of the oedipal child are generally overcome, as the school-age child develops a variety of defense mechanisms, including introjection, projection, and the turning of passive into active to avoid guilt feelings. With time, more refined defense mechanisms are acquired, enabling the child to assert a more autonomous sense of self (Bornstein, 1951).

Fantasy activity reaches its peak during this period, becoming extraordinarily complex and extensive. Most significant is the child's development of a relationship with the outer world. In this regard, self-regulation enables the child to achieve a broader range of emotional, cognitive,

and social competencies. Children also exhibit an awareness of their own gender and the gender of others during this period. Jacklin (1989) suggests that gender is represented internally by schemata that organize large amounts of information. Several important characteristics are associated with gender at this time. For example, boys seem drawn to sport activities that involve competition and dispute (Gilligan, 1982). In contrast, girls appear to be attracted by the demands of socialization and are more apt to participate in activities that involve mutuality and cooperation. It should be emphasized, however, that these are generalities; many girls are drawn to competitive activities and many boys pursue cooperative activities.

Of relevance to the case just discussed, latency-age children pass through a phase referred to as the "Interpretation of Rules" stage, in which the child becomes more sensitive to the spirit of rules and engages in subjective moral judgments (Piaget, 1948). Moreover, the latency-age child displays the capacity for contemplation and introspection, manifested by serious reflection upon one's actions (Kohlberg, 1969). In particular, the child assesses whether his or her behavior pleases peers as well as those in authority. These tendencies seemed particularly prominent in Sam, who appeared to be struggling with his peer relationships. In effect, Sam seemed unable to play cooperatively with peers; instead he imposed his will on others.

Differences in gender development at this age may be summarized by saying that boys develop instrumental functions involved in achieving specific ends, while girls evolve more expressive functions that implicate descriptions of the world and involve interpersonal relationships. In accord with this conclusion, girls tend to excel verbally, while boys display a greater aptitude in such areas as science and math.

COGNITIVE DEVELOPMENT

The child's cognitive development also undergoes substantial change during the latency-age period. According to Piaget (1948), this is the era of concrete operations. Essentially, the child has relinquished the egocentric thought patterns of the preschool period and embarked upon the mastery of important operations that enhance objectivity. Flexible and reversible mental operations now become common for the child, and the ability to *de-center* is noted. Mussen, Conger, Kagen, and Huston (1984) explain that decentering is the ability to focus attention on several aspects of an object or event simultaneously and to understand the relationship among these dimensions. Classification and conservation are two further hallmarks of intellectual achievement at this time. *Classification* may be defined as the capacity to group objects or concepts into one category. For example, the child comes to understand that George Washington and Abraham Lincoln belong in the same category as presidents of the United States. *Conservation* is the ability to recognize constant qualities and quantities of material, despite the fact that the material undergoes dramatic change in shape or appearance. Thus the child can understand that water and ice are two versions of the same substance. Other aspects of concrete operations become prominent during this period, including composition, associativity, and reversibility. Composition involves combining elements in order to achieve another class of items—for example, red triangles and blue triangles lead to the class of triangles, in general. Associativity involves combinations in different sequences in order to achieve similar results, and reversibility involves being able to return to an earlier point during mental processing.

Combined, these intellectual skills enhance the child's ability to master reading and arithmetic skills. In addition, these capacities are prerequisites to meaningful social interaction. Also associated with the achievement of objective mental operations comes an understanding of the finality, universality, and inevitability of death.

Researchers are convinced that the child's ability to exercise these cognitive skills is largely contingent upon his or her experience in the home environment with caregivers. This factor has bearing on the case example discussed in this chapter. Specifically, the mother complained that Sam seemed to adhere to rules that applied only to him. She also indicated that at times Sam resisted the admonitions of authority figures, such as his father, who told the child to finish his homework before he watched television. The comment that Sam's mother made about her own stepfather is also noteworthy. She indicated that he was a willful individual who did the opposite of what people told him to do. These comments provide further

insights concerning the developmental changes Sam is most likely experiencing at this time. In particular, he seems to be grappling with many of the intellectual challenges that occur during the period of concrete operations. Children of this age are especially concerned about the meaning of rules. Such issues as: "To whom do the rules apply?" "Are the rules uniformly enforced against everyone?" and "Do the rules infringe upon my autonomy?" are especially important. However, Sam's resistance to following the rules is also significant. It is possible that his rebellious behavior may be due not to an internal problem of cognitive maturation but to an environmental influence. Indeed, the child's mother may be reenacting issues from her own childhood—such as her stepfather's independence—in her relationship with her son. This intergenerational transmission of deviational authority patterns and patterns of compliance should be investigated further.

Other cognitive tendencies are also present in latency-age children. For example, as Dweck and Reppucci (1973) noted, attributional style and self-concept are notable characteristics of latency-age children. Psychologically adaptive children of this age also display a mastery orientation, meaning that they attribute success to their own abilities and do not "give up" when confronted with task failure. By 8 years of age, mastery-oriented children appear to possess an internal coping mechanism for overcoming failure and achieving the positive affect associated with accomplishment. However, children with psychological difficulties may display an opposite tendency—learned helplessness—which causes them to respond in an exaggerated and debilitated fashion to even the most minimal setbacks. Clinicians should be alert to these responses. Another cognitive tendency that emerges at this time is the proclivity to use comparative terms (Secord & Peevers, 1974). "I ride my bike" has now been replaced by "I can ride my bike better than my brother."

From the clinician's perspective, the important point to remember is that the child is formulating a perception of reality that integrates subjective impressions with objective data. That is, the child has mastered the narcissistic tasks of the preschool years—many of which involved physiologic functioning and the assertion of a sense of self—and has begun to interact with the external world enthusiastically. Through this interaction, the child recognizes the degree to which he or she is a constituent of society and must conform to the regulations of adults. As a result of this advance in cognitive skills, clinicians evaluating children of this age should be aware of the child's ability to accept and, indeed, welcome the application of rules to play activities. When a child of this age challenges authority figures, further investigation may be warranted. This form of challenging was evident in Sam. The therapist was thus requested to determine if the boy's inability to cooperate was due to lack of cognitive skill or to problems in his home environment.

SOCIAL MATURATION

No change is more apparent in the child during the latency years than the acclimation to the school environment and to social exchange with peers. Several dimensions of the school environment exert a significant effect on the child. First, the clinician should consider the degree to which the school environment conforms to the cultural expectations engendered within the child's family. Next, the school imposes certain social expectations on the child. The child's ability to meet these expectations should be considered. The third dimension of school involves the learning interaction that occurs between the student and teacher. In this regard, the therapist should ask whether the child is able to follow instructions and adhere to the teacher's directives. Finally, school is the domain within which the child confronts and learns to deal with peer interaction. In contrast to the home setting, school requires that the child conform to rules established by teachers and the school administration. Moreover, in the home the child may enjoy a special status based on his or her birth order as oldest child (and therefore leader) or youngest child (and therefore the coddled baby), whereas in the school environment the child is among equals and needs to relinquish preconceived notions about how he or she should be treated.

In general, then, during the school-age years the major arena of the child's functioning shifts away from the home to the school. Children now spend the majority of their time in the company of people to whom they are unrelated. As a result, each child constructs a social persona, a sense of self that is defined in terms of the ability to sustain meaningful relationships with others. Forming friendships with peers thus assumes utmost significance. Children of this age regard friends as helpmates with whom to share mutual interests (Damon, 1977). Moreover, peer relationships bolster the child's cognitive skills regarding competition, compromising and learning the rules of various activities. Harter (1982) describes this process by noting that the child begins to separate from the family in order to achieve a sense of union with peers.

During this period the child is transformed into a social creature. Several theorists have traced the permutations of interactional skill that occur as the child begins experimenting with his or her social identity. For example, Sullivan (1953) proposes that the latency-age child gradually replaces the standards of the family with his or her own judgment. In the early school period, Sullivan notes that the child enters the phase of social subordination, during which authority figures such as teachers—as opposed to parents—come to be the primary rule makers. Social accommodation follows, a phase during which the child acknowledges and accepts differences in others. Initially, children are intolerant of differences, but eventually they become tolerant of respected authority figures, such as teachers. With time, the child moves to the phase Sullivan has labeled the differentiation of authority figures in which teachers and parents are compared and contrasted. Next the child abandons egocentrism and embraces the conventional attitudes of peers. Finally, Sullivan posits that the child attains the capacity to view him- or herself objectively in a group. At this juncture the child's ability to balance internal impressions with external events becomes most pronounced.

Grunebaum and Solomon (1982) also have examined the transition from preschool to school-age functioning and have described a series of stages comparable to those of Sullivan. According to these researchers, during the preschool years the child is in the stage of unilateral partnership. When the child progresses to the latency years, bilateral partnerships and cooperative activities become prominent. Finally, preadolescence is typified by chumship and consensual exchange.

Although the emphasis of the latency years is on peer interaction, not all children progress through these stages of social development without trauma. Studies indicate that latency-age children generally fall into 5 categories based on their aptitude for initiating and maintaining social relationships: popular, average, rejected, neglected, and controversial. In one study, Boivin and Begin (1989) determined that "rejected" children either possess low self-esteem or, while they may view themselves positively, are perceived as being aggressive and defensive by others. Nonetheless, during the latency years, peer interactions tend to dominate and altruism toward others, particularly those in one's group, increases (Mussen & Eisenberg-Berg, 1977; Rushton, 1980).

The child's peer reputation is also likely to be of significance. Various studies have shown that peer relations during the latency years can predict future adaptation. In particular, this correlation has been established for school dropouts, criminal behavior, and psychopathology (Parker & Asher, 1987). According to Morison and Masten (1991), peer reputation assessed during the latency years also has substantial significance for predicting adolescent judgment. The clinician may gain information about the child's peer reputation from parent and teacher interviews as well as by observing the child interact in a diagnostic peer group.

An awareness of the child's developmental accomplishments in the areas of physiology, cognition, and social integration is therefore likely to help the clinician in formulating a diagnosis. Specifically, the clinician should be alert to deviations from the norm in these areas. In other words, does the child display an appropriate amount of compliance with the rules and regulations imposed by the external world, or does the child possess an unduly rebellious attitude? Finally, does the child exhibit appropriate social interactions with peers, or is the child a "loner," isolated from friends?

Assessment Techniques in the Latency-Age Child

Armed with a knowledge of the developmental peaks that characterize the latency years, the clinician may begin assessing the child. Significantly,

children of latency age—in contrast to younger children—have attained a fairly advanced level of verbal functioning and also will be less prone to retreat to fantasy or pretend behavior to express strong emotions. Thus the clinician should engage in a substantial amount of verbal interaction with the child. Of course, the child may be sufficiently agile with language to disguise emotions. Nevertheless, an astute clinician should be able to detect this form of defense. In addition, the clinician should not resort to fantasy unless the child conveys an incident of extreme stress or trauma. That is, the clinician should be aware that the child's regression to fantasy play may indicate that the child is experiencing anxiety about a particular situation.

CLINICAL INTERVIEWS

The core techniques advocated for use with latency-age children are history-taking and the mental status examination; both are performed in the context of clinical interviews. Parents also should be interviewed both alone and with the child. The child may be given the choice of being seen alone first or being present during the parental interview. General factual data, such as age, gender, race, pregnancy history, infant status at birth, achievement of developmental milestones and medical history, are obtained most effectively through specific inquiries addressed to the parents (Cox, Rutter, & Holbrook, 1981). In contrast, emotional information and material relating to family interaction is best gathered through flexible, open-ended questions.

The clinical interview should commence with a description of the presenting problem, as articulated from both the parents' point of view and the child's point of view. The child's developmental history, family history, school history, and medical history should follow. The clinician should pay particular attention to events in the child's life that have involved separations, losses, illnesses, accidents, and deaths. Moreover, because of the distinctive developmental attainments of the school-age child, the clinician should explore areas pertinent to that age group. In particular, the clinician should determine whether the child's gender identity is appropriate, whether the child complies with social directives, whether the child is able to learn in school, and whether the child interacts adaptively with peers. Moreover, the clinician should devote equal time to asking questions and to listening to responses. Not only is the content of the response significant in this regard, but the tone of voice used and the affect displayed also may provide helpful insights about the child's psychiatric status.

Interviews with the school-age child should take place at a leisurely pace in a nonthreatening atmosphere. It is advisable to have a variety of evocative games available during the session. The format of the session should be unstructured, meaning that no specific tasks will need to be accomplished; rather, the clinician and child should get acquainted in an improvised atmosphere that offers the child sufficient leeway to explore significant issues.

A rapport should be established with the child so that the full benefits of the interview may be attained. To promote this sense of rapport, the clinician should not intrude upon the child's physical space in the waiting room. Rather, the clinician should approach the child calmly and introduce him- or herself. Next, the child should be invited into the interview room. The clinician may wish to take a seat, in order that the child does not feel threatened by the towering figure of an adult. Once in the interview room, the clinician should point out some objects to orient the child and should identify a convenient place for both to sit. The clinician should not sit behind a desk, since the artificial barrier of the furniture may symbolize a psychological barrier for the child. The clinician should then ask the child's name and whether he or she knows the purpose of the visit. Subsequently, the clinician should provide his or her own view of the goals of the session.

The clinician also may wish to offer some direction. A comment such as "We can work together to figure out what's bothering you" is often helpful for initiating discussion. The clinician should reveal the extent of his or her knowledge of the child as disclosed by the parents and should assure the child of confidentiality. Throughout the interview the clinician should observe the child carefully. Needless to say, observation does not mean staring or using a probing gaze. Taking notes also should be avoided, since it may deter candid disclosures. The clinician should adopt a personable style and use open-ended questions to coax forth material. A modicum of patience is advised. It may take the child a few minutes to feel comfortable enough with the clinician to reveal deeply felt emotions. The clinician should conceal any signs of impatience or frustration. A calm demeanor and a friendly but nonintrusive attitude are conducive to obtaining confidential disclosures from the child.

Throughout the entire interview process, the clinician should be alert to both transference and countertransference responses. If the child displays an exaggerated emotional response to the clinician, it is likely that a transference reaction has been triggered. Aggression, hostility, and extreme withdrawal with no evident precipitating cause may be indications that an emotional displacement has occurred. The clinician also should be alert to countertransference responses. Some typical countertransference reactions include a feeling of repulsion awakened by the child, feelings of anxiety without an identifying source, and feelings of depression whenever a session with a particular child begins. In essence, any powerful emotional reaction that is aroused by the child is likely to be countertransferential. To deal effectively with these responses, the clinician should keep in mind certain principles. First, strong emotional urges—such as the desire to act out or regress with the child—must not be exhibited during the session. Second, the clinician needs to identity the source of the countertransference reaction. Occasionally the clinician may achieve this understanding by reviewing the patient's notes and concentrating on the source of the problem. When this technique does not work, however, the clinician should seek the insight of a supervisor.

In Sam's case, the child's willingness to cooperate with the clinician after receiving reassurance suggested that the origins of the child's disruptive behavior might lie in his social experience, as opposed to stemming from a developmental deficit.

MENTAL STATUS EXAMINATION

Besides the clinical interview, a mental status examination should be performed. This examination includes a description of physical appearance, including stigmata, gait, dress, and mannerisms; the child's response to separation from the parents; the child's mode of relating to others; spatial and temporal orientation; central nervous system functioning, including gross motor coordination and fine motor coordination. Right-left discrimination, wrist-rotation movements, finger-tapping movements, eye tracking, hopping on one foot exercises, and reading and writing difficulties may facilitate the assessment of central nervous system functioning. Speech and language skills also should be investigated. In particular, the clinician should be alert to an impoverished vocabulary, an excessive use of certain words, the failure to use descriptive words, and a tendency to remain taciturn. In addition, the clinician should distinguish between expressive and receptive language problems. Problems with expression refer to the child's ability to use language appropriately to initiate communication with others. Receptive problems, in contrast, refer to difficulties the child may encounter when attempting to understand the verbal communications of others. For example, the child may have a sensory impairment (e.g., deafness), neurological damage (e.g., cerebral palsy), be mentally retarded, have a developmental delay, or refuse to listen to others because of a behavioral disorder. Each of these possibilities should be explored by the clinician.

The child's intelligence and memory should be reviewed during the mental status examination as well. Intelligence may be approximated based on informal criteria. For example, the clinician should focus on the extent of the child's vocabulary, the level of comprehension manifested, and the degree of curiosity displayed. One effective method for testing the child's memory capacity is to use basic arithmetic computations. For example, a cognitively healthy 8-year-old child can recall 5 digits forward and 2 or 3 digits backward, while a 10-year-old child can recall 6 digits forward and 4 digits backward. The clinician should be patient when performing these tests, however, since some hesitation by the child may reflect anxiety.

The child's ability to engage in logical thought and to generate accurate perceptions about him- or herself and the world are additional areas that warrant exploration during the mental status examination. Stream of thought should reflect coherent ideas, should be relatively rapid in pace, and should flow easily. In contrast, disordered thought may involve illogical cause-effect sequences. When the pace of thinking is impaired, the child probably will display retarded thought patterns or seem confused, as if the

thoughts are "flying away." Disorder in the flow of the thought patterns is evidenced by repetitions or blocking. The child suddenly forgets what he or she is about to say and "loses his or her train of thought." As with speech and language problems, when a problem with thought or perception is encountered, the clinician should explore all possible sources for the disorder, including psychological, genetic, organic, or endocrine causes, and should systematically rule out each cause.

The mental status examination of the latency-age child also needs to consider the domain of subjective impressions. For instance, one key question involves whether the child has experienced any auditory or visual hallucinations. In this regard, the clinician should ask: "Do you ever think you hear something, but nothing is there?" and "Do you ever think you see something, but nothing is there?" Hallucinations are important clinical signs, and their underlying etiologies should be considered by the clinician. Among the causes of hallucinations to be reviewed are drug ingestion, a seizure disorder, a metabolic disorder, infectious processes, a situation of extreme stress and anxiety, a mood disorder, or schizophrenia. Related to hallucinations are episodes of suicidal ideation. Significant inquiries in this area focus on the child's wishes or impulses to engage in self-destructive acts as well as behaviors that possess the lure of danger. Pertinent questions include: "Do you ever want to hurt yourself?" and "Do you like to do dangerous things?" These kinds of inquiries are helpful in coaxing forth information that may be relevant for determining the scope of any suicidal thought patterns.

Fantasy is an area related to the latency-age child's perceptual impressions. Clinicians may use a variety of techniques to gain access to the child's fantasy domain. Analyzing the child's spontaneous play is one such technique, although the school-age child may be hesitant about engaging in symbolic play while in the clinician's presence. Other techniques are more ingenious and better suited to the child's developmental status. For example, the clinician may ask the child to describe a dream. Winkley (1982) advocates asking the question: "If you could have three wishes, what would they be?" Coaxing the child to draw a picture is another effective method for obtaining insight about the child's fantasies (Burns, 1982; Klepsch & Logie, 1982). The clinician should remember that gaining access to the child's fantasy world may be a slow and arduous process. For some children a strong therapeutic alliance is a prerequisite before they divulge their innermost perceptions. Moreover, older children may be more adept at using powerful defensive operations to disguise emotion. Therefore, clinicians are advised to be assertive when exploring the child's fantasy material.

The affective expression of the child is yet another area to be investigated during the mental status examination. Although the clinician should attempt to discern the full scope of the child's emotional repertoire, certain emotions are more important to investigate than others. In particular, negative emotions such as anger, depression, apathy, guilt, and anxiety warrant special attention. If these emotions surface during the interview or are manifested in a persistent manner, the clinician should ask the child directly about these affects.

The risk of suicidal behavior may be present in children of this age. In the case of children who seem sad or whose histories include verified instances of either self-destructive or overly aggressive behavior, the presence of suicidal ideation should be explored in a systematic fashion. When the child recounts overt suicidal ideation or self-destructive behavior, the clinician should assess the circumstances leading up to the episode. Was this behavior planned or impulsive? Why did the child undertake such a course of action? Most significantly, the clinician may wish to investigate whether the child understands the implications of death. For example, does the child understand that death is permanent and irreversible? Because self-destructive manifestations have such dire consequences for children, the clinician should be exceptionally thorough when making these inquiries. For example, the clinician is advised to ask precise questions about the present episode and the motivation underlying the episode and should inquire about previous suicidal thoughts and behaviors and about any related experience. Evidence of depression should be investigated too, with attention to appetite, sleep patterns, and changes in relationships with peers. Clinicians should note that when the child communicates a clear intent to hurt him- or herself, and when factors such as family support and peer relationships reveal problems, the child may be at risk for self-destructive behavior. Other risk factors include

hopelessness about the future, poor judgment, and poor impulse control.

Assessing the child's interpersonal abilities is vital for determining the level of the child's functioning. The clinician should explore three primary areas in particular. First, how does the child get along with family members, including parents and siblings? The clinician should determine if the child has a favorite family member as well as a least favorite. Interpersonal relations with peers also should be explored. The clinician may ask the child to describe his or her friends and to discuss his or her best friend. Finally, the child's perceptions about teachers should be explored. Teachers are authority figures, and the child's attitude in this regard will be apt to reveal how he or she deals with authority.

During every assessment, an effort should be made to explore the child's defense profile. As with other areas of functioning, the best mode of investigation is thorough inquiry. In this regard, the clinician might ask the child whether he or she has any problems. A negative response would suggest denial. Observing the child drawing an object may provide information concerning an obsessive or a compulsive tendency. For example, does the child erase and rearrange frequently? Is the drawing neat to the point of being fastidious? Similar strategies may help discern the presence of other defenses.

A comprehensive psychiatric evaluation of the child permits the clinician to arrive at a viable explanation for the child's signs and symptoms. The mental status examination should reflect consideration of all the developmental factors affecting the child—including somatic, cognitive, socioaffective, and motivational factors. From this comprehensive portrait, the clinician attains a multidimensional perspective on the child that leads to the formulation of an accurate diagnosis and effective treatment goals. If the clinician cannot coherently explain findings at the conclusion of a mental status examination, the assessment probably has not been complete.

During the evaluation, the clinician's primary task is to assess the child's level of functioning; however, it is also important for the clinician to forge an alliance with the child. A rapport of this type is especially critical because it facilitates the evaluation as well as the transition into treatment. To reinforce this alliance, the clinician should be as candid about the interview process as possible. If interviews are conducted, the clinician should inform the child in advance of the procedure to be followed. During the final interview session, the clinician should share with the child and family the main findings and consider their point of view about the procedures of the next stage of the process. The clinician may also reinforce the theme of confidentiality and ask the child if there is anything he or she does not want the parents to know. The clinician also should ask whether the child has any further comments about the interview process. At such times, children often express emotions that have been pent up inside during the interview process. These comments are often of significant importance.

Although the mental status examination generally occurs in an unstructured environment, occasionally the clinician may wish to conduct a structured interview with the child using standardized tests, questionnaires, and rating scales. Many diagnostic instruments are useful screening tools that may be helpful in evaluating the child's functioning. Structured interviews help the clinician focus on a particular area. Among the most popular structured interviews are the Diagnostic Interview for Children and Adolescents (Herjanic & Campbell, 1977; Herjanic et al., 1975) and the Diagnostic Interview Schedule for Children developed by Costello, Edelbrock, Dukan, Kalas, and Klaric (1984). Clinicians should be flexible about using these structured instruments, although—if used properly—they are likely to significantly enhance diagnostic insight about the child.

One adjunctive procedure that may be employed in a child of this age is use of the diagnostic peer group. As has been noted, children of the middle childhood years possess a remarkable array of developmental competencies, including physiological, emotional, and cognitive skills. No form of assessment can better display the child's skill at integrating these advances than the peer group.

When using a peer group evaluation, the clinician should be alert to several phenomena pertinent to the child's developmental skills. First, has the child attained the physiological maturity expected by this age? That is, is the child of comparable size as peers, and do physical movements and coordination abilities indicate physical growth commensurate with age. Related to physiologic maturity is gender identity. In this regard, the clinician should be alert to the tendency of the latency-age child to exhibit gender-related activities. For example, do girls engage in cooperative play while boys manifest competitive behavior? Gender guidelines should not be utilized rigidly, but they do offer a basic indication of the child's status.

The cognitive achievements of the latency-age child are also likely to emerge forcefully in the peer group setting. In particular, the proclivity for adherence to rules is likely to find expression as the child interacts with peers. Moreover, the child's ability to use classification skills and to engage in fine motor activities are additional qualities effectively tested in a social environment. Opportunities for the observation of the child's social skills are a further advantage of the peer group. Does the child engage easily with peers and seek to establish friendships, or do anomalous tendencies emerge, such as the tendency to withdraw or to dominate others? Finally, the child's ability to engage in fantasy should be evaluated. By this age, fantasy activity has peaked. Although the child may not be as enamored of make-believe behavior as earlier, other areas (social skills, vocabulary) have progressed substantially, enabling the child to use fantasy appropriately for the purposes of escape. Therefore, this tendency should be evaluated.

Conclusion

Evaluating a latency-age child can be a formidable task for the clinician. As noted, such children have essentially achieved a developmental plateau. That is, they are no longer undergoing the rapid changes of the infancy and preschool years; nor have they yet begun to experience the dramatic physiologic changes of adolescence. Nonetheless, during this period of time the child first negotiates an equilibrium between the world of inner perceptions and the domain of external objective reality. This is also the time when children become entranced with rules, perhaps using such organizers as a way of imposing order on the world. Another significant change that occurs at this time concerns the child's social maturation: For the first time, the child attains a social identity in the school environment. Peer relationships—or the lack thereof—become important criteria for evaluating the child's psychological health. In addition, this is the age when gender identity becomes evident. In this context, gender identity does not refer so much to an awareness of one's sexuality but rather to the sense that one belongs to a certain group—male or female—and that certain behaviors are associated with one's group.

The evaluation of a latency-age child strives to clarify the status of developmental functioning in light of these advances. The focus of the evaluation will be on clinical interviews conducted both with the parents present and alone with the child. During an interview with the child alone, the clinician is advised to use both inquiry and observational techniques to conduct the mental status examination. In some instances, a series of interviews may be required. In addition, at times standardized tests in the form of structured interviews will be helpful for obtaining certain information concerning the child.

Above all, the clinician should focus on establishing a relationship of trust in order to clarify the nature of developmental functioning in all areas. As a result of such a relationship, the clinician will be more likely to obtain an optimal amount of information and compliance.

REFERENCES

Boivin, M., & Begin, G. (1989). Peer status and self-perception among early elementary school children: The case of the rejected children. *Child Development, 60,* 591–596.

Bornstein, B. (1951). On latency. *Psychoanalytic Study of the Child, 6,* 279–285.

Burns, R. C. (1982). *Self-growth in families. Kinetic family drawings (K-F-D). Research and applications.* New York: Brunner/Mazel.

Costello, A. J., Edelbrock, C. S., Dulcan, M. K., Kalas, R., & Klaric, S. H. (1984). *Development and Testing of the NIMH Diagnostic Interview Schedule for Children on a clinical population: Final report* (Contract #RFP-DB-81-0027). Rockville, MD: Center for Epidemiological Studies, National Institute of Mental Health.

Cox, A., Rutter, M., & Holbrook, D. (1981). Psychiatric interviewing techniques. V: Experimental study: Eliciting factual information. *British Journal of Psychiatry, 139,* 29.

Damon, W. (1977). *The world of the child.* San Francisco: Jossey-Bass.

Dweck, C. S., & Reppucci, N. D. (1973). Learned helplessness and reinforcement responsibility in children. *Journal of Personality and Social Psychology, 25,* 109–116.

Gilligan, C. (1982). *In a different voice: Psychological theory and women's development.* Cambridge, MA: Harvard University Press.

Grunebaum, H., & Solomon, L. (1982). Toward a theory of peer relationships. II: On the stages of social development and their relationship to group psychotherapy. *International Journal of Group Psychotherapy, 32,* 283–307.

Harter, S. (1982). The perceived competence scale for children. *Child Development, 53,* 87–97.

Herjanic, B., & Campbell, W. (1977). Differentiating psychiatrically disturbed children on the basis of a structured interview. *Journal of Abnormal Child Psychology, 5,* 127–134.

Herjanic B., Herjanic M., Brown F., & Wheatt, T. (1975). Are children reliable reporters? *Journal of Abnormal Child Psychology, 3,* 41–48.

Jacklin, C. N. (1989). Female and male: Issues of gender. *American Psychology, 44,* 127–133.

Klepsch, M., & Logie, L. (1982). *Children draw and tell.* New York: Brunner/Mazel.

Kohlberg, L. (1969). Stage and sequence: The cognitive-development approach to socialization. In D. A. Goslin (Ed.), *Handbook of socialization theory and research* (pp. 347–480). Chicago: Rand-McNally.

Minuchin, P. (1977). *The middle years of childhood.* Belmont, CA: Brooks/Cole.

Morison, P., & Masten, A. S. (1991). Peer reputation in middle childhood as a predictor of adaptation in adolescence: A seven-year follow-up. *Child Development, 62,* 991–1007.

Mussen, P. H., Conger, J. J., Kagen, J., & Huston, A. C. (1984). *Child development and personality.* New York: Harper & Row.

Mussen, P. H., & Eisenberg-Berg, N. (1977). *Roots of caring, sharing, and helping: The development of prosocial behavior in children.* San Francisco: W. H. Freeman.

Parker, J. G., & Asher, S. R. (1987). Peer relations and later personal adjustment: Are low-accepted children at risk? *Psychological Bulletin, 102,* 357–389.

Pfeffer, C. (1986). *The suicidal child.* New York: Guilford Press.

Piaget, J. (1948). *The moral judgement of the child.* New York: Free Press.

Rushton, J. P. (1980). *Altrusim, socialization, and society.* Englewood Cliffs, NJ: Prentice-Hall.

Sullivan, H. S. (1953). *The interpersonal theory of psychiatry.* New York: W. W. Norton.

Secord, P. F., & Peevers, B. H. (1974). The development and attribution of person concepts. In T. Mis-chel (Ed.), *Understanding other persons* (pp. 117–142). Oxford: Blackwell.

Winkley, L. (1982). The implication of children's wishes. Research note. *Journal of Child Psychology/Psychiatry, 23,* 477.

20 / The Prepubertal Child: Assessment, Evaluation, and Diagnosis

Paul V. Trad

Introduction

When evaluating the child of prepubertal age, the clinician is dealing with an individual who has achieved a separate identity and whose sense of self is distinct from that of other family members. Of course, younger children are also individuals, but they feel strongly bound to and influenced by the wishes of their parents. This tendency is modified during the late latency years, however. The child's body begins to change, and, for the first time, peer judgments assume paramount significance, while the appraisals of parents or teachers may be viewed with skepticism. The child who acts out at this age may be doing so simply because he or she believes that his or her body is changing too slowly or too quickly, or because he or she is not accepted by the clique of popular children. The family's inability to accept and acclimate to changes in the child's body also may lead to acting out behavior.

The evaluation of such a child should take these developmental factors into consideration. Although the clinician should listen carefully to the parent's explanation of problems encountered with the child, it is recommended that the child be interviewed separately. During the interview, the clinician should first establish a sense of rapport with the child by listening patiently. The child should be treated as a mature preadolescent, and the clinician should be careful not to impose as much authority as might be the case with a younger child. The clinician may have to tolerate initial silence or hostility by the child who views the clinician as yet another intrusive adult. But the clinician should not be deterred by this attitude and should persevere.

Patience is likely to be rewarded in these cases. The clinician should assure the child that confidentiality will be maintained. The primary components of the mental status examination should be based on observation and inquiry. In certain instances, standardized measures may be advisable. Above all, however, the clinician is apt to find that the child's verbal disclosures will be abundant. From these prolific disclosures, a comprehensive perception of the child may be obtained leading to an accurate diagnosis.

Case History

The following case example may serve as an illustration of the process of assessment of an older grade-school child. Roger G., a 10½-year-old black male, was referred for a psychiatric evaluation by his teacher because of a progressive deterioration in school performance.

HISTORY OF PRESENTING PROBLEM

This child presented with a variety of problems. First, Roger's mother complained that her son "doesn't make sense." According to the mother, the child mumbles to himself and often seems "lost in his own world." She is especially concerned that Roger may have inherited a form of mental illness from his father, a paranoid schizophrenic. Second, Roger's school performance has recently deteriorated dramatically. Beginning at least 2 months before presentation, a marked decline in the child's performance on standardized tests was noted. Third, Roger's teacher also noted that the child appeared to be "depressed and irritable." At school, he was withdrawn. "He doesn't mix with the others," his teacher said, and she attributed the tendency of the other children to ostracize Roger to his small physical stature. Intermittent biting of his fingers began approximately 4 months prior to presentation. Moreover, nocturnal enuresis is reported to occur 2 to 3 times each week. Finally, the mother reports that the child has a history of being overly sensitive to criticism, cries easily, and has difficulty maintaining peer relationships. According to the mother, Roger has few friends, no close friends, and often plays alone.

DEVELOPMENTAL AND MEDICAL HISTORIES

Roger is the product of an unplanned, full-term pregnancy that was complicated by maternal hypertension. The mother's blood pressure normalized prior to the birth. Spontaneous vaginal delivery was complicated by meconium aspiration. Presumably, this accounts for Apgar scores of 5 and 10 at 1 minute and 5 minutes after birth, respectively. Roger's birth weight was 5 pounds, 7 ounces. When the child was 6 weeks old, he was admitted to the hospital with diarrhea and fever of unknown origin; both conditions resolved after a few days.

Roger's mother reports that she had been told by a gynecologist that she would be unable to bear children because of pelvic inflammatory disease; she was therefore "shocked" to learn that she was pregnant. Although Roger's father was excited about the pregnancy, he became withdrawn and taciturn as the delivery date approached. "At one point, he suspected that I had slept with another man and that the baby was not his," Roger's mother reported. While Roger's mother denies that she experienced postpartum depression after the birth, she says that she frequently envisioned herself lying in a coffin. The duration and significance of this psychological state are not known. Nor did the mother seek psychiatric treatment.

At 9 months of age, Roger developed asthma and subsequently experienced episodes of respiratory distress that mandated hospitalization. He is currently treated with an aerosol agent. Roger's mother reports that some of the children at school have teased her son because he occasionally uses a nasal inhalant and is physically small for his age. The mother also reports that the child is allergic to chocolate, milk, and fish, although specific reactions to these foods have not been confirmed. Roger's inability to eat certain foods has led to some teasing by classmates, who apparently have referred to the child as a "mama's boy."

There is no history of developmental delay with this child. According to his mother, Roger was a happy baby who achieved all developmental milestones on schedule. He sat up at 5 months, began standing at 9 months, spoke his first word ("mama") at 11 months, and was speaking in complete sentences by 2½ years. He was breast-fed during the first 3 months of life and toilet-trained between ages 2 and 3 years. He was enrolled in day care center at age 2½ years and began kindergarten at 4 years.

FAMILY ASSESSMENT

Roger is an only child. His mother is one of 8 siblings. She allegedly had an incestuous relationship with one of her older brothers. This older brother also set fire to the family home when he was a teenager. Roger's mother reports that several of her siblings have problems with substance abuse and that her father was an alcoholic who received no treatment for his drinking problem. The maternal grandmother is reported as being "serious and not affectionate."

Roger's mother comments that she herself began drinking heavily while she was still a teenager and often frequented bars with her sister. However, she says she stopped using alcohol at age 18 when she married her first husband. This man apparently used cocaine and was physically abusive to her; she divorced him 3 years later. Shortly thereafter, she married Roger's father, a man 7 years younger than herself. Roger's mother states that even at the beginning of her relationship with Roger's father, she was aware that "what he says seems twisted ... but I can usually understand him." Roger's father worked at a construction site for 5 years before being laid off when Roger was just a few months old. At that time, the father left the household to seek work in a different part of the country.

During her husband's absence, Roger's mother entered psychotherapy for treatment of her depression. A few months later, her husband returned. He worked sporadically until he experienced an episode of paranoia. He was placed in a psychiatric hospital and diagnosed with paranoid schizophrenia. Upon his release from the hospital, Roger's father took antipsychotic medication and remained stable for several months. However, according to the mother, her husband subsequently disappeared. In turn, she became depressed again. "I couldn't shake the feeling of hopelessness." Rather than seek treatment, however, she prayed with members of her fundamentalist church. According to Roger's mother, the prayer meetings helped and eventually her depression lifted.

MENTAL STATUS EXAMINATION

Roger presented as a thin and short Afro-American male, casually attired, and wearing thick eyeglasses. He was very small in stature for his age. Initially, he would not meet with the interviewer without his mother being present; he clung to her dress and behaved like a much younger child. He appeared to be shy and soft-spoken, but as the interview progressed, he became more relaxed. After several minutes, he agreed that his mother could leave and that he would speak alone with the therapist. By this time, he was easily engaged.

Roger displayed no evidence of psychomotor agitation or retardation. After initial hesitation, he made appropriate eye contact. His stream of thought was coherent and goal-directed. Although he spoke at a normal pace, after several minutes a loosening of verbal associations began to occur and the therapist was unable to follow his thought processes. When provided with an opportunity to clarify the meaning of his verbal productions, however, the child became intelligible and coherent. Roger's mood was generally euthymic, although he openly acknowledged that sometimes he experienced sadness and loneliness, feelings he attributed to teasing from his peers. Roger said he was teased because he was not as big as the other boys, he wore glasses, and he wasn't good at

sports. A broad range of affect was observed in the child.

Roger displayed no evidence of delusional beliefs. He acknowledged, however, that at night he sometimes became afraid that monsters would visit him. When pressed further, he appeared capable of distinguishing between fantasy and reality. His thought content focused primarily on two themes: being the object of his classmates' scorn and concern that he did not have a father. He confided at one point that sometimes he wanted to "put a knife in my heart" because he felt so bad about being teased. The child's play activities were adaptive, although unenthusiastic. However, his drawings of human figures suggested the possibility of gender-role confusion, since the "person" he drew had a female head and torso but was male from the waist down. In addition, Roger gestured to a substantial degree with his hands and his gestures often had an effeminate quality.

DIAGNOSTIC PEER GROUP

When placed in a group of peers for the purposes of evaluation, several of the initial diagnostic impressions regarding Roger's physical and social skills were confirmed. For example, while the child initially approached some boys of his age, he immediately retreated when the other boys rebuffed his efforts at friendship. One boy roughly pushed Roger and called him a "shrimp." Rather than challenge this appellation, Roger withdrew to a corner without protest and spent several minutes crying and biting his nails. He refused to accept comfort from the clinician at this time.

Roger then remained isolated from his peers for almost 20 minutes. He found an easel and paint and appeared content to play by himself. After a half hour had elapsed, however, he was evidently lonely. Gazing around, he finally joined a group of girls playing with a doll house. Within a few minutes, the girls appeared to have accepted Roger, who played with them contentedly until the end of the session.

DIAGNOSTIC IMPRESSION

Axis I: Adjustment Disorder
            Sexual and Gender Identity Disorder
Axis II: Deferred
Axis III: Asthma
            Enuresis

Axis IV: Paternal Schizophrenia, Familial Substance
          Abuse
Axis V: 51

A course of individual treatment was recommended in this case to further explore the impending adolescence of this child and his adjustment to the gender changes attendant to puberty. Sessions were also advised for Roger's mother in order that she be able to achieve a better understanding of the developmental transformations her son was undergoing.

Developmental Factors Affecting the Prepubertal Child

During the latency years of development, most children experience a degree of stability in terms of their developmental aptitude. That is, while maturational change proceeds throughout all the years of middle childhood, the change is gradual, cumulative, and, from the child's point of view, tends to be predictable. In other words, the child may reliably envision that the following year he or she will most likely grow several inches or be able to read at a more advanced grade level. A dramatic transition occurs, however, in the midst of the late latency years. The child is now on the verge of adolescence and puberty, triggering physical changes as well as a host of cognitive and social changes.

Puberty signifies a form of physical maturation that culminates in the ability to engage in sexual reproduction (Petersen & Taylor, 1980). In actuality, the onset of puberty is not precipitous; instead, it is a lengthy process that involves the awakening of myriad hormonal systems that have been present but dormant since infancy (Tanner, 1962). Although—from a medical perspective—the process may be lengthy, from the child's perspective puberty tends to be a sudden and, because its effect differs from anything the child has experienced previously, an unpredictable sequence of events. Physical changes caused by the onset of puberty may awaken self-consciousness in the child.

The implications of puberty are diverse and affect several developmental domains simultane-

ously. First, it is important to emphasize that although there are norms, puberty begins at different ages for different children. As a general rule, girls undergo pubertal changes 2 years earlier than boys; but even within the female population, pubertal alterations may begin as early as 10 years of age or as late as the midteen years (Tanner, 1962). As a result, pubertal changes may be experienced as being traumatic for the child who matures early as well as a source of pain and stress for the child whose maturational clock is slower than that of his or her peers.

Because of the dramatic physiologic changes that attend puberty and the uncertain age of onset, the expectation of puberty becomes a significant social issue for children during the late latency years. For perhaps the first time, children become aware of physical differences not noticed previously in size and appearance among their peers. Moreover, these differences may acquire exaggerated importance because of their diverse nature and the child's sensitivity. For example, girls are often physically taller than boys during the years of late latency—a phenomenon that may cause confusion, embarrassment, and even fear since the child has difficulty predicting which changes will occur next. In addition, the child will need to adapt psychologically to both primary sex changes and secondary sex changes, with the latter having a direct bearing on reproductive capabilities. Petersen (1988) has noted that two aspects of pubertal change may effect the child's psychological well-being—pubertal status and pubertal timing. Both of these phenomena significantly affect the social status with peers as well as impact on the child's sense of self.

Boxer and Petersen (1986) have noted that the impending changes accompanying puberty may be influenced by the child's psychological processing. That is, as children become more cognizant of the physiologic changes likely to occur to their bodies in the imminent future, they may—through both thought and action—influence these changes. Modifying one's diet to affect metabolic functioning is, for example, one method that has been used to prevent or hasten the onset of puberty. As Frisch (1980, 1983) notes, a particular metabolic level is necessary to trigger pubertal events. Girls with anorexia nervosa consume so little food that the metabolic rate is altered, thereby interrupting or preventing the onset of the menstrual cycle. Moreover, if anorectic behavior patterns begin at an early enough age and persist for a long enough period of time, a form of stunted growth may result (Garfinkel & Garner, 1982). Thus, in the late-latency child, physiological processes are by no means segregated from psychological and social processes.

Besides the imminence of puberty, other key developmental changes also occur during the years of the late-latency period. For example, the child's ability to engage in abstract thinking becomes more sophisticated and refined (Keating & Clark, 1980). This is the age when the child acquires the capacity to understand the perspectives of others. Nonetheless, a concurrent focus on the self also flourishes at this time (Elkind, 1975). One reason for the increased self-awareness is that the child becomes sensitive to the physiological changes occurring to him- or herself and to peers. This enhanced self-awareness may cause the child to experience greater sensitivity to criticism from others as well as more introspective behavior. Acceptance or rejection by peers becomes a key issue during this epoch. Researchers have shown that peer acceptance leads to a host of adaptive prosocial behaviors, including cooperation and nonaggressive tendencies (Coie, Dodge, & Coppotelli, 1982; French & Waas, 1985). Social competence in school is also related to classroom achievement, according to Wentzel (1991). In contrast, rejected children may manifest a broad spectrum of aberrant social behaviors, including withdrawal from peers.

During this transitional period, the child tends to acquire a self-critical attitude. Some studies have shown that the self-image of preadolescents and early adolescents is more negative and less stable than during both early childhood and the late teen years (Abramowitz, Petersen, & Schulenberg, 1984; Simmons, Rosenberg, & Rosenberg, 1973). Perceptions of one's physical attractiveness assumes prominence at this time. For girls the feeling of being unattractive physically may have overwhelmingly negative psychological effects, while for boys less than optimal skill in sports and physical prowess may trigger feelings of debilitation. Small physical size impairing athletic ability may have been a key factor in the case discussed in this chapter. Depressive affect tends to become manifest in girls of this age for the first time, an outcome that may be attributed to multiple variables, including genetics, hormones and environmental factors. In one study conducted by Richards et al. (1990), a sample of 284 male and female adolescents was studied. The researchers found that the girls in the study exhibited a poorer body image and less satisfaction with their weight. In contrast, boys had a more positive body image and were significantly more satisfied with their weight. As a result, clinicians evaluating children during the late-latency years should be more attuned to signs of depressed affect in girls than in boys. Moreover, the clinician should be cognizant that these negative perceptions often will be tied to the child's image of her physical status, appearance, and development.

Another phenomenon that tends to begin during the late-latency years may be referred to as a proliferation of the sense of identity. By the time a child is 2 years old, a coherent and intact sense of self generally has emerged (Stern, 1985). This identity tends to remain stable until the late-latency years. At that time, the child is confronted with a variety of changes that all converge at once—physiological, social, psychological—each of which seems to require a different and more sophisticated response. As a result, there is a greater tendency to segment aspects of one's functioning and to evolve different "selves," each of which is ascendant and assumes priority in a particular domain. Offer and Sabshin (1984), for instance, refer to the onset of adolescence as a critical period for the evolution of the self. The child's improved ability to engage in abstract thought with the advent of formal operations skill results in a more complex understanding of the sense of self. Physiological and social changes also exert a dramatic impact on the way in which the child views him- or herself in terms of others. For example, bodily changes to the child or his or her peers bring the issue of sexuality to the forefront, while other physiological changes, such as increased stature, mean that the child will be granted more independence by the family.

In order to understand aberrant attitudes in the prepubertal child, the clinician should be familiar with the response of normal children of this age. For example, normal children of late-latency age are likely to take pride in their physiological development and to have positive feelings regarding puberty. Normal children also have a positive view of their social identity. They believe they are capable of making friends easily and will be successful in social endeavors. The clinician evaluating children of this age should therefore be cognizant of the implications of change for late-latency children. In particular, the clinician should clarify the child's attitude toward physiological, social, and psychological change. The manner in which these developmental advances affect the sense of self often will reveal the etiology of maladaptive behavior patterns.

Assessment Techniques in the Prepubertal Child

The assessment of the prepubertal child is an enormous challenge to the clinician. As a preliminary matter, the clinician should keep in mind that he or she and *not* the child—no matter how sophisticated or mature—is in charge of conducting the interview. While younger children may present difficulties because they cannot communicate well with the clinician verbally, with children of late-latency age an opposite problem may prevail. That is, the child may use language to be less than candid with the clinician, to set the agenda for the exchange, and to disguise genuine emotions.

One of the first issues that should be addressed with a child of this age is confidentiality. To what extent should the clinician reveal material the parents have provided, and how should the clinician express confidentiality to the child? The best approach concerning this issue is one of candor, if for no other reason than that the child probably will be able to discern if the clinician is not telling the truth or is concealing some information. If a child of this age senses that material is being concealed, establishing rapport with him or her subsequently will be almost impossible. Thus the clinician should rephrase the parents' key remarks. The clinician also should tell the child that while the parents will generally be kept apprised of the child's progress, specific material will not be revealed, unless the child specifically wants that material revealed.

The primary instrument of assessment with the late-latency child remains the clinical interview.

The clinician should begin this interview by asking the child to express his or her views concerning the parent's remarks or to discuss the issues that are bothering him or her. Early in the interview it is important for the clinician to establish a rapport with the child. Thus the clinician should convey genuine interest in the content of the child's remarks, should listen carefully to these remarks without being judgmental, and should make a special effort to be candid. At the same time, however, the clinician should not attempt to be the child's pal or buddy. Some clinicians err in thinking that they have to prove themselves to the late-latency child. Common miscalculations include overidentification with the prepubertal child's dress or talk, as if the clinician is a buddy who may be confided in; on the contrary, the clinician should not overidentify with the child in any respect. Nor should the clinician talk down to or belittle the child. It is important to remember that children of this age are especially sensitive. Their burgeoning sexuality and the imminent changes in their bodies may make them particularly wary of an adult authority figure whose task is to probe their consciousness. The clinician will do best to treat the child seriously without relinquishing the role of a beneficent authority.

During the interview, the clinician should give the child his or her undivided attention, patience, and a sympathetic ear. If the clinician experiences boredom, impatience, or uncertainty, these feelings generally connote a countertransference response that should be thoroughly examined.

Children of this age may be embarrassed about opening up and disclosing sensitive information to an adult. Yet at the same time they often are desperate to obtain the opinions of an adult on an issue of significance to them. To circumvent this delicate situation, the preadolescent child may prefer to speak in terms of a third person. For example, the child may say something to the effect of "... my friend got into trouble because he ..." or "... a girl in my class tried ..." When this kind of third-person inquiry is posed, the clinician should reply in a clinically honest but emotionally neutral fashion. The child most likely knows that the clinician is not being fooled and vice versa. Yet going along with this charade is important for bolstering the child's sense of esteem. It allows the child to raise issues about the self that would evoke shame or embarrassment if spoken of directly. This is one method that allows the preadolescent to "test" the extent to which he or she is being accepted, protected, and taken seriously by the clinician.

The clinician also should be prepared to endure an initially challenging relationship with the prepubertal child. Indeed, the preteen may be overt in his or her hostility, refuse to talk, or berate the clinician. It is important to remember that the child of this age is beginning to reexamine his or her relationship with the parents and, ultimately, to rebel against the parents' authority. Thus, the clinician will need to convey interest, patience, and resilience. Again, the clinician should recognize that this is the child's strategy for determining how much the clinician is to be trusted. Comments like "Am I right in assuming that you are pretty angry about being here today? Why don't you share some of that anger with me because maybe I can help" are often persuasive and eventually coax the child to begin opening up.

Although the clinician may permit the child some latitude, ultimately he or she also should be careful about not permitting the child to control the interview process. This is a bad precedent to set, because once the child understands that he or she can manipulate the session, that control will not be relinquished without a struggle. Therefore, silences should not be allowed to continue for too long because they may degenerate into a futile power struggle. Moreover, the clinician should not be dogmatic about the length of the interview or about what will take place during it. The need for a session to last 50 minutes should not be viewed as mandatory. Preadolescents may find the toys in the interview room to be somewhat patronizing, since they may wish to be treated more seriously by the adult figures in their lives. The prepubertal child's interest in the opinions of others—especially peers—also may make him or her more receptive to listening to and sharing perceptions with a sympathetic adult. As a result, it may be helpful to vary the format of the interview. The clinician can suggest a walk, for example. Walking also helps the prepubertal child avoid maintaining eye contact with the clinician, a condition that may be intimidating for the child.

As a general principle, the clinician should be available to listen to the late-latency child. Above all, children of this age wish to be understood, and eventually they will begin talking and disclosing substantial information. Moreover, the primary means by which these children will reveal information is through conversation. Therefore, the clinician will need to rely heavily on listening skills. On occasion, the child also may ask for the clinician's opinion. The clinician's goal at these times should be to offer support and convey understanding to the preadolescent child. This attitude will go a long way toward establishing a rapport.

Although listening is important, the clinician should realize as well that children of this age need to address some difficult issues. In particular, the clinician should inquire about sensitive areas such as hallucinations, suicide, drug use, and sexual behavior. Such questions should be asked in a matter-of-fact manner. With regard to these issues, the clinician should again keep in mind the sensitive developmental status of the prepubertal child and recognize that the child may be eager to keep certain information from parents.

Because the late-latency stage is such an awkward developmental period, clinicians often may find that preadolescents evoke strong countertransference responses. For example, a clinician may feel the need to solicit the child's approval, may overidentify with the child—especially concerning the child's feelings toward the parents—or may feel threatened by the child. The clinician should remember that the years of preadolescence are difficult ones because the child is grappling with his or her sexual identity, with separation from the parents, and with the acceptance of peers. Therefore, any strong countertransference issues evoked by the child's arrogance, competitiveness, seductiveness, or negativism should be clarified thoroughly by the clinician and not be permitted to intrude into the child's evaluation and treatment.

In assessing the preadolescent child, the clinician should review all of the major factors that are considered in any mental status examination. For example, the child's physical appearance, posture, psychomotor functioning, orientation to time and place, ability to relate adaptively to others, speech and language skills, memory, intelligence, quality of thought and perception, fantasy material, affective display, drive behavior, and defensive operations all should be evaluated. In certain cases, the clinician may wish to use a standardized diagnostic test to assess a particular area of the child's functioning. Moreover, diagnostic peer groups are often valuable adjunctive tools for determining the degree to which the child is capable of interacting adaptively with peers.

It is advised that the clinician keep in mind, at all times, the primary developmental issues confronting these children. On the verge of puberty, many of them are concerned about their physical development and their status with peers. The clinician should be sensitive to these issues throughout the mental status examination, communicating an acknowledgment of the child's maturity as well as a sense of support.

Conclusion

The years of late latency are highly sensitive ones for the child beginning to mature sexually. During this time, the child may become acutely sensitive about his or her body and about the perceptions of peers. This sensitivity may emerge in a variety of ways. The child may become disruptive at school or demonstrate an almost opposite response by becoming taciturn and withdrawn. Needless to say, either attitude may present a challenge to the clinician. The clinician should first strive to form an alliance with the child. Listening to the child's inquiries and answering the child's questions in a serious manner conducive to establishing a rapport is vital. Evaluation with this age group requires the child to be given appropriate leeway, while at the same time, the clinician should assert sufficient authority.

Since preadolescent children rarely engage in fantasy play, a good deal of emphasis will fall on the clinical interview. These preadolescents generally will be prepared to talk to an adult and to use verbal expression for the purpose of conveying their emotions. The clinician should take advantage of the child's verbal ability as an opportunity to observe and to evaluate the customary elements of the mental status examination.

REFERENCES

Abramowitz, R. H., Petersen, A. C., & Schulenberg, J. E. (1984). Changes in self-image during early adolescence. In D. Offer, E. Ostrov, & K. Howard (Eds.), *Patterns of adolescent self-image* (pp. 19–28). San Francisco: Jossey-Bass.

Boxer, A. M., & Petersen, A. C. (1986). Pubertal change in a family context. In G. K. Leigh & G. W. Peterson (Eds.), *Adolescents in families* (pp. 73–103). Cincinnati: South-Western Publishing.

Coie, J. D., Dodge, K. A., & Coppotelli, H. (1982). Dimensions and types of status: A cross-age perspective. *Developmental Psychology, 18*, 557–570.

Elkind, D. (1975). Perceptual development in children. *American Scientist, 63* (5), 533–541.

French, D. C., & Waas, G. A. (1985). Behavior problems of peer-neglected and peer-rejected elementary-age children: Parent and teacher perspectives. *Child Development, 56*, 246–252.

Frisch, R. E. (1980). Fatness, puberty, and fertility. *Natural History, 89*, 16.

Frisch, R. E. (1983). Fatness, puberty, and fertility: The effects of nutrition and physical training on menarche and ovulation. In J. Brooks-Gunn & A. C. Petersen (Eds.), *Girls at puberty: Biological and psychosocial perspectives* (pp. 29–49). New York: Plenum Press.

Garfinkel, P. E., & Garner, D. M. (1982). *Anorexia nervosa: A multidimensional perspective.* New York: Brunner/Mazel.

Keating, D. P., & Clark, L. V. (1980). Development of physical and social reasoning in adolescence. *Developmental Psychology, 23*, 23–30.

Offer, D., & Sabshin, M. (1984). *Normality and the life cycle: A critical integration.* New York: Basic Books.

Petersen, A. C. (1988). Adolescent development. *Annual Review of Psychology, 39*, 583–607.

Petersen, A. C., & Taylor, B. (1980). The biological approach to adolescence. In J. Adelson (Ed.), *Handbook of adolescent psychology* (pp. 117–155). New York: John Wiley & Sons.

Richards, M. H., Boxer, A. W., Petersen, A. C., & Albrecht, R. (1990). Relation of weight to body image in pubertal girls and boys from two communities. *Developmental Psychology, 26*, 313–321.

Simmons, R. G., Rosenberg, M. F., & Rosenberg, M. C. (1973). Disturbance in self-image at adolescence. *American Sociological Review, 38*, 553–568.

Stern, D. N. (1985). *The interpersonal world of an infant: A view from psychoanalysis and developmental psychology.* New York: Basic Books.

Tanner, J. M. (1962). *Growth at adolescence.* Springfield, IL: Charles C. Thomas.

Wentzel, K. R. (1991). Relations between social competence and academic achievement in early adolescence. *Child Development, 62*, 1066–1078.

SECTION III
Syndromes of the Grade-School Child

21 / Impact of Divorce on School-Age Children: Assessment and Intervention Strategies

Vivienne Roseby and Judith Wallerstein

Children of grade-school age have been studied within a wide range of psychological, sociological, and educational perspectives, both at the time of the breakdown of their parents' marriage and during the years that follow. By and large, however, these efforts have not addressed clinical issues. Findings from large-scale quantitative as well as long-term clinical studies have raised grave concerns about the impact of divorce on these children (Wallerstein & Blakeslee, 1989; Zill & Schoenborn, 1990). Moreover, by the late 1980s, over one fourth (27%) of all children in the United States between the ages of 5 and 11 had experienced their parents' divorce (Zill, personal communication). Nevertheless, there has been little theoretical or technical explication as to how these research findings and observations from many diverse settings could translate into such clinical strategies as assessment or treatment.

One major difficulty that has hampered both assessment and treatment is the lack of theoretical clarity about how children of divorce can be distinguished from groups that are more familiar to the clinician. Attempts have been made to carry over theoretical formulations from other seemingly similar life events, such as parental death. But time and time again, the accumulated knowledge of the past two decades has shown that divorce represents a unique experience. Growing up within the divorced family confronts a child with an array of novel challenges: the encounter with new relationships, such as with the visiting or joint-custody parent; the need to resolve inner conflicts; and the issue of negotiating divorce-specific psychological tasks and external challenges. Often enough, these are new not only to the child and the family but to the clinician as well. Moreover, it has become increasingly clear that the divorced family does not represent a truncated version of the intact family; it is, rather, a new family form that requires theoretical and clinical understanding in its own right (Wallerstein, 1991).

A second obstacle to our understanding of children's needs has been the failure to define parental divorce in ways that capture the dynamic process of continuous and unpredictable change that the children experience. Lacking prospective studies, children are not identified as "children of divorce" until the separation or legal dissolution of the marriage has taken place. As a result, parental divorce has been understood as a single traumatic experience and viewed from the perspective of critical life events. In fact, divorce is a multistage process of radically changing relationships that may occupy the major portion of a child's life (Wallerstein, 1983).

The first, preseparation phase begins in the failing marriage, often many years before children are first identified as "children of divorce." Many children attain this status after living within a chaotic family marked by verbal and/or physical aggression throughout the preseparation phase. Others grow up amid the silence of bitter alienation that comes from long-standing failures of empathy and intimacy between parents. For many children of divorce, therefore, the central and defining divorce experience may be embedded within events that have occurred long before the moment of actual separation that ushers in the acute and most widely recognized phase of the divorce process. This acute phase is marked by intense feeling, heightened disorganization, and diminished parenting. The stress may be further exacerbated by violent parental conflict, often in families where no violence has occurred before. Some families will remain fixated at the acute phase for many years. Most, however, will enter a postacute phase of disequilibrium that lasts several years and is characterized by marked permeability of the family's boundaries. In the final phase of the divorce process, the family will clarify existing boundaries and restabilize or take on an entirely new form as one or both parents remarry.

Clearly, children's divorce adjustment spans

many years in which crucial changes will occur in all areas of their development. Nonetheless, except for the California Children of Divorce Study (Wallerstein & Kelly, 1980), a developmental framework rarely has been applied to the description and analysis of the impact of divorce on children. Other longitudinal studies, including the work of sophisticated researchers such as Hetherington (Hetherington, Cox & Cox, 1985) and Furstenberg (Furstenberg & Seltzer, 1986), have made no allowance for the effect of developmental changes on symptoms in children. Thus, for example, Hetherington (Hetherington, Cox, & Cox, 1985) reported that 2 years after the divorce, the moderate to severe symptoms initially observed in a preschool sample had abated. She did not tie these observed changes in any way to the progression of these children into latency, and concluded from her work that the effect of divorce endures approximately 2 years. The general use of cross-sectional designs also has failed to provide a window into the associated developmental issues.

Our purpose here is to address some broad clinical implications of the reported findings and specifically to invoke the developmental framework with reference to clinical and treatment issues. We have found that an amalgam of concepts from the traditionally separate domains of psychoanalytic and social cognitive developmental psychology yields the most broadly applicable framework. All of our clinical knowledge indicates that children's subjective interpretation of events, shaped by their perception and understanding, is central to the way in which experience is integrated. Understanding, therefore, is intimately related to the ways in which the child's moral sensibilities, capacity for relationships, and identity will develop; these may be modified in treatment in ways that are ego-syntonic. We propose, therefore, that such an amalgam of cognitive and psychoanalytic developmental theories may provide a useful, heuristic perspective.

Within this framework we propose three clinical subgroups with suggestions for differential treatment of children and their parents. We discuss the indications for group and individual treatment for children and present a newly designed group treatment model that is tailored to address the developmental and clinical needs that these children present.

The Young Grade-School Child

The young grade-school child (approximately 6 to 8 years of age) is likely to be fully engaged in an array of complex and formidable intrapsychic, cognitive, moral, social and educational tasks. Among others, these include the critical issues of consolidating gender identity. Since clinical training generally emphasizes the child's emotional development, we call particular attention here to cognitive advances that interweave complexly with other domains of the child's life as he or she enters what Erikson has described as "a most decisive stage" in which foundations for learning and achievement will be laid.

As the child enters into the world beyond the family, there are associated advances in his or her cognitive ability to differentiate self and others in progressively less behavioral and increasingly psychological terms. These advances fall under the rubric of interpersonal reasoning (Selman, 1980), a capacity that matures with the child's ability to infer and accommodate perspectives beyond his or her own. In the early grade-school years, the child has an evolving capacity to hold in mind one perspective (in relation to his or her own) at a time (Selman, 1980). This advance is set in motion when, for the first time, the child is able to differentiate thoughts and feelings from behavior. From that point on, the child becomes increasingly sensitive to his or her own thoughts and feelings as well as ever more aware that others have an internal life as well. Still limited in his or her new capacities, the young grade-school child continues to use behavioral and situational cues in order to make sense of the internal life of others. As the child's interpersonal reasoning matures, however, there is an increased capacity to conserve perspectives and to understand the ways in which internal life may differ from and influence behavior. When these advances occur, concepts of motivation, intentionality, and interpersonal conflict can be more clearly understood.

Mindful of the complexities of these challenges to the grade-school child, clinicians have stressed the special importance of assuring external continuity during these years. In the nature of things, these newly consolidating ego functions are fragile, and environmental discontinuity (in the form of marital breakup) may easily evoke overwhelming anxieties that interrupt the child's inner growth and compromise his or her freedom to negotiate relationships in the world beyond the family orbit. As a result, both the child's capacities and readiness to cope with developmental tasks are placed at risk. The child's affective responses contribute to the difficulty in maintaining recent developmental achievements. Acute reactions are characterized by grief and sadness and a longing for the departed parent. The child is centrally preoccupied with feelings of rejection by the parent who has left home for reasons he or she can only imagine with great pain. Fears of abandonment by the remaining parent are also central. The child frequently responds with constriction, displacement of aggression, and, of course, threatened regression.

The young grade-school child's limited ability to integrate more than one perspective at a time, or to understand behavior as internally motivated, contributes significantly to his or her suffering. Understanding is necessarily confused and fragmented because the child lacks the capacity simultaneously to accommodate and to make sense of both sides of the parental conflict in psychological terms. Instead, the child's understanding of events is framed in terms of a propositional conviction that one parent left the other in response to some identifiable provocation. From this perspective, it is not difficult to understand that the child may come to fear that he or she may have caused the provocation and may yet anger the remaining parent and be similarly abandoned. Ironically, the very fact of the child's developmental progress may increase the youngster's pain, because he or she is increasingly aware of thoughts and feelings and is less able to utilize denial to buffer the suffering. The young grade-school child usually lacks the capacity to plan for his or her own relief with sublimated activities and thus has less access to more active and independent strategies to relieve anxiety and painful feelings.

The Older Grade-School Child

Psychoanalytic theory has generally dealt with the grade-school years as the single stage of latency. Cognitive developmental theory, on the other hand, has identified significant changes in children's capacities for reasoning about relationships that begin at age 8 or 9 and accelerate into early adolescence. The evolving ability of the later latency child (approximately 9 to 12 years of age) to infer and coordinate two perspectives allows the child to understand that both parents may be responsible for the conflict between them. Moreover, the older latency child also is able to conserve events in his or her mind over time. As a result, he or she is able to understand that the failure of the relationship may be attributable to long-standing unhappiness rather than to one precipitating event. These cognitive advances are constrained, however, by the child's still-immature grasp on the link between internal feelings and external events. The notion persists that rearranging the external world would undo the feelings that underlie the failed relationship (Roseby, 1988). Not surprisingly, therefore, the child believes that parents could take themselves in hand, resolve the conflict with alacrity, and avoid the divorce. Fueled by the same belief, children often become actively preoccupied in trying to resolve the conflict by their own thoughts and actions, as if it were actually their assignment (Wallerstein, 1985). These heroic efforts to change the fact of the separation, which the child fancies are taken in the interests of his or parents, meet with repeated disappointment. Inevitably the child becomes angry.

During the acute phase of the divorce, the older child's anger is characteristically intense and object-directed. The older grade-school child's ability to express anger directly may be attributed partially to his or her increased understanding that two opposing feelings can be held toward the same person. Anger, therefore, is no longer experienced as annihilating (Roseby, 1988). At the same time, the child may experience new freedom to express angry and aggressive impulses because the parents' own moral authority falters under the stress of the separation. At this vulnerable time, children may witness abusive and even violent behavior between parents who would never have tolerated these breaches in themselves or their children in the preseparation family. The child's confusion about right and wrong deepens if each parent claims the moral high ground and blames the other in a way that disrupts the child's sense of what is true. Thus, the loss of moral direction and control that often characterizes the separation can place the child's conscience development at risk (Johnston & Roseby, 1996).

Feelings of shame about the family collapse are central to the older grade-school child's response. These feelings may be partially understood in terms of the child's emerging ability to infer the perspective of another in relation to self; this, in turn, can bring an acute and painful awareness of the judgments of others as well as a wish to conceal one's own inner distress. Much of what is inferred about the judgments of others, however, represents a projection onto the outside world of the child's sense that his or her parents are failing at a central task of adulthood and that they are powerless to rescue themselves.

Ironically, cognitive advances in older grade-school children bring new sources of pain and difficulty. The older child suffers because he or she is now able to perceive both sides of the battle and is unable to take sides without betraying one or the other parent. As a result, the child faces intense loneliness. One way in which the youngster attempts to resolve such conflicts of loyalty and the accompanying anxiety of feeling alone is by aligning strongly with one parent against the other. This alignment serves to reduce confusion, consolidate a badly shaken sense of identity, and assure a source of support within the fragile context of the child's fragmented family. Shame also may be reduced by taking this more active stance, and anger can be mobilized readily against the nonaligned parent. For these older children, the alignment with one parent against the other represents a complexly organized, ego-syntonic coping behavior that binds a number of significant conflicts and attendant anxieties. If the alignment is allowed to consolidate over time, the child's integrity and potential for individuation and identity achievement are placed at serious risk. It may be relevant to note here that the parent alienation syndrome referred to by Gardner (1987) treats the child as a helpless or passive victim in the parents' plan for vengeance. This formulation fails to recognize the complex, multifaceted interaction of the child's anxiety and anger with their counterparts in the parent or parents (Johnston & Roseby, 1995).

Additional risks are posed as the child's anger and confused preoccupation with the events of parental divorce spill over into the school setting, where performance can be adversely affected.

Without timely intervention, the child is left vulnerable to a downward spiral at home and at school with each decrement exacerbating the loss that went before. Lacking a foundation for the future, the child may fixate or regress. Alternatively, though unprepared in every way, the child may show a precocious move into early adolescence.

Gender Differences in Coping Responses

Reports on the effects of parental separation and divorce on children almost uniformly, indicate that, until adolescence, overt disturbances are more evident in boys. Girls, on the other hand, are reported to be more resilient in latency, showing fewer adjustment difficulties and recovering relatively quickly. Several recent studies have found this pattern of gender differences beginning in the predivorce phase of the marriage and thereafter, and continuing throughout the separation and postdivorce process. For example, in the mid-1980s, a psychological study of 180 children showed that many years prior to the divorce, young boys (but not girls) in families that later divorced often showed serious behavior problems (Block, Block, & Gjerde, 1986). Similarly, Cherlin and colleagues found in two studies that boys often were symptomatic during the predivorce years as well as after the divorce and were altogether significantly more troubled than boys in intact families (Cherlin et al., 1991). The apparent resilience of girls, contrasted with the vulnerability of boys, appears to continue throughout the child's grade-school years. In a large, national school-based study, for example, Guidubaldi and colleagues evaluated first-, third-, and fifth-grade children who had been in a divorced family for a median of 4 years. In the initial study, the children were compared to children in intact families; they were reevaluated 2 and 3 years later (Guidubaldi & Perry, 1985; Guidubaldi, Perry & Cleminshaw, 1984). Boys in mother-custody homes were found to have significantly (and increasingly over time) more problematic behaviors in all areas than boys from intact families. Specifically, these boys were consistently rated most poorly by teachers and school psychologists, showed less appropriate behavior in school, put forth less work effort, evidenced less happiness, and had a higher frequency of behavior problems. In contrast, the girls showed fewer adverse effects and were, increasingly over time, indistinguishable from girls in intact families.

Various explanations have been offered for findings indicating that boys seem to have greater difficulty adjusting to their parents' divorce than do girls. The divorce research findings with regard to boys are in accord with studies in other areas that consistently show that grade-school-age boys are more likely to be referred for learning difficulties, reading delays, and behavioral problems of all types (Weiner, 1982). These conclusions, which long predate divorce research, suggest that boys may have constitutional and maturational vulnerabilities to stress. Kalter and Rembar (1981) reported that preadolescent boys of divorce had significantly higher rates of behavior problems in conjunction with lower rates of subjective psychological symptoms; accordingly, these authors suggested that boys have "a proclivity for the behavioral expression of conflict" (p. 98). Others have hypothesized that mother custody may stimulate a "coercive cycle" of interaction that has been observed between boys and their custodial mothers (Hetherington & Clingempeel, 1988). The view that boys may be more vulnerable in the custody of their mothers is supported by findings that indicate that boys in father custody show more socially competent behavior, high self-esteem, lower anxiety, and fewer behavior problems than boys in mother custody (Camara & Resnick, 1988; Santrock & Warshak, 1979).

In fact, preadolescent boys who live in the custody of their fathers show markedly similar adjustment patterns to preadolescent girls who live in the custody of their mothers. At first glance this may suggest that, for the grade-school-age child, the opposite-sex parent is peripheral to the central developmental tasks of that period. From this perspective, Chase-Landsdale and Hetherington (1989) have concluded that girls in non-remarried mother-custody families appear to recover completely during the elementary years, benefitting from a close and companionate relationship with their mothers until adolescence. At this time, the authors suggest, the quality of the mother-daughter interaction deteriorates as the girls begin to

separate, and the youngsters then become symptomatic.

The appearance of adjustment difficulties at adolescence in girls of divorce has been widely reported. In a 10-year follow-up of children of divorce, Wallerstein (1985), for example, found a significant number of young women who were caught in a cycle of low self-esteem, multiple short-lived relationships with men, and intense anxiety about being betrayed or abandoned. Kalter and colleagues also have found increased promiscuity and relationship difficulties in adolescent girls of divorced families as well as lower self-esteem, higher rates of juvenile deliquency, and more negative feelings about men and marriage (Kalter, Riemer, Brickman, & Chen, 1985). Similarly, Hetherington (1972) found that adolescent girls, 13 to 17 years old, in mother-custody families were more provocative with males than girls from intact families and engaged in earlier dating and sexual intercourse. A follow-up study of these girls in the first year of marriage found that they, more than girls from intact or widowed families, were more likely to marry young, to be pregnant at marriage, and to select husbands who were less educated and less emotionally and economically stable (Hetherington & Parke, 1987). Large-scale, nationally representative samples provide similar evidence that adult women from divorced families were more likely than those from intact families to have married early, to have experienced premarital pregnancy, and to be divorced (Glenn & Kramer, 1985; Mueller & Pope, 1977).

Our clinical experience with girls from divorced families has led us to conclusions at considerable variance to those of other researchers. These colleagues speak to the recovery of girls during these school-age years within the framework of the protective mother-daughter relationship. Our observations show a conscious effort by little girls to conform to their mother's expectations out of fear that failure to do so will result in banishment from the family.

CASE EXAMPLES

Mary T.: Mary T. was 12 when we first saw her. Her parents had separated 3 years earlier. Mary dressed in shapeless baggy clothing and was consumed by her long-standing interest in baseball. Worried that Mary was an oddball who was increasingly rejected by her classmates, her mother hoped that she would benefit from participating in a group for children of divorce. In assessment interviews, Mary spoke warmly of her relationship with her mother and identified no areas of conflict or disagreement between them. She seemed to have trouble even confiding that she preferred a different baseball team other than her mother's favorite. Although Mary saw her father at irregular and infrequent intervals, she sometimes chose not to visit him, saying that she preferred time alone with her mother. Although Mary communicated indifference in most every area, she admitted to being hurt by her classmates' recent habit of saying "There's boys, there's girls, and then . . . there's Mary." Clinical findings showed enormous underlying anxiety, held in strict control by an almost phobic clinging to the mother. These findings were reinforced by Rorschach data that showed extreme emotional constriction and a rigid tendency to turn inward as well as a limited capacity to see whole objects or to understand relationships among others. Like so many of these girls, Mary was asymptomatic in school except for her poor social adjustment.

Patricia Y.: Patricia Y. was 9 when she was referred to our center. Her parents had separated 2 years earlier; they thought that she was doing well but wondered if a group for children of divorce might not be of value. Patricia was very chatty during her interviews and talked almost without a break about her friends and their activities. She worried that she sometimes got too giddy and sociable in some of her classes but thought she was getting the problem under control. Patricia acknowledged that she had been sad about the divorce early on, but understood now that it was for the best since "if they were together, they would fight all the time." Her teachers described her as achieving, competent, and well liked by her peers. They complained only of her mild difficulty coping with failure and a continual tendency to seek the attention of her peers. Despite this reassuring picture, the clinician saw a highly anxious child who was warding off anxiety, depression, and a fear of abandonment by constant activity, clowning, and nonstop talking. Patricia's Rorschach protocol presented a world full of watchful eyes, ears, and teeth. Most striking in the projected material was a sense of this child's pained search for affirmation and real contact as she strove, with marked disregard for form, to distort almost every percept into some semblance of a human face.

Both these girls show a pattern that we have seen repeatedly, namely, indications in clinical material and projective data of an anxiety-laden interior world that simply do not show up in behavior or as symptoms. As a result, these inner difficulties are not reported in studies that rely on teacher or parent observation or on self-report measures. Where these studies record good adjustment, close clinical observation shows hyperconformity and a premature assumption of the quiescent feminine role. This facade covers a profound conviction that being good will placate the powerful mother. Clinically put, the central configuration in the mother-daughter relationship is a child in libidinal retreat from oedipal attachment, propelled by an anxiety-driven sense of the mother as an omnipotent and potentially engulfing figure. A common unconscious fantasy is of mother as a powerful witch. The development of the girl at this time often represents a compromised holding pattern. The foundation of her developmental progress is seriously weakened by her relinquishing her oedipal attachment to father and regressing to a primary attachment to the preoedipal mother. This unconscious choice may draw the child into the protection of a truly companionate mother-daughter relationship during latency. At adolescence, however, girls frequently are reported to have serious difficulties with separation from their mother, which subsequently inhibits development of identity achievement and intimacy.

Assessment

For children of divorce, an assessment of treatment needs takes place in the context of unpredictable and shifting circumstances that do not necessarily reflect the past nor predict the future. Diagnosis necessarily conveys a fluid temporal picture, because the understanding of the child is set in such an unpredictable environment.

Children affected by divorce range from those whose developmental course is intact to those with consolidated psychopathology who are burdened with serious developmental delays. We distinguish three categories: (1) competent children who have achieved a reasonably solid developmental foundation and can draw upon age-appropriate capacities to deal with the crisis; (2) fragile children who present with more mixed developmental achievements, often layering age-appropriate gains in intellectual and physical domains over a fragile early foundation for trust and inner integration; (3) seriously disturbed children whose developmental course has been disrupted or distorted by their psychopathology.

It is important to bear in mind that observations by parents are influenced by their own response to the divorce and that their ability to perceive the child's needs as separate from their own is likely to be impaired. Teachers' observations can be valuable because there often are significant discrepancies between the child's functioning at school and at home. Access to the child's internal experience can be enhanced by the use of projective tests. These tests may be especially useful with constricted children who, because of fears of abandonment and worry about loyalty to both parents, may severely limit their output during clinical interviews. The Rorschach has particular value because it is least likely to alert the child's conscious defensiveness.

COMPETENT CHILDREN

The crisis of marital rupture can occur in the life of a child of grade school age who is developmentally on course. He or she then draws on resources and achievements that have been forged in the successful negotiation of the preceding stages. Like Dorothy in *The Wizard of Oz,* the child may call upon his or her courage, brains, love, and trust in others to stay on the yellow brick road. Most of these children have a sense, born of their experience, that adults will provide both a safe place and moral guidance. When they fail, as the Wizard did, the child is able to use his or her self-confidence and capacity for entitled indignation. Children with a well-consolidated sense of trust often are able to seek and find support in emotional connections outside the family. For healthy children, these connections will be increasingly strengthened as they mature, providing distraction and opportunities for involvement in age-appropriate activities that help them to manage their feelings. The preadolescent child's increasingly well-organized ego structures allow him or her to distinguish fantasy and reality as well as to encapsulate, isolate, and postpone the intrusion of potentially overwhelming material into the interior world.

Paradoxically, children who are developmentally on target are likely, at divorce, to present with acute adjustment reactions. Because they are most able to access a range of emotions, they are more likely to be intensely aware of anger, fear, abandonment; again, because they have a greater capacity not to be overwhelmed by these feelings, they are more able to give these expression. Symptomatic differences between younger and older grade-school children are most apparent within this category because these competent children draw upon the most well-developed and, therefore, most differentiated capacities for coping. It is important for the clinician to note that longitudinal studies show clearly that the early symptomatic response in relatively healthy children, however severe, does not predict outcome over the subsequent years (Wallerstein & Blakeslee, 1989). It is equally important to note that although the achievements and capacities of these children have the potential to tip the balance in favor of mastery and continued developmental progress, they are nevertheless placed at risk by the disorganizing and unpredictable effects of the acute and postacute phases of the divorce. If parenting does not restabilize and refocus on the child fairly rapidly at this time, the child's resources may become depleted, derailing developmental progress and undermining past achievements.

CASE EXAMPLE

Colin Q.: On Colin Q.'s sixth birthday, his parents separated. His father flew to the East Coast to begin drug and alcohol treatment, and Colin remained on the West Coast with his mother. Colin's parents, confused about how to explain their separation, told him very little. Mr. Q.'s use of drugs and alcohol mostly took place away from home; Colin had little knowledge of this aspect of his father's very troubled behavior. Colin had often accompanied Mr. Q., who was a photographer, to his assignments.

Colin's mother was furious with her ex-husband. He had left her with multiple debts and a business in shambles. She was also very concerned about her son. She said "he's like a firecracker . . ." at home, challenging her with "You can't tell me what to do. . . ." Colin's first-grade teacher was not complaining. She said that Colin was doing fine except for a one-time explosive tantrum. Yet Colin's mother felt that she was losing control of a child with whom she had been very close. She could no longer hold and comfort him when she felt he most needed her, although he would sometimes break down and cry in her arms after angrily fending her off. Colin's father visited very irregularly, although he often talked to his son by telephone.

When Colin was first seen, he showed no wish for conversation, turning his full attention instead to the dart board and basketball hoop. During this demonstration of skill and strength, Colin told us "My dad taught me how to throw like this . . ." then added sadly, "My mom doesn't play very well." Colin's longing came through with stark clarity as he talked with pride about his father's skills as a photographer: "I wish my dad could come to school with me and bring his proof sheets and it would say right on them that he's the boss of his agency!" Later he confided "You know, my dad kind of lied to me when I was 6; he said he was going to the beach and then he went to New York." But Colin acknowledged no anger toward his dad, only confusion and a wish for his return. Since he had been told very little about the separation, Colin was left with a sense of anger and humiliation about being bypassed and left by the very person with whom he was struggling to identify. Bereft of his father's presence in the ongoing oedipal triangle and left alone with his mother, Colin now struggles to set appropriate distance between his emerging male self and his mother.

The divorce places this well-developed child on the horns of a serious inner dilemma that effectively isolates him from both his mother and father at a critical time. Colin's anger toward his father is fueled at once by the abandonment and irregular visits as well as by the child's sense of betrayal at having been kept in the dark. This rage, however, comes into conflict with Colin's intense love, sorrow, and longing for his beloved father and with his developmental need for his father's presence as an identification figure. Colin's relationship with his mother is equally problematic. He is torn by his need for her, his loneliness, his wish for comfort, and his anxiety about undoing the distance between his emerging masculine self and the oedipal as well as the preoedipal attachment. Colin's anger at his mother defends against the longing to be with her, but also arises from his belief, born of his developmental level of understanding, that she is responsible for sending his father away from him.

In spite of his inner struggles, Colin maintains his fragile conscience and a sense of justice and fair play. In a massive soldier battle with the therapist, Colin at first seems inclined to annihilate one and all. In the end, however, he leaves one soldier to be resurrected so that there can be a standoff one-to-one. "You did your best," he says. "It's only fair." Paradoxically, as we have noted, Colin's well-developed sense of right and wrong contributes to his confusion and humiliation. He is unable to understand how or why his parents have failed him. Nor can he understand his rage. His weeping and confiding to his mother that he does not know why he gets so mad after a severe tantrum are profoundly moving.

Like other competent children, Colin draws on a history of solid developmental achievement that fuels his capacity to keep his feelings under control and to use the school structure to continue to learn. Nevertheless, he cannot be expected to defend against the threatened regression indefinitely. If his parents fail to reestablish a stable and reliable structure, their child may easily give way. Colin's rage may place his development at risk in many domains. If his anger further intrudes upon his academic work and his relationships, he may become caught in a downward spiral in which his own sense of humiliation, helplessness, and peer rejection invade his capacity to concentrate and maintain the foundations of learning and achievement. An escalation of his defensive efforts to draw a line between himself and his mother can lead to a deterioration of the only support Colin presently has. If this occurs, he is likely to become an increasingly angry, alienated child at risk for consolidation of moderate to severe behavioral difficulties. We conclude that even for a well-developed, psychologically intact child, a prolonged period of instability, coupled with the psychological injuries inherent in the divorce, can have the potential for generating serious problems.

FRAGILE CHILDREN

A second category identifies children whose developmental course has been tenuously achieved, in part because of the psychological frailties of one or both parents. While the predivorce family structure may have provided a marginal holding environment, the child's capacities for spontaneity, for trust in relationships with others, and for inner integrations are somewhat impaired. During the grade-school years, however, consolidating and new ego functions can become the child's stepping-stones for growth. He or she may perform competently in the classroom, in sports, or in other areas requiring intellectual or physical mastery. What evolves is a delicate equilibrium in which the child's tenuous interpersonal adjustment is balanced by other skills. Given a stable and continuous family structure, this fragile internal organization has the capacity to sustain development. When, however, the external world comes apart, these children's potential for mastery is undermined by their already depleted capacities in the interpersonal realm. Furthermore, these children are likely to lack Colin's confidence in adults' ability to set things in order and to be just and fair. Complicating the picture is an increased likelihood that the vulnerabilities or frank psychopathology of parents in these families will be exacerbated and lead to acting-out and unremitting conflict between the parents (Johnston & Roseby, 1996). These circumstances are latent in all divorce situations, but present a particular array of hazards in the families of these already burdened children. The hazards are threefold and are not mutually exclusive. The child's development and adjustment may be threatened by the temporary or more lasting disruption of the child-rearing function that accompanies the marital rupture; by the psychopathological solutions adopted by parents and children to control painful affects and anxieties stirred by the marital separation; and by the increased salience of the long-standing psychopathology of one or both parents in the parent-child relationship. All have implications for long-term suffering and psychological maladjustment in these children. All can be magnified when incorporated into a custody or visitation plan or into a lifestyle that increases the hazards to the child.

CASE EXAMPLE

Tanya M.: Tanya M., whose parents had separated 4 years earlier, was first seen at our center when she was 9 years old. Mrs. M. was a psychologically fragile woman whose first child had been killed in a boating accident. Mrs. M. blamed herself for her child's death. Her psychological functioning, which had been marginal throughout, continued to be dominated by her preoccupation with this tragedy. Some years later she became pregnant with Tanya during an affair with Mr. M., who reluctantly married her. The marriage was troubled from the start. Mr. M. described his former wife as dependent and controlling, and he withdrew both physically and emotionally, leaving Mrs. M. with almost exclusive control of Tanya's parenting. Mr. M. felt "that he knew nothing about children," and Mrs. M. felt justified

in keeping her daughter very strictly under her control and supervision. Mrs. M. focused her anxieties on Tanya's physical health, worrying about symptoms that she imagined at different times to be cancer or other life-threatening illnesses. She believed that Tanya had severe food allergies and prescribed strict dietary regimens for her daughter. Mr. M. implemented his wife's instructions and accepted the role of boy-father.

When Mr. M. left the marriage after a long retreat into silence, Mrs. M. was devastated. Her unresolved grief for the child who had died was reactivated by the separation, and every subsequent contact with Mr. M. brought intolerable feelings of helpless rage. Mrs. M. resisted Tanya's visits to her father, claiming that he could not parent her safely. Mr. M. was viewed as the toxic, dangerous parent, which in large part seemed to be a projection of her own self-image. Mr. M. reacted passively at first but gradually took a more independent role with his daughter, encouraging her to engage in more age-appropriate activities and to worry less. This terrified Mrs. M., and she became more controlling than ever.

After 4 years, the parents sought help with their bitter conflict about Tanya's visitation. When she was first seen, Tanya seemed markedly unchildlike, very solemn and constricted. She spoke very little, making use instead of the sand tray. In her play, two dinosaurs repeatedly teamed up to bury a third, which Tanya would then anxiously dig out and begin again. In conjoint sessions with her father, Tanya was alternately hostile and patronizing. In conjoint sessions with her mother, Tanya was anxious and placating, frequently requesting confirmation and approval for her activity and behavior, which was flatly given but never offered spontaneously. There was a lifeless quality in the interaction between mother and daughter. For Tanya, the central hazards were clear. The separation had left her mainly in the care of a chronically depressed and phobic mother who was intent on removing the father and any other adults from Tanya's life.

In the context of a treatment group, Tanya expressed a wish that "my mother will never leave me." Further, she made it clear that she experienced her father as insensitive and inattentive. Although Tanya's capacities for individuation from her mother were seriously compromised, the developmental tasks of the grade-school years offered opportunities for growth. Tanya was both intelligent and creative. She was competent and well behaved at school and accomplished in dance. She performed regularly with a major urban dance group. Tanya's emotional constriction and anxiety did not impede her in these areas. The dance group provided another milieu that supported her talent. Overall, however, Tanya's developmental achievements remained markedly variable. As she moved into adolescence, with its demands for separation, Tanya was poised on the verge of a powerful, regressive alignment with her mother against her father. Without intervention, Tanya's prospects for maintaining developmental progress into early adolescence are clearly at risk.

SERIOUSLY DISTURBED CHILDREN

A third category identifies children who come to the divorce crisis already suffering with consolidated psychopathology, often because the parents have consciously and unconsciously denied the child's difficulty or maintained a fantasy that when the marriage improves, the child will recover. For these children, the marital separation is not the psychologically salient event but rather an exacerbating factor. The child's acute responses are woven into the structure of his or her illness.

CASE EXAMPLE

Edward O.: Edward O., whose parents had separated when he was 8 years old, was first seen at our center when he was 9. His parents were in their 40s and well established in intellectually demanding fields. Both agreed that Mr. O. had suffered from lifelong depression. When Edward was 5, the father's depression had culminated in a suicide attempt. Three years later, Mr. O. left his wife. Edward was first seen immediately after the separation, at which time a psychiatrist had diagnosed him as severely depressed and recommended long-term psychotherapy. This assessment came on the heels of a similar recommendation by the school psychologist. A year later we contacted Mr. and Mrs. O. to offer a group intervention to Edward. At that time we learned from Mrs. O. that Edward had seen a therapist only a few times before the treatment was discontinued. Mrs. O. said, "He seemed fine after a couple of sessions, and he really wasn't opening up to the therapist."

Nevertheless, Edward came to the group. In that setting it became quickly apparent that his emotional development was seriously arrested and that he had little or no capacity for affection or friendship. His developmental achievements were narrowly limited to the intellectual realm so that, in school, he was considered to be on course academically. However, his teachers said that he was poorly tolerated by his peers and chronically isolated. In group he was as isolated as he was at school. When asked to write adjectives to describe himself he wrote "nothing, nothing, nothing. . . ." When feelings surfaced in the course of group activities such as role-playing, Edward quickly regressed into rambling, incoherent commentaries in which the intrusion of primary thinking was striking: ". . . there's a rabid dog that was

so angry he got into a chocolate bar and then the man ate the rabid dog. ." In group he would sometimes discourse at length about archeology and history. Edward communicated his pain with heart-rending clarity in an anonymous letter to parents that was developed in the last group session. His contribution read "I'm a person. I'm not an alien. I have feelings. I'm a deadhead."

At the termination of group, the clinician again recommended long-term treatment for Edward. In that interview the parents' denial was once again apparent. Mrs. O. made it clear that she believed her son's difficulties were inherited from his father. She felt that Mr. O. had added to Edward's burden by attempting suicide and abandoning the marriage. She told us that she was terrified that Edward would turn out like his father and consistently tried to "cheer him up . . . teach him to look on the bright side of things . . . to buck up." This message, directed at the son, was also clearly intended for the father, who maintained a morose silence during the conjoint interviews. He agreed that Edward might have inherited his depression but countered that the boy had spent too much time in the company of his mother. Mr. O. believed that Edward needed treatment but was unable to challenged his former wife effectively with any conviction, stopping in midsentence and shrugging his shoulders resignedly.

The severity of Edward's psychopathology is rooted in difficulties that began years before the marriage ended and may have further consolidated around the father's suicide attempt. Although the marital separation may have further confirmed the terrors that this poorly individuated child had lived with for most of his life, it cannot be seen as the psychologically salient event for him.

Treatment Strategies

SEQUENTIAL USE OF GROUP AND INDIVIDUAL TREATMENT

In our work with this range of competent to seriously disturbed children and their parents, we have found that carefully timed group work can be uniquely valuable for a number of reasons. First, group treatment seems to be more acceptable to divorcing parents, who are particularly vulnerable to feeling shamed and incompetent and often resist suggestions for individual psychotherapy for their children. Their resistance seems to reflect both a wish to deny that the children may be having difficulty and a fear of being pushed aside by the therapist as the individual treatment relationship develops. A suggestion for group treatment, however, is usually received more positively. Parents frequently express the belief that shared experiences in group treatment will help their child to feel more normal and less isolated. This belief, which may be valid in its own right, also appears to reflect the parents' hope that group will help their child to blame them less and repair the child's view of them as uniquely failing in their efforts to hold the family together. Many children also enter group treatment with a greater sense of pleasure and ease, finding in the company of others a refuge from the perceived loyalty demands and expectations of grown-ups. Within this protected setting, the group offers children opportunities to find support in emotional connections outside the family and to engage in pleasurable, age-appropriate activity that buffers suffering and restores a sense of hope and possibility. Group work also is designed to help children realistically understand and acquire appropriate psychological distance from the parental conflict. Children's capacities to make use of the group work will depend on their overall developmental maturity.

The competent children, like Colin Q., tend to engage in structured group activities and discussions quite fully, allowing their feelings, conflicts, and cognitive confusion to surface. For these children, the task of working through can begin in group and be completed with the support of parents and clinical follow-up as needed. If, however, the supplementary work with parents fails to restore adequate parenting, then individual psychotherapy is needed to help the child to complete the process of working through.

Children with a more mixed developmental profile, such as Tanya M., generally use the group work somewhat differently. Typically, they will participate in group activity and discussion with every appearance of being competent, if not pseudomature, group members. At this level of engagement, the children's conceptual understanding of the parental conflict and their role in it improves markedly. However, their impaired capacity for trust mitigates against finding or feeling enough real connection to support deeper work within the group. Not surprisingly, these highly

defended children are most likely to benefit from supplementary individual therapy (and a longer course of work with parents) to help them to repair and maintain their developmental course. Interestingly, the group work appears to enhance their progress in individual treatment. This unanticipated outcome may be due to the fact that the group setting allows the more fragile children to hear about and identify with the conflicts and anxieties that other, less impaired children are able to express. This experience provides a powerful antidote for the secret shame of children who tend to believe that they only appear to be normal and competent while in reality they are interpersonally inadequate aliens. When their shame is thus reduced, the children are less hypervigilant and more able to make use of a therapeutic alliance in individual treatment. After a period of individual work these children frequently are able to find valuable, age-appropriate support from their peers in a second group experience.

For seriously disturbed children, such as Edward O., early engagement in group work may be experienced as supportive and does help the therapist who is leading the group to assess their insight into their functioning. Functioning more rapidly and accurately than individual work allows. This insight can provide essential and timely leverage in the supplementary work with parents. Nevertheless, the potential benefits of the group always must be weighed against the possibility that the child will experience overwhelming affect and deepen his or her defensive constriction. Generally, group work is most likely indicated after a period of individual treatment in which the child can achieve some inner integration. At that point it is possible for some of these very disturbed children to feel more supported and less overwhelmed by the group process. Finally, group treatment should be delayed for any child who needs immediate intervention for symptoms that are in the process of consolidating. School avoidance, for example, is frequently seen in children who are concerned that further catastrophe, such as abandonment by the in-home parent, will occur in their absence. School avoidance represent a type of acute reactive symptom that children in any diagnostic category may develop. If not brought under control very quickly, these symptoms can spiral into a pattern of consolidating difficulties and symptoms that take on a life of their own and are then extremely difficult to modify.

Clearly, the combined use of group and individual approaches to treatment must be carefully timed to address each child's unique needs and capacities. We continue to investigate the indications, contraindications, and timing considerations for group and individual treatment methods in our work with these children and their families.

THE ROLE OF PARENTS WHEN CHILDREN ARE IN GROUP TREATMENT

The efficacy of a group treatment approach depends in large part on the establishment of a positive treatment relationship with both parents. The significance of this issue is consistently overlooked in the majority of school-based groups, in which parents are afforded no role in the child's treatment beyond giving permission (Pedro-Carroll, Cowen, Hightower, & Guare, 1986). Supports and risks within the child's environment should be assessed to identify lacunae that will need to be addressed in the present as well as in the future. Many parents will need a certain amount of educational guidance to help to restore the diminished parenting and undo or prevent the early dysfunctional responses to the marital rupture that can threaten the child's psychological development. A further goal is to distance the child from psychopathological relationships that may have existed during the failing marriage. When direct work with parents does not suffice, the clinician-parent relationship that has developed can be used to facilitate a referral for group and/or individual psychotherapy for the child.

The combined use of group treatment for children and work with parents, conducted by the same clinician, creates a powerful therapeutic interplay between the two strategies. The clinician's experience of the child in group brings insight into the child's perceptions, conflicts, and related anxieties, which often differ dramatically from parents' expectations. Fortunately, in drawings, role-plays, and other structured activities, the children tend to express themselves in group with startling clarity. When children give permission to share this material, these dramatic and unedited productions can mobilize parents into awareness in ways that the more remote psychological language of the clinician cannot. The resulting enhancement of parents' understanding of their children, and the need to protect them appropriately, can serve to focus the work with parents and heighten its seriousness.

Eleven-year-old Vick had experienced his parents' first divorce, their remarriage, and their second divorce. The parents described a happy, well-adjusted child. In individual interviews Vick talked placidly about his situation, giving no outward indication that he was sad or angry. This presentation was sharply contradicted by a drawing Vick completed in group in which both parents pointed accusing fingers at a weeping child. The caption read "This is all your fault." Although Vick's parents were profoundly upset by the drawing, it catalyzed their understanding of his distress and provided the clinician with much-needed leverage to restore their parenting.

MANAGEMENT ISSUES IN THE TREATMENT WITH PARENTS

Our experience suggests that intervention during the acute phase is optimal, preferably 3 to 6 months postseparation, when the situation is still fluid and many decisions have not yet been consolidated. Unlike ordinary child-centered work, in dealing with divorce, the clinician has greater responsibility for the agenda of the intervention. In part this is because parents often are unaware of the vulnerable psychological condition of the children or of one partner, and in part because divorcing families bring multiple, conflicting agendas. The clinician also carries the responsibility for determining the question of who now constitutes the family. In divorcing families it is not unusual for nonparent adults, such as a parent's lover, new spouse, or a grandparent, to assume significant control over the child and, frequently, over the biological parent as well. Failure to include these powerful figures in the treatment process is likely to undermine the work from the outset.

In divorce work, it is also profoundly important for the clinician to maintain therapeutic neutrality in the conflict between the parents. This is especially difficult with this population, where transference displacements from the present crisis, as well as from the past, significantly influence the reactions of both clinician and client (Wallerstein, 1991). The clinician should communicate from the outset his or her intent to represent the issues from the child's point of view, and to work with each parent on behalf of the child. This open statement to parents sometimes provides the therapist with the only leverage he or she may ever have.

In work with divorcing families, termination of treatment does not represent a definitive end point. Instead, when current presenting issues are resolved, the treatment alliance with the child and family explicitly shifts to an on-call position. The need for the therapist to continue as a benign presence over the years exists because the children and their families experience multiple changes, and there are frequent crises along the way. This approach resembles a family practice model in which intensive treatment is followed by periodic checkups and additional treatment if the child's condition so indicates (Wallerstein, 1991).

STRATEGIES WITH PARENTS

In cases where the child is developmentally on course and parents are able to maintain adequate focus on their child's well-being, the treatment with parents may include only brief supportive work and a built-in follow-up. Selected issues that place the child at some risk in the evolving family can be identified early on. Because the divorce process continues for many years beyond the point of separation, typically involving multiple and unpredictable changes, regularly scheduled follow-up and availability at critical times is a crucial (though frequently ignored) component of work with all divorcing families.

In the case of Colin Q., whose case has already been described, a central strategy in the work with parents was a brief but intensive series of meetings between Mrs. Q. and her former husband. He was requested to travel from the East Coast for the purpose. In these meetings the parents were helped to understand the meaning of their child's intermittent rages as well as his sense of grief and loss. This understanding would provide the necessary leverage for change. These relatively healthy parents were able to identify and label the issues that were unresolved between them. They were able to agree that these would have to be kept separate from their interaction around the child, and they were able to create a conflict-free zone in which to negotiate on Colin's behalf. Following this clarification of the obstacles

to coparenting and the effects of their failure to cooperate, the parents were helped to discuss their divorce with Colin and to structure a visitation plan upon which he could begin to rely.

More intensive work with parents is required on behalf of more fragile children. Concurrent group treatment for parents and children can be an appropriate and parsimonious next step. Other strategies for adults in highly polarized families have been detailed elsewhere (Johnston & Campbell, 1988). In many cases this approach, combined with built-in follow-up, will suffice. In other cases, the work with parents will serve to clarify that they cannot be mobilized on behalf of their child. Ongoing treatment for the child is then recommended. In our experience, the child's participation in group can facilitate the transition into individual work because he or she can bring to it a clearer understanding of the therapeutic process, a more consolidated sense of the psychological issues that are troubling, and a more practiced access to the language of feeling.

Tanya M.'s parents participated separately in a series of meeting with other parents of children who were in group treatment. This provided a supportive milieu in which Mrs. M. was gradually helped to articulate her exhaustion. In subsequent individual meetings with Mrs. M., this admission provided leverage for the clinician to begin to share the burden of this mother's conscious concern about her child's safety and to relieve her unconscious guilt. In separate meetings, Mr. M. was helped toward a better understanding of the meaning of his former wife's controlling behavior and an appreciation that the mother's fears were becoming all too real to the daughter. We suggested minimally threatening ways to invite Tanya into a relationship without arousing the fears of the mother. This, we told him, would have to be the basis from which he gently invited his daughter into a relationship with him. With this fragile beginning, which took 6 months, the parents were helped to develop a series of agreements in which safety concerns were carefully identified and agreed upon. Mr. M. became able to respond more sensitively to the very real anxieties that his daughter carried with her. In group, and later at home, Tanya grew more clear and articulate about her own needs, separate from those of her mother. Movement in this brief work, however, was restricted by Mrs. M.'s very limited capacity for insight and change. The clinician's positive, if always tenuously maintained, relationship with each parent and Tanya's good progress and pleasure in the group were best used to help each parent accept Tanya's need for long-term treatment. An empathic and informed referral could then be made to a clinician who could negotiate in the delicate middle ground on behalf of this child.

For children in whom psychological difficulties are well consolidated, the central and very difficult task of the work with parents often is to help them focus on the needs of their child so that the recommendation for individual psychotherapy can be accepted and followed through. This effort often challenges all of the clinical skills that can be brought to bear.

After a series of conjoint meetings with Edward O.'s parents, for example, the clinician focused her efforts on work with the father. This decision was made in part because there was no strategic leverage to help the mother with her panic-driven denial. The father was responsive to the therapist's strong assertion that the child's depression might lead to a repetition of his father's lifelong suffering. In the course of five very difficult interviews, the father was moved both by the therapist's implied concern for father's own unhappiness, which had almost led to suicide, and by her obvious and very personal worry about Edward. As a result, he was able to take the initiative on behalf of his son. He accepted the clinician's referral for long-term treatment for Edward and contacted the therapist himself. Only at that point did the clinician recontact the mother, who needed to remain at a clear psychological remove. The clinician fully supported the mother in her need for both denial and distance, and the mother was only encouraged not to block the treatment. As a result, this very disturbed little boy was able to begin the long-term work that was necessary for his recovery.

An Experimental Group Treatment Strategy

MANAGEMENT ISSUES

The group method that we have developed and refined to meet the particular needs of these chil-

dren provides for 10 weekly sessions. Older grade-school children meet for 1½ hours per week, whereas the younger children meet for just 1 hour. The group meetings are held at our center in a conference room that is large enough to permit a range of group activities and small enough to maintain the group's sense of focus and cohesion. The groups range in size from 5 to 8 members, with an equal number of girls and boys or are of exclusively one gender.

Separate groups are offered for younger and older grade-school children because we have found major differences in their cognitive capacities. While the treatment goals for both age groups remain constant, the activities, tempo, and duration of the sessions are tailored to accomodate the differences. When siblings fall into the same age category, the decision to treat them together or separately rests with the clinician. In some cases siblings can benefit from the comfort each brings to the other in the course of the group experience. In other cases each child may need a separate place in which to work, particularly those who come from families where boundaries between members are not clear.

A thorough psychological evaluation of the child is conducted before he or she enters the group. The Rorschach is the centerpiece of our assessment process for three reasons: (1) the unstructured nature of the test tends to bypass the expectable defensiveness of school-age children, who are not, generally, forthcoming in direct interviews; (2) the test is a comprehensive instrument that can provide information about the kinds of interpersonal difficulties these children are most likely to experience; and (3) using the Exner comprehensive scoring system (Exner, 1986) allows for reliable normative comparisons. These data are supplemented by observations of projective play and behavioral checklists that are completed by parents and teachers. In this type of short-term work, these data can greatly enhance the leader's ability to empathize, prompt appropriately, and generally structure the experience in a therapeutically focused manner. When combined with clinical experience of the child in group, the initial assessment data provide crucial feedback to parents, so that they can better understand, empathize with, and protect their children. Clinical assessment is ongoing throughout the intervention and, together with more formal posttreatment assessment, provides the basis for developing follow-up treatment and support plans for individual children.

The decision to use one or two group leaders depends on the availability of resources, the training and experience of the leaders, and the specific needs of the children in the group. Experienced single leadership can be quite successful, particularly with more mature groups. However, coleadership becomes essential when a child's acting out is likely to disrupt group process. In such a case, one leader can be available to support the disruptive child, while the other maintains the group's focus and emotional tone. Discussion between the coleaders also can provide the children with a model of negotiation and conflict resolution between adults. In our model of group work, the group leader conducts the initial and final evaluations, works with both the child's parents through the course of the group, and sees the child and the family at structured intervals thereafter. When the group is coled, the responsibility for these interventions can be divided so that each child and family has the opportunity to develop a primary and continuous relationship with one of the leaders. In our experience this approach helps the child to see the leader(s) as a trusted and neutral figure who remains constant when the child's world is in flux. This view of the leader(s) can enhance his or her relationship with the group members, and that relationship can in turn support the child's capacity to work in a way that no other ingredient can.

GROUP THEORY BASE AND TREATMENT STRATEGIES

We have found it necessary to depart from traditional approaches in developing treatment strategies for children of divorce. With this population, a central clinical goal is to strengthen the child's capacity to make sense of the interpersonal world, because one of the major effects of divorce is that children begin to see the world as inchoate. A related goal is to help the child understand that his or her family relationships do not represent all personal relationships, and that different and more positive experiences may be possible in adulthood. A third goal is to empower the child to hold a view of self, others, and events that may differ from the one that may be imposed by adults in conflict. The different visions that the adults have sought to impose on the child may have al-

ready distorted his or her developing conceptions of self, of morality, and of relationships. These children require opportunities to test the reality of perceptions, feelings, and fantasies, to reconstruct a moral code that may have become distorted, to expand psychological understanding of self and others, and to attain an appropriate psychological distance from what they have experienced in their own families.

For grade-school-age children, a structured peer group can provide a developmentally appropriate context within which to address these crucial tasks. A group provides an effective way to achieve a variety of goals: to undo the child's sense of isolation, to restore his or her sense of pleasure in the company of peers, and to provide a window of hope into the world outside the family. The group milieu can become a place of safety, an alternative culture within which the children can explore their own shaken sense of the interpersonal world of adults. The group leader can come to represent a benevolent adult who defines and supports a moral order.

In order to be effective, the therapeutic strategies of group should address the grade-school-age child's greater ease with activity rather than with language. The child's premature use of language to describe his or her traumatic experience has the dangerous potential of triggering a regression in which language and the experience itself are fused. Within this context, the child may experience using words as reliving the memory, releasing impulses and overwhelming feelings.

Activities can and should be structured to permit group members to titrate their approach to painful issues as they freely select a balance between watchfulness and participation. The experience of choice is particularly central for these children, many of whom have been robbed of their sense of control by life events and for whom control over feelings is a salient developmental issue. Additionally, group activities should capture the child's imagination and provide a sense of pleasure (all too often a foreign experience for these youngsters). For the group leader, the technical challenge is to maintain the group's serious therapeutic agenda without forestalling the children's enjoyment and real freedom to contribute to and modify the group experience.

The goals and strategies of the experimental group approach described here draw upon an amalgam of psychoanalytic theory and the cognitive-developmental theory of interpersonal understanding (Roseby & Johnston, 1995) *Interpersonal understanding* is defined as the way in which children understand and reason about themselves, other people, and the interactions between them (Selman, 1980). The development of interpersonal understanding parallels the child's capacity to move beyond the boundaries of his or her own perspective and to infer the perspective of others. This maturation of cognitive skills increasingly enables the child to differentiate self and other, to understand the psychological meaning of what we do and why we do it, and to construct a working theory of family relationships. Group activities focus on improving the child's capacity to differentiate inner experience and outward presentation so that ego boundaries can be strengthened. The activities also help children to understand relationships in their own families, especially when those relationships involve change and conflict. Above all, the work attempts to link conceptual considerations of what is trustworthy, fair, and reliable in people and in relationships to children's underlying conflicts and feelings about these issues. All of these concerns shape children's interpretation and integration of their experience in the family and are central to children's developing capacities for relationships, identity formation, and morality.

Group Treatment Strategies

SELF-DEFINITION

One of the first things that the leader and children create together is a color-feeling chart, which is used throughout the course of the group as a communication tool. The chart includes a list of feelings that the children generate with the leader's help. Each feeling is then assigned, by group consensus, a corresponding color. The leader helps the children to use appropriate blends of color to identify complex emotions. The children may add to the group chart at any time, and some develop their own individual color-feeling keys, which may vary with each activity.

The color-feeling chart is an important tool in activities that are designed to help the children differentiate their internal self from their external representation. In this process self-boundaries

may be strengthened. In the first group session children are invited to imagine a place within themselves that takes the form of a private room to which they each have exclusive and protected access. The room may be of any size, shape, color, location, and may contain whatever the child wishes. When the image is in place, the children make drawings of their rooms using the color-feeling chart to identify feelings associated with areas or objects in the room. In subsequent sessions, the leader uses guided imagery to help children symbolically enter this "inner room" and use it as a safe place in which to identify private wishes and hopes for the future. Over the course of the group, children add to these initial drawings, which seems to function as a concrete representation of their expanding self-awareness.

Nine-year-old Chris D. drew a treehouse that could be reached by a rope ladder which remained under the exclusive control of the occupant. Danielle U. created a room that expanded with each session as she added items that she felt were important to her. These included art supplies and earplugs.

Interestingly, the children seem to generalize from these activities directly into other aspects of their lives. Parents frequently reported that, at home, the children showed a new interest in the arrangement of their rooms, moving furniture and making plans for more privacy. Other parents told us that children had requested locked diaries. Katie R.'s mother told us that her daughter came home from school after being picked on by her friend Caitlin and said, "I just went into my private space to think what I wanted to do about Caitlin." Mrs. R. described the incident to us after hearing about the private space activities in group. "I recognized it instantly . . . this was the most active position I had heard from Katie . . . so unlike her . . . I thought it came from out of the blue . . . but it didn't."

Internal states and external representations also are clarified and differentiated by activities in which these aspects of self are concretely represented. For example, group members create masks that represent their external presentation (and often, their defensive style). These masks are used later in role-plays during which children are prompted to consider safe persons (or pets) and/ or times when they might remove the mask and communicate their real thoughts and feelings.

Twelve-year-old Sandra M., for example, made a smiling mask without eyes for a role-play in which she was required to visit her father and stepmother, although she wanted to stay home with her mother. In the first role-play Sandra wore the mask for the duration of the visit. When the leader invited her to consider a safe person in this situation, Sandra decided to show her brother the furious face beneath the smiling mask. For Sandra, this provided a new awareness of her behavior and her choices in relationships with other people. Later Sandra gave the leader permission to show the mask to her parents and discuss it with them. Mr. and Mrs. M. were deeply upset by this stark indication that Sandra believed she needed a facade in her family and that they had accepted her facade without seeing the child beneath. These powerful feelings, which are aroused in parents by the children's work in group, provide leverage for the therapist to move the parents toward greater empathy and awareness.

In a related activity, children are asked to recall a family incident during which they felt that they had to hide what they were really feeling. They are then helped to remember how they felt inside and what they showed on the outside. Following this, children are given two pieces of paper that are stapled together, one on top of the other. On each is drawn the outline of a human figure. Children are asked to use the color-feeling chart to color the figure on the bottom sheet with the inner feelings. The figure on the top sheet is colored in to show the child from the outside. Patricia Y., like many children, filled in the inner figure with a whirl of color, while the external figure was completed with clothes and a bland face. Younger and more disturbed children often complete only one figure as they struggle with the distinction between inner and outer self. Nevertheless, they have the opportunity to listen to other children who are able to complete both figures and share their meaning.

In group sessions each of these activities is reinforced by the role-playing that follows. As the children both prepare for their roles and subsequently review them, deciding what the person felt and how the person acted, the youngsters have the opportunity to explore further the relation between behavior and inner thoughts and feelings. As children begin to understand these distinctions, they begin to feel less vulnerable and more capable of psychological distance from their parents' conflict. Differentiation of feelings from behavior also allows the leader to address moral issues as he or she helps the children to understand that feelings are never wrong, but that there are right and wrong ways to act on them.

ROLE-PLAYING

Structured role-playing and role-switching activities have long been a useful tool for working through issues in the psychoanalytic treatment of children; these modalities also have been associated consistently with advances in children's perspective-taking and interpersonal understanding (Chandler, 1973; Roseby & Deutsch, 1985; Shantz, 1983). Role-playing, therefore, is a central strategy in this treatment approach. Projective drawings of situations that are commonly experienced by children of divorce are used to evoke experiences that the children need to work through.

In order to maximize the children's sense of safety and control, the role of director is offered to whomever provides material for a role-play. The director's job is to select the role-players and to help each to identify the feelings and appropriate behaviors for the role. Vignettes are videotaped and reviewed within the group. Role-playing, role-switching, and video review all provide opportunities to experience and coordinate increasingly complex and different perspectives of the events in the vignette. It is expected that children will experience the issues at the level of complexity that they are developmentally capable of accommodating. During the role-playing and in discussions during the videotape review, the leader prompts the group members to reality-test their feelings, perceptions, and fantasies about the role-play material. The leader also uses the role-playing to help children to identify issues of right and wrong in the roles they play and to consider revisions in their own theories of fairness, justice, and morality.

After the divorce, 11-year-old Daniel had been the object of a bitter custody battle, which had left his parents furious and uncooperative. When the group was shown a picture of a child caught between two adults, Daniel selected group members to act out the following scene. Daniel is at his father's house, and the father is busy at his desk. Daniel's mother is working at her house. Suddenly

197

Daniel remembers that he left his homework at his mother's and, in a panic, asks his father to take him to get it. The father tells his son that he is far too busy, and anyway, it's his mother's job. The mother says essentially the same thing to Daniel, who is left at the end without his homework, feeling sad, angry, and worried about what will happen at school the next day.

At this point, Daniel spontaneously set up a second role-play. He is at school. His teacher publicly berates him about the homework as classmates watch and giggle. Daniel says that he feels "embarrassed and furious." Following this, the group leader invited Daniel to re-create the role-play according to his own sense of fairness. In response, Daniel chooses to play the role of teacher while another child plays him. In the role of teacher, Daniel says to the child playing him: "This is not your fault. Your parents are to blame. I want a conference with them!" Daniel now selects two children to play his parents. Daniel, still in the role of teacher, berates them furiously for putting their son in a terrible position. During the review of the videotape, the leader helped the group to clarify the feelings of the role-players and the unfairness of Daniel's position. The leader also invited the children to talk about what would happen if Daniel let his parents know how furious he really was with them. This required consideration of which parent was experienced as safe and under what conditions. In flat tones that belied his pain, Daniel said he was sure that neither of his parents cared about his real feelings. When the session was over, the leader planned with Daniel how she would talk with his parents about the issues that had come up in the role-play. The leader then used this material to help the parents to understand the effect that their bitter conflict had on the daily experience of their child.

Eight-year-old Lynette's parents were in the midst of an amicable divorce at the time the child was seen in group. Both parents agreed that she had shown few, if any, noticeable adjustment reactions, but they worried that more might be going on beneath the surface. In individual interviews Lynette was cooperative but unable to tell the interviewer very much about herself. In group, however, when the leader invited the children to remember a time when they wished they could have been a superhero, Lynette volunteered a telling role-play. Choosing to play herself, she directed others in the group to take the roles of her parents in the following remembered incident: Lynette was being taken back to her mother's house after visiting her father. At the door to the mother's house, it became clear that the father had mixed up the return time. An argument ensued during which Lynette's normally affable father slapped her mother across the face. This ended the role-play. Lynette could not tolerate talking about her feelings of fear and confusion but freely discussed her wish to be Superwoman who always knew the right time, the right place to be, and the way to get there. When the leader asked what would happen in the second role-play if she could really be Superwoman, Lynette correctly remembered the return time and flew back to her mother's house. The slapping did not occur because her father did not have to bring her home at all.

When the children discussed the video of Lynette's role-play, the leader asked them to think about whether Lynette could in fact manage without her parents' help, and if she did, if this would help to keep them under better control. In work with the parents, the therapist used this particular memory, which neither parent had talked about, to increase their awareness of Lynette's emotional constriction and her fantasies about the power of undemanding, good behavior to ward off anger and undo its effects.

RELATIONSHIP AND ROLE DEFINITION

Role boundaries often are unclear in divorced families, where children become easily enmeshed in their parents' troubles. The leader helps younger children to move toward a sense of autonomy by working with the group to develop a list of "jobs" that are appropriate for different family members. The "jobs" provide a concrete metaphor that the children can use to clarify emotional and intellectual boundaries. For children, "jobs" include role-defining behaviors such as "playing with friends" and "learning in school," and for parents may include behaviors such as "protecting the children" and "setting up fair rules in the house." Older children are helped to codify a set of rules about behavior in relationships, in particular behavior of parents toward children. Both the list of jobs and the code for relationships can help children to articulate moral issues as they discuss what is fair and expectable in the role-play material.

Toward the end of group, the leader helps each child to create a family sculpture (Satir, 1972) that represents that youngster's view of family relationships as they currently exist. Children also are asked to create a fantasy sculpture of their families as they wish they could be. Both sculptures are videotaped. During review and discussion of the videotapes, the leader prompts the children to articulate their expectations about relationships in their families that they have expressed in the sculpture. The sculpture of the wished-for family provides the children with opportunities to review, revise, and reconstruct their ideas about family relationships. The leader helps the children to clarify that their revised expectations and ideas about relationships may not affect the current family, which they do not have the power to change, but can become the foundation for their own families when they are adults.

Eight-year-old Nina Y. would not create a sculpture without the smiling mask that she had made in the previous session. She viewed the mask as an integral part of herself. When the leader asked Nina if there was anyone with whom it was safe to remove the mask, she replied instantly and firmly, "No one is safe. Only my cat is safe." Nina's ability to articulate her sense of danger and consider the possibility of protective strategies represented a major step forward for this child. Unfortunately, her parents could acknowledge their child's experience of danger only by blaming each other, so that no real change in their relationship was possible. The work with these, as with many character-disordered, parents focused almost exclusively on helping each to accept and support a referral for supplemental, individual psychotherapy for Nina. (For a comprehensive disscusion of the treatment of highly conflicted character disordered parents, see the work of Johnston and Roseby, 1996.)

During the final session of the group, the children serve as a panel of experts, giving advice to other children of divorce who send in "letters" that the leaders have developed to reflect specific concerns the group has identified over time. The panel is videotaped and dramatized as a television talk show, with one child in the role of host. Children develop a title for the show; *The Wide World of Divorce from the Kids' Point of View* is one ex-

ample. The type of questions for the panel may include: "My parents cannot agree about how much time I spend with each of them. Sometimes I feel like I have to decide, but that's really hard. What should I do?" "My mother blames my dad for everything that goes wrong and I wish that she would stop. What can I do about this?" Or, "When my mom's boyfriend sleeps over I have to find a friend's house to stay at and I hate asking! I wish my mom would just stay home." Almost invariably the child whose issues are reflected in the question will choose to respond as expert. When this activity is introduced, the leader underscores the seriousness of the task by explaining that, in fact, clinicians learn from children's understanding most of all. We sincerely consider them to be experts in the field of children and divorce, and we need to listen to what they have to tell us.

Summary

A developmental framework provides a coherent approach to clinical understanding and treatment strategies in work with grade-school-age children of divorce and with their parents. This is true, in part, because a developmental framework can accommodate the fact that divorce actually represents a long-term experience that profoundly influences the child's entire growing-up process. Our approach is designed to address the complex way in which the child's evolving understanding shapes the very nature of his or her experience and becomes a central determinant of interpersonal behavior and intrapsychic functioning. These relationships between developmental lines must be bridged in order fully to capture the intricacies of diagnosis and treatment.

Major cognitive and emotional differences, as well as differences in social relationships, distinguish the responses of younger and older grade-school children. Additionally, there are major differences by gender. By and large, girls have been described as well adjusted in latency and compared favorably to boys, whose difficulties have been widely reported. Our own observations differ sharply from this view. We believe that, in many cases, girls who seem well adjusted are in fact presenting a conforming facade that masks serious anxiety and emotional constriction. These hidden fears and inhibitions silently erode the foundations of gender consolidation and autonomy achievement. Subsequently, as the research clearly indicates, these lacunae become apparent in adolescence.

All of the children are placed at risk by the unpredictable years of change that precede and frequently follow divorce. The forces at work during these years have the potential to skew or inhibit the child's development across many domains. In the nature of things, children come to the moment of divorce with different levels of vulnerability. We have used these differences to identify three categories of children with different treatment needs: competent children who are developmentally on course and have access to a reasonable repertoire for coping and mastery; more fragile children who present with variable development achievements (often the developmental pattern reflects new growth in latency-specific tasks that is only tenuously supported by a fragile early foundation for inner integration and trust in relationships); and children whose developmental course has been seriously disrupted by the consolidation of severe psychopathology. Each of these categories can be linked to different histories within the predivorce family and sometimes to a

greater or lesser capacity for recovery. We have discussed the timing and potential benefits of group and individual treatment for children in each of the diagnostic categories. Finally, we have described a theory-driven group treatment model for grade-school children that is embedded in the context of work with both parents. This model of group work uses structured activities such as role-playing, family sculpting, and mask making to help children to achieve a more mature, psychologically differentiated conception of self, of morality, and of relationships. In turn, these conceptual advances are used to support the child's intrapsychic working through of conflicts and affects associated with these issues.

In work with parents, the goals are to restore diminished parenting and prevent dysfunctional relationships from consolidating in the post-divorce family. These goals often are tempered by the recognition that many parents who come to divorce are psychologically fragile and may have been traumatized by the failure of the marriage. Not all will recover, but the child's future adjustment depends on establishing and maintaining an environment that will allow development to proceed throughout and beyond the grade-school years.

REFERENCES

Block, J. H., Block, J., & Gjerde, P. F. (1986). The personality of children prior to divorce. *Child Development, 57,* 827–840.

Camara, K. A., & Resnick, G. (1988). Interpersonal conflict and cooperation: Factors moderating children's post-divorce adjustment. In E. M. Hetherington & J. D. Arasteh (Eds.), *Impact of divorce, single-parenting, and stepparenting on children* (pp. 169–195). Hillsdale, NJ: Erlbaum.

Chandler, M. J. (1973). Egocentrism and antisocial behavior: The assessment and training of social perspective-taking skills. *Developmental Psychology, 9,* 323–326.

Chase-Landsdale, P. L., & Hetherington, E. M. (1990). The impact of divorce on life-span development: Short and long-term effects. In P. B. Baltes, D. L. Featherman, & R. M. Lerner (Eds.), *Life-span development and behavior* (Vol. 10. pp. 105–150). Hillsdale, NJ: Lawrence Erlbaum.

Cherlin, A. J., Furstenberg, Jr., F. F., Chase-Landsdale, P. L., Kiernan, K. E., Robins, P. K., Morrison,

D. R., & Teitler, J. O. (1991). Longitudinal studies of effects of divorce on children in Great Britain and the United States. *Science, 252,* 1386–1389.

Exner, J. (1986). *The Rorschach: A comprehensive system. Volume 1: Basic foundations* (2nd ed.). New York: John Wiley & Sons.

Furstenberg, F. F., & Seltzer, J. A. (1986). Divorce and child development. In P. A. Adler & P. Adler (Eds.), *Sociological studies of child development* (Vol. 1, pp. 137–160). Greenwich, CT: JAI Press.

Gardner, R. A. (1987). *The parental alienation syndrome and the difference between fabricated and genuine child sexual abuse.* Cresskill, NJ: Creative Therapeutics.

Glenn, N. D., & Kramer, K. B. (1985). The psychological well-being of adult children of divorce. *Journal of Marriage and the Family, 47,* 905–912.

Guidubaldi, J., Perry, J. D., & Cleminshaw, H. K. (1984). The legacy of parental divorce: A nationwide study of family status and selected mediating variables on children's academic and social competencies. In B. B. Lahey & A. E. Kazdin (Eds.), *Advances in clinical child psychology* (Vol. 7, pp. 109–151). New York: Plenum Press.

Hetherington, E. (1972). Effects of father absence on personality development in adolescent daughters. *Developmental Psychology, 7*(3), 313–326.

Hetherington, E. M. (1989). Coping with family transitions: Winners, losers and survivors. *Child Development, 60,* 1–14.

Hetherington, E. M., & Arasteh, J. D. (Eds.). (1988). *Impact of divorce, single-parenting and stepparenting on children.* Hillsdale, NJ: Erlbaum.

Hetherington, E. M., & Clingempeel, W. G. (1988, March). Coping with remarriage: The first two years. Symposium conducted at the Conference on Human Development, Charleston, SC.

Hetherington, E., Cox, M., & Cox, R. (1985). Long-term effects of divorce and remarriage on the adjustment of children. *Journal of the American Academy of Child Psychiatry, 24,* 518–530.

Hetherington, E. M., & Parke, R. (1987). *Contemporary readings in child psychology.* New York: McGraw-Hill.

Inannotti, R. (1978). Effect of role-taking experiences on role taking, empathy, altruism and aggression. *Developmental Psychology, 14*(2), 119–124.

Johnston, J., & Campbell, L. (1988). *Impasses of divorce: The dynamics and resolution of family conflict.* New York: Free Press.

Johnston, J., Campbell, L., & Mayes, S. (1985). Latency children in post-separation and divorce disputes. *Journal of American Academy of Child Psychiatry, 24*(5), 563–574.

Johnston, J., & Roseby, V. (1995, July). *Parental alienation in young adolescents of custody disputes: Developmental psychopathology and treatment implications.* Paper presented at the Fourth International Congress for Adolescent Psychiatry, Athens, Greece.

Johnston, J., & Roseby, V. (1996). *In the name of the child.* New York: The Free Press.

Kalter, N., & Rembar, J. (1981). The significance of a child's age at the time of parental divorce. *American Journal of Orthopsychiatry, 51*(5), 538–544.

Kalter, N., Riemer, B., Brickman, A., & Chen, J. (1985). Implications of parental divorce for female development. *Journal of American Academy of Child Psychiatry, 24*(5), 538–544.

Kurdek, L., Blisk, D., & Siesky, A. (1981). Correlates of children's long-term adjustment to their parents' divorce. *Developmental Psychology, 17*(5), 565–579.

Longfellow, C. (1979). Divorce in context: Its impact on children. In G. Levinger & O. Moles (Eds.), *Divorce and separation* (pp. 287–306). New York: Basic Books.

McKinnon, R., & Wallerstein, J. S. (1988). A preventive intervention program for parents and young children

in joint custody arrangements. *American Journal of Orthopsychiatry, 58*(2), 168–178.

Mueller, C., & Pope, H. (1977). Marital instability: A study of its transmission between generations. *Journal of Marriage and the Family, 39*(1), 83–94.

Pedro-Carroll, J. L., Cowen, E. L., Hightower, D., & Guare, J. C. (1986). Preventive intervention with latency-aged children of divorce: A replication study. *American Journal of Community Psychology, 14*(3), 277–290.

Roseby, V. (1988). Short & long term effects of interpersonal understanding training on fourth and fifth grade children of divorce. Unpublished doctoral dissertation, University of Wisconsin, Madison.

Roseby, V., & Deutsch, R. (1985). Children of separation and divorce: Effects of a social role-taking group intervention on fourth and fifth graders. *Journal of Clinical Child Psychology, 6*(2), 15–20.

Roseby, V., & Johnston, J. (1995). Clinical interventions with children of high conflict and violence. *American Journal of Orthopsychiatry, 65*(1), 48–59.

Santrock, J., & Warshak, R. (1979). Father custody and social development in boys and girls. *Journal of Social Issues, 35*(4), 112–125.

Satir, V. (1972). *Peoplemaking.* Palo Alto, CA: Science and Behavior Books.

Selman, R. (1980). *The growth of interpersonal understanding.* New York: Academic Press.

Shantz, C. (1983). Social cognition. In J. H. Flavell & E. M. Markman (Eds.), *Handbook of child psychology: Vol. 3. Cognitive development* (pp. 495–555). New York: John Wiley & Sons.

Wallerstein, J. S. (1983). Children of divorce: The psychological tasks of the child. *American Journal of Orthopsychiatry, 53*(2), 230–243.

Wallerstein, J. S. (1985). Children of divorce: Preliminary report of a ten-year follow-up of older children and adolescents. *Journal of the American Academy of Child Psychiatry, 24*(5), 545–553.

Wallerstein, J. S. (1991). The long-term effects of divorce on children: A review. *Journal of the American Academy of Child and Adolescent Psychiatry, 30*(3), 349–360.

Wallerstein, J. S., & Blakeslee, S. (1989). *Second chances: Men, women and children a decade after divorce.* New York: Ticknor & Fields.

Wallerstein, J. S., & Kelly, J. B. (1980). *Surviving the breakup: How children and parents cope with divorce.* New York: Basic Books.

Weiner, I. B. (1982). *Child and adolescent psychopathology.* New York: John Wiley & Sons.

Zill, N., & Schoenborn, C. A. (1990). Developmental, learning and emotional problems: Health of our nation's children, 1988. *Advance Data from Vital and Health Statistics of the National Center for Health Statistics, 190.*

22 / The Impact of Physical, Sexual, and Emotional Abuse

Arthur H. Green

Introduction

Physical abuse and neglect of children and adolescents are major public health problems in many countries throughout the world. In the United States, it was estimated that more than 1,036,000 children were abused or neglected in 1994, and 1,271 children died that year as a result of their maltreatment (National Committee to Prevent Child Abuse, 1995). Although the maltreatment of children has occurred throughout history, it was not defined as a medical problem until 1962, when Kempe, Silverman, Steele, Droegemueller, and Silver (1962) described the "battered child syndrome." Several years later, the first psychiatric studies of abusing parents and their child victims appeared in the literature (Galdston, 1965; Silver, 1968; Steele and Pollock, 1968).

Physical Abuse

Physical abuse has been defined by the Child Abuse Prevention, Adoption, and Family Services Act of 1988 (Public Law 100-294) as "the physical injury of a child under 18 years of age by a person who is responsible for the child's welfare." This includes staff members of facilities providing out-of-home care for children. Most state laws define child physical abuse as the infliction of injury on a person under 18 years of age by a parent or legally responsible caregiver, or allowing such injury to take place.

The possibility of physical abuse must be considered in every child who presents with an injury. Helfer (1975) estimated that 10% of all childhood accidents treated in emergency rooms were consequences of physical abuse. A careful history and physical examination should be performed if an injury is suspected to have been inflicted. While no single physical finding or diagnostic procedure

can confirm the diagnosis of physical abuse with absolute certainty, the presence of the following signs and symptoms derived from the history, physical examination, and observation of the child and parent(s) is suggestive of an inflicted injury:

- Unexplained delay in bringing the child for treatment following the injury
- A history that is contradictory or incompatible with the physical findings
- A history of repeated suspicious injuries
- The parent blaming the injury on the child, a sibling, or a third party
- A history of numerous hospitalizations for prior injuries
- A lack of parental concern about the injury
- Premature and unrealistic expectations of the child by the parent
- The child's accusing the caregiver of the abuse.

PHYSICAL FINDINGS IN CHILD PHYSICAL ABUSE

"Typical" injuries frequently associated with physical abuse are bruises on the buttocks and lower back and bruises in the genital area or inner thigh, which may be inflicted as punishment for soiling or wetting or for resisting toilet training. Bruises of a special configuration, such as hand marks, grab marks, and pinch marks, usually indicate abuse, while bruises and soft tissue injuries at different stages of healing are signs of repeated physical abuse. Certain types of burns are typically inflicted, such as multiple cigarette burns, scalding of the hands or feet, and burns of the perineum or buttocks. Multiple fractures at different stages of healing, spiral fractures caused by a forcible twisting of an arm or leg, and multiple rib fractures caused by blows to the chest or back are reliable indicators of inflicted injury. Radiological evidence of abuse includes subperiosteal hemorrhages, epiphyseal separations, metaphyseal fragmentation, periosteal shearing, and periosteal calcifications.

Additional signs of inflicted trauma are eye injuries, including retinal hemorrhage, dislocated lens, and detached retina; ear injuries such as twisting injuries of the lobe; bruises of the pinna, and ruptured tympanic membrane with hemmorhage and hematoma formation. Cephalhematoma is a typical result of hairpulling.

PSYCHOPATHOLOGY AND PSYCHOLOGICAL IMPAIRMENT IN PHYSICALLY ABUSED CHILDREN

Anxiety Disorders: Pathhological expressions of anxiety, consisting of sleep disturbances, nightmares, increased separation anxiety, phobic behavior, and psychosomatic complaints, may be observed in children who are victims of ongoing physical abuse. The child may be hypervigilant and appear to be anxious and frightened in the presence of the abusing parent. This phobic response may be generalized to other unfamiliar adults. Physically abused children tend to reenact the abuse experiences in play and fantasy in a compulsive, driven manner, which often fails to relieve their anxiety. Some of the abused children satisfy criteria from the fourth edition of the *Diagnostic and Statistical Manual of Mental Disorders* (*DSM-IV;* American Psychiatric Association, 1994) for posttraumatic stress disorder (Green, 1985), displaying autonomic hyperarousal, flashbacks, a marked avoidance of situations evoking memories of their abuse, and a foreshortened future. The symptoms of anxiety may diminish rapidly when children feel secure and protected from the abusive caregivers. On the other hand, long-standing exposure to traumatic abuse might result in chronic posttraumatic stress disorder.

Depression and Low Self-Esteem: Green (1978a) regarded the fragile self-image and low self-esteem in physically abused children as an end result of chronic physical and emotional scarring, humiliation, and scapegoating compounded by each new episode of abuse. These children appeared to internalize the negative feeling their parents expressed toward them. Oates (1986) found that abused children scored significantly lower on the Piers-Harris Self-Concept Scale than did normal children. Gaensbauer and Sands (1979) described social and affective withdrawal, diminished capacity for pleasure, and a proneness toward negative affects such as distress, sadness, and anger in a group of abused infants. Green

(1978a) observed that physically abused children were frequently sad, depressed, and self-deprecatory. Green (1978b) also documented that 40% of a research population of physically abused children displayed self-destructive behavior in the form of self-mutilation, suicide attempts, or suicidal ideation. Allen and Tarnowski (1989) documented a higher incidence of depression and hopelessness in a group of physically abused children than in nonabused controls. The abused children also exhibited a more external locus of control, indicating a perception that their actions have little impact on environmental events. Deykin, Alpert, and McNamarra (1985) reported that adolescents who made suicide attempts were more frequently victimized by physical abuse than nonattempters.

While the self-destructive behavior might be regarded as an expression of compliance with the hostile wishes of the abusing parent, the child's self-injury or provocation of abuse from the environment also might be defensive in nature, providing the child with a means of mastery and control over more frightening and often more traumatic parental beatings that occur spontaneously and without warning.

Increased Aggression: Bullying and assaultive behavior have frequently been described in abused children of all ages. In a day care setting, George and Main (1979) observed that abused toddlers from 1 to 3 years of age physically assaulted their peers twice as often as the nonabused controls. They also assaulted their caregivers. Livingston (1987) documented a diagnosis of conduct disorder in 87% of a population of abused children who were psychiatric inpatients, while Lewis, Shanok, Pincus, and Glaser (1979) described a high incidence of physical abuse in delinquent and violent adolescents. According to Green (1978a), the impaired impulse control in abused children is overdetermined. These children form a basic identification with their violent parents, which facilitates the use of "identification with the aggressor" as a major defense against feelings of anxiety and helplessness. Loss of impulse control is further enhanced by the presence of neurological impairment. Victims of physical abuse are also at risk for battering their future offspring (Green, 1980).

Paranoid Reactions and Mistrust: Physically abused children's prolonged exposure to parental assault and rejection undermine their ability to achieve basic trust (Green, 1978a). These children expect similar maltreatment from other adults and parental figures, and learn to regard all relationships as potentially abusive. Ounstead (1972) described the syndrome of "frozen watchfulness," referring to the expression of hypervigilance and fearfulness in the infant or young child who scans the environment for potentially abusive individuals. This early hypervigilance might be a precursor to subsequent paranoid reactions.

Cognitive and Developmental Impairment: Physically abused children frequently demonstrate cognitive and intellectual impairment on standardized IQ and developmental tests (Martin, 1972; Morse, Sahler, and Friedman, 1970; Smith, 1975). In controlled studies, Oates (1986) and Sandgrund, Gaines, and Green (1974) reported depressed IQ scores in abused children compared with nonabused controls. In the Sandgrund study, 25% of the abused children had IQs of less than 70. While some abused children sustain cognitive damage as a result of their maltreatment, it is possible that many of them might have demonstrated cognitive deficits prior to the abuse, which may have constituted a risk factor in provoking maltreatment. Speech and language impairment in abused children might be caused by an inhibition of these functions if the child is frequently beaten for crying or vocalizing.

Central Nervous System Impairment: Retrospective studies of central nervous system functioning of abused children have documented neurological impairment (Baron, Bejar, & Sheaff, 1970; Morse et al., 1970; Smith & Hanson, 1974), but the causes of this dyfunction are not completely understood. Martin (1972) reported that many abused children with skull fractures and subdural hematomas were neurologically intact, while abused children without head injury displayed neurological deficits. Green, Voeller, Gaines, and Kubie (1981) found that 52% of abused children without obvious head injury were neurologically impaired, compared with 14% of the nonabused controls. However, the abused sample was not more damaged than a neglected, nonabused comparison group. This suggests that the noxious physical and psychological environment associated with maltreatment and neglect, such as perinatal trauma, poor infant and child care, nutritional deficiency, and abnormal sensory stimulation, may be more damaging to the central nervous system than the physical assault itself.

Sexual Abuse

Sexual abuse may be defined as the use of a child for sexual gratification by an adult. *Incest* refers to the sexual exploitation of a child by another family member who is related to the victim by blood or law. Sexual abuse usually involves genital contact and may range in severity from gentle fondling to forcible rape resulting in physical injury. Girls are victimized most commonly by exhibitionism, fondling, genital contact, masturbation, and vaginal, oral, or anal intercourse by a male perpetrator. Boys usually are abused by a male offender, and are typically subjected to fondling, mutual masturbation, fellatio, and anal intercourse.

Finkelhor and Hotaling (1984) project the annual number of new cases of sexual abuse in the United States to be 150,000 to 200,000 if extrafamilial sexual abuse cases and unreported cases are included. Retrospective surveys of women estimate that 38% (Russell, 1983) and 45% (Wyatt, 1985) of community populations of randomly selected women had unwanted sexual contact during childhood.

PHYSICAL FINDINGS IN CHILD SEXUAL ABUSE

A physical examination should be performed immediately if the alleged molestation took place within 72 hours, or if there is a possibility of pregnancy or a sexually transmitted disease. If more than 72 hours elapsed after the alleged molestation, there in less urgency about scheduling the examination.

The examination of females should include observations of the labia majora, labia minora, and vaginal vestibule, encompassing the urethra, periurethral glands, hymenal membrane, hymenal orifice, Bartholin's glands, fossa navicularis, anus, and rectum. The examination of males should include the anus, rectum, penis, and scrotum. The use of a colposcope may facilitate the examination by providing magnification for better visualization of scar tissue and vascular changes. Typical findings of acute trauma are lacerations, petechiae, edema, and contusions. Hymenal tears may indicate penile penetration. Trauma also may produce scar tissue and adhesions (synechiae), which distort the shape of the hymenal membrane. Other signs of chronic sexual abuse are clefts or bumps on the hymenal membrane, labial adhesions, widening of the hymenal orifice, and rounding of the hymenal edge. Signs of anal trauma include hematomas, fissures, prolapse of anal tissue, pigmentation, anal skin tags, hemorrhoids, and scar tissue. Chronic anal penetration may produce changes in anal sphincter tone.

When the child is examined within 72 hours of the alleged molestation, clothing, hair, and debris should be saved to check for the presence of semen in the vagina and anus and on the child's body and clothing. Cultures of the vagina, anus, and throat should be taken routinely to detect the presence of sexually transmitted diseases such as gonorrhea, *Chlamydia trachomatis*, venereal warts (*Condyloma acuminata*), and *Herpes simplex*. A serology should be obtained for the diagnosis of syphilis.

PSYCHOPATHOLOGY IN SEXUALLY ABUSED CHILDREN

A recent study by Merry and Andrews (1994) reported that 63.5% of 66 sexually abused children evaluated with The Diagnostic Interview Schedule for Children warranted an Axis I diagnosis on *DSM-III-R*. The adverse impact of sexual abuse is strikingly similar to that of physical abuse in a number of ways. Sexually abused children exhibit types of pathological anxiety, depression, and mistrust similar to what is encountered in their physically abused peers. However, certain more specific sequelae are unique to sexually abused children, consisting of pathological alterations in sexual behavior and gender identity. Sexually abused children also lack the cognitive and neurological impairment commonly associated with physical assault.

Anxiety Disorders: Fearfulness and anxiety-related symptoms have frequently been described in sexually abused children as an immediate or short-term response to the trauma. Sleep disturbances, insomnia, and nightmares have been documented in sexually abused children by Lewis and Sarrell (1969), Kempe and Kempe (1978), and

Sgroi (1982). Somatic complaints and psychosomatic disorders were observed by Adams-Tucker (1982) and Browning and Boatman (1977). Sgroi (1982) described fear reactions of female sexual abuse victims extending to phobic avoidance of all males. Just as with victims of physical abuse, sexually abused children often satisfy criteria for posttraumatic stress disorder. Goodwin (1985) described fear, startle reactions, repetition, reenactments, flashback to the trauma, explosive anger, and ego constriction in sexually abused children. Kiser, Ackerman, Brown, and Edwards (1988) observed posttraumatic stress disorder in 9 of 10 children from 2 to 6 years old who were sexually abused in a day care setting, while McLeer, Deblinger, Atkins, Foa, and Ralphe (1988) reported that 48% of sexually abused children evaluated at a child psychiatry outpatient clinic met *DSM-III-R* criteria for posttraumatic stress disorder.

Depression and Low Self-Esteem: Depressive symptoms frequently have been reported in sexually abused children. MacVicar (1979) found that sexually abused adolescents were the most vulnerable to depression. Livingston (1987) reported that 10 of 13 sexually abused child psychiatric inpatients manifested major depressive disorder with psychotic features as measured by the Diagnostic Interview Schedule for Children. Sansonnet-Hayden, Haley, Marriage, and Fine (1987) reported that sexually abused adolescent inpatients exhibited more severe depressive symptoms and more suicide attempts based on the Diagnostic Interview Schedule for Children. Friedrich, Urquiza, and Beilke (1986) documented that 46% of a sample of 671 sexually abused girls had elevated scores on the internalizing scale of the Child Behavior Checklist, indicating fearful, inhibited, depressed, and overcontrolled behavior.

Mistrust: Sexually abused children are unable to establish trusting relationships with adults based on the father's breach of his parental role and the mother's failure to protect the child from incest (Herman, 1981). Through the process of generalization, other adults become tainted with the unpredictable and sexually exploitative characteristics of the offender.

Hysterical and Dissociative Symptoms: Goodwin, Zouhar, and Bergman (1989) observed six cases of hysterical seizures in adolescents who had been victims of incest. Gross (1979) also reported four cases of incest related hysterical seizures. Hysterical symptoms may represent the child's attempt to "wall off" traumatic memories of the sexual abuse through such primitive defenses as denial, splitting, and isolation of affect. The most extreme dissociative reactions may lead to multiple personality disorder. Kluft (1985) and Putnam (1984) described multiple personality disorder in sexually abused children, while Goodwin (1989) observed it in adult incest survivors. Some signs of early dissociation in children are the presence of an imaginary companion, excessive fantasizing and daydreaming, forgetfulness with periods of amnesia, sleepwalking, and "blackouts."

Disturbances in Sexual Behavior and Gender Identity: It might be expected that premature exposure to coercive and frightening sexual activity would have an adverse impact on the child's psychosexual development and future capacity for sexual intimacy. Sexual acting out and hypersexuality frequently have been described in the sexual abuse literature (MacVicar, 1979; Sgroi, 1982). Brant and Tisza (1977) postulate that these children provoke further sexual contact both as a means of obtaining pleasure and need satisfaction and as a technique for mastering the sexual abuse trauma. Yates (1982) described the eroticization of preschool children by incest. These young children were orgastic and maintained a high level of sexual arousal. They failed to differentiate affectionate from sexual relationships and became aroused by routine physical or psychological closeness. The promiscuity of these children sometimes extends into prostitution (James & Meyerding, 1977).

Recent studies have demonstrated problems in gender identity and sexual object choice in both boys and girls who have been sexually victimized. Aoisa-Karpas, Karpas, Pelcovitz, and Kaplan (1991) documented problems of gender identity in adolescent girls aged 12 to 19 who had been sexually abused. With regard to their choice of male fantasy roles in early childhood play, the abuse victims reported greater male identification for gender role behavior compared to nonabused psychiatric and nontreated controls. The authors suggest that these adolescent sex abuse victims experience difficulties in the formation and consolidation of a stable female identity due to an identification with a more dominant incestuous father rather than with the disengaged mother. In a simi-

lar study by Cosentino (1991), sexually abused girls experienced extreme unhappiness with their gender and a strong preference to become a boy. They participated more actively in rough-and-tumble play, had a greater interest in traditionally masculine clothing, and manifested a greater tendency to associate with male peers than a comparison group of nonabused girls. Many of the sexually abused girls rejected their female genitalia. Studies of adult women who were sexually victimized during childhood (Fromuth, 1986; Gundlach, 1977) documented a significant relationship between their sexual abuse and subsequent participation in homosexual activity. These studies suggest that the homosexual outcome in female victims of sexual abuse is related to a generalized avoidance of sexual activity with males.

Disturbances in gender identity also have been reported in sexually abused boys (Meyer & Dupkin, 1985; Zucker & Kuksis 1990) and in adult males with a history of sexual abuse during childhood (Dimock, 1988; Myers, 1989). The gender-disordered boys are effeminate and wish to become girls. The adult male survivors of child sexual abuse demonstrate a damaged sense of masculinity and frequent sexual dysfunction. They often exhibit compulsive sexual behavior. Heterosexual survivors of childhood sexual victimization are often homophobic, with an irrational dread of homosexuality. On the other hand, victims of childhood sexual abuse are more likely to become involved in subsequent homosexual activity (Finkelhor & Hotaling, 1984).

Emotional Abuse

Emotional abuse has been defined in the *Study of the National Incidence and Prevalence of Child Abuse and Neglect* (U.S. Department of Health and Human Services, 1988) as follows:

- Close confinement (tying or binding and other forms): Tortuous restriction of movement, as by tying a child's arms or legs together or binding a child to a chair, bed, or other object, or confining a child to an enclosed area as a means of punishment.
- Verbal or emotional assault: Habitual patterns of belittling, denigrating, scapegoating, or other nonphysical forms of overtly hostile or rejecting treat-

ment, as well as threats of other forms of mal-treatment (beating, sexual assault, abandonment, etc.).

- Other or unknown abuse: Overtly punitive, exploitative, or abusive treatment other than that specified under other forms of abuse, or unspecified abusive treatment. This includes attempted or potential physical or sexual assault, deliberate withholding of food, shelter, sleep, or other necessities as a form of punishment, economic exploitation, and unspecified abusive actions.

Social researchers have offered additional definitions of emotional abuse. Garbarino, Guttman, and Seeley (1986) regard emotional abuse as a pattern of psychically destructive behavior inflicted by an adult upon a child. They postulated five forms of emotional abuse: (1) rejecting—devaluing or depreciating the child; (2) terrorizing—threatening or intimidating the child; (3) ignoring—failing to respond appropriately to the child; (4) isolating—limiting the child's contact with peers and adults outside of the family; and (5) corrupting—socializing the child in conflict with prevailing moral standards, reinforcing aggressive, sexual, or criminal behaviors. Hart, Germain, and Brassard (1987) introduced similar operational definitions of psychological abuse: (1) spurning (rejecting), (2) terrorizing, (3) isolating, (4) corrupting/exploiting, and (5) denying emotional responsiveness (ignoring).

INCIDENCE OF EMOTIONAL ABUSE

In 1994, The *National Committee to Prevent Child Abuse* (1995) study estimated the incidence of emotional abuse to be 30,000 in the United States.

PSYCHOPATHOLOGY IN EMOTIONALLY ABUSED CHILDREN

Hart et al. (1987) described a wide range of negative consequences of psychological maltreatment based on clinical case studies and empirical research. The negative behaviors include poor appetite, lying and stealing, encopresis and enuresis, low self-esteem, emotional instability, reduced emotional responsiveness, excessive dependency, underachievement, failure to thrive, pathological aggression, and suicidal behavior. Extreme antisocial behavior, leading to psychopathy and serial murder, has been attributed to psychological neglect that denied children emotional responsiveness and bonding.

Erickson, Egeland, and Pianta (1989) compared children of psychologically unavailable mothers to normal controls. Kindergarten teachers rated the children in the psychologically unavailable group as more aggressive, unpopular, nervous, and overactive than the controls on the Achenbach Child Behavior Checklist. These children also received higher scores on the externalizing scale of the Achenbach and were lower in social competence than children in the control group. They also scored lower on the block design subtest on the Wechsler Preschool and Primary Scale of Intelligence.

Neglect

In contrast to abuse as an act of "commission," neglect of children is considered to be an act of "omission." Neglect is perpetrated by caregivers who fail to fulfill their caregiver obligations to children (Giovannoni, 1988). As defined by the U.S. Department of Health and Human Services (1988), neglect may be broken down into the three categories of physical, educational, and emotional neglect.

PHYSICAL NEGLECT

Physical neglect consists of the caregiver's failure to provide health care or delaying health care for the child when recommended by a health care professional. Physical neglect also includes inadequate supervision and abandonment of a child or expulsion of a child from the home without adequate arrangement for care by others. Additional types of physical neglect include the failure to provide adequate food, clothing, or shelter, and reckless disregard of the child's safety, such as driving with a child while intoxicated.

EDUCATIONAL NEGLECT

Educational neglect includes permitting a child to be absent excessively from school, failing to enroll a child in school, or keeping a school-age child home for nonlegitimate reasons (e.g., to work or to care for a sibling). A final category of educational neglect pertains to the caregiver's refusal to obtain or allow recommended remedial educational services or neglect in following through with a special educational program for a child.

EMOTIONAL NEGLECT

Emotional neglect is defined by the 1988 National Center on Child Abuse Study as "a parent providing inadequate nurturance/affection, exposing a child to chronic or extreme spouse abuse, permitting a child to abuse drugs or alcohol, permitting other maladaptive behavior, or refusing a child psychological care."

PSYCHOPATHOLOGY IN NEGLECTED CHILDREN

The harmful sequelae of neglect and maternal deprivation in infants and young children living in institutions have been described in the pioneering studies of Bowlby (1951), Goldfarb (1945), and Spitz (1945). These children displayed physical and developmental retardation, especially in the area of speech and language, and were impaired in their ability to form human attachments. Researchers felt these symptoms were caused by the unavailability of a consistent caregiver in the institutional setting.

Subsequent studies by Coleman and Provence (1957) and Prugh and Harlow (1962) documented similar types of deprivation leading to impaired development in children living at home as a result of inadequate maternal care. The most common sequelae of neglect in these children, as described by Marans and Lourie (1967), Malone (1967), Rutter (1972), and Green (1980) are developmental delay, pathological object relationships, and difficulties in attachment. Egeland and Sroufe (1981) and Gaensbauer and Harmon (1982) demonstrated anxious/avoidant attachment in neglected infants and toddlers. Maternal unavailability gives rise to diminished initiative and enjoyment in play. Inadequate verbal stimulation contributes to speech and language delays. Neglected children also exhibit poor self-care and accident-proneness in an attempt to provoke a response from the neglectful environment. Many neglected children display poor impulse control

and conduct disorders, which may ultimately lead to delinquency and antisocial behavior (Polansky, Chambers, Buttenwieser, and Williams, 1981).

Several research studies have documented intellectual impairment in neglected youngsters. Polansky et al. (1981) and Sandgrund et al. (1974) reported significantly lower IQ scores in neglected children compared with normal controls. The Sandgrund study found that 20% of the neglected children were retarded, with IQs below 70. Green et al. (1981) reported significant neurological impairment in these same neglected children on the basis of a pediatric neurological examination including electroencephalograms and perceptual motor testing designed to elicit soft signs of central nervous system impairment. The neurological deficits were attributed to poor prenatal and infant care, insufficient or excessive sensory stimulation, poor nutrition, and inadequate medical care.

INTERVENTION IN CHILD MALTREATMENT

The immediate goal of intervention with families involved in child maltreatment is to modify the noxious family environment so that the child is no longer at risk for abuse or neglect. Crisis intervention and treatment of the child and family should commence as soon as possible in order to strengthen and stabilize the family unit and prevent placement of the child. The child should be removed from the home only as a last resort, such as when the abuse or neglect cannot be controlled, or when the maltreating parents are unwilling or unable to follow through with the treatment program while the child is still at risk. The focus of intervention should be on the parents, the child(ren), and the environmental stressors that contribute to the maltreatment.

INTERVENTION WITH MALTREATING PARENTS

Intervention with the parents must deal with any serious psychopathology, including substance abuse, that might contribute to abusive or neglectful child-rearing practices. In addition, parenting education that will enable the parents to utilize nonabusive and nonstigmatizing forms of discipline instead of relying on abusive and neglectful techniques must be provided. The therapist must be able to engage in a supportive, non-judgmental relationship with the parents, while satisfying some of their unmet dependency needs. The parents must learn to recognize and relinquish pathological parenting styles based on exploitation, role reversal, and scapegoating, and avoid the tendency to reenact their own childhood abuse and neglect. Group therapy and family therapy also have proven effective for maltreating parents (Daro, 1988).

INTERVENTION WITH MALTREATED CHILDREN

Maltreated children require complete medical, developmental, and psychiatric evaluation to assess their risk for behavioral and emotional disorders, developmental delays, and learning problems. Most maltreated children will require crisis intervention and short-term psychotherapy or play therapy, in order to help them cope with feelings of betrayal, stigmatization, depression, anger, and heightened anxiety, including posttraumatic stress disorder. Some children will require long-term therapy. Group therapy has been useful with maltreated children. In groups with similarly traumatized peers, they can share their experiences of abuse and neglect in a supportive and understanding milieu. A major treatment goal with maltreated children is to help them to verbalize their repressed memories and affects associated with their abuse or neglect, so they will be less likely to reenact their experiences in the next generation.

INTERVENTION TO REDUCE ENVIRONMENTAL STRESS

The importance of a stressful environment as a catalyst for maltreatment is predicated on the high percentage of low socioeconomic status, multiproblem families in child abuse registers throughout the country (American Humane Association, 1979; Gil, 1970). Environmental stress usually interacts with parent personality variables and child behaviors to potentiate child maltreatment. Environmental stress includes events that widen the discrepancy between the limited child-rearing capacity of the parents and the burden of child rearing in a given family. Diminished capacity for child care may occur when a spouse becomes physically or emotionally unavailable, or when ties with parents or important relatives are severed due to estrangement, illness, or death. Increased child-rearing burdens may consist of the physical or emotional illness of a child, the birth of another child, or the responsibility for the additional care of children of friends or relatives. Other stressors in the environment contributing to maltreatment are large family size, work-related pressures, unemployment, and concrete aspects of poverty—a lack of money, inadequate housing, overcrowding, family disorganization, high crime rate, and unsafe neighborhoods.

The provision of supportive and advocacy services can reduce the numerous environmental stressors experienced by maltreating families. A therapist or social worker may assume an advocacy role in the parents' numerous encounters with municipal and community agencies, such as the welfare department, protective service agency, schools, housing administration, and the courts. The advocate also may help arrange for child care, day care, or nursery programs. Home-making assistance might be required to help with cooking, cleaning, and child care during times of stress when the family is overburdened. The advocate also might assist the family in obtaining medical and dental care and family planning counseling. Job training and job placement are additional types of services that can help families achieve a measure of independence. Legal assistance might be provided to the family to help in their dealings with the family court or with law enforcement personnel. A hot line for emergencies and home visiting are also important outreach modalities that may stabilize a family under stress.

These interventions are directed toward parents, children, and the maltreating environment. These efforts usually are carried out by specialized multidisciplinary treatment programs for abused and neglected children and their families; as a rule, such programs are based in hospitals, communities, or social agencies. Mental health professionals play a major role in the provision and coordination of these services.

REFERENCES

Adams-Tucker, C. (1982). Proximate effects of sexual abuse in childhood: A report on 28 children. *American Journal of Psychiatry, 139,* 1252–1256.

Allen, D. M., & Tarnowski, K. J. (1989). Depressive characteristics of physically abused children. *Journal of Abnormal Child Psychology, 17,* 1–11.

American Psychiatric Association. (1994). *Diagnostic and statistical manual of mental disorders* (4th ed.). Washington, DC: Author.

Aoisa-Karpas, C., Karpas, R., Pelcovitz, D., & Kaplan, S. (1991). Gender identification and sex role attribution in sexually abused adolescent females. *Journal of the American Academy of Child and Adolescent Psychiatry, 30,* 266–271.

American Humane Association. (1979). *National survey of reported cases of child abuse and neglect, 1977.* Denver: Author.

Baron, M., Bejar, R., & Sheaff, P. (1970). Neurological manifestations of the battered child syndrome. *Pediatrics, 45,* 1003–1007.

Bowlby, J. (1951). Maternal care and mental health. *Bulletin of the World Health Organization, 31,* 355–533.

Brant, R., & Tisza, V. (1977). The sexually misused child. *American Journal of Orthopsychiatry, 47,* 80–90.

Browning, D. H., & Boatman, B. (1977). *Incest: Children at risk. American Journal of Psychiatry, 134,* 69–72.

Coleman, R., & Provence, S. A. (1957). Developmental retardation (hospitalism) in infants living in families. *Pediatrics, 19,* 285–292.

Cosentino, C. E. (1991). Gender role behavior and sexual behavior in girls who were sexually abused. Unpublished doctoral dissertation, New York University, New York.

Daro, D. (1988) *Confronting child abuse: Research for effective program design.* New York: Free Press.

Deykin, E., Alpert, J., & McNamarra, J. (1985). A pilot study of the effect of exposure to child abuse or neglect on suicidal behavior. *American Journal of Psychiatry, 142,* 1299–1303.

Dimock, P. (1988). Adult males sexually abused as children. *Journal of Interpersonal Violence, 3,* 203–221.

Egeland, B., & Sroufe, A. (1981). Attachment and early maltreatment. *Child Development, 52,* 44–52.

Erickson, M. E., Egeland, B., & Pianta, R. (1989). The effects of maltreatment on the development of young children. In D. Cicchetti & V. Carlson (Eds.), *Child maltreatment: Theory and research on the causes and consequences of child abuse and neglect* (pp. 647–684). Cambridge: Cambridge University Press.

Finkelhor, D., & Hotaling, G. (1984). Sexual abuse in the national incidence study of child abuse and neglect. *Child Abuse & Neglect, 8,* 22–32.

Friedrich, W. N., Urquiza, A. J., & Beilke, R. (1986). Behavioral problems in sexually abused young children. *Journal of Pediatric Psychology, 11,* 47–57.

Fromuth, M. E. (1986). The relationship of childhood sexual abuse with later psychological and sexual adjustment in a sample of college women. *Child Abuse & Neglect, 10,* 5–15.

Gaensbauer, T., & Harmon, R. (1982). Attachment behavior in abused/neglected and premature infants: Implications for the concept of attachment. In R. N. Emde & R. J. Harmon (Eds.), *Attachment and affiliative systems* (pp. 245–279). New York: Plenum Press.

Gaensbauer, T., & Sands, K. (1979). Distorted communication in abused/neglected infants and their potential impact on caretakers. *Journal of the American Academy of Child Psychiatry, 18,* 236–250.

Galdston, R. (1965). Observations on children who have been physically abused and their parents. *American Journal of Psychiatry, 122,* 440–443.

Garbarino, J., Guttman, E., & Seeley, J. (1986). *The psychologically battered child.* San Francisco: Jossey-Bass.

George, C., & Main, M. (1979). Social interactions of young abused children: Approach, avoidance, and aggression. *Child Development, 50,* 3306–318.

Gil, D. (1970). *Violence against children.* Cambridge, MA: Harvard University Press.

Giovannoni, J. (1988). Overview of issues on child neglect. In *Child neglect monograph: Proceedings from a symposium* (pp. 1–6). Washington, DC: Clearinghouse on Child Abuse and Neglect Information.

Goldfarb, W. (1945). Psychological privation in infancy and subsequent adjustment. *American Journal of Orthopsychiatry, 102,* 247–255.

Goodwin, J. (1985). Post-traumatic symptoms in incest victims. In: S. Eth & R. Pynoos (Eds.), *Post-traumatic stress disorder in children* (pp. 157–168). Washington, DC: American Psychiatric Association Press.

Goodwin, J. (1989). Recognizing multiple personality disorder in adult incest victims. In J. Goodwin (Ed.), *Sexual abuse: Incest victims and their families* (pp. 160–181). Chicago: Year Book Medical Publishers.

Goodwin, J., Zouhar, M. S., & Bergman, R. (1989). Hysterical seizures in adolescent incest victims. In J. Goodwin (Ed.), *Sexual abuse: Incest victims and their families* (pp. 125–132). Chicago: Year Book Medical Publishers.

Green, A. H. (1978a). Psychopathology of abused children. *Journal of the American Academy of Child Psychiatry, 17,* 92–103.

Green, A. H. (1978b). Self destructive behavior in battered children. *American Journal of Psychiatry, 135,* 579–586.

Green, A. H. (1980). *Child maltreatment: A handbook for mental health and child care professionals.* New York: Jason Aronson.

Green, A. H. (1985). Children traumatized by physical abuse. In S. Eth & R. Pynoos (Eds.), *Post-traumatic stress disorder in children* (pp. 135–154). Washington, DC: American Psychiatric Press.

Green, A. H., Voeller, K., Gaines, R. W., & Kubie, J. (1981). Neurological impairment in battered children. *Child Abuse and Neglect, 5,* 129–134.

Gross, M. (1979). Incestuous rape: A cause for hysterical seizures in four adolescent girls. *American Journal of Orthopsychiatry, 49,* 704–708.

Gundlach, R. H. (1977). Sexual molestation and rape reported by homosexual and heterosexual women. *Journal of Homosexuality, 2,* 367–384.

Hart, S. N., Germain, R., & Brassard, M. R. (1987). The challenge: To better understand and combat psychological maltreatment of children and youth. In M. R. Brassard, R. Germaine, & S. N. Hart (Eds.), *Psychological maltreatment of children and youth* (pp. 3–24). New York: Pergamon Press.

Helfer, R. E. (1975). The diagnostic process and treatment programs (DHEW publication No. OHD 75-69). Washington, DC: U.S. Department of Health, Education, and Welfare, National Center for Child Abuse and Neglect.

Herman, J. (1981). *Father-daughter incest.* Cambridge, MA: Harvard University Press.

James, J., & Meyerding, J. (1977). Early sexual experience as a factor in prostitution. *American Journal of Psychiatry, 134,* 1381–1385.

Kempe, C. H., Silverman, F. N., Steele, B. F., Droegemueller, W., & Silver, H. (1962). The battered child syndrome. *Journal of the American Medical Association, 181,* 17–24.

Kempe, R., & Kempe, C. H. (1978). *Child abuse.* Cambridge, MA: Harvard University Press.

Kiser, L. J., Ackerman, B. J., Brown, E., & Edwards, N. B. (1988). Post-traumatic stress disorder in young children: A reaction to pourported sexual abuse. *Journal of the American Academy of Child and Adolescent Psychiatry, 27,* 645–649.

Kluft, R. (1985). *Childhood antecedents of multiple personality.* Washington, DC: American Psychiatric Press.

Lewis, D. O., Shanok, S. S., Pincus, J. H., & Glaser, G. H. (1979). Violent juvenile delinquents: Psychiatric, neurological, psychological, and abuse factors. *Journal of the American Academy of Child Psychiatry, 18,* 307–319.

Lewis, M., & Sarrell, P. (1969). Some psychological aspects of seduction, incest and rape in childhood. *Journal of the American Academy of Child Psychiatry, 8,* 606–619.

Livingston, R. (1987). Sexually and physically abused children. *Journal of the American Academy of Child and Adolescent Psychiatry, 26,* 413–415.

MacVicar, K. (1979). Psychotherapy of sexually abused girls. *Journal of the American Academy of Child Psychiatry, 18,* 342–353.

Malone, C. A. (1967). Developmental deviations considered in the light of environmental forces. In E. Pavenstedt (Ed.), *The drifters: Children of disorganized lower class families* (pp. 125–161). Boston: Little, Brown.

Marans, A. E., & Lourie, R. (1967). Hypotheses regarding the effects of child rearing patterns on the disadvantaged child. In J. Hellmuth, (Ed.), *The disadvantaged child* (pp. 19–41). New York: Brunner/Mazel.

Martin, H. (1972). The child and his development. In C. Kempe & R. Helfer (Eds.), *Helping the battered child and his family* (pp. 93–114). Philadelphia: Lippincott.

McLeer, S. V., Deblinger, E., Atkins, M., Foa, E., & Ralphe, D. (1988). Post-traumatic stress disorder in sexually abused children. *Journal of the American Academy of Child and Adolescent Psychiatry, 27,* 650–654.

Merry, S. N., & Andrews, L. K. (1994) Psychiatric status of sexually abused children 12 months after disclosure of abuse. *Journal of the American Academy of Child and Adolescent Psychiatry, 33,* 939–944.

Meyer, J. K., & Dupkin, C. (1985). Gender disturbance in children: An interim clinical report. *Bulletin of the Meninger Clinic, 49,* 236–239.

Morse, W., Sahler, O., & Friedman, S. (1970). A 3-year follow-up study of abused and neglected children. *American Journal of Diseases of Children, 120,* 439–446.

Myers, M. F. (1989). Men sexually assaulted as adults and sexually abused as boys. *Archives of Sexual Behavior, 18,* 203–215.

National Committee to Prevent Child Abuse. (1995). *Current trends in child abuse reporting and fatalities: The results of the 1994 annual 50 state survey.* Chicago: Author.

Oates, K. (1986). *Child abuse and neglect: What happens eventually?* New York: Brunner/Mazel.

Ounsted, L. (1972). Essay on developmental medicine. In B. Mandelbrote & M. G. Gelder (Eds.), *Psychological aspects of medical practice* (p. 130). London: Staples.

Polansky, N. A., Chambers, M., Buttenwieser, E., & Williams, D. P. (1981). *Damaged parents: An anatomy of child neglect.* Chicago: University of Chicago Press.

Prugh, D. G., & Harlow, R. G. (1962). "Masked deprivation" in infants and young children. In *Deprivation of maternal care: A reassessment of its effects* (pp. 201–221). Geneva: World Health Organization.

Putnam, F. (1984), The psychophysiologic investigation of multiple personality disorder. *Psychiatric Clinics of North America, 7,* 31–40.

Russell, D. (1983). Incidence and prevalence of intrafamilial and extrafamilial sexual abuse of female children. *Child Abuse and Neglect, 7,* 133–146.

Rutter, M. (1972). Maternal deprivation reconsidered. *Journal of Psychosomatic Research, 16,* 241–250.

Sandgrund, A., Gaines, R. W., & Green, A. (1974). Child abuse and mental retardation: A problem of cause and effect. *American Journal of Mental Deficiency, 79,* 327–330.

Sansonnet-Hayden, H., Haley, G., Marriage, K., & Fine, S. (1987). Sexual abuse and psychopathology in hospitalized adolescents. *Journal of the American Academy of Child and Adolescent Psychiatry, 26,* 753–757.

Sgroi, S. (1982). *Handbook of clinical intervention in child sexual abuse.* Lexington, MA: Lexington Books.

Silver, L. (1968). The psychological aspects of the battered child and his parents. *Clinical Proceedings of The Children's Hospital in the District of Columbia, 24,* 355–364.

Smith, S. M. (1975). The battered child syndrome. London: Butterworths.

Spitz, R. A. (1945). Hospitalism: An inquiry into the genesis of psychiatric conditions of early childhood. *Psychoanalytic Study of the Child, 1,* 53–74.

Steele, B., & Pollock, C. A. (1968). A psychiatric study of parents who abuse infants and small children. In R. E. Helfer & C. H. Kempe (Eds.), *The battered child,* (pp. 103–147). Chicago: University of Chicago Press.

U.S. Department of Health and Human Services. (1988). *Study findings: Study of the national incidence and prevalence of child abuse and neglect.* Washington, DC: Author.

Wyatt, G. E. (1985). The sexual abuse of Afro-American and white American women in childhood. *Child Abuse and Neglect, 9,* 507–519.

Yates, A. (1982). Children eroticized by incest. *American Journal of Psychiatry, 139,* 482–485.

Zucker, K. J., & Kuksis, M. (1990). Gender dysphoria and sexual abuse: A case report. *Child Abuse & Neglect, 14,* 281–283.

23 / Bereavement of the Grade-School Child

Erna Furman

History of the Disorder

Bereavement is defined as the loss of a loved one through death. Since the human infant requires extensive nursing and nurturing, relationships are the sine qua non of human survival and growth during childhood, and they continue to play a major part in the lives of adults. And since death is a part of life, it has always, sooner or later, ruptured these relationships and caused the surviving partner to be bereaved. The death of a loved one has been acknowledged as an important event in all cultures at all times. Most social groups have evolved special ceremonies and customs to assist the bereaved. By contrast, the individual's inner, psychic task of coming to terms with the death of a loved one has been studied only this century, beginning with Freud's *Mourning and Melancholia* (1915/1955).

Death and bereavement, however, are such painful facts and pose such a threat to our innermost selves that, despite their universality and frequency, study of the psychological aspects has been halting and understanding often beclouded by unconscious defenses (Gorer, 1965; Mitford, 1962; Stern, 1968a, 1968b). This has been especially true in regard to bereavement in childhood, where it can make the most powerful impact. The defenses of some adults led them to minimizing this impact by denying children's capacity to understand death or to experience the feelings evoked by it. More recently, other researchers have minimized the impact of death by being overly active and didactic in the unspoken hope of "getting it over with" quickly and efficiently.

Truly understanding and helping a bereaved person, especially a child, make special demands on the professional mental health worker. However skilled and experienced we may be, we need to realize that the problems of death and bereavement cannot be mastered intellectually without our inevitable and necessary emotional involvement. This implies empathizing with each bereaved individual's specific experiences and feelings, coming to terms with them in ourselves, and accepting the limitations of our helplessness in the face of death. Since no two patients, deaths, or bereavements are quite alike, each will strike different chords in us and require us to come to terms, with each patient afresh, in a new way. If we succeed sufficiently in this never-ending difficult task, we can achieve that essential middle ground between the extremes of emotional overinvolvement and cool distance, so well expressed in the words of St. Francis: "There but for the grace of God go I"; it is not me, but it could be.

Comparative Nosology

DESCRIPTION OF THE BEREAVEMENT TASK

The mental work of bereaved individuals consists of adapting themselves psychically to the permanent external unavailability of the deceased loved one. Laymen as well as professionals often refer to this as *mourning*. Actually, mourning is only one part of the wider bereavement task (E. Furman, 1974). It differs in intensity and duration, depending on the nature of the relationship to the deceased, and consists of three successive and partly overlapping parts: (1) Understanding and accepting the death of a loved one; (2) the mourning process itself; and (3) resuming and continuing with one's life.

Understanding and accepting a loved one's death implies knowing what dead means, understanding the cause and circumstances of the particular death and how and where the bodily remains of the deceased were disposed of—buried or cremated. It implies also an inner acceptance of these facts. At the same time, during this often insufficiently appreciated initial phase, bereaved people need to assure themselves that they and their surviving loved ones will not die in the foreseeable future. On the contrary, their bodily and emotional needs will be sufficiently assured to make their continuing life worth living.

The process of mourning encompasses two simultaneous aspects. One is detachment, the painful repeated confrontation between longing for the deceased and finding him or her externally unavailable. This period helps people to resign themselves and to loosen and detach many of the inner ties to the memory image of the lost loved one and the relationship with him or her. Detachment is accompanied by a variety of intense feelings, including sadness, anger, guilt, pain, and is therefore often the stage of bereavement best rec-

ognized by bereaved individuals and by those around them. The second aspect, identification, proceeds silently and often goes unnoticed. It consists of bereaved people taking into themselves aspects of the dead loved one's personality and integrating them permanently as a part of themselves; for example, a widow may take over her dead husband's activities or some of his likes and habits. Insofar as the internalized parts fit the bereaved individual's personality and serve adaptively, they can enrich him or her and, at the same time, soothe the distress of detachment.

Resuming and continuing the course of living is the last stage. When mourning has proceeded enough to free energy for renewed investment in people and activities, bereaved people begin to resume their work and interests and, depending on their stage in life, may build new relationships—for example, a young widower may remarry, an old one may decide to remain single. This phase rekindles the anguish of detachment as the new and lost relationships are compared or as the new aloneness is again contrasted with the lost shared life.

When one phase of the bereavement task has been mastered to a sufficient extent, the next one is initiated spontaneously. Special difficulties may arise during each phase or be due to unresolved problems from preceding phases. At best and especially with major bereavements, that is, those of important, intensively invested relationships, mastery does not mean "over and done with"; nor does it imply the end of anguish and struggle. It merely implies the ability to progress phase-appropriately in life, without undue interference by the burden of a failed or insufficiently worked through psychic task. There is no real end to mourning. Anniversaries or special life situations may at any time revive old feelings and memories and may require more working through.

DEVELOPMENT OF THE CAPACITY TO MOURN

For a long time children's capacity to mourn was denied and disputed (Wolfenstein, 1966, 1969), even after clinical cases demonstrated it (Barnes, 1964; R. A. Furman, 1964a, b, 1967). While this was in part due to poorly understood data, it stemmed largely from our difficulty with facing death as adults and with fulfilling the important role we have to assume to assist children in mastering bereavement. With such help, children from nursery school age on are developmentally capable of mourning as adults can. In some instances even youngsters in their second and third years of life could be helped to do so (E. Furman, 1974).

This holds true even with the most incisive and difficult bereavement, namely the death of a child's parent. The incomparable hardship of a parental bereavement is related to two factors: First, children's relationships with their parents are so closely and intensely invested that all their other relationships pale by comparison. Adults, by contrast, maintain several meaningful relationships (spouse, parents, relatives, friends, children, colleagues). Second, the parent is not only children's most important loved and loving person, he or she is also a part of the children, functioning for them, fostering the growth of their functions, and, through their relationship, providing a model and means of integrating new personality structures that ultimately enable children to live independently. In children's earliest years, parents even meet all of their bodily needs; during the school years, parents become internalized as children's conscience, values, attitudes, and interests; during adolescence they serve as the model for children's growing identity as a sexual adult, parent, and breadwinner. Thus, a parent's death confronts children with a double loss, that of a uniquely close relationship and that of a part of the self. Only a parent's loss of a child comes close to the depth of this relationship, in that parents also view their children as part of themselves; however, the parent's personality can function without the child (E. Furman, 1980).

A child can mourn the loss of a loved one, even of a parent, if the living parent or parent substitute fulfills those functions that the child has not yet developed sufficiently. In terms of the first phase of the bereavement task, school-age children usually know what dead means in concrete terms as well as how the bodily remains are disposed of, but they rely on adults to understand the specific cause and circumstances of the death. Since parents, not to mention siblings, of growing children are rather young, their deaths are untimely and harrowing, caused by violence (acci-

dents, murders) or pernicious disease (cancer, heart failure, mental illness leading to suicide). Despite the fright these circumstances engender for adult and child, they need to be clarified truthfully. Adults cannot mourn when they are deprived of this information—for example, when soldiers are missing in action. At the same time, adults need to meet children's bodily and emotional needs and assure them that neither the children nor they themselves will die for a long time. This reassurance constitutes children's equivalent of the adult's need for financial security and support of friends and relatives. It helps them feel that life will still be ongoing and worthwhile.

During the second phase, that of mourning proper, school-age children need empathy and support in order to tolerate the intense mixed feelings accompanying detachment. Children also need help with identification as they may select to take in attributes of the deceased that deeply impressed them but are maladaptive, such as symptoms of the deceased loved one's terminal illness (weakness, stomach pains), or personal problems (argumentativeness or harshness) (R.A. Furman, 1967).

For school-age children, the third phase of resuming the course of living involves building a new relationship after a parent's death. Sometimes children may, on their own, find partial new relationships among relatives or neighbors, or with a sports coach. But new relationships are not invested just because they are available. Children may not really relate even to a grandparent or stepparent who cares for them until the children are internally ready. Sometimes, however, children may be ready when nobody is available. The arrival of a stepparent depends on the surviving parent's readiness, not on the child's (E. Furman, 1974).

EPIDEMIOLOGICAL DATA

Children encounter death almost daily from early on, in the form of withering plants, killed insects and worms, dead animals by the roadside, funeral processions, news of others' deaths, and TV programs. These encounters can be used to develop a concept of death and its causes as well as of ways of disposal of the dead (E. Furman, 1990). Such understanding can then be used in coping with meaningful losses, which are also much more common than is usually appreciated. Among these are the many deaths of pets, grandparents, and siblings, especially through perinatal death (E. Furman, 1979; Leon, 1990). According to the 1971 U.S. Bureau of the Census, 4.7% of children under 18 years of age have lost either their father or mother through death. This percentage has varied but slightly during the preceding and following 20 years.

Clinical Presentation and Diagnostic Assessment

OVERT SIGNS/SYMPTOMS OF BEREAVEMENT WORK

To ascertain clinically whether children who have suffered a meaningful loss through death are grappling with their bereavement task, we need to explore with them and their family how each phase has been addressed. To start with, have the children demonstrated an understanding and acceptance of the concrete aspects of death, about the exact causes and circumstances of this death and of the burial or cremation? Have the children, in words and/or behavior, asked whether they and their caregivers will die? Do the children feel reasonably assured on this score? Have they shown concern about who will care for them and questioned and tested their commitment, as through demands for services, such as buying things, going places, special foods? Have the adults understood and addressed the children's questions helpfully and, if so, have the children felt sufficiently relieved to begin the second phase, mourning proper?

Mourning proper may evidence itself in thinking and talking about the deceased, sadness and reproaches against self and others, crying or overwhelming sobbing and rage. But children may not express overt tears and anguish; they often fear the seeming loss of bodily control, which reminds them of incontinence (R.A. Furman, 1968). Do the children insist on, or shy away from, activities that were a part of the lost relationship? Are they angry and irritable? Is there evidence of adaptive or maladaptive identification with the deceased?

Do the children appear preoccupied, joyless, and feeling low or inadequate? Children also may lose recently acquired functions that still depended on the dead parent's participation; for example, school achievements may lapse when there is no parent to share them with. The caring adults need to recognize and discuss this with children, saying "I know how hard it is to do the work and to enjoy it without Mom. But we can spend extra time on it together and remember how pleased she would be to see you do well and have fun."

Allowing for a measure of overlap, are there as yet signs of the third phase, of resuming the course of living? Are periods of acute mourning becoming intermittent and interspersed with times of regained pleasure in play and activities? Are there signs of wishing for, seeking out, and relating with potential new loved ones, or of painful comparison between the new and lost relationship? Have the newly invested and surviving adults recognized the children's conflict and respected their continuing psychic ties to the deceased? Or have they insisted on usurping that place in the children's love?

Last but not least, have additional stresses interfered with the bereavement work? Such stresses may have stemmed from without, including separation at the time of the bereavement or following it, move to a new house with loss of school and friends, a diminished standard of living, and especially loss of other family members, such as mother going to work or placement of siblings in day care or other homes. Stresses operating within children may include the state of their bodily and mental health at the time of the bereavement. The bereavement task makes such intense demands on the personality that it cannot be handled when energy is drained off by bodily illness or tied up in emotional lags and symptoms.

RELATIONSHIP TO OTHER DISORDERS

The psychic responses to losses other than of loved ones and other than through death are often equated with mourning. Some apply the term *mourning* to partial, temporary, or potentially reversible absences of the loved one, as in separation, divorce, emotional withdrawal, or depression of the loved one. Some use it with developmental losses, as in the baby's weaning or the adolescent's detachment from infantile ties to parents (Nagera, 1970). Many connect it with relationships that never existed, such as an adopted child's "loss" of the biological mother he or she never knew or the "loss" of the imagined healthy baby when a defective one was born (Solnit & Stark, 1961). The term *mourning* often is also applied to losses that do not even involve a loved one but represent parts of an individual's own personality or belongings, such as loss of home, country, or fortune; loss of limb through amputation; loss of a function such as vision or motility through illness; loss of youth through aging; or loss of ideals and status.

These kinds of losses, although similar in some respects to the loss of a loved one through death, differ greatly in others and are coped with by different mental means (E. Furman, 1974). The partial, temporary, and potentially reversible losses of loved ones are not coped with by mourning because they lack the special finality of death. Unless this unique reality is the cause of the loss, comprehended and acknowledged as such, mourning proper cannot take place. This fact does not imply that the other losses are less hard or more readily worked through. On the contrary, death, for all its threat to us and for all our helplessness in the face of it, does not imply a rejection or insufficient caring, and it happens only once. It never exposes us to the repeated dashed hopes and unbearable frustrations that so often accompany separations. For example, children who lost one parent through death and another through divorce could be helped to master their bereavement but not the separation from the living but unavailable parent (Goldman, 1974).

As to the losses of parts of the self, including the mental image of persons who were never really known, while the loss may well be irrevocable, there is another crucial difference. We can love parts of ourselves but they cannot love us back. Only a real relationship provides the mutuality of loving and being loved. Losses of a part of ourselves lower our self-love and self-regard and require a painful readjustment of our self-image, but they differ from the loss of a relationship and its related bereavement task. It is therefore more accurate and clinically helpful to restrict the term *mourning* to the loss of a loved one through death.

Another common confusion obtains in connecting mourning with depression. Children who are developmentally capable of engaging in the bereavement task—that is, children from nursery school age on—do not normally respond to the death of a loved one with a reactive depression, even though they may experience periods of feeling low, apathetic, or self-reproachful. In instances where bereaved schoolchildren are clinically primarily depressed or apathetic (a difficult differential diagnosis in itself) and do not proceed with the psychic bereavement work, their response usually indicates either a defense against sadness and/or a belated reaction to a variety of early infantile experiences that were triggered by the current bereavement (Fleming, 1974; E. Furman, 1974; Gut, 1989; McCann, 1974; Rosenbaum, 1974; Schiff, 1974).

PATTERNS OF PEER RELATIONSHIPS

Schoolchildren's peer relationships may be affected by bereavement. Most obviously, the preoccupation with the bereavement work and attendant diminished pleasure in pursuits may lead to some withdrawal from peers or to lack of pleasure in being with them. By contrast, increased engagement with peers and heightened excitement—as opposed to calm content—in play and activities with them tends to indicate a defensive turning away from the bereavement task and a defensive reversal of affect, from feeling sad and low to feeling pseudohappy and excited.

Children almost never use peers, even if they are real friends, for help with a bereavement the way they use caring adults. On the contrary, bereaved children often shun peers or at least avoid discussing the bereavement with them. To an extent this may serve as a temporary respite from inner pain. Mostly however, and especially when a parent dies, this avoidance is related to children's diminished self-regard vis-à-vis their peers, their feeling that the others are worthier and that by lacking a parent they do not measure up, are not a "regular guy." Some children are even ashamed of being orphans and resent the fact being known or talked about.

Like the death of a contemporary in adult life, the death of a peer or of a peer's parent represents a special threat to oneself, even if he or she was not meaningfully invested. Children therefore need extra adult help to deal with the heightened concern for their own safety (E. Furman, 1978; R. A. Furman, 1968).

PATTERNS OF PLAY

During the latency years, children do not usually utilize imaginary symbolic play in coping with a bereavement, and such play does not shed light on children's psychic struggle with the death, unless children are in therapy and favor this means of communication with the therapist. Children often utilize structured play, such as puzzles and board games, as a means of respite from the bereavement task or as a defense against it. Certain kinds of imaginary and structured forms of play also may be used to re-create and relive the relationship with the deceased if the particular play used to be fondly shared.

PSYCHODYNAMIC FORMULATION

Patterns of Defense: As already mentioned, the ability to master a bereavement requires (1) the achievement of a certain developmental level of personality functioning, one normally already surpassed by the school-age child; (2) sufficient bodily and mental health to enable all parts of the personality to draw on its optimal resources of energy; (3) lack of or at least minimal experience of additional external stresses; (4) assurance of continued bodily and emotional well-being; and (5) phase-appropriate assistance with all parts of the bereavement task by the surviving parent or parent substitutes.

Even with all these factors operative, children normally use defenses at times to "cushion" the psychic stress. For example, denial may be used to stave off the horror of the real cause and circumstances of a death (such as a murder), or the pain of the finality of death (as when a child believes in reunion with the deceased), or the threat of one's own death. Many defenses, including reversal of affect, may ward off painful feelings. Displacement of anger to the living may serve to protect the needed inner loving tie to the deceased. It is important to assess whether these defenses are only temporary and/or are paralleled by genuine understanding and feeling at other times, as well as the extent to which caring adults empathically help children with tolerating the inner and outer reality or perhaps actually share or support the defenses.

Ego Functioning and Strengths: The available strengths a person has to tolerate a variety of unpleasurable feelings and to be able to face, understand, and accept stressful realities are of great help in coping with a bereavement. Developing these functions and valuing them in oneself depends, of course, primarily on the educational approach of the parents and on the model of their own comparable strengths. Thus, some parents, from early on, use the opportunity of brief separations to support their children's ability to bear and express sadness, longing, anger, disappointment. They also use children's observations of death in plants and insects to assist them in acquiring a basic concept of death. Inquiring into the ways in which feelings and reality are handled in minor situations and with uncomfortable realities other than death often affords insight into the parents' as well as children's attitudes and coping mechanisms with a bereavement.

Superego: When children experience too much difficulty with the detachment aspect of bereavement, they may unconsciously make excessive use of the aspect of identification. Augmented by unrecognized anger at the deceased, such "wholesale" identification may lead to harsh superego introjects, which may show in unreasonably high self-expectation in achievement, self-control, and morality as well as in extreme guilt, lowered self-esteem, and self-punishment or fear of punishment with even minor lapses or transgressions (Meiss, 1952). Bereaved children's relentless hard work, overachieving, and excellent behavior are sometimes viewed as the positive outcome of a bereavement. These manifestations actually tend to mask a pathology based on psychic conflict with a harsh superego introject.

COMPARISON WITH PRESENTATION OF BEREAVEMENT IN OTHER STAGES OF LIFE

Apart from the different and usually most serious predicament of a bereavement during the first 2 to 3 years of age, children and adults psychically cope with bereavements in the same manner, and all face similar concerns and hardships although, as mentioned earlier, the stressful impact of a parental bereavement in childhood has no equivalent in adulthood. The other difference, namely children's need of the caring adults' help, is only relative. The older the children, the less they require the assistance of their surviving loved ones, but even adults normally require considerable support. Mourning alone is nearly impossible (Kroeber, 1964).

Since mastering a bereavement is difficult at best, adults tend to encounter as many hurdles as children do. Often a child's mourning is handicapped by a parent's inability to mourn, and often children master a bereavement whereas adults cannot (E. Furman, 1974).

Etiology/Pathogenesis

BIOLOGICAL ASPECTS

There is as yet no evidence of genetic influences on the psychic bereavement task. Nor is there evidence of specific neurochemical components triggering or accompanying the bereavement work. Also, affective and behavioral manifestations related to mourning are not indicative of cyclothymic disease and need to be distinguished from it. As discussed earlier, manifestations of depression tend to be defensive and/or related to a variety of very early experiences rekindled by the bereavement. Temporary depressive affect and related behavior also may represent a healthy means of self-protection and further, rather than impede, the personality's ability to engage in the bereavement work in time, after a necessary respite (Gut, 1989).

The use of drugs, especially with children, is contraindicated, not only because of their potential noxious side effects (Ambrosini, Rabinovich, & Puig-Antich, 1984; Kovacs, Feinberg, Crouse-Novak, Paulauskas, & Finkelstein, 1984; Kovacs et al., 1984) but particularly because they aim to suppress the full intense experience of feelings. Feelings are a crucial means of coping with a bereavement. Their psychic unavailability to the bereaved personality interferes with its ability to master the bereavement.

TRAUMATIC ASPECTS

As mentioned, traumatic deaths, so common with children and their parents, have a very stressful and potentially traumatic effect on the bereaved—not only due to the cause and circumstances of the death but also to the manner in which the bereaved learns about it, as by witnessing it him- or herself and/or being involved in

it, as may happen with car crashes (Schiff, 1974) or suicides (E. Furman, 1981), or by finding out about it totally unprepared. Even partial mastery of these traumata is very painful and difficult and tends to delay or prevent the unfolding of the bereavement work (E. Furman, 1986).

PSYCHOSOCIAL ASPECTS

All societies, cultural groups, and religions have evolved their own rites and beliefs to deal with death and bereavement. Notably, none of them deny the concrete aspects of death. Verification of the death and forms of disposal of the bodily remains are always part of the traditional rituals. Yet often psychosocial aspects serve to soften or countermand the threat and anguish of death for the survivors; these include belief in afterlife, return of the deceased, or reincarnation. School-age children are able to understand such beliefs as long as they also are helped to know clearly the concrete aspects of death and as long as neither they nor their loved ones misuse the spiritual to deny the concrete.

FAMILIAL ASPECTS

In the United States, families can, to a considerable extent, choose their own ways of dealing with a death. The rites and beliefs they feel most comfortable with are usually the most helpful to them (E. Furman, 1976). Schoolchildren benefit from being respected participants at funeral rites if caring adults assist them in explaining and preparing for all aspects and remain emotionally available to them throughout. Sometimes families want to "protect" children, either by keeping them away or by telling them beliefs they, the adults, do not hold, such as the dead going to heaven. In these ways the adults really protect a part of themselves, confuse the young, and create an unhelpful emotional barrier between themselves and the children that interferes with mourning. By contrast, children may welcome sharing in beliefs that the adults truly hold, as long as the concrete death also is acknowledged.

VULNERABILITY

Apart from the factors already discussed, schoolchildren's main vulnerability is their still considerable developmental dependence on their parents—the parents' ability to assist them phase-appropriately with their bereavement work, to meet their bodily needs, and to remain emotionally available.

Morbidity

EFFECTS ON CHILDREN'S FUNCTIONING/ DEVELOPMENT

A failed or insufficiently completed bereavement work never shows in any specific pathology but "hides" in every variety of symptoms, neurotic, delinquent, or developmental (E. Furman, 1974; Shoor & Speed, 1963). Moreover, manifest problems, including maturational arrest, may not surface until the child's personality is faced with the conflicts of the next developmental phase, when the necessary energy is unavailable for the new challenges of growth because it is still tied up in coping with the loss (Machlup, 1974). For example, trouble with a bereavement at 6 years of age may emerge in apparently unrelated symptoms only in the prepubertal age of 11 or 12. This underlines the most serious potential impairment, namely failure of progressive personality development. This danger is often overlooked, especially as smooth outward adjustment may be mistaken for mental health. Loud manifest symptoms following a bereavement at least indicate a measure of active psychic struggle and are, in a sense, a call for help.

IMPACT ON FAMILY/INTERPERSONAL/SOCIAL ENVIRONMENT AND COMORBIDITY

Family and school are inevitably affected by children's difficulties, but they often also contribute to children's pathology in the case of a bereavement. This holds true when the adults either cannot mourn themselves or are unable to empathize with and support children's mourning at each phase of the bereavement task.

SEQUELAE AND PROGNOSIS

Many studies have substantiated the varied, mostly unhappy effects in adulthood of an unmastered childhood bereavement (Dorpat, 1971; Hilgard & Newman, 1959; Hilgard, Newman, &

Fisk, 1960). In the case of early parent loss, however, there is an aftermath even when the bereavement was mastered as best possible, especially when a child then grows up in a single-parent family and, for inner or outer reasons, has no opportunity to invest a new relationship. The lack of loving and being loved by two parents unhappily affects many areas of personality functioning and growth (E. Furman & R. A. Furman, 1989).

Treatment

PSYCHOLOGICAL AND SOCIAL TREATMENT

Children benefit most when they are helped at the time of their bereavement and in the months following it. Their best helpers are their parents or parent substitutes. Professional assistance during this period is, if indicated, best extended to the parents, alerting them to their essential role and exploring with them how they can best fulfill it with their child. Most parents experience difficulties and make mistakes in helping their child. As long as they can acknowledge their trouble and correct mistakes, their halting and imperfect help is preferable to direct therapeutic intervention because it maintains feelingful communication with the parents and assures children that even adults find coping with death and bereavement difficult and have to struggle with these issues honestly in themselves.

Therapeutic peer groups are sometimes helpful to schoolchildren but should be used in addition to, not instead of, empathic understanding with the family.

If a bereavement was not mastered and contributed to later pathology, individual psychotherapy or analysis is indicated, depending on the rigidity of the defenses, available tolerance of anxiety, and extent of personality impairment. Even then, the parents need to be worked with so that parent/child communication regarding the death can be reestablished.

EDUCATIONAL HANDLING

Educational measures serve well before a bereavement happens. As discussed, this involves developing a tolerance for uncomfortable feelings, especially related to separation, and the ability to perceive and understand unpleasant realities, including the concrete aspects of death.

MILIEU TREATMENT

Outpatient treatment is indicated, and ongoing contact with the family is so important that it should be maintained even if the child's difficulties require temporary inpatient placement.

Current Developments and Research

Since the 1970s there has been much new appreciation of children's reactions to death and bereavement. Many studies have extended the new understanding to various forms of bereavement, and attempts to apply knowledge have proliferated. Many hospitals, hospices, social and community agencies, funeral homes, and schools now address the needs of bereaved children with the help of short-term programs. The New York–based Foundation of Thanatology works to coordinate nationwide efforts to achieve greater awareness and access to help for all.

The persisting marked denial of death that occurs throughout this country is an area that has been studied very little. Even those who deal with death of children, as do the staff in pediatric hospitals (E. Furman, 1984), frequently fail to face up to the true meaning of death. This area is in need of further research.

REFERENCES

Ambrosini, P. J., Rabinovich, H., & Puig-Antich, J. (1984). Biological factors and pharmacologic treatment in major depressive disorder in children and adolescents. In H. S. Sudak, A. B. Ford, & N. B. Rushforth (Eds.), *Suicide in the young* (pp. 81–95). Littleton, MA: John Wright PGS.

Barnes, M. J. (1964). Reactions to the death of a mother. *Psychoanalytic Study of the Child, 19,* 334–357.

Dorpat, T. L. (1971). Psychological effects of parental suicide in surviving children. *Bulletin of the Philadelphia Association for Psychoanalysis, 21* (1), 45–46.

Fleming, E. (1974). Lucy. In E. Furman (Ed.), *A child's parent dies* (pp. 219–232). New Haven, CT: Yale University Press.

Freud, S. (1955). Mourning and melancholia. In J. Strachey, (Ed. and Trans.), *The standard edition of the complete psychological works of Sigmund Freud* (Vol. 14, pp. 237–258) London: Hogarth Press. (Original work published 1915).

Furman, E. (1974). *A child's parent dies.* New Haven, CT: Yale University Press.

Furman, E. (1976). Commentary on J. B. Schowalter's How do children and funerals mix? *Journal of Pediatrics, 89* (1), 143–145.

Furman, E. (1978). Helping children cope with death. *Young Children, 33* (4) 25–32.

Furman, E. (1979). Newborn death: Care of the parents. Audio-Digest Foundation, Continuing Education Series. *Pediatrics, 25,* (18).

Furman, E. (1980). The death of a newborn: Assistance to parents. In E. J. Anthony & C. Chiland (Eds.), *The child in his family: Preventive child psychiatry in an age of transitions. Yearbook of the International Association of Child Psychiatry and Allied Professions, 6* (pp. 497–506). New York: John Wiley & Sons.

Furman, E. (1981). Treatment-via-the-parent: A case of bereavement. *Journal of Child Psychotherapy, 7,* 89–102.

Furman, E. (1984). Helping children cope with dying. In L. H. Suszycki, A. H. Kutscher, & D. Fisher (Eds.), *Social work and terminal care. The Foundation of Thanatology Series* (Vol. 2, pp. 15–23). New York: Praeger.

Furman, E. (1986). On trauma: When is the death of a parent traumatic? *Psychoanalytic Study of the Child, 41,* 191–208.

Furman, E. (1990). Plant a potato—Learn about life (and death). *Young Children, 46,* 15–20.

Furman, E., & Furman, R. A. (1989). Some effects of the one-parent family on personality development. In D. R. Dietrich & P. C. Shabad (Eds.), *The problem of loss and mourning; Psychoanalytic Perspectives* (pp. 129–157). Madison, CT: International Universities Press.

Furman, R. A. (1964a). Death and the young child: Some preliminary considerations. *Psychoanalytic Study of the Child, 19,* 321–333.

Furman, R. A. (1964b). Death of a six-year-old's mother during his analysis. *Psychoanalytic Study of the Child, 19,* 377–397.

Furman, R. A. (1967). A technical problem: The child who has difficulty in controlling his behavior in analytic sessions. In E. R. Geleerd (Ed.), *The child ana-*

lyst at work (pp. 59–84). New York: International Universities Press.

Furman, R. A. (1968). Additional remarks on mourning and the young child. *Bulletin of the Philadelphia Association of Psychoanalysis, 18* (2), 51–64.

Goldman, M. W. (1974). Addie. In E. Furman (Ed.), *A child's parent dies* (pp. 140–148). New Haven, CT: Yale University Press.

Gorer, G. (1965). *Death, grief, and mourning.* Garden City, NY: Doubleday.

Gut, E. (1989). *Productive and unproductive depression.* New York: Basic Books.

Hilgard, J. R. & Newman, M. F. (1959). Anniversaries in mental illness. *Psychiatry, 22,* 113–121.

Hilgard, J. R., Newman, M. F., & Fisk, F. (1960). Strength of adult ego following childhood bereavement. *American Journal of Orthopsychiatry, 30,* 788–798.

Kovacs, M., Feinberg, T. L., Crouse-Novak, M. A., Paulauskas, S. L., & Finkelstein, R. (1984). Depressive disorders in childhood. I. A longitudinal prospective study of characteristics and recovery. *Archives of General Psychiatry, 41,* 229–237.

Kovacs, M., Feinberg, T. L., Crouse-Novak, M., Paulauskas, S. L., Pollock, M., & Finkelstein, R. (1984). Depressive disorders in childhood. II. A longitudinal study of the risk for a subsequent major depression. *Archives of General Psychiatry, 41,* 643–649.

Kroeber, T. (1964). *Ishi, last of his tribe.* Berkeley, CA: Parnassus.

Leon, I. (1990). *When a baby dies: Psychotherapy for pregnancy and newborn loss.* New Haven, CT: Yale University Press.

Machlup, M. R. (1974). Seth. In E. Furman (Ed.), *A*

child's parent dies (pp. 149–153). New Haven, CT: Yale University Press.

McCann, M. E. (1974). Geraldine. In E. Furman (Ed.), *A child's parent dies* (pp. 69–87). New Haven, CT: Yale University Press.

Meiss, M. (1952). The oedipal problem of a fatherless child. *Psychoanalytic Study of the Child, 7,* 216–229.

Mitford, J. (1962). *The American way of death.* New York: Simon & Schuster.

Nagera, H. (1970). Children's reactions to the death of important objects: A developmental approach. *Psychoanalytic Study of the Child, 25,* 360–400.

Rosenbaum, A. L. (1974). Hank and Sally. In E. Furman (Ed.), *A child's parent dies* (pp. 129–139). New Haven, CT: Yale University Press.

Schiff, E. J. (1974). Jim. In E. Furman (Ed.), *A child's parent dies* (pp. 88–95). New Haven, CT: Yale University Press.

Shoor, M., & Speed, M. (1963). Delinquency as a manifestation of the mourning process. *Psychiatric Quarterly, 37,* 540–558.

Solnit, A. J., & Stark, M. H. (1961). Mourning and the birth of a defective child. *Psychoanalytic Study of the Child, 16,* 523–537.

Stern, M. M. (1968a). Fear of death and trauma. *International Journal of Psycho-Analysis, 49* (2–3), 457–461.

Stern, M. (1968b). Fear of death and neurosis. *Journal of the American Psychoanalytic Association, 16* (1), 3–31.

Wolfenstein, M. (1966). How is mourning possible? *Psychoanalytic Study of the Child, 21,* 93–123.

Wolfenstein, M. (1969). Loss, rage and repetition. *Psychoanalytic Study of the Child, 24,* 432–462.

24 / Pervasive Developmental Disorder

Margaret E. Hertzig

Origins, Classification, and Differential Diagnosis

Pervasive developmental disorder (PDD) entered the psychiatric nomenclature in 1980 (American Psychiatric Association [APA], 1980) to designate conditions characterized by distortions in the development of multiple, basic psychological functions in prepubertal children. The term reflects 40 years of clinical and investigative effort stimulated by Kanner's (1943) publication entitled "Autistic Disturbances of Affective Contact." Although not the first to describe severe disturbances of the development of language and social skills in young children, Kanner's particularly clear and incisive account of 11 children whose extreme social withdrawal, idiosyncratic and delayed use of language, restriction of interests, and insistence on sameness he believed constituted a specific syndrome remains a model of clinical investigation.

Although Kanner observed that some of the manifestations of early infantile autism (Kanner,

1943) were similar to schizophrenia, as it was then thought to occur during childhood, he considered his cases unique because their extreme aloneness was evident from the very beginning of life. He believed that these children were of normal intelligence but acknowledged that previously many had been viewed as feebleminded. He also thought that their families were characterized by coldness and formality (refrigerator parents) and suggested that faulty parenting was implicated in pathogenesis. Nevertheless, he asserted that "these children have come into the world with an innate inability to form the usual, biologically provided affective contact with people just as other children come into the world with innate physical or intellectual handicaps" (p. 43). The major symptoms of impaired communication, rigidities, stereotypies, and insistence on sameness developed in the service of "[an] all-powerful need for being left undisturbed" (p. 36). Thus, Kanner set the stage for controversy about the syndrome, its specificity, its relation to other disorders of early childhood as well as its etiology, pathogenesis, and longitudinal course.

As confirmatory reports began to appear, early infantile autism came to be designated as the earliest form of schizophrenia (Bender, 1947). Efforts to distinguish further among severely disordered young children led to the proliferation of additional syndromes: the atypical child (Rank, 1955), symbiotic psychosis (Mahler & Gosliner, 1955), childhood psychosis (Creak, 1963), and autistic psychopathology (Asperger, 1944). Neither of the two earlier editions of the *Diagnostic and Statistical Manual (DSM) of Mental Disorders* (APA, 1952, 1968) provided guidelines for distinguishing among them. In *DSM-II*, the designation "childhood schizophrenia" included all conditions "manifested by autistic atypical and withdrawn behavior; failure to develop identity separate from the mother's; and general unevenness, gross immaturity and inadequacy in development" (APA, 1968, p. 35). During this period, as well, clinical investigation and treatment were guided primarily by efforts to demonstrate the psychogenic etiology of the various childhood psychoses (Bettelheim, 1967; Szurek & Berlin, 1973).

By the 1970s a growing body of evidence (Kolvin, 1971) indicated clear differences between "psychoses" beginning before the age of 5 years and those beginning later in childhood. These studies provided the basis for the establishment of distinctions between schizophrenia and PDD. In *DSM-III*, diagnostic criteria for the diagnosis of schizophrenia were the same for adults, adolescents, and those rare cases that began before puberty. Pervasive developmental disorder was the term developed to describe conditions characterized by distortions in the development of basic psychological functions thought to be involved in development of language and social skills, including attention, perception, reality testing, and motor movement (APA, 1980).

In *DSM-III*, PDD, despite its designation as a developmental disorder, was listed on Axis I (that section of the multiaxial classification reserved for clinical syndromes) and subdivided into infantile autism, childhood-onset PDD, atypical PDD, and residual states. Infantile autism and childhood-onset PDD differed principally in age of onset and severity of symptomatology. The criteria for infantile autism were very similar to those originally specified by Kanner: onset before 30 months of age, pervasive lack of responsiveness to others, gross deficits in the development and organization of language, and bizarre responses to aspects of the environment occurring in the absence of delusions, hallucinations, loosening of associations, and incoherence as in schizophrenia. Childhood-onset PDD included children in whom the onset of gross and sustained impairment in social relationships began after 30 months of age. Three of the following 7 symptoms were required for the diagnosis: excessive anxiety, constricted or inappropriate affect, resistance to change, oddities of motor movements, abnormalities of speech, hyper- or hyposensitivity to sensory stimuli, or self-mutilization, also occurring in the absence of delusions and hallucinations, incoherence, or marked loosening of associations. Atypical PDD was to be applied to children whose multiple developmental distortions could not be classified as either infantile autism or childhood-onset PDD.

In 1987 the psychiatric nomenclature underwent further revision (APA, 1987). In this edition of the *DSM*, PDD was more properly listed on Axis II along with other disorders of development and personality. The criteria derive from the findings of the epidemiologically based studies of Wing and her colleagues (Wing & Attwood, 1987) who concluded that "Kanner's syndrome [*DSM-III*] is not a unique specific condition, but a small segment of a spectrum of disorders" (p. 8). Although the concept of pervasive developmental disorder was retained in *DSM-III-R*, its characteristics now included "qualitative impairment in the development of reciprocal social interaction, in the development of verbal and non-verbal communication skills, and in imaginative activity, often accompanied by a markedly restricted repertoire of activities and interests which frequently are stereotyped and repetitive" (APA, 1987, p. 33).

The manual recognized only one subgroup of the general PDD category—autistic disorder—noting that this disorder is the most severe and prototypical form of PDD. Recognizing that affected children may exhibit markedly different symptom pictures, the criteria for autistic disorder have shifted from a simple catalog of descriptive criteria (monothetic) to a menulike scheme that requires the presence of a minimum number of criteria in each of three distinct areas of function. To meet criteria an individual must exhibit at least 8 of 16 specific symptoms, including 2 of the 5 that describe abnormalities in reciprocal social interaction, 1 of the 6 that encompass impairment in communication and imaginative activity, and 1 of the 6 that reflect a markedly restricted repertoire of activities and interests. Pervasive developmental disorder not otherwise specified (PDD-NOS) is to be used when there is a qualitative impairment of social interaction and communicative skills but the criteria for autistic disorder are not met. In contradistinction to the requirements of *DSM-III* (APA, 1980), neither onset before 30 months of age nor the absence of hallucinations, delusions, or loosening of associations is required for the diagnosis.

DSM-III-R criteria for autistic disorder provided a different and broader definition than *DSM-III*. While the sensitivity of *DSM-III-R* criteria for DSM-III cases of PDD was high, *DSM-III-R* criteria were less specific. The concept of autism was broadened to include children previously diagnosed as atypical PDD who, although they may display qualitative impairments of social interaction, communication, and a markedly restricted repertoire of activities and interests, are not pervasively unresponsive to other people (Hertzig, Snow, New, & Shapiro, 1990).

DSM-IV (APA, 1994) introduced further changes in the definition of autism and PDD intended to provide for greater simplicity and compatibility with the tenth edition of the *International Classification of Diseases* (*ICD-10*), as well as with the assessment of experienced clinicians. While the general format of the *DSM-III-R* definition has been retained, individual items have been reworded in accordance with the results of field trials conducted to determine specific items and thresholds for diagnosis. Furthermore, an age at onset criterion—prior to age 3—has been introduced.

Three additional conditions also listed in *IDC-10* are included in *DSM-IV* under the PDD rubric: Rett's disorder, childhood disintegrative disorder, and Asperger's disorder. Rett's disorder, reported to occur most frequently in girls, is characterized by normal head circumference at birth and apparently normal psychomotor development through the first 6 through 18 months of life, followed by a progressive deceleration of head growth, loss of previously acquired purposeful hand movements, emergence of characteristic handwringing behavior, loss of social engagement, poorly coordinated gait or trunk movements, marked delay and impairment of expressive and receptive language, and severe retardation (Van Acker, 1991).

The diagnosis of childhood disintegrative disorder is suggested for children who meet the behavioral criteria for autistic disorder but who have had an apparently normal developmental course for at least the first 2 years of life. Such children are described as having displayed age-appropriate verbal and nonverbal communication, social relationships, play and adaptive behavior, followed by clinical significant loss of previously acquired skills in at least two of the following areas: expressive and/or receptive language, social skills or adaptive behavior, bowel or bladder control, play, or motor skills. Although this disorder is quite rare, the rationale for its inclusion is that it: (1) has distinctive clinical features, (2) appears to have a worse prognosis than autistic disorder, and (3) is an important topic for research (Task Force on *DSM-IV*, APA, 1991). Differentiating between cases meeting these criteria and those of autistic disorder who have had a period of normal development may prove difficult in practice.

The principle characteristics of Asperger's disorder, which takes its name from Asperger's (1944) description of a group of socially isolated children, include the presence of gross and sustained impairment in social interaction and restricted, repetitive, and stereotyped patterns of behavior, interests, and activities occurring in the absence of clinically significant general delay in language and cognitive development (APA, 1994). The essential differences between Asperger's disorder and autism are considered to lie in the greater degree of social unresponsiveness, the higher frequency of deviant language development, and the lack of symbolic play seen in autistic children. The child with Asperger's disorder has been described as developing warm relationships with parents but having difficulties in social interactions with peers. Although affected children may perseverate and lack the ability to initiate and sustain conversation, echolalia, pronominal reversal, idiosyncratic use of speech, jargon, and neologisms are rare. Symbolic play is observed although it is usually repetitive and stereotypic (Szatmari, 1991). Considerable difficulty may be anticipated in distinguishing between Asperger's disorder and autistic disorder as it occurs in some individuals with good cognitive ability (Klin, 1994; Klin, Volkman, Sparrow, Cicchetti, & Rourke, 1995; Ozanoff, Pennington, & Rogers, 1991; Szatzmari, Archer, Fisman, Streiner, & Wilson, 1995).

Not only is the clinician increasingly required to distinguish among children within the group of pervasive developmental disorders, but differential diagnosis includes consideration of other developmental and psychiatric conditions as well. The key to distinguishing the pervasive developmental disorders from other conditions affecting development and behavior is the simultaneous presence of impairment in social interaction, communication, and restriction of interest and activities. The identification of pervasive developmental disorder depends on observation of the total pattern of behavior. The major differential diagnosis in young pervasively developmentally disordered children, once a hearing loss has been ruled out, is between autism and mental retardation in low-functioning children and autism and developmental language disorder in higher-functioning ones. Retarded children who are not autistic usually display appropriate sociability and good nonverbal communication. Diagnostic problems may arise if mental age is below 20 months, which is too low for pretend play to have developed. Profoundly retarded individuals often display simple motor stereotypies, such as rocking or finger flicking, but observation of social responsivity may allow for differential diagnosis. Children with developmental language disorders are frequently socially immature, but nonautistic children with receptive and expressive language problems are eager to communicate, are sociable, and develop pretend play. Children with congenital or early-onset hearing impairments have problems in acquiring speech and may be socially withdrawn and behaviorally difficult, but if not autistic, they use gestures to communicate, develop pretend play, and are interested in other children. Social and behavioral problems usually improve when hearing problems are addressed with hearing aids and/or the introduction of alternative methods of communication. Children with severe visual impairments of congenital or early onset may also appear autistic. Such children tend to twist and turn their hands near their eyes, lack eye contact, have restricted facial expressivity, and seek sensory input through touch, taste, smell, and movement. Careful observation of patterns of social, communicative, and imaginative behavior is required for diagnosis (Wing & Attwood, 1987).

Some of the behaviors displayed by children with pervasive developmental disorders are similar to those seen in other psychiatric conditions. Many children with pervasive developmental disorders are restless and distractible and in this regard resemble children with attention deficit hyperactivity disorder. The ticlike behaviors, compulsive shouting, swearing, and echoing of words, sounds, and actions sometimes seen in children with PDD resemble the symptoms of Tourette's disorder, and the repetitive routines of many pervasively developmentally disordered people have obvious similarities to patterns of thought and behavior seen in obsessive compulsive disorder. A careful history documenting the early onset of symptoms reflecting impairments in socialization, communicative behavior, and patterns of restricted and repetitive activities should establish the diagnosis (Wing & Attwood, 1987).

The language characteristics of older verbal pervasively developmentally disordered individuals include evidence of concrete, perseverative, impoverished, circumstantial, and obsessional thinking delivered in a flat monotonic, mechanical style that can sometimes appear to be quite similar to the language characteristics of schizophrenics (Rumsey, Rapoport, & Sceery, 1985). However, the full *DSM-IV* criteria sets for pervasive developmental disorder and schizophrenia clearly distinguish between the two conditions (Green et al., 1984). Nevertheless, *DSM-III* schizophrenia has been described, albeit rarely, in older individuals with well-documented histories of autism (Petty, Ornitz, Michelman, & Zimmerman, 1984).

EPIDEMIOLOGY

Epidemiologic studies conducted before the publication of *DSM-III* (Wing & Gould, 1979) estimated the prevalence rate of Kanner's autism to be between 2 and 5 per 10,000. More recent investigations, utilizing *DSM-III* criteria for infantile autism, have essentially confirmed these estimates (Burd, Fisher, & Kerbeshian, 1987). No estimates of the prevalence of autistic disorder as defined by *DSM-IV* criteria are available. However, the combined prevalence of infantile autism and "autisticlike" conditions, similar to PDD as defined in both *DSM-III* and *DSM-III-R*, ranges from 21 per 10,000 (Wing & Gould, 1979) to 11 per 10,000 (Burd, Fisher, & Kerbeshian, 1987). No epidemiologic studies based on *DSM-IV* criteria have been conducted as yet.

Autism occurs more frequently in boys, with the estimated male to female ratio for all PDD (*DSM-III* criteria) being 2.7:1 (Burd, Fisher, & Kerbeshian, 1987). The sex ratio is more equal when autism is associated with organic brain disease or severe mental retardation (Wolf, 1991). Some investigations have confirmed Kanner's (1943) original observation that parents of autistic children come from higher socioeconomic groups than the general population (Cox, Rutter, Newman, & Bartak, 1975). However, these findings appear to reflect patterns of referral rather than a genuine difference. More recent epidemiologically based studies (Wing, 1980) do not support the view that autistic children come from higher social classes.

Although pervasive developmental disorder can be associated with any level of intelligence, about 40% of autistic children have an IQ below 50 and only 30% score above 70 on standardized tests (Wing & Gould, 1979).

Clinical Characteristics from Infancy to Adulthood

The longitudinal course of the pervasive developmental disorders, most particularly autism, and the range of symptomatic expression at each age stage of development are now well studied. In the great majority of cases, onset is reported before 3 years of age, although milder impairments may not be detected until school entrance (Wing & Attwood, 1987). In addition, rarely occurring cases of childhood disintegrative disorder most often begin after 3 years of age. Three modes of onset have been described: (1) "always different," (2) a period of normal development followed by a definite downward developmental turning point or "setback," and (3) a gradual failure to progress normally. No systematic relation between mode of onset and clinical picture has been described (DeMyer, 1979).

Wing and Gould (1979) used variations in social impairment to develop a descriptive subclassification of children with pervasive developmental disorder, distinguishing among aloof, passive, and active-but-odd groups at each age stage of development. Although these subtypes are strongly related to IQ, they are a useful way of describing the developmental course of PDD. Wing (Wing & Attwood, 1987) suggested that individual socialization patterns are consistent over time. However, there is some evidence that, particularly for autistic individuals with higher levels of functioning, a progression from aloofness, to passive acceptance, to active-but-deviant ways of seeking interaction may be a more typical course (Paul, 1987). For those whose IQs are in the retarded range, the shift from aloofness to passivity is common, and active-but-odd social interactions are generally not observed.

Failure to acquire language at the expected age is the most frequent presenting complaint for children with pervasive developmental disorder who come to clinical notice during the preschool period (Rapin, 1991). Although all autistic children have marked difficulties in both verbal and nonverbal communications, these impairments are most severe among the aloof group (Wing & Attwood, 1987). Their understanding of spoken language is also significantly impaired. Lack of response to speech may lead to a suspicion of deafness, but this diagnosis frequently is rejected even before formal assessment of hearing, because the children often display an ability to react to sounds that seem to have particular meaning for them. Poor eye contact, active visual avoidance, passive facial expression, and lack of social gestures, such as waving or nodding, also are noticeable. About one half of all autistic people, especially those who are mentally retarded, remain mute throughout their lives. When speech does develop, it is usually preceded by an increased interest in attending to speech and improved comprehension of language. Typical abnormalities include delayed and inappropriate echoing, reversal of pronouns, repetitiveness, literalness of meaning, idiosyncratic use of words and phrases, as well as intonation that is monotonous, mechanical, or singsong in quality. Although speech tends to be better in the passive and active-but-odd groups during the preschool period, similar abnormalities are observed.

Most aloof children do not engage in symbolic play. Although they manipulate objects, they do not seem able to pretend that toys represent real things. Passive children may participate in imaginative games that are organized by others, typically accepting the assigned role of "baby" in a game of house. Children who are active but odd may build and rebuild the same imaginary system of roads or pretend to be an animal or superhero over and over again (Wing & Attwood, 1987). During the preschool period repetitive stereotyped activities are prominent among all three social groups. Those whose IQs are low tend to engage in simple actions, such as finger flicking, arm flapping, or body rocking, but the more able may display more complex repetitive behavior, such as organizing objects into lines or patterns, following a lengthly bedtime ritual, or insisting on taking exactly the same route to school each day. Difficult, socially inappropriate behavior can occur in response to interference with repetitive routines and a lack of understanding of instructions and the rules of social behavior.

The school years are often a period of relative calm in the lives of pervasively developmentally disordered children and their families. Many of the behaviors that were most disturbing earlier in life tend to lessen in frequency and intensity. Nevertheless, ritualistic behaviors and peculiar cir-

cumscribed interests may persist well into adulthood. Most children learn to perform many activities of daily living and adjust, although often with difficulty, to the demands and expectations of others. Autistic children tend to become increasingly social during the middle childhood years. Even the most aloof and cognitively impaired display clear-cut signs of attachment to parents and other familiar people, and are increasingly accepting of the social overtures of others. More cognitively and communicatively able children may initiate social interactions by asking stereotypic questions or giving long monologues about topics of their particular specialized area of interest. Among speaking autistic children, echolalia begins to be replaced by more spontaneous speech, although difficulties in initiating and maintaining conversation persist. Some socially passive or aloof children whose IQs are in the normal to mildly impaired range can make academic progress in regular classroom settings, but most pervasively developmentally disordered youngsters require placement in special classes. Somewhere between 6 and 9% of autistic children begin to demonstrate an extraordinary ability to perform calendrical or numerical calculations or display other idiot savant talents (O'Connor & Hermelin, 1988).

For many pervasively disordered individuals, the adolescent years often are characterized by slow but steady progress in the acquisition of social and communicative skills. Many tolerate quite calmly the advent of menstruation and increased sexual drive. A recent study of sexual knowledge and experience in high-functioning adolescents and young adults with autism has revealed less experience, but equivalent knowledge and interest in sexual matters as a similarly aged moderately retarded comparison group (Ousley & Mesibov, 1991). Nevertheless, exhibitionism or public masturbation may pose management problems. Some autistic people show marked improvement during adolescence that frequently is sustained into adulthood (Kanner, Rodriguez, & Achenden, 1972). However, somewhere between 10 and 35% undergo serious regression, with no obvious precipitating factor other than puberty itself. If such deterioration does occur, it appears to level off and not to progress further during the adult years (Rutter, 1985). Approximately one fifth of autistic children develop seizures by age

18, with the peak onset being between 11 and 14 years. Seizures are more likely in autistic people with severe retardation than in those of normal nonverbal intelligence (Rutter, 1983).

Long-term follow-up studies of autistic children suggest that the natural history of the disorder is one of gradual symptomatic improvement with persistent social impairment (Kanner et al., 1972; Lotter, 1974; Rumsey et al., 1985; Rutter, 1970). However, in adult life, some two thirds of autistic individuals continue to be completely unable to care for themselves, whereas only 5 to 17% develop sufficiently to be able to work independently and lead some kind of social life. IQ and language skills are the best predictors of adult functioning. If a child's nonverbal IQ is below 50 or 60, it is virtually certain that he or she will remain severely handicapped. If IQ is above that level but gross language impairments persist beyond 5 years of age, the individual may make a fair social adjustment and be able to live and work in sheltered supervised settings. Children whose intelligence is in the normal range and who have developed communicative language by 5 years of age have a 50-50 chance of achieving a good social outcome in adulthood. Even those who have progressed well may lack social skills and an ability to empathize with others (Kanner et al., 1972; Rumsey et al., 1985). However, a very few can do surprisingly well despite serious childhood abnormalities. Szatmari (Szatmari, Bartolucci, Bremner, Bond, & Rich, 1989) found that among 16 autistic children with a mean IQ of 92, 4 had "recovered" at a mean age of 26 years, living independent lives with long-term relationships, and 1 had married. However, in this series as in others, the majority of cases were characterized by persisting social impairment and poor occupational achievement. The severity of early symptoms of social unresponsivity, deviant language, and bizarre behavior were not related to outcome.

Theories of Autism

BIOLOGICAL STUDIES

Kanner's (1943) original suggestion that autism is inborn stimulated investigation of biologic correlates. Genetic influences in the etiology of au-

tism are increasingly recognized. Studies of the familial aggregation of autism have contributed to increased recognition of the etiologic importance of genetic factors. In most case series and population-based studies, the prevalence of autism in the siblings of autistic children has been estimated to be about 2 to 3%—a rate 50 to 100 times greater than the expected rate of autism in the population. When the frequency with which families who have a severely handicapped child decide not to have further children after the birth of the proband is taken into account—so-called stoppage rules—the recurrence risk of autism is estimated as 8.6% (Folstein & Piven, 1991). A population-based twin study carried out in Great Britain examined 21 same-sexed twin pairs that included at least 1 autistic child. Ten of these pairs were monozygotic, and 4 of the monozygotic cotwins were diagnosed as having autism, whereas none of the dizygotic cotwins met criteria. However, 9 of the 10 monozygotic twins were concordant for milder cognitive impairment and language delay, suggesting that autism could be the severest form of inherited language and congitive difficulties (Folstein & Rutter, 1977). Ritvo and colleagues (Ritvo, Freeman, Mason-Brothers, Mo, & Ritvo, 1985) collected 61 families with autistic twins who volunteered for study. Forty-seven families provided sufficient records to make a diagnosis. Forty met research diagnostic criteria for autism with 95.7 concordance in the monozygotic twins (22 of 23) and 23.5% of the dizygotic group (4 of 17). Sample selection may have contributed to the very high concordance in this study. However, cognitive-processing difficulties were found in 10.3% of siblings, a finding consistent with the view that there may be a subgroup of autistic children with a genetic etiology and variable penetrance. The results of more recent studies examining personality characteristics, language, and psychiatric disorder in the relatives of autistic individuals suggest that a variety of different abnormalities aggregate in their families and that they also may be manifestations of an underlying genetic liability to autism (Folstein & Piven, 1991).

Autism also has been described to occur in association with several single-gene disorders, including tuberous sclerosis (autosomal dominant), untreated phenylketonuria (autosomal recessive), and perhaps neurofibromatosis (autosomal dominant). Associations with a variety of chromosomal abnormalities including Down's syndrome, Klinefelter's syndrome (Folstein & Piven, 1991), as well as partial trisomy of chromosome 15 (Gilberg et al, 1991) have been described. The fragile X marker also has been reported to be significantly associated with the syndrome of autism. This X-linked mental retardation syndrome is the second most common known genetic cause of mental retardation. Affected males may show such physical characteristics as macro-orchidism, square prognathous jaw, high arched narrow palate, and large ears. A pooled estimate of prevalence, based on the screening of 614 autistic males reported in 12 studies, was 7.7%. The relationship between autism and fragile X may be mediated by the level of cognitive impairment. In reports that include information about IQ, autistic subjects with fragile X tend to be among the most mentally retarded members of the samples. Studies that incorporate nonautistic IQ-matched control groups do not support a direct association between autism and fragile X (Folstein & Piven, 1991).

The available evidence suggests that problems during pregnancy, delivery, and the neonatal period may be more frequent in children who later develop autism as compared with nonautistic children. However, perinatal difficulty is associated with a wide variety of developmental disabilities and is not specific to autism (Nelson, 1991).

Increasingly sophisticated methodologies are being applied to the study of the structure and the function of the nervous system of individuals with autism and pervasive developmental disorder. While findings of nonspecific abnormalities were characteristic of early studies, the results of more recent investigations tend to be more consistent. Structural changes in the cerebral cortex, thalamus, basal ganglia, and brainstem have been variably identified in the brains of autistic individuals through the use of neuroradiologic techniques. Ventricular enlargement also has been noted in some autistic children. One of the more consistent findings is that of a reduction in cerebellar tissue, greatest in the neocerebellar regions within the vermis and hemispheres. This reduction has been interpreted as resulting from developmental hypoplasia rather than damage following full development, and may serve as a temporal marker to identify the events that damage the developing brain in autism (Courchense, 1991).

Microscopic neuroanatomic abnormalities in the cerebellum, cerebellar circuits, and limbic system have been described in four brains of individuals with clinically well-documented autism. The types of abnormalities, which included variable but consistent bilateral symmetrical loss of Purkinje's cells, increased cell-packing density with reduced neuronal cell size, and an absence of obvious gliosis, are considered to be consistent with a curtailment of the normal development of portions of the limbic system and cerebellar circuits. Associated preservation of olivary neurons suggests that the process causing these abnormalities began or occurred before birth (Bauman, 1991).

While the findings of neuroanatomic and neuroimaging studies tend to point to abnormalities in the limbic system and cerebellum in autism, physiologic studies are more likely to reveal abnormalities of the cerebral cortex, most particularly the association cortex. Electroencephalographic studies of autistic persons have reported a significant incidence of abnormalities involving the cerebral cortex. Preliminary positron emission tomography data reveal increased glucose metabolism in all areas of the association cortex and in related subcortical structures. Abnormalities in cerebral cortical energy metabolism also have been found in a preliminary ^{31}P nuclear magnetic resonance spectroscopy study of the dorsal prefrontal cortex (Minshew, 1991). Moreover, MRI studies have revealed autistic adolescents and adults to have enlarged brains as a consequence of both greater brain tissue volume and greater lateral ventricle volume (Piven et al., 1995).

Studies of neurotransmitters, including dopamine, norepinepherine, and acetylcholine, have been inconclusive. However, hyperserotenemia has been a consistent finding in about one third of all autistic children. Studies of serotonin receptors and serotonin levels show a persistent diminution of receptor sites. A challenge test, based on the fenfluramine-serotonin relationship, indicates that central serotonergic responsivity is reduced in autistic adults (McBride et al., 1988).

In summary, there is little doubt that the pervasive developmental disorders are associated with abnormal function—and perhaps structure—of the central nervous system. Nevertheless, the multiplicity of possible etiological factors makes the search for relationships between identified abnormalities and the linguistic, cognitive, and interpersonal disabilities of affected persons difficult indeed. On the level of the organization of the central nervous system, several model systems, including dysfunction of central vestibular connections (Ornitz, 1985), temporal lobe dysfunction (DeLong, 1978), and left-hemispheric dysfunction (Prior, 1979), have been suggested as possible mechanisms underlying the brain-behavior relationships in autism. More recently Goodman (1989) has suggested that attempts to explain autism in terms of just one underlying neurological or psychological deficit may be misguided. Rather, autism may involve multiple functional deficits due to multiple coexistent neurological deficits. Comparison with related conditions such as Asperger's disorder and the developmental dysphasias leads Goodman to suggest that the autistic syndrome may result from the coexistence of at least two distinct constellations of functional impairments: deficits in mechanical language skills, as in the developmental dysphasias, and deficits in social relatedness, play, and nonverbal communication, as in Asperger's disorder. Although clearly preliminary, such considerations provide direction for further hypothesis-bound research, in the course of which biologic investigators may be better able to link the unique behavioral features of autism to the findings generated by the application of new techniques for defining the architecture and function of the central nervous system.

PSYCHOLOGICAL STUDIES

The detailed examination of the organization of psychological functions in autism also has been dominated by the search for a single defining mechanism. The cognitive and linguistic attributes of autistic children have been the most extensively investigated, perhaps because of the early recognition of their importance as predictors of later functional level. For the past two decades, autism has been viewed primarily as a cognitively based disorder in which socially deviant behavior emerges secondarily (Fein, Pennington, Markowitz, Braverman, & Waterhouse, 1986). Autistic children vary greatly in their intellectual performance, but the IQ scores of individuals are moderately consistent over time. Cognitive performance is not fully explainable in terms of motivational factors, but rather varies systematically in accordance with task difficulty and the nature of task demand. The IQ scores of autistic children are found to differ from mental-age-matched controls in showing a distinctive pattern of deficits in verbal sequencing and abstraction skills contrasted with rather good performance in visuospatial and rote memory skills (Rutter, 1983).

The language of speaking autistic children is not only delayed but deviant as well. Young autistic children echo far more than normally developing 2- and 3-year-olds, but their echoing is not productive or generative as in normal language acquisition. Although autistic children designate adequately, they do not develop grammatical complexity and flexibility. Poorly contextualized remarks, irrelevancies, and pat repetitions of phrases—delayed echolalia—account for their being taken as odd. Reaction time for echoes is significantly less than for other responses, suggesting that the echo serves as a social closure device, a pragmatic technique, that derives from a perceived need to take turns in communicating. The language difficulties of autistic children do not stem primarily from a syntactic deficit but rather involve the use of language in dialogues (Shapiro, 1977).

In more recent years the affective and social components of autistic behavior have once again become a focus of investigation (Fein et al., 1986). The natural spontaneous expression of positive affect is diminished in autistic children (Snow, Hertzig, & Shapiro, 1987), as is the frequency with which they use emotionally expressive gestures (Hermelin, 1982). Moreover, their ability to imitate and analyze affective cues in controlled task situations also is deficient (Hertzig, Snow, & Sherman, 1989), as is the ability to sustain joint attention and to initiate social-emotional approach behaviors (Mundy, 1995). Hobson (1991) has suggested that the essence of autism is an impairment in affectively patterned intersubjective personal relations. Alternatively Baron-Cohen (1991) views the affective impairments of autistic persons as part of a more general cognitive deficit: an impairment in the capacity to infer what is in the minds of others—that is, a lack of a "theory of mind." Regardless of interpretation, it is becoming increasingly clear that "the stimuli that pose difficulties for autistic children are those that carry emotional or social meaning" (Rutter, 1983, p. 528). Nevertheless, autistic children, particularly those who are high-functioning, exhibit considerable variability in the degree to which they are able to perceive themselves and others. A recent study examined relationships between perceived self-competence, intellectual ability, emotional understanding, and parent report of social adaptation in 18 nonretarded autistic children. Children who perceived themselves as less socially competent demonstrated stronger intellectual capacities, greater understanding of other's emotional experiences, and were better able to access their own emotions than were those who perceived themselves as more socially competent. However, parents considered children who perceived themselves as less socially competence to be more socially adaptive and to express more interest and less sadness and fear than did those who perceived themselves as more socially competent (Capps, Sigman, & Yirmiya, 1995).

Diagnostic Assessment

The pervasive developmental disorders are etiologically heterogeneous behavioral syndromes. Consequently, the diagnostic evaluation and workup of a child suspected of having a PDD requires the input from a number of different professionals whose contributions are necessary to explore questions of etiology and identify associated conditions that may require treatment, as well as to define developmental level and cognitive and communicative abilities. The child psychiatrist often functions to integrate information from a variety of different sources and to interpret findings to parents. Pervasively disordered children usually first come to clinical notice during the preschool years, although higher-functioning children may not be seen until after school entrance. The child psychiatrist also may be called upon to assess older children to clarify diagnosis and to evaluate the adequacy of ongoing treatment.

Assessment begins with careful history taking including a systematic review of perinatal and developmental events, family history, descriptions of previous treatment and responses to medication, and in older children, educational placement, school functioning, and behavior. Parents' descriptions of day-to-day behavior should be ampli-

fied to include details of patterns of social interaction, communicative style, patterns of play, and stereotypies and rigidities. Direct observation of the child provides an opportunity for the informal assessment of developmental level, communicative abilities, sociability, and imaginative play. Behavioral scales, while not a substitute for interview and direct observation, can assist in focusing on those symptom areas most relevant to diagnosis (APA, 1989).

Neurologic consultation is indicated to assist in the identification of potentially treatable neurologic conditions. The physical examination includes a search for signs of specific illness associated with autistic symptomatology, such as fragile X syndrome, tuberous sclerosis, or congenital rubella. In choosing how extensively to evaluate a pervasively disordered child, a distinction must be made between tests that are important to treatment planning and those that are done for the purpose of increasing knowledge. A wake and sleep electroencephalogram is indicated, particularly if there is a history of behavioral regression and loss of language. An electroencephalogram with frequent paroxysmal discharges might warrant a trial of anticonvulsants. The therapeutic yield from neuroimaging studies, computed tomography, and magnetic resonance imaging is low, and parents need to know that even if a structural abnormality of the brain is discovered, such a finding is unlikely to alter management or to further clarify diagnosis. The need to sedate a young or uncooperative child must be weighed against the advantage of waiting until such tests can be performed without sedation. Unless the history or physical examination points to a particular diagnosis, or symptoms appeared after 3 years of age or are progressive, blind testing for metabolic errors is unlikely to be helpful. However, because of the genetic implications for other family members, testing for fragile X and genetic counseling should be offered (Rapin, 1991).

Measurement of IQ, adaptive functioning, and speech and language assessment are central to treatment planning. In addition, these measures provide a framework for the consideration of prognosis. Appropriate referrals to specialists experienced in working with children with developmental disabilities are required. The selection of the proper instrument to measure IQ is guided by the child's general level of functioning and communicative ability, and some estimate of nonverbal intelligence needs to be provided.

The evaluation of communicative ability is directed toward providing answers to the following general questions: How does the child communicate? What does the child communicate? Why does the child communicate? And where, when, to whom, and under what conditions does the child communicate? Developmental level is well described by the results of the Vineland Adaptive Behavior Scales (Sparrow, Balla & Cicchetti, 1984), which yields standard scores, percentile ranks, stanines, adaptive levels, and age equivalents in four domains (communication, daily living skill, socialization, and motor skills) and an adaptive behavior composite. The Vineland does not require the direct administration of tasks to an individual, but rather scoring is based on the responses of parents or caregivers to questions posed during a semistructured interview, thus circumventing many of the problems associated with interpreting results of direct testing of uncooperative and/or nonverbal children.

Assessment of the PDD child also must take into consideration the concerns, resources, and priorities of the family. The clinician needs not only to gather information but also to establish a working partnership with parents based on a sensitivity to their needs and an appreciation of the difficulties of their situation. The results of assessment procedures should be fully shared. Questions of long-term prognosis often arise, and while it is not either necessary or wise to be definitive, careful specification of current patterns of function provide a basis for developing understanding of the chronicity of the disorder. Parents must come to recognize, grieve, and ultimately accept the fact that their child has a severe developmental disorder with long-term consequences. However, coping with a developmentally disordered child is a process that unfolds over years, and opportunities for continued discussion need to be provided. Parents need not fully accept their child's incapacities, nor is it necessary for them to abandon hope. Rather, the clinician should strive to help parents develop a realistic awareness of the child's neurologic and developmental impairments, sufficient to allow the provision of appropriate care at home and to facilitate participation in ongoing education and treatment.

Treatment and Education

Practically the entire psychiatric armamentarium has been offered to autistic and pervasively developmentally disordered children at one or another point in time. Psychoanalysis, behavior modification, dyadic and triadic treatments, speech and language therapy, directed communication, sign language, holding therapy, language-based approaches to learning, and neurodevelopmentally directed therapies, including perceptual retraining as well as pharmacotherapies, all have been applied. The overwhelming finding is that humane management leads to better outcome than when the child is permitted to regress. Special educational opportunities are the cornerstone of the management and treatment of the pervasive developmental disorders. Systematic comparison of the progress made by autistic children in three different educational settings, however, found that the best results were obtained by the unit that used extensive, specifically targeted teaching in a well-controlled classroom that provided an organized and structured program with individualized educational goals and techniques appropriate to the level of handicap. Least progress was made in a permissive environment in which regressive techniques dominated (Bartak & Rutter, 1973; Rutter & Bartak, 1973).

The goals of treatment for pervasively developmentally disordered children include the (1) fostering of normal development, (2) promotion of learning, (3) reduction of rigidities and stereotypies and other maladaptive behaviors, and (4) reduction of family distress. Pervasively developmentally disordered children require a multimodal approach that includes a focus on the development of socialization and communication skills. Goals must be individualized and consistent with IQ. Behavioral approaches often are useful in reducing or eliminating nonspecific maladaptive behaviors, such as tantrums, aggression, and bedwetting, as well as in the facilitation of communicative skills.

An increasing number of programs, most particularly for young autistic children, are providing a particular form of behavior therapy, intensive behavioral analysis, in an effort to ameliorate or even reverse the symptoms of autism. This highly structured intervention, which is administered one-to-one for up to 40 hours per week, utilizes a variety of behavioral techniques including prompting, modeling, and generalization, systematically reinforced with food, praise, smiles, or tokens. Parents are active participants and progress is monitored through the collection of extensive data. Replication of the initially encouraging results of a small-scale controlled study (Lovaas, 1987; McEachin, Smith, & Lovaas, 1993) as well as the report of two cases (Perry et al., 1995) is clearly indicated (Shapiro & Hertzig, 1995).

Communication therapies and social skills training approaches are becoming increasingly well specified. Individual psychotherapy is generally possible only with verbal adolescents and adults. An approach that emphasizes the understanding of real-life problems and situations as well as the development of effective coping strategies can be helpful to individuals who may experience considerable anxiety and frustration or are confused about the nature of their disability (Marcus & Campbell, 1989, Mesibov, 1989).

No drugs specifically affect autism and the pervasive developmental disorders. Nevertheless, pharmacotherapy may play an important part in the development of an individualized treatment program. Hyperactivity, stereotypies, withdrawal, aggressive behavior toward others, self-mutilation, irritability, and temper tantrums are among the target symptoms that may respond to drug treatment. When effective, medication may improve the autistic child's responsivity to educational and psychosocial interventions. Pharmaco-

therapy is indicated only if it makes sufficient impact on maladaptive behavior to outweigh the possible short-term and long-term side effects (most particularly tardive dyskinesia in association with neuroleptics). Consequently, the administration of medication must be preceded by the establishment of a stable behavioral baseline and procedures for evaluating effectiveness. The effectiveness and safety of a wide range of pharmacologic agents has been examined, including hallucinogens, antidepressants, lithium, thyroid hormone, megavitamins, stimulant medications, antiserotoninergic agents including fenfluramine, and levodopa, naltrexone, and the neuroleptics. The most consistently positive findings have been reported for the high-potency neuroleptics, most particularly haloperidol, use of which is associated with considerable decrease of symptoms without untoward effects on learning. Early reports of the efficacy of fenfluramine have not been sustained (Campbell, 1989).

Education and treatment of the pervasively developmentally disordered child cannot occur in a vacuum. Attention to the changing needs of parents and siblings is a critical part of any intervention program. Pervasive developmental disorder imposes a lifelong handicap, and the families of affected individuals require a long series of guiding experiences as they cope with the ongoing stresses of participation in the care and treatment of a handicapped child and adolescent and plan effectively for the residential and vocational needs of a still significantly impaired adult (Mesibov, 1989).

REFERENCES

American Psychiatric Association. (1952). *Diagnostic and statistical manual of mental disorders*. Washington, DC: Author.

American Psychiatric Association. (1968). *Diagnostic and statistical manual of mental disorders* (2nd ed.). Washington, DC: Author.

American Psychiatric Association. (1980). *Diagnostic and statistical manual of mental disorders* (3rd ed.). Washington, DC: Author.

American Psychiatric Association. (1987). *Diagnostic and statistical manual of mental disorders* (3rd ed., rev.) Washington, DC: Author.

American Psychiatric Association. (1991). *DSM-IV options book: Work in progress 9/1/91*. Washington, DC: Author.

American Psychiatric Association. (1994). *Diagnostic

and statistical manual of mental disorders*. (4th ed.). Washington, DC: Author.

Asperger, H. (1944). Die "autistichen Psychopathen" Kindesalter. *Archive Psychiatrika Nervenkrantz*, 117, 76–136.

Baron-Cohen, S. (1991). The development of a theory of mind in autism; Deviance and delay? *Psychiatric Clinics of North America, 14*, 33–52.

Bartak, L., & Rutter, M. (1973). Special educational treatment of autistic children: A comparative study. I: Design of study and characteristics of units. *Journal of Child Psychology and Psychiatry, 14*, 161–179.

Bauman, M. L. (1991). Microscopic neuroanatomic abnormalities in autism. *Pediatrics, 87* (5, Pt. 2), 791–796.

Bender, L. (1974). Childhood schizophrenia: A clinical

study of 100 schizophrenic children. *American Journal of Orthopsychiatry, 17,* 40–56.

Bettelheim, B. (1967). *The empty fortress. Infantile autism and the birth of the self.* New York: Free Press.

Burd, I., Fisher, W., & Kerbeshian, J. (1987). A prevalence study of pervasive developmental disorder in North Dakota. *Journal of the American Academy of Child and Adolescent Psychiatry, 26,* 700–703.

Campbell, M. (1989). Pharmacotherapy. In *Treatment of psychiatric disorders. A task force report of the American Psychiatric Association* (Vol. 1, pp. 226–248). Washington, DC: American Psychiatric Association.

Capps, L., Sigman, M., & Yirmiya, N. (1995). Self-competence and emotional understanding in high-functioning children with autism. *Developmental Psychopathology, 7,* 137–149.

Courchesne, E. (1991). Neuroanatomic imaging in autism. *Pediatrics, 87* (5, Pt. 2), 781–770.

Cox, A., Rutter, M., Newman, S., & Bartak, L. A. (1975). A comparative study of infantile autism and specific developmental receptive language disorder. II: Parental characteristics. *British Journal of Psychiatry, 126,* 146–159.

Creak, M. (1963). Childhood psychosis: A review of 100 cases. *British Journal of Psychiatry, 109,* 84–89.

DeLong, G. R. (1978). A neuropsychological interpretation of infantile autism. In M. Rutter & E. Schopler (Eds.), *Autism: A reappraisal of concepts and treatment* (pp. 207–218). New York: Plenum Press.

DeMyer, M. K. (1979). *Parents and children in autism.* Washington, DC: V.H. Winston.

Fein, D., Pennington, B., Markowitz, P., Braverman, M., & Waterhouse, L. (1986). Towards a neuropsychological model of infantile autism. *Journal of the American Academy of Child and Adolescent Psychiatry, 25,* 198–212.

Folstein, S. E., & Piven, J. (1991). Etiology of autism: Genetic influences. *Pediatrics, 87* (5, Pt. 2), 767–773.

Folstein, S. E., & Rutter, M. (1977). Infantile autism: A genetic study of twin pairs. *Journal of Child Psychology and Psychiatry, 18,* 297–321.

Gilberg, C., Steffenburg, S., Wahlstrom, J., Gilberg, I. C., Sjostedt, A., Martinsson, T., Lkiedgren, S., & Eeg-Olofsson, O. (1991) Autism associated with marker chromosome. *Journal of the American Academy of Child and Adolescent Psychiatry, 30,* 489–493.

Goodman, R. (1989) Infantile autism: A syndrome of multiple primary deficits. *Journal of Autism and Developmental Disorders, 19,* 409–424.

Green, W. H., Campbell, M., Hardesty, A. S., Grega, D. M., Padron-Gayol, M., Shell, J., & Erlenmeyer-Kimling, L. (1984). A comparison of schizophrenic and autistic children. *Journal of the American Academy of Child Psychiatry, 23,* 399–409.

Hermelin, B. (1982). Thoughts and feelings. *Australian Autism Review, 1,* 10–19.

Hertzig, M. E., Snow, M. E., New, E., & Shapiro, T. (1990). DSM-III and DSM-III-R diagnosis of autism and PDD in nursery school children. *Journal of the American Academy of Child and Adolescent Psychiatry, 29,* 123–126.

Hertzig, M. E., Snow, M. E., & Sherman, M. (1989). Affect and cognition in autism. *Journal of the American Academy of Child and Adolescent Psychiatry, 28,* 195–199.

Hobson, R. P. (1991). What is autism? In M. M. Konstantareas & J. H. Beitchman (Eds.), *Psychiatric Clinics of North America, 14,* 1–18.

Kanner, L. (1943). Autistic disturbances of affective contact. *Nervous Child, 2,* 217–250.

Kanner, L., Rodriguez, A., & Ashenden, B. (1972). How far can autistic children go in matters of social adaptation? *Journal of Autism and Childhood Schizophrenia, 2,* 9–33.

Klin, A. (1994). Asperger syndrome. *Child and Adolescent Psychiatric Clinics of North America, 3,* 131–148.

Klin, A., Volkman, F. R., Sparrow, S., Cicchetti, D. V., & Rourke, B. B. (1995) *Journal of Child Psychiatry and Psychology, 36,* 1127–1140.

Kolvin, I. (1971). Studies in the childhood psychoses: I. Diagnostic criteria and classifications. *British Journal of Psychiatry, 118,* 381–384, 385–395.

Lotter, V. (1974). Social adjustment and placement of autistic children in Middlesex: A follow-up. *Journal of Autism and Childhood Schizophrenia, 4,* 11–32.

Lovaas, O. I. (1987). Behavioral treatment and normal educational and intellectual functioning in young autistic children. *Journal of Consulting and Clinical Psychology, 55,* 3–9.

Mahler, M., & Gosliner, B. J. (1955). On symbiotic child psychosis. Genetic, dynamic and restitutive aspects. *Psychoanalytic Study of the Child, 10,* 195–212.

Marcus, L. M., & Campbell, M. (1989). Diagnosis and evaluation for treatment planning. In T. B. Karasu (Chairperson), *Treatment of psychiatric disorders. A task force report of the American Psychiatric Association* (Vol. 1, pp. 180–191) Washington, DC: American Psychiatric Association.

McBride, P. A., Anderson, G. M., Hertzig, M. E., Sweeney, J. A., Kream, J., Cohen, D. J., & Mann, J. J. (1988). Serotonergic function in male young adults with autistic disorder. *Archives of General Psychiatry, 46,* 213–221.

McEachin, J. J., Smith, T., & Lovaas I. O. (1993). Long-term outcome for children with autism who received early intensive behavioral treatment. *American Journal of Mental Retardation, 97,* 359–373.

Mesibov, G. B. (1989). Other treatment modalities. In T. B. Karasu (Chairperson), *Treatment of psychiatric disorders. A task force report of the American Psychiatric Association* (Vol. 1, pp. 266–274). Washington, DC: American Psychiatric Association.

Minshew, N. J. (1991). Indices of neural function in autism: Clinical and biologic implications. *Pediatrics, 87* (5, Pt. 2), 774–780.

Mundy, P. (1995). Joint attention and social-emotional approach behavior in children with autism. *Development and Psychopathology, 7,* 61–82.

Nelson, K. B. (1991). Prenatal and perinatal factors in the etiology of autism. *Pediatrics, 87* (5, Pt. 2), 761–766.

O'Connor, N., & Hermelin, B. (1988). *Journal of Child Psychology and Psychiatry, 29,* 391–396.

Ornitz, E. M. (1985). Neurophysiology of infantile autism. *Journal of the American Academy of Child Psychiatry, 24,* 251–262.

Ousley, O. Y., & Mesibov, G. B. (1991). Sexual attitudes and knowledge of high-functioning adolescents and adults with autism. *Journal of Autism and Developmental Disorders, 21,* 471–481.

Ozonoff, S., Pennington, B., & Rogers, S. (1991) Executive function deficits in high-functioning autistic individuals: Relationship to theory of mind. *Journal of Child Psychology and Psychiatry, 32,* 1081–1105.

Paul, R. (1987). Natural history. In D. J. Cohen, A. Donnellon, & R. Paul (Eds.), *Handbook of autism and pervasive developmental disorders* (pp. 121–130). Silver Springs, MD: V. H. Winston.

Perry, R., Cohen, I., & DeCarlo, R. (1995). Case study: Deterioration, autism, and recovery in two siblings. *Journal of the American Academy of Child and Adolescent Psychiatry, 34,* 232–237.

Petty, L. K., Ornitz, E. M., Michelman, J. D., & Zimmerman, E. G. (1984). Autistic children who become schizophrenic. *Archives of General Psychiatry, 41,* 129–135.

Pivan, J., Arndt, S., Baley, J., Havercamp, S., Andreasen, N. C., & Palmer, P. (1995). An MRI study of brain size in autism. *American Journal of Psychiatry, 152,* 1145–1149.

Prior, M. (1979). Cognitive abilities and disabilities in infantile autism: A review. *Journal of Abnormal Child Psychology, 7,* 359–380.

Rank, B. (1955). Intensive study and treatment of preschool children who show personality deviation or "atypical development" and their parents. In G. Caplan (Ed.), *Emotional problems of early childhood* (pp. 491–501). New York: Plenum Press.

Rapin, I. (1991). Autistic children: Diagnosis and clinical features. *Pediatrics, 87* (5, Pt. 2), 751–760.

Ritvo, E. R., Freeman, B. J., Mason-Brothers, A., Mo, A., & Ritvo, A. M. (1985). Concordance for the syndrome of autism in 40 pairs of affected twins. *American Journal of Psychiatry, 42,* 74–77.

Rumsey, J. M., Rapoport, J. L., & Sceery, W. R. (1985). Autistic children as adults: Psychiatric, social and behavioral outcomes. *Journal of the American Academy of Child Psychiatry, 24,* 465–473.

Rutter, M. (1970). Autistic children: Infancy to adulthood. *Seminars in Psychiatry, 2,* 435–450.

Rutter, M. (1983). Cognitive deficits in the pathogenesis of autism. *Journal of Child Psychology and Psychiatry, 24,* 513–531.

Rutter, M. (1985). Infantile autism and other pervasive developmental disorders. In M. Rutter & L. Herzov (Eds.), *Child and adolescent psychiatry: Modern approaches* (2nd ed., pp. 545–566). London: Blackwell.

Rutter, M., & Bartak, L. (1973). Special education treatment of autistic children: A comparative study: II. Follow-up findings and implications for services. *Journal of Child Psychology and Psychiatry, 14,* 241–270.

Shapiro, T. (1977). The quest for a linguistic model to study the speech of autistic children. Studies on echoing. *Journal of the American Academy of Child Psychiatry, 16,* 608–629.

Shapiro, T., & Hertzig, M. E. (1995). Letter to the editor, Applied behavioral analysis: Astonishing results. *Journal of the American Academy of Child and Adolescent Psychiatry, 34,* 1255.

Snow, M. E., Hertzig, M. E., & Shapiro, T. (1987). Expression of emotion in young autistic children. *Journal of the American Academy of Child and Adolescent Psychiatry, 26,* 836–838.

Sparrow, S., Balla, D. A., & Cicchetti, D. V. (1984). *The Vineland Adaptive Behavior Scales.* Circle Pines, MN: American Guidance Service.

Szatmari, P. (1991). Asperger's syndrome: Diagnosis, treatment, and outcome. In M. M. Konstantareas & J. H. Beitchman (Eds.), *Psychiatric Clinics of North America, 14,* 81–94.

Szatmari, P., Archer, L., Fisman, S., Streiner, D. L., & Wilson, F. (1995). Asperger's syndrome and autism: Differences in behavior, cognition. *Journal of the American Academy of Child and Adolescent Psychiatry, 34,* 1662–1671.

Szatmari, P., Bartolucci, G., Bremner, R., Bond, S., & Rich, S. (1989). A follow-up study of high-functioning autistic children. *Journal of Autism and Developmental Disorders, 19,* 213–225.

Szurek, S. A., & Berlin, I. N. (Eds.), (1973). *Clinical studies in childhood psychoses. 25 years in collaborative treatment and research. The Langley Porter children's service.* New York: Brunner/Mazel.

Wing, L. (1980). Childhood autism and social class: A question of selection. *British Journal of Psychiatry, 137,* 410–417.

Wing, L., & Attwood, A. (1987). Syndromes of autism and atypical development. In D. J. Cohen, A. Donnellon, & R. Paul (Eds.), *Handbook of autism and pervasive developmental disorders* (pp. 3–19). Silver Springs, MD: V. H. Winston.

Wing, L., & Gould, J. (1979). Severe impairments of social interaction and associated abnormalities in children: Epidemiology and classification. *Journal of Autism and Developmental Disorders, 9,* 11–30.

Wolf, S. (1991). Childhood autism: Its diagnosis, nature and treatment. *Archives of Diseases in Childhood, 66,* 737–741.

Van Acker, R. (1991). Rett syndrome: A review of current knowledge. *Journal of Autism and Developmental Disorders, 21,* 381–406.

25 / Learning Disabilities: Developmental Disorders

Edward Greenblatt and Rena Matison Greenblatt

Background

HISTORY OF THE DISORDER

The term *learning disabilities* was first used in the late 1950s and early 1960s to describe a discrepancy or difference between academic skill acquisition and intellectual capabilities as measured by standardized tests. That is, a learning-disabled child is of average or above-average intelligence but cannot perform adequately in school in one or more areas. This difficulty in performance results from unknown causes but usually is attributed to a possible central nervous system dysfunction.

Congenital word blindness and *strephosymbolia* (or twisted symbols) were the original terms used to describe one type of learning disability (Morgan, 1896; Orton, 1925, 1928). Today this disability would be referred to as a developmental dyslexia. In his seminal work, Orton attributed this disability to problems in cerebral dominance, implying that the difficulty was neurologically based.

The cluster of similar deficits found in brain-damaged patients and in the learning disabled provided further support for a neurological basis for learning disabilities. Strauss and Lehtinen (1947) used the term *minimal brain damage* to describe the subclinical damage in the learning impaired. Later Clements (1966) coined the term *minimal brain dysfunction (MBD) syndrome* to distinguish functional from structural deficits. The MBD syndrome includes children of near-average, average, or above-average intelligence with certain mild to severe learning or behavioral difficulties that are associated with central nervous system dysfunction. The impairment may affect perception, conceptualization, language, or memory, or it may impinge on control of attention, impulse, or motor function. However, unlike minimal brain damage syndrome (Strauss & Leh-

tinen, 1947), MBD does not include other major brain syndromes such as the epilepsies, mental retardation, deafness, blindness, or autism; it may however, include genetic determinants and early sensory deprivation as causative factors (Clements, 1966). Today, the term *MBD* usually is associated with behavioral disorders (i.e., attention-deficit hyperactivity disorder [ADHD] without learning disabilities) rather than with disorders of academic skill acquisition or learning disabilities. (Note that throughout the chapter, ADHD is used to include the former term *attention deficit disorder*.)

At first learning disabilities were defined as a retardation, disorder, or delayed development or lag in speech, language, reading, spelling, writing, or arithmetic resulting from a possible cerebral dysfunction and/or emotional or behavioral disturbance (Kirk, 1962). Later, when the term was defined in Public Law (PL 94–142), emotional or behavioral factors were excluded as causal factors. According to this definition: "the term includes such conditions as perceptual handicaps, brain injury, minimal brain damage, dyslexia, and developmental aphasia [but] does not include children who have learning problems which are primarily the result of visual, hearing, or motor handicaps, of mental retardation, or environmental, cultural or economic disadvantage" (U.S. Office of Education, 1977, p. 42478).

More recently, the National Joint Committee on Learning Disabilities (NJCLD), an organization comprising major professional and parent groups, has modified this definition to acknowledge co-occuring factors. The NJCLD sees "learning disabilities" as "a generic term that refers to a heterogeneous group of disorders manifested by significant difficulties in the acquisition and use of listening, speaking, reading, writing, or mathematical abilities." According to the NJCLD, learning disabilities are "presumed to be due to central

235

nervous system dysfunction" (in Kavanaugh & Truss, 1988, p. 550).

Emotional difficulties, social skills impairment, socioenvironmental influences, and ADHD are included among various factors that can occur concomitantly with a learning disability, although it is clearly stated that the learning disability is not the direct result of these factors (in Kavanaugh & Truss, 1988, pp. 541–542).

EPIDEMIOLOGY AND PREVALENCE

The Centers for Disease Control (1987) estimate that learning disabilities occur in 5 to 10% of the population. In most large population studies, there is a higher prevalence of learning disabilities among individuals with low socioeconomic status and males. Yet in order to establish a true estimate of how many are affected, a more uniform definition and diagnostic criteria are needed. If, for example, fewer exclusionary criteria are used in defining a learning disability, the prevalence rate will be higher. Similarly, if a greater number of academic areas are measured for deficient performance, the prevalence rate will be higher.

Prevalence rate is also significantly increased within specific groups. Thus, children with such neurological disorders as Tourette's disorder, neurofibromatosis, or seizure disorder show a higher incidence of learning disabilities. Children of normal intelligence with cerebral palsy or a history of head trauma may evidence a learning disability. In these cases, the prognosis for the learning disability is more guarded (Spreen, 1988).

Psychiatrically disturbed children are another group that seems particularly vulnerable to learning disabilities. Although it has been documented that children with learning disabilities frequently develop secondary social, emotional, and family problems (Silver, 1989), the reverse is certainly true. Studies of children and adolescents with conduct disorder and young adults diagnosed with a personality disorder show that about one third of these individuals also have an underlying learning disorder (Hunt & Cohen, 1984). Similar findings have been documented in studies of adolescent boys in detention centers (Berman & Siegal, 1976; Robbins, et al., 1983).

In a recent study, Greenblatt, Mattis, and Trad (1990) found that there was a greater prevalence of learning disabilities in a group of over 500 children from a psychiatric hospital compared with the national average. The prevalence was greater for an arithmetic disability than for a reading disability. The group was further divided according to patient status (i.e., inpatient, outpatient, or day hospital). The inpatient children were considered more acutely or severely disturbed than either the outpatient or day hospital children, while the day hospital children were considered to have a more chronic disorder than the other two groups. The prevalence of learning disabilities did not differ for inpatient and outpatient children, but it did significantly differ for day hospital children. Thus, chronicity but not severity of a psychiatric illness appears to be associated with learning disabilities.

Various psychiatric groups have been studied to determine whether prevalence rate is influenced by specific diagnoses. In particular, Silver (1981) found that ADHD is the most frequently occurring concurrent disorder, with 20 to 25% of learning-disabled children and adolescents also exhibiting ADHD.

Estimates of prevalence also have been made by calculating the number of persons receiving special educational services. The percentage of all school-age children receiving these services for learning disabilities as defined by PL 94–142 was 4.73% in 1985–86 (U.S. Dept. of Ed., 1987) and again nearly 5% in 1988–89 (U.S. Dept. of Ed., 1989). In 1989–90, the percentage of 6- to 21-year-olds identified as learning disabled was 3.6 in the school-age resident population (U.S. Dept. of Ed., 1991). In 1993–94, the percentage of 6- to 21-year-olds with learning, disabilities who were serviced was 4.1% (U.S. Dept. of Ed., 1995). Nearly 50% of school-age students identified with a handicapping condition were learning disabled. The number of students receiving services increases rapidly from age 6 to 11 and then decreases gradually to age 16. Although substantial numbers of children are identified as learning disabled in the early grades, fewer are identified in junior and senior high school. It may be that the older children already have been remediated. However, as Shaywitz, Escobar, Shaywitz, Fletcher, and Makuch (1992) suggest, dyslexia may be part of a continuum of reading ability rather than a discrete impairment, and some children may be reclassified as no longer impaired in later grades. The data reflect predictable year-to-year variability rather than actual improvement since these children received no remediation.

Clinical Presentation and Diagnostic Assessment

Learning disabilities belong to the covert group of disorders. Outside of the school environment, overt signs and symptoms may not be as obvious as in other disorders. Symptoms may manifest themselves when the child is confronted with activities of daily living that require the use of the deficient area of ability. For example, the child may have difficulty in determining whether he or she has received the correct change when purchasing items in a store. The learning-disabled individual also may have difficulty following directions or may reverse the numbers in a telephone number or address. In more severe and rare cases, the child may have difficulty traveling from place to place.

In school, when confronted with the disability, the child may lose interest in learning, which may then affect concentration and behavior, with the child becoming restless or withdrawn. If, the youngster has some other disorder besides the learning disability, the symptoms of the other disorder may be more evident. For example, a youngster with both ADHD and a learning disability probably will evidence those symptoms associated with hyperactivity first. In part, this occurs because the onset of hyperactivity is evident during the preschool years.

PATTERNS OF PEER RELATIONSHIPS

Children with learning disabilities tend to be less well liked and accepted than their peers (Bryan & Bryan, 1981; Schumaker & Hazel, 1984a). They also perceive their social acceptance and self-worth to be lower than that of their peers (La Greca & Stone, 1990). In addition, how they perceive their learning disability is positively related to their academic self-concept and self-esteem (Heyman, 1990). That is, if they understand and accept their learning disability, they will feel better about their school performance and have greater self-esteem. Children with learning disabilities have difficulty choosing socially acceptable behaviors, discriminating social cues, and assuming role-taking skills (Schumaker & Hazel, 1984a).

Peer Relations: Peer relationships may be impaired in part as a result of the child's difficulty in taking the other's point of view. According to Piagetian theory, this occurs because of an impairment in cognitive development. The ability to see things from another's perspective usually is achieved between the ages of 7 and 12 (Voyat, 1982). An impairment in this ability may result in a perceived lack of empathy, which could affect social acceptance. As a result of their difficulty in taking the other's perspective, these children may be perceived as unfriendly.

By adolescence, however, the individual with learning disabilities usually has friends and engages in appropriate activities with them (Deshler & Schumaker, 1983). This suggests that the learning-disabled adolescent has achieved coordination of perspectives, the cognitive ability to see things from another's perspective. As the youngster reaches adolescence and peers become increasingly important in the tasks of self-definition and separation from parents, he or she continues to use face-saving tactics, such as avoiding tasks that confront him or her with the disability. An example of such a defensive maneuver is the so-called failure syndrome: "I can't do it, so why bother trying?"

Linguistic processing deficits may make it more difficult for the child both to understand what is said and to make an appropriate response. Children with learning disabilities tend to view social interactions as more unfriendly than do their peers without disabilities (Weiss, 1985). They tend to miss the more subtle social cues in the interpretation of social situations. Moreover, although children with learning disabilities understand socially appropriate behavior, they do not put this understanding into action (Bryan, 1982). Thus, they are more likely to be rejected by peers (Bryan, 1974, 1976).

Although deficits in linguistic functioning and poor communication are most frequently associated with poor psychosocial abilities, difficulties in nonverbal functioning also play a role. A child with perceptual processing problems, for example, may have problems reading nonverbal cues such as facial expression (Osman, 1982) and body language cues. Children whose performance IQ (PIQ) is lower than verbal IQ (VIQ) are at a greater risk for severe psychopathology (Fuerst, Fisk, & Rourke, 1990). The syndrome of nonverbal learning disabilities, which includes factors other than the VIQ/PIQ discrepancy, tends to eventuate in significant psychosocial dysfunction (Rourke, 1989).

Patterns of Play: Because the learning-disabled child may have difficulty with certain aspects of symbolic representation, imagery, or classification, play may be impaired, for play requires the ability to imagine and pretend, as well as to use language and ideas in a symbolic way. Play also may require attention to rules, and the child with a learning disability may have difficulty following the rules of the game, sharing, or taking turns (Silver, 1989).

Etiology

GENETICS

Studies indicate that a high percentage of children with learning disabilities have a family history of learning disabilities, suggesting the presence of genetic factors in etiology (Bannatyne, 1971; Mattis, French, & Rapin, 1975). There is also a higher prevalence of learning disabilities in the family members of learning-disabled children than in the general population. Twin studies also lend support to a hypothesis of a genetic etiology (Decker & Vandenberg, 1985). The incidence of both members of a pair of dizygotic twins having a learning disability is greater than that for monozygotic twins (LaBuda, DeFries, & Pennington, 1990).

According to the Colorado Reading Project, which studied individuals with dyslexia and their family members (DeFries, 1985), reading disabilities appear to be highly heritable. Five to 10% of school-age children are affected, with the ratio of boys to girls 3:1 or 4:1 (Rutter, 1978). Higher visual-spatial ability (or PIQ) versus low verbal ability (VIQ) has been associated with a familial type

of reading disability (Owen, 1978). However, the reverse pattern of low PIQ and high VIQ, associated with neurological dysfunction, does not appear to be familial in nature (Boder, 1971).

Further evidence for a familial link comes from Pennington and Smith (1988), who have described the relationship of phonological impairment to the phenotype associated with specific developmental dyslexia. They also describe a linkage between dyslexia and chromosome 15 heteromorphisms.

When Vogler, DeFries, and Decker (1985) measured familial risk for dyslexia in the Colorado Reading Project sample, they found the risk to sons of affected fathers to be 40% and the risk to sons of affected mothers to be 35%, a 5- to 7-fold increase in risk over that found in sons without affected parents. The risk to daughters of an affected parent of either sex was 17 to 18%, a 10- to 12-fold increase over that found in daughters without affected parents.

Environmental factors appear to play a role as well, as indicated by an epidemiological study (Berger, Yule, & Rutter, 1975). The prevalence rate of learning disabilities among urban children in London was 10%, compared with 4% on the rural Isle of Wright. Environmental toxins, such as lead, are related to neural development and subsequent cognitive functioning (Needleman, 1986; Needleman, Leviton, & Bellinger, 1982).

NEUROPSYCHOLOGICAL ASPECTS

One approach to learning disabilities is to see all types as aspects of a unitary disorder rather than classifying the types on the basis of information-processing abilities and/or etiology (Satz & Morris, 1981). Bender's (1958) maturational lag hypothesis, Cruickshank's (1977) perceptual deficit hypothesis, and Vellutino's (1978) verbal mediation hypothesis all adopt this approach. The disorder is presumed to result respectively from a developmental lag, a perceptual deficit, or a verbal processing problem.

A maturational lag is seen as differentially affecting those cognitive skills that are typically developed at a particular age. Thus, visual-perceptual and cross-modal sensory integration are delayed in young children who are "maturationally immature," while linguistic skills may be delayed in older children. Developmental dyslexia is seen as a disorder in central processing, the nature of which varies with the chronological age of the child.

The etiology of reading disabilities also has been traced to deficits in visual perception. Yet there may be deficits in short-term memory in a given sensory domain (e.g., visual or auditory). One view of reading disabilities proposes that there is a failure in phonetic processing, affecting phonetic representations in short-term memory. Individuals with learning disabilities therefore may need to apply conscious effort and attention to a task that others may do automatically. This deficit would be consistent with an automatization failure or an inability to learn rules (Sternberg & Wagner, 1982). The preponderance of research supports the hypothesis that learning disabilities constitute different syndromes.

The syndromes of learning disabilities are heterogeneous and are based partially on exclusionary criteria. However, it is also useful to use "inclusionary" criteria and define the abilities that may be impaired in order for a youngster to be considered learning disabled. To this end, subtypes have been delineated within several of the developmental syndromes. One of the most important studies is by Mattis, French, and Rapin (1975) on the three syndromes of dyslexia. They were able to classify a sample of 82 children with dyslexia. Of these, 29 were developmental dyslexics and 53 were brain-damaged dyslexics. A third group of brain-damaged readers was included as a control group ($N = 31$).

Mattis et al. (1975) found that children with dyslexia exhibited one of three clinical syndromes: a language disorder, an articulation and graphomotor discoordination syndrome, or a visuo-perceptual disorder. The prevalence rate was 39%, 37%, and 16%, respectively, for each syndrome. Children with a language disorder demonstrated a verbal/performance IQ discrepancy with VIQ significantly lower and an anomia or word-finding difficulty. This word-finding difficulty and verbal learning difficulty affected the acquisition of a "look-and-say vocabulary." Recognition vocabulary is usually stressed before a phonics approach, so these children were delayed before beginning to learn with a phonics approach. In addition, they probably were not able to reliably retrieve the letter name that went with the sound, thus further impairing their learning of phonics.

Children with the articulatory and graphomotor discoordination syndrome demonstrated articulation and graphomotor deficits but normal acoustosensory and language processes. Those with the visuo-perceptual disorder syndrome had a VIQ greater than their PIQ and impaired visual-perceptual processes. Thus, children with similarly severe deficits in reading showed different patterns of impairment in higher cortical functions.

Later, in a nonclinical referred sample of younger (mean age 9 years) black and Hispanic children (Mattis, 1978), the same three subtypes were identified. However, the prevalences of each were somewhat different for the language disorder subtype (63%), articulatory and graphomotor discoordination syndrome (10%), and visual-perceptual disorder (5%). In the first study, no subjects fit into overlapping categories. However, in the later study, some children presented with more than one syndrome.

Denckla (1972) identified three subtypes similar to Mattis's syndromes: a specific language disturbance subtype, a specific visuo-spatial disability subtype, and a discontrol subtype. Approximately 7% of Denckla's subjects did not clearly fit into any one category or exhibited the characteristics of more than one subtype.

Both Mattis and Denckla based their subtypes on cognitive, neuropsychological distinctions. Another type of classification is based on achievement variables (Satz & Morris, 1981). Boder (1973) examined achievement patterns of 92 boys and 15 girls with developmental dyslexia and did a qualitative analysis of how each child read and spelled; she did not include a control group. She identified three subtypes of children: a dysphonetic group (67%), a dyseidetic group (10%), and a mixed dysphonetic-dyseidetic group (23%). The dysphonetic group had difficulty "analyzing the phonetic or sound properties of words and symbols." The dyseidetic group had difficulty with the visual properties of letters and words. Finally, the third subtype, the mixed dysphonetic-dyseidetic group, showed impairment "both in phonetic word-analysis skills and in perceiving whole words as visual gestalts" (p. 112).

Satz and Morris (1981) identified different learning-disabled groups from a larger population using different clustering procedures. This statistical approach produced nine subgroups, including global language, specific language-naming, global language and perceptual, and visual-perceptual-motor. They examined these subtypes for positive neurological and familial-genetic determinants.

Petrauskas and Rourke (1979) found three subtypes based on statistical analysis of neuropsychological test performance. One was similar to the language disorder and another to the articulatory and graphomotor discoordination syndrome previously identified by Mattis et al. (1975). The third subtype, linguistic, sequencing, and finger localization, was not similar to previously identified subtypes. Overall, however, the subtypes found across several studies are similar: a language disorder subtype, a visual-perceptual disorder subtype, and a subtype involving some kind of motor skill. (See Table 25.1.)

It is clear that dyslexics may be impaired in a variety of cognitive functions including language and phonemic abilities, visuo-perceptual and visuo-motor integration or coordination, visual and intersensory memory, and other functions such as organizational abilities (Levin, 1990). Reading failure may result from a deficit in a variety of subskills because reading requires an integration of input, output, and mediating processes (Mattis et al., 1975). In other words, reading problems can occur for more than one reason since reading requires a number of cognitive functions. For example, spatial abilities are required for a sight reading vocabulary while auditory-acoustic abilities are necessary for sounding out words. An impairment in any one function can have a deleterious effect on the ability to read.

Reading and spelling may be seen as separate functions, although they share many cognitive elements (Yule & Rutter, 1976). In fact, although children may be impaired in both reading and spelling, impairment in one without the other is found as well (Levin, 1990). Reading may be accomplished by visual clustering strategies, but spelling requires phonological analysis as well (Bryant & Bradley, 1985).

Overall, a learning disability is viewed as an impairment in several neuropsychological processes, involving brain function rather than brain structure. Although some workers choose to see the impairment as related to damage to a specific brain region (Galaburda & Kemper, 1978; Galaburda, Sherman, Rosen, Aboitiz, & Geschwind, 1985), it is more useful to view it as a functional impairment because there is plasticity of function in the developing child's brain. Levin (1990), for example, sees the organizational deficits he found in 9-year-old children as related to frontal lobe dysfunction. Bakker and Licht (1986) describe reading as a developmental process, in which there is a change from primarily right-hemisphere or visuo-perceptual strategies to left-hemisphere or linguistically based strategies. Thus, the young child (ages 5 to 7) uses visuo-perceptual strategies until the graphemes or letters can be identified automatically. Then the child (age 9 to 11) switches to higher-order concept formation skills and semantic and language-based strategies. The primacy of the different hemispheres at different ages has been documented by electrophysiologic studies. This relates to Orton's (1925, 1928) original hypothesis that developmental dyslexia is associated with problems in cerebral dominance.

TABLE 25.1

Subtypes of Learning Disabilities

Disability Subtype	Mattis, French & Rapin (1975)	Petrauskas & Rourke (1979)	Satz & Morris (1981)
Language	Language disorder	Language disorder	Global language Specific language—Naming
Visual-Perceptual	Visuospatial perceptual disorder	Linguistic, sequencing, and finger localization deficiencies, and acid pattern	Global language and perception
Motor Skill	Articulatory and graphomotor discoordination	Articulatory and graphomotor discoordination	Visual-perceptual Motor

VULNERABILITY

Kavale and Forness (1996) did a meta-analysis of studies examining the social skills of students with learning disabilities. They found that about "75% of students with learning disabilities manifest social skills deficits that distinguish them from comparison samples" (p. 226). The social skills deficits occur across different raters (teachers, peers, self) and across many dimensions of social competence. The authors believe that the deficits can be best viewed as a part of the learning disability constellation rather than as warranting a change in the definition of a learning disability.

Social interaction problems of children with learning disabilities include withdrawal and problems with aggression and conduct (Quay, 1979). Youngsters with learning disabilities tend to experience more anxiety, withdrawal, depression, and low self-esteem than their peers (Cullinan, Epstein, & Lloyd, 1981). Depression appears to be more common in adolescents with learning disabilities than in children (Maag & Behrens, 1989). Attentional problems, however, decrease as the children grow older.

Geisthardt and Munsch (1996) report that adolescents with learning disabilities tend to use a cognitive avoidance coping strategy more than their nondisabled peers when dealing with a school stressor. Furthermore, those students with learning disabilities tend to rely less on their peers for social support "when dealing with an academic stressor or with an interpersonal problem" (p. 287).

The quality of family functioning of boys with learning disabilities was a strong predictor of later academic and social success (Hartzell & Compton, 1984). Families of children with reading problems are less effective communicators when making joint decisions than families of normally achieving boys (Peck & Stackhouse, 1973). In addition, families of children with learning disabilities lived in an atmosphere that tended to be both less organized and emotionally stable than that of other families (Owen, Adams, Forrest, Stolz, & Fisher, 1971). Often, when there is a familial basis to the learning disability, the parent may be so identified with the child that he or she has difficulty dealing with the child's limitations and pressures the child to succeed.

Dyson (1996) has found that the functioning of families of children with learning disabilities and the self-concept of the siblings were comparable to those of families of children without learning disabilities. However, parents do experience greater stress than do parents of nondisabled children. Few problems exist in sibling relationships, although the families do have difficulties with adaptation and, therefore, family intervention is suggested.

Relationship to Other Disorders

Often a differential diagnosis must be made between a learning disability and attention deficit hyperactivity disorder (Duane, 1989), conduct disorder, and other emotional disorders. These disorders may or may not co-occur with the diagnosis of learning disability. ADHD and conduct disorder often go along with learning disabilities in prevalence (Shaywitz, Schnell, Shaywitz, & Towle, 1986; Shaywitz & Shaywitz, 1988).

Conduct-disordered individuals with learning disabilities may lack the know-how to get themselves out of difficult situations. Furthermore, low self-esteem resulting from poor school performance may result in a tendency to act out. Children also may seek the approval of peers. Youths with learning disabilities generally tend to exhibit behavior problems, although there are age and sex differences (Epstein, Cullinan, & Lloyd, 1986). For example, females tend to internalize their problems. An elevated rate of psychiatric diagnoses, particularly conduct disorder and depression, is associated with reading disorders. Depression is often a concomitant of developmental nonverbal learning disorders as well (Johnson, 1988).

The emotional problems associated with the learning disability may be understood from several theoretical viewpoints. Consider Erikson's (1963, 1968) description of latency-age achievements as revolving around the conflict of industriousness versus inferiority. During this stage, the child works effectively at producing, or he or she feels inferior. For example, during the grade-school years, identity issues become increasingly salient as the child's schoolwork and performance become more important. Thus, a child with a learning disability may have difficulty achieving a sense of being productive as reflected in Erikson's stage of industry versus inferiority. Difficulties arise when the mother does not allow independence and when the father is competitive. This problem may become exacerbated still further in the learning-disabled child.

Psychoanalytic and Piagetian theories can be amalgamated in relating the shift from primary to secondary process thinking and from preoperational to concrete-operational thinking. Although these two types of thinking are not equivalent, there are certain similarities. For example, in concrete operational thinking as in secondary process thinking, children think more logically and their thinking is not based so much on perception as on logical operations.

Although other disorders may co-occur with the learning disability, the learning disability is not considered the cause of these other disorders. That is, it has an independent existence and is organically based. For example, ADHD is not a learning disability but a related disorder (Silver, 1990).

Morbidity

EFFECTS ON CHILDREN'S FUNCTIONING

The behavioral or emotional difficulties associated with the learning disability may reflect the individual's way of coping with the learning disability. Associated defenses and emotional difficulties may include regression, projection, withdrawal, phobias, somatic complaints, poor self-esteem, and passive-aggressive and impulsive behavior (Silver, 1989). In addition, some children use the diagnosis as an excuse not to try. Clowning is another defensive reaction. Although humor can be used constructively, clowning may be done in an effort to deny feelings of lack of self-worth and depression (Silver, 1989). Parents may first deny the reality of the child's disability, then they may feel guilty or angry about it. They may expect more of the child than he or she is capable of, stating that they feel the child is "lazy."

PROGNOSIS

Much of the research on prognosis comes from follow-up studies of clinical samples or prospective studies on high-risk samples. These studies point to an unfavorable prognosis with continued academic failure and increased risk for "a damaged self-concept" and undesirable behaviors (Deshler, 1978, pp. 63, 61). A longitudinal study suggests that intervention between the second and fifth grade may be important in order to reduce the prospect of repeated failure and the emotional effects associated with it as children progress through the elementary grades. The research confirms other cross-sectional and prospective work showing that as learning-disabled children get older, their deficit in achievement increases compared with peers.

Spreen (1988), in his review, states that outcome is dependent on the severity of the learning disability at school age, intelligence, neurological impairment, and socioeconomic status of parents. Occupational outcome seems related to the occupational and educational status of the father. In his longitudinal study, Spreen found that all learning-disabled subgroups showed a greater amount of maladjustment and antisocial behavior than control subjects. Female subjects also showed a greater incidence of social and personality problems as compared to male subjects. The emotional, behavioral, and adjustment problems reached a peak during late adolescence and then seemed to decrease as the individual goes through young adulthood. However, Spreen notes that the prognosis or outcome, as applied to an individual child, has little validity at this time. In addition, he indicates that intervention was not a significant factor. However, it should be noted that severity is a confounding variable since the more severely impaired persons with learning disabilities are likely to be the ones to get remediation. Furthermore, a large number of different intervention approaches were used.

The results of outcome studies depend on the variables used. For example, when education is among the variables, the outcome is good for adults with learning disabilities. When performance on tests of basic skill functioning are the criteria for outcome, the picture is not as good. Research studies have not clearly documented the emotional-behavioral outcome of individuals with learning disabilities. Adults may have mastered methods for compensating for a learning disability by avoiding tasks that confront them with the impairment. The findings on the efficacy of treatment are somewhat unclear as well and dependent on the methodology of the study (Horn, O'Donnel, & Vitulano, 1983). These methodological issues include criteria for initial subject selection, inclusion of control groups, initial severity of the learning disability, and demographic characteristics such as age and sex. For example, boys tend to do better than girls in outcome studies (Berger, Yule, & Rutter, 1975).

More epidemiological studies are needed, as these have the advantage of investigating total child populations and thus avoiding biases in sample selection. It can be argued that children selected from different referral sources have inherent differences. For example, children who are retarded in reading and referred to a neurologist are different from those referred to a child psychiatrist or remedial teacher, speech therapist, or educational psychologist (Yule & Rutter, 1976). Children referred to a psychiatrist will most likely have more notable psychiatric problems, thus setting up a bias in the sample.

Assessment and Treatment

The goal of classification of reading disabilities is to relate the different subgroups to etiology and to identify treatment approaches. If subgroups can be identified, remediation can be tailored for each group. Furthermore, if potential reading problems can be identified early, then methods of learning to read can be tailored for the child with the potential problem.

Treatment for youngsters with learning disabilities includes remedial, psychological, and social methods. Individuals with learning disabilities often undergo psychotherapy to help them with their low self-esteem or with other psychological concomitants of the learning disability. Work with the family of children with learning disabilities is necessary to help effect a change in the family system, which often depends on the targeted patient and focuses on maintenance of the disability. Group therapy is a supportive means for children with learning disabilities, as it helps them feel that they are not alone in their disability and learn other coping mechanisms. Peer tutoring counteracts the child's tendency to avoid difficult tasks

and to escape embarrassment in front of a peer in the event of failure. Biological treatments such as nutritional methods and vitamin therapy have not been proven to be effective.

EDUCATIONAL ASSESSMENT

When referring a child for assessment, the parent or educator generally observes that the child is having difficulty learning in some domain. Referral questions may include why the child cannot read at grade level, why writing skills are so poorly developed, and what instructional approaches would best address the child's strengths and limitations. Early assessment is important because the sooner the child is assessed, the sooner an appropriate intervention can begin. However, boys tend to be referred more frequently than girls in the early elementary school years, possibly because the combination of behavioral problems and the learning disability makes early identification easier and more obvious. In addition, there is a higher prevalence of boys with learning disabilities in the early years.

The psychologist, upon receiving the referral from the psychiatrist, pediatrician, school, or parent, generally inquires into the specifics of the referral. In addition, he or she takes a developmental history from the psychiatrist and the parents. If a differential diagnosis is being made between ADHD and a learning disability, the psychologist may request that the teacher and parent complete the Conner's teacher's rating scale (Pelham, Milich, Murphy, & Murphy, 1989) to get a sense of whether there is a behavior problem in both the home and the school or in just one situation. The rating scale also indicates whether the child has difficulty in attention and related problems. A history is obtained through an interview with the parents. Important information to be procured includes the prenatal and perinatal history, medical problems of mother during pregnancy as well as drug use, pre- and postnatal nutritional factors, the timing of developmental milestones such as walking and talking, duration of childhood friendships, significant traumas (including losses or moves), changes of school in childhood, history of learning disabilities or emotional problems in the family, and educational level and socioeconomic status of the parents. In addition, the family attitude toward the child with a learning disability and the parents' expectations are important to assess.

Tests may include an intelligence test, an achievement test, a test of reading comprehension, a writing sample, and tests of memory, attention, language, somatosensory processes, motor processes, and personality functioning. After examining the intelligence test for patterns of impairment, the psychologist can decide which areas need further assessment. He or she forms a hypothesis about the areas of difficulty and then, using selected tests, begins to test the hypothesis. Another approach that some psychologists use is to administer an entire battery of tests, such as the Halstead-Reitan Battery (Reitan & Davison, 1974).

The criterion often used for designating a child as learning disabled is a score of 2 years below grade level or age on a standardized achievement test. However, a 2-year discrepancy is not equivalent across grades or subjects (Reynolds, 1980). A 2-year discrepancy between reading level and actual grade level reflects a more severe impairment in the lower grades as compared to the upper grades (Reynolds, 1980). It is therefore recommended that a standard score be used instead of a grade-equivalent score.

Children as young as kindergarten age can be identified as predisposed to develop a learning disability if they do not exhibit a general developmental readiness in perception, cognition, language, and memory (Satz & Van Nostrand, 1973). A delay on developmental tests may reflect a developmental unreadiness or immaturity—although Fisk and Rourke (1979) suggest that it is a deficit, not a delay, and that it will not be outgrown. In either case, it is important to identify these children at an early age, when their central nervous system is still plastic and the children can benefit from remediation and the child is less subject "to the shattering effects of repeated academic failure" (Satz, Friel, & Rudegeair, 1976, p. 133). Problems in preschool have been demonstrated to affect the child in second and third grades. For example, children who had been identified with depressed scores on developmental tests during kindergarten were found to be learning disabled in the early grades (Satz & Van Nostrand, 1973).

Gordon (1968) points to the importance of understanding the quality and style of intellectual functioning of preschoolers for planning educational experience and measuring educational growth. Psychologists assessing individuals with learning disabilities should use such a qualitative approach. Furthermore, instruction must be adapted to individual learning behaviors—learning style, cultural style, or behavioral style—in order to reduce school failure (Gordon, 1991). When tailoring recommendations for remediation, this concept can be applied to individuals with learning disabilities.

Coordination and communication between the psychologist, teacher, parent, and mental health practitioner is, of course, essential for the proper treatment of the child. The results of psychological testing, for example, must be explained in a way that is understandable and relevant to school personnel.

Disadvantaged Populations

Disadvantaged children, as a group, appear to arrive at school less prepared than their advantaged classmates (Gordon, 1970). Yet according to PL 94-142, children who have learning problems that are primarily the result of environmental, cultural, or economic disadvantage should not be labeled learning disabled. In practice, however, 38% of 314 school psychologists surveyed in a national sample do not comply with this clause (Harris, Gray, Davis, Zaremba, & Argulewicz, 1988). The authors speculate that the psychologists do not comply so that more children will be serviced.

Moreover, an economically disadvantaged child may be learning disabled as well. In fact, certain aspects of home life may affect the capacity for intellectual growth. Predictors of early school adjustment were investigated using an ethnically diverse cohort of kindergartners and first graders (Reynolds, Weissberg, & Kasprow, 1992). Prior adjustment and sociodemographic factors explained the majority of the variance in adjustment. Independent of these factors, parent involvement and life-event variables also were found to be important. That is, parent involvement in school appears to be helpful to the child. Life-event variables were defined as parental drug abuse, poor nutrition, living in a single-parent home, or death of a parent. Since early behavior has been shown to be associated with later school and social competence (Reynolds, 1991), early intervention appears to be essential.

Some educational programs attempt to compensate for deprivation by targeting the entire deprived population. Such programs might include compensatory education, remediation, and extracurricular activities (Hellmuth, 1970). However, programs of this nature have failed to provide long-term improvement for the disadvantaged child. This has led to hypotheses that attempt to explain the learning failure of such children. Gordon (1970) focuses on motivational differences between lower- and middle-class children. The decreased motivation in disadvantaged children is usually consistent with what the children have perceived is available to them. That is, although they want immediate rewards for themselves, they often do not get immediate satisfaction or feedback from their environment (Gordon, 1970). Motivational deficits may result from ". . . the children's histories of failure-based experience in academic settings, low expectation for success, and deficits in perceived self-efficacy which results in the avoidance of situations and tasks in which they feel failure is possible" (Gresham, 1987, p. 284).

There have been other hypotheses as to why children from economically disadvantaged homes have difficulties with learning. Poor nutrition and health care have an adverse effect on the learning capacities of young children (Birch & Gussow, 1970). For example, maternal malnutrition and pregnancy and birth complications have been related to learning disabilities (Creevy, 1986). Furthermore, sensory overstimulation, which has been associated with learning disabilities, may occur in disadvantaged homes (Kavale, 1988).

Remediation

Much of the research on remediation has failed to show significant or sustainable improvements. In her review, Richardson (1989) concludes that "no one discipline . . . and no single technique or method of remediation has yet or will by itself solve the broad problem of learning disabilities" (p. 16).

Although no one technique or remedial approach has been successful, research has shown that a combination of approaches may be useful

(Wade & Kass, 1987). Furthermore, there is controversy in the field as to whether to remediate the deficit or bolster the strength of the individual with a learning disability—the latter approach would serve to help the child compensate for the deficit. Reynolds (1992) adheres to a strength model of remediation in which task analysis and diagnostic achievement testing delineate the specifics of what to teach.

Several workers point to the importance of basing remedial approaches on theoretical knowledge and research. So, for example, Korhonen (1991) believes remedial approaches should be specific to the targeted subtype of learning disability. Other techniques include information processing approaches that may be applied for effective remediation (Kolligian & Sternberg, 1987). Also, cross-age tutoring (tutoring of younger by older children) was successful in increasing positive social behaviors and academic achievement in spelling for boys with learning disabilities (Trapani & Gettinger, 1989).

Research shows that students must be taught strategies for solving academic problems; it is helpful if these approaches include self-monitoring, goal-orientation, and a structured method (Kavale, 1988). The literature indicates that although most teachers use process-type remediation—for example, auditory reception of visual perception—it is not as effective as direct academic training. Children with learning impairments were given a treatment program consisting of phonemic awareness exercises aimed at reducing the risk of dyslexia (Korkman & Peltomaa, 1993). The treatment was effective in improving the acquisition of reading and spelling.

Finally, communication to coordinate all efforts of individuals working with the learning-disabled students and communication between student and teacher is important in facilitating remedial efforts (Deshler, Schumaker, Lenz, & Ellis, 1984; Taylor, Adelman, & Kaser-Boyd, 1983).

Current Developments

New research findings on dyslexia focus on a dysfunction in the processing of information. The basis of the condition is considered to be a failure in the proper timing of the affected sensory system.

One recent research study demonstrates that there is a defect in the timing of one of the two visual pathways, the magnocellular system (Livingstone, Rosen, Drisland & Galaburda, 1991). This system consists of large cells that are responsible for low-contrast, depth-perception, and stereoscopic vision. These processes, which are recognized as fast processes due to large neural cells, operate more slowly in dyslexics. Using autopsied brains, it was found that these cells were smaller in persons with dyslexia than in normal readers. Tallal (1980; Tallal, Stark, & Mellits, 1985) has observed that the fast components of the auditory system are similarly impaired, making it difficult to distinguish between certain phonemes. Similarly, the sense of touch also may be impaired. When two fingers are touched in rapid succession, the individual senses only a single touch.

Since all of these processes are involved in reading and can be impaired, the timing of the sense processes involved in reading may possibly affect reading itself. This fact may address one component of the problem involved in different types of dyslexia. However, the visuo-perceptual form of dyslexia involves an actual misperception of letters, not just a distortion, such as a wavy image.

Learning Disorders, Motor Skills Disorders, and Communication Disorders

According to the fourth edition of the *Diagnostic and Statistical Manual of Mental Disorders* (*DSM-IV*; American Psychiatric Association [APA] 1994), the learning disorders include the following subgroups: learning disorders consisting of reading disorder, mathematics disorder, disorder of written expression and learning disorder not otherwise specified; motor skills disorder, which includes developmental coordination disorder and communication disorders, which are comprised of expressive language disorder, mixed receptive expressive language disorder, and phonological disorder.

The learning disorders (previously academic skills disorder—*DSM-III-R;* APA, 1987) may be diagnosed if achievement in the particular academic skill area (reading, mathematics or written expression) or activities of daily living requiring these skills is significantly below that expected given the person's age, measured intelligence, and age-appropriate education. Moreover, if the child evidences a sensory deficit, the academic difficulties are more than would be expected from the sensory deficit alone. The learning disorder not otherwise specified category is for learning disorders that do not meet criteria for any of the specific disorders just described. Thus, an individual may have difficulty in all of the academic areas, significantly compromising his or her academic achievement.

The motor skills disorder category is comprised of developmental coordination disorder. As with the other disorders, performance in daily activities that require the activity is significantly below what would be expected given the individual's chronological age and measured intelligence. This may manifest itself in several ways: delays in the achievement of developmental motor milestones, clumsiness, difficulty in performing sports, and poor graphomotor performance. Furthermore, the disturbance is not a result of a medical condition or a pervasive developmental disorder. If mental retardation is present, the disturbance in motor skills is in excess of that which would usually be associated with the mental retardation.

For the category of communication disorders, if mental retardation, a speech-motor, or sensory deficit or environmental deprivation is present, the deficits are in excess of those usually associated with these difficulties. An expressive language disorder manifests itself clinically when the child has difficulty expressing him- or herself. For example, he or she may have a limited vocabulary, exhibit an anomia, make tense errors, or produce sentences not appropriate in complexity for his or her age. These difficulties significantly interfere with academic or work-related achievement and with social communication. Scores on standardized tests of expressive language are significantly below those obtained from standardized measures of nonverbal intellectual ability and receptive language development. Furthermore, criteria are not met for mixed receptive expressive language disorder or a pervasive developmental disorder.

In mixed receptive-expressive language disorder, a receptive language deficit also is present. Thus, difficulties with both receptive and expressive language significantly interfere with the individual's functioning. Performance on standardized measures of both receptive and expressive language are significantly below performance on standardized measures of nonverbal intelligence.

A person diagnosed with a phonological disorder manifests a failure to use developmentally expected speech sounds appropriate for his or her age and dialect. For example, the individual may substitute one sound for another or omit sounds. An individual diagnosed with stuttering manifests a disturbance in the normal fluency and time patterning of normal speech. This disturbance interferes with academic or occupational achievement or with social communication.

CASE EXAMPLE

In the following example, a clinical description of a latency-age girl is presented to illustrate how a learning disability impacts on a youngster of this age. In addition, the process of test referral and evaluation is demonstrated. Although not all aspects of the actual test report are included, those important for the demonstration of learning disability in a latency age child are addressed.

Case I: Lynn was referred for neuropsychological assessment because she was having difficulty in school, particularly in the areas of reading comprehension and mathematics. Lynn is a 9½-year-old, right-handed girl who is one of three children. One of her sisters is three years older and the other is three years younger than she.

Lynn was born at full term by cesarean section. Motor development was normal but language development was slow. Although Lynn had friendships of long duration, she was manipulative and always succeeded in getting "her own way."

Lynn fell and sustained a mild concussion when she was 7½ years old. She did not lose consciousness. Moreover, Lynn's difficulties in school predated this concussion.

On intake, Lynn's parents stated that her strengths are in conceptual areas, abstracting, memory, and fine and gross motor coordination. However, her vocabulary is limited and she does not grasp information as readily when it is presented auditorily rather than visually. There is no family history of learning disabilities or intellectual or cognitive difficulties.

When Lynn was in the third grade, she refused to go to school for a period of 6 weeks to 2 months. She ex-

hibited psychosomatic symptoms and held her body rigid, thereby impairing her mother's ability to dress her for school. It is interesting that Lynn did not dress herself. At this time, Lynn began psychotherapy. She has made dramatic improvements this past year.

Lynn is a petite, attractive young girl. Her eye contact is good, she is pleasant and smiles readily. At first, Lynn was anxious about the testing but she quickly adjusted and became engaged with the tasks and the examiner. Her verbalizations during testing were extensive.

On testing, Lynn's IQ was within the average range. Her Verbal IQ was 103, her Performance IQ 93 and Full Scale IQ 99. There was some discrepancy between verbal and nonverbal functions, with nonverbal functions slightly lower. Academic achievement in spelling and arithmetic was consistent with Lynn's intellectual abilities. However, academic achievement in reading was lower than her capabilities.

Lynn's reading comprehension also was significantly lower than her intellectual ability. Language abilities were normal with the exception of naming or word finding. Although sound blending was normal, speech sound discrimination was impaired; however, it did not seriously interfere with spelling.

All of the part processes necessary for reading were present. Lynn's spelling was good and she used a phonetic approach. However, her naming and word-finding ability was deficient. Reading comprehension was poor and Lynn had impaired reading decoding skills. Lynn does not have a general language comprehension problem but her reading is impaired. She has a mild anomia (word-finding difficulty), which is handicapping but by itself not limiting. With proper remediation, Lynn should be able to overcome her word-finding difficulty so that it does not affect her learning.

Lynn does not seem to utilize her psychological resources to mobilize energy to overcome her learning difficulties. Instead, she uses her energy to avoid situations and behave in a histrionic manner. This was evident when she refused school and exhibited somatic symptoms.

Summary: Personality issues are a contributing factor to Lynn's learning difficulties. These difficulties can be overcome if Lynn receives the proper remedial help and if she can muster the psychological resources necessary to attempt to overcome her language disability. Continued therapy is necessary in this respect.

It is recommended that Lynn begin language training in a resource room. Vocabulary and word-finding skills may be improved using a technique that allows Lynn to associate different words with one another in a semantic network. In this way, she will increase her vocabulary, and this will then help her word-finding skills. Lynn's strong phonic approach can be used to her advantage in helping her to improve her reading skills.

This case illustrates how a learning disability impacts on a child's ability to perform in school and to attain good reading skills. In addition, the learning disability is associated with psychological symptoms, such as school refusal and psychosomatic symptomotalogy. By not attending school, Lynn did not have to be directly confronted by her learning disability. The secondary gain was her ability to stay home with her mother.

It can be inferred that the mother's acquiescing to dress Lynn and her inability to allow this petite girl to separate may also have contributed to Lynn's choice of symptomatology. Thus, this case illuminates the interaction of psychological and cognitive factors in the manifestation of a learning disability in a school age youngster.

The following clinical description illustrates the importance of correct assessment of a learning and language disability for proper school placement. In this case, the differential diagnosis was between mental retardation and a learning disability in a youngster of 6 years who is just beginning his grade-school years. This can be an important period for proper assessment and placement since it is the time that the child learns to read.

Case II: Bob was referred for neuropsychological assessment because he was having difficulty in school. His class of language-impaired youngsters no longer employs an aide and now has an 8:1 student:teacher ratio. The school personnel recommended placing him in a class for mentally retarded children so that he might have the benefit of a teacher's aide. Bob's parents would like to know what type of school program is appropriate for him.

Bob is a 6-year-old, right-handed boy who is the younger of two children. His older brother is 8 years old.

Bob's mother reports that there were no difficulties in pregnancy or delivery. Bob has a history of ear infections, which may have contributed to a history of severe delays in language development. Bob's social development was normal.

The timing of developmental milestones was variable. According to his parents, crawling and turning over were on time but Bob did not walk until he was 17 months of age. Language development was severely delayed. Fine motor coordination was normal while gross motor coordination was slightly impaired. Bob was toilet trained when he was 4 years old. Bob is very sensitive to odors and has been reported to vomit in school. He also has reportedly urinated in his pants while in school. According to his parents, these behav-

iors do not occur at home. Bob frequently jumps off bars on the playground and is seemingly unaware of danger. Bob's parents report that his attention span is short but that he can stay with a task if it interests him or if he is given individual encouragement.

Bob is an attractive young boy. His eye contact is good, he is very good-natured and smiles readily. At first, Bob became inattentive when difficult tasks were presented to him. However, with encouragement, he was cooperative and eager to please. He was somewhat fidgety and restless during the testing sessions. However, he was able to find an appropriate outlet for his motor activity. Bob's working style can be somewhat impulsive; this together with his restlessness are symptoms that are consistent with hyperactivity. Bob was appropriately interested in the whereabouts of his mother, and he was able to monitor his own tolerance for work by asking for a break when needed.

Bob's IQ is within the average range or 2 points below that range depending on which instrument is used. On the Wechsler Preschool and Primary Scale of Intelligence, his Verbal IQ was 87, his Performance IQ was 91 and Full Scale IQ was 88. Bob's auditory processing appeared deficient during the administration of the verbal subtests. For example, when he was asked to define "moth," he responded, "Santa lives in the north." This auditory processing deficiency did not affect the performance subtests that do not require language. As a result, his performance IQ is within the average range. The Raven's Coloured Progressive Matrices was administered to get an assessment of problem-solving ability and intellectual potential that would be free of verbal factors. Bob's score was at the 62.5%, which is equivalent to an IQ of 105.

Academic achievement was not consistent with Bob's intellectual capabilities. Arithmetic, in particular, was lower than his capabilities at the 1%, with a standard score of 65. Reading and spelling were lower than the IQ measured by the non–language-mediated test. However, performance on reading and spelling were not significantly lower than the scores attained on the WPPSI where language factors were taken into account.

Bob's language abilities were impaired in sentence repetition, word finding, verbal fluency, syntactic comprehension, and auditory discrimination. Color naming, body part naming, and articulation of sounds and single words were normal.

Bob's expressive abilities appear better than his receptive language abilities. The impairment in auditory discrimination suggests that Bob has a deficiency in auditory information processing. That is, Bob hears a word but it may get distorted as the word gets encoded. This is handicapping but not by itself limiting. A language disorder makes the acquisition of language arts in a school setting difficult, influencing the early acquisition of reading skills. With proper remediation, Bob should be able to compensate for his language disorder and learning disability so that it does not adversely affect his learning.

Bob is able to utilize psychological resources to overcome his language disorder and learning disability. He is able to feel pride in his own accomplishments and to look to others for encouragement. However, Bob tends to avoid tasks that he finds difficult and to favor tasks with which he is comfortable. Therefore, his favored tasks—for example, drawing—should be used as a reward when he has accomplished a more difficult task.

Bob's drawing abilities and perceptual abilities are within normal limits. Motor testing showed some motor overflow.

Bob needs a class setting with intensive language therapy. A classroom for children with mental retardation would be an inappropriate placement for him. His intellectual capacities place him within the average range, especially when his language disability is taken into account. Bob is already demonstrating a learning disability in that his arithmetic achievement is lower than his capabilities. If Bob begins to get his educational needs met, he will be able to compensate for his language difficulties and for his learning disability. Like many learning-disabled youngsters of his age, Bob needs approval for tasks well done and help and encouragement on difficult ones.

Bob needs individual attention in school in order to help him bring his achievement up to the level of his intellectual potential. He also needs intensive remediation. It would be important to use short commands and sentences when addressing him. Furthermore, it would be helpful to have him repeat a word to be sure he understands it. With appropriate classroom placement and appropriate remediation, Bob should be able to compensate for his language and learning disability and develop his academic achievement so that it is commensurate with his capabilities. Early intervention is the key to success with a youngster of this age. In addition, encouragement of his efforts is critical so that he does not begin to feel that he is a failure.

This case illustrates the importance of psychological assessment to ensure a proper school placement for children who may not fit perfectly in the school setting. A proper assessment can help the school mainstream the child, if possible, and best address his or her needs. Such an assessment can help with early diagnosis, which is important for remediation in order to prevent school failure with its concomitant loss of self-esteem (Boder, 1973).

REFERENCES

American Psychiatric Association. (1980). *Diagnostic and statistical manual of mental disorders* (3rd ed.). Washington, DC: Author.

American Psychiatric Association. (1987). *Diagnostic and statistical manual of mental disorders* (3rd ed., rev.). Washington, DC: Author.

American Psychiatric Association. (1994). *Diagnostic and statistical manual of mental disorders* (4th ed.). Washington, DC: Author.

Bakker, D. J., & Licht, R. (1986). Learning to read: Changing horses in mid-stream. In G. T. Pavlidis & D. F. Fisher (Eds.), *Dyslexia: Neuropsychology and treatment* (pp. 87–95). London: John Wiley & Sons.

Bannatyne, A. (1971). *Language, reading and learning disabilities.* Springfield, IL: Charles C. Thomas.

Bender, L. (1958). Problems in conceptualization and communication in children with developmental alexia. In P. M. Hoch & J. Zubin (Eds.), *Psychopathology of communication* (pp. 155–176). New York: Grune & Stratton.

Berger, M., Yule, W., & Rutter, M. (1975). Attainment and adjustment in two geographical areas: II. The prevalence of specific reading retardation. *British Journal of Psychiatry, 126,* 510–519.

Berman, A., & Siegal, A. (1976). Adaptive and learning skills in delinquent boys. *Journal of Learning Disabilities, 9,* 583–590.

Birch, H. G., & Gussow, J. D. (1970). *Disadvantaged children: Health nutrition and school failure.* New York: Grune & Stratton.

Boder, E. (1971). Developmental dyslexia: Prevailing diagnostic concepts and a new diagnostic approach. In H. R. Myklebust (Ed.), *Progress in learning disabilities* (vol. 2, pp. 293–321). New York: Grune & Stratton.

Boder, E. (1973). Developmental dyslexia: Prevailing diagnostic concepts and a new diagnostic approach. *Bulletin of the Orton Society, 23,* 106–118.

Bryan, T. H. (1974). Peer popularity of learning disabled children. *Journal of Learning Disabilities, 7,* 621–625.

Bryan, T. (1982). Social skills of learning disabled children and youth: An overview. *Learning Disability Quarterly, 15,* 332–333.

Bryan, T. H. (1976). Peer popularity of learning disabled children: A replication. *Journal of Learning Disabilities, 9,* 307–311.

Bryan, T. H., & Bryan, J. (1981). Some personal and

social experiences of learning disabled children. In B. Keogh (Ed.), *Advances in special education* (Vol. 3, pp. 147–186). Greenwich, CT: JAI Press.

Bryant, P., & Bradley, L. (1985). *Children's reading problems.* Oxford, England: Blackwell.

Centers for Disease Control. (1987). Assessment of the number and characteristics of persons affected by learning disabilities. In *Interagency committee in learning disabilities: Learning disabilities: A report to the U.S. Congress* (p. 107). Washington, DC: U.S. Department of Health and Human Services.

Clements, S. D. (1966). *Task force one: Minimal brain dysfunction in children.* National Institute of Neurological Disease and Blindness, Monograph No. 3. Washington, DC: U.S. Department of Health, Education and Welfare.

Creevy, D. C. (1986). The relationship of obstetrical trauma to learning disabilities: An obstetrician's view. In M. Lewis (Ed.), *Learning disabilities and prenatal risk* (pp. 91–124). Urbana: University of Illinois Press.

Cruickshank, W. M. (1977). Myths and realities in learning disabilities. *Journal of Learning Disabilities, 10,* 51–64.

Cullinan, D., Epstein, M. H., & Lloyd, J. (1981). School behavior problems of learning disabled and normal girls and boys. *Learning Disability Quarterly, 4,* 163–169.

Decker, S. N., & Vandenberg, S. G. (1985). Colorado twin study of reading disability. In D. B. Gray & J. F. Kavanaugh (Eds.), *Biobehavioral measures of dyslexia* (pp. 123–136). Parkton, MD: York Press.

DeFries, J. C. (1985). Colorado reading project. In D. B. Gray & J. F. Kavanaugh (Eds.), *Biobehavioral measures of dyslexia* (pp. 107–122). Parkton, MD: York Press.

Denckla, M. B. (1972). Clinical syndromes in learning disabilities: The case for "splitting" vs. "lumping." *Journal of Learning Disabilities, 5,* 401–406.

Denckla, M. B. (1975). Minimal brain dysfunction and dyslexia: Beyond diagnosis by exclusion. In M. E. Blaw, I. Rapin, & M. Kinsbourne (Eds.), *Topics in child neurology* (pp. 243–261). New York: Spectrum Publications.

Deshler, D. (1978). Psychoeducational aspects of learning disabled adolescents. In L. Mann, L. Goodman, & J. L. Wiederholt (Eds.), *Teaching the learning disabled adolescent* (pp. 47–74). Boston: Houghton Mifflin.

Deshler, D. D., & Schumaker, J. B. (1983). Social skills of learning disabled adolescents: Characteristics and intervention. *Topics in Learning and Learning Disabilities, 3,* 15–23.

Deshler, D. D., Schumaker, J. B., Lenz, B. K., & Ellis, E. (1984). Academic and cognitive interventions for LD adolescents: II. *Journal of Learning Disabilities, 17,* 170–179.

Duane, D. D. (1989). Neurobiological correlates of learning disorders. *Journal of the American Academy of Child Psychiatry, 28,* 314–318.

Dyson, L. L. (1996). The experiences of families of children with learning disabilities: Parental stress, family functioning, and sibling self-concept. *Journal of Learning Disabilities, 29,* 280–286.

Epstein, M. H., Cullinan, D., & Lloyd, J. W. (1986). Behavior-problem patterns among the learning disabled: III. Replication across age and sex. *Learning Disability Quarterly, 9,* 43–54.

Erikson, E. H. (1963). *Childhood and society* (2nd ed.). New York: W. W. Norton.

Erikson, E. H. (1968). *Identity, youth and crisis.* New York: W. W. Norton.

Fisk, J. L., & Rourke, B. P. (1979). Identification of subtypes of learning-disabled children at three age levels: A neuropsychological, multivariate approach. *Journal of Clinical Neuropsychology, 1,* 289–310.

Fuerst, D. R., Fisk, J. L., & Rourke, B. P. (1990). Psychosocial functioning of learning-disabled children: Relations between WISC verbal IQ—performance IQ discrepancies and personality subtypes. *Journal of Consulting and Clinical Psychology, 58,* 675–680.

Galaburda, A. M., & Kemper, T. L. (1978). Cytoarchitectonic abnormalities in developmental dyslexia: A case study. *Annals of Neurology, 6,* 94–100.

Galaburda, A. M., Sherman, G. F., Rosen, G. D., Aboitiz, F., & Geschwind, N. (1985). Developmental dyslexia: Four consecutive patients with cortical anomalies. *Annals of Neurology, 18,* 222–223.

Geisthardt, C., & Munsch, J. (1996). A comparison of adolescents with and without learning disabilities. *Journal of Learning Disabilities, 29,* 287–296.

Gordon, E. W. (1968). Introduction. In J. Hellmuth (Ed.), *Disadvantaged child: Head start and early intervention* (pp. 8–14). New York: Brunner/Mazel.

Gordon, E. W. (1970). Problems in the determination of educability in populations with differential characteristics. In J. Hellmuth (Ed.), *Disadvantaged child* (Vol. 3, pp. 249–267). New York: Brunner/Mazel.

Gordon, E. W. (1991). Human diversity and pluralism. *Educational Psychologist, 26,* 99–108.

Gresham, F. M. (1987). Social competence and motivational characteristics of learning disabled students. In M. C. Wang, M. C. Reynolds, & H. J. Walberg (Eds.), *Advances in Education* (p. 284). New York: Pergamon Press.

Greenblatt, E., Mattis, S., & Trad, P. V. (1990). Learning disabilities in a child psychiatric population. *Journal of Developmental Neuropsychology, 6,* 71–83.

Harris, J. D., Gray, B. A., Davis, J. E., Zaremba, E. T., & Argulewicz, E. N. (1988). The exclusionary clause and the disadvantaged: Do we try to comply with the law? *Journal of Learning Disabilities, 21* (9), 581–583.

Hartzell, H. E., & Compton, C. (1984). Learning disability: 10-year follow-up. *Pediatrics, 74,* 1058–1064.

Hellmuth, J. (Ed.). (1970). *Disadvantaged child* (Vol. 3). New York: Brunner/Mazel.

Heyman, W. B. (1990). The self-perception of a learning disability and its relationship to academic self-concept and self-esteem. *Journal of Learning Disabilities, 23,* 472–475.

Horn, W. F., O'Donnell, J. P., & Vitulano, L. A. (1983).

Long-term follow-up studies of learning-disabled persons. *Journal of Learning Disabilities, 16,* 542–555.

Hunt, R. D., & Cohen, D. J. (1984). Psychiatric aspects of learning disabilities. *Pediatric Clinics of North America, 31,* 471–497.

Johnson (1988). Review of research in specific reading, writing and mathematical disorders. In J. F. Kavanaugh & T. J. Truss, Jr. (Eds.), *Learning disabilities: Proceedings of the national conference* (pp. 79–163). Parkton, MD: York Press.

Kavale, K. A. (1988). Learning disability and cultural-economic disadvantage: The case for a relationship. *Learning Disability Quarterly, 11,* 195–210.

Kavale, K. A. & Forness, S. R. (1996). Social skill deficits and learning disabilities: A meta-analysis. *Journal of Learning Disabilities, 29,* 226–237.

Kavanaugh, J. F., & Truss T. J., Jr. (Eds.). (1988). *Learning disabilities: Proceedings of the national conference.* Parkton, MD: York Press.

Kirk, S. A. (1962). *Educating exceptional children.* Boston: Houghton Mifflin.

Kolligian, J., & Sternberg, R. J. (1987). Another look at intelligence and learning disabilities: A reply to Reynolds' "rap." *Journal of Learning Disabilities, 20,* 325–326.

Korhonen, T. T. (1991). Neuropsychological stability and prognosis of subgroups of children with learning disabilities. *Journal of Learning Disabilities, 24,* 48–57.

Korkman, M., & Peltomaa, A. R. (1993). Preventative treatment of dyslexia by a preschool training program for children with language impairments. *Journal of Clinical Child Psychology, 22,* 277–287.

LaBuda, M. C., DeFries, J. C., & Pennington, B. F. (1990). Reading disability: A model for the genetic analysis of complex behavioral disorders. *Journal of Counseling and Development, 68,* 645–651.

La Greca, A. M., & Stone, W. L. (1990). LD status and achievement: Confounding variables in the study of children's social status, self-esteem, and behavioral functioning. *Journal of Learning Disabilities, 23,* 483–490.

Levin, B. E. (1990). Organizational deficits in dyslexia: Possible frontal lobe dysfunction. *Developmental Neuropsychology, 6,* 95–110.

Licht, R., Kok, A., Bakker, D. J., & Bouma, A. (1986). Hemispheric distribution of ERP components and word naming in pre-school children. *Brain and Language, 27,* 101–116.

Livingstone, M. S., Rosen, G. D., Drisland, F. W., & Galaburda, A. M. (1991). Physiological and anatomical evidence for a magnocellular defect in developmental dyslexia. *Proceedings of the National Academy of Science, 88,* 7943–7947.

Maag, J. W., & Behrens, J. T. (1989). Depression and cognitive self-statements of learning disabled and seriously emotionally disturbed adolescents. *Journal of Special Education, 23,* 17–27.

Mattis, S., French, J., & Rapin, I. (1975). Dyslexia in children and young adults: Three independent neuropsychological syndromes. *Developmental Medicine and Child Neurology, 17,* 150–163.

Mattis, S. (1978). Dylexia syndromes: A working hypothesis that works. In A. L. Benton & D. Pearl (Eds.), *Dyslexia: An appraisal of current knowledge* (pp. 43–58). New York: Oxford University Press.

Morgan, W. P. (1896). A case of congential word-blindness. *British Medical Journal, 2,* 1378.

Needleman, H. L. (1986). Prenatal exposure to pollutants and neural development. In M. Lewis (Ed.), *Learning disabilities and prenatal risk* (pp. 19–27). Urbana: University of Illinois Press.

Needleman, H. L., Leviton, A., & Bellinger, D. (1982). Lead-associated intellectual deficit. *New England Journal of Medicine, 306,* 367.

Orton, S. T. (1925). Word blindness in school children. *Archives of Neurology and Psychiatry, 14,* 581–615.

Orton, S. T. (1928). Specific reading disability, strephosymbolia. *Journal of the American Medical Association, 90,* 1095–1099.

Osman, B. B. (1982). *No one to play with: The social side of learning disabilities.* New York: Random House.

Owen, F. W. (1978). Dyslexia-genetic aspects. In A. L. Benton & D. Pearl (Eds.), *Dyslexia: An appraisal of current knowledge* (pp. 265–284). New York: Oxford University Press.

Owen, F. W., Adams, P. A., Forrest, T., Stolz, L. M., & Fisher, S. (1971). Learning disorders in children, sibling studies. *Monograph of the Society for Research in Child Development, 36* (4, Serial No. 144).

Peck, B. B., & Stackhouse, T. W. (1973). Reading problems and family dynamics. *Journal of Learning Disabilities, 6,* 506–511.

Pelham, W. E., Milich, R., Murphy, D. A., & Murphy, H. A. (1989). Normative data on the IOWA Conners teacher rating scale. *Journal of Clinical Child Psychology, 18,* 259–262.

Pennington, B. F., & Smith, S. D. (1988). Genetic influences on learning disabilities: An update. *Journal of Consulting and Clinical Psychology, 56,* 817–823.

Petrauskas, R., & Rourke, B. (1979). Identification of subgroups of retarded readers: A neuropsychological multivariate approach. *Journal of Clinical Neuropsychology, 1,* 17–37.

Public Law 94-142. *Education for All Handicapped Children Act of 1975.* (23 August 1977). 20 U.S.C. 1401 et seq.: *Federal Register, 42* (163), 42474–42518.

Quay, H. C. (1979). Classification. In H. C. Quay & J. S. Werry (Eds.), *Psychopathological disorders of childhood* (2nd ed, pp. 1–42). New York: John Wiley & Sons.

Reitan, R. M., & Davison, L. A. (1974). *Clinical neuropsychology: Current status and applications.* Washington, DC: Winston and Sons.

Reynolds, A. J. (1991). Early schooling of children at risk. *American Educational Research Journal, 28,* 392–422.

Reynolds, A. J., Weissberg, R. P., & Kasprow, W. J. (1992). Prediction of early social and academic adjustment of children from the inner city. *American Journal of Community Psychology, 20,* 599–624.

Reynolds, C. R. (1980). The fallacy of "two years below grade level for age" as a diagnostic criterion for reading disorders. *Journal of School Psychology, 19,* 350–358.

Reynolds, C. R. (1992). Two key concepts in the diagnosis of learning disabilities and the habilitation of learning. *Learning Disability Quarterly, 15,* 2–12.

Richardson, S. O. (1989). Specific developmental dyslexia: Retrospective and prospective views. 39th Annual Conference of the Orton Dyslexia Society: Samuel Torrey and June Lyday Orton Memorial Lecture. *Annals of Dyslexia, 39,* 3–23.

Robbins, D. M., Beck, J. C., Pries, R., Cags, Jacobs, D., & Smith, C. (1983). Learning disability and neuropsychological impairment in adjudicated, unincarcerated male delinquents. *Journal of the American Academy of Child Psychiatry, 22,* 40–46.

Rourke, B. P. (1989). *Nonverbal learning disabilities: The syndrome and the model.* New York: Guilford Press.

Rutter, M. (1978). Prevalence and types of dyslexia. In A. L. Benton & D. Pearl (Eds.), *Dyslexia: An appraisal of current knowledge* (pp. 3–28). New York: Plenum Press.

Satz, P., Friel, J., & Rudegeair, R. (1976). Some predictive antecedents of specific reading disability: A two-, three- and four year follow-up. In J. R. Guthrie (Ed.), *Aspects of reading acquisition* (pp. 111–140). Baltimore: Johns Hopkins University Press.

Satz, P., & Morris, R. (1981). Learning disability subtypes: A review. In F. J. Pirozzolo & M. C. Wittrock (Eds.), *Neuropsychological and cognitive processes in reading* (pp. 109–141). San Diego: Academic Press.

Satz, P., & Van Nostrand, G. (1973). Developmental dyslexia: An evaluation of a theory. In P. Satz & J. Ross (Eds.), *The disabled learner; early detection and intervention* (pp. 121–148). Rotterdam: Rotterdam University Press.

Schumaker, J. B., & Hazel, J. S. (1984a). Social skills assessment and training for the learning disabled: Who's on first and what's on second: Part I. *Journal of Learning Disabilities, 17,* 422–431.

Schumaker, J. B., & Hazel, J. S. (1984b). Social skills assessment and training for the learning disabled: Who's on first and what's on second? Part II. *Journal of Learning Disabilities, 17,* 492–499.

Shaywitz, S. E., Excobar, M. D., Shaywitz, B. A., Fletcher, J. M., & Makuch, R. (1992). Evidence that dyslexia may represent the lower tail of a normal distribution of reading ability. *New England Journal of Medicine, 326,* 145–150.

Shaywitz, S. E., Schnell, C., Shaywitz, B. A., & Towle, V. R. (1986). Yale children's inventory (YCI): An instrument to assess children with attention deficits and learning disabilities: I. Scale development and psychometric properties. *Journal of Abnormal Child Psychology, 14,* 347–364.

Shaywitz, S. E., & Shaywitz, B. E. (1988). Attention deficit disorder: Current perspectives. In J. F. Kavanaugh & T. J. Truss, Jr. (Eds.), *Learning disabilities: Proceedings of the national conference* (pp. 369–523). Parkton, MD: York Press.

Silver, L. B. (1981). The relationship between learning disabilities, hyperactivity, distractible and behavioral problems. *Journal of the American Academy of Child Psychiatry, 20,* 385–397.

Silver, L. B. (1989). Psychological and family problems associated with learning disabilities: Assessment and intervention. *Journal of the American Academy of Child Psychiatry, 28,* 319–325.

Silver, L. B. (1990). Attention deficit-hyperactivity disorder: Is it a learning disability or a related disorder? *Journal of Learning Disabilities, 7,* 394–397.

Spreen, O. (1988). *Learning disabled children growing up: A follow-up into adulthood.* New York: Oxford Press.

Sternberg, R. J., & Wagner, R. K. (1982). Automatization failure in learning disabilities. *Topics in Learning Disabilities, 2,* 1–11.

Strauss, A. A., & Lehtinen, L. E. (1947). *Psychopathology and education of the brain-injured child* (Vol. 1) New York: Grune & Stratton.

Tallal, P. (1980). Auditory temporal perception, phonic, and reading disabilities in children. *Brain and Language, 9,* 182–198.

Tallal, P., Stark, R. E., & Mellits, D. (1985). The relationship between auditory temporal analysis and receptive language development: Evidence from studies of developmental language disorder. *Neuropsychologia, 23,* 527–534.

Taylor, L., Adelman, H. S., and Kaser-Boyd, N. (1983). Perspectives of children regarding their participation in psychoeducational decisions. *Professional Psychology Research and Practice, 14,* 882–894.

Trapani, C., & Gettinger, M. (1989). Effects of social skills training and cross-age tutoring on academic achievement and social behaviors of boys with learning disabilities. *Journal of Research and Development in Education, 23,* 1–9.

U.S. Department of Education. (1987). *Ninth annual report to Congress on the implementation of the Education of the Handicapped Act.* Washington, DC: Author.

U.S. Department of Education. (1989). To assure the free appropriate public education of all handicapped children. *Eleventh annual report to Congress on the implementation of the Education of the Handicapped Act.* Washington, DC: Author.

U.S. Department of Education. (1991). *Thirteenth annual report to Congress on the implementation of the individuals with Disabilities Education Act.* Washington, DC: Author.

U.S. Department of Education. (1995). To assure the free appropriate public education of all children with disabilities. Seventeenth annual report to Congress on the implementation of the Individuals with Disabilities Education Act. Washington, DC: Author.

U.S. Office of Education. (1977). Education of all handicapped children: Implementation of part B of the Educational of the Handicapped Act. *Federal Register, 42*, 42474–42518.

Vellutino, F. R. (1978). Toward an understanding of dyslexia: Psychological factors in specific reading disability. In A. L. Benton & D. Pearl (Eds.), *Dyslexia: An appraisal of current knowledge* (pp. 61–111). New York: Oxford University Press.

Volger, G. P., DeFries, J. C., & Decker, S. N. (1985). Family history as an indicator of risk for reading disability. *Journal of Learning Disabilities, 18*, 419–421.

Voyat, G. E. (1982). *Piaget systematized*. Hillsdale, NJ: Erlbaum.

Wade, J., & Kass, C. E. (1987). Component deficit and academic remediation of learning disabilities. *Journal of Learning Disabilities, 20*, 441–447.

Weiss, E. (1985). Learning disabled children's understanding of social interaction of peers. *Journal of Learning Disabilities, 17*, 612–615.

Yule, W., & Rutter, M. (1976). Epidemiology and social implications of specific reading retardation. In R. M. Knights & D. J. Bakker (Eds.), *The Neuropsychology of Learning Disorders*. Baltimore: University Park Press.

26 / Posttraumatic Stress Disorder in Children

Sandra Kaplan and David Pelcovitz

Background

HISTORY

Systematic research into the nature of children's reactions to trauma is of relatively recent vintage. In the late 1800s and early 1900s there was interest in children's reactions to parental loss and the association of this loss with intellectual and developmental retardation, particularly when children were placed in institutional care (Langmeier & Matejacek, 1973). However, these investigations focused on the quality of the children's physical surroundings rather than trying to understand the psychological mechanisms underlying grief and trauma (Benedek, 1985). Although Freud and Burlingham (1943) provided clinical descriptions of children's response to the trauma of World War II, their emphasis was on the response of the parents, rather than of the child. Block, Silver, and Perry (1956) published the first report specifically describing the effects of a natural disaster on children. Their description of children's reactions to a tornado included reexperiencing (repetitive playing of a "tornado game") and hyperarousal as indicated by irritability and sensitivity to noise. Unlike most current studies, Block et al. relied exclusively on data gathered from parents rather than on direct interview and observation of the children. It was not until the 1980s that systematic study of children's reaction to trauma was undertaken by researchers such as Terr (1979) regarding the reactions of children who were kidnapped and buried in a bus, and by Pynoos and Eth's work with witnesses of violence (1986). Unlike previous work in this area, these studies emphasized children's unique cognitive and emotional responsiveness to trauma, rather than parental perceptions. With the publication of the third revised edition of the *Diagnostic and Statistical Manual of Mental Disorders* (*DSM-III-R;* American Psychiatric Association [APA], 1987) and *DSM-IV* (APA, 1994) there was, for the first time, formal recognition in the psychiatric nomenclature that children, like adults, can show the effects of posttraumatic stress disorder (PTSD). (See Table 26.1.)

EPIDEMIOLOGY

In the largest epidemiologic investigation of the prevalence of PTSD in adults, Helzer, Robins, and McEvoy (1987) included diagnosis of PTSD in the St. Louis site of the Epidemiologic Catchment Area Survey of the prevalence of psychiatric disorders. The authors found a history of PTSD in 1% of the total population. The occurrence of behavioral problems before age 15 was a risk factor for the development of PTSD later in life. To date, there have been no reliable studies regard-

TABLE 26.1

Diagnostic Criteria for Posttraumatic Stress Disorder

A. The person has been exposed to a traumatic event in which both of the following were present:

    (1) the person experienced, witnessed, or was confronted with an event or events that involved actual or threatened death or serious injury, or a threat to the physical integrity of self or others

    (2) the person's response involved intense fear, helplessness, or horror. **Note:** In children, this may be expressed instead by disorganized or agitated behavior

B. The traumatic event is persistently reexperienced in one (or more) of the following ways:

    (1) recurrent and intrusive distressing recollections of the event, including images, thoughts, or perceptions. **Note:** In young children, repetitive play may occur in which themes or aspects of the trauma are expressed.

    (2) recurrent distressing dreams of the event. **Note:** In children, there may be frightening dreams without recognizable content.

    (3) acting or feeling as if the traumatic event were recurring (includes a sense of reliving the experience, illusions, hallucinations, and dissociative flashback episodes, including those that occur on awakening or when intoxicated). **Note:** In young children, trauma-specific reenactment may occur.

    (4) intense psychological distress at exposure to internal or external cues that symbolize or resemble an aspect of the traumatic event

    (5) physiological reactivity on exposure to internal or external cues that symbolize or resemble an aspect of the traumatic event

C. Persistent avoidance of stimuli associated with the trauma and numbing of general responsiveness (not present before the trauma), as indicated by three (or more) of the following:

    (1) efforts to avoid thoughts, feelings, or conversations associated with the trauma

    (2) efforts to avoid activities, places, or people that arouse recollections of the trauma

    (3) inability to recall an important aspect of the trauma

    (4) markedly diminished interest or participation in significant activities

    (5) feeling of detachment or estrangement from others

    (6) restricted range of affect (e.g., unable to have loving feelings)

    (7) sense of a foreshortened future (e.g., does not expect to have a career, marriage, children, or a normal life span)

D. Persistent symptoms of increased arousal (not present before the trauma), as indicated by two (or more) of the following:

    (1) difficulty falling or staying asleep

    (2) irritability or outbursts of anger

    (3) difficulty concentrating

    (4) hypervigilance

    (5) exaggerated startle response

E. Duration of the disturbance (symptoms in Criteria B, C, and D) is more than 1 month.

F. The disturbance causes clinically significant distress or impairment in social, occupational, or other important areas of functioning.

Specify if:

    Acute: if duration of symptoms is less than 3 months

    Chronic: if duration of symptoms is 3 months or more

Specify if:

    With Delayed Onset: if onset of symptoms is at least 6 months after the stressor

NOTE. From *Diagnostic and Statistical Manual of Mental Disorders*, 4th ed., American Psychiatric Association, 1994, pp. 427 to 429. Washington, D.C.: Author. Copyright 1994 by the American Psychiatric Association. Reprinted with permission.

ing the prevalence of PTSD in children. In general, the highest percentages of PTSD have been reported in studies of survivors of sexual abuse—ranging from 20.7% (Deblinger, McLeer, Atkins, Ralphe, & Foa, 1989) to 90% (Kiser et al., 1988). These studies have been mostly of adult survivors. Relatively lower prevalence rates have been reported for children exposed to war—27.5% (Saigh, 1487)—and to environmental disaster—55% (Yule & Udwins, 1991), 60% (Martini, Ryan, Nakayama, & Ramenofsky, 1989). Conclusions regarding the actual prevalence of PSTD in childhood cannot be generated based on existing studies, which vary widely in instruments used to measure PTSD and have relied on the use of samples referred for treatment.

Clinical Presentation and Diagnostic Assessment

SYMPTOMS OF PTSD IN CHILDHOOD

Since the inclusion of posttraumatic stress disorder (PTSD) in *DSM-III* in 1980, there has been a significant increase in systematic investigation of this phenomenon both in children and adults. Posttraumatic disorder is characterized by a constellation of *DSM-IV* (APA, 1994) symptoms in response to a traumatic event "outside the range of normal human experience" clustering in three categories: reexperiencing of the traumatic event, autonomic arousal, and avoidance as manifested by a supression or numbing of emotional responsiveness. In the original description of PTSD (*DSM-III;* APA, 1980), no mention was made of this disorder in children; nor were descriptions given of the differences of symptoms in children and adults. *DSM-IV*, however, gives specific examples of how PTSD symptomatology may present in children as compared to adults.

Although, as in other diagnostic categories, there are many similarities between adult and childhood manifestations of PTSD, numerous differences have been reported. In the reexperiencing cluster of symptoms, children are less likely to experience classic flashbacks (Pynoos & Nader, 1988). Child survivors of unanticipated single events are also hypothesized to be different from

adults in their ability to recall details of events vividly (Pynoos & Eth, 1986; Terr, 1991). Terr describes one of the universal responses of children to trauma, regardless of type, as vivid, repeated visual memories of the traumatic event. These memories, which are most likely to be experienced by children when they are not busy, may at times also be experienced as tactile or olfactory. Also in this category are repetitive dreams (generally seen in children over age 5) that may vividly re-create the trauma or, more likely, may take a disguised form. Children also may show signs of reexperiencing the trauma through traumatic play (Terr, 1981a) or more directly through repetitive reenactments.

Avoidance of reminders of the traumatic event are most obviously seen when children refuse to talk about the event or are unable to remember important aspects as a result of traumatic amnesia. Terr (1991) reports that massive denial, psychic numbing, and dissociation are associated with long-term traumatic processes such as abuse, rather than single traumatic events. In contrast to the more obvious manifestations of reexperiencing symptoms, these sequelae of long-term trauma may be more difficult to diagnose, since they tend to be egosyntonic, as they are the result of years of attempting to cope with long-term abuse. It is therefore important to realize that children, particularly if, as a result of chronic abuse, they have never known what it is like to feel truly "alive," will not be able to articulate feeling "numb." Rather, this form of avoidance may manifest itself through withdrawal from previously enjoyable activities, as in withdrawing from contact with friends. The *DSM-IV* (1994) criteria specify that, in children, avoidance may manifest itself through regression—loss of previously acquired skills, such as toilet training or language. Terr (1991) hypothesizes that a sense of foreshortened future is one of the universal reactions of children to both acute or chronic types of trauma. Therefore, it is important to question traumatized children about future plans, such as career plans and plans for marriage.

The arousal symptoms mentioned in *DSM-IV* (1994) are consistent with the most common descriptions of symptoms seen in traumatized children. Sleep difficulties, hypervigilance, difficulty concentrating in school, and irritability have all been reactions to trauma described both in the child abuse literature abuse and in descriptions of children's reactions to unanticipated single events.

In some instances, the deterioration in children's school performance following traumatic events may lead to their meeting the criteria for attention deficit hyperactivity disorder (ADHD). It is not yet known whether this type of ADHD is identical to non–trauma-related ADHD. It should be noted, however, that in a minority of children, school performance possibly may improve (Pynoos & Nader, 1988).

In their view of developmental differences in children's reactions to trauma, Green et al. (1991) summarize the varied manifestations of traumatic reactions as a function of the child's age. Preschool children tend to show global, disorganized reactions, including both trauma-specific and generalized fears, regression clinginess, and irritability. Parental functioning and family cohesiveness are more important predictors of outcome for children at this age than at any other (Bloch et al., 1956). In school-age children somatic concerns, sleep difficulties, and school problems predominate (Gleser, Green, & Winget, 1981). Adolescents, who have more sophisticated cognitive understanding of the implications of traumatic episodes, have responses very similar to PTSD as seen in adults. Perhaps, because of adolescents' increased awareness, they tend to show a greater incidence of overall emotional disturbance when compared to younger survivors (e.g., Gleser et al., 1981).

TRAUMATIC EXPOSURE ETIOLOGIES

Traumatic etiologies of PTSD symptomatology in children that have been studied include: intrafamilial child physical or sexual abuse; extrafamilial child sex abuse; serious physical illness; crimes witnessed by children outside of their families, such as school shootings, and crimes inflicted upon family members by nonfamily members, such as maternal rape by an intruder; natural or man-made induced environmental disaster experiences, such as earthquakes, floods, or nuclear reactor errors; and the witnessing of war. Tables 26.2 to 26.9 summarize studies of posttraumatic stress disorder symptomatology following exposure to various traumatic experiences.

PATHOGENESIS

Posttraumatic stress disorder is the only diagnosis (other than adjustment disorders) that, by definition, is caused by exposure to an external stressor. Barlow (1988) hypothesizes that PTSD develops when, in response to an overwhelming traumatic event, an individual who is biologically and psychosocially at risk for this disorder develops persistent avoidance of all stimuli (including thoughts and feelings) associated with the trauma. As with other anxiety disorders, over time the trauma victim develops a sense that avoidance of the feared thoughts and feelings reminiscent of the event, coupled with intrusive reexperiencing phenomena, are proceeding in an uncontrollable manner. A vicious cycle of anxious apprehension and avoidance ultimately results in PTSD.

Although a sizable number of children may develop PTSD in response to exposure to very traumatic events, many, if not most, children will not develop symptoms of the full-blown disorder. To understand what places children at risk for developing PTSD, it is important to look at the nature of the stressor, individual factors, and posttrauma family and social support.

NATURE OF THE STRESSOR

The nature of the traumatic event provides important clues as to how much a child is placed at risk for developing PTSD. Events that put an individual's life in danger, intentionally inflicted physical injury, exposure to grotesque sights, and the violent or sudden death of family members (particularly if the child witnesses the incident) have all been associated with increased risk for PTSD (Green, 1990). In general, the more a traumatic event is tied to a man-made as opposed to natural disaster, the more difficult will be the period of recovery (Green et al., 1991). Pynoos et al. (1987) found that proximity to violence was significantly related to PTSD severity in a group of children who experienced a sniper attack on their school's playground. Similarly, children in a "high-exposure" group following a bus accident were at increased risk for PTSD (Milgram et al., 1988), as were those with the highest levels of life threat following the collapse of a dam (Green et al., 1991).

Bereavement is another major aspect of trauma that greatly increases the challenge of coping with traumatic events. The combination of loss of a family member or friend and exposure to a traumatic event is particularly difficult to resolve. Gleser et al. (1981) showed a significant correlation between degree of loss following a dam collapse and children's level of psychological impairment 2 years later. In addition to death or injury of family members or friends, property loss is another aspect of trauma that is important to consider. Children who lose favorite toys and clothing in fires or other disasters may have more difficulty dealing with the effects of the disaster than those whose possessions are not affected. Exposure to widespread community destruction is particularly important to consider (Phifer & Norris, 1989). If following a major disaster the child's surrounding community is no longer able to provide a feeling of cohesion and support, then the likelihood of posttraumatic symptoms becoming chronic may be increased (Erikson, 1976).

Posttraumatic Stress Disorder and Sexual Abuse

A number of clinicians and researchers have linked sexual abuse, both extrafamilial and intrafamilial, to increased risk for PTSD. In investigations of PTSD in victims of sexual assaults (including extrafamilial), this diagnosis has been found to be twice as prevalent than is found in victims of other crimes (Kilpatrick, Saunders, Vernon, Best, & Von, 1987). When researchers have relied on referred samples, very high rates of PTSD have generally been found in incest victims. Lindberg and Distad (1985) found PTSD in all 17 patients who were survivors of incest, and Donaldson and Gardner (1985) reported PTSD in 96% of 26 women who were receiving therapy for the sequelae of sexual abuse. Similarly, in a referred sample of 31 sexually abused children, McLeer, Deblinger, Atkins, Foa, and Ralphe (1988) report a 48.4% incidence of PTSD, ranging from 75% of children abused by their fathers to 25% of those abused by trusted adults. However, when the rela-

tive prevalence of PTSD in victims of incest is looked at more systematically using nonclinical samples, it is clear that a significant proportion of victims do not meet the criteria for this disorder. Greenwald and Leitenberg (1990) found 4% of 54 women in a nonclinical sample of sexual abuse victims reported moderate PTSD symptomatology currently, and only 17% may have met criteria in the past. In Kilpatrick et al.'s (1987) investigation of 126 adult survivors of child sexual abuse, the current incidence was 10% and the lifetime history of PTSD was 36%.

Finkelhor (1987) criticized exclusive reliance on the PTSD diagnosis for sexual abuse victims. He noted that PTSD is a more appropriate diagnosis for "events," such as crimes or combat, and may be a less relevant diagnosis for incest, which is more of a process that frequently is not accompanied by violence or threats. Furthermore, a PTSD diagnosis does not address symptoms frequently reported in the literature on sequelae of child abuse such as self-blame, revictimization, and sexual difficulties.

As with sexual abuse, victims of intrafamilial physical abuse grow up in a situation that may not be directly analogous to the high-magnitude stressors usually associated with PTSD. Victims of adolescent physical abuse often live in an environment that is so dominated by violence that they are exposed to an ongoing process rather than a discrete "event." Even more than is true with survivors of incest, the violence physical abuse victims encounter may be viewed as part of their parents' childrearing style rather than as a traumatic event outside the range of normal human experience.

In one of the only published studies investigating PTSD symptoms in victims of physical child abuse, Deblinger et al. (1989) report that 6.9% of the physically abused children ($n = 29$), 20.7% of the sexually abused children, most of whom were also physically abused (20 out of 29), and 10.3% of the nonabused comparison children ($n = 29$) met the *DSM-III-R* criteria for PTSD as diagnosed by a symptom checklist. This study had several limitations, including use of a referred sample of abused children; reliance on a checklist rather than on structured interviews; and the overlap between physical and sexual abuse in the sex abuse sample. Furthermore, both the physical abuse and sex abuse samples contained subjects who were victimized by family members as well as victims who were assaulted by nonrelatives.

Kiser, Heston, and Millsap (1991) studied 49 victims of sexual and/or physical abuse who had symptoms characteristic of PTSD based primarily on clinician ratings and 40 victims of sexual and or/physical abuse who did not show evidence of PTSD symptoms. Findings suggested that two distinct symptom pictures emerged. One was consistent with the reexperiencing, arousal, and avoidance criteria seen in patients with PTSD; the other was characterized by higher levels of behavioral difficulties (as measured by the Child Behavior Checklist and the Youth Self Report), including delinquency, aggression, anxiety, and depression. The generalizability of this study is limited, because the researchers combined physical and sexual abuse victims and did not rely on structured interviews for diagnosis of PTSD. However, the findings are intriguing, as they raise the possibility that a significant percentage of abuse victims may respond by exhibiting symptoms not explained by a PTSD diagnosis. (See Tables 26.2 to 26.4.)

PTSD and Chronic Illness

Although several researchers recently have explained the behavioral and emotional symptoms associated with chronic illness in children in the context of posttraumatic stress disorder (Nir, 1985; Stuber, Nader, Yasuda, Pynoos, & Cohen, 1991), there have been few studies of the prevalence of this disorder in chronically ill populations. In fact, according to *DSM-III-R* (1987) guidelines, criteria for PTSD individuals who are "chronically ill" do not technically meet the requirements for inclusion in the A criterion—that of experiencing an event "outside the range of usual human experience" (p. 250). In one of the few studies investigating the prevalence of PTSD in children with chronic illness, Stuber et al. (1991) found that children undergoing bone marrow transplantation showed a variety of symptoms suggestive of PTSD, particularly denial, avoidance, and intrusive symptomatology. Interestingly, the symptoms tended to intensify over time. The *DSM-IV* PTSD field trials recently addressed the

question of the prevalence of PTSD in chronic illness as part of a broader investigation of whether changes need to be made in criterion A of the disorder. Using structured interviews, PTSD was present (current + lifetime) in 40% of the adolescent cancer survivors, 56% of their mothers, 17% of the adult cancer survivors, and 11% of the physical abuse victims. In all of the cancer samples, the PTSD was related to the cancer and *not* to other high-magnitude stressors. Requirements for criterion A in *DSM-IV* have been modified in a manner that now allows for a PTSD diagnosis in response to life-threatening illness.

The high prevalence rate of PTSD in adolescent cancer survivors and their mothers is not surprising in light of the combination of life threat and painful intensive treatments. Chronic illness in adolescence is a traumatic event associated with several risk factors for developing PTSD, including life threat and painful procedures. There is also evidence that when an event is particularly unexpected, PTSD is more likely to develop. The "surprise" inherent in having to deal with an illness more typically associated with adults may make childhood chronic illness particularly likely to result in posttraumatic symptomatology. Cella, Mahon, and Donavan (1991) studied PTSD in adult cancer patients and found that when recurrence of cancer was a complete surprise, they were more at risk for developing intrusive and avoidant stress response symptoms. (See Table 26.5.)

PTSD Symptoms Following Exposure To Nonsexual Assault Crimes

Children have been studied who have been kidnapped (Terr, 1979), held hostage (Jessee, Strickland, & Ladewig, 1992), and who have witnessed shootings (Jessee et al., 1992; Malmquist, 1986; Ornitz & Pynoos, 1989; Pynoos et al., 1987; Pynoos & Nader, 1990). Findings indicated that severity of children's PTSD symptomatology varied with time held hostage (Jessee et al., 1992), length of exposure to a shooting and proximity to the shooting (Nader, Pynoos, Fairbanks, & Frederick, 1990). Pynoos et al. (1987) found that children's PTSD symptoms increased with level of

TABLE 26.2

PTSD Symptomatology in Children Subjected to Infrafamilial Child or
Adolescent Physical or Sexual Abuse

Author, Date	Type of Trauma	Subjects	Measures	Results
Deblinger, McLeer, Atkins, Ralphe, & Foa. (1989)	Physical and sexual abuse	87 children, 3–13 years. Mean age: 8.8 years. 29 were sexually abused (20 also were physically abused); 29 were physically but not sexually abused; 29 were nonabused. Children were inpatients at the Child Inpatient Unit at the Medical College of Pennsylvania.	Nine 22-item symptom checklists, composed of 17 items drawn from *DSM-III-R* criteria plus 5 symptoms frequently cited in the child sexual abuse literature	20.7% of the sexually abused children, 6.9% of the physically abused children, and 10.3% of the non-abused children met diagnostic criteria for PTSD.
Deblinger, McLeer, & Henry (1990)	Sexual abuse	19 females, age 3–16 years. Mean age: 7.7 years	Interview, Child Behavior Checklist (CBCL), Child Depression Inventory (CDI), State-Trait Anxiety Inventory (STAIC)	Cognitive behavioral treatment resulted in significant improvements across all PTSD subcategories
Famularo, Kinscherff, & Fenton (1990)	Severe maltreatment: physical and/or sexual abuse	24 children diagnosed with PTSD according to *DSM-III* criteria. 15 girls, 9 boys, 5–13 years. Mean age: 9.1 years.	Clinical interview, record review, inventory encompassing *DSM-III* criteria and items in the PTSD Reaction Index	Acute PTSD group showed: greater difficulty falling asleep, nightmares, hypervigilance, exaggerated startle response. Chronic PTSD subjects showed detachment or estrangement from others, restricted affect, dissociative episodes.
Kiser, Heston, & Millsap (1991)	Physical/sexual abuse	89 children & adolescents. 40 were physically abused; 25 were sexually abused; 24 were physically and sexually abused.	CBCL, Youth Self-Report (YSR), Personality inventory for children (PIC), FES, Family Adoptability and Cohesion Scales III	55% of subjects developed symptoms characteristic of PTSD. Those who did not develop PTSD symptoms exhibited more anxiety, depression, externalizing behaviors, and overall problems.
McLeer, et al. (1988)	Sexual abuse	31 children, 25 girls, six boys, 3–16 years. Mean age: 8.4 years. 12 abused by father,	Interview, self-esteem inventory (SEI), STAIC, CDI, CBCL	48.4% met *DSM-III-R* criteria for PTSD.

TABLE 26.2

(*continued*)

Author, Date	Type of Trauma	Subjects	Measures	Results
		8 by a trusted adult, 6 by an older sibling, and 3 by a stranger.		
Sanders & Giolas (1991)	Childhood stress, physical/sexual abuse, and trauma	47 adolescents, 13–17 years. 35 girls, 12 boys.	Dissociative Experiences Scale, child abuse and trauma questionnaire	Scores on the Dissociative Experiences Scale correlated significantly with self-reported physical abuse or punishment, sexual abuse, psychological abuse, neglect, and negative home atmosphere but not with abuse ratings made from hospital records.

acquaintance and that those children highly exposed, by virtue of proximity to violence, were more likely to have intrusive thoughts, emotional constriction, difficulty concentrating, avoidance, and sleep disturbances. Terr (1983 a, b) reported that children kidnapped on a bus continued to have a sense of foreshortened future and of philosophical pessimism, and conscious suppressional avoidance of thoughts of their kidnapping 4 years after the event. (See Table 26.6.)

PTSD Symptoms Following Exposure to Environmental Disasters

Children's reactions to trauma have been studied following: fires (Jones and Ribbe, 1991; McFarlane, 1987); blizzards and floods (Burke, Borus, Burns, Millstein, & Beasley, 1982; Burke, Moccia, Borus, & Burns, 1986; Earls, Smith, Reich, & Jung, 1988; Green et al., 1991; Newman, 1976); a nuclear power plant accident (Handford et al., 1986); and a boating accident (Martini, Ryan,

Nakayama, & Ramenofsky, 1990). Children's posttraumatic symptomatology following these disasters varied with: the level of parental posttraumatic disorder symptomatology (Earls et al., 1988; Green et al., 1991; Handford et al., 1986; Martini et al., 1990; McFarlane, 1987); gender, with girls more likely to develop symptomatology (Burke et al., 1986; Green et al., 1991); separation from parents (McFarlane, 1987); proximity to and level of exposure to disaster (Burke et al., 1982; Jones & Ribbe, 1991; Newman, 1976); the presence of preexisting childhood disorders (Earls et al., 1988; Martini, Ryan, et al., 1990); and age of child, with older children having more symptoms (Green et al., 1991; Handford et al., 1986) (See Table 26.7.).

PTSD Symptomatology in Children Exposed to War

Children studied following exposure to war also have been reported to have posttraumatic disor-

TABLE 26.3

PTSD Symptomatology in Children Subjected to Intrafamilial Child or Adolescent Physical or Sexual Abuse: Long-Term Effects

Author, Date	Type of Trauma	Subjects	Measures	Results
Chu & Dill (1990)	Physical and/or sexual abuse	98 female inpatients. Mean age: 34 years	Dissociative Experiences Scale (DES), SCL-90-R, Life Experiences Questionnaire	Childhood abuse by family members was clearly related to a higher level of dissociative symptoms in adulthood. Childhood physical abuse but not sexual abuse was related to general psychiatric symptoms in adulthood.
Greenwald & Leitenberg (1990)	Sexual abuse	54 women, sexually abused as children, 23–61 yrs. Mean age: 35 years.	Questionnaire based on *DSM-III-R,* modeled after SCL-90-R (subjects rated each symptom on a 5-point Likert Scale)	20% of the subjects currently suffer from mild PTSD; 41% had suffered from mild PTSD sometime in the past. Moderate abuse perpetrated by fathers was associated with more severe symptoms than was abuse perpetrated by nonfamily members. Completed sexual intercourse was associated with more severe PTSD symptoms.
Lindberg & Distad (1985)	Childhood incest	17 women, age 24 to 44		Met *DSM-IV* criteria for PTSD. Symptoms: anxiety, nightmares, insomnia, depression, anger, guilt. Average range of incidence: 7 years.

der symptoms. Severity of children's symptoms has been related to length of exposure to war violence (Baker, 1990). In a 3-year follow-up of 27 Cambodian students who were in a concentration camp, 48% had posttraumatic stress disorder (Kinzie, Sack, Angell, Clark, & Ben, 1989). Adjustment following exposure to war has been hypothesized to be enhanced by early interventions, which include abreaction (Dreman & Cohen, 1990) or behavioral techniques (Saigh, 1987). (See Table 26.8.)

PTSD Symptomatology in Children Exposed to Mixed Types of Trauma

In a study of 19 children diagnosed as having borderline personality disorder, 36.8% met criteria for posttraumatic stress disorders (Famularo, Kinscherff, & Fenton, 1991). Sixty-three children studied after experiencing varied types of trauma before age 9 had symptoms, including greater

TABLE 26.4

PTSD Disorder Symptomatology in Children and Women Subjected to Extrafamilial Child Sexual Abuse

Author, Date	Type of Trauma	Subjects	Measures	Results
Kiser, Ackerman, & Brown (1988)	Repeated sexual abuse in day care	10 children, 2–6 years. 5 boys, 5 girls	FES, FILE DAS, MCMI, Minnesota Child Development Inventory, Personality Inventory for Children, Child Behavior Checklist	Fell under type II classification (repeated trauma) associated with denial, psychic numbing, rage, mistrust of people, and fearfulness. Did not demonstrate loss of time perspective and omen formation.
Kramer & Green (1991)	Sexual assault	30 women. 53% 18–34 years. 40% under 18 years.	2 semistructured interviews, one within 72 hours of the assault and a follow-up interview 6–8 weeks postassault.	73.3% met full *DSM-III* criteria for a PTSD diagnosis. 80% reported intrusive symptoms and 76.7% reported avoidant symptoms.

TABLE 26.5

PTSD Symptomatology in Children with Cancer

Author, Date	Type of Trauma	Subjects	Measures	Results
Stuber et al. (1991)	Bone marrow transplant	Six children, 3 girls, 3 boys. 3 3/4–6 3/4 years. Mean age: 4.9 years.	Interview, PTSD reaction index, Play performance scale.	Symptoms of PTS: pronounced denial, avoidance, and reexperiencing. Perceived life threat affected the intensity of symptoms.

anger, passivity in decision making, misperceptions of reality with poor judgment, and less ability to seek intimacy than were reported on norms when tested with the Rorschach (Holaday, Armsworth, Swank, & Vincent, 1992). Also, in children exposed to varied types of traumatic experiences, Terr (1991) reported compulsive posttraumatic stress symptomatology and distortions of time and time-related phenomena, including omen formation, a foreshortened sense of future, and confusion of memories of time sequencing during the trauma (Terr, 1983c). (See Table 26.9.)

Vulnerability Factors of Victims

A number of demographic characteristics have been associated with increased risk for developing PTSD. Perhaps reflecting the general tendency of girls to show relatively higher prevalence rates of anxiety disorders, researchers have found that girls may be at increased risk for developing posttraumatic symptoms (e.g., Gleser et al., 1981, Green et al., 1991). In contrast to adults, where the older the trauma survivor, the less likely he or

TABLE 26.6

PTSD Disorder in Children Who Experienced Nonsexual Assault Crimes

Author, Date	Type of Trauma	Subjects	Measures	Results
Jesse, Strickland, & Lodewig (1992)	Held hostage in elementary school for up to 13 hours	101 children, 47 females, 54 males. 6–12 years	Behavioral Problem Checklist completed by teachers and some parents at 5 days, 4 months, and 1 year posttrauma	Negative school behavior and parent-reported symptoms (temper tantrums, fear of dark, desire to talk about the event) increased over time and were positively related to amount of time child was held hostage.
Malmquist (1986)	Witnesses of parental murder	16 children, 5–10 years	Clinical evaluation for *DSM-III* PTSD; Impact of Events Scale.	All met PTSD criteria. Most common: intrusive thoughts and psychophysiological symptoms. Least common: numbing response.
Nader et al. (1990)	Sniper attack on school playground.	100 of the original 159 children	PTSD Reaction Index	Greater exposure to attack continued to predict more severe and greater number of PTSD symptoms. New findings included a greater number of somatic complaints among children at high and moderate levels of exposure.
Ornitz & Pynoos (1989)	Sniper attack	6 children, 2 boys, 4 girls. 8–13 years. Met *DSM-III* criteria and exhibited excessive startle responses and hypervigilance.		Responses to startle modulation indicated that children with PTSD experienced a significant loss of inhibitory modulation of startle response 17–21 months after event. May reflect that traumatic experience induced long-lasting alteration in brainstem circuits subserving startle modulation.
Pynoos et al. (1987)	Sniper attack	159 children. 50.3% male, 49.7% female. 50% Black, 50% Hispanic, 5–13 years. Mean age: 9.2 years	PTSD Reaction Index, Coddington Life Events Scale	Posttraumatic stress symptoms did occur. Age, sex, or ethnicity did not influence type or severity of symptoms. As exposure increased, so did number of PTSD symptoms correlated

TABLE 26.6

(continued)

Author, Date	Type of Trauma	Subjects	Measures	Results
				between proximity to the violence and type and number of symptoms.
Terr (1979)	Chowchilla school bus kidnapped, held for 27 hours	23 children, 17 females, 6 males. Age 5–14	Clinical interviews, 5–8 months posttrauma.	All children had moderate-severe posttraumatic symptoms: dreams (23 subjects); kidnap-related and "mundane" fears (23); personality change (19); reenactment (14); posttraumatic play (11); visual and/or time misperception during event (8); hallucinations during event (3).
Terr (1983a)	4-year follow-up on Chowchilla kidnap victims	25 children (16 females, 9 males), 9–17 years, randomly selected from public schools then matched to Chowchilla children for age, sex, ethnicity	Clinical interviews	All children continued to present with posttraumatic symptoms. New findings were embarrassment connected with victimization; conscious suppressional avoidance of thoughts of event; denial and/or repression of earlier symptoms though not of actual event; psychophysiological symptoms related to event; sense of foreshortened future.
Terr (1983b)		23 children (16 females, 9 males), 9–17 years, randomly selected from public schools then matched to Chowchilla children for age, sex, ethnicity	Clinical interviews	Chowchilla children had expectations for shortened life span; greater intensity of ordinary fears; and less concern about future global or local events. Interest in world events was more narrowly limited to personal, trauma-related concerns.

TABLE 26.7

PTSD Symptomatology in Children Exposed to Environmental Disasters

Author, Date	Type of Trauma	Subjects	Measures	Results
Burke et al. (1982)	Blizzard and flood in Revere, MA	64 children, 31 females, 33 males. 6–7 years	Connors Parent Questionnaire given 6 months preflood as part of Head Start program and 5-months postflood.	Children at higher risk for posttrauma problems were: boys whose overall Anxiety score increased post-flood; children previously assessed as having special needs; and younger children living closest to flooded area. High level of parental denial of children's posttraumatic problems.
Burke et al. (1986)	Blizzard and flood in Revere, MA	47 5th graders, mixed male and female. 19 from flooded and evacuated area; 28 from nonflooded area.	"Story about Coming Winter" written 10 months after flood.	Girls from flooded area showed greatest distress: had greater depression, anxiety, fear of harm from external forces, preoccupation with death, and less sense of power over own fate than nonflooded girls and flooded and nonflooded boys.
Earls et al. (1988)	Severe flooding in Missouri	32 children, 16 females, 16 males. 6–17 years. 26 parents of these children.	Modified DICA and DICA-P, Home Environment Interview for Children and HEIC-P; School reports including Child Behavior Checklist: 1 year postflood	No child met full PTSD criteria. Most common PTSD symptoms were reported by children who were given diagnosis of preexisting disorder. Greater PTSD symptoms also associated with greater parental symptomatology.
Green et al. (1991)	Buffalo Creek dam collapse and flood	Retrospective review of data gathered 2 years after trauma	PTSD worksheet modeled on *DSM-III-R* criteria.	37% given "probable" diagnosis. Commonly endorsed items: distress at reminders, restricted social range, restricted affect, irritability. Fewer symptoms in youngest children and greater symptoms in girls. Contributing factors to PTSD symptoms were life threat, gender, parental psychopathology, and

265

TABLE 26.7

(continued)

Author, Date	Type of Trauma	Subjects	Measures	Results
				irritable/depressed family.
Handford et al. (1986)	Three Mile Island accident	35 children, 19 females, 16 males. 6–19 years. 67 parents of these children living an average of 7.5 miles from Three Mile Island	Structured and unstructured interviews of parents and children; Behavior Problem Checklist; Children's Manifest Anxiety Scale; Kinetic Family Drawing	Realistic recognition of danger of accident was not evident in children below 8 years 5 months; understanding increased with age. Children consistently self-reported more fear and anxiety than parents reported for them. Intensity of reaction in mother-father was related to discrepancy in mood and reaction to the event.
Holaday et al. (1992)	Rape, accidents or extreme loss, etc.	63 children, 16 female, 47 males. 7–17 years. Trauma occurred before age 9 (confirmed by parent or guardian)	Rorschach scores on 10 variables compared to Exner norms	Compared to norms, traumatized children had greater anger, passivity in decision making, misperception of surrounding reality leading to displays of poor judgment; less ability to seek intimacy, express feelings, and tolerate stress; less self-esteem.
Jones & Ribbe (1991)	Residential fire	Study 1: 8 child and adolescent victims, 4–16 years, 12 adult victims, 21–68 years.	Study 1: child and adult questionnaires identifying reactions to residential fires (FQ-A; FQ-C), semistructured diagnostic interview (DICA-6R-A).	Study 1: fire victims expressed several symptoms related to PTSD.
		Study 2: 38 boys, 14–19 years, in a private boarding school. 25 were residents in a recent dormitory fire; 13 were nonresidents	Study 2: Interview, State-trait Anxiety Inventory (STAI), Horowitz Impact of Events Scale (HIES), and DICA-6R-A	Study 2: HIES data indicate that a residential fire is capable of producing high levels of stress symptomatology in both resident and nonresident groups. No statistically significant differences in PTSD symptomatology as measured by the HIES

TABLE 26.7

(continued)

Author, Date	Type of Trauma	Subjects	Measures	Results
				were found in resident and nonresident groups.
Martini, Ryan, Nakayama, & Ramenofsky (1990)	Pittsburgh Regatta accident	56 children injured in the accident, 3–9 years, with injuries of varying severity.	Kiddie SADS-P, Pre-School Symptom Self-report (PRESS), PTSD reaction index-child revision, family environment scale, STAIC, CDI, FES, FILE, CBCL	Presence or severity of PTSD symptoms not related to seriousness or nature of injury. Instead, symptoms resulted from level of family stress, coping styles of patient and family, positive psychiatric history in child/family, and experience in having dealt effectively with stressful episodes in the past.
McFarlane (1987)	Severe Australian bushfire	808 children, 47.2% female; 52.8% male. Median age: 8.2 years	Modified Rutter Parent and Teacher questionnaires, given 2, 8, and 26 months postfire	All posttraumatic phenomena persisted over 26 months. Phobic disorder was most strongly predictive of posttraumatic phenomena. Primary contributors to greater posttraumatic phenomena were separation from parents following fire; continuing maternal preoccupation with fire; and changed family functioning.
McFarlane (1987)	Australian bushfire	183 families with children between 7–12 years surveyed after 8 months. 26 months after the fire, a sample of 103 families was obtained.	Family functioning questionnaire	Fire-affected group showed an increased level of "irritable distress" at both 8 and 26 months. A major cause was posttraumatic phenomena in mothers and in fathers.
McFarlane (1988)	Australian bushfire	50 firefighters representing the 7 high-risk subgroups	GHQ 4 months after disaster, structured interview, GHQ 8 months after disaster, GHQ 11 and 29 months after disaster. IES, DIS after 42 months	8 of 15 subjects who had definite or borderline PTSD at 8 months remained symptomatic 3 years later. Disturbance of attention and concentration found to be best predictor of chronic PTSD.

TABLE 26.7

(continued)

Author, Date	Type of Trauma	Subjects	Measures	Results
				Depression and panic reported by 67% of PTSD group after 8 months.
Newman (1976)	Buffalo Creek dam collapse and flood	8 children under 12 years 1 female, 7 males. Median age: 6 at time of trauma.	Developmental data obtained from mothers and school records. Interviews with children using drawing and storytelling 2 years posttrauma.	Major factors contributing to nature and severity of impairment were developmental level at time of trauma, perceptions of family reactions, and degree of exposure to flood. Children showed modified sense of reality and power of self, greater vulnerability to stress, early awareness of death.

she is to develop PTSD (Gleser et al., 1981; Janoff-Bulman, 1992), there is some evidence that older children, who better understand the meaning of a traumatic event, may be more likely to develop PTSD than younger children (Green et al., 1991). Demographic variables that may be associated with resilience in the face of traumatic incidents are intelligence, high socioeconomic status, and temperament (Crittenden, 1985).

The extent to which pretrauma personality factors predispose children to PTSD is unknown. Studies conducted primarily on adults suggest that acute reactions are determined mostly by the exposure to and intensity of the traumatic event. If PTSD symptoms persist, psychological difficulties are more likely (McFarlane, 1989).

SOCIAL AND FAMILY FACTORS

Since the earliest studies of posttraumatic adjustment of children, it has been recognized that parental reactions are crucial predictors of the child's functioning. Particularly in young children, the higher the level of parental anxiety and distress, the more likely will it be that the child will develop PTSD (Bromet & Connell, 1984; Green et al., 1991). There is also evidence that a family

psychiatric history of anxiety and depression places individuals at risk for PTSD (Davidson, Swartz, & Storch, 1985). Finally, as in other areas of childhood adjustment, social supports have been found to be important buffers against the stress of traumatic events (Bromet & Connell, 1984).

Biological Stress Disorder Responses

To date, most biological studies of PTSD have been conducted on adults, not children.

Autonomic hyperactivity to combat stimuli (Pitman et al., 1990) has been demonstrated in combat-related PTSD patients. In a study of Vietnam veterans with PTSD compared to veterans without PTSD (Pitman et al., 1990), PTSD patients showed analgesic response to stimuli reminiscent of the original trauma, with a decrease in pain intensity ratings after exposure to a videotape depicting a combat scene.

Decreased platelet basal cyclic adenylate cyclase levels and decreased reactivity to isoproterenol and forskolin stimulation also were found

TABLE 26.8

PTSD Symptomatology in Children Exposed to War

Author, Date	Type of Trauma	Subjects	Measures	Results
Baker (1990)	Intifada	796 Palestinian children	Observed symptoms, rating scale, Nowicki-Strickland Locus of Control Scale for Children, Cooper-Smith Self-Esteem Inventory	Significant psychological and behavioral problems included disobedience, fighting with others, disturbing others, irresponsibility, jealousy, difficulty in awakening, disturbances of sleep, depression, fear of leaving house, fear of soldiers. Subjects possessed a relatively high level of self-esteem and appeared more internally controlled than other groups of children.
Dreman & Cohen (1990)	Death of parent(s) resulting from terrorist activities	4 children, then aged 6–11 years (2 case studies, each involving 2 children)		10-year follow-ups indicated poor long-term adjustment and psychopathology indicative of unresolved trauma.
Kinzie et al. (1989)	Cambodian students in concentration camp	3-year follow-up of 27 of the Cambodian students	SADS, DIS, Social Adjustment and Life Events scales, Beck Depression Inventory and Impact of Events Scale	PTSD was still prevalent (48%), including 5 new cases. Depression persisted in 41% of students. Avoidance behavior was common, even among those without PTSD diagnoses.
Kinzie et al. (1986)	Lived for 4 years in Pol Pot concentration camps, 27 months as refugees in Thailand; in U.S. for 2 years at time of study	40 Cambodian students, 15 females, 25 males. 14–20 years. Trauma occurred at age 8–12.	Semistructured interviews including questions from SADS and DIS on affective disorders, PTSD and other anxiety disorders.	50% met *DSM-III* PTSD criteria. Most common: intrusive mental states and avoidance. Mild but prolonged depressive symptoms also common. Symptoms more frequent and severe when the student did not live with family member.
Krell (1988)	Japanese concentration camps	2 case studies: 48-year-old man and 46-year-old woman, both child survivors of Dutch origin who were victims of		Both child victims succumbed to emotional illness, such as repeated and intrusive memories years later. Affective disorders precipitated

TABLE 26.8

(continued)

Author, Date	Type of Trauma	Subjects	Measures	Results
		Japanese concentration camps		by randomly recalled memories triggered by contemporary events.
Sack et al. (1986)	Cambodian students in concentration camp	40 Cambodian students compared to Control group of 6 Cambodian students in U.S. before Pol Pot	Home interviews, teacher ratings, Children's Global Assessment Scale	Compared to 6 escapees, 40 subjects reported more distress with school grades, peers, and themselves than reported by caregivers. Teacher reports of students with psychiatric diagnoses indicated more withdrawal and daydreaming than disruptive behavior.
Saigh (1991)	War-related traumatic episodes	230 Lebanese children, 9–12 years, who met *DSM-III* criteria for chronic PTSD	Children's PTSD inventory, Revised Children's Manifest Anxiety Scale (RCMAS), CDI, Connor's Teacher Rating Scale (CTRS).	Each group scored significantly higher on the RCMAS, CDI, and CTRS than the non-clinical controls, but there were no differences between the four types of PTSD cases.

in PTSD-diagnosed patients (Lerer, Bleich, Solomon, Shaleva, & Ebstein, 1990).

In a study of autonomic functioning in children, Ornitz and Pynoos (1989) reported that children who experienced a sniper attack had a loss of inhibitory modulation of startle response 17 to 21 months after the shooting.

Assessment of PTSD in Children

As in evaluating other areas of children's functioning, assessment of PTSD in children requires a combination of direct interview and observation of the child as well as reliance on parent and teacher reports. In PTSD as other anxiety disorders, it is important to recognize that parents and teachers may underreport symptomatology because of not being "tuned in" to the child's post-traumatic difficulties (Earls et al., 1988; Handford

et al., 1986). In recent years, a number of specific interviews and instruments for measurement of PTSD in children have been developed. Structured clinical interviews with both children's and parent versions include the Diagnostic Interview for Children and Adolescents—Revised (Reich, Shayka, & Taibleson, 1991) and the Diagnostic Interview Schedule for Children, supplemental module, (Fisher & Kranzler, 1990). A major caveat in using structured interviews is that, since the screening questions for assessing whether a child has been exposed to traumatic events are generally not very specific regarding type of traumatic life event, there tends to be a high rate of false negatives. In interviewing children and parents, it is important to ask specifically about exposure to a variety of upsetting experiences to ensure that other significant events have been discussed.

The PTSD Reaction Index (Pynoos et al., 1987) is the most commonly used measure of PTSD in children; it has versions for interviewing the child

TABLE 26.9

PTSD Symptomatology in Children Exposed to Mixed Trauma

Author, Date	Type of Trauma	Subjects	Measures	Results
Famularo et al. (1991)	Witnessing or experiencing physical assaults, sexual abuse, or natural disaster.	19 children, ages 7–14 diagnosed as Borderline Personality Disorder; 3 diagnosed as PTSD by *DSM-III-R*.	DICA-C-R	78.9% reported a significant traumatic experience. 36.8% met PTSD criteria.
Holaday et al. (1992)	Rape, accidents or extreme loss, etc.	63 children 7–17 years, 16 females, 47 males. Trauma occurred before age 9 (confirmed by parent or guardian)	Rorschach scores on ten variables compared to Exner norms.	Compared to norms, traumatized children had greater anger, passivity in decision making, misperception of surrounding reality leading to displays of poor judgment, and less ability to seek intimacy, to express feelings, and to tolerate stress, and less self-esteem.
Terr (1981a)	Mixed trauma	16 traumatized children, 8 females, 8 males. 7 months to 17 years	Clinical interviews	Discusses 11 characteristics of compulsive posttraumatic "play."
Terr (1983c)	Mixed life-threatening traumas	30 subjects, 7 months to 69 years. 20 of these (13 females, 7 males) traumatized under age 18	Clinical interview, from 5 days–12½ years posttrauma	Following distortions of time and time-related phenomena noted: omen formation (20 subjects); foreshortened sense of future (11 subjects); sense of time lengthening during trauma (6 subjects); confusion of time sequencing during trauma, and similar time-skew phenomena.

and for interviewing the parent. This measure, which was originally based on *DSM-III* criteria, has been through numerous revisions, and there is currently a version modified for use with *DSM-III-R* criteria (Applebaum & Burns, 1991). The advantage of this assessment instrument is that, unlike other instruments, which tend to be adult measures revised downward, this instrument is based on clinical and theoretical considerations that take into account the unique aspects of a child's reactions to trauma as opposed to those of an adult.

A number of self-administered paper-and-pencil questionnaires measuring PTSD symptoms may be helpful with older children and adolescents. The Impact of Events Scale (Zilberg, Weiss, & Horowitz, 1982), useful as a screen of current levels of intrusive and avoidant symptomatology, has been utilized in several studies of PTSD prevalence in children. The Symptom Checklist-90-Revised, which can be administered to adolescents (Derogatis, 1977), and the Child Behavior Checklist (Achenbach & Edelbrock, 1983), which is filled out by parents, have both been adapted as screens for posttraumatic symptomatology (Saunders, Mandoki, & Kilpatrick, 1996; Wolfe, Gentile, & Wolfe, 1989). More recently, several scales have emerged that are designed to measure specifically the impact of trauma on children. Although still in the early stages of development, the Trauma Symptom Checklist for Children (Lanktree & Briere, 1990) and the Children's Impact of Traumatic Events Scale Revised (Wolfe, Wolfe, Gentile, & LaRose, 1989) both show promise as measures attuned to the developmentally unique manifestations of children's reactions to trauma.

These measures should prove helpful in evaluating posttraumatic symptoms in older children and adolescents. Preschooler assessment should place heavier reliance on parent reports as well as on observation of the child's play and drawings. Pynoos and Eth (1986) describe a clinical interview with young children based on children's drawings related to the traumatic event and on stories they make up regarding the drawing. Terr (1981a) describes methods for evaluating children's play in a manner that allows for determining the presence of intrusive and/or avoidant symptomatology. For example, the presence of intrusive symptoms can be inferred if the child engages in traumatic play characterized by repetitively reenacting aspects of the trauma with no symbolic signs that he or she is achieving mastery.

Treatment

Horowitz's (1986) dynamically oriented psychotherapy is often used to treat PTSD in adults. The treatment is based on the clinician establishing a supportive relationship with the survivor, which helps the patient "dose" the reexperience of the traumatic event in a gradual manner. Emphasis is placed on gradually helping patients organize and express their memories and feelings regarding the trauma in a manner that facilitates their viewing the traumatic event as something bad that hap-

pened to them, rather than as an indication that they are stigmatized or destined to be revictimized. The treatment of children is more complex, since active efforts need to be made to involve parents, and since the reliance on less verbally mediated techniques (e.g., art or play therapy) may be necessary.

The relative efficacy of different treatment strategies for childhood PTSD has not received much systematic study. Here and in other disorders, therapists with behavioral orientations are most likely to assess (Saigh, 1987) treatment outcome systematically. Exposure-based behaviorally oriented treatments of children systematically reexpose them to thoughts and images of the trauma until the anxiety associated with the trauma is extinguished (Saigh, 1987). There are also reports of cognitive-behavioral treatments of PTSD in child sexual abuse survivors (Deblinger et al., 1989).

Regardless of theoretical orientation, clinicians agree that treatment at some point needs to include active exploration of the child's memories, feelings, and associations to the traumatic episode. Efficacious treatment of childhood trauma victims requires validation of the child's feelings of anger, shame, guilt, and sadness, while at the same time enabling him or her to confront, rather than to avoid, memories of the traumatic incident.

Many clinicians feel that group therapy is the most effective modality for helping children through this process. In a survey of 36 incest-treatment professionals, Forseth and Brown (1981) report that group therapy was deemed the treatment of choice. However, group therapy may not be appropriate for all traumatized children, particularly those who are ADHD or borderline (Mandell & Damon, 1989). A general guideline for the lack of suitability of group treatment is that children who are not able to function in a classroom setting without major support will be more likely to require individual treatment.

A number of authors have highlighted the need for parallel treatment for parents of trauma victims. There are a number of reasons for this in the case of sex abuse. Frequently mothers of sex abuse victims have themselves been victimized. Therefore, they are at risk for sabotaging treatment through their denial or anxiety unless they receive the group support. Other advantages include helping parents respond more appropriately to material that children bring home from group.

The goals of treatment of traumatized children

TABLE 26.10

PTSD Childhood PTSD Treatment Studies

Author, Date	Type of Trauma	Subjects	Measures	Results
Davidson et al. (1991)	Post-childhood traumatic stress disorder; pharmacological treatment	5 subjects, 4 females, 1 male. 26–42 years. All diagnosed with PTSD. Treated with 20–80 mg. fluoxetine/day for 8–32 weeks.	Impact of Events Scale, Intrusive and Avoidant scores especially noted.	Fluoxetine associated with marked improvement of intrusive symptoms in all cases.
Doyle & Bauer (1989)		10 children, 2 females, 8 males, 8–15.1 years, in a day and residential treatment center for emotionally disturbed youth. Diagnosed with PTSD.		Authors present a "Seven-Objective Recovery Treatment Model" for working through and integrating traumatic experience.
Friedrich (1991)	4 case studies: (1) Domestic violence including kidnapping following parents' divorce: 12-year-old boy; (2) stabbing of mother by father: 4-year-old boy; (3) sexual abuse: 9-year-old girl; (4) near drowning: 11-year-old boy			Hypnosis useful in forming a positive therapeutic alliance. Symptom stabilization and removal achieved in all cases. In addition, hypnosis allowed subjects to uncover painful events and integrate them into their lives in a therapeutic manner.
Galante & Foa (1986)		300 1st through 4th grade children traumatized by earthquake in Central Italy		Most important treatment features found to be family support; prompt reestablishment of daily routine; structured opportunity to discuss and work through disaster experiences and fears.
Pynoos & Eth (1986)		Technique for interviewing children ages 3–16 who are recent witnesses to traumatic violence. Used 200 children at time of publication.		3-stage, approximately 90-minute interview that enables child to release emotion in safe, holding environment, relive and describe experience initially using drawing and storytelling, focus on "worst moment," fantasies, fears, guilt, to achieve a sense of mastery over trauma and discuss pragmatic and interpersonal current and future concerns related to trauma.

may vary based on the type of trauma. However, commonalities include validating expression of feelings surrounding the traumatic incident (James, 1989) and reducing feelings of responsibility and guilt. This latter goal needs to be undertaken with an understanding that children may need to hold on to some feelings of responsibility as a mechanism for feeling less helpless (Janoff-Bulman, 1992). It needs to be accomplished in the context of empowering the child against future victimization; among incest survivors, for example, this would include teaching sex abuse prevention strategies. Other goals are integrating conflicted feelings toward the perpetrator (in the case of interpersonal of victimization), and mobilizing of family support for the victim (Trepper & Barrett, 1989).

James (1989) makes the important point that therapy of traumatized children may need to be sequenced over time. Even after termination of an initial course of treatment, it may be necessary to have the child return at later developmental stages to "work through" the meaning of the trauma in light of a new stage of development. For example, the sexual impact of incest may not become fully apparent until an abused child becomes sexually active as an adolescent. These considerations need to be balanced with a sensitivity to the need not to see children in such long-term therapy that they come to internalize permanent views of themselves as "victims."

Friedrich (1991) reported that hypnosis allowed child trauma victims to uncover painful events and to integrate them into their lives in a therapeutic manner with resulting symptom reduction. (See Table 26.10 for specific treatment studies.)

Biological Treatments

Antidepressant medication, including tricyclic antidepressants (Davidson, Roth & Newman, 1991; Lerer, 1987), monamine oxidose inhibitors (Davidson et al., 1985), and fluoxetine have been utilized to treat posttraumatic stress disorder in adults (Davidson, et al., 1991). To date, there have been no research reports regarding the use of antidepressant medication for treating children with PTSD symptomatology.

Impairment and Long-term Effects After Traumatic Experiences

In all studies, severity of impairment from PTSD symptomatology varies with: severity of trauma (Green et al., 1991; Nader et al., 1990); proximity and degree of exposure to site of the traumatic incident (Burke et al., 1982; Pynoos et al., 1987; Pynoos & Nader, 1990); gender (Burke et al., 1982), with females more often having symptomatology; and age of the child, with older children suffering more impairment (Green et al., 1991). Preexisting psychiatric disorders (Earls et al., 1988) and the severity of parental symptomatology (Earls et al., 1988) are also variables associated with greater impairment in children following traumatic exposure.

REFERENCES

Achenbach, T., & Edelbrock, C. (1983). *Manual for the Child Behavior Checklist and Child Behavior Profile.* Burlington: University of Vermont, Department of Psychiatry.

American Psychiatric Association. (1980). *Diagnostic and statistical manual of mental disorders* (3rd ed.) Washington, DC: Author.

American Psychiatric Association. (1987). *Diagnostic and statistical manual of mental disorders* (3rd ed., rev.) Washington, DC: Author.

American Psychiatric Association. (1994). *Diagnostic and statistical manual of mental disorders* (4th ed.) Washington, DC: Author.

Applebaum, D., & Burns, G. (1991). Unexpected childhood death: Post-traumatic stress disorder in surviving siblings and parents. *Journal of Clinical Child Psychology, 20,* 114–120.

Baker, A. (1990). The psychological impact of the Intifada on Palestinian children in the Occupied West Bank and Gaza: An exploratory study. *American Journal of Ortheopsychiatry, 60* (4), 496–505.

Barlow, D. (1988). *Anxiety and its disorders: The nature and treatment of anxiety and panic.* New York: Guilford Press.

Benedek, E. (1985). Children and psychic trauma: A brief review of contemporary thinking. In S. Eth &

R. Pynoos (Eds.), *Post-traumatic stress disorder in children* (pp. 1–16). Washington, DC: American Psychiatric Association Press.

Block, D., Siber, E., & Perry, S. (1956). Some factors in the emotional reaction of children to disaster. *American Journal of Psychiatry, 113,* 416–422.

Bromet, E., & Connell, M. (1984). Mental health of children near the Three Mile Island reactor. *Journal of Preventive Psychiatry, 2,* 275–301.

Burke, J. F., Borus, J. F., Burns, B. J., Millstein, K. H., & Beasley, M. C. (1982). Changes in children's behavior after a natural disaster. *American Journal of Psychiatry, 139* (8), 1010–1014.

Burke, J. D., Moccia, P., Borus, J. F., & Burns, B. J. (1986). Emotional distress in fifth-grade children ten months after a natural disaster. *Journal of the American Academy of Child Psychiatry, 25* (4), 536–541.

Cella, D., Mahon, S. M., & Donavan, M. (1991). Cancer recurrence as a traumatic event. *Behavioral Medicine, 16,* 15–22.

Chu, J. A., & Dill, D. L. (1990). Dissociative symptoms in relation to childhood physical and sexual abuse. *Journal of the American Academy of Child and Adolescent Psychiatry, 147* (7), 887–892.

Crittenden, P. M. (1985). Maltreated infants: Vulnerability and resilience. *Journal of Child Psychology and Psychiatry, 26,* 85–96.

Davidson, J., Roth, S., & Newman, E. (1991). Fluoxetine in post-traumatic stress disorder. *Journal of Traumatic Stress, 4* (3), 419–423.

Davidson, J., Swartz, M., & Storck, M. (1985). A diagnostic and family study of post-traumatic stress disorder. *American Journal of Psychiatry, 142,* 90–93.

Deblinger, E., McLeer, S. V., Atkins, M. S., Ralphe, D., & Foa, E. (1989). Post-traumatic stress in sexually abused, physically abused, and nonabused children. *Child Abuse & Neglect, 13,* 403–408.

Deblinger, E., McLeer S. V., & Henry D. (1990). Cognitive behavioral treatment for sexually abused children suffering post-traumatic stress: Preliminary findings. *Journal of the American Academy of Child and Adolescent Psychiatry, 29,* 747–752.

Derogatis, L. (1977). *SCL-90 administration, scoring & procedure manual—I for the revised version.* Baltimore: Johns Hopkins University School of Medicine.

Donaldson, M. A., & Gardner, R. (1985). Diagnosis and treatment of traumatic stress among women after childhood incest. In C. R. Figley (Ed.), *Trauma and its wake* (pp. 356–377). New York: Brunner/Mazel.

Doyle, J. S., & Bauer, S. K. (1989). Post-traumatic stress disorder in children: Its identification and treatment in a residential setting for emotionally disturbed youth. *Journal of Traumatic Stress, 2* (3), 275–288.

Dreman, S., & Cohen, E. (1990). Children of victims of terrorisms revisited: Integrating individual and family treatment approaches. *American Journal of Orthopsychiatry, 60* (2), 204–209.

Earls, F., Smith, E., Reich, W., & Jung, K. (1988). Investigating psychopathological consequences of a disaster in children: A pilot study incorporating a structured diagnostic interview. *Journal of the American Academy of Child and Adolescent Psychiatry, 27,* 90–95.

Erikson, K. (1976) *Everything in its path: Destruction of community in the Buffalo Creek flood.* New York: Simon and Schuster.

Famularo, R., Kinscherff, R., & Fenton, T. (1990). Symptom differences in acute and chronic presentation of childhood post-traumatic stress disorder. *Child Abuse and Neglect, 14,* 439–444.

Famularo, R., Kinscherff, R., & Fenton, T. (1991). Post traumatic stress disorder among children clinically diagnosed as borderline personality disorder. *Journal of Nervous and Mental Disease, 179,* 428–431.

Finkelhor, D. (1987). The trauma of child sexual abuse: Two models. *Journal of Interpersonal Violence, 2* (4), 348–366.

Fisher, P., & Kranzler, E. (1990). *Post-traumatic stress disorder: Supplemental module for the DISC-2.1.* New York: New York State Psychiatric Institute.

Forseth, L., & Brown, A. (1981). A survey of intrafamilial sexual abuse treatment centers: Implications for intervention. *Child Abuse and Neglect, 5,* 177–186.

Freud, A., & Burlingham, D. (1943). *War and children.* London: Medical War Books.

Friedrich, W. N. (1991). Hypnotherapy with traumatized children. *International Journal of Clinical and Experimental Hypnosis, 39* (2), 67–81.

Galante, R., & Foa, D. (1986). An epidemiological study of psychic trauma and treatment effectiveness for children after a natural disaster. *Journal of the American Academy of Child Psychiatry, 25* (3), 357–363.

Gleser, G., Green, B., & Winget, C. (1981) *Prolonged psychosocial effects of disaster: A study of Buffalo Creek.* New York: Academic Press.

Goodwin, J. (1985). Post-traumatic symptoms in incest victims. In S. Eth & R. S. Pynoos (Eds.), *Post-traumatic stress disorder in children* (pp. 157–168). Los Angeles: American Psychiatric Association.

Green, B. (1990). Defining trauma: Terminology and generic stressor dimensions. *Journal of Applied Social Psychology, 20,* 1632–1642.

Green, B., Korel, M., Grace, M., Vary, M., Leonard, A., Gleser, G., & Smitson-Cohen, S. (1991). Children and disaster: Age, gender, and parental effects on PTSD symptoms. *Journal of the American Academy of Child and Adolescent Psychiatry, 30* (6), 945–951.

Greenwald, E., & Leitenberg, H. (1990). Post traumatic stress disorder in a nonclinical and nonstudent sample of adult women sexually abused as children. *Journal of Interpersonal Violence, 5,* 217–228.

Handford, H. A., Mayes, S., Mattison, R., Humphrey, F., Bagnoto, S., Bixler, E., & Kales, J. (1986). Child and parent reaction to the Three Mile Island nuclear accident. *Journal of the American Academy of Child and Adolescent Psychiatry, 25,* 346–356.

Helzer, J., Robins, L., & McEvoy, L. (1987). Post-traumatic stress disorder in the general population: Findings of the Epidemiologic Catchment Area Survey. *New England Journal of Medicine, 317,* 1630–1634.

Holaday, M., Armsworth, M. W., Swank, P. R., & Vincent, K. R. (1992). Rorschach responding in traumatized children and adolescents. *Journal of Traumatic Stress, 5* (1), 119–129.

Horowitz, M. (1986). *Stress response syndromes.* New York: Jason Aronson.

James, B. (1989). *Treating traumatized children: New insight and creative interventions.* Lexington, MA: Lexington Books.

Janoff-Bulman, R. (1992) *Shattered assumptions: Towards a new psychology of trauma.* New York: Free Press.

Jessee, P. O., Strickland, M. P., & Ladewig, B. H. (1992). The after effects of a hostage situation on children's behavior. *American Journal of Orthopsychiatry, 62* (2), 309–312.

Jones, R. T., & Ribbe, D. P. (1991). Child, adolescent, and adult victims of residential fire. *Behavior Modification, 15,* 560–580.

Kilpatrick, D. G., Saunders, B. E., Vernon, L. J., Best, C. L., & Von, J. M. (1987). Criminal victimization: Lifetime prevalence, reporting to police, and psychological impact. *Crime and Delinquency, 33,* 479–489.

Kilpatrick, D. G., Saunders, B. E., Amick-McMullan, A., Best, C. L., Veronen, L., & Resnick, H. S. (1989). Victim and crime factors associated with the development of crime-related post-traumatic stress disorder. *Behavior Therapy, 20,* 199–214.

Kinzie, J. D., Sack, W., Angell, R., Clark, G., & Ben, R. (1989). A three year follow-up of Cambodian young people traumatized as children. *Journal of the American Academy of Child and Adolescent Psychiatry, 28* (4), 501–504.

Kinzie, J. D. Sack, W. H., Angell, R. H., Manson, S., & Ben, R. (1986). The psychiatric effects of massive trauma on Cambodian children: I. The children. *Journal of the American Academy of Child Psychiatry, 25* (3), 370–376.

Kiser, L. J., Ackerman, B. J., & Brown, E. (1988). Post-traumatic stress disorder in young children: A reaction to purported sexual abuse. *Journal of the American Academy of Child and Adolescent Psychiatry, 27,* 645–649.

Kiser, L. J., Heston, J., & Millsap, P. A. (1991). Physical and sexual abuse in childhood: relationship with post-traumatic stress disorder. *Journal of the American Academy of Child and Adolescent Psychiatry, 30,* 776–783.

Kramer, T., & Green, B. (1991). Posttraumatic stress disorder as an early response to sexual assault. *Journal of Interpersonal Violence, 6* (2), 160–173.

Krell, R. (1988). Survivors of childhood experiences in Japanese concentration camps. *American Journal of Psychiatry, 145,* 383–384.

Langmeier, J., & Matejcek, Z. (1973). *Psychological deprivation in childhood.* New York: Halsted Press.

Lanktree, C., & Briere J. (1990). *Early data on the Trauma Symptoms Checklist for Children (TSC-C).* Paper presented at the annual meeting of the American Psychological Association, Boston, MA.

Lerer, B., Bleich, A., Solomon, Z., Shaleva, A., &

Ebstein, R. (1990). Platelet adenylate cyclase activity as a possible biological marker for post traumatic stress disorder. In M. Wolf & A. Mosnaim (Eds.), *Post traumatic stress disorder. Etiology, phenomenology and treatment* (pp. 149–156). Washington, DC: American Psychiatric Press.

Lindberg, F. H., & Distad, L. J. (1985). Post-traumatic stress disorders in women who experienced childhood incest. *Child Abuse & Neglect,* 329–334.

Malmquist, C. P. (1986). Children who witness parental murder: Post traumatic aspects. *Journal of the American Academy of Child Psychiatry, 25* (3), 320–325.

Mandell, J. G., & Damon, L. (1989). *Group treatment for sexually abused children.* New York: Guilford Press.

Martini, D. R., Ryan, C., Nakayama, D., & Ramenofsky, M. (1989). Psychiatric Regatta accident. *Journal of the American Academy of Child and Adolescent Psychiatry, 27,* 650–654.

Martini, D. R., Ryan C., Nakayama D., & Ramenofsky, M. (1990). Psychiatric sequelae after traumatic injury: The Pittsburgh Regatta Accident. *Journal of the American Academy of Child and Adolescent Psychiatry, 29* (1), 70–75.

McFarlane, A. C. (1987). Post traumatic phenomena in a longitudinal study of children following a natural disaster. *Journal of the American Academy of Child and Adolescent Psychiatry, 26* (5), 764–769.

McFarlane, A. (1989). The aetiology of post-traumatic morbidity: Predisposing, precipitating, and perpetuating factors. *British Journal of Psychiatry, 154,* 221–228.

McLeer, S. V., Deblinger, E., Atkins, M. S., Foa, E. B., & Ralphe, D. L. (1988). Post-traumatic stress disorder in sexually abused children. *Journal of the American Academy of Child and Adolescent Psychiatry, 27,* 650–654.

Milgram, N., Toubiana, Y., Klingman, A., Raviv, A. & Goldstein, I. (1988). Situational exposure and personal loss in children's acute and chronic stress reactions to a school bus disaster. *Journal of Traumatic Stress, 1,* 339–352.

Nader, K., Pynoos, R., Fairbanks, L., & Frederick, C. (1990). Children's PTSD reactions one year after a sniper attack at their school. *American Journal of Psychiatry, 147,* 1526–1530.

Newman, C. J. (1976). Children of disaster: Clinical observations at Buffalo Creek. *American Journal of Psychiatry, 133* (3), 306–312.

Nir, Y. (1985). Post-traumatic stress disorder in children with cancer. In S. Eth & R. Pynoos (Eds.) *Post-traumatic stress disorder in children* (pp. 121–132). Washington, DC: American Psychiatric Association Press.

Ornitz, E. M., & Pynoos, R. S. (1989). Startle modulation in children with post traumatic stress disorder. *American Journal of Psychiatry, 146,* 866–870.

Phifer, J., & Norris, F. (1989). Psychological symptoms in older adults following natural disaster: Nature, timing, duration, and course. *Journal of Gerontology: Social Sciences, 44,* S206–S217.

276

Pitman, R., Orr, S., Vanderkolk, B., Greenberg, M., Meyerhoff, J., & Mougey, E. (1990). Analgesia: A new dependent variable for the biological study of post traumatic stress disorder. In M. Wolf & A. Mosnaim (Eds.), *Posttraumatic stress disorder: Etiology, phenomenology, and treatment.* Washington, DC: American Psychiatric Association Press.

Pynoos, R. S., & Eth, S. (1986). Witness to violence: The child interview. *Journal of the American Academy of Child and Adolescent Psychiatry, 25,* 306–319.

Pynoos, R. S., Frederick, C., Nader, K., Arroyo, E., Steinberg, A., Eth, S., Nunez, F., & Fairbanks, L. (1987). Life threat and post traumatic stress in school age children. *Archives of General Psychiatry, 44,* 1057–1063.

Pynoos, R. S., & Nader, K. (1988). Psychological first aid and treatment approach to children exposed to community violence: Research implications. *Journal of Traumatic Stress, 1,* 445–473.

Pynoos, R. S., & Nader, K. (1990). Children's exposure to violence and traumatic death. *Psychiatric Annals, 20* (6), 334–344.

Reich, W., Shayka, J., & Taibleson, C. (1991). *Diagnostic Interview for Children and Adolescents— Revised.* St. Louis, MO: Washington University, Division of Child Psychiatry.

Sack, W. H., Angell, R. H., Kinzie, D., & Ben, R. (1986). The psychiatric effects of massive trauma on Cambodian children: II. The family, the home, and the school. *Journal of the American Academy of Child Psychiatry, 25* (3), 377–383.

Saigh, P. (1987). In vitro flooding of childhood posttraumatic stress disorders: A systematic replication. *Professional School Psychology, 2,* 133–144.

Saigh, P. (1991). The development of posttraumatic stress disorder following four different types of traumatization. *Behavior Research and Therapy, 29,* 213–216.

Sanders, B., & Giolas, M. (1991). Dissociation and childhood trauma in psychologically disturbed adolescents. *American Journal of Psychiatry, 148,* 50–54.

Saunders, B., Mandoki, K., & Kilpatrick, D. (1996). Development of a crime-related post-traumatic stress disorder scale for women within the Symptom Checklist-90-Revised. *Journal of Traumatic Stress.*

Schwartz, E., & Kowalski, J. (1991). Post traumatic stress disorder after a school shooting: Effects of symptom threshold selection and diagnosis by DSM-III, DSMIII-R, or proposed DSM-IV. *American Journal of Psychiatry, 148,* 592–597.

Stuber, M. L., Nader, K., Yasuda, P., Pynoos, R., & Cohen, S. (1991). Stress responses after pediatric bone marrow transplantation: Preliminary results of prospective longitudinal study. *Journal of the American Academy of Child and Adolescent Psychiatry, 30* (6), 952–957.

Terr, L. C. (1979). Children of Chowchilla: A study of psychic trauma. *Psychoanalytic Study of the Child, 34,* 552–623.

Terr, L. C. (1981a). Forbidden games. *Journal of the American Academy of Child Psychiatry, 20,* 741–760.

Terr, L. C. (1981b). "Forbidden games." Post-traumatic child's play. *Journal of the American Academy of Child and Adolescent Psychiatry, 34,* 547–623.

Terr, L. C. (1983a). Chowchilla revisited: The effects of psychic trauma four years after a school-bus kidnapping. *American Journal of Psychiatry, 140,* (12), 1543–1550.

Terr, L. C. (1983b). Life attitudes, dreams and psychic trauma in a group of "normal" children. *Journal of the American Academy of Child Psychiatry, 22* (3), 221–230.

Terr, L. C. (1983c). Time sense following psychic trauma: A clinical study of ten adults and twenty children. *American Journal of Orthopsychiatry, 53* (2), 244–261.

Terr, L. (1991). Childhood traumas: An outline and overview. *American Journal of Psychiatry, 148,* 10–20.

Trepper, T. S., & Barrett, M. J. (1989). *Systemic treatment of incest.* New York: Brunner/Mazel.

Wolfe, V., Gentile, C., & Wolfe, D. (1989). The impact of sexual abuse on children: A PTSD formulation. *Behavior Therapy, 20,* 215–228.

Wolfe, V., Wolfe, D., Gentile, C., & LaRose, L. (1989). *Children's impact of traumatic events scale—revised.* Unpublished manuscript, University of Western Ontario.

Yule, W., & Udwin, O. (1991). Screening child survivors for post-traumatic stress disorder: Experiences from the "Jupiter" sinking. *British Journal of Clinical Psychology, 30,* 131–138.

Zilberg, R., Weiss, D., & Horowitz, M. (1982). Impact of Events Scale—Revised. *Journal of Consulting and Clinical Psychology, 50,* 407–414.

27 / Dissociative Disorders in Childhood

Joyanna L. Silberg

Research into the dissociative disorders in adulthood has increased exponentially in the last 10 years, particularly in response to the increasing identification of patients suffering from multiple personality disorder, now termed dissociative identity disorder. Although retrospective patient accounts (Dell & Eisenhower, 1990) suggest that the condition has its onset in early childhood, research tracking dissociative phenomena in childhood and their evolution to more serious disorders has been sparse.

The fourth edition of the *Diagnostic and Statistical Manual of Mental Disorders* (*DSM-IV*; American Psychiatric Association, 1994) classifies the following dissociative disorders: depersonalization disorder, dissociative amnesia, dissociative fugue, dissociative identity disorder (DID) (formerly termed multiple personality disorder [MPD]), and dissociative disorder not otherwise specified (DDNOS).

Depersonalization experiences have been documented in childhood (Fast & Chetnik, 1976; Salfield, 1958; Shimizu & Sakamoto, 1986), but not depersonalization disorder. These children describe feelings of unreality, estrangement, and visual-perceptual distortions. These feelings may be precursors to depersonalization disorder, which is diagnosed most often after the age of 15 (Nemiah, 1989). Only one case of dissociative fugue in a child has been documented (Akhtar & Brenner, 1979), and pediatric case reports of dissociative amnesia appear to be exclusively adolescents (Keller & Shaywitz, 1986).

DID (MPD) and DDNOS have received the most attention of the *DSM-IV* dissociative disorders. (Volume III of the *Handbook of Child and Adolescent Psychiatry* contains a full description of diagnostic features of these disorders.) Current research on childhood DID (MPD) and DDNOS includes 4 several reported case series (Fagan & McMahon, 1984, Hornstein & Putnam, 1992; Hornstein & Tyson, 1991; Kluft, 1985; Putnam, Hornstein, & Peterson, 1996; Silberg, 1996a) and a

few case reports (Malenbaum & Russell, 1987; Weiss, Sutton, & Utecht, 1985). These case reports describe a group of youngsters with an abundance of affective, anxiety, conduct and posttraumatic symptoms who developed dissociative defenses as a means of protecting themselves within an unpredictable, chaotic, and abusive environment.

Putnam, Helmers, and Trickett (1993), Fagan and McMahon (1984), and Kluft (1985) have offered symptom checklists that helped describe the symptom picture of these children. Symptoms in these checklists include: trancelike, day dreaming spells; dramatic fluctuations in skills or behavior; internal experiences of "dividedness"; inner voices or vivid imaginary companions (termed *process* symptoms [Putnam, 1991]; aggressive, anti-social, sexual, or self-injurious behavior; fearfulness, night terrors, and other PTSD symptoms; intermittent depression; and amnesia or disavowal of behaviors).

Many childhood cases do not display a fully developed dissociative identity disorder (multiple personality disorder) with well-defined alternate identities. Within the younger samples, more youngsters seem to display precursors to DID (MPD) (Fagan & McMahon, 1984; Hornstein & Putnam, 1992) with abundant passive influence experiences and hallucinated inner voices but without the full pattern of amnesia or switches to alter states seen in the older population. The frequency of DID (MPD) diagnoses, as opposed to DDNOS, appears to increase with age (Hornstein & Putnam, 1992; Putnam et al., 1996). In recognition of the unique features of childhood cases of dissociative disorders, Peterson (1991) has proposed adding a new category of dissociative disorder of childhood within the *Diagnostic and Statistical Manual*. Initial field trial results suggest that this new category does describe a unique population (Peterson & Putnam, 1993).

Childhood cases that do satisfy DID (MPD) criteria—"two or more distinct identities or per-

sonality states (each with its own relatively enduring pattern of perceiving, relating to, ... and
thinking about the environment and self)" (APA,
1994, p. 487)—have fewer alternate personalities
(two to five) (Vincent & Pickering, 1988) than
adults or adolescents (Dell & Eisenhower, 1990).
The intensity of self-destructive behaviors
may not be as profound as with older patients,
and the sex ratio is closer to 1:1 (Vincent &
Pickering, 1988), unlike the adolescent samples,
which favor females by 2:1 (Dell & Eisenhower,
1990).

Diagnosis

The diagnosis of (DID) MPD or DDNOS in
childhood is a difficult one, as many of the features of the disorder may suggest other, more frequently occurring childhood conditions, and
many child clinicians are unfamiliar with dissociative phenomenology. Diagnostic evaluation
should include interviewing an informant about
strange fluctuations in behavior, unusual forgetfulness, and observed dazed states especially in
youngsters known to have traumatic histories.
Putnam et al. (1993) have introduced the Child
Dissociative Checklist, an observer-report screening measure with established discriminant validity, which may be helpful in gathering observational information about the child. When
observing the child, careful attention should be
paid to wandering attention, trances, blank stares,
and sudden switches in affects, behavior, or style
and content of speech or play. I have found direct
questions about inner experiences and imaginary
playmates to be helpful as well. Preliminary research suggests that pathological fantasy playmates as seen in childhood DID or DDNOS
can be differentiated from normal fantasy playmates, as normal children do not feel bothered or
controlled by their imaginary friends (Silberg,
1996b). Educational information to the child
about dissociative defenses ("Some children who
live in scary places find the only place that they
feel safe is in their own head") also can stimulate
disclosure by helping the youngster feel that he or
she is not alone.

Recent research has documented features on
psychological testing, such as dissociative coping,
depersonalized imagery, and emotional confusion,
that give clues to underlying dissociative pathology. Dissociative children demonstrate unique behaviors during the testing, such as unusual motor
movements, trance states, fluctuating approach to
tests, and forgetting or denial of responses (Silberg, 1994).

Treatment

Treatment of childhood MPD and dissociative
disorders has been discussed by Kluft (1984), Hornstein and Tyson (1991), James (1989), McMahon
and Fagan (1993), Shirar (1996), and Silberg and
Waters (1996). Kluft's series of latency-age youngsters with MPD demonstrated the effectiveness of
hypnotherapy, which was used to address alter
states rapidly, encourage communication, and facilitate integration through images appealing to
youngsters. These techniques have shown favorable results in those youngsters studied (Kluft,
1984; Weiss et al., 1985).

Fagan and McMahon (1984) and James (1989)
have described the use of play therapy techniques, which are useful with dissociative children, as well. James (1989) advocates structured
cognitive strategies involving active mastery over
the abuse experience and cognitive exploration
of feeling states that are dissociated. Waters and
Silberg (1996) emphasize multisensory experiences for learning the concept of personality integration and the importance of each dissociated
"part" attaching to a nurturing parent.

Although adept individual therapeutic techniques involving hypnosis, play therapy, or guided
imagery are important, the context of the child's
behavior must be understood and the systems in
which the child lives must be addressed therapeutically as well. A basic tenet for all therapy with
childhood dissociative patients is assuring safety
through appropriate referral to protective services
for children in ongoing abusive situations.

Educational programming for children with a
dissociative disorder best occurs in an environment where teachers can be sensitive to therapeu-

tic issues and have some familiarity with the diagnosis. My experience suggests it is helpful to have teachers work with youngsters to help predict rapid changes and identify cues in the environment that have led to switching. In some cases, actively processing and commenting to the child about changes observed helps refocus the child to the task at hand.

At times, treatment may require inpatient hospitalization. Hornstein and Tyson (1991) describe the purpose of hospitalization as protection from abusive families or self-injurious behavior, as a protected environment for difficult abreactive work, and as a way to enlist the family in active treatment while diffusing crises. They describe six steps in inpatient treatment: insuring safety, establishing trust, assisting ego functioning, encouraging communication between alters or split-off parts, integration, and follow-up. Hornstein and Tyson emphasize that in the inpatient setting, all staff who deal with the dissociative youngster are encouraged to take a matter-of-fact, empathic, and accepting approach to the alternate personality presentations. This accepting response in the milieu helps to facilitate integration of the personality and helps break down further the rigid dissociative boundaries the youngsters have constructed.

Whatever techniques are used, the early reported cases suggest that brief childhood treatment can yield positive results (Fagan & McMahon, 1984; Kluft, 1984). However, once the youngster reaches adolescence, the disorder becomes increasingly more resistant to treatment

(Dell & Eisenhower, 1990). The most important factor associated with treatment success for children or adolescents is the availability of consistent parenting during the course of treatment (Silberg & Waters, 1996).

Currently, the field of dissociative disorders in childhood is undergoing a rapid expansion. Within child protective settings, the prevalence of dissociative symptomatology is beginning to be recognized (30% of an outpatient abused cohort; Rodberg, Bagly & Welling, 1990; 73% of a severely traumatized cohort in an emergency diagnostic center; Waterbury, 1991). Within general psychiatric settings, the frequency of dissociative disorders also has recently been recognized (5% of child and adolescent psychiatric inpatients, Hornstein & Tyson, 1991; Silberg, 1991). Current psychiatric interest in childhood dissociation is increasing rapidly as evidenced by the number of books (Peterson, in press; Shirar, 1996; Silberg, 1996c), chapters (Peterson, 1996; Silberg, Stipie, & Taghizadeh, 1996), and articles (Jacobsen, 1995; Putnam et al., 1996) devoted to this topic. Research on posttraumatic stress disorder (PTSD) in childhood has undergone a resurgence as well (Schwarz & Perry, 1994; Terr, 1988). As research in the fields of child abuse, PTSD, and dissociative disorders begins to converge over the next decade, child clinicians should be in a better position to diagnose, treat, and understand dissociative phenomena in children and the developmental course of youngsters with severely traumatic histories.

REFERENCES

Akhtar, S., & Brenner, I. (1979). Differential diagnosis of fugue-like states. *Journal of Clinical Psychiatry, 40,* 381–385.

American Psychiatric Association. (1994). *Diagnostic and statistical manual of mental disorders* (4th ed.). Washington, DC: Author.

American Psychiatric Association. (1987). *Diagnostic and statistical manual of mental disorders* (3rd ed., rev.). Washington, DC: Author.

Dell, D. F., & Eisenhower, J. W. (1990). Adolescent multiple personality disorder: A preliminary study of eleven cases. *Journal of American Academy of Child & Adolescent Psychiatry, 29* (3), 359–366.

Fast, I., & Chetnik, M. (1976). Aspects of depersonalization—derealization in the experience of children. *International Review of Psycho-Analysis, 3,* 483–490.

Fagan, J., & McMahon, P. P. (1984). Incipient multiple

personality in children. *Journal of Nervous and Mental Disease, 172,* 26–36.

Hornstein, N. L., & Putnam, F. W. (1992). Clinical phenomenology of child and adolescent dissociative disorders. *Journal of the American Academy of Child and Adolescent Psychiatry, 31* (6), 1077–1085.

Hornstein, N. L., & Tyson, S. (1991). Inpatient treatment of children with multiple personality/dissociation disorders and their families. *Psychiatric Clinics of North America—MPD, 4* (3), 631–648.

Jacobsen, T. (1995). Case study: Is selective mutism a manifestation of dissociative identity disorder? *Journal of the American Academy of Child and Adolescent Psychiatry, 34,* 863–866.

James, B. (1989). *Treating traumatized children: New insights and creative interventions.* Lexington, MA: Lexington Books.

Keller, R., & Shaywitz, B. A. (1986). Amnesia or fugue state: A diagnostic dilemma. *Journal of Developmental and Behavioral Pediatrics, 7* (2), 131–132.

Kluft, R. P. (1984). MPD in childhood. In B. G. Braun, (Ed.), *Psychiatric Clinics of North America—MPD, 7,* 121–134.

Kluft, R. P. (1985). Childhood multiple personality disorder: Predictors, clinical findings and treatment results. In R. P. Kluft (Ed.), *Childhood antecedents of multiple personality* (pp. 167–196). Washington, DC: American Psychiatric Press.

Malenbaum, R., & Russell, A. T. (1987). Multiple personality disorder in an eleven-year-old boy and his mother. *Journal of the American Academy of Child and Adolescent Psychiatry, 26* (3), 436–439.

McMahon, P. P. & Fagan, J. (1993). Play therapy with children with multiple personality disorder. In R. P. Kluft & C. G. Fine (Eds.), *Clinical perspectives on multiple personality disorder* (pp. 253–276). Washington, DC: American Psychiatric Press.

Nemiah, J. C. (1989). Dissociative disorders, hysterical neurosis; dissociative type. In H. I. Kaplan & B. J. Sadock (Eds.), *Comprehensive textbook of psychiatry* (Vol. 5, pp. 1028–1044). Baltimore: Williams & Wilkins.

Peterson, G. (1991). Children coping with trauma: Diagnosis of "dissociative identity disorder." *Dissociation, 4* (3), 152–164.

Peterson, G. (1996). Early onset. In J. L. Spira (Ed.), *Treating dissociative identity disorder* (pp. 135–173). San Francisco: Jossey-Bass.

Peterson, G. (In press) *Dissociative disorders in youth: A primer.* Washington, DC: American Psychiatric Press.

Peterson, G., & Putnam, F. W. (1993, October). *Dissociative disorder of childhood (DDoC): Field trial results.* Paper presented at the 10th International Conference on Multiple Personality/Dissociative States, Rush Presbyterian—St. Luke's Medical Center, Chicago.

Putnam, F. W. (1991). Dissociative disorders in children and adolescents: A developmental perspective. *Psychiatric Clinics of North America—MPD, 14* 519–531.

Putnam, F. W., Hornstein, N., & Peterson, G. (In press.) Clinical phenomenology of child and adolescent dissociative disorders: Gender and age effects. *Child and Adolescent Psychiatric Clinics of North America, 5.*

Putnam, F. W., Helmers, K., & Trickett, P. K. (1993). Development, reliability, and validity of a child dissociation scale. *Child Abuse and Neglect, 17,* 731–741.

Rodberg, G., Bagly, C. & Welling, D. (1990). *Dissociative disorders and abused children.* Proceedings of the 7th International Conference on Multiple Personality/Dissociative States, Chicago, IL.

Salfield, D. (1958). Depersonalization and altered disturbances in childhood. *Journal of Mental Science, 104,* 472–476.

Schwarz, E. D., & Perry, B. (1994). The post-traumatic response in children and adolescents. *Psychiatric Clinics of North America, 17,* 311–326.

Shimizu, M., & Sakamoto, S. (1986). Depersonalization in early adolescence. *Japanese Journal of Psychiatry and Neurology, 40,* 603–608.

Shirar, L. (1996). *Dissociative children: Bridging the inner and outer worlds.* New York: W. W. Norton.

Silberg, J. L. (1991, November). *Differential diagnosis of dissociative disorders in children.* Paper presented at the 8th International Conference on Multiple Personality/Dissociative States, Rush Presbyterian—St. Luke's Medical Center, Chicago.

Silberg, J. L. (1994, November). *Psychological testing features associated with dissociative diagnoses in children and adolescents.* Paper presented at the 11th International Conference on Multiple Personality/Dissociative States, Rush Presbyterian—St. Luke's Medical Center, Chicago, IL.

Silberg, J. L. (1996a). Psychological testing with dissociative children and adolescents. In J. L. Silberg (Ed.), *The dissociative child: Diagnosis, treatment, and Management.* Baltimore: Sidran Press.

Silberg, J. L. (1996b). Interviewing strategies for assessing dissociative disorders in children and adolescents. In J. L. Silberg (Ed.), *The dissociative child: Diagnosis, treatment, and management.* Baltimore: Sidran Press.

Silberg, J. L. (Ed.) (1996c). *The dissociative child: Diagnosis, treatment and management.* Baltimore: Sidran Press.

Silberg, J. L., Stipic, D., & Taghizadeh, F. (1996). Dissociative disorders in children and adolescents. In J. D. Noshpitz (Ed.), *Handbook of child and adolescent psychiatry.* New York: John Wiley & Sons.

Silberg, J. L., & Waters, F. S. (1996). Factors associated with positive therapeutic outcome. In J. L. Silberg (Ed.), *The dissociative child: Diagnosis, treatment and management.* Baltimore: Sidran Press.

Terr, L. (1988). What happens to early memories of trauma? A study of 20 children under age 5 at the time of documented traumatic events. *Journal of the American Academy of Child and Adolescent Psychiatry, 27* (1), 96–104.

Vincent, M., & Pickering, M. R. (1988). Multiple personality in childhood. *Canadian Journal of Psychiatry, 33,* 524–529.

Waterbury, M. (1991, November). Abuse histories and prior diagnosis in 123 inner-city children with dissociative disorders. Paper presented at the 8th International Conference on Multiple Personality/Dissociative States, Rush Presbyterian—St. Luke's Medical Center, Chicago, IL.

Waters, F. S., & Silberg, J. L. (1996). Promoting integration in dissociative children. In J. L. Silberg (Ed.), *The dissociative child: Diagnosis, treatment and management.* Baltimore: Sidran Press.

Weiss, M., Sutton, P. J., & Utecht, A. J. (1985). Multiple personality in a 10-year-old girl. *Journal of the American Academy of Child Psychiatry, 24* (4), 495–501.

28 / Sleep and Its Disorders in the Grade-School Child

Charles P. Pollak

Normal Sleep

Sleep changes as dramatically throughout life, as the brain from which it arises. While the most rapid changes take place during the neonatal and early childhood periods, a rapid pace of change is maintained through adolescence.

The neonate displays approximately four-hour cycles of feeding, sleep, and wakefulness (Morath, 1974). Sleep accounts for about two thirds of the neonate's existence. Feeding and other social and environmental interactions occur during the remaining waking intervals. In 1953 Aserinsky and Kleitman discovered that the sleep phases were themselves organized into cycles consisting of two components: one in which the infant was behaviorally quiescent and displayed high-voltage, slow electroencephalogram (EEG) waves; and one in which the infant was behaviorally asleep but made rapid, isolated movements of the eyes and face while displaying low-voltage, fast EEG waves resembling those of wakefulness. (See also Aserinsky & Kleitman, 1955.) The cycles of non–rapid eye movement sleep (NREMS) and REM sleep (REMS) last about 50 to 60 minutes and were soon found to be present in changing amounts throughout the human life span.

Starting at birth, the EEG of NREMS becomes progressively more differentiated. Sleep spindles develop during the first few months and high-voltage slow waves develop later in the first year (slow-wave sleep, SWS). Along with the changes in NREMS, a circadian or approximately 24-hour rhythm of sleep can increasingly be discerned and eventually dominates the sleep-waking pattern (Kleitman & Engelmann, 1953; Pollak, 1994).

NREM-REM cycles lengthen to an adult duration of 90 to 110 minutes and acquire a bipolar organization: The early-night cycles are rich in

The bibliographic assistance of Joanne Koven, M.D., is gratefully acknowledged.

SWS, and later cycles contain more REMS (Coble, Kupfer, Reynolds, & Houck, 1987). As NREMS comes to dominate the early part of the sleep period, the infant increasingly "falls into" NREM rather than REM sleep.

Changes in sleep over the latency years (6 to 11 years) of healthy children were studied in the sleep laboratory by Coble et al. (1987). The time spent in bed by the children decreased from 9.7 hours to 8.2 hours, the time spent asleep decreased from 9.1 hours to 7.8 hours, and sleep efficiency (percent of time in bed spent sleeping) remained high (about 95%). Time spent in SWS decreased from 130 minutes (24% of sleep) to 98 minutes (21%). The decrease in SWS is paralleled by a linear decrease in quantitative EEG slow-wave activity, from about 4 to 24 years of age (Feinberg et al., 1990). Measures of the duration and intensity of REMS were more variable among children and showed little or no tendency to decrease.

The outstanding change in sleep during childhood, then, is decreased time spent sleeping, especially time spent in slow-wave sleep. The function of SWS in children is unknown. It may serve to conserve energy, as it does in other small mammals, or it may be an epiphenomenon of evolving cortical activity. Slow (1–3 Hz) waves are most abundant during early childhood when the cortex is developing rapidly, and decrease in parallel with subsequent decreases in cortical metabolic rate, thickness, and synaptic density (Feinberg et al., 1990). The regressive changes may result from "pruning" of underused neural connections (Rakic, Bourgeois, Eckenhoff, Zecevic, & Goldman-Rakic, 1986).

SLEEP NEED

Current theories of sleep regulation include a circadian factor and a homeostatic sleep drive (Borbely, 1982). Homeostatic regulation implies that there is a certain amount (duration) of sleep to which the organism tends to return after a disturbance. This accords with the everyday notion that children "need" a certain amount of sleep and make up for lost sleep by sleeping longer at the first opportunity.

Because of night-to-night variations, many days of observation, including at least one weekend, are needed to determine long-term sleep need. Ideally, sleep need would be quantified electrophysiologically, but cost limits the number of nights that can be recorded. The studies of Coble et al. (1987) mentioned earlier, for example, were limited to 3 consecutive nights, and data from the first night were discarded owing to "first-night effect," which is attributed to the novelty of the laboratory environment. Ambulatory methods for recording sleep in the child's home environment remain technically challenging. Available information on long-term sleep need therefore is based on parental observations and records. Even so, few studies are available. The 18- to 36-month-old children of well-educated parents were observed to sleep 12 hours a day (9 to 11 hours at night plus a 2-hour afternoon nap) (Crowell, Keener, Ginsburg, & Anders, 1987). Six-year-old Swedish children sleep for 9.5 hours (Klackenberg, 1982). Gass and Strauch (reported by Richman, 1987) found that 3- to 6-year-old Swiss children slept 11 hours 40 minutes on average. After starting school at age 7, they retired later and slept less, presumably compensating on weekends or in the daytime, since sleepiness appears to be uncommon in prepubertal children (Carskadon et al., 1980).

A child's sleep need may be estimated by having the family maintain a sleep log that includes an estimate of total nightly sleep for at least 10 days. If the child maintains alert wakefulness in the daytime and does not seem irritable, the average nightly duration of sleep is then the best available estimate of the child's sleep need.

Some children who are assessed by this method will be found to need less sleep than available age norms or oral traditions would predict. In such cases, and especially if the child is bothered by delay in falling asleep or is wakeful later in the night, the scheduled sleep period should be reduced to approximate the calculated mean sleep length; longer bedrest periods may result in delayed onset of sleep or prolonged intervals of nocturnal wakefulness, while shorter bedrest periods may deprive the child of needed sleep. The disorders discussed in this chapter are included in the fourth edition of the *Diagnostic and Statistical Manual of Mental Disorders* (American Psychiatric Association, 1994), and the full range of pediatric sleep disorders is reviewed in a recent textbook (Ferber & Kryger, 1995).

Sleep Disorders of Childhood

GENERAL GUIDELINES FOR EVALUATION

The evaluation of a child with a sleep problem always should begin with a detailed history of the problem. Usually it is important to obtain a description of the child's 24-hour day, including details about the events of the evening, the period around bedtime, and the events that take place during the night. The parents' responses to the behavior are especially important in young children. Family members who observe the child while asleep may provide the crucial observations, for example, of breathing difficulty or abnormal movements. The child's own experience may provide crucial information. It is important, for example, whether dreams can be described in detail and whether the child is amnesic for a dramatic, partial arousal in which he or she screamed or ran out of the room.

In cases of difficulty falling asleep, difficulty maintaining sleep, or daytime sleepiness, the history should be complemented by a log of the child's sleep pattern kept for at least 1 week and preferably 2. Essential information includes: bedrest periods (times into and out of bed), sleep periods (including any daytime naps), medications, and noteworthy events. Graphical logs provide the information in the most easily interpreted format and are available from Metrodesign Associates (90 Clinton Street, Homer, NY 13077; tel. 607-749-4492). In addition to systematizing the parents' observations and the child's experiences, sleep logs provide the parents with some perspective on the problem. Thus, a problem of night waking that seems intolerable at the time it is taking place may be seen to be occasional, limited to certain days of the week, or brief in duration. It is common for parents who call a sleep disorders center in desperation to fail to come in after keeping a log for several weeks.

Sleep logs should make disorders of sleep timing (delayed sleep phase syndrome, inconsistent bedrest schedules) immediately apparent. They are also useful in monitoring the child's response to a treatment regimen.

INDICATIONS FOR REFERRAL TO A SLEEP DISORDERS CENTER

Sleep disorders centers offer expertise in sleep disorders medicine and laboratory facilities for quantitative, physiological assessment during sleep. Many centers can provide guidance on diagnostic and management issues as well as direct case evaluation or management. Sleep laboratory assessment (polysomnography) is essential in suspected cases of sleep apnea, narcolepsy, and nocturnal seizures. Certification of the sleep disorders center and laboratory gives assurance that minimal standards of quality are being met. Further information can be obtained from the Association of Professional Sleep Societies (1610-14th Street Northwest, Suite 300, Rochester, MN 55901).

It is probably fair to say that no child remains entirely free of sleep disturbance. Deciding what constitutes a "disorder" therefore must be somewhat arbitrary. For example, the sharing of a bed by child and parent is more symptomatic of stress in families of higher socioeconomic status (Lozoff, Wolf, & Davis, 1984; Rosenfeld, Wenegrat, Haavik, Wenegrat, & Smith, 1982).

Broadly speaking, sleep disorders can be divided into those that represent disturbances of central nervous function and those that represent conflict between the child, with his or her immature nervous system, and the environment, primarily the family and school (Ferber, 1990). In both cases, the sleep problems are specific to the child's stage of development; thus, disorders of childhood differ from those of both infancy and adolescence, but neither demarcation is sharp.

The most characteristic sleep disorders of childhood are behaviors that are inappropriate to the sleeping state, termed *parasomnias*. They include sleep terrors, sleepwalking, and nocturnal enuresis. Parasomnias arise in childhood and decline or end before adolescence; their course roughly parallels the development and regression of slow-wave sleep and may be a by-product of

that normal maturational process. Many represent partial arousals, in the sense that motor and autonomic functions but not cortical ones are activated.

Insomnias usually are thought of as adult sleep problems, but they occur throughout childhood. Narcolepsy and other disorders that manifest as excessive sleepiness are more characteristic of adolescence but also may be encountered in late childhood and therefore will be discussed herein.

Parasomnias

NIGHT TERRORS AND CONFUSIONAL AROUSALS

Night terrors (pavor nocturnus) superficially resemble nightmares in that sleep is interrupted by a distressful awakening. The child may sit up in bed, scream, and look terrified. Screaming may continue for many minutes. Heart rate sharply increases, and the child may sweat profusely. Characteristically, the child is unresponsive to name calling and even shaking and may recall little when finally awakened in the morning. If the child is able to produce a verbal description, it is usually that of a simple image or emotion—"a monster was after me!"—and detailed description is lacking.

Ferber (1989b) has distinguished confusional arousals (Broughton, 1968) from night terrors by their earlier occurrence in infants and toddlers, absence of a look of terror, and prolonged duration up to 30 to 40 minutes. The child is wide-eyed and is described as more confused-looking than frightened. There is moaning, crying, and thrashing. The child fails to recognize the parents and resists attempts to provide comfort. Autonomic activation occurs and events are associated with slow-wave sleep (Ferber & Boyle, 1983). It seems unlikely that such events represent a distinct disorder; more likely, the mechanism of sleep terror is being expressed in a younger brain.

Night terrors occur in 1 to 3.5% of children ages 3 to 16 years (Beltramini & Hertzig, 1983; Kales et al., 1980; Klackenberg, 1987; Kurth, Gohler, & Knaape, 1965). Typical sleep terror peaks at 5 to 7 years and appears to be rare or nonexistent before age 3 years or after 9. Klackenberg (1987) found that children with night terrors usually develop somnambulism later. Children may bolt from the bed and run dangerously (Ferber, 1989a), but in our experience such combined episodes of terror and sleepwalking are more often described by patients in their late teens or 20s.

Polygraphic sleep recordings show that events arise abruptly from slow-wave sleep during the first 4 hours of sleep and are accompanied by sharp increases of heart and respiratory rate and sweating. EEG slow waves continue to be generated during behavioral and autonomic arousal; the lack of cortical activation explains the inability to respond coherently to people or to recall the events. Such events therefore represent partial, abnormal arousals (Broughton, 1968).

The most remarkable feature of sleep terrors is their dramatic suddenness of onset. Partial episodes consisting of equally sudden but less intense movements and autonomic activation may be recorded in the sleep laboratory during asymptomatic nights. Brief arousals preceded by EEG slow waves occur with greater frequency in children with sleep terror or somnambulism (Halasz, Ujszaszi, & Gadoros, 1985).

The decision to perform polysomnography should depend on the frequency of events and the likelihood that the behaviors represent nocturnal epileptic seizures. Events that occur less than 1 to 3 times a week are so unlikely to occur on the particular nights on which a laboratory recording is performed that the effort and expense might not be worthwhile. The occurrence of partial events on otherwise uneventful nights is helpful but is diagnostically only suggestive, and the absence of evidence of seizure activity is less reassuring if the behavioral events are infrequent. Partial complex seizures are a rare cause of sleep terror–like behavior. If nocturnal episodes are frequent, daytime seizures are also probable and make diagnosis easier. If seizures are rare and exclusively nocturnal, polysomnography nevertheless should be considered, because more numerous, subclinical electrographic or behavioral seizures may be found.

Sleep terrors respond promptly to bedtime benzodiazepines such as lorazepam and diazepam, but suppressing them offers no known benefit to the child, and residual side effects on daytime performance and mood from the medication may develop. Medication therefore should be used only if the sleep terrors have been frequent (for several

weeks or longer) and are highly disturbing to the family. Even children with longstanding or frequent night terrors may have long symptom-free periods, making intermittent pharmacotherapy feasible.

SLEEPWALKING

Sleepwalking (somnambulism) is more common than sleep terror and develops later in childhood. It has been reported in 40% of children ranging from 6 to 16 years and nearly 17% of 12-year-olds, the age of highest prevalence (Klackenberg, 1987). Onset is most often between 4 to 6 years of age, followed by 7 to 10 years (Cirignotta, Zucconi, Mondini, Lenzi, & Lugaresi, 1983). It is rare or nonexistent before age 4 and much less common after age 9. Sleepwalking may be slightly more common in boys. Most children sleepwalk infrequently (much less than once a month), but some walk frequently and over a period of 5 years or longer. Yet their sleep is normal at other times. Many had night terrors or bed-wetting at an earlier age (Klackenberg, 1987).

The behavior of the sleepwalking child varies from a bland event in which the child moves from the bed to another part of the room, to a much more active, even violent, escape from the bed and running without regard to obstacles that may be in the way. There may be partial awareness of the environment, as shown by the child's ability to negotiate turns of hallways and objects strewn on the floor, but the risk of colliding with an object or stumbling on stairs is high. Children have crashed into glass windows and walked out of the house into a street with traffic. Severe injuries have occurred. Autonomic activation is usually less intense than in sleep terrors. Memory for episodes often is absent, but there may be dim recall of the behavior or of the need to escape.

Sleep recordings made during such events have shown continued slow-wave activity while the child is in motion. In this respect, sleepwalking resembles night terror. Polysomnograms of sleepwalkers between episodes differ from those of controls: Hypersynchronous delta EEG waves are increased, there are more interruptions of slow-wave sleep, and more time is spent in SWS (Blatt, Peled, Gadoth, & Lavie, 1991).

Diagnostic considerations include automatisms associated with partial complex seizures, Tourette's disorder (discussed later), REM behavior disorder, and sleep apnea. If a detailed history and examination suggests these possibilities, polysomnography should be carried out. Our clinical experience is that children are referred for evaluation in a sleep disorders center much less often than are patients in their teens or 20s.

Neither sleepwalking nor sleep terror presents risks to the child other than that of injuries resulting from out-of-bed behaviors, but those risks can be high in children who tend to run or whose movements are violent. Glass and sharp objects therefore should be removed from the child's room and adjoining areas of the house. Access to staircases should be limited. If there is a history of violence, it may be safer to have the child sleep alone (Oswald & Evans, 1985).

Sleepwalking may be suppressed with benzodiazepines, such as lorazepam or diazepam. Decisions regarding their use should be based on an assessment of the injury risk and the costs of residual daytime drug effects. A treatment trial may be necessary for a final decision. As with sleep terrors, consideration should be given to intermittent use of medication, because episodes of sleepwalking may cluster in time.

PANIC DISORDER

Panic disorder is increasingly recognized in children, who may present with school phobia and refusal, separation anxiety, depression or somatic symptoms such as abdominal pain, "seizures," or hyperventilation (Alessi & Magen, 1988; Berg, 1967; Black & Robbins, 1990; VanWinter & Stickler, 1984; Vitiello, Behar, Wolson, and McLeer, 1990). Attacks consist of palpitations, weakness, trembling, sense of impending death or insanity, shortness or breath, dizzyness, and others (Garland & Smith, 1991; Vitiello et al., 1990). Attacks may begin as early as 5 years of age (Vitiello et al., 1990). In adults, panic attacks may occur during sleep and have much in common with night terrors and arise from NREMS but not SWS (Hauri, Friedman, & Ravaris, 1989; Lesser, Poland, Holcomb, & Rose, 1985; Mellman & Uhde, 1989). Sleep panic has been noted in children only rarely (Black & Robbins, 1990). However, several cases of combined panic disorder, night terrors, and somnambulism have recently been described in two 10-year-old boys (Garland & Smith, 1991). All symptoms responded to imipramine. Such cases

suggest that panic disorder and the parasomnias may share a common pathogenesis. Sodium lactate infusions, which induce panic in waking panic patients, arouse panic patients when infused during sleep, suggesting that the pathogenesis may include inappropriate activation of brainstem arousal mechanisms (Koenigsberg, Pollak, Fine, & Kakuma, 1992). So far, however, sleep lactate infusions have not induced sleep terror or somnambulism. Further investigations of the relationship between parasomnias and anxiety disorders may shed light on both.

NIGHTMARES

Children who awaken in distress are usually presumed to have had a "bad dream." This can be confirmed only in the verbal child. Dream descriptions that contain much visual imagery, scene shifts, and bizarreness are usually presumed to arise from REM sleep, since such reports often can be elicited from children awakened from REM sleep (Foulkes, 1982). Furthermore, classical nightmares tend to occur during the later hours of sleep, when REM-sleep periods are longer and more filled with eye movements. The distinction between REMS- and SWS-related dreams is by no means absolute, however, as traumatized children may have anxiety dreams in both forms of sleep (Terr, 1981).

Nightmares are very common among the patients of pediatricians and child psychiatrists (41% of 6- to 10-year-olds and 22% of 11-year-olds) and among school children and adolescents in general (9.7%, [Simonds & Parraga, 1982]). Often they are associated with emotional stress, such as parental divorce and the events leading up to it (Mack, 1970). Occasionally nightmares are a sign of past trauma (Terr, 1981, 1983), and they may herald the onset of schizophrenia or other psychotic disorder. Hartmann (1984) has found that adults with lifelong, frequent nightmares are open, trusting, creative types who are vulnerable to mental illness. Nightmares also may develop when REMS-suppressing medications, such as tricylic antidepressants, are withdrawn or, less often, as a toxic drug effect. Fortunately, medications prone to induce nightmares (antihypertensive agents, including beta blockers, and antiparkinsonian drugs) are not used often in children.

Nightmares may be suppressed with REMS-inhibiting drugs such as tricylic antidepressants, but this is rarely appropriate in young children. Instead, attention should be directed toward the probable cause.

REM BEHAVIOR DISORDER

REM behavior disorder is a recently described parasomnia, in which complex, often violent, behavior is enacted during polygraphically confirmed REMS (Schenck, Bundlie, Ettinger, & Mahowald, 1986). Most patients are older men, but abnormal movements during REMS have been described in a 10-year-old girl with a brainstem astrocytoma and her 8-year-old brother (Schenck, Bundlie, Smith, et al., 1986). Diagnosis requires polysomnography, usually for multiple nights. The resulting disruptions of sleep can be controlled with clonazepam, a potent benzodiazepine.

BED-WETTING

Urinary continence is achieved later during sleep than during wakefulness. As in any maturational process, the age at which dryness is achieved varies. An important factor is whether the child's parents were enuretic; if they were, the child is much more likely to be late in achieving continence. Also, because of natural variation in the age at which nocturnal continence is achieved, age-based definitions of pathological bed-wetting (nocturnal enuresis) are somewhat arbitrary. Most authors use the age of 5 to 6, when voluntary control over voiding has become neurologically possible. However, 10 to 18% of children of that age continue to wet at least occasionally (reviewed by Ferber, 1989a). Klackenberg (1987) found that primary enuresis (unbroken history of enuresis from infancy) did not persist beyond age 8. Secondary cases invariably begin before age 7 to 8 and may continue into later childhood. He also found that bed-wetters often become sleepwalkers, as already mentioned, supporting earlier proposals that these parasomnias, as well as night terrors, have a common neurophysiological basis.

Age alone is not a sufficient reason to treat enuresis. Some clinicians choose simply to treat those children for whom (or for whose families) the behavior represents a problem (Nino-Murcia & Keenan, 1987). The urgency of treatment will of course depend on the attitudes of the parents, who may be sensitized by a personal history of the problem, as well as social pressures such as those arising when children wish to sleep at a friend's house or at a summer camp.

Most cases respond to behavioral treatments, and these should be tried first, unless the initial history points to any organic disorders. Behavioral treatments include bladder training exercises to increase functional bladder capacity, exercises to increase the tone of the external urethral sphincter, conditioning of arousal to wetness and ultimately to sensation of bladder fullness, and reinforcement of motivation with rewards. Techniques and treatment programs have been described by several authors (Ferber, 1985; Starfield, 1972). If the response to such measures is limited, if organic disorders have been ruled out of consideration, and if the age of the child or the personal social consequences of bed-wetting are judged to merit it, symptomatic treatment with medications such as imipramine, 10 to 75 mg at bedtime, or intranasal arginine vasopressin (desmopressin, dDAVP) may be considered. Intermittent use of imipramine when the child sleeps away from home can be beneficial and safe (Ferber, 1989a). Medication also can be used for periods of several months to "buy time" until a more permanent remission develops.

Organic disorders are uncommon causes of nocturnal enuresis (Starfield, 1972) but they should be considered, especially if specific symptoms are present. These symptoms include a variety of functional and anatomic disturbances of bladder function requiring urological evaluation, urinary tract infections in girls, diabetes mellitus and diabetes insipidus, allergic disorders, obstructive sleep apnea, nocturnal epilepsy, Tourette's disorder (discussed later), and the effects of dopamine receptor antagonists and sodium valproate (reviewed in Nino-Murcia & Keenan, 1987).

In addition to urological, neurological, and medical evaluations, polysomnography should be performed to detect sleep apnea and nocturnal seizures. Enuresis may be detected easily in the sleep laboratory using a moisture-sensitive signal generator. The sleep stage during which enuresis occurs is of little diagnostic value. Bed-wetting was once grouped with sleep terror and somnambulism as a SWS-related parasomnia, but it has become apparent that enuretic episodes occur during all sleep stages in proportion to their abundance (Kales, Kales, Jacobson, Humphrey, & Soldatos, 1977; Mikkelsen & Rapoport, 1980).

SLEEP TALKING (SOMNILOQUY), HEAD BANGING, TEETH GRINDING (BRUXISM)

The common parasomnias of sleep talking, head banging, and teeth grinding are not specifically associated with slow-wave sleep as are night terrors and sleepwalking. Their frequencies have been ascertained by Klackenberg (1987). Over half of infants younger than 12 months engage in rhythmic movements at bedtime; these are among the earliest "abnormal" behaviors to develop (Klackenberg, 1987). Head banging is a repetitive thrusting of the head into the mattress or headboard. It is rarely epileptiform in origin (Guilleminault & Sylvestri, 1982). Head turning consists of less violent, rhythmic side-to-side movements, which continue to occur in 3% of 8-year-olds. Body rocking is performed on the knees and elbows and may be combined with head banging. These rhythmic movements and others, such as finger sucking and hair twiddling, are often performed by children to help themselves fall asleep (Werry, Carlielle, & Fitzpatrick, 1983). Similar stimulation is provided by maternal rocking. Children also take soft animals, blankets, and many other types of objects to bed to comfort themselves, especially in privileged homes (reviewed by Richman, 1987).

Teeth grinding (nocturnal bruxism) occurs in 4 to 6% of 4- to 5-year-olds and is especially common in children with temper tantrums. Klackenberg (1987) also found that about 8% of 4- to 5-year-olds have been heard to talk in their sleep; often they go on to develop somnambulism one year or more later. Sleep-talking is not associated with a particular sleep stage (Arkin, Antrobus, Baker, & Jackler, 1972).

NOCTURNAL SEIZURES

Epileptiform EEG activity is promoted by sleep, and some epileptic children seize predominantly or even exclusively during the night. The events are often complex in nature and may be mistaken for nonepileptiform sleep disorders. For example, sleepwalking sometimes may be of epi-leptiform origin (Pedley & Guilleminault, 1977), and complex partial seizures of both temporal and frontal origin may be misinterpreted as nightmares (Stores, 1991).

Recognition of nocturnal epilepsy depends on awareness of the possibility, starting with parents' descriptions of nocturnal events. The most suggestive feature is the repetition of stereotypical behaviors, such as nonfunctional posturings of the trunk or extremities. Focal onset is especially valuable but is unlikely to be witnessed by family members, who are alerted by the child's ictal sounds or movements and tend to describe the more dramatic aspects of the events. Laboratory EEG and video recordings can be decisive. The yield of such recordings may be much higher than family observations would suggest, because even numerous partial events go unobserved. Responsiveness to anticonvulsant medications is evidence of the epileptiform nature of abnormal nocturnal behaviors but is not of absolute diagnostic value. The paroxysmal nocturnal dystonia described by Lugaresi, Cirignotta, and Montagna (1986), for example, usually responds well to the anticonvulsant carbamazepine but has not been associated conclusively with epileptiform EEG activity.

Insomnias

Insomnia—difficulty falling or staying sleep—is not rare during childhood (Richman, 1987). The common sleep problems from birth to 3 years are resisting going to bed, settling down to sleep, and night waking (Richman, 1981). Such problems may continue into early childhood. Many young toddlers (21%) wake at night, and older ones (24 to 29 months) more often take over 30 minutes to fall asleep (14%) (Crowell, Keener, Ginsburg, & Anders, 1987). Problems increase even more at later ages, reaching 26% in 3-year-olds (Earls, 1980). Difficulty falling sleep has been reported for 28.5% of 6- to 10-year-olds (Salzarulo & Chevalier, 1983), and 10 to 23% of 10- to 13-year-olds (Bearpark & Michie, 1987; Morrison, McGee, & Stanton, 1992). Over one third of 10- 13-year-olds reported waking at least once a night (Anders, Carskadon, Dement, & Harvey, 1978).

Problems in falling asleep are associated with

"positive" parental responses (holding the child until it falls asleep, cosleeping) (Ungerer, Sigman, Beckwith, Cohen, & Parmake, 1983), and recent evidence suggests that such difficulty in children is associated with insecure attachment in their mothers (Benoit, Zeanah, Boucher, & Minde, 1992). Large numbers of children from 4 to 12 years of age have fears at night of which the parents are unaware (reviewed by Richman, 1987). For example, children may fear sleep because they confuse it with death (Connell, Persley, & Sturgess, 1987). Sleep-phobic children who are at a developmental age (10 to 11 years) when the universality of death is being confronted may refuse to lie in their own beds, may refuse to allow others to sleep while they are awake, and often can be put to bed only after they have fallen asleep in their daytime clothing. Anxiety dreams are common. Such children have separation anxiety resulting from early separation trauma, and a recent death often precipitates phobic avoidance of sleep. Brief psychotherapy focused on clarifying the concept of death is often effective.

AFFECTIVE DISORDERS

Several surveys have associated sleep difficulty with family problems and depression (Richman, 1981) and with disturbances of mood (depression, anxiety, tension), inattention, and disorders of conduct (Marks & Monroe, 1976; Morrison et al., 1992; Price, Coates, Thoresen, & Grinstead, 1978). A wide variety of sleep problems are reported to occur with greater frequency among psychiatric outpatients (Simonds & Parraga, 1984).

Depressed adolescents complain of sleep difficulty, just as depressed adults do (Puig-Antich, 1980; Puig-Antich et al., 1982; Ryan, 1987), but they are less likely to display the changes in sleep architecture that are associated with major depression in adults. These abnormalities include disturbances of sleep initiation and maintenance, including a tendency to awaken too early. The interval from sleep onset to the first REM sleep period is often short, the first REM period may be long, and slow-wave sleep tends to be delayed from the first sleep cycle to the second. The sleep of depressed adolescents, by contrast, does not differ from that of matched nondepressed controls in any of these respects, as shown by at least three independent investigators (Kupfer, Coble,

Kane, Petti, & Conners, 1979; Puig-Antich, 1980; Young, Knowles, MacLean, Boag, & McConville, 1982). Depressed children whose sleep does differ from that of controls tend to be more severely depressed (Dahl et al., 1991) and are more likely to be suicidal or inpatients (Dahl et al., 1990; Emslie, Rush, Weinberg, Rintelmann, & Roffwarg, 1990; Robbins & Alessi, 1985).

The failure to find objective correlates of the subjective complaints has been explained by limited sensitivity of current sleep recording techniques or by maturational factors that protect the sleep of children and mask the abnormalities (Dahl et al., 1990). Surprisingly, only one objective sleep abnormality, early-morning awakening, could be explained by the combined effect of depression and age from 15 to 64 years (Mendelson, Garnett, & Gillin, 1981). An intriguing characteristic of the sleep of young depressives is that it can be extended almost twice as long as that of nondepressed controls (Hawkins, Taub, & Van de Castle, 1985).

DELAYED SLEEP PHASE SYNDROME

A child or adolescent who complains of difficulty falling asleep but little difficulty staying asleep should be suspected of having the delayed sleep phase syndrome (Weitzman et al., 1981). This syndrome is probably the most common cause of chronic difficulty initiating sleep in young people. The condition can be viewed as a discrepancy between the hours of the 24-hour day when sleep is biologically possible and the hours at which it is socially necessary. Delays in falling asleep are explained by bedtimes that are biologically too early. Similarly, the desired times of waking may occur before sleep has run its course, leading to difficulty getting up on time to get to school or work. The child may struggle with the family member appointed to get him or her out of bed in the morning, and tardiness and absenteeism from school are common.

Although the underlying mechanism of delayed sleep phase syndrome is not yet understood, the relative lateness of the biological "window" during which sleep is possible is consistent with the finding of time-isolation studies that the biological clock governing sleep and other rhythms in normal people runs slow in terms of solar time. This can be seen from the progressive delay of sleep periods chosen by subjects on the basis of endogenous signals rather than knowledge or time or schedules. The mean period of sleep and other biological rhythms usually lies between 24.0 and 25.0 hours (Weaver, 1979). As a result, a "tug" is exerted on the usual, 24-hour daily routine, to which normal people often "give in" on weekends and vacations, as seen by their tendency to go to bed and arise later than during the working week. The delayed sleep phase syndrome can be viewed as an exaggeration of this tendency, with social and psychological consequences. To summarize, this syndrome can be understood as an inability to oppose the tendency of sleep to become progressively more delayed. It has not been determined whether the tendency to delay is increased.

Experience has shown that patients with delayed sleep phase syndrome are able to *delay* the period of sleep by several hours per day, making it possible to treat the disorder by delaying the sleep period until the sleep coincides with a target schedule. A patient who falls asleep between 3:00 and 5:00 A.M. and arises after 12:00 noon, for example, is first instructed to follow a regular schedule for several days. The schedule should meet two requirements: It should correspond to the usual hours of sleep; and it should provide enough time to meet the age-appropriate daily sleep quota, but not more time than is needed. In the example, the schedule might be to sleep from 4:30 A.M. to 12:30 P.M. Compliance with the schedule is demonstrated by having the patient complete a sleep log each morning. When it has been determined that the patient is able to comply with a regular sleep schedule, the sleep period is delayed by 3 hours a day. In the example, starting on Friday night, the sleep period is delayed to 7:30 A.M. to 3:30 P.M.; on Saturday, 10:30 A.M. to 6:30 P.M.; . . . ; on the following Wednesday, 10:30 P.M. to 6:30 A.M. The final, target schedule is decided in advance by striking a compromise between the desire to socialize or do homework in the evening and the need to arrive at school on time in the morning. Once the target schedule has been attained, the sleep schedule must not be allowed to vary by more than about 1 hour; otherwise, the sleep period may again become "trapped" at a late hour, and the series of schedule delays may need to be repeated.

Some adolescents are unable to conform to any regular sleep schedule, even if it is tailored to their most frequent hours of sleep. In such cases, major psychiatric problems are often present.

OTHER TYPES OF INSOMNIA

Several psychiatric disorders not yet mentioned may be associated with severe sleeplessness in children. They include incipient schizophrenia in teenagers (Easson, 1979), mania (Dahl et al., 1990), and psychosocial dwarfism (Wolff & Money, 1973).

Several neurological disorders also should be considered. Tourette's disorder starts around 7 years of age (Jankovic & Rohaidy, 1987) with motor and vocal tics. Tics also can be detected during all stages of sleep, and most patients report that their sleep is disturbed (Comings & Comings, 1987; Jankovic & Rohaidy, 1987). Tourette's disorder also may be associated with sleep terrors, sleepwalking, and bed-wetting (Barabas, Matthews, & Ferrari, 1984; Comings & Comings, 1987). Attention deficit disorder often is associated with Tourette's and may itself be associated with a variety of sleep problems (Simonds & Parraga, 1984). Sleep disturbances are also more common among epileptics, partly as an effect of the central nervous disorder, partly the effect of the drugs chronically used to control seizures (Dadmehr, Congbalay, Pakalnis, & Drake, 1987). Boys with Duchenne muscular dystropy awaken frequently at night; surprisingly, this is not because of respiratory insufficiency (Redding, Okamoto, Guthrie, Rollevson, & Milstein, 1985). The same is true of the Prader-Willi syndrome (Vela-Bueno et al., 1984). Sleep disturbances associated with characteristic polysomnographic features develop in dystonia musculorum deformans (Jankel, Niedermeyer, Graf, & Kalsher, 1984).

Additional considerations include narcolepsy, which often is associated with discontinuity of nocturnal sleep; and sleep apnea, which may present with insomnia if the apnea-induced arousals last long enough to result in full wakefulness and memory of the event. Sleepiness is the usual presenting sleep problem in these disorders but occasionally may be overshadowed by sleep disturbance.

Finally, in evaluating insomnia, the use of stimulant drugs, including caffeine, must be considered. Based on body weight, children may consume as much caffeine in cola drinks, which contain about 20 milligrams of caffeine per 12 ounces, as adults do in coffee (Snyder & Sklar, 1984).

The Sleepy Child

Children are normally never sleepy before bedtime, a fact that attests to the overwhelming influence of the circadian timing system on sleep and wakefulness by the time the child is 1 to 2 years of age and especially after afternoon naps have been given up at around age 5. Daytime sleepiness may develop, however, if the circadian organization of sleep and wakefulness is impaired or lost, as in narcolepsy, or if the child has been deprived of nighttime sleep. Sleep loss may occur if the sleep schedule is irregular or has been shifted (as in east-west travel), if a disease process interferes with the continuity or depth of sleep, or if sleep has been deliberately prevented.

Sleepiness means an impairment of the ability to remain awake in the daytime. It should not be confused with tiredness or with changes in activity level, which may reflect muscular fatigue, depression, or medical illness.

The prevalence of sleepiness among young children is not known. It appears to increase markedly during adolescence, when 25% report needing more sleep than they previously had (Carskadon et al., 1980; Morrison, McGeer, & Stanton, 1992).

Sleepiness occasionally may be manifested by automatic behavior, in which the child may behave in a confused, disorganized fashion and speak incoherently or about matters irrelevant to those at hand. The state is not altogether different from sleepwalking. Unlike that state, however, EEG recordings show brief episodes of light sleep (Guilleminault, Billiard, Montplaisir, & Dement, 1975). If automatic behavior cannot be dispelled by sleeping, absence or complex partial status epilepticus should be considered (Stores, 1991).

Nocturnal epilepsy can result in sleepiness because of repeated disturbances of sleep, and sedating anticonvulsant drugs also may induce sleepiness (Collaborative Group, 1986).

A complete medical history should be taken on the sleepy child. About one third of children with Epstein-Barr viral infection, presenting as infectious mononucleosis or Guillain-Barre syndrome, go on to have chronic sleepiness, which may last for years (Guilleminault & Mondini, 1986).

Finally, it should be kept firmly in mind that sleepiness is the most predictable consequence of sleep deprivation. This is illustrated by the following case.

CASE EXAMPLE

A 14-year-old boy presented with a history of mononucleosis at age 12 followed by unremitting daytime sleepiness that was threatening his school performance. The sleepiness had failed to improve with increasing doses of dextroamphetamine prescribed, under family pressure, by a pediatrician who referred him for presumed narcolepsy. The boy was found not to have the specific symptoms of narcolepsy or of any other medical or neurological disorder that might explain pathological sleepiness. He was asked to keep a sleep log, which showed that he was spending only 7 hours a night in bed. This was explained by his drive to be successful in school. He was active in several sports and was taking a heavy course load that required him to stay up late to study. He was instructed to increase the period of bedrest to 8 hours and eventually to 8.5 hours. The result was that sleepiness disappeared over the next 2 to 3 weeks. Dextroamphetamine was withdrawn without any ill effects, and he remains a highly successful student.

SLEEP APNEA SYNDROMES

Sleep apnea syndromes are the most readily diagnosed, dangerous, and treatable sleep disorders. In these syndromes, breathing during sleep either ceases or becomes too shallow to maintain normal levels of oxygen and carbon dioxide. Typically, a sleep-associated loss of respiratory drive is followed after a few seconds by partial or complete closure of the naso- and oropharyngeal airway (Weitzman et al., 1978), making efforts to breathe ineffective. As a result of abnormal blood gases and activation of thoracic stretch receptors, the child awakens, takes a few breaths, and returns to sleep within seconds. Such cycles of apnea and compensatory hyperpnea typically last 15 to 20 seconds and are accompanied by cycles of bradycardia and tachycardia. Sleep is interrupted as often as apneic cycles occur, which may be hundreds of times a night. As a result, both the organization and continuity of sleep are profoundly disrupted, resulting in severe daytime sleepiness.

If the obstructive element is prominent, the child may struggle to breathe during the night, thrashing about in bed or sitting up or sleeping on all fours to lessen the obstruction. Loud snoring and vocalizations may be heard as each obstructive cycle ends in an explosive intake of breath.

The most common cause of obstructive sleep apnea in children is enlargement of the lymphoid tissues of the pharynx. If adenoidal enlargement is prominent, the child may breathe with open mouth with the tongue partially protruded, and he or she appears dull. As sleepiness develops, intelligence and school performance may indeed become impaired, and growth and development lags (Kravath & Pollak, 1976). In severe cases, right heart disease develops because of hypoxia-induced, nocturnal pulmonary hypertension. A child suspected of obstructive sleep apnea should be referred immediately for definitive diagnosis and treatment. Tonsillectomy/adenoidectomy is usually curative. Nonsurgical treatments for obstructive sleep apnea are also available, with nasal positive airway pressure machines being the safest and most effective.

Children also may be predisposed to nocturnal airway obstruction by craniofacial malformations that displace the tongue posteriorly or compromise the nasopharyngeal airway. Surgery to correct incomplete closure of the nasopharynx during speech and swallowing has led to the death of children during sleep (Kravath, Pollak, Borowiecki, & Weitzman, 1980).

Despite the seriousness of severe sleep apnea, nonobstructive respiratory pauses lasting more than 5 seconds are common in children and usually require no treatment (Carskadon et al., 1978).

Sleep also may be disturbed by asthma or by obstructive pulmonary disorders, such as cystic fibrosis, which decrease nocturnal oxygen saturation and tidal volume, especially during REMS, but are not prominently associated with sleep apnea (reviewed by Gaultier, 1987). Asthmatic children awaken frequently and may experience shortness of breath during the night and become sleep deprived (Kales et al., 1970). Desaturation may be corrected with nocturnal oxygen therapy, and theophylline can reduce both apneas and desaturation episodes (Avital et al., 1991).

Treatment decisions should be based on an accurate diagnosis, which requires monitoring of the breathing pattern for an entire night. Physiological measures should include airflow, respiratory effort (thoracic/abdominal movements), arterial oxygen saturation, end-tidal carbon dioxide, and electrocardiogram.

NARCOLEPSY

Narcolepsy usually presents as an abnormal tendency to sleep in the daytime. Typically, the problem comes to notice when a high school student is observed to be sleepy in the classroom or repeatedly falls asleep. Confronted with the behavior, the child is at a loss to explain it, since the sleepiness is present even after a full and normal night's sleep. Schoolwork suffers, and the child may lose rapport with teachers if they interpret sleepiness as a sign of irresponsible sleep habits or lack of interest in school work. Such behavior is often called "laziness" by parents and others, and the child may accept the characterization. Visits to the doctor may be of little avail, as unusual viral or metabolic illnesses are more likely to be considered than the more common causes of sleepiness covered in this chapter.

Within weeks, months, or years, the child experiences sudden weakness of some part of the body, usually the knees, or the whole body when laughing or expressing another emotion, usually anger. Such episodes of *cataplexy* may be profuse and dramatic during the early years of the illness but usually moderate with age. In some case, the lessening of cataplexy is explained by the child's development of strategies to avoid expressing laughter and other prepotent emotions. The long-term effects of this on personality development are unknown, and treatment of cataplexy with 25 milligrams imipramine should be considered. Imipramine has a nearly immediate and strong preventive action in most cases. It may be given three to four times a day if cataplexy is frequent; otherwise, the child may be instructed to carry a few tablets to take in situations in which emotions that trigger cataplexy are anticipated.

Additional symptoms of narcolepsy may develop. Sleep paralysis is the brief, total loss of muscle strength as the child is falling asleep or waking up. This is often frightening to children, especially if associated with hypnogogic hallucinations, which are usually visual. Most frightening are hallucinations of a stranger in the house, to which the child is unable to respond by moving or by calling out. Automatic behavior often is associated with narcolepsy, occurring when an affected child is struggling to stay awake.

Finally, while patients with narcolepsy do not describe themselves as insomniac, nighttime sleep usually is interrupted by multiple, brief awakenings. The presence of both daytime sleep episodes and nighttime awakenings has suggested that the control of the sleep-wake cycle may be weak (Kripke, 1976). This concept is supported by the finding that adult narcoleptics who have been isolated from time cues in a special laboratory and sleep in accordance with their own inner sense of time do not obtain more sleep than normal controls, even when naps are included. The daytime sleep tendency therefore represents the need to sleep at abnormally short intervals more than any increased need for sleep (Pollak, Moline, & Wagner, 1987).

An important advance was the discovery that narcoleptics usually enter REMS soon after falling asleep ("sleep-onset REM period"; Dement, Rechtschaffen, & Gulevich, 1966). Not only is this observation diagnostically useful, but it helps to understand the symptoms of narcolepsy as misplaced components of normal REM sleep. REM sleep is itself a constellation of neurophysiological components, including activated cerebral cortex and dreaming; bursts of rapid, conjugate eye movements; atonic skeletal musculature; and changes in multiple autonomic functions. The episodes of cataplexy and sleep paralysis have the same neurophysiological basis as REM atonia. Hypnogogic hallucinations appear to be homologous to dreams during REMS.

The diagnosis of narcolepsy rests on the presence of certain symptoms: the daily need for one or more naps, despite adequate nocturnal sleep, and cataplexy, even if mild or rare. Additional symptoms (sleep paralysis, hypnogogic hallucinations, nocturnal awakenings) are not decisive. Obstructive sleep apnea should be ruled out when snoring or other symptoms are reported and before further diagnostic consideration is given to narcolepsy. The diagnosis of narcolepsy may be established by the Multiple Sleep Latency Test (Mitler et al., 1979). A series of four or five nap opportunities are presented at 2-hour intervals in the sleep laboratory. Onset of sleep within 5 minutes on average is evidence of pathological sleep tendency, and multiple rapid entries into REM sleep are diagnostic of narcolepsy if sleep apnea and other causes of sleep disruption such as shift-work are not a consideration.

Nearly all (99%) of the known cases of narcolepsy are associated with certain serotonin serotypes (DR2 and DQ1; Juji, Satake, Honda, & Doi, 1984; Langdon, Welsh, van Dam, Vaughan, & Parker, 1984; Mignot et al., 1994). Since these are present in about 15% of nonnarcoleptic American Caucasians, however, HLA testing is useful only to rule out the diagnosis of narcolepsy. This is important in children who are sleepy but do not display other symptoms of narcolepsy and seem more likely to be sleepy for other reasons, especially if the parents or child have been inappropriately led to believe narcolepsy is responsible. Accurate diagnosis is vital, because narcolepsy is a lifelong disorder that will almost certainly require long-term treatment with stimulant drugs, several of which are controlled substances.

Once the diagnosis of narcolepsy has been established, the success of long-term management will depend on initial counseling of both the child and family. Goals of counseling include:

1. Explaining the syndrome of narcolepsy, its expected effects on everyday life, its prognosis, and its management.

2. Convincing the patient to accept the presence of a lifelong disorder, without inducing a sense of despair or hopelessness.

3. Encouraging napping once or several times a day, preferably at scheduled times to preempt involuntary sleep episodes. This may be life-saving in adolescents who drive.

4. Initiating a medication regime of stimulant medication for nearly all patients, because regular napping is an unrealistic goal for many and because a few naps a day may not eliminate all sleepiness. A reasonable and well-tolerated regimen is 18.75 to 75.0 milligrams pemoline in the morning. This may be supplemented by 5 milligrams methylphenidate or 5 milligrams dextroamphetamine, once or twice in late morning or early afternoon.

5. Setting appropriate educational and occupational goals. Higher education is not precluded if

symptoms can be controlled adequately by medication and scheduled naps.

KLEINE-LEVIN SYNDROME

The Kleine-Levin syndrome is a rare but highly distinctive disorder of sleep and eating (Critchley, 1962; Smolik & Roth, 1988). Often after a viral illness, an adolescent boy begins to spend long periods sleeping, awakening at long intervals to urinate and to eat voraciously. While awake, he may be sexually aggressive, autistic, mute, socially regressed, or mentally slow and confused. After two to four weeks, the episode ends, and the boy returns to his old self. Several months later, another episode occurs, and so on with diminishing severity for several years, until the disorder fades out without further consequences.

In addition to the classical form of the disorder found in pubertal boys, variant hypersomnia/hyperphagia syndromes have been described in girls. Diagnostic considerations typically include encephalitis, brain tumor, recurrent depression, bipolar disorder, schizophrenia, and drug abuse. Most cases underwent extensive testing before the true diagnosis became apparent. EEG abnormalities have been demonstrated during episodes. Neurologic examination, EEG, cerebrospinal fluid examination and computed tomography or magnetic resonance imaging scans of the brain are typically normal between episodes. Postmortem material has suggested an abnormality of brainstem serotonergic mechanisms (Koerber et al., 1984). The etiology is unknown. Increasing clinical evidence links Kleine-Levin syndrome with cyclical affective disorders (Cawthron, 1990).

Summary

It should come as no surprise that sleep changes as the brain matures. REM sleep is abundant during the early postnatal period and is partly replaced by NREM sleep as the latter becomes progressively more differentiated. The resulting REM-NREM sleep cycles progressively lengthen and modulate into a circadian sleep-wake rhythm. Later in childhood, the duration of slow-wave sleep decreases and, with it, sleep as a whole. A wide spectrum of sleep disorders may develop as these maturational changes take place.

Parasomnias are behaviors and experiences inappropriate to sleep. They may be horrific for the child (nightmares) or parents (sleep terrors), or they may be dangerous (sleepwalking) or embarrassing (bed-wetting). While they respond well to medication, they eventually regress in most cases.

Insomnia often points to an underlying affective disorder or other primary psychiatric disorder. Pure difficulty initiating sleep may be largely explained by anomalous timekeeping by the biological clock.

Chronic sleepiness develops when the continuity of sleep is repeatedly broken (sleep apnea) or when the circadian organization of sleep and wakefulness is partially lost (narcolepsy).

Specialty consultation and laboratory services for the disorders discussed in this chapter are available from a growing number of sleep disorders centers.

REFERENCES

Alessi, N. E., & Magen, J. (1988). Panic disorder in psychiatrically hospitalized children. *American Journal of Psychiatry, 145,* 1450–1452.

American Psychiatric Association. (1994). *Diagnostic and statistical manual of mental disorders (4th ed.).* Washington, DC: Author.

Anders, T. F., Carskadon, N. A., Dement, W. C., & Harvey, K. (1978). Sleep habits of children and the identification of pathologically sleepy children. *Child Psychiatry and Human Development, 9,* 56–62.

Arkin, M. A., Antrobus, J. S., Baker, J., & Jackler, F. (1972). A comparison of the content of mentation reports elicited after nonrapid eye movement associated sleep utterance and WREN "silent" sleep. *Journal of Nervous and Mental Disease, 155,* 427–435.

Aserinsky, E., Kleitman, N. (1953). Regularly occurring periods of eye motility and concomitant phenomena during sleep. *Science, 118,* 273–274.

Aserinsky, E., & Kleitman, N. (1955). A motility cycle in sleeping infants as manifested by ocular and gross bodily activity. *Journal of Applied Physiology, 8,* 11–18.

Avital, A., Steljes, D. G., Pasterkamp, H., Kryger, M., Sanchez, I., & Chernick, J. (1991). Sleep quality in asthmatic children treated with theophylline or sodium cromoglycate. *Journal of Pediatrics, 119,* 979–984.

Barabas, C., Matthews, V. S., & Ferrari, M. (1984). Disorders of arousal in Gilles de la Tourette's syndrome. *Neurology, 34,* 815–817.

Bearpark, H. M., & Michie, P. T. (1987). Prevalence of sleep/wake disturbances in Sydney adolescents. *Sleep Research, 16,* 304.

Beltramini, A. V., & Hertzig, N. E. (1983). Sleep and bedtime behavior in preschool-aged children. *Pediatrics, 71,* 153–158.

Benoit, D., Zeanah, C. H., Boucher, C., & Minde, K. K. (1992). Sleep disorders in early childhood: Association with insecure maternal attachment. *Journal of the American Academy of Child and Adolescent Psychiatry, 31,* 86–93.

Berg, I. (1967). School phobia in children of agoraphobic women. *British Journal of Psychiatry, 128,* 86–89.

Black, B. & Robbins, D. R. (1990). "Panic disorder in children and adolescents." *Journal of the American Academy of Child and Adolescent Psychiatry, 29,* 36–44.

Blatt, I., Peled, R., Gadoth, N., & Lavie, P. (1991). The value of sleep recording in evaluating somnambulism in young adults. *Electroencephalography and Clinical Neurophysiology, 78,* 407–412.

Borbely, M. (1982). A two-process model of sleep regulation. *Human Neurobiology, 1,* 195–204.

Broughton, R. (1968). Sleep disorders: Disorders of arousal? *Science, 159,* pp. 1070–1078.

Carskadon, M. A., Harvey, K., Dement, W. C., Guilleminault, C., Simmons, F. B., & Anders, T. F. (1978). Respiration during sleep in children. *Western Journal of Medicine, 128,* 477–481.

Carskadon, M. A., Harvey, K., Duke, P., Anders, T. F., Litt, I. F., & Dement, W. C. (1980). Pubertal changes in daytime sleepiness. *Sleep, 2,* 453–460.

Cawthron, P. (1990). A disorder unique to adolescence? The Kleine-Levin syndrome. *Journal of Adolescence, 13,* 401–406.

Cirignotta, F., Zucconi, N., Mondini, S., Lenzi, P. L., & Lugaresi, E. (1983). Enuresis, sleep walking and nightmares: An epidemiological survey in the Republic of San Marino. In B. Lugaresi (Ed.), *Sleep/ wake disorders: Natural history, epidemiology and long-term evolution* (pp. 237–241). New York: Raven Press.

Coble, P. A., Kupfer, D. J., Reynolds, C. F., & Houck, P. (1987). EEC sleep of healthy children 6 to 12 years of age. In C. Guilleminault (Ed.), *Sleep and its disorders in children* (pp. 29–41). New York: Raven Press.

Collaborative Group for Epidemiology of Epilepsy. (1986). Adverse reactions to antiepileptic drugs: A multicenter survey of clinical practice. *Epilepsia, 27,* 323–330.

Comings, D. E., & Comings, B. C. (1987). A controlled study of Tourette syndrome. VI. Early development, sleep problems, allergies, and handedness. *American Journal of Human Genetics, 41,* 822–838.

Connell, H. M., Persley, G. V., & Sturgess, J. L. (1987). Sleep phobia in middle childhood—a review of six cases. *Journal of the American Academy of Child and Adolescent Psychiatry, 26,* 449–452.

Critchley, N. (1962). Periodic hypersomnia and megaphagia in adolescent males. *Brain, 85,* 627–657.

Crowell, J., Keener, M., Ginsburg, N., & Anders, T. (1987). Sleep habits in toddlers 18 to 36 months old. *Journal of the American Academy of Child and Adolescent Psychiatry, 26,* 510–515.

Dadmehr, N., Congbalay, D. R., Pakalnis, A., & Drake, N. E. (1987). Sleep and waking disturbances in epilepsy. *Clinical Electroencephalography, 18,* 136–141.

Dahl, R. E., Puig-Antich, J., Ryan, N. D., Nelson, B., Dachille, S., Cunningham, S. L., Trubnick, L., & Klepper, T. P. (1990). EEG sleep in adolescents with major depression: The role of suicidality and inpatient status. *Journal of Affective Disorders, 19,* 63–75.

Dahl, R. E., Ryan, N. D., Birmaher, B., Al-Shabbout, M., Williamson, D. E., Neidig, M., Nelson, B., & Puig-Antich, J. (1991). Electroencephalographic sleep measures in prepubertal depression. *Psychiatry Research, 38,* 201–214.

Dement, W., Rechtschaffen, A., & Gulevich, G. (1966). The nature of the narcoleptic sleep attack. *Neurology* (Minneapolis), *16,* 18–33.

Easson, W. M. (1979). The early manifestations of adolescent thought disorder. *Journal of Clinical Psychiatry, 40,* 469–475.

Earls, F. (1980). Prevalence of behavior problems in three year old children. *Archives of General Psychiatry, 37,* 1153–1157.

Emslie, C. J., Rush, A. J., Weinberg, W. A., Rintelmann, J. W., & Roffwarg, H. P. (1990). Children with major depression show reduced rapid eye movement latencies. *Archives of General Psychiatry, 47,* 119–124.

Feinberg, T., March, J. D., Flach, K., Maloney, T., Chern, W. J., & Travis, F. (1990). Maturational changes in amplitude, incidence and cyclic pattern of the 0 to 3 hz (delta) electroencephalogram of human sleep. *Brain Dysfunction, 3,* 183–192.

Ferber, R. (1985). *Solve Your Child's Sleep Problems.* New York: Simon and Schuster.

Ferber, R. (1989a). Sleep-associated enuresis in the child. In W. C. Dement (Ed.), *Principles and practice of sleep medicine* (pp. 643–647). Philadelphia: W. B. Saunders.

Ferber, R. (1989b). Sleepwalking, confusional arousals, and sleep terrors in the child. In W. C. Dement (Ed.), *Principles and practice of sleep medicine* (pp. 640–642). Philadelphia: W. B. Saunders.

Ferber, R. (1990). Sleep schedule-dependent causes of insomnia and sleepiness in middle childhood and adolescence. *Pediatrician, 17,* 13–20.

Ferber, R., & Boyle, M. P. (1983). Confusional arousals in infants and toddlers (not quite pavor nocturnus). *Sleep Research, 12,* 241.

Ferber, R., & Kryger, M. 1995. *Principles and Practice of Sleep Medicine in the Child.* Philadelphia: W. B. Saunders.

Foulkes, D. (1982). *Children's dreams: Longitudinal studies.* New York: John Wiley & Sons.

Garland, E. J., & Smith, D. H. (1991). Simultaneous prepubertal onset of panic disorder, night terrors, and somnambulism. *Journal of the American Academy of Child and Adolescent Psychiatry, 30,* 553–555.

Gaultier, C. (1987). Respiration during sleep in children with chronic obstructive pulmonary disease and asthma. In C. Guilleminault (Ed.), *Sleep and its disorders in children* (pp. 225–229). New York: Raven Press.

Guilleminault, C., Billiard, N., Nontplaisir, I., & Dement, W. C. (1975). Altered states of consciousness in disorders of daytime sleepiness. *Journal of Neurological Science, 26,* 377–393.

Guilleminault, C., & Mondini, S. (1986). Mononucleosis and chronic daytime sleepiness. A long-term follow-up study. *Archives of Internal Medicine, 146,* 1333–1335.

Guilleminault, C., & Sylvestri, R. (1982). Disorders of arousal and epilepsy during sleep. In P. Passouant (Ed.), *Sleep and epilepsy* (pp. 513–531). New York: Academic Press, 1982.

Halasz, P., Ujszaszi, J., & Gadoros, J. (1985). Are microarousals preceded by electroencephalographic slow wave synchronization precursors of confusional awakenings? *Sleep, 8,* 213–218.

Hartmann, E. (1984). *The nightmare: The psychology and biology of terrifying dreams.* New York: Basic Books.

Hauri, P., Friedman, M., & Ravaris, C. L. (1989). Sleep in patients with spontaneous panic attacks. *Sleep, 12,* 323–337.

Hawkins, D. R., Taub, I. N., & Van de Castle, R. L. (1985). Extended sleep (hypersomnia) in young depressed patients. *American Journal of Psychiatry, 142,* 905–910.

Jankel, W. R., Niedermeyer, E., Craf, N., & Kalsher, N. (1984). Polysomnography of torsion dystonia. *Archives of Neurology, 41,* 1081–1083.

Jankovic, J., & Rohaidy, H. (1987). Motor, behavioral and pharmacologic findings in Tourette's syndrome. *Canadian Journal of Neurological Science, 14,* 541–546.

Juji, T., Satake, M., Honda, Y., & Doi, Y. (1984). HLA antigens in Japanese patients with narcolepsy. All the patients were DR2 positive. *Tissue Antigens, 24,* 316–319.

Kales, A., Kales, J. D., Jacobson, A., Humphrey, F. J., & Soldatos, C. R. (1977). Effects of imipramine on enuretic frequency and sleep states. *Pediatrics, 60,* 431–436.

Kales, A., Kales, J. D., Sly, R. M., Scharg, M. B., Tan, T., & Preston, T. A. (1970). Sleep pattern of asthmatic children: All-night electroencephalographic studies. *Journal of Allergy, 46,* 301–308.

Kales, A., Soldatos, C. R., Bixler, E. O., Ladda, R. L., Charney, D. S., Weber, G., & Schweitzer, P. K. (1980). Hereditary factors in sleepwalking and night terrors. *British Journal of Psychiatry, 137,* 111–118.

Klackenberg, G. (1982). Sleep behavior studied longitudinally: Data from 4–16 years on duration, night awakening and bedtime. *Acta Paediatrica Scandinavica,* 501–596.

Klackenberg, C. (1987). Incidence of parasomnias in children in a general population. In C. Guilleminault (Ed.), *Sleep and its disorders in children* (pp. 99–113). New York: Raven Press.

Kleitman, N., & Engelmann, T. G. (1953). Sleep characteristics of infants. *Journal of Applied Physiology, 6,* 269–282.

Koenigsberg, H. W., Pollak, C. P., Fine, J., & Kakuma, T. (1992). Lactate sensitivity in sleeping panic disorder patients. *Biological Psychiatry, 32,* 539–542.

Koerber, R. K., Torkelson, R., Haven, G., Donaldson, J., Cohen, S. M., & Case, M. (1984). Increased cerebrospinal fluid S-hydroxytryptamine and 5-hydroxyindoleacetic acid in Kleine-Levin syndrome. *Neurology, 34,* 1597–1600.

Kravath, R. E., & Pollak, C. P. (1976). Lymphoid obstruction of the airway in children: A threat to sleep, breath and life. *Pediatric Research, 10,* 462.

Kravath, R., Pollak, C., Borowiecki, B., & Weitzman, E. D. (1980). Obstructive sleep apnea and death associated with surgical correction of velopharyngeal incompetence. *Journal of Pediatrics, 96,* 645–648.

Kripke, D. (1976). Biological rhythm disturbances might cause narcolepsy. In C. Guilleminault, W. C. Dement, & P. Passouant (Eds.), *Narcolepsy. Advances in sleep research, Vol. 3* (pp. 475–483). New York: Spectrum Publications.

Kupfer, D. J., Coble, P., Kane, J., Petti, T., & Conners, C. K. (1979). Imipramine and EEG sleep in children with depressive symptoms. *Psychopharmacology, 60,* 117–123.

Kurth, V. E., Gohier, I., & Knaape, H. H. (1965). Untersuchungen uber der pavor nocturnus bei kindern. *Psychiatry, Neurology, and Medical Psychology, 17,* 1–7.

Langdon, N., Welsh, K. I., van Dam, M., Vaughan, R. W., & Parkes, D. (1984). Genetic markers in narcolepsy. *Lancet, 2,* 1178–1180.

Lesser, I. M., Poland, R. E., Holcomb, C., & Rose, D. E. (1995). Electroencephalographic study of nighttime panic attacks. *Journal of Nervous and Mental Disease, 173,* 744–746.

Lozoff, B., Wolf, A. W., & Davis, N. S. (1984). Co-sleeping in families with young children. *Pediatrics, 74,* 171–182.

Lugaresi, E., Cirignotta, F., & Montagna, P. (1986). Nocturnal paroxysmal dystonia. *Journal of Neurology, Neurosurgery and Psychiatry, 49,* 375–380.

Mack, J. E. (1970). *Nightmares and the human conflict.* Boston: Little, Brown.

Marks, P. A., & Monroe, U. (1976). Correlates of adolescent poor sleepers. *Journal of Abnormal Psychology, 85,* 243–246.

Mellman, T. A., & Uhde, T. W., (1989). Sleep panic attacks: New clinical findings and theoretical implications. *American Journal of Psychiatry, 146,* 1204–1207.

Mendelson, W. B., Garnett, D., & Gillin, J. C. (1981).

Single case study. Flurazepam-induced sleep apnea syndrome in a patient with insomnia and mild sleep-related respiratory changes. *Journal of Nervous and Mental Disorders, 169,* 261–264.

Mignot, E., Lin, X., Arrigoni, J., Macaubas, C., Olive, F., Hallmayer, J., Underhill, P., Guilleminault, C., Dement, W. C., & Grumet, F. C. (1994). DQBI°0602 and DQA1°0102 (DQ1) are better markers than DR2 for narcolepsy in Caucasian and black Americans. *Sleep, 17,* S60–S67.

Mikkelsen, E. J., & Rapoport, J. L. (1980). Enuresis and sleep. *Urologic Clinics of North America, 7,* 361–377.

Mitler, M. M., van den Hoed, J., Carskadon, M. A., Richardson, G., Park, R., Guilleminault, C., & Dement, W. C. (1979). REM sleep episodes during the multiple sleep latency test in narcoleptic patients. *Electroencephalography and Clinical Neurophysiology, 46,* 479–481.

Morath, M. (1974). The four-hour feeding rhythm of the baby as a free-running endogenously regulated rhythm. *International Journal of Chronobiology, 2,* 39–45.

Morrison, D. N., McGee, R., & Stanton, W. R. (1992). Sleep problems in adolescence. *Journal of the American Academy of Child and Adolescent Psychiatry, 31,* 94–99.

Nino-Murcia, C., & Keenan, S. A. (1987). Enuresis and sleep. In C. Guilleminault (Ed.), *Sleep and its disorders in children* (pp. 253–267). New York: Raven Press.

Oswald, I., and Evans, J. (1985). On serious violence during sleep walking. *British Journal of Psychiatry, 147,* 688–691.

Pedley, T. A., & Guilleminault, C. (1977). Episodic nocturnal wanderings responsive to anticonvulsant drug therapy. *Annals of Neurology, 2,* 30–35.

Pollak, C. P. (1994). Regulation and sleep rate and circadian consolidation of sleep and wakefulness in an infant. *Sleep, 17,* 567–575.

Pollak, C. P., Moline, M. L., & Wagner, D. R. (1987). Sleep times in narcoleptic subjects isolated from time cues. Fifth International Congress of Sleep Research. *Sleep Research, 16,* 406 (Copenhagen, Denmark).

Price, V. A., Coates, T. J., Thoresen, C. E., & Grinstead, O. A. (1978). Prevalence and correlates of poor sleep among adolescents. *American Journal of Diseases of Children, 132,* 583–586.

Puig-Antich, J. (1980). Affective disorders in childhood. A review and perspective. *Psychiatric Clinics of North America, 3,* 403–424.

Puig-Antich, J., Goetz, R., Hanlon, C., Tabrizi, M. A., Davies, H., & Weitzman, B. (1982). Sleep architecture and REM sleep measures in prepubertal major depressives during an episode. *Archives of General Psychiatry, 39,* 932–939.

Rakic, P., Bourgeois, J.-P., Eckenhoff, M. F., Zecevic, N., & Goldman-Rakic, P. S. (1986). Concurrent overproduction of synapses in diverse regions of the primate cerebral cortex. *Science, 232,* 232–235.

Redding, S. I., Okamoto, G. A., Guthrie, R. D.,

Rollevson, D., & Nustein, J. M. (1985). Sleep patterns in nonambulatory boys with Duchenne muscular dystropy. *Archives of Physical and Medical Rehabilitation, 66,* 818–821.

Richman, N. (1981). A community survey of characteristics of one to two year olds with sleep disruptions. *Journal of the American Academy of Child and Adolescent Psychiatry, 20,* 281–291.

Richman, N. (1987). Surveys of sleep disorders in children in a general population. In C. Guilleminault (Ed.), *Sleep and its disorders in children* (pp. 115–127). New York: Raven Press.

Robbins, D. R., & Alessi, N. E. Depressive symptoms and suicidal behavior in adolescents. *American Journal of Psychiatry, 142,* 588–592.

Rosenfeld, A. A., Wenegrat, A. O., Haavik, D. K., Wenegrat, B. C., & Smith, C. R. (1982). Sleeping patterns in upper-middle-class families when the child awakens ill or frightened. *Archives of General Psychiatry, 39,* 943–947.

Ryan, N. R. (1987). The clinical picture of depression in children and adolescents. *Archives of General Psychiatry, 44,* 854–861.

Salzarulo, P., & Chevalier, A. (1983). Sleep problems in children and their relationship with early disturbances in waking-sleeping rhythms. *Sleep, 6,* 45–51.

Schenck, C. H., Bundlie, S. R., Ettinger, M. C., & Mahowald, M. W. (1986). Chronic behavioral disorders of human REM sleep: A new category of parasomnia. *Sleep, 9,* 293–308.

Schenck, C. H., Bundlie, S. R., Smith, S. A., Ettinger, M. G., & Mahowald, M. W. (1986). REM behavior disorder in a 10 year old girl and aperiodic REM and NREM sleep movements in an 8 year old brother. *Sleep Research, 15,* 162.

Simonds, J. F., & Parraga, H. (1982). Prevalence of sleep disorders and sleep behaviors in children and adolescents. *Journal of the American Academy of Child Psychiatry, 21(4),* 383–388.

Simonds, J. F., & Parraga, H. (1984). Sleep behaviors and disorders in children and adolescents evaluated at psychiatric clinics. *Journal of Developmental and Behavioral Pediatrics, 5,* 6–10.

Smolik, P., & Roth, B. (1988). Kleine-Levin syndrome. Etiopathogenesis and treatment. *Acta Univsitatis Carolinae Medica, 128.*

Snyder, S. H., & Skiar, P. (1984). Behavioral and molecular actions of caffeine: Focus on adenosine. *Journal of Psychiatric Research, 18,* 91–106.

Starfield, B. (1972). Enuresis: Its pathogenesis and management. *Clinical Pediatrics, 11,* 343–350.

Stores, G. (1991). Confusions concerning sleep disorders and the epilepsies in children and adolescents. *British Journal of Psychiatry, 158,* 1–7.

Terr, L. (1981). Psychic trauma in children: Observations following the Chowchilla school-bus kidnapping. *American Journal of Psychiatry, 138,* 14–19.

Terr, L. (1983). Life attitudes, dreams, and psychic trauma in a group of "normal" children. *Journal of the American Academy of Child Psychiatry, 22,* 221–230.

Ungerer, J. A., Sigman, M., Beckwith, L., Cohen, S.

E., & Parmalee, A. H. (1983). Sleep behavior of pre-term children at three years of age. *Developmental Medicine & Child Neurology, 25,* 297–304.

VanWinter, J. T., & Stickler, G. B. (1984). Panic attack syndrome. *Journal of Pediatrics, 105,* 661–665.

Vela-Bueno, A., Kales, A., Soldatos, C. R., Dobladez-Blanco, B., Campos-Castello, J., Espino-Hurtado, P., & Olivan-Palacios, J. (1984). Sleep in the Prader-Willi syndrome. Clinical and polygraphic findings. *Archives of Neurology, 41,* 294–296.

Vitiello, B., Behar, D., Wolson, S., & McLeer, S. V. (1990). Diagnosis of panic disorder in prepubertal children. *Journal of the American Academy of Child Adolescent Psychiatry, 29,* 782–784.

Weitzman, E. D., Czeisler, C. A., Coleman, R. N., Spielman, A. J., Zimmerman, J. C., Dement, W., Richardson, C., & Pollak, C. P. (1981). Delayed sleep phase syndrome: A chronobiologic disorder associated with sleep onset insomnia. *Archives of General Psychiatry, 38,* 737–746.

Weitzman, E. D., Pollak, C. P., Borowiecki, B., Burack,

B., Shprintzen, R., & Rakoff, S. (1978). The hyper-somnia-sleep apnea syndrome: Site and mechanism of upper airway obstruction. In C. Guilleminault (Ed.), *Sleep apnea syndromes* (pp. 235–246). New York: Alan R. Liss.

Werry, J. S., Carlielle, J., & Fitzpatrick, B. A. (1983). Rhythmic motor activities (stereotypies) in children under five: Etiology and prevalence. *Journal of the American Academy of Child Psychiatry, 22,* 329–336.

Wever, R. A. (1979). *The circadian system of man: Results of experiments under temporal isolation.* New York: Springer-Verlag.

Wolff, C., & Money, I. (1973). Relationship between sleep and growth in patients with reversible somato-tropin deficiency (psychosocial dwarfism). *Psychological Medicine, 3,* 18–27.

Young, W., Knowles, J. B., MacLean, A. W., Boag, L., & McConville, B. J. (1982). The sleep of childhood depressives: Comparison with age-matched controls. *Biological Psychiatry, 17,* 1163–1168.

29 / Obsessive Compulsive Disorder

Henrietta L. Leonard, Susan E. Swedo, Albert John Allen, and Judith L. Rapoport

Introduction

Increased attention in the past decade has demonstrated that obsessive compulsive disorder (OCD) in children and adolescents is not uncommon. However, historical references are limited to single-case reports or small series of pediatric patients. Janet first described a 5-year-old with obsessive compulsive behavior in 1903, writing: "no reassuring satisfies: the patient must be forever verifying his honesty, cleanliness, sanity, perceptions, and what he did last." He likened obsessions to "mental tics"; thus one was conscious of their existence but had lost voluntary control over these thoughts. In 1935 Kanner reported that some children suffering from OCD had "constricted" premorbid personalities and had been raised with an "overdose of parental perfectionism" (Kanner, 1962).

Others have noted both similarities and differ-

ences between the pediatric and adult OCD patients. In 1942 Berman described four cases of obsessive compulsive disorder and noted the similarity of the content of their obsessions (sexual thoughts, counting, fear harm coming to others, and doubts) to that seen in adults. Despert's (1955) work presented 68 cases and noted that the OCD children were distinguishable from psychotic children and were acutely aware of the abnormality of their thoughts.

Anna Freud made the distinction between obsessive compulsive phenomena and the "pre-ego" repetitions of young children. "Even well defined obsessional symptoms, such as bedtime ceremonials or counting compulsions, are found in children with otherwise uncontrolled, restless, impulsive personalities . . ." (A. Freud, 1965, p. 151). Judd's (1965) report of 5 cases noted normal premorbid behavior and no obviously intrusive or strict parents. Adams's (1973) book described 49 obsessive compulsive children and reported that precipitating events were not common and that boys were more likely than girls to be afflicted.

Early estimates of the prevalence of pediatric OCD ranged from 0.2 to 1.2% and were based on psychiatric clinic patient samples (Berman, 1942; Hollingsworth, Tanguay, Grossman, & Pabst, 1980; Judd, 1965). In the only general-population survey of children, Rutter, Tizard, and Whitmore (1970) found a 0.3% prevalence among over 2,000 10- and 11-year-olds on the Isle of Wight. Flament et al.'s (1988) epidemiological survey estimated OCD rates of 1% (current) and 1.9% (lifetime) in adolescents (when weighted to reflect sampling design).

Clinical Presentation

PHENOMENOLOGY

Obsessive compulsive disorder is defined in the fourth edition of the *Diagnostic and Statistical Manual of Mental Disorders* (*DSM-IV*; American Psychiatric Association, 1994) by the presence of obsessions (recurrent and persistent ideas) and/ or rituals (repetitive, purposeful, and intentional behaviors that are performed in response to an obsession) that cause marked distress, are time-consuming, or significantly interfere in the person's life. In adults, the person recognizes his or her behavior as excessive or unreasonable. However, young children may not identify their thoughts or behaviors as such, and this difference was acknowledged and integrated into *DSM-IV* (APA, 1994). Compulsive eating, drinking, gambling, shopping, or sexual behavior are not considered to be part of this disorder.

Over 100 children and adolescents with severe primary OCD have been evaluated at the National Institute for Mental Health (NIMH), and they provide a large clinical data base to help to understand this unusual disorder. Seventy consecutive cases have been described in detail (Swedo, Rapoport, Leonard, Lenane, & Cheslow, 1989). These 47 boys and 23 girls had a mean age of onset of 10 years of age; 7 of the patients had had the onset of their OCD prior to the age of 7 years. In general, boys had a prepubertal onset of obsessive compulsive (OC) symptoms (mean age 9), while girls had their onset around puberty (mean age 11 years). The male:female ratio changed with age, with the earliest age of onset having the greatest male predominance.

Interestingly, the clinical symptoms manifested in childhood OCD are virtually identical to those seen in adults (Rapoport, 1986). In the NIMH sample, the most common rituals were excessive washing (85%), repeating (51%), checking (46%), touching (20%), counting (18%), ordering/arranging (17%), and hoarding (11%). The most common obsessions were concerns of germs or contaminants (40%), fears that harm would come to self or others (24%), scrupulosity (excessive religiosity or scrutiny of one's thoughts or actions) (13%), or forbidden thoughts (4%). Counting and mental ordering/arranging also was reported. A similar presentation has been reported by others (Riddle et al., 1990; Thomsen & Mikkelsen, 1991). The illness is typically characterized by a waxing and waning course, sometimes exacerbated by some psychosocial stress. It was not unusual for children to hide their rituals, and often parents do not become aware of the behaviors until children can no longer conceal them.

Typically, multiple obsessions and compulsions were present at any one time (Rettew et al., 1992). In 90% of the cases, the symptoms changed over time, although no clear pattern of specific symptom progression over time could be found. "Pure obsessives" were rare, but "pure ritualizers" were fairly common. In particular, some very young boys either denied the presence of accompanying obsessions or had difficulty labeling the precipitant for the ritualized behavior. This might be explained by their level of cognitive development, such that they may be unable to develop an abstract explanation for why they carry out their driven and seemingly bizarre behavior.

Those attempting to hide their illness, and the less severely ill patients, often are difficult to recognize. One might be suspicious of an OCD diagnosis if parents report the child spends excessive unproductive hours on homework, repeatedly erases (to the point of holes in the paper), retraces over letters and words, or rereads lines and paragraphs such that it becomes difficult to complete any assignment. Other clues might include: large water and utility bills from excessive showering or clothes washing, toilets plugged with toilet paper, red and chapped hands, being unable to tolerate others coming into one's room or touching one's things, and avoidance of certain activities or places for unknown reasons.

DEVELOPMENTAL RITUALS

Clearly, normal developmental rituals of childhood must be distinguished from the compulsions of OCD. Around age 2½, some ritualistic behavior becomes evident in most children. Young children want things done "just so," and elaborate bedtime rituals are the rule (Gesell, Ames, & Ilg, 1974). Such ritualistic behavior, such as ordering, arranging, and bedtime rituals, can be understood in terms of anxiety about separation and developmental issues of mastery and control. In general, developmental rituals are usually gone by age 8 or 9 (Van Amerongen, 1980) and are replaced by collecting, hobbies, and "focused interests." Typically, the content of the OCD ritual does not resemble that of the developmental ritual, or it occurs at an inappropriately late age (e.g., bedtime rituals in a 3-year-old are expected, but when present in a 14-year-old may indicate OCD). However, parents of OCD children recall significantly more "marked" patterns of early ritualistic behavior than do parents of normal controls (Leonard, Goldberger, Rapoport, Cheslow, & Swedo, 1990). This could be an artifact of recall, and prospective studies are necessary.

PSYCHODYNAMIC FORMULATION

Obsessive compulsive neurosis, well described in the 1909 publication of the case of the "Rat Man" by Sigmund Freud (1909/1955), has received a great refocus of attention in the last decade. Psychoanalytic theory suggests that the specific OC symptom has meaning, stemming from an unconscious dynamic conflict. The obsessional adult might utilize defenses of reaction formation, intellectualization, isolation of affect, undoing, and magical thinking in order to control his or her thoughts (Esman, 1989). The ritual would prevent experiencing of uncomfortable or forbidden feelings. Freud's works do not make a clear distinction between what is now known as the obsessive compulsive personality (OCP) and the disorder (OCD). Early descriptions of obsessional defenses might best describe those of the OCP individual.

It is even more difficult to delineate clearly such a dynamic formulation for children, as they are struggling with developmental issues of separation/individuation and trying to master and control their environment. Despite some uniqueness of each child's symptoms, the behaviors do fall into the relatively few categories, as previously described (e.g., washing, checking, counting, etc.). Interestingly, they are consistent across cultures in the world.

CASE EXAMPLES

Contamination Fears and Washing: K.W., age 8, was brought to the National Institute of Mental Health (NIMH) by his parents after 2 years of excessive hand washing. He would spend four hours or more per day washing and rewashing his hands, which caused him to be late to school and to stay up late at night. K.W.'s hands were chapped and bleeding from the washing, and he would not allow any lotion to be put on his hands for fear of "contamination." He walked around with his hands up in the air in a "surgeon's position" for fear of contacting anything dirty. He was no longer able to touch doorknobs, flush toilets, touch anyone else, or play with his dog or in any contact sports. K.W. responded to clomipramine (at 3 milligrams [mg] per kilogram [kg]) and not desipramine during the NIMH double-blind study with a dramatic decrease (85%) in his washing and avoidance rituals. K.W. was maintained on clomipramine for 1½ years and spent only 20 minutes per day washing his hands. Although traces of the rituals remained, they did not interfere in his life (e.g., he could play with his dog). When the patient's clomipramine was blindly substituted with desipramine, he relapsed within three weeks and was returned to his maintenance clomipramine dosage.

Repetition: J.R., age 17, would have to retrace his steps from the car into the house in a very elaborate and specific manner (two steps forward, look to the sky, three steps backward, glance to the left and think a good thought). It took 20 minutes to go a distance that normally should have taken seconds. His complex ritual made him the object of neighborhood curiosity. If interrupted or prevented from completing his elaborate walking ritual, he became enraged and inconsolable. J.R. had a good response (70%) to clomipramine but not desipramine during the NIMH double-blind study, such that he completely stopped his repeating rituals. Although he acknowledged still having the thought to do so, he was able to resist them with little effort. J.R. was maintained on clomipramine (at 3 mg per kg per day) and developed tachycardia (without any other electrocardiographic changes) and orthostatic hypotension. When his dosage was dropped (to 2 mg per kg per day) and 1,000 mg per day of L-tryptophan was added to augment the clomipramine, the tachycardia resolved, but he was unable to maintain his clinical response. (Of note, L-tryptophan is no longer used as an augmenting agent for OCD.) J.R. was switched to fluoxetine, 60 mg per day, and had an excellent response without side effects.

Scrupulosity: W.S. is a 17-year-old boy who prayed about four hours per day. Although he came from a very religious family, they became quite concerned about what they perceived as excessive prayer. W.S. would ruminate over past deeds for hours, tortuously reviewing them and wondering if he had done something wrong. He began to go to confession three times per day seeking forgiveness for imagined misdeeds and would repeatedly ask his parents if he had done anything wrong and if he were going to hell. Although W.S. experienced a decrease in symptomatology on clomipramine, he chose not to continue on the medication, for he was not distressed enough by his praying to want it treated.

Somatic Preoccupation: A recent presentation of OCD is the preoccupying fear that one might have AIDS. K.T., a 17-year-old girl, believed that she had contracted AIDS from having touched a sterile, packaged syringe on the ground at a carnival. This conviction that she had AIDS later transformed into fearing that she had herpes and rabies. K.T. was able to totally lose her obsession about AIDS on clomipramine (3 mg per kg per day) after 4 weeks of treatment. She remained on clomipramine maintenance for 6 months. When the medication was discontinued, her symptoms did not return. She has been symptom-free for 2 years now.

Etiology

Biological data have implicated neurophysiologic, neuroanatomic, neuroimmunological, and genetic factors in the etiology of OCD. The "serotonin hypothesis of OCD" has been primarily based on controlled treatment trials, which have shown the specificity and efficacy of the serotonin reuptake inhibitors (clomipramine, fluoxetine, sertraline, fluvoxamine) (Goodman et al., 1990). Speculations that dopaminergic disregulation may also be involved (Swedo & Rapoport, 1990; Goodman et al., 1990) are based on the association of OCD and Tourette's disorder (Pauls, Towbin, Leckman, Zahner, & Cohen, 1986), and the use of dopamine blocking agents (haloperidol) as an augmenting agent in the treatment of OCD (McDougle et al.,

1994). However, cerebrospinal fluid studies have had inconsistent results, suggesting that it is far more complicated than simply the disregulation of two neurotransmitters. An adult study found no difference in the 5-hydroxyindoleacetic acid (5-HIAA) (serotonin metabolite) between OCD patients and normal controls, although it correlated with treatment response (Thoren et al., 1980). In the only studies of cerebrospinal fluid in pediatric OCD patients, pretreatment 5-HIAA was higher than that of disruptive behavior control children (Kruesi et al., 1990) and correlated with 3 of 7 measures of improvement following 5 weeks of clomipramine treatment (Swedo et al., 1992), supporting a role for serotonergic disregulation.

Hormonal disregulation also may play a role in the etiology of OCD. Boys are more likely to have a prepubertal onset of OCD than are girls, and many patients report an exacerbation of their symptoms at puberty (Swedo, Rapoport, et al., 1989). In a large epidemiologic study, the 11 OCD boys were shorter than both the normal and psychiatric controls and had a flatter growth pattern, thus suggesting the possibility of a subtle neuroendocrine dysfunction in OCD (Hamburger, Swedo, Whitaker, Davies, & Rapoport, 1989). These observations coupled with reports of changes in OCD symptoms during pregnancy and the postpartum period suggest that further study is necessary to understand the role that hormones may play.

Evidence suggesting a frontal lobe–basal ganglia abnormality is supported by the comorbidity of OCD in basal ganglia illnesses and by findings from brain imaging studies. There is an increased rate of OCD in several illnesses of the basal ganglia; specifically, Tourette's disorder (Pauls et al., 1986), postencephalitic Parkinson's disease (von Economo, 1931), and Huntington's chorea (Cummings & Cunningham, 1992). In brain imaging studies, Luxenberg et al. (1988) found smaller caudate volumes on computerized tomography (CT) scans in 10 male adults with childhood-onset OCD when compared to controls. Swedo, Schapiro, et al. (1989) reported orbital frontal regional hypermetabolism and alterations in the left anterior cingulate in adults with childhood-onset OCD.

The most interesting work in the field of pediatric OCD concerns the recent evidence that tics and/or OCD may be mediated via autoimmune mechanisms, and suggests that assessment and treatment would be very different from what was previously thought (Swedo, 1994; Swedo, Leonard, & Kiessling; 1994; Swedo et al., 1993). An increased incidence of OCD in pediatric patients with Sydenham's chorea, an autoimmune inflammation of the basal ganglia triggered by Group A beta-hemolytic streptococcal (GABHS) infection, suggests that Sydenham's chorea may be a medical model for OCD (Swedo et al., 1993). Conversely, some patients with tics and/or OCD experience a dramatic onset or a dramatic exacerbation after GABHS infection, which is hypothesized to be due to a similar underlying pathophysiology as that seen with Sydenham's chorea (Allen, Leonard, & Swedo, 1995; Swedo et al., 1993, 1994). Thus, in any child with abrupt onset or dramatic exacerbation of symptoms, a careful medical history concerning any bacterial or viral illnesses should be obtained, as well as inquiry into a family history of autoimmune illnesses, including rheumatic fever and Sydenham's chorea. Ongoing systematic work at the NIMH is studying whether immunomodulatory therapy and/or antibiotic prophylaxis is effective and necessary for these children.

Observations of some specific obsessive compulsive symptoms (washing, picking, evening, licking, and hair-pulling), coupled with data from animal models, have led to a hypothesis that OCD may be a "grooming behavior gone awry" (Swedo, 1989). The most compelling of these grooming behaviors, trichotillomania (the act of pulling out one's own hair), is considered part of the "OCD spectrum disorders." Trichotillomania patients report an overwhelming urge to carry out the behavior, and the pulling responds to clomipramine therapy (Swedo, Leonard, et al., 1989). The relationship of the "spectrum disorders" to OCD remains controversial at this time.

GENETIC STUDIES

Systematic studies have concluded that there is a genetic component for many patients with OCD. Lenane, Swedo, Leonard, Pauls, and Rapaport (1990) reported that 20% of the parents (9% of mothers and 25% of fathers) of pediatric OCD probands met criteria for a lifetime diagnosis of OCD. The dissimilarity between the primary

OCD symptom of the child and that of his or her parent suggested that a modeling/learning hypothesis did not account for this familial transmission. Riddle et al. (1990) reported a similar result; 71% of 21 childhood OCD patients had a parent with either OCD (19%) or OC symptoms (52%).

Several lines of evidence have reported a relationship between OCD and Tourette's disorder (and less severe tic disorders). There is an increased rate of tics in OCD probands (Swedo, Rapaport, et al., 1989; Riddle et al., 1990; Leonard et al., 1992) and, conversely, a high rate of OCD in Tourette's patients (Pauls, Raymond, Stevenson, & Leckman, 1991). Pauls and colleagues (1986, 1991) reported an increased rate of OCD in the first-degree relatives of Tourette's probands over that of the control sample of adoptee relatives, regardless of whether the Tourette's proband had OCD or not. These family study results, in addition to the observed increased association of the two disorders in Tourette's and OCD probands, have led Pauls and colleagues (1986) to hypothesize that some forms of OCD may represent alternative expressions of the gene(s) responsible for Tourette's. Initially, transmission had been proposed to be an autosomal dominant model with variable penetrance and sex-influenced specificity; however, that is still under investigation. Despite this compelling relationship between the two disorders, however, it is still unknown what proportion of OCD probands have a genetic vulnerability and which environmental and/or psychosocial factors may precipitate or exacerbate the illness.

NEUROLOGICAL AND NEUROPSYCHOLOGICAL FINDINGS

In general, the majority of the pediatric OCD probands do not have gross or clinically impairing neurological or neuropsychological abnormalities. Typically, pediatric OCD probands had a full-scale IQ in the average to high-average range (Keller, 1989). In general, the OCD children's performance on neuropsychological measures was close to those of controls; however, on a select subset of tests, there were increased errors (Cox, Fedio, & Rapoport, 1989). Errors on the Sylus Maze, Money's Road Map, and Wisconsin Card Sort were felt to be consistent with frontal lobe and/or caudate lesions (Cox et al., 1989), although conclusions cannot be drawn without larger studies.

On stressed neurological examination of 54 pediatric OCD patients, over 80% (44) had some positive "soft" neurological finding. There were 8 individuals with left hemisyndrome, 13 cases of neurodevelopmental "immaturity," and 18 cases of choreiform syndrome (Denckla, 1989). This high rate of "soft signs" is generally consistent with that reported in the adult literature (Hollander et al., 1990). The subtle neurological findings on stressed neurological examination and on neuropsychological testing are suggestive of underlying abnormalities and merit further study.

Differential Diagnosis

The differential diagnosis of OCD most commonly includes depressive and/or anxiety disorders with obsessional features. The ruminations of major depression typically would have a different content than that characteristically seen in OCD. Theoretically, the anxiety from separation anxiety and from overanxious and generalized anxiety disorder might resemble that of OCD, if the principal fear happened to be fear of harm coming to self or others. The distinction between OCD and phobias would be made based on the specific content of the fear (e.g., snakes). Phobics are usually not symptomatic when away from the feared object, while typically an OCD patient will still worry. Rarely, psychosis may be comorbid with OCD. If the obsessions or compulsions are particularly bizarre, yet they are seen by the patient as reasonable, a comorbid diagnosis of psychosis might be considered.

Stereotypies seen in those with mental retardation, pervasive developmental disorder, and autism may resemble OCD rituals in that they are repetitive ritualized behaviors. Although little is known about the cognitive process behind these actions, typically it has been assumed that stereotypies are not associated with an obsession. Interestingly, stereotypies may also respond to the serotonin reuptake inhibitor clomipramine, as do the rituals of OCD (Gordon, Rapoport, Ham-

burger, State, & Mannheim, 1992). This raises interesting theoretical questions about their possibly similar underlying pathophysiology.

The ritualized eating and exercise patterns of anorexics, as well as the inconstant preoccupation with food and calories, may resemble those of OCD patients. However, they typically deny any distress or that there is any problem at all. In contrast, the bulimic patient (usually female) may recognize that her binging and purging behaviors are abnormal but feel compelled to perform them. The compulsive nature of these symptoms and the increased incidence of a history of anorexia in adult OCD patients (Kasvikis, Tsakiris, & Marke, 1986) suggest a relationship between these disorders that invites further investigation.

As OCD and tic disorders frequently are associated, it is important to attempt to distinguish between rituals and tics, as each has different treatments. Rituals are distinguished from motor tics in that they are purposeful, intentional, and in response to a cognition, for example, "I may be kidnapped if I don't do things in threes." Motor tics, although they can be complex and many dispel an "urge" or tension, are not typically initiated by a thought or accompanied by anxiety. Touching, tapping, spitting, and licking behaviors may be either a compulsive ritual or a motor tic depending on their character and the accompanying cognition. Occasionally classifying the behavior is problematic; interesting new data suggest that patients may have a premonitory sensory feeling preceding the tic (Leckman, Walker, & Cohen, 1993).

Morbidity

IMPACT ON CHILDREN

By *DSM-IV* definition (APA, 1994), the obsessions and compulsions of OCD must cause marked distress, be time-consuming, or significantly interfere in the person's functioning. Children feel compelled to carry out their ritual despite the fact that it may be senseless. Younger children may not recognize the irrationality of their worries, a fact that has been acknowledged in the diagnostic criteria in *DSM-IV*. Certainly, our experience with over 100 children with OCD has confirmed that young children may not recognize their thoughts as senseless.

OCD children often become withdrawn and isolated, feel overwhelmed by distressing obsessions, and/or fear that they are losing their mind. Typically, although they had normal peer relationships prior to the illness, OCD children may avoid friends and activities directly because of the content of their obsessions (i.e., fearing contamination) or indirectly because they are preoccupied with carrying out their rituals. Patterns of play may be altered; some sports and games may be given up, because children can no longer do them because of obsessions and compulsions. At ages where crucial developmental stages shape character structure, self-esteem, and level of intimacy in relationships, these children frequently are isolated from peers and their families, thus putting them at great risk of not successfully mastering these important tasks.

The time-consuming rituals may prevent children from participating in their peer activities and scholastic responsibilities. Children observed with raw and chapped hands from overwashing or retracing steps around the schoolyard may be perceived as unusual and people to be avoided. Many children and adolescents have had to give up their normal activities (i.e., quit the swim team because the pool has become contaminated, quit football because one would get dirty, or stop going to school to avoid using public bathrooms). One patient was forced to carry every book around with him at school in order to avoid using his locker, which required endless rechecking. Other children with previously outstanding school performance found themselves unable to complete tests and homework because they had to reread lines, retrace over letters, or erase repeatedly to make it all "right."

IMPACT ON THE FAMILY

Families quickly feel a significant impact of the OCD rituals: Children wake parents up in the middle of the night to go recheck the doors, toilets are plugged up from excessive paper, utility bills skyrocket from excessive showering and clothes washing, families can not leave on a trip because the child has to keep rechecking things, or the child attempts to pull the family into repeated praying and confessing or seeks reassurance for

his or her doubts. At first, the parents wonder why their child is behaving so strangely. Even when the illness is diagnosed, many parents cannot understand why their child just can't stop the behavior (Lenane, 1989). Relatives may underestimate the problem and impose their own ideas and suggestions on the family.

Not being drawn into participating in the rituals presents a major difficulty for parents. It is not at all unusual for the child to ask the parent to check, to do the laundry, to repeat things "just so," or to give endless reassurance. Parents may want to respond to the child's demands, in order to seemingly decrease his or her anxiety. Family therapy can help educate the family about what is part of the OCD illness. For example, "I can't clean my room, because if I start I can't stop." Parents struggle with the balance between being empathic and not becoming overinvolved in the child's illness and enabling the symptoms.

Additionally, the effect of the patient's illness on the siblings cannot be overlooked. Siblings may be burdened and unfairly expected to understand what is going on with the patient—the extra attention he or she gets and the way the household may revolve around the child's rituals. (For a detailed discussion of family issues, see Lenane, 1989.)

COMORBIDITY

In the 70 children studied at the NIMH reported in 1989, comorbidity was common, and only 18 (26%) had no other psychiatric diagnosis (Swedo, Rapoport, et al., 1989). At initial presentation, the children and adolescents had the following current diagnoses: tic disorder (30%) (lifetime history 57%), major depression (26%), specific developmental disability (24%), simple phobia (17%), overanxious disorder (16%), adjustment disorder with depressed mood (13%), oppositional disorder (11%), attention deficit disorder (10%), conduct disorder (7%), and separation anxiety disorder (7%) (Leonard et al., 1992; Swedo, Rapoport, et al., 1989). Riddle and colleagues (1990) confirmed that associated psychopathology was common: 38% received an anxiety disorder diagnosis; 29% received a mood disorder diagnosis; and tics were observed in 24%. Comorbidity is common and additional treatment may be required.

Only 11% of the children with OCD could be diagnosed as having obsessive compulsive personality disorder, thus speaking to the differences between the two disorders (Swedo et al., 1989a). The diagnosis of personality disorders in children is obviously problematic since character is an evolving process and perfectionistic behavior can be seen in either OCD or OCP. In OCP, the child would typically be perfectionistic, rigid, and often have high expectations for self, which seemingly should not be egodystonic.

PROGNOSIS

Follow-up studies of adult OCD patients generally have reported continued symptoms for most. For example, Kringlen (1965) found that 72% of 85 adults had impaired occupational functioning at 10-year follow-up. There are very few follow-up studies of pediatric OCD cases. Warren (1960) reported that in a 7-year reevaluation of 15 youths with "obsessive compulsive state," 2 (13%) had no symptoms, 8 (53%) had mild to moderate symptoms, and 5 (33%) were "severely handicapped" with 1 having been leukotomized. Hollingsworth, et al. (1980) reported 1½- to 14-year follow-up on 10 of 17 patients with severe obsessive compulsive neurosis; only 3 (30%) were symptom free, and 1 of the children had had an acute schizophrenic reaction. In Flament et al.'s (1990) reevaluation of 25 of 27 (93%) patients 2 to 7 years after initial evaluation, 17 (68%) still met criteria for OCD, and comorbidity was common. Bolton, Collins, and Steinberg (1983) found that of 15 OCD adolescents who had received behavior therapy, 7 of 14 (50%) had no symptoms, 5 (35%) had mild to moderate symptoms, and 1 (7%) was severely affected. To see whether a community-based population of OCD adolescents (from an epidemiologic study) differed from those in clinic-based studies, Berg, Rapoport, Whitaker, et al. (1989) followed up such a group 2 years after initial contact. Thirty-one percent (5 of 16) of those who had initially met criteria for OCD still did so, and only 12% (2 of 16) had no OCD features of any form (Berg, Rapoport, Whitaker, et al., 1989). Most interesting was that the 2 (12%) adolescents who had been originally diagnosed with OCD met criteria for OCP at follow-up. Thus the relationship between OCD and OCP remains problematic and deserves ongoing study.

In the largest systematic follow-up study of pediatric OCD patients, 54 patients were reevaluated at 2- to 7-year follow-up (Leonard et al., 1993). This recent study was unique in that patients had access to the serotonin reuptake inhibitor medications (which had not been commercially available previously) and to behavior therapy. Twenty-three (43%) of the subjects still met diagnostic criteria for OCD, and only 6 (11%) were totally asymptomatic, supporting previous reports of the chronicity and intractability of the illness. Thirty-eight (70%) were on psychoactive medication at the time of follow-up. As a group, they were improved from baseline, although 10 (19%) were unchanged or worse. Of the 5 (9%) who were rated as worse than at baseline, all had severe comorbid disorders at follow-up that had not been present at baseline, which may have contributed in part to their poor outcome. From the results, it might be inferred that treatment interventions can improve long-term outcome; however, without concurrent untreated control groups, it cannot be said whether the interventions were specifically responsible. Thus, with intensive treatment, most pediatric OCD patients can expect substantial improvement but not complete remission with time.

Treatment

PSYCHODYNAMIC TREATMENT

"Freud spoke of 'obsessional neurosis' as the 'most interesting and repaying subject of analytic research. But as a problem,' he wrote, 'it had not yet been mastered.' Sixty years later we are in the same position" (Esman, 1989, p. 319). Freud made it possible to understand the ruminations and rituals of the obsessional patient in a developmental and interpersonal context (Esman, 1989). However, it is currently debated whether the symptoms really are derivatives of intrapsychic conflicts.

Until recently, the disorder has, for the most part, been refractory to the more traditional psychodynamically oriented treatments. Nevertheless, psychotherapy may be an important adjunctive treatment in a comprehensive approach. Psychotherapy may address the associated anxiety and depressive symptoms, increase coping skills, focus on improving family relationships, and help a child who may have withdrawn from peer activities. The illness impacts on most children's lives in a variety of ways; getting "back on track" becomes an important goal that can be focused on in psychotherapy. Family therapy is often necessary to reestablish boundaries between members that have been altered by the patient's behaviors and to explain how the others are affected by the illness.

PSYCHOPHARMACOLOGIC TREATMENT

Pharmacotherapy is an important treatment intervention in children with OCD and the new class of medications has changed the recommendations and prognosis (Leonard et al., 1993; March, Leonard, & Swedo, 1995). The serotonin reuptake inhibitors—clomipramine, fluoxetine, sertraline, paroxetine, and fluvxamine—are the most effective class of medications for treatment of OCD in adults. (For a recent review of pharmacotherapy, see March et al., 1995.) So far only clomipramine and fluoxetine have been studied systematically in pediatric patients, although the other drugs are under study.

The first serotonin reuptake inhibitor trial for children with OCD was completed by Flament and colleagues (1985). They reported that clomipramine was significantly superior to placebo in a 10-week (5-week active medication), placebo-controlled, double-blind crossover study. Seventy-five percent of the patients had a moderate to marked improvement during the trial, and only 16% were unchanged. These results were supported by a large 8-week multicenter double-blind parallel comparison of clomipramine and placebo. The 31 patients on clomipramine had a mean reduction in OCD severity score of 37% compared to 8% in the 29 receiving placebo (De-Veaugh-Geiss et al., 1992). Clomipramine proved superior to desipramine in a large 10-week controlled trial (5 weeks each medication) in 48 children with OCD (Leonard et al., 1989). Dosages targeted 3 mg per kg per day and did not exceed 5 mg per kg per day. In general, clomipramine was well tolerated with expected anticholinergic side effects (Leonard et al., 1989). Ongoing clinical management typically would include periodic monitoring of electrocardiograms, vital signs, and liver functions.

Fluoxetine, a selective serotonin reuptake in-

hibitor has been reported to be safe, effective, and reasonably well tolerated in children and adolescents with OCD (both with and without Tourette's disorder) (Riddle et al., 1992). Often lower initial dosages than those recommended for adults are used. Often medication might be increased slowly, as with the long half-life of the parent and metabolite, steady state is not reached for weeks, and it is not completely eliminated from the system for at least 6 weeks after discontinuation.

The selective serotonin reuptake inhibitors offer an advantage in their side effect profile and their broad therapeutic index over that seen with the tricyclic antidepressants. Their advantage of few anticholinergic side effects and limited cardiovascular toxicities are particularly relevant for the pediatric population (March et al., 1995). As mentioned, currently trials of fluvoxamine, sertraline, and paroxetine in children with OCD are under way, and results similar to those in adults are expected. Augmentation strategies often are tried for children who are partial responders to an adequate dose of a serotonin reuptake inhibitor (Leonard et al., 1994). It is not known how long maintenance therapy is required for children and adolescents with OCD who respond to medication. Although periodic tapering should be attempted to determine the continued necessity for medication, for many responders long-term maintenance appears required. A double-blind desipramine substitution study of long-term clomipramine-maintained responders found that 8 of 9 desipramine-substituted patients relapsed within 2 months, in comparison to 2 of 11 subjects who were not substituted (Leonard et al., 1991). However, even those on continued long-term clomipramine maintenance had continued OC symptoms, which varied in severity over time. With the refinement of behavioral treatment for children (March, 1995; March, Mulle, & Herbel, 1994), this concomitant behavioral treatment potentially might decrease the long-term necessity of medication maintenance.

BEHAVIORAL TREATMENT

Behavior therapy is considered one of the treatments of choice in children with OCD. Although it has been clinically successful for many, systematic studies have not been done. In general, the exposure-with-response-prevention technique, which is used in adults (Marks, 1987), is applicable to the pediatric population (Berg, Rapoport, & Wolfe, 1989; March et al., 1994). Children need to be very motivated and capable of understanding and following directions. Bolton et al. (1983) used response prevention in 15 OCD adolescents and achieved a "very good" response in 11. March and Mulle (1993) have developed a systematic manual for cognitive behavior therapy for children with OCD. (See March, 1995; March et al., 1994 for reviews.) Thus, behavior therapy should be tried either with or without concomitant medication, but exposure with response prevention should be the specific approach.

PATIENT SUPPORT GROUPS AND INFORMATION

For many patients, connecting with other individuals with OCD proves to be reassuring. The Obsessive Compulsive Foundation (P.O. Box 70, Milford, CT 06460) is an active patient support organization that can distribute educational materials and put individuals in touch with doctors familiar with treating the disorder and local support groups. Additionally, the Obsessive Compulsive Information Center (8000 Excelsior Drive, Suite 302, Madison, WI 53717-1914) is an excellent source of information on the illness and its treatment.

Current Research Questions

Despite the recent attention that childhood-onset OCD has received, many questions remain unanswered. What is the long-term prognosis of this illness? Are other medications safe and effective for the treatment of OCD in this pediatric population? What are the causes of this illness? Why does a child get one specific symptom rather than another? Perhaps the most challenging question is to understand how neurobiology, learning, environmental (bacterial and viral) triggers, and emotional conflicts interact together to determine this illness, as its etiology remains unknown.

REFERENCES

Adams, P. L. (1973). *Obsessive children.* New York: Penguin Books.

Allen, A. J., Leonard, H. L., & Swedo, S. E. (1995). Case study: A new infection-triggered, autoimmune subtype of pediatric OCD and Tourette's syndrome. *Journal of the American Academy of Child and Adolescent Psychiatry 34,* 307–311.

American Psychiatric Association. (1994). *Diagnostic and statistical manual of mental disorders (4th ed.).* Washington, DC: Author.

Berg, C. Z., Rapoport, J. L., & Wolff, R. P. (1989). Behavioral treatment for obsessive-compulsive disorder in childhood. In J. L. Rapoport (Ed.), *Obsessive-compulsive disorder in children and adolescents,* (pp. 169–185). Washington, DC: American Psychiatric Association.

Berg, C. Z., Rapoport, J. L., Whitaker, A., Davies, M., Leonard, H., Swedo, S. E., Braiman, S., Lenane, M. (1989). Childhood obsessive compulsive disorder: A two-year prospective follow-up of a community sample. *Journal of the American Academy of Child and Adolescent Psychiatry 28* (4), 528–533.

Berman, L. (1942). Obsessive-compulsive neurosis in children. *Journal of Nervous and Mental Disease, 95,* 26–39.

Bolton, D., Collins, S., & Steinberg, D. (1983). The treatment of obsessive-compulsive disorder in adolescence: A report of fifteen cases. *British Journal of Psychiatry, 142,* 456–464.

Cox, C. S., Fedio, P., & Rapoport, J. L. (1989). Neuropsychological testing of obsessive-compulsive adolescents. In J. L. Rapoport (Ed.), *Obsessive-compulsive disorder in children and adolescents* (pp. 73–86) Washington, DC. American Psychiatric Press.

Cummings, J. L., & Cunningham, K. (1992). Obsessive-compulsive disorder in Huntington's disease. *Biological Psychiatry, 31,* 263–270.

Denckla, M. B. (1989). Neurological examination. In J. L. Rapoport (Ed.), *Obsessive-compulsive disorder in children and adolescents* (pp. 107–118). Washington, DC: American Psychiatric Press.

Despert, L. (1955). Differential diagnosis between obsessive-compulsive neurosis and schizophrenia in children. In P. H. Hoch & J. Zubin (Eds.), *Psychopathology of childhood.* (chap. 14). New York, Grune & Stratton.

Deveaugh-Geiss, J., Moroz, G., Biederman, J., Cantwell, D., Fontaine, R., Greist J. H., Reichler, R., Katz, R., & Landau, P. (1992). Clomipramine hydrochloride in childhood and adolescent obsessive-compulsive disorder—A multicenter trial. *Journal of the American Academy of Child and Adolescent Psychiatry, 31,* 1.

Esman, A. H. (1989). Psychoanalysis and general psychiatry: Obsessive-compulsive disorder as paradigm. *Journal of the American Psychoanalytic Association, 37* (2), 319–336.

Flament, M. F., Koby, E., Rapoport, J. L., Berg, C., Zahn, T., Cox, C., Denckla, M., & Lenane, M. (1990). Childhood obsessive compulsive disorder: A prospective follow-up study. *Journal of Child Psychology and Psychiatry, 31,* 363–380.

Flament, M. F., Rapoport, J. L., Berg, C. J., Sceery, W., Kilts, C., Mellstrom, B., & Linnoila, M. (1985). Clomipramine treatment of childhood compulsive disorder. *Archives of General Psychiatry, 42,* 977–983.

Flament, M. F., Whitaker, A., Rapoport, J. L., Davies, M., Berg, C. Z., Kalikow, K., Sceery, W., & Shaffer, D. (1988). Obsessive compulsive disorder in adolescence: An epidemiological study. *Journal of the American Academy of Child and Adolescent Psychiatry, 27* (6), 764–771.

Freud, A. (1965). *Normality and pathology in childhood.* New York: International University Press.

Freud, S. (1955). Notes on a case of obsessional neurosis. In J. Strachey (Ed. and Trans.), *The standard edition of the complete psychological works of Sigmund Freud* (vol. 10, pp. 153–318). London: Hogarth Press. (originally published 1909.)

Gesell, A., Ames, L. B., & Ilg, F. L. (1974). *Infant and child in the culture today.* New York: Harper & Row.

Goodman, W. K., McDougle, C. J., Price, L. H., Riddle, M. A., Pauls, D. L., & Leckman, J. F. (1990). Beyond the serotonin hypothesis: A role for dopamine in some forms of obsessive compulsive disorder? *Journal of Clinical Psychiatry, 51* (Suppl.), 36–43.

Gordon, C. T., Rapoport, J. L., Hamburger, S. D., State, R. C., & Mannheim, G. B. (1992). Differential response of seven subjects with autistic disorder to clomipramine and desipramine. *American Journal of Psychiatry, 149* (3), 363–366.

Hamburger, S. D., Swedo, S., Whitaker, A., Davies, M., & Rapoport, J. L. (1989). Growth rate in adolescents with obsessive-compulsive disorder. *American Journal of Psychiatry, 46,* 652–655.

Hollander, E., Schiffman, E., Cohen, B., et al. (1990). Signs of central nervous system dysfunction in obsessive-compulsive disorder. *Archives of General Psychiatry, 47,* 27–32.

Hollingsworth, C. E., Tanguay, P. E., Grossman, L., & Pabst, P. (1980). Long-term outcome of obsessive compulsive disorder in childhood. *Journal of the American Academy of Child Psychiatry, 19,* 134–144.

Janet, P. (1903). *Les obsessions et la psychiatrie* (Vol. 1). Paris: Felix Alan.

Judd, L. (1965). Obsessive compulsive neurosis in children. *Archives of General Psychiatry, 12,* 136–143.

Kanner, L. (1962). *Child psychiatry* (3rd ed.) Springfield, IL: Charles C. Thomas. (Originally published 1935.)

Kasvikis, Y. G., Tsakiris, F., & Marks, I. M. (1986). Women with obsessive compulsive disorder fre-

quently report a past history of anorexia nervosa. *International Journal of Eating Disorders, 5,* 1069–1075.

Keller, B. (1989). Cognitive assessment of obsessive-compulsive children. In J. L. Rapoport (Ed.), *Obsessive-compulsive disorder in children and adolescents* (pp. 33–39). Washington, DC: American Psychiatric Press.

Kringlen, E. (1965). Obsessional neurotics: A long-term follow-up. *British Journal of Psychiatry, 111,* 709–722.

Kruesi, M. J. P., Rapoport, J. L., Hamburger, S., Hibbs, E., Potter, W. Z., Lenane, M., & Brown, G. L. (1990). CSF monoamine metabolites, aggression and impulsivity in disruptive behavior disorders of children and adolescents. *Archives of General Psychiatry, 47,* 419–426.

Leckman, J. T., Walker, D. E., & Cohen, D. J. (1993). Premonitory urges in Tourette's Syndrome. *American Journal of Psychiatry, 150,* 98–102.

Lenane, M. (1989). Families and obsessive compulsive disorder. In J. L. Rapoport (Ed.), *Obsessive compulsive disorder in children and adolescents* (pp. 237–249). Washington, DC: American Psychiatric Press.

Lenane, M., Swedo, S., Leonard, H., Pauls, D., & Rapoport, J. (1990). Psychiatric diagnoses in first degree relatives of children and adolescents with obsessive compulsive disorder. *Journal of the American Academy of Child and Adolescent Psychiatry, 29* (3), 407–412.

Leonard, H. L., Goldberger, E. L., Rapoport, J. L., Cheslow, D. L., & Swedo, S. E. (1990). Childhood rituals: Normal development or obsessive compulsive symptoms. *Journal of the American Academy of Child and Adolescent Psychiatry, 29,* 17–23.

Leonard, H. L., Lenane, M. C., & Swedo, S. E. (1993). Obsessive compulsive disorder. *Child and Adolescent Psychiatric Clinics of North America, 2* (4), 655–666.

Leonard, H. L., Lenane, M. C., Swedo, S. E., Rettew D. C., Gerson, E. S., & Rapoport, J. L. (1992). Tics and Tourette's disorder: A 2- to 7-year followup of 54 obsessive-compulsive children. *American Journal of Psychiatry, 149,* 1244–1251.

Leonard, H. L., Swedo, S. E., Rapoport, J. L., Koby, E. V., Lenane, M. C., Cheslow, D. L., & Hamburger, S. D. (1989). Treatment of childhood obsessive compulsive disorder with clomipramine and desipramine: A double-blind crossover comparison. *Archives of General Psychiatry, 46,* 1088–1092.

Leonard, H. L., Swedo, S. E., Lenane, M. C., Rettew, D. C., Cheslow, D. C., Hamburger, S. D., & Rapoport, J. L. (1991). A double-blind desipramine substitution during long-term clomipramine treatment in children and adolescents with obsessive compulsive disorder. *Archives of General Psychiatry, 48,* 922–927.

Leonard, H. L., Swedo, S. E., Lenane, M. C., Rettew, D. C., Hamburger, S. D., Bartko, J. J., & Rapoport, J. L. (1993). A two to seven year follow-up study of

54 obsessive compulsive children and adolescents. *Archives of General Psychiatry, 50,* 429–439.

Leonard, H. L., Topol, D., Bukstein, O., Hindermarsh, D., Allen, A. J., & Swedo S. E. (1994). Clonazepam as an augmenting agent in the treatment of childhood onset obsessive compulsive disorder. *Journal of the American Academy of Child and Adolescent Psychiatry, 33,* 792–794.

Luxenburg, J. S., Swedo, S. E., Flament, M. F., Friedland, R., Rapoport, J., & Rapoport, S. (1988). Neuroanatomic abnormalities in obsessive-compulsive disorder detected with quantitative X-ray computed tomography. *American Journal of Psychiatry, 145,* 1089–1093.

March, J. S. (1995). Cognitive-behavioral psychotherapy for children and adolescents with obsessive-compulsive disorder: A review and recommendations for treatment. *Journal of the American Academy of Child and Adolescent Psychiatry, 34,* 7–18.

March, J. S., & Mulle, K. (1993). *How I ran OCD off my land: A guide to cognitive-behavioral psychotherapy for children and adolescents with obsessive-compulsive disorder.* Program in Child and Adolescent Anxiety Disorders, Department of Psychiatry, Division of Child and Adolescent Psychiatry, Duke University Medical Center, Box 3527, Durham, NC.

March, J. S., Mulle, K., & Herbel, B. (1994). Behavioral psychotherapy for children and adolescents with obsessive-compulsive disorder: An open trial of a new protocol-driven treatment package. *Journal of the American Academy of Child and Adolescent Psychiatry, 33,* 333–341.

March, J. S., Leonard, H. L., & Swedo, S. E. (1995). Pharmacotherapy of obsessive-compulsive disorder. In M. Riddle (Ed.), *Child and adolescent psychiatric clinics of North America: Pediatric psychopharmacology. I,* (Vol. 4, No. 1, pp. 217–236). Philadelphia: W.B. Saunders.

Marks, I. M. (1987). *Fears, phobias, and rituals. Panic anxiety and their disorders.* Oxford: Oxford University Press.

McDougle, C. J., Goodman, W. K., Leckman, J. F., Lee, N. C., Heninger, G. R., & Price, L. H. (1994). Haloperidol addition in fluvoxamine-refractory OCD: A double-blind placebo controlled study in patients with and without tics. *Archives of General Psychiatry, 51,* 302–308.

Pauls, D. L., Raymond, C. L., Stevenson, J. M., & Leckman, J. F. (1991). A family study of Gilles de la Tourette syndrome. *Human Genetics, 48,* 154–163.

Pauls, D. L., Towbin, K. E., Leckman, J. F., Zahner, G. E. P., & Cohen, D. J. (1986). Gilles de la Tourette's syndrome and obsessive compulsive disorder: Evidence supporting a genetic relationship. *Archives of General Psychiatry, 43,* 1180–1182.

Rapoport, J. L. (1986). Annotation: Childhood obsessive compulsive disorder. *Journal of Child Psychology and Psychiatry, 27,* 289–296.

Rettew, D. C., Swedo, S. E., Leonard, H. L., et al. (1992). Obsessions and compulsions across time in 79 children and adolescents with obsessive compulsive disorder. *Journal of the American Academy of Child and Adolescent Psychiatry, 31,* 1050–1056.

Riddle, M. A., Scahill, L., King, R., Harden, M. T., Anderson, G. M., Ort, S. I., Smith, J. C, Leckman, J. F., & Cohen D. J. (1992). Double-blind, crossover trial of fluoxetine and placebo in children and adolescents with obsessive compulsive disorder. *Journal of the American Academy of Child and Adolescent Psychiatry, 31,* 1062–1069.

Riddle, M. A., Scahill, L., King, R., Hardin, M. T., Towbin, K. E., Ort, S. I., Leckman, J. F., & Cohen, D. J. (1990). Obsessive compulsive disorder in children and adolescents: Phenomenology and family history. *Journal of the American Academy of Child and Adolescent Psychiatry, 29* (5), 766–772.

Rutter, M., Tizard, J., & Whitmore, K. (1970). *Education, health and Behavior.* London: Longmans.

Swedo, S. E. (1989). Rituals and releasers: An ethological model of obsessive-compulsive disorder. In J. L. Rapoport (Ed.), *Obsessive-compulsive disorder in children and adolescents* (pp. 269–288). Washington, DC: American Psychiatric Press.

Swedo, S. E. (1994). Sydenham's chorea: A model for childhood autoimmune neuropsychiatric disorders. *Journal of the American Medical Association, 272,* 1788–1791.

Swedo, S. E., Leonard, H. L., & Kiessling, L. S. (1994). Speculations on antineuronal antibody-mediated neuropsychiatric disorders of childhood. Commentaries. *Pediatrics, 93,* 323–326.

Swedo, S. E., Leonard, H. L., Kruesi, M. J. P., Rettew, D. C., Listwak, S. J., Berretini, W., Stipetic, M., Hamburger, S., Gold, P. W., Potter, W. Z., & Rapoport, J. L. (1992). Cerebrospinal fluid neurochemistry in children and adolescents with obsessive compulsive disorder. *Archives of General Psychiatry, 49,* 29–36.

Swedo, S. E., Leonard, H. L., Rapoport, J. L., Lenane, M. C., Goldberger, E. L., & Cheslow, D. L., (1989). A double-blind comparison of clomipramine and desipramine in the treatment of trichotillomania. *New England Journal of Medicine, 321,* 497–501.

Swedo, S. E., Leonard, H. L., Schapiro, M. B., Casey, B. J., Mannheim, G. B., Lenane, M. C., & Rettew, D. C. (1993). Sydenham's chorea: Physical and psychological symptoms of St. Vitus's Dance. *Pediatrics, 91,* 706–713.

Swedo, S. E., & Rapoport, J. L. (1990). Neurochemical and neuroendocrine considerations of Obsessive Compulsive Disorders in childhood. In: S. I. Deutsch, A. Weizman, & R. Weizman (Eds.), *Application of basic neuroscience to child psychiatry* (pp. 275–284). New York: Plenum Press.

Swedo, S. E., Rapoport, J. L., Leonard, H., Lenane, M., & Cheslow, D. (1989). Obsessive-compulsive disorder in children and adolescents: Clinical phenomenology of 70 consecutive cases. *Archives of General Psychiatry, 46,* 335–341.

Swedo, S. E., Schapiro, M. B., Grady, C. L., Cheslow,

D. L., Leonard, H. L., Kumar, A., Friedlard, R., Rapoport, S. I., & Rapoport, J. L. (1989). Cerebral glucose metabolism in childhood-onset obsessive compulsive disorder. *Archives of General Psychiatry, 46*, 518–523.

Thomsen, P. H., & Mikkelsen, H. U. (1991). Children and adolescents with obsessive-compulsive disorder: the demographic and diagnostic characteristics of 61 Danish patients. *Acta Psychiatrica Scandinavica, 83*, 262–266.

Thoren, P., Asberg M., Cronholm, B., et al. (1980). Clomipramine treatment of obsessive-compulsive disorder: I. A controlled clinical trial. *Archives of General Psychiatry, 37*, 1281–1285.

Van Amerongen, S. T. (1980). Latency and prepubertal children. In J. D. Noshpitz (Ed.), *Basic handbook of child psychiatry* (Vol. 3). New York Basic Books.

von Economo, C. (1931). *Encephalitis lethargic, its sequelae and treatment.* Oxford: Oxford University Press.

Warren, W. (1960). A study of adolescent psychiatric inpatients and the outcome six or more years later. *Journal of Child Psychology and Psychiatry, 6*, 141–160.

30 / The Cyclic Mood Disorders in Latency-Age Children: Bipolar Disorder and Cyclothemia

Javad Kashani and Mark Henigan

Introduction

As with dysthymia, the cyclic mood disorders are gradually being recognized in school-age children. While some argue that mood swings and emotional turmoil are a typical response to the developmental problems posed by adolescence (Lefkowitz & Tesiny, 1980), the middle school years generally are not characterized by such distress. The child whose disruptiveness and extremes of mood cannot be adequately managed by psychotherapy, appropriate milieu, antidepressant medication, and parenting and behavioral techniques should call to mind the possibility of bipolar disorder.

Weller, Weller, Tucker, and Fristad (1986) performed a retrospective survey of the literature for possible manic episodes in 6- to 12-year-old children and examined each case description for *Diagnostic and Statistical Manual of Mental Disorders,* third edition (*DSM-III;* American Psychiatric Association [APA], 1980) criteria of manic syndrome. They found that approximately half of the children who fulfilled the criteria had received a diagnosis other than mania, suggesting that as a result of clinician expectations, the diagnosis was excluded a priori. This interpretation was bolstered by the fact that almost all of the children who were given a diagnosis of mania by the original author qualified for the diagnosis by the relatively stringent study criteria. The earliest cases were published in the 19th century (Weller, Weller, & Fristad, 1986a), demonstrating that the disorder in children is not new, although the diagnosis may be novel. The *DSM-IV* criteria (APA, 1994) are similar to those of *DSM-III-R* (APA, 1987). In both sets of criteria, the only distinction made between children or adolescents and adults is that of allowing irritable rather than depressed mood in the former as a criterion for depression. Weinberg and Brumback (1976) suggested a similar refinement for mania for the Feighner criteria in that elevated mood (euphoria) could manifest as (1) denial of problems or illness, or (2) inappropriate feelings of well-being, inappropriate cheerfulness, or giddiness and silliness. In addition, they suggested that irritability should include "agitation (particularly belligerence, destructiveness, and antisocial behavior)" and that increased activity include intrusiveness and "motor driven." Their criteria for depression also make several distinctions between adults and children. None of these recommendations has ever been acted upon in the formulation of consensus (*DSM*) criteria.

The *DSM-IV* (1994) descriptions of bipolar syndromes are significantly different from those in previous *DSMs*. For instance, hypomanic episode is presented as a separate entity and not merely a mild presentation of manic episode. In addition, the distinction between Type I and Type II of bipolar disorder is formalized rather than being optional, suggesting a greater degree of confidence in these subcategories. To be diagnosed with Bipolar I, full-blown depressive and manic episodes must be present, while Bipolar II requires only hypomanic episodes.

The diagnostic criteria for manic episode in *DSM-IV* include a distinct period of abnormally and persistently elevated, expansive, or irritable mood for one week, during which time 3 of the following 7 symptoms (4 if mood disturbance is exclusively irritable) must be present:

1. Inflated self-esteem or grandiosity
2. Decreased need for sleep
3. Pressure of speech or more talkative than usual
4. Flight of ideas
5. Distractibility
6. Increased goal-directed activity or psychomotor agitation
7. Excessive involvement in pleasurable activities that have a high potential for painful consequences

As a result of mood changes, impairment in functioning must be present in occupational or social activities or in relationships with others, hospitalization must become necessary to prevent harm to self or others, or psychotic features must be present, and the symptoms must not result from direct physiological effects of a psychoactive substance (either therapeutic or abused), other treatment, or a general medical condition. Finally, treatment-induced (e.g., by medication, electroseizure therapy, or phototherapy) "manic-like" episodes are not to be used to support the diagnosis of bipolar I disorder.

Cyclothymia represents a still greater problem in childhood diagnosis. The *DSM-IV* criteria for cyclothymic disorder require a duration of 1 year in children and adolescents (2 years in adults) with numerous hypomanic and depressive episodes that, respectively, do not reach the severity of frank mania or major depression. However, no study has yet established the existence of cyclothemia in childhood. Second, its status as a diagnosis even in adults is poorly defined, having been "upgraded" from personality disorder to an Axis I condition in *DSM-III* (Carlson, 1990). Akiskal (1995) and Akiskal and colleagues (1979, 1983) discuss in careful detail the complexity inherent

in this distinction and indicate that, while not necessarily causative, certain temperaments may precede a frank bipolar disorder either as a subsyndromal expression of the disorder or as a result of growing up in an environment dominated by serious psychopathology in adult caretakers. Carlson (1995) cautions against extrapolating too freely from our experiences with adults.

Historical Background

Anthony and Scott (1960), in their classic paper on the subject, reviewed the literature on the diagnosis of manic-depressive psychosis in children, which they were careful to describe as both age 12 or younger and as not yet exhibiting any pubertal secondary sex characteristics. They point out that developmental effects on the presentation of signs and symptoms are most problematic when considering mania, which rarely occurs in children in its typical adult form (i.e., elevated mood, grandiosity, flight of ideas). For this reason they assemble a strict set of criteria for undeniable diagnosis of the disorder and then present their case of a 12-year-old boy that amply satisfies those criteria. Two concerns with their approach are the requirement for full-blown psychotic symptoms in order to make the diagnosis and their belief that the cycles of variation in mood must lengthen as the disorder progresses. Their insistence that familial loading be present demonstrates how serious they were about making their diagnosis unassailable, thereby ending the argument over whether bipolar disorder occurs in childhood. They note the paucity of published cases in early childhood but posit the disorder's existence in an as yet unrecognized form based on psychodynamic evidence.

The difficulty of diagnosing bipolar disorder in a clinical climate dominated by attention deficit hyperactivity disorder (ADHD) likely explains much of the underdiagnosis. (This problem is discussed at length later in the section on comorbidity.) Bowden and Sarabia (1980) also emphasized the tendency to choose other diagnoses in order to avoid giving children a socially negative label and to avoid a diagnosis that would demand the use of medication. Unfortunately, because psychotic symptoms often accompany severe episodes of mood disorder, the diagnosis of schizophrenia often is substituted later in the course of the illness. This situation is especially troubling because such a diagnosis tends to make the patient and those involved in his or her care pessimistic and delays effective treatment with antimanic and mood-stabilizing medications. Bowden and Sarabia also make a case for the validity of the Research Diagnostic Criteria (RDC) for the diagnosis of bipolar disorder in adolescents, although they have reservations about applying them to preadolescents. They list a number of features from which a bipolar diagnosis can be suspected, including the tendency to be episodic in contrast to the more tonic hyperactivity of ADHD, the strong positive evidence of a family history of the illness, episodic variation in functioning, episodic aggressive behavior associated with an elevated or irritable mood, biphasic mood shifts with periods of good functioning as well, and an energetic and outgoing premorbid personality without obvious pathology.

Carlson and Strober (1978) discussed the misdiagnosis for a period of almost 4 years of a girl who had her first episode of affective disorder at 12 years of age. The diagnosis given during her first evaluation was of adjustment disorder; during her second, schizophrenia; only with her third episode did she receive a bipolar diagnosis. According to the authors, the diagnosis of adjustment disorder is used too freely and the girl's second period of overt illness was clearly a psychotic depression; they assert that bipolar disorder should have been diagnosed much earlier. This is a difficult issue, particularly when many clinicians believe that the diagnosis of adjustment disorder benefits the patient by not labeling him or her prematurely when insufficient data are available to support a firm diagnosis of a primary psychiatric disorder. These clinicians believe that, without a diagnosis that has ample historical justification, the dangers of instituting pharmacotherapy far outweigh the unproven advantages of beginning such therapy in childhood or early adolescence. The analysis is complicated still further by the frequent lack of reliable histories or of adequate records of previous treatment (or, for that matter, of any records at all). This issue deserves extensive study by our profession.

Ballenger, Reus, and Post (1982) found a higher prevalence of symptoms of schizophrenia in 9 manic adolescents than in 12 manics over the age of 30, all of whom had concurrent symptoms of mania. This suggests that bipolar disorder with psychotic features is a common presentation in this age group. Had the psychotic features been the diagnostic focus, the core affective disorder might have been missed altogether. Although this study had several methodological flaws, it possessed the rare strength of lengthy follow-up and was buttressed with a convincing literature review. *Thus, it would seem prudent, after ruling out states resulting from drug ingestion, to approach psychotic children and adolescents first as potentially suffering from bipolar disorder, settling on the diagnosis of schizophrenia or other primarily psychotic illness only if no mood disorder can be discovered.* Several other reports consistent with this point of view have been published in recent years (e.g., Akiskal & Weller, 1989; Rogeness, Riester, & Wicoff, 1982). Sylvester, Burke, McCauley, and Clark (1984) reported a similar presentation in two prepubertal children, one of whom was managed easily with lithium. The other experienced a recrudescence of mania despite apparently "adequate" serum levels.

Isaac (1991) utilized slightly truncated *DSM-III-R* criteria for manic episodes to determine the lifetime prevalence of the diagnosis among the 5 students in a classroom for severely emotionally disturbed children. The criteria were well satisfied for all 5 children. Since they had all received years of treatment and repeated evaluations and had yet to receive the bipolar diagnosis, Isaac suggested that the disorder may be relatively common in severely disturbed children. In these children the presentation of mania was mixed or dysphoric rather than the elated, expansive, grandiose sort of picture that the word *manic* initially calls to mind. The children also exhibited an uneven pattern with periodic exacerbations and subsequent intervals where comorbid, and possibly secondary, behavior problems predominated. Unfortunately, it was not possible to initiate treatment for bipolar disorder, so the question of whether children respond to therapies useful in adults with the disorder remains unanswered. It was also clear that the issue of environmental effects could not be separated easily from the diagnostic classification and the atypical presentation since all of the children had a family history of bipolar disorder or cyclothymia (4 of 5 in a parent), 2 had been abused, and 1 had experienced exacerbations of his condition in the spring for 2 consecutive years.

Akiskal and Weller (1989) presented an analysis adapted from a 1985 study by Akiskal et al., which quantified the disorders "misdiagnosed" in a group of preadolescents, adolescents, and young adults who were children or younger siblings of patients who had already received the diagnosis of bipolar disorder. All members of this group had been referred for evaluation of affective symptoms rather than simply because of pedigree. Misdiagnoses included: adjustment disorder, 35%; conduct disorder, 15%; schizophrenia, 15%; overanxious disorder, 11%; attention deficit hyperactivity disorder, 9%; separation anxiety disorder, 9%; and mental retardation, 6%.

Natural History/Epidemiology

Few population studies of bipolar symptomatology in younger persons exist. An evaluation (Carlson & Kashani, 1988) of 150 randomly selected 14- to 16-year-olds with a structured interview (Diagnostic Interview for Children and Adolescents [DICA], Parent and Child Versions), which also examined the observations of their parents, yielded a group of 20 adolescents who endorsed 4 or more manic symptoms (*DSM-III* criterion level for manic syndrome) lasting at least 2 days. (Only 11 had symptoms lasting at least 1 week, a DICA criterion for an "episode.") Members of this group also were found to be more dysphoric, impulsive, and emotionally labile and to suffer from significantly higher rates of attention deficit, conduct, and anxiety disorders as well as psychotic symptoms when compared to the remaining sample. In addition, the 20 adolescents were perceived by the interviewers to need treatment and endorsed far more symptoms than did their parents. In fact, the parents of only 1 of the 20 concurred with the adolescent's report. However, this should not be assumed to invalidate these adolescents' self-reports, since it is consistent with findings in suicidal children and adolescents (Kashani, Goddard,

& Reid, 1989). The authors also point out that based on impairment of functioning—the *DSM-III-R* distinction between mania and hypomania—all 20 adolescents would be diagnosed as hypomanic.

Strober et al. (1995) studied 54 adolescents admitted consecutively to a university inpatient service with a diagnosis of RDC bipolar I disorder and subsequently given structured clinical evaluations every 6 months for 5 years. They found recovery from index episodes of pure mania or mixed states to be rapid but from pure depression, slow. Subjects hospitalized with mixed or cycling illness were at higher risk for relapse. Thus, polarity at first admission suggests prognosis.

A significant factor that has contributed to the problem of underdiagnosis is the delay between the onset of an affective disorder and the onset of sufficient dysfunction to motivate the person to seek psychiatric evaluation. This is a particular problem for children and adolescents, since a delay of only a few years may move them from adolescence into adulthood or from childhood into adolescence. This fact exacerbates the underdiagnosis of childhood-onset bipolar disorder since apparently there are fewer cases in this age group and since the diagnosis is less apparent by dint of a lower "index of suspicion," the relative lack of sophisticated verbal skills in younger individuals, and because there is still little accumulated history, a vital part of recognition of most disorders. Egeland, Blumenthal, Nee, Sharpe, and Endicott (1987) studied the reliability of a variety of age-of-onset indices to assess the reliability, and implicitly the validity, of age estimates for the diagnosis of affective disorders in children. They were able to demonstrate that the indices were all intrinsically reliable indicators of onset but that the first noticeable symptoms preceded impairment by approximately 8 years, on average. In addition, bipolarity was correlated with an earlier age of onset, with Bipolar I subjects having a median age of onset almost 4 years earlier than subjects with "pure" unipolar disorder. These findings are complicated further by the assertion of Sibisi (1990) that the ascertainment of cases with early onset would be artificially elevated by the presence of numerous individuals who had survived many years with the disorder while the brief life span of persons with onset in, for example, their 70s would render their impact on the numbers appreciably less unless only cases with onset during a defined calendar period were compared. Utilizing records of the national health registry for the period 1982 to 1986, Sibisi also found that almost no 10- to 14-year-old female patients were admitted for the first time for manic-depressive psychosis, while 0.6 first admissions of males in that age range per year occurred. Taking into account the total of 940.8 lifetime first admissions for mania, this would yield only 0.06% of patients with onset in this age group. Since it is reasonable to expect even fewer cases below the age of 10, this appears to deviate significantly (by an order of magnitude) from the report of Kraepelin (1921) of 0.4% of his manic patients professing onset before that age. However, if Egeland, Blumenthal, et al.'s (1987) statistics are used roughly to adjust Kraepelin's finding from age at which affective symptoms first caused impairment (definite onset) to age of first hospitalization, a difference of approximately 10 years, we find that his 0.4% corresponds to onset before age 20 (10 years + 10 years) for which Sibisi found 50.8 first admissions per year ([0.6 males per year, age 10–14] + [24.6 females per year, age 15–19] + [25.6 males per year, age 15–19]). This yields a "corrected" estimate of 5.2% (50.8/940.8) with onset before age 10. These derived estimates (0.06% and 5.2%) flank Kraepelin's, suggesting that researchers are in the same region but have yet to suppress the conceptual and methodological noise surrounding this issue.

Family/Genetic Studies

Despite recent claims that the (or, more likely, "a") genetic locus for bipolar disorder had been determined (Egeland et al., 1987), there is still no consensus on the issue. There is, however, no argument with the familial transmission of liability for the disorder. Studies that have addressed this issue fall into two broad categories: studies of relatives of probands with childhood-onset bipolar disorder, and studies of the offspring of bipolar probands. The former suffer from the potential for retrospective distortion and the difficulty of compiling complete pedigrees, while the latter are more difficult to administer and tend to create

heuristic dilemmas because of the problem of subjects lost to follow-up who take with them not only their own data but bring into question the meaning of the data of remaining subjects.

Dwyer and DeLong (1987) evaluated the first- and second-degree relatives of 20 probands with juvenile-onset bipolar disorder and found rates of 27 and 14%, respectively, for unipolar and bipolar affective illness. In all of the families there was significant affective illness on one or both sides. In addition, elevated rates of anxiety disorders, alcoholism, and sociopathy were found. The authors presented evidence that the diagnosis describes the same disorder in both adults and children and that early onset may indicate a more severe course. Rice et al. (1987) studied the first-degree relatives of 187 childhood bipolar probands with structured interviews and structured family history instruments. The control group consisted of unipolar probands and their families. The morbid risk of bipolar disorder in relatives of bipolar probands was 5.7% while it was only 1.1% for the controls. No gender effects were found.

Strober et al. (1988) compared a group of adolescent probands with bipolar disorder with a control group of probands with schizophrenia utilizing a variety of structured interviews for both probands and their parents as well as clinical observation during an inpatient evaluation and subsequent initiation of treatment. Neither group included any adoptees. In contrast to Dwyer and DeLong (1987), there was no increase in diagnoses of substance abuse, anxiety disorders, or antisocial personality in relatives. Relatives of bipolar probands had a nearly 15% risk of both bipolar and unipolar depression, for a total of almost 30% for major affective disorders, in contrast to 4.2% for relatives of schizophrenic probands; the latter figure is consistent with previous estimates for relatives of normal controls. The relevance of these findings to latency-age children is underscored by the finding that relatives of bipolar probands who had prepubertal onset of their disorder had almost double the risk of major affective disorder and four times the risk of Bipolar I disorder of those with probands having adolescent onset. Finally, the response to lithium treatment of the early-onset probands was only 40% at 6 weeks of treatment contrasted with 80% response in the adolescent-onset group. These findings support those of Dwyer and DeLong (1987) and indicate a much greater degree of familial loading with prepubertal onset and a more severe course. A number of significant factors may have contributed to Dwyer and DeLong's results, including the longer period of illness in the prepubertal-onset probands (which has been found to correlate to relatively poor response to lithium) and the possibility that juvenile onset signifies a distinct pathological entity from adolescent bipolar disorder.

The second approach to family study allows closer examination of the developmental effects of growing up in a bipolar household and its interaction with genetic vulnerabilities. LaRoche et al. (1985) found that 23% (9) of 39 children of bipolar parents earned *DSM-III* diagnoses, with dysthymia in 7 of the 9 and anxiety disorders of childhood and adolescence in the other 2. In addition, 5 of the 30 with no diagnosis were described as having cyclothymic personality traits, although the paper provides no operational definition of the term. The degree of genetic loading was not found to be related to pathology in the children while marital adjustment of the nonbipolar spouse was, particularly when the bipolar parent was the mother. A follow-up study (LaRoche et al., 1987) of 37 offspring of the original 39 found a similar proportion to have *DSM-III* diagnoses (24.3%), the majority of which were still affective (6 of 9). However, the diagnoses were less homogeneous. They included cyclothymic disorder (2), major depressive episode (1), dysthymic disorder (1), adjustment disorder with depressed mood (2), adjustment disorder with anxious mood (1), separation anxiety disorder (1), and enuresis (1). Both of the subjects diagnosed with cyclothymic disorder were in their 20s, the time usually considered typical for the emergence of bipolar symptoms. This is not entirely consistent with the previously noted findings of Egeland et al., who found median ages of onset of noticeable affective symptoms of 14.7 years for bipolar I and 12.5 for bipolar II with median ages of fulfillment of RDC major affective disorder criteria, treatment, and hospitalization in the early to mid-20s.

The genetic locus and mode of inheritance have been hotly debated topics. It now seems clear that no one locus is responsible for the disorder in all pedigrees. Hays and Field (1989) reported on three families in which stuttering was apparently closely linked with bipolar disorder, suggesting that the bipolar locus was probably the same in

all three. A possible association between bipolar disorder and heterozygous beta-thalassemia also has been reported in the psychiatric literature and should raise the index of suspicion for the former in patients of Mediterranean descent.

Comorbidity and Primary Psychiatric Differential Diagnosis

While the diagnosis of bipolar disorder in children is probably missed more frequently than it is made correctly, overdiagnosis is also a serious danger. Children so diagnosed are likely to receive treatment with potent psychotropic medications and to have important psychosocial problems overlooked. After being treated for ADHD and subsequently for bipolar disorder, a child described by Jemerin, Roebuck, and Philips (1988) was given a possible diagnosis of posttraumatic stress disorder with "explosive outbursts after his abandonment at age 2." The relationship of his behavior to the interrelated problems of family dysfunction, insecure attachment, being raised by a mother who suffered from an apparent major affective disorder (diagnosed as bipolar), and being a "difficult" baby all must be taken into account. Diagnosing bipolar disorder in a child who is exhibiting disruptive behavior and whose mother has a history of the illness is an easy trap. This case report demonstrates the importance of a thorough diagnostic evaluation that does not slight the possible influence of a child's environment.

Another pitfall is placing too much emphasis on treatment response to medication. It is important to beware of regarding response to lithium as diagnostic of bipolar disorder since there is strong evidence that it is nonspecific (DeLong & Aldershof, 1987). The reinforcing effect of having observed many difficult patients respond to lithium with a decrease in aggressive behavior might lead to systematic error. However, careful use of the current diagnostic criteria will likely avoid most such misdiagnoses.

Fristad, Weller, and Weller (1992) provided evidence for the use of the Mania Rating Scale (Young, Biggs, Ziegler, & Meyer, 1978) in children and adolescents. Their work validates applying the manic syndrome described in adults to children and adolescents, thus making the instrument tentatively available both for assisting diagnosis and for monitoring the illness in young patients.

In addition to the problem of establishing the correct diagnosis to begin with, the frequent comorbidity of other psychiatric maladies with bipolar disorder must be recognized. Since the distinction is not clear among many childhood disorders (and many adult diagnoses as well), the following discussions of several diagnoses and diagnostic categories are presented to aid in the process.

ADHD

Individuals with attention deficit hyperactivity disorder present both diagnostic challenges and a potential source of insight into the nature of bipolar disorder. The diagnostic problems are highlighted by the work of Biederman et al. (1987), who found that 9% of 22 children with ADHD had lifetime diagnoses of bipolar disorder. Nieman and DeLong (1987) used a diagnostic instrument, the Personality Inventory for Children (PIC), to evaluate 20 children with the established diagnosis of mania and 20 with ADHD. The test correctly classified all of the manic subjects while incorrectly classifying 20% of the subjects with ADHD as manic-depressive. The authors recommended augmenting the PIC with appropriate phenomenological, symptom history, and family history data to focus the diagnosis more precisely. A report by Schmidt, Delaney, Jensen, Levinson, and Lewitt (1986) discussed the differential response to methylphenidate in mania and ADHD, and described what they termed a "[methylphenidate] challenge." They posited a response in manic children similar to that observed in adult manics with an exacerbation of "flight of ideas, talkativeness, elation and when present, manic grandiosity and paranoia" (Janowsky & Davis 1980). They hypothesized that in hyperactive children, an overall improvement in symptomatology would likely occur, although they noted that increased talkativeness was probable based on previous reports. The possibility of an adverse reaction to methylphenidate consisting of irritability, anxiety, formication (according to Stedman [1982], a tactile "sensation as of ants running over the skin"), or psychotic symptoms should be kept in mind (Dulcan, 1990), since these may confound the differential diagnosis. No controlled study of such psychostimulant "challenge" tests has yet appeared in the literature. However, case reports of induction of mania by trials of stimulants in children being treated for ADHD (e.g., Koehler-Troy, Strober, & Malenbaum, 1986) support the underlying principle of this approach if not its clinical utility as a diagnostic tool. The only other report of methylphenidate given for such a reason (Schmidt et al., 1986) describes not only the exacerbation of symptoms as expected in mania but also an electrodermal response, which indicates autonomic hyperactivity.

ANXIETY DISORDERS

Anxiety in children may manifest as hyperactive (i.e., restless) behavior, although such a presentation is admittedly more common when there is an associated affective disturbance. The case described by Jemerin et al. (1988), discussed earlier, is one of the most instructive.

AUTISM AND MENTAL RETARDATION

A handful of reports has been published describing manic or bipolar symptomatology in children and adolescents with autism, always in conjunction with mental retardation. McCracken and Diamond (1988) reported on five such adolescents, all of whom exhibited cyclic mood with episodes of mania and four of whom exhibited psychotic features including thought disorder (4) and auditory (3) and visual (1) hallucinations. Three of the five responded to lithium. Kerbeshian, Burd, and Fisher (1987) outlined features that may be useful to identify children with autism and lithium-responsive symptoms including: "a family history of bipolar illness; extreme hyperactivity not responsive to a stimulant; a definite cyclic component to symptomatic behaviors; sustained laughter, irritability, or giddiness that is not stereotypic; and/or the presence of many or all of the symptom criteria for bipolar disorder" (p. 404). They point out that in this population, many patients do not have the expressive ability required to produce four of the *DSM-III-R* criterion B symptoms for mania and that almost none would have a baseline level of functioning sufficient to allow for a recognizable decrement in "occupational functioning or in usual social activities or relationships," thus failing criterion C. For this reason they recommend focusing on the affective components of their presentations when dealing with irritable autistic children. Notably, the two cases they presented both responded well to lithium. Steingard and Biederman (1987) contributed cases of 7- and 20-year-old patients who responded well to lithium despite little response to neuroleptics alone. This is significant because neuroleptics are usually at least partially effective in calming the agitated states in developmentally disordered individuals; the presumably bipolar symptoms of these patients thus may have constituted a phenomenon distinct from such agitation.

Rivinus and Harmatz (1979) systematically studied the response to lithium of 5 mentally retarded children in a single-blind fashion over a period of 3 years. The subjects had symptoms suggestive of a major affective disorder as outlined by the authors. Suggestive symptoms for mania included: increased vocalization, motor activity, aggressiveness and sleeplessness, and decreased appetite lasting over a week. Depressive symptoms included: mutism, decreased motor activity, withdrawal, sleeplessness or excessive sleep, and decreased appetite lasting over a week. Significant response to treatment occurred, which argues for the development of "adapted" criterion sets for these disorders in retarded population.

VIOLENT BEHAVIOR AND CONDUCT DISORDER

In children, mania can be manifested as aggressiveness. Therefore, it is important to keep the manic syndrome in mind when evaluating patients with a history of violent, assaultive, or otherwise angry and aggressive behavior. Miller (1986) hypothesizes that it is cyclic mood that particularly predisposes bipolar patients to such disturbances because it not only involves the irritability of depression and the grandiose, agitated, impulsive behavior of mania but carries with it the unpredictable destabilization produced by one extreme affect alternating with the other. The picture is somewhat clouded by the decrease in aggressive behaviors found by Campbell et al. (1984) in "treatment-resistant" children with conduct disorder given lithium carbonate. Whether there is a mood disorder comorbid with conduct disorder in many of the children in Campbell's sample or if lithium has a nonspecific effect on aggression is not clear. However, basing diagnosis on drug effects is often misleading and can be depended on to supply no more than hints about the nature of psychiatric disorders and their underlying pathology. Kovacs and Pollock (1995) studied the relationship between bipolar disorder and conduct disorder in 26 youth with bipolar disorder, 8 to 13 years old, systematically evaluated using *DSM-III* (APA, 1980) for as long as 12 years. They found a lifetime rate of comorbidity with conduct disorder of 69% with 54% comorbidity during episodes of bipolar illness. Conduct disorder developed before bipolar disorder in 11 subjects and afterward in 7. The clinical course may be slightly worse in patients with comorbidity. However, the difference between the groups was most significant for a high rate of paternal substance abuse for patients suffering comorbid conduct disorder and a high rate of maternal mania for those without such comorbidity.

TICS AND TOURETTE'S DISORDER

Comings and Comings (1987b) studied a group of 246 patients with Tourette's syndrome (TS), 17 with ADD, 15 with ADD and TS, and 47 controls using a variety of standard diagnostic instruments to estimate the presence and lifetime history of depressive or manic syndromes in each group. They were able to demonstrate the association of both syndromes to TS with only a relatively small contribution attributable to ADD. They also presented evidence of a strong linkage between the gene for TS and at least one locus responsible for the presence or expression of manic depression in that "dozens" of carriers of the "TS gene" who manifested either no or mild motor or vocal tics nonetheless had received the diagnosis of depression or manic depression elsewhere. Their findings are particularly provocative because only two previous reports of the association of TS with major affective disorders are present in the literature (Bleich, Bernout, Apter, & Tyano, 1985; Penna & Lion, 1975). A subsequent paper (Kerbeshian &

Burd, 1988) described the efficacy of lithium in 5 of 10 children and adolescents with TS, all of whom also had bipolar symptomatology. They conceived of lithium as a probe with which they hoped to dissect the diagnostic categories in order to gain insight into the underlying neurophysiology of TS, bipolar disorder, and ADHD. They found a negative relationship between response to lithium and the diagnosis or family history of ADHD, as well as with the combination of psychotic symptoms and the absence of grandiosity. They concluded that TS may be a stage in the development of more clearly defined adult psychiatric disorders. Comings and Comings (1987a) noted the typical natural history of comorbid TS in children as following the diagnosis of ADHD by 2.4 years. They recommended that children with disruptive behavior with significant disturbance of mood, the presence of tics, and the absence of grandiosity be followed closely for the future development of thought disorder. In view of an earlier study of 250 TS sufferers by Comings and Comings (1985), which found 54% to suffer from ADHD and 61% to have significant discipline problems and/or anger problems, children with Tourette's disorder are clearly at high risk.

ALCOHOL ABUSE AND DEPENDENCE

Famularo, Stone, and Popper (1985) presented data on 10 children who met the criteria for *DSM-III* alcohol abuse or dependence by age 13. All but one suffered from a major affective disorder. The single exception had the diagnosis of atypical psychosis, which is often the label given to children during their first manic episodes. Six children received the diagnosis of bipolar disorder. Of the six, four completed adequate trials of lithium, three achieving an excellent, and one a good, response to the medication.

CASE EXAMPLE

An 8-year-old girl recently hospitalized by one of the authors (MHH) illustrates the interplay among several of the above factors. She was referred to a private psychiatric hospital after threatening to kill herself as well as her mother and brother. She was sleeping only three to four hours a night, was very hyperactive, had lost five pounds during the past 2 months (despite a voracious

appetite), and had severe problems with inattention in the classroom. She had previously picked up and thrown her maternal grandmother by wrapping her arms around her grandmother's legs and lifting. Shortly after her mother had undergone abdominal surgery, the child struck her in the abdomen with her fist as she walked by, calling the act "an accident" and then laughing. She also had tried to cut her wrist with a plastic knife and had been suspended from school for the last 2½ months of the previous academic year for assaulting a teacher. She was oppositional with all adults. She had been diagnosed with ADHD by educational psychologists 6 months before the hospitalization and then had been placed on oral methylphenidate, 15 milligrams, each morning and noon, by a pediatrician, reportedly with an improvement in her ADHD symptoms. She and her mother had seen a succession of psychologists for individual and conjoint family therapy regarding the child's problems. Numerous relatives, both female and male, had histories of alcohol and drug dependence, difficulties in school, and problems with law enforcement authorities; several had been treated in forensic psychiatric facilities, with at least one receiving a definite diagnosis of bipolar disorder within the last few years. Her mother also had been diagnosed as suffering from a depressive disorder of possibly bipolar type and had children fathered by several different men. During the initial interview, the child seemed ashamed to meet the gaze of the examining psychiatrist and spent much of the time describing apparent auditory and visual hallucinations with a histrionic style that earlier had convinced the admissions clerk that they were merely attention-seeking ploys. Although smiling much of the time, she exuded an anxious dysphoria and described a mixed mood. She exhibited high-average to above-average intellect but was disorganized and easily distracted. There was no evidence that she was attending to hallucinations during the interview. Indeed, she frequently sought the attention of her mother, who appeared haggard and did not participate in her child's inpatient treatment, instead taking "time off."

On the ward, she exhibited a high activity level and little sense of give and take with her peers. She was often irritable when she was not engaged in frenetic, clowning behavior, which appeared to be a means of distracting herself from more dysphoric affects. She was observed to apparently attend to visual hallucinations, at which time she described a "ghost" hovering above one of her peers. Discontinuation of methylphenidate with the substitution of imipramine to treat depressive and ADHD symptoms and subsequent addition of lithium carbonate yielded, in a supportive and structured milieu, a cheerful and well-behaved child who performed well in the hospital classroom where she had previously been the primary source of disruption.

Etiologies of Mania

In the area of etiology we find yet another topic that has so far received little attention in the literature. Theorists have perhaps been reluctant to hypothesize about childhood cyclic mood disorders because the issue would largely involve conceptions of pathology in adults being tested in children, while clinicians who work mostly with adults may seldom be in a position to evaluate child populations.

PSYCHOANALYTIC THEORIES

Bleiberg (1991) provides an excellent review of mood disorders in children and adolescents, which argues for continued attention to psychodynamic formulations not as etiologic explanations of the disturbances but as crucial to understanding the presentation of mood disorders, particularly in regard to developmental factors, and to the selection of an appropriate approach to psychotherapy. He is not shy about discussing the shortcomings of previous psychoanalytic theories of childhood mood disorders, or more frequently the lack of such theories. Rather, he points out the valuable advances in our understanding of childhood development resulting from the work of psychoanalysts and psychoanalytically informed researchers.

NEUROCHEMICAL AND STRUCTURAL THEORIES

Dewan, Haldipur, Lane, et al. (1988) performed comprehensive quantitative computed tomography of the brains of 26 patients with *DSM-III* bipolar disorder and 22 controls and found increased third ventricular size and increased periventricular and anterior cortical white matter density. Similar findings have been reported in patients with schizophrenia and are thought by the authors likely to represent characteristics shared by psychotic disorders rather than being

specific to bipolar disorder. The other important feature associated with bipolarity in this study was increased density of the right temporal lobe, which had been previously noted in Alzheimer's disease but not in psychosis. Numerous studies using a variety of methodologies have suggested nondominant temporal lobe involvement in bipolar disorder. In a companion study, Dewan, Haldipur, Boucher, et al. (1988), compared electroencephalograms, the Halstead-Reitan Neuropsychological Battery, premorbid personality adjustment, family history of affective disorder, positive and negative symptoms, employment history, and response to lithium carbonate treatment in computed tomography (CT) positive and CT negative patients from the previous sample; not a single significant correlation was found. Besides looking at the CT findings, they examined lateral ventriculomegaly, because previous studies have found this abnormality associated with a bipolar diagnosis. They discussed explanations for their negative findings in detail. Most significant are the questions of whether recognizable structural abnormalities precede or follow clinical manifestations and whether the CT findings reported are stable in individual patients. Few reports examining biological etiology in children were found. In a pilot study of magnetic resonance imaging of the brain of 8- to 16-year-olds with a *DSM-III-R* (APA, 1987) diagnosis of mania, Botteron, Vannier, Geller, Todd, and Lee (1995) found ventricular enlargement or asymmetry or white matter abnormalities in 4 of 8 manic subjects and 1 of 5 controls. They note the importance of establishing the parameters of normal development since ventricular size was correlated positively with age in both manic and control subjects.

GENERAL MEDICAL DIFFERENTIAL DIAGNOSIS

The differential diagnosis of manic and bipolar syndromes is much less well defined in children and adolescents than in adults. This is a result of the recent recognition of these syndromes as well as the lower base rate of causative general medical disorders in younger populations. Thus it may be several years before the differential has been adequately enlarged by case reports and collections. The paper by Larson and Richelson (1988) summarized organic mania in adults and may be a good starting point for medical investigation of new-onset mania in children as well.

Organic Mood Disorders: Organic disorders of mood are generally believed to be relatively rare in childhood. Larson and Richelson (1988) reviewed the organic causes of mania and noted that the organic mania usually appeared in persons older than 35 years of age, while late adolescence through the mid-20s is the typical period of onset for the first episode of mania in the development of bipolar disorder (primary idiopathic mania). However, they also make the point that organic mania and the manic onset of bipolar disorder can be indistinguishable clinically and in their response to lithium. For this reason it would seem prudent to evaluate first-onset mania, even in children, with the following:

1) careful elicitation of the history regarding current medical symptoms, recent infections, use of medications or drugs of abuse, and past history and family history of psychiatric disorders; 2) complete medical examination, in conjunction with a neurologic consultation if unexplained neurologic deficits are present; 3) computed tomography of the head, electroencephalography, and determination of serum thyroxine [high sensitivity], vitamin B$_{12}$, and [red blood cell] folate levels; and 4) screening for drugs and toxins. Additional studies should be ordered if abnormalities are found. (p. 909)

In the treatment of organic mania, the underlying pathology should be addressed first; antimanic agents, primarily lithium, should be considered to manage the psychiatric manifestations.

Trauma is an occasional cause of mania. Joshi, Capozzoli, and Coyle (1985) describe the case of a 10-year-old girl who had suffered a closed-head traumatic brain injury at the age of four when she was struck by a car. After recovering from a coma of 1 week's duration, she developed persistent hyperactivity, impulsivity, distractibility, irritability, and grandiosity. Serious problems with destructiveness, cruelty to animals, and fire-setting appeared. Treatment with psychostimulants was unsuccessful. Manic behaviors became progressively more evident until treatment with lithium was instituted; she rapidly returned to a euthymic state. Trials of carbamazepine and sodium valproate had to be terminated due to a generalized pruritic rash and deteriorating psychiatric condition respec-

tively. An important prospective study of head-injured children by Brown, Chadwick, Shaffer, Rutter, and Traub (1981), utilizing orthopedically injured controls, found significant psychiatric morbidity only in the group who suffered post-traumatic amnesia lasting a week or more (severe). The mildly head-injured children seem to have had behavior problems pretraumatically that may have predisposed them to the injuries and that did not worsen with follow-up. Approximately half of the severely head-injured children developed psychiatric disorders not present prior to the injury and that were not correlated with the severity of physical disability. Although no distinctive patterns of symptomatology emerged from the study, several of the children described as disinhibited also might have been characterized as manic or hypomanic. For example, of these children, two were noted to undress at home at inappropriate times (one would then dance in the living room to music on the record player), one was overly talkative, and one child (not described as disinhibited) developed a psychosis with "agitation, flight of ideas, ideas of reference, [and] silly giggling" (p. 74). Of course, these symptoms are impossible to evaluate adequately without the full psychiatric interview. It is also not clear what diagnostic criteria formed the basis for the interviews of the parents and children.

In one 5-year-old girl, tuberous sclerosis that eventually caused major motor epilepsy was described (Khanna & Borde, 1989). A definite right temporal lobe focus of epileptiform activity was found on EEG. The girl responded to carbamazepine with a decrease in seizures and an increase in "irritable, abusive, and demanding" behavior. The addition of haloperidol led to marked improvement in her behavioral symptoms.

Reported cases of treatment-induced manic or depressive syndromes in children and adolescents are limited to those caused by medication. They include episodes attributed to amitriptyline (hypomania: Kashani, Hodges, & Shekim, 1980), fluoxetine (Achamallah & Decker, 1991), and carbamazepine (mania: Myers & Carrera, 1989; Pleak, Birmaher, Gavrilescu, Abichandani, & Williams, 1988; Reiss and O'Donnell, 1984). Pleak et al. (1988) point out the strong similarity between the molecular structure of carbamazepine and imipramine thereby invoking the antidepressant-induced manic "switch" that has been reported in adults. Some researchers have hypothesized that such a response merely uncovers a propensity to develop bipolar disorder. Others argue that antidepressant use does not lead to an increase in subsequent manic episodes over what would be expected in persons treated with other means.

As noted earlier, the case described by Jemerin et al. (1988) likely represents the effects of severe family dysfunction on children and may merit only an adjustment disorder diagnosis or a "V code." Most clinicians are familiar with such chaotic behavior in children from families with disturbed relationships, but often the child must be evaluated in a controlled environment for a period of time so that an appropriate baseline may be established. The symptomatic behaviors almost invariably return when the child is again exposed to family influences. Table 30.1 lists differential diagnoses of mania in children and adolescents.

Treatment

While the "biological" nature of bipolar disorder is well accepted, it is important not to narrow our vision of treatment to somatic therapies any more than to treat patients with a bipolar diagnosis with psychotherapy alone. Again, the case described by Jemerin et al. (1988) is instructive in that the diagnosis itself could not be made accurately without venturing into realms inaccessible to pharmacologic treatment. Thus the approach should be bal-

TABLE 30.1

Differential Diagnosis of Mania in Children and Adolescents

	Bipolar Disorder	Attention Deficit Hyperactivity Disorder	Schizophrenia and Psychotic Disorder Not Otherwise Specified	Organic Mania
Usual Onset Age	late adolescence?	before age 7	young adult	adult
Premorbid Personality	energetic, outgoing, no obvious psychopathology	often normal although may be irritable	schizoid, withdrawn in about 1/4 of patients	no typical pattern
Onset Rate	rapid	insidious	rapid	rapid
Course	episodic	continuous	episodic	continuous
Elevated, Expansive, or Irritable Mood	present	frequent	varies with type	present
Psychosis	frequent	absent	present	frequent
Organic Factor	absent	absent	absent	present
Bipolar Family History	present	absent	absent	absent
Response to Lithium	usually good to excellent	poor	poor	variable
Goal-Directed Behavior	frequent	absent	may be present	may be present
Overactivity or Restlessness	present	present	may be present	present
Short Attention Span	present	present	may be present	present
Distractibility	variable	present	may be present	variable
Impulsivity	present	present	may be present	present

NOTE. From M. H. Henigan, ms. in preparation, 1996. Reprinted with permission.

anced and may be provided by an individual psychiatrist or a multidisciplinary team. However, there is relatively little research to guide treatment selection. Kafantaris's (1995) recent review of the literature on the treatment of bipolar disorder in children and adolescents found no adequately controlled studies of any component of the biopsychosocial treatment of mania. The following summary of studies is intended provide a rational basis for clinical decision making.

SOMATIC TREATMENT OF BIPOLAR DISORDER

Pharmacologic Treatment: Lithium has been the mainstay of the pharmacotherapy of bipolar disorder in adults for many years. Similar effectiveness has been found in children. Varanka, Weller, Weller, and Fristad (1988) treated 10 prepubertal 6 to 12-year olds with a *DSM-III* diagnosis of manic episode with psychotic features. All of the children improved substantially in both manic and psychotic symptoms in an average of 11 days following the rapid initiation of lithium therapy. No systematic follow-up was done. On the other hand, DeLong and Aldershof (1987) followed 196 children with *DSM-III* diagnoses of bipolar affective disorder ($n = 59$), emotionally unstable character disorder (EUCD; $n = 11$), attention deficit disorder (ADD; $n = 19$), unipolar depression ($n = 29$), conduct disorder ($n = 33$), or a family history of a lithium-responsive parent ($n = 7$) for as long as 10 years. Double-blind placebo-controlled and open discontinuation trials were used to demonstrate efficacy. Lithium was persistently effective for at least two-thirds of the bipolar, ADD, and EUCD groups as well as mixed groups involving a combination of affective disorder and behavior. It was also effective over a study period of 7 to 48 months for a group of neurologically disordered children with either rage or aggressiveness and encopresis. As a result of their studies, the authors conclude that a trial of lithium therapy should be provided for treatment-resistant children manifesting certain clinical features, diagnosis notwithstanding, including: cyclic affective extremes, especially hateful hostile anger, and manic overexcitement; a family history of affective disorder, especially bipolar; aggressiveness; and prominent neurovegetative disorders, especially hyperphagia, hyperdipsia, salt-craving, and encopresis. The question of whether these problems (including the neurovegetative disorders) share a common pathological core is unexplored.

Weller, Weller, and Fristad (1986) provided a guide for rapid initiation of lithium therapy in prepubertal children that is based on weight with the goal of achieving a serum lithium level of 0.6 to 1.2 within a few days. Advantages include more rapid achievement of therapeutic effect and fewer phlebotomies. In a subsequent paper (Weller et al., 1987), the authors discuss the technique of monitoring lithium levels in the saliva, which has many potential advantages in children. Spencer et al. (1990) review the current status of saliva lithium monitoring and point out that even after establishing a strong correlation between serum and saliva levels in a patient, it is important also to monitor the clinical status and fluid intake closely because little reasearch was reported that assesses how effective the method is in avoiding toxicity. Usable guidelines may be available eventually.

Carbamazepine has long been used as a drug of second choice for mania in adults and has been used for disorders marked by poor impulse control as well. It has been used in children most often for behavior disorders thought to be the result of neurologic damage and partial complex ("temporal lobe") seizure activity. An excellent review of its use in child psychiatry has been published (Evans, Clay, & Gualtieri, 1987). More than in adult psychiatry, carbamazepine should likely be reserved for patients who fail to respond to lithium, because its efficacy has been less well documented and because adverse behavioral reactions to it are more common than with lithium. As noted earlier, carbamazepine has been responsible for cases of iatrogenic mania, presumably because of its structural similarity to the tricyclic antidepressants. Although anticonvulsants other than carbamazepine have been used successfully to treat adult mania, so far there have been no controlled studies in children with mood disorders (Gadow, 1991).

Electroseizure Therapy: Despite its poor public image, electroseizure therapy still is used to treat a number of conditions. The technique has undergone dramatic improvement, making it an attractive choice in geriatric depression due to a favorable side effect profile when compared to most antidepressants. Experience in children has been much more limited. Bertagnoli and Borchardt

(1990) reviewed the literature on the topic and concluded that it is an effective treatment for children with bipolar disorder and depression, with the unexplored potential to produce rapid clearing of symptoms in otherwise treatment-resistant cases. They point out, however, the continued need to be vigilant for complications and to respond to them appropriately.

PSYCHOTHERAPEUTIC TREATMENT

Little has been written specifically on psychotherapy of childhood bipolar disorder, particularly mania.

One exception to this dearth of psychotherapeutic literature is a psychoanalytic/psychodynamic paper by Kestenbaum and Kron (1987). In their excellent synthesis of the literature and case studies, they emphasize the importance of an integrated rather than eclectic approach to the treatment of bipolar disorder in children and adolescents, an approach they feel is most appropriate to the medically and analytically or psychodynamically trained psychiatrist. They discuss one patient whom one of the authors first saw for psychoanalysis at age 10 and describe certain features of patients with bipolar disorder that have been prominent in their experience with treatment in a psychoanalytic/medical setting. These include family history of bipolar disorder, a significantly lower performance IQ than verbal IQ with much subtest scatter, and specific symptoms including temper tantrums, compulsive rituals, dysphoria, mood lability, obsessional preoccupation, problems with learning, hyperactivity, and impulsivity. These findings are similar to those noted by Akiskal et al. (1983). Specific psychotherapeutic issues with these patients included poor self-esteem covered by a "veneer" of narcissism and grandiosity and manifested by extreme sensitivity to criticism, resultant powerful use of denial, extreme sensitivity to loss, a need to understand the biological basis and course of their illness as well as the anticipated effects of medication, a need to know the stresses that can trigger an affective episode (e.g., "work pressures, menses, exhaustion"), and a need to learn to monitor their emotional state and to respond appropriately to regulate their behavior and to seek further psychiatric attention promptly. The goal of such therapy is not only to resolve problems arising from previous experience but to give patients the tools they need to collaborate most ably in their care.

FAMILY SYSTEMS APPROACHES TO TREATMENT

Weber, Simon, Stierlin, and Schmidt (1988) maintain that families in which bipolar illness flourishes operate on an either/or and all-or-nothing basis utilizing assumptions that lead to dilemmas that stimulate either manic or depressive reactions. Such a system leads family members to perceive events in extremes, with some members at each pole as well as some who seem to undergo transformations from one end of the behavioral spectrum to the other. To counterbalance the manic individual, some or all of the family members must aggregate at the depressive/controlled pole to preserve family integrity. However, the tension between conflicting roles leads all members to feel threatened at one time or another, with persons at each pole attempting to sway the balance lest their own sense of control be lessened. Children ally themselves with an adult figure to avoid being overwhelmed and to find some security in the chaos. Despite the apparent disruptive influence of severe affective episodes, they serve to mobilize the will of both groups of family members, actually serving to unify the family around the "sick" person, only to be destabilized again. The therapeutic techniques utilized by Weber et al. center on exploring the pattern of dynamics in the family, specifically focusing on restrictive patterns. The therapist's goal is to preserve therapeutic neutrality as each group attempts to draw him or her to its side.

CASE EXAMPLE

Some principles just discussed are illustrated by an exceptionally intelligent 11-year-old boy who was brought for consultation because of his poor response to current medication and the inability of his current physician to provide individual or family therapy. He was being treated with imipramine for ADHD and would develop irritability and episodes of crying when he forgot to take it. He frequently exhibited increased hyperactivity and defensiveness, getting up from bed late at night and walking around the house crying uncontrollably even when taking the medication regularly. At school he got into trouble for talking even though he always had been considered something of a loner. Both sides of the family contained numerous relatives who were severely mentally ill, most with mood disorders or alcohol dependence, some of whom were maintained on psychotropic medications. His mother noted that he had an exceptional imagination and had written "fantastic stories." He fulfilled the criteria for major depression. However, on further questioning, he was discovered to have periods of excessive activity with grandiose plans and an expansive mood that could rapidly deteriorate into tearful irritability if he became frustrated. Addition of lithium carbonate and consolidation of his imipramine doses to bedtime led to a rapid resolution of all symptoms including those previously attributed to ADHD. Concurrent family therapy began to relieve feelings of alienation between family members, which appeared to derive from the parents' experiences of growing up in households dominated by severe mood disorders. Individual therapy was focused on building self-esteem and cognitive methods of combatting the boy's negative perceptions of himself and his surroundings.

Directions for Future Investigation

In order to firmly establish the diagnostic criteria for mania and bipolar disorder in children and adolescents, it will be important to conduct naturalistic studies of young people with a genetic predisposition for these disorders. A number of relatively small-scale, more focused studies have been done. However, a large longitudinal project with reviews of psychiatric status performed at developmentally relevant intervals would be invaluable. Because such a project would be so expensive and would require the time of many researchers and a multitude of research subjects, it would have to study developmental manifestations of psychopathology for a variety of disorders. A systematic retrospective study of symptom development in patients already diagnosed with bipolar disorder would provide candidate criteria for a consensus definition of the syndromes, which could then be tested for validity, reliability, and distinguishability from recognized disorders in children. Only by such an empirical approach can we expect to see consistent enough application of criteria for bipolar disorder to change clinical practice significantly.

An interesting letter to the *Journal of the American Academy of Child and Adolescent Psychiatry* (Picker, Solomon, & Gertner, 1990) noted a strong susceptibility to the thyroid suppressant properties of lithium in two half brothers, suggesting that a study of parent-to-child transmission might allow us to avoid cases of iatrogenic hypothyroidism in children with relatives who have had such a reaction.

The subjective description of symptoms by children and adolescents is a little-researched area that poses significant problems in the diagnosis of many disorders. In its most refined form, study of this topic involves linguistic sophistication. On the other hand, the initial field studies would require only the willingness to listen and to correlate descriptions with standard diagnostic instruments.

Finally, controlled studies of the efficacy of various treatments for these disorders are of extreme importance to provide a rational basis for treatment selection.

While this description of research topics is brief, there are important unresearched questions concerning every phase of the study of cyclic mood disorders in children.

REFERENCES

Achamallah, N. S., & Decker, D. H. (1991). Mania induced by fluoxetine in an adolescent patient. *American Journal of Psychiatry, 148,* 1404.

Akiskal, H. S. (1995). Developmental pathways to bipolarity: are juvenile-onset depressions pre-bipolar? *Journal of the American Academy of Child and Adolescent Psychiatry, 34,* 754–763.

Akiskal, H. S., Downs, J., Jordan, P., Watson, S., Daugherty, D., & Pruitt, D. B. (1985). Affective disorders in referred children and younger siblings of manic-depressives. *Archives of General Psychiatry, 42,* 996.

Akiskal, H. S., Hirschfeld, M. A., & Yerevanian, B. I. (1983). The relationship of personality to affective disorders. *Archives of General Psychiatry, 40,* 801–810.

Akiskal, H. S., Khani, M. K., & Scott-Strauss, A. (1979). Cyclothymic temperamental disorders. *Psychiatric Clinics of North America, 2,* 527–554.

Akiskal, H. S., & Weller, E. B. (1989). Mood disorders and suicide in children and adolescents. In H. I.

Kaplan & B. J. Sadock (Eds.), *Comprehensive textbook of psychiatry* (5th ed., pp. 1981–1994). Baltimore: Williams and Wilkins.

American Psychiatric Association. (1980). *Diagnostic and statistical manual of mental disorders* (3rd ed.), Washington, DC: Author.

American Psychiatric Association. (1987). *Diagnostic and statistical manual of mental disorders* (3rd ed., rev.). Washington, DC: Author.

American Psychiatric Association. (1994). *Diagnostic and statistical manual of mental disorders* (4th ed.). Washington, DC: Author.

Anthony, J., & Scott, P. (1960). Manic-depressive psychosis in childhood. *Child Psychology and Psychiatry, 1,* 53–72.

Ballenger, H. C., Reus, V. I., & Post, R. M. (1982). The "atypical" picture of adolescent mania. *American Journal of Psychiatry, 139,* 602–606.

Bertagnoli, M. W., & Borchardt, C. M. (1990). A review of ECT for children and adolescents. *Journal of the American Academy of Child and Adolescent Psychiatry, 29,* 302–307.

Biederman, J., Munir, K., Knee, D., Armentano, M., Autor, S., Waternaus, C., & Tsuang, M. (1987). High rate of affective disorder in probands with attention deficit disorder and in their relatives: A controlled family study. *American Journal of Psychiatry, 144,* 330–333.

Bleiberg E. (1991). Mood disorders in children and adolescents. *Bulletin of the Menninger Clinic, 55,* 192–204.

Bleich, A., Bernout, E., Apter, A., & Tyano, S. (1985). Gilles de la Tourette syndrome and mania in an adolescent. *British Journal of Psychiatry, 146,* 664–665.

Botteron, K. N., Vannier, M. W., Geller, B., Todd, R. D., & Lee, B. C. P. (1995). Preliminary study of magnetic resonance imaging characteristics in 8- to 16-year-olds with mania. *Journal of the American Academy of Child and Adolescent Psychiatry, 34,* 742–749.

Bowden, C. L., & Sarabia, F. (1980). Diagnosing manic-depressive illness in adolescents. *Comprehensive Psychiatry, 21,* 263–269.

Brown, G., Chadwick, O., Shaffer, D., Rutter, M., & Traub, M. (1981). A prospective study of children with head injuries: III. Psychiatric sequelae. *Psychological Medicine, 11,* 63–78.

Campbell, M., Small, A. M., Green, W. H., Jennings, S. J., Perry, R., Bennett, W. G., & Anderson, L. (1984). Behavioral efficacy of haloperidol and lithium carbonate. *Archives of General Psychiatry, 41,* 650–656.

Carlson, G. A. (1990). Annotation: Child and adolescent mania—diagnostic considerations. *Journal of Child Psychology and Psychiatry, 31,* 331–341.

Carlson, G. A. (1995). Identifying prepubertal mania. *Journal of the American Academy of Child and Adolescent Psychiatry, 34,* 750–753.

Carlson, G. A., & Kashani, J. H. (1988). Manic symptoms in a non-referred adolescent population. *Journal of Affective Disorders, 15,* 219–226.

Carlson, G. A., & Strober, M. (1978). Affective disorder in adolescence: Issues in misdiagnosis. *Journal of Clinical Psychiatry, 39,* 59–66.

Comings, D. E., & Comings, B. G. (1987a). A controlled study of Tourette Syndrome. I. Attention deficit disorder, learning disorders, and school problems. *American Journal of Human Genetics, 41,* 701–741.

Comings, B. G., & Comings, D. E. (1987b). A controlled study of Tourette syndrome. V. Depression and mania. *American Journal of Human Genetics, 41,* 804–821.

Comings, D. E., & Comings, B. G. (1985). Tourette Syndrome: Clinical and psychological aspects of 250 cases. *American Journal of Human Genetics, 37,* 435–450.

DeLong, G. R., & Aldershof, A. L. (1987). Long-term experience with lithium treatment in childhood: Correlation with clinical diagnosis. *Journal of the American Academy of Child and Adolescent Psychiatry, 26,* 389–394.

Dewan, M. J., Haldipur, C. V., Boucher, M. F., Ramachandran, T., & Major, L. F. (1988). Bipolar affective disorder: II. EEG, neuropsychological, and clinical correlates of CT abnormality. *Acta Psychiatrica Scandinavica, 77,* 677–682.

Dewan, M. J., Haldipur, C. V., Lane, E. E., Ispahani, A., Boucher, M. F., & Major, L. F. (1988). Bipolar affective disorder: I. Comprehensive quantitative computed tomography. *Acta Psychiatrica Scandinavica, 77,* 670–676.

Dulcan, M. K. (1990). Using psychostimulants to treat behavioral disorders of children and adolescents. *Journal of Child and Adolescent Psychopharmacology, 1,* 7–20.

Dwyer, J. T., & DeLong, G. R. (1987). A family history study of twenty probands with childhood manic-depressive illness. *Journal of the American Academy of Child and Adolescent Psychiatry, 26* (2), 176–180.

Egeland, J. A., Blumenthal, R. L., Nee, J., Sharpe, L., & Endicott, J. (1987). Reliability and relationship of various ages of onset criteria for major affective disorder. *Journal of Affective Disorders, 12,* 159–165.

Egeland, J. A., Gerhard, D. S., Pauls, D. L., Sussex, J. N., Kidd, K. K., Allen, C. R., Hostetter, A. M., & Housman, D. E. (1987). Bipolar affective disorders linked to DNA markers on chromosome 11. *Nature, 325,* 783–787.

Evans, R. W., Clay, T. H., & Gualtieri, C. T. (1987). Carbamazepine in pediatric psychiatry. *Journal of the American Academy of Child and Adolescent Psychiatry, 26,* 2–8.

Famularo, R., Stone, K., & Popper, C. (1985). Preadolescent alcohol abuse and dependence. *American Journal of Psychiatry, 142,* 1187–1189.

Fristad, M. A., Weller, E. B., & Weller, R. A. (1992). The mania rating scale: Can it be used in children? A preliminary report. *Journal of the American Academy of Child and Adolescent Psychiatry, 31,* 252–257. Erratum (1992). *Journal of the American Academy of Child and Adolescent Psychiatry, 31,* 1001.

Gadow, K. D. (1991). Clinical issues in child and adolescent psychopharmacology. *Journal of Consulting and Clinical Psychology, 59*, 842–852.

Hays, P., & Field, L. L. (1989). Postulated genetic linkage between manic-depression and stuttering. *Journal of Affective Disorders, 16*, 37–40.

Henigan M. H., manuscript in preparation, 1996.

Isaac, G. (1991). Bipolar disorder in prepubertal children in a special educational setting: Is it rare? *Journal of Clinical Psychiatry, 52*, 165–168.

Janowsky, D. S., & Davis, J. M. (1980). Cholinergic mechanism in mania and depression. In R. H. Belmaker, & H. M. van Praag (Eds.). *Mania, an evolving concept.* New York: Spectrum.

Jemerin, J. M., Roebuck, K., & Philips, I. (1988). Bipolar disorder in a six-year-old boy: A diagnosis by proxy. *Journal of the American Academy of Child and Adolescent Psychiatry, 27*, 133–137.

Joshi, P., Capozzoli, J. A., & Coyle, J. T. (1985). Effective management with lithium of a persistent, post-traumatic hypomania in a 10-year-old child. *Developmental and Behavioral Pediatrics, 6*, 352–354.

Kafantaris, V. (1995). Treatment of bipolar disorder in children and adolescents. *Journal of the American Academy of Child and Adolescent Psychiatry, 34*, 732–741.

Kashani, J. H., Goddard, P., & Reid, J. C. (1989). Correlates of suicidal ideation in a community sample of children and adolescents. *Journal of the American Academy of Child and Adolescent Psychiatry, 28*, 912–917.

Kashani, J. H., Hodges, K. K., & Shekim, W. O. (1980). Hypomanic reaction to amitriptyline in a depressed child. *Psychosomatics, 21*, 867–868.

Kerbeshian, J., & Burd, L. (1988). Differential responsiveness to lithium in patients with Tourette disorder. *Neuroscience & Biobehavioral Reviews, 12*, 247–250.

Kerbeshian, J., Burd, L., & Fisher, W. (1987). Lithium carbonate in the treatment of two patients with infantile autism and atypical bipolar symptomatology. *Journal of Clinical Psychopharmacology, 7*, 401–405.

Kestenbaum, C. J., & Kron, L. (1987). Psychoanalytic intervention with children and adolescents with affective disorders: A combined treatment approach. *Journal of the American Academy of Psychoanalysis, 15*, 153–174.

Khanna, R., & Borde, M. (1989). Mania in a five-year-old child with tuberous sclerosis. *British Journal of Psychiatry, 155*, 117–119.

Koehler-Troy, C., Strober, M., & Malenbaum, R. (1986). Methylphenidate-induced mania in a prepubertal child. *Journal of Clinical Psychiatry, 47*, 566–567.

Kovacs, M., & Pollock, M. (1995). Bipolar disorder and comorbid conduct disorder in childhood and adolescence. *Journal of the American Academy of Child and Adolescent Psychiatry, 34*, 715–723.

Kraepelin, E. (1921). *Manic-depressive insanity and paranoia.* Edinburgh: Livingstone.

LaRoche, C., Cheifetz, P., Lester, E. P., Schibuk, L., DiTommaso, E., & Engelsmann, F. (1985). Psychopa-

thology in the offspring of parents with bipolar affective disorders. *Canadian Journal of Psychiatry, 30*, 337–343.

LaRoche, C., Sheiner, R., Lester, E., Benierakis, C., Marrache, M., Engelsmann, F., & Cheifetz, P. (1987). Children of parents with manic-depressive illness: A follow-up study. *Canadian Journal of Psychiatry, 32*, 563–560.

Larson, E. W., & Richelson, E. (1988). Organic causes of mania. *Mayo Clinic Proceedings, 63*, 906–912.

Lefkowitz, M. M., & Tesiny, E. P. (1980). Assessment of childhood depression. *Journal of Consulting and Clinical Psychology, 48*, 43–50.

McCracken, J. T., & Diamond, R. P. (1988). Bipolar disorder in mentally retarded adolescents. *Journal of the American Academy of Child and Adolescent Psychiatry, 27*, 494–499.

Miller, D. (1986). Affective disorders and violence in adolescents. *Hospital & Community Psychiatry, 37*, 591–596.

Myers, W. C., & Carrera, F. (1989). Carbamazepine-induced mania with hypersexuality in 9-year-old boy. *American Journal of Psychiatry, 146*, 400.

Nieman, G. W., & DeLong, R. (1987). Use of the Personality Inventory for Children as an aid in differentiating children with mania from children with attention deficit disorder with hyperactivity. *Journal of the American Academy of Child and Adolescent Psychiatry, 26*, 381–388.

Penna, M. W., & Lion, J. R. (1975). Gilles de la Tourette's syndrome and depression: A case report. *Diseases of the Nervous System, 36*, 41–43.

Picker, W., Solomon, G., & Gertner, J. M. (1990). Lithium side effect [Letter to the editor]. *Journal of the American Academy of Child and Adolescent Psychiatry, 29*, 489.

Pleak, R. R., Birmaher, B., Gavrilescu, A., Abichandani, C., & Williams, D. T. (1988). Mania and neuropsychiatric excitation following carbamazepine. *Journal of the American Academy of Child and Adolescent Psychiatry, 27*, 500–503.

Reiss, A. L. (1985). Developmental manifestations in a boy with prepubertal bipolar disorder. *Journal of Clinical Psychiatry, 46*, 441–443.

Reiss, A. L., & O'Donnell, D. J. (1984). Carbamazepine-induced mania in two children: Case report. *Journal of Clinical Psychiatry, 45*, 272–274.

Rice, J., Reich, T., Andreasen, N. C., Endicott, J., Van Eerdewegh, M., Fishman, R., Hirschfeld, R. M. A., & Klerman, G. L. (1987). The familial transmission of bipolar illness. *Archives of General Psychiatry, 44*, 441–447.

Rivinius, T. M., & Harmatz, J. S. (1979). Diagnosis and lithium treatment of affective disorder in the retarded: Five case studies. *American Journal of Psychiatry, 136*, 551–554.

Rogeness, G. A., Riester, A. E., & Wicoff, J. S. (1982). Unusual presentation of manic depressive disorder in adolescence. *Journal of Clinical Psychiatry, 43*, 37–39.

Schmidt, K., Delaney, M. A., Jensen, M., Levinson,

D. F., & Lewitt, M. (1986). Methylphenidate challenge in a young boy. *Biological Psychiatry, 21,* 1107–1109.

Sibisi, C. D. T. (1990). Sex differences in the age of onset of bipolar affective illness. *British Journal of Psychiatry, 156,* 842–845.

Spencer, E. K., Campbell, M., Adams, P., Perry, R., Choroco, M. C., Padron-Gayol, M., & Small, A. M. (1990). Saliva and serum lithium monitoring in hospitalized children. *Psychopharmacology Bulletin, 26,* 239–243.

Stedman, T. L. (1982). *Stedman's Medical Dictionary.* Baltimore: Williams & Wilkins.

Steingard, R., & Biederman, J. (1987). Lithium-responsive manic-like symptoms in two individuals with autism and mental retardation. *Journal of the American Academy of Child and Adolescent Psychiatry, 26,* 932–935.

Strober, M., Morrell, W., Burroughs, J., Lampert, C., Danforth, H., & Freeman, R. (1988). A family study of bipolar I disorder in adolescence: Early onset of symptoms linked to increased familial loading and lithium resistance. *Journal of Affective Disorders, 15,* 255–268.

Strober, M., Schmidt-Lackner, S., Freeman, R., Bower, S., Lampert, C., & DeAntonio, M., (1995). Recovery and relapse in adolescents with bipolar affective illness: A five-year naturalistic, prospective follow-up. *Journal of the American Academy of Child and Adolescent Psychiatry, 34,* 724–731.

Sylvester, C. E., Burke, P. M., McCawley, E. A., &

Clark, C. J. (1984). Manic psychosis in childhood: Report of two cases. *Journal of Nervous and Mental Disease, 172,* 12–15.

Varanka, T. M., Weller, R. A., Weller, E. B., Fristad, M. A. (1988). Lithium treatment of manic episodes with psychotic features in prepubertal children. *American Journal of Psychiatry, 145,* 1557–1559.

Weber, G., Simon, F. B., Stierlin, H., & Schmidt, G. (1988). Therapy for families manifesting manic-depressive behavior. *Family Process, 27,* 33–49.

Weinberg, W. A., & Brumback, R. A. (1976). Mania in childhood: Case studies and literature review. *American Journal of Diseases of Children, 130,* 380–385.

Weller, E. B., Weller, R. W., & Fristad, M. A. (1986). Lithium dosage guide for prepubertal children: A preliminary report. *Journal of the American Academy of Child and Adolescent Psychiatry, 25,* 92–95.

Weller, E. B., Weller, R. W., Fristad, M. A., Cantwell, M., & Tucker, S. (1987). Saliva lithium monitoring in prepubertal children. *Journal of the American Academy of Child and Adolescent Psychiatry, 26,* 173–175.

Weller, R. A., Weller, E. B., Tucker, S. G., & Fristad, M. A. (1986). Mania in prepubertal children: Has it been underdiagnosed? *Journal of Affective Disorders, 11,* 151–154.

Young, R. C., Biggs, J. T., Ziegler, V. E., & Meyer, D. A., (1978). A rating scale for mania: Reliability, validity and sensitivity *British Journal of Psychiatry, 133,* 429–435.

---

31 / **Dysthymic Disorder in Latency-Age Children**

Javad Kashani and Mark Henigan

Introduction

Chronic smoldering depression in children undoubtedly has been with us for many years, as the sad countenances of waifs toiling in sweatshops in the early industrial revolution so clearly bear witness. That such a state is often endured for a lifetime is also clear. The onset of this disorder, as conceptualized by most psychiatrists, is in childhood. Akiskal (1983) and, later, Kocsis and Frances (1987) argued that childhood onset should be made one of the criteria for diagnosis, thus eliminating the subtype of late onset and "purifying" the category. The debate about whether dysthy-

mia is a subsyndromal form of major depression or a distinct diagnostic entity is far from resolved, partly because the criteria probably encompass a variety of syndromes with depressive characteristics that share a chronic course but that differ in their pathophysiology.

Description

The most widely accepted current diagnostic criteria are those of the *Diagnostic and Statistical Manual of Mental Disorders* (4th ed.) *DSM-IV;*

American Psychiatric Association [APA], 1994), supplied with childhood age-specific features incorporated. Table 31.1 presents these criteria.

Early or late onset distinguishes those cases that begin before age 21 from those beginning at that age or later. This distinction is not of direct value in the diagnosis of childhood and adolescent dysthymia, since all such cases obviously have early onset. However, because the relationship between early- and late-onset cases will provide evidence of (or cast doubt upon) the validity of the diagnosis in younger age groups, it is of considerable heuristic value and will be examined later.

These criteria resulted from significant revision of those in *DSM-III-R* (APA, 1991). Specific concerns that were addressed include the omission of

TABLE 31.1

300.4 Dysthymic Disorder (or Depressive Neurosis)

A. Depressed mood for most of the day, for more days than not, as indicated either by subjective account or observation by others, for at least 2 years. **Note:** In children and adolescents, mood can be irritable and duration must be at least 1 year

B. Presence, while depressed, of at least two (or more) of the following:
   (1) poor appetite or overeating
   (2) insomnia or hypersomnia
   (3) low energy or fatigue
   (4) low self-esteem
   (5) poor concentration or difficulty making decisions
   (6) feelings of hopelessness

C. During a 2-year period (1 year for children or adolescents) of the disturbance, the person has never been without the symptoms in Criteria A and B for more than 2 months at a time.

D. No Major Depressive Episode has been present during the first 2 years of the disturbance (1 year for children and adolescents); i.e., the disturbance is not better accounted for by chronic Major Depressive Disorder, or Major Depressive Disorder, In Partial Remission.
Note: There may have been a previous Major Depressive Episode provided there was a full remission (no significant signs or symptoms for 2 months) before development of the Dysthymic Disorder. In addition, after the initial 2 years (1 year in children and adolescents) of Dysthymic Disorder, there may be superimposed episodes of Major Depression, in which case both diagnoses may be given when the criteria are met for a Major Depressive Episode.

E. There has never been a Manic Episode, a Mixed Episode, or a Hypomanic Episode, and criteria have never been met for Cyclothymic Disorder.

F. The disturbance does not occur exclusively during the course of a chronic Psychotic Disorder, such as Schizophrenia or Delusional Disorder.

G. The symptoms are not due to the direct physiological effects of a substance (e.g., a drug of abuse, a medication) or a general medical condition (e.g., hypothyroidism).

H. The symptoms cause clinically significant distress or impairment in social, occupational, or other important areas of functioning. . . .
Specify (for most recent 2 years of Dysthymic Disorder):

With Atypical Features

A. Mood reactivity (i.e., mood brightnens in response to actual or potential positive events)

B. Two (or more) of the following features:
   (1) significant weight gain or increase in appetite
   (2) hypersomnia
   (3) leaden paralysis (i.e., heavy, leaden feelings in arms or legs)
   (4) long-standing pattern of interpersonal rejection sensitivity (not limited to episodes of mood disturbance) that results in significant social or occupational impairment

C. Criteria are not met for With Melancholic Features or With Catatonic Features during the same episode.

NOTE. From *Diagnostic and Statistical Manual of Mental Disorders*, 4th ed., American Psychological Association, 1994. Washington, D.C.: Author. Copyright 1994 by the American Psychological Association. Reprinted with permission.

many of the symptoms thought to be characteristic of the disorder, the failure to establish the symptom threshold empirically (i.e., the number or severity of symptoms required to make the diagnosis), and the appropriateness of the *DSM-III-R* distinctions among the syndromes of major depression and dysthymia. "Double depression" (a major depressive episode superimposed on dysthymia) has been relegated to a "course specifier" under the rubric of major depressive disorder. However, the two diagnoses are not considered mutually exclusive. Also, the conception of some cases of dysthymic disorder as being "related to a preexisting, chronic, nonmood Axis I or Axis III disorder, e.g., Anorexia Nervosa, Somatization Disorder, a Psychoactive Substance Dependence Disorder, an Anxiety Disorder, or rheumatoid arthritis" has apparently been shorn of close connections to Axis I depressive disorders and given separate form under the diagnoses of substance-induced mood disorder and mood disorder due to a general medical condition.

CHARACTERISTICS OF DYSTHYMIA: SUBCATEGORIES AND COMPARISON WITH OTHER DEPRESSIVE DISORDERS

The following sections examine the concept of dysthymia across a number of dimensions. One section looks at the relationship between dysthymic disorder and other depressive disorders to establish its position within the nosology of mood disorders, while others review the evidence for developmental variation in presentation, caution against diagnosis based on a limited period of observation (because of affective variation in the individual dysthymic patient), and emphasize the dangers inherent in the cornucopia of diagnostic systems and tests currently available. Finally, there is a brief description of the social consequences of dysthymia for the affected child followed by a brief summary of its clinical features.

Variation among Diagnostic Categories: Stark (1990) presented data for numerous symptoms and specific descriptors for children from grades 4 to 7 with major depressive disorder (MDD, $n = 11$), dysthymic disorder (DD, $n = 15$), or depressive disorder not otherwise specified (DDNOS, $n = 35$) compared with 179 children without such diagnoses. His data demonstrate the diverse signs and symptoms of depressive illness

and the importance of not focusing on a rigid diagnostic category as sufficient to indicate the seriousness of a depression. We cannot afford to be complacent with the implications of our current nosology. For example, while 11% of the children with DDNOS thought about suicide (compared with 27% and 7% of those with MDD and DD, respectively), 3% of them performed acts of self-harm, while none of the children in other categories did so. Thus, the group to which we naturally might have ascribed the least potential for harm appears to be the one associated with the greatest risk. While such statistics have limited value due to the small numbers of subjects, they illustrate both the dearth of reliable data on the phenomenology of childhood depression and provide a warning to us as clinicians to take this group of disorders seriously no matter which specific diagnosis is made based on descriptive methods.

McConville, Boag, and Purohit (1973) produced a classification system for childhood depression based on interpersonal style and self-esteem that has partially worked out implications for choice of psychotherapeutic intervention. They postulate three categories of depression, D-1, D-2, and D-3, and a mixed group, D-1/D-2, which they evaluated by studying 75 children with severe depressive symptoms. The D-1 group exhibited predominantly affective disturbance while the D-2 group was distinguished by negative self-esteem. Besides a mixed affective/negative self-esteem category (D-1/D-2), a D-3 group was identified that was characterized by guilt. Although rare, the D-3 group carried a high risk of suicide and often was associated with auditory hallucinations.

Variation among Age Groups: At the time this was written no study was found in the literature that examined variation of the presentation of dysthymia among age groups; MDD has been studied on that dimension. Ryan et al. (1987) evaluated clinically referred samples of 95 children and 92 adolescents using Research Diagnostic Criteria (RDC) for major depressive disorder and found that while most depressive symptoms occurred with similar frequencies in the two groups, prepubertal children exhibited more depressed appearance, somatic complaints, psychomotor agitation, separation anxiety, phobias, and hallucinations while the adolescents exhibited more anhedonia, hopelessness, hypersomnia, weight change, use of alcohol and illicit drugs, and lethality of suicidal method, although severity of suicidal thinking and intent were not significantly different. While the authors concluded that depression is phenomenologically more similar than different in these two groups, they reported potentially significant differences that exist and should be taken into account both in diagnosis and evaluation of response to treatment.

Distinction between Early and Late Subtypes: Few studies have examined the subtyping of dysthemic disorder by age of onset or primary versus secondary origin. Klein, Taylor, Dickstein, and Harding, et al. (1988b) compared primary dysthymics with early and late onset retrospectively for numerous variables and found the early-onset group to have a more serious course with higher levels of depression, higher rates of superimposed major depressive episodes and anxiety disorders, more familial loading, and more frequent seeking of treatment. In another study Klein et al. (1988a) compared primary early-onset dysthymics with patients having primary nonbipolar nonchronic major depression and again found the dysthymic group to have more severe depressive pathology with more comorbid personality disorders and substance abuse as well as a strong family history of affective and antisocial personality disorders. They functioned more poorly and had a weaker social support system. Thus, Klein et al.'s findings suggest that early-onset dysthymia represents a particularly "biological" disorder with a poor prognosis.

Variation within the Individual Patient: One frequently encountered problem in the diagnosis of depressive disorders is the variability of both depressive symptoms and appearance. Observers who see children manifest euthymia at times only to appear profoundly depressed when under stress often are uncertain of the accuracy of the diagnosis and may even make the error of interpreting such variation as "proof" that the child is manipulating his or her caregivers. This problem was addressed in adults by Hall, Sing, and Romanoski (1991), who studied 9 depressed inpatients and 9 nondepressed persons (5 members of nursing staff and 4 patients with paraphilias) with hourly assessment of their moods for 12 hours. They found significantly more variability in the depressed individuals. They also analyzed the data to detect cyclic variation over periods briefer than

a day (termed *ultradian* variation) and found the period to be the same for both groups (4 to 8 hours) while the amplitude of cycles (i.e., the degree of mood change) was significantly greater for the depressed group. This information underscores the need to augment our clinical assessments with data from parents, teachers, and other adults who have the opportunity to interact with children over periods longer than an hour.

Variation Due to Classification Scheme or Diagnostic Instrument: McConville and Bruce (1985) examined the several approaches to classification of depressive illness in children as well as the possible contributions to be made by structured interviews and rating scales. They found these methods to produce grossly similar diagnoses but still to vary in sensitivity, selectivity, and core concept (e.g., "biological" vs. "psychodynamic") enough to raise serious questions about whether research based on them is generalizable and whether data and results from studies using similar but not identical diagnostic operational definitions are more than superficially comparable.

Effects on Social Functioning: It is reasonable to hypothesize that the social functioning of depressed children is frequently disturbed by many features of this group of disorders. Loss of interest in activities and a decrease in the energy available for involvement in social interaction could interfere directly, while impaired concentration and self-confidence might decrease the effectiveness of the depressed child in such interactions. The view of the self as a failure could distort the child's cognition so that potential reward and encouragement from others would not be interpreted accurately, thus neutralizing their reinforcement value. Brumback, Dietz-Schmidt, and Weinberg (1977) noted the presence of each of the following impairments in socialization in nearly two thirds of a sample of 42 depressed children: decreased group participation, less friendly or outgoing, socially withdrawing, and loss of usual social interests. By 1980 Petti, Bornstein, Delamater, and Connors suggested "improving peer interactions" as a significant therapeutic focus in the multimodal treatment of chronically depressed prepubertal children. They emphasized the need to develop social skills adequate to succeed upon return home since the patient they described had difficulty maintaining eye contact with those to whom she was speaking, exhibited discomfort when complimented by peers and markedly blunted affect in general, and used only maladaptive responses (aggression or withdrawal) when provoked by her peers. Stark (1990) notes a lack of popularity of depressed children, which he attributes to a disturbance of social skills comprised of "a skills deficit, a disturbance in cognitions surrounding social situations, and greater attention to physiological arousal" (pp. 159–160). Treatment of these problems is discussed later.

Clinical Presentation: Dysthymia is a chronic low-grade depressive disorder characterized by fewer, but often no less pronounced, symptoms than major depression. It may include depressed or irritable mood, low self-esteem, feelings of hopelessness, and a number of vegetative symptoms (including changes in sleep and appetite, low energy or fatigue, and impaired concentration or decision making) and is often comorbid with a number of other disorders, as will be discussed later. In most cases it appears to have both a biological substrate and environmental precipitants.

Natural History/Epidemiology

One general population study of depression based on *DSM-III* criteria found a point prevalence of MDD of 1.8% and of minor depressive disorder (mDD) of 2.5% in a sample of 641 children 9 years of age (Kashani et al., 1983). Minor depression is an RDC concept that has no precise equivalent in *DSM-IV* (1994); likely it includes children who now would be diagnosed with dysthymic disorder or depressive disorder not otherwise specified. Previous studies had not been designed to evaluate specifically for depression, used nonstandard diagnostic approaches, and/or had too few subjects. There were no differences between depressed and nondepressed groups in gender, socioeconomic status, teacher reports of behavior problems, or cognitive or motor deficits.

Kovacs, Feinberg, Crouse-Novak, Paulauskas, and Finkelstein (1984) conducted a longitudinal prospective study of 65 children ages 8 to 13 who suffered from the *DSM-III* depressive disorders of major depression, dysthymic disorder, and adjustment disorder with depressed mood (ADDM) who had been referred from outpatient child psychiatric or pediatric departments. They utilized a control group of 49 children with nonaffective psychiatric diagnoses such as attention deficit, conduct, and oppositional disorders. They found major depression to resolve rarely in the first 3 months with a peak rate of resolution between 15 and 18 months after onset and the maximal rate of recovery of 92% at 1½ years. Dysthymia required more than 6 years to attain a peak recovery rate of 89%. ADDM was associated with a significant degree of remission in the first 3 months with peak recovery rate between 6 and 9 months, by which time 90% were recovered. Mean age of onset was approximately 2 years earlier in dysthymic disorder than in major depressive disorder, with no significant difference between the latter and ADDM. Earlier age at onset of either disorder predicted a more prolonged course in MDD and DD but not in ADDM. On the other hand, gender was unrelated to rate of recovery for MDD and DD, while a weak trend toward earlier recovery from ADDM was noted for males. Treatment was uncontrolled but did not affect recovery from DD or ADDM; it appeared to delay remission in MDD. The depressed sample was predominantly female in contrast to the control group, which contained more males. Finally, the stressors that often are advanced as etiologic agents in depression were no more common in the depressed group than among the controls, suggesting that they are more related to mental illness than a specific diagnostic category. The most important message here is that depressive illnesses in children often persist long enough to disrupt a child's development. Therefore, they deserve our urgent attention.

Next, Kovacs, Feinberg, Crouse-Novak, Paulauskas, and Pollock (1984) examined the risk of a subsequent major depression in the same cohort and discovered that both MDD and DD carried a high risk of future episodes of MDD (0.72 and 0.69 in the 72 months following resolution of the last episode of MDD or the onset of DD, respectively), while ADDM and control disorders were associated with only a 5% risk over the 8½-year follow-up. These findings revealed that in children the occurrence of "double depression" is a typical feature of the course of dysthymic disorder rather than being a severe exception. The close relationship of MDD and DD as well as their similarities in such parameters as just noted raises the question of whether these two disorders actually are different manifestations of the same pathophysiology. This question is complicated by the fact that only 38% of Kovacs et al.'s patients with MDD had a preexistent DD.

Family/Genetic Studies

A large and rapidly growing body of research has examined the effects of different environmental characteristics on the personalities of children. One of the most readily available populations for evaluation is the offspring of psychiatric patients.

McConville and Bruce (1985) noted in their sample of psychiatrically hospitalized children that approximately 50% had been rejected by their families. Positive family histories of depression were most common among the patients suffering from "predominantly guilt depressions" (D-3, 100%), while 67% of the children with "predominantly affectual depressions" (D-1) and 58% of the mixed "affectual" and "negative self-esteem" (D-1/D-2) had such a history, in contrast with only 30% of the pure "negative self-esteem" patients (D-2).

On a different tack, Wisner and Perel (1991) found low serum concentrations of 10-hydroxynortriptyline in 2 of 4 infants of nursing mothers treated with nortriptyline. Such data raise the question of what effects such exposure might have on the developing brain, particularly one that may already be genetically predisposed to mood disorders.

Comorbidity

SUBSTANCE ABUSE

Kashani, Keller, Solomon, Reid, and Mazzola (1985) looked specifically at double depression and found more alcohol-dependent and amphetamine-abusing adolescents with that diagnosis than would have been predicted based on the statistics for the entire sample of substance-abusing youth evaluated in the study.

ANXIETY DISORDERS

Kovacs, Feinberg, Crouse-Novak, Paulauskas, and Finkelstein (1984) found no evidence that anxiety disorders influence the recovery from or the relapse into a major depressive episode. In addition, neither MDD nor a superimposed anxiety disorder altered the cumulative probability of recovery from dysthymia.

CONDUCT DISORDER

Adolescent depressive disorders are similar to conduct disorder (CD) in a number of ways. The irritable mood often seen in adolescent depression can be difficult to distinguish from the angry, defiant behavior typical of conduct disorder. In addition, frank agitation might manifest as poorly controlled aggression in an adolescent already prone to use physical means of dealing with conflict. Conduct disorder in males may to some extent correspond to affective disorders in females, considering the proportions of each gender affected, the shared comorbidity with substance abuse, and the elevated risk of suicide in both groups. Both disorders also appear to involve abnormal functioning of central serotonergic and noradrenergic pathways (Richelson, 1990; Sakanian, 1981). Such arguments are essentially speculative, however, and have seldom been the primary focus of research.

Alessi, McManus, Grapentine, and Brickman (1984) evaluated 71 juvenile offenders (40 male, 31 female) using multiple instruments, including the Schedule for Affective Disorders and Schizophrenia (SADS) (*not* the K-SADS), RDC, and *DSM-III* criteria as well as the Hamilton Rating Scales (HRS), Carroll Self-Rating Scale (CSRS), and Global Rating Scale for Depression (GRS). They diagnosed 11 (15%) with active major depressive disorder, 6 (11%) with major depressive disorder in remission, and 9 (13%) with minor depressive disorder, then compared the 11 from the delinquent sample with 40 psychiatrically hospitalized adolescents with MDD. They found the delinquent group to have a significantly higher percentage of secondary, endogenous, and agitated depression subtypes. The secondary depression was related to alcohol and other substance abuse in all of the delinquent adolescents. If the diagnosis of antisocial personality disorder had been allowed despite age less than 18 years, fully 8 of the delinquents would have qualified for that subtype. It is also interesting that the type of conduct disorder (i.e., socialized or undersocialized, aggressive or nonaggressive) was not related to the types of affective and other diagnoses in these adolescents. Thus, antisocial behavior does not appear to be the result of depression. The study was hampered by small numbers, especially of delinquent subjects, and by failure to define a group that fit closely the concept of dysthymia.

Kovacs, Paulauskas, Gatsonis, and Richards (1988) studied the same group of children from which they drew samples for the previously noted papers (1984a, 1984b) and found many symptoms of depressive and conduct disorders to overlap, making it difficult to decide to which syndrome children should be assigned or whether they were simultaneously symptomatic of both. At some time during the study, 24 (23%) of the 104 children in the sample earned the diagnosis of conduct disorder. The conduct disorder was comorbid in 17 children (16%) but had its initial onset after remission of the depression in another 7 (7%). There was no association between type of depressive disorder and type or presence of conduct disorder. Depression appears to have been the primary disorder in two thirds of the subjects with the comorbid diagnoses. Such comorbidity was noted to carry a high potential for disruption of social adjustment.

Etiological Theories

EARLY CHILDHOOD EXPERIENCE

The variable contribution of childhood experience to the course and character of depressive disorders is underscored by the work of Alnaes and Torgersen (1989), who provided retrospective evidence that chronic depression is a distinct entity from acute major depression for a number of variables. For example, relationship problems with the mother involving overly strict or overprotective parenting were more common in dysthymic or cyclothymic patients, as were competitiveness with siblings and a recollection of themselves as isolated, dependent, nervous, restless, or weak. Patients with acute major depression were more

likely to have experienced trauma in childhood. This fact has led researchers to question whether dysthymia is more akin to a personality disorder than to a primary affective syndrome (Akiskal et al., 1980), a distinction made even more difficult to evaluate by the nearly identical diagnostic symptom criteria for the two afflictions (i.e., major depression and dysthymia) (APA, 1980). Kaufman's study (1991) of 56 7- to 12-year-old children found 18% (10) to meet criteria for major depression while 25% (14) met the criteria for dysthymia; 14% (8) satisfied the criteria for both disorders. This means that 80% of her sample with major depression also suffered from dysthymia. What is especially valuable about Kaufman's work is that her sample was not composed exclusively of offspring of parents with a history of affective illness, as were the subjects in prior studies. Thus, her data support an abusive environment as a risk factor in the development of depression, possibly independent of family history. It could be argued, however, that the majority of families in which abuse occurs are at high risk for parental psychiatric illness.

One of the classic psychological mechanisms postulated to explain depressive disorders is "learned helplessness" (Seligman, 1975), which is based on experiments in which animals subjected repeatedly to a noxious stimulus from which they could not escape subsequently would make no effort to escape the stimulus even when it was possible, seeming to believe that their situation was hopeless; in other words, they seemed to "give up." A more contemporary version of this model is the attributional vulnerability model, which is discussed later in the section on cognitive theories.

PSYCHOANALYTIC THEORIES

René Spitz (1946) described the progressive withdrawal and physical deterioration of infants who were deprived of maternal care for a period of months. Characteristics included: apprehension, sadness, weepiness; lack of contact, rejection of environment, withdrawal; retardation of development, retardation of reaction to stimuli, slowness of movement, dejection, stupor; loss of appetite, refusal to eat, loss of weight; and insomnia as well as a depressed facial expression. Spitz's explanation of this syndrome involved trauma to the tender rudimentary ego as a result of object loss. Today most psychiatrists would perceive in this a disruption of attachment with a resulting reactive attachment disorder. This pathogenesis resulting from an *actual* object loss also distinguishes such "anaclitic" depression from descriptions of depression by other analytic theorists who deal with losses that are symbolic or fantasized, thus perhaps limiting the generality of the syndrome. Melanie Klein, a more controversial psychoanalyst and a disciple of Abraham, considered depression in children a universal phenomenon:

Analytic experience of healthy children of various ages has convinced me that even though their ego reacts in a normal way they too have to face great quantities of anxiety, severe unconscious guilt and deep depression and that in some cases the only thing that distinguishes their difficulties from those of the neurotic child is that they are able to deal with them in a more confident and active manner. (M. Klein, 1932, pp. 153–154)

This implies that Klein did not conceive of a "disorder" of depression so much as depression as a result of normal intrapsychic dynamics that most other analysts considered impossibly precocious.

Perhaps the classic conceptualization of depression in latency-age children comes from Bibring (1953), who viewed depression as an ego state rather than the result of conflict between the ego and superego: "the emotional expression . . . of a state of helplessness and powerlessness of the ego, irrespective of what may have caused the breakdown of the mechanisms which established self-esteem" (p. 54). This view opened the way for consideration of a depressive diagnosis even in young children. According to Bibring, the source of the feelings of helplessness could be found in stages of development besides the oral stage, although that stage is particularly prone to such feelings by its nature, involving "the need to get affection, to be loved, to be taken care of, to get the 'supplies,' or by the opposite defensive need: to be independent, self-supporting" (p. 53). He noted the loss of self-esteem engendered by failure of what he considered more anally oriented narcissistic goals such as "the wish to be good, not to be resentful, hostile, defiant, but to be loving, not to be dirty, but to be clean, etc." (p. 53). The inability to achieve these aspirations would be associated with a sense of inability to control impulses, aggressive as well as libidinal, with resultant guilt over this failure, perhaps lending theoretical credence to the notion that mood in child-

hood depressive illness may be either depressed *or* irritable. Finally, Bibring saw the phallic stage as associated with "the wish to be strong, superior, great, secure, not to be weak and insecure" (p. 52), the frustration of which would lead to feelings of inadequacy and inferiority. The central theme, in any case, is the loss of self-esteem.

A more recent formulation of psychoanalytic thought sharing many common themes with Bibring's is expressed by Milrod (1988), who first describes depression as loss-induced rage that is turned on the self representation, as distinguished from sadness (including grief and mourning) at the loss of a love object. Mood is described as an ego state that pervades the psyche to a degree dependent on the capacity of the ego to discharge the tension in a more focused manner. Mood colors both self and object representations and serves to discharge excessive psychic tension that the ego cannot manage. The hostility toward self in depression is expressed as guilt and/or diminished self-esteem. In this view two depressive mechanisms can be distinguished. The narcissistic injury may occur on the level of the ego, as when the person does not live up to his or her expectations, or may involve the guilt from the superego if the individual fails to achieve the ethical standards of the ego ideal. A third form of depression described by Milrod involves a symbiotic relationship with an ambivalent love object, which forms the basis of the person's self-esteem and which must be revered even if the self must be denigrated to maintain the object in its elevated status. This relationship eventually can deplete the libido, leading to melancholia in which the self and object are introjected as ego and superego respectively, with the superego continuing to punish the self.

ATTACHMENT THEORY

Lyons-Ruth (1991) discussed the apparent connection between disorganized attachment and psychopathology through preschool age. One study (Lyons-Ruth, 1989) found such an attachment pattern to be associated with increased behavior problems overall and hostile/aggressive behavior toward peers in particular. The mothers of these children were more likely to have been chronically depressed during the children's early years of life and therefore to have shown their children less closeness and warmth. Lyons-Ruth (1991) also stated that "Current evidence supports the position that patterns of emotional regulation are negotiated with caregivers from the first year of life, and that aspects of these early regulating structures are carried into new relationships over time" (p. 272). Rutter (1985) points out that "maltreatment and severe punishment" do not prevent attachment. This fact suggests that such children accept a worldview containing little hope and that might predispose to depression. Radke-Yarrow, Cummings, Kuczynski, and Chapman (1985) pointed out that some of the "huddling on the floor" behaviors of insecurely attached (ambivalent/avoidant) children noted in a previous report might represent sadness. Much basic work remains to be done to establish connections between disrupted attachment and later psychopathology.

COGNITIVE THEORY

Hammen, Adrian, & Hiroto (1988) performed a 6-month follow-up of 79 children and adolescents ages 8 to 16 at high risk due to maternal depression. Their approach was based on a "reformulation" of the learned helplessness model in cognitive behavioral terms. It hypothesizes that depression develops as a result of causal attributions made by the depressed person to explain negative outcomes. Their study examined the influence of the subjects' attributional styles on their subsequent risk for depressive episodes and found no effect, although a correlation was found involving the interaction of attributions and life events with *nonaffective* diagnoses.

NEUROENDOCRINE THEORIES

Some of the earliest attempts to explain depression with a biochemical model involved the biogenic amines norepinephrine (NE) and serotonin (5-HT) since tricyclic antidepressants and monocamine oxidase inhibitors were discovered to increase the synaptic concentration of these neurotransmitters by preventing their reuptake or degradation, respectively. Reserpine, on the other hand, was found to deplete biogenic amines in lab animals and to produce depression in a significant proportion of humans. These findings led to the simplistic notion that deficiencies of the biogenic amines were the cause of depression while excess led to mania. Another conceptualization hypothe-

sized two categories of depression, one being deficient in norepinephrine, the other in serotonin. These ideas have not survived closer scrutiny and are being replaced by theories that emphasize adaptation of brain neurotransmitter receptors. In fact, our knowledge of neurotransmitter- and receptor-related activities has done far more to clarify the physiology of side effects than of therapeutic effects (Richelson, 1990).

The conceptualization of affective disorders as arising from dysfunction of the hypothalamic-pituitary axis has achieved moderate popularity in adult psychiatry but has been little explored in children. The dexamethasone suppression test has been the most prominent assessment of such dysfunction, although its use is fraught with ambiguity and confounding influences (APA Task Force on Laboratory Tests in Psychiatry, 1987). Its uncritical and poorly reasoned use by some psychiatrists has led many clinicians to consider it to be a discredited procedure (Carroll, 1985). While it appears to be of limited utility for diagnostic purposes, it yielded the provocative finding that rates of cortisol nonsuppression were similar in major depression and dysthymia, which supports the inclusion of dysthymia on a continuum with a depressive disorder more widely accepted to have a biologic component (Petty, Asarnow, Carlson, and Lesser, 1985). On the other hand, Woodside, Brownstone, and Fisman (1987) found elevated rates of nonsuppression in major affective disorders (10 of 12) and adjustment disorders (3 of 18) while scores on the Children's Depression Inventory were elevated to a similar degree for children with major depression and conduct disorders, suggesting that the inventory measured nonspecific distress rather than depression per se. This finding was echoed by Steingard, Biederman, Keenan, and Moore (1990), who found similar rates of nonsuppression in children and adolescents with major depressive disorder and attention deficit hyperactivity disorder and an even higher rate in those with both disorders concurrently.

DIFFERENTIAL DIAGNOSIS

Akiskal (1983) stirred the pot and brewed a rich controversy by constructing a nosology of dysthymias. He examined the tendency to view depressed persons as suffering from either an affective or a personality disorder and pointed out that all chronic depressions necessarily share the same etiology even though they might descriptively be called dysthymia. He notes that a common tendency is to see the brooding, narcissistic person with depression as having character pathology without a biological basis when, in fact, the patient may present with a comorbid subsyndromal mood disorder that might well respond to somatic therapies. He recalled a previous follow-up study of 100 patients with "neurotic depression" for 3 to 4 years and found that 36% developed melancholic episodes and that half of those "changed polarity." He examined several validating criteria, particularly family history, rapid-eye-movement latency, and response to medication and concluded that 4 distinct groups existed: (1) late-onset primary depressions with residual chronicity, (2) chronic secondary dysphorias with age of onset determined by the primary insult (largely long-standing incapacitating medical diseases), (3) early-onset character-spectrum disorders arising from disturbed early object relationships (which do not respond to antidepressant treatment), and (4) subaffective dysthymic disorders (which respond to antidepressant treatment). The latter groups are the "characterologic depressions"—those involving disturbance of personality, the disturbance being intrinsic in the "character-spectrum" ("personality") disorders and, in the subaffective disorders, secondary to the presence of a subsyndromal biological depression. This approach has formed the basis of much of subsequent debate on dysthymia.

Primary Psychiatric Disorders: Because drugs and alcohol are available to many children, substance abuse involving alcohol and virtually all other drugs must be considered, although for some substances the abstinence syndrome may be more likely to lead to a depressed presentation (e.g., amphetamines and cocaine), while others often produce such an appearance even during periods of active use (e.g., alcohol, marijuana, minor tranquilizers, and opiates). In addition, the potential for comorbidity should be kept in mind (Herrington, Jacobson, and Benzer, 1987).

Personality Disorders/Neurosis: As noted, Akiskal has defined a group of persons with dysthymia as suffering from a "character spectrum" disorder; the fact that clinicians often consider these to be borderline and other personality disorders tends to promote therapeutic nihilism on the part of the clinician and continued depression

in the affected individual. According to Akiskal, often there is no clear demarcation between the subtypes based on initial clinical presentation (Akiskal, et al., 1980); this fact suggests that clinicians might best keep an open mind about the value of somatic therapies in individual patients.

Mood Disorders Related to General Medical Disorders and Substance Abuse: Since children with depressive presentations often come from less than optimal life circumstances, it is important to rule out general medical causes for their symptoms. A physical examination focusing on neurological function is essential. A complete blood count with differential, electrolytes, serum calcium, blood urea nitrogen, serum creatinine, and blood glucose also may be of value in ferreting out causative or contributory medical illness that might not be obvious from the physical exam alone. Some of the medical causes of depressive symptoms in children are infection (including infectious mononucleosis and *Mycoplasma pneumoniae* and other pneumonias), uremia, hyperglycemia, and rheumatologic disorders (e.g., systemic lupus erythematosus). No systematic study of depression in children was found in the literature that addresses the issue of organic differential diagnosis, presumably because the syndrome is thought to be almost exclusive to the adult (and particularly geriatric) population.

Lozoff and Brittenham (1986) described numerous behavioral abnormalities that may be caused by iron deficiency, including affective manifestations such as withdrawal from or hesitance with the examiner, increased fearfulness, unhappiness in all or part of the examination sessions, easy fatigability or restlessness, increased body tension, increased body contact with their mothers, as well as nonaffective manifestations. These data come from infant studies performed in Central and South America and are bolstered by research with rats; screening children with depressive presentations for iron deficiency and anemia is strongly recommended.

Treatment

Treatment of depressive disorders in children should embrace all of the modalities that are available. In addition to individual, family, and pharmacologic therapies, many schools offer groups for students who have been identified as being depressed. Careful evaluation of interests and abilities may provide the basis for more rational goal setting and thus improved self-esteem and increased satisfaction from life activities. Hospitalization or an alternative placement may become necessary if the risk of self-harm becomes significant or if the home environment is nonsupportive or even hostile; however, intensive in-home intervention is becoming available in many parts of the country and may be preferable in those situations where it can be productive and safe for all involved. Finally, approaches to prevention of depressive disorders in children genetically and environmentally at risk because of parental depression should become a part of public health policy. Such preventive interventions have been discussed by LaRoche (1986).

Treatment selection in childhood depression is a nearly unexplored territory. McConville and Bruce (1985) utilized their subtypes to distinguish treatment styles, largely based on the way each child interacted with his or her therapist. They found the D-1 (primarily affectual) patients to develop an intense relationship based on early childhood parenting experiences that emphasized contact comfort. These children initially exhibited improved mood and expression of affection with decreased wishes to die. As therapy progressed, these children expressed fearful themes of being harmed or killed by the therapist or by "frightening fantasy figures." During the final stage of therapy described, these children became less demanding and more able to accept affection on others' terms as their self-esteem improved. Only 17% of these children were treated with antidepressant medication (imipramine).

The D-2 (negative self-esteem) children more often had an essential mistrust of the therapist. Overcoming this necessitated a highly structured and consistent nurturing approach that gradually allowed the child to see the therapist as a safe object for emotional investment. This progress was interspersed with frequent periods of anger and rejection of the therapist as doubts about the reliability of their relationship were rekindled. In later phases, the children became more vulnerable and clinging and began to internalize new cognitive schemata. Group therapy appeared to espe-

cially suitable for this group. Only 14% of these children were treated with antidepressants. However, this group showed the least improvement on a 1-to-4 assessment scale and contained 58% of those children requiring further placement after hospitalization.

The mixed D-1/D-2 group exhibited combinations of the themes noted for each of the two categories. Fifty-eight percent were treated with antidepressants. This group contributed 42% of those requiring further placement.

The D-3 group (guilt) demanded both supportive and self-destruction limiting interventions initially with a variety of therapies eventually being used. One hundred percent were treated with imipramine. It could be hypothesized that this group included more "biologic" depressives, particularly given the high frequency of positive family history of depression, the psychotic symptoms, and the relative success of their treatment, which included antidepressant medication.

It is unclear how much of this treatment specificity is attributable to the environment and to the therapists' training. In addition, the validity of the criteria for use and the adequacy of dosing of antidepressant medication in this study are open question that weaken its generalizability.

SOMATIC THERAPIES

Pharmacologic Treatment: Antidepressant treatment of depressed children has evolved slowly over the years since the diagnosis first began to be used. Unfortunately, relatively few of the agents available for use in adults have been evaluated in well-controlled protocols, and so far those tried have yielded discouraging results (Gadow, 1991). Gadow points out, however, that all such studies have involved methodological problems, such as small sample size, which make them difficult to use as a basis for therapeutics. Rancurello (1986) suggests that clinicians are driven into the trap of the "one disorder—one drug myth" by pressures to use their time as efficiently as possible. In children who respond poorly or not at all to standard antidepressants, cautious use of newer pharmacologic alternatives with documentation of the need for novel therapy may be a reasonable option, particularly given the potential long-term consequences of depressive disorders.

Tingelstad (1991) summarizes clearly the risk of

sudden death in children taking tricyclic antidepressants. In all three of the cases that had been
reported by that time, the agent involved was desipramine and the probable cause of death was a
cardiac dysrhythmia despite therapeutic or subth-
erapeutic plasma levels of the drug. Two of the
three children had risk factors for cardiac dysfunction (a history of paroxysmal atrial tachycardia and
family history of sudden death in one, and a history of maternal death due to congestive heart
failure in the other). Tingelstad's recommendations are listed in Table 31.2

Electroseizure Therapy: This procedure generally has been reserved for depressive episodes
more severe than those discussed in this section.
There are no literature reports of its use in dysthymic disorder or depressive disorder not otherwise
specified in children or adolescents. Slater and
Roth (1969) noted that it produced dramatic improvement in dysthymia at times.

PSYCHOTHERAPIES

Cognitive-Behavioral Therapy: After a thorough review of the treatment-outcome literature,
Stark (1990), enlarging and elaborating the interventions of Kendall (1977, 1981), has assembled
a number of cognitive techniques specifically
designed for use with middle-school-age (i.e., approximately 8- to 10-year-old) children. He concentrates on approaches that define the vocabulary of mood and then engage the child in games
that build on the newly developed communication
skills. Storytelling techniques are described that
extend the mere telling with the drawing of cartoons to allow the child to illustrate and elaborate
basic methods of such therapeutic activities as
identification of maladaptive cognitions and self-
monitoring. Such concrete methods allow relatively abstract concepts to be communicated and
the work of therapy to be observed by the therapist,
thus providing the data needed to make decisions
regarding the direction of treatment.

*Integrative Approaches—Psychoanalytic/Psy-
chodynamic/Family Systems:* School-age children
span a developmental spectrum that for practical
purposes begins at the preschool level and generally does not extend deeply into the adolescent
realm. Shafii and Shafii (1992) offer treatment approaches to the psychodynamic therapy of different age groups of children and adolescents. The
preschool child (ages 3 to 6 years) is approached

TABLE 31.2

*Tricyclic Antidepressant Therapy Pretreatment
Screening and Treatment Monitoring*

Pretreatment Screening

Medical History
  cardiac dysrhythmia
  heart disease
  syncope
  hearing loss (Congenital deafness is associated with
    prolonged QT syndromes.)
Family History
  heart disease
  sudden cardiac death
12-Lead EKG (If significant dysrhythmia is noted,
    obtain 2-minute rhythm strip.)
  rate
  PR interval (should be no more than 0.20 seconds)
  QRS duration (should be no more than 0.12
    seconds)
  QT_c (should be no more than 0.45 seconds)
  ST segment and T-wave morphologies

Treatment Monitoring

12-Lead EKG (see above)
  PR interval (less than 0.20 seconds)
  QRS duration (less than 0.12 seconds)
Serum Antidepressant Levels (no greater than
  300 ng/ml for desipramine)

using play therapy with warmth and a permissive
atmosphere in which the child may freely express
emotions. These emotions are then reflected to
the child in a manner that promotes insight and
confidence that the actions will not threaten parental nurturance, the loss of which is seen as the
common underlying concern in depressed preschoolers. This assurance in parental love and
support allows the child to develop solutions to his
or her problems, which then may be tested both
in therapy and in the world at large. Depressed
preschool children are thought to overutilize the
defenses of suppression, repression, introjection,
and reaction formation. By such a nondirective
approach, the child is encouraged to become an
independent problem solver. At the same time,
the parents are engaged in some form of conjoint
therapy or parenting training. Family therapy is
used to integrate the changes being made by the
various family members.

School-age children (ages 7 to 12 years) present
more complex issues in that such "latency-age"
children are grappling with the developmental
tasks of moderation of the "oedipal, sexual, and

aggressive wishes and fantasies toward their parents through the intensification of the defense mechanisms of repression, suppression, and denial" (Shafii & Shafii, 1992, p. 165). Transference of intense emotions from the parents to the therapist occurs at the same time the child develops the defenses of rationalization and isolation of affect, all of which make the school-age child much less open. It is the prominent, rigid, and dysfunctional use of certain of these defenses that distinguishes the child with an affective disorder from a normal child. A flexible mixture of active and quiet, structured and free-form therapeutic approaches provides the greatest opportunity for development of rapport and the lowering of these defenses. It is also important to avoid abstraction, because the majority of children in this age group are still functioning on a relatively concrete level. On the other hand, they have the ability to think categorically and to separate personal problems from those belonging to others.

In our experience, family therapy of the preschooler requires a deft ballet in which the therapist, after developing a therapeutic alliance with both the parents and the child, alternately confronts the parents (usually to the delight of the child, who finally feels that he or she has an adult ally) and communicates to the child the responsibilities that he or she must assume in order to maintain and continue change within the family. Humor is a vital component of such treatment, as is the willingness of the therapist to present himself or herself as a fallible human being. This encourages the child and each family member to embrace the process of change despite its implication of personal responsibility for the dysfunction exhibited by the child. Alternately supporting and confronting the participants in family therapy provides each person with the impetus and the nurturance required to expose one's human side without immediately retreating into the safety of the defenses that sustain dysfunction within the family. Therapeutic tasks of an interpersonal nature also can serve to stabilize the new interactions that arise in such a family approach. Often these tasks are most effective when they are paradoxical or seemingly irrational, challenging the very nature of the rules under which the family previously operated (i.e., the "second-order change" of Watzlawick, Weakland, & Fisch, 1974). These "old" rules often lead to progressive escalations of the child's behaviors and parental responses in a spiraling power struggle. An example is the child with poor self-esteem who persists in trying to prove that he is a "bad" child. Such paradoxical tasks might be for the parents to no longer discuss "the problem" of their child, even in private, choosing instead to discuss him only from a positive perspective and to react to misbehaviors by identifying the motive ("You're not trying to make me mad, are you?"). This serves to confound the game in which the child has previously succeeded in eliciting only negative and pessimistic responses.

Social Skills Training: As noted earlier, remedying deficits in social skills can play an important part in the successful treatment of depressed children. Petti et al. (1980) used a group setting to provide "both positive and negative feedback about [the patient], an appropriate outlet for her feelings, and an arena to test out alternative ways of behaving" (p. 694). Stark (1990) suggests a procedure where the therapist models desired behaviors, discusses relevant situations, and allows the child to role-play the behaviors with corrective feedback. Cognitive restructuring as well as relaxation and positive imagery training are used to aid the child in integrating the new behaviors and to cope with the anxiety associated with putting them into practice.

INTEGRATION OF TREATMENTS

In our experience, treatment of depressive disorders in latency-age children in inpatient settings virtually always requires simultaneous use of antidepressant medication, individual psychotherapy, and family therapy (or preparation for out-of-home placement if an abusive home environment exists). The modalities appropriate to each child should be pursued as soon as possible to obtain the maximum benefit from inpatient time. Outpatients, depending both on the severity and the apparent basis of the depression, may be amenable to either psychotherapy or family therapy alone, although it is our clinical experience that family therapy usually should be emphasized when resources are limited.

Directions for Future Investigation

Estimates of the disease-free interval between episodes of major depressive disorder in adults vary greatly (Kovacs, Feinberg, Crouse-Novak, Paulauskas, Pollock and Fiukelstein, 1984), probably due to procedural differences and definitions (ascertainment methods also are likely significant), making comparisons of data from various studies unacceptably weak. This uncertainty identifies fertile ground for an enterprising and patient researcher to conduct a comprehensive longitudinal study using consistent definitions and methodology across age groups in order to better clarify the meanings of the diagnostic criteria at various developmental stages—truly a daunting proposal.

Such a longitudinal study of a large group of children could use multiple instruments, one to evaluate the hypotheses of each etiological or conceptual model (i.e., cognitive, psychoanalytic, family systems), with specific attention to genetic and biological factors and to family functioning and the psychological makeup of the child. These instruments would be developed most productively with similar or equivalent forms for each significant age group, in order to allow the comparison of results through the stages of maturation. The easiest approach would be the longitudinal analysis of specific symptoms. All of this would, of course, be helped if we first develop respected and universally accepted criteria for childhood depression. The need for longitudinal study designs that respect passage through multiple overlapping developmental stages and include the influences of family, peers, and culture is the core difficulty in research in childhood depressive disorders.

Research looking at biologic variables in depressive disorders of childhood is just beginning. Current problems include the association of markers such as the dexamethasone suppression test with specific depressive diagnoses or symptoms, the relationship between depression and immune function, and abnormalities of cortical function in depression, either electrical (determined by electroencephalography or magnetoencephalography) or metabolic (determined by positron emission tomography or similar imaging techniques). Alessi et al. (1984) suggested evaluating the dexamethasone suppression test in conduct-disordered adolescents, particularly including a significant number with depressive disorders, both in hopes of elucidating the pathophysiology of each of the two disorders and in identifying those juvenile offenders most likely to benefit from specific forms of pharmacotherapy.

Even the clinically vital issue of efficacy of treatments has not yet been evaluated adequately. To establish the role of tricyclic antidepressants in the effective treatment of childhood depressive disorders would do a great service to the field of child psychiatry.

REFERENCES

Akiskal, H. S. (1983). Dysthymic disorder: Psychopathology of proposed chronic depressive subtypes. *American Journal of Psychiatry, 140,* 11–20.

Akiskal, H. S., Rosenthal, T. L., Haykal, R. F., Lemmi, H., Rosenthal, R. H., & Scott-Strauss, A. (1980). Characterological depressions: Clinical and sleep EEG findings separating "subaffective dysthymias" from "character spectrum disorders." *Archives of General Psychiatry, 37,* 777–783.

Alessi, N. E., McManus, M., Grapentine, W. L., & Brickman, A. (1984). The characterization of depressive disorders in serious juvenile offenders. *Journal of Affective Disorders, 6,* 9–17.

Alnaes, R., & Torgersen, S. (1989). Characteristics of patients with major depression in combination with dysthymic or cyclothymic disorders: Childhood and precipitating events. *Acta Psychiatrica Scandinavica, 79,* 11–18.

American Psychiatric Association. (1980). *Diagnostic and statistical manual of mental disorders* (3rd ed.). Washington, DC: Author.

American Psychiatric Association. (1987). *Diagnostic and statistical manual of mental disorders* (3rd ed., rev.). Washington, DC: Author.

American Psychiatric Association Task Force on DSM-IV. (1991). *DSM-IV options book: Work in progress (9/1/91).* Washington,

American Psychiatric Association. (1994). *Diagnostic and statistical manual of mental disorders* (4th ed.). Washington, DC: Author.

APA Task Force on Laboratory Tests in Psychiatry. (1987). The dexamethasone suppression test: An overview of its current status in psychiatry. *American Journal of Psychiatry, 144,* 1253–1262.

Bibring, E. (1953). The mechanism of depression. Cited in M. Mendelson (1960). *Psychoanalytic concepts of depression* (pp. 52–56). Springfield, IL: Charles C Thomas.

Brumback, R. A., Dietz-Schmidt, S. G., & Weinberg, W. A. (1977). Depression in children referred to an educational diagnostic center: Diagnosis and treatment and analysis of criteria and literature review. *Diseases of the Nervous System, 38,* 529–535.

Carroll, B. J. (1985). Dexamethasone suppression test: A review of contemporary confusion. *Journal of Clinical Psychiatry, 46*(2, Sec. 2), 13–24.

Gadow, K. D. (1991). Clinical issues in child and adolescent psychopharmacology. *Journal of Consulting and Clinical Psychology, 59,* 842–852.

Hall, D. P., Sing, H. C., & Romanoski, A. J. (1991). Identification and characterization of greater mood variance in depression. *American Journal of Psychiatry, 148,* 1341–1345.

Hammen, C., Adrian, C., & Hiroto, D. (1988). A longitudinal test of the attributional vulnerability model in children at risk for depression. *British Journal of Clinical Psychology, 27,* 37–46.

Herrington, R. E., Jacobson, G. R., & Benzer, D. G. (1987). *Alcohol and drug abuse handbook.* St. Louis: Warren H. Green.

Kashani, J. H., Keller, M. B., Solomon, N., Reid, J. C., & Mazzola, D. (1985). Double depression in adolescent substance users. *Journal of Affective Disorders, 8,* 153–157.

Kashani, J. H., McGee, R. O., Clarkson, S. E., Anderson, J. C., Walton, L. A., Williams, S., Silva, P. A., Robins, A. J., Cytryn, L., & McKnew, D. H. (1983). Depression in a sample of 9-year-old children: Prevalence and associated characteristics. *Archives of General Psychiatry, 40,* 1217–1223.

Kaufman, J. (1991). Depressive disorders in maltreated children. *Journal of the American Academy of Child and Adolescent Psychiatry, 30,* 257–265.

Kendall, P. C. (1977). On the efficacious use of verbal self-instructional procedures with children. *Cognitive Therapy and Research, 1,* 331–341.

Kendall, P. C. (1981). Cognitive-behavioral interventions with children. In B. B. Lahey & A. E. Kazdin (Eds.), *Advances in clinical child psychology* (Vol. 4, pp. 53–90). New York: Plenum Press.

Klein, D. N., Taylor, E. B., Dickstein, S., & Harding, K. (1988a). Primary early-onset dysthymia: Comparison with primary nonbipolar nonchronic major depression on demographic, clinical, familial, personality, and socioenvironmental characteristics and short-term outcome. *Journal of Abnormal Psychology, 97,* 387–398.

Klein, D. N., Taylor, E. B., Dickstein, S., & Harding, K. (1988b). The early-late onset distinction in DSM-III-R dysthymia. *Journal of Affective Disorders, 14,* 25–33.

Klein, M. (1932). *The psychoanalysis of children,* trans. A. Strachey. International Psycho-Analytical Library, No. 22). London: Hogarth Press and Institute of Psycho-Analysis.

Kocsis, J. H., & Frances, A. J. (1987). A critical discussion of DSM-III dysthymic disorder. *American Journal of Psychiatry, 144,* 1534–1542.

Kovacs, M., Feinberg, T. L., Crouse-Novak, M. A., Paulauskas, S. L., & Finkelstein, R. (1984). Depressive disorders in childhood: I. A longitudinal prospective study of characteristics and recovery. *Archives of General Psychiatry, 41,* 229–237.

Kovacs, M., Feinberg, T. L., Crouse-Novak, M. A., Paulauskas, S. L., Pollock, M., & Finkelstein, R. (1984). Depressive disorders in childhood: II. A longitudinal study of the risk for a subsequent major depression. *Archives of General Psychiatry, 41,* 643–649.

Kovacs, M., Paulauskas, S., Gatsonis, C., & Richards, C. (1988). Depressive disorders in childhood: III. A longitudinal study of comorbidity with and risk for conduct disorders. *Journal of Affective Disorders, 15,* 205–217.

LaRoche, C., (1986). Prevention in high risk children of depressed parents. *Canadian Journal of Psychiatry, 31,* 161–165.

Lozoff, B., & Brittenham, G. M. (1986). Behavioral aspects of iron deficiency. *Progress in Hematology, 14,* 23–53.

Lyons-Ruth, K. (1989). *From birth to five: Developmental pathways of the young child at social risk.* Paper presented at the Bunting Institute Colloquium Series, Radcliffe College, Cambridge, MA.

Lyons-Ruth, K. (1991). Rapprochement or approchement: Mahler's theory reconsidered from the vantage point of recent research on early attachment relationship. *Psychoanalytic Psychology, 8,* 1–23.

McConville, B. J., Boag, L., & Purohit, A. (1973). Three types of childhood depression. *Canadian Psychiatric Association Journal, 18,* 133–138.

McConville, B. J., & Bruce, R. T. (1985). Depressive illnesses in children and adolescents: A review of current concepts. *Canadian Journal of Psychiatry, 30,* 119–129.

Milrod, D. (1988). A current view of the psychoanalytic theory of depression: With notes on the role of identification, orality, and anxiety. *Psychoanalytic Study of the Child, 43,* 83–99.

Petti, T. A., Bornstein, M., Delamater, A., & Conners, C. K. (1980). Evaluation and multimodality [*sic*] treatment of a depressed prepubertal girl. *Journal of the American Academy of Child Psychiatry, 19,* 690–702.

Petty, L. K., Asarnow, J. R., Carlson, G. A., & Lesser, L. (1985). The dexamethasone suppression test in depressed, dysthymic, and nondepressed children. *American Journal of Psychiatry, 142,* 631–633.

Radke-Yarrow, M., Cummings, E. M., Kuczynski, L., & Chapman, M. (1985). Patterns of attachment in two- and three-year-olds in normal families and families with parental depression. *Child Development, 56,* 884–893.

Rancurello, M. (1986). Antidepressants in children: Indications, benefits, and limitations. *American Journal of Psychotherapy, 15,* 377–392.

Richelson, E. (1990). Antidepressants and brain neurochemistry. *Mayo Clinic Proceedings, 65,* 1227–1236.

Rutter, M. (1985). Attachment and the development of

social relationships. In M. Rutter and M. Herzov (Eds.), *Child and adolescent psychiatry: Modern approaches* (pp. 267–279). Oxford: Blackwell Scientific Publications.

Ryan, N. D., Puig-Antich, J., Ambrosini, P., Rabinovich, H., Robinson, D., Nelson, B., Iyengar, S., & Twomey, J. (1987). The clinical picture of major depression in children and adolescents. *Archives of General Psychiatry, 44,* 854–861.

Sahakian, B. J. (1981). The neurochemical basis of hyperactivity and aggression induced by social deprivation. In D. O. Lewis (Ed.), *Vulnerabilities to delinquency.* New York: Spectrum Publications.

Seligman, M. E. P. (1975). *Helplessness: On depression, development, and depth.* San Francisco: W. H. Freeman.

Shafii, M., & Shafii, S. L. (1992). Dynamic psychotherapy of depression. In *Clinical guide to depression in children and adolescents.* Washington, DC: American Psychiatric Press.

Slater, E., & Roth, M. (1969). *Clinical psychiatry* (3rd ed.). Baltimore: Williams and Wilkins.

Spitz, R. A. (1946). Anaclitic depression: An inquiry into the genesis of psychiatric conditions in early childhood, II. *Psychoanalytic Study of the Child, 2,* 313–342.

Stark, K. D. (1990). *Childhood depression: School-based intervention.* New York: Guilford Press.

Steingard, R., Biederman, J., Keenan, K., & Moore, C. (1990). Comorbidity in the interpretation of dexamethasone suppression test results in children: A review and report. *Biological Psychiatry, 28,* 193–202.

Tingelstad, J. B. (1991). The cardiotoxicity of the tricyclics. *Journal of the American Academy of Child and Adolescent Psychiatry, 30,* 845–846.

Watzlawick, P., Weakland, J. H., & Fisch, R. (1974). *Change: Principles of problem formation and problem resolution* New York: W. W. Norton.

Wisner, K. L., & Perel, J. M. (1991). Serum nortriptyline levels in nursing mothers and their infants. *American Journal of Psychiatry, 148,* 1234–1236.

Woodside, D. B., Brownstone, D., & Fisman, S. (1987). The dexamethasone suppression test and the children's depression inventory in psychiatric disorders in children. *Canadian Journal of Psychiatry, 32,* 2–4.

32 / Psychopathology and Suicidal Behavior

Cynthia R. Pfeffer

Suicidal behavior in children is a symptom that is defined as any self-destructive behavior with an intent to cause serious harm to self or death (Pfeffer, 1986). In general, suicidal behavior should be differentiated from other risk-taking behaviors, such as impulsive behavior, substance abuse, and anorexia. It also should be distinguished from repetitive stereotyped behaviors, such as headbanging, compulsively, cutting one's skin, or pulling out one's hair. These behaviors have other determinants and usually are not conscious efforts to cause death.

A main aspect of the criteria for defining suicidal behavior is intentionality to cause serious harm or possibility for death. Children can describe suicidal intent, noted by such statements as: "I want to kill myself"; "I want to die and I will try to hang myself." Children younger than 10 to 12 years of age may not comprehend the finality of death; nonetheless, most children have concepts about death even though such concepts may be quite immature.

Suicidal behavior implies a goal. The goal is to die. Despite what children actually comprehend about the finality of death, they are able to enact methods to achieve their goal, that is, to die. Toward this end, they can carry out initiatives such as running into traffic, jumping from high places, ingesting harmful substances, hanging, or shooting in efforts to cause their own death.

The motivation for suicidal behavior often is associated with intense feelings of guilt, shame, hopelessness, and helplessness. In children such states may be precipitated by different factors from those in older individuals. For example, guilt implies a sense of having committed a breach of conduct that then involves a penalty. Shame, a closely related concept, involves a very painful emotion excited by being conscious that others know of one's guilt. Children are developmentally dependent on adults for basic sustenance and socialization. Children know that social norms or rules are established by adults; hence, when a child violates the perceived adult expectations, he or she may expect a punishment.

Because children's feelings of guilt or shame are highly determined by these perceptions of external authority, it is likely that children who experience aberrant home environments may perceive chronic intense states of guilt, shame, and a poor sense of self-esteem. When parents lack skills or are unavailable to provide a consistent pattern to a child's home life, the youngster's fear of harsh punishment or confusion about adult expectations may be intense. These problems may be specific attributes of a potentially suicidal child's social system.

Epidemiology of Childhood Suicidal Behavior

The incidence of suicide in the United States among children ages 5 to 14 years and teenagers and young adults ages 15 to 24 years has increased markedly subsequent to World War II, especially among white males. (See Table 32.1.) As noted in the table, the rate of suicide for 5 to 14-year-olds more than doubled from 1968 to 1988, although

TABLE 32.1

Youth Yearly Suicide Rates Per 100,000 Individuals

Year	Rate for 5- to 14-year-olds	Rate for 15- to 24-year-olds
1968	0.3	7.1
1977	0.5	13.6
1980	0.4	12.4
1982	0.6	12.1
1984	0.6	12.2
1987	0.7	12.9
1988	0.7	13.2

NOTE. Adapted from: National Center for Health Statistics (1984a, 1984b, 1985, 1986, 1990)

these rates are substantially lower than for youths who are 15 to 24 years old.

A number of hypotheses have been proposed about factors underlying these increases in suicide rates. Most agree that the increase is not a genetically related phenomenon, because genetic mutations arising in large populations require extensive time periods before their effects are observable. Since these epidemiological trends parallel similar increases in depression, substance abuse, delinquency, and eating disorders (Klerman, 1989), it appears more likely that societal factors may be involved. The period since World War II has been one of technological expansion with associated features of increased mobility, changes in social role functioning and family life, and enhanced independent role functioning among children. The number of divorces and remarriages, with resultant changes in family structure and interactions, has increased greatly. In many respects, recent social trends are characterized by greater exposure to violence and less setting of limits on youth with resultant increased opportunities to engage in problematic behaviors. For example, there is increased access to drugs and firearms, especially among adolescents and young adults. These are important correlates of youth suicide (Brent, Perper, Allman, 1987). Specifically, in 1988 (Fingerhut, Kleinman, Godfrey, & Rosenberg, 1991), the age-specific rate of firearm suicides for 10- to 14-year-olds was 0.8 per 100,000 (125 children). This rate is comparable to the age-specific suicide rate of 0.7 per 100,000 (112 children) associated with all other lethal methods. Since the mid-1950s media, especially television, have greatly influenced the exposure to violence in society. Recent reports suggest that among vulnerable teenagers, media portrayal of suicide may precipitate suicidal enactment (Hafner & Schmidtke, 1989; Philips, Carstensen, & Paight, 1989).

Specific rates of nonfatal suicidal acts among children are not known, but estimates suggest that the ratio of suicide to suicide attempt is 1:100. Clinical studies suggest that 6 to 12% of preadolescents in the general community report recent suicidal ideation or attempts and that 1% of these children report a suicide attempt in their lifetimes (Kashani, Goddard, & Reid, 1989; Pfeffer, Plutchik, Mizruchi, & Lipkins, 1986). In contrast, approximately 25% of preadolescents attending psychiatric outpatient services and close to 80%

admitted to psychiatric hospitals report suicidal ideation or attempts within six months of admission to psychiatric treatment.

Suicide rates may be lowest in preadolescents because these children are developmentally immature with regard to biological correlates, social role independence, natural course of psychiatric disorders, and cognitive or motor skills needed to plan and carry out complex suicidal methods.

Clinical Characteristics of Children Who Commit Suicide

Several methods have been employed to study childhood and adolescent suicide, involving the use of medical, school, social agency, and medical examiner records or gathering information by interviewing people who knew the youngster who committed suicide. The latter approach is commonly referred to as the psychological autopsy method, because it is primarily a postmortem assessment of the youth suicide victim. Because of the low rate of suicide among children under 15 years of age, most studies of youth suicide report on adolescents. Another method of study, one that has the advantage of evaluating characteristics of a youth suicide victim directly, is a prospective research design of youths who are at high risk for committing suicide. An important limitation of this method is that the number of expected suicides in a given population of youth under study is always too low to permit meaningful statistical analyses. Despite the rising rates of youth suicide in recent times, the incidence of suicide is relatively low.

An important characteristic noted in all studies of preadolescents who commit suicide is that at the time of death, they are experiencing significant psychiatric symptomatology. Indeed, these children are rarely normal or devoid of psychological morbidity. For example, the first record review study (Shaffer, 1974) of such children reported on 31 youngsters who were 14 years or younger when they committed suicide in England and Wales from 1962 to 1968. While this is one of the few studies devoted to children and young

adolescents, no youngster was below 12 years old and most were 13 or 14 years old with a ratio of 2.3:1 boys to girls.

This study highlights important psychosocial characteristics of young suicide victims. For example, the most frequent methods used to commit suicide were carbon monoxide gas (45%), hanging (17%), drug overdose (15%), and firearms (10%). The most frequent precipitant of suicide was a "disciplinary crisis" that involved a violation such as truancy from school or antisocial behavior that eventuated in school punishment or court action. These events evidently may have intensified feelings of humiliation, blame, guilt, worthlessness, helplessness, and hopelessness that became stimuli for suicide.

Symptoms of antisocial behavior and affective symptoms were prevalent among these children. Specifically, 5 (17%) children had only antisocial symptoms, 17 (57%) had both antisocial and affective symptoms, 4 (15%) had only affective symptoms, and 4 (15%) had neither of these constellations of symptoms. Fourteen (46%) children had a previous history of suicidal ideation, threats, or attempts. The intense and significant effects of a disciplinary crisis with its attendant state of fear, humiliation, and other feelings are suggested by the finding that children who committed suicide after such a crisis were less likely to have had a previous history of suicidal behavior than those whose suicide occurred after other types of precipitants. This study was limited by the fact that there were no comparison children who did not commit suicide.

Another unique report (Corder & Haizlip, 1984) focused entirely on children who were younger than 10 years old when they committed suicide. This case study described two 9-year-old boys who committed suicide by shooting themselves and one 7-year-old boy who died by self-poisoning. The authors hypothesized that the suicides of these children were related to problems in family relationships in which stresses, such as losses, resulted in damage to the frail self-esteem of both child and parents. These children appeared to have had an unusual precocity in school or sports and spent a great deal of time with adult relatives. The family perceived these children as being able to handle important losses in a manner similar to adults. As a result, when crises over loss

344

developed in the families, these children were not provided with emotional support. However, the suicides did not occur at times of sudden intense crisis but resulted after a gradual intensification of more chronic stress. The children's specially perceived qualities appeared to wane, they could no longer maintain their feelings of infantile omnipotence, and, as a result, intense feelings of hopelessness pervaded. The authors proposed that these children represented a subgroup of suicidal children, "special" children who experience threats to their self-esteem within inflexible, enmeshed families that are attempting to adapt to loss or change.

In the first study to compare prepubertal and young adolescent child suicidal victims who were younger 14 years with adolescent suicide victims who were 15 to 19 years old, Hoberman and Garfinkel (1988) used medical examiner reports to gather data. Methods of committing suicide were different among the 209 older and 21 younger individuals. Approximately 52% of the younger suicides hanged themselves or used firearms (42%), while the older youths used firearms (44%) or carbon monoxide (17%).

The younger suicide victims were more likely to have been angry (40%) or nervous (40%), symptoms suggestive of conduct and anxiety disorders, while the older youths appeared to be sad (49%) with evidence of mood and substance abuse disorders. School problems and arguments with parents were more important stressors for the younger suicide victims, but arguments with parents or boy- or girlfriends were likely stressors for the older suicide victims.

Other psychological autopsy studies (Shaffer, 1988; Shafii, Carrigan, Whittinghill, & Derrick, 1985) that involve predominantly adolescents and nonsuicidal comparison individuals suggest that psychopathology, usually in the form of depression or conduct disorder, is an important characteristic of the suicide victims. Use of firearms, especially when intoxicated by drugs or alcohol, is a frequent method of suicide among the adolescents (Brent, Perper, & Allman, 1987). It is notable that Kuperman, Black, and Burns (1988) identified an excessive number of suicide victims among child psychiatric patients who were studied during a 4- to 15-year record-linkage follow-up, thereby illustrating the important association between severe psychosical factors and suicide. The diagnoses most often associated with suicide were schizophrenia, organic mental disorder, and personality/conduct disorder.

Clinical Features of Childhood Nonfatal Suicidal Behavior

Research with children who think about or attempt suicide has focused on specific patient and nonpatient populations. The findings provide an overview about the possible variability in expression of suicidal tendencies among children. One of the most extensive comparative studies involving over 300 subjects was conducted by Pfeffer et al. (1986). Altogether the study population included 106 child psychiatric inpatients, 101 child psychiatric outpatients, and 101 children selected from the community. All children were 6 to 12 years old. The severity of suicidal behavior was greatest among the inpatients and lowest among the community sample. Approximately 54% of the inpatients, 9% of the outpatients, and 3% of the nonpatients threatened or attempted suicide within the six months prior to being interviewed. Furthermore, there was a significant difference between the suicidal behavior of the mothers of the inpatients, outpatients, and nonpatients. Approximately 11% of the mothers of the inpatients had attempted suicide and 1 committed suicide; none of the mothers of the outpatients or nonpatients either attempted or committed suicide.

Other differences were reported regarding suicidal behavior in these three groups of children. Inpatient children with psychiatric diagnoses of major depressive disorder, adjustment disorder, especially with depressed mood, and specific developmental disorder were at higher risk for suicidal behavior. Outpatient children who had a major depressive disorder, dysthymic disorder, or borderline personality disorder were more likely to report suicidal behavior. No specific psychiatric disorder was associated with suicidal behavior in the community sample; on the other hand, all the suicidal children in the community sample did have a psychiatric disorder.

345

Overall, factors such as symptoms of psychopathology, preoccupations with death, and symptoms of recent and past depression were associated with suicidal behavior (Pfeffer, Solomon, Plutchik, Mizruchi, & Weiner, 1982).

Myers, Burke, and McCauley (1985) verified the important relationship between mood disorders and prepubertal and young adolescent suicidal behavior in a record review of 348 children, ages 5 to 13, admitted to a psychiatric inpatient unit. Other factors that were associated with suicidal behavior were assaultive behavior, a positive family history of depression, more intense recent stressful life events, and family violence.

Appreciating that violent tendencies may be an important factor for certain suicidal children, Pfeffer, Plutchik, and Mizruchi (1983) explored whether subtypes of suicidal children could be identified based on their degree of violent propensities. Diagnostic distinctions were noted. Among nonassaultive-nonsuicidal children, neurotic disorders, such as overanxious or phobic disorders and chronic depression, predominated, whereas organic brain syndrome was the least prevalent. Affective disorder was most prevalent among suicidal-only children, and borderline personality disorder was most prevalent among the assaultive-suicidal children. Specific developmental disorder was most frequent among assaultive-only children. Assaultive-only and assaultive-suicidal children experienced significantly more parental violence than the other children. In addition, more suicidal behavior was reported among the parents of the assaultive-suicidal and suicidal-only children than among other children. This study supported the idea of at least two subtypes of suicidal children. One type, consisting of children with suicidal but not violent behavior, includes children with relatively stable ego and cognitive functioning who decompensate and become depressed under the influence of extreme environmental stress. The other subtype, children who are assaultive and suicidal, exhibit ego deficits involving impulsivity and poor reality testing and have family tendencies toward violence and suicidal behavior. An important finding of this study is that some suicidal children show intense depression, but others exhibit relatively less depression but more intense aggression.

Many other reports provide ample evidence that a variety of symptoms of psychopathology such as depressive symptoms, aggressive symptoms, and anxiety symptoms (Kashani et al., 1989) are associated with suicidal behavior in children. However, these relationships are extremely complex. Some studies (Brent et al., 1986; Pfeffer et al., 1982) suggest that the severity of depressive symptoms is associated with severity of suicidal tendencies. However, other reports (Carlson & Cantwell, 1982) propose that there is no direct continuous relationship between depressive symptoms and severity of suicidal tendencies; instead, they find that, in contrast to those who think about suicide, children who attempt suicide have less depressive symptomatology.

Kosky, Solburn, and Zubrick (1986) explored the distinctions between depressed, suicidal children and depressed nonsuicidal children. Although there were no differences between groups of children for any symptom of depression or conduct disorder, the groups did differ in respect to intrafamilial conflict. Compared to the nonsuicidal depressed children, the suicidal depressed children were more likely to have disturbed child-father and child-sibling relationships. Child-mother relationship problems existed in both groups. Family relationship problems among the suicidal children were more likely to involve persistent discord, with persecution, hostility, and abuse directed toward the suicidal child. This study demonstrated that disturbed family relations were more important risk factors for suicidal behavior than whether the parents had separated or whether the child experienced problems with peer relationships or with school pressure.

In other studies, the intensity of stress experienced by suicidal children, compared to nonsuicidal, depressed children, and nondepressed, nonsuicidal children with other types of psychopathology, was identified to be greater and more chronic (Cohen-Sandler, Berman, & King, 1982). These stresses were particularly high for events related to family problems and change as well as for abuse directed toward the child (Rosenthal, Rosenthal, Doherty, & Santora, 1986).

Pfeffer (1981) proposed a family model for suicidal risk of children that concurs with the empirical data. She proposed that children who report suicidal tendencies live in family milieus that are rigid and inflexible with regard to change, limit setting, and expectations. In such families, prominent conflicts and features of primitive fantasies and attitudes are projected onto the potentially suicidal child. In time, that youngster comes to feel confused, guilty, helpless, and unable to cope. In effect, there follows an insufficient differentiation of self from parental influences and a failure to establish the child's stable and separate identity. This, in turn, may lead to an enhanced vulnerability to suicidal behavior. Such children often feel they do not have sufficient support from others, are not able to plan appropriate behavior, become overwhelmed, and imagine that the best means of escape from this intolerable situation is to commit suicide.

Others (Kazdin, French, Unis, Esveldt-Dawson, & Sherich, 1983) noted that hopelessness is a more important correlate of childhood suicidal behavior than is depression. Family constellations beset by extreme discord or abuse and violence toward the child engender states of symptomatic depression in children. However, when stress is intense, a child's coping mechanisms often are so overwhelmed or depleted, and the child's positive sense of self is so dissipated, that hopelessness becomes a major precipitant for suicidal behavior (Asarnow, Carlsen, & Guthrie, 1987).

tensified by a past history of suicidal behaviors. Where children have strong adaptive skills, do not have symptoms of psychopathology, and experience empathy and an appropriately consistent environment, they are protected from suicidal tendencies.

Other models, such as genetic or biological models, have not been subject to empirical testing with respect to children. Studies of adults using family history, twin, and adoption methodology suggest that suicidal behavior tends to be inherited (Roy, 1989). This appears to be especially the case when suicidal behavior co-occurs with affective disorders among relatives.

Studies of adults suggest that neurotransmitter and neuroendocrine factors are part of an underlying propensity for suicidal behavior (Mann, De-Meo, Keilp, & McBride, 1989). For example, disturbances in serotonin metabolism are associated with increased risk for suicidal behavior. In particular, studies report reduced levels of 5-hydroxyindoleacetic acid (5-HIAA), a serotonin metabolite, in the cerebrospinal fluid of suicide attempters and victims. This finding was especially associated with a history of violence in suicidal subjects.

Putative Models for the Pathogenesis of Childhood Suicidal Behavior

Different perspectives can be emphasized that suggest varied theoretical models for risk of suicidal behavior in children. Research with suicidal preadolescents focuses mostly on psychosocial factors that may be useful in understanding their role in a sociocultural-psychosocial-developmental model. It is assumed that the level of childhood suicidal risk results from an equilibrium between risk and protective factors. (See Table 32.2.) From a sociocultural perspective, modern society with its enhanced technology, mobility, and associated increase in identified psychopathology offers a stressful macroscopic milieu that impinges on the functioning of individuals. Risk for suicidal behavior in children is heightened by loss of social support, problems in family functioning, and aberrations in familial attachment responses. A child's vulnerability is in-

Prognosis of Suicidal Children

Relatively little research information has been acquired about the likelihood of preadolescents with a history of suicidal behavior to express repeated suicidal behavior or to commit suicide. In a comprehensive longitudinal study, Pfeffer et al. (1991) observed prepubertal children with a history of suicidal ideation or attempts. Such youngsters were significantly more likely to repeat suicidal behavior during a six- to eight-year follow-up period than were nonsuicidal children to report a first episode of suicidal behavior in the same period. No deaths occurred, suggesting that suicidal children grow up. However, within six to eight years of follow-up, approximately 30.8% of 26 prepubertal children with histories of suicidal ideation or attempts reported further suicide attempts. The degree of morbidity of such children is illustrated by the high prevalence of mood, conduct, and substance abuse disorders during the follow-up period. These data suggest that suicidal

TABLE 32.2

Equilibrium Between Risk and Protective Factors For Suicidal Behavior in Children

Increased Suicidal Risk	Risk Factors	Level of Childhood Suicidal Risk	Protective Factors	Decreased Suicidal Risk
	1. Child's Severity of Past or Present Suicidal Ideation or Acts		1. Absence of Psychopathology	

	2. Loss of Social Support
	  a. Death
	  b. Parental separation/divorce
	  c. School changes
	  d. Peer problems
	  e. Abandonment
			2. Presence of Social Support
			  a. Empathy
			  b. Consistent availability
			  c. Limit setting
			  d. Environmental structure	

	3. Problems in Family Functioning
	  a. Affective disorders
	  b. Suicidal behavior
	  c. Alcohol or substance abuse
	  d. Interpersonal conflicts
	  e. Violence
			3. Child's Adaptive Skills
			  a. Realistic appraisal of stress
			  b. Plan alternative solutions
			  c. High frustration tolerance
			  d. Self-esteem
			  e. High impulse control
			  f. Hope	

	4. Attachment Aberations
	  a. Sexual abuse
	  b. Physical abuse			

NOTE. Reprinted, with permission, from "Suicidal Behavior in Young Children," by C. R. Pfeffer, 1991, *Briefings, 1,* 4.

children are not normal youngsters who are only responding to stress by means of suicidal behavior; instead they experience various elements of morbidity that heighten their vulnerability and impair their future functioning.

Treatment of Suicidal Children

Treatment of children who are potentially at imminent risk for suicidal behavior necessitates a time-intensive and clearly defined process that involves a therapist's methodical attention to changes in the child's clinical state and flexible availability to the child and family (Pfeffer, 1986). It is essential that therapeutic intervention be focused not only on the potentially suicidal child but also on the family, especially because by the very nature of developmental necessity, young children are dependent on family support (Pfeffer, 1986).

At present, there are no controlled treatment studies of suicidal children. Pfeffer and colleagues (1992) reports that prepubertal suicidal child psychiatric inpatients, compared to nonsuicidal children selected from the community, have significantly higher rates of psychiatric hospitalization, residential treatment, and outpatient and day hospital care during a six- to eight-year follow-up period. This study highlights the fact that suicidal children may require multiple types of intervention for long periods of time.

Treatment must focus on diminishing acute suicidal tendencies and associated risk factors involving psychiatric symptoms; problems in social relationships with family, friends, and others; and improving coping skills in order to enable the child to endure more adequately various environmental stresses (Pfeffer, 1986). Because of the complex features of childhood suicidal behavior, treatment should integrate psychodynamic, cognitive, psychopharmacological, and family interventions. Psychotherapy with the child should focus on understanding motives for suicidal behavior, developing alternate ways of managing current situations, appraising psychiatric symptoms and decreasing their severity, and improving self-esteem, social relations, and perception of hope. Often medication may be prescribed for specifically targeted psychiatric symptoms. For example, impulsivity, inattention, and hyperactivity may be treated with a psychostimulant, while depression may be treated with an antidepressant; both agents are employed as adjunctive interventions to individual psychotherapy. A neuroleptic medication may be useful to ameliorate psychotic thinking. Many suicidal children are withdrawn, have impaired peer relations, and suffer from poor self-esteem. Group treatment may be useful to provide a forum to discuss how a child's perceptions agree with those of others, to develop better skills in interactions with peers, and to discuss mutual life experiences.

In general, the family is the basis for social support and physiological needs. Family intervention, especially with parents, is of almost equal importance to individual intervention with the child. The scope of such treatment involves meeting jointly with the child and parents to identify conflicts, to determine ways of settling disputes, and to foster parental support needed to promote adequate development of the child. Parent guidance is needed, so that they can both foster a better atmosphere for communication between them and their child and develop effective ways of assisting their child with problems that arise from school activities, peer relationships, and family interactions. Frequently, the parents themselves may require additional specific psychotherapeutic and psychopharmacological intervention to alleviate psychiatric symptoms or disorders.

An important clinical decision that frequently has to be made is whether to psychiatrically hospitalize a suicidal child. The need for hospitalization arises when the child's behavior is not predictable, when a child displays intense suicidal preoccupation and either plans to or has made a serious suicide attempt, or when other psychiatric symptoms are severe enough to create severe impairment of functioning. Other factors determining the need for psychiatric hospitalization involve presence of poor or minimal social support (especially within the family), ongoing abusive experiences, or lack of adequate compliance with treatment recommendations.

Psychiatric hospitalization provides a structured, consistent atmosphere in which intensive study and close observation of the child can occur. In such an environment, multiple types of intervention, such as individual, group, activity, family, psychological, and school, are provided. Thus, psychiatric hospitalization offers multimodal and more intense treatment than outpatient care.

Since suicidal children are at significant risk for repeated suicidal episodes and associated psychopathologies, follow-up is essential. As part of follow-up care, children and their families need to be taught how to recognize signs of impending risk. They should be made aware of the possibility of recurrence of symptoms and of the need to consult with medical professionals immediately to determine whether treatment is indicated. Therapists may wish to develop mechanisms for follow-up visits that may enable checks on the clinical state of the child. This may be accomplished by planned future contact with children and their parents.

In recent years, the need for national efforts toward suicide prevention has been recognized. One approach has been the development of programs within the schools to educate children and adolescents about suicidal behavior and to instruct them in ways to identify signs of risk in self and peers. The basic premise of such programs is to teach youngsters how to seek help after identifying signs of suicidal behavior. While such programs have been widely implemented, there has been little systematic evaluation of their effects. A number of reports (Shaffer, Garland, Vieland, Underwood, & Busner, 1991; Spirito, Overholser, Ashworth, Morgan, & Benedict-Drew, 1988) suggest that such school-based suicide prevention programs have not been successful. It is impossible to evaluate whether suicide has been prevented because the incidence of suicide within a defined location is so low. Moreover, it has been suggested that youngsters with a history of suicidal behavior were disturbed by such programs and that, ultimately, these negative effects may hamper the prevention of suicidal behavior. In fact, only a select group of students were affected in the program's intended ways. Girls were more likely to feel that the programs were helpful, that they learned to recognize features of suicidal risk, and that they would assist others in seeking help. In contrast, boys were more upset by the discussions of suicidal behavior and remarked that they would not recommend the programs to others. These reports suggest that methods to reduce suicidal risk among youths might well focus on vulnerable youths rather than on youths in the general population, who are at very low risk. The most important lesson to be learned is that evaluation

studies of interventions for suicidal behavior among children are needed.

Finally, a family history of suicidal behavior may increase risk for childhood suicidal behavior (Ness & Pfeffer, 1990). Research is needed to explore the long-term course of children who are bereaved as a result of suicide and to identify appropriate means to prevent their possible future suicidal behavior.

REFERENCES

Asarnow J. R., Carlson G. A., & Guthrie D. (1987). Coping strategies, self-perceptions, hopelessness, and perceived family environments in depressed and suicidal children. *Journal of Consulting and Clinical Psychology, 55*, 361–366.

Brent D. A., Kalas, R., Edelbrock, C., Costello, A. J., Dulcan, M. K., & Conover, N. (1986). Psychopathology and its relationship to suicidal ideation in childhood and adolescence. *Journal of the American Academy of Child Psychiatry, 25*, 666–673.

Brent, D. A., Perper, J. A., & Allman, C. J. (1987). Alcohol, firearms, and suicide among youth: Temporal trends in Allegheny County, Pennsylvania, 1960 to 1983. *Journal of the American Medical Association, 257*, 3369–3372.

Carlson, G. A., & Cantwell, D. P. (1982). Suicidal behavior and depression in children and adolescents. *Journal of the American Academy of Child Psychiatry, 21*, 361–368.

Cohen-Sandler, R., Berman, A. L., & King, R. A. (1982). Life stress and symptomatology: Determinants of suicidal behavior in children. *Journal of the American Academy of Child Psychiatry, 21*, 178–186.

Corder, B. F., & Haizlip, T. M. (1984). Environmental and personality similarities in case histories of suicide and self-poisoning by children under ten. *Suicide and Life-Threatening Behavior, 14*, 59–66.

Fingerhut, L. A., Kleinman, J. C., Godfrey, E., & Rosenberg, H. (1991). Firearm mortality among children, youth and young adults 1–34 years of age, trends, and current states: United States, 1979–88. *Monthly vital statistics report.* (Vol. 39, no. 11, suppl.). Hyattsville, MD: National Center for Health Statistics.

Hafner, H., & Schmidtke, A. (1989). Do televised fictional suicide models produce suicides? In C. R. Pfeffer (Ed.)., *Suicide among youth: Perspectives on risk and prevention* (pp. 117–142). Washington, DC: American Psychiatric Press.

Hoberman, H. M., & Garfinkel, B. D. (1988). Completed suicide in children and adolescents. *Journal of the American Academy of Child and Adolescent Psychiatry, 27*, 689–695.

Kashani, J. H., Goddard, P., & Reid, J. C. (1989). Correlates of suicidal ideation in a community sample of children and adolescents. *Journal of the American Academy of Child and Adolescent Psychiatry, 28*, 912–917.

Kazdin, A. E., French, N. H., Unis, A. S., Esveldt-Dawson, K., & Sherick, R. B. (1983). Hopelessness, depression, and suicidal intent among psychiatrically disturbed inpatient children. *Journal of Consulting and Clinical Psychology, 51*, 504–510.

Klerman, G. L. (1989). Suicide, depression, and related problems among the Baby Book cohort. In C. R. Pfeffer (Ed.), *Suicide among youth: Perspectives on risk and prevention* (pp. 63–81). Washington, DC: American Psychiatric Press.

Kosky, R., Solburn, S., & Zubrick, S. (1986): Symptomatic depression and suicidal ideation: A comparative study with 628 children. *Journal of Nervous and Mental Disease, 174*, 523–528.

Kuperman, S., Black, D., & Burns, T. (1988). Excess suicide among formerly hospitalized child psychiatry patients. *Journal of Clinical Psychiatry, 49*, 88–93.

Mann, J. J., DeMeo, M. D., Keilp, J. G., & McBride, P. A. (1989). Biological correlates of suicidal behavior in youth. In C. R. Pfeffer (Ed.)., *Suicide among youth: Perspectives on risk and prevention* (pp. 185–203). Washington, DC: American Psychiatric Press.

Myers, K. M., Burke, P., & McCauley, E. (1985). Suicidal behavior by hospitalized preadolescent children on a psychiatric unit. *Journal of the American Academy of Child Psychiatry, 24*, 474–480.

National Center for Health Statistics. (1984a). Advance report final mortality statistics, 1977. *Monthly vital statistics report* (Vol. 28, no. 1, suppl.). Hyattsville, MD: Public Health Service.

National Center for Health Statistics. (1984b). Advance report final mortality statistics, 1982. *Monthly vital statistics report* (Vol. 33, no. 9, suppl.). Hyattsville, MD: Public Health Service.

National Center for Health Statistics. (1985). Final report of mortality statistics, 1983. *Monthly vital statistics report* (Vol. 3). Hyattsville, MD: Public Health Service.

National Center for Health Statistics. (1986). Annual summary of births, marriages, divorces, and deaths.

United States 1985. *Monthly vital statistics report* (Vol. 34, no. 13). Hyattsville, MD: Public Health Service.

National Center for Health Statistics. (1990). Advance report of final mortality statistics, 1988. *Monthly vital statistics report* (Vol. 39, no. 7, suppl.). Hyattsville, MD: Public Health Service.

Ness, D. E. & Pfeffer, C. R. (1990). Sequelae of bereavement resulting from suicide. *American Journal of Psychiatry, 147,* 279–285.

Pfeffer, C. R. (1981). The family system of suicidal children. *American Journal of Psychotherapy, 35,* 330–341.

Pfeffer, C. R. (1986). *The suicidal child.* New York: Guilford Press.

Pfeffer, C. R. (1991). Suicidal behavior in young children. *Briefings, 1,* 3–6.

Pfeffer, C. R., Klerman, G. L., Hurt, S. W., Lesser, M., Peskin, J. R., & Siefker, C. A. (1991). Suicidal children grow up: Demographic and clinical risk factors for adolescent suicide attempts. *Journal of the American Academy of Child and Adolescent Psychiatry, 30,* 609–616.

Pfeffer, C. R., Peskin, J. R., & Siefker, C. A. (1992). Suicidal children grow up: Psychiatric treatment during follow-up. *Journal of the American Academy of Child and Adolescent Psychiatry, 31,* 679–685.

Pfeffer C. R., Plutchik R., & Mizruchi M. S. (1983). Suicidal and assaultive behavior in children: Classification, measurement, and interrelations. *American Journal of Psychiatry, 140,* 154–157.

Pfeffer, C. R., Plutchik, R., Mizruchi, M. S., & Lipkins, R. (1986). Suicidal behavior in child psychiatric inpatients and outpatients and in nonpatients. *American Journal of Psychiatry, 143,* 733–738.

Pfeffer, C. R., Solomon, G., Plutchik, R., Mizruchi, M. S., & Weiner, A. (1982). Suicidal behavior in latency-age psychiatric inpatients: A replication and cross-validation. *Journal of the American Academy of Child Psychiatry, 21,* 564–569.

Phillips, D. P., Carstensen, L. L., & Paight, D. J. (1989). Effects of mass media news stories on suicide, with new evidence on the role of story content. In C. R. Pfeffer (Ed.), *Suicide among youth: Perspectives on risk and prevention* (pp. 101–116). Washington, DC: American Psychiatric Press.

Rosenthal, P. A., Rosenthal, S., Doherty, M. B., & Santora, D. (1986). Suicidal thoughts and behaviors in depressed hospitalized preschoolers. *American Journal of Psychotherapy, 40,* 201–212.

Roy, A. (1989). Genetics and suicidal behavior. In C. R. Pfeffer, *Suicide among youth: Perspectives on risk and prevention* (pp. 165–185). Washington, DC: American Psychiatric Press.

Shaffer, D. (1974). Suicide in childhood and early adolescence. *Journal of Child Psychology and Psychiatry, 15,* 275–291.

Shaffer, D. (1988). The epidemiology of teen suicide: An examination of risk factors. *Journal of Clinical Psychiatry, 49,* 36–41.

Shaffer, D., Garland, A., Vieland, V., Underwood, M., & Busner, C. (1991). The impact of curriculum-based suicide prevention programs for teenagers. *Journal of the American Academy of Child and Adolescent Psychiatry, 30,* 588–596.

Shafii, M., Carrigan, S., Whittinghill, J. R., & Derrick, A. (1985). Psychological autopsy of completed suicide in children and adolescents. *American Journal of Psychiatry, 142,* 1061–1064.

Spirito, A., Overholser, J., Ashworth, S., Morgan, J., & Benedict-Drew, C. (1988). Evaluation of a suicide awareness cirriculum of high school students. *Journal of the American Academy of Child and Adolescent Psychiatry, 27,* 705–711.

33 / **Oppositional Defiant Disorder**

Stewart Gabel

Background

Oppositional disorder became a new category in the classification of mental disorders with the publication of the third edition of the *Diagnostic and Statistical Manual of Mental Disorders* (DSM-III) more than a decade ago (American Psychiatric Association [APA], 1980). Along with a slight change in name to oppositional defiant disorder (ODD), and minor changes in the associated information and diagnostic criteria, the disorder continues to be represented in *DSM-III-R* (APA, 1987) and in *DSM-IV* (APA, 1994). This conceptualization in *DSM-III, DSM-III-R,* and *DSM-IV* has occurred despite a lack of broadly accepted empirical evidence supporting ODD as a distinct disorder that is apart from conduct disorder (CD) with which it is usually compared (Reeves, Werry, Elkind, & Zametkin, 1987; Werry, Reeves, & Elkind, 1987).

The representation of ODD in *DSM-III, DSM-*

III-R, and *DSM-IV* does reflect, however, the clinical awareness that large numbers of children are seen in mental health practice who have temper outbursts and oppositional, defiant, negative, resistant, and hostile interactions with others, commonly adults, but who do not violate basic rights of others or engage in major behavioral problems, such as severe aggression, fire setting, and cruelty to animals that are more characteristic of CD. These former types of children often qualify for a diagnosis of ODD when their behaviors are more common than would be expected for youth of the same developmental age.

ODD, along with CD (and attention deficit hyperactivity disorder [ADHD] in *DSM-III-R*) form the group of disruptive behavior disorders in *DSM-IV*. This group often is considered together as externalizing disorders, in that they characteristically are manifested by externally directed maladaptive behaviors (e.g., hyperactivity, impulsivity, aggression, defiance to rules) in contrast to the internalizing disorders, such as anxiety and depression, which are manifested more by internal feeling states and discomfort experienced by the individual him- or herself. Earlier, in some classifications the externalizing disorders, including ODD, were considered as behavioral disorders and the internalizing disorders as neurotic or emotional disorders; such characterizations are used less often today.

This chapter reviews research available on ODD, including the question of whether it is a distinct disorder or an aspect of CD as the latter presently is conceptualized. Unfortunately, a great deal is not known about this disorder from the perspectives of family background, associated features, etiology, course, and prognosis. Chapter 34 reviews the much larger literature on conduct disorder. That chapter should help readers to understand at least some youths with ODD, the apparently sizable (but unknown) number who progress to a conduct disorder diagnosis.

Classification, Clinical Description, and Developmental Course

The clinical description of ODD as a distinct disorder derives from its inclusion in the *DSM-III*,

DSM-III-R, and *DSM-IV* classifications. Earlier empirically derived categories of behavioral disorders in childhood (see Quay, 1979, 1986) had not described this disorder (Wells & Forehand, 1985). Achenbach (1991), however, currently considers the "aggressive behavior" factor of the Child Behavior Checklist, a widely used behavioral rating instrument with empirically derived behavioral dimensions, as generally reflecting descriptively either the solitary aggressive type of CD or the ODD category of *DSM-III-R*.

Rey (1993) has reviewed the literature on ODD and concluded that there is some empirical support for an oppositional defiant disorder diagnosis which would include an aggressive but not delinquent dimension. Lahey et al. (1994) assessed the results of *DSM-IV* field trials for ODD and CD, finding improved internal consistency and test-retest agreement compared to *DSM-III-R* definitions.

DSM-III-R and *DSM-IV* describe youths with ODD as displaying a pattern of negative, hostile, and defiant behavior that is more common than usually seen in youth of the same mental age. These children, while not violating basic rights of others, as do conduct-disordered youngsters, commonly engage in arguments with adults, lose their tempers, swear, and seem angry, resentful, and annoyed by others around them. They are defiant and blame others for their own problems. These children's problems are most commonly manifested in the home environment and with their parents, although manifestations in other environments (e.g., school) and with other adults or peers also occur.

On clinical interview, these youths often seem to be rather nondisclosing about themselves or their difficulties, and attribute their problems and their noncompliance with adult requests to what others have done to annoy or frustrate them. Parents often describe home environments with a great deal of arguing and attempted coaxing of the children to perform chores, do tasks on time, and conform to household rules. These children's resistance, negativism, and refusal to comply with requests often suggest a power struggle or struggle for control between them and their parents (or others). Psychodynamically oriented clinicians sometimes understand these issues further as defensive struggles in developmentally problematic areas such as attachment, separation, or the development of psychological independence.

The more severely affected of the group present much as would conduct-disordered youths, with poor verbal skills, little reflection and insight, and a strong tendency to deny involvement in behavior that is greatly disturbing to their parents, while also blaming and criticizing parents or others for what has been done to or has happened to them. (Chapter 34 has a more complete description of the clinical presentation that would apply to at least some of these youths.)

Youths with ODD are not psychotic and, unless there is a coexistent psychiatric disorder, display no abnormality of appearance, mood, thought process, or speech on examination. A common associated feature is attention deficit hyperactivity disorder (ADHD) (*DSM-III-R*); these youths, by parent or teacher report (and perhaps in clinical evaluation), may show the hyperactivity, impulsivity, and inattention characteristic of ADHD. They also commonly manifest delaying tactics, resistance to adult requests, and difficulty separating from therapists initially or during the course of their clinical assessment and treatment (Gabel, Oster, & Pfeffer, 1988). *DSM-III-R* and *DSM-IV* state that associated features include poor self-esteem and mood lability. Older children with ODD may use illegal psychoactive substances, alcohol, or tobacco.

Using the *DSM-III-R* and *DSM-IV* descriptions, ODD is said to begin by age 8 years and to be more common in males than in females before puberty. In many cases it may evolve into conduct disorder or mood disorder. *DSM-III* considers continuity with passive-aggressive personality disorder an outcome in some cases, but there is no mention of this possible outcome in *DSM-III-R*. Table 33.1 provides the specific diagnostic criteria for ODD in *DSM-IV*.

Given the lack of empirical literature on ODD and the large number of children seen in clinical settings who conform to an ODD diagnosis, the following case example is provided to highlight particular characteristics of some ODD youths.

CASE EXAMPLE

A is a 6-year-old boy brought for evaluation by his mother because of noncompliant behavior at home and in school. Early development was unremarkable although A was described as "all boy" from the end of his first year onward because of active and impulsive behavior. A's mother noted increasing noncompliant behavior, stubbornness, refusal to follow her directions, and occasional aggression toward her around A's fourth birthday, a time that coincided with increasing marital difficulties, alleged infidelity on the part of the father,

TABLE 33.1
Diagnostic Criteria for 313.81 Oppositional Defiant Disorder

A. A pattern of negativistic, hostile, defiant behavior lasting at least 6 months, during which four (or more) of the following are present:
   (1) often loses temper
   (2) often argues with adults
   (3) often actively defies or refuses to comply with adults' requests or rules
   (4) often deliberately annoys people
   (5) often blames others for his or her mistakes or misbehavior
   (6) is often touchy or easily annoyed by others
   (7) is often angry and resentful
   (8) is often spiteful or vindictive

   Note: Consider a criterion met only if the behavior occurs more frequently than is typically observed in individuals of comparable age and developmental level.

B. The disturbance in behavior causes clinically significant impairment in social, academic, or occupational functioning.

C. The behaviors do not occur exclusively during the course of a Psychotic or Mood Disorder.

D. Criteria are not met for Conduct Disorder, and, if the individual is age 18 years or older, criteria are not met for Antisocial Personality Disorder.

NOTE. From *Diagnostic and Statistical Manual of Mental Disorders* (4th ed.) (pp. 93–94), by American Psychiatric Press, 1994; Washington, DC: Author. Copyright 1994 by American Psychiatric Press. Reprinted with permission.

and ultimate divorce when A was about 4½ years old. The mother herself had been depressed for some time around marital issues and the divorce. The father, who had been actively involved with A and who had been considered the more effective disciplinarian in the home, had less and less contact with A as the marriage deteriorated and as he moved out of the home. Family history indicated mild learning problems in the father, but no history of severe hyperactivity, aggression, conduct disorder, or antisocial personality.

At the time of evaluation, A's behavior was consistent in home, school, and neighborhood settings. He was described as bossy, wanting his own way, demanding attention, and acting aggressively toward others when they seemed to receive more attention from adults than he did. A seemed to take opportunities to challenge his mother's or the teacher's authority, to "talk back," and to defy or refuse instructions from others, adults or peers.

On several occasions in his preschool program and then again during his kindergarten year, A had to be removed from the classroom when he became disruptive and aggressive in refusing to get into line with other children, play cooperatively, or attend to particular tasks. A's difficulties seemed especially prominent when changes in structure or routine were imposed on him, such as when the need arose to get ready for Sunday school or to go home after a day's outing. Early academic readiness and testing in the school environment had revealed no major problems, although receptive language was a relative weakness.

A's behavior at home was similar to his behavior in school, although he seemed to have many difficulties around separation in the home environment. A became most noncompliant and angry when his mother went out with female friends during the daytime or in the evening and with occasional male friends at night. He also seemed to challenge her authority more than he would do with other adults, and would verbally question her love for him and tell her that she would leave him.

A's behavior with his father was more easily managed, and the boy showed only minimal signs of noncompliance during paternal visits. His mother felt that he was afraid of his father and therefore complied better with him, although she did not allege excessive physical discipline or threats by the father against the child.

A's range of playmates in the neighborhood had become modestly restricted by the time of the evaluation because two neighbors would not allow A to play with their children (three boys) because of excessive fighting and arguing over rules and turns in games. Other children, who were perhaps more "easygoing" by the mother's description, had less difficulty with A, and he played more harmoniously with them.

During the course of the evaluation, several points emerged. A was a likable, energetic, moderately active boy who was not clinically depressed but who smiled little and at times seemed quite sad. He displayed none of the more severe behaviors of CD, such as fighting with weapons, fire setting, or cruelty to animals. His cognitive development was broadly normal. He separated from his mother for the individual evaluation with slight difficulty, but soon seemed to enjoy time with the examiner when playing games that he chose and when arranging toys, such as military figures, in the order he wanted (often in two battle lines, one on his side of the table and one on the examiner's). He was loath to discuss himself, his feelings, possible problems at home, or his knowledge of his parents' marital difficulties or divorce. When these topics were raised, he became angry, silent, and sometimes openly defiant. He would not clean up the office when asked to do so (even with earlier reminders), but would delay or seem not to hear the clinician's requests until they were repeated several times.

A's mother and father were seen separately. She was a professional woman in her late 20s who had been married briefly as a teenager. A was her only child. The mother admitted alternating between her rage at A's defiant and noncompliant behavior, and her indulgence and love for him as her only child. She wanted to make sure that he did not suffer or have any further misfortune happen to him. A's mother also was quite depressed and had been depressed for almost two years around the family and marital issues. She denied earlier episodes of mood disorder.

A's father was in his mid-30s. He too had been married once before. He described A's mother as a "nag" who was never satisfied. He felt that his life was moving better since the divorce, both professionally and socially. He felt A's mother "babied" A and never followed through on her instructions, demands, or discipline. He said that he had not seen A very much because of his anger at his former wife and not wanting to be around her, as well as his need to establish his own life after the divorce. He enjoyed the time he spent with A (several hours twice each week) but seemed to have little desire to have more contact.

A's principal diagnosis, by *DSM-III-R* criteria (APA, 1987) was ODD although some elements of ADHD also were present.

The treatment centered around clarification and exploration with the parents about earlier periods in their lives, the marital relationship, and the effects of their lingering feelings about one another on A and their management of him. His probable reactions to the family turmoil, marital separation, and relative loss of contact with his father also were explored. The mother's own depression and resultant inconsistent emotional availability to A was discussed with her, and she ultimately entered treatment herself. Joint sessions between A and his father and between A and his mother were held to discuss, in an age-appropriate manner, issues around the divorce and each parent's individual feelings for A and their expectations and hopes at this time. These sessions, which neither parent wanted to occur with both of them present, allowed each to express to A their commitment to him and to attempt to relieve him of any guilt related to feelings about his participation in the divorce. A behavioral program was also developed with the mother and with A's school teacher. This program strongly emphasized reinforcement for desirable behavior and appropriate consequences for aggressive and disruptive behavior.

Through these interventions, A's behavior gradually improved across settings. After several months of treatment, his mother described him as happier, more able to play with peers, and better able to follow the teacher's directions. His anger and noncompliance at home were markedly improved, although occasional defiance when fatigued or at times of separation or change in routine still occurred.

The publication of *DSM-III* and *DSM-III-R* spawned a great deal of research into the nosology and diagnosis of various childhood disorders. The publication of *DSM-IV* has spurred further efforts to clarify the nature of the disruptive behavior disorders and their relationships to one another.

Lahey, Frick, Loeber, Tannenbaum, et al. (1990, cited in Loeber, Lahey, & Thomas, 1991) used a set of 64 factor analytic studies based on assessments of over 23,000 children and adolescents in an attempt to clarify further the nosology of the disruptive behavior disorders. They extracted a bipolar scale with all ODD symptoms plus aggressive CD symptoms at one pole (called "overt") and all other CD symptoms along with substance abuse at the opposite pole (called "covert"). They then extracted a second bipolar dimension in which "destructiveness to property" and "nondestructiveness to property" poles were found. These findings, although preliminary, raise the possibility of a more meaningful future classification of "disruptive behavior" problems into four groups: (1) behaviors that are overt and nondestructive (ODD behaviors but expanded from the *DSM-III-R* and *DSM-IV* criteria); (2) behaviors that are overt and destructive (e.g., aggression); (3) behaviors that are covert and destructive (e.g., fire setting); and (4) behaviors that are covert and nondestructive (e.g., truancy). Figure 33.1 presents this newer, highly tentative classification, which is in need of confirmation through additional studies.

Several important topics, are related to the concept of ODD in comparison to CD, such as the issues of age of onset and developmental course, need further research and clarification. Are these distinct disorders with differing pathways? Are they manifestations of the same disorder with different behaviors at different ages? Are they distinct disorders with some overlap in etiology and/or manifestations?

Loeber et al. (1991) describe a different developmental course for many ODD symptoms compared to many CD symptoms. ODD symptoms, unlike CD symptoms, emerge most commonly in the preschool period. At this time they often are considered normative. Deviance occurs when these behaviors increase in frequency or intensity compared to established or presumed norms; when the behaviors persist into later periods (e.g., into or beyond grade-school age); and when additional behavior problems emerge later (e.g., conduct problems).

Overall, from a developmental perspective, ODD symptoms begin during the preschool period and generally decrease during school age; CD symptoms rarely begin during the preschool period, but the prevalence of these symptoms (e.g., theft, drug use) increases with age. An early onset of CD symptoms (e.g., in the preschool period) puts the child at increased risk for severe CD. In most cases ODD probably precedes the onset of CD. The usual pathological developmental pathway is for ODD to emerge first (in the preschool period), followed by mild CD symptoms slightly later and serious CD symptoms still later. ODD therefore predicts CD (Loeber et al., 1995). When CD symptoms emerge, ODD symptoms do not cease but rather coexist with the CD symptoms. Therefore, nearly all youth fulfilling criteria for CD also fulfill criteria for ODD, although the reverse clearly is not true. Aggression is a particularly important symptom in predicting boys with ODD who later are more likely to be diagnosed as having CD (Loeber et al., 1991).

Etiology

When considered as a distinct entity apart from CD, there is little information about the biological or psychosocial etiology of ODD. The discussion of etiology in Chapter 34 should be relevant for most cases of ODD that progress to CD.

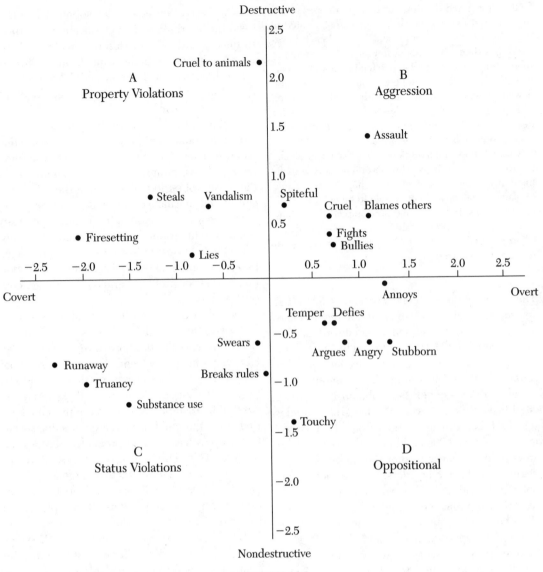

FIGURE 33.1

Results of the meta-analysis of factor analyses of disruptive child behavior.

From "Diagnostic Conundrum of Oppositional Defiant Disorder and Conduct Disorder," by R. Loeber, B. B. Lahey, and C. Thomas, 1991, *Journal of Abnormal Psychology, 100,* p. 382. Copyright 1991 by Benjamin B. Lahey.

Lahey, Frick, Loeber, Hart, et al., (1990, cited in Loeber et al., 1991) did find that CD boys, compared with ODD boys (as defined earlier) were not as intelligent and were from less advantaged families. These boys had the strongest family histories suggestive of antisocial personality; boys in the ODD group also had substantial family histories of antisocial personality disorders, but less than in the CD group. Loeber et al. (1991) comment that "the evidence indicates that the diagnoses of ODD and CD have similar correlates, with the difference being that those boys who progress to more frequent or serious disruptive behaviors are from families with more antisocial behavior and other handicaps than those whose disruptive behavior remains less serious" (p. 386).

Differential Diagnosis

The differential diagnosis of ODD, as this disorder is described using *DSM-III-R* and *DSM-IV* criteria, is fairly straightforward. (It should be noted, however, that *DSM-III-R* and *DSM-IV* criteria for ODD are somewhat more restrictive in terms of behavior, such as mild aggression, than factor analytic studies suggest might be warranted for an ODD-type disorder.)

Most CD boys (there is little information on girls with CD) also exhibit symptoms of ODD; for this reason, a CD diagnosis preempts an ODD diagnosis. Features of ODD may be seen during the course of psychotic disorders or mood disorders (such as dysthymia). In such cases, the additional diagnosis of ODD is not given. As noted earlier, ADHD commonly is an associated diagnosis whose essential features usually can be distinguished from symptoms of ODD, although sometimes behaviors of the ADHD child (such as inattention to activities, not maintaining on task behavior, or making distracting sounds) may seem defiant, resistant, or provocative, symptoms that are associated with ODD.

Morbidity

DSM-III-R states that symptoms such as low self-esteem, mood lability, use of illegal psychoactive substances or of legal psychoactive substances (e.g., alcohol) before the legal age are associated features of ODD.

Overall, compared to CD boys, ODD boys appear to have greater intelligence, more social advantage, and less conflict with school and judicial systems. Both CD and ODD boys have high degrees of comorbidity with ADHD, with ODD boys showing less comorbidity with depression than the CD group (Loeber et al., 1991).

Perhaps the most important issues with regard to the sequelae and prognosis of ODD involve its relationship with and development into CD (Loeber et al., 1995). As noted, ODD symptoms usually persist in boys who go on to develop CD. Loeber et al., (1991) also have found that aggressive ODD youth are more likely to develop CD over time compared to nonaggressive ODD youth. Aggression is an extremely important predictor of later, serious, more diversified antisocial behavior that can serve as an important marker of greater risk among ODD boys. Information about the long-term prognosis of CD youth is found in Chapter 34.

It is not known if ODD youth who do not progress to CD have other pathological developmental pathways. Those youngsters who are not overtly aggressive (often girls) sometimes appear clinically to be "passive-aggressive" in style. Whether, as suggested in *DSM-III*, some of these youths will later exhibit symptoms of passive-aggressive personality disorder remains to be elucidated by future research, as does the *DSM-III-R* contention that the disturbance may evolve into a mood disorder.

Treatment

Probably the most demonstrably successful psychotherapeutic intervention for CD has been parent management training (PMT) (Patterson, 1982), which is reviewed in Chapter 34. Patterson, DeBaryshe, and Ramsey (1989) have noted that treatment for antisocial youth apparently is most effective for preadolescent boys and less so for adolescents.

There appear to be few systematic intervention studies specifically designed for ODD youth. Loeber et al. (1991) consider Patterson's (1982) PMT as having been applied successfully with boys who essentially have ODD symptoms (probably including milder forms of physical aggression) and to be promising for such preadolescent youth.

PMT is a treatment approach based on social learning principles. The child's positive and negative behaviors are assumed to develop and be maintained because of known or unknown reinforcements for those behaviors. "Coercive behavior," in Patterson's (1982) sense, includes behaviors such as hitting, screaming, and nagging that are intended to elicit a response from others (e.g., attention). These behaviors are maintained because of the reinforcement they have received. Changing these behaviors and developing more prosocial behavior involve the appropriate use of positive reinforcement for desired behavior (e.g., helping with chores, not yelling when requesting something from parents versus screaming one's demands), and appropriate consequences, including time out from social interaction for negative behaviors, such as hitting others. Through a series of parent training sessions, parents are trained to apply these contingencies with their child. Commonly, target behaviors are defined, reinforcers and consequences are decided upon, and parents are asked to keep written records of change or lack of change in the behaviors targeted as the contingencies are applied.

A variety of effective psychopharmacological approaches are available for treatment of ADHD when it is associated with CD. (See Chapter 34 for a review.) Similar principles would apply to the treatment of ADHD in association with ODD. Since many ADHD youths treated with psychostimulants exhibit a decrease in aggressivity and improved social interaction, ODD symptoms also may improve with simultaneous psychostimulant treatment of comorbid ADHD. As with CD, multimodal treatment for many ODD youth with ADHD probably is indicated.

Current Developments and Research Issues

Among the important tasks facing researchers interested in the disruptive behavior disorders is to clarify further whether the ODD diagnosis is a valid one and truly describes a disorder with its own course and correlates. While evidence reviewed in this chapter suggests that ODD has a distinct behavioral profile, its validity as a distinct disorder would be enhanced if particular characteristics, etiology, or prognosis could be demonstrated for ODD children in comparison with youths who have CD. Longitudinal and developmental studies, along the lines of that described by Loeber and Lahey (1989) for CD youth, should be considered. (See Chapter 34.) Such studies would help to clarify if the correlates of onset, maintenance, desistance from ODD symptoms, for examples, are similar to those of CD youth.

Further, longitudinal studies would help to clarify whether alternative pathways exist for ODD youth who do not develop CD. Little information is available on disruptive behavior disorders in girls compared to boys. Do girls with ODD have different developmental pathways than boys? In females are other disorders, such as mood disorders or passive-aggressive personality disorder, more likely developmental outcomes, given that aggressive behavior is so much more common in boys than girls?

As with conduct disorder, more effort needs to be directed toward knowing what might be effective prevention for ODD, whether it is a separate entity, an early manifestation of CD, or a variant of CD. There is almost no research in this area, while there is great interest and many infant and preschool intervention programs seem well suited to provide not only early treatment for the behavioral disorders of infants and preschoolers but also to study more systematically prevention efforts for current or future siblings of children in treatment. Further directions for research are discussed in Chapter 34.

REFERENCES

Achenbach, T. M. (1991). *Manual for the Child Behavior Checklist/4–18 and 1991 Profile.* Burlington: University of Vermont, Department of Psychiatry.
American Psychiatric Association. (1980). *Diagnostic and statistical manual of mental disorders* (3rd ed.). Washington, DC: Author.
American Psychiatric Association. (1987). *Diagnostic and statistical manual of mental disorders* (3rd ed., rev.). Washington, DC: Author.
American Psychiatric Association. (1994). *Diagnostic and statistical manual of mental disorders* (4th ed.). Washington, DC: Author.
Gabel, S., Oster, G., & Pfeffer, C. R. (1988). *Difficult moments in child psychotherapy.* New York: Plenum Press.
Lahey, B. B., Applegate, B., Barkley, R. A., Garfinkel, B., McBurnett, K., Kwerdyk, L., Greenhill, L., Hynd, G. W., Frick, P. J., Newcorn, J., Biederman,

J., Ollendick, T., Hart, E. L., Perez, D., Waldman, I., & Shaffer, D. (1994). DSM-IV field trials for oppositional defiant disorder and conduct disorder in children and adolescents. *American Journal of Psychiatry, 151*, 1163–1171.

Lahey, B. B., Frick, B. J., Loeber, R., Hart, E. L., Hanson, K. L., & Jansevics, R. (1990). *The distinction between oppositional and conduct disorder: II. Cross validation of the meta-analytic review.* Unpublished manuscript. University of Georgia, Athens. Cited in R. Loeber, B. B. Lahey, & C. Thomas (1991), Diagnostic conundrum of oppositional defiant disorder and conduct disorder. *Journal of Abnormal Psychology, 100*, 379–390.

Lahey, B. B., Frick, B. J., Loeber, R., Tannenbaum, B. A., VanHorn, Y., & Christ, M. A. G. (1990). *Oppositional and conduct disorder: I. A meta-analytic review.* Unpublished manuscript. University of Georgia, Athens. Cited in R. Loeber, B. B. Lahey, & C. Thomas (1991), Diagnostic conundrum of oppositional defiant disorder and conduct disorder. *Journal of Abnormal Psychology, 100*, 379–390.

Loeber, R., Green, S. M., Keenan, K., & Lahey, B. B. (1995). Which boys will fare worse? Early predictors of the onset of conduct disorder in a six-year longitudinal study. *Journal of the American Academy of Child and Adolescent Psychiatry 34*, 499–509.

Loeber, R., & Lahey, B. B. (1989). Recommendations for research on disruptive behavior disorders of childhood and adolescence. In B. B. Lahey & A. E. Kazdin (Eds.), *Advances in clinical child psychology* (vol. 12, p. 221–251). New York: Plenum Press.

Loeber, R., Lahey, B. B., & Thomas, C. (1991). Diagnostic conundrum of oppositional defiant disorder and conduct disorder. *Journal of Abnormal Psychology, 100*, 379–390.

Patterson, G. R. (1982). *Coercive family process.* Eugene, OR: Castalia Publishing Co.

Patterson, G. R., DeBaryshe, B. D., & Ramsey, E. (1989). A developmental perspective on antisocial behavior. *American Psychologist, 44*, 329–335.

Quay, H. C. (1979). Classification. In H. C. Quay & J. S. Werry (Eds.), *Psychopathological disorders of childhood* (2nd ed., pp. 1–42). New York: John Wiley & Sons.

Quay, H. C. (1986). Classification. In H. C. Quay & J. S. Werry (Eds.), *Psychopathological disorders of childhood* (3rd ed., pp. 1–34). New York: John Wiley & Sons.

Reeves, J. C., Werry, J. S., Elkind, G. S., & Zametkin, A. (1987). Attention deficit, conduct, oppositional, and anxiety disorders in children: II. Clinical characteristics. *Journal of the American Academy of Childhood and Adolescent Psychiatry, 26*, 144–155.

Rey, J. M. (1993). Oppositional defiant disorder. *American Journal of Psychiatry, 150*, 1769–1778.

Wells, K. C., & Forehand, R. (1985). Conduct and oppositional disorders. In P. H. Bornstein & A. E. Kazdin (Eds.), *Handbook of clinical behavior therapy with children* (pp. 218–265). Homewood, IL: Dorsey.

Werry, J. S., Reeves, J. C., & Elkind, G. S. (1987). Attention deficit, conduct, oppositional, and anxiety disorders in children: I. A review of research on differentiating characteristics. *Journal of the American Academy of Child and Adolescent Psychiatry, 26*, 133–143.

34 / **Conduct Disorder in Grade-School Children**

Stewart Gabel

Background

The evaluation and treatment of conduct problems and antisocial behavior are major components of the practice of child and adolescent psychiatry. Youths presenting for treatment with these problems are very common, although exact frequency rates depend on sample, setting, and criteria used in defining the disturbance.

Shamsie (1981) estimates that from one half to two thirds of all children and adolescents referred to mental health centers exhibit antisocial behavior as a predominant problem. A recent study reviewing admission diagnoses and preadmission variables in children and adolescents treated in day hospitals and as inpatients found that conduct disorder was the most common admission diagnosis, being present in 23% of the youths, and that operationally defined severe aggressive/destructive behavior occurring 6 to 12 months prior to admission was found in slightly over one third of the group (Gabel & Shindledecker, 1991). Another study found that nearly 50% of boys and

40% of girls admitted to psychiatric treatment at the University of Iowa Child Psychiatry Clinic and Ward, a tertiary care center, had diagnoses of aggressive conduct disorder (Stewart, deBlois, Meardon, & Cummings, 1980).

Prevalence rates of conduct disorder in the community of grade-school-age children vary somewhat depending on the sample. Rutter, Tizard, and Whitmore (1970) found that conduct disorder occurred in about 4% of 10- to 11-year-old English youth on the Isle of Wight, a percentage somewhat less than half that estimated for the same age group in an inner-city London borough (Rutter, Cox, Tupling, Berger, & Yule, 1975). Szatmari, Boyle, and Offord (1989) relied on criteria from the third edition of the *Diagnostic and Statistical Manual of Mental Disorders* (*DSM-III;* American Psychiatric Association [APA], 1980) and reported that 2.6% of males and 1.0% of females ages 4 to 11 years in a community sample of youth in Canada had a "pure" form of conduct disorder without an accompanying attention deficit disorder with hyperactivity diagnosis; 3.7% of males and 1.2% of females in the same age range had a "mixed" form, showing both conduct disorder and attention deficit disorder with hyperactivity diagnoses.

Studying data about individuals in the criminal justice system allows a somewhat different perspective on the impact of antisocial behavior on children and families. The prison population in the United States more than doubled in the decade from 1980 through the end of 1989 (Bureau of Justice Statistics, 1990). If we consider federal and state prisoners along with country and local jail inmates together, more than 1 million individuals currently are incarcerated in the United States. Indeed, now more than 4 million individuals (2.2% of the adult population in the United States) are under some form of correctional supervision (jail, prison, probation, parole) (Bureau of Justice Statistics, 1991).

Figures are not available to determine the number of children who currently have, who have had, or who will have an incarcerated parent during their childhood years. Considering that more than 1 million individuals are incarcerated, the number may well be in the millions. These children and adolescents are at risk to develop antisocial behavior and conduct disorder themselves, given the known increased likelihood parental

criminality and incarceration confer on youth for the development of conduct problems and antisocial behavior (Robins, West, & Herjanic, 1975).

A recent study at a day hospital program for children ages 5 to 12 years found that nearly 40% had a parent who had been incarcerated at some time in the past. These children, who were from disadvantaged homes themselves, appeared to be more aggressive and to have more conduct problems than their peers in treatment who did not have a history of parental incarceration, although not to a statistically significant degree in the small sample of 26 children studied. The children were, however, significantly more likely to have had histories of parental substance abuse and to have been involved in incidents of suspected child abuse/maltreatment than their peers in treatment without a history of parental incarceration (Gabel & Shindledecker, 1992).

All of this suggests that the problems of conduct disorder, antisocial behavior, and aggression are among the most important social and mental health issues facing our society at the present time. These problems appear very much tied to other problems variously regarded as either "social" or "mental health," depending on one's perspective—problems such as parental substance abuse and child abuse/maltreatment. The misery and lost productivity in personal, familial, and social terms as the result of conduct disorder and antisocial behavior clearly are incalculable.

It therefore is not surprising that vast amounts of attention and resources from diverse sectors of society (e.g., mental health, social service, criminal justice) have been devoted to the understanding and at times remediation of these problems. Indeed, the prevention and treatment of conduct problems and juvenile delinquency has been a cornerstone in the development of child psychiatry as a discipline; major prevention, treatment, and research projects, such as the Cambridge-Somerville Youth Study in Massachusetts, were developed to address these issues in the early decades of the 20th century. The clinical and research efforts directed to the topics of conduct disorder, aggression, and antisocial behavior in youths have yielded a great deal of information about these problems. Unfortunately, as will become apparent in succeeding pages, although much more is known now about these problems, effective treatment approaches in general remain to be discovered and applied helpfully to large groups of youth and families.

Classification, Diagnostic Assessment, and Developmental Course

CLASSIFICATION AND DIAGNOSTIC ASSESSMENT

Most empirical studies of emotional and behavioral problems in large numbers of youths have identified a distinct type of behavioral disorder that has varied in its label but that conforms to the designation of what is here termed *conduct disorder* (Quay, 1986).

Youth with conduct disorder act in ways that apparently disregard social norms and rules of behavior that are deemed appropriate for their age. Many act aggressively. These youths may fight, steal within or outside the home, lie, threaten others, disrupt activities, destroy property, provoke fights, blame others, not attend classes in school, run away from home, stay out late at night, set fires, and be cruel to animals. They may mistreat siblings and peers, disregard the feeling of others, use alcohol to excess and while under the legal drinking age, use substances such as glue ("glue sniffing") to become "high," use illicit drugs, engage in sexual behavior at an early age or promiscuously, be a part of a delinquent group or gang, and have no or very few friends.

Investigators have attempted to further classify conduct disorder based on empirical approaches using statistical techniques that allow large numbers of behaviors to be considered along a variety of behavioral dimensions conceptualized individually or in profiles. While some disagreement exists, and particular labels vary, two types of conduct disorder generally have been found (Quay, 1986; Werry, Reeves, & Elkin, 1987).

In the commonly used Child Behavior Checklist (CBCL) (Achenbach, 1991a, b), for example, two factors, labeled "aggressive behavior" and "delinquent behavior," comprise what might be considered the behavioral components of a conduct disorder designation. The "aggressive behavior" factor involves many of the previously noted behaviors such as arguing, lying, fighting, threatening, destroying property, having temper outbursts, and so on. The "delinquent behavior" factor includes behaviors often found among somewhat older youths, such as running away from home, associating with negative peer models, vandalism, and using illicit drugs.

Interestingly, clinicians also have consistently described a group of youngsters with "conduct disorder" based, in part, on the experience of evaluating and treating many youths with different features. The psychiatric classification embodied in the American Psychiatric Association's *Diagnostic and Statistical Manuals* (*DSMs*) uses a categorical rather than dimensional approach to classification, however. Recent *DSMs* nonetheless have grouped conduct disorder into types that have had some apparent relationship to the empirically derived syndromes conceptualized along a dimensional framework (Werry et al., 1987).

DSM-II (APA, 1968), for example, contained the diagnoses of "unsocialized-aggressive reaction," "runaway reaction" and "group-delinquent reaction" within the behavior disorders of childhood and adolescence section. The first of these diagnoses resembles the empirically derived "aggressive behavior" factor of the CBCL (Achenbach, 1991a) and similar syndrome designations of other rating scales. The last two of these diagnoses together describe important features of the "delinquent behavior" factor.

DSM-III (APA, 1980) contained the type of conduct disorder termed "undersocialized aggressive," which again appears to relate to the "aggressive behavior" factor of the CBCL. The socialized forms of conduct disorder in *DSM-III* (APA, 1980) resemble broadly the CBCLs "delinquent behavior" dimension.

DSM-III-R (APA, 1987) contained the "solitary aggressive" type of conduct disorder, which appears to relate to the "aggressive behavior" factor of the CBCL (Achenbach, 1991a). The "group type" of conduct disorder in *DSM-III-R* appeared to relate to the "delinquent behavior" factor of the CBCL (Achenbach, 1991a, p. 181).

DSM-IV (APA, 1994) has classified conduct disorder into two types based on age of onset. The "childhood onset" type is diagnosed when at least one criterion has occurred prior to age 10. The "adolescent onset" type is diagnosed when no criterion has occurred before age 10. *DSM-IV* describes four groups of conduct problems: aggression to people and animals, destruction of property, deceitfulness or theft, and serious violations of rules. The specific behaviors in these groups are similar to those in *DSM-III-R*, which did not divide specific behaviors into groups. The childhood-onset and adolescent-onset types in *DSM-IV* appear to correspond broadly to the solitary aggressive and group types in *DSM-III-R*. The current *DSM-IV* classification therefore supports the view that conduct disorder may be considered within two groups based partly on gender (males more common in early-onset types), age of onset, severity, and course.

This relative agreement between empirically derived dimensions and what traditionally have been more clinically derived diagnoses should not be overstated, however, since there clearly are important differences within the empirically derived approaches and when comparing the more clinically and empirically conceived systems (Werry et al., 1987). The *DSM-III* (APA, 1980) types of undersocialized nonaggressive conduct disorder and socialized nonaggressive conduct disorder, for example, do not seem to have adequate approximations to principal dimensions derived from empirical studies (Quay, 1986).

Furthermore, there is relatively less research on youths who comprise the "group" or adolescent-onset types of conduct disorder as distinct entities than on youths who conform to the "solitary aggressive" or childhood-onset types of conduct disorder in *DSM-III-R* and *DSM-IV* respectively. Studies of conduct disorder often have considered youths who might have these separate types as one group, thus possibly obscuring important differences between the groups (Quay, 1986). Rutter and Giller (1983), in fact, have argued that the validity of subtypes of conduct disorder remains to be established. They also point out that questions involving which characteristics of youths are actually most meaningful in distinguishing and validating the subgroups have not been answered.

In their descriptions of different types of conduct disorder, for example, clinicians commonly emphasize the importance of a youngster's feelings of remorse or guilt for behavioral deviance (such as stealing) and the presence of a social conscience. These characteristics, which influence treatment decisions (Kernberg & Chazen, 1991), are not emphasized in current diagnostic systems.

The *DSM-III-R* (APA, 1987) classification emphasizes the two recognized types of conduct disorder and also includes an "undifferentiated" type for those cases in which features cannot be classified as either the solitary aggressive or group type. *DSM-III-R* states that this undifferentiated type actually may be larger than the other two specifically defined types, thus emphasizing that many cases of conduct disorder are difficult to classify (Rapoport & Ismond, 1990).

Due to the relative lack of research on the two designated types considered independently (Quay, 1986), the remainder of this chapter will not differentiate between the types of conduct disorder except as indicated.

ASSOCIATED FEATURES

Children with conduct disorder that is diagnosed during the grade-school years commonly have had a long history of prior behavioral and learning difficulties. Problems related to hyperactivity, inattentiveness, delayed development, learning difficulties, and oppositional, resistant, and defiant behavior often have been noted. These children (largely boys) often come from families with long histories of marital discord; turmoil in family relationships; parental antisocial behavior, criminality, substance abuse, and psychopathology; and child abuse/maltreatment.

A number of issues and questions merit emphasis in relation to the association of conduct disorder in grade-school boys with other types of psychopathology, with family variables, and with learning problems. These points are important to stress here because they may influence the severity of the disorder, its development, and its prognosis. They are important to consider prior to and during the assessment procedures.

One question that is heavily debated is whether a pure form of conduct disorder exists at all, or whether it actually is a disorder that includes symptoms similar to those of attention deficit hyperactivity disorder (ADHD) (*DSM-IV*; APA, 1994; Loeber, Brinthaupt, & Green, 1990; Reeves, Werry, Elkind, & Zametkin, 1987; Taylor, Schacher, Thorley, & Wieselberg, 1986; Werry et al., 1987). A number of studies have found that boys with pure conduct disorder in grade-school populations are far less common than boys with

ADHD symptoms plus conduct disorder symptoms (Loeber, et al., 1990; Werry et al., 1987).

Symptoms associated with these two disorders appear to be interdependent (Loeber et al., 1990; Shapiro & Garfinkel, 1986). Through their own study and a review of other studies, Loeber et al. (1990) have attempted to discover contextual features that might help to differentiate hyperactive, impulsive, inattentive (HIA) behavior from conduct problems, given the recognized co-occurrence of ADHD symptoms in conduct-disordered boys.

The following are among the social and family factors that appear to relate mostly to conduct problems rather than to HIA behaviors: poor supervision; lack of maternal warmth; maternal criticism; maternal rejection; poor and inconsistent parenting; poor marital relationship; separation from the parent; paternal alcoholism; and paternal substance abuse. Delinquency in the family and parental antisocial personality also appear to be related mainly to conduct problems, although parental criminality was related to HIA behavior also. Below-average intelligence, school problems, and low self-evaluation of academic skills may be found in both groups of boys but seem overall to be related more to HIA boys than to conduct-problem boys. Truancy is more related to conduct-problem boys than to HIA boys (Loeber et al., 1990).

DSM-III (APA, 1980) described and named another disorder whose symptoms overlap those of conduct disorder. Oppositional defiant disorder (*DSM-IV*; APA, 1994) appears commonly as a precursor to conduct disorder and often is found in younger children. It is not yet clear, however, whether oppositional defiant disorder is an early or less severe form of conduct disorder or whether it can be differentiated from conduct disorder by factors such as differential prognosis and treatment response (Frick, et al., 1991; Loeber, Lahey, & Thomas, 1991a; Reeves et al., 1987). (See Chapter 33 for a further discussion of these issues.)

Other psychiatric symptoms sometimes found in youths with behavioral problems such as conduct disorder include depression and anxiety (Woolston, et al., 1989), as well as other "internalizing disorders" (Curry, Pelissier, Woodford, & Lochman, 1988). These relationships will be discussed further in the section on the association of conduct disorder with other psychiatric diagnoses.

It generally is recognized that school difficulties and impaired academic performance are common in conduct-disordered boys. Recent studies suggest that these difficulties may be multiple in origin. Lower intelligence (Farrington, Loeber, & Van Kammen, 1990), adverse family environments (Loeber et al., 1990; Reeves et al., 1987; Werry et al., 1987) as well as associated neurocognitive deficits associated with ADHD symptoms in the majority of these youngsters (Loeber et al., 1990; Reeves et al., 1987; Werry et al., 1987) would be expected to interfere with or decrease academic achievement.

CLINICAL EVALUATION

The optimal evaluation of youths with a suspected conduct disorder involves gathering information from a variety of sources and conducting an individual and family evaluation. Numerous rating scales and structured interviews with adequate reliability are available to help differentiate conduct disorder from other psychiatric problems, to assess its comorbidity with other psychiatric disorders, and to assess the relative severity of its presentation.

Rating scales and structured interviews by or responded to by parents are very helpful but should be supplemented by standardized teacher assessment of the child. Rating scales and interviews for the youth him- or herself also are available and are likely to provide additional information, including areas of divergence with parent and teacher reports. It is important to assess these youngsters' peer relationships and social competence. Standard rating forms, such as the parent form of the CBCL (Achenbach, 1991a) provide information on these areas; both the parent and teacher forms (Achenbach, 1991a, b) provide information on academic performance. Actual peer ratings may be helpful in assessing relationships but usually are obtained mainly in research settings. A recently developed semistructured interview given to grade-school children who are asked about their own social relationships (peers, friendships) offers another means to assess these dimensions by direct query of the child (Kernberg, Clarkin, Greenblatt, & Cohen, 1992).

The individual clinical interview and family evaluation of these youths add additional information about relationships in the family and strengths and weaknesses of individual members as well as an appraisal of family coping skills. Children of the grade-school age with conduct disorder are mainly boys. When seen for initial evaluation, these youths often do not reveal or discuss internal feeling states or reactions to any significant degree. The youngsters commonly convey a pseudomaturity in the interview, seem relatively nonverbal, nonreflective, and nonintrospective. They may disclaim having negative feelings about interpersonal issues that would be troubling to most of their age mates. They do not easily discuss attachments to others, including family members. They may, however, reveal angry, vindictive thoughts and feelings in reaction to what others reportedly have done to them. These youths appear to have a limited repertoire of feeling states, attitudes, or thoughts in response to events in their lives. On questioning, they commonly do not acknowledge their participation in the behavioral difficulties that usually are the reason for referral, although they may be quick to point out what others, such as peers, have done to them to result in fights or disciplinary action taken by authority figures, such as teachers or principals.

As a group, youths with conduct disorder exhibit an impulsive, activity-oriented style. Many are hyperactive; some are clearly depressed. Those with learning difficulties and developmental delays may be obviously cognitively limited compared to age mates. A small number may have brief psychotic experiences and hallucinations.

These youngsters ask readily what rewards they can have while also, at other times, disclaiming that any restrictions or punishments are meaningful to them or that restrictions on them will be upsetting. This disclaimer is in contrast to aggressive outbursts that often follow limit setting or denial of requests.

Offer and colleagues (Offer, Ostrov, & Howard, 1981) have studied delinquent and other adolescents empirically using a specially designed questionnaire. They emphasize the poor self-image and low self-esteem of delinquent adolescents, pointing out that these youths, compared with normals, are more unhappy, confused, ashamed, and empty, while also being more hostile. While these studies were on adolescents, the findings seem true for the grade-school age group being considered here as well.

In interviews, conduct-disturbed youths convey a lack of warmth and interpersonal relatedness. Psychoanalytic clinicians have described these youths as having denied their feelings, acted mainly for gratification, repressed their anxiety around punishment or interpersonal loss, and projected blame and guilt onto others.

From the psychoanalytic perspective, considering especially the contributions of ego psychology and object relations theory, Kernberg and Chazen (1991) have emphasized the subjective experience of these youths, who

express themselves through action, rather than words, . . . prefer not to use language to communicate, to share experiences, or to express feelings. In their own view of events they tend not to perceive the connections between motive, action, and consequence. . . . authority figures, including parents and teachers, are frequently experienced as interfering and unfairly punitive. . . . Their play tends to be concrete, repetitive, unimaginative, and aggressive. These children show a narrow range of expressed feelings and hardly ever express happiness and enjoyment. (pp. 2–3)

Such children, in structural psychoanalytic terms, "have ego deficits in the following areas: cognitive functioning, attention, impulse control, judgment, modulation of affects, language, and tolerance for anxiety and frustration. In the domain of the id, aggression predominates at the expense of integration of impulses with libidinal or affectionate feelings" (Kernberg & Chazen, 1991, p. 5).

These youths also have significant superego deficits, with little capacity for guilt or remorse. "They find it difficult to understand that peers have motivations, characteristics, and preferences different from their own. . . . Conduct disorder children share a core feeling of being unloved and uncared for. . . . their subjective representational world is constructed around the premise of rejection and abandonment" (Kernberg & Chazen, 1991).

Some psychoanalytic approaches have emphasized the narcissistic vulnerability of youths with aggression and conduct disorder as a central concept. Willock (1986) speaks of these youths as feeling disregarded, not cared for, and repugnant.

He describes boys with aggressive conduct disorder as shielding feelings of anger and alienation behind their defiant and aggressive postures. Internally they feel unwanted, not loved, and not appreciated, that others do not care for them or for what happens to them. They feel disregarded. Because of this alienation and perceptions of disregard and isolation, they act, often aggressively, to ward off these internal feeling states.

These children's antisocial behavior and defiance, therefore, reflect attempts to keep from awareness feelings of being unloved (Willock, 1986). Because they feel that they are not cared about or cared for, these youths act as if they do not care about what others do either or about important relationships. Defiance and disregard for adult rules and values act to reverse their internal feelings of not being valued themselves. Therefore, aggressive, conduct-disordered youths exhibit, in disguised form, the manifestations of their narcissistic vulnerability.

Other approaches, including cognitive and social information processing studies also have described aspects of the internal experience of these youth (Akhtar & Bradley, 1991; Dodge, 1986). These are described in more detail in the section on morbidity.

DEVELOPMENTAL COURSE

The study of developmental pathways for the expression of particular disorders is an extremely important area from the perspectives of prevention, treatment, and research (Loeber, 1990, 1991a; Loeber, Stouthamer-Loeber, Van Kammen, & Farrington, 1991; Patterson, DeBaryshe, & Ramsey, 1989). As noted earlier, the findings on relationships among family variables, academic performance, and psychiatric diagnosis in conduct disorder, for example, would be especially useful if they could be pinpointed in relation to variables such as onset, maintenance, severity, and desistance of conduct problems.

Loeber, Stouthamer-Loeber, Van Kammen, and Farrington (1991) have performed a large-scale study (as part of the Pittsburgh Youth Study) to learn whether particular variables covary with "offending behavior" in male youths on both concurrent and longitudinal bases. Loeber et al. studied boys in a community sample who initially were in first, fourth, and seventh grades (considered respectively the youngest, middle, and oldest samples) at entry. These youths were evaluated at 6-month intervals for 2 years. At the time of the report, they were in third, sixth, and ninth grades. The modal ages of the groups then were 8, 11, and 14 years respectively. A series of measures given to the child, parent, and teacher was used to assess variables such as behavior, school performance, and family characteristics. Loeber et al. developed an "offense seriousness classification" based on a number of the boys' own, the caregivers', and teacher reports. They developed a "dynamic classification of offenders," utilizing seven groups of youngsters. These were: stable nondelinquents, stable moderates, stable highs, starters, escalators, deescalators and desistors.

Loeber, Stouthamer-Loeber, Van Kammen, and Farrington et al. found that initiating offending behavior occurred more commonly between ages 7 and 8 than between 10 and 11 or 13 and 14 years. Escalation was more common in the boys who were 10 to 11 and 13 to 14 years of age than in the 7- to 8-year-olds. The percentages of youths in the stable moderate and stable high offending behavior groups increased with age, occurring most commonly in the 13- to 14-year-olds. Deescalators also increased across the age groups, and the desistors increased from 7 to 8 years to 10 to 11 years and then stabilized. Overall, the youngest groups showed the greatest initiation of offending behavior; escalation was most notable for the middle and old samples; and deescalation was prevalent in the oldest group. Figure 34.1 presents the relationships.

Loeber, Stouthamer-Loeber, Van Kammen, and Farrington (1991) also studied the relationship of numerous variables which were important correlates of delinquency in the literature in relation to the three age groups. Figure 34.2 shows variables of similar strength across the age groups, variable strength across the age groups, and decreasing and increasing strength from the youngest to oldest boys.

From a developmental perspective, correlates of initiation of offending, escalation of offending, and desistance of offending also are important. Figures 34.3, 34.4, and 34.5 indicate the variables that are associated with these processes across the age groups studied. The figures also indicate the variables that are most important specific age groups.

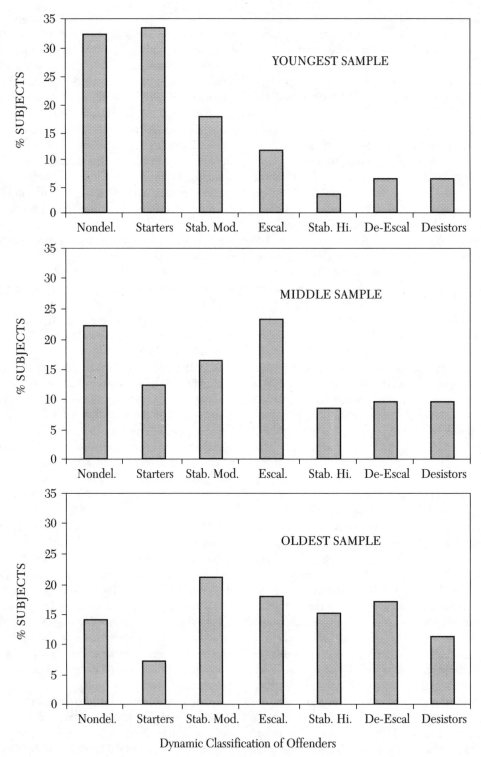

FIGURE 34.1

Percent of boys in each of the categories of the dynamic classification of offenders

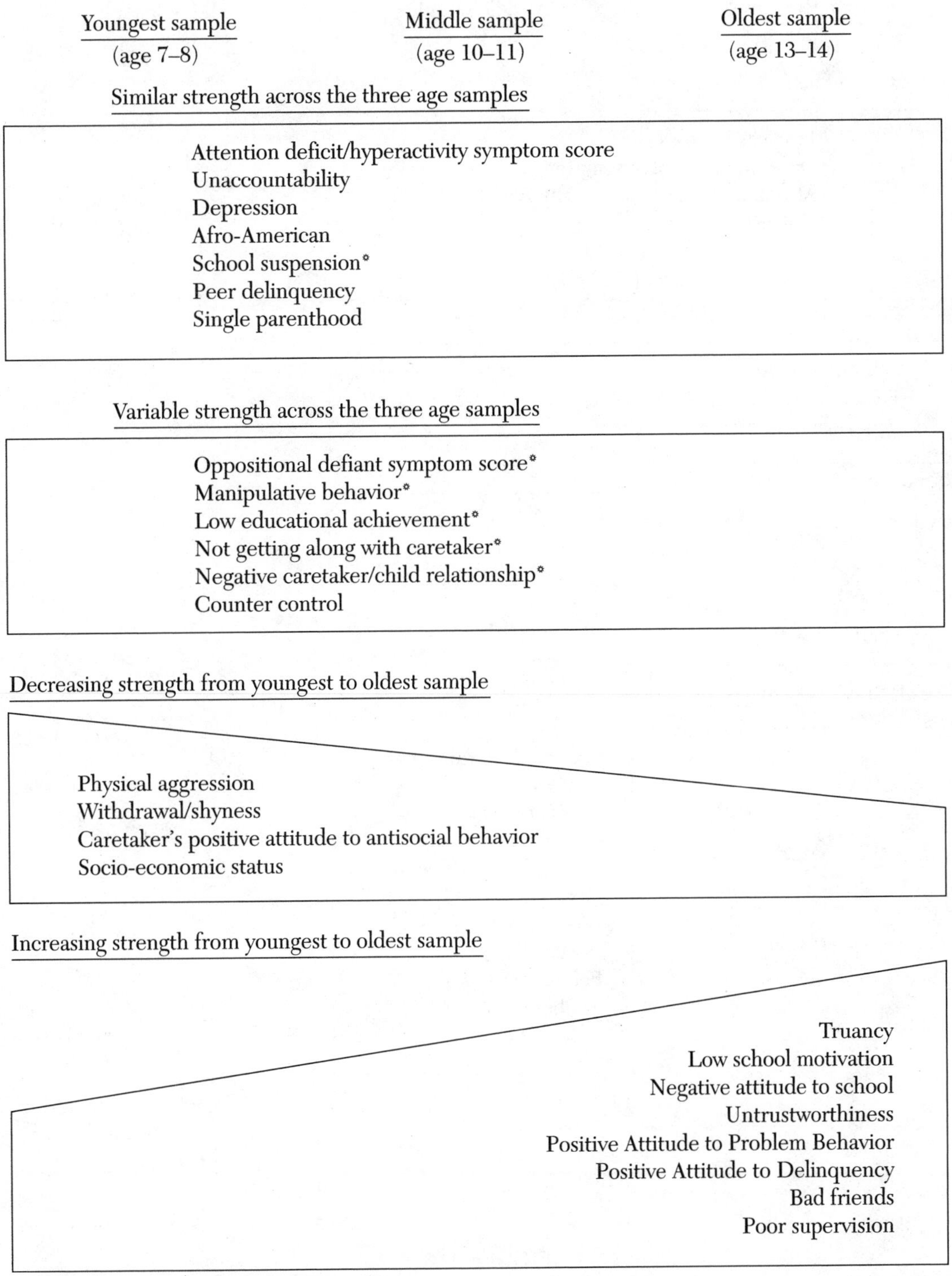

Youngest sample (age 7–8)	Middle sample (age 10–11)	Oldest sample (age 13–14)

Similar strength across the three age samples

Attention deficit/hyperactivity symptom score
Unaccountability
Depression
Afro-American
School suspension°
Peer delinquency
Single parenthood

Variable strength across the three age samples

Oppositional defiant symptom score°
Manipulative behavior°
Low educational achievement°
Not getting along with caretaker°
Negative caretaker/child relationship°
Counter control

Decreasing strength from youngest to oldest sample

Physical aggression
Withdrawal/shyness
Caretaker's positive attitude to antisocial behavior
Socio-economic status

Increasing strength from youngest to oldest sample

Truancy
Low school motivation
Negative attitude to school
Untrustworthiness
Positive Attitude to Problem Behavior
Positive Attitude to Delinquency
Bad friends
Poor supervision

°Strongest relationship for middle sample.

FIGURE 34.2

Strength of the correlates of the dynamic classification of offenders for the three samples

NOTE. From "Initiation, Escalation, and Desistance in Juvenile Offending and Their Correlates," by R. Loeber, M. Stouthamer-Loeber, W. Van Kammen, and D. P. Farrington, 1991, *Journal of Criminal Law and Criminology, 82.* Copyright 1991 by R. Loeber. Originally published by the Northwestern University School of Law. Reprinted with permission.

Youngest sample (age 7–8)	Middle sample (age 10–11)	Oldest sample (age 13–14)

Across-age effects

Physical aggression
Oppositional defiant symptom score
Attention deficit/hyperactivity symptom score
Untrustworthiness
Truancy
Negative caretaker-child relationship

School suspension
Positive attitude to problem behavior
Peer delinquency

Poor supervision
Bad friends

Age-specific effects

Withdrawal/ shyness

Depression
Low caretaker
    enjoyment of child
Not getting along with
    caretaker
Low socio-economic
    status
Poor communication
    about child's
    activities

Low school motivation
Counter control
Afro-American

FIGURE 34.3

Correlates of initiation of offending for the three samples

NOTE. From "Initiation, Escalation, and Desistance in Juvenile Offending and Their Correlates," by R. Loeber, M. Stouthamer-Loeber, W. Van Kammen, and D. P. Farrington, 1991, *Journal of Criminal Law and Criminology, 82*. Copyright 1991 by R. Loeber. Originally published by the Northwestern University School of Law. Reprinted with permission.

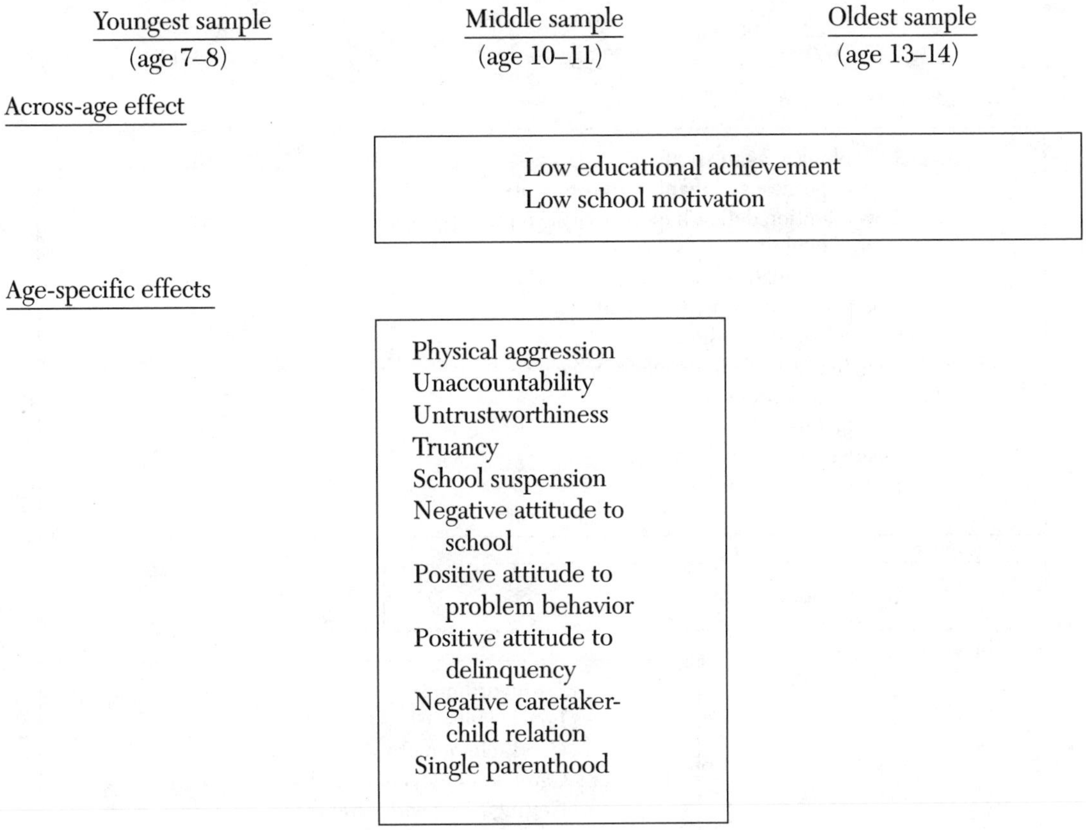

Youngest sample
(age 7–8)

Middle sample
(age 10–11)

Oldest sample
(age 13–14)

Across-age effect

| Low educational achievement |
| Low school motivation |

Age-specific effects

Physical aggression
Unaccountability
Untrustworthiness
Truancy
School suspension
Negative attitude to
    school
Positive attitude to
    problem behavior
Positive attitude to
    delinquency
Negative caretaker-
    child relation
Single parenthood

FIGURE 34.4

Correlates of escalation in offending for the three samples

NOTE. From "Initiation, Escalation, and Desistance in Juvenile Offending and Their Correlates," by R. Loeber, M. Stouthamer-Loeber, W. Van Kammen, and D. P. Farrington, 1991, *Journal of Criminal Law and Criminology, 82*. Copyright 1991 by R. Loeber. Originally published by the Northwestern University School of Law. Reprinted with permission.

Loeber, Stouthamer-Loeber, Van Kammen, and Farrington (1991) drew several tentative conclusions from their data. Initiation of offending is very high among the youngest group of boys. Escalation in seriousness of offenses also was high in the younger group as well as the middle group. Desistance was greatest among the middle and older group of boys. Whether in escalation or desistance, boys who moved in their grouping seemed to move to adjacent rather than nonadjacent levels of offense seriousness over time. As boys grew older, the predictability of their future offense status improved. That is, youths solidify into either delinquent or prosocial behavior as they get older.

Correlates of initiation of offending included several disruptive behaviors, such as physical aggression, negative caregiver-child interactions, poor supervision, and lack of involvement with the child. Internalizing disturbances, such as depression, also were important correlates of offending behavior, as were peer influences. Escalation of offending behavior was related to school functioning, disruptive behavior, family functioning, and attitudinal variables, such as acceptance of deviant behavior. Desistance of offending behavior correlated with low social withdrawal and also with low disruptive behavior. Stricter discipline, better motivation, and attitudinal factors also were important, at least in the two older samples.

While Loeber, Stouthamer-Loeber, Van Kammen, and Farrington (1991b) have assessed characteristics of children and families that were associated with antisocial behavior in boys at three

Youngest sample (age 7–8)	Middle sample (age 10–11)	Oldest sample (age 13–14)

Across-age effects

Low physical aggression
Low oppositional defiant symptom score
Low attention deficit/hyperactivity symptom score
Accountability
Low manipulative behavior
Good educational achievement
Low school suspension
Negative attitude to problem behavior
Low peer delinquency
Few bad friends
Positive caretaker-child relationship
Low countercontrol

Low withdrawal/shyness

Trustworthiness
Low truancy
Good school motivation
Caretaker enjoyment of child
Getting along with caretaker
Strict discipline

Age-specific effects

Postive attitude to
  school
Two-parent family

Neg. attitude to del.
Good communication
  about child's activ.

Low depression
Positive attitude to
  school
Good supervision

FIGURE 34.5

Correlates of desistance in offending for the three samples

NOTE. From "Initiation, Escalation, and Desistance in Juvenile Offending and Their Correlates," by R. Loeber, M. Stouthamer-Loeber, W. Van Kammen, and D. P. Farrington, 1991, *Journal of Criminal Law and Criminology, 82.* Copyright 1991 by R. Loeber. Originally published by the Northwestern University School of Law. Reprinted with permission.

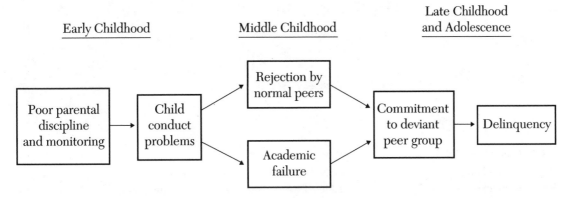

FIGURE 34.6

A developmental progression for antisocial behavior

NOTE. From "A Developmental Perspective on Antisocial Behavior," by G. R. Patterson, B. D. DeBaryshe, and E. Ramsey, 1991, *American Psychologist, 44.* Copyright 1991 by the American Psychological Association. Reprinted by permission.

distinct epochs based on various self and other reports, Patterson (1982) and Patterson et al. (1989) have provided another developmental model that is conceptualized within a social learning framework. It is based on their own and others' research on developmental trends in antisocial behavior, the latter's stability over time, and its relationship to family management practices. This model is based both on measures to assess antisocial behavior and on home video recordings of family interactions.

Patterson et al.'s (1989) model emphasizes that the path to chronic delinquency for boys is preceded by predictable stages involving an interaction between the child and his social environment. The first stage in the process begins with training of the child in antisocial behavior by family members. Patterson et al. argue that parents of antisocial boys are noncontingent in their use of both positive reinforcement for prosocial behavior and in effective punishment for behavior that is deviant. This inept parenting allows numerous interactions between the child and the parents that essentially reinforce coercive behavior by the child (e.g., temper outbursts, yelling, crying, screaming). The child uses these tactics in order to force other family members to give him what he wants or to cease behavior that disturbs him. As the process continues, escalation occurs and physical attacks (on either side) may ensue. After having received training in its development and maintenance, eventually the child controls other members of the family through his coercive behavior. While training the child to be coercive, the family does not train prosocial behavior, which such families respond to inappropriately or not at all.

These types of parenting practices and family interaction patterns reportedly account for 30 to 40% of the variance in antisocial behavior exhibited by several hundred grade-school boys in four different samples.

Patterson et al. (1989) hypothesize that the next stage in the development of chronic delinquency on the part of coercive boys involves academic failure as well as rejection by the normal peer group. This group of investigators points out that antisocial youth have poor academic achievement, possibly based in part on noncompliant behavior. They do not attend to tasks, remain in their seats, or complete homework assignments compared to more successful students.

These boys also are rejected by normal peers. They are deficient in social and cognitive skills related to peer group interactions and to the understanding of peer group norms.

The next developmental stage toward chronic delinquency for these youths, is membership in deviant peer groups. Poor parental supervision and monitoring of the youths also contribute, as does rejection by normal peers and academic problems, to the choice of a deviant peer group. In the deviant peer group, adolescents receive attitudes and models for further antisocial behavior, including drug use and delinquent behavior. This process is diagramed in Figure 34.6.

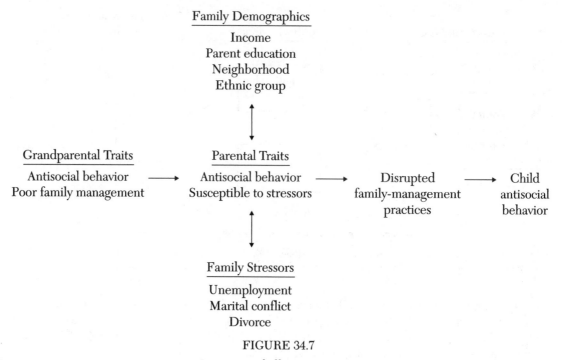

FIGURE 34.7

Disruptors of effective parenting

NOTE. From "A Developmental Perspective on Antisocial Behavior," by G. R. Patterson, B. D. DeBaryshe, and E. Ramsey, 1991, *American Psychologist, 44.* Copyright 1991 by the American Psychological Association. Reprinted by permission.

The developmental model proposed by Patterson et al. (1989) has as its central tenet the notion that family management practices contribute to the onset, maintenance and decline of antisocial behavior. A number of variables that are termed *disruptors* may negatively affect parenting skill—that is, adversely influence parent management practices. Examples of potential disruptors include demographic variables, such as socioeconomic status, parental education, occupation, unemployment, parental history of antisocial activity (in which parents themselves also have been trained in antisocial behavior), family violence, marital conflict, and divorce. In this model, the effect of poor socioeconomic conditions on the development of antisocial behavior is mediated through family management practices that are in part reflective of social class (e.g. more physical discipline, authoritarian parenting, less verbal stimulation used by lower-class parents).

Figure 34.7 shows the interaction between potential disruptors and parent management practices that, when impaired, may lead to antisocial behavior on the part of male youths.

Etiology

Researchers have studied possible causes and correlates of conduct disorder and juvenile delinquency for much of the 20th century. This section reviews findings in several areas.

FAMILY AND ENVIRONMENTAL INFLUENCES

Investigators have had a long-standing interest in the relationship between family and environment with antisocial behavior in youth. Because of their importance in the development of research on conduct disorder in children and adolescents, I will briefly review historically important studies as well as more current research.

Glueck and Glueck (1950), in a classic study, matched 500 delinquent boys with 500 nondelinquent boys in the Boston, Massachusetts, area on four dimensions: age, general intelligence, national (ethnic-racial) origin, and residence in underprivileged neighborhoods. They compared delinquent boys who were inmates of a state correctional school with nondelinquents attending community schools. They found that both the mothers and fathers of the delinquent boys were significantly more likely to have had mental retardation, emotional disturbance, drunkenness, and criminality than were the mothers or fathers of the nondelinquent boys.

The delinquent boys' homes were less cohesive, less effective in supervisory practices, and less organized than the nondelinquent boys' homes. More parents of delinquent boys had poor marital relations; often these parents were incompatible and quarreled more than the parents of the nondelinquent boys.

More than one half of the fathers and about one quarter of the mothers of the delinquent boys were characterized as indifferent, hostile, or rejecting toward their sons. Parent management practices in this group overall were more harsh, punitive, and erratic.

McCord and McCord (1963) also studied variables in the family environment, including parental role model, parental attitudes toward the child, and parental discipline methods in relationship to delinquency. They studied the parents of boys originally followed through the Cambridge-Somerville Youth Study, which was developed in the first half of this century. Boys from lower- and lower-middle-class homes in disorganized urban areas who were referred as predelinquents were matched with control boys considered "normal" by teachers and community officers. The average age of the boys was 7 years. Subsequently the groups were divided into treatment and control groups. Treatment began in 1939 and continued for about five years on average. Counselors visited the boys and their families and obtained a great deal of information about them. In 1955 trained workers read the case records and recorded pertinent information. Criminal records also were obtained on both parents and subjects. The subjects then averaged 27 years of age.

McCord and McCord (1963) found that both paternal rejection of the son and a paternal model of deviance were associated with criminality in the son. Criminal rates were particularly high in those boys whose fathers were criminals and acted in a rejecting manner to their sons. Maternal affection was related to a decrease in the son's criminality, whereas maternal passivity or rejection was associated with an increase in the son's criminal tenden-

cies, as were maternal criminality, alcoholism, and promiscuity. Consistent discipline decreased the likelihood of the son's criminality.

Robins and Lewis (1966) also studied the relationship between parental antisocial behavior and deviance in children using former child guidance clinic patients (now grown), most of whom had themselves been referred for treatment of antisocial behavior years earlier. The original study involved white children who were on average 13 years of age when first seen. Interviews, police and court records, and school records all were used for information to determine arrest record and school completion. Information about the former patients' own parents (the new subjects' grandparents) also was acquired, partly from the child guidance clinic records of their sons.

Robins and Lewis (1966) found that the presence of antisocial relatives of the original patients' sons was important in predicting the sons' juvenile arrests. A significant association existed between having either a parent or grandparent who was antisocial with the sons' failure to graduate from high school and having had a juvenile arrest. Robins and Lewis concluded that the continuity of antisocial behavior appears to be related to antisocial behavior in the child's constellation of adult relatives.

Robins, West, and Herjanic (1975) later studied the relationship of criminality in different generations in a sample of black individuals. They followed up a group of black urban boys into adulthood and elicited information about the children, spouses, and parents of these now-adult males. The original study had involved over 200 black elementary school boys in St. Louis. At the time of the study, many of the adult males had children old enough (18 years) to be included in the study.

Robins et al. (1975) found that arrest of the father was a powerful predictor of juvenile delinquency for both male and female offspring. Considering boys and girls together, the strongest predictor of delinquency (occurring in 50% of the cases) was the arrest of both parents. However, even when both parents had been arrested and had been delinquent as youngsters, only 67% of the juveniles were delinquent.

Robins (1978) later added to some of this data by reporting on antisocial behavior in four groups of males of different eras, places of residence, and races. One group was all white, one all black, and two racially mixed. The first two groups already have been discussed. The third group was a random sample of military men who had left Vietnam in 1971 and were being followed up to learn more about predictors of continued heroin usage in men who had been to Vietnam. The fourth group was nonveterans, matched with the Vietnam veterans on a number of dimensions.

Based on the data from these four groups, Robins (1978) concluded that adults who were highly antisocial had in two thirds or more cases children who were antisocial. More than 90% of highly antisocial adults had had some childhood antisocial behavior. Most highly antisocial children do not become highly antisocial adults, however. Depending on the criteria used, not much more than 50% highly antisocial children became highly antisocial adults. Childhood antisocial behaviors, not family variables, were the best predictors of severe antisocial behavior in adulthood. Social class was not important in predicting antisocial adult outcome compared to childhood antisocial behavior and other family variables that were studied.

Rutter (1978) also reported on the relationship among family, area, and school influences on conduct disorder, using data from a series of epidemiological studies he and colleagues performed. (See also Rutter, 1971.) The studies involved interviews, teacher ratings, and researcher observations and were conducted in London and on the Isle of Wight, with latency-age children and adolescents. Several findings related to family variables contributed to psychiatric disorder and conduct problems. Severe marital discord (i.e., unhappy, quarrelsome, disruptive home environments) was associated with psychiatric disorder in children. Paternal criminality also was important. Three times as many fathers of children with psychiatric disorders had been in prison compared to the number of fathers of children without psychiatric disorder who had been in prison. Mental disorder in mothers of children with psychiatric disorders was very high, although not always significantly associated with child psychiatric disorder. A warm and positive relationship with one parent seemed to have a protective effect; children with a good relationship with at least one parent had less than one third the rate of conduct disorder as children who did not have such a relationship, even when the former also were brought up in a markedly discordant home environment.

Farrington (1978) studied a group of over 400 male children in England using a longitudinal design, beginning when the boys were age 8. The research was part of the Cambridge Study in Delinquent Development, and the youths were mainly white and working class. They and their families were assessed at a number of different points over many years using a variety of measures and sources. Assessment of the boys' aggressiveness, parent practices and discipline, supervision, separations the boys had experienced, IQ and educational achievement, peer ratings, and physical characteristics all were obtained. The findings indicated that aggressiveness was fairly stable over time. Aggressiveness at 8 to 10 years, 12 to 14 years, and 16 to 18 years was significantly associated with violent delinquency (which occurred generally at age 17 to 18 years and in a subgroup of the youngsters). Several factors that were assessed at age 8 to 10 years independently predicted later violent delinquency. These included harsh, cold, disharmonious parents, parents who were criminals, poor supervision by parents, separation of the child from parents up to age 10 (usually due to parental desertion and thought to reflect marital disharmony), the child's own characteristics of "daring" and low IQ.

These findings are in general quite consistent and in agreement with findings by different investigators working in the United States. The home environment, the marital relationship, parenting practices and characteristics, and a role model of criminality all have been associated with the development of antisocial behavior in youth. The child's own characteristics, such as severe aggressive and antisocial behavior, also play a role and in some cases (e.g., Robins, 1978) may be more important.

Overall, more recent cross-sectional and longitudinal studies both in this country and in England (see Farrington & West, 1981) have supported the findings of earlier research on the effects of the home environment, parenting practices, and parental deviance in their relationship to conduct disorder and juvenile delinquency. These studies, such as the research conducted by Loeber, Stouthamer-Loeber, Van Kammen, and Farrington (1991) and Lahey et al. (1995) also have emphasized correlates of changes in conduct problems and delinquency over time and at different ages. They have clarified types of offending behavior in relation to family factors and other variables (Farrington, 1987; Farrington & Hawkins, 1991).

Given the focus on home and family environment in the genesis of conduct disorder, more recent research efforts have emphasized particular areas of concern (e.g., child abuse) and/or have tried to elucidate more specific pathway mechanisms, developmental sequences, and microsocial interactive family processes that may produce a pattern of conduct disorder in youth (Loeber, Stouthamer-Loeber, Van Kammen, and Farrington, 1991; Patterson, 1982; Patterson et al., 1989).

Child Abuse/Maltreatment and Physical Harm: A great deal of attention has focused on possible relationships between family violence and child abuse/maltreatment with aggression, antisocial behavior, and other psychiatric disorders in children (Emery, 1982). Widom (1989a) has provided an extensive review of the literature in this area; she has not clearly demonstrated a linkage between child abuse or neglect and conduct problems in childhood, although in a research study she herself conducted Widom (1989b) does find support for the view that child abuse or neglect is associated with later adult criminality and violence.

Dodge, Bates, and Pettit's (1990) findings challenge Widom's (1989a) review. In their recent prospective study, young children were assessed for aggressive behavior several months after they had been evaluated in terms of their social information processing and after their mothers had given histories of prior episodes of physical harm against the children. The sample consisted of 309 4-year-olds who were identified at preregistration for kindergarten and followed subsequently. Children's aggressive behavior was assessed through ratings by the teacher on a standard behavior checklist during kindergarten, peer in the school environment, and trained observations in playground and classroom situations.

Dodge et al. (1990) found that among both boys and girls, who were physically harmed in early life were more likely to act aggressively toward peers than those who had not been harmed. These findings remained true even after consideration of various family variables and the child's own health related or temperament factors. Children who had been physically harmed had different styles of processing social information from children who

had not been physically harmed. They were not as attentive to relevant social cues; they were more likely to attribute hostile intent to others; and they were less likely to develop competent solutions to problematic interpersonal events. A child's pattern of social information processing when assessed at 5 years of age therefore predicted his or her aggressive behavior several months later; the latter could be predicted by whether the child had been physically harmed earlier. Dodge et al. argue that their findings "are consistent with the hypothesis that early physical harm has its effect on a child's aggressive behavioral development largely by altering the child's patterns of processing social information" (p. 250).

Parental Substance Abuse: Some studies, but not others, have found parental substance abuse, specifically alcoholism, to be related to conduct disorder in youth. (See Tharinger & Koranek, 1988; West & Prinz, 1987; Woodside, 1988, for reviews). The relationship between other substances of abuse by parents and conduct problems in their children has not been studied in any detail, although a recent study by Gabel and Shindledecker (1992) suggests that parental abuse of illicit substances may be more important than alcohol abuse in its relationship to aggressive or antisocial behavior in youth.

As with child abuse or maltreatment, it is important to learn mediating mechanisms that might contribute to conduct disorder in youth of substance-abusing parents. Genetic, familial, environmental, and parenting practices all have been offered as possible contributants to the development of behavioral disorder in children of alcoholics (Woodside, 1988). Child abuse or maltreatment also may be an important link in many cases. Gabel and Shindledecker (1991), for example, found significant associations between substance abuse in parents and suspected child abuse or maltreatment in their children. Since substance abuse itself is an extremely broad and heterogenous entity, however, the issue may be whether subgroups of substance abusers (such as those who abuse particular substances or those who have associated antisocial personality or violent behavior) are more likely also to abuse or maltreat their children.

The relationship among child abuse, parental substance abuse, and parental psychopathology remains somewhat clouded, with most studies arguing that individuals who have committed child abuse do not have specific psychiatric disorders (Wolfe, 1987). Others have disagreed and argue that family violence is strongly associated with psychiatric disorder. Bland and Orn (1986), for example, found significant relationships between psychiatric disorder and family violence, with high rates of violent behavior occurring in those in whom alcoholism was combined with antisocial personality disorder or with recurrent depression. Based on standardized interviews of 1,200 residents of the city of Edmonton, Canada, these investigators found that almost half of all individuals who were abusive of children had definite or possible antisocial personality disorder, recurrent depression, or alcohol abuse and/or dependence.

From clinical perspectives, children who have been abused or maltreated often come from families that are dysfunctional and in which parents themselves have significant substance abuse and/or other psychiatric disorders.

Parental Psychiatric Disorder, Social and Environmental Adversity: Based on the preceding text, we may ask whether parental psychiatric disorder and adverse home environments are related in their ability to produce conduct disorder in youth. Research has considered this question and the issue of socioeconomic and environmental factors in relation to adverse parenting and childhood behavioral disorder.

Rutter and Quinton (1984) studied the children of a group of adult psychiatric patients in England. They found that spouses of these patients had an increased rate of psychiatric disorders and that family discord was particularly high in the families. Children had increased rates of psychiatric problems, often of the conduct problem variety. Youth who were exposed to parents with personality disorders and to home environments with family discord and hostility seemed to be at greatest risk. Rutter and Quinton argue that "family discord and hostility constitute the chief mediating variable in the association between parental mental disorder and psychiatric disturbance in the children" (p. 877). Family discord was not the only mechanism involved, however. Parental personality disorder increased the risk to the child even after accounting for hostile behavior, such as irritability, quarreling, and aggression.

Canino, Bird, Rubio-Stipec, Bravo, and Alegria (1990) studied a community sample of families in Puerto Rico having children between 4 and 16 years of age. They too found that parental psychopathology was significantly related to behavioral disorder in children, a relationship that was maintained even after accounting for negative family environment.

Another variable studied frequently in relation to conduct disorder in youth is socioeconomic and environmental adversity, a recognized factor having a significant overall relationship to psychiatric disorder (Bruce, Takeuchi, & Leaf, 1991). Conclusions on the impact of socioeconomic and environmental factors in contributing to conduct problems have been mixed. After considering the importance of individual and family factors, Robins (1978), as noted, found little contribution of social class to adult antisocial behavior in several samples. Olweus (1980) found no relationship between levels of boys' aggression and socioeconomic factors in the family.

Dodge et al. (1990), in a study cited earlier, state that "child abuse is relatively likely to occur in a context of poverty, deprivation, and marital conflict, even though instances of abuse were reported in all family contexts. But it appears that the experience of physical abuse raises one's risk for developing chronic aggressive behavior beyond the risk afforded by these other factors" (p. 1682).

The risk for aggression in the young children studied by Dodge et al. (1990) did not seem to be related to environmental or family variables such as low socioeconomic status or single parenthood. Rather, as others argue (Patterson, 1982), the presence of these variables is more likely to disturb adequate parenting practices, which then contributes to the development of aggression or conduct problems.

In the same context, Offord, Alder, and Boyle (1986) studied the relationship between sociodemographic variables and conduct disorder in a sample of youth ages 4 to 16 years in Ontario, Canada. Being a welfare recipient and living in subsidized housing were related to conduct disorder. Offord et al. also argue, however, that the relationship between conduct disorder and low socioeconomic conditions probably is not direct. Variables such as disturbed family functioning and marital discord, which are more likely in poverty areas, appear to be mediators involved in the development of conduct problems in youth.

GENETIC, TRAIT AND PSYCHOPHYSIOLOGICAL RELATIONSHIPS

Several studies have suggested that aggressive and/or antisocial behavior may reflect innate or genetic tendencies in individuals. This area has been difficult to study, given the known relationship between antisocial and criminal behavior in parents and antisocial behavior in their sons, which appears at least in part to be mediated by psychosocial and familial risk factors (Farrington, 1978; Farrington, Gundry, & West, 1975). Nonetheless, an impressive array of studies has accumulated to suggest that nonenvironmental variables may contribute strongly to antisocial or conduct-disordered behavior. One such group of studies has evaluated the stability of antisocial behavior and aggressive behavior over time and in some cases over generations. While such studies do not prove biological, genetic, or trait etiologies for antisocial or aggressive behavior, given that family or environmental influences also may endure over time, the results have been impressive.

Trait Studies: Loeber (1982; Loeber, Stouthamer-Loeber, Van Kammen, and Farrington 1991), for example, in comprehensive reviews, has studied the long-term stability of antisocial behavior. He concludes that frequent early antisocial behavior places youths at greater risk for later, more chronic antisocial behavior. Youthful chronic offenders commonly have exhibited antisocial behavior at early ages. Furthermore, while patterns or type of antisocial behavior tend to become more covert (e.g., theft) rather than more overt (e.g., fighting) in preadolescence or adolescence, there remains considerable stability in antisocial behavior overall for youths who have been identified as antisocial in their early years. High rates of antisocial behavior and a variety of antisocial behaviors also appear related to the persistence of antisocial behavior over time.

Olweus (1979, 1984) has reviewed literature bearing on the stability of aggressive behavioral patterns in males. Despite the variability in the studies' methodology, he found a high degree of stability in aggression over time, which was similar to the stability usually found in intellectual assessments. Huesmann, Eron, Lefkowitz, and Walder (1984) also have reported on the stability of aggressive behavior. They collected data on aggressiveness in over 600 individuals, their parents, and

their children. They too comment on the similarity of the stability of aggressive behavior to the stability of measured intellectual capacity. In subjects followed from age 8 to age 30, they estimated the stability of aggression to be about 0.50 for males and 0.35 for girls. Huesmann et al. also found that early aggression patterns predicted later more serious antisocial behavior, findings consistent with those of others cited earlier. Lower levels of aggression, on the other hand, lessen the risk in conduct problems and severe drug use (Brook, Whiteman, Cohen, Shapiro, & Balka, 1995).

Aggression as a behavior often is a component of a conduct disorder diagnosis. "Aggressivity" also may be considered a "trait." Other "traits," such as "impulsivity" and "sensation-seeking" (or "stimulation-seeking") behavior, often have been linked with conduct disorder or antisocial personality disorder. Quay (1965) has described the psychopath as

> highly impulsive, relatively refractory to the effects of experience in modifying his socially troublesome behavior, and lacking in the ability to delay gratification. His penchant for creating excitement for the moment without regard for later consequences seems almost unlimited. He is unable to tolerate routine and boredom, while he may engage in antisocial, even vicious, behavior his outbursts frequently appear to be motivated by little more than a need for thrills and excitement. (p. 371)

(See also Quay, 1977.)

Zuckerman, Kolin, Price, and Zoob (1964) have developed a scale intended to operationally define and assess the concept of "optimal stimulation" for an individual. The resultant measure was termed the Sensation Seeking Scale (SSS) and has been used mainly with adult populations. High scores on the SSS have been noted in individuals with various psychiatric disorders, including antisocial characteristics and drug abuse (Zuckerman, Buchsbaum, & Murphy, 1980). The SSS has four factors: thrill and adventure seeking, experience seeking, disinhibition, and boredom susceptibility. Russo et al. (1991) recently have developed a modification of the SSS for children. Two factors on this scale correspond to the boredom susceptibility and the thrill- and adventure-seeking factors of the adult scale. The boredom susceptibility factor has been found to correlate with conduct disorder in boys.

377

These studies of "trait" characteristics suggest that distinct profiles based on the manner an individual perceives and responds to his or her environment may be developed for youths who have different psychiatric diagnoses. Aggressivity, impulsivity, sensation seeking, behavioral disinhibition, and hyperactivity are all terms that commonly have been applied to conduct-disordered boys.

Psychophysiological Studies: Psychophysiological studies provide another means of comparing antisocial or conduct disordered individuals with others who have different or no psychiatric diagnoses. Autonomic variables, such as skin conductance and heart rate, provide easily accessible measures. When compared with prosocial children, antisocial children have been found to have significantly lower resting heart rates in a number of studies, a finding that may relate to a lowered emotional impact of certain potentially punishing social situations or to a lack of fear in the face of what would be considered dangerous for others (Raine & Jones, 1987).

In one study, using a population of 101 male schoolchildren ages 14 to 16 years—older than the primary group of interest in this chapter—Raine, Venables, and Williams (1990) studied psychophysiological measures related to three biological response systems: electrodermal (skin conductance), cardiovascular (heart rate) and cortical (electroencephalographic activity). Approximately 10 years later, they searched national records for indications of criminal offenses committed by these youth. Seventeen of the 101 youths had criminal records. Compared to the noncriminal controls, these young men had significantly lower resting heart rates, lower skin conductance activity, and more slow-frequency electroencephalographic activity.

Raine et al. (1990) hypothesize that their findings of reduced arousal in the youths who became criminals is "consistent with the view that the genetic predisposition to criminality may find its expression through ANS [autonomic nervous system] and CNS [central nervous system] underarousal . . . a diffuse brainstem arousal mechanism may be dysfunctional in criminals" (p. 1006).

Adoption Studies: Adoption studies have been used to investigate the issue of genetic influences on antisocial behavior or conduct disorder in youths. Cadoret, Cain, and Crowe (1983), for example, found that antisocial behavior in adolescent adoptees was related to both genetic factors and to environmental conditions, such as disturbance in the adoptive home.

Cadoret and Stewart (1991), in a more recent study, reported on the interwoven effects of biological endowment and environment. These investigators studied nearly 300 male adoptees, ages 18 to 40 years, and their adoptive families. The adoptees had been separated from their biological parents at birth and placed with adoptive parents who were nonrelatives. Adoption records allowed separation of adoptee biological parent groups into those showing psychiatric problems or behavioral disturbances and those showing no problems. Adoptive parents also were queried about adoptees' early lives through a structured interview. Particular areas of interest were attention deficit, hyperactivity, and aggressivity in the adopted children and their relationship to home, family, and environmental circumstances.

Cadoret and Stewart (1991) found that criminality/delinquency in a biological parent related significantly to attention deficit hyperactivity disorder (ADHD) in the adopted male child. Biological parent alcohol problems, psychiatric problems, or mental retardation did not relate to ADHD. Biological parent criminality/delinquency also predicted adult antisocial personality when the adoptee was placed in a lower socioeconomic status (SES) home. SES, without the biological parent history of criminality/delinquency, was unrelated to adult adoptee antisocial personality. Aggressivity and ADHD in the histories of the adopted child were significantly correlated, but aggressivity as a child, and not ADHD, was correlated with antisocial personality in the adult adoptee. ADHD alone did not predict adult antisocial personality.

These findings have some similarity to nonadoptee studies of biological parents and their children with attention deficit disorders in which there appears to be distinct subgroups of children with attention deficit disorder (ADD/ADHD). Those ADD/ADHD children who have associated conduct problems are more likely to have parent/family backgrounds that are characterized by increased rates of antisocial problems and antisocial personality disorder than is true of ADD/ADHD children without conduct problems (Biederman, Munir, & Knee, 1987; Lahey et al., 1988).

378

BIOCHEMICAL STUDIES

Numerous behavioral scientists have studied the relationship of biochemical measures to behavior. Aggression, for example, has been studied on a number of occasions, especially with regard to a possible association with elevated testosterone levels. Studies in animals tend to be more supportive of this hypothesized relationship than studies in humans, which have been inconsistent in their results (Parke & Slaby, 1983).

There recently also has been interest in biological psychiatry regarding various neurotransmitters, their metabolites and enzymes regulating their concentration, as possible contributants to a variety of psychiatric disorders, including conduct problems and antisocial behavior in adults and in children. The study of individuals who exhibit impulsive, antisocial, or aggressive behavior has centered on one monoamine neurotransmitter, serotonin (5HT), and two enzymes, dopamine beta hydroxylase (DBH) and monoamine oxidase (MAO). Serotonin (5HT) is converted to 5-hydroxyindoleacetic acid (5-HIAA) by MAO deamination in central nervous system neurons. Dopamine is converted through the activity of MAO and other enzymes to homovanillic acid (HVA). Dopamine is also converted to another neurotransmitter, norephinphrine (NE), by DBH in central nervous system and peripheral nervous system neurons. NE is then metabolized partly by MAO to 3-methoxy-4-hydroxphenylglycol (MHPG) in the brain and to vanillymandelic acid (VMA) in peripheral nervous system neurons.

A number of studies in adults have found a relationship between decreased serotonin levels and aggressive and violent behavior (Coccaro et al., 1989; Linnoila, DeJong, & Virkkunen, 1989; Mann, 1987; Virkkunen, DeJong, Bartko, Goodwin, & Linnoila, 1989; Virkkunen, DeJong, Bartko, & Linnoila, 1989).

Serotonin levels have not been studied frequently in children, although Kruesi et al. (1990) have reported reduced 5-HIAA cerebrospinal fluid (CSF) levels in children and adolescents with "disruptive behavior disorders" (a group that includes attention deficit hyperactivity disorder, oppositional defiant disorder and conduct disorder).

These investigators studied CSF levels of 5HT and various metabolites in 29 children and adolescents with disruptive behavior disorders who had been recruited from community sources. They also studied the same parameters in a group of youth with diagnoses of obsessive compulsive disorder. All subjects were evaluated with a structured interview for diagnostic purposes and given additional measures to assess variables such as impulsivity and aggression.

Kruesi et al. (1990) found significant negative correlations with age-corrected 5-HIAA levels for youths within the disruptive behavior disorders group on reports of aggression toward others. They also found low levels of 5-HIAA in the disruptive behavior disorders group compared to matched controls with obsessive compulsive disorder. No significant relationship was found between impulsivity and CSF 5-HIAA levels.

Altered MAO activity has been reported in various studies of psychopathology in adults. Low MAO levels have been found in individuals with high scores on the SSS (Zuckerman, 1989; Zuckerman et al., 1980). In children, studies with MAO have had mixed results. Stoff et al. (1989) found a correlation between high levels of platelet MAO and poor performance on a laboratory assessment of impulsivity. Bowden, Deutsch, and Swanson (1988), however, found that MAO was lower in boys with both ADD and undersocialized conduct disorder (UCD) (*DSM-III*) (APA, 1980) than in boys with only ADD not associated with UCD.

Another group of studies has evaluated differential activity levels of DBH in relation to undersocialized conduct disorder. These studies are based on the premise that low DBH activity would be associated with altered (reduced) noradrenergic functioning, given that DBH facilitates the conversion of dopamine to NE in the central and peripheral nervous systems. As reviewed by Rogeness, Javors, Maas, and Macedo (1990), on a theoretical basis, individuals with high levels of noradrenergic functioning would be expected to be very sensitive to signals of impending punishment and to be overly anxious and inhibited. They also would be more likely to have increased attachment behavior and difficulty with separation. Low levels of noradrenergic functioning would be associated with characteristics such as impulsivity, daring, and fearlessness as well as with lessened attachment behavior and decreased sociability. UCD therefore would be associated with low DBH activity (low noradrenergic functioning).

Anxiety disorders and some depressive disorders would be associated with high DBH activity (high noradrenergic functioning).

Rogeness and colleagues (Rogeness, Crawford, & McNamara, 1989; Rogeness, Hernandez, Macedo, & Mitchell, 1982; Rogeness et al., 1984; Rogeness, Hernandez, Macedo, Amrung, & Hoppe, 1986; Rogeness, Javors, Maas, Macedo, & Fischer, 1987; Rogeness, Maas, Macedo, Harris, & Hoppe, 1988; Rogeness et al., 1990) have tested this hypothesis by studying peripheral DBH levels as well as various NE metabolites in blood and urine, in conduct-disordered boys.

Rogeness et al. (1984), for example, compared 20 hospitalized, psychiatrically disturbed boys who had near-zero levels of plasma DBH (≤ 6 micromoles/minute/liter) with 20 hospitalized psychiatrically disturbed boys who had higher levels of DBH (≥ 15 micromoles/min/L). They found that diagnoses of UCD and borderline personality disorder were significantly more common in the near-zero-DBH group. By various criteria, boys in this group also were significantly more aggressive than the boys with higher levels of DBH.

Subsequent studies by Rogeness and coworkers (Rogeness et al., 1986; Rogeness, Javors, Maas, Macedo, & Fischer, 1987) again reported that boys with near-zero levels of DBH had an increase in diagnoses of UCD. More recent studies by the same group (Rogeness et al., 1988, 1989, 1990) using hospitalized boys have continued to support the hypothesis presented.

In a study mentioned earlier, Bowden et al. (1988) studied platelet MAO levels and plasma DBH levels in 48 nonhospitalized boys ages 6 to 14 years with ADD and in 24 healthy controls. One sixth of the boys with ADD also met criteria for UCD. Levels of DBH were lower in the ADD boys with UCD than in the controls. DBH and MAO levels did not differ when considering the whole sample of ADD boys in comparison with control subjects. The subgroup of ADD boys with UCD symptoms had significantly lower platelet MAO and plasma DBH values than the subgroup of ADD boys without UCD.

Pliszka, Rogeness, Renner, Sherman, and Broussard (1988) studied whether the findings of low DBH in conduct-disorder children could be generalized to older male adolescents who were in a juvenile detention center. They compared a sample of 27 male adolescents who all met criteria for conduct disorder with a sample of 17 male adolescents at a mental health clinic who had anxiety or depressive disorders. The study failed to generalize Rogeness et al.'s earlier (1984, 1986) work to the older nonpsychiatric hospital group of conduct-disturbed males in whom a finding of low DBH levels was uncommon.

Pliszka, Rogeness, and Meandro (1988) also attempted to generalize Rogeness et al.'s (1984, 1986) findings to a less severely disturbed group of boys who were in the approximate age range of the earlier studies. They measured plasma DBH levels, platelet MAO, and plasma MHPG levels in 42 boys, ages 7 to 14, seen at a community mental health clinic. The boys were placed into one of four categories that were based on their primary *DSM-III* (APA, 1980) diagnosis. No significant differences between groups were found with respect to DBH, MHPG, or MAO levels.

In summary, these findings in children suggest that low CSF 5-HIAA levels may be associated with disruptive behavior disorders and that peripheral DBH levels are low in some children with UCD. Disturbances in other measures of the dopaminergic/noradrenergic neurotransmitter system also have been found in this latter group. The findings for DBH activity appear strongest in severely disturbed hospitalized youth and more questionable in other groups.

Further research in this area is crucial because of the important leads toward understanding brain function and the development of treatment options that are suggested. The findings related to serotonin (Kruesi et al., 1990) are consistent with adult studies. While confined to hospitalized samples, the findings of Rogeness et al. (1990) related to noradrenergic functioning receive some support from theories of antonomic and central nervous system underarousal in conduct-disordered youth, as described earlier (Raine et al., 1990).

INTERACTIONAL THEORIES

Most investigators would agree that a variety of factors in children, in families, and perhaps in society contribute to the development of conduct disorder. Researchers, however, often must focus on one or a group of similar variables as hypothesized contributants to the development of antisocial behavior and therefore do not actively pursue an "interactional" approach in their research.

Lewis and colleagues (e.g., Lewis, Shanok,

Pincus, & Glaser, 1979; Lewis, Pincus, Lovely, Spitzer, & Moy, 1987; Lewis, Lovely, et al., 1988; Lewis, Pincus, et al., 1988; Lewis, Lovely, Yaeger, & Femina, 1989), on the other hand, while studying adolescents (not the primary age group of interest in this chapter), provide a useful example of an interactional model. They have emphasized the relationship between various factors, such as a history of child abuse and family violence, psychiatric disorder in the youth, cognitive and neuropsychological impairments, soft neurological signs, and psychomotor symptoms, as contributing together to the development of violent delinquents. Furthermore, employing this interactional or "biopsychosocial model," at least within a sample of known violent delinquent adolescents, appears to allow the prediction of adult violent offenses far better than knowledge of juvenile aggression alone (Lewis et al., 1989).

Differential Diagnosis

As indicated in Table 34.1, the differential diagnosis of conduct disorder by *DSM-IV* (APA, 1994) criteria usually is fairly straightforward. Antisocial behavior in the last 12 months during which the youngster has demonstrated 3 or more of the behaviors listed qualifies for the diagnosis. One of the behaviors must have been present in the last 6 months. Based on the number of conduct problems and/or their harmful effect on others, severity is assessed (i.e., mild, moderate or severe). Associated features were described earlier.

Relatively few disorders might be confused with conduct disorder by *DSM-IV* (APA, 1994) criteria. Isolated acts of antisocial behavior that do not have the repetitive and persistent pattern of conduct disorder generally do not qualify for that diagnosis. Oppositional defiant disorder has some similar features to conduct disorder but is a less severe disorder and often occurs in younger children. It does not involve violation of the basic rights of others or age-appropriate social rules or norms of behavior. Youth with bipolar disorder may exhibit antisocial behavior during manic periods, but the manic episodes usually are recognizable by other typical criteria.

A relatively small number of youth with psychotic symptoms may pose diagnostic dilemmas.

Burke, Del Beccaro, McCauley, and Clark (1985) found that 7 of 25 children (28%) under age 13 years admitted to an inpatient unit who had hallucinations not due to an organic brain syndrome had a conduct disorder. Some clinicians feel that youngsters of this type merit an additional diagnosis of psychotic disorder, not otherwise specified, by *DSM-IV* (APA, 1994) criteria. Their apparent relatedness, better reality testing, and only transient psychotic episodes help to rule out a more pervasive psychotic disorder, such as schizophrenia.

Other severely disturbed children manifest conduct problems as well as stress related severe regressive behavior, marked periodic anxiety, brief episodes of psychosis, including hallucinations, mild thought disorder, inattentiveness, and hyperactivity. These youngsters do not fit well into the current *DSM-IV* (APA, 1994) classification. They sometimes fulfill criteria for conduct disorder, attention deficit hyperactivity disorder, and personality disorder, and all three diagnoses sometimes are given. Other clinicians consider these youngsters to be borderline children or to also have a diagnosis of psychotic disorder, not otherwise specified by *DSM-IV* criteria.

Finally, as noted earlier, a number of disorders commonly coexist with conduct disorder and should be included in a comprehensive diagnostic evaluation. These include attention deficit hyperactivity disorder (which, as noted earlier, probably is present in the majority of severely conduct-disordered youth of grade-school age) and specific developmental disorders (e.g., learning disabilities, the most studied of which is reading disorder). Other disorders, such as major depressive episodes or dysthymic disorder, may coexist with conduct disorder and should be diagnosed when present (Loeber et al., 1994).

Morbidity

Children with severe antisocial behavior in the grade-school years exhibit a broad range of abnormalities in relation to themselves, their families, their peers, their academic productivity, and their society that is not captured sufficiently by diagnostic labels such as conduct disorder. Here I describe in more detail various aspects of the associ-

TABLE 34.1

Diagnostic Criteria for 312.8 Conduct Disorder

A. A repetitive and persistent pattern of behavior in which the basic rights of others or major age-appropriate societal norms or rules are violated, as manifested by the presence of three (or more) of the following criteria in the past 12 months, with at least one criterion present in the past 6 months:

Aggression to people and animals
(1)   often bullies, threatens, or intimidates others
(2)   often initiates physical fights
(3)   has used a weapon that can cause serious physical harm to others (e.g., a bat, brick, broken bottle, knife, gun)
(4)   has been physically cruel to people
(5)   has been physically cruel to animals
(6)   has stolen while confronting a victim (e.g., mugging, purse snatching, extortion, armed robbery)
(7)   has forced someone into sexual activity

Destruction of property
(8)   has deliberately engaged in fire setting with the intention of causing serious damage
(9)   has deliberately destroyed others' property (other than by fire setting)

Deceitfulness or theft
(10)   has broken into someone else's house, building, or car
(11)   often lies to obtain goods or favors or to avoid obligations (i.e., "cons" others)
(12)   has stolen items of nontrivial value without confronting a victim (e.g., shoplifting, but without breaking and entering; forgery)

Serious violations of rules
(13)   often stays out at night despite parental prohibitions, beginning before age 13 years
(14)   has run away from home overnight at least twice while living in parental or parental surrogate home (or once without returning for a lengthy period)
(15)   is often truant from school, beginning before age 13 years

B. The disturbance in behavior causes significant impairment in social, academic, or occupational functioning.

C. If the individual is age 18 years or older, criteria are not met for Antisocial Personality Disorder.

Specify type based on age at onset:
   Childhood-Onset Type: onset of at least one criterion characteristic of Conduct Disorder prior to age 10 years
   Adolescent-Onset Type: absence of any criteria characteristic of Conduct Disorder prior to age 10 years

Specify severity:
   Mild: few if any conduct problems in excess of those required to make the diagnosis **and** conduct problems cause only minor harm to others
   Moderate: number of conduct problems and effect on others intermediate between "mild" and "severe"
   Severe: many conduct problems in excess of those required to make the diagnosis **or** conduct problems cause considerable harm to others

NOTE. From *Diagnostic and Statistical Manual of Mental Disorders* (4th ed.) (pp. 90–91), by American Psychiatric Press 1994, Washington, DC: Author. Copyright 1994 by American Psychiatric Press. Reprinted with permission.

ated and comorbid characteristics of conduct-disordered youth and also discuss the prognosis of these youth into adulthood.

RELATIONSHIP TO OTHER PSYCHIATRIC DISORDERS

As noted earlier, there is considerable controversy about whether ADHD and conduct disorder are separate disorders or aspects of the same childhood disorder (Werry et al., 1987). There clearly exists a group of youngsters with both diagnoses according to standard criteria. In clinic referral samples, the majority of male youths with severe conduct disorder diagnoses appear to have associated ADHD (Reeves et al., 1987; Werry et al., 1987).

Szatmari, Boyle, and Offord (1989) addressed the question of the prevalence of each of these two disorders in relatively pure form, as well as the prevalence of their overlap, in a large community survey sample in the Ontario Child Health Study. As noted earlier, these researchers found that 2.6% of boys ages 4 to 11 years had pure conduct disorder; 5.1% had pure ADDH; and 3.7% had both disorders (mixed group). In girls, 1.0% of the 4- to 11-year-old group had pure conduct disorder; 2.2% had pure ADDH; and 1.2% had both disorders.

Szatmari et al. (1989) found that 42% of boys ages 4 to 11 with ADDH also had conduct disorder; 59% of boys in this age range with conduct disorder had ADDH. Thirty-six percent of girls ages 4 to 11 with ADDH also had conduct disorder; 56% of girls in this age range with conduct disorder had ADDH. Clearly, there is a great deal of overlap between these conditions, whether they are considered one disorder or two.

From clinical perspectives, those youngsters having both disorders present additional challenges since they have conduct disorder, a condition associated more commonly with family dysfunction and psychosocial disadvantage, as well as ADDH, a condition associated more commonly with developmental disorders and maturational impairments.

Another commonly associated problem in conduct-disordered youth of grade-school age is depression, although precise estimates of the prevalence of depression in children of this age range who are referred for treatment because of conduct problems is not clear.

Curry et al. (1988) found that a group of youths including boys ages 6 to 11 years who were identified as having seriously violent or assaultive behavior had similar rates of internalizing disorders (e.g., depression) as samples of youth referred primarily for mental health services. Assaultive children "showed an average degree of internalizing behavior problems equal to the mental health samples. These internalizing problems, however, were more often linked with predominant externalizing problems in the assaultive than in the mental health sample" (p. 23).

Chiles, Miller, and Cox (1980) studied depression in a population of 13- to 15-year-old adolescents admitted to a correctional faculty. Twenty-three percent had a major depressive disorder. Eppright, Kashani, Robison, and Reid. (1993) found high rates of personality disorders in incarcerated juveniles diagnosed by adult personality disorder criteria.

A number of studies have assessed the prevalence of conduct disorder in children being evaluated primarily for depressive disorders. Puig-Antich (1982) found that one third of preadolescent boys fulfilling criteria for major depression also fulfilled *DSM-III* (APA, 1980) criteria for conduct disorder. Kovacs, Paulauskas, Gatsonis, and Richards (1988) found that 16% of children ages 8 to 13 years who were part of a study of depressive disorders in childhood had a conduct disorder diagnosis during their index depressive episodes.

Walker et al. (1991) evaluated the impact of a comorbid diagnosis of anxiety disorder (overanxious disorder, separation anxiety disorder, or both), by *DSM-III-R* (APA, 1987) criteria on the impairment and social adjustment of boys with conduct disorder. These youths were part of a longitudinal study of 177 boys between 7 and 12 years of age who had been referred to outpatient clinics. The sample consisted of 68 boys (33%) with a conduct disorder diagnosis. Of these 68 boys, 42 (62%) had as associated anxiety disorder, a percentage higher than expected based on other samples. Interestingly, Walker et al. (1991) found that boys with diagnoses of conduct disorder and anxiety disorder were less impaired socially than boys having a conduct disorder without a comorbid anxiety disorder diagnosis. Perhaps this was related to a broader range of social responses available to conduct-disordered youth who also are anxious.

FAMILY INTERACTION PATTERNS

Earlier we discussed the important influences parental behavior and characteristics may have on the development of prosocial versus antisocial behavior. Child abuse/maltreatment, parental substance abuse, and family violence have been cited as possible contributants to later antisocial or aggressive behavior in youth. Although less research has been done on the possible effects of deviant child behavior that may produce deviant parental behavior (e.g., child abuse), it is recognized clinically that parent-child behaviors commonly are interactive and that some children are more likely to be viewed negatively or mistreated than others.

The interaction between antisocial and aggressive behavior in youths and aversive behavior or cognitions in parents has been described in a number of contexts. Campbell, Breaux, Ewing, and Szumowski (1986) studied preschool children who were hyperactive and aggressive at age 3 years. These child behaviors were associated with maternal behavior that was negative and directive. Children in whom problems persisted when studied again at ages 4 and 6 years were more likely to have had problematic maternal-child interactive patterns at initial evaluation. Campbell et al. comment that a

troubled family climate may contribute to aggression and hyperactivity in some children either directly or indirectly through its influence on child-rearing practices and maternal attitudes; active and aggressive child behavior may exacerbate ongoing family difficulties directly and may also influence the quality of the mother-child relationship in families already stressed by external circumstances. (pp. 232–233)

Morris et al. (1988) also emphasize the possibly interactive effects of parental style with children's difficulties in a study assessing problem solving, behavioral interactions, and cognitive attributions in fathers of aggressive and well-behaved sons. Morris et al. videotaped problem-solving sessions between fathers and sons. They also elicited fathers' thoughts about the sessions and had fathers rate their family environments. These investigators found that fathers of nonaggressive sons were more efficient in problem solving, modeled more constructive behaviors in the problem-solving task, and considered their families more cohesive, expressive, and less conflicted than fathers of aggressive sons. They themselves had fewer critical thoughts about their boys. Fathers of aggressive sons had more thoughts about their sons, but these commonly reflected negative attitudes toward them. These fathers also had more negative thoughts about their families. Again, it is not certain whether the aggression in the child leads to negative parental attributions or if negative parental characteristics are modeled by the aggressive child.

It is interesting to note that Patterson (1982) has found that depression in mothers of antisocial boys may improve on successful treatment of the boys' conduct disturbance. This raises the question of whether the child's behavioral disorder contributes to the onset or maintenance of the mother's depression. Usually the process is conceptualized differently, with the parent's depression felt to contribute to the onset of the conduct disturbance. It may be that both processes are operative.

INTELLECTUAL AND ACADEMIC DIFFICULTIES

Numerous studies have documented intellectual deficits, learning problems, learning disabilities, poor classroom behavior, inattentiveness in classrooms, and poor academic orientation in conduct-disordered and antisocial children. (See Kazdin, 1987a, b; Loeber et al., 1990; Loeber & Patterson, 1981, for reviews.)

Rutter and colleagues (Rutter et al., 1970; Rutter, Tizard, Yule, Graham, & Whitmore, 1976) studied educational and psychiatric disorders in 9- to 12-year-old children on the Isle of Wight in the mid-1960s. About 4% of the children were found to have specific reading retardation, which was defined as reading at least 28 months below what would be expected based on age and IQ. One third of this group had significant antisocial behavior. The pattern suggested that the antisocial behavior sometimes developed as a maladaptive response to the educational difficulties. A later study of 10-year-olds in an inner-city London borough also found a strong association between reading retardation and conduct disturbance.

The association between academic difficulties and conduct disorder therefore is well established on one level, but what is less clear is whether the association is in part actually between academic underachievement and ADHD, a common comorbid diagnosis in conduct-disordered youth. McGee, Williams, and Silva (1984), for example, divided a large sample of 7-year-old children into "aggressive only," "hyperactive only," "aggressive-hyperactive," and "problem-free" groups. All of the problem groups had some degree of cognitive impairment but its nature differed. There was a general cognitive deficit in both hyperactive groups, with specific reading retardation in the "hyperactive-aggressive" group but not in the "pure-aggressive" group.

More recently, Frick et al. (1991) studied boys ages 7 to 12 years who had predominantly disruptive behavior disorders and who were seen in outpatient settings. Conduct disorder and attention disorder/attention deficit disorder groups did not differ from boys without disruptive behavior disorder diagnoses on IQ but did differ on a number of academic achievement measures. Further analysis indicated that after controlling for the co-occurrence of conduct disorder and attention deficit hyperactivity disorder, only the latter and not conduct disorder was associated with academic underachievement.

INTERPERSONAL RELATIONS AND SOCIAL SKILLS

Children with aggressive behavior and conduct disorder commonly have poor peer relations and social skill deficits. Indeed Patterson et al. (1989) have argued that peer rejection follows developmentally from antisocial behavior. Kazdin (1987a) and Loeber and Patterson (1981) cite several studies indicating that aggressive or antisocial children are rejected by playmates and classmates. Such youths interact poorly with adults also and commonly are considered socially immature. Patterson (1986) points out that it is difficult to teach social skills to noncompliant children who do not follow implicit or explicit rules for behavior. Rejection by peers is important since the rejected child does not form appropriate models for cooperative, mutually beneficial relationships in the future.

Walker, Shinn, O'Neill, and Ramsey (1987) studied fifth-grade boys at high risk for antisocial behavior in comparison with a control group of boys who were not antisocial based on assessments that included direct observations in academic settings, peer interactions, school record review, and teacher ratings of social skills. Antisocial boys differed from nonantisocial boys on direct observation in several ways. They spent more time in free play and less time in structured games and activities; they had similar rates of positive social behavior, but more negative verbal and physical social behavior with peers; they initiated negative interactions with peers about 10 times more often than nonantisocial controls. Teacher ratings found antisocial boys to have poorer adjustment and social behavior than boys who were not antisocial.

COGNITIVE PROCESSING AND ATTRIBUTIONS

A number of investigators have studied the cognitive styles or attributions of aggressive and antisocial children, assuming quite understandably that deviant externalizing behavior would be accompanied by disturbed internal processing of personally and socially relevant information.

Dodge (1986) has been influential in developing this approach and has formulated a social information processing model to describe social problem-solving and interactional skills along with their deficits in aggressive children. Akhtar and Bradley (1991) summarize various steps that are involved in competent social interactions. These cognitive steps include: encoding, interpretation, response search with decision making, enactment, and evaluation. These authors reviewed the literature to determine whether aggressive children showed deficits in these areas.

Aktar and Bradley (1991) conclude that aggressive children as a group have difficulties in all of these areas. These youths often do not encode relevant environmental cues; they are more likely to assign hostile intentions to peers; they generate less effective and fewer solutions to problematic situations; they seem to pursue goals in social situations that are not appropriate; they are less able to enact and perform numerous social behaviors successfully; and they appear to display an egocentrism in their evaluation of the environment's response to their behavior.

Huesmann and Eron (1984) also have used a cognitive, information-processing approach to aid in understanding how aggression "as a characteristic way of solving social problems usually emerges early in life" (p. 243). They hypothesize that social behavior is governed to a large extent by "cognitive scripts, schemas, and strategies that have been stored in memory and are used as guides for behavior. These strategies must be encoded, rehearsed, stored, and retrieved in much the same way as are other strategies for intellectual behaviors" (p. 244).

Huesmann and Eron (1984) studied children's fantasies as a form of cognitive rehearsal for aggressive behavior. They interviewed and tested several hundred children who were first and third graders at the start of the study. Scales from a children's fantasy measure were used to assess rehearsal of aggressive behavior. Children's daydreams, night dreams, and imaginary play all were included in the information used to develop fantasy scores. Huesmann and Eron found positive correlations between aggressive fantasies and peer nominations for aggression. More aggressive children fantasized more about aggression, an internal act that these researchers argue serves as a cognitive rehearsal for further aggressive behavior.

INTERACTING NEUROLOGICAL, PSYCHIATRIC, AND/OR NEUROPSYCHOLOGICAL DEFICITS

As noted earlier, Lewis and coworkers (e.g., Lewis et al., 1989; Lewis, Pincus, Feldman, Jackson, and Bard, 1986) have argued for an understanding of violent delinquents that is based on the interaction of environmental factors (e.g., child abuse, family violence) with intrinsic variables that predispose youths to violent behavior. Intrinsic factors that produce a variety of dysfunctions in these youths include a history of head injury, major and minor neurological impairments, neuropsychological deficits (as an indicator of central nervous system dysfunction), and severe psychiatric disorder with frequent psychotic features. These comorbid neurological and psychiatric features, together with a history of violence in the youth's own experience, are useful in predicting severe violence perpetrated in adolescence or in adulthood by certain delinquents or adult criminals.

LONGER-TERM OUTCOME AND PROGNOSIS

The longer-term (adolescent, adult) outcome of grade-school-age boys with conduct disorder has been studied on a number of occasions. Given the frequent association of attention deficit hyperactivity disorder with conduct disorder that has been noted earlier (Reeves et al., 1987; Werry et al., 1987), the question of outcome must be addressed with the understanding that hyperactivity and conduct disorder probably occurred together in a number of studies of "conduct-disordered" youth.

Interestingly, however, it also must be pointed out that hyperactivity in grade-school boys may be a risk factor for the later development of conduct disorder even when conduct disorder is not present during the grade-school period itself. Gittelman, Mannuzza, Shenker, and Bonagura (1985) studied 101 males ages 16 to 23 years who had been given diagnoses of hyperactivity when they were 6 to 12 years of age. Their outcome was compared with findings in 100 normal controls. Structured interviews were administered to subjects and to their parents. Thirty-one percent of the probands compared to 3% of the controls showed a full attention deficit disorder with hyperactivity

syndrome. Twenty-seven percent of the probands compared to 8% of the controls had an antisocial/conduct disorder, and 19% of the probands compared to 7% of the controls had a substance abuse disorder. These results were statistically significant.

In another study using the same population, Mannuzza, Gittelman Klein, Horowitz Konig, and Giampino (1989) found that significantly more probands compared to controls had been arrested, convicted, or incarcerated. Having an antisocial/conduct disorder diagnosis at follow-up almost entirely accounted for this increased risk of criminal behavior.

Another study by Mannuzza, Klein et al. (1991) used a different cohort of 94 hyperactive boys of essentially the same age. The findings were consistent with the earlier report. Attention deficit disorder, antisocial disorders, and substance abuse disorders all were significantly more common in the probands compared to the control group.

Mannuzza, Gittelman Klein, and Addalli (1991) also reported on the follow-up of a group of 50 former hyperactive boys (ages 16 to 23 years at the time of this study) from the above cohorts and compared their outcome with their nonhyperactive brothers' outcome and with matched controls. The prevalence of antisocial disorders was not significantly different in probands and their brothers, but the severity of the antisocial behavior, as indicated by more conduct problems in different settings, did significantly differentiate the groups.

These studies of Gittelman et al. (1985) and Manuzza et al. (1989), Manuzza, Gittelman Klein et al. (1991), and Manuzza, Klein et al. (1991) were developed initially on groups of hyperactive youth. Boys were not accepted into the studies if the primary reason for their referral was aggressive behavior. This designation was not always performed in a systematic manner, however, as Manuzza et al. point out. Some youths initially diagnosed as hyperactive may have had preexisting or comorbid conduct disorder, although the number of such youths apparently was extremely small.

While these follow-up studies of hyperactive boys suggest an increased long-term risk for antisocial behavior and substance abuse, it seems probable that such youths are not at greatest risk for the most severe forms of antisocial behavior in adolescence or adulthood. This assumption is based on studies indicating that early onset and greater degree of conduct problems in childhood increases the risk for more severe antisocial behavior in subsequent years (Loeber, 1982; 1991b).

Other studies focusing specifically on antisocial behavior in grade-school children would be expected to show an even greater prevalence of and more severe antisocial behavior in adolescence and adulthood. Robins and colleagues (Robins, 1970, 1978; Robins & Lewis, 1966; Robins & Ratcliff, 1979) have described the outcome and prognosis of youths with early forms of antisocial behavior in the United States in a number of publications. Other investigators, such as Farrington and West (1981) and Farrington and Hawkins (1991), have described the outcome of youth in England.

Robins (1978) has concluded that antisocial behavior appears to be a verifiable syndrome in males. It rarely occurs in adulthood without having been preceded by serious antisocial behavior earlier in childhood. While serious adult antisocial behavior almost always has been preceded by antisocial behavior in childhood, most antisocial boys (about 50% or slightly higher) do not become severely antisocial adults. Many of the latter group, however, do demonstrate some antisocial behavior.

Robins and Ratcliff (1979), in a study using data from a sample of black youths, addressed further the question of the origins of antisocial behavior in relation to individual, family, and social variables. They conclude that social class of rearing does not seem to be important in predicting severe antisocial behavior found in adults. Milder forms of antisocial behavior may be related to social conditions or social class, however. They suggest that "milder antisocial behavior in men reared in deprived environments is pathological only by middle-class standards, but that severely antisocial behavior, as indicated by a failure to conform over a broad range of functioning . . . is pathological in every social stratum and has it origins chiefly within the person and his family" (p. 115).

Information about whether antisocial behavior in childhood predicts other (nonantisocial) adult psychiatric disorders has been scanty. Robins and Price (1991) recently have addressed this question in both men and women, the latter an understudied group of both youths and adults with antisocial behavior. These investigators used data from interviews conducted as part of the National Institute of Mental Health Epidemiologic Catchment Area Program in which over 19,000 adults ages 18 years and over from several cites in the United States participated between 1980 and 1984. Robins and Price examined the relationship between conduct problems in childhood (as assessed by number of behavior problems) with several *DSM-III* psychiatric disorders found in adults. They were particularly interested to learn whether childhood conduct problems were related to nonexternalizing disorders (e.g., somatization, anxiety, depression) as well as externalizing disorders, such as antisocial personality and substance abuse.

Robins and Price (1991) found that the rates of externalizing disorders (adult antisocial behavior, drug and alcohol disorders) increased in both sexes as the number of childhood conduct problems increased. Fourteen percent of men had externalizing disorders with no history of childhood conduct problems; 76% of adult men had externalizing disorders with five or more childhood conduct problems. Less than 4% of women had externalizing disorders with no history of conduct problems; 50% of women with five or more childhood conduct problems had adult externalizing disorders.

Robins and Price (1991) also found that, as expected, externalizing disorders were more common in males than in females. The predictive power of childhood conduct problems was nonetheless similar for adult males and females. Additionally, while childhood conduct problems had a direct and strong link to externalizing disorders, they also were related to the nonexternalizing disorders, an effect that was mediated largely through the development of externalizing disorders. This was especially true for men. "The more conduct problems, the more externalizing disorders, and the more externalizing disorders present, the more likely the person is to subsequently develop other disorders as well" (p. 130). In other words, severe childhood antisocial behavior predicts adult antisocial behavior, which makes an individual more likely also to have non–conduct-disorder-type problems (e.g., depression).

Treatment

The treatment of severe conduct disorder in youths generally has been disappointing. Given the huge numbers of children and families involved and the enormous costs to individual, family, and society, the lack of apparently effective treatments for conduct disorder must rank as a major disappointment in the history of psychotherapeutic efforts with children and adolescents. This is not to say that all treatments or all treatment approaches have failed, because this clearly is not the case. It is rather to emphasize that, to date, few treatments have been shown to be effective for conduct disorder and antisocial behavior in youths. One problem is the lack of well-controlled studies that would help to determine the relative efficacy of various treatment approaches, of which there are several broad groups.

Several sources, including Dumas (1989), Kazdin (1987a, b); and Rutter and Giller (1983), provide reviews of individual, family, community, or correctional approaches. While it is not always possible to separate out treatment approaches or outcome in the child and adolescent groups, whenever possible we focus on treatment for children in the grade-school range (5 or 6 to 12 years old). Table 36.2 provides a brief synopsis of major treatment approaches that have been employed for conduct-disordered and antisocial youth.

INDIVIDUAL, FAMILY, AND GROUP APPROACHES

Many verbally oriented therapies have been used with conduct-disordered youth. There is little evidence to suggest that traditional individual psychodynamically oriented or play therapy, group therapy, or family therapy is effective in conduct disorder or antisocial behavior in youths. As Kazdin (1987a) points out, treatments that probably are applied most often in clinical settings—individual, group, and family therapy—have not been tested adequately in controlled studies.

The pitfalls of continuing treatments and intervention efforts whose efficacy has not been established is illustrated by the long-term follow-up of boys enrolled in the Cambridge Somerville project, an ambitious attempt to prevent juvenile delinquency among high-risk elementary-school–aged youths that was started more than half a century ago (McCord, 1978).

In this project, selected boys from high-delinquency areas were assigned randomly to either experimental or control groups. Boys in the experimental group were provided with counseling, additional social service involvement and remedial education if needed, summer camp experiences, and general advocacy for their own and their family's needs. Counseling occurred about twice per month for 2 to 8 years. In general, both counselors and the youths themselves felt the program had been helpful, although systematic evaluations have not demonstrated benefits. Indeed, McCord (1978) found that on a number of variables, the experimental group fared worse than the control group.

Based on the disappointing outcome studies of this project and others intended to prevent delinquency through counseling, Rutter and Giller (1983) conclude: "In view of the consistently negative results from both large and small scale studies (most of which were well planned and several with random assignment), it is clear that this form of long-term unfocused counselling is without value as a method of preventing delinquency" (p. 284). The same authors also review studies of psychotherapy outcome with adolescents who already are delinquent or disruptive. They conclude that "the balance of evidence . . . suggests that counselling and psychotherapy are not particularly effective methods of intervention for most delinquents" (p. 285). This is not to say that some delinquents would not benefit from various forms of psychotherapy, but that for delinquent youths generally, this approach has not been shown to be beneficial.

Kernberg and Chazen (1991) recently have described a treatment approach that combines individual psychodynamic treatment, parent management training, and group therapy that they feel is suitable for certain conduct-disordered youth, specifically those who are more socialized. The effort to combine treatment modalities (multimodal treatment) in difficult to treat youth seems worthwhile. It is hoped that controlled outcome research from this psychodynamically oriented but multimodal approach will be forthcoming.

Functional family therapy (FFT) (Barton & Alexander, 1981; see Kazdin, 1987a) is another

TABLE 34.2

Therapeutic Focus and Processes of Major Classes of Treatment for Antisocial Behavior

Treatment type	Focus	Key processes
Child focused		
Individual psychotherapy	Focus on intrapsychic bases of antisocial behavior, especially conflicts and psychological processes that were adversely affected over the course of development.	Relationship with the therapist is the primary medium through which change is achieved. Treatment provides a corrective emotional experience by providing insight and exploring new ways of behaving.
Group psychotherapy	Processes of individual therapy, as noted above. Additional processes are reassurance, feedback, and vicarious gains by peers. Group processes, such as cohesion and leadership, also serve as the focus.	Relationship with the therapist and peers as part of the group. Group processes emerge to provide children with experiences of others and opportunities to test their own views and behaviors.
Behavior therapy	Problematic behaviors presented as target symptoms. Prosocial behaviors are trained directly.	Learning new behaviors through direct training, modeling, reinforcement, practice, and role playing. Training in the situations (e.g., at home and in the community) in which the problematic behaviors occur.
Problem-solving skills training	Cognitive processes and interpersonal cognitive problem-solving skills that underlie social behavior.	Teach problem-solving skills to children by engaging in a step-by-step approach to interpersonal situations. Use of modeling, practice, rehearsal, and role playing to develop problem-solving skills. Development of an internal dialogue or private speech that uses the processes of identifying prosocial solutions to problems.
Pharmacotherapy	Designed to affect the biological substrates of behavior, especially in the light of laboratory-based findings on neurohumors, biological cycles, and other physiological correlates of aggressive and emotional behavior.	Administration of psychotropic agents to control antisocial behavior. Lithium carbonate and haloperidol have been used because of their antiaggressive effects.
Residential treatments	Means of administering other techniques in day treatment or residential setting. Foci of other techniques apply.	Processes of other techniques apply. Also, separation of the child from parents or removal from the home situation may help reduce untoward processes or crises that contribute to the clinical problem.
Family focused		
Family therapy	Family as a functioning system rather than the identified patient serves as focus. Interpersonal relationships, organization, and roles and dynamics of the family.	Communication, relationships, and structure within the family and processes as autonomy, problem solving, and negotiation.

TABLE 34.2

(continued)

Treatment type	Focus	Key processes
Parent management training	Interactions in the home, especially those involving coercive exchanges.	Direct training of parents to develop prosocial behavior in their children. Explicit use of social-learning techniques to influence the child.
Community based		
Community-wide interventions	Focus on activities and community programs to foster competence and prosocial peer relations.	Develop prosocial behavior and connections with peers. Activities are seen to promote prosocial behavior and to be incompatible with antisocial behavior.

NOTE. From "Treatment of Antisocial Behavior in Children: Current Status and Future Directions," by A. E. Kazdin, 1987, *Psychological Bulletin, 102.* Copyright 1987 by the American Psychological Association. Reprinted by permission.

treatment approach that has been used with conduct-disordered youth. It differs from several other forms of family therapy in that it conceptualizes problems within the context of the functions these problems serve in the family system. In FFT, this family systems approach is joined with a more behavioral family approach based on social learning theory.

In the few studies in which FFT has been applied in treatment with delinquent adolescents, it has been quite effective and superior to other types of family therapy (e.g., psychodynamically oriented). Whether it will continue to be effective in the hands of other therapists/researchers or with grade-school groups remains to be determined.

Two additional verbally oriented treatment approaches are worthy of note. Parent management training (PMT; Patterson, 1982) is recognized for its efficacy with a sizable group of school-age conduct-disordered youths; problem-solving skills training (PSST) has an established theoretical base and some research to suggest it may be useful. The description of these two approaches relies on Kazdin (1987a).

Parent Management Training (PMT): Parent management training is a form of treatment in which parents are taught (trained) to interact more effectively with their children in order to reduce deviant (antisocial) behavior and to increase prosocial behavior. Patterson (1982) has advanced the view that children learn antisocial and aggressive behavior through maladaptive parent-child interactions. Commonly, this process develops through a series of coercive interactions in which, for example, the parents respond to persistent coercive child behaviors (yelling, aggressive behavior toward a sibling) by yielding to the demands of the child. In this way parents themselves are negatively reinforced when the child's aversive behavior ceases, but they also inadvertently positively reinforce the child's aggressive or threatening behavior. Thus, the parents are caught in a "reinforcement trap" in which, by yielding to the child, they are temporarily reinforced themselves but also set up future coercive and at times escalating interchanges.

PMT is intended to alter these types of interchanges between parents and children and to increase reinforcement for prosocial behavior. Several parental behaviors are encouraged through "training" sessions—establishing appropriate, consistently enforced, rules; providing positive reinforcement for desired behaviors, providing appropriate mild punishment for undesirable behavior (e.g., time out from parental attention for persistent yelling).

PMT is a technique based on social learning principles. While children commonly are included in sessions and often are asked about desired reinforcers and how the program is proceeding, the focus of the training program is parents, not children. Techniques such as positive reinforcement, the use of social contingencies (e.g., time out), and contracting are described, modeled, and role-played.

PMT has been assessed in many studies with children having varying degrees of dysfunction. Studies have included aggressive children of different ages, with large numbers in the grade-school years. Favorable evaluations have been found through parent and teacher reports and through direct observation in home and in school environments. Improvement has at times been striking, bringing deviant children's behavior to normative ranges and persisting for a year or more of follow-up. Child behaviors that were not the focus of training also have shown improvement. Sibling behavior, although also not the focus of treatment, sometimes improves as well. Psychopathology in the mother, particularly depression, has decreased after PMT, suggesting that PMT may alter favorably several problems in dysfunctional families.

Factors that contribute to positive outcome with PMT include duration of treatment (more substantial benefits with certain populations may require 50 to 60 hours of treatment), specific training for parents in social learning principles, and greater therapist skill and training. Negative outcome with PMT is more likely with greater family dysfunction (e.g., parental psychopathology), socioeconomic disadvantage, and in insulated mothers with few social supports outside the home. In general, PMT has been a carefully evaluated and effective treatment approach for many antisocial and aggressive children. Some severely disturbed children and families may not benefit. The demands PMT makes of dysfunctional families for mastering educational materials, observing their children at home, and implementing behavioral procedures in the home environment may be beyond the parents' capacity.

Problem-solving Skills Training (PSST): PSST is an approach that emphasizes cognitive processes within the child that are felt to underlie behavioral deviance. It is based on the empirically established recognition that children with aggressive behavior (as well as other types of behavior problems) have distorted cognitive processes (i.e., perceptions, attributions, or problem-solving skills) compared to children without these behavior problems. Hostile intent, for example, is more commonly attributed to others by aggressive than nonaggressive children, thus apparently making it more likely that actual behavioral aggression will occur in the face of relative ambiguity. Aggressive children also are less able than nonaggressive children to take others' perspectives or to empathize with others.

PSST attempts to help youngsters with behavioral problems develop more adaptive cognitive processes and problem-solving skills (e.g., generating alternative solutions to problematic situations, developing means-ends thinking) and to better recognize reasons for their behavior.

PSST, when applied to conduct-disordered children, has had several variations. Essentially, however, the approach emphasizes thought processes rather than actual behavior. Step-by-step approaches to solving interpersonal problem situations are taught to the children. Self-statements that direct attention to particular aspects of a problems or to a task are reviewed. Structured tasks involving games or stories are used, and, over time, cognitive problem-solving skills are applied to actual life situations. The therapist is actively involved in the treatment, and behavioral procedures such as modeling and reinforcement are employed, as is role playing.

While PSST has been shown to be effective on laboratory task performances, it has not been used extensively with clinical populations of conduct-disordered youth, although some outcome research has been encouraging. Further study of this cognitive-based treatment approach is needed.

PHARMACOTHERAPY

There has been little systematic research into the pharmacotherapy of conduct disorder in youths when considered apart from ADHD. As indicated earlier, probably only a minority of severe cases of conduct-disordered youths in the preadolescent age range do not also fulfill criteria for ADHD. Given this perspective, a discussion of the pharmacotherapy of conduct disorder must consider the following questions: (1) What are effective psychopharmacological treatments for ADHD? (2) Do these treatments affect overlapping symptoms of conduct disorder, such as aggressivity, that also commonly occur in ADHD youths who do or do not have conduct disorder diagnoses? and (3) Are there effective psychopharmacological treatments for preadolescent conduct-disordered youths who do not have associated ADHD?

The psychopharmacological treatment of ADHD probably is the most widely researched psychopharmacological treatment in child and adolescent psychiatry. Psychostimulants such as methylphenidate, dextroamphetamine sulfate, and magnesium pemoline have a history of generally safe, effective use in children with hyperactive behavior and ADHD symptoms.

Dulcan (1990) recently has reviewed the use of psychostimulants in youth. (See also Chapter 40 herein.) With the use of psychostimulants in ADHD children, improvement occurs in about 75% of cases. Target symptoms such as excessive motor activity, inattention, impulsivity, and distractibility are all improved, as is short-term memory and accuracy and speed in various academic tasks. Reduced oppositional behavior and aggressivity also are commonly noted, as is increased compliance with adult requests. More positive behavior toward parents and teachers has been found, as have reciprocal positive responses from parents and teachers toward the psychostimulant-treated child. Other psychopharmacologic treatments, such as desipramine and clonidine, also have been useful for hyperactive children, but experience with these latter medications is more limited. (See Biederman, Baldessarini, Wright, Knee, & Harmatz, 1989; Hunt, Capper, & O'Connell, 1990).

Psychostimulant treatment of ADHD youths clearly favorably affects target symptoms, such as aggressivity and impulsivity, which also are found in conduct-disordered youth. Although, from theoretical perspectives, it is important to clarify the diagnostic relationship between ADHD and conduct disorder, from clinical perspectives at present it often is advisable to treat conduct-disordered youths who have an ADHD diagnosis with psychostimulant medication initially. In many cases, conduct-disordered (or is it the ADHD?) symptoms and interpersonal relationships will improve along with the expected reduction of hyperactivity and inattentiveness that is expected in "pure" ADHD.

Klorman et al.'s (1988) research has supported this clinical stance. They used methylphenidate with different groups of ADHD children ages 6 to 12 years who did and did not have noncompliant or aggressive behavior, such as defiance, quarrelsomeness, and uncooperativeness. They found comparable improvement in the groups based on parent and teacher ratings, laboratory tasks, and event-related potentials.

It should be noted, however, that while ADHD youths with associated conduct disorder may benefit from psychostimulant treatment and show reductions in "conduct" problems, these youngsters are greatly in need of other nonpharmacological therapies, such as education and parent management training, as well.

Fewer psychopharmacological treatments have been studied in youths when the main focus of research interest has been on conduct disorder itself. Campbell et al. (1984) studied 61 hospitalized children (57 boys and 4 girls) between the ages of 5 and 13 years who had diagnoses of conduct disorder, undersocialized aggressive, using *DSM-III* (APA, 1980) criteria. These youths had been unresponsive to outpatient management. The children were given placebo for two weeks. Those who remained acceptable for the study (e.g., no significant improvement on placebo) were randomly assigned to haloperidol, lithium carbonate, or placebo for 4 weeks. A variety of behavioral and laboratory measures were obtained in this double-blind study. Results indicated that both the lithium- and the haloperidol-treated groups were significantly and similarly improved compared to placebo in several areas, including hyperactivity, aggression, and hostility. In general, lithium had fewer untoward side effects than haloperidol, which was associated with excessive sedation in some of the children. The lithium-treated group had a notable weight gain. The optimal dosage for the children receiving haloperidol ranged from 1.0 to 6.0 milligrams (mg) per day, or 0.04 to 0.21 mg per kilogram per day. The optimal dosage for the children receiving lithium ranged from 500 to 2,000 mg per day.

INPATIENT HOSPITALIZATION, RESIDENTIAL TREATMENT CENTERS, AND DAY TREATMENT PROGRAMS

Blotcky, Dimperio, and Gossett (1984) reviewed follow-up information from 24 reports that involved children under 12 years of age (some studies including inpatient and residential settings). Ten variables were identified and related to long-term outcome: "intelligence, organicity, diagnosis, symptom pattern, age at admission, sex, family functioning, treatment, after care and follow-up" (p. 1500). Children with more severe personality disorders, antisocial or bizarre symptoms, neurological dysfunction, and below-average intelligence had poorer long-term outcomes. More competent family system on discharge, completion of inpatient treatment goals, and the patient's continuance in appropriate aftercare were associated with improved outcome.

Pfeiffer and Strzelecki (1990) extended Blotcky et al.'s (1984) review by adding more recent reports. They also developed statistical procedures to aid further in the outcome evaluation. Their review, which includes 34 studies involving both children and adolescents, concludes that neurological dysfunction (organicity), psychotic disorder, or undersocialized aggressive conduct disorder diagnoses and bizarre or antisocial symptoms were important predictors of poor outcome. Better family functioning, planned discharge, completion of the treatment program, and involvement in aftercare related to better outcome.

The reviews just noted emphasize the importance of antisocial or conduct-disordered behavior in predicting poor outcome for severely disturbed inpatient youths, many of whom presumably received a variety of intensive treatment approaches while living outside of the home environment.

Day treatment for children of the grade-school age is another approach that commonly employs more than one treatment strategy at the same time (e.g., individual, group) along with the efforts of several mental health disciplines and special education approaches. The setting may be hospital, school, or community based but most commonly involves a program of several hours per day for the child, 5 days per week (i.e., the usual school week). A number of studies have described patient/student characteristics, although outcome has not been studied frequently. It is clear that conduct-disordered youth make up a large percentage of day treatment children (Gabel & Shindledecker, 1991).

Gabel, Finn, and Ahmad (1988) studied the characteristics and outcome of one day hospital sample of 52 children ages 4 to 12 years who were discharged between 1981 and 1985. They also defined preadmission variables as hypothesized predictors of outcome. These preadmission variables were severe aggressive/destructive behavior and suicidal ideation/threats/behavior occurring within 6 months of admission and parental sub-stance abuse and suspected child abuse/maltreatment at any time in the child's life.

Gabel et al. (1988) found that severe aggressive/destructive behavior was the most important predictor of poor outcome, which was defined as recommendations for residential treatment or inpatient hospitalization on discharge. This outcome variable was felt to be especially important for day treatment, where goals generally are to try to maintain children in the community if at all possible. In this study, severe aggressive/destructive behavior prior to admission and an admission diagnosis of conduct disorder (which also predicted poor outcome) were significantly related, although the severe aggressive/destructive behavior variable was more important in predicting outcome.

A later study by Gabel, Swanson, and Shindledecker (1990a) did not replicate these findings for severe aggressive/destructive behavior at two other day treatment programs studied, although this variable showed a trend toward significance in predicting outcome at the other hospital-based day treatment program in the study.

Gabel, Swanson, and Shindledecker (1990b) later studied outcome of a new population of discharged patients from the same day hospital program as in the original study (Gabel et al., 1988), using essentially the same preadmission variables in both studies. Several changes had been made in treatment efforts at the day hospital since the earlier study, however, including the greater use of medication for ADHD and conduct-disordered youths and a broader behavioral approach. Outcome for the severely aggressive/destructive children in the program improved dramatically in the second sample. While the changes had not been systematic or performed in a controlled manner, thereby not allowing definitive statements about whether changes in treatment had resulted in the improved outcome, the authors expressed cautious optimism that multimodal day treatment efforts might be a useful treatment approach for some aggressive or conduct-disordered children from dysfunctional homes.

MULTIMODAL AND BROAD-BASED TREATMENT APPROACHES

Severe conduct disorder in youths generally is a chronic condition having multiple areas of impairment (e.g., academic, interpersonal, familial). Given this picture, it can be argued that interventions that focus on only one aspect of this broadbased disorder may have little overall impact on its course and outcome (Kazdin, 1987a). It is a challenge to provide different types of targeted interventions that have empirical support and standardized approaches. Carefully planned and implemented multimodal approaches may have considerable value, however.

Satterfield, Satterfield, and Schell (1987), for example, report that a subgroup of hyperactive boys previously treated only with medication and brief counseling were found to be at risk for delinquency in adolescence compared to normal controls. Using multimodal treatment, however (a combination of methylphenidate plus "intensive cognitive-behavioral-interpretative treatments based upon an individual treatment plan for each child" (p. 57), Satterfield et al. found significantly lower indicators of delinquency in adolescents who had begun treatment in school-age years with multimodal therapy compared to those in the mainly medication treatment group. Tremblay et al. (1991) also report on favorable outcome for disruptive boys using a multimodal approach including parent training, social skills training, and other elements.

Concluding Comments, Additional Issues

The problems of conduct disorder, violence, and antisocial behavior in youths are among the most pressing mental health and social issues confronting the United States and other parts of the world. The broad scope of these problems, their multidimensional aspects, and their diverse etiologies argue against unidimensional approaches toward solution. While the problems often are described broadly as "conduct disorder," greater specificity requires further clarification and delineation of subtypes that may then be used beneficially in the study, prevention, and treatment of this disorder.

The social perspectives of conduct disorder at this time are daunting. Although Robins (1978) has argued that severe and early forms of conduct

disorder (the type with which this chapter has been most concerned) seem more related to personal and family characteristics than to social class of rearing, others (e.g., Boyle & Offord, 1990; Farrington, 1987) have emphasized the importance of social deprivation and poverty.

Patterson (1982) described a useful model that encompasses these different views on the effects of poverty when he speaks of "disruptors" of effective parenting. Family breakup, child abuse, substance abuse, for example, all are more common in lower socioeconomic groups and are likely to impact on individual families as "disruptors" of effective parent management procedures that then render boys more likely to manifest antisocial behavior.

Conduct disorder should be understood not only in terms of its individual manifestations and associated characteristics, its familial correlates, and its relationship to social disruptors of parenting, however, but also in terms of its developmental course and outcome. The stability of aggressive and antisocial behavior is striking, making early recognition, identification, and intervention crucial.

This view of the broad scope of conduct disorder in youths, and the variables that impact it over a developmental course, is intended to highlight the complexity of the problem and to emphasize the need for intervention and research within its various dimensions and along its long developmental course. (See Loeber and Lahey, 1990.)

Kazdin (1987b) has reviewed prevention efforts with regard to conduct disorder. He emphasizes the need for greater discrimination in assessing the effectiveness of prevention programs. Several approaches, along relational, behavioral, and other domains, have been tried in communities and in schools, with overall unproven efficacy at this point. Kazdin's review indicates that some programs may have had harmful effects, increasing the likelihood of antisocial behavior in some youths, while perhaps decreasing the likelihood of other types of psychopathology in youths who manifested other types of problems at the outset of the program. Further, several programs seem to have had beneficial effects during the course of the prevention effort but failed to have effects powerful enough to sustain improvement on cessation of the program.

Farrington (1987) has studied several hundred

males in London as part of the Cambridge Study in Delinquent Development. He emphasizes another crucial area for research. Very little is known about "protective factors" that might decrease the likelihood of youths developing antisocial and delinquent behavior. In the main, protective factors appear to be the reverse of early precursors of severe antisocial and criminal behavior that have been described earlier. Interestingly, boys from potentially criminogenic backgrounds who, in grade school, were considered nervous and withdrawn, appear less likely to become severely antisocial than boys from similar backgrounds who were aggressive and antisocial at an early age.

Additional research is needed also on the predictors, development, and outcome of conduct disorder and delinquency in females, a relatively neglected topic.

Future progress in the prevention and treatment of conduct disorder seems most likely to come from carefully designed empirical efforts targeted toward several of this disorder's various dimensions (e.g., biological characteristics, social skills deficits) and from efforts directed toward particular high-risk groups (e.g., those in poverty situations). (See Boyle & Offord, 1990; Farrington, 1987.) These efforts should be based on firm conceptual grounds, adhere to accepted research principles, and use standardized and reproducible measures and techniques in order to maximize the likelihood of obtaining meaningful results that can guide future research and intervention.

It also seems crucial to recognize the long-term and severe disabilities of many children and families when youths are identified as having conduct disorder. Kazdin (1987a) has suggested the poten-tial value of considering conduct disorder within a "medical model" that recognizes the disorder as a long-term ongoing condition that potentially has several manifestations along its course and that needs ongoing professional involvement. Keith (1988) also has emphasized the need for continued involvement with antisocial adolescents over several years, providing a number of treatment options, depending on need.

It must be noted, however, as Kazdin (1987a) has pointed out, that mental health efforts by themselves, whether they are screening, assessment, broader evaluation, intervention, or follow-up, cannot be expected to solve the enormous problem of conduct disorder and antisocial behavior in youths.

In this author's view, society contains within itself the breeding grounds for antisocial behavior through the "disruptors" of parental and family functioning (e.g., parental substance abuse, child abuse/maltreatment) that effectively work to reduce youths' attachment to social norms and development of socially oriented behavior. While some forms of antisocial and violent behavior likely would exist even with much improved social and family conditions, greater strides toward lessening antisocial behavior in youths depend on improving the social conditions that impact children and families adversely in so many areas. An extremely important role for mental health researchers and clinicians, therefore, is to bring their understanding of the various dimensions of conduct disorder in youths to the broader social arena where public policies that impact the mental health of youths are determined.

REFERENCES

Achenbach, T. M. (1991a). *Manual for the Child Behavior Checklist/4–18 and 1991 Profile*. Burlington: University of Vermont, Department of Psychiatry.

Achenbach, T. M. (1991b). *Manual for the Teacher's Report Form and 1991 Profile*. Burlington: University of Vermont, Department of Psychiatry.

Akhtar, N., & Bradley, E. F. (1991). Social information processing deficits of aggressive children: Present findings and implications for social skills training. *Clinical Psychology Review, 11,* 621–644.

American Psychiatric Association. (1968). *Diagnostic and statistical manual of mental disorders* (2nd ed.). Washington, DC: Author.

American Psychiatric Association. (1980). *Diagnostic and statistical manual of mental disorders* (3rd ed.). Washington, DC: Author.

American Psychiatric Association. (1987). *Diagnostic and statistical manual of mental disorders* (3rd ed., rev.). Washington, DC: Author.

American Psychiatric Association. (1994). *Diagnostic and statistical manual of mental disorders* (4th ed.). Washington, DC: Author.

Barton, C., & Alexander, J. F. (1981). Functional family therapy. In A. S. Gurman & D. P. Kniskern (Eds.), *Handbook of family therapy* (pp. 403–443). New York: Brunner/Mazel.

Biederman, J., Baldessarini, R. J., Wright, V., Knee, D., & Harmatz, J. S. (1989). A double-blind placebo controlled study of desipramine in the treatment of ADD: I. Efficacy. *Journal of the American Academy of Child and Adolescent Psychiatry, 28,* 777–784.

Biederman, J., Munir, K., & Knee, D. (1987). Conduct and oppositional disorder in clinically referred children with attention deficit disorder: A controlled family study. *Journal of the American Academy of Child and Adolescent Psychiatry, 26,* 724–727.

Bland, R., & Orn, H. (1986). Family violence and psychiatric disorder. *Canadian Journal of Psychiatry, 31,* 129–137.

Blotcky, M. J., Dimperio, T. L., & Gossett, J. T. (1984). Follow-up of children treated in psychiatric hospitals: A review of studies. *American Journal of Psychiatry, 141,* 1499–1507.

Bowden, C. L., Deutsch, C. K., & Swanson, J. M. (1988). Plasma dopamine-beta-hydroxylase and platelet monomine oxidase in attention deficit disorder and conduct disorder. *Journal of the American Academy of Child and Adolescent Psychiatry, 27,* 171–174.

Boyle, M. H., & Offord, D. R. (1990). Primary prevention of conduct disorder: Issues and prospects. *Journal of the American Academy of Child and Adolescent Psychiatry, 29,* 227–233.

Brook, J. S., Whiteman, M., Cohen, P., Shapiro, J., & Balka, E. (1995). Longitudinally predicting late adolescent and young adult drug use: Childhood and adolescent precursors. *Journal of the American Academy of Child and Adolescent Psychiatry, 34,* 1230–1238.

Bruce, M. L., Takeuchi, D. T., & Leaf, P. J. (1991). Poverty and psychiatric status. Longitudinal evidence from the New Haven epidemiological catchment area study. *Archives of General Psychiatry, 48,* 470–474.

Burke, P., Del Beccaro, M., McCauley, F., & Clark, C. (1985). Hallucinations in children. *Journal of the American Academy of Child and Adolescent Psychiatry, 24,* 71–75.

Bureau of Justice Statistics Bulletin. (1990). *Prisoners in 1989.* Washington, DC: U.S. Department of Justice.

Bureau of Justice Statistics Bulletin. (1991). *Correctional population in the United States, 1989.* Washington, DC: U.S. Department of Justice.

Cadoret, R. J., Cain, C. A., & Crown, R. R. (1983). Evidence for gene-environment interaction in the development of adolescent antisocial behavior. *Behavior Genetics, 13,* 301–310.

Cadoret, R. J., & Stewart, M. A. (1991). An adoption study of attention deficit/hyperactivity/aggression and their relationship to adult antisocial personality. *Comprehensive Psychiatry, 32,* 73–82.

Campbell, S. B., Breaux, A. M., Ewing, L. J., & Szumowski, E. K. (1986). Correlates and predictors of hyperactivity and aggression: A longitudinal study of parent-referral problem preschoolers. *Journal of Abnormal Child Psychology, 14,* 217–234.

Campbell, M., Small, A. M., Green, W. H., Jennings, S. J., Perry, R., Bennett, W. G., & Anderson, L. (1984). Behavioral efficacy of haloperidol and lithium carbonate. A comparison in hospitalized aggressive children with conduct disorder. *Archives of General Psychiatry, 41,* 650–656.

Canino, G. J., Bird, H. R., Rubio-Stipec, M., Bravo, M., & Alegria, M. (1990). Children of parents with psychiatric disorders in the community. *Journal of the American Academy of Child and Adolescent Psychiatry, 29,* 398–406.

Chiles, J. A., Miller, M. L., & Cox, G. B. (1980). Depression in an adolescent delinquent population. *Archives of General Psychiatry, 37,* 1179–1184.

Coccaro, E. F., Siever, L. J., Klar, H. M., Marrer, G., Cochrane, K., Cooper, T. B., Mohs, R. C., & Davis, K. L. (1989). Serotonergic studies in patients with affective and personality disorders. *Archives of General Psychiatry, 46,* 587–599.

Curry, J. F., Pelissier, B., Woodford, D. J., & Lochman, J. E. (1988). Violent or assaultive youth: Dimensional and categorical comparisons with mental health samples. *Journal of the American Academy of Child and Adolescent Psychiatry, 27,* 226–232.

Dodge, K. A. (1986). A social information processing model of social competence in children. In M. Perlmutter, (Ed.), *Minnesota symposium on child psychology:* Vol. 18 (pp. 77–125). Hillsdale, NJ: Erlbaum.

Dodge, K. A., Bates, J. E., & Pettit, G. S. (1990). Mechanisms in the cycles of violence. *Science, 250,* 1678–1683.

Dulcan, M. K. (1990). Using psychostimulants to treat behavioral disorders of children and adolescents. *Journal of Child and Adolescent Psychopharmacology, 1,* 7–20.

Dumas, J. E. (1989). Treating antisocial behavior in children: Child and family approaches. *Clinical Psychology Review, 9,* 197–222.

Emery, R. E. (1982). Interparental conflict and the children of discord and divorce. *Psychological Bulletin, 92,* 310–330.

Eppright, T. D., Kashani, J. H., Robison, B. D., & Reid J. C. (1993). Comorbidity of conduct disorder and personality disorders in an incarcerated juvenile population. *American Journal of Psychiatry, 150,* 1233–1236.

Farrington, D. P. (1978). The family backgrounds of aggressive youths. In L. A. Hersov, M. Berger, & D. Shaffer, (Eds.), *Aggression and antisocial behavior in childhood and adolescence* (Vol. 1, pp. 73–93). New York: Pergammon Press.

Farrington, D. P. (1987). Early precursors of frequent offending. In J. Q. Wilson & G. C. Loury (Eds.), *From children to citizen: Vol. 3. Families, schools and delinquency prevention* (pp. 27–50). New York: Springer-Verlag.

Farrington, D. P., Gundry, G., & West, D. J. (1975). The familial transmission of criminality. *Medical Science and Law, 15,* 177–186.

Farrington, D. P., & Hawkins, J. D. (1991). Predicting participation, early onset and later persistence in officially recorded offending. *Criminal Behavior and Mental Health, 1,* 1–33.

Farrington, D. P., Loeber, R., & Van Kamman, W. B. (1990). Long-term criminal outcomes of hyperactive-impulsive-attention deficit and conduct problems in childhood. In L. N. Robins & M. R. Rutter (Eds.), *Straight and devious pathways to adulthood* (pp. 62–81). New York: Cambridge University Press.

Farrington, D. P., & West, D. J. (1981). The Cambridge study in delinquent development. In S. A. Mednick & A. E. Baert (Eds.), *Prospective longitudinal research: An empirical basis for the primary prevention of psychosocial disorders* (pp. 137–145). Oxford: Oxford University Press.

Frick, P. J., Lahey, B. B., Kamphaus, R. W., Loeber, R., Christ, M. A. G., Hart, E. L., & Tannenbaum, L. E. (1991). Academic underachievement and the disruptive behavior disorders. *Journal of Consulting and Clinical Psychology, 59,* 289–294.

Frick, P. J., Lahey, B. B., Loeber, R., Stouthamer-Loeber, M., Green, S., Hart, E. L., & Christ, M. A. G. (1991). Oppositional defiant disorder and conduct disorder in boys: Patterns of behavioral covariation. *Journal of Clinical Child Psychology, 20,* 202–208.

Gabel, S., Finn, M., & Ahmad, A. (1988). Day treatment outcome with severely disturbed children. *Journal of the American Academy Child and Adolescent Psychiatry, 27,* 479–482.

Gabel, S., & Shindledecker, R. (1991). Aggressive behavior in youth: Characteristics, outcome and psychiatric diagnoses. *Journal of the American Academy of Child and Adolescent Psychiatry, 30,* 982–988.

Gabel, S., & Shindledecker, R. (1992). Incarceration in parents of day hospital youth: Relationship to parental substance abuse and suspected child abuse/maltreatment. *International Journal of Partial Hospitalization, 8,* 77–87.

Gabel, S., & Shindledecker, R. (1993). Parental substance abuse: General and specific aspects of its relationship to severe aggression and/or antisocial behavior in youth. *American Journal on Addictions, 2,* 48–58.

Gabel, S., Swanson, A. J., & Shindledecker, R. (1990a). Outcome in children's day treatment: Relationship to preadmission variables. *International Journal of Partial Hospitalization, 6,* 129–137.

Gabel, S., Swanson, A. J., & Shindledecker, R. (1990b). Aggressive children in a day treatment program: Changed outcome and possible explanations. *Child Abuse and Neglect, 14,* 515–523.

Gift, T. E., Strauss, J. S., Ritzler, G. A., Kokes, R. F., & Harder, D. W. (1986). Social class and psychiatric outcome. *American Journal of Psychiatry, 142,* 222–225.

Gittelman, R., Manuzza, S., Shenker, S., & Bonagura, J. (1985). Hyperactive boys almost grown up. I. Psychiatric status. *Archives of General Psychiatry, 42,* 937–947.

Glueck, S., & Glueck, E. (1950). *Unraveling juvenile delinquency.* New York: Commonwealth Fund.

Huesmann, L. R., & Eron, L. D. (1984). Cognitive processes and the persistence of aggressive behavior. *Aggressive Behavior, 10,* 243–251.

Huesmann, L. R., Eron, L. D., Lefkowitz, M. M., & Walder, L. O. (1984). Stability of aggression over time and generations. *Developmental Psychology, 20,* 1120–1134.

Hunt, R. D., Capper, L., & O'Connell, P. (1990). Clonidine in child and adolescent psychiatry. *Journal of Child and Adolescent Psychopharmacology, 1,* 87–102.

Kazdin, A. E. (1987a). Treatment of antisocial behavior in children: Current status and future directions. *Psychological Bulletin, 102,* 187–203.

Kazdin, A. E. (1987b). *Conduct disorders in childhood and adolescence.* Beverly Hills: Sage Publications.

Keith, C. R. (1988). Community treatment of violent youth: Seven years of experience with a class action suit. *Journal of the American Academy of Child and Adolescent Psychiatry, 27,* 600–604.

Kernberg, P. F., & Chazen, S. E. (1991). *Children with conduct disorders. A psychotherapy manual.* New York: Basic Books.

Kernberg, P. F., Clarkin, A. J., Greenblatt, E., & Cohen, J. (1992). The Cornell Interview of peers and friends: Development and validation. *Journal of the American Academy of Child and Adolescent Psychiatry, 31,* 483–489.

Kovacs, M., Paulauskas, S., Gatsonis, C., & Richards, C. (1988). Depressive disorders in childhood III. A longitudinal study of comorbidity with and risk for conduct disorders. *Journal of Affective Disorders, 15,* 205–217.

Klorman, R., Brumaghim, J. T., Salzman, L. F., Strauss, J., Borgstedt, A. D., McBride, M. C., & Loeb, S. (1988). Effects of methylphenidate on attention-deficit hyperactivity disorders with and without aggressive-noncompliant features. *Journal of Abnormal Psychology, 97,* 413–422.

Kruesi, M. J. P., Rapoport, J. C., Hamburger, S., Hibbs, E., Potter, W. Z., Lenane, M., & Brown, G. L. (1990). Cerebrospinal fluid monomaine metabolites, aggression, and impulsivity in disruptive behavior disorders of children and adolescents. *Archives of General Psychiatry, 47,* 419–426.

Lahey, B. B., Loeber, R., Hart, E. L., Frick, P. J., Applegate, B., Zhang, Q., Green, S. M., & Russo, M. F. (1995). Four-year longitudinal study of conduct disorder in boys: Patterns and predictors of persistence. *Journal of Abnormal Psychology, 104,* 83–93.

Lahey, B. B., Piacentini, J. C., McBurnett, K., Stone, P., Hartdagen, S., & Hynd, G. (1988). Psychopathology in the parents of children with conduct disorder and hyperactivity. *Journal of the American Academy of Child and Adolescent Psychiatry, 27,* 163–170.

Lewis, D. O., Lovely, R., Yaeger, C., & Femina, D. D. (1989). Toward a theory of the genesis of violence: A follow-up study of delinquents. *Journal of the American Academy of Child and Adolescent Psychiatry, 28,* 431–436.

Lewis, D. O., Lovely, R., Yaeger, C., Ferguson, G., Friedman, M., Sloane, G., Friedman, H., & Pincus, J. H. (1988). Intrinsic and environmental characteristics of juvenile murderers. *Journal of the American Academy of Child and Adolescent Psychiatry, 27,* 582–587.

Lewis, D. O., Pincus, J. H., Bard, B., Richardson, E., Prichey, L. S., Feldman, M., & Yaeger, C. (1988). Neuropsychiatric, psychoeducational, and family characteristics of 14 juveniles condemned to death in the United States. *American Journal of Psychiatry, 145,* 584–589.

Lewis, D. O., Pincus, J. H., Feldman, M., Jackson, L., & Bard, B. (1986). Psychiatric, neurological, and psychoeducational characteristics of 15 death row inmates in the United States. *American Journal of Psychiatry, 143,* 838–845.

Lewis, D. O., Pincus, J. H., Lovely, R., Spitzer, E., & Moy, E. (1987). Biopsychosocial characteristics of matched samples of delinquents and non delinquents. *Journal of the American Academy of Child and Adolescent Psychiatry, 26,* 744–752.

Lewis, D. O., Shanok, S. S., Pincus, J. H., & Glaser, G. H. (1979). Violent juvenile delinquents. Psychiatric, neurological, psychological, and abuse factors. *Journal of the American Academy of Child Psychiatry, 18,* 307–319.

Linniola, M., DeJong, J., & Virkkunen, M. (1989). Family history of alcoholism in violent offenders and impulsive fire setters. *Archives of General Psychiatry, 46,* 613–616.

Loeber, R. (1982). The stability of antisocial and delinquent behavior: A review. *Child Development, 53,* 1431–1446.

Loeber, R. (1990). Development and risk factors for juvenile antisocial behavior and delinquency. *Clinical Psychology Review, 10,* 1–41.

Loeber, R. (1991a). Questions and advances in the study of developmental pathways. In D. Cicchetti & S. Toth (Eds.), *Models and integrations. Rochester symposium on developmental psychopathology: Volume 3* (pp. 97–114). Rochester, NY: University of Rochester Press.

Loeber, R. (1991b). Antisocial behavior: More enduring than changeable? *Journal of the American Academy of Child and Adolescent Psychiatry, 30,* 393–397.

Loeber, R., Brinthaupt, V. P., & Green, S. M. (1990). Attention deficits, impulsivity and hyperactivity with or without conduct problems: Relationships to delinquency and unique contextual factors. In R. J. McMahon & De V. Peters (Eds.), *Behavior disorders of adolescence. Research, intervention, and policy in clinical and school settings* (pp. 39–61). New York: Plenum Press.

Loeber, R., & Keenan, K. (1994). The interaction between conduct disorder and its comorbid conditions: Effects of age and gender. *Clinical Psychology Review, 14,* 497–523.

Loeber, R., Lahey, B. B. (1989). Recommendations for research on disruptive behavior disorders of childhood and adolescence. In B. B. Lahey & A. E. Kazdin (Eds.), *Advances in clinical child psychology: Vol. 12* (pp. 221–251). New York: Plenum Press.

Loeber, R., Lahey, B. B., & Thomas, C. (1991). Diagnostic conundrum of oppositional defiant disorder and conduct disorder. *Journal of Abnormal Psychology, 100,* 379–390.

Loeber, R., & Patterson, G. R. (1981). The aggressive child: A concomitant of a coercive system. *Advances in Family Intervention, Assessment and Theory, 2,* 47–87.

Loeber, R., Stouthamer-Loeber, M., Van Kammen, W., & Farrington, D. P. (1991). Initiation, escalation and desistance in juvenile offending and their correlates. *Journal of Criminal Law and Criminology, 82,* 36–82.

Mann, J. J. (1987). Psychobiologic predictors of suicide. *Journal of Clinical Psychiatry, 48* (12, Suppl.), 39–43.

Mannuzza, S., Gittelman Klein, R., & Addalli, K. A. (1991). Young adult mental status of hyperactive boys and their brothers: A prospective follow-up study. *Journal of the American Academy of Child and Adolescent Psychiatry, 30,* 743–751.

Mannuzza, S., Gittelman Klein, R., Horowitz Konig, P., & Giampino, T. L. (1989). Hyperactive boys almost grown up. IV. Criminality and its relationship to psychiatric status. *Archives of General Psychiatry, 46,* 1073–1079.

Mannuzza, S., Klein, R. G., Bonagura, N., Malloy, P., Giampino, T. L., & Addalli, K. A. (1991), Hyperactive boys almost grown up. V. Replication of psychiatric status. *Archives of General Psychiatry, 48,* 77–83.

McCord, J. (1978). A thirty year follow up of treatment effects. *American Psychologist, 33,* 284–289.

McCord, J., & McCord, W. (1963). The effects of parental role model on criminality. In N. J. Smelser & W. T. Smelser (Eds.), *Personality and social systems* (pp. 194–202). New York: John Wiley & Sons. (Reprinted from *Journal of Social Issues, 14,* 66–75, 1958.)

McGee, R., Williams, S., & Silva, P. A. (1984). Behavioral and developmental characteristics of aggressive, hyperactive and aggressive-hyperactive boys. *Journal of the American Academy of Child Psychiatry, 23,* 270–279.

Morris, P. W., Horne, A. M., Jessell, J. C., Passmore, J. L., Walker, J. M., & Sayger, T. V. (1988). Behavioral and cognitive characteristics of fathers of aggressive and well-behaved boys. *Journal of Cognitive Psychotherapy: An International Quarterly, 2,* 251–265.

Offer, D., Ostrov, E., & Howard, K. I. (1981). *The adolescent. A psychological self-portrait.* New York: Basic Books.

Offord, D. R., Alder, R. J., & Boyle, M. H. (1986). Prevalence and sociodemographic correlates of conduct disorder. *American Journal of Social Psychiatry, 4,* 272–278.

Olweus, D. (1979). Stability of aggressive reaction patterns in males: A review. *Psychological Bulletin, 86,* 852–875.

Olweus, D. (1980). Familial and temperamental determinants of aggressive behavior in adolescent boys: A causal analysis. *Developmental Psychology, 16,* 644–660.

Olweus, D. (1984). Development of stable aggressive reaction patterns in males. *Advances in the Study of Aggression, 1,* 103–137.

Parke, R. D., & Slaby, R. H. (1983). The development of aggression. In P. H. Mussen (Ed.), *Handbook of child psychology: Vol. 4. Socialization, Personality and Social Development* (4th ed., pp. 547–641). New York: John Wiley & Sons.

Patterson, G. R. (1982). *Coercive family practice.* Eugene, OR: Castalia Publishing Co.

Patterson, G. R. (1986). Performance models for antisocial boys. *American Psychologist, 41,* 432–444.

Patterson, G. R., DeBaryshe, B. D., Ramsey, E. (1989). A developmental perspective on antisocial behavior. *American Psychologist, 44,* 329–335.

Pfeiffer, S. U., & Strzelecki, S. C. (1990). Inpatient psychiatric treatment of children and adolescents: A review of outcome studies. *Journal of the American Academy of Child and Adolescent Psychiatry, 29,* 847–853.

Pliszka, S. R., Rogeness, G. A., & Medrano, M. A. (1988). DBH, MHPG and MAO in children with depressive, anxiety and conduct disorders: Relationship to diagnosis and symptom ratings. *Psychiatric Research, 24,* 35–44.

Pliszka, S. R., Rogeness, G. A., Renner, P., Sherman, J., & Broussard, T. (1988). Plasma neurochemistry in juvenile offenders. *Journal of the American Academy of Child and Adolescent Psychiatry, 27,* 588–594.

Puig-Antich, J. (1982). Major depression and conduct disorder in prepuberty. *Journal of the American Academy of Child Psychiatry, 21,* 118–128.

Quay, H. C. (1965). Psychopathic personality as pathological stimulation-seeking. *American Journal of Psychiatry, 122,* 180–183.

Quay, H. C. (1977). Psychopathic behavior. Reflections on its nature, origins and treatment. In I. C. Uzgiris & F. Weizman (Eds.), *The structuring of experience* (pp. 317–383). New York: Plenum Press.

Quay, H. C. (1986). Classification. In H. C. Quay and J. S. Werry (Eds.), *Psychopathological disorders of childhood* (3rd ed., pp. 1–34). New York: John Wiley & Sons.

Raine, A., & Jones, R. (1987). Attention, autonomic arousal, and personality in behaviorally disordered children. *Journal of Abnormal Child Psychology, 15,* 583–599.

Raine, F., Venables, P. H., & Williams, M. (1990). Relationships between central and autonomic measures of arousal at age 15 years and criminality at age 24

years. *Archives of General Psychiatry, 47,* 1003–1007.

Rapoport, J. L., & Ismond, D. R. (1990). *DSM-III-R training guide for diagnosis of childhood disorders.* New York: Brunner/Mazel.

Reeves, J. C., Werry, J. S., Elkind, G. S., & Zametkin, A. (1987). Attention deficit, oppositional, and anxiety disorders in children. II. Clinical characteristics. *Journal of the American Academy of Child and Adolescent Psychiatry, 26,* 144–155.

Robins, L. N. (1970). The adult development of the antisocial child. *Seminars in Psychiatry, 2,* 420–434.

Robins, L. N. (1978). Sturdy childhood predictors of adult antisocial behavior: Replications from longitudinal studies. *Psychological Medicine, 8,* 611–622.

Robins, L. N., & Lewis, R. G. (1966). The role of the antisocial family in school completion and delinquency: A three-generation study. *Sociological Quarterly, 7,* 500–514.

Robins, L. N., & Price, R. K. (1991). Adult disorders predicted by childhood conduct problems. Results from the NIMH epidemiologic catchment area project. *Psychiatry, 54,* 116–132.

Robins, L. N., & Ratcliff, K. S. (1979). Risk factors in the continuation of childhood antisocial behavior into adulthood. *International Journal of Mental Health, 7,* 96–116.

Robins, L. N., West, P. A., & Herjanic, B. L. (1975). Arrests and delinquency in two generations: A study of Black urban families and their children. *Journal of Child Psychology and Psychiatry, 16,* 125–140.

Rogeness, G. A., Crawford, L., & McNamara, A. (1989). Plasma dopamine-B-hydroxylase and preschool behavior in children with conduct disorder. *Child Psychiatry and Human Development, 20,* 149–156.

Rogeness, G. A., Hernandez, J. M., Macedo, C. A., Amrung, S. A., & Hoppe, S. K. (1986). Near zero plasma dopamine-beta-hydroxylase and conduct disorder in emotionally disturbed boys. *Journal of the American Academy of Child Psychiatry, 25,* 521–527.

Rogeness, G. A., Hernandez, J. M., Macedo, C. A., & Mitchell, E. L. (1982). Biochemical differences in children with conduct disorder socialized and undersocialized. *American Journal of Psychiatry, 139,* 307–311.

Rogeness, G. A., Hernandez, J. M., Macedo, C. A., Mitchell, E. L., Amrung, S. A., & Harris, W. R. (1984). Clinical characteristics of emotionally disturbed boys with very low activities of dopamine-beta-hydroxylase. *Journal of the American Academy of Child Psychiatry, 23,* 203–208.

Rogeness, G. A., Javors, M. A., Maas, J. W., & Macedo, C. A. (1990). Catecholamines and diagnoses in children. *Journal of the American Academy of Child and Adolescent Psychiatry, 29,* 234–241.

Rogeness, G. A., Javors, M. A., Maas, J. W., Macedo, C. A., & Fischer, C. (1987). Plasma dopamine-beta-hydroxylase, HVA, MHPG, and conduct disorder in emotionally disturbed boys. *Biological Psychiatry*, 22, 1155–1158.

Rogeness, G. A., Maas, J. W., Javors, M. A., Macedo, C. A., Harris, W. R., & Hoppe, S. K. (1988). Diagnoses, catecholamine metabolism and plasma-dopamine-beta-hydroxylase. *Journal of the American Academy of Child and Adolescent Psychiatry*, 27, 121–125.

Russo, M. F., Lahey, B. B., Christ, M. A. G., Frick, P. J., McBurnett, K., Walker, J. L., Loeber, R., Stouthamer-Loeber, M., & Green, S. (1991). Preliminary development of a sensation seeking scale for children. *Personality and Individual Differences*, 12, 339–405.

Rutter, M. (1971). Parent-child separation: Psychological effects on the children. *Journal of Child Psychology and Psychiatry*, 12, 233–260.

Rutter, M. (1978). Family, area and school influences in the genesis of conduct disorders. In L. A. Hersov, M. Berger, & D. Shaffer (Eds.), *Aggression and antisocial behavior in childhood and adolescence* (Book Suppl. to the *Journal of Child Psychology and Psychiatry*, No. 1). New York: Pergamon Press.

Rutter, M., Cox, A., Tupling, C., Berger, M., & Yule, W. (1975). Attainment and adjustment in two geographical areas. I. The prevalence of psychiatric disorder. *British Journal of Psychiatry*, 126, 493–509.

Rutter, M., & Giller, H. (1983). *Juvenile delinquency: Trends and perspectives*. New York: Guilford Press.

Rutter, M., & Quinton, D. (1984). Parental psychiatric disorder: Effects on children. *Psychological Medicine*, 14, 853–880.

Rutter, M., Tizard, J., & Whitmore, K. (Eds.). (1970). *Education, health and behavior*. London: Longman.

Rutter, M., Tizard, J., Yule, W., Graham, P., & Whitmore, K. (1976). Research report: Isle of Wight Studies 1964–1974. *Psychological Medicine, 6*, 313–332.

Satterfield, J. H., Satterfield, B. T., & Schell, A. M. (1987). Therapeutic interventions to prevent delinquency in hyperactive boys. *Journal of the American Academy of Child and Adolescent Psychiatry*, 26, 56–64.

Shapiro, S. K., & Garfinkel, B. D. (1986). The occurrence of behavior disorders in children: The interdependence of attention deficit disorder and conduct disorder. *Journal of the American Academy of Child Psychiatry, 26*, 809–819.

Shamsie, S. J. (1981). Antisocial adolescents: Our treatments do not work—Where do we go from here? *Canadian Journal of Psychiatry, 26*, 357–364.

Stewart, M. A., deBlois, C. S., Meardon, J., & Cummings, C. (1980). Aggressive conduct disorder of children. The clinical picture. *Journal of Nervous and Mental Disease, 168*, 604–610.

Stoff, D. M., Friedman, E., Pollock, L., Vitiello, B., Kendall, P. C., & Bridger, W. H. (1989). Elevated platelet MAO is related to impulsivity in disruptive behavior disorders. *Journal of the American Academy of Child and Adolescent Psychiatry, 28*, 754–760.

Szatmari, P., Boyle, M., & Offord, D. R. (1989). ADDH and conduct disorder: Degree of diagnostic overlap and differences among correlates. *Journal of the American Academy of Child and Adolescent Psychiatry, 28*, 865–872.

Taylor, E., Schacher, R., Thorley, G., & Wieselberg, M. (1986). Conduct disorder and hyperactivity: I. Separation of hyperactivity and antisocial conduct in British child psychiatry patients. *British Journal of Psychiatry, 149*, 760–770.

Tharinger, D. J., & Koranek, M. E. (1988). Children of alcoholics—at risk and unserved: A review of research and service roles for school psychologists. *School Psychology Review, 17*, 166–191.

Tremblay, R. E., McCord, J., Boileau, H., Carlibois, P., Gagnon, C., LeBlanc, M., & Larivee, S. (1991). Can disruptive boys be helped to become competent? *Psychiatry, 54*, 148–161.

Virkkunen, M., DeJong, J., Bartko, J., Goodwin, F., & Linnoila, M. (1989). Relationship of psychobiological variables to recidivism in violent offenders and impulsive fire setters. A follow-up study. *Archives of General Psychiatry, 46*, 600–603.

Virkkunen, M., DeJong, J., Bartko, J., & Linnoila, M. (1989). Psychobiological concomitants of history of suicide attempts among violent offenders and impulsive fire setters. *Archives of General Psychiatry, 46*, 604–606.

Walker, H. M., Shinn, M. R., O'Neill, R. E., & Ramsey, E. (1987). A longitudinal assessment of the development of antisocial behavior in boys: Rationale, methodology, and first-year results. *Remedial and Special Education, 8*, 7–16, 27.

Walker, J. L., Lahey, B. B., Russo, M. F., Frick, P. J., Christ, M. A. G., McBurnett, K., Loeber, R., Stouthamer-Loeber, M., & Green, S. M. (1991). Anxiety, inhibition, and conduct disorder in children: I. Relation to social impairment. *Journal of the American Academy of Child and Adolescent Psychiatry, 30*, 187–191.

Werry, J. S., Reeves, J. C., & Elkind, G. S. (1987). Attention deficit, conduct, oppositional, and anxiety disorders in children: I. A review of research on differentiating characteristics. *Journal of the American Academy of Child and Adolescent Psychiatry, 26*, 133–143.

West, M. O., & Prinz, R. J. (1987). Parental alcoholism and childhood psychopathology. *Psychological Bulletin, 102*, 204–218.

Widom, C. S. (1989a). Does violence beget violence? A critical examination of the literature. *Psychological Bulletin, 106*, 3–28.

Widom, C. S. (1989b). Child abuse, neglect, and adult behavior: Research design and findings on criminality, violence and child abuse. *American Journal of Orthopsychiatry, 59*, 355–367.

Willock, B. (1986). Narcissistic vulnerability in the hyperaggressive child: The disregarded (unloved, uncared for) self. *Psychoanalytic Psychology, 3*, 59–80.

Wolfe, D. A. (1987). *Child abuse. Implication for child development and psychopathology*. Newbury Park, CA: Sage Publications.

Woodside, M. (1988). Research on children of alcoholics: Past and future. *British Journal of Addiction, 83*, 785–792.

Woolston, J. L., Rosenthal, S. L., Riddle, M. A., Sparrow, S. S., Cicchetti, D., & Zimmerman, L. D. (1989). Childhood comorbidity of anxiety/affective disorders and behavior disorders. *Journal of the American Academy of Child and Adolescent Psychiatry, 28*, 707–713.

Zuckerman, M. (1989). Personality in the third dimension: A psychobiological approach. *Personality, Individual Differences, 10*, 391–418.

Zuckerman, M., Buchsbaum, M. S., & Murphy, D. L. (1980). Sensation seeking and its biological correlates. *Psychological Bulletin, 88*, 187–214.

Zuckerman, M., Kolin, E. A., Price, L., & Zoob, I. (1964). Development of a sensation seeking scale. *Journal of Consulting Psychology, 28*, 477–482.

35 / Acute and Chronic Brain Syndrome in the School-Age Child

Elisabeth Guthrie

Definition of Brain Syndromes

Affect, cognition, and behavior are the product of an integrated and well-functioning brain. When an aspect of the brain's environment is significantly changed, its function deviates from the routine. The degree to which brain functions are altered by a pathophysiologic insult will depend on that the nervous system's current state, the nature and extend of the insult, and the interventions that follow. Even the most subtle brain syndromes may present early with changes in mental status. For the purposes of this chapter, the term "organic brain syndrome" refers to any deviation in mental status or behavior that is attributable to a pathophysiological process; "encephalopathy" is used interchangeably with that term.

By definition, acute brain syndromes differ from chronic brain syndromes in the duration of observable symptoms. Certain insults, such as toxic ingestion and infectious processes, may be more likely to result in acute encephalopathic changes. Other pathology, such as tumors and inborn errors of metabolism, result in more chronic outcomes. A chronic brain syndrome may ensue from an acute encephalopathic process. Individuals with preexisting chronic brain syndromes are usually more susceptible to further neurological deterioration when acutely stressed (Carter & Gold, 1974). Occasionally, subtle, short-lived disturbances in brain function may go undiagnosed.

Chronic brain syndromes in children, however, have a greater likelihood of being diagnosed, as the cognitive and motoric challenges of childhood afford more opportunity for clinical presentation.

The School-Age Brain

Children are particularly susceptible to organic brain syndromes. Delirium with fever, heightened sensitivity to drug side effects, and a relative proclivity toward seizures in response to noxious stimuli are examples of the increased susceptibility of the pediatric brain to acute stress.

The cerebral cortex in childhood has a greater capacity to compensate for interhemispheric losses than that of the adult, presumably due to its relative functional immaturity. An example of this capacity is the transfer of cortically specific tasks, such as language functions, from one hemisphere to the other following focal injury, something the mature brain is much less capable of doing. While the developmental immaturity of the pediatric brain bodes well in the face of unilateral injury, this same quality makes the child's brain more vulnerable to damage from diffuse injury (Rutter, 1983).

The morbidity associated with brain syndromes in the school-age population is not only a function of neuronal immaturity but also reflects the fact that the child is at the mere beginning of his or her education. Disruption of the brain's potential to perceive, integrate, retain, and respond to stimuli profoundly affects a child's capacity to learn.

Mechanisms of Injury in Brain Syndromes

The central nervous system has the highest metabolic demands of any organ in the human body. In view of the fact that a child's brain is proportionally larger than that of the adult, the fractional energy requirements are even greater in childhood. Neurons expend energy in the maintenance of membrane potentials; in the synthesis, storage, and secretion of neurotransmitters; and in the production of cellular structures. The brain requires a minimum of 5 milligrams glucose and 3.3 milliliters oxygen per minute per 100 grams of tissue to sustain its baseline level of activity. Disruption of the supply, bioavailability, or utilization of these essential substrates, as occurs, for example, with hypoxia, hypoglycemia, shock, or inflammation, will result in central nervous system dysfunction (Plum & Posner, 1982).

Fluid and electrolyte balance are also critical in maintaining the integrity of the nervous system. The brain is 80% water by weight. Large or acute osmolar shifts result in encephalopathy via a variety of pathophysiologic mechanisms. Relative hypo-osmolality occurs following organic insults resulting in the inappropriate secretion of antidiuretic hormone or when excessively aggressive rehydration results in water intoxication. Hyperosmolar states may be seen in cases of severe diarrhea and diabetic ketoacidosis (Krane, Rockoff, Wallman, & Wolfsdorf, 1984). Both conditions result in fluid shifts between the intracellular and intravascular compartments of the brain. The blood-brain barrier is selectively permeable and accommodates more slowly to changes in electrolyte concentrations. Hypo- and hyperosmolar states directly impair the integrity of the blood-brain barrier, resulting in brain shrinkage or cerebral edema (Devivo, 1996).

Inflammation of the brain also results in direct tissue damage. Inflammation may occur secondary to compartmental osmolar shifts, resulting in hemorrhages and thrombosis, or due to infection, immune reactions, or trauma. The ensuing damage may include demyelination, destruction of oligodendrocytes, glial formation, and scarring; any or all of these may occur focally or diffusely, depending on the nature of the insult. Commonly the end result is impaired dendritic communication and brain dysfunction.

Traumatic Brain Injury

Injury to the head is a frequent occurrence in childhood. Approximately 5 million incidents of pediatric head trauma occur yearly (Yudofsky & Hales, 1992). Moving vehicle accidents, falls, sports injuries, gunshot wounds, and child abuse are among the major sources of severe head injury. Children with intellectual impairment and impulse control disorders are at increased risk for accidents due to poor judgment. Consequently, children with preexisting brain syndromes are overrepresented among the head injured population. Several factors appear to exert a profound effect on children's recovery from head injury. These factors include children's preaccident behavior, as mentioned, as well as their age, psychosocial status, and the parental reaction to injury. The psychosocially disadvantaged younger child who was behaviorally difficult prior to injury and whose parents tend to be overindulgent has the poorest prognosis for outcome (Brown, Chadwick, Shaffer, Rutter, & Traub, 1981; Kriel, Krach, & Panser, 1989).

Certain areas of the brain are particularly vulnerable to specific types of trauma. Direct impact occurs with moving vehicle accidents, and, while all areas of the brain may be injured, the frontal lobes are involved most frequently. Disturbances of frontal lobe functioning present with prominent personality and behavioral changes, including disorderliness, argumentativeness, anxiety, and suspiciousness. In prefrontal-frontal syndromes, cognitive functioning typically is preserved, whereas personality and judgment demonstrate profound alterations. The temporal lobes are particularly vulnerable to the shearing forces generated by acceleration-deceleration injuries.

In contrast to frontal lobe injuries, damage to the temporal and parietal areas results in a significant cognitive change. Concentration, integration of information, the use of language, abstractions, calculations, and the ability to categorize, generalize, and prioritize are only some examples of the areas of neuropsychological deficits that may occur following temporal and parietal lobe damage. Memory and learning are profoundly impaired with this type of injury, with younger children generally being more susceptible to long-term memory deficits than adolescents (Chadwick, Rutter, Brown, Shaffer, & Traub, 1981; Ghajar & Hariri, 1992; Johnston & Gerring, 1992; Rosman, 1994; Rutter, Chadwick, Shaffer, & Brown, 1980).

Closed Head Injury

Closed head injury occurs when there is trauma to the head and the cranium remains intact. Trauma to underlying brain tissue varies with the nature and localization of the injury sustained. Contusion, lacerations, contrecoup effects, subdural bleeding, and shearing injuries are frequent complications (Menkes & Till, 1995a; Rusonis, 1990). Loss of consciousness often occurs and frequently is followed by a posttraumatic amnestic period. The duration of this posttraumatic amnestic period has been shown to be prognostic of residual cognitive deficits (Chadwick et al., 1981; Filley, Cranberg, Alexander, & Hart, 1987).

Subdural bleeding occurs supratentorially 5 to 10 times more frequently than epidural bleeds (Johnston & Gerring, 1992). The precipitating trauma giving rise to subdurals often is minimal, with loss of consciousness occurring in a minority of individuals (Johnston & Gerring, 1992; Menkes & Till, 1995a; Rusonis, 1990). Subdural collections occur when veins transversing the subdural space from the cortex to the underlying surface of the dura are torn. Blood oozes into the subdural space, where clot and eventual cyst formation occur. Alterations in intracranial pressure reflect the changes in cyst size and are evidenced clinically in fluctuations in consciousness and other symptoms. Nonspecific complaints of headache, dizziness, diplopia, personality changes, and memory impairments are seen in children and ad-

olescents with chronic subdurals. Diagnosis often is confounded by the diffuse and variable nature of these complaints. Electroencephalogram findings are rarely helpful but may reveal low voltages and slow waves on the same side as the subdural. Computed tomography (CT) scans and occasionally magnetic resonance imaging are needed to confirm the diagnosis. Surgical intervention is almost always indicated and involves opening the dura and suctioning the subdural collection (Menkes & Till, 1995a).

An epidural hematoma results from disruption of a major vascular channel, such as the middle meningeal artery or a large venous sinus, that rapidly accumulates a potentially lethal blood clot between the dura and inner table of the skull. The resultant increase in intracranial pressure presents as an acute change in mental status that progresses rapidly to coma and death if not attended to on an emergency basis. Neurosurgical evacuation of the clot along with identification and control of the bleeding source can be lifesaving interventions if implemented early, prior to the onset of coma (Menkes & Till, 1995a; Rosman, 1994).

Open Head Injury

Open head injuries are distinguished from closed head injuries by their pathophysiology and complications. Fractures, penetrating wounds, local trauma, and intracranial hematomas, with associated problems of infection and thrombosis, are seen in open injuries to the head. Increased intracranial pressure, which is a frequent complication of closed head injury, is uncommon in open head trauma. Consciousness is preserved in the majority of cases, making the posttraumatic amnestic period of less prognostic value. School-age children who survive gunshot wounds to the head have been shown to have greater deficits in adaptive behavior and attention than a control group of youths with closed head injuries (Ewing-Cobbs, Thompson, Milner, & Fletcher, 1994). Epilepsy is a complication in 50% of open head injuries, as compared to only 5% of closed head trauma (Johnston & Gerring, 1992; Rosman, 1994).

Toxic/Metabolic Encephalopathy

Toxic encephalopathy may result from endogenous substrate deficiencies, inborn errors of metabolism, organ failure, or exogenous poisoning from drugs and other agents. Delirium is the typical clinical presentation of an acute metabolic brain syndrome. The manifest features of delirium include fluctuating consciousness, impaired memory, inattention, disorientation, and perceptual distortions. Psychomotor agitation or retardation and abnormalities in sleep/wake cycles are common findings. Electroencephalogram findings mirror the clinical picture, revealing gross abnormalities in cortical activity. Chronic metabolic encephalopathy presents a picture of deteriorating cognitive and intellectual skills and delayed or regressed development.

Substrate Deficiency

Anoxia and hypoxia may result in organic brain syndromes via a variety of mechanisms. Anoxic anoxia is due to an absolute decreased availability of oxygen, due either to environmental factors such as high altitudes or to impaired pulmonary diffusion. Pediatric examples of respiratory disease compromising diffusion include bronchopulmonary dysplasia and cystic fibrosis. Evidence of either acute delirium or chronic dementia may ensue, depending on the severity and duration of anoxia. Total ablation of the oxygen supply to the brain will result in a loss of consciousness in a matter of seconds. After 4 minutes of no oxygen, brain cells begin to die. Conditions that lower the brain's metabolic demands, such as coma and hypothermia, serve to buffer the lethal effects of anoxic and ischemic insults (Plum & Posner, 1982).

Anemic anoxia, as the name suggests, refers to oxygen insufficiency secondary to decreased hemoglobin bioavailability. Acute anemic anoxia may be seen in cases of smoke inhalation or methanol ingestion, where the oxygen molecule is displaced by carbon monoxide or methyl hemoglobin, with a resultant drop in the cerebral blood flow oxygen saturation. A deterioration in mental status is heralded by an acute change in consciousness. Severe anemia, as seen in some cases of sickle cell disease, may result in a slower decline in central nervous system functioning. Memory, intellect, and psychomotor changes are subtle and may be detectable only on neuropsychological testing.

Hypoglycemia is not uncommon in diabetics and children with galactosemia. Extremely low blood sugar has its greatest clinical impact on cortical brain function, producing a picture of delirium, social impropriety, irritability, or withdrawal. Convulsions are often a symptom of hypoglycemia, and focal deficits may be seen on neurological examination. The brainstem usually is unaffected. Other important metabolic causes of organic brain syndromes in the child with diabetes include ketoacidosis, lactic acidosis, hyponatremia, hypophosphatemia, and hyperosmolar coma (Plum & Posner, 1982).

Inborn Errors of Metabolism

Many inborn errors of metabolism affect the brain's function. Only those disorders presenting with symptoms of organic brain syndrome in the school-age years will be outlined here. In general, gray matter diseases tend to present with disturbances in intellect and behavior more frequently than disorders of white matter. The lipidoses are diseases of the gray matter, where excess lipid is accumulated in neuronal tissue. Juvenile Gaucher's disease, also known as Type 3, is a deficiency of glucocerebroside-B-glucosidase, and may present in the school-age years. It is associated with central nervous system deterioration, mental confusion, motor impairments, and progressive spasticity. In the juvenile-onset variety of Niemann-Pick disease, sphingomyelinase deficiency results in abnormalities of bahavior and intellectual decline. Ceroid lipofuscinoses, also known as Spielmeyer-Vogt disease, present with mild ataxia, dystonia, dementia, and behavioral changes. Sanfilippo's syndrome is a mucupolysaccharidois characterized by disordered degradation of keratan sulfate resulting in deteriorating cognitive function during the school-age years (Chutorian & Paulakis, 1992).

Leukodystrophies are white matter diseases

usually associated with demyelination. Metachromatic leukodystrophy appears in an infantile and a juvenile form; both are due to the impaired metabolism of arylsulfatase A, with consequent accumulation of sulfatide. The older child with this disorder will demonstrate psychotic mental processes, including thought disorders and delusions, as well as dementia (Naylor & Alessi, 1989). Adrenoleukodystrophy is an X-linked abnormality of myelination that presents clinically with emotional lability, behavioral disturbances, and dementia (Kitchin, Cohen-Cole, & Mickel, 1987).

Aminoacidopathies such as phenylketonuria and maple syrup disease generally result in mental retardation if not diagnosed early in infancy. Urea cycle disorders are episodic in nature, presenting in early childhood and through the school-age years with transient and intermittent encephalopathy. Huntington's chorea may present during the school-age years. The presence of chorea in a child with cognitive or other psychiatric dysfunction should alert the clinician to a possible diagnosis of Huntington's. Wilson's disease, or hepatolenticular degeneration, is an inherited disorder of copper metabolism affecting multiple organ systems including the brain. Overt manifestations may occur in childhood if the hepatic dysfunction is severe enough. Psychiatric and neurological symptoms usually present later in the course of the disease and are characterized by behavioral disturbances, dysarthria, deterioration in school performance, personality changes, and even psychosis. Wilson's is a treatable condition, so the prompt diagnosis is of paramount importance. Acute intermittent porphyria is a disorder of heme synthesis that may cause a school-age child to display episodic bouts of bizarre behavior, abdominal pain, and occasionally seizures. Ingestion of certain drugs, particularly barbiturates, sulfonamides, and alcohol, is thought to aggravate attacks in many cases.

Exogenous Toxins

As stated earlier, children are particularly sensitive to untoward effects of medications; occasionally even therapeutic dosages of common drugs may result in symptoms of an organic brain syndrome. Other causes of metabolic encephalopathy from exogenous agents include overdosage with medications and exposure to environmental poisons. Table 35.1 lists numerous pediatric drugs that have been associated with delirium. Certain individuals are more susceptible to drug side effects than others, and this susceptibility is compounded by other systemic stresses, such as fever, pain, and sensory deprivation.

Approximately 1 million poisonings occur yearly in the under-6-year-old population; the vast majority of these are accidental. While the number drops significantly in the later school-age years, the incidence remains high among cognitively impaired children. There is also a significant increase in the occurrence of intentional overdosing in later childhood. The drugs most often implicated in toxic encephalopathy secondary to accidental or volitional overdosing are aspirin and tricyclic antidepressants. Salicylate poisoning results in the uncoupling of oxidative phosphorization resulting in hyperthermia, tachycardia, tachypnea, and hypoglycemia. The child who has ingested a large amount of aspirin appears acutely confused and agitated, as the salicylate effect is compounded by the central nervous system response to fever and hypoglycemia. Tricyclic antidepressant overdosing results in an anticholinergic delirium. Disorientation, hallucinations, fever, impaired visual accommodation, and flushing are clinical features.

TABLE 35.1

Common Pediatric Drugs Associated with Delirium

ACTH	Ibuprofen
Acyclovir	Indomethacin
Aminophylline	Isoniazid
Amphetamines	Opiates
Amphotericin	Phenergan
Antihistamines	Phenobarbital
Antispasmodics	Phenytoin
Benzodiazepam	Propanolol
Clonidine	Rifampicin
Corticosteriods	Salicylates
Digitalis	Tricyclic Antidepressants
Diphenhydramine	Valproate

Industrial pollutants have deleterious effects on a child's central nervous system. Carbon monoxide, lead, and organophosphates are common examples of noxious agents. The toxic effects of carbon monoxide poisoning include anemic anoxia, described earlier (Zimmerman & Truxal, 1981). Lead poisoning, or plumbism, is a public health concern that affects a significant proportion of preschoolers, but residual or undiagnosed cases are common in the school-age population. Sources of lead abound in daily urban life and include water, food, air pollution, and paint, among others. Low levels of lead intoxication result in microcytic anemia, as lead interferes with the biosynthesis of heme. Moderate to high levels of lead poisoning may be reflected clinically by poor learning, inattention, apathy, aggressive behavior, and hyperactivity. Lead levels greater than 120 micrograms per deciliter result in lead deposition in nervous tissue and encephalopathic changes (Bagnurst et al., 1992). Organophosphates are encountered in pesticides and reversibly inhibit acetylcholinesterase. Toxic symptoms include headache, blurry vision, dizziness, and confusion followed by respiratory and gastrointestinal complications. The temporal onset of symptoms is directly related to the mode of exposure; inhalation causes almost immediate distress, ingestion has a somewhat slower onset, and dermal absorption gives rise to a delay of up to 24 hours.

except for its temporal association with epidemic viral illnesses, resembles a toxic encephalopathy (Lichenstein et al., 1983). An accompanying fatty infiltration of organs results in grossly abnormal liver function tests, hyperammonemia, and hypoglycemia; this in turn creates additional disturbances for the central nervous system. Cerebral edema is the most lethal complication of Reye's syndrome, resulting in transtentorial and cerebellar herniation. Decreased aspirin administration among children, early intensive management of the acute illness with the use of intracranial monitors, and various means of life support have greatly diminished the death toll from this disease (Stumpf, Parker, & Angelini, 1985).

Renal disease results in greater electrolyte disturbances and disorders of osmolality. The detrimental effects of electrolyte abnormalities and osmolar shifts were discussed earlier. Clinically children with renal failure demonstrate a progressive picture of dementia, motor incoordination, ataxia, and bulbar disturbances that are correlated with increased levels of serum phosphate, alkaline phosphatase, and parathyroid hormone. Cases of dialysis-related encephalopathy have been described and present with features of dementia (Foley, Polinsky, Gruskin, Baluarte, & Grover, 1981). Electroencephalograms in both renal and hepatic failure have been remarkable for progressive slowing and increased paroxysmal activity.

Organ Failure

Infectious Causes

Liver and kidney failure are the two major organ-related causes of toxic encephalopathy. Hepatic failure may be due to any insult that compromises the liver's capacity to detoxify blood and sustain an adequate blood sugar level. Early stages of liver failure cause personality changes, lethargy, lability, and memory impairment, which is followed by increasingly disturbed levels of consciousness, and eventual unresponsiveness.

Reye's syndrome is an acute organic brain syndrome whose pathogenesis is unknown; however, it often occurs following an Influenza B or varicella infection, and has been associated with salicylate use. It is characterized by a deterioration in mental functioning and persistent vomiting, and,

Infections of the central nervous system result in a variety of inflammatory reactions that usually produce an acute change in cerebral function. Meningitis, an inflammation of the meninges, generally is accompanied by a pleocytosis of the cerebrospinal fluid. In bacterial meningitis, spinal fluid cultures tests positive for bacterial growth; in aseptic meningitis, there are clinical signs and symptoms of meningitis plus cerebrospinal fluid pleocytosis, but bacterial cultures are negative; this generally implies a viral etiology. Encephalitis is an inflammation of the brain tissue itself and is most commonly viral in origin. As the name indicates, meningoencephalitis is an inflammation of both brain tissue and its surrounding meninges.

While tissue damage often occurs in an unpredictable fashion, specific infectious agents tend to cause some particular types of cellular destruction. Bacterial pathogens tend to inflame meningeal and ependymal tissue, resulting in transudates and exudates, and frequently in abscess formation. Rickettsiae typically invade perivascular areas resulting in granulomata and vascular endothelial proliferation. Viral infections commonly result in ganglion destruction, lymphocytic infiltration, and microgliosis (American Academy for Pediatrics, 1991).

In the school-age population, the incidence of bacterial meningitis is a function of host immunocompetency and pathogen factors. Approximately 80 infants per 100,000 are afflicted with meningitis within the first year of life. By the school-age years, this incidence drops dramatically, to only 2 per 100,000. Pathogens most commonly involved are *Streptococcus pneumoniae, Neisseria meningitidis,* and *Haemophilis influenza.*

The organisms usually enter the bloodstream via the upper respiratory tract and from there go on to seed the meninges, resulting in meningeal inflammation. Inflammation of the choroid plexus results in decreased transport of glucose to the brain. Hypoglycorrhachia, or decreased cerebrospinal fluid glucose, is compounded by the increased energy demands of brain tissue reacting to meningeal inflammation and the metabolic requirements of invading bacteria and leukocytes. Decreased cerebral blood flow as a result of infection may in turn lead to tissue acidosis and impairment of oxygenation. Electrolyte disturbances are associated with depolarization of neurons and abnormal electrical activity. Invasion of the meninges by bacterial pathogens results in perivascular infiltration of polymorphonucleocytes, a meningeal exudate, ventriculitis, and increased intracranial pressure. Vasculitis may result in necrotizing arteritis and venous thrombosis with subsequent formation of subdural hemorrhages and transudate collections (Prober, 1996).

Clinically the child with bacterial meningitis will present with an acute febrile illness and complaints of headache, malaise, nausea, and vomiting. Photophobia, nuchal rigidity, and seizures may be evident on physical examination, while mental status changes include confusion, lethargy, and irritability. Management of the acute infection with appropriate antibiotic therapy results in a mortality rate of less than 8% (Feigin, McCracken, & Klein, 1992; Quagliarello & Scheld, 1992).

Over half of the children surviving bacterial meningitis suffer some central nervous system morbidity. Focal signs, syndrome of inappropriate antidiuretic hormone output, and a depressed level of consciousness at time of presentation are the most reliable predictors of permanent sequelae following meningitis. Complications vary depending on the causative organism; they include obstructive hydrocephalus, seizures, ataxia, hearing loss, and behavioral problems. Long-term impairments of purulent meningitis include cognitive inpairment as evidenced on psychometric testing in a significant number of cases (Jiang, Liu, Wu, Zheng, & Liu, 1990; Pomeroy, Holmes, Dodge, & Feigin, 1990; Taylor et al., 1990).

Subacute, chronic meningitis may occur in Lyme disease as well as tuberculosis and fungal and other opportunistic infections found in immunocompromised hosts. These children typically have generalized chronic headache and deteriorating coordination as well as insidious changes in mental status and personality. Central nervous system infection with *Borrelia burgdoferi,* the spirochete responsible for Lyme disease, can lead to a variety of clinical presentations. Both the infecting organism and the host responses produce neurological symptoms that appear late in the clinical course of the infection. The spirochete enters the body via the bite of a tick endemic to three geographic areas in the United States: *Ixodes damini* in the Northeast and Midwest, *Ixodes pacificus* on the West Coast. Generally, a localized rash will develop within 8 to 20 days of the bite, followed by a septicemia associated with joint pains, pleuritis, carditis, and neuritis (Rahn & Malawista, 1991). If left untreated, further neurological involvement may ensue with the appearance of dementia, psychomotor retardation, seizures, and hallucinations. Approximately 10% of individuals infected with Lyme disease will develop neurological complications; the presence of the HLA DR2 histocompatibility gene is thought to increase the likelihood of developing neuroborreliosis. Neuropathological findings include meningitis, encephalitis, and cranial neuritis; less frequent findings include pseudotumor cerebri, optic atrophy, demyelinating processes, or unilateral blindness. Diagnosis is confirmed by identification of the spirochete with enzyme linked immunosorbent assay of the spinal fluid. Patients with neurological symptoms who do not improve on oral antibiotic treatment warrant intravenous therapy (Halperin et al., 1989; Lecomte, Mihout, & Humbert, 1989).

Viral Encephalitis

Viral infections of the brain fall into four general categories: acute, slow, postinfectious, and chronic degenerative, of which acute and postinfectious are the most pertinent in childhood. Viruses enter the central nervous system via the blood or neuronal tissue. With hematogenous access, inflammation of the gray matter results from endothelial disturbances; neuronal access occurs from peripheral interneuronal communications.

Each year approximately 20,000 cases of viral encephalitis are reported, the majority of which are transient and mild. Acute infections are characterized clinically by a febrile illness and headache, accompanied by changes in consciousness and behavior. Cortical involvement results in seizures and focal findings on neurological examination. Unlike bacterial meningitis, in viral encephalitis meningeal signs are rare. Postinfectious encephalitis presents days to weeks following a viral syndrome and is characterized by vague complaints, insidious personality changes, and a spinal fluid analysis that is remarkable for increased protein and mononuclear cells. Demyelination is thought to be a prominent histopathological finding in the afflicted central nervous system. Acquired immunodeficiency syndrome (AIDS) is a significant cause of chronic viral infections of the central nervous system. In children its presentation may vary greatly, from chronic developmental delay to a more fulminant course, which is outlined later. Some viruses demonstrate a tropism for specific areas of the central nervous system, for example, the rabies virus involves the limbic system whereas mumps infection attacks the ependymal cells (Whitney, 1990).

Arboviruses, *Herpes simplex*, rabies virus, influenza B, and varicella are among the viral agents most frequently implicated in acute pediatric encephalitis. Arboviruses incidentally infect humans via arthropod vectors, such as mosquitoes, ticks, and blood-sucking flies, that are endemic to the Gulf, eastern, central and southern United States. Eastern Equine and Lacrosse viruses have a greater disease potential among the pediatric population. Infection with the Eastern Equine Virus is associated with a 50 to 75% mortality and a morbidity of 80% among survivors. Lacrosse viral infection has a mortality rate of less than 1% and a correspondingly lower incidence of neurological sequelae. Therapeutic interventions are entirely supportive; no licensed vaccines exist in this country.

Herpes simplex virus, or HSV, is a ubiquitous large DNA virus that exists in two types, HSV 1 and HSV 2, which have distinct genomes and antigenicity. The virus is transmitted person to person and is more common in socially disadvantaged pediatric populations. After the neonatal period, pediatric infection with HSV 2 is highly suggestive of sexual transmission. In central nervous system infection, a dramatic deterioration in mental status and behavior occurs leading to stupor and coma. Spinal fluid findings are often unhelpful, and diagnosis rests on biopsy of the temporal lobes, which are involved most frequently. Treatment of encephalitis includes acyclovir and vidarabine; however, unless intervention is initiated exceedingly early, outcome in HSV encephalitis is generally very poor (Gordon, Selnes, Hart, Hanley, & Whitley, 1990; Rautonen, Koskiniemi, & Vaheri, 1991).

Rabies virus is a rhabdovirus that exists in a large animal reservoir and is transmitted to humans via saliva, either from a bite or by licking open wounds. The incubation period in humans averages 2 months, with ranges from 8 days to 1 year. The virus's tropism for the limbic system accounts in good part for the intense and extreme anxiety and other affective symptoms associated with the onset of this illness. The disease is almost always fatal despite immunoprophylactic interventions, and prevention is best achieved through animal vaccination.

The human immunodeficiency virus (HIV) is transmitted to children in a number of ways. While only about 20% of infants born to HIV-positive women will become infected, this mode of transmission accounts for the majority of pediatric AIDS cases. The minority of school-age cases can be accounted for by transfusion therapy and, rarely, sexual contact. Between 20 to 60% of children infected with HIV will have neuropsychological deficits and disturbances of fine motor coordination. The term "HIV-associated progressive encephalopathy of childhood" has been proposed to describe central nervous system dysfunction in children with the AIDS virus. Symptoms of HIV-associated encephalopathy include developmental delay, loss of milestones, acquired microcephaly, movement disorders, and ataxia. Other mental status changes seen to varying degrees in pediatric AIDS include cognitive slowing, dementia, social withdrawal, apathy, emotional lability, inattention, and behavioral outbursts. Opportunistic and other uncommon infections of the central nervous system are a serious complication in pediatric AIDS and will precipitate or compound a preexisting encephalopathy (Belman, 1990, 1992; Vandersteenhoven et al., 1992). Pediatric HIV infections of the central nervous system are less likely to give rise to secondary neoplastic processes than in adult AIDS. Continuous zidovudine treatment of HIV-associated progressive encephalopathy of childhood has demonstrated significant clinical improvement in neurological functioning. Even children who appeared cognitively intact prior to treatment demonstrated improvement on standardized IQ testing following AZT administration. This suggests that the HIV virus may have subclinical effects on intellectual functioning in otherwise neurologically asymptomatic children (Pizzo et al., 1988).

Slow viruses are viruses that infect the central nervous system and remain dormant for months to years but, when activated, result in a progressive and often fatal illness. Kuru, Creutzfeldt-Jakob dementia, and progressive multifocal leukoencephalopathy are extreme rarities in children. Subacute sclerosing panencephalitis occurs years following exposure to a measleslike agent; this occurs most typically in rural areas and affects males much more frequently than females. The child often first presents with subtle personality changes and antisocial behavior, which progresses to seizures, ataxia, cognitive deterioration, and dyskinesias, and ultimately to a decerebrate vegetative state. As a result, the diagnosis is usually not made until late in the disease. Since the measles vaccination campaigns in the 1970s, a decline in subacute sclerosing panencephalitis has been noted.

Autoimmune Cerebritis

Although uncommon, autoimmune disease does affect children and can present with neurological symptoms, including mental status changes. Systemic lupus erythematosus occurs 8 times more frequently in females than males. It usually presents with skin manifestations and arthritis, but personality changes, mood disturbances, and outright psychosis have been reported. Therapy for systemic lupus erythematosus entails treatment with steroids, which, in turn may result in further mental status changes (Schaller, 1996).

Other systemic autoimmune disorders seen in childhood that may result in encephalopathy include polyarteritis nodosa and rheumatoid arthritis. While rare, polyarteritis nodosa may present with multiple nerve involvement simultaneously or over the course of the disease, seizures and hemiplegia. Up to 65 of patients with juvenile rheumatoid arthritis may develop encephalopathic signs and symptoms (Ozen, Besbas, Saatei, & Bakkaloglu, 1992).

Postinfectious encephalitis also is considered to be an autoimmune disorder of the central nervous system. As described previously, these are relatively acute conditions that occur late in the course of an infection, typically varicella or measles, and virus is not isolated from the cerebrospinal fluid. The incidence has been estimated at 1/10,000 for varicella and 1/1000 for measles (Koskiniemi & Vaheri, 1989).

Neoplasms

The incidence for brain tumors in childhood is 2.4 per 100,000 and peaks during the school-age years. Brain tumors represent the most common solid tumor of this age group and are second only to leukemia as a cause of childhood cancer. The majority of pediatric brain tumors are midline and infratentorial, arising in the cerebellum, third or fourth ventricle, and brainstem. The signs and symptoms produced are variable and depend on the tumor's location and growth rate as well as the brain's capacity to accommodate. Even after a child has become symptomatic, many central nervous system neoplasms go undiagnosed for months. Increased intracranial pressure is a frequent complication of pediatric tumors that accounts for many nonspecific signs. Generalized symptoms include headache, lethargy, vomiting, and personality and behavioral changes. The headache is a prominent symptom during the first six months and then may subside. It is typically made worse by reclining or when performing Valsalva's maneuver. Personality and behavioral changes include irritability, affective lability, anxiety, apathy, listlessness, mental slowing, and maladjustment.

Focal neuropsychiatric symptoms depend on the nature and location of the tumor. Midline neoplasms affecting the corpus callosum may present with amnesia, apathy, akinesia, and dementia; those affecting the hypothalamic-pituitary axis will give rise to neuroendocrine dysfunction. Frontal lesions are rare in children; when they do occur, the children are likely to display psychiatric symptomatology. Most individuals with frontal lobe tumors manifest personality changes, affective lability, and IQ variation. Temporal lobe tumors frequently are associated with psychiatric complaints including anxiety, depression, hallucinations, and complex perceptual distortions that often correlate with electroencephalogram abnormalities. Specific cognitive impairments such as agnosia, apraxia, and aphasia often are associated with parietal lobe lesions. Occipital lobe tumors are rare and generally result in visual hallucinations or impairment (Menkes & Till, 1995b).

Nomenclature for childhood tumors is a function of location and histology. Infratentorial tumors include cerebellar neoplasms, which are typically medulloblastomas or astrocytomas, the latter more often diagnosed in the school-age child. Supratentorial lesions are often cerebral or optic gliomas and craniopharyngiomas. Ependymomas occur in the fourth ventricle; pinealomas most commonly arise in the third ventricle.

Treatment of brain tumors in childhood is asso-ciated with significant morbidity that frequently compounds a preexisting brain syndrome or gives rise to a new bout of encephalopathy. This neurodevelopmental decline is a function of the neurologic deficits arising from the combined effects of the tumor, sensorimotor impairments, surgical interventions, chemotherapeutic complications, and radiation (Friedman, Horowitz, & Oakes, 1991). Radiotherapy has been directly implicated in intellectual deterioration. This decline in IQ is a function of age and radiation field, with younger children and whole-brain irradiation having the worst outcome. Children under the age of 7 who undergo brain radiotherapy for tumors demonstrate an IQ that averages 25 points below their expected norm. Efforts to delay radiation therapy with preradiation chemotherapy in hopes of minimizing this complication have met with some success (Mulhern et al., 1989). Leukoencephalopathy is a late, rare complication of central nervous system radiotherapy that gives rise to dementia, motor deficits, ataxia, and seizures. Anatomically, it represents a loss of oligodendroglia and myelin. This appears on a CT scan as hypodense areas, enlarged ventricles, periventricular hyperintensity, and calcification of the basal ganglia. Oncogenesis, or the occurrence of radiation-induced tumors, is a tragic complication of brain irradiation. Children who have undergone radiotherapy for intracranial neoplasms are at sevenfold greater risk for the development of secondary central nervous system tumors (Albright, 1993; Mulhern et al., 1989).

Congenital Malformations

It is rare for congenital malformations to become symptomatic during the school-age years. However, it does occur; examples include central nervous system malformations such as Arnold-Chiari deformity, Dandy-Walker syndrome, and vascular anomalies. Arnold-Chiari malformations occur in the cerebellum and lower brainstem and are associated with noncommunicating (obstructive) hydrocephalus. Dandy-Walker also results in intermittent obstructive hydrocephalus on the basis of cystlike lesions located in the fourth ventricle and posterior fossa. Both anomalies present with signs and symptoms of increased intracranial pressure (Fishman, 1996).

Vascular anomalies may be congenital or acquired. Arteriovenous malformations, cavernous sinus anomalies, venous angiomas, capillary telangiectasia, and aneurysms result in a redistribution of blood flow that gives rise to "steal" phenomena, pressure effects, subarachnoid hemorrhaging and thrombosis. The symptoms produced are a function of the anomalies size, location and cerebral hemodynamics.

Congenital neurocutaneous syndromes occasionally present in the school-age period with central nervous system involvement. The most common are neurofibromatosis, tuberous sclerosis, and Sturge-Webb. Seizures occur in the majority of patients with tuberous sclerosis. Brain tumors, especially optic gliomas, are found in 15% of subtype NF1; bilateral acoustic neuromas confirm the diagnosis of NF type 2 (Roach, 1992).

Summary

Acute and chronic brain syndromes in the school-age child may result from traumatic, metabolic, infectious, neoplastic, or congenital insults. The mechanisms of neuronal injury vary depending on the nature of the insulting agent. Pathophysiological disturbances of the central nervous system are reflected in mental status and behavioral changes that may be acute or chronic, generalized, or specific. In view of their neurological and developmental immaturity, children are more susceptible to organic brain syndromes and their sequelae. The child psychiatrist is often the first professional to assess these disorders. Any change in mental functioning or mental illness refractory to appropriate treatment should raise the suspicion of an organic brain syndrome. A thorough neurologic and pediatric assessment is indicated to determine if an organic process is responsible for affective, cognitive, or behavioral changes.

REFERENCES

Albright, A. L. (1993). Pediatric brain tumors. *CA: A Cancer Journal for Clinicians, 43* (5), 272–288.

American Academy for Pediatrics. (1991). Report of the committee on infectious disease (22nd ed.) Elk Grove Village, IL: Author.

Bagnurst, P. A., McMichael, A. J., Wigg, N. R., Vimpani, G. V., Robertson, E. P., Roberts, R. J., & Tong, S.-L. (1992). Environmental exposure to lead and children's intelligence at the age of seven years. *New England Journal of Medicine, 327,* 1279–1284.

Belman, A. L. (1990). AIDS and pediatric neurology. *Neurology Clinics, 8,* 591–603.

Belman, A. L. (1992). Acquired immunodeficiency syndrome and the child's central nervous system. *Pediatric Clinics of North America, 39* (4), 691–714.

Brown, G., Chadwick, O., Shaffer, D., Rutter, M., & Traub, M. (1981). A prospective study of children with head injuries: III. Psychiatric sequelae. *Psychological Medicine, 11,* 63–78.

Carter, S., & Gold, A. P. (1974). *Neurology of infancy and childhood.* New York: Appleton-Century-Crofts.

Chadwick, O., Rutter, M., Brown, G., Shaffer, D., & Traub, M. (1981). A prospective study of children with head injuries: II. Cognitive sequelae. *Psychological Medicine, 11,* 49–61.

Chutorian, A., & Paulakis, S. (1992). Psychiatric symptoms in progressive disorders of the nervous system. In D. M. Kaufman, G. E. Solomon, & C. R. Pfeffer, *Child and adolescent neurology for psychiatrists.* Baltimore: Williams & Wilkins.

Devivo, D. (1996). Acute encephalopathies of childhood. In A. M. Rudolf (Ed.), *Rudolf's pediatrics* (20th ed.). Stanford, CT: Appleton Lange.

Ewing-Cobbs, L., Thompson, N. M., Milner, M. E., & Fletcher, J. M. (1994). Gunshot wounds to the brain in children and adolescents: Age and neurobehavioral development. *Neurosurgery, 35* (2), 225–233.

Feigin, R. D., McCracken, G. H., & Klein, J. O. (1992). Diagnosis and management of meningitis. *Pediatric Infectious Disease Journal, 11,* 785.

Fishman, M. A. (1996). Disturbances in neural tube closure and spine and cerebrospinal fluid dynamics. In A. M. Rudolf (Ed.), *Rudolf's pediatrics* (20th ed.), Stanford, CT: Appleton-Lange.

Foley, C. M., Polinsky, M. S., Gruskin, A. B., Baluarte, H. J., & Grover, W. D. (1981). Encephalopathy in infants and children with chronic renal disease. *Archives of Neurology, 38,* 656–659.

Friedman, H. S., Horowitz, M., & Oakes, W. J. (1991). Tumors of the central nervous system: Improvement in outcome through a multimodality approach. *Pediatric Clinics of North America, 38* (2), 381–391.

Ghajar, J., & Hariri, R. J. (1992). Management of pediatric head injury. *Pediatric Clinics of North America, 39* (5), 1093–1125.

Gordon, B., Selnes, O. A., Hart, J., Hanley, D. F., &

Whitley, R. J. (1990). Long-term cognitive sequelae of acyclovir-treated Herpes simplex encephalitis. *Archives of Neurology, 47*, 646–647.

Greenspan, A. I., & MacKenzie, E. J. (1994). Functional outcome after pediatric head injury. *Pediatrics, 94* (4), 425–432.

Halperin, J. J., Luft, B. J., Anand, A. K., Roque, C. T., Alvarez, O., Volkman, D. J., & Dattwyler, R. J. (1989). Lyme neuroborreliosis: Central nervous system manifestations. *Neurology, 39*, 753–759.

Jiang, Z. D., Liu, X. Y., Wu, Y. Y., Zheng, M. S., & Liu, H. C. (1990). Long-term impairments of brain and auditory functions of children recovered from purulent meningitis. *Developmental Medicine and Child Neurology, 32*, 473–480.

Johnston, M. V., & Gerring, J. P. (1992). Head trauma and its sequelae. *Pediatric Annals, 21*, 362–368.

Kitchin, W., Cohen-Cole, S. A., & Mickel, S. F. (1987). Adrenoleukodystrophy: Frequency of presentation as a psychiatric disorder. *Biological Psychiatry, 22*, 1375–1387.

Koskiriemi, M., & Vaheri, A. (1989). Effects of measles, mumps, rubella vaccination on pattern of encephalitis in children. *Lancet, 1*, 31–34.

Kriel, R. L., Krach, L. E., & Panser, L. A. (1989). Closed head injury: Comparison of children younger and older than 6 years of age. *Pediatric Neurology, 5*, 296–300.

Krane, E. J., Rockoff, M. A., Wallman, J. K., & Wolfsdorf, J. I. (1984). Subclinical brain swelling in children during treatment for diabetic ketoacidosis. *New England Journal of Medicine, 312* (18), 1147–1151.

Lecomte, F., Mihout, B., & Humbert, G. (1989). Neurological manifestations of Lyme disease and treatments. *Biomedicine and Pharmacotherapy, 43*, 409–413.

Lichenstein, P. K., Henbill, J. E., Daugherty, C. C., Farrell, M. K., Sokol, R. J., Rothbaum, R. J., Suchy, F. J., & Balisteri, W. F. (1983). Grade I Reye's syndrome: A frequent cause of vomiting and liver dysfunction after varicella and upper respiratory tract infection. *New England Journal of Medicine, 309*, 133–139.

Menkes, J. H., & Till, K. (1995a). Postnatal trauma and injuries by physical agents. In J. H. Menkes, *Textbook of child neurology* (5th ed.). Baltimore: Williams & Wilkins.

Menkes, J. H., & Till, K. (1995b). Tumors of the nervous system. In J. H. Menkes (Ed.), *Textbook of child neurology* (5th ed.). Baltimore: Williams & Wilkins.

Mulhern, R. K., Horowitz, M. E., Kovnar, E. H., Langston, J., Sanford, R. A., & Kun, L. E. (1989). Neurodevelopmental status of infants and young children treated for brain tumors with preirradiation chemotherapy. *Journal of Clinical Oncology, 7* (11) 1660–1666.

Naylor, M. W., & Alessi, N. E. (1989). Pseudoarylsulfatase: A deficiency in a psychiatrically disturbed adolescent. *Journal of the American Academy of Child and Adolescent Psychiatry, 28*, 444–449.

Ozen, S., Besbas, N., Saatei, U., & Bakkaloglu, A. (1992). Diagnostic criteria for polyarteritis nodosa in childhood. *Journal of Pediatrics, 120*, 206–209.

Pizzo, P. A., Eddy, J., Falloon, J., Balis, F. M., Murphy, R. F., Moss, H., Wolters, P., Brouwers, P., Jarosinski, P., Rubin, M., Braler, S., Yarchoan, R., Brunetti, A., Maha, M., Nusinoff-Lehrman, S., & Poplack, D. G. (1988). Effect of continuous intravenous infusion of zidovudine (AZT) in children with symptomatic HIV infection. *New England Journal of Medicine, 319*, (14), 889–896.

Plum, F., & Posner, J. B. (1982). Metabolic brain diseases causing coma. In *The diagnosis of stupor and coma* (3rd ed.). Philadelphia: F. A. Davis Company.

Pomeroy, S. L., Holmes, S. J., Dodge, P. R., & Feigin, R. D. (1990). Seizures and other neurological sequelae of bacterial meningitis. *New England Journal of Medicine, 323*, 1651–1657.

Prober, C. G. (1996). Infections of central nervous system. In R. E. Behrman, R. M. Kliegman, & A. N. Arvin (Eds.), *Nelson textbook of pediatrics* (15th ed.). Philadelphia: W. B. Saunders.

Quagliarello, V., & Scheld, W. M. (1992). Bacterial meningitis: Pathogenesis, pathophysiology, and progress. *New England Journal of Medicine, 327*, 864.

Rahn, D. W., & Malawista, S. E. (1991). Lyme disease: Recommendations for diagnosis and treatment. *Annals of Internal Medicine, 114* (6), 472–481.

Rautonen, J., Koskiniemi, M., & Vaheri, A. (1991). Prognostic factors in childhood encephalitis. *Pediatric Infections Disease Journal, 10*, 441.

Roach, E. S. (1992). Neurocutaneous syndromes. *Pediatric Clinics of North America, 39* (4), 591.

Rosman, P. N. (1994). Acute brain injury. In K. F. Swaiman (Ed.), *Pediatric neurology* (2nd ed., Vol. 2). St. Louis: C. V. Mosby.

Rusonis, E. S. (1990). Adolescents with closed head injury. *Medical Clinics of North America, 74* (5), 1311–1319.

Rutter, M. (1983). *Developmental neuropsychiatry.* New York: Guilford Press.

Rutter, M., Chadwick, O., Shaffer, D., & Brown, G. (1980). A prospective study of children with head injuries: 1. Design and methods. *Psychological Medicine, 10*, 633–645.

Schaller, J. G. (1996). Systemic lupus erythematosus. In R. E. Behrman, R. M. Kliegman, & A. M. Arvin (Eds.), *Nelson textbook of pediatrics* (15th ed.). Philadelphia: W. B. Saunders.

Stumpf, P. A., Parker, W. D., & Angelini, C. (1985). Carnitine deficiency, organic acidemias and Reye's syndrome. *Neurology, 35*, 1041–1045.

Taylor, H. G., Mills, E. L., Crampi, A., du Berger, R., Walters, G. V., Gold, R., MacDonald, N., & Michaelis, R. H. (1990). The sequelae of Haemophilus influenza meningitis in school-age children. *New England Journal of Medicine, 323*, 1657–1663.

Tilley, C. M., Cranberg, L. D., Alexander, M. P., & Hart, E. J. (1987). Neurobehavioral outcome after closed head injury in childhood and adolescence. *Archives of Neurology, 44,* 194–198.

Vandersteerhoven, J. J., Dhaibo, G., Boyko, O. B., Hulette, C. M., Anthony, D. C., Kenny, J. F., & Wilfert, C. M. (1992). Progressive multifocal leukoencephalopathy in pediatric acquired immunodeficiency syndrome. *Pediatric Infectious Disease Journal, 11,* 232–237.

Whitney, R. J. (1990). Viral encephalitis. *New England Journal of Medicine, 323* (4), 242–250.

Yudofsky, S., & Hales, R. (1992). *Textbook of neuropsychiatry* (2nd ed.). Washington, DC: American Psychiatric Press.

Zimmerman, S. S., & Truxal, B. (1981). Carbon monoxide poisoning. *Pediatrics, 68,* 215–224.

36 / Mental Retardation in the Grade-School Child

Edwin J. Mikkelsen

Historical Observations

Descriptions of mental retardation date to antiquity; however, it was only after the Middle Ages that organized efforts to assist the mentally retarded were instituted in Western cultures. An interesting lineage of leaders in the treatment and education of the mentally retarded revolves around the "Wild Boy of Averyron," who was found in France in 1801. In some ways the story actually began in the mid-1600s when Vincent DePaul created a refuge for the mentally retarded at the Bicetre. Over a century later, Jean Marie Itard studied there before becoming a teacher of the deaf in Paris. It was to the physician Itard that the "Wild Boy" was brought for further study. Eventually Itard expanded his work with the mentally retarded and began to train students of his own. One of those students was Edward Seguin, who introduced Itard's principles of education to the United States when, in 1848, he became involved with the Massachusetts Experimental School for the Teaching and Training of Idiots. This facility, later known as the Fernald School, was to become the training ground for many of the future leaders in the field of mental retardation (Tanguay & Russell, 1991).

Progress in the education and treatment of the mentally retarded has not been made linearly. During the early part of the 20th century, the eugenics movement, forced sterilization, and the creation of large custodial institutions in the United States impacted negatively on the lives of thousands of mentally retarded individuals. In Germany, the Nazis systematically exterminated large numbers of mentally retarded individuals.

The modern era of the care and treatment of the mentally retarded dates to 1964 when Congress, under the leadership of President John F. Kennedy, passed the Mental Retardation and Developmental Disabilities Act. Since that time slow but consistent gains have been made in the deinstitutionalization of the mentally retarded into community residences that are integrated into the general community. Again, it should be noted that this progress has not been linear and varies greatly from state to state.

Definition

The most widely accepted definition of mental retardation is that offered by the American Association on Mental Retardation (1992), which states that:

mental retardation refers to substantial limitations in present functioning. It is characterized by significantly subaverage intellectual functioning, existing concurrently with related limitations in two or more of the following applicable adaptive skill areas: communication, self-care, home living, social skills, community use, self-direction, health and safety, functional academics, leisure, and work. Mental retardation manifests before age 18. (p. 5).

The phrase "significantly subaverage intellectual functioning" is further defined as:

an IQ standard score of approximately 70 to 75 or below, based on assessment that includes one or more individually administered general intelligence tests developed for the purpose of assessing intellectual functioning. These data should be reviewed by a multidisciplinary team and validated with additional test scores or evaluative information (p. 5)

Thus, while intelligence is central to the diagnosis, the definition also refers to the manifestation of the impaired intellectual functioning in "adaptive skill areas." This aspect of the definition stresses the importance of looking beyond intelligence scores alone, which could produce too narrow a focus. It also points to the limitations of intelligence tests. Most states have adapted the AAMR criteria; thus eligibility for clinical services and other public assistance hinges not only on the intelligence quotient alone but also on adaptive abilities.

The often-quoted phrase "Intelligence is what intelligence tests measure" implies the shortcoming of standardized tests in determining cognitive and mental abilities. Nevertheless, the standardized instruments, such as the Wechsler Intelligence Scales for Children (WISC-III, age range 6 to 16 years) and the Stanford Binet (age range 2 to 18 years), provide the best available means of assessing cognitive ability. Within the general category of mental retardation, four subcategories have been developed along the parameter of measured intelligence as follows: mild (IQ 50–55 to approximately 70); moderate (IQ 35–40 to 50–55); severe (IQ 20–25 to 35–40); and profound (IQ below 20 or 25) (American Psychiatric Association, 1994).

Epidemiology

The expected bell-shape curve for the distribution of intelligence does not materialize in actual population studies as there are relatively more individuals at the lower end of intellectual functioning than there are at the higher IQ levels. Thus, the curve has an elongated left-hand tail (indicating lower scores) as compared to the right-hand tail

(Tanguay & Russell, 1991). The most likely explanation for this observation is that those with extremely high IQs derive solely from genetic diversity whereas those who test in the retarded range represent two groups, those who have lower IQs on a genetic basis as well as those whose retardation has been contributed to by organic factors present prenatally, at birth, or during early development (Mikkelsen, 1987). The prevalence of mental retardation ranges from 1 to 3%, with the figure of 2 to 2.5% being generally accepted (Zigler & Hodapp, 1987).

The vast majority of mentally retarded individuals will fall in the mild range (89%) with far fewer in the moderate group (7%) and only 4% in the severe and profound categories combined (Tanguay & Russell, 1991). The male-to-female ratio is 3:2.

Etiology

As alluded to already, the number of mentally retarded individuals exceeds the number of individuals who would be expected by genetic variation alone. Heredity is thought to account for 45 to 80% of the variation in intelligence (Zigler & Hodapp, 1986). In one study specific genetic abnormalities were reported to account for more than 25% of children referred for assessment of developmental delay (Fryns, 1987).

Approximately one third of those cases attributed to a genetic abnormality are accounted for by Down syndrome and fragile X syndrome (Bregman & Hodapp, 1991). Phenylketonuria is another common genetic condition linked to mental retardation with a frequency of 1 in 11,500 live births (Tanguay & Russell, 1991). Screening in developed countries has decreased the actual impact of this disorder, but screening and dietary intervention is far from universal, especially in Third World countries.

The major nongenetic causes of intellectual deficiency can be classified under the categories of infectious, traumatic, toxic, and nutritional (Mikkelsen, 1987). Medical factors may be more prevalent in cases of mild impairment. In this regard Bregman and Hodapp (1991) cite a study that reported medical factors as causing intellectual impairment in 30 to 42% of a sample of 295 mildly impaired children. The primary medical factors are those related to prematurity, low birthweight, and physical trauma at birth (i.e., hypoxia, intracranial hemorrhage).

Social factors also may play a role in the evolution and severity of mental retardation. Socioeconomic factors have been found to correlate with development in premature infants (Bregman & Hodapp, 1991). Repeated social rejection also may negatively effect the degree of competence and skills achieved by mentally retarded individuals (Zigler & Hodapp, 1987).

Evaluation and Diagnosis

Although intelligence testing confirms the diagnosis of mental retardation, the developmental delays and difficulties with adaptive functioning bring most children for evaluation. Typically, parents notice that their child is not developing at the same rate as other children and request an assessment. However, a significant proportion of children are not diagnosed until they begin school and their difficulties become more manifest in the classroom.

While, in general, virtually all cases are detected by the early grade-school years, the clinician should not automatically assume that this is the case. Mental retardation should remain in the differential diagnosis if the clinician has concerns about the child's cognitive abilities. A recent example is provided by a 15-year-old boy who was in the ninth grade in an inner-city school. The boy was referred for severe aggressive acting-out behavior. His mother complained that he could not even read at a first-grade level. Although he had been held back twice in grade school, he was receiving only basic remedial help with reading. Intelligence testing revealed a full-scale IQ of 68, which actually made him eligible for services from the Department of Mental Retardation as well as more extensive support from the educational system.

The major differential diagnoses to be considered when mental retardation is suspected are severe learning disabilities that make the child appear more intellectually impaired than he or she

is, a language disorder, and a pervasive developmental disorder.

Psychopathology

There is no doubt that persons with mentally retardation are more vulnerable to develop psychiatric illness than the general population. Bregman (1991) has systematically reviewed many of the studies concerning the incidence of psychopathology in this population and notes that "between one-third and two-thirds of the individuals in these representative community samples exhibited a significant degree of psychopathology, a rate several times higher than that found among non-mentally retarded comparison groups" (p. 861). There is, of course, variability across studies due to differences in methods as well as random chance variation, but the overall impression is still quite striking.

The patterns of psychopathology seen are related to intellectual level to a certain extent. In the severe to profoundly retarded, the pervasive developmental disorders and autism are the most frequently cited coexisting conditions (Gillberg, Persson, Grufman, & Themner, 1986). The most frequently cited disorders in the higher-functioning groups are an increased rate of schizophrenia with an incidence of 2 to 3% (Bregman, 1991; Reid, 1989) and increased risk of affective illness (Bregman, 1991; Sovner & Desnoyers-Hurley, 1983). However, persons with mental retardation are not limited to developing just these disorders; they are subject to the entire range of psychiatric disorders.

The increased risk of psychopathology in mentally retarded persons is in most cases multidetermined. The primary factors that need to be considered as major contributors to dysfunction are organic, psychodynamic, family related, and cultural.

ORGANIC FACTORS

The incidence of seizure disorder is substantially higher in mentally retarded populations. Three to 6% of mildly retarded children will have experienced a seizure as opposed to 0.7% of the general population (Corbett, Harris, & Robinson, 1975). Certainly in many cases the seizure disorder may be not be causally linked to the behavioral disturbance per se, but the high prevalence rates for seizures do suggest a greater degree of cerebral dysfunction in this population. The higher incidence of hyperactivity and poor concentration that is observed in retarded persons also are likely related to organic factors.

Certain conditions, such as fragile X syndrome and the Prader-Willi syndrome, are accompanied by extremely high rates of psychopathology whereas Down syndrome individuals have relatively lower rates of psychopathology (Silverstein et al., 1985). In general, diffuse organic dysfunction is more of an issue in the severe and profoundly retarded population.

PSYCHODYNAMIC FACTORS

Psychodynamic factors vary according to intellectual level, but they are more important among severe to profoundly retarded people than is generally recognized. In this group the issues will be more basic and fundamental, such as loss and attachment.

CASE EXAMPLE

A profoundly retarded boy engaged in severe self-injury by bitting the flesh on his forearms to the point that there were always open lesions. Carbamazepine administration virtually extinguished the behavior. This nonverbal boy was involved in a foster grandparent program that brought retired senior citizens into the institution for a few hours a day. Several months after he began the carbamazepine, the foster grandparent program was abruptly terminated. Despite the boy's apparent excellent pharmacological response and the observation that he had often appeared to be oblivious to the foster grandmother's presence, he began to bite himself again after she did not visit for three consecutive days. The behavior continued until the program was resumed several weeks later. A subsequent attempt to withdraw the carbamazepine produced similar results, suggesting that both psychodynamic and organic factors were involved in the genesis and treatment of the behavior.

As intelligence rises, the psychodynamic factors become more complex. Zigler and Hodapp (1987) have discussed the effects of repeated failure on the development of mentally retarded children. If the increased dependency of retarded children becomes a character trait, it can become a major impediment to their development. Higher-functioning mentally retarded children will likely become acutely aware of their deficiencies as their younger siblings and children in the neighborhood develop skills that they do not possess. These observations can naturally lead to anger, depression, and diminished self-esteem. I also have been impressed with what can best be described as an existential depression as the children grapple with the question of why they are different from others and begin to see how much more limited their lives will be than those around them. These issues are similar to those seen in some children with severe physical limitations.

EDUCATIONAL AND SCHOOL EXPERIENCE

While the role of the educational system is also discussed in the section on treatment considerations, it is discussed here because of the negative impact that educational experiences can have on the developing child if not managed appropriately. While this is true for all children, it is even more important for children with developmental disabilities.

Educators have a difficult task teaching children with cognitive limitations and severe learning disabilities. They must strike a balance between challenging children to work up to the limits of their potential while not presenting them with so many experiences of failure that they do not feel continually frustrated. Although the balance often is successfully struck, in many situations children are either undereducated or overly frustrated. Many of those developmentally impaired children who are continually confronted with failure tend to evolve into a chronic demoralized dysthymic state. Another subgroup evolves into an angry oppositional conduct-disordered presentation.

Of equal importance to the educational experience is the social experience with their peers. Grouping developmentally impaired children with normal peers has advantages. However, it also brings with it the risk of scapegoating and victimization. Even normally developing children can be quite unsure of their abilities and can project their own uncertainties and vulnerabilities onto the retarded child in the classroom. The teasing and ridicule that ensue can border on the sadistic. Besides overt hostility toward the impaired child, more subtle affronts on self-esteem arise as the developmentally impaired child continually compares his or her skills unfavorably to those of the normal child. Although these concerns are present at all levels of developmental impairment, they take on an added dimension in those children who are mildly retarded, the largest subgroup, as they are often more keenly aware of their deficiencies than those with more severe impairments.

Thus, teachers must be constantly vigilant that neither the educational program nor the social milieu of the classroom becomes a detrimental rather than a constructive force in the child's development.

FAMILY ISSUES

The birth of a mentally retarded child places an extreme strain on even a well-functioning family system. Wolfensberger (1968) described three primary issues that parents of a handicapped child must deal with: (1) the initial disappointment and shock, (2) a rethinking of long-term expectations and goals for the child and, (3) the reality of practical problems that will occur on an ongoing basis (Corbett, 1985). Despite these stressors, the incidence of divorce and/or behavioral disturbance in the parents and siblings does not appear to be greater than that of the general population (Caldwell & Guze, 1960; Carr, 1974; Corbett, 1985).

CULTURAL FACTORS

It is difficult to quantify the day-to-day effects of cultural stigmatization on the development of the mentally retarded child. This stigmatization can range from the subtle effects of being stared at (if physical anomalies also are present) to outright harassment. At the other extreme, well-meaning individuals may inadvertently foster overdependence or cause embarrassment through overly solicitous behavior.

Treatment Considerations

BEHAVIORAL APPROACHES

Historically behavioral approaches have represented the predominant intervention for behav-

ioral problems manifested by mentally retarded children. Behavioral approaches also have been the most intensively and rigorously studied treatment modalities (Lennox, Miltenberger, Spengler, & Erfanian, 1988; Matson & Gorman-Smith, 1986). According to Bregman (1991), the behaviors most frequently treated with this approach are "aggression, noncompliance, hyperactivity, destructive and disruptive behavior, self-injury and stereotype" (p. 864). In general, these approaches attempt to increase the frequency of adaptive behaviors through positive reinforcement with the goal of simultaneously decreasing negative target behaviors. Direct efforts to decrease negative target behaviors through various punishment techniques have been used widely but currently are considered to be controversial (Matson & Taras, 1989).

EDUCATIONAL APPROACHES

Historically many mildly retarded children were not diagnosed until they began school. Improvements in early detection and the development of early intervention programs have led to the earlier delivery of appropriate services for many children. However, there are still some developmentally impaired children whose difficulties are not fully appreciated until they begin school. Thus, the educational system still has an important role in detection and diagnosis. As children age, fully delineating the nature and extent of the cognitive deficit becomes more possible. Ongoing thorough evaluation of children's abilities is a key component of effective educational planning.

Those with mild mental retardation traditionally have been thought of as the "educable" subgroup of the developmentally impaired in terms of their ability to acquire traditional academic skills. As these children become older, increasing attention needs to be devoted to vocational, general living, and social skills development, as many of this group can live independently or with minimal support if appropriately prepared. The emphasis on the practical also provides individuals with a degree of immediate positive reinforcement that may be lacking with the acquisition of more abstract skills.

As noted earlier, the educational environment carries with it the potential for both significant positive as well as negative impact on the emotional growth and development of the mentally retarded child. The primary challenge facing the special needs educator is that of balancing the need to challenge and motivate these children to perform to their fullest potential without overly frustrating them with repeated experiences of failure.

The educator also has to attend to the social milieu of the classrooms and broader school setting. No discussion would be complete without mention of the concept of "mainstreaming" (Zigler & Hodapp, 1987). This term refers to the placement of developmentally impaired children in classrooms that also serve nonhandicapped children. The rationale for this is that placement in a more normalized environment will facilitate the intellectual and social growth of the developmentally impaired child. While this theoretical concept has widespread appeal, investigations into its actual benefit have been inconclusive (Zigler & Muenchow, 1979). My own experience in evaluating the emotional status of developmentally impaired children has indicated that the attitudes and individual characteristics of the child's educators are more important factors than the theoretical tenets that they ascribe to.

PSYCHODYNAMIC APPROACHES

Individual and family psychotherapy is probably the most overlooked treatment approach for the mentally retarded population. Many psychotherapists remain unaware of the richness of the emotional life of mentally retarded people and underestimate the value of this approach. This is especially true for the mild and moderately retarded (Hurley, 1989). Bregman (1991, p. 865) has delineated the goals of psychotherapy for mentally retarded persons as follows:

1. The expression and resolution of dysphoria, anger, and resentment related to realistic cognitive limitations and to experiences of social stigmatization and rejection
2. The enhancement of self-esteem and personal competence within realistic boundaries
3. The development of a greater capacity to recognize, process, and resolve internalized conflict adaptively
4. The ability to assume greater personal independence and emancipation from family and others
5. A broadening of the social skills and competencies

necessary for successful social group acceptance and participation

Certain issues arise during psychotherapeutic work with mentally retarded persons of which therapists must be aware to work effectively with this population (Mikkelsen, 1994). For example, the retarded individual's diminished capacity for abstract thinking may limit the scope of potential insight and slow the progress of the therapy. The goals of the therapy should be relatively concrete and introduced gradually. Many mentally retarded individuals have experienced repeated interpersonal losses. These experiences can make them reticent to enter into a therapeutic relationship. This reticence can be easily mistaken for a by-product of limited intelligence. The therapist also must grapple with the demands of establishing an empathic relationship. Their acute awareness of their deficiencies often makes the situation of higher-functioning, mildly retarded individuals more poignant. The therapist may respond to these issues by an overly sympathetic approach or by distancing him- or herself from the core existential issues. Once the therapist has worked through and dealt with the special issues that may be involved with a given individual, psychotherapy can prove to be as effective and gratifying as it is with any other population.

PSYCHOPHARMACOLOGICAL APPROACHES

The historical overuse of antipsychotic medication to control negative behaviors in the mentally retarded population through sedation has led many professionals in the field to an understandable but unfortunate bias against psychotropic medication. This antimedication bias is beginning to abate somewhat as research into the pharmacological treatment of behavioral disorders in the mentally retarded population becomes more specific and credible.

In general, psychotropic medication will be used to treat either a diagnosed psychiatric disturbance that is occurring comorbidly in a mentally retarded individual or will be used on an empirical basis to treat a specific behavior, such as aggression or self-injurious behavior (Mikkelsen, 1986; Ratey et al., 1986). As would be expected, the former approach is more apt to be used in mildly retarded persons while the latter approach is more common in those with severe to profound retardation. A complete review of the range of psychopharmacological agents employed in the treatment of the retarded is beyond the scope of this chapter. Studies of the efficacy of antipsychotic medication for the pervasive developmental disorders have been reviewed by Mikkelsen (1982), and Bregman (1991) has prepared an extensive review of the literature concerning the use of psychotropic medication in the mentally retarded population.

Current Trends and Future Direction

In many states the deinstitutionalization of mentally retarded persons is moving forward at a rapid rate. In general, this movement is proving more successful than it did for mentally ill persons. As retarded individuals require a greater level of basic care usually they are not removed from an institution until a definite community placement and support system has been identified. Thus, they are more likely to move into a staffed community residence and are less likely than mentally ill persons to appear on the streets or in homeless shelters.

The trend toward community treatment and deinstitutionalization has had a marked impact on the school-age mentally retarded child and his or her parents. Far fewer children are being institutionalized today than was the case in past years. While this is certainly desirable, it does place additional strain on families whose child may have a concomitant behavioral problem and on the schools that are required to provide educational services. There is a growing recognition that if families are to meet the challenge of successfully caring for their mentally retarded child at home, they will require greater respite and in home support resources.

REFERENCES

American Association on Mental Retardation. (1992). *Mental Retardation: Definition, classification, and systems of supports* (9th ed.) Washington, DC: Author.

American Psychiatric Association. (1994). *Diagnostic and statistical manual of mental disorders* (4th ed. 1994). Washington, DC: Author.

Bregman, J. D. (1991). Current developments in the understanding of mental retardation. Part II: Psychopathology. *Journal of the American Academy of Child and Adolescent Psychiatry, 30* (6), 861–872.

Bregman, J. D., & Hodapp, R. M. (1991). Current developments in the understanding of mental retardation Part I: Biological and phenomenological perspectives. *Journal of the American Academy of Child and Adolescent Psychiatry, 30* (5), 707–719.

Caldwell, B. M., & Guze, S. B. (1960). A study of the adjustment of parents and siblings of institutionalized and non-institutionalized retarded children. *American Journal of Mental Defiency, 64,* 845–861.

Carr, J. (1974). The effect of the severely subnormal on their families. In A. M. Clarke & A. B. D. Clarke (Eds.), *Mental deficiency: The changing outlook* (pp. 807–839). London: Methuen.

Corbett, J. A. (1985). Mental retardation: Psychiatric aspects. In M. Rutter & L. Hersov (Eds.), *Child and adolescent psychiatry: Modern approaches* (2nd ed., pp. 661–678.) London: Blackwell Scientific Publications.

Corbett, J. A., Harris, E., & Robinson, R. (1975). Epilepsy. In J. Wortis (Ed.), *Mental retardation and developmental disabilities: Vol. 7.: An annual review* (pp. 79–111). New York: Brunner/Mazel.

Fryns, J. P. (1987). Chromosomal anomalies and autosomal syndromes. *Birth Defects, 23,* 7–32.

Gillberg, C., Persson, E., Grufman, M., & Themner, U. (1986). Psychiatric disorders in mildly and severely mentally retarded urban children and adolescents: Epidemiological aspects. *British Journal of Psychiatry, 149,* 68–74.

Hurley, A. D. (1989). Individual psychotherapy with mentally retarded individuals: A review and call for research. *Research in Developmental Disabilities, 10,* 261–275.

Lennox, D. B., Miltenberger, R. G., Spengler, P., & Erfanian, N. (1988). Decelerative treatment practices with persons who have mental retardation: A review of five years of the literature. *American Journal of Mental Retardation, 92,* 492–501.

Matson, J., & Gorman-Smith, D. (1986). A review of treatment research for aggressive and disruptive behavior in the mentally retarded. *Applied Research in Mental Retardation, 7,* 95–103.

Matson, J., Taras, M. E. (1989). A 20-year review of punishment and alternative methods to treat problem behaviors in developmentally delayed persons. *Research in Developmental Disabilities, 10,* 85–104.

Mikkelsen, E. J. (1982). Efficacy of neuroleptic medication in pervasive developmental disorders of child-hood. *Schizophrenia Bulletin 8* (2), 320–332.

Mikkelsen, E. J. (1986). Low dose haloperidol for stereotypic self-injurious behavior in the profoundly retarded. *New England Journal of Medicine, 315* (6), 398–399.

Mikkelsen, E. J. (1987). Organic mental disorders. In R. Michels & J. O. Cavenar (Eds.), *Psychiatry* (3rd ed., chap. 34). Philadelphia: J.P. Lippincott Co. Basic Books.

Mikkelsen, E. J. (1994). Is psychotherapy useful for the mentally retarded? *Harvard Mental Health Letter 11* (2), F8.

Ratey, J. J., Mikkelsen, E. J., Smith G. B., Upadhyaya, A., Zuckerman, H. S., Martell, D., & Sorgi, P. (1986). Betablockers in the severely and profoundly mentally retarded. *Journal of Clinical Psychopharmacology, 6,* 103–107.

Reid, A. (1989). Schizophrenia in mental retardation: Clinical features. *Research in Developmental Disabilities, 10,* 241–249.

Silverstein, A. B., Ageno, D., Alleman, A. C., Derecho, K. T., Gray, S. B., & White, J. F. (1985). Adaptive

behavior of institutionalized individuals with Down syndrome. *American Journal of Mental Deficiency, 89,* 555–558.

Sovner, R., & Desnoyers-Hurley, A. (1983). Do the mentally retarded suffer from affective illness? *Archives of General Psychiatry, 40,* 61–67.

Tanguay, P. E., & Russell, A. T. (1991). Mental retardation. In M. Lewis (Ed.), *Child and adolescent psychiatry: A comprehensive textbook* (pp. 508–516). Baltimore: Williams & Wilkins.

Wolfensberger, W. (1968). Vocational preparation and occupation. In A. A. Baumeister (Ed.), *Mental retardation appraisal, rehabilitation and education* (pp. 329–400). London: University of London Press.

Zigler, E., & Hodapp, R. M. (1986). *Understanding mental retardation.* Cambridge: Cambridge University Press.

Zigler, E., & Hodapp, R. M. (1987). Mental retardation. In R. Michels & J. Cavenar (Eds.), *Psychiatry* (2nd ed., chap. 28). Philadelphia: J. P. Lippincott.

Zigler, E., Muenchow, S. (1979). Mainstreaming: The proof is in the implementation. *American Psychologist, 34,* 993–996.

37 / Developmental Language Disorders in School-Age Children

Lauren Hummel and Carl Feinstein

Developmental language disorders are a topic of considerable importance to child and adolescent psychiatry. Estimates of the prevalence of these conditions in school-age children range from 5 to 20% (Cantwell and Baker, 1991; Silva, 1987; Tallal, 1988). Furthermore, it is now well established that these commonly occurring disorders greatly increase vulnerability to psychiatric disorder and, indeed, are found in a high proportion of children referred for psychiatric treatment (Cantwell & Baker, 1991). Approximately one half of school-age children with developmental language disorder also suffer from psychiatric disorder (Beitchman et al., 1986; Cantwell & Baker, 1987). Most

studies of psychiatrically disordered school-age children similarly find that approximately one half have a speech or language disorder (Mack & Warr-Leeper, 1992; Prizant et al., 1990). Even in public school programs for school-age children with mild to moderate behavior disorders, 71% have been found to have language deficits (Miniutti, 1991).

Despite the well-documented association between psychiatric disorders and language disorders, many language-disordered school-age children referred to child psychiatric settings still arrive with their language disorder unrecognized. Within the mental health setting, language disorders frequently are not discovered or are acknowledged only as a peripheral problem. There appear to be three reasons for this relative neglect. First, in most school-age children, the manifestations of language disorders are subtle. Their detection requires a clinician with some training in this area

This work was supported by Child and Adolescent Mental Health Academic Award 1KO7MH00766 from the National Institute of Mental Health. Additional support was provided by Program Project NS 20489 from the National Institute of Neurologic Diseases and Strokes, U.S. Public Health Service.

The authors wish to acknowledge the thoughtful critique by Paula Menyuk, Ph.D., of initial drafts of this chapter.

plus a high index of suspicion. Second, the potential detrimental effects of these disorders on academic and psychosocial functioning have only begun to be widely recognized. Third, few specialized treatment protocols adjust psychotherapeutic interventions to the language level of the child. Therefore, many mental health professionals do not recognize what difference it makes in their clinical practice if their patients are language disordered.

This chapter concentrates on providing information useful in identifying language disorder in school-age children and in recognizing its many deleterious effects on psychosocial adaptation. We begin by presenting definitions of linguistic functioning and of developmental language disorder. Next we provide a brief overview of normal language development as a framework within which to evaluate possible clinical abnormalities. Following this, we review the types of language difficulties that may be clinically observed in school-age children. Against this backdrop, we discuss the impact of language difficulties on academic and social functioning. We conclude with a brief discussion of etiologic considerations and current trends in assessment and intervention.

Language: Definitions of Terms

Communication may be defined as the successful transmission of meaning. In this context, language is a symbol system that is used to communicate with others. It can occur in spoken, written, and gestural modalities. Communication by spoken language is commonly augmented by paralinguistic (e.g., intonation) and nonlinguistic (e.g., facial expressions or gestures) means. Language is commonly analyzed in terms of form, content, and use. (Bloom & Laley, 1978).

Language form may be described in terms of 5 rule-governed systems: phonological, morphological, syntactic, semantic, and pragmatic. Phonology refers to the set of rules determining which speech sounds in which combinations are appropriate to a given language, such as English or Swahili. Phonological rules differentiate words on the basis of sounds (e.g., "*l*ip" from "*l*ap" and "*s*it" from *s*ip"). Morphology refers to the set of rules

by which units of speech sound (morphemes) modify the meaning of words ("walk" from "walk*ed*" and "I walk" from "he walk*s*," "*un*happy" from "happy"). Syntax refers to the set of rules governing how words and word phrases may be ordered correctly to form standard sentences in a given language (e.g., "the farmer plants seeds" would be correct in English; whereas "seeds farmer plant" is intelligible but incorrect syntax). A variety of syntactically correct sentences (e.g., the child fed the cat, the cat was fed by the child) may convey close to the same meaning in a different form. Semantics refer to the set of rules that govern the coding of meaning into single words (lexical semantics) and the ordering of combinations of words to convey different meanings (relational semantics). A simple example of relational semantics might be the distinction between "the man bit the dog" and "the dog bit the man," where the ordering of the noun elements determines the meaning.

Language use is governed by strategies, rules, and customs for effective communication commonly called pragmatics. The competent application of pragmatics allows messages to be conveyed and the intentions served by words (e.g., to greet, comment, to be polite, or tell a story to a given person or audience) to be achieved. Pragmatics also govern conversation, so that conversational partners can achieve listener and speaker roles, effectively alternate these roles, and repair miscommunications. Pragmatic strategies frequently involve taking into account the situation or perspective of the listener, so that sufficient contextual information is included for the communication to be understood. Ineffective pragmatics lead to breakdowns in communication, as when a person starts a story from the middle without providing background information, or when a listener ignores turn-taking rules and interrupts a speaker.

Communication Disorders

The American Speech, Language, Hearing Association defines Communication Disorder as: ". . . an impairment in the ability to receive, send, process, and comprehend concepts or verbal nonverbal and graphic symbol systems . . ." (American

Speech, 1993). The associated ASHA definitions of Speech Disorder and Language Disorder are as follows:

specific disorders delineated in *DSM-IV* are expressive language disorder, mixed receptive-expressive language disorder, phonological disorder, stuttering, and communication disorder not otherwise specified. The *DSM-IV* definitions of these disorders are presented in Tables 37.2 to 37.6. Disorders of reading and written expression are classified under learning disorders, although clearly they have much to do with language and communication.

There are several notable changes in the *DSM-IV* classification as compared to the third revised edition of the *DSM* (*DSM-III-R*, APA, 1987). All the communication disorders are coded on Axis I instead of Axis II. Mixed Receptive-Expressive Language Disorder replaces the *DSM-III-R* diagnosis of Developmental Receptive Language Disorder, because more recent thinking is that language disorders are invariably accompanied by expressive deficits. The diagnostic category Pho-nological Disorder in *DSM-IV* replaces the *DSM-III-R* category of Developmental Articulation Disorder. Phonological Disorder, unlike its predecesor, includes (although not explicity stated as such in the formal criteria) both articulation and cognitive processing of speech sounds. *DSM-IV* departs significantly from the *DSM-III-R* in that dysarthria, apraxia, or other neurological disorder, sensory deficit, mental retardation, and environmental deprivation are no longer exclusion criteria in *DSM-IV*. These problems may be present, so long as the degree of language deficit is greater than can be accounted for by their presence alone. Another difference from the *DSM-III-R* is that, in *DSM-IV*, communication disorders may either be developmental or acquired.

Early Language Development

When infants first communicate, it is to influence the behavior of others, to establish joint atten-

TABLE 37.1

Speech Disorder and Language Disorder

A. *A SPEECH DISORDER* is an impairment of the articulation of speech sounds, fluency and/or voice.

   1. AN ARTICULATION DISORDER is the atypical production of speech sounds characterized by omissions, additions or distortions that may interfere with intelligibility.

   2. A FLUENCY DISORDER is an interruption in the flow of speaking characterized by atypical rate, rhythm, and repetitions in sounds, syllables, words, and phrases. This may be accompanied by excessive tension, struggle behavior, and secondary mannerisms.

   3. A VOICE DISORDER is characterized by the abnormal production and/or absences of vocal quality, pitch, loudness, resonance, and/or duration, which is inappropriate for an individual's age or sex.

B. *A LANGUAGE DISORDER* is impaired comprehension and/or use of spoken, written and/or other symbol systems. The disorder may involve (1) the form of language (phonology, morphology, syntax), (2) the content of language (semantics), and/or (3) the function of language in communication (pragmatics) in any combination.

   1. Form of Language
      a. PHONOLOGY is the sound system of a language and the rules that govern the sound combinations.
      b. MORPHOLOGY is the system that governs the structure of words and the construction of word forms.
      c. SYNTAX is the system governing the order and combination of words to form sentences and the relationships among the elements within a sentence.

   2. Content of Language
      a. SEMANTICS is the system that governs the meaning of words and sentences.

   3. Function of Language
      a. PRAGMATICS is the system that combines the above language components in functional and socially appropriate communication.

TABLE 37.2

Diagnostic Criteria for 315.31 Expressive Language Disorder

A. The scores obtained from standardized individually administered measures expressive language development are substantially below those obtained from standardized measures of both nonverbal intellectual capacity and receptive language development. The disturbance may be manifest clinically by symptoms that include having a markedly limited vocabulary, making errors in tense, or having difficulty recalling words or producing sentences with developmentally appropriate length or complexity.

B. The difficulties with expressive language interfere with academic or occupational achievement or with social communication.

C. Criteria are not met for Mixed Receptive-Expressive Language Disorder or a Pervasive Developmental Disorder.

D. If Mental Retardation, a speech-motor or sensory deficit, or environmental deprivation is present, the language difficulties are in excess of those usually associated with these problems.

Coding Note: If a speech-motor or sensory deficit or a neurological condition is present, code the condition on Axis III.

NOTE. From *Diagnostic and Statistical Manual of Mental Disorders*, 4th ed., American Psychiatric Association, 1994. Washington, D.C.: Author, p. 58. Copyright 1994 by the American Psychiatric Association. Reprinted with permission.

TABLE 37.3

Diagnostic Criteria for 315.31 Mixed Receptive Expressive Language Disorder

A. The scores obtained from a battery of standardized individually administered measures of both receptive and expressive language development are substantially below those obtained from standardized measures of nonverbal intellectual capacity. Symptoms include those for Expressive Language Disorder as well as difficulty understanding words, sentences, or specific types of words, such as spatial terms.

B. The difficulties with receptive and expressive language significantly interfere with academic or occupational achievement or with social communication.

C. Criteria are not met for a Pervasive Developmental Disorder.

D. If Mental Retardation, a speech-motor or sensory deficit, or environmental deprivations is present, the language difficulties are in excess of those usually associated with these problems.

Coding Note: If a speech-motor or sensory deficit or a neurological condition is present, code the condition on Axis III.

NOTE. From *Diagnostic and Statistical Manual of Mental Disorders*, 4th ed., American Psychiatric Association, 1994. Washington, D.C.: Author, pp. 60–61. Copyright 1994 by the American Psychiatric Association. Reprinted with permission.

TABLE 37.4

Diagnostic Criteria for 315.39 Phonologial Disorder

A. Failure to use developmentally expected speech sounds that are appropriate for age and dialect (e.g., errors in sound production, use, representation, or organization such as, but not limited to, substitutions of one sound for another [use of /t/ for target /k/ sound] or omissions of sounds such as final consonants).

B. The difficulties in speech sound production interfere with academic or occupational achievement or with social communication.

C. If Mental Retardation, a speech-motor or sensory deficit, or environmental deprivation is present, the speech difficulties are in excess of those usually associated with these problems.

Coding Note: If a speech-motor or sensory deficit or a neurological condition is present, code the condition on Axis III.

NOTE. From *Diagnostic and Statistical Manual of Mental Disorders*, 4th ed., American Psychiatric Association, 1994. Washington, D.C.: Author, p. 63. Copyright 1994 by the American Psychiatric Association. Reprinted with permission.

TABLE 37.5

Diagnostic Criteria for 307.0 Stuttering

A. Disturbance in the normal fluency and time patterning of speech (inappropriate for the individual's age), characterized by frequent occurrences of one or more of the following:
   1) Sound and syllable repetitions.
   2) Sound prolongations.
   3) Interjections
   4) Broken words (e.g., pauses within a word)
   5) Audible or silent blocking (filled or unfilled pauses in speech).
   6) Circumlocutions (word substitutions to avoid problematic words).
   7) Words produced with an excess of physical tension.
   8) Monosyllabic whole-word repetitions (e.g., "I-I-I-I see him").

B. The disturbance in fluency interferes with academic or occupational achievement or with social communication.

C. If a speech-motor or sensory deficit is present, the speech difficulties are in excess of those usually associated with these problems.

Coding Note: If a speech-motor or sensory deficit or a neurological condition is present, code the condition on Axis III.

NOTE. From *Diagnostic and Statistical Manual of Mental Disorders*, 4th ed., American Psychiatric Association, 1994. Washington, D.C.: Author, p. 65. Copyright 1994 by the American Psychiatric Association. Reprinted with permission.

TABLE 37.6

Diagnostic Criteria for 307.9 Communication Disorder Not Otherwise Specified

This category is for disorders in communication that do not meet criteria for any specific Communication Disorder; for example, a voice disorder (i.e., an abnormality of vocal pitch, loudness, quality, tone, or resonance).

NOTE. From *Diagnostic and Statistical Manual of Mental Disorders*, 4th ed., American Psychiatric Association, 1994. Washington, D.C.: Author, p. 65. Copyright 1994 by the American Psychiatric Association. Reprinted with permission.

tion, and to engage their caregivers socially (Bruner, 1981). Prior to the development of spoken language, infants use gesture, facial expression, vocalization, and intonational contour to communicate and express a wide range of affects (Menyuk, 1988).

By the end of the first year of life, children have begun to acquire language as a representational system: In the course of this advance, the ability to comprehend precedes the ability to express. The first words acquired are commonly those with which children have the most experience, such as the names of specific people and objects (e.g., "mommy," "daddy," "shoe"), action words (e.g., "up"), and attributes or values (e.g., "good," "dirty") (Menyuk, 1988). These words are understood and used initially in the context of familiar events.

Although infants communicate first about the here and now, an advance occurs toward the second year of life, to include past and present. This transition is accompanied by an increase in both the rate of lexical acquisition and the production of two-word utterances (Menyuk, 1988). By the age of 4, children have progressed from single words and short phrases to sentences, have acquired a substantial vocabulary, and have begun to demonstrate conversational and narrative skills. By 5 years of age children "show the first signs of being able to utilize language skills in the same way adults do: to talk with one another concerning events, ideas, objects, or relationships with sufficient clarity so that the listener—with no previous awareness of the speaker's content—can comprehend the meaning of the speaker" (Weiner, 1989, p. 7).

Language Development in the Early School Years

During the early elementary school years, children's narrative skills and their ability to participate in conversation continue to develop. They begin to tell stories containing characters, initiating events, and conveying the response of the characters to those events (Westby, Van Dongen, & Maggart, 1989). Lexical knowledge becomes more adultlike (Menyuk, 1988) as does the comprehension and use of nonliteral language, such as metaphors and jokes (Bernstein, 1989a). During this period, children progressively develop the ability to use and understand complex sentences such as those containing embedding (e.g., "The boy who sat on the couch was crying") and acquire specific morphemes (e.g., the derivational morpheme *-er,* which changes the verb [catch] to a noun [catcher]) (Bernstein, 1989a, p. 134).

Much of language development occurring after children reach the age of 6 depends on their development of metalinguistic awareness (Wallach & Miller, 1988), which refers to the dual recognition that, first, language is a product of the mental activities of both the self and the other, and, second, to the ability to observe and reflect consciously on its attributes. Metalinguistic awareness is needed for discussing conversational rules (e.g., "It's not polite to interrupt"), talking about phonological aspects of words (e.g., "What's the first sound in cat?"), relating spoken words to written words (e.g., "What does that sign say?"), recognizing and employing synonyms and antonyms, distinguishing between standard and nonstandard grammatical forms (e.g., double negations, "is not" versus "ain't," etc.), and understanding jokes and puns. The elementary school language arts curriculum assumes that school-age children have already achieved a foundation of metalinguistic awareness and proceeds to build on it in order to promote mastery of more sophisticated language skills.

Language Development in Ages 9 through 12

Language development through the middle and later school-age years is a gradual and incremental process (Nippold, 1988a), in the course of which the role of written language becomes progres-

sively more important. Literary styles emerge that are significantly different from the spoken vernacular. Syntax development during this period involves the acquisition of the ability to understand and apply low-frequency syntactic structures, to form unique combinations of structures, and to adapt syntax use to a wide variety of contexts (Scott, 1988). More dramatic still are the changes that occur during this period in pragmatic conversational skills, such as topic maintenance, the use and understanding of specific types of indirect speech acts (e.g., lying, humor, sarcasm), and awareness of communicative behavior (Menyuk, 1988).

Recognizing Language Disorders

Language disorder is a heterogeneous condition. It takes many forms, with a wide variety of possible impairments occurring singly or, more frequently, in combination (Cantwell & Baker, 1991). Three broad types of language-impaired children are commonly described: children who comprehend significantly more than they produce (expressively impaired), children whose expressive fluency disguises poor comprehension (receptively impaired), and children who seem significantly impaired in both expressive and receptive domains (Tallal, 1988). Although these three groupings are widely recognized and incorporated into both *DSM-III-R* and *DSM-IV* (APA, 1987, 1994), no empirically validated classification of childhood language disorders has been established clearly. Distinct patterns of phonological, morphological, syntactic, semantic, and pragmatic performance within each group have not been identified (Morris, 1988; Rapin & Allen, 1988). What follows here is a very brief account of impairments that have been noted to occur commonly in school-age children. Mental health clinicians who detect these problems should request a formal assessment of language functioning, to rule out, confirm, or more precisely describe the form of language disorder.

A factor that greatly complicates recognition of language disorders in school-age children is that, even though such conditions are frequently chronic in course, the language abilities of language-impaired children nevertheless undergo considerable development. Deficits in one or another language skill fade developmentally as the child grows older, to be replaced by deficits at some higher level of functioning that would be normative for the child's more advanced chronological age. Thus, as these children grow older, their impairments may become more subtle, affecting higher-order functions that are less easily perceived in routine conversations. Many signs and symptoms of developmental language disorder fall into this category. Thus, overt symptoms of this kind in a preschool or early school-age child may take form as delayed onset of language development, greatly reduced utterance length, and limited vocabulary. However, in the same child at age 10 or 12, these problems may no longer be present or as obvious (Wallach & Liebergott, 1984). But this child might now have impairments in other areas, such as in following complicated directions, inferential verbal reasoning deficits, word retrieval problems, and pragmatic difficulties that interfere with academic functioning or optimal participation in peer group activities. For the older school-age child, language impairment might not be noticed in spoken language but manifested instead as poor performance in reading and writing. Thus, while the language of the language-disordered child does improve over time, the later manifestations of the impairment still leave these children at a relative disadvantage compared to peers.

Symptoms of Developmental Language Disorders

In terms of language form, syntactic problems may be manifested by difficulty comprehending and producing longer sentences, such as those that require coordination of information from two or more simpler sentences (e.g., "John and Mary liked ice cream"); or that contain multiple modifiers (e.g., *the big round red apple*); or that contain embedding (e.g., "I saw a boy wearing a red hat"). Other children have difficulty understanding even short sentences with more complex syntax (e.g., "Joe was hit by Bill") (Menyuk, 1988).

Such children have trouble understanding verbal or written material that conveys abstract ideas or relationships, and have difficulty communicating complex thoughts. These children may speak in short or even telegraphic sentences and find it very hard to convey a coherent sequence of ideas, subjects, feelings, or events.

Problems that some language-impaired children have with language content are evident in poorly developed lexical knowledge or difficulty calling up specific words. Although they may know the names of common objects, their knowledge of the various relationships between words, such as categories or classification (e.g., apples and grapes as fruit, trains and airplanes as forms of transportation, etc.) may be limited. Such children may make imprecise word choices or rely on nonspecific referents such as "that" or "guy." They do not readily appreciate that words can have multiple meanings, and consequently they fail to understand apparently "simple" directions (e.g., "I want a quiet line"). Preadolescents with a history of language acquisition difficulties have to struggle to grasp metaphors such as "Anger ate him up" (Nippold & Fey, 1983). Not infrequently, language-impaired children do poorly in recalling stories or other longer narratives, or they may have difficulty drawing inferences or grasping the significant themes (Crais & Chapman, 1987).

In terms of social use of language, language-impaired children may produce disorganized narratives and/or fail to provide sufficient information to be understood out of context (Westby et al., 1989).

The pragmatic deficits of some language-impaired children will be described further as these deficits relate to the impact of language disorders on social functioning.

Relationship of Language Disorders to Learning Disorders

Language disorders and learning disorders frequently are referred to as distinct entities without reference to each other, as if they were separate conditions; in fact, however, this distinction has little empirical support (Feinstein & Aldershof,

1991). Children diagnosed as language disordered in the preschool or early school-age years often are found years later at follow-up to be learning disordered (Aram & Hall, 1989; Cantwell & Baker, 1991; Silva, 1987; Stevenson et al., 1985). Conversely, evaluation of learning-disordered school-age children often reveals an underlying language disorder (Silva, 1987; Stevenson & Richman, 1978). In fact, many such children have specific deficits both in language and in other cognitive areas (Mattis, 1975; Morris, 1986; Nussbaum, 1986).

Children with language deficits are consistently found to be at increased risk for reading problems (Catts, 1993). Since reading and writing are basically language functions, it is not surprising that significant impairment in any linguistic domain is likely to impede the school-age child's ability to learn to read and write. For example, some poor readers have difficulty recognizing or producing phonological sequences or utilizing phonological structure to recognize words and to spell (Catts, 1989). Other poor readers may have difficulty in such areas as word association tasks, word retrieval, comprehension and use of morphological units and syntactic structures, narrative production, recalling details from stories, answering inferential questions about stories, and comprehending figurative language.

The Impact of Language Disorders on Social Functioning

Since communication is central to social functioning, it follows that children whose communication is impaired by language deficits are at increased risk for difficulties in their social adaptation. To date a considerable body of research documents that childhood language impairment may adversely affect the parent-child relationship in a variety of ways, namely by decreasing overall communication, by making the child less "readable" to the parents, and by influencing parents toward a more directive and intrusive pattern of interaction with the child, (Van Kleeck and Richardson, 1988).

There is emerging evidence that language deficits impact on social interactions even in the preschool years. Rice, Sell, and Hadley (1991) found that the preferred conversational partners of preschool children were peers with normally developing language as opposed to peers with speech and language impairments. In addition, Gertner, Rice, and Hadley (1994) reported that children with normally developing language were more popular than children with specific language impairment and children who lacked English proficiency. Language impairment may adversely affect social interaction with peers by directly hindering speaking to or comprehending others or, in more subtle fashion, by interfering with such social skills as the ability to appreciate the reciprocal nature of communication (e.g., taking listener and speaker roles), the ability to regulate discourse (e.g., requesting clarification), the ability to "code switch" or modify speech relative to the age and status of the communicative partner, and the ability to employ a wide range of speech acts, such as requesting, greeting, and refusing (Tallal, 1988). As suggested by Gertner et al. (1994), "it is likely that children with language limitations will not have a circle of friends with whom to experience socioverbal interactions" (p. 922).

Numerous difficulties in the social use of language have been documented in children with psychiatric disorders. These include violations of conversational "rules" and failure to provide background information (Baltaxe & Simmons, 1988). Children with co-occurring language and psychiatric disorders may respond to stress by displaying increased difficulty, accessing partially developed linguistic capacities that might otherwise be within their repertoire. Thus, when the adaptive need for language is greatest (e.g., to verbally express disagreement, to request clarification, to elaborate alternative solutions to problems, or to negotiate), these children are at a disadvantage. Misunderstanding is then more likely to occur, and the repair of communication breakdowns is more difficult.

Language-disordered children are less likely to be among those chosen as friends by classmates and, as they grow older, less frequently invited to socialize by peers or be involved in extracurricular activities. Language-based difficulties in acquiring both vocabulary and syntactic and semantic structures may hinder children's ability to learn new peer slang and idiomatic expressions, causing them to miss out on innuendos, jokes, puns, and sarcastic remarks. The ability to talk over problems and the verbal fluency necessary to engage in age-typical bantering may be reduced (Donahue and Bryan, 1984). As reported by Henry, Reed, and McAllister (1995), normally achieving adolescents have been found to value most those communication skills that can be associated with characteristics of empathy, perspective taking, and vocal tone comprehension. Children who lack these skills are likely to be at risk for social isolation.

Some school-age language-impaired children have difficulty learning the rules or objectives of sports or games, or generalizing rules from one game to another. Language-impaired children are likely to have difficulty resolving conflicts, and experimental evidence suggests they may use persuasion less often than their peers (Stevens & Bliss, 1995).

The Impact of Language Disorders on School Behavior

Between kindergarten and second grade, children with comprehension problems are likely to have difficulty in understanding verbal instruction from the teacher. Their classroom participation may be reduced secondary to problems in both verbal expression and comprehension (Bashir, 1989). Children with phonologic problems are likely to do poorly at phonological decoding of words, an important skill in learning to read and spell. Relative to peers, these children will experience failure at the very outset of their lives as students.

As children progress through school, instructional language becomes increasingly detached from the here and now and ever more closely linked to events depicted in texts or, at any rate, not directly experienced in the classroom. Many language-impaired children who are able to understand what is said when it is accompanied by actual objects or clear referents such as pictures will have difficulty when these supports are not available. As the proportion of classroom time devoted to language-based learning activities increases, these children may develop attentional or behavioral problems. They also may do less well as learning becomes more discussion-based, as opposed to experientially based. Children with

inadequate language skills may fail to grasp the gist of classroom discussions or may lack the necessary conversational skills to participate in the exchanges. They may appear off-task, inattentive, or disorganized.

In the fourth grade new literacy demands begin. These include the use of instructional language composed of increasingly complex vocabulary and sentence structure, and the requirement that children demonstrate inferential understanding of texts (Bashir, 1989). Many language-impaired children can be expected to have difficulties meeting these expectations. As a consequence they will begin to fall behind in other academic subjects besides language arts, such as science and social studies, fall off the learning curve of their peers, and develop secondary self-esteem and motivational problems. Children who had begun to fall behind in the earlier grades continue to lag, and those who had initially managed to "keep up" now begin to experience failure.

By the time language-disordered youngsters reach adolescence, the adverse effects on their academic skills and knowledge, in conjunction with cumulative damage to their self-esteem and motivation, have created a very adverse high-risk situation. Of equal importance, a serious mismatch has come into play between the demands of the secondary school curriculum and the learning characteristics of language-disordered teenagers (Ehren & Lenz, 1989). Many of these youngsters continue to be impaired in their capacities to employ higher-level syntax, semantics, and pragmatics; unfortunately, mastery of these skills is required to negotiate the junior and senior high school curriculums successfully.

It is likely that in adolescence two general groupings of students with language disorders may be identified: those whose language disorder and learning problems were identified during primary school and whose problems persist; and those never previously identified, who struggled through elementary school but who are unable to cope with the secondary school curriculum (Ehren and Lenz, 1989). In either case, these adolescents suffer badly in high school. Many begin to fail, whereas others are placed in low-level or remedial classes recognized by everyone as of lower status.

Recent studies of adolescent psychiatric populations also find a high rate of language impairment (Feinstein, Aldershof, Seifer, Trecartin, &

Fey, 1991). Such evidence led the National Institute of Deafness and other Communication Disorders to convene a workshop that addressed correlations between communication disorders and juvenile behaviors in 1994. Although research in this area is quite limited, there is little doubt that, among the ranks of high school dropouts, a significant number bear the burden of a developmental language disorder. Among those teenagers who become delinquent, there is considerable evidence that many are developmentally language disordered (Lewis, 1991).

Etiological Considerations

The etiology of language disorders generally has been studied from both environmental and biological perspectives. The main thrust of the environmental perspective suggests that insufficient linguistic exposure or an impoverished social environment may result in impaired language development. Puckering and Rutter (1987) reviewed studies relative to this perspective and concluded that "certain very adverse conditions can retard the development of language. [but] . . . even after gross deprivation [language] will recover in a more enhancing environment" (p. 123). However, poor language development in younger children may lead to adverse educational tracking or to negative sociological or psychological consequences that further detract from the language environment.

Two current theories seek to explain the postulate that minority and disadvantaged children lag in language proficiency (Terrell & Terrell, 1983). The first (and dominant) view states that legitimate dialectal differences exist among various sociocultural groups and that language competence can be assessed only in the context of a child's sociocultural language milieu. The second view states that children from minority sociocultural backgrounds whose mastery of the standard language develops to a level below the expectation for the general population are, at the least, language disadvantaged both at school and then later when facing subsequent life opportunities. Current thinking in linguistics and among speech and language professionals (Taylor, 1988) asserts that dialects of all sociocultural groups must be considered on their own terms as valid and equal language systems. Nevertheless, it appears that the formal language of instruction and textbooks, especially in the higher school grades, may be culturally mismatched to the linguistic styles of many minority and low socioeconomic-status youngsters, placing these youngsters at greater risk for lower academic achievement or for actual failure.

The biological approach to the etiology of language disorders speaks of delay, damage, abnormalities, or disruption to the developing brain. It includes consideration of hereditary factors that recently have been identified in at least a subset of children with developmental language disorder (Bashir, Kuban, Kleinman, & Scavuzzo, 1983; Goodman, 1987; Heywood & Canavan, 1987; Tallal, 1988). Tallal (1988) summarized studies that indicate that many language-impaired children have significant temporal-perceptual deficits that can be linked to phonological deficits (such as the ability to discriminate and sequence specific speech sounds that incorporate rapidly changing acoustic spectra). Menyuk (1988) discussed alternative explanations for the processing difficulties of language-impaired children. She suggests that these stem from difficulties with storing and retrieving information from working memory. Other than the hereditary hypothesis, various biological theories, ranging from nonspecific neurodevelopmental delay, to birth-related brain damage, to specific cortical lesions or anatomic abnormalities, have been postulated as etiologies, but much research remains to be done before these suggested etiologic mechanisms can be applied to large numbers of children in clinical practice (Feinstein & Aldershof, 1991).

In some studies, chronic otitis media with effusion occurring in early childhood has been linked to speech and language problems (Paul, Lynn & Lohr-Flanders, 1993). However, the relationship between persistent otitis media and speech and language problems is not yet resolved (Grievink, Peters, van Bon, & Schilder, 1993). One theory states that the unstable speech signal resulting from an early hearing loss, whether fluctuating or chronic, interferes with the child's developing ability to segment speech sounds during a critical neuromaturational period. This, in turn, leads to a language disorder. A second view maintains that temporary early hearing in the context of childhood brain plasticity does not lead to permanent language deficits (Friel-Patti, 1990).

Assessment

The major components of communicative and language functioning are encountered in naturalistic contexts, during the informal clinical evaluation, and during psychometric testing. Therefore, valid comprehensive evaluation of childhood language functioning requires a systematic assessment of each of these realms. Examination of speech production alone is not sufficient to determine whether a child is language impaired. While some, particularly younger, children with language disorders have concomitant speech articulation disorders, many language-impaired children exhibit normal articulation (Tallal, 1988, p. 183). Conversely, children with immature motor speech may have normal language skills otherwise (Cantwell & Baker, 1991).

Tallal (1988) recommends that differential diagnosis of language impairment be conceptualized as a three-tier process: (1) Establishing that the child is demonstrating significant delay in developing language at or near the expected age; (2) determining whether the language delay is the primary disorder or is secondary to other developmental disorders (e.g., mental retardation, hearing loss, autism); and (3) determining the nature of the language disorder and its associated characteristics and subtype. These subtypes may include receptive and/or expressive language disorder with or without concomitant articulation disorder, perceptual/motor impairments, memory disorder, emotional disturbances, or academic achievement problems.

In the past, the identification of language disorder relied largely on psychometric testing. The most widely used diagnostic criteria for language disorder, including the *DSM* system (APA, 1987, 1994), are based on discrepancies of one or two standard deviations on standardized tests between nonverbal intelligence and language abilities. Hence, this has seemed to be a sensible approach. As a means for identifying language disorder, however (as distinct from studying the specific language profile in a given child), it is becoming clear that the discrepancy-based psychometric approach is flawed. Language functioning should be evaluated based on actual language performance in real-life contexts, such as school, home, or peer environments, rather than on inferences about language knowledge based on standardized office procedures (Lahey, 1990).

A second type of criticism concerns the significant technical problems involved in interpreting language scores, or performance IQ/language discrepancies. While school systems use equivalence scores that generate "language age," many authors consider the method problematic (Lahey, 1990). For example, when a child is 4 years old, a language equivalent age of 3 certainly represents a greater problem than that of a 13-year-old with a language age of 12, although both might be scored as having a 1-year delay. In language assessment, referring to a standardized "normal" population when assessing a child who is a product of a specific subcultural language environment and educational system also is problematic. Another technical problem concerns how to interpret the significance of a discrepancy between two psychometric tests (as in performance IQ versus language test). The standard error of measurement of the respective tests is not always taken into account, and often data are unavailable to guide determination as to what constitutes a significant difference in scores between any two tests.

Perhaps more serious than technical problems are unresolved issues of validity and clinical interpretation of test scores. No empirical guidelines exist for interpreting discrepant nonverbal IQ language scores when the language score is not low in itself (e.g., the child with a nonverbal IQ of 130 and a language quotient of 110). Most important, however, are impressive recent research findings that nonverbal IQ/language score discrepancies do not correctly classify many children as language disordered when these same children have been found independently to have significant language deficits by experienced speech pathologists (Aram & Morris, 1991).

In general, referral to a speech/language pathologist is indicated for any child with obvious difficulties in either expressive or receptive language, interactive communication, or significant academic difficulties. A common first step in the language assessment process is a brief screening procedure, which can take the form of informal observation or administration of a standardized screening protocol, such as the Clinical Evaluation of Language Fundamentals Revised Screening Test (Semel, Wiig, & Secord, 1989). A less formal but time-efficient method utilized by some clinicians is story retelling (e.g., Culatta et al., 1983). This method has been found effective for kindergarten screening (Vail, 1984). Speech/language pathologists are trained to identify and differentially diagnose language disorders using a combination of standardized tests plus an analysis of naturalistic data. Naturalistic data may include observations of connected speech, interactive discourse samples, imaginative play skills, parent and teacher reports, and, whenever possible, actual observation in real-life contexts. Attention is paid to the type of language used by caregivers interacting with the child being assessed.

For the school-age child, the current trend in speech/language assessment is to evaluate clinically the areas of functioning most relevant to academic and social success. Evaluation protocols may include assessment of a child's metalinguistic awareness, ability to answer and ask questions, comprehend and formulate simple and complex sentences, comprehend simple and complex vocabulary as contextual supports vary, comprehend and produce paragraphs and stories, produce coherent organized messages, and assume listener and speaker roles (Simon, 1984, 1991). Nelson (1994) described curriculum-based assessment and intervention, an emerging approach. This involves: analyzing the language and communication expectations of the regular curriculum; identifying points of match and mismatch between the curriculum and the target student; and designing intervention strategies that support student's attempts to make sense of what is going on, to communicate competently, and to learn (p. 105).

Treatment

The treatment needs of language-impaired school-age children vary depending on the severity of the disorder and the problems that accompany it. Priorities for treatment include improving communication patterns, increasing opportunities for play and social interaction, and maximizing the child's potential for learning in academic and interpersonal contexts. The older a child is before being properly diagnosed, the more likely he or she is to have experienced academic and social failure. For such children, psychotherapeutic pro-

motion of self-esteem and confidence as a learner and social participant may be needed. In view of the high rate of psychiatric disorders in language-impaired children, individual or family psychotherapy may become essential components of a multidisciplinary intervention.

For the school-age child, the primary focus of speech/language intervention is to promote competence as a communicator. Therefore, speech/language pathologists consult with teachers and other caregivers so that educational programming can be adjusted to the child's language level. Direct intervention techniques emphasize developing basic concepts, teaching strategies for comprehending and formulating information in various contexts (e.g., paraphrasing, rehearsal), developing speaker and listener roles, promoting narrative development, and promoting development of metalinguistic awareness (Simon, 1991; Wallach & Miller, 1988). Clearly, these are not solely the province of the speech/language pathologist; they require an integrated team approach.

Although speech/language pathologists have used other service delivery options in the past (e.g., individual and small group therapy outside the classroom), there is increasing emphasis on conducting language intervention within the framework of a classroom-based service delivery model (Miller, 1989). Several types of classroom-based language programs exist, including self-contained classes taught by language specialists, team teaching, one-to-one intervention with goals based on ongoing classroom activities, consultation, and staff and program development (Miller, 1989). Other options include classroom-based groups led by the speech/language pathologist and individual strategy-based therapy in clinical settings.

For children with combined language and psychiatric disorders, the goals of speech/language therapy are to enhance the child's language and communicative competence and to promote development of successful relationships with adults and peers (Hummel & Prizant, 1993). Many children need to learn to identify, label and communicate their feelings and to develop strategies for anticipating and solving problems such as reviewing picture schedules with caregivers (Audet & Hummel, 1990). Often children need to learn to use others to help them cope with difficult situations by requesting assistance. Clearly speech/language treatment with these children requires on-going input from a psychoeducational team to determine the relative contribution of biological, social, emotional, and family factors to the child's communicative and behavioral functioning. Professionals who employ verbal psychotherapy techniques probably are not fully aware of the child's linguistic limitations. As a consequence, the therapists make excessive language demands of their patients, which compromises treatment. Consultation with a speech/language pathologist is a useful component of both individual therapy and milieu therapy with such children.

Conclusion

Developmental language disorders are common and significant impairments in children. These conditions potentially have harmful effects on parent-child interaction, social development, academic achievement, and school behavior. The rate of co-occurrence of developmental language disorder and psychiatric disorder in children is very high, necessitating a close, collaborative relationship among the disciplines of child psychiatry, psychology, speech/language pathology, and education, for effective identification and treatment. Further research is sorely needed to clarify the interactive influences of linguistic development, socioemotional development, and educational practices on language-impaired children. Pathways that lead to combined psychiatric and language disorder require further elucidation. Prevention of psychiatric disorders in this high-risk population should be an important priority. Systematic research is needed to identify linguistically appropriate treatment approaches for the large numbers of psychiatrically disordered children with co-occurring language impairment.

REFERENCES

American Psychiatric Association. (1987). *Diagnostic and statistical manual of mental disorders* (3rd ed., rev.). Washington, DC: Author.

American Psychiatric Association. (1994). *Diagnostic and statistical manual of mental disorders* (4th ed.). Washington, DC: Author.

American Speech, Language, and Hearing Association. (1993). Definitions of communication disorder and variations. *ASHA, 35* (Supp. 10), 40–41.

Aram, D., & Ruben, R. J. (1994). *Report of the Workshop on Communication Disorders and Juvenile Behaviors* (June 14–15 1994, Bethesda, MD). National Institute on Deafness and Other Communicative Disorders.

Aram, D., & Hall, N. (1989). Longitudinal follow-up of children with pre-school communication disorders; treatment implications. *School Psychology Review, 18,* 487–501.

Aram, D., & Morris, R. (1991). Validity of discrepancy criteria for identifying children with developmental language disorder (abstract). *Journal of Clinical and Experimental Neuropsychology, 13* (1).

Audet, L., & Hummel, L. (1990). A framework for assessment and treatment of language learning disabled children with psychiatric disorders. *Topics in Language Disorders, 10* (4), 57–74.

Baltaxe, C., & Simmons, J. (1988). Pragmatic deficits in emotionally disturbed children and adolescents. In R. Schiefelbusch & L. Lloyd (Eds.), *Language perspectives: Acquisition, retardation and intervention* (pp. 223–253). Austin, TX: Pro-Ed.

Baltaxe, C., & Simmons, J. (1990). The differential diagnosis of communication disorders in child and adolescent psychopathology. *Topics in Language disorders, 10* (4), 17–31.

Bashir, A. (1989). Language intervention and the curriculum. *Seminars in Speech and Language, 10* (3), 181–191.

Bashir, A., Kuban, K., Kleinman, S., & Scavuzzo, A. (1983). Issues in language disorders: Considerations of cause, maintenance and change. In J. Miller, D. Yoder, & R. Schiefelbusch (Eds.), *Contemporary issues in language intervention* (pp. 92–106). Trenton, NJ: BC Decker.

Beitchman, J., Nair, R., Clegg, M., et al. (1986). Prevalence of psychiatric disorders in children with speech and language disorders. *Journal of the American Academy of Child Psychiatry, 25,* 528–535.

Bernstein, D. (1989a). Language development: The school-age years. In D. Bernstein & E. Tiegerman, (Eds.), *Language and communication disorders in children* (2nd ed., pp. 133–139). Columbus, OH: Merrill.

Bernstein, D. (1989b). The nature of language and its disorders. In D. Bernstein & E. Tiegerman, (Eds.), *Language and communication disorders in children* (2nd ed., pp. 1–24). Columbus, OH: Merrill.

Bloom, L., & Lahey, M. (1978). *Language development*

and language disorders. New York: John Wiley & Sons.

Brinton, B., Fujiko, M., Winkler, E., & Loeb, D. (1986). Responses to requests for clarification in linguistically normal and language-impaired children. *Journal of Speech and Hearing Disorders, 51* (4), 370–378.

Bruner, J. (1981). The social context of language acquisition. *Language and Communication, 1,* 155–178.

Cantwell, D., & Baker, L. (1991). *Psychiatric and developmental disorders in children with communication disorder.* Washington, DC: American Psychiatric Press.

Catts, H. (1989). Phonological processing deficits and reading disabilities. In A. Kamhi & H. Catts (Eds.), *Reading disabilities: A developmental language perspective* (pp. 101–131). Boston: College-Hill.

Catts, H. W. (1993). The relationship between speech-language impairments and reading disabilities. *Journal of Speech and Hearing Research, 36,* 948–958.

Catts, H, & Kamhi, A. (1986). The linguistic basis of reading disorders: Implications for the speech-language pathologist. *Journal of Speech and Hearing Research, 16,* 329–341.

Committee on Language, Speech and Hearing Services in the Schools. (1982). Definitions Communication Disorders and Variations, *Journal of the American Speech and Hearing Association, 24* (11), 949–950.

Committee on the Status of Racial Minorities. (1983). Position statement on social dialects. *Journal of the American Speech and Hearing Association, 25* (9), 23–24.

Crais, E., & Chapman, R. (1987). Story recall and inferencing skills in language/learning-disabled and nondisabled children. *Journal of Speech and Hearing Disorders, 52* (1), 50–55.

Culatta, B., Page, J., & Ellis, J. (1983). Story retelling as a communicative performance screening tool. *Language, Speech and Hearing Services in Schools, 14* (2), 66–74.

Doherty, M., & Hummel, L. (1990). Conceptual models: Broadening diagnostic perspectives on communication disorders in emotionally and behaviorally disordered children. *Topics in Language Disorders, 10* (4), 32–41.

Donahue, M. (1983). Learning disabled children as conversational partners. *Topics in Language Disorders, 4* (1), 15–27.

Donahue, M., & Bryan, T. (1984). Communicative skills and peer relations of learning disabled adolescents. *Topics in Language Disorders, 4* (2), 10–21.

Ehren, B., & Lenz, B. (1989). Adolescents with language disorders: Special considerations in providing academically relevant language intervention. *Seminars in Speech and Language, 10* (3), 192–204.

Feinstein, C., Aldershof, A., Seifer, R., Trecartin, J., & Feil, L. (1991). Language impairment in psychiatrically disordered adolescents [Abstract]. *Scientific Proceedings of the American Academy of Child and Adolescent Psychiatry, 7,* 67–68.

Friel-Patti, S. (1990). Otitis media with effusion and the development of language: A review of the evidence. *Topics in Language Disorders, 11* (1), 11–22.

Gertner, B. L., Rice, M. L. & Hadley, P. A. (1994). Influence of communicative competence on peer preference in a preschool classroom. *Journal of Speech and Hearing Research, 37,* 913–923.

Goodman, R. (1987). The developmental neurobiology of language. In W. Yule & M. Rutter (Eds.), *Language development and language disorders* (pp. 129–145). Philadelphia: J. B. Lippincott.

Graybeal, C. (1981). Memory for stories in language-impaired children. *Applied Psycholinguistics, 2,* 269–283.

Grievink, E. H., Peters, S. A. F., Van Bon, W. H. J., & Schilder, A. G. M. (1993). The effects of early bilateral otitis media with effusion on language ability: A prospective cohort study. *Journal of Speech and Hearing Research, 36,* 1004–1012.

Henry, F. M., Reed, V. A., & McAllister, L. L. (1995). Adolescents' perceptions of the relative importance of selected communication skills in their positive peer relationships. *Language, Speech and Hearing Services in Schools, 26,* 263–272.

Heywood, C. A., & Canavan, A. G. M. (1987). Developmental neuropsychological correlates of language. In W. Yule & M. Rutter (Eds.), *Language development and language disorders* (pp. 146–158). Philadelphia: J. B. Lippincott.

Hummel, L. J., & Prizant, B. M. (1993). A socioemotional perspective for understanding social difficulties of school age children with language disorders. *Language, Speech and Hearing Services in Schools, 24,* 216–224.

Johnston, J. (1988). Specific language disorders in the child. In N. J. Lass, I. V. McReynolds, J. L. Northern, & D. E. Yoder (Eds.), *Handbook of speech-language pathology and audiology* (pp. 685–715). Philadelphia: B. C. Decker.

Kamhi, A. (1989). Causes and consequences of reading disabilities. In A. Kamhi & H. Catts (Eds.), *Reading disabilities: A developmental language perspective* (pp. 67–99). Boston: College-Hill.

Kamhi, A., & Catts, H. (1989). Language and reading: Convergences, Divergences and Development. In A. Kamhi & H. Catts (Eds.), *Reading disabilities: A developmental language perspective* (pp. 1–34). Boston: College-Hill.

Kamhi, A., & Catts, H. (1989). Reading disabilities: Terminology, definitions, and subtyping issue. In A. Kamhi & H. Catts (Eds.), *Reading disabilities: A developmental language perspective* (pp. 35–66). Boston: College-Hill.

Kamhi, A., & Catts, H. (Eds.) (1989). Reading disabilities: A developmental language perspective. Boston: College-Hill.

Kinney, D. K., Yurgelun-Todd, D. A., & Woods, B. T. (1991). Hard neurologic signs and psychopathology in relatives of schizophrenic patients. *Psychiatry Research, 39,* 4553.

Lahey, M. (1990). Who shall be called language disordered? Some reflections and one perspective. *Journal of Speech and Hearing Disorders 55*, 612–620.

Lahey, M., & Edwards, J. (1995). Specific language impairment: Preliminary investigation of factors associated with family history and with patterns of language performance. *Journal of Speech and Hearing Research, 38*, 630–642.

Larson, V., & McKinley, N. (1985). General intervention principles for language-impaired adolescents. *Topics in Language Disorders, 5* (3), 70–77.

Leiven, B. (1984). Interaction style and children's language learning. *Topics in Language Disorders, 4*, 15–23.

Lewis, D. O. (1991). Conduct disorder. In M. Lewis (Ed.), *Child and adolescent psychiatry* (pp. 561–572). Baltimore: Williams & Wilkins.

Mack, A. E., & Warr-Leeper, G. A. (1992). Language abilities in boys with chronic behavior disorders. *Language, Speech and Hearing Services in Schools, 23*, 214–223.

Mattis, S., French, J., & Rapin, I. (1975). Dyslexia in children and young adults: Three independent neuropsychological syndromes. *Developmental Medicine & Child Neurology, 17*, 150.

McLean, J. (1983). Historical perspectives on the content of child language programs. In J. Miller, D. Yoder, & R. Schiefelbusch (Eds.), *Contemporary issues in language intervention* (pp. 115–126). Trenton, NJ: B. C. Decker.

Menyuk, P. (1988). *Language development, knowledge and use.* Glenview, IL, Scott, Foresman & Co.

Menyuk, P. (1991). Metalinguistic abilities and language disorder. In J Miller (Ed.), *Research on child language disorders,* (pp. 387–397). Austin, TX: Pro-Ed.

Menyuk, P., Chesnick, M., Liebergott, J., Korngold, B., D'Agnostino, R., & Belanger, A. (1991). Predicting reading problems in at-risk children. *Journal of Speech and Hearing Research, 34*, 893–903.

Miller, L. (1989). Classroom-based language intervention. *Language, Speech, Hearing Services in the Schools, 20* (2), 153–169.

Miniutti, A. (1991). Language deficiencies in inner city children with learning and behavioral problems. *Language, Speech and Hearing Services in Schools, 22*, 31–38.

Morris, R. (1988). Classification of learning disabilities: Old problems and new approaches. *Journal of Consulting and Clinical Psychology, 56*, 789–794.

Morris, R., Blashfield, R., & Satz, P. (1986). Developmental classification of reading-disabled children. *Journal of Clinical and Experimental Neuropsychology, 8*, 371–392.

Nelson, N. (1984). Beyond information processing: The language of teachers and textbooks. In G. Wallach & K. Butler (Eds.), *Language, learning disabilities in school age children.* (pp. 154–178). Baltimore: Williams & Wilkins.

Nelson, N. (1988). The nature of literacy. In M. Nippold (Ed.), *Later language development: Ages nine through nineteen* (pp. 11–28). Boston: College-Hill.

Nelson, N. (1994). Communication-based language assessment and intervention across the grades. In G. P. Wallach & K. G. Butler (Eds.), *Language learning disabilities in school-age children and adolescents: Some principles and applications* (pp. 104–131). New York: Macmillan.

Nippold, M. (1988a). Introduction. In M. Nippold (Ed.), *Later language development: Ages nine through nineteen* (pp. 1–10). Boston: College-Hill.

Nippold, M. (1988b). The literate lexicon. In M. Nippold (Ed.), *Later language development: Ages nine through nineteen* (pp. 29–47). Boston: College-Hill.

Nippold, M., & Fey, S. (1983). Metaphoric understanding in preadolescents having a history of language acquisition difficulties. *Language, Speech, Hearing Services in the Schools, 14* (31), 171–180.

Nussbaum, N. L., Bigler, E. D., & Koch, W. (1986). Neuropsychologically derived subgroups of learning-disabled children: Personality/behavioral dimensions. *Journal of Research and Development in Education, 19*, 57–67.

Paul, R., Lynn, T. F., & Lohr-Flanders, M. (1993). History of middle ear involvement and speech-language development in late talkers. *Journal of Speech and Hearing Research, 36*, 1055–1062.

Peck, O. (1989). Assessment of social communicative competence: Evaluating environments. *Seminars in Speech and Language, 10* (1), 1–15.

Prizant, B., Audet, L., Burke, G., Hummel, L., Maher, S., & Theadore, G. (1988, November). *Therapeutic considerations in serving children with communication disorders and emotional/behavioral disorders.* Mini seminar presented at American Speech-Language-Hearing Association Annual Convention, Boston, MA.

Prizant, B., Audet, L., Burke, G., Hummel, L., Maher, S., & Theadore, G. (1990). Communication disorders and emotional/behavioral disorders in children and adolescents. *Journal of Speech and Hearing Disorders, 55* (2), 179–192.

Prizant, B., & Wetherby, A. (1990). Toward an integrated view of early language and communication development and socioemotional development. *Topics in Language Disorders, 10* (4), 1–16.

Puckering, C., & Rutter, M. (1987). Environmental influences on language development. In W. Yule & M. Rutter (Eds.), *Language development and language disorders* (pp. 103–128). Philadelphia: J. B. Lippincott.

Rapin, I., & Allen, D. A. (1988). Syndromes in developmental dysphasia and adult aphasia. In F. Plum (Ed.), *Language communication, and the brain* (pp. 57–75). New York: Plenum Press.

Rice, M. L., Sell, M. A., & Hadley, P. A. (1991). Social interactions of speech and language-impaired children. *Journal of Speech and Hearing Research, 34*, 1299–1307.

Roberts, J., & Schuele, C. (1990). Otitis media and later

academic performance: The linkage and implications for intervention. *Topics in Language Disorders, 11* (1), 43–62.

Roth, F., & Spekman, N. (1984). Higher-order language processing and reading disabilities. In A. Kamhi & H. Catts (Eds.), *Reading disabilities: A developmental language perspective* (pp. 159–197). Boston: College-Hill.

Sameroff, A. (1987). The social context of development. In N. Eisenburg (Ed.), *Contemporary topics in development* (pp. 273–291). New York: John Wiley & Sons.

Savich, P. (1983). Improving communicative competence: The role of metapragmatic awareness. *Topics in Language Disorders, 4* (1), 38–48.

Scott, C. (1988). Spoken and written syntax. In M. Nippold (Ed.), *Later language development: Ages nine through nineteen* (pp. 49–95). Boston: College-Hill.

Semel, E., Wiig, E., & Secord, N. (1989). *Clinical evaluation of language fundamentals—revised screening test.* San Antonio, TX: The Psychological Corporation-Harcourt Brace Jovanovich.

Silva, P. A. (1987). Epidemiology, longitudinal course and some associated factors: An update. In W. Yule & M. Rutter (Eds.), *Language development and disorders* (pp. 1–15). Philadelphia: J. B. Lippincott.

Simon, C. (1984). Functional-pragmatic evaluation of communication skills in school-age children. *Language, Speech, Hearing Services in the Schools, 20* (2), 153–169.

Simon, C. (1985a). *Communication skills and classroom success assessment of language learning disabled students.* San Diego: College-Hill.

Simon, C. (1985b). *Communication skills and classroom success therapy methodologies for learning disabled students.* San Diego: College-Hill.

Simon, C. (1991). Introduction: Communication skills and classroom success: Some considerations for assessment and therapy methodologies. In C. S. Simon (Ed.), *Communication skills and classroom success: Assessment and therapy methodologies for language and learning disabled students* (pp. 1–77). Eau Claire, WI: Thinking Publications.

Stevens, L. J., & Bliss, L. S. (1995). Conflict resolution abilities of children with specific language impairment and children with normal language. *Journal of Speech and Hearing Research, 38*, 599–611.

Stevens, M. (1988). Pragmatics. In M. Nippold (Ed.), *Later language development: Ages nine through nineteen* (pp. 247–262). Boston: College-Hill.

Stevenson, J., & Richman, N. (1978). Behavior, language and development in three-year old children. *Journal of Autism and Childhood Schizophrenia, 8*, 299–313.

Stevenson, J., Richman, N., & Graham, P. (1985). Behavior problems and language abilities at three years and behavioral deviance at eight years. *Journal of Child Psychology and Psychiatry, 26*, 215–230.

Tallal, P. (1988). Developmental language disorders. In J. Kavanagh, & T. Truss (Eds.), *Learning disabilities: Proceedings of the national conference* (pp. 181–272). Parkton, MD: York Press.

Taylor, O. (1988). Speech and language differences and disorders of multicultural populations. In N. J. Lass, L. V. McReynolds, J. L. Northern, & D. E. Yoder (Eds.), *Handbook of speech-language pathology and audiology* (pp. 939–958). Philadelphia: B. C. Decker.

Taylor, O., Payne, K., & Anderson, N. (1987). Distinguishing between communication disorders and communication differences. *Seminars in Speech and Language, 8* (4), 415–427.

Terrell, S., & Terrell, F. (1983). Distinguishing linguistic differences from disorders: The past, the present and future of nonbiased assessment. *Topics in Language Disorders, 3* (3), 1–7.

Vail, B. (1984). Story retelling as a screening tool. *Language, Speech and Hearing Services in Schools, 15* (2), 140.

Van Kleek, A., & Richardson, A. (1988). Language delay in the child. In N. J. Lass, L. V. McReynolds, J. L. Northern, & D. E. Yoder (Eds.), *Handbook of speech-language pathology and audiology* (pp. 655–684). Philadelphia: B. C. Decker.

Wallach, G. (1980). So you want to know what to do with the language disabled child above the age of six. *Topics in Language Disorders, 1* (1), 99–111.

Wallach, G., & Butler, K. (1984). *Language learning disabilities in school age children.* Baltimore: Williams & Wilkins.

Wallach, G., & Liebergott, J. (1984). Who shall be called "Learning disabled." Some new directions. In G. Wallach & K. Butler (Eds.), *Language learning disabilities in school age children* (pp. 1–14). Baltimore: Williams & Wilkins.

Wallach, G., & Miller, L. (1988). *Language intervention and academic success.* Boston: College-Hill.

Weiner, L. (1989). The background for K-Talk. *Clinically Speaking, 8* (1), 3–7.

Westby, C. (1985). Learning to talk and talking to learn. Oral literate language differences. In C. Simon (Ed.), *Communication skills and classroom success* (pp. 181–213). San Diego: College-Hill.

Westby, C., Van Dongen, R., & Maggart, Z. (1989). Assessing narrative competence. *Seminars in Speech and Language, 10* (1), 63–76.

Wetherby, A., & Prizant, B. (1989). The expression of communicative intent. *Assessment Guidelines: Seminars in Speech and Language Disorders, 10*, 77–91.

38 / Normal and Disturbed Speech Development

Clyde L. Rousey

From birth until death, humans produce sounds, which offer a unique record of both normal development and unresolved life stresses. Understanding both normal development and disordered production of sound has been attempted from a neurological, educational, linguistic, cognitive, and psychological point of view.

This chapter briefly reviews the proposals advanced by neurologists, educators, linguists, and psychologists. A more detailed presentation integrates literature common to speech pathology and audiology with Mahler, Pine, and Bergman's (1975) and Stern's (1985) psychological constructs around early infant development, Erikson's (1950) exposition of infantile sexuality, and the ideas proposed by Wallerstein (1983) and Kernberg (1992) about defense mechanisms and defensive behavior. In this chapter, the term *speech* refers to individual sounds that, when combined in varying orders, produce a *spoken language* peculiar to a given culture or nationality. Speech and language are considered as independent behaviors.

Neurological Factors Affecting Speech Development

Early neurologists such as Broca (1861), Wernicke (1874), and Head (1926) noted what they termed *speech disturbances* in their patients following stroke, head trauma, or congenital defects. In the context of how speech is defined in this chapter, they were referring to spoken language. They concluded that the individual's neurological status was of prime importance in "speech" development and usage. This notion was further extended in the work of Penfield and Roberts (1959) and Luria (1966). Most persons who have a neurologi-

The author gratefully acknowledges the helpful comments and suggestions of Carol G. Rousey, Ph.D.

cal orientation regarding speech and language assume that any disorder of communication must reflect some dysfunctional medical or neurological state (Darby, 1981a; Darley, Aronson, & Brown, 1975).

Education and Speech Development

From an educator's point of view, speech development and usage reflect the learning subsequent to acoustic and environmental stimulation. Both normal and disordered speech sounds are considered a learned skill capable of modification by elocution lessons or by speech teaching. In George Shaw's Bernard play *Pygmalion*, for example, Professor Henry Higgins used this approach in his efforts to teach Eliza Doolittle proper speech. This point of view is also the rationale for providing speech therapy in the public schools as one part of special education.

Linguistic and Cognitive Factors Affecting Speech Development

The third approach to speech development and speech disorders resulted from the influence of Skinner (1957) and Chomsky and Halle (1968). As a result of their efforts, the focus shifted from a primary concentration on individual sounds to a study of rules of grammar and syntax. The search continues for a neurological area related to the various rules used in language (Bishop, 1993). The production of individual speech sounds has been considered an early form of language that also should follow rules. The concepts of distinctive features (Singh, 1976) and phonological processes (Stoel-Gammon & Dunn, 1985) advocate a cognitive/linguistic understanding of the rules governing the use of sounds.

Psychological Factors Affecting Speech Development

A BRIEF REVIEW OF PSYCHOLOGICAL IDEAS

Freud (1901/1960) contributed an early account of the influence of dynamic factors on pathologies of speech. Apart from that, however, little psychological attention was devoted to this realm until the work of Moses (1954). Although he was a laryngologist, Moses felt he could identify neurotic issues and conflicts in the voices of the professional singers who were his patients. Working with children who were involved in a long-term research study dealing with coping skills, Rousey and Moriarty (1965) analyzed the relationships between their speech patterns and their psychological life. A comprehensive statement of this emerging theory was first proposed by Rousey (1971).

In recent years Darby (1981a, b) presented the work of researchers utilizing a more biologically oriented notion of personality. Cantwell and Baker (1991) published work trying to apply psychiatric thinking to the high incidence of speech disorders in child and adult psychiatric populations. Later efforts in this same direction were made in England by Gravell and France (1991) and in the United States by Prizant and Meyer (1993). Rousey and Rousey (1993) developed a computerized psychological report based on understanding speech development and disorders from a psychodynamic view. Their report (RAP-Rousey Assessment of Personality) is similar to what is generated by the computerized Minnesota Multiphasic Personality Inventory (MMPI). Levy and Rousey (1976) have demonstrated how use of the RAP concepts can be an important element in predicting the outcome of treatment.

BASIC CONSTITUENTS OF SPEECH BEHAVIOR

To understand how speech sounds can be conceptualized within a psychodynamic framework requires some basic information about the param-eters of speech behavior. The sounds of speech are categorized as either vowels or consonants.

Vowels are made by producing a sound in the larynx that is then emitted through the oral cavity in a relatively unobstructed manner. Phoneticians describe vowels as being either front, mid, or back, depending on the place in the oral cavity where the sound is configured (Carrell & Tiffany, 1960). Other dimensions of vowels include whether they are made in the high, mid, or low positions of the oral cavity, and whether they are stressed (tense) or unstressed (lax). Vowel sounds also have subjective aspects such as pitch, loudness, and quality.

Consonants, in contrast to vowels, result from specific obstructions in the front, mid, or back portions of the oral cavity secondary to tongue or lip placement. Unlike vowels, they do not require phonation on all sounds. For example, the /th/ sound as in *th*anks is made without any sound produced in the larynx, while the /th/ sound as in *th*em requires phonation.

While there are a limited number of vowels and consonants in conventional spelling, acoustically, 25 consonants and 21 vowels and diphthongs are found in American English. Rousey (1974) further elaborated the resulting permutations and combinations of the individual sounds plus the variations in voice quality and auditory perception of sound as a supplementary means for psychiatric assessment.

VOWELS AND CONSONANTS IN THE FIRST YEAR

To understand speech development psychologically, the order of appearance of vowels and consonants in the normally developing child must be recognized. During the first 6 months of life, the predominant sounds made are vowels and semivowels (Irwin, 1948). Semivowels have some aspects of both vowels and consonants. A few consonants (e.g., *m* and *p*) are present in the first few months of life. In the last 6 months of the first year, all of the remaining consonants appear that will be needed for later spoken language (Irwin, 1947). As will be discussed later, the order of appearance of sounds can be conceptualized as being related to psychological development as hypothesized by Mahler (1975), Stern (1985), and Erikson (1950).

VOWELS AND CONSONANTS AFTER THE FIRST YEAR

From the beginning of the second year and lasting until around age 6, the time of correct usage of consonants in spoken language among the general population is irregular and often inconsistent (Smit, Hand, Freilinger, Bernthal, & Bird, 1990; Templin, 1957). On the other hand, from the beginning vowels are almost always used correctly. The irregular pattern of correct usage of consonants mentioned earlier has been understood as a reflection of normal developmental variations in mental development or motor control of the speech mechanism. In contrast, I propose this irregular pattern is important in understanding the relationships between vowel disturbances and primary process and between consonant disturbances and disturbed object relationships.

ANATOMICAL NECESSITIES FOR SPEECH AND HEARING

Normal speech can be produced with or without teeth and with very little tongue mobility, or even when parts of the tongue are removed secondary to accident or cancer. Contrary to popular notions, there is no scientific substantiation to the claim that either a mild hearing loss of 30 decibels or transient hearing loss secondary to middle ear infections really can affect the development of speech and language (Grievink, Peters, van Born, & Schilder, 1993).

It will be recalled that Freud's (1923/1961) earliest drawing of the ego contained an "ear." This suggests he felt a relationship might exist between hearing and emotional growth. Since Freud's time, this possibility has received indirect support by anatomical studies of the auditory tracts, which have been shown to have synaptic connections both with the cortex and with subcortical structures believed associated with basic affect states, such as aggression and sexuality (LeDoux, 1992). Further, the auditory tracts gradually mature in terms of handling complex auditory data (i.e., intensity, frequency, and timing). While the association between this maturation and psychological development has yet to be demonstrated by a coordinated anatomical, physiological, and psychological study, it is a theoretical possibility. With the foregoing information in mind, we now turn to how speech and hearing development parallels psychological development.

Psychodynamic Understanding of Speech Development

It is my position that both speech development and most speech disorders (excluding strokes and head injuries or disturbances of speech secondary to cancer, cleft palate, etc.) can be understood theoretically and explained as auditory manifestations of psychological health or distress. As proposed by Mahler and her colleagues (1975) and taking into account some of the modifications of her work as proposed by Stern (1985), the various phases in the psychological birth of the infant can serve as a framework for understanding the close early relationship between speech and psychological development. Stern's criticism of Mahler's use of the term *autism* is supported by the following discussion of the infant's early use of speech sounds. Therefore, in keeping with Stern's suggestion, the term *emergence* is substituted for Mahler's term *autistic phase*.

SPEECH AND THE "EMERGENT PHASE"

As previously noted, vowels are the predominant element of speech found in the first 6 months of life. Vowels are sounds produced and expressed in such a manner that there is no stoppage or containment provided by the speech articulators. I believe this production of sound is analogous to the relatively unrestrained discharge of affect that occurs in the infant at birth and during the first few weeks of life. In other words, the initial production of vowel sounds is assumed to be the auditory manifestation of libidinal and aggressive instinctual needs and their derivatives. The fact that vowels can be either tense or lax appears to parallel how the expression of instinctual needs often is described (i.e., active or passive).

While the instinctual needs (or, in the present context, vowels) can be thought of as impervious to outside stimuli, observational research suggests otherwise and thus supports Stern's (1985) conclusions. I initially noted this phenomenon in the course of recording an infant's birth cry. Anxious to ensure a good recording, the attending obstetrician vigorously and repeatedly slapped the infant's buttocks, causing the cry to become more intense and to change the quality and type of vowels produced. While it is unlikely that the infant had any conscious control over the type and quality of the sound, it was evident to any listener that a change in affect was being expressed by the change in voice (i.e., vowels) being used subsequent to the obstetrician's actions. This capacity to express affects vocally is readily apparent to parents who listen to their child when the infant is satisfied (after feeding) or in distress (needing a diaper change). These observations appear to be in accord with the contentions of Wolff (1959) and Fantz (1961) regarding the impact of external stimuli on instinctual expressions.

My own clinical experience supports the notion that front vowels express libidinal feelings or their derivatives (such as satisfaction/pleasure), while back vowels express aggression or its derivatives (such as protest/anger). Mid vowels are conceived of as expressive of the ability to integrate and modulate the two foregoing drives.

SPEECH DEVELOPMENT AND THE SYMBIOTIC PHASE

The cooing sounds made by the infant after the satiation of hunger or while being held by the mother or father marks the beginnings of the speech component of the symbiotic phase. It is seen as an early indication that the child is trying to "connect" with someone. This "connection" must have tactile as well as auditory components by virtue of the fact that even profoundly deaf children engage in vocal behavior the first few months of life. The cooing sounds in hearing infants likely serve as a form of auditory self-stimulation and thus are associated with the development of normal narcissism. The impact of reduced or absent auditory stimulation in deaf and hard-of-hearing children on the development of normal narcissism needs further study.

The appearance of semivowels in the first 6 months marks the earliest beginnings of object relationships. One semivowel of importance in terms of developing object relations is the l sound as in the word *lady*. Cinefluoradiographic evaluation amply demonstrates that the tongue movement needed to produce this sound is quite similar to what is required for effective nursing. I feel that if the infant's early psychological nurturance has been adequate, this sound should be produced clearly and correctly. If not, recognition of this speech disturbance by the alert pediatrician or child mental health practitioner could be an

early warning sign that the ensuing differentiation phase may be compromised.

SPEECH DEVELOPMENT AND THE DIFFERENTIATION SUBPHASE

Around 5 to 6 months the emerging speech sounds include numerous consonants. The use of speech sounds (both vowels and consonants) as a kind of auditory transition behavior is now evident, especially when the child is alone in the crib during times of waking up or before beginning a nap. The primary function of consonants, to contain and shape vowels and allow differential verbal responses, parallels the psychological task of differentiating and responding to important persons in the environment. Thus, problems in object relationships during the last 6 months of the first year are regarded as capable of leaving traces in disturbed consonant production. These traces can be observed easily in the spoken words that first appear around the first year of life.

By noting whether consonant errors are made in the initial, medial, or final position, I believe it is possible to infer additional details regarding both normal and disturbed object relationships. Disturbances in initial consonants (e.g., *low*, *see*) are hypothesized to relate to conflicts over maternal or maternallike interactions that have occurred in the first 6 to 8 months. Disturbances in final consonants (e.g., bu*t*, u*p*) are hypothesized as being related to conflicts over paternal or paternallike interactions in the months 9 to 10 of the first year. Disturbances in medial consonants (e.g., a*ll*ow, bo*th*er) are hypothesized as related to problems in integration of early drives and drive derivatives with maternal and paternal object relationships. Validation of these concepts can be gathered both in clinical work and in studies of the development of object relationships.

SPEECH DEVELOPMENT AND THE PRACTICING SUBPHASE

In this phase, at approximately 12 to 18 months, the child's production of sounds begins to be submerged in the first word and developing use of language. This period marks the first time that most parents become aware that their child's verbal productions do not sound usual. This recognition presents a chance for the child development specialist to recognize early signs of developmental psychological conflicts that originate in the first year of life.

During the practicing subphase, the child likes to be read to and experience how the correct blending of vowels and consonants in spoken language can be soothing. Reading to a child thus is not only cognitively stimulating but also emotionally reassuring. Little wonder that parents are advised to hold their child while reading bedtime or nap stories. The lack of such interaction can have negative consequences in both the emotional and cognitive life of the child. A soothing imprint of the mother's and father's voice will be laid down at this time and stand the child in good stead later. In adolescence, as the child enjoys hearing the parent's approval and support in outside school or sport activities, the verbal traces may return again. This verbal imprint is also the basis for the comfort adults feel when making a long-distance call and hearing the voice of loved ones. This listening experience appears to be a symbolic "recalling" of the earlier lullabies heard during the emergent and symbiotic stages.

SPEECH DEVELOPMENT AND THE RAPPROCHEMENT SUBPHASE

As displayed in speech development, this subphase, from about 18 to 36 months, is characterized by the use of all the previously made consonants and vowels in spoken language. The seemingly irregular pattern of errors that occur in spoken language is a function of both ongoing vicissitudes in object relationships and, more important, the arousal of old, unresolved conflicts that originated in the first year of life. I believe these irregular patterns of errors are at least partially the basis for what Freud termed *slips of the tongue*.

SPEECH DEVELOPMENT AND THE INDIVIDUALITY AND OBJECT CONSTANCY SUBPHASE

Consonant difficulties, such as a frontal lisp (i.e., saying *thun* for *sun*) and dysfunction of the speech mechanism (the presence of a tongue thrust) are hypothesized as reflecting children's coming to grips with oedipal issues as well as their developing sense of self. This hypothesis is based on the disappearance of the tongue thrust in most

persons and the parallel theoretical resolution of oedipal issues around age 5. Clinically, the continued presence of a tongue thrust in older children and adults is found in individuals who have been able to sublimate their competitiveness in business or sports or, in a maladaptive sense, in persons who violate the laws of society. One clinical difference I have noted between the two groups is the presence of good reality testing in those able to sublimate and impaired reality testing in those who violate society's laws.

SPEECH DEVELOPMENT IN LATENCY AND ADOLESCENCE

At this point we leave the comparison of speech development with the phases described by Mahler and her colleagues. There are relatively few problems with normal speech production in latency, from approximately 6 to 12 years. To the extent that speech production is an expression of psychological development, this is to be expected. That is, the normal submerging of infantile conflicts in the interest of learning that occurs in latency should be accompanied by a reduction in speech sound errors. I believe that the continued presence of speech problems in latency and adolescence (from about 12 to 17 years) signals significant emotional distress requiring psychological intervention. The popular notion that children have outgrown their speech disorder may be better understood as children having transferred the expression of their inner conflicts to other aspects of cognition and behavior. Symptom substitution does occur in children who are treated behaviorally for their speech problem (Rousey & Diedrich, 1974).

Speech Development and Infantile Sexuality

Another way of understanding the psychological meanings of speech development is to approach it from the vantage point of psychosexual development. Since, by 1 year of age, a child has already demonstrated the ability to make all of the vowels and consonants, the failure to use these sounds in spoken language may be understood as an expression of unresolved conflicts. Heretofore, phoneticians and linguists have regarded the failure to make sounds correctly as a reflection of failure or delay in cognitive or motoric maturation. From my own psychological viewpoint, these same data can be understood as a lag in the resolution of some early trauma that now becomes tied to other crises in the normal development of infantile sexuality. Thus, rather than reflecting maturation of motor skills, the fact that sounds seem to be "mastered" in groups at certain periods can alternatively be understood as the time the general population works through the psychological traumas sustained in the first year of life. Elsewhere, Rousey (1979) using Erikson's (1950) discussion of infantile sexuality suggested that the consonantal sounds of speech were related to various periods as follows:

Stage	Sounds
Oral respiratory-sensory stage	*m, p, w, h, y* as in *y*ellow, *l, n,* and *t*
Oral biting stage	*b, f, k, g,* and *d*
Anal-expulsive stage	*ch* as in *ch*urch; *j* as in *j*udge
Anal-retentive stage	*s, r, sh,* and *z* as in a*z*ure
Phallic stage	*th* as in *th*anks; *v, z,* and the *th* as in *th*em

Many of these assumptions have been validated in clinical studies (Filippi & Rousey, 1971; LaFon & Rousey, 1970; Mehrhof & Rousey, 1971; Rousey, 1974; Rousey & Averill, 1963; Rousey & Toussieng, 1964). In addition, Kernberg and Rousey (1970) and Fleming and Rousey (1974) utilized speech errors to measure change independently in the course of psychotherapy.

Defense Mechanisms and Defensive Behavior

A final way to understand speech and auditory perceptual development is to use Wallerstein's (1983) and Kernberg's (1992) contributions regarding the differences between defense mechanisms and defensive behavior. Their conceptualization makes it possible to dissect the meanings

of speech disturbances and auditory perceptual distortions of sound as presented on the sound localization test (Rousey & Rousey, 1993).

SPEECH AS DEFENSIVE BEHAVIOR

Speech disturbances generally fall into one of three classes: substitutions of one sound for another, omission of a sound that should be present, or distortion of a consonant or vowel. If a speech disturbance is regarded as a symptom of psychopathology rather than a cognitive act, it is possible to conceive of the speech problem as defensive behavior and to understand the resulting conflicts and compromise that are exhibited. A further virtue of understanding speech disorders as defensive behavior is that it provides another cue to the alert clinician as to the presence of psychological conflict. Utilization of the schema proposed in this chapter should correlate with other observable clinical behavior. If it does not, then the therapy process is in danger of being terminated prematurely (Levy & Rousey, 1976).

The compromises included in the defensive behavior exhibited by a speech problem can be illustrated by the child who has a sound substitution of "f" for the voiceless "th." In this instance the child might pronounce the word both as *bof*. Recalling the previous discussion of which certain sounds are related to which stages of infantile sexuality will help pinpoint the areas of conflict which are contained in this speech disorder. Since the /f/ sound is associated with the oral biting stage while the voiceless /th/ sound is associated with the phallic stage, the compromise exhibited in this speech error is between the child's conflict over a sense of paternal psychological absence and the resulting rage over this absence. This inference is buttressed by the study of LaFon and Rousey (1970) demonstrating that such a sound substitution is common in situations where the father is psychologically or physically absent. While such an analysis is possible for other speech disturbances, the space limitations of this chapter preclude such a presentation.

DEFENSE MECHANISMS AND AUDITORY BEHAVIOR

As mentioned, Freud originally had an ear in his drawing of the ego. Because of the previously noted neural interconnections between the auditory tracts and the areas of the brain dealing with affect, it is possible to hypothesize the presence of some of the classic mechanisms of defense and defensive behavior. This area is assessed by use of a hearing test first devised by Rousey (1974), which samples a person's auditory localization of a simultaneously and binaurally presented pure tone. Much the same as in the administration of the Rorschach, the person is given the opportunity to report the sound as emanating from any place on the body, in the body or outside of the body. From a strictly anatomical standpoint, a person should logically locate the sound either in both ears or in some part of the head.

Clinical observation of the test responses of children below 3 years of age supports the assumption that interpretation of sound localization needs to be done with caution because of the magical thinking common to children. The approach presented offers another way to study the development of some of the classic defenses in young children and in that sense should provide complementary information to Kernberg's (1992) study of the development of defenses.

In clinical practice, use of this measure allows the detection of the defense mechanisms of projection, denial, and splitting. The following illustrations relating localization of sounds to defense mechanisms have both face validity as well as being validated in clinical assessments (Rousey, 1974) by Rousey, Morrison, and Deacon (1994) over the course of the past 15 years. Specific defenses and the assumptions relating them to sound localization responses are explicitly stated so that other clinicians and researchers can subject them to their own clinical and empirical validation process.

Projection: This defense mechanism is signaled by the person reporting hearing a simultaneously and binaurally presented pure tone as coming from a distance of greater than 2 feet outside of the head. In more seriously disturbed patients, the sound may be localized as coming from the walls of the test room, trees, and elsewhere.

Denial: This defense mechanism is evidenced by the person reporting hearing a simultaneously and binaurally presented pure tone as coming from one ear only. It is important to be certain by appropriate audiological tests that there is no evidence of a significant unilateral hearing loss.

Splitting: This defense mechanism is present when a simultaneously and binaurally presented pure tone is located outside of the head but no more than 2 feet away.

Somatization: This defensive behavior involves the localization of a binaurally presented tone at some site within the person's body rather than the ears or head. For example, it is clinically observable that ulcer patients often report the sound as being somewhere inside their stomach.

Summary

This chapter has integrated information from the disciplines of psychology, audiology, and speech pathology in an effort to illustrate how speech development and use of hearing can be utilized to understand psychological development. Such a conceptualization has important implications for the mental health practitioner in that new ways are opened for both clinical assessment and evaluation of psychological change resulting from therapy that are independent of either the patient or therapist. As such, it may have unexpected benefits in the context of society's need for accountability of mental health treatment. From the present conceptualization, it is probable that some of the most effective speech therapy is accomplished unwittingly by good psychotherapy. The hypotheses proposed in this chapter need continued research and scrutiny by both clinicians and researchers.

REFERENCES

Bishop, J. (1993, October 12). Stroke patients yield clues to brain's ability to create language. *The Wall Street Journal*, pp. A1, A4.

Broca, P. (1861). Remarques sur le siege de la faculte du langage articule, suives d'une observation d'aphemie. *Bulletin de la Societe Ancitomique de Paris, 36,* 350–357.

Cantwell, D., and Baker, L. (1991). *Psychiatric and de-*

velopmental disorders in children with communication disorders. Washington, DC: American Psychiatric Press.

Carrell, J., & Tiffany, W. (1960). *Phonetics: Theory and application to speech improvement.* New York: McGraw-Hill.

Chomsky, N., & Halle, M. (1968). *The sound pattern of English.* New York: Harper & Row.

Darby, J. (Ed.). (1981a). *Speech evaluation in medicine.* New York: Grune & Stratton.

Darby, J. (Ed.). (1981b). *Speech evaluation in psychiatry.* New York: Grune & Stratton.

Darley, F., Aronson, A., & Brown, J. (1975). *Motor speech disorders.* Philadelphia: W. B. Saunders.

Erikson, E. (1950). *Childhood and society.* New York: W. W. Norton.

Fantz, R. (1961, May). The origin of form perception. *Scientific American,* pp. 66–72.

Filippi, R., & Rousey, C. (1971). Positive carriers of violence among children: Detection by speech deviations. *Mental Hygiene, 55,* 157–161.

Fleming, P., and Rousey, C. (1974). Qualification of psychotherapy change by study of speech and hearing patterns. In C. Rousey (Ed.), *Psychiatric assessment by speech and hearing behavior* (pp. 196–210). Springfield, IL: C. C. Thomas.

Freud, S. (1961). The ego and the id. In J. Strachey (Ed. and Trans.), *The standard edition of the complete psychological works of Sigmund Freud* (hereafter *Standard edition*), (Vol. 19, pp. 3–66). London: Hogarth Press. (Original work published 1923.)

Freud, S. (1960). Slips of the tongue. In *Standard edition* (vol. 6, pp. 53–105). (Original work published 1901.)

Gravell, R., & France, J. (1991). *Speech and communication problems in psychiatry.* New York: Chapman and Hall.

Grievink, E., Peter, S., van Bon, W., and Schilder, A. (1993). The effects of early otitis media with effusion on language ability: A prospective cohort study. *Journal of Speech and Hearing Research, 36,* 1004–1012.

Head, H. (1926). *Aphasia and kindred disorders of speech.* New York: Macmillan.

Irwin, O. (1947). Infant speech: Consonantal sounds according to place of articulation. *Journal of Speech and Hearing Disorders, 12,* 397–401.

Irwin, O. (1948). Infant speech: Development of vowel sounds. *Journal of Speech and Hearing Disorders, 13,* 31–34.

Kernberg, P. (1992, October). *Outline of mechanisms of defense: development and research perspectives.* Paper presented at A celebration of the mind: The 50th anniversary of the Topeka Institute for Psychoanalysis, Topeka, KS.

Kernberg, P., & Rousey, C. (1970). Variations in speech sounds during psychotherapy: An independent indicator of change. *Journal of the American Academy of Child Psychiatry, 9,* 762–777.

LaFon, D., & Rousey, C. (1970). Residues of early father-child conflict. *Journal of Nervous and Mental Disease, 150,* 366–370.

LeDoux, J. (1992). Brain mechanisms of emotion and learning. *Current Opinion in Neurobiology, 2,* 191–197.

Levy, E., and Rousey, C. (1976). *Treatment failure after dispute about diagnosis.* Unpublished manuscript.

Luria, A. (1966). *Higher brain functions in man.* New York: Basic Books.

Mahler, M., Pine, F., & Bergman, A. (1975). *The psychological birth of the infant.* New York: Basic Books.

Mehrhof, E., & Rousey, C. (1971). Speech difficulties symptomatic of destructive behavior toward self or others. *Journal of Nervous and Mental Disease, 152,* 63–71.

Moses, P. (1954). *The voice of neurosis.* New York: Grune & Stratton.

Penfield, W., & Roberts, L. (1959). *Speech and brain mechanisms.* Princeton, NJ: Princeton University Press.

Prizant, B., & Meyer, E. (1993). Socioemotional aspects of language and social-communication disorders in young children. *Journal of Speech-Language Pathology, 2,* 56–71.

Rousey, C. (1971). *Slips of the tongue revisited.* Unpublished manuscript, The Topeka Institute for Psychoanalysis. Topeka, KS.

Rousey, C. (1979). Disorders of speech. In: J. Noshpitz (Ed.), *Basic handbook of child psychiatry; Vol. 2. Disturbances of Development* (pp. 464–474). New York: Basic Books.

Rousey, C. (1989). Reality testing and judgment. *Bulletin of the Menniger Clinic, 53,* 149–153.

Rousey, C. (Ed.). (1974). *Psychiatric assessment by speech and hearing behavior.* Springfield, IL: C. C. Thomas.

Rousey, C., & Averill, S. (1963). Speech disorders among delinquent boys. *Bulletin of the Menninger Clinic, 27,* 177–184.

Rousey, C., & Diedrich, W. (1974). *Tracking symptom substitution.* Unpublished manuscript.

Rousey, C., and Moriarty, A. (1965). *Diagnostic implications of speech sounds.* Springfield, IL: C. C. Thomas.

Rousey, C., & Rousey, W. (1993). *RAP (Rousey assessment of personality): A computerized clinical report.* Topeka, KS. Private publication of Drs. Rousey and Rousey, Ltd. P.O. Box 4929, Topeka, KS 66604.

Rousey, C., & Toussieng, P. (1964). Contributions of a speech pathologist to the psychiatric examination of children. *Mental Hygiene, 4,* 107–114.

Rousey, C., Morrison, D., & Deacon, D. (1994). *Choosing successful executives.* Manuscript submitted for publication and available to clinicians and research organizations.

Singh, S. (1976). *Distinctive features: Theory and validation.* Baltimore, MD: University Park Press.

Skinner, B. F. (1957). *Verbal behavior.* New York: Appleton-Century-Crofts.

Smit, A., Hand, L., Freilinger, J., Bernthal, J., & Bird, A. (1990). The Iowa articulation norms project and its Nebraska replication. *Journal of Speech and Hearing Disorders, 55,* 779–798.

443

Stern, D. (1985). *The interpersonal world of the infant.* New York: Basic Books.

Stoel-Gammon, C., and Dunn, C. (1985). *Normal and disordered phonology in children.* Baltimore, MD: University Park Press.

Templin, M. (1957). *Certain language skills in children.* Institute of Child Welfare Monograph series (No. 26). Minneapolis: University of Minnesota Press.

Wallerstein, R. (1983). Defense and structure of the mind. *Journal of the American Psychoanalytic Association 131 (Suppl.),* 201–225.

Wernicke, C. (1874). *Der aphasiche symptomencomplex.* Breslau: Cohn and Weigart.

Wolff, P. (1959). Observations on newborn infants. *Psychosomatic Medicine, 21,* 110–118.

39 / Separation Anxiety Disorder

John J. Stine, Paula K. Rauch, and Eugene V. Beresin

Separations are woven into the fabric of life. Coping with losses, whether they are transient or permanent, is part of a lifelong developmental process. From a toddler's venturings away from mother's protective body to an octogenarian burying a beloved wife, every human being is repeatedly challenged by a series of good-byes. In latency, children are confronted with the separations inherent in attending school and falling asleep, along with sleep-over parties, invitations to visit relatives, school trips, baby-sitters, and camp. For most children, these separations and their subsequent reunions are taken in stride, but for the child with separation anxiety disorder (SAD), every day is fraught with a sense of danger. This chapter examines our understanding of the etiology and risk factors associated with separation anxiety disorder and the treatment of affected latency aged children.

Separation anxiety is a normal phase of development. It begins in the latter half of the first year of life, and peaks between 15 and 21 months of age, and wanes in the third year of life (Rosetti-Ferreira, 1975). In order to experience the distress of separation, an infant must both recognize and feel attached to a special caregiver. When this developmental phenomenon is absent, some form of pathology exists—for example, a pervasive developmental disorder or a reactive attachment disorder. The intensity of normal separation anxiety is determined by both nature and nurture, that is, by the infant's physiologic reactivity, genetics, parental attunement, and experience of loss and separation.

Historical Perspective

Historically, John Bowlby and Mary Ainsworth are the founders of attachment theory. Bowlby incorporated concepts from animal ethology and expanded the psychoanalytic notion of attachment as an instinctual process in which biological needs are gratified, to include a primary social relationship factor between a mother and an infant (Bowlby, 1978). Ainsworth introduced a scientific methodology to the evolving understanding of normal attachment. She and her colleagues created a standard situation in the course of which they observed and systematically scored the behavior of 1-year-old in a prescribed sequence, with mother and/or a stranger present and/or absent. The infants were most curious about the play environment when their mothers were present and least curious when the mothers were absent and the strangers were present. The infants' level of exploration increased again when the absent mothers were returned but did not regain the level of curiosity exhibited prior to the mother leaving. Ainsworth interpreted these data to mean that secure attachment to mother enables an infant to explore and experience the environment most freely and that threats or perceived threats to attachment, such as the mother's absence in the experimental paradigm, result in inhibition of exploration in the form of quiet or noisy distress (Ainsworth & Bell, 1970).

Beginning with the publication of the third revised edition of the *Diagnostic and Statistical Manual of Mental* Disorders (*DSM-III-R*, American Psychiatric Association [APA], 1987), the term separation anxiety disorder (SAD) has been used to describe children who display signs and symptoms of anxiety triggered by actual, anticipated, or symbolic separations from important "attachment figures." These anxiety symptoms can range from vague somatic complaints, mild apprehension, reluctance to function away from home and refusal to go to camp or social activities, on the one hand, to severe sleep disorders, complete school refusal, and severe, incapacitating panic reactions in the face of even the slightest threat of separation from a parental figure on the other.

Thanks to the pioneering clinical research of Adelaide Johnson, Mary Ainsworth, Margaret Mahler, and John Bowlby, there is a general consensus that the underlying psychobiological mechanism in this disorder is related to abnormalities in the developmental processes of psychological attachment and separation. Later in this chapter we explore in more detail how the views of these investigators about the etiological mechanisms of this disorder both converge and differ.

Comparative Nosology

Many children with separation anxiety disorder were formerly diagnosed as suffering from "school phobia," "school avoidance," or "school refusal," because they presented with problems attending school. Continuing clinical experience with this patient population has revealed not only the typical underlying psychodynamic problems of dependency, separation fears, and preoedipal conflicts but often a history of chronic, subclinical separation anxiety prior to the acute episode that brought the children to clinical attention.

Consequently, cases formerly diagnosed as school phobia (SP) are currently diagnosed as sep-

aration anxiety disorder. This chapter discusses SP as a special category of SAD.

In contrast, the term *school avoidance* (SA) is a more general term to describe the behavior of a child who avoids or who cannot attend school. School avoidance can best be regarded as a final common pathway of behavior that can be caused by a spectrum of disorders, including separation anxiety disorder (or "school phobia"), a bona fide simple or social phobia to some object of situation at school, a severe avoidance disorder of childhood, panic disorder, behavior disorder, or psychotic disorder. These conditions are described in more detail in their respective chapters.

DEVELOPMENTAL NOSOLOGICAL ISSUES

In current usage, the term *separation anxiety* can be confusing. It can refer both to increases in anxiety that are a result of normative developmental processes (e.g., psychological and cognitive differentiation in infancy or the separation-individuation phase of early childhood) or, alternatively, to anxiety associated with psychopathology. More confusion results from the fact that abnormal degrees of separation anxiety may be seen not only in separation anxiety disorder but in other childhood disorders, such as pervasive developmental disorders and borderline states. In order to resolve these problems, some clinicians suggest that the term *separation reaction* be used to refer to normal developmental phenomena and that *separation anxiety* be confined to describing a symptom of psychopathology that may be the result of one of a number of psychiatric disorders, including separation anxiety disorder.

EPIDEMIOLOGICAL DATA

Anxiety disorders, including SAD, are the most prevalent form of childhood psychopathology in both normal and patient populations. Kashani and Orvaschel (1990), for example, found that 21% of children and adolescents in a community study had some sort of anxiety disorder, with SAD and Overanxious Disorder being the most common.

According to *DSM-IV* (APA, 1994), SAD is considered "not uncommon" and has an equal sex ratio; other studies find a slightly increased prevalence in girls. Current epidemiological studies of children in grade school agree on a general prevalence rate of between 4 and 5%. Costello (1989), for example, surveyed a general pediatric population in the United States and found a weighted 1-year prevalence rate of 4.1%. This is in close agreement with a study of Puerto Rican children ages 4 to 16 years by Bird, Gould, Yager, Staghezza, and Canino (1989) that found a 4.7% weighted prevalence rate.

In adolescents between the ages of 12 and 18, Bowen, Offord, and Boyle (1990) found a prevalence of 2.4%, with 6:1 female to male ratio. This supports the common clinical observation that while the prevalence of SAD generally decreases with advancing age, the disorder increases in girls. Bird et al. (1989) found that SAD was most prevalent in the 6 to 11-year age group and becoming less frequent as children grow older, and Last et al. (1987) found that the mean age of clinical presentation of children with SAD was 9.1 years.

Between 30 and 40% of cases show significant comorbidity with other anxiety disorders, depression, and externalizing psychiatric disorders (Bowen et al., 1990). This parallels the more general observation that children with anxiety disorders have a significantly increased number of problems, including depression, acting out, and physiological complaints (Kashani & Orvaschel 1990).

Clinical Presentation and Diagnostic Assessment

OVERT SIGNS AND SYMPTOMS

SAD can present with a wide spectrum of symptoms and signs of anxiety that are triggered by concerns about separation. The *DSM-IV* criteria for the diagnosis require the presence of at least 3 of the following 8 major categories of problems. These must be present before the age of 18 and persist for a period of more than 2 weeks.

1. recurrent excessive distress when separation from home or major attachment figures occurs or is anticipated
2. persistent and excessive worry about losing, or about possible harm befalling, major attachment figures
3. persistent and excessive worry that an untoward

event will lead to separation from a major attachment figure (e.g., getting lost or being kidnapped)
4. persistent reluctance or refusal to go to school or elsewhere because of fear of separation
5. persistent and excessive fear or reluctance to be alone or without major attachment figures at home or without significant adults in other settings
6. persistent reluctance or refusal to go to sleep without being near a major attachment figure or to sleep away from home
7. repeated nightmares involving the theme of separation
8. repeated complaints of physical symptoms (such as headaches, stomachaches, nausea, or vomiting) when separation from major attachment figures occurs or is anticipated. (APA, 1994, p. 113)

In fact, somatic symptoms of unknown etiology can be the presenting symptoms of SAD in the pediatrician's office and may result in multiple negative medical workups until the underlying disorder is suspected. For example, Livingston, Taylor, and Crawford (1988) studied somatic complaints in 95 consecutively psychiatrically hospitalized 6 to 12-year-old children. He found a strong association between complaints of abdominal pain and palpitations and separation anxiety. More recently, Last and Strauss (1989) studied 158 anxiety-disordered children in an outpatient clinic and found that 78% of separation anxiety disordered children reported somatic complaints. There was also a statistically higher prevalence of somatic complaints in children with separation anxiety who developed school refusal.

RELATIONSHIP TO OTHER DISORDERS

Separation anxiety and separation reactions are considered to be part of the normal process of psychological development in childhood and occur frequently in otherwise normal children and adolescents. Clinicians and researchers continue to debate whether SAD represents the extreme expression of an essentially normal developmental presence, or whether it is a qualitatively different psychological state. For diagnostic purposes, in order to establish the presence of SAD, it is important to demonstrate that the symptoms are severe enough to interfere with psychological and social functioning.

In the realm of psychopathology, has definite

but still imprecisely defined relationships with other anxiety disorders, including school avoidance, school phobia, general anxiety disorder, and panic disorder. These relationships are hard to define for the following reasons. First, there is considerable but inconsistent comorbidity among these conditions; in short, they frequently appear together but in no one consistent pattern or combination. For example, about 33% of children with SAD also suffer from overanxious disorder of childhood (Last et al., 1987). Second, there is considerable overlap between the signs and symptoms that are used to define their presence in clinical and research situations. Third, psychodynamically oriented clinicians often invoke common psychological factors to explain the origin of all of these problems: Most often, pathologically high levels of separation anxiety are posited as a common causative dynamic mechanism. Fourth, biological research offers converging evidence about common underlying temperamental, genetic, or neurophysiological etiological factors for many of the anxiety disorders of childhood (Hirshfeld et al., 1992). For all these reasons, it remains unclear whether they represent truly distinct entities or merely variants of one underlying disorder.

There is considerable controversy as to whether these anxiety disorders of childhood are continuous with anxiety disorders of adulthood. To date, epidemiological research devoted to this issues has yielded contradictory findings.

Finally, there is also some anecdotal evidence of an association between separation anxiety disorder and psychosomatic disorders, such as ulcerative colitis (Sperling, 1967).

PATTERNS OF PEER RELATIONSHIPS

Children with SAD are reported to be usually well liked by peers, to have age-appropriate social skills, and to function well when in an emotionally secure setting. However, they are either reluctant to or refuse to sleep away from home; they often will refuse invitations from friends to sleep over or oppose parental attempts to induce them to go to sleep-away camp. When school refusal is part of the clinical picture, on school days, such children typically appear in severe distress until allowed to stay home, at which point their acute anxiety rapidly abates. They often spend the rest of the school day hiding at home, and then, once school

is out, they interact with their peers in a seemingly normal, happy fashion.

However, albeit typical of the child with pure SAD, this description may not be universally applicable. Clinical observations of patients with coexisting depressions or multiple anxiety disorders often reveal more infantile and withdrawn children who avoid social interactions and alienate peers. This occurs because of their apathy, irritability, and lack of social skills, compounded by their severe dependency at an age when most children take pride in a growing sense of their own autonomy, individuality, and adventuresomeness.

PATTERNS OF PLAY

Children with SAD who are observed in play therapy often express their underlying preoccupations via symbolic fantasy play. Themes of abandonment, fears of separation, and fantasies of subsequent disasters befalling children and their parents are frequently the repetitive content of doll and puppet play or may be repetitively re-enacted in dramatic fantasy play. One 8-year-old boy with severe SAD, for example, compulsively played out episodes that were loosely based on the *Wizard of Oz* and that featured a family of murderously sadistic witches who tortured lost children and then attacked each other. These stories symbolized both the terrible dangers that he feared when alone and the enormous rage that he felt toward his mother and sister when he felt ignored by them.

Objective Measures

One interesting adjunct to interview data is the comparison of psychophysiological parameters of anxiety with the child's self-report. In one study, facial muscle tension and skin tone conductance were measured in 8-year-olds who were confronted with anxiety-provoking visual stimuli (photographs of snakes with fangs bared). The self-reports of distress by the anxious and normal children in this study were not significantly different, but the psychophysiologic parameters were significantly different between the two groups

(Turner, Beidel, & Epstein, 1991). These results highlight the limits of self-report for anxiety in children less than 10 years old. It would be particularly interesting to learn whether anxiety self-report data would be any more accurate if this study were repeated with older latency-age children.

One attempt to translate a child's inner experience of anxiety into an objective measurement tool is the Revised Fear Survey Schedule for Children (FSSC-R) (Last & Strauss, 1989), which asks children about an array of specific fears. The nonnormative fears of separation anxiety disorder children as elicited in the FSSC-R can be useful in that they may help differentiate these children from normal and overanxious disorder children. The SAD children most often complained of fears of getting lost, sick, or hurt, as opposed to overanxious disorder children, who had more fears of being teased or criticized. The presence of school fears was not significantly different between the separation anxiety group and the social phobia group (Last & Strauss, 1987). The FSSC-R also offers the clinician a host of special fears about which to inquire as opposed to vague questions about feeling-states that may be impossible for the young latency-age child to answer.

Etiology and Pathogenesis

PSYCHODYNAMIC FORMULATION

Latency-age children with SAD are attempting to cope with severe fears of separation and object loss that most of their peers successfully mastered in the preschool years. The SAD youngsters often are painfully aware that their anxieties force them into regressive and infantile patterns of behavior; consequently, despite their intense suffering, a sense of deep shame often leads them consciously and unconsciously to suppress, repress, deny, or minimize their problems.

In general, for the majority of children with SAD, basic ego functioning is intact. This includes age-adequate reality testing, secondary process thinking, impulse control, and the control and modulation of affects. Object relations usually have progressed well beyond the establishment of object constancy. Many children with SAD have well-endowed personalities supplemented by many strengths and talents that have been fostered and developed by parents who are often child-oriented. At the same time, both the parents and the child are overly dependent and enmeshed with each other. However, ego functioning and ego strengths will vary depending on such factors as the developmental history of the individual child, patterns of comorbidity, and the types of co-existing family psychopathology.

In children with SAD, self-esteem is often fragile, however, because of their sense of shame over their symptomatology, especially if it is chronic in nature. The child with SAD often suffers from intense unconscious guilt generated by a punitive superego that reacts even more harshly to forbidden impulses and wishes than does the rigid and sadistic superego of the normal latency-age child. Many of the typical conscious fears of robbers, bodily injury, or calamitous events are overdetermined and are the result of both the projection of the child's hostile wishes toward the parent and the projection of his or her unconscious guilty wishes for punishment. As a result, some children with SAD can be extremely sensitive and easily upset by criticism and harshness from authority figures, because they experience such treatment as a punishment, a confirmation of their unconscious sense of being bad and a confirmation of their worst fears about separation.

Ken: Ken, for example, at age 11, still remembered crying, trembling, and vomiting uncontrollably every morning when it was time to leave for school during first grade. Although he had been referred for treatment because of "poor academic motivation," he gradually revealed a lifelong history of severe separation anxiety, which was periodically exacerbated when his teachers were critical of him. In addition, he literally was never able to tolerate anyone yelling at him, because it made him feel depressed, worthless, and unlikable.

Although he now passively aggressively resisted his mother's attempts to force him to do his schoolwork, he was scrupulously polite and pleasant with her and felt bad and guilty when he had the slightest angry, critical, or rebellious feeling. It took a great deal of emotional support from his therapist before Ken was able to discuss his lifelong anger at his mother and his conviction that her critical, angry tone was in some way his just deserts for his "rebelliousness."

SAD may be divided into two major psychodynamic categories. In the one instance, the latency-age child has continually suffered from a chronic

448

form of the disorder since the preschool years; on the other, the child has experienced a recent, acute outbreak of symptomatology (Sperling, 1967). In all cases, there is an underlying "anxious attachment" or hostile-dependent relationship between the patient and primary object (usually mother). However, some cases are precipitated by acute psychologically traumatic events, while in others, separation anxiety is induced primarily by a chronically anxious and fearful parent. In all types, the children unconsciously fear separation and abandonment as a punishment for forbidden, unconscious oral, anal, or phallic forms of libidinal and aggressive wishes. Simultaneously, they must struggle to contain enormous rage at the mother for not being constantly at their disposal as a reassurance against the fantasy of abandonment.

In the chronic form, preoedipal conflicts and unconscious mechanisms of defense more typical of the younger, preoedipal child are most prominent. These defenses include turning passive into active, reaction formations, doing and undoing, projection of anger, and partial discharge of the impulses via acting out. They may be manifested by such behaviors as daytime fighting with counterphobic qualities, bedtime rituals, and clinging or overly compliant behavior toward the parents.

Bobby: Bobby, age 7, for example, had never mastered his fears of being away from his mother, although he could attend school reluctantly. He would play with children if they came to his house. Each night as bedtime approached, he would become increasingly cooperative and compliant, would cling piteously to his mother, insist on endless drinks of water, demand bedtime stories, or complain of gastrointestinal disorders.

In contrast to this, during the day, he would act in a tough, hypermasculine manner, performing dangerous acrobatic feats in the schoolyard and alienating his peers by fighting and bullying. He attempted to deal with his anger at his mother by utilizing a number of mechanisms simultaneously: displacement (verbally attacking girls on the school bus), splitting (he talked about his mother as perfect while complaining that his teacher was cold, mean, and uncaring), and projection (he worried constantly that his mother disliked him and had repetitive nightmares about evil witches attacking him).

In the acute type, the child has been able to mobilize ego defenses sufficiently to partially master these underlying fears and conflicts and to move more or less successfully through the phallic-oedipal and into the latency phase of de-

velopment. In such cases, symbolic or actual traumatic events during middle childhood may not only activate fears of separation and abandonment directly but simultaneously intensify unconscious oedipal conflicts to an unbearable extent. This may precipitate a defensive intrapsychic regression from the postoedipal stage back to separation conflicts and fears that have remained as fixation points in psychic development.

BIOLOGICAL ASPECTS

Some investigators and clinicians maintain that much of separation anxiety can best be understood as a natural consequence of the "biologically programmed" attachment behaviors of the normal infant. They have observed similar behavioral sequences of protest, despair, and detachment in both human and monkey infants that have been separated from their mothers. In addition, upon reunion, infants of both species show similar increases in the frequency of clinging and attachment behaviors. Consequently, it is argued that separation reactions are genetically determined, instinctive behavioral reaction patterns that have evolved through natural selection and have intrinsic survival value. According to this view, separation anxiety can be intensified to clinically pathological proportions by life experiences, especially those that occur in the first 3 years of life before psychological object constancy has been achieved. (See Bowlby, 1973.) Bowlby maintains that from 7 months to the fourth year of life even relatively brief separations of mother and infant can have a traumatic although sometimes subtle impact upon future development of the infant. Signs of this impact can range from chronic symptoms of depression and developmental regressions to heightened shyness, anxiety, and inhibition manifested only when the child is in new situations.

It is important to note that this theoretical position does not attempt to eliminate psychosocial factors from etiological theory. However, it does maintain that separation anxiety is the result of biologically determined behavioral patterns interacting with social learning and psychological mechanisms of defense against forbidden internal impulses (Bowlby, 1973, p. 185). According to this formulation, traumatic life events involving actual or threatened separation from attachment figures, especially in early childhood, can predispose an individual to a lifelong pattern of "anxious attachment," dependency, and subclinical levels of separation anxiety. This constitutes a predisposition to the development of a separation anxiety disorder under the impact of subsequent life stresses.

Despite the fact that no direct evidence currently exists about the role of genetic factors, given the increased familial prevalence of SAD and other anxiety disorders, the possibility of a genetically transmitted, heightened vulnerability to separation anxiety in some children seems to have face validity. To date, however, no neurochemical or neuropsychological abnormality has been discovered that might serve as a biological "marker" for this disorder.

An important corollary to an etiologic understanding of separation anxiety disorder is the concept of a vulnerable or at-risk child for the disorder. Thomas and Chess (1981) introduced the concept of temperamental traits that are present early in childhood and that persist throughout development. Temperament is a constellation of traits, some of which may predispose to separation difficulty, such as a tendency toward withdrawal rather than approach, greater tactile sensitivity, and less adaptability. Kagan (1984) carried the concept of temperament to its physiologic roots; he described the "behaviorally inhibited" anxious child, who enters the world more threatened by external stimuli, more sensitive to loss of the secure object, and more inhibited in his or her exploration of the new situation as compared to the average child. The behaviorally inhibited children Kagan identifies have more rapid heart rates than do less inhibited children and often slow their heart rates in response to solitary, cognitive tasks during which they presumably feel least threatened by environmental cues. It is as if these children are specially attuned to interpret as threatening input that for other children is benign. Perhaps these children are born primed for anxiety disorders, thus highlighting the role of "nature" in the development of separation anxiety disorder.

Primate research supports the human findings of physiologic vulnerability to anxiety and a predisposition to a particular kind of lifelong temperament. In a fashion all too reminiscent of the behaviorally inhibited children, rhesus monkeys with increased noradrenergic activity are more anxious, behaviorally inhibited, and sensitive to cues of punishment, as compared to monkeys with lower levels of noradrenergic activity (Charney & Redmond, 1983). The presence of increased anxietylike behavior in rhesus monkeys remains consistent from early life into adulthood (Suomi, 1986).

TRAUMATIC FACTORS

Clinically, separation anxiety disorder often occurs after a life stress that involves a loss, such as the death of a relative or pet, an illness, or environmental changes, such as moving to a new school or neighborhood. However, a careful history often reveals a lifelong sensitivity to separation with subclinical levels of separation anxiety. Bowlby (1973) cites multiple studies that find that "anxious attachment" (i.e., high levels of separation anxiety) is highly correlated with a history of actual separations, especially before the third birthday; hostile, critical, or rejecting parents, and unstable pathological family interactions. He stresses that separation anxiety may be heightened in children who are regularly exposed either to actual threats of abandonment as part of parental attempts at discipline or to parental quarreling that stimulates fantasies of abandonment. Such threats may be overlooked during clinical evaluations because the clinician may focus exclusively on intrapsychic factors or because of parental reluctance to reveal such disciplinary tactics. Bowlby refers to Newson and Newson's study (1968) that indicates that over 25% of 600 English parents admitted to regularly threatening children with actual abandonment. Similarly, Sears, Maccoby, and Levin (1967) interviewed hundreds of American mothers and found that 25 to 50% of them made moderate to considerable use of threats of withdrawal of love and/or abandonment as part of their child-care practices. Bowlby's point is well taken: Clinicians should be more aware of the possibility that ongoing, reality factors such as these are contributing to the maintenance of a SAD so that appropriate interventions can be directed toward coexisting family pathology.

FAMILIAL FACTORS

Clinical observation and clinical research have long implicated the quality of the mother-child relationship as an important variable affecting the degree of separation anxiety in a child as well as an important predictor of separation anxiety disorder. For example, Adelaide Johnson and her colleagues (Johnson, Falstein, Szuerk, & Svendsen, 1941) distinguished between two different types of school refusal, those due to truancy and those due to "school phobia." In the latter type, both child and mother were found to be suffering from severe, mutually reinforcing separation anxieties that often seemed to have been activated by real or symbolic object loss which had occurred recently in the mother's life. The multigenerational nature of this type of separation anxiety was demonstrated by the repeated finding that these mothers usually had highly dependent and overly close relationships with their own mothers and had unconsciously encouraged a similar pattern of dependency and anxious reactivity in their school-phobic children (Eisenberg, 1958).

Subsequently, Margaret Mahler and her research group described the process of psychological separation, individuation, and rapprochement, which constitutes an intermediate developmental stage between infantile dependency on the one extreme, and the establishment and consolidation of psychological object constancy and autonomy in the child, on the other (Mahler, Pine, & Bergman, 1975). During this period heightened separation anxiety, which normally occurs between 18 and 30 months of life, is observed universally.

The severity of this anxiety was reported to be affected by two factors. One was the occurrence of stressful environmental events and the quality of the mother-child relationship. Of special importance was the mother's emotional availability and her capacity for empathic response to the child's needs during this normal developmental crisis. Mahler's clinical research strongly implies that a child's failure to transverse this phase of development successfully sets the stage for both a lifelong vulnerability to separation anxiety and the subsequent development of psychopathology.

According to *DSM-IV* (APA, 1994), SAD is more common in first-degree biological relatives of probands with SAD than in the general population. The risk for anxiety disorders is many times greater in the children of anxious parents than in the children of normal controls. A genetic vulnerability to anxiety disorders or states is also supported by data that demonstrate an increased concordance between monozygotic twins as compared to dizygotic twins. Clearly genetics alone are not sufficient to predict anxiety disorders, since the concordance for undifferentiated anxiety disorders between monozygotic twins remains less that 50% (Turner et al., 1991). The genetics of anxiety have to be teased out of the complex interplay between a child's biology on the one hand and his or her experience of the world when living with anxious caregivers or siblings on the other. In addition, mothers of children with SAD show a very high prevalence of emotional disorders (Last et al., 1987), including generalized anxiety disorders (47.4%), posttraumatic stress disorder (15.8%), agoraphobia (5.3%), and affective disorder (78.9%).

Many children with SAD tend to come from families that are close-knit, caring, and centripetal, and that may have several additional members who suffer from a range of anxiety disorders. Although there is little statistical data available, there is abundant anecdotal clinical evidence that emotionally impaired family members often stimulate SAD in offspring by either implied or actual threats of abandonment as a discipline technique, by modeling anxious behaviors that reinforce anxiety about separation, or by teaching their children by attitude or example that the world outside the family home is too dangerous to be explored.

VULNERABILITY

The broad range of epidemiological and clinical studies just discussed enables us to construct a profile of the children who are most vulnerable to developing a separation anxiety disorder. The most vulnerable children will come from families in which many members suffer from anxiety disorders. They will have at least one parent, usually the mother, who suffers from separation anxiety disorder and who often uses tacit or over threats of abandonment as a disciplinary technique. There will be a developmental history of lifelong problems with excessive separation anxiety, and the actual outbreak of the disorder is preceded by real or symbolic losses, such as illnesses or death of people who are psychologically important to the children. It seems intuitively likely that children with all of these characteristics (in addition to coexisting emotional disorders) would be highly vulnerable to the development of separation anxiety disorder.

Phenomenology of SAD in Other Stages of Life

Key differences in the way this disorder appears at different ages are determined by the acute or chronic nature of the condition and the degree to which the patient's personality style and life patterns have been affected by and organized around separation anxiety. Usually, the preschool and latency-age child presents with acute and obvious symptoms that are precipitated by traumatic events by the stress that emerges from the normal development demands of attending school, socializing, attending camp, and taking part in other recreational activities.

In contrast, adolescents and adults with chronic SAD may have organized their lives so as to avoid most symbolic or real separations, often with the aid and unconscious encouragement of their pathogenic, anxiety-inducing families. These behavioral patterns are frequently rationalized as entirely normal and have become ego-syntonic. For example, some adolescents with SAD are permitted to stay home frequently from school because of "chronic illness," lack of academic "interest," or the need to take care of chronically ill family members. Similarly, some adults with chronic SAD remain as close to home as possible; they confine themselves to their immediate neighborhood and limit their social interactions in order to stay in close proximity with their own attachment figures. Such individuals rarely come to clinical attention unless they are suffering with other acute emotional disorders. Sometimes they become acutely anxious because of changes in their life patterns that reawaken separation fears. In such cases, mood disorders and panic attacks with agoraphobia are frequent presenting problems.

Psychological and Social Treatments

INDIVIDUAL PSYCHOTHERAPY

Psychotherapeutic treatment of SAD has been strongly influenced by the pioneering studies of school phobia by Adelaide Johnson and her associates. These investigators discovered that many cases of school avoidance were caused by severe and mutually reinforcing separation anxiety disorders in children and their mothers. Consequently, individual therapy for both the child and the affected parent was strongly recommended, usually with different therapists. Although this remains a basic treatment model for SAD, there have been many case reports of successful individual treatment of children with SAD via the modalities of intensive psychotherapy or child psychoanalysis (Geleerd, 1967; McDevitt, 1967; Sperling, 1967). In these reports treatment for the parent seems to be minimal. It may be speculated that excellent results reported in these cases may reflect minimal effects of parental psychopathology.

FAMILY THERAPY

Family therapists have focused increased attention on the types of pathogenic family systems that induce and maintain separation anxiety in both the identified patient as well as other family members. The work of this school of therapists extends the concepts of Johnson and her colleagues; more than that, it alerts the clinician to another important possibility, namely that because many of the members of the extended, multigenerational family may be overinvolved and enmeshed with each other, the mutually reinforcing separation anxiety of child and mother may be reinforced in turn by these additional family members. In such cases, structural family therapy may be an invaluable part of the treatment plan (Minuchin, 1974).

BEHAVIORAL INTERVENTIONS

Multiple case reports and single case studies have appeared over the past decades describing the successful treatment of SAD and other anxiety disorders with the use of behavioral techniques. These include such methods as in vivo desensitization, contingency management, flooding and cognitive-behavioral therapy (Klein & Last, 1989). Behavioral approaches such as in vivo desensitization, operant conditioning, and contracting often are used in conjunction with medication in order to help a school-phobic child return to school as rapidly as possible. Using the end point of a return to school as the outcome criterion, clinicians using these techniques report excellent, short-term results. However, these studies are often single case reports, usually lack long-term follow-up, and usually do not assess global personality functioning before and after treatment. As a result, we lack reliable statistical data about treatment efficacy. Treatment efficacy is even harder to judge in applying behavioral techniques to other forms of separation anxiety, because the pervasive nature of the disorder makes treatment evaluation difficult.

EDUCATIONAL INTERVENTIONS

There are several important educational interventions with the school-avoidant child who suffers from SAD. First, at the time of the acute onset of the disorder, it is an important priority to help the child return to school as soon as possible. This is because the longer one delays, the more anxious such children tend to become about returning to school. This anxiety often is secondarily reinforced as they fall further behind in their schoolwork and bear the additional worry about academic failure.

Children with acute SAD may require the presence of school personnel coming to their home to help them make the transition to school, or they may require the temporary presence of a parent in the school to help them overcome their paralyzing anxiety.

In contrast, children with chronic, severe SAD who have not attended school for a lengthy period of time may be too anxious and educationally impaired to be able to return to a class at their grade level. They may require a variety of alternative educational interventions, ranging from home tutoring to special class placement. In short, some means must be found to help them overcome educational gaps that may have resulted from poor school attendance while they were severely symptomatic. Some may even require placement in a special school or in long-term milieu treatment before they are able to return to the educational mainstream. It is important to stress that these interventions are not primary treatment modalities that will result in definitive cure; they are, rather, ancillary supportive techniques within an overall treatment plan. They should be selected and implemented with great care and follow-up lest they

unwittingly reinforce an anxious child's sense of self as deviant, impaired, or chronically and hopelessly ill.

BIOLOGICAL TREATMENT

Biological treatment for SAD is largely limited to the use of tricyclic antidepressants. The use of imipramine in SAD is supported by Gittleman-Klein and Klein's study (1971, 1973). Here the medication demonstrated its superiority to placebo in treating children with school phobia. The approach involved a 6-week treatment course using doses up to 200 milligrams per day combined with behaviorally oriented psychotherapy. Campbell and Spencer (1988) cite Reicher's personal communication that children with panic disorder also respond to tricyclic antidepressants. However, subsequent studies of tricyclic treatment of school-phobic children with clomipramine (Berney, Kolvin, Bhate, et al., 1981), imipramine, and alprozolam (Bernstein, Garfinkel, & Borchardt, 1987) and imipramine treatment of separation anxiety disordered children (Klein, Koplewicz, & Kanner, 1992) have failed to demonstrate that drugs are therapeutically superior to placebo; in fact, significant therapeutic responses to placebo have been noted in these studies. Moreover, Klein et al.'s 1992 study documented that a significant number of children showed substantial clinical improvement in response to progressive in vivo desensitization behavioral techniques rather than to drug therapy. However, despite the conflicting research evidence about the efficacy of these drugs, a majority of clinicians use them on an empirical basis, usually as part of multimodal treatment plan that may include some combination of family, individual, and behavioral therapies.

Alprozolam has been used widely and successfully in adult populations to treat panic attacks and other anxiety disorders thought to be related to underlying separation anxiety. One unpublished pilot study demonstrates its efficacy in children with SAD who are unresponsive to psychotherapy (Klein, reported in Klein & Last, 1989); aside from that report, however, no research data about its efficacy in children are available. In addition, because of increasing concerns about the potential for abuse, addiction, drug tolerance, and rebound effects, alprazolam and other benzodi-azapines currently are not recommended for the treatment of SAD in children and adolescents.

MILIEU TREATMENT

Because a major goal of treatment is rapid nor-malization of functioning in as many areas of life as possible, milieu treatment is reserved for care-fully selected cases. Usually such patients come from severely emotionally impaired families that have had difficulty in fully supporting the treat-ment plan. In addition, these children have had long-standing problems and impaired global func-tioning. The decision for milieu treatment is also based on the degree to which the child's function-ing is impaired. When this reaches a critical level, initial placement in a protective, structured set-ting is required in order to prevent a further breakdown of functioning during the initial phases of treatment. A day hospital setting or an inpatient setting may be especially useful for those children with SAD who also suffer from se-vere mood disorders and panic attacks. In such cases there is a crucial need for structure, readily available and consistent emotional support, and even protection against suicidal impulses during the initial phases of treatment.

Current Developments, Research, and Unanswered Questions

In recent years, a series of epidemiological studies have demonstrated a high prevalence of anxiety disorders in normal populations. Moreover, these studies have begun to delineate some of the unique characteristics of children with SAD that differentiate them from children with other types of anxiety disorders. However, many questions re-main unanswered at this time.

From a descriptive point of view, we still lack substantive longitudinal profiles of children with SAD and more complete knowledge of outcome, both with and without treatment. As a result, clini-cians still find it hard to predict the clinical course of the disorder and are thus handicapped when making treatment recommendations. Long-term follow-up studies of the clinical course of children with SAD (with and without treatment) are sparse and methodologically flawed. However, they give the overall impression that, even with psychother-apeutic treatment, only a minority of children grow up to be adults who are free from emotional difficulties. The majority continue to suffer pre-dominately from anxiety disorders, personality problems, and impaired social and occupational functioning (Gittleman, 1986). In addition, chil-dren with chronic SAD onset of school avoidance in adolescence have a poorer outlook (Coolidge, Willer, Tessman, & Waldfogel, 1960).

Although epidemiological research initially seemed to demonstrate that SAD is one of a num-ber of different and distinct anxiety disorders, research findings increasingly show that there is significant overlap of symptoms and diagnostic criteria between all of the anxiety disorders of childhood. Moreover, current research discloses that in a significant number of patients, the anxi-ety disorders seem to show considerable comor-bidity and that the diagnostic profile of a partic-ular patient may change over time. Further research is clearly needed to clarify how stable these diagnoses are and to test whether SAD is actually a precursor of adult disorders such as panic disorder and agoraphobia. Longitudinal studies also are needed to test the psychoanalytic developmental hypothesis that severe separation anxiety disorder in early childhood may be a pre-cursor to severe character pathology (Mahler et al., 1975). Additionally, in view of the high preva-lence of comorbidity between the anxiety dis-orders and mood disorders, further research is in-dicated to test whether the current diagnostic classification of the anxiety disorders is scientifi-cally valid and offers clinically and therapeutically useful constructs. Continued neurobiological and genetic research into possible biological markers for separation anxiety would be useful in investi-gating possible etiological factors.

Finally, as with all of the emotional disorders of childhood, well-designed and well-controlled re-search studies of all current modalities of treat-ment are important research priorities. In the meantime, it seems clear that anxiety disorders are the product of a complex interplay of nature and nurture. Good treatment is a mosaic, balanc-ing individual psychotherapy, behavioral therapy, parent guidance, family therapy, and medication to meet the needs of the individual child and family. No modality alone has been shown to be either the treatment of choice or ineffective. It becomes the task of the therapist to help the child, family, and the social network bear the unreasonable anxiety, so that the child can grow to master his or her fears and continue to move forward in development.

REFERENCES

Ainsworth, M. D. S., & Bell, S. M. (1970). Attachment exploration and separation illustrated by the behavior of one year olds in a strange situation. *Child Development, 41,* 49–67.

American Psychiatric Association. (1987). *Diagnostic and statistical manual of mental disorders* (3rd ed., rev.). Washington, DC: Author.

American Psychiatric Association (1994). *Diagnostic and statistical manual of mental disorders* (4th ed.). Washington, DC. Author.

Berney, T., Kolvin, I., Bhate, S. R., et al. (1981). School phobia: A therapeutic trial with clomipramine and short-term outcome. *British Journal of Psychiatry, 138,* 110–118.

Bernstein, G. A., Garfinkel, B. D., & Borchardt, C. M. (1987). *Imipramine versus Alprazolam for school phobia.* Paper presented at the annual meeting of the American Academy of Child and Adolescent Psychiatry, Washington, DC.

Bird, H. R., Gould, M., Yager, T., Staghezza, B., & Canino, G. (1989). Risk factors for maladjustment in Puerto Rican children. *Journal of the American Academy of Child and Adolescent Psychiatry, 28,* 847–850.

Bowen, R., Offord, D., & Boyle, M. (1990). The prevalence of overanxious disorder and separation anxiety disorder: Results from the Ontario Child Health Study. *Journal of the American Academy of Child and Adolescent Psychiatry, 29,* 753–758.

Bowlby, J. (1973). *Attachment and Loss. Volume 2. Separation-Anxiety and Anger.* New York: Basic Books.

Bowlby, J. (1978). The nature of the child's ties to the mother. *International Journal of Psycho-analysis, 39,* 350–373.

Campbell, M., & Spencer, E. (1988). Psychopharmacology in child and adolescent psychiatry: A review of the past five years. *Journal of the American Academy of Child and Adolescent Psychiatry, 27,* 269–279.

Charney, D. S., & Redmond, D. E. (1983). Neurobiological mechanisms in human anxiety: Evidence supporting noradrenergic hyperactivity. *Neuropharmacology, 22,* 1531.

Coolidge, J. S., Willer, M. L., Tessman, E., & Waldfogel, S. (1960). School phobia in adolescence: A manifestation of severe character disturbance. *American Journal of Orthopsychiatry, 30,* 599–607.

Costello, E. (1989). Child psychiatry disorders and their correlates: A primary care pediatric sample. *Journal of the American Academy of Child and Adolescent Psychiatry, 28,* 851–855.

Eisenberg, L. (1958). School phobia: A study of the communication of anxiety. *American Journal of Psychiatry, 114,* 712–718.

Geleerd, E. (1967). Intrapsychic conflicts as observed in child analysis. In E. R. Geleerd (Ed.), *The child analyst at work.* New York: International Universities Press.

Gittleman, R. (1986). Childhood anxiety disorders: Correlates and outcome. In R. Gittleman (Ed.), *Anxiety disorders of childhood* New York: Guilford Press.

Gittelman-Klein, R., & Klein, D. F. (1971). Controlled imipramine treatment of school phobia. *Archives of General Psychiatry, 25,* 204–207.

Gittelman-Klein, R., & Klein, D. F. (1973). School phobia: Diagnostic considerations in the light of imipramine effects. *Journal of Nervous and Mental Disease, 156,* 199–215.

Hirshfeld, D., Rosenbaum, J., Biederman, J., Bolduc, E., Faraone, S., Snidman, N., Reznick, J. S., & Kagan, J. (1992). Stable behavioral inhibition and its association with anxiety disorder. *Journal of the American Academy Child and Adolescent Psychiatry, 31,* 103–111.

Johnson, A., Falstein, E., Szuerk, S., & Svendsen, M. (1941). School phobia. *American Journal of Orthopsychiatry, 11,* 702–708.

Kagan, J. (1984). Guiding themes in human development. In J. Kagan (Ed.), *The nature of the child* (pp. 3–26). New York: Basic Books.

Kashani, J., & Orvaschel, H. (1990). A community study of anxiety in children and adolescents. *American Journal of Psychiatry, 147,* 313–318.

Klein, R., Koplewicz, H., & Kanner, A. (1992). Imipramine treatment of children with separation anxiety disorder. *Journal of the American Academy of Child and Adolescent Psychiatry, 31,* 21–28.

Klein, R., & Last, C. (1989). *Anxiety disorders in children.* Newbury Park, CA: Sage Publications.

Last, C. G., Hersen, M., Kazdin, A. E., Finkelstein, R., et al. (1987). Comparison of DSM III separation anxiety and overanxious disorders: Demographic characteristics and patterns of comorbidity. *Journal of the American Academy of Child and Adolescent Psychiatry, 26,* 527–531.

Last, C. G., Strauss, C. C., & Francis, G. (1987). Comorbidity among childhood anxiety disorders. *Journal of Nervous and Mental Disease, 175* (12), 726–730.

Last, C. G., & Strauss, F. G. (1989). Assessing severity in anxiety disordered children with a revised fear survey schedule for children (FSSC-R). *Journal of Clinical Child Psychology, 18* (2), 137–141.

Livingston, R., Taylor, J., & Crawford, L. (1988). A study of somatic complaints and psychiatric diagnosis in children. *Journal of the American Academy of Child and Adolescent Psychiatry, 27,* 185–187.

Mahler, M. S., Pine, F., & Bergman, A. (1975). *The psychological birth of the human infant.* New York: Basic Books.

McDevitt, J. (1967). A separation problem in a three-year old girl. In E. R. Geleerd (Ed.), *The child analyst at work.* New York: International Universities Press.

Minuchin, S. (1974). *Families and family therapy.* Cambridge, MA: Harvard University Press.

Newson, J., & Newson, E. (1968). *Four-year old in an urban community.* London: Allen and Unwin.

Rossetti-Ferreira, M. D. (1985). Adult-child and peer interaction during brief separations. *British Journal of Developmental Psychology, 3* (2), 163–173.

Sears, R. R., Maccoby, E. E., & Levin, H. (1967). *Patterns of child rearing.* Evanston, IL: Rowe Peterson.

Suomi, S. J. (1986). Anxiety-like disorders in young nonhuman primates. In R. Gittleman (Ed.), *Anxiety disorders of childhood.* New York: Guilford Press.

Sperling, M. (1967). School phobias: Classification, dynamics and treatment. *Psychoanalytic Study of the Child, 22,* 375–401.

Thomas, A., & Chess, S. (1981). The role of temperament in the contributions of individuals to their development. In R. M. Lerner & N. A. Busch-Rossnagel (Eds.), *Individuals as Producers of Their Development* (pp. 231–254). New York: Academic Press.

Turner, S. M., Beidel, D. C., & Epstein, S. H. (1991), Vulnerability and risk for anxiety disorder. *Journal of Anxiety Disorders, 5* (2).

40 / Attention Deficit Hyperactivity Disorder

Barbara J. Coffey

Historical Overview

Attention deficit hyperactivity disorder has been recognized for over 100 years in the scientific literature; although our understanding of this disorder has increased significantly since that time, the etiology and pathophysiology remain elusive. In 1902 Dr. George Still described these children in his lecture to the Royal Academy of Physicians (Still, 1902). Later, children who became ill with von Economo's encephalitis developed motor activity and inattention. In the 1930s, children with impulsivity, motoric overactivity, and inattention were described as having "organic drivenness"; shortly afterward, such a group of organically impaired children with overactivity, impulsivity, and inattention became candidates for the first trial of psychostimulants by Charles Bradley (Bradley, 1937; Kahn & Cohen, 1934).

The description of these clusters of symptoms consolidated, over the next few decades, becoming in the 1960s and 1970s "hyperactivity," "hyperkinetic syndrome," and "minimal brain damage." The latter term was used to denote the fact that most of these children had no overt, gross neurological lesions but instead tended to have minor physical anomalies and poor motor coordination. Unfortunately, the validity of these classification hypotheses was not determined empirically at the time (Wender, 1971).

Nosology/Current Description

Most recently, a descriptive nosology has developed and operationalized definitions have replaced less precise and reliable criteria. The third edition of the *Diagnostic and Statistical Manual of Mental Disorders* (*DSM-III;* American Psychiatric Association [APA], 1980) brought a new perspective on this clinical syndrome. Attention deficit disorder (ADD) could be diagnosed with or without hyperactivity, introducing the concept that the activity component may be separate, or different, from the problem with inattention and impulsivity. Questions regarding the validity of ADD without hyperactivity as a separate diagnostic category arose (Lahey & Carlson, 1991).

The definition in the third revised edition of

the *Diagnostic and Statistical Manual of Mental Disorders* (*DSM-III-R*, APA, 1987) incorporated both inattention and motoric overactivity in the description of the syndrome as attention deficit hyperactivity disorder (ADHD). Criteria for the severity of attention deficit hyperactivity disorder were developed and reflected degree of impairment in the child's school and social functioning.

The other diagnostic category in this edition was undifferentiated ADHD, a "residual category in which the predominant feature is the persistence of developmentally inappropriate and marked inattention that is not a symptom of another disorder" (APA, 1987, p. 95).

DSM-III-R represented an advance over *DSM-III* and previously developed classification systems. Field trials for the disruptive behavior disorders in *DSM-III-R* took place at 10 sites throughout the United States and included 550 children evaluated by 72 clinicians. For the first time, instead of by committee consensus the criteria for *DSM-III-R* were developed with an attempt to empirically validate their accuracy. Previously validated item pools from *DSM-III* were tested for sensitivity and specificity in a move toward a polythetic format. Odds ratios were calculated based on individual items' sensitivity and specificity, using clinical diagnosis of ADHD as the criterion. The odds ratios were generally high, indicating good power of discrimination. Threshold for cut-off (minimal number of symptoms) was set using sensitivity and specificity values, with 8 of 14 having the highest total predictive value (Spitzer, Davies, & Barkley, 1990).

The polythetic approach utilized in *DSM-III-R* implied that a dimensional rather than a categorical classification system provided a theoretical foundation (Fletcher, Morris, & Francis, 1991). Factor analysis of *DSM-III* items revealed that they fell into two dimensions: inattention-restless and impulsive-hyperactive (Barkley, 1990c). These factors have served as the foundation for the development of the criteria in the fourth edition of the *Diagnostic and Statistical Manual* (*DSM-IV*, 1994).

The *DSM-IV* definition separates the two dimensional categories described in this syndrome and hence allows for subtyping the disorder. These criteria also incorporate developmental considerations.

Children with attention deficit hyperactivity disorder are characterized by short attention span; restless movement and activity; poor modulation of impulses, particularly aggressive ones; and lack of socially acceptable behavior for their peer group. The core deficits occur in modulation and inhibition of motor, cognitive, affective, and social functions. Modulation and control of internal states as well as interaction with the environment in the form of parents, teachers, and peers is problematic.

The clinical manifestations of ADHD change with the unfolding of development. Often parents describe these children as having been excessively active in utero; as infants, they were irritable, difficult to soothe, and poor sleepers. In early childhood, these children are typically hyperactive, restless, impulsive, and destructive; they do not respond to discipline. They cannot easily sustain play sequences and are frequently destructive with their toys and clothes. Parents experience these children as unrewarding to parent and engage in more directive and negative interactions with them as compared to parents of children without ADHD (Mash & Johnston, 1982).

Children with ADHD often are first diagnosed in the school-age period. The developmental expectation for school-age children is that they sit still, follow rules and regulations, master cognitive tasks such as reading, math, and language, and pay attention for sustained periods. Children with ADHD are unable to master these age-appropriate demands for competence and are extremely vulnerable to failure. They are restless, disorganized, disruptive, and unrewarding to teach. They frequently forget assignments and lose materials, often failing to complete or hand in homework. Teachers see them as lazy, underachieving, and overtly defiant.

On the playground, these children are loud, disruptive, and act like bullies with peers. They are aggressive and tend to butt in on other children's activities, with little awareness or sensitivity to others' feelings.

Frequently physically and verbally aggressive, they tend to externalize conflicts and blame others for their problems. Gradually, these children become socially isolated as their peers tire of their aggressive and insensitive behavior.

Over time, with repeated experiences of failure in the classroom, socially, and in self-control at home, self-esteem suffers. Failure to accomplish

TABLE 40.1

Diagnostic Criteria for Attention Deficit Hyperactivity Disorder in DSM-IV

A. Either (1) or (2):
   (1) six (or more) of the following symptoms of **inattention** have persisted for at least 6 months to a degree that is maladaptive and inconsistent with developmental level:

   Inattention:
   (a) often fails to give close attention to details or makes careless mistakes in schoolwork, work, or other activities
   (b) often has difficulty sustaining attention in tasks or play activities
   (c) often does not seem to listen when spoken to directly
   (d) often does not follow through on instructions and fails to finish scholwork, chores, or duties in the workplace (not due to oppositional behavior or failure to understand instructions)
   (e) often has difficulty organizing tasks and activities
   (f) often avoids, dislikes, or is reluctant to engage in tasks that require sustained mental effort (such as schoolwork or homework)
   (g) often loses things necessary for tasks or activities (e.g., toys, school assignments, pencils, books, or tools)
   (h) is often easily distracted by extraneous stimuli
   (i) is often forgetful in daily activities

   (2) six (or more) of the following symptoms of **hyperactivity-impulsivity** have persisted for at least 6 months to a degree that is maladaptive and inconsistent with developmental level:

   Hyperactivity:
   (a) often fidgets with hands or feet or squirms in seat
   (b) often leaves seat in classroom or in other situations in which remaining seated is expected
   (c) often runs about or climbs excessively in situations in which it is inappropriate (in adolescents or adults, may be limited to subjective feelings of restlessness)
   (d) often has difficulty playing or engaging in leisure activities quietly
   (e) is often "on the go" or often acts as if "driven by a motor"
   (f) often talks excessively

   Impulsivity:
   (g) often blurts out answers before questions have been completed
   (h) often has difficulty awaiting turn
   (i) often interrupts or intrudes on others (e.g., butts into conversations or games)

B. Some hyperactive-impulsive or inattentive symptoms that caused impairment were present before age 7 years.

C. Some impairment from the symptoms is present in two or more settings (e.g., at school [or work] and at home).

D. There must be clear evidence of clinically significant impairment in social, academic, or occupational functioning.

E. The symptoms do not occur exclusively during the course of a Pervasive Developmental Disorder, Schizophrenia, or other Psychotic Disorder and are not better accounted for by another mental disorder (e.g., Mood Disorder, Anxiety Disorder, Dissociative Disorder, or a Personality Disorder).

NOTE. From *Diagnostic and Statistical Manual of Mental Disorders*, 4th ed., pp. 83–85. American Psychiatric Association, 1994, Washington, DC: Author. Copyright 1994 by the American Psychiatric Association. Reprinted by permission.

the primary tasks of development in the school-age period—achievement of competence in the classroom, mastery of impulse control, emotional separation from parents, and the establishment of satisfying relationships with peers—can result in a variety of emotional reactions, including anger, sadness, and depression. Chronic experiences of anger and depression in the context of social isola-tion, stressed parental relationships, and genetic vulnerabilities may put the ADHD child at risk for the development of additional clinical syndromes, including conduct disorder and/or depression.

Although the tendency to be motorically active diminishes in adolescence, the inner restlessness and distractibility persist. Learning difficulties persist, as well, although usually by this phase of development, educational and other special interventions have been introduced. Stimulus-seeking and risk-taking behavior become particularly problematic at this developmental phase, since these youth have little capacity for careful judgment. Childhood conduct disorder places the adolescent at high risk for adult antisocial disorder and substance abuse (Klein & Mannuzza, 1991).

Adults with ADHD symptoms that persist are at extremely high risk for antisocial, substance abuse, and legal difficulties. Mastery of adult developmental tasks, such as stable work or career choice, interpersonal intimacy in the form of marriage or committed personal relationships, and generativity in the form of parenting or other nurturant activity, is severely compromised. Adults with ADHD cannot stably involve themselves in ongoing, meaningful work and interpersonal relationships, and frequently move, lose or quit jobs, and disrupt their relationships (Wender, 1987).

Epidemiology

Attention deficit hyperactivity disorder is a relatively common disorder. Estimates of its prevalence range from 1 to 10%, depending on the diagnostic criteria and measures utilized and the population studied. Estimates are lower (1–2%) when diagnosis is based on multiple sources (Rasbury, 1988). The *DSM-IV* describes a prevalence of about 3 to 5% of school-age children (APA, 1994). In 1987, an epidemiologic study in Baltimore revealed that about 6% of the elementary school population was on stimulants (Safer & Krager, 1988). The ratio of males to females is reported to range between 3 and 10:1. Recently reports of an increase in the number of girls with ADHD have decreased the ratio to approximately 3 to 1 (APA, 1994).

Cross-cultural studies have revealed a slightly lower prevalence when compared to the United States, and diagnostic criteria contribute to the variance. Taylor and Sandberg (1984) noted a 20-fold difference in diagnostic rate between the United States and the United Kingdom. Prendergast and associates (1988) studied diagnoses given to 36 boys ages 6 to 11 using teams of clinicians and researchers from the United States and United Kingdom. *International Classification of Diseases-9* diagnoses of hyperactive syndrome were less frequent than ADHD was by *DSM-III* criteria. Diagnosticians in the United Kingdom preferred the diagnosis of conduct disorder and American diagnosticians preferred ADHD when both problems co-occurred.

A prevalence of ADHD in 9% of boys and 3% of girls was found in the Ontario Child Health Study of children ages 4 to 16 in each of four administrative regions (Szatmari, Offord, & Boyle, 1989b). During the survey, it was determined that these children were more impaired in a variety of developmental spheres, including school performance, extracurricular activities, and relationships with others, as compared to normals (Szatmari, Offord, & Boyle, 1989a).

McGee and coworkers (1990) found a prevalence of 2% of ADD and residual ADD in New Zealand. A prevalence of about 11% was found in a pediatrics population of 1000 children ages 3 to 12 in India (Bhatia, Nigam, Bohra, & Malik, 1991). In a study of 914 children in Hong Kong from a nonreferred population of school-age children, teachers rated conduct, hyperactivity, and inattention highly (Luk, Leung, & Lee, 1988).

Associated Features/Comorbidity

A diverse but consistent spectrum of associated features occur in relation to ADHD and have generated considerable literature and some controversy. As a heterogenous disorder, ADHD can perhaps be subtyped by its associated features or comorbidity. Coexisting conduct and oppositional disorder, learning disabilities (specific developmental disorders), and emotional disorders such as depression and anxiety have been described in association with ADHD (Biederman, Newcorn, & Sprich, 1991; Biederman, Faraone, et al., 1993; Shaywitz, & Shaywitz, 1991).

The conceptual model for understanding comorbidity and ADHD relates directly to questions regarding the validity of the clinical syndrome. Is ADHD one syndrome with numerous subgroups with a common etiology, or is it truly a heterogenous disorder and final common pathway for a variety of etiologies? Do comorbid patterns of association define subtypes? How do referral patterns bias the face validity of the syndrome? Which symptoms should be seen as the core deficits (hyperactivity-impulsivity vs. inattention-distractibility) and which are associated features? In an extensive literature review of comorbidity and ADHD, Biederman, Newcorn et al. (1991) summarize a number of hypotheses for patterns of comorbidity. These include:

1. They are the same entities with phenotypic variability expression.
2. They are separate and distinct clinical entities.
3. There are common vulnerabilities, either genetic (genotype) or psychosocial (adversity), or both.
4. There are distinct subtypes within a heterogenous group (i.e., attention deficit hyperactivity disorder plus comorbid disorder may be a subtype of attention deficit hyperactivity disorder).
5. One syndrome represents an early manifestation of the comorbid disorder (i.e., an attention deficit hyperactivity disorder is an early manifestation of a conduct or mood disorder).
6. One syndrome increases the risk for the development of the other (i.e., attention deficit hyperactivity disorder increases the risk for conduct or mood disorder).

Data from family studies and long-term prospective studies of individuals at risk will address this question.

Disruptive Behavior Disorders

The association between conduct disorder and oppositional defiant disorder and ADHD has long been described in the literature. Controversy exists as to whether these syndromes are essentially indistinguishable or whether they are separate and independent (Szatmari, Boyle, & Offord, 1989). Thirty to 70% of patients with ADHD have been reported to have conduct or oppositional defiant disorder (Anderson, Williams, McGee, & Silva, 1987; August, Stewart, & Holmes, 1983; Biederman, Faraone, Keenan, & Tsuang, 1991; Biederman, Munir, & Knee, 1987; Bird et al., 1988; Epstein, Shaywitz, Shaywitz, & Woolston, 1991; Faraone, Biederman, Keenan, & Tsuang, 1991; Farrington, Loeber, & Van Kammen, 1989; Gittelman, Mannuzza, Shenker, & Bonagura, 1985; Klorman et al., 1988; Lahey, Green, & Forehand, 1980; Lahey et al., 1988; Loeber, Brinthaupt, & Green, 1988; Loney, 1987; Mannuzza,

Gittelman-Klein, Horowitz-Konig, & Giampino, 1989; McGee, Williams, & Silva, 1985; Milich, Offord, Sullivan, Allen, & Abrams, 1979; Reeves, 1987; Sandberg, Wieselberg, & Shaffer, 1980; Shapiro & Garfinkel, 1986; Stewart, Cummings, Singer, & De Blois, 1981; Szatmari, Boyle, & Offord, 1989; Taylor, schachar, Thorley, & Weiselberg, 1986; Thorley, 1984).

Disparities in referral patterns contribute to differences in comorbidity. A recent study by Epstein, Shaywitz, Shaywitz, and Woolston (1991) of referral patterns to child neurologists, pediatricians, psychologists, and psychiatrists demonstrated that diagnoses of learning disability and ADHD were made in 85 to 92% of the referrals made to the pediatricians, neurologists, and psychologists and in only 27% of those referred to child psychiatrists. Conversely, over three-quarters of the referrals to the child psychiatrists were for oppositional defiant disorder, conduct disorder, or other psychiatric-behavioral problems, as compared to 0 to 15% to the other clinicians (Epstein et al., 1991).

Evidence in favor of conduct disorder and ADHD constituting one disorder include similarities in symptoms, outcome, and stimulant response (Biederman, Newcorn et al., 1991; Campbell & Werry, 1986; Quay, 1986). Evidence in favor of the independence of ADHD and conduct disorder include family history data and outcome studies; aggression and not hyperactivity per se predicts a poorer prognosis in terms of greater likelihood of antisocial outcome (Biederman, Newcorn et al., 1991; Loney, Kramer, & Milich, 1981).

Faraone and associates (1991) studied the family history of 457 first-degree relatives of 73 ADHD patients ages 6 to 17, 26 psychiatric controls, and 26 normal controls referred to a tertiary care pediatric psychopharmacology clinic. Twenty-four (33%) of the probands met criteria for conduct disorder, 33 (45%) met criteria for oppositional defiant disorder, and 16 (22%) had ADHD alone. Mannuzza and team (1989) compared 372 clinically referred patients ages 16 to 23 to a control group and demonstrated that in the first cohort, 45% of ADD patients had conduct disorder vs. 16% of controls; in the second cohort, 59% of ADD patients had conduct disorder vs. 18% of controls.

Numerous other studies have demonstrated a high association between conduct disorder and

ADHD, including those from nonreferred populations. Bird and colleagues (1988), in an epidemiologic study in Puerto Rico of 386 4- to 16-year-olds, showed that 57% of cases with ADHD had conduct disorder and/or oppositional defiant disorder.

SPECIFIC LEARNING DISABILITIES/ DEVELOPMENTAL DISORDERS

The association between ADHD and learning disabilities has long been noted in the literature, ranging from 10 to 92% (Biederman, Newcorn et al., 1991). Recent reports estimate that 10% to 25% of children with ADHD have comorbid learning disorders (Richters et al., 1995). ADHD and learning disabilities overlap on many characteristics, and questions of independence of each have been raised. (McGee & Share, 1988; Prior & Sanson, 1986; Silver, 1981). Although learning problems occur as a result of the inattention, disorganization, and lack of planful activity with ADHD, not all ADHD children have the specific cognitive-perceptual deficits that characterize specific developmental disorders. Both conditions can lead to classroom failure, but most literature appears to point to their independence (Biederman, Newcorn, et al., 1991).

Recent studies have attempted to address the question of the independence of learning disabilities and ADHD. August and Garfinkel (1990) studied 115 boys with ADHD who were referred to an outpatient child psychiatry clinic. These patients were grouped according to the presence or absence of a specific developmental disorder in reading. Criteria for the reading disability were 1 standard deviation below the mean on the Wide Range Achievement Test in reading or spelling and 1 standard deviation below the Peabody Picture Vocabulary IQ. Of the 115 subjects with ADHD, 45 (39%) met criteria for reading disability; most of these subjects had reading and spelling delays.

While both groups showed similar scores on the Conners hyperactivity and conduct factors, the ADHD plus reading disability group showed a specific cognitive impairment in rapid word naming (August & Garfinkel, 1990).

Felton and Wood (1989) undertook a series of studies to differentiate ADD from reading disability. With age, gender, and intellectual ability controlled for, cognitive deficits associated with reading disability differentiated the group. Measures of naming and phonological awareness were significantly impaired. Other investigators have found similar results (Denckla & Rudel, 1976; Felton, Wood, Brown, Campbell, & Harter, 1987). Some investigators have questioned the differences and challenged the results of some of these studies (Share & Schwartz, 1988).

Learning disabilities, defined as being at least 2 years behind in reading, spelling, mathematics, or written language, were found in 80% of 11-year-olds with ADHD by the Anderson team (Anderson, Williams, McGee, & Silva, 1987). Dykman and Ackerman (1991) studied 182 clinic-referred children with ADHD (*DSM-III*); more than 82 met the criteria for specific reading disorder. The group with the reading disorder was differentiated from the group with the ADD without reading disorder and a control group on laboratory measures of sustained attention and impulse control (coding and arithmetic on Wechsler Intelligence Scale for Children-Revised). Stimulant response, however, did not differentiate the groups.

Approached from the perspective of learning disability as the primary problem, a significant proportion of children with specific developmental disorders have ADHD. A study by Cantwell and Baker (1991) of 600 speech- and language-impaired children ages 1 to 16 showed that of those 42 who had specific developmental disorders at initial presentation, 40% also had ADHD, the most common associated form of psychopathology. At follow-up of 300 subjects 4 to 5 years later, 30% had learning disabilities and ADDH was present in 53%. This study showed a strong association between learning disabilities and disruptive behavior disorders. Others have found similar results (Love & Thompson, 1988).

EMOTIONAL DISORDERS

Investigators recently have described the co-existence of mood and anxiety disorders with ADHD in referred and nonreferred populations (Biederman, Newcorn, et al., 1991); others have not found such an association (Klein & Mannuzza, 1991). Estimates of the frequency of major mood disorders co-occurring with ADHD range from 3 to 75%; 15 to 20% may be most common (Alessi & Magen, 1988; Anderson et al., 1987; Biederman, Munir, et al., 1987; Bird et al., 1988; Bohline, 1985; Brown, Borden, Clinderman, & Jenkins, 1988; Brown & Sexon, 1988; Gittelman et al., 1985; Jensen, Burke, & Garfinkel, 1988; Keller et al., 1988; Mannuzza et al., 1989; McClellan, Rubert, Reichler, & Sylvester, 1990; Staton & Brumback, 1981; Stewart & Morrison, 1973; Strober et al., 1988; Weinberg et al., 1989; Weiss, Hechtman, Milroy, & Perlman, 1985; Woolston et al., 1989). This association has been noted in studies of depression, dysthymia, bipolar disorder, and ADHD. (Biederman, Newcorn et al., 1991; Bohline, 1985; Brown et al., 1988; Munir et al., 1987). As is discussed later, family history studies have contributed evidence for such an association, and some case reports of follow-up studies have noted an association (Dvoredsky & Stewart, 1981). To some degree, diagnostic criteria and differential diagnostic considerations can easily confound the issue.

Follow-up studies of ADHD and major affective disorders indicate that both groups carry a substantial risk for poor prognosis (Brent et al., 1988; Kovacs, Feinberg, Crouse-Novack, & Paulauskas, 1984; Kovacs, Paulauskas, Gatsonis, & Richards, 1988). Comorbidity of both conditions in one individual potentially carries a graver prognosis in terms of morbidity and mortality than in those without comorbidity.

Estimates of the coexistence of anxiety disorders with ADHD run up to 25 to 30% in clinical and nonreferred populations (Anderson, 1987; Biederman, 1991; Bird, 1988; Gittelman, 1985; Lahey, Schaughency, Hynd, Carlson, & Nieves, 1987; Last, Strauss, & Francis, 1987; Mannuzza, 1989; Munir, Biederman, & Knee, 1987; Pliszka, 1989; Sylvester, Hyde, & Reichler, 1987; Woolston et al., 1989). Family studies also have contributed evidence for an association. Again, differential diagnosis may be confounding, particularly in relation to studies of ADD without hyperactivity (Lahey & Carlson, 1991; Lahey et al., 1987).

COMORBIDITY WITH OTHER DISORDERS

Attention deficit hyperactivity disorder has been found to occur in association with a variety of medical conditions. Children with mental retardation have been found to have ADHD at higher rates than normals in some studies. Relationship with IQ is complicated by increased rates of psychopathology in general below 50 and lack of appropriate or standardized instruments for use in the developmentally delayed population (Bie-

derman, Newcorn et al., 1991; Varley & Trupin, 1982).

Four of 14 preschool children with Down syndrome were noted to have attention deficits in a study by Green, Dennis, and Bennets (1989).

Soft neurological signs represent a group of nonfocal abnormalities that are thought to result from neurological immaturity. Soft central nervous system signs have been reported to be common in children with ADHD (Denckla & Rudel, 1978; Mikkelsen, Brown, Minichiello, Millican, & Rapoport, 1982; Paulsen, 1982). A recent study by Vitiello and team (Vitiello, Stoff, Atkins, & Mahoney, 1990) of 31 boys ages 6 to 13 years referred to a child psychiatry service for disruptive behavior and 45 controls examined the relationship between central nervous system soft signs and measures of impulsivity. Controlling for age and number of tests, the authors found a significant correlation between soft central nervous signs and impulsivity as measured by the Matching Familiar Figures Test and Continuous Performance Test. This occurred in the absence of a correlation with general intelligence.

Other authors have described increased incidence of minor physical anomalies in children with ADHD. In a study of hyperactive boys, Rapoport, Quinn, and Lamprecht (1974) noted multiple minor physical anomalies.

Attention deficit hyperactivity disorders have been described in 50 to 60% of patients with Tourette's disorder (Cohen, Bruun, & Leckman, 1988; Comings & Comings, 1987). Evidence for a genetic relationship between ADHD and Tourette's disorder has been controversial; some investigators believe that the association can be accounted for on a genetic basis, while others do not (Comings & Comings, 1984; Pauls et al., 1986).

Associations between ADHD and allergy and ADHD and otitis media in the previous year have been noted (Adesman, Altshuler, Lipkin, & Walco, 1990; Marshall, 1989).

Family History/Genetics

A genetic or familial contribution to ADHD has been postulated for many years; 25 years ago Morrison and Stewart (1971) reported that close relatives of hyperactive children were more likely to have had a history of hyperactivity in childhood themselves as compared to a control group.

August and Stewart (1982) reported an association between conduct and antisocial problems in children with ADHD and antisocial personality and alcohol abuse in close relatives. It was the aggression and conduct problems in childhood that predicted adult antisocial problems, not the ADHD itself. Similarly, Biederman, Faraone, Keenan, Knee, and Tsuang (1990) found that relatives of children with ADD who had childhood ADD were at higher risk for antisocial disorders than relatives without childhood ADD. Lahey, Piacentini, and coworkers (1988) found that biological parents of ADDH children were not associated with any particular psychiatric disorder unless conduct disorder was present. Parents of conduct disorder/ADDH children were more likely to show antisocial behavior. Schachar and Wachsmuth (1990) found similar results; ADHD complicated with conduct disorder predicts higher rates of adult psychopathology, but without conduct disorder does not. (Schachar & Wachsmuth, 1989).

Twin and adoption studies reveal a significant genetic-familial contribution to the development of ADHD. For example, Goodman and Stevenson (1989) investigated the heritability of certain measures of hyperactivity and inattentiveness in a large group of nonreferred 13-year-old twins. This included 127 both recognized and unrecognized identical monozygotic twins and 111 dizygotic twins. For all measures of inattentiveness and hyperactivity drawn from standardized instruments, monozygotic twins showed higher (51%) concordances than same-sex dizygotic twins (33%). This was particularly noteworthy in the case of measures of attentiveness in which both recognized and unrecognized monozygotic twins showed in the correlation, controlling for expectancy bias. Genetic factors accounted for 30 to 50% of the variance in measures of childhood hyperactivity and attentiveness in this study.

Recent studies have demonstrated that biological mothers of ADHD children run a 15 to 20% risk and biological fathers a 20 to 30% risk of having the syndrome themselves. Siblings run approximately a 26% risk (Barkley, 1990e).

Cadoret and Stewart (1991) reported on a study of two samples of 285 males, ages 18 to 40, who had been adopted at birth; both groups contained samples of adoptees whose biological parents had records of psychiatric or behavioral problems and

those that did not. Adoptive families also were classified by those with alcohol problems, those with antisocial problems, and those with psychiatric problems in parents, siblings, or other close relatives. Results analyzed by a loglinear model indicated that ADHD alone did not predict adult antisocial personality disorder. However, a biological parent with criminality or delinquency predicted ADHD in adopted-away sons. ADHD also was significantly correlated with aggressivity, which in turn predicted high likelihood of adult antisocial personality. These findings do not agree with those of Lahey and coworkers, who studied a referred population.

A study by Biederman, Faraone and colleagues (1990) of 457 first-degree relatives of 73 probands with ADHD demonstrated that the morbidity risk for ADD was 25% compared to a risk of about 5% in relatives of psychiatric controls and about 5% in relatives of normal controls. This remained the case when gender was controlled for.

Familial association between ADHD and emotional disorders has been investigated recently as part of an ongoing study of the genetics of the disorder at Massachusetts General Hospital. Results indicate that ADD and affective disorders may share a familial association.

In a study of 73 clinically referred probands with ADD and 26 normal controls, 24, or 33%, met criteria for an affective disorder (major depression, bipolar disorder, or dysthymia). Among 264 first-degree relatives of the 73 ADD probands, 27% met criteria for an affective disorder (bipolar disorder, major depressive disorder, or dysthymia) as compared to 4% of 92 relatives of normal controls. The presence of ADD in a relative did not increase the risk for an affective disorder in that relative, indicating that ADD and depression did not cosegregate among relatives of ADD probands (Biederman, Faraone, Keenan, & Tsuang, 1991).

The same team investigated the familial association between ADD and anxiety disorders in the same clinical population of 73 ADD probands and 26 normal controls. Twenty-two (30%) met criteria for one or more comorbid anxiety disorders, including avoidant disorder, obsessive-compulsive disorder, overanxious disorder, separation anxiety, and phobic disorder. Among 356 first-degree relatives, the risk for anxiety disorders was 31% in the mothers, 18% in fathers, and 2 to 8% in siblings. The presence of ADD in a relative increased the risk of an anxiety disorder in that relative, demonstrating that ADD and anxiety disorders did cosegregate among close relatives of ADD probands (Biederman, Faraone, Keenan, Steingard, & Tsuang, 1991).

Etiology/Pathophysiology

Despite significant advances in the understanding of ADHD in terms of nosology, genetics, and long-term course, etiology and pathophysiology have remained elusive. Much data have accumulated in recent years regarding prenatal, toxic-environmental, neurophysiological, neuroanatomic, and biochemical factors that may contribute; a brief review follows.

PRENATAL/OBSTETRICAL FACTORS

In general, epidemiological studies have not found a significant correlation between prenatal or obstetrical complications and ADHD when socioeconomic status and other factors are controlled for (Barkley, 1990a). However, a number of studies have indicated that hypoxic insults to the brain at birth are associated with attention deficits and hyperactivity (Cruikshank, Eliason, & Merrifield, 1988; O'Dougherty, Nuechterlein, & Drew, 1984). ADHD symptoms are seen more often in children with seizure disorders, as well (Holdsworth & Whitmore, 1974). Some investigators have demonstrated a higher prevalence of obstetrical complications, including fetal distress, abnormal labor, toxemia, and forceps delivery (Hartsough & Lambert, 1985; Minde, Webb, & Sykes, 1968). Studies have suggested that low birthweight or young maternal age may be a risk factor for ADHD (Nichols & Chen, 1981). Maternal cigarette smoking during gestation also has been reported to be a risk factor for ADHD (Nichols & Chen, 1981; Streissguth et al., 1984).

POSTNATAL, TOXIC ENVIRONMENTAL FACTORS

Some studies suggest that elevated blood lead levels in children are associated with a greater risk for ADHD. When confounding factors are controlled for, this association is not as strong (Fergusson, Fergusson, Howrood, & Kinzett, 1988; Gittelman & Eskinazi, 1983; Needleman et al., 1979).

Early malnutrition places children at risk for the development of ADHD. In a study of children on Barbados who experienced severe malnutrition during the first year of life, 60% demonstrated symptoms of ADD later on at the ages of 5 to 11 in a follow-up (Galler, Ramsly, Soliman, & Lowell, 1983).

NEUROPHYSIOLOGICAL/ PSYCHOPHYSIOLOGICAL AND COGNITIVE FACTORS

Some studies suggest patterns of autonomic underarousal in children with ADHD. Lowered levels of reticular activating system excitation in ADHD were reported by Satterfield and Dawson in 1971. Other studies have reported decreased galvanic skin response conductance or rapid heart rate deceleration in hyperactive children. Unfortunately, methodologic difficulties limit these studies' generalizability (Barkley, 1990a; Satterfield & Dawson, 1971).

Recently, more methodologically sophisticated studies have examined the nature of the neurophysiology of attention in clinical populations of ADHD children. Event related potentials (ERPs), a measure of endogenous brain activity, are thought to reflect different cognitive processes in the brain. Satterfield, Schell, and team (1990) studied 20 children with ADHD and 20 normal controls in a discrimination task of selective attention. Three different potentials were examined in the study: the first, N2, which represents the capacity to respond differentially to novel stimuli, an involuntary function, is associated with the orienting response. A second potential, Nd (processing negativity), is thought to reflect processing of the attended channel only, and a third potential, P3b (P3 or P300), is thought to reflect cognitive processes involving updating of the schema imposed on information feedback. Findings indicated that N2 and Nd were significantly different in ADHD children from those in normal controls. These findings suggest that ADHD children have compromised orienting response to novel stimuli and abnormalities in the processing of attended stimuli in the frontal lobes.

In a longitudinal study over 2 years by the same

team, further abnormalities were found in auditory and visual ERPs. Nd (processing negativity) and P3b (revision or updating of memory) abnormalities were found as were developmental differences between 6 and 8 years. Interpretation of the data indicated that the abnormal P3b reflected inadequate attention to relevant stimuli in the attended channel, rather than general distractibility, due to high levels of stimuli that were difficult to filter out. The authors speculated that the low P3b response in ADHD patients may be related to decreased locus coeruleus activity normally triggered by novel stimuli (Satterfield et al., 1990).

Other investigators have noted similar abnormalities in P3b waves and have speculated that children with ADD are weak in information processing and in motor processes involving memory. Klorman (1991) reviewed this topic, particularly noting the positive effects of stimulants' enlargements of the P3b wave.

Many investigators have attempted to define the nature of the attentional dysfunction in children with ADHD through neuropsychological and other cognitive tasks. A study of 20 children ages 6 to 12 with ADHD and 20 matched controls examined performance on several standardized measures of frontal lobe function, including the Wechsler Intelligence Scale for Children—Revised (WISC-R), the Wisconsin Card Sorting Test, and a variety of tests of verbal and performance fluency. The presence of learning disabilities was controlled for by exclusion criteria. ADHD children showed impairments in the Information, Arithmetic, Digit span, Block design, and Coding Subtests of the WISC-R; the Distractibility and Vigilance sections of the Gordon Diagnostic System; reading comprehension on verbal learning and memory on the Brown-Peterson and California verbal learning tests; however, they showed nearly normal performance on measures of frontal lobe function on letter, design, and category fluency and the Wisconsin Card Sorting Test. Only more rule violations on letter and design, but not category, fluency differentiated patients from controls (Loge, Staton, & Beatty, 1990).

Swanson and colleagues investigated the nature of two theoretical attentional systems in the brain through cued reaction time testing in a study of 28 ADHD children and 27 normals. Both normals and ADHD children performed similarly in early covert shift of visual-spatial attention as measured

by reaction time patterns. However, later overt shift of attention based anteriorly was found to be abnormal in ADHD children, suggesting a failure to sustain focused attention (Swanson et al., 1991). Others have found no deficits in sustained attention between patients and controls when children with ADHD were subdivided on a continuum of pervasiveness of hyperactivity (Van der Meere, Wekking, & Sergeant, 1991).

NEUROANATOMICAL FACTORS

Few gross anatomical differences in brain structure have been found on computerized tomography scan or magnetic resonance imaging to date between ADHD patients and normals (Barkley, 1990a). Cortical atrophy was found in 24 adults with ADHD, but methodological problems confounded the data (Nasrallah et al., 1986).

Recent studies of regional cerebral blood flow have been promising. Lou and coworkers (1984) studied 11 ADHD children's emission computed tomography scans after xenon 133 inhalation. All 11 had hypoperfusion of the frontal lobes, particularly white matter, and 7 of 11 had hypoperfusion of the caudate nuclei. High cerebral blood flow was found in the primary sensory regions of the occipital and temporal cortices. This study was also compounded by methodological problems, including small sample size.

Zametkin and associates (1990) investigated cerebral glucose metabolism in 25 male adults with histories of hyperactivity in childhood and residual symptoms, who were biological parents of children with ADHD, and 50 normal control patients. Positron emission tomography scanning was undertaken during the subjects' performance of a computerized auditory-attention task. Global cerebral glucose metabolism was about 8% lower in the adults with hyperactivity as compared to the normals. Glucose metabolism was significantly reduced in half of the specific regions of the brain examined, including the premotor and the superior prefrontal cortex. These areas are thought to be involved in the processing of attention and motor activity.

A small magnetic resonance imaging study of 7 ADHD children and 10 normal controls revealed significant morphological differences between groups. Although all the scans were read as normal, children with ADHD had smaller corpus callosi, particularly in the splenium, genu, and anterior to the splenium areas. These regions are thought to be important in connecting right and left occipital, parietal, frontal, and posterior temporal regions. The authors speculated that abnormalities in corticogenesis could account for these differences (Hynd et al., 1991).

NEUROTRANSMITTER/BIOCHEMICAL FACTORS

Investigations of central, peripheral blood, and urinary metabolites of neurotransmitters have contributed a variety of data. Dysfunctions of norepinephrine and dopamine have been implicated but, to date, no conclusive evidence has been found (Voeller, 1991; Zametkin, 1987). Studies of cerebrospinal fluid in ADHD children showed decreased dopamine when compared to normal controls (Raskin, Shaywitz, Shaywitz, Anderson, & Cohen, 1984). Studies of norepinephrine and serotonin have been conflicting, showing both elevated and lowered levels (Ionescu, Kiehl, Ona, & Wichmann-Kunz, 1990; Zametkin et al., 1985). A study of imipramine binding to platelets failed to differentiate between normals and controls (Weizman, Bernhout, Weitz, Tyano, & Rehavi, 1988).

Studies of platelet monoamine oxidase activity have also been conflicting. A recent study, controlling for undersocialized conduct disorder, demonstrated that lowered levels of plasma dopamine-beta hydroxylase and platelet monoamine oxidase were associated with the conduct disorder, not ADHD alone (Bowden, Deutsch, & Swanson, 1988). Other studies show an association with the impulsivity (Stoff et al., 1989). Elevated plasma levels of dopamine and epinephrine but not norepinephrine were found in an investigation of 12 ADHD children (Ionescu, et al., 1990). Lower levels of plasma amino acids in ADHD patients, including phenylalanine, tyrosine, tryptophan, histidine, and isoleucine, were found as compared to normal controls, suggesting impairment in amino acid transport and/or absorption (Bornstein et al., 1990).

In a study suggesting that disruptive behavior disorders potentially can be classified by biological characteristics, children with low dopamine-beta hydroxylase output in 24-hour urine showed stronger correlations with ADD than those with elevated dopamine-beta hydroxylase. Children

with socialized conduct disorders had elevated 24-hour urinary norepinephrine and 3-methoxy-4-hydroxymandelic acid (VMA) output (Rogeness et al., 1989).

In a small study of endocrinological function involving dopamine and norepinephrine pathways, Jensen and Garfinkel (1988) tested pituitary response to growth hormone challenge. Prepubertal ADHD children had a blunted growth hormone response to levodopa; postpubertal ADHD children also have a low or abnormal response to clonidine challenge. The authors' interpretation of these data was that there is an interaction of two monoamine systems at work in this disorder. A study of urinary free cortisol, as a measure of adrenal function, in 19 boys ages 7 to 16 with disruptive behavior disorders and 19 controls did not differentiate between the two groups (Kruesi, Schmidt, Donnelly, Hibbs, & Hamburger, 1989).

Peptides are speculated to have biological activity in the brains of some patients with psychiatric disorders. Hole and coworkers (1988) studied excretion of peptide containing complexes in the urine of 104 patients ages 1 to 23 with attention deficit disorders with and without hyperactivity and 36 controls. Several patterns emerged. Sixty-four patients showed increases of benzoic acid-glycoprotein-peptide complexes in middle and late peaks; all of these patients were diagnosed as having ADDH. Thirty-five patients showed no uric acid late-peak complexes; 32 of this group met criteria for ADD without hyperactivity. Although some overlaps occurred, the authors concluded that there was a correlation between clinical diagnoses of hyperactivity and patterns of urinary peptide-containing complexes.

Biochemical effects of stimulant medication have been investigated in ADHD. Zametkin and Hamburger (1988) treated 11 boys ages 6 to 12 with ADHD for 2 weeks with methylphenidate, 0.74 milligrams per kilogram per day. Changes were measured in urinary excretion during this time. Urinary 3-methoxy-4-hydroxyphenylethylene glycol (MHPG) excretion was not changed by methylphenidate, replicating earlier studies.

Methylphenidate challenge was used to assess central monoamines hypothesized to be involved in ADHD in a recent study. Plasma growth hormone and prolactin were dependent measures; growth hormone release is under the control of dopamine, norepinephrine, and serotonin systems, whereas prolactin release involves both dopamine and serotonin mechanisms. In this study, Shaywitz and team challenged 14 boys ages 7 to 12 with ADD with three different doses of methylphenidate and placebo. Prolactin response was increased after methylphenidate at all doses as compared placebo. No consistent change in growth hormone was found following lower or higher dose of methylphenidate (Shaywitz et al., 1990).

ANIMAL MODELS

Over the years, a number of animal models have been proposed to further the understanding of possible biochemical and neuroanatomical deficits in ADHD.

Damage to dopamine-containing pathways in neonatal rats leads to motoric hyperactivity and attention deficits corrected by stimulants (Shaywitz et al., 1990). Pregnant rats injected with methylazoxymethanol, an antimitotic agent, gave birth to offspring with cortical hypoplasia. These experimental rats showed increased motor activity and learning impairments (Mercugliano, Hyman, & Batshaw, 1990). In another model, offspring of rats exposed to methylmercury chloride showed performance impairments, suggesting dysfunction in the tactile-kinesthetic system (Elsner, 1991). Spontaneously hypertensive rats show increased motor activity in the field and in the cage; low to medium doses of methylphenidate produced stimulation in both experimental and control animals, but effects were more pronounced in the controls (Wultz, Sagvolden, Moser, & Moser, 1990).

Another investigator proposed a model of ADHD involving the locus coeruleus system. The author proposes that the locus coeruleus is driven by a defective alpha-2-mediated somatic or dendritic agonist system, in which epinephrine is the primary neurotransmitter. The threshold for orienting to novel stimuli is reduced due to dysfunction in this part of the brainstem (Mefford & Potter, 1989).

Finally, in a comprehensive review on the neurobiology of ADHD, Zametkin and Rapoport (1985) hypothesize inhibitory influences of frontal cortical activity, mostly norepinephrine, acting on lower striatal structures, driven by both direct dopamine agonists and controlled or modulated by higher structures sensitive to adrenergic agents.

Differential Diagnosis

For a variety of reasons, differential diagnosis is challenging in patients with symptoms and signs of ADHD. First, although rare, treatable medical causes of impulsivity and hyperactivity must be delineated so that proper treatment can take place. Medical conditions such as seizures, metabolic dysfunction, perceptual disturbances and lead intoxication are among those conditions that must be ruled out. Rarely, generalized resistance to thyroid hormone may increase risk for ADHD, but this is not common among clinical referrals (Elia, Gulotta, Rose, Marin, & Rapoport, 1994; Hauser et al., 1993 Spencer et al., 1996). Adverse side effects of medication, such as phenobarbital and theophylline, can include hyperactivity and restlessness.

From the psychiatric perspective, differential diagnosis must address primary clinical syndromes and possible comorbid conditions. ADHD and primary disorders of vigilance must be differentiated (Weinberg & Brumback, 1990). Major mood disorders (including major depression, bipolar disorder, and dysthymia) and anxiety disorders can be difficult to differentiate and frequently co-occur. Despite overlapping criteria, juvenile mania can be differentiated by the severity of aggressive dyscontrol and mood instability (Wozniak et al., 1995). Children with posttraumatic stress disorders may present with motoric hyperactivity, impulsivity and distractibility. Children with pervasive developmental disorders frequently show signs of ADHD as a component of multiplex developmental disorders (Cohen, Paul, & Volkmar, 1986).

Evaluation/Diagnostic Workup

Comprehensive evaluation of children with attention deficit hyperactivity disorders must include a thorough and detailed history, clinical psychiatric examination and mental status exam, history and observational data from school teachers, physical examination, neurological screening, and laboratory testing, including behavior rating sales.

The psychiatric history should include history of the pregnancy, prenatal exposure to illnesses, alcohol, cigarettes, or other toxins, obstetrical complications, and postnatal exposure to environmental toxins such as lead paint or severe malnutrition. Exposure to abuse, particularly physical violence or sexual contact, must be determined. Family history of ADHD, antisocial disorders, alcohol abuse, and affective and anxiety disorders must be obtained.

Ideally, clinical examination of the child should include unstructured interviews, semistructured techniques, and direct behavior observation in the classroom, if possible.

Direct reports from teachers are necessary in order to assess classroom academic performance, attentional capacity, and impulsivity. Data on classroom structure and setting should be obtained at this time.

Physical exam should occur as part of a thorough assessment, through the child's pediatrician or specifically arranged. Baseline height, weight, and vital signs should be included. Specific neurological assessment should include any history of neurological trauma, soft signs, or minor physical anomalies if present, and any abnormal movements, including tics and dystonias.

Specific laboratory tests, such as complete blood count with differential, chemistry screening, and electrocardiogram, may be useful for children who are candidates for medication.

Educational and cognitive evaluations may be indicated for those children who are underachieving in school. Neuropsychological tests may be helpful to assess specific problems but are not clinical diagnostic instruments (Barkley & Grodzinsky, 1994). Similarly, Continous Performance Tests (computer-based tests of selective attention and vigilance) are useful primarily as research tools but not in routine clinical practice (Abikoff & Klein, 1992; Barkley, 1990b).

Behavioral rating scales can be useful in the assessment of children with ADHD (Barkley, 1990b). A variety of behavioral scales that can be applied to clinical settings have been used in research on ADHD. These scales include the Achenbach Child Behavior Checklist (Parent, Youth and Teacher Forms); the Conners Parent and Teacher Rating Scales; the Eyberg Child Behavior Inventory; the Home Situations Questionnaire; the School Situations Questionnaire; the Child Attention Problems Scale; the Academic Performance Rating Scale; the ADHD Rating Scale; Attention Deficit Disorders Evaluation Scale; and several others.

Studies have indicated the utility of using multiple rating scales concurrently or multidimensional scales (Zelko, 1991). School performance may be assessed using the Yale Children's Inventory, which shows two different domains of relevance to the child's school functioning—Behavioral and Cognitive domains, both of which overlap with the Attention Scale (Shaywitz, Shaywitz, Schnell, Towle, & McPhil, 1988). Other rating scales useful in the classroom setting include the IOWA-Conners Rating Scale; the Swanson Nolan and Pelham (SNAP) Rating Scale; Social Skills Rating System for social competency and peer rating scale, including the Pupil Evaluation Inventory (Atkins & Pelham, 1991). Computer-based diagnostic systems such as the Language Performance Test and Gordon Diagnostic System also may have a role in evaluation in this population (Gordon, 1986; Irwin, Bilinski-Mettelman, 1989).

Given the complexity of symptomatology in ADHD and likelihood of comorbidity, rating scales can provide useful quantified data.

In general, multimethod assessment is recommended utilizing multiple informants, observation, and instruments. A multistage identification screening procedure was examined in a nonreferred epidemiologic sample of 1,490 elementary-school-age children in a recent study. Stage 1 comprised teacher screening using the Achenbach Child Behavior Checklist (CBCL) Teacher Rating; Stage 2 involved screening of positive cases on the teacher form with the parent version of the CBCL. Positive parent screened cases were then given the Diagnostic Interview for Children and Adolescents, Revised—Parent version (DICA R-P) structured psychiatric interview as part of Stage 3. Results indicated that about 11% were identified at Stage 1; of those 163 cases, 115 were entered into Stage 2. Seventy (60%) were screened positive on parent ratings, and 64

(90%) were identified positively by DICA R-P as having ADHD. The authors called attention to the moderate convergence of teachers' and parent ratings and recommended "multiple gating procedures for research and clinical settings" (August, Ostrander, & Bloomquist, 1992). Examining this issue from another perspective, Biederman, Keenan, and Faraone (1990) found in a clinical sample of 43 ADD children, using the DICA, that there was a 90% probability that the teacher report would yield a positive diagnosis if the parent report was positive.

Treatment: Overview

Treatment strategies are designed to address the behavior, cognitive, social, and family problems that are characteristic of ADHD. In general, multimodal treatment is recommended, including pharmacologic intervention, parent education and training, cognitive/behavioral approaches, educational intervention, and social skills training (Pelham & Murphy, 1986). Although pharmacological treatment has been studied extensively in this population, empirical support for parent training, cognitive/behavioral approaches, and social skills training has been relatively lacking (Anastopoulos & Barkley, 1990). Other techniques such as family therapy, relaxation treatment, and biofeedback have been described in the literature but have not yet been investigated systematically (Donney & Poppen, 1989; Lee, 1991; Zeigler & Holden, 1988).

Although only a limited number of studies have been conducted, parent training intervention has produced improvement in ADHD children's behavior. Barkley recommends a combination of parental education concerning the nature of ADHD and 8 to 12 time-limited parent counseling sessions. (Patients must be between the ages of 2 and 11 for this approach to work.) Barkley's outline for treatment sessions includes:

1. Program orientation and review of ADHD.
2. Understanding parent-child relations and principles of behavioral management.
3. Enhancement of parental attending skills.

4. Positive reinforcement of appropriate behavior and parental efficiency with commands.
5. Establishment of a home token system.
6. Review of home token system using response cost.
7. Use of time-out strategies.
8. Extending time-out to other behavior and settings.
9. Booster sessions with individual parents or in a group setting.

This cognitive/behavioral approach also can be incorporated into a family perspective and used with adolescents (Anastopoulos & Barkley, 1990).

Parent training strategies have been applied to preschool children and found to be effective, particularly with regard to ADHD symptomatology, internalizing symptomatology, parental confidence in their management ability, and the parent-child relationship in general (Erhardt & Baker, 1990; Strayhorn & Weidman, 1989).

Cognitive training encompasses a variety of approaches, such as self-instruction, modeling, self-monitoring, self-reinforcement, and problem solving. Goals are to improve self-regulation and problem-solving strategies. According to a review of studies of cognitive training, there is no evidence that cognitive training alone, without medication, improved academic performance (Anastopoulos & Barkley, 1990).

Some investigators believe that cognitive training is not effective, particularly as an intervention to improve academic performance (Abikoff, 1991). Long-term studies are needed.

Other investigators have concluded that cognitive-social learning treatment is no more effective than pharmacotherapy alone (Gittelman, 1983). In an attempt to address the question of whether combined treatment is more effective than pharmacotherapy alone, investigators assessed the effects of low-dose and high-dose stimulants and a combination of behavioral treatment. Results indicated that there was no evidence of the superiority of any combined conditions over stimulants alone; however, the parent training self-control (PT/SC) plus low-dose stimulant combination was as effective as the high-dose alone or the high-dose PT/SC condition as measured by teacher ratings of symptomatology (Horn et al., 1991).

Anastopoulos, DuPaul, and Barkley (1991) recommended a combination of stimulant and parent training intervention in order to effectively address symptoms acutely and also to maintain efficacy over time. Although other investigators have found that prior to treatment intervention, parents see stimulants as less socially acceptable than behavior modification, posttreatment evaluations suggest improvement in parents' attitudes toward stimulants (Liu, Robin, Brenner, & Eastman, 1991). Other investigators have suggested that combined management, stimulant, and multimodal intervention may yield more positive outcome (Hechtman, 1985; Pelham et al., 1993).

Educational and classroom consultation constitute another important treatment strategy, since many children with attention deficit disorders have problems with academic performance. Target symptoms include a variety of behaviors: disruptive behavior in class, inattention, specific academic deficits, lack of motivation, and productivity in homework and other outside-of-class assignments. Treatment interventions can target teachers, peers, parents, and patients. Classroom modifications designed to facilitate positive attention and eliminate distraction serve as a foundation for educational intervention. Special educational services, including consultation with special education teachers, utilization of resource rooms or learning centers, and substantially separate classrooms, are useful. Communication and collaboration between teachers and parents is essential, and behavioral strategies can provide a bridge between home and school (Pfiffner & Barkley, 1990).

Since the majority of children with ADHD have some degree of impairment in self-esteem and difficulty with peer relations, social skills training may be utilized as an adjunct to other primary treatment interventions. Goals of such programs include increased awareness of the impact of behavioral difficulties on others and alteration of social behaviors. Although there is little empirical support for the usefulness of this strategy, social skills training may be considered for ADHD children showing signs of the consequences of social rejection, such as aggression, social isolation, and oppositionality. Social skills training sessions can take place in structured groups over 18 to 20 sessions. Content includes orientation, social entry skills, conversational skills, conflict resolution and problem-solving skills, and anger-control training. In addition, traditional psychotherapy may be useful to address the impairments in self-esteem (Guevremont & Barkley, 1990).

Pharmacotherapy

STIMULANTS

Pharmacotherapy has been the most extensively studied intervention (Barkley, 1977; Barkley, 1990e; Greenhill, 1995). First reported in 1937 by Charles Bradley, stimulants have been in the cornerstone of treatment of ADHD since the late 1950s, when methylphenidate was first marketed. Recent studies indicate that 2 to 6% of elementary school students are receiving stimulants (Safer & Krager, 1988). Approximately 75% of treated patients with ADHD respond to stimulants. Specific behavioral symptoms that are stimulant-responsive include motoric overactivity, impulsivity, distractibility, aggressive behavior, oppositionality, and off-task behavior. Specific cognitive symptoms that are ameliorated by stimulants include enhanced performance on vigilance tasks, fine motor coordination, reaction time, impulsivity, short-term memory, learning efficiency and productivity. Improved peer and parent-child interactions also have been reported on stimulants. More recently, small but significant medication effects on academic performance have been observed (Barkley, 1990e; Rapport, DuPaul, Stoner, & Janest, 1986). Pharmacological effects are primarily short term; longer-term effectiveness, such as changes in IQ or achievement, has not been proven unequivocally.

Norepinephrine and dopamine neurotransmitter systems are postulated to play a role in the mechanism of therapeutic action of stimulants, but the exact nature is not known. Stimulants cause release of dopamine and norepinephrine at the synaptic cleft and interfere with reuptake. Methylphenidate (Ritalin) and dextroamphetamine (Dexedrine) facilitate release of dopamine from different storage sites, which may account for their slight differential responsivity. Methylphenidate is metabolized quickly, with peak blood levels at 1 to 2 hours, and has an elimination half-life of 2 to 4 hours; dextroamphetamine and pemoline (Cylert) peak after 2 to 3 hours and has an elimination half-life of 6 to 7 hours. Pharmacokinetic studies indicate a wide interindividual variability in blood levels (Stevenson & Wolraich, 1989). For the most part, a dose-response curve of improvement exists. Sustained-release preparations of methylphenidate and dextroamphetamine produce a flatter pharmacokinetic curve but appear to have similar efficacies. Some children will do better on one form or the other.

Stimulants have been studied in several special populations. Evidence for stimulants' efficacy in adolescence is accumulating; several recent studies have documented their usefulness in children 12 to 19 (Klorman, Brumaghim, Fitzpatrick, & Borgstedt, 1990). Some evidence suggests that efficacy can be maintained despite the presence of comorbid conditions such as conduct/oppositional disorders and mood disorders. Reduction of aggression in adolescents with conduct disorders and ADHD has been documented (Kaplan, Busner, Kupietz, Wasserman, & Segal, 1990). A trial of low-, medium-, and high-dose methylphenidate in African American adolescents revealed that the most beneficial response in terms of behavioral and academic measures occurred at the higher levels, but a significant linear increase in diastolic blood pressure occurred simultaneously (Brown & Sexson, 1988).

Other investigators have found that patients with ADHD and other comorbid conditions such as anxiety disorders respond less robustly to stimulants than do patients with "pure ADHD" (Plizska, 1989).

Developmentally disabled and autistic patients probably are frequently treated with stimulants, but there are very few systematic studies of their efficacy or of their side effect profiles in this population. Some investigators have found that mentally retarded children respond at similar rates and with similar improvement on target behaviors as do nonretarded children (Handen, Breaux, Gosling, Ploof, & Feldman, 1990; Payton, Burkhart, Hersen, & Helsel, 1989). Those retarded patients with higher IQs and developmental levels may respond at a higher rate than the more intellectually impaired (Aman, Marks, Turbott, Wilsher, & Werry, 1991).

A recent study of a small group of autistic children with ADHD showed improvement in target symptoms on doses of 10 to 50 milligrams per day of methylphenidate (Birmaher, Quintana, & Greenhill, 1988).

Stimulants are generally well tolerated by the majority of patients; serious or major long-term toxicity is infrequent. Most common side effects that occur in patients include decreased appetite, insomnia, headaches, and stomachaches (Klein et al., 1988; Wilens & Biederman, 1992). A study of 83 children with ADHD on 0.6 milligrams per kilogram or 1.0 milligrams per kilogram per day of methylphenidate demonstrated that only 3 children (3.6%) had to be withdrawn from medication due to adverse effects (Barkley, McMurray, Edelbrock, & Robbins, 1990).

The effects of stimulants on growth have been conflicting. Recent prospective studies have demonstrated reduced growth velocity with methylphenidate in terms of weight, but no reduction in final height, and growth rebound off of the drug. Other shorter-term studies have shown no clear-cut effects on growth (Gittelman-Klein & Mannuzza, 1988; Vincent, Varley, & Leger, 1990).

Some populations may potentially be at higher risk for adverse effects. A recent small double-blind placebo-controlled study of side effects of methylphenidate in 27 mentally retarded children demonstrated that 22% required medication withdrawal because of motor tics or social withdrawal (Handen, Feldman, Gosling, Breaux, & McAuliffe, 1991). Another study showed an increase in diastolic blood pressure in African American adolescents on stimulants (Brown & Sexson, 1989).

Hepatotoxicity has been reported in pemoline (Pratt & Dubois, 1990).

PHARMACOLOGICAL ALTERNATIVES

Reviews of pharmacologic treatment of ADHD reveal that approximately 25% of patients are not responsive to one of the three available stimulants (Barkley, 1990b). A variety of alternative pharmacologic treatments have been studied, including tricyclic antidepressants such as desipramine, nortriptyline, and imipramine; clonidine; bupropion; buspirone; bromocriptine; nomifensine; and fenfluramine (Balon, 1990; Biederman, 1988; Casat, Pleasants, Schroeder, & Parler, 1989; Cavanagh, Clifford, & Gregory, 1989; Donnelly et al., 1989; Gualtieri & Evans, 1988; Gaultieri, Keenan, & Chandler, 1991; Riddle, Hardin, Cho, Woolston, & Leckman, 1988; Shekim, Masterson, Cantwell, Hanna, & McCracken, 1989; Shekim,

Antun, Hanna, McCracken, & Hess, 1990; Spencer et al., 1996; Wender & Reimherr, 1990; Wilens et al., 1993).

Empirical support exists for the usefulness of the tricyclic antidepressants, particularly desipramine and nortriptyline (Spencer, Biederman, Kerman, Steingard, & Wilens, 1993; Wilens et al., 1993). Relative benefit vs. risk ratios must be weighed in decision making. These medications are indicated as a second-line choice for patients with uncomplicated ADHD who are not stimulant responders and for those patients who have clinically significant comorbidity with mood and anxiety disorders or tic disorders (Riddle et al., 1988; Spencer et al., 1993; Wilens et al., 1993). They confer the advantage of less frequent dosing but have a more complicated side profile. Cardiovascular effects include prolongation of cardiac conduction and repolarization (Biederman et al., 1989b; Biederman, Baldessarini et al., 1993). Five cases of unexplained sudden death in children treated with desipramine have been reported, but no causal relationship has been established (Popper & Zimnitzky, 1995). Recent evidence suggests that desipramine in a therapeutic range is associated with only slightly elevated risk of sudden death beyond natural occurrence (Biederman, Thisted, Greenhill, & Ryan, 1995).

Clonidine may be useful in highly aroused, hyperactive children (vs. primarily inattentive) children with ADHD and in children with a combination of ADHD and tics or Tourette's disorder (Hunt, Cappen, & O'Connell, 1990; Steingard, Biederman, Spencer, Wilens, & Gonzalez, 1993). It also may be efficacious in combination with stimulants for patients with ADHD who are partial stimulant responders or who have comorbid tics. As an alpha-adrenergic agonist used to treat hypertension, clonidine requires blood pressure and electrocardiogram monitoring. It has a gradual onset of therapeutic effects over several weeks to months. Side effects include sedation, hypotension, nausea, and dry mouth. A transdermal form is available for children who cannot comply with the oral preparation or who experience significant sedation (Hunt et al., 1990). Guanfacine, a longer-acting alpha-adrenergic agonist, may be used alternatively for patients who are candidates for clonidine; its side effect profile may be more favorable (Chappell et al., 1995).

Preliminary results of open trials suggest bu-propion's usefulness as an alternative in child and adult populations (Casat, Pheasants, Schroeder, & Parler, 1989; Simeon, Ferguson, Van Wyck, & Flett, 1986; Wender & Reimherr, 1990). Monoamine oxidase inhibitors also have been used to treat this population (Zametkin et al., 1985).

Long-Term Course

A number of prospective follow-up studies of hyperactive children have been conducted over the past 20 years. A rich body of data has accumulated regarding adolescent and adult outcome, clarifying the natural history of the ADHD and its long-term prognosis (Barkley, Fischer, Edelbrock, & Smallish, 1990; Biederman et al., 1996; Weiss & Hechtman, 1993).

Evidence for continued psychopathology and academic and cognitive problems in adolescence converges from all U.S. studies and from cross-cultural data. About half to two-thirds of children with ADHD will show signs in adolescence and at least half will continue to show signs in adulthood (Abikoff & Klein, 1992; Barkley et al., 1990; Biederman et al., 1996; Weiss & Hechtman, 1993).

Satterfield and team (1982) reported that, as adolescents, hyperactive children had a higher rate of arrest and incarceration than a control group (36 to 58% vs. 9% to 11% for arrest and 25% vs. 1% for incarceration). Lambert (1988) reported on a study of 166 children who had been diagnosed as hyperactive in childhood, 74 psychiatric controls, and 127 normal controls. Outcome data at 17 or 18 in adolescence was available from more than one source in 64% of the cases. Using two different sets of criteria for diagnosis, adolescents with a history of hyperactivity had a poorer educational prognosis in terms of school failure, special education, or dropouts. They also had greater rates of conduct problems and use of cigarettes.

An 8-year U.S. prospective study of 123 hyperactive and 66 normal controls revealed that at a mean age of 15 at follow-up, 72% met *DSM-III-R* criteria for ADHD, vs. 3% of controls; about 60% met *DSM-III-R* criteria for oppositional defiant disorder vs. 12% of controls; and 44% met criteria for conduct disorder vs. 2% of controls.

Antisocial behavior was significantly more frequent in hyperactive children at adolescence than in controls in the form of drug possession, use, or sale; theft/shoplifting, physical fighting, and assaults; and possession or the use of a weapon (Barkley et al., 1990).

Klein reported that over two-thirds of the New York sample of 101 hyperactive boys had confirmed evidence of ADDH until age 15, and nearly half had evidence of a conduct disorder in adolescence. In the Montreal study, about a quarter of the patients in adolescence had antisocial behavior (Klein & Mannuzza, 1991). The same group found increased risk of antisocial problems in adolescence independent of the presence of conduct disorder (Abikoff & Klein, 1992).

Studies in New Zealand and Great Britain have demonstrated similar results. McGee and associates followed 21 "pervasively hyperactive" preschool children and 2 control groups from a large nonclinical setting over 12 years. At follow-up, at age 15, 50% of the hyperactive children manifested signs of a *DSM-III* disorder as compared to 5 to 24% of the control and remaining groups. Thirty-five percent were reading disabled vs. 10 to 17% in the other groups. Only 25% were symptom-free at follow-up (McGee, Partridge, Williams, & Silva, 1991).

Adolescent males with ADHD particularly those with comorbid oppositional defiant disorder or conduct disorder, were more likely to have driving record problems; other investigators have reported increased risk for suicidal behavior (Weiss & Hechtman, 1993).

Biederman et al. (1996) recently reported that in a 4-year prospective follow-up assessment of 128 children and adolescents ages 6 to 17 with ADHD, 85% showed persistence of the disorder and 15% remitted. Predictors of persistence were comorbidity with mood, conduct, and anxiety disorders, familiality of the disorder, and psychosocial adversity.

In general, adults with a history of childhood ADHD have elevated risk for continued psychopathology and antisocial and substance abuse disorders (Biederman, Faraone et al., 1993; Mannuzza, Klein, & Addalli, 1991; Mannuzza, Klein, Bessler, Malloy, & LaPadula, 1993; Weiss & Hechtman, 1993). Prospective naturalistic studies have reported results on these children followed into young and middle adulthood. Evidence suggests that about half have continued impairments in the areas of attentional functioning, peer and marital relationships, self-esteem, and work records (Mannuzza et al., 1993).

Prospective follow-up has demonstrated that formerly hyperactive children were significantly more likely than control groups to manifest antisocial personality disorders in adulthood (Klein & Mannuzza, 1991; Weiss, Hechtman, Milroy, & Perlman, 1985). Klein and Mannuzza (1991) found that formerly hyperactive patients were more likely to have evidence of ADHD, antisocial problems, and substance abuse (nonalcohol). Those patients who had continued evidence of ADHD were more likely to develop antisocial personality disorders followed by substance abuse disorders. In addition, ADHD patients were more likely to have been arrested (39 vs. 20% of controls), convicted (28 vs. 11% controls), and put in jail (9 vs. 1% of controls). Significantly, ADHD alone without conduct or antisocial disorder was not associated with increased risk of criminal behavior.

The Montreal group found no differences in self-reported criminal behavior at mean ages of 19 and 25 years. At 15-year follow up, the 61 probands were divided into two groups: one with no or mild ongoing ADHD symptoms and one with moderate to severe symptoms. Those without continuing symptoms did not differ from controls, but those with symptoms of a moderate to severe nature manifested more antisocial problems, emotional difficulties, and alcohol use (Greenfield, Hechtman, & Weiss, 1988).

Although the Iowa group noted no difference in police contacts between 22 patients and their siblings in their early 20s, there was a significant difference reported in rates of incarceration (Loney, Whaley-Klahn, Kosier, & Conboy, 1983).

A study of 56 adults referred for evaluation of adult ADHD revealed that 51 (91%) met *DSM-III* criteria and Utah criteria for ADHD, residual state. Unfortunately, no specific data were available regarding percentage of those with diagnosed childhood ADHD. Interestingly, the majority of these adults had comorbid psychiatric disorders, including 64% with histories of current affective disorders, 30% with alcohol abuse, 34% with drug abuse, and 53% with generalized anxiety disorder (Shekim, Asarnow, Hess, Zaucha, & Wheeler, 1990). Other studies have demonstrated high comorbidity with mood disorders, anxiety disorders, substance abuse, and antisocial personality disorder (Biederman, Boldessarini, et al., 1993).

Conclusion

ADHD is a relatively common childhood-onset psychiatric disorder that frequently continues into adolescence and adulthood. Children with ADHD are at risk for mood and anxiety disorders, and some are at later risk for antisocial personality disorder, substance abuse disorders, and criminality in adulthood. As children and adolescents, these patients are at risk for learning problems in the form of specific developmental disorders in reading and mathematics and academic failure. Peer and family relationships are difficult and disturbed, and these children are at risk for chronically low self-esteem and demoralization through the life cycle. Data are accumulating to suggest central nervous system dysfunction, possibly of frontal lobes, involving a cascade of interacting neurotransmitter and possibly neuropeptide systems that results in a complex picture of behavioral disinhibition at many levels.

Evaluation requires a comprehensive view of the child through multiple sources of information, including school and parents. Treatment should be comprehensive, with pharmacotherapy as the cornerstone and including parent training and counseling, cognitive/behavioral intervention, social skills groups, and family work.

REFERENCES

Abikoff, H. (1991). Cognitive training in ADHD children: Less to it than meets the eye. *Journal of Learning Disabilities, 24* (4), 205–209.

Abikoff, H., & Klein, R. G. (1992). Attention deficit hyperactivity and conduct disorder: comorbidity and implications for treatment. *Journal of Consulting and Clinical Psychology, 60,* 881–892.

Adesman, A. R., Altshuler, L. A., Lipkin, P. H., & Walco, G. A. (1990). Otitis media in children with learning disabilities and in children with attention deficit disorder with hyperactivity. *Pediatrics, 85,* 442–446.

Alessi, N. E., & Magen, J. (1988). Comorbidity of other psychiatric disturbances in depressed, psychiatrically hospitalized children. *American Journal of Psychiatry, 145,* 1582–1584.

Aman, M. G., Marks, R. E., Turbott, S. H., Wilsher, C. P., & Werry, J. N. (1991). Clinical effects of methylphenidate and thioridazine in intellectually subaverage children. *Journal of American Academy of Child and Adolescent Psychiatry, 30* (2), 246–256.

American Psychiatric Association. (1980). *Diagnostic and statistical manual of mental disorders* (3rd ed.). Washington, DC: Author.

American Psychiatric Association. (1987). *Diagnostic and statistical manual of mental disorders* (3rd ed., rev.). Washington, DC: Author.

American Psychiatric Association. (1994). *Diagnostic and statistical manual of mental disorders* (4th ed.). Washington, DC: Author.

Anastopoulos, A., & Barkley, R. A. (1990). Counseling and training parents. In R. A. Barkley (Ed.), *Attention deficit hyperactivity disorder—A handbook for diagnosis and treatment* (pp. 397–431). New York: Guilford Press.

Anastopoulos, A. D., DuPaul, G. J., & Barkley, R. A. (1991). Stimulant medication and parent training therapies for attention deficit-hyperactivity disorder. *Journal of Learning Disabilities, 24* (4), 210–218.

Anderson, J. C., Williams, S., McGee, R., & Silva, P., (1987). DSM-III disorders in preadolescent children: Prevalence in a large sample from the general population. *Archives of General Psychiatry, 44,* 69–76.

Atkins, M. S., & Pelham, W. E. (1991). School-based assessment of attention deficit-hyperactivity disorder. *Journal of Learning Disabilities, 24* (4), 197–204.

August, G. J., & Garfinkel, B. D. (1990). Comorbidity of ADHD and reading disability among clinic-referred children. *Journal of Abnormal Child Psychology, 18* (1), 29–45.

August, G. J., Ostrander, R., & Bloomquist, M. J. (1992). Attention deficit hyperactivity disorder: An epidemiological screening method. *American Journal of Orthopsychiatry, 62* (3), 386–408.

August, G. J., & Stewart, M. (1982). Is there a syndrome of pure hyperactivity? *British Journal of Psychiatry, 170,* 305–311.

August, G. J., & Stewart, M. A. (1983). Familial subtypes of childhood hyperactivity. *Journal of Nervous and Mental Disease, 171,* 362–368.

August, G. J., Stewart, M. A., & Holmes, C. S. (1983). A four-year follow-up of hyperactive boys with and without conduct disorder. *British Journal of Psychiatry, 132,* 192–198.

Barkley, R. A. (1977) A review of stimulant drug research with hyperactive children. *Journal of Child Psychology and Psychiatry, 18,* 137–165.

Barkley, R. A. (1990a). A critique of current diagnostic criteria for attention deficit hyperactivity disorder: Clinical and research implications. *Journal of Developmental and Behavioral Pediatrics, 11,* 343–352.

Barkley, R. A. (1990b). A review of stimulant research with hyperactive children. *Journal of Child Psychology, 5,* 331–369.

Barkley, R. A. (1990c). Associated problems, subtyping, and etiologies. In R. A. Barkley (Ed.), *Attention deficit hyperactivity disorder—A handbook for diagnosis and treatment* (pp. 74–105). New York: Guilford Press.

Barkley, R. A. (1990d). Behavior rating scales. In R. A. Barkley (Ed.), *Attention deficit hyperactivity disorder—A handbook for diagnosis and treatment* (pp. 278–326). New York: Guilford Press.

Barkley, R. A. (1990e). The family of ADHD children in attention deficit hyperactivity disorder. In R. A. Guilford (Ed.), *Attention deficit hyperactivity disorder—A handbook for diagnosis and treatment* (pp. 130–168). New York: Guilford Press.

Barkley, R. A., Fischer, M., Edelbrock, C. S., & Smallish, L., (1990). The adolescent outcome of hyperactive children diagnosed by research criteria: I. An 8-year prospective follow-up study. *Journal of American Academy of Child and Adolescent Psychiatry, 29* (4), 546–557.

Barkley, R. A., & Grodzinsky, G. M. (1994) Are tests of frontal lobe functions in the diagnosis of attention deficit disorders? *Clinical Neuropsychologist, 8,* 12111–12139.

Barkley, R. A., McMurray, M. B., Edelbrock, C. S., & Robbins, K. (1990). Side effects of methylphenidate in children with attention deficit hyperactivity disorder: A systematic, placebo-controlled evaluation. *Pediatrics, 86* (2), 184–192.

Barkley, R. A., McMurray, M. B., Edelbrock, C. S., et al. (1989). The response of aggressive and nonaggressive ADHD children to two doses of methylphenidate. *Journal of American Academy of Child and Adolescent Psychiatry, 28,* 873–881.

Baton, R. (1990). Buspirone for attention deficit hyperactivity disorder? *Journal of Clinical Psychopharmacology, 10* (1), 77.

Bhatia, M. S., Nigam, V. R., Bohra, N., & Malik, S. C. (1991). Attention deficit disorder with hyperactivity among pediatric outpatients. *Journal of Child Psychology and Psychiatry, 32* (2), 297–306.

Biederman, J. (1988). Pharmacological treatment of adolescents with affective disorder and attention deficit disorder. *Psychopharmacology Bulletin, 24* (1), 81–87.

Biederman, J., Baldessarini, R. J., Goldblatt, A., Lapey, K. A., Doyle, A., & Hesslein, P. S. (1993). A naturalistic study of 24 hour electrocardiographic recordings and echocardiographic findings in children and adolescents treated with desipramine. *Journal of the American Academy of Child and Adolescent Psychiatry, 32,* 805–813.

Biederman, J., Baldessarini, R. J., Wright, V., Knee, D., & Harmatz, J. S. (1989). A double-blind placebo controlled study of desipramine in the treatment of ADD: I. Efficacy. *Journal of the American Academy of Child and Adolescent Psychiatry, 28* (5), 777–784.

Biederman, J., Baldessarini, R. J., Wright, V., Knee, D., Harmatz, J. S., & Goldblatt, A. (1989). A double-blind placebo controlled study of desipramine in the treatment of ADD: II. Serum drug levels and cardiovascular findings. *Journal of the American Academy of Child and Adolescent Psychiatry, 28* (6), 903–911.

Biederman, J., Faraone, S. V., Keenan, K., Knee, D., & Tsuang, M. T. (1990). Family-genetic and psychosocial risk factors in DSM-III attention deficit disorder. *Journal of the American Academy of Child and Adolescent Psychiatry, 29* (4), 526–533.

Biederman, J., Faraone, S. V., Keenan, K., Steingard, R., & Tsuang, M. T. (1991). Familial association between attention deficit disorder and anxiety disorders. *American Journal of Psychiatry, 148,* 251–256.

Biederman, J., Faraone, S. V., Keenan, K., & Tsuang, M. T. (1991). Evidence of familial association between attention deficit disorder and major affective disorders. *Archives of General Psychiatry, 48,* 633–642.

Biederman, J., Faraone, S., Milberger, S., Curtis, S., Chen, L., Marrs, A., Ouellette, C., Moore, P., & Spencer, T. (1996). Predictors of persistence and remission of ADHD into adolescence: Results from a four-year prospective followup study. *Journal of the American Academy of Child and Adolescent Psychiatry, 35,* 343–351.

Biederman, J., Faraone, S., Spencer, T., Wilens, T., Norman, D., Lapey, K. A., Mick, E., Lehman, B. K., & Doyle, A. (1993). Patterns of psychiatric comorbidity, cognition, and psychosocial functioning in adults with attention deficit hyperactivity disorder. *American Journal of Psychiatry, 150,* 1792–1798.

Biederman, J., Keenan, J., & Faraone, S. V. (1990). Parent-based diagnosis of attention deficit disorder predicts a diagnosis based on teacher report. *Journal of American Academy of Child and Adolescent Psychiatry, 29* (5), 698–701.

Biederman, J., Munir, K., & Knee, D., (1987). Conduct and oppositional disorder in clinically referred children with attention deficit disorder and: A controlled family study. *Journal of American Academy of Child and Adolescent Psychiatry, 26,* 724–727.

Biederman, J., Munir, K., Knee, D., Armentano, M. A., Autor, S., Waternaux, C., & Tsuang, M., (1987). High rate of affective disorders in probands with attention deficit disorder and in their relatives: A controlled family study. *American Journal of Psychiatry, 144,* 330–333.

Biederman, J., Newcorn, J., & Sprich, S. (1991). Comorbidity of attention deficit hyperactivity disorder with conduct, depressive, anxiety, and other disorders. *American Journal of Psychiatry, 148,* 564–577.

Biederman, J., Thisted, R. A., Greenhill, L. L., & Ryan, N. (1995). Estimation of the association between desipramine and the risk for sudden death in 5 to 14 year old children. *Journal of Clinical Psychiatry, 56,* 87–93.

Bird, H. R., Canino, G., Rubio-Stipec, M., Gould, M. S., Ribera, J., Sesman, M., Woodbury, M., Huertas-Goldman, S., Pagan, A., Sanchez Lacay, A., & Moscosoz N. (1988). Estimates of the prevalence of childhood maladjustment in a community survey in Puerto Rico. *Archives of General Psychiatry, 45,* 1120–1126.

Birmaher, B., Quintana, H., & Greenhill, L. L. (1988). Methylphenidate treatment of hyperactive autistic children. *Journal of the American Academy of Child and Adolescent Psychiatry, 27* (2), 248–251.

Bohline, D. S. (1985). Intellectual and affective characteristics of attention deficit disordered children. *Journal of Learning Disorders, 18,* 604–608.

Bornstein, R. A., Baker, G. B., Carroll, A., King, G., Wong, J. T. F., & Douglass, A. B. (1990). Plasma amino acids in attention deficit disorder. *Psychiatry Research, 33,* 301–306.

Bowden, C. L., Deutsch, C. K., & Swanson, J. M. (1988). Plasma dopamine-B-hydroxylase and platelet monoamine oxidase in attention deficit disorder and conduct disorder. *Journal of American Academy of Child and Adolescent Psychiatry, 27* (2), 171–174.

Bradley, C. (1937). The behavior of children receiving Benzedrine. *American Journal of Psychiatry, 27,* 248–251.

Brent, D. A., Perper, J. A., Goldstein, C. E., Kolko, D. J., Allan, M. J., Allman, C. J., & Zelenak, J. P. (1988). Risk factors for adolescent suicide: A comparison of adolescent suicide victims with suicidal inpatients. *Archives of General Psychiatry, 45,* 581–588.

Brown, R. T., Borden, K. A., Clingerman, S. R., & Jenkins, P., (1988). Depression in attention deficit-disordered and normal children and their parents. *Child Psychiatry and Human Development, 18,* 119–132.

Brown, R. T., & Sexson, S. B. (1988). A controlled trial of methylphenidate in black adolescents. *Clinical Pediatrics, 27* (2), 74–81.

Brown, R. T., & Sexson, S. B. (1989). Effects of methylphenidate on cardiovascular responses in attention deficit hyperactivity disordered adolescents. *Journal of Adolescent Health Care, 10,* 179–183.

Cadoret, R. J., & Stewart, M. A. (1991). An adoption study of attention deficit/hyperactivity/aggression and their relationship to adult antisocial personality. *Comprehensive Psychiatry, 32* (1), 73–82.

Campbell, S. B., & Werry, J. S. (1986). Attention deficit disorder (hyperactivity). In H. C. Quay & J. S. Werry (Eds.), *Psychopathologic disorders of childhood.* New York: John Wiley & Sons.

Cantwell, D. P., & Baker, L. (1991). Association between attention deficit-hyperactivity disorder and learning disorders. *Journal of Learning Disabilities, 24* (2), 88–95.

Casat, C. D., Pheasants, D. Z., Schroeder, D. H., & Parler, D. W. (1989). Bupropion in children with attention deficit disorder. *Psychopharmacology Bulletin, 25* (2), 198–201.

Cavanagh, R., Clifford, J. S., & Gregory, W. L. (1989). The use of bromocriptine for the treatment of attention deficit disorder in two chemically dependent patients. *Journal of Psychoactive Drugs, 21* (2), 217–220.

Chappell, P. B., Riddle, M. A., Scahill, L., Lynch, K. A., Schultz, R., Arnsten, A., Leckman, J. F., & Cohen, D. J. (1995). Guanfacine treatment of comorbid attention-deficit disorder and Tourette's syndrome: Preliminary clinical experience. *Journal of the American Academy of Child and Adolescent Psychiatry, 34,* 1140–1146.

Cohen, D. J., Bruun, R. D., & Leckman, J. F. (1988). *Tourette's syndrome and tic disorders: Clinical understanding and treatment.* New York: John Wiley & Sons.

Cohen, D., Paul, R., & Volkmar, F. (1986). Issues in the classification of pervasive and other developmental disorders: Toward DSM-IV. *Journal of American Academy of Child and Adolescent Psychiatry, 25,* 213–220.

Comings, D. E., & Comings, B. G. (1984). Tourette syndrome and attention deficit disorder with hyperactivity: Are they genetically related? *Journal of American Academy of Child Psychiatry, 23,* 138–146.

Comings, D. E., & Comings, B. G. (1987). A controlled study of Tourette syndrome. I: Attention deficit disorder, learning disorders, and school problems. *American Journal of Human Genetics, 41,* 701–741.

Comings, D. E., & Comings, B. G. (1988). Tourette's syndrome and attention deficit disorder. In D. Cohen, R. Bruun, & J. Leckman (Eds.), *Tourette's syndrome and tic clinical disorders: Clinical understanding and treatment* (pp. 119–136). New York: John Wiley & Sons.

Comings, D. E., & Comings, B. G. (1990). A controlled family history study of Tourette's syndrome. I: Attention-deficit hyperactivity disorder and learning disorders. *Journal of Clinical Psychiatry, 51* (7), 275–280.

Cruikshank, B. M., Eliason, M., & Merrifield, B. (1988). Long-term sequelae of cold water near-drowning. *Journal of Pediatric Psychology, 13,* 379–388.

Denckla, M. B., & Rudel, R. G. (1976). Naming of object drawings by dyslexic and other learning disabled children. *Brain and Language, 3,* 1–16.

Denckla, M. B., & Rudel, R. G. (1978). Anomalies of motor development in hyperactive boys. *Annals of Neurology, 3,* 231–233.

Donnelly, M., Rapoport, J. L., Potter, W. Z., Oliver, J., Keysor, C. S., & Murphy, D. L. (1989). Fenfluramine and dextroamphetamine treatment of childhood hyperactivity. *Archives of General Psychiatry, 46,* 205–212.

Donney, V. K., & Poppen, R. (1989). Teaching parents to conduct behavior relaxation training with their hyperactive children. *Journal of Behavior Therapy and Experimental Psychiatry, 20* (4), 319–325.

Dvoredsky, A., & Stewart, M. (1981). Hyperactivity followed manic depressive disorder: Two case reports. *Journal of Clinical Psychiatry, 42,* 212–214.

Dykman, R. A., & Ackerman, P. T. (1991). Attention deficit disorder and specific reading disability: Separate but often overlapping disorders. *Journal of Learning Disabilities, 24* (2), 96–103.

Elia, J., Gulotta, C., Rose, S. R., Marin, G., & Rapoport, J. (1994). Thyroid function and attention-deficit hyperactivity disorder. *Journal of the American Academy of Child and Adolescent Psychiatry, 33,* 169–172.

Elsner, J. (1991). Tactile-kinesthetic system of rats as an animal model for minimal brain dysfunction. *Archives of Toxicology, 65,* 465–473.

Epstein, M. A., Shaywitz, S. E., Shaywitz, B. A., & Woolston, J. L. (1991). The boundaries of attention deficit disorder. *Journal of Learning Disabilities, 24,* 78–86.

Erhardt, D., & Baker, B. L. (1990). The effects of behavioral parent training on families with young hyperactive children. *Journal of Behavior Therapy and Experimental Psychiatry, 21* (2), 121–132.

Faraone, S. V., Biederman, J., Keenan, K., & Tsuang, M. T. (1991). Separation of DSM-III attention deficit disorder and conduct disorder: Evidence from a family-genetic study of American child psychiatric patients. *Psychological Medicine, 21,* 109–121.

Farrington, D. P., Loeber, R., & Van Kammen, W. B. (1989). Long-term criminal outcomes of hyperactivity-impulsivity-attention deficit and conduct problems in childhood. In L. N. Robins & M. R. Rutter (Eds.), *Straight and devious pathways to adulthood.* New York: Cambridge University Press.

Felton, R. H., & Wood, F. B. (1989). Cognitive deficits in reading disability and attention deficit disorder. *Journal of Learning Disabilities, 22* (1), 3–13.

Felton, R. H., Wood, F. B., Brown, I. B., Campbell, S. K., & Harter, M. R. (1987). Separate verbal memory and naming deficits in attention deficit disorder and reading disability. *Brain and Language, 31,* 171–184.

Fergusson, D. M., Fergusson, I. E., Howrood, L. J., & Kinzett, N. G. (1988). A longitudinal study of dentine lead levels, intelligence, school performance, and behavior. *Journal of Child Psychology and Psychiatry, 29,* 811–824.

Fletcher, J. M., Morris, R. D., & Francis, D. J. (1991). Methodological issues in the classification of attention-related disorders. *Journal of Learning Disabilities, 24,* 72–77.

Galler, J., Ramsly, F., Soliman, G., & Lowell, W., (1983). The influence of early malnutrition on subsequent behavioral development. II. Classroom Behavior. *Journal of American Academy of Child Psychiatry, 22* (1), 16–22.

Gittelman, R. (1983). Hyperkinetic syndrome: Treatment issues and principles. In M. Rutter (Ed.), *Developmental neuropsychiatry* (pp. 437–452). New York: Guilford Press.

Gittelman, R., & Eskinazi, B. (1983). Lead and hyperactivity revisited. *Archives of General Psychiatry, 40,* 827–833.

Gittelman, R., Mannuzza, S., Shenker, R., & Bonagura, M. (1985). Hyperactive boys almost grown up. *Archives of General Psychiatry, 42,* 937–947.

Gittelman-Klein, R., Landa, B., Mattes, J. A., & Klein, D. F. (1988). Methylphenidate and growth in hyperactive children controlled withdrawal study. *Archives of General Psychiatry, 45,* 1127–1130.

Gittelman-Klein, R., Mannuzza, S., (1988). Hyperactive boys almost grown up—III. Methylphenidate effects on ultimate height. *Archives of General Psychiatry, 45,* 1131–1134.

Goodman, R., & Stevenson, J. (1989). A twin study of hyperactivity II. The aetiological role of genes, family relationships and perinatal adversity. *Journal of Child Psychology and Psychiatry, 30* (5), 691–709.

Gordon, M. (1986). *Instruction manual for the Gordon Diagnostic System.* DeWitt, NY: Gordon Diagnostic System.

Green, J. M., Dennis, J., & Bennets, L. A. (1989). Attention disorder in a group of young Down's syndrome children. *Journal of Mental Deficiency Research, 33,* 105–122.

Greenfield, B., Hechtman, L., & Weiss, G. (1988). Two subgroups of hyperactives as adults: Correlations of outcome. *Canadian Journal of Psychiatry, 33* (6), 505–508.

Greenhill, L. L. (1995). Attention-deficit hyperactivity disorder: The stimulants. *Child and Adolescent Psychiatric Clinics of North America, 4,* 123–168.

Gualtieri, C. T., & Evans, R. W. (1988). Motor performance in hyperactive children treated with imipramine. *Perceptual and Motor Skills, 66,* 763–769.

Gualtieri, C. T., Keenan, P. A., & Chandler, M. (1991). Clinical and neuropsychological effects of desipramine in children with attention deficit hyperactivity disorder. *Journal of Clinical Psychopharmacology, 11* (3), 155–159.

Guevremont, D., & Barkley R. A. (1990). Social skills and peer relationship training. In R. A. Barkley (Ed.), *Attention deficit hyperactivity disorder: A handbook for diagnosis and treatment* (pp. 540–572). New York: Guilford Press.

Handen, B. L., Breaux, A. M., Gosling, A., Ploof, D. L., & Feldman, H. (1990). Efficacy of methylphenidate among mentally retarded children with attention deficit hyperactivity disorder. *Pediatrics, 86* (6), 922–930.

Handen, B. L., Feldman, H., Gosling, A., Breaux, A. M., & McAuliffe, S. (1991). Adverse side effects of methylphenidate among mentally retarded children with ADHD. *Journal of American Child and Adolescent Psychology, 30* (2), 241–245.

Hartsough, C. S., & Lambert, N. M. (1985). Medical factors in hyperactive and normal children: Prenatal, developmental, and health history findings. *American Journal of Orthopsychiatry, 55,* 190–210.

Hauser, P., Zametkin, A. J., Martinez, P., Vitiello, B., Matochik, J. A., Mixson, A. J., & Weintraub, B. D. (1993). Attention deficit hyperactivity disorder in people with generalized resistance to thyroid hormone. *New England Journal of Medicine, 328,* 997–1001.

Hechtman, L. (1985). Adolescent outcome of hyperactive children treated with stimulants in childhood: A review. *Psychopharmacology Bulletin, 21,* 178.

Hechtman, L., & Weiss, G. (1986). Controlled prospective fifteen year follow-up of hyperactive adults: Nonmedical drug and alcohol use and antisocial behavior. *Canadian Journal of Psychiatry, 31,* 557–567.

Holdsworth, L., & Whitmore, K. (1974). A study of children with epilepsy attending ordinary schools: I. Their seizure patterns, progress, and behavior in school. *Developmental Medicine and Child Neurology, 16,* 746–758.

Hole, K., Linggaerde, O., Morkrid, L., Boler, J. B., Saelid, G., Diderichsen, J., Ruud, E., Reichelt, K. L. (1988). Attention deficit disorders: A study of peptide-containing urinary complexes. *Developmental and Behavioral Pediatrics, 9* (4), 205–212.

Horn, W. F., Ialongo, N. S., Pascoe, J. M., Greenberg, G., Packard, T., Lopez, M., Wagner, A., & Puttler, L. (1991). Additive effects of psychostimulants, parent training, and self-control therapy with ADHD children. *Journal of American Academy of Child and Adolescent Psychiatry, 30* (2), 233–240.

Hunt, R. D., Capper, L., & O'Connell, P. (1990). Clonidine in child and adolescent psychiatry. *Journal of Child and Adolescent Psychopharmacology 1,* 87–101.

Hynd, G. W., Semrud-Clikeman, M., Lorys, A. R., Novey, E. S., Eliopulos, D., & Lyytinen, H. (1991). Corpus callosum morphology in attention deficit-hyperactivity disorder: Morphometric analysis of MRI. *Journal of Learning Disabilities, 24,* 3.

Ionescu, G., Kiehl, R., Ona, L., & Wichmann-Kunz, F., (1990). Abnormal plasma catecholamines in hyperkinetic children. *Society of Biological Psychiatry, 28,* 547–550.

Irwin, M., & Bilinski-Mettelman, B. (1989). Pitfalls of the continuous performance test. *Developmental and Behavioral Pediatrics, 10* (5), 284–285.

Jensen, J. B., Burke, N., & Garfinkel, B. D. (1988). Depression and symptoms of attention deficit disorder with hyperactivity. *Journal of American Academy of Child and Adolescent Psychiatry, 27,* 742–747.

Jensen, J. B., & Garfinkel, B. D. (1988). Neuroendocrine aspects of attention deficit hyperactivity disorder. *Endocrinology of Neuropsychiatric Disorders, 17,* 111–129.

Kahn, E., & Cohen, L. (1934). Organic drivenness: A brain stem syndrome and experience with case reports. *New England Journal of Medicine, 210,* 748–756.

Kaplan, S. L., Busner, J., Kupietz, S., Wassermann, E., & Segal, B. (1990). Effects of methylphenidate on adolescents with aggressive conduct disorder and ADDH: A preliminary report. *Journal of American Academy of Child and Adolescent Psychiatry, 29* (5), 719–723.

Keller, M. B., Beardslee, W., Lavori, P. W., Wunder, J., & Samuelson, H. (1988). Course of major depression in non-referred adolescents: A retrospective study. *Journal of Affective Disorders, 15,* 235–243.

Klein, R. G., & Mannuzza, S. (1991). Long-term outcome of hyperactive children: A review. *Journal of American Academy of Child and Adolescent Psychiatry, 30* (3), 383–387.

Klorman, R. (1991). Cognitive event-related potentials in attention deficit disorder. *Journal of Learning Disabilities, 24* (3), 130–140.

Klorman, R., Brumaghim, J. T., Fitzpatrick, P. A., & Borgstedt, A. D. (1990). Clinical effects of a controlled trial of methylphenidate on adolescents with attention deficit disorder. *American Academy of Child and Adolescent Psychiatry, 29,* (5), 702–709.

Klorman, R., Brumaghim, J. T., Salzman, L. F., Strauss, J., Borgstedt, A., McBride, M., & Loeb, S. (1988). Effects of methylphenidate on attention deficit hyperactivity disorder with and without aggressive/noncompliant features. *Journal of Abnormal Psychology, 97,* 413–422.

Kovacs, M., Feinberg, T. L., Crouse-Novack, M. A., Paulaskas, S., & Finkelstein, R. (1984). Depressive disorders in childhood. I: A longitudinal prospective study of characteristics and recovery. *Archives of General Psychiatry, 41,* 229–237.

Kovacs, M., Paulauskas, S., Gatsonis, C., & Richards, C. (1988). Depressive disorders in childhood. III: A longitudinal study of comorbidity with and risk for conduct disorders. *Journal of Affective Disorders, 15,* 205–217.

Kruesi, M. J. P., Schmidt, M. E., Donnelly, M., Hibbs, E. D., & Hamburger, S. D. (1989). Urinary free cortisol output and disruptive behavior in children. *Journal of American Academy of Child and Adolescent Psychiatry, 28* (3), 441–443.

Lahey, B. B., Green, K. D., & Forehand, R. (1980). On the independence of rating hyperactivity, conduct problems, and attention deficits in children: A multiple regression analysis. *Journal of Consulting and Clinical Psychology, 48,* 566–574.

Lahey, B. B., & Carlson, C. L. (1991). Validity of the diagnostic category of attention deficit disorder without hyperactivity: A review of the literature. *Journal of Learning Disabilities, 24* (2), 110–120.

Lahey, B. B., Pelham, W. E., Schaughency, E. A., Atkins, M. S., Murphy, H. L., Hynd, G. W., Russo, M., Hartdagen, S., & Lorys-Vernon, A., (1988). Dimensions and types of attention deficit disorder. *Journal of American Academy of Child and Adolescent Psychiatry, 27,* 330–335.

Lahey, B. B., Piacentini, J. C., McBurnett, K., Stone, P., Hartdagen, S., & Hynd, G. (1988). Psychopathology in the parents of children with conduct disorder and hyperactivity. *Journal of American Academy of Child and Adolescent Psychiatry, 27,* (2), 163–170.

Lahey, B. B., Schaughency, E. A., Hynd, G. W., Carlson, C. L., & Nieves, N. (1987). Attention deficit disorder with and without hyperactivity: Comparison of behavioral characteristics of clinic-referred children. *Journal of American Academy of Child and Adolescent Psychiatry, 26,* 718–723.

Lambert, N. M. (1988). Adolescent outcomes for hyperactive children. *American Psychologist, 43* (10), 786–799.

Last, C. G., Strauss, C. C., & Francis, G. (1987). Comorbidity among childhood anxiety disorders. *Journal of Nervous and Mental Disease, 175,* 726–730.

Lee, S. W. (1991). Biofeedback as a treatment for childhood hyperactivity: A critical review of the literature. *Psychological Reports, 68,* 163–192.

Liu, C., Robin, A. L., Brenner, S., & Eastman, J. (1991). Social acceptability of methylphenidate and behavior modification for treating attention deficit hyperactivity disorder. *Pediatrics, 88* (3), 560–565.

Loeber, R., Brinthaupt, V. P., & Green, S. M. (1988). Attention deficits, impulsivity, and hyperactivity with or without conduct problems: Relationships to delinquency and unique contextual factors in behavior disorders of adolescence. In R. J. McMahon & R. D. Peters (Eds.), *Research intervention and policy in clinical and school settings.* New York: Plenum Press.

Loge, D. V., Staton, R. D., & Beatty, W. W. (1990). Performance of children with ADHD on tests sensitive to frontal lobe dysfunction. *Journal of American Academy of Child and Adolescent Psychiatry, 29* (4), 540–545.

Loney, J. (1987). Hyperactivity and aggression in the diagnosis of attention deficit disorder. In B. B. Lahey & A. E. Kazdin (Eds.), *Advances in clinical child psychology.* New York: Plenum Press.

Loney, J., Kramer, J., & Milich, R. S. (1981). The hyperactive child grows up: Predictors of symptoms, delinquency and achievement at follow-up. In K. D. Gadow & J. Loney (Eds.), *Psychosocial aspects of drug treatment for hyperactivity.* Boulder, CO: Westview Press.

Loney, J., Whaley-Klahn, M. A., Kosier, T., & Conboy, J. (1983). Hyperactive boys and their brothers at 21: Predicators of aggressive and antisocial outcomes. In K. T. VanDusen & S. A. Mednich (Eds.), *Prospective studies of crime and delinquency* (pp. 111–206). Boston: Klerner, Nijhoff Publishers.

Lou, H., Henriksen, L., & Bruhn, P. (1984). Focal cerebral hypoperfusion in children with dysphasia and/or attention deficit disorder. *Archives of Neurology, 41,* 825–829.

Love, A. J., & Thompson, M. G. G. (1988). Language disorders and attention deficit disorders in young children referred for psychiatric services: Analysis of prevalence and a conceptual synthesis. *American Orthopsychiatric Associates, Inc.,* 52–64.

Luk, S. L., Leung, P. W. L., & Lee, P. L. M. (1988). Conners' teacher rating scale in Chinese children in Hong Kong. *Journal of Child Psychology and Psychiatry, 29* (2), 165–174.

Mannuzza, S., Gittelman-Klein, R., Horowitz-Konig, P., & Giampino, T. L. (1989). Hyperactive boys almost grown up. IV: Criminality and its relationship to psychiatric status. *Archives of General Psychiatry, 46,* 1073–1079.

Mannuzza, S., Klein, R. G., & Addalli, K. A. (1991). Young adult mental status of hyperactive boys and their brothers: A prospective followup study. *Journal of the American Academy of Child and Adolescent Psychiatry, 30,* 743–751.

Mannuzza, S., Klein, R. G., Bessler, A., Malloy, P., & LaPadula, M. (1993). Adult outcome of hyperactive boys: Educational achievement, occupational rank, and psychiatric status. *Archives of General Psychiatry, 50,* 565–576.

Marshall, P. (1989). Attention deficit disorder and allergy: A neurochemical model of the relation between the illnesses. *Psychological Bulletin, 106* (3), 434–446.

Mash, E. J., & Johnston, C. (1982). A comparison of the mother-child interactions of younger and older hyperactive and normal children. *Child Development, 53,* 1371–1381.

McClellan, J. M., Rubert, M. P., Reichler, R. J., & Sylvester, C. E. (1990). Attention deficit disorder in children at risk for anxiety and depression. *Journal of American Academy of Child and Adolescent Psychiatry, 29* (4), 534–539.

McGee, R., Feehan, M., Williams, S., Partridge, F., Silva, P. A., & Kelly, J. (1990). DSM-III disorders in a large sample of adolescents. *Journal of American Academy of Child and Adolescent Psychiatry, 29* (4), 611–619.

McGee, R., Partridge, F., Williams, S., & Silva, P. (1991). A twelve-year follow-up of preschool hyperactive children. *Journal of American Academy of Child and Adolescent Psychiatry, 30* (2), 224–232.

McGee, R., & Share, D. (1988). Attention deficit disorder, hyperactivity and academic failure: Which comes first and what should be treated? *Journal of American Academy of Child and Adolescent Psychiatry, 27* (3), 318–325.

McGee, R., Williams, S., & Silva, P. H. (1985). Factor structure and correlates of ratings of inattention, hyperactivity and antisocial behavior in a large sample of 9-year-old children from the general population. *Journal of Consulting and Clinical Psychology, 53,* 480–490.

Mefford, I. N., & Potter, W. Z. (1989). A neuroanatomical and biochemical basis for attention deficit disorder with hyperactivity in children: A defect in tonic adrenaline mediated inhibition of locus coeruleus stimulation. *Medical Hypotheses, 29,* 33–42.

Mercugliano, M., Hyman, S. L., & Batshaw, M. L. (1990). Behavioral deficits in rats with minimal cortical hypoplasia induced by methylazoxymethanol acetate. *Pediatrics* [Suppl. *Behavioral Deficits and Cortical Hypoplasia*], 432–436.

Mikkelsen, E. J., Brown, G. L., Minichiello, M. D., Millican, F. K., & Rapoport, J. L. (1982). Neurologic status in hyperactive, enuretic, and normal boys. *Journal of American Academy of Child Psychiatry, 21,* 75–81.

Milich, R., Widiger, T. A., & Landau, S. (1987). Differential diagnosis of attention deficit and conduct disorders using conditional probabilities. *Journal of Consulting Clinical Psychology, 55,* 762–767.

Minde, K., Webb, G., & Sykes, D. (1968). Studies on the hyperactive child. VI. Prenatal and perinatal factors associated with hyperactivity. *Developmental Medicine and Child Neurology, 10,* 355–363.

Morrison, J., & Stewart, M. (1971). A family study of the hyperactive child syndrome. *Biological Psychiatry, 3,* 189–195.

Munir, K., Biederman, J., & Knee, D. (1987). Psychiatric comorbidity in patients with attention deficit disorder: A controlled study. *Journal of American Academy of Child and Adolescent Psychiatry, 26,* 844–848.

Nasrallah, H., Loney, J., Olsen, S., McCalley-Whitters, M., Kramer, J., & Jacoby, C. (1986). Cortical atrophy in young adults with a history of hyperactivity in childhood. *Psychiatric Research,* 241–246.

Needleman, H. L., Gunnoe, C., Leviton, A., Reed, R., Peresie, H., Maher, C., & Barrett, P. (1979). Deficits in psychologic and classroom performance of children with elevated dentine lead levels. *New England Journal of Medicine, 300,* 689–695.

Nichols, P. L., & Chen, T. C. (1981). *Minimal brain dysfunction: A prospective study.* Hillsdale, NJ: Lawrence Erlbaum.

O'Dougherty, M., Nuechterlein, K. H., & Drew, B. (1984). Hyperactive and hypoxic children: Signal detection, sustained attention, and behavior. *Journal of Abnormal Psychology, 93,* 178–191.

Offord, D. R., Sullivan, K., Allen, N., & Abrams, N. (1979). Delinquency and hyperactivity. *Journal of Nervous and Mental Disease, 167,* 734–741.

Pauls, D. L., Hurst, C. R., Kruger, S. D., Leckman, J. L., Kidd, K. K. & Cohen, D. J. (1986). Gilles de la Tourette's syndrome and attention deficit disorder with hyperactivity: evidence against a genetic relationship. *Archives of General Psychiatry, 43,* 1177–1179.

Paulsen, K. (1982). Reflection-impulsivity and level of maturity. *Journal of Psychology, 99,* 109–112.

Payton, J. B., Burkhart, J. E., Hersen, M., & Helsel, W. J. (1989). Treatment of ADDH in mentally retarded children: A preliminary study. *Journal of American Academy of Child and Adolescent Psychiatry, 28* (5), 761–767.

Pelham, W. E., Carlson, C., Sams, S. E., Vallano, G., Dixon, J., & Hoza, B. (1993). Separate and combined effects of methylphenidate and behavior modification on boys with attention deficit hyperactivity disorder in the classroom. *Journal of Consulting and Clinical Psychology, 61,* 506–515.

Pelham, W. E., & Murphy, H. A. (1986). Attention deficit and conduct disorders. In M. Herson (Ed.), *Pharmacological and behavioral treatment: An integrative approach* (pp. 108–148). New York: John Wiley & Sons.

Pfiffner, L. J., & Barkley, R. A. (1990). Educational placement and classroom management. In R. A. Barkley (Ed.), *Attention deficit hyperactivity disorder: A handbook for diagnosis and treatment* (pp. 498–539). New York: Guilford Press.

Pliszka, S. R. (1989). Effect of anxiety on cognition, behavior, and stimulant response in ADHD. *Journal of American Academy of Child and Adolescent Psychiatry, 28* (6), 882–887.

Popper, C. W., & Zimnitzky, B. (1995). Sudden death putatively related to desipramine treatment in youth: A fifth case and a review of speculative mechanisms. *Journal of Child and Adolescent Psychopharmacology, 5,* 283–300.

Pratt, D. S., & Dubois, R. S. (1990). Hepatotoxicity due to pemoline (Cylert): A report of two cases. *Journal of Pediatric Gastroenterology and Nutrition, 10* (2), 239–241.

Prendergast, M., Taylor, E., Rapoport, J. L., Bartko, J., Donnelly, M., Zametkin, A., Ahearn, M. B., Dunn, G., & Wieselberg, H. M. (1988). The diagnosis of childhood hyperactivity U.S.-U.K. cross-national study of DSM-III and ICD-9. *Journal of Child Psychology and Psychiatry, 29* (3), 289–300.

Prior, M., & Sanson, A. (1986). Attention deficit disorder with hyperactivity: A critique. *Journal of Child Psychology and Psychiatry, 27,* 307–319.

Quay, H. C. (1986). Conduct disorder. In H. C. Quay & J. S. Werry (Eds.), *Psychopathologic disorders of childhood.* New York: John Wiley & Sons.

Rapoport, J. L., Quinn, P. O., & Lamprecht, F. (1974). Minor physical anomalies and plasma dopamine betahydroxylase activity in hyperactive boys. *American Journal of Psychiatry, 121,* 386.

Rapport, M., DuPaul, G., & Stoner, G. J. (1986). Comparing classroom and clinic measures of attention deficit disorder. Differential, idiosyncratic and dose response effects of methylphenidate. *Journal of Consulting and Clinical Psychology, 54,* 334–341.

Rasbury, W. C. (1988). Attention deficit disorder: An overview. *Henry Ford Hospital Medical Journal, 36* (4), 212–216.

Raskin, L. A., Shaywitz, S. E., Shaywitz, B. A., Anderson, G. M., & Cohen, D. J. (1984). Neurochemical correlates of attention deficit disorder. *Pediatric Clinics of North America, 31,* 387–396.

Reeves, J. C., Werry, J. S., Elkind, G. S., & Zametkin, A. (1987). Attention deficit, conduct, oppositional, and anxiety disorders in children. II: Clinical characteristics. *Journal of American Academy of Child and Adolescent Psychiatry, 26,* 144–155.

Richters, J. E., Arnold, L. E., Jensen, P. S., Abikoff, H., Conners, C. K., Greenhill, L. L., Hechtman, L., Hinshaw, S. P., Pelham, W. E., & Swanson, J. M. (1995). NIMH collaborative multisite multimodal treatment study of children with ADHD: Background and rationale. *Journal of the American Academy of Child and Adolescent Psychiatry, 34,* 987–1000.

Riddle, M. A., Hardin, M. T., Cho, S. C., Woolston, J. L., & Leckman, J. F. (1988). Desipramine treatment of boys with attention deficit hyperactivity disorder and tics: Preliminary clinical experience. *Journal of American Academy of Child and Adolescent Psychiatry, 27* (6), 811–814.

Riddle, M. A., Nelson, J. C., Kleinman, C. S., Rasmusson, A., Leckman, J. F., King, R. A., & Cohen, D. J.

(1991). Sudden death in children receiving nor-pramin: A review of three reported cases and commentary. *Journal of American Academy of Child and Adolescent Psychiatry, 30* (1), 104–108.

Rogeness, G. A., Maas, J. W., Javors, M. A., Macedo, C. A., Fischer, C., & Harris, W. R. (1989). Attention deficit disorder symptoms and urine catecholamines. *Psychiatry Research, 27,* 241–251.

Safer, D. J., & Krager, J. M. (1988). A survey of medication treatment for hyperactive/inattentive students. *Journal of the American Medical Association, 260* (15), 2256–2258.

Sandberg, S. T., Wieselberg, M., & Shaffer, D. (1980). Hyperkinetic and conduct problem children in a primary school population: Some epidemiologic considerations. *Journal of Child Psychology and Psychiatry, 21,* 293–311.

Satterfield, B., & Dawson, M. (1971). Electrodermal correlates of hyperactivity in children. *Psychophysiology, 8,* 191–197.

Satterfield, J. H., Hoppe, C. M., & Schell, A. M. (1982). A prospective study of delinquency in 110 adolescent boys with attention deficit disorder and 88 normal adolescent boys. *American Journal of Psychiatry, 139,* 195–198.

Satterfield, J. H., Schell, A. M., Nicholas, T., & Backs, R. W. (1988). Topographic study of auditory event-related potentials in normal boys and boys with attention deficit disorder with hyperactivity. *Society for Psychophysiological Research, 25* (5), 591–606.

Satterfield, J. H., Schell, A. M., Nicholas, T. W., Satterfield, B. T., & Freese, T. E. (1990). Ontogeny of selective attention effects on event-related potentials in attention-deficit hyperactivity disorder and normal boys. *Biological Psychiatry, 28,* 879–903.

Schachar, R., & Wachsmuth, R. (1990). Hyperactivity and parental psychopathology. *Journal of Child Psychology and Psychiatry, 31,* 3, 381–392.

Shapiro, S. K., & Garfinkel, H. D. (1986). The occurrence of behavior disorders in children: The interdependence of attention deficit disorder and conduct disorder. *Journal of American Academy of Child Psychiatry, 25,* 809–819.

Share, D. L., & Schwartz, S. (1988). A note on the distinction between attention deficit disorder and reading disability: Are there group-specific cognitive deficits? *Brain and Language, 34,* 350–352.

Shaywitz, B. A., & Shaywitz, S. E. (1991). Comorbidity: A critical issue in attention deficit disorder. *Journal of Child Neurology, 6* [Suppl.] S13–S20.

Shaywitz, B. A., Shaywitz, S. E., Sebrechts, M. M., Anderson, G. M., Cohen, D. J., Jatlow, P., & Young, J. G. (1990). Growth hormone and prolactin response to methylphenidate in children with attention deficit disorder. *Life Sciences, 46* (9), 625–633.

Shaywitz, S. E., Shaywitz, B. A., Schnell, C., Towle, V. R., & McPhil, M. (1988). Concurrent and predictive validity of the Yale children's inventory: An instrument to assess children with attentional deficits and learning disabilities. *Pediatrics, 81* (4), 562–571.

Shekim, W. O., Antun, F., Hanna, G. L., McCracken, J. T., & Hess, E. B. (1990). S-Adenosyl-L-Methionine (SAM) in adults with ADHD, RT: Preliminary results from an open trial. *Psychopharmacology Bulletin, 26* (2), 249–253.

Shekim, W. O., Asarnow, R. F., Hess, E., Zaucha, K., & Wheeler, N. (1990). A clinical and demographic profile of a sample of adults with attention deficit hyperactivity disorder, residual state. *Comprehensive Psychiatry, 31* (5), 416–425.

Shekim, W. O., Masterson, A., Cantwell, D. P., Hanna, G. L., & McCracken, J. T. (1989). Nomifensine maleate in adult attention deficit disorder. *Journal of Nervous and Mental Disease, 177* (5), 296–299.

Silver, L. B. (1981). The relationship between learning disabilities, hyperactivity, distractibility, and behavioral problems. *Journal of American Academy of Child Psychiatry, 20,* 385–397.

Simeon, J., Ferguson, H., VanWyck, & Flett, J. (1986). Bupropion effects interaction deficit and conduct disorders. *Canadian Journal of Psychiatry, 31,* 581–585.

Spencer, T., Biederman, J., Kerman, K., Steingard, R., & Wilens, T. (1993). Desipramine treatment of children with attention deficit hyperactivity and tic disorder or Tourette's syndrome. *Journal of the American Academy of Child and Adolescent Psychiatry, 32,* 354–360.

Spencer, T., Biederman, J., Wilens, T., Harding, M., O'Donnell, D., & Griffin, S. (1996). Pharmacotherapy of attention deficit hyperactivity disorder across the life cycle. *Journal of the American Academy of Child and Adolescent Psychiatry, 35,* 409–432.

Spitzer, R. L., Davies, M., Barkley, R. A. (1990). The DSM-III-R field trial of disruptive behavior disorders. *Journal of American Academy of Child and Adolescent Psychiatry, 29* (5), 690–697.

Staton, R. D., & Brumback, R. A. (1981). Non-specificity of motor hyperactivity as a diagnostic criterion. *Perceptual and Motor Skills, 52,* 323–332.

Steingard, R., Biederman, J., Spencer, T., Wilens, T., & Gonzalez, A. (1993). Comparison of clonidine response in the treatment of attention-deficit hyperactivity disorder with and without comorbid tic disorders. *Journal of the American Academy of Child and Adolescent Psychiatry, 32,* 350–353.

Stevenson, R. D., & Wolraich, M. L. (1989). Stimulant medication therapy in the treatment of children with attention deficit hyperactivity disorder. *Pediatrics Clinics of North America, 36* (5), 1183–1197.

Stewart, M. A., Cummings, C., Singer, S., & DeBlois, C. S. (1981). The overlap between hyperactive and unsocialized aggressive children. *Journal of Child Psychology and Psychiatry, 22,* 35–45.

Stewart, M. A., & Morrison, J. R. (1973). Affective disorders among the relatives of hyperactive children. *Journal of Child Psychology and Psychiatry, 14,* 209–212.

Still, F. (1902). The Coulstonian lectures on some abnormal physical conditions in children. *Lancet, 1,* 1008–1012, 1077–1082, 1163–1168.

Stoff, D. M., Friedman, E., Pollock, L., Vitiello, B.,

Kendall, P. C., & Bridger, W. H. (1989). Elevated platelet MAO is related to impulsivity in disruptive behavior disorders. *Journal of American Academy of Child and Adolescent Psychiatry, 28* (5), 754–760.

Strayhorn, J. M., & Weidman, C. S. (1989). Reduction of attention deficit and internalising symptoms in preschoolers through parent-child interaction training. *Journal of American Academy of Child and Adolescent Psychiatry, 28* (6), 888–896.

Streissguth, A. P., Martin, D. C., Barr, H. M., Sandman, B. M., Kirchner, G. L., & Darby, B. L. (1984). Intrauterine alcohol and nicotine exposure: Attention and reaction time in 4-year-old children. *Developmental Psychology, 20,* 533–541.

Strober, M., Morrell, W., Burroughs, J., Lampert, C., Danforth H., & Freeman, R., (1988). A family study of bipolar I disorder in adolescence: Early onset of symptoms linked to increased familial loading and lithium resistance. *Journal of Affective Disorders, 15,* 255–268.

Swanson, J. M., Posner, M., Potkin, S., Bonforte, S., Youpa, D., Fiore, C., Cantwell, D., & Crinella, F. (1991). Activating tasks for the study of visual-spatial attention in ADHD children: A cognitive anatomic approach. *Journal of Child Neurology, 6,* 119–127.

Sylvester, C. E., Hyde, T. S., & Reichler, R. J. (1987). The diagnostic interview for children and personality inventory for children in studies of children at risk for anxiety disorders or depression. *Journal of American Academy of Child and Adolescent Psychiatry, 26,* 718–723.

Szatmari, P., Boyle, M., & Offord, D. R. (1989). ADDH and conduct disorder: Degree of diagnostic overlap and differences among correlates. *Journal of American Academy of Child and Adolescent Psychiatry, 28,* 865–883.

Szatmari, P., Offord, D. R., Boyle, M. H. (1989a). Correlates, associated impairments and patterns of service utilization of children with attention deficit disorder: Findings from the Ontario child health study. *Journal of Child Psychiatry, 30* (2), 205–217.

Szatmari, P., Offord, D. R., & Boyle, M. H. (1989b). Ontario child health study: Prevalence of attention deficit disorder with hyperactivity. *Journal of Child Psychiatry, 30* (2), 219–230.

Taylor, E., Everitt, B., Thorley, G., Schachar, R., Rutter, M., & Weiselberg, M. (1986). Conduct disorder and hyperactivity. II: A cluster analytic approach to the identification of a behavioral syndrome. *British Journal of Psychiatry, 149,* 768–777.

Taylor, E., & Sandberg, S. (1984). Hyperactive behavior in English school children: A questionnaire survey. *Journal of Abnormal Child Psychology, 12,* 143–156.

Taylor, E., Schachar, R., Thorley, G., & Weiselberg, M. (1986). Conduct disorder and hyperactivity. I: Separation of hyperactivity and antisocial conduct in British child psychiatric patients. *British Journal of Psychiatry, 149,* 760–767.

Thorley, G. (1984). Hyperkinetic syndrome of childhood: Clinical characteristics. *British Journal of Psychiatry, 144,* 16–24.

Van Der Meere, J. J., Wekking, E., & Sergeant, J.

(1991). Sustained attention and pervasive hyperactivity. *Journal of Child Psychology and Psychiatry, 32* (2), 275–284.

Varley, C. K., & Trupin, E. W. (1982). Double-blind administration of methylphenidate to mentally retarded children with attention deficit disorder: A preliminary study. *American Journal of Mental Deficiency, 86,* 560–566.

Vincent, J., Varley, C. K., & Leger, P. (1990). Effects of methylphenidate on early adolescent growth. *American Journal of Psychiatry, 147* (4), 501–502.

Vitiello, B., Stoff, D., Atkins, M., & Mahoney, A. (1990). Soft neurological signs and impulsivity in children. *Developmental and Behavioral Pediatrics, 11* (3), 112–115.

Voeller, K. K. S. (1991). Toward a neurobiologic nosology of attention deficit hyperactivity disorder. *Journal of Child Neurology, 6,* S2–S8.

Weinberg, W. A., & Brumback, R. A. (1990). Primary disorder of vigilance: A novel explanation of inattentiveness, daydreaming, boredom, restlessness, and sleepiness. *Journal of Pediatrics, 116* (5), 720–725.

Weinberg, W. A., McLean, A., Snider, R. L., Nuckols, A. S., Rintelmann, J. W., & Erwin, P. R. (1989). Depression, learning disability and school behavior problems. *Psychological Reports, 64,* 275–283.

Weiss, G., & Hechtman, L. (1993). *Hyperactive children grown up: ADHD in children, adolescents and adults* (2nd ed.). New York: Guilford Press.

Weiss, G., Hechtman, L., Milroy, T., & Perlman, T., (1985). Psychiatric status of hyperactives as adults: A controlled prospective 15-year follow-up of 63 hyperactive children. *Journal of American Academy of Child Psychiatry, 24,* 211–220.

Weizman, A., Bernhout, E., Weitz, R., Tyano, S., Rehavi, M. (1988). Imipramine binding to platelets of children with attention deficit disorder with hyperactivity. *Society of Biological Psychiatry, 23,* 491–496.

Wender, P. H. (1971). *Minimal brain dysfunction in children.* New York: John Wiley & Sons.

Wender, P. H. (1987). *The hyperactive child adolescent and adult: attention deficit disorder through the life span.* New York: Oxford University Press.

Wender, P. H., & Reimherr, F. W. (1990). Bupropion treatment of attention-deficit hyperactivity disorder in adults. *American Journal of Psychiatry, 147,* 1018–1040.

Wilens, T. E., & Biederman, J. (1992). The stimulants. *Psychiatric Clinics of North America, 15,* 191–222.

Wilens, T., Biederman, J., Geist, D. E., Steingard, R., & Spencer, T. (1993). Nortriptyline in the treatment of ADHD; a chart review of 58 cases. *Journal of the American Academy of Child and Adolescent Psychiatry, 32,* 343–349.

Woolston, J. L., Rosenthal, S. L., Riddle, M. A., Sparrow, S., Cicchetti, D., & Zimmerman, L. (1989). Childhood comorbidity of anxiety/affective disorders and behavior disorders. *Journal of American Academy of Child and Adolescent Psychiatry, 28,* 707–713.

Wozniak, J., Biederman, J., Kiely, K., et al. (1995). Mania-like symptoms suggestive of childhood-onset bipolar disorder in clinically referred children. *Journal of the American Academy of Child and Adolescent Psychiatry, 34*, 867–876.

Wultz, B., Sagvolden, T., Moser, E. I., & Moser, M. B. (1990). The spontaneously hypertensive rat as an animal model of attention deficit hyperactivity disorder: Effects of methylphenidate on exploratory behavior. *Behavioral and Neurological Biology, 53*, 88–102.

Zametkin, A. J., & Hamburger, S. D. (1988). The effect of methylphenidate on urinary catecholamine excretion in hyperactivity: A partial replication. *Society of Biological Psychiatry, 23*, 350–356.

Zametkin, A. J., Nordahl, T. E., Gross, M., King, A. C., Semple, W. E., Rumsey, J., Hamburger, S., & Cohen, R. M. (1990). Cerebral glucose metabolism in adults with hyperactivity of childhood onset. *New England Journal of Medicine, 323* (30), 1361–1366.

Zametkin, A., & Rapoport, J. (1985). Neurobiology of attention deficit disorder with hyperactivity: Where have we come in 50 years? *Journal of American Academy of Child and Adolescent Psychiatry, 26* (5), 676–686.

Zametkin, A., Rapoport, J., Murphy, L., Linnoila, D. L., Karoum, M., Potter, W., & Ismond, D. (1985). Treatment of hyperactive children with monoamine oxidase inhibitors. II. Plasma and urinary monoamine findings after treatment. *Archives of General Psychiatry, 42*, 969–973.

Zelko, F. A. J. (1991). Comparison of parent-completed behavior rating scales: Differentiating boys with ADD from psychiatric and normal controls. *Developmental and Behavioral Pediatrics, 12* (1), 31–37.

Ziegler, R., & Holden, L. (1988). Family therapy for learning disabled and attention-deficit disordered children. *American Journal of Orthopsychiatry, 58* (2), 196–210.

41 / Elective Mutism

Eleanor B. Krolian and John J. Stine

A small group of children come to the attention of mental health professionals and pediatricians because of their remarkable refusal to speak to most people except immediate family members and, in some cases, peers. In most social settings outside the house, however, although they are able to speak and comprehend the spoken word, they are steadfastly silent.

Background

HISTORY OF THE DISORDER

Initial references to elective or selective mutism date to 1877, when Kussmaul (1877) used the term *aphasia voluntaria* to classify mentally intact people who elected not to speak. Tramer, in 1934, described children who refused to speak in certain settings and with selected people as suffering elective mutism.

COMPARATIVE NOSOLOGY

Controversy exists as to whether elective mutism is simply an uncommon symptom associated with more frequently observed disturbances, such as an oppositional or panic disorder, or whether it properly should be regarded as a distinct diagnostic disorder. As in previous decades, clinicians and researchers have attempted to define the boundaries of the disorder more narrowly.

The fourth edition of the *Diagnostic and Statistical Manual of Mental Disorders* (DSM-IV; American Psychiatric Association, 1994) delineates elective mutism as a separate diagnostic category to be distinguished from communication disorders, pervasive developmental disorder, and psychotic disorders.

EPIDEMIOLOGY

Few detailed epidemiological studies of this disorder exist, and most lack sufficient rigor to provide valid statistical results. In one of the more thorough research studies, Fundudis, Kolvin, and Garside (1979) found only 2 cases of elective mutism in a population of 3,300 7-year-old children (a prevalence of 0.8 per 1,000). Bradley and Sloman (1975) report a prevalence of less than 0.5 of 1%. Over a 12-year period, among all referrals to a child psychiatry service, Wilkins (1985) discovered only 24 cases of elective mutism. In 3 of those 24 cases, however, the onset of the mutism occurred after 10 years of age. Additionally, these 3 children were mute at home, not at school or in other social settings, raising doubt as to whether elective mutism, as narrowly defined, was the most appropriate diagnosis.

The disorder typically first presents itself between ages 3 to 5, though the onset may occur as late as age 7. The disorder is more common in girls, although the difference does not appear to be statistically significant. While it appears to be relatively evenly spread across socioeconomic groups, some authors have found it more common among lower socioeconomic levels. This finding appears to be a function of the researchers' inclusion of non-English-speaking immigrant children in their sample. It is unclear whether the absence of expressive language in such a population is due to elective mutism or the temporary effects of a language barrier. There is no information on distribution of this disorder based on racial or ethnic groupings.

Kolvin and Fundudis (1981) studied birth order and family size and report that family size did not differ between elective mutes and controls but that the electively mute children were born significantly early in their sibship. No statistical data are offered on the occurrence of elective mutism or behaviors associated with the disorder in more than one child in a sibling group, but anecdotal information by various authors indicates that it is not infrequent (Halpern, Hammond, & Cohen, 1971; Mora, DeVault, & Schopler, 1962; Wilkins, 1985).

Clinical Presentation and Diagnostic Assessment

OVERT SIGNS AND SYMPTOMS

The electively mute child is one who exhibits partial speech avoidance in most all social interactions outside of the home and, predominantly, with nonfamily members. The refusal to speak can range from offering only occasional monosyllabic utterances to total silence; characteristically, it is maintained with great tenacity in the face of external enticements to speak. First observation usually coincides with the child's entry into school, al-

though in some cases there is an insidious history of shyness and limited speech usage. The disorder frequently is accompanied by school refusal, fears of separation from an overly attached and overprotective mother, and varying degrees of negative and controlling behavior.

Kolvin and Fundudis (1981) report that bowel and bladder control problems are not uncommon in these children. In their study of 24 elective mutes, 17% were encopretic and 42% were enuretic versus 2% and 15% respectively in the control group. Other anecdotal reports in the literature also refer to episodic wetting and soiling by these children.

Electively mute children are typically anxious, withdrawn, and difficult to engage. Facial expressions and body gestures often exude negativism, and these children can be quite stubborn in their silent refusal to comply with common demands. Certain electively mute children will appear to enjoy the attention that these symptoms elicit; by and large, these children are not shy.

PEER RELATIONSHIPS AND PATTERNS OF PLAY

There is a paucity of information in the literature about the nature, quality, or duration of these children's peer relationships. We can speculate that a chronically silent child is gravely disadvantaged in seeking out, developing, and maintaining age-appropriate and progressive peer relationships. Initially, peers may attempt to communicate with the child in benign and engaging ways, but, with repeated rejection, more hostile or sadistic means may be used, and the child may become a scapegoat. Expectably, peers eventually may give up their attempts to engage with the silent child, thus reinforcing the mutist's feelings of isolation from the world outside the immediate family.

The literature is noteworthy in its lack of descriptions of patterns of play in these children. Electively mute children seem to maintain an interest in peers, but the nature and manifestation of this interest is unclear. Some of these children will preferentially talk with and play with peers while avoiding interactions with adults. In Chethiks (1975) case study of a 6½-year-old girl, the child never spoke to the therapist, although her mutism abated in all other settings. The child's improvement was clearly attributable to the intensive therapy and occurred in spite of her continued muteness in session.

PSYCHODYNAMIC FORMULATION

A broad range of dynamic issues underlie this condition, depending on patterns of comorbidity, age of onset, and familial factors. The cases reported in the literature tend to represent the most disturbed end of the spectrum. Predictably, the predominant clinical picture seems to be that of children who are fixated at the preoedipal level of development.

The degree of neediness and dependency that these children exhibit, as well as by their fears of abandonment, demonstrate oral fixation. There is also substantial evidence of anal-retentive and passive-aggressive tendencies, as seen in the stubborn withholding of speech, the need for control, and the refusal to comply with demands. One of the authors (E.K.) treated an 8-year-old boy who clearly manifested these issues.

Paul was admitted for day hospital treatment at 8 years. He had not spoken outside the home since age 4, when his mother was briefly hospitalized. He was fearful that she would not return home and subsequently was excessively clingy. Because of his separation anxiety, his mother needed to remain at the day hospital program each day for several weeks after admission. In the course of his therapy, Paul's need for control became obvious. In one session, he moved all of the therapist's personal belongings out of the office. I noted that it looked like I was moving out and he acknowledged this with a satisfied grin. When asked who was moving in, he pointed to himself and gleefully slammed the door shut. Later, as a thief he named "Hitler Jones," he would steal and hoard all the items on my desk but return them just before being caught.

Level of Ego Functioning and Superego Involvement: Case reports describe a wide range of disturbance in ego functioning. Some children seem to exhibit defects in autonomous ego functioning, especially in expressive language and cognitive functioning. Others show additional impairments in object relations, impulse control, reality testing, and the use of a maladaptive defense constellation.

Ann, a 7½-year-old girl, was treated by one of the authors (E.K.) upon her admission to the day hospital after a year of outpatient psychotherapy. During her outpatient treatment, she spoke twice to her therapist,

once to say "The devil's inside me and I'm going to get you." Her first-grade teacher observed that Ann would frequently bite her hand or stick objects in her mouth to avoid speaking. Her muteness had a distancing and cold quality that tended to push others away, and she frequently was on the periphery of activity. Attempts by peers to engage Ann often had a sadistic flavor, as with one older female patient, who would tickle and gently pinch Ann until she would say "I love you." Early in our sessions Ann would scornfully throw things in my hair and then silently laugh as if she had humiliated me. She would boldly rifle through the contents of my desk drawers with a chilling disregard of my presence in the room. These reflections of primitive grandiosity and desires for total domination and control of others suggested an immature capacity for object relations indicative of a severe arrest in ego development.

By and large, there is very little evidence that superego conflict plays a prominent or easily recognized role in the conflict in these children. The primary focus is more on the issue of control than on a later sense of guilt or issues of conscience.

Patterns of Defense: Typically, no unique constellation of defenses seems to be employed by electively mute children. This is due to a number of factors, including the frequent appearance of comorbid conditions, a wide variation in the level of ego functioning these children display, and differences in their characterological styles ranging from shy and withdrawn to oppositional and aggressive. Additionally, the often impenetrable silence itself limits clinicians' ability to analyze and interpret the behavior and defenses with any degree of certainty, since confirmation from the children is lacking. In treatment, therapists must process the silence as both a communication and a defense.

Given these qualifications, three defenses appear to be associated with the disorder: identification with the aggressor, and regression, and turning against the self. It should be noted that these defenses are primarily immature and narcissistic in nature.

The literature and clinical experience confirm that families of electively mute children frequently are socially isolated. One parent, often the mother, models the hostile withholding of speech. By identifying with the silent parent, the child attempts to avoid loss of the parent while simultaneously gaining control over the aggressive characteristic of that parent.

In some cases the silence may have a regressive

rather than oppositional quality to it. The silence may represent a retreat to an earlier preverbal level of development as a means of escaping instinctual tension. Precipitating events for this regression include any separation from the parent (e.g., attending school) and a demand for social interaction outside the family.

The more disturbed electively mute child often exhibits difficulty in the expression and adequate regulation of aggression. Management of aggressive impulses is achieved by changing the object of the aggression from another person to the self. This is seen in the following clinical example (from a case previously cited):

Several months into treatment in the course of a session, Ann picked a bouquet of flowers and promptly shoved them into my face. She then tried to force her wrist into my mouth indicating that I should bite her. Unsuccessful at this, she grabbed my hand and repeatedly attempted to have me slap her face.

This example also illustrates the primitive narcissistic defense of omnipotent control, as seen in Ann's exaggerated and grandiose attempt to control the adult in her environment.

As stated previously, the silence of these children frequently represents a maladaptive attempt to manage aggression. Many clinicians view silence as a displaced expression of aggression. Supporting this is the common clinical finding that when these children do begin to speak, they tend to exhibit more direct, unmodulated expressions of aggression.

When Paul began to use speech more freely in sessions and in the milieu, his self-description was of a "mad bomber." A torrent of aggressive affect was unleashed. He spoke excessively, loudly, and with much cursing. The staff was able to help him begin to modulate his aggressive feelings and gain better control as these feelings were put into words.

PRESENTATION IN LATER LIFE

This disorder has not been reported in adults, and there are no systematic studies following these children into adulthood. Crumley (1990) reports on the 20-year follow-up of an 8½-year-old boy who presented with elective mutism. At the time of follow-up, the patient was verbal but still expressed great anxiety in dealing with people, fear of the unexpected, and a hesitancy to be the first to begin a conversation. The author suggested that the most accurate diagnosis may have been panic disorder leading to elective mutism.

Kaplan and Escoll (1973) report on a form of elected silence beginning in adolescence. This mutism differs from childhood-onset elective mutism in (1) age of onset was after 12 years; (2) the silence extended to family members; (3) the presence of conduct-disordered behavior, suicidal acts, or conversion reactions; (4) the predominance of oedipal and genital issues; and (5) no prior history or speech disturbances. The authors considered these cases to be an unusual manifestation of the diagnosis of hysterical personality disorder.

Etiology

Multiple endogenous factors must be considered in the etiology of elective mutism. Clearly there are temperamental underpinnings; these children can be unusually shy, silently oppositional, and "slow to warm up" (Thomas, Chess, & Birch, 1968). Moodiness, anxiousness, and aggressive negativism are frequently part of the personality patterns.

NEUROPSYCHOLOGICAL ASPECTS AND THE ROLE OF TRAUMA

Neuropsychological examinations of these children reveal a wide spread in intellectual functioning. Kolvin and Fundudis (1981) found a mean I.Q. of 85 and Wilkins reported a mean I.Q. of 100.3, both necessarily based on performance testing. Delay in speech development and articulation irregularities are consistently reported in the literature, but no specific hearing abnormalities appear to be present. The prevalence or nature of specific learning disabilities in this population is not known and warrants investigation.

Several authors believe that a traumatic event at the time of speech formation or in response to inadequate or irregular speech production may contribute to the onset of the disorder (Laybourne, 1979). Parker (Parker, Olsen, & Throckmorton, 1960) reports on a history of trauma to the mouth at the time of speech formation. Browne, Wilson, and Laybourne (1963) refer to the reduced use of speech in a 22-month-old after a sudden hospitalization for acute giant urticaria.

Trauma may play a part in the development or maintenance of the disorder in later grade-school years as well. Such trauma could include being required to speak in front of a large group or being compelled to maintain a family secret.

FAMILIAL AND PSYCHOSOCIAL FACTORS

Problems within the marital and family system are seen consistently as playing a significant role in the development and maintenance of elective mutism. These families exhibit a high incidence of social dysfunction, particularly in the areas of aggression and excessive shyness. Social isolation, suspiciousness, and distrust of those outside the immediate family also are seen as predisposing familial factors. Often there is some degree of psychiatric disturbance in one or both parents, ranging from maternal depression to character pathology. The mothers are frequently reported to be both rejecting and overprotective and demanding, whereas the fathers are often passive or uninvolved.

Goll (1979) proposes that mutists' families, lacking confidence in the outside world, insulate themselves from social contact. When the child is called upon to interact with the larger social group (e.g., in school), his or her loyalty to the family collides with the requirement to engage with the outside world, and the mutism unfolds.

Examination of the mother-child relationship in these families reveals an excessive closeness in which the child is frequently abusive and controlling toward the parent. The presence of a poor marital relationship often further encourages the overdependence between mother and child.

DIFFERENTIAL DIAGNOSIS

Mental retardation or pervasive development disorder initially may be mistaken for elective mutism. In contrast to the electively mute child who selectively uses language for purposes of communication, children with severe forms of these disorders may be unable to use language at all and will show even more widespread impairments of cognitive and ego functioning.

Children with expressive language disorders may avoid talking in public situations because of conditioned anxiety about their relative difficulty in communicating. A speech and language evaluation may clarify the diagnosis by disclosing generalized and severe problems of language processing and usage.

In avoidant disorder of childhood, the child initially may be reluctant to speak to those outside of the family; as the youngster habituates to a novel or unfamiliar situation, he or she eventually will warm up and begin to communicate verbally. In some cases, the avoidant disorder and elective mutism may occur together.

In contrast to the child with elective mutism who shows a generalized refusal to speak outside the family, the child with social phobia reacts with anxiety and avoidance to one or more *specific* situations in which he or she may be exposed to scrutiny; as a rule, the child refuses or is unable to speak only in these given contexts. The differential diagnosis is more difficult when the socially phobic child fears many social situations, such as a generalized fear of being asked questions or required to speak in public. Indeed, some clinical pictures of elective mutism may be determined by dynamics similar to those underlying social phobia.

In separation anxiety disorder, anxiety is linked to separation from important figures rather than to an encounter with new situations or people. The child with severe separation anxiety disorder may indeed also avoid talking with people outside the family setting. However, verbal interactions with others may become completely normal when significant attachment figures are present.

Rarely, a child with overanxious disorder may be so frozen with anxiety that he or she is literally unable to interact verbally outside of the psychological comfort zone of family and home. However, in such cases there is a premorbid history of normal language and speech usage in all settings, and the clinical picture is dominated by pervasive anxiety, worry, and fearfulness.

The child with major depressive disorder may be mute and withdrawn as part of the severe depressive state but will have a history of normal verbal communication patterns outside of the family until the onset of recent illness.

Children with adjustment disorder with social withdrawal also show a normal premorbid pattern of language and speech usage; however, there will be a history of specific psychosocial stressor and the clinical course of the problems will have endured less than 6 months.

MORBIDITY

The electively mute child's ability to develop normally in the academic and social spheres is impeded by the protracted presence of failed communication. Many children are referred for special education placements because of their inability to learn and participate in a conventional manner in normal classroom settings. The mutism also reinforces social isolation. The family frequently views their refusal to speak and oppositional behavior as disruptive. Not uncommonly, they end up being scapegoated by peers because of their willful avoidance of verbal interaction.

Comorbidity: In examining comorbidity, the various cases reflect a wide range of patterns. In some cases purer form of the disorder is reported, while others show comorbidity, especially with oppositional and panic disorder, separation anxiety disorder, social phobia, and, in some instances, depression.

PROGNOSIS

There is no clear consensus on the course and prognosis of this unusual disorder. The prognosis is poor where there are multiple problems, such as neurological impairment, thought disorders, and low intelligence. Kolvin and Fundudis (1981) indicate that where there is no improvement in response to therapy by age 10, a more intractable form of elective mutism is present. Of 8 children in their study who had not improved by age 10, only 1 had made any progress at the time of follow-up. Again, the trend toward improvement also was seen to be greater in those cases where parental personality problems were not an issue. The persistence of the disorder through adolescence can be accompanied by behavior in the prepsychotic to psychotic range. In treating this disorder, early intervention on multiple levels is essential and tends to result in a better outcome.

Treatment

The treatment of elective mutism has been undertaken in many different clinical settings and by means of a number of modalities, each claiming its own degree of success.

MILIEU TREATMENT

Outpatient treatment alone is generally not effective in treating this disorder.

Significant emphasis has been placed on removing the child from the home for treatment on an inpatient psychiatric unit. The results of this strategy vary; sometimes there are reports of improvement and sometimes there are accounts of further trauma based on the separation. Day hospital treatment has been described as a milieu that offers both an intensive treatment setting and an optimal degree of distance between the child and the disturbed family. In such a setting, individual, group, and family therapy can be utilized in conjunction with behavioral techniques and special education services to provide a comprehensive treatment approach (Krolian, 1988).

BEHAVIOR MODIFICATION

Behavioral intervention is specifically focused on extinguishing the mutism and enhancing the scope, volume, and frequency of the spoken word. The mutism is viewed as a learned behavior, and it is the direct and immediate target of behavior modification strategies.

A thorough functional analysis of the child's speech problem is considered essential to the formulation of a comprehensive treatment strategy (Labbe & Williamson, 1984; Sanok & Ascione, 1979). Such an assessment entails establishing a baseline of the child's speech across various settings and defining with whom the child does and does not speak. Accurate diagnosis of the presence of elective mutism versus, for instance, reluctant speech or the absence of speech in all settings is also critical in treatment planning. Neither intrapsychic nor familial factors is determinative in constructing a behavioral treatment approach (Sanok & Ascione, 1979).

Several authors have undertaken evaluative reviews of behavioral techniques, methodological issues, and the clinical outcome of studies reported in the literature. The predominant treatment techniques reported are stimulus fading with positive reinforcement (e.g., reinforcement for the production of speech in situations where the child was previously silent); positive reinforcement with extinction or response cost (e.g., losing reinforcers for not speaking); and shaping (e.g., imitating behaviors that approximate speech, such as mouthing words). Sanok and Ascione (1979) highlight the need for programmed generalization of speech so that spontaneous as well as prompted speech is produced. Additionally, nonreinforcement of nonverbal responses should accompany reinforcement of verbal responses. Labbe and Williamson (1984) report improvement in speech production in the 29 cases they reviewed; however, they note that more controlled group outcome studies and the use of single-case methodology are needed to evaluate reported results objectively.

The reports of successful clinical outcomes based on improved speech production do not reflect whether improvement also was obtained in some of the significant collateral problems associated with the disorder, such as excessive shyness, negativism, and oppositional behavior.

FAMILY, INDIVIDUAL, AND GROUP TREATMENT

Family therapists view the disorder as a form of family neurosis and utilize family therapy in conjunction with individual treatment of the child. Psychodynamically oriented psychotherapy, as described by Chethik (1975) and Ruzicka and Sackin (1974), focuses on the psychogenic origins of the disorder and the importance of the resolution of core conflicts. For many of these authors, the main focus of the individual treatment is not the silence; rather it is the importance of understanding the silence as an expression of past experience and conflict. Attempts to focus initially on the mutism often lead to increased controlling and oppositional behavior, thus intensifying the silence. The therapist must view the silence as well as all other mannerisms, facial expressions, and motor activity as communications to be explored, clarified, and, when appropriate, interpreted.

Great flexibility is needed in treating this group of children since their level of object relations and ego development can vary so widely. In some cases the child initially cannot tolerate the closeness of being confined to an office for sessions; in such cases, treatment should take place outdoors or in waiting areas. Providing the child with the opportunity to use telephones, tape recorders, or musical instruments to facilitate the production of sound can be helpful. One child treated by one of the authors (E.K.) began to communicate by producing different animal sounds and recording them on tape.

Group psychotherapy has not been described in the literature to date. The nearest approximation to group work with these children is the array of behavioral treatment interventions in classroom settings.

BIOLOGICAL INTERVENTIONS

There are very few reports on psychopharmacological intervention in treating elective mutism. In a case report by Kummer (1953), the child's mutism was considered to be secondary to hypothyroidism and improved with hormonal replacement therapy. In a single-case study, Golwyn and Weinstock (1990) report on the successful use of phenelzine in alleviating the mutism in a 7-year-old girl with a 2-year history of mutism. The authors postulate "that dopamanergic systems may regulate talkativeness as well as movement and activity" (p. 385) in a number of conditions, including elective mutism. However, the phenelzine simply may have reduced the child's anxiety, enabling her to speak. Although results of this case study are promising, they do not address the question of whether the medication is affecting the specific disorder or a symptom of the disorder.

Future Considerations

Efforts by clinicians and researchers to define more clearly the nature, scope, and duration of this unusual and rare disorder continue. More systematic case studies with adequate control groups and detailed longitudinal follow-up are warranted. A closer examination of patterns of family functioning is also needed. For instance, how is verbal interaction conducted within the home? What does and does not get communicated among family members? How does the family view the verbal expression of emotion? Additionally, observational reports on the nature of peer relationships and patterns of play would provide a broader picture of the level of object relations these children attain. Retrospective reports from previously electively mute children would be helpful in gaining a deeper understanding of the child's subjective experience of his or her silence and withdrawal. Clearly, much uncharted territory remains in understanding this strangely silent group of children.

REFERENCES

American Psychiatric Association. (1994). *Diagnostic and statistical manual of mental disorders* (4th ed.). Washington, DC: Author.

Bradley, S., & Sloman, L. (1975). Elective mutism in immigrant families. *Journal of the American Academy of Child Psychiatry, 14,* 510–514.

Browne, E., Wilson, V., & Laybourne, P. (1963). Diagnosis and treatment of elective mutism in children. *Journal of the American Academy of Child Psychiatry, 2,* 605–617.

Chethik, M. (1975). The intensive treatment of an elective mute. *Journal of the American Academy of Child Psychiatry, 12,* 482–498.

Crumley, F. E. (1990). The masquerade of mutism. *Journal of the American Academy of Child Psychiatry, 29,* 318–319.

Fundudis, T., Kolvin, I., & Garside, R. F. (1979). *Speech retarded & deaf children: Their psychological development.* London: Academic Press.

Goll, J. (1979). Role structure & subculture in families of elective mutists. *Family Process, 18,* 55–68.

Golwyn, D. H., & Weinstock, R. C. (1990). Phenelzine treatment of elective mutism: A case report. *Journal of Clinical Psychiatry, 51,* 384–385.

Halpern, W. I., Hammond, J. and Cohen, R. (1971) A Therapeutic Approach to Speech Phobia: Elective Mutism Re-examined. *Journal of the American Academy of Child Psychiatry, 10,* 94–107.

Kaplan, S. L., & Escoll, P. (1973). Treatment of two silent adolescent girls. *Journal of the American Academy of Child Psychiatry, 12,* 59–71.

Kolvin, I., & Fundudis, T. (1981). Elective mute children: Psychological, development and background factors. *Journal of Child Psychology & Psychiatry, 22,* 219–232.

Krolian, E. B. (1988). Speech is silver, but silence is golden: Day hospital treatment of two electively mute children. *Clinical Social Work Journal, 16,* 355–377.

Kummer, R. (1953). Betrachtungen zum problem des freiwilligen Schweigens. *Zeitschrift fuer Forschung und Praxis, 5,* 79–83.

Kussmaul, A. (1877). Die Stoerungen der sprache. Ther. Leipzig: Vogel.

Labbe, E. E., & Williamson, D. A. (1984). Behavioral treatment of elective mutism: A review of the literature. *Clinical Psychology Review, 4,* 273–292.

Laybourne, P. C. (1979). Elective mutism. In J. D. Noshpitz (Ed.), *Basic Handbook of Child Psychiatry. Vol. 2: Disturbances in Development* (pp. 475–481). New York: Basic Books.

Mora, G., DeVault, S., & Schopler, E. (1962). Dynamics and psychotherapy of identical twins with elective mutism. *Journal of Child Psychology and Psychiatry, 3,* 41–52.

Parker, E. B., Olsen, T. F., & Throckmorton, M. C. (1960). Social casework with elementary school children who do not talk in school. *Social Work, 5,* 64–70.

Ruzicka, B. B., & Sackin, H. D. (1974). Elective mutism: The impact of the patient's silent detachment upon the therapist. *Journal of the American Academy of Child Psychiatry, 13,* 551–561.

Sanok, R. L., & Ascione, F. R. (1979). Behavioral interventions for elective mutism. *Child Behavior Therapy, 1,* 49–68.

Thomas, A., Chess, S., & Birch, H. G. (1968). *Temperment and behavior disorders in children.* New York: New York University Press.

Tramer, M. (1934). Elektiver Mutisms us bei Kindern. *Zeitschrift fur Kinderpsychiatrie, 1,* 30–35.

Wilkins, R. (1985). A comparison of elective mutism and emotional disorders in children. *British Journal of Psychiatry, 146,* 198–203.

42 / Typical and Atypical Eating Disorders in School-Age Children

Hans Steiner

The preparation of food, the act of eating, and the rituals associated with consumption are among the most powerful of human interactions. Throughout the life span, disturbances in our relationships with those most important to us often are accompanied by disturbances in how we perform the functions of preparing and ingesting food. Food and drink satisfy such immediate needs that it is quite easy to understand how these acts acquire surplus meaning. Food is perhaps the most powerful symbol of acceptance and love. The concrete act of handing down nourishment is easily turned into a symbol of the inculcation of values from one generation to the next. Thus eating and feeding easily become a battleground of conflicts between parent and child.

Developmentally, school-age children usually do not present the dramatic disorders that can be found in either the preschooler (such as pica or failure to thrive) or the adolescent (anorexia nervosa, bulimia). In this sense, typical eating disorders are rare among school-age children. However, the most recent research has helped us understand that many traits that later seem to put children at risk for developing eating disorders originate in the preschool years, persist through school age, and lead to problems as adolescence begins. The clinician has a unique opportunity to identify early risk in these children, monitor adequate functioning, and prevent future disability.

the currently available information on normative data on the development of eating behaviors).

Concerning the psychosocial aspects of eating, very few normative data are available, but I will draw on my clinical experience to point out some relevant factors. As with most behaviors in children of this age, eating is a fairly ritualistic activity, bound by concrete expectations and thinking. A child's repertoire of foods is limited; often considerable encouragement is required to persuade children to try new foods. Strong tastes are usually experienced as disgusting and are avoided. Children in this age group often have favorite foods, but they are fairly narrow in range. Often concrete ideas prevail about the specific effects of certain foods, such as: If it tastes bad it must be bad for you; if it tastes good it must be good for you. Family meals are more civilized than with preschool youngsters; school-age children are quite able to track and engage in dinner conversation. Still, parents of school-age children should be prepared for the occasional return to the messy eating styles of the preschool-age child. To school-age children, sharing and turn taking are important when it comes to dividing up dessert. Family dynamics around mealtime assume more and more the function of pairing the feeding process with the passing on of familial values. The ritual gathering of family around certain favorite foods often forms the nidus of later happy remembrances of childhood.

Developmental Aspects of Eating in the School-Age Child

By age 5, most children establish complete self-feeding at mealtimes. With increasing age, the number of mealtime-specific behaviors increases, while noneating behavior decreases (Hammer, 1992; see also that same chapter for a summary of

Definitions

Eating disorders represent clinical syndromes, where we observe the cooccurrence of pathological thoughts and emotions concerning appearance, eating and food, eating behavior that is deviant, and alterations in body composition and functioning that are the direct result of these symptoms. These disorders are classical "psycho-somatic" syndromes in the sense that psychological and somatic functioning are inextricably intertwined, affect each other profoundly, and need to be treated jointly to lead to permanent improvement. Classical eating disorders such as anorexia nervosa and bulimia clearly fit into this category, but so do food phobias and disturbances of eating based on delusional thinking. Obesity, in contrast, by itself does not, as the psychological component typical of anorexia, for example, is lacking.

Review of the Literature

Disturbances in appetite are extremely common in school-age children. Many illnesses and psychopathological disturbances are accompanied by altered regulation of hunger and satiety. All such problems need to be considered in the differential diagnosis of eating problems in this age group.

Some empirical studies are relevant to eating disorders in school-age children (Attie & Brooks-Gunn, 1989; Button, 1990; DiNicola, Roberts, & Oke, 1989; Fabian & Thompson, 1989; Hill, Weaver, & Blundell, 1990; Levine, Smolak, & Murnen, 1990; Maloney, McGuire, Daniels, & Specker, 1989; Marchi & Cohen, 1990; Shore & Porter, 1990; Slade, Dewey, Kiemle, & Newton, 1990; Stein & Reichert, 1990; Winkler & Vacc, 1989). All studies to date are methodologically flawed from the point of view of providing definitive information. Few employ a state-of-the-art, two-phase screening procedure consisting of a self-report index of disordered eating and a follow-up screening via a structured or unstructured clinical interview for those with high scores on the self-report instrument (Killen et al., 1992, 1993). Most of the studies report baseline data only, with no follow-up, thus putting in question the predictive validity of the categories of disordered eating.

Despite the flaws in the available studies, a fairly consistent picture can be gleaned from them. Throughout elementary school, children seem to be very aware of wanting to be thinner (45%). Thirty-seven percent try some form of weight loss and 6.9% score in the anorexic range on an adapted version of the Eating Attitude Test

(EAT). There were few significant differences between boys and girls: Both sexes were equally concerned. No further diagnostic follow-up is available, so the predictive validity of these high frequencies on the EAT is uncertain (Maloney et al., 1989). Findings such as these, common in the literature, suggest that the degree of concern among school-age children is so common as to be almost normative in this particular age group. Given that only a very small minority of these children will in fact develop eating disorders, additional factors must operate that influence some children to remain regressively preoccupied with weight and thinness, while others rather smoothly outgrow the preoccupations or, more precisely, do not manifest the preoccupation in eating disorders. Such a sequence is also suggested by the finding of our research group at Stanford (Hensala & Steiner, 1990) that a sample of normal school-age children showed significant degrees of body-image distortion on the Askevold body-image marking procedure, regardless of sex. Compared to adolescents without eating disorders, these distortions in body image were significantly larger. Again, this sequence suggests that body-image problems in children and adolescents are common but lead to problems in only a small proportion of normal children. Therefore, additional factors must be operating.

The factors suggested by the literature are: internalizing dimensions of pathology, problems in the family environment, and negative relationship to body (Attie & Brooks-Gunn, 1989); low self-esteem (Button, 1990); concerns about current shape (Levine, Smolak, & Murnen, 1990); depression, teasing history, and body esteem (Fabian & Thompson, 1989); onset of puberty and especially early sexual maturation (Killen et al., 1992); and maternal preoccupation with restricting dietary intake (Hill, Weaver & Blundell, 1990). These factors are diverse, and the list is by no means exhaustive. Many of them need replication and testing in prospective designs. But some of these factors—low self-esteem, negative relationship to body, concerns about current shape—seem to suggest that children who have problems with self-regulation (i.e., the ability to integrate multiple external and internal demands into a socially acceptable compromise) in fact are more vulnerable to developing eating disorders later. Cross-sectional studies of very young anorexics and bulimics with very short duration of illness confirm such an association (Steiner, 1990; Strober, 1980). Most likely several other factors are operating as well, such as special characteristics of the family.

Descriptions of concurrent family environments point to special characteristics, such as discomfort in discussing problems with parents (Larson, 1991); dietary concerns of mothers (Hill et al., 1990); and negative family characteristics comparable to those described by depressed children of their families (Thienemann & Steiner, 1993). The Stanford research group also studied the retrospective reports of mothers of eating-disordered patients on their feeding practices during infancy, and compared these to feeding practices with other siblings in the same family as well as similar reports in non–eating-disordered adolescents. Feeding practices were reported as constant regarding either sibling, but two factors differed between mothers of eating disorders and controls: the degree of reliance on scheduled feedings and the inappropriately early introduction of solids, suggesting that feeding was rigid and inappropriate at times. However, from our study it was also clear that not all children who were exposed to such feedings turned out to develop eating disorders (Steiner, Smith, & Rosenkrantz, 1991). This finding most likely means that an additional set of constitutional factors (among others) plays an important role in the development of eating problems. Our group has described the co-occurrence of special temperamental variables that distinguish groups of anorexic and bulimic adolescents. Anorexic patients exhibited characteristics more consistent with inhibition, anxiety, and control; while bulimic patients were more dysphoric, affectively labile, and less orderly in their daily routines (Shaw & Steiner, 1990). Killen's group also has identified affective lability as a risk factor for the development of bulimia (Killen et al., 1993). However, at this time, none of these factors has been tested in a truly adequate prospective design, following an adequate number of children. Only one available study has looked at the question of early childhood antecedents of eating disorders in a lagged design, where the different overlapping cohorts were followed prospectively for several years, and all three cohorts allowed the study of the entire range of childhood development from 0 to 18. This study found that maladaptive eating patterns

between the ages of 1 and 10 do seem to increase the likelihood of problems in adolescence. Picky eating and digestive problems seem to relate to preanorexic behavior. Pica and meals characterized by fighting in childhood, both indicating eating-related family struggles and problems in the self-regulation of eating, relate to bulimia (Marchi & Cohen, 1990).

Currently, our best information is that the classic eating disorders—anorexia nervosa and bulimia—are uncommon in the school-age group. In the Eating Disorders Clinic at Packard Children's Hospital at Stanford, we have evaluated approximately 900 patients in the past 14 years. Of these, about 10% were preadolescent children as assessed by Tanner Staging, ranging in age from 6 to 11 years. All of these children had either anorexia nervosa or unspecified eating disorders; there were no bulimic patients in this group. School-age children who were clinically diagnosable showed the same descriptive characteristics as older children with eating disorders, but their psychological characteristics were different. They were significantly more pseudomature and defensive than older patients and had fewer stressful life events prior to the onset of their eating disorder (Steiner & Sanders, 1994). This suggests that school-age children who develop eating disorders are perhaps less resilient, more compliant, and less resourceful, so that it takes only the threat of oncoming separation from the family to produce symptoms.

In the past, obesity in children, adolescents, and adults has been thought to reflect an eating disorder. The fourth edition of the *Diagnostic and Statistical Manual of Mental Disorders* (American Psychiatric Association, 1994) does not list obesity as an eating disorder. As only a few data that support such a classification at this point, this syndrome is not included in this chapter. (The reader is referred to the excellent summary chapters by Hammer, 1990 & 1993.) Voracious eating and shortened mealtimes have been described in obese individuals, but these are observed only in concurrent data sets, and it is not clear what drives what—that is, fat accumulation, the altered eating pattern, or vice versa. Currently obesity is seen as the result of decreased caloric expenditure and increased caloric intake in some patients (Maloney & Ruedisueli, 1993). Obese patients clearly expend fewer calories because they move less, but, again, it is not clear from the data as to whether this is an antecedent or a consequence of their body composition. There is some evidence that heritability of obesity is about 70 to 80%, as assessed in children adopted away at birth (Stunkard, Harris, Pedersen & McClearn, 1990). Such studies, however, are also incomplete, not having adequately controlled family characteristics of the adoptive set. But for the purposes of this discussion, such findings on heritability of obesity leave only a few cases as related to other factors, such as potential eating disorders. There is no question, though, that the obese child suffers a great deal of discrimination and ridicule in our society (Hammer, 1992). Such treatment of children leads to secondary complications in a high number of them—such as social stigma, ridicule, peer isolation, and rejection. From a psychiatric point of view, dysthymia, depression, and anxiety disorders such as social phobias may well be related to such treatment. The child psychiatrist needs to be ready to consult appropriately under these circumstances and guide the child and the parents to a more appropriate and not unnecessarily restrictive handling of the child's eating. It is possible that some forms of obesity may be the result of nonpurging bulimia (Maloney & Ruesdisueli, 1993; McCann & Agras, 1990), and *DSM-IV* now includes this syndrome as a new entity. There is some evidence that a subset of adult obese people have hyperphagia, not accompanied by purgation. This subset of "nonpurging" bulimics needs special attention and tracking, as their behavior will lead to obesity and usually will require treatment. In adults, such patients respond to the same interventions as do purging bulimics, with comparable success rates. In children, such interventions have not been tested systematically. In our Eating Disorders Program at Stanford, we have encountered some such patients and have treated them with limited success with behavioral interventions or tricyclic antidepressants. These children are an understudied group and deserve further attention.

Regarding school-age children who develop classic eating disorders, definitive information regarding their outcome is unavailable due to flaws in research designs (Fosson, Knibbs, Bryant-Waugh, & Lask, 1987; Hawley, 1985; Jacobs & Issacs, 1986; Swift, 1982). The literature is mixed, assigning either a worse or better outcome to the very young patient with an eating disorder. Our own clinical experience suggests that classifying eating disordered patients by Tanner Stage rather than chronological age is more useful in predicting outcome. Differentiating patients in this way separates those who react to the threat of puberty from those who experienced puberty, reacted to it, and regressed. As would be expected, there appears to be a difference in their respective courses. The patients developing anorexia earlier have a slower, longer course. This is not surprising, given our finding that such patients tend to be less resilient, less resourceful, and more defensive than older patients. They have in fact never faced the changes in their bodies induced by puberty, and they anticipatorily avert the experience altogether. This pattern of responses to the unfamiliar can be found throughout their course of illness and makes intervention difficult and prolonged. By contrast, postpubertal anorexic patients have experienced major changes in their lives, have struggled with them to some extent, and have then recoiled. Nevertheless, they have been able to acquire a certain amount of experience of dealing with the unfamiliar, which then comes in handy as they approach other problem areas of their lives in the course of illness. At 3-year follow-up, most of the postpubertal-onset anorexics do quite well, while prepubertal-onset ones are just beginning to struggle with some major issues in their lives. However, ultimately, on 8-year follow-up, a similar outcome is found in both age groups (Steiner & Sanders, 1994). Much of the different rates of recovery in the two groups seems to be related to the younger groups' need for lengthy preparation to face the problems related to their disorder, while the older group enters such an enterprise more readily and with much less encouragement and pressure.

CASE EXAMPLES

The following cases are representative of the kinds of eating disorders encountered in our clinic at Packard Children's Hospital at Stanford. We will discuss them briefly to provide concrete material for the clinician.

B.J., 7-year-old with Anorexia Nervosa: B.J. was a 7-year-old girl referred by her pediatrician for a 20% weight loss in 3 months. Approximately 8 months before the weight loss, the child began avoiding desserts. Subsequently, she progressively limited the size of her meals until she was eating only vegetables and fruit. She was intensely preoccupied with the fat content of foods as well as the healthiness of her own eating and that of others. She insisted that her abdomen was too big and needed reduction and was very concerned about children at her school who were overweight and being teased. At the culmination of her weight loss period, she was almost constantly exercising—swimming, running, and biking vigorously. Friendly requests by the parents, reassurances that she was not overweight, fell on deaf ears. Throughout this difficult time, the patient continued to do very well at school, obtaining As. However, what was increasingly apparent was that she was becoming progressively more isolated and withdrawn. At home, she began to withdraw from other family members and was highly critical of the dietary habits of her family, especially her older pubertal sister, whom she reduced to tears by calling a fat pig.

Precipitant for the current episode of anorexia nervosa was the death of the maternal grandmother by cancer and emaciation. The patient was very attached to her grandmother and witnessed her death. Family history was negative for other psychiatric illnesses. Her older sister seemed to have a mild depressive diathesis and, fairly typical of upper-class families, members of her family were weight and health conscious. Both parents were successful lawyers. The mother had worked part time but increased her work commitment to almost full time near the time of the patient's first hospitalization. On admission, the patient had a pronounced drive for thinness, both by clinical exam and Eating Disorders Inventory subscale, and had an active body image distortion of 32% on the Askevold measure and by clinical examination. She was extremely dissatisfied with her looks, despite the fact that she was drawn and emaciated, and she was constantly active. When asked how she would react to having to gain weight, she flat out refused and became very anxious and clingy, insisting on being held on her mother's lap. Later in therapy she revealed that one of her prime concerns regarding growing up was that she would be "too heavy and too big for Mummy's lap." In addition to these mentioned findings, psychometrics revealed a high trait anxiety score on the Spielberger Trait Anxiety Inventory—a measure of chronic levels of anxiety (64th percentile)—a moderate elevation on the Children's Defense Rating Scale—a measure of a child's tendency to defensively conceal information (12)—and an overall elevated Eating Disorder Inventory—a 8-subscale measure of the core features of eating disorders—score (39) with peaks on the drive for thinness, perfectionism, lack of interoceptive awareness, and maturity fears subscales. On the Defense Style Questionnaire, she showed a strong emphasis on reaction formation and pseudoaltruism as well as a moderate elevation of im-

mature defenses, such as passive aggressiveness, somatization, inhibition, and withdrawal.

The child was hospitalized on two occasions, once for initial weight rehabilitation, a second time for passive suicidal behavior on the anniversary of her grandmother's death. The multimodal treatment regimen, standard for our program and described previously (Palla & Litt, 1988; Steiner, 1982; Steiner, Mazer, & Litt, 1990) consisted of the following: (1) pediatric supervision of refeeding, weight gain, and medical vital sign stability; (2) behavioral program for weight gain, rewarding gains between 0.2 and 0.5 kilograms per day and prescribing bedrest and isolation for weight loss; (3) individual and family psychotherapy, based on psychodynamic principles; and (4) participation in the milieu program while hospitalized. This included daily groups, occupational and recreational therapy, and a twice-weekly special eating disorders group. The goal of the treatment is to increase weight at a stable rate, while at the same time exploring with family and patient relevant, contributing, interpersonal, and intrapsychic factors that either precipitated or maintained the eating disorder. This program is continued as an outpatient program on a weekly basis.

B.J.'s response in terms of weight gain and medical stabilization during the first hospitalization was rapid, as is usually the case in our program. As with many patients in this age group, progress in terms of the family's and the patients' understanding of what brought about the problem lagged far behind the rate of improvement in weight. This fact usually leads to a renewed crisis in the near future, and in this case the patient was rehospitalized within 6 months after discharge. During this second hospitalization, we were able to more fully understand her reaction to her grandmother's death: B. J. felt that she needed her grandmother around to take care of her, since her mother was so busy at work, and she was worried that she would not adequately be cared for with her grandmother gone. The mother had indeed found it necessary to work part time outside of the home just prior to her mother's death, and there was some discussion about her even increasing her work hours to full time. After 9 months B.J. returned to normal functioning in the home and at school, resuming her former social activities. Her weight was normal for age and height, and she showed no more body concerns. Occasionally she commented on the eating habits of others, but not intrusively so. There was also a shift in her defense style: The peak in the internalizing neurotic defenses remained, but there was a decrease in immature defenses to age-inappropriately low levels. Similarly, she showed an age-inappropriate peak in mature defenses, which she emphasized to a degree compatible with young adulthood. Defensiveness remained high on both occasions of testing. We took this to mean that the patient had returned to her premorbid level of adjustment. During the treatment, B.J. had expressed enough of her concerns about dependency to grieve more appropriately for the death of her grandmother, to no longer feel required to be symptomatic in terms of her eating. However, she had not substantially altered her adaptive stance vis-à-vis her parents: She remained intent on pleasing them even more than before and was even more hesitant to bring up conflict and controversy. Both parents and patient decided at this point that they had benefited sufficiently from treatment and terminated, despite our pointing out that B.J. retained many indicators of a pseudomature adjustment and remained at risk for developing eating problems during adolescence. We felt that she had not acquired any new means of negotiating conflict and handling stressful events, and that she had simply returned to her old adaptive stance and had increased her efforts at being successful at it, to the detriment of her own needs. In all probability, such a stance would not allow her to navigate successfully through the treacherous waters of adolescence. We acknowledged that much discomfort had been raised by our bringing up the issue of mother's employment, but we saw this as an opportunity to work on new ways of resolving conflict in the family, prior to the advent of puberty, where even more complex issues would be raised. Neither parent saw any alternative course of action necessary to their current plan. The patient agreed. Both parents were somewhat dismissive of the patient's initial complaint regarding mother's work hours, emphasizing that the patient was being taken care of properly and that the treatment team was overly concerned. Both parents were unable to take the worries seriously and explore further the origin of B.J.'s feelings, however irrational they deemed them to be.

This patient's presentation is fairly typical of eating disorders in this age group. Her course of treatment is somewhat atypical in that the parents prematurely ended treatment despite our warnings about possible future risks. In our experience, such a patient is very likely to experience relapse in puberty.

A.S., 6-year-old with an Anorexia Nervosa–by-Proxy: A.S. was a 6-year-old girl whose mother presented her daughter to the clinic. In the preliminary screening information, mother completed a developmental inventory and a symptom checklist. On these, all items suggesting anorexia nervosa were endorsed. No family history was given regarding psychiatric illness. On presentation in the clinic, we encountered a somewhat anxious child who had some problems separating from her mother. Her weight was slightly below the ex-

pected range for her age. When mother recounted her symptoms in the presence of the child, the patient passively listened. Once separated, she demonstrated no drive for thinness, body dissatisfaction, or body image distortion. More notable was the mother's appearance and eating history. She worked as a model in an agency and had at least one course of treatment for anorexia nervosa. Currently she was not symptomatic, but she reacted to her child's eating behavior in an exaggerated and projective fashion. The mother's interpersonal relationships were quite unstable and unsatisfying. Professionally, she was not as successful as she had been in previous years and financial problems impacted the life of the family. The child had some problems with school avoidance, for which a treatment referral was made.

Five years later the patient reappeared in clinic, again referred by her mother, who had diagnosed the child as having anorexia. The child had some but not all diagnostic features of the illness: She was at the 73rd percentile of ideal body weight and was premenstrual. Tanner Stage was 2 for breast (showing some budding), 1 for genitalia (showing prepubertal status). On a Slade Observer Rating (a 22-item standardized observer scale of eating behavior, consisting of 3 factors: restriction, purgation, and activity level) of her eating, she scored 12 (14 ± 6 characterizes an anorexic patient). Elements of restriction and excessive exercise were present. She had no body image distortions or drive for thinness on either clinical examination or by Eating Disorders Inventory. She professed to welcome weight gain, but prescriptions of weight gain (between 1–2 pounds per week is expected in most patients and easily achievable) in our clinic by the pediatric staff did not result in such in the course of 3 weeks. There was no evidence of purgation. She was highly defensive and protective of her overly close relationship with her mother. The mother herself was highly symptomatic in terms of her own eating disorder but was not in treatment. The stressors in the household had worsened considerably. The mother was on Aid to Families with Dependent Children and had declared bankruptcy. She had several live-in boyfriends who exploited her financially, but there was no evidence of abuse or sexual misconduct. The patient was very much aware of all the problems but steadfastly refused to attribute any responsibility to her mother. She, like her mother, saw herself and her mother as victims of the situation. After our referral, they had terminated the treatment for school avoidance for financial reasons after 3 months. Once again they were engaged in treatment but were lost to follow-up when they dropped out after 3 weeks. A referral to Child Protective Services resulted in no further action on behalf of the child.

In this case, the patient clearly mirrored the mother's eating disorder symptoms. The 5 years between contact showed how the child internalized the mother's psychopathology, but only to the degree that she fulfilled some of the criteria for anorexia. In cases of atypical eating disorders, it is important that the clinician keep in mind the possibility of parental pathology. This case bordered on a Munchausen's-by-proxy syndrome. We did not feel that it was such because the mother, although worried about her child's eating, did nothing actively to curtail the child's eating or generate symptoms.

T.M., 9-year-old with Posttraumatic Stress Disorder, Conversion Discord, and Separation Anxiety Disorder: T.M.'s case shows the overlap between conversion disorders and anorexia. This child was a first-generation American of Iranian parents who had fled their country after the Islamic revolution. She was conceived and born in this country, the youngest in a family of 7 girls and 3 boys. Her family kept a very traditional Muslim household, while the patient was fully acculturated. The presenting problem was one of failure to grow and make age-appropriate weight gain. She had lost only about 5 pounds at referral, but her height had begun to fall off the growth curve. Fourteen months prior to the clinic visit, the patient suddenly avoided all chewable food for no apparent reason. She seemed fearful of it. She would ingest only liquids and pureed food, but just prior to referral, she restricted herself to water only. The family noticed that she was quite anxious and jumpy; her parents were asked to keep her home from school because she was so disruptive in class. At the time of the clinic visit, she was being tutored at home. At night, she was extremely fearful and refused to sleep alone. Thus she slept in her mother's bed. She was vigilant about other people's eating, would join the family at the table and watch intently what everybody ate, but would not herself partake. She was preoccupied with not eating, but the encouragement and bribery the family offered were not sufficient to motivate her to eat. The mother's pride was considerably injured at the thought that her daughter would not eat her special ethnic foods, even the ones that she prepared specially for the child. The patient repeatedly was observed to chew food, then surreptitiously spit it into a napkin and dispose of it. There also was a history of fears of heights, elevators, and escalators. There was no evidence of panic attacks.

On examination, T.M. was a sad and anxious-appearing child who clung intensely to her mother and on the first visit and refused to be examined. Over the course of 4 weeks, we obtained all the relevant information. She did not have any drive for thinness and body image distortion, but she did have pronounced maturity fears. Trait anxiety was high (STAI-X-2: 82nd percentile), and she was very defensive (MCSDS-26). Her Eating Disorders Inventory showed the following elevations in the anorectic norm: perfectionism, interpersonal distrust, and maturity fears.

The patient described repetitive and intrusive thoughts about ingesting solids, reported nightmares of choking, and manifested hyperarousal around rituals of eating, such as family meals and food advertisements on television. We diagnosed T. M. as suffering from posttraumatic stress disorder and began a series of exploratory interviews centering on possible traumata in the child's life. Sexual abuse was ruled out, and after 5 sessions, the patient revealed a sequence of events that she had previously kept from the parents because she felt guilty and responsible. While baby-sitting her 2-year-old nephew, she had given the child a piece of hard candy. The child aspirated and became cyanotic. At this moment, the child's mother entered, performed a Heimlich maneuver, and saved the child. Our patient watched from an adjacent room, paralyzed and helpless, certain that she had caused the little boy's death. Her mother did not suspect the patient as the source of the candy, but thought the child had found it on the floor. Following the Heimlich maneuver, a vessel in the boy's pharynx ruptured and he bled profusely. By this time, many family members were present and much confusion and commotion ensued. Finally, an ambulance arrived and took the boy to safety. Our patient began avoiding solids 2 weeks after the incident.

Treatment was uncomplicated catharsis, aided by some focused parent intervention. After 6 months and a desensitization program, the patient was back in school, performing well, eating, and growing normally.

This case superficially presented very similar to classic anorexia nervosa. The child clearly had a premorbid anxious disposition, a feature often found in anorexia nervosa. However, the mental content of her food avoidance was quite different from an eating disorder altogether. The cultural dimensions of the case delayed a quick diagnosis. Her family was not well acculturated and tolerated her socially phobic responses too readily because they fit with some of their cultural expectations for women. The child had a very traditional relationship with her parents, and her guilt about her "transgression" also played a role in the late detection of the problem. The family's social isolation also contributed in other ways: as they were not accustomed to seeking mental health services or even looking for psychiatric explanations of behavioral difficulties, there was some delay in bringing the child to proper attention of specialists, and her symptoms probably coalesced to classic posttraumatic stress disorder.

Future Directions

It is clear that eating disturbances, even some classical ones, do appear among school-age children, although they are rare. More important is the fact that many other psychopathological and pediatric syndromes can mimic such disorders and need to be ruled out. Furthermore, there is some indication that in this age group, children at risk for later developing eating disorders can be identified and possible future problems prevented. While currently information to do this with great certainty is lacking, the prevention of eating disorders is a very active area of study, and in the near future, much more useful data should be available (Steiner, Sanders, & Ryst, 1995).

REFERENCES

American Psychiatric Association (1994). *Diagnostic and statistical manual of mental disorders* (4th ed.). Washington, DC: Author.

Attie, I., & Brooks-Gunn, J. (1989). Development of eating problems in adolescent girls: A longitudinal study. *Developmental Psychology, 25,* 70–79.

Button, E. (1990). Self-esteem in girls aged 11–12: Baseline findings from a planned prospective study of vulnerability to eating disorders. *Journal of Adolescence, 13,* 407–413.

DiNicola, V. F., Roberts, N., & Oke, L. (1989). Eating and mood disorders in young children. *Psychiatric Clinics in North America, 12 (4),* 873–893.

Fabian, L., & Thompson, J. K. (1989). Body image and eating disturbances in young females. *International Journal of Eating Disorders, 8,* 63–74.

Fosson, A., Knibbs, J., Bryant-Waugh, R., & Lask, B. (1987). Early onset anorexia nervosa. *Archives of Disease in Childhood, 62,* 114–118.

Hammer, L. D. (1990). Obesity. In M. Green & R. Haggerty (Eds.), *Ambulatory pediatrics.* Philadelphia: W.B. Saunders.

Hammer, L. D. (1992). The development of eating behavior in childhood. *Pediatric Clinics of North America, 39,* 379–394.

Hammer, L. D. (1993). Child and adolescent obesity. In R. E. Behrman (Ed.), *Textbook of Pediatrics, Update 1* (pp. 1–11). Philadelphia: W.B. Saunders.

Hawley, R. M. (1985). The outcome of anorexia nervosa in younger subjects. *British Journal of Psychiatry, 146,* 657–660.

Hensala, J., & Steiner, H. (1990). Body image distortions occur as a function of age rather than diagnosis. *Scientific Proceedings, 37th Annual Meeting of the American Academy of Child and Adolescent Psychiatry, 6,* 51.

Hill, A. J., Weaver, C., & Blundell, J. E. (1990). Dieting concerns of 10-year old girls and their mothers. *British Journal of Clinical Psychology, 29,* 346–348.

Jacobs, B. W., & Issacs, S. (1986). Pre-pubertal anorexia nervosa: A retrospective controlled study. *Journal of Child Psychiatry and Psychology, 27,* 237–250.

Killen, J. D., Hayward, C., Litt, I., Hammer, L. D., Wilson, D. M., Miner, B., Taylor, C. B., Varady, A., & Shisslak, C. (1992). Is puberty a risk factor for eating disorders? *American Journal of Diseases of Children, 146,* 323–325.

Killen, J. D., Taylor, C. B., Hammer, L. D., Litt, I., Wilson, D. M., Rich, T., Hayward, C., Simmonds, B., Kraemer, H., & Verady, A. (1993). An attempt to modify unhealthful eating attitudes and weight regulation practices of young adolescent girls. *International Journal of Eating Disorders, 13,* 369–384.

Larson, B. J. (1991). Relationship of family communication patterns to eating disorder inventory scores in adolescent girls. *Journal of the American Dietetic Association, 91,* 1065–1067.

Levine, M. P., Smolak, L., & Murnen, S. K. (1990). Dieting and disordered eating during early and middle adolescence: Do the influences remain the same? *International Journal of Eating Disorders, 9,* 501–512.

Maloney, M. J., McGuire, J., Daniels, S. R., & Specker, B. (1989). Dieting behavior and eating attitudes in children. *Pediatrics, 84 (3),* 482–489.

Maloney, M. J., & Ruedisueli, G. (1993). The epidemiology of eating problems in nonreferred children and adolescents. *Child and Adolescent Psychiatric Clinics of North America, 2,* 1–13.

Marchi, M., & Cohen, P. (1990). Early childhood eating behaviors and adolescent eating disorders. *Journal of the American Academy of Child and Adolescent Psychiatry, 29,* 112–117.

McCann, U. D., & Agras, W. S. (1990). Successful treatment of non-purging bulimia nervosa with desipramine: A double blind placebo-controlled study. *American Journal of Psychiatry, 147,* 1509–1513.

Palla, B., & Litt, I. (1988). Medical complications of eating disorders in adolescents. *Pediatrics, 81,* 613–623.

Shaw, R. S., & Steiner, H. (1990). Stability of temperament measure during state disturbances. *Scientific Proceedings, 37th Annual Meeting of the American Academy of Child and Adolescent Psychiatry, 6.*

Shore, R. A., & Porter, J. E. (1990). Normative and reliability data for 11 to 18 year olds on the Eating Disorder Inventory. *International Journal of Eating Disorders, 9,* 201–207.

Slade, P. D., Dewey, M. E., Kiemle, G., & Newton, T. (1990). Update on SCANS: A screening instrument for identifying individuals at risk of developing an eating disorder. *International Journal of Eating Disorders, 9,* 583–584.

Stein, D. M., & Reichert, P. (1990). Extreme dieting behaviors in early adolescence. *Journal of Early Adolescence, 10,* 108–121.

Steiner, H. (1982). Anorexia nervosa. *Pediatrics in Review, 4,* 125–129.

Steiner, H. (1990). Defense styles in eating disorders. *International Journal of Eating Disorders, 9,* 141–151.

Steiner, H., Sanders, M., & Ryst, Erika. (1995). Precursors and risk factors of juvenile eating disorders. In H.-C. Steinhausen (Ed.), *Eating disorders in adolescence* (pp. 95–125). New York: de Gruyter.

Steiner, H., Mazer, C., & Litt, I. F. (1990). Compliance and outcome in anorexia nervosa. *Western Journal of Medicine, 153,* 133–139.

Steiner, H., & Sanders, M. (1994). *Psychopathologic characteristics of prepubertal anorexics.* Unpublished manuscript.

Steiner, H., Smith, C., Rosenkrantz, R., & Litt, I. F. (1991). The early care and feeding of anorexics. *Child Psychiatry & Human Development, 21,* 163–167.

Strober, M. (1980). Personality and symptomatological features in young, nonchronic anorexia nervosa patients. *Journal of Psychosomatic Research, 24,* 353–359.

Stunkard, A. J., Harris, J. R., Pedersen, N. L., & McClearn, G. E. (1990). The body-mass index of twins who have been reared apart. *New England Journal of Medicine, 322,* 1483–1487.

Swift, W. J. (1982). The long-term outcome of early onset anorexia nervosa: A critical review. *Journal of the American Academy of Child Psychiatry, 21,* 38–46.

Thienemann, M., & Steiner, H. (1993). Family environment of eating disordered and depressed adolescents. *International Journal of Eating Disorders, 14,* 43–48.

Winkler, M. R., & Vacc, N. A. (1989). Eating-disordered behavior of girls. *Elementary School Guidance & Counseling, 24,* 119–127.

43 / The Array of Phobic Disorders

John J. Stine

Background

When discussing the phobic disorders, there can be considerable confusion for two reasons. First, a variety of terms have been used for describing different types of phobias. Second, phobias have been treated as part of the symptoms of a more general anxiety disorder in some nosological systems and as a separate, specific diagnostic entity in other systems.

In this chapter, the term *simple phobia* is used to describe a specific disorder characterized as an isolated fear of a single, specific object that is persistent and intense enough to interfere with normal functioning (in contrast to common childhood fears) and that causes the patient to avoid the feared object. The patient does not specifically suffer from a fear of separation (as in separation anxiety disorder), a fear of having a panic attack (as in panic disorder with or without agoraphobia), a fear of strangers (as in avoidant disorder), or a fear of embarassment or shyness in a social situation (as in social phobia). Separation anxiety disorder, panic disorder, and avoidant disorders are discussed in separate chapters. Simple phobia is the main subject of this chapter; social phobia is treated as one of its special variants.

HISTORY OF THE DISORDER

The term *phobia* has been in common usage for many centuries to describe a feeling of fear characterized by dread and horror. With its adjectival ending, it had been used to describe voluminous lists of feared objects and situations during the era when psychiatrists spent much effort in cataloging and attempting to classify emotional disorders. For many years, however, phobias were not uniformly considered to be discrete psychopathological disorders but part of the diffuse symptomatology of many disorders, such as neuresthenia and anxiety neurosis.

In 1909, Sigmund Freud made a major conceptual step forward when he published the first extensive case history of a phobic child. This was important both as a landmark clinical discription and as a theoretical statement about the relationship between phobia and unconscious mental conflicts involving the Oedipus complex: In addition, it was an important nosological advance because Freud conceptualized phobia as a disorder distinct from the anxiety neurosis and caused by psychological factors. Despite the fact that Freud made this nosological distinction at the beginning of this century, anxiety disorders of childhood continued to be classified under the general term *anxiety neurosis* until the publication of the third edition of the *Diagnostic and Statistical Manual of Mental Disorders (DSM-III)* in 1980 by the American Psychiatric Association. Phobias were so classified largely because of the influence of psychoanalytic theory, which conceptualized different types of childhood anxiety disorders as symptom variants of a single, underlying neurotic disorder stemming from unresolved oedipal conflicts.

Beginning with *DSM-III*, however, anxiety disorders of childhood have been divided into overanxious disorder, separation anxiety disorder, and avoidant disorder. Phobia has been conceptualized as a totally separate disorder that can be diagnosed at any age, using essentially identical diagnostic criteria. This change was made in an attempt to remove any theoretical bias about the etiology of these conditions and to encourage the application of an epidemiological and medical model to the study of anxiety in childhood.

In some ways this has been a useful advance. For example, it has given us valuable information about developmental, phenomenological, and longitudinal aspects of different types of anxiety. However, researchers have repeatedly found a high degree of overlap between symptoms of anxiety disorders and a high degree of comorbidity among the anxiety states. Therefore, it still remains an open question as to whether the anxiety disorders are symptom variants of a single psychological or biological disorder whose expression is determined by other psychological and environmental variables.

COMPARATIVE NOSOLOGY

Descriptive Nosology: Currently, phobic disorders are characterized by the presence of anxiety that is experienced when the person confronts a feared object or situation. These disorders differ from common fears in that the phobic patient also seeks to avoid the feared object.

Confusion exists in child development, academic psychology, and clinical psychiatry literatures because different authors use terms such as phobia, phobic reactions, fears, and anxieties as if they were interchangeable. In modern psychiatric usage, phobic disorders are characterized by anxiety that is experienced when the person confronts a feared object or situation. According to the *APA Psychiatric Glossary* (1969), phobia is defined as an obsessive, persistent, unrealistic, and intense fear of an object or situation. These disorders differ from common fears in that the phobic patient also seeks to avoid the feared object. Similarly, in a more recent definition, the third revised edition of the *Diagnostic and Statistical Manual (DSM-III-R;* APA, 1987), simple (or specific) phobia is an excessive, unrealistic, persistent fear of a circumscribed object or situation, exposure to which produces anticipatory anxiety and/or an anxiety response. The feared object is avoided or endured with intense anxiety.

The fourth edition of the *Diagnostic and Statistical Manual (DSM-IV;* APA, 1994) further clarifies diagnostic criteria in several ways. First, the nature of the phobia is made more precise by the use of the diagnostic term *Specific Phobia* and the elimination of "Simple Phobia" from the nosology. This emphasizes that the phobic response is to clearly discernible and circumscribed stimuli (Criterion A). Second, the immediate nature of the anxiety response is stressed (Criterion B). Third, it recognizes that children, unlike most adolescents and adults, may not have the capacity to recognize that their fear is excessive or unreasonable (Criterion C) and may not have the capacity to recognize or describe themselves as anxious; they may react instead by crying, freezing, clinging, or having tantrums (Criterion B).

This definition is consonant with the definition of phobia used by many behaviorists. For example, Marks (1983), cited by Morris and Kratochwill (1983), defines phobia as a subcategory of fear that is out of proportion to demands of the situation, cannot be explained or reasoned away, is beyond voluntary control, and leads to avoidance of the feared situation.

The psychoanalytic definition of the term *phobia* emphasizes the same phenomenological criteria of intense, irrational anxiety and an intense need to avoid the phobic object or situation. However, in addition, psychoanalysts view the overt symptoms of phobia more broadly as manifestations of an anxiety neurosis that is generated by unresolved conflicts of the Oedipus complex as well as by preexisting, unresolved preoedipal problems that may foster neurotic development. Moreover, psychoanalysts view the development of a phobia as the product of a typical constellation of ego defenses against the emergence into consciousness of "forbidden" instinctual impulses, fantasies, and feelings. These include the defenses of externalization, displacement, projection, reversal, and avoidance, which will be discussed in more detail later in this chapter. In contrast, the term *fear* generally is used to describe normal, age-appropriate reactions to real or imagined dangers; *phobia* is used to describe a pathological degree of anxiety about situations or objects that are avoided. It is important to note, however, that, as mentioned, some authors may use these terms interchangeably.

Finally, some patients may develop "phobic reactions" or symptoms as part of the clinical picture of more pervasive and more severe disorders, such as mood disorders, pervasive developmental disorders, or borderline personality disorders. These reactions may have the same phenomenology or psychodynamics as a classical phobia but should not be the primary diagnosis. It is also not always clear from a clinical or theoretical point of view whether such reactions should be diagnosed as a comorbid state (and placed on Axis I in *DSM-III-R*) or whether they should be viewed as part of the more pervasive emotional disturbance.

Developmental Issues in Nosology: It has been repeatedly documented that children suffer from multiple, often transient fears from early childhood through adolescence and that these fears are nearly universally prevalent. Although most researchers and clinicians refer to these phenomena as normal fears and worries, it is useful to remember that some psychodynamically oriented clinicians may refer to them as normal or developmentally appropriate phobic reactions. These fears include the fears of the dark, of monsters, or of animals that are seen commonly in children between the ages of 2 and 6 years old. Psychoanalysts often refer to them as normal phobic reactions because they view these fears as derivatives of the normal working through of the oedipal and preoedipal conflicts, using the same intrapsychic mechanisms as a phobic disorder but in the service of healthy, normal development.

EPIDEMIOLOGICAL DATA

Simple phobias are regarded as common in the general population, but people with this condition rarely come to clinical attention unless their symptoms are severe and markedly impair functioning. Agras et al. (1969), for example, studied a random population of 325 adults and children, of whom 7.5% suffered from phobias. Only 0.2% of that population was severely functionally impaired by phobic anxiety and relatively few of them had ever sought any form of treatment. In contrast, 74.5% of the phobic probands were found to be mildly disabled.

Representative studies of child populations disclose a prevalence of simple phobia ranging from between 2.4 and 4.3 to 9.2%, while social phobia had a prevalence of about 1% (Anderson, Williams, McGee, & Silva, 1987; Costello, 1989; Kashani & Ovraschel, 1990). In adolescent populations, the prevalence of simple phobia ranged from $3.6 \pm \frac{1}{2}$% with a 2.9:1 female-to-male ratio (MGee et al., 1990). All of these studies agree that girls have about twice the prevalence rate of boys for these disorders.

The majority of phobias have their onset in childhood and run a mild, chronic course; in general, the prevalence decreases with advancing age. Burke, Burke, Regier, and Rae (1990) examined the reported age at onset of phobic disorders in a large cohort of five community populations, using data from the National Institutes of Mental Health Epidemiologic Catchment Area program. Using life table survival methods to calculate hazard rates, they found that the rate of onset of phobias (combining agoraphobia, social phobia, and simple phobia began to rise dramatically in early childhood and that the highest hazard rate was between 5 to 9 years of age. Despite this, the mean onset was at about 13 years of age for both sexes, indicating a large number of phobias also begin in adulthood. This apparent contradiction can be explained by examining data from Agras et al.'s epidemiological study (1969). The study indicates that, while most types of phobias do begin in childhood, fears and phobias of crowds, death, illness, and separation frequently begin in adulthood and are quite prevalent in middle age. In addition, social phobias tend to begin in late latency and early adolescence.

There is also general agreement that fears are quite common in children of all ages. One classic epidemiological study (Jersild, Markey, & Jersild, 1933) found that the vast majority of normal children between 5 and 12 years of age suffered from at least one fear; boys usually were afraid of bodily injury while girls usually were afraid of the dark, solitude, and strange sights or noises. In another study, Lapouse and Monk (1959) found that mothers of 43% of 6- to 12-year-olds reported that their children had many (over 7) fears and worries. More recently, Bell-Dolan et al. (1990) found that between 11.3 and 22.6% of children between 5 and 18 years reported subclinical phobic symptoms (fears of crowds, heights, the dark, insects, etc.) without being sufficiently disturbed to be diagnosed as suffering from a phobic disorder. The 10 most common fears reported in several studies were being hit by a car, not being able to breathe, a bombing attack, getting burned in a fire, falling from a high place, burglars, earthquakes, death, snakes, and getting poor grades (Bernstein & Borchardt, 1991).

Some data indicate that the prevalence of fears may be influenced by population variables. For example, Lapouse and Monk (1959) found a greater prevalence of fears in girls (50%) than in boys (36%), in 6- to 8-year-olds (48%) than in 9- to 12-year-olds (37%), in black children (63%) than in white children (44%), and in poor children (50%) than in middle-class ones (36%). Finally, the presence of multiple fears and worries did not seem to be correlated with other forms of psychopathology. (See also Fyer et al., 1990.)

Both clinically and for research purposes, normal multiple fears are distinguished from a phobic disorder by the degree of impairment in daily functioning and in the severity and degree of distress felt by the patient.

Clinical Presentation and Diagnostic Assessment

OVERT SIGNS/SYMPTOMS

The child with a specific phobia typically presents with the sudden onset of severe phobic anxiety or the sudden intensification of preexisting anxiety. In many cases with an acute onset, the phobic anxiety is preceded by a variable period of nonspecific anxiety more typical of overanxious disorder of childhood. In Freud's famous case description "A Phobia in a Five-Year-Old Child," for example, Little Hans had a nightmare and had an episode of separation anxiety while taking a walk with his nursemaid in which he suddenly began to cry and insisted on returning home to be comforted by his mother. This occurred several days before he became overwhelmed with a specific fear of being bitten by a horse to the extent that he refused to leave the house (Freud, 1909/1963).

Like Little Hans, children with specific phobias present with the following diagnostic signs and symptoms:

1. Persistent fear of a circumscribed specific stimulus (object or situation) other than fears of a panic attack. In social phobia, the child specifically fears humiliation and embarrassment in certain social situations, such as reciting in front of the class at school, participating in sports events, or going to birthday parties.
2. During some phase of the disturbance, exposure to the specific phobic stimulus almost always provokes an immediate anxiety response. This diagnostic criteria is usually best elicited while taking the initial history from the child's parents, who almost always go through a period of trying to force the child to confront the phobic object. Often the child's reaction of crying, panic, and avoidance in response to this maneuver convinces parents of the need for professional intervention. This part of the history needs to be taken with great tact and sensitivity, as some parents may feel guilty and defensive about having tried to force their child to confront the object.
3. The object or situation is totally avoided or endured only with intense anxiety. Children characteristically cry, tremble, look acutely unhappy, sad, or distressed, plead with parents to remove them from the phobic situation. Or they may seek to run away, as when a child has a dog or cat phobia. As stressed in *DSM-IV* (APA, 1994), some

children may freeze, cling to caregivers, or have tantrums. They also may suffer from severe anticipatory anxiety, ruminating and spend sleepless nights worrying about how to avoid phobic objects and situations. Although some children can be intimidated, forced, or persuaded to endure the phobic situation, they invariably report both severe anticipatory anxiety and severe anxiety while encountering the phobic object. This is an important diagnostic distinction from overanxious disorder, in which the chronically worried child's anticipatory anxiety may decrease and even become extinguished with continued exposure to the feared situation (Beidel, 1991).

4. The fear and avoidant behavior significantly interferes with normal routines, social activities, and/ or relationships with others. This is important but not totally reliable criteria in distinguishing between a collection of fears and a phobic disorder. For example, some severely phobic children superficially appear to be functioning normally because their parents actively assist them in totally avoiding phobic objects, even to the extent of altering the family's lifestyle. Such parents may themselves be fearful, phobic individuals who use denial and avoidance as major coping devices in their own lives. Such children often are brought to clinical attention because they suffer from a comorbid disorder or are going through an acute crisis, such as an acute social phobia in school that cannot be rationalized away in the usual manner.

5. The phobic patient recognizes that his or her fear is excessive or unreasonable. This criterion is not always useful with younger children whose relatively undeveloped capacities for self-observation may be further compromised by severe anxiety, sometimes of paniclike proportion: They may initially insist that school is a dangerous place, that dogs can really bite, or that heights can be dangerous. Part of the intitial therapeutic process with such children may involve providing them with enough emotional support so that they can be helped to see the excessive nature of their fears.

6. For both children and adolescents, *DSM-IV* (APA, 1994) indicates that the duration of the disorder must be at least 6 months to establish the diagnosis and that the disorder not be better explained by the presence of other anxiety disorders, such as obsessive compulsive disorder, separation anxiety disorder, or posttraumatic stress disorder. This issue will be discussed further in the section on differential diagnosis.

RELATIONSHIP TO OTHER DISORDERS

Because of the very high prevalence in the general population of fears, phobias, and other anxiety disorders, it is reasonable to hypothesize a high statistical association between phobias and many other forms of psychopathology in both child and adult populations. This association has been substantiated in a number of population studies.

At least two other, more specific relationships seem to exist. First, at least 30% of phobias in a general adult population are associated with panic disorder, mostly because of linkage between agoraphobia and panic disorder (Weissman & Merikangas, 1986). This association is not directly applicable to child populations, however, because of the later average age of onset for both of these disorders. Second, there is an often-noted clinical pattern in which children may suffer from some or many of the symptoms of overanxious disorder of childhood both prior to the outbreak or after the remission of a phobic disorder. This fact is consonant with both psychoanalytic and biological etiological theories: In both conceptual models, a phobia is but one of several possible manifestations of a more global, underlying problem that generates maladaptive levels of anxiety.

PATTERNS OF PEER RELATIONSHIPS

Children with phobias traditionally are described as functioning very well as long as their phobic anxieties are not mobilized. When comfortable, they can be friendly, outgoing, and academically and socially successful. This is especially true with the many children who suffer from multiple fears or mild phobic disorders, particularly in early childhood through midlatency.

With advancing age, however, children with multiple, severe fears and several anxiety disorders may become severely incapacitated both socially and academically, depending on the degree to which their anxieties cause them to avoid important life experiences. For example, Kashani and Orvaschel (1990) found that 8-year-old children with anxiety disorders and normal controls had similar patterns of peer and social relationships and similar rates of success. In contrast, 17-year-olds with anxiety disorders had significantly poorer peer relationships and much higher rates of problems with their families than did normal controls. Moreover, as anxious children move into adolescence, they show fewer fears of strangers and separation experiences but increasing fears about adequacy and interpersonal and social relationships.

Descriptively, children with phobias and other anxiety disorders can show two major pathways of personality development. In the first, phobic children may become increasingly dependent, demanding, clinging, and irritable with their families. Their personality frequently becomes constricted with the passage of time; as a result, they often become sensitive, begin to avoid play and competitive situations, and develop compliant, dependent, and passive personality traits. Many times a sense of hopelessness and neurotically based anergy leads to a picture of coexisting depression. In the second pathway, children seek to master their fears and phobias by aggressive, maladaptive behaviors, plunging headlong into situations that they formerly feared and avoided. They gradually suppress and then repress their fears and may develop a neurotic behavior disorder that utilizes counterphobic defense mechanisms. These are discussed later.

PATTERNS OF PLAY

Children with phobic disorders may show several characteristic play patterns that serve an intrapsychic, adaptive function. One of the many normal functions of play is an attempt to master fears and internal conflicts by repeated symbolic reenactments in which the children repeat actively in play what they fear to experience passively in real life (A. Freud, 1936). From the time a toddler begins to acquire the cognitive capacity to utilize symbolism, the psychodynamically informed observer can readily observe characteristic play patterns that help the child to master fears, from using dolls to reenact visits to the doctor to dramatic fantasy play about monsters, murderers, and kidnappers. Depending on the level of anxiety and extent of the disorder, children with phobias often reenact the feared situation in a driven, repetitive manner. In contrast to the normal child, repetitive play does not help phobic children to master their anxiety symbolically and emotionally: instead, their play has a repetitive, unsatisfying quality because it provides only a par-

tial discharge of feelings instead of gradual psychic mastery and closure.

Children with higher levels of anxiety may attempt to cope by total avoidance of the phobic object or situation in word, fantasy, and play, seeking a mental universe totally free of phobic anxiety. In play therapy, such children may flood the session with copious symbolic play activity that totally avoids their real problem and that can serve as a formidable resistance to the psychotherapeutic process unless confronted and interpreted actively by the therapist.

A third play pattern is seen most typically with children who present with a neurotic behavior disorder. Their play reflects their unconscious identification with the active, aggressive role in feared situations. One such child, for example, in playing out his fears about repeated hospitalizations, took active, open pleasure in compulsively reenacting the role of a laughing, sadistic witch who lured children to a gingerbread house where they were mutilated and thrown into an isolated, lonely room to die.

Finally, children with social phobias may use symbolic play in the service of wish fulfillment in order to express their frustrated exhibitionistic wishes to be the admired center of everyone's attention. One 8-year-old girl with a performance phobia, for example, would repeatedly play out fantasy games about a beautiful, brilliant girl who would captivate her teachers and win the love of all the boys with her singing and dancing.

PSYCHODYNAMIC FORMULATION

Defenses: The typical unconscious defense mechanisms in phobias can be illustrated in a brief psychodynamic description of Freud's prototypical phobic patient, Little Hans (Freud, 1909/ 1963). The presenting symptom in this case was the child's inability to go out on the street because of an overwhelming fear of being bitten by one of the cart horses that were commonly used for transportation during that era. Prior to the acute outbreak of his phobia, Hans showed many indications of age-typical curiosity about sex, girls, and reproduction, along with a romantic, possessive interest in his mother's love and affection, all of which we would consider normal derivatives of the positive oedipal complex.

Freud postulated that the phobia began at the

point when Hans began to be overwhelmed by overly intense longings for his mother, accompanied by mounting rivalrous, aggressive feelings toward his father and fears of paternal retaliation. As this process developed, Hans first experienced increased anxiety, which resulted in a nightmare. As his inner turmoil increased further, he had an episode of crying while taking a walk and insisted that his nursemaid take him back to his mother to be comforted. This episode probably was the result of an intrapsychic projection of his anger onto the outer world, so that he experienced it as ominous and threatening. With the actual outbreak of the phobia, this projected anger was displaced more specifically onto horses and reversed so that Hans experienced himself as a potential passive victim rather than the active source of aggression. In addition, the defense mechanism of libidinal regression altered Hans's wish to be a powerful horse and knock his father to the ground into a wish to bite. This aggressive wish was then further transformed by being reversed and then projected onto the horse; thus Hans became additionally fearful of being bitten. Finally, the defense mechanism of avoidance came into play, so that Hans sought to alleviate his severe anxiety by refusing to go out of the house lest he see a horse.

In addition to these defense mechanisms, children with phobias may utilize the defense mechanism of identification with the aggressor. As a result, they unconsciously adopt the role of the object onto which they have previously projected their own anger and aggressive impulses. The degree with which the phobic child enacts this identification in play, fantasy, and behavior varies considerably. Little Hans, for example, would enact the role of a horse in dramatic fantasy play and occasionally would "playfully" butt his father in the stomach. On the other hand, some children, such as the girl mentioned earlier, repetitively take on the role of a sadistic, aggressive, and dangerous object and play out sadistic fantasies with great enjoyment. At the other end of the spectrum, other children demonstrate their use of this defense mechanism in their everyday behavior by bullying younger children, torturing animals, and an attitude of blustering bravado. Prominent use of this defense mechanism also is seen in children whose phobias have been triggered by actual physical traumata, such as physical or sexual abuse. Phobic children who use this mechanism

prominently are at risk for developing a neurotic behavior disorder.

A closely allied defense mechanism is that of counterphobic behavior, in which children seek to master fears and phobias by forcing themselves to do what scares them the most. For example, one 6-year-old phobic child whose fear of sports-related injuries had been constantly reinforced by a psychotic nursemaid would rush out headlong onto the rink during ice-skating lessons. Refusing to listen to instructions, he would rapidly become disorganized, overly excited, and motorically hyperactive until his parents would become frightened and remove him from the situation.

Ego Functioning and Ego Strengths: Ego functioning and strengths are important variables in determining the symptomatic expression of the phobia and the child's general level of functioning. About 75% of phobic children are only mildly impaired by their disorder. Like Little Hans, their ego functioning is intact in the areas of reality testing, impulse control, affect modulation, secondary process thinking, object relationships, and their general capacity to adapt to the demands of reality. Whether their problem is conceptualized as based on a relatively mild neurosis or conditioned fear responses, they function well in many areas of their lives. Like Little Hans, they can be appealing, intelligent children who relate well to adults and peers, are curious, enjoy learning, and may have the capacity to establish excellent subliminatory channels for their impulses.

Children with social phobias may have many of the same personality characteristics but may have great difficulty in relating to adults or peers in settings that mobilize their phobic anxiety; here they may appear anxious, shy, withdrawn, and inhibited so that their capacity for age-appropriate, pleasurable, and reciprocal object relationships is not immediately apparent.

Children with more severe phobic disorders usually retain normal basic ego functioning. However, those children who have had significant difficulties in resolving their preoedipal conflicts or who have been severely traumatized will have greater difficulty in modulating their aggressive, angry feelings, even before the outbreak of the phobia. Consequently, they may be more prone to master phobic anxiety by identification with the aggressor or counterphobic defense mechanisms.

Finally, children with additional psychopathology, especially those in the process of developing a borderline personality disorder, may present with a phobia but may have more compromised ego functioning. Such comorbid psychopathology often makes both diagnosis and treatment more difficult processes for the clinician.

Self: Phobic children usually have a well-established sense of the self and a firm sense of self-object differentiation. When phobias run a protracted course and significantly interfere with daily activities of living, phobic children's self-esteem can be progressively impaired because of shame over their inability to control their feelings and overcome their problems. Many phobic children are embarrassed over the extent of their anxieties even though they frequently rationalize their reactions as similar to those of their friends. In clinical interviews, they often will minimize the number and extent of their fears or seek to avoid the topic completely.

Superego: Clinical descriptions of superego functioning in elementary-school-age phobic children differ depending on the presence of coexisting psychopathology (e.g., neurotic depression) and the child's age. Age is a very important variable to consider because the superego normally begins to consolidate at the beginning of this period of life and then gradually undergoes important developmental changes over the next several years. As a result, younger children in the midst of oedipal phase conflicts will control their impulses less because of guilt and more because of fears of disapproval, punishment, or retaliation for their wishes. It is with increasing age and resolution of oedipal conflicts that self-control comes gradually under the influence of the superego by means of internalized, consistent feelings of guilt and shame, and by idealized standards of behavior.

If the phobia is considered to be the result of a neurotic conflict, the phobic symptom can be analyzed as a complex compromise formation involving a forbidden wish, the ego defenses, the demands of the real world, and both the child's fear of punishment and his or her sense of guilt for experiencing that wish. In general, phobic children defend against experiencing any guilty feelings by unconsiously projecting their sexual, exhibitionistic, and aggressive feelings onto the phobic object. In older children, the feared consequences of contact with the phobic object can represent not just a fantasy of retaliation but can acquire the additional unconscious meaning of a well-deserved punishment for wishes that mobilize intense guilt and shame.

For example, one 10-year-old girl abruptly quit drama school after years of acting lessons because of the acute onset of a performance phobia. Her anxiety began following her mother's hospitalization, when she felt herself thrust into the pleasurable role of the "woman of the house," especially at the frequent dinners that her successful father continued to give for family, friends, and business associates. Her frequent nightmares and daydreams of being humiliated while onstage represented both a fear of and a wish to be punished for her pleasure in dressing up and taking her mother's place at the dinner table as well as for her sexual fantasies about her father.

PRESENTATION OF SYNDROME AT DIFFERENT STAGES OF LIFE

In general, a phobia presents a similar clinical picture at all stages of life, although the content of the fear may change. Thus, preschool children may be afraid of the dark, animals, strangers, or injury, while school-age children additionally may present with fears of robbers, monsters, death, and environmental threats. In adolescence, performance and social phobias become more prominant, while adults may present with agoraphobias, travel phobias, and fears of separation. Unlike adolescents and adults, younger children may not be able to realize the irrational nature of their fears. Finally, adults may have found ways to organize their lives in the service of avoiding the phobic objects and minimizing the seriousness of their problems that are impossible for young children to do.

Etiology/Pathogenesis

BIOLOGICAL ASPECTS

Ethological theory, as articulated by John Bowlby, represents one set of important and coherent hypotheses about the biological basis for fears and simple phobias. Bowlby (1973) points out that the majority of children show a similar constellation of fears during early childhood; these include fears of separation from attachment figures, strange situations, objects and people, darkness, being alone, sudden noises and movements, rapid approach, animals, height, and anything that is associated with pain. In addition, these same fears can be observed in nonhuman infant primates. Bowlby argues that these fears are biological patterned responses to situations that represent indicators of the potential and quite realistic dangers that exist in a natural, primitive environment and that their presence has been genetically determined through the evolutionary process of natural selection.

According to this line of reasoning, the common fears of childhood—fear of strange situations, separation from mother, sudden rapid approach of objects, loud noise, the dark, heights, animals—are not intrinsically pathological but are instead biologically programmed, normal indicators of potential danger situations. Phylogenetically, they have positive, adaptive functions that would tend to increase survival in naturalistic, primitive, and dangerous settings. They become pathological only when they are absent or too easily, rapidly, and inappropriately activated. In Bowlby's model, a predisposition to inappropriate activation may be further reinforced by psychodynamic conflicts and especially by environmental influence, including traumatic events and chronically stressful personal relationships.

This conceptual model is interesting because it is compatible with a wide variety of possible intervening mechanisms, including genetic or neurochemically lowered thresholds of activation that may determine why only some children's fears develop into phobias and why only certain objects become stimuli for phobic anxiety for certain children. It may help us to clarify the problem of symptom choice in psychoanalytic theory—the vexing question of why some children develop certain types of phobias and not others. Alternatively, it may serve to clarify an equally difficult problem in the learning theory model of phobia—why some children can be conditioned so easily, rapidly, and unexpectedly to fear and stay fearful of a commonly experienced object as the result of a single unpleasurable exposure, a fact that flies in the face of empirical experience with operant conditioning.

NEUROPSYCHOLOGICAL ASPECTS

Several major behavioral theories seek to account for the development of phobias, including classical or Pavlovian conditioning, operant conditioning, and social-learning theory.

The earliest experimental evidence that classical conditioning might play an etiological role in a phobia is Watson and Raynor's case study (1920) of "Little Albert." The experimenters were able to condition a fear response to a white rate in this 11-month-old child by pairing exposure to the rat with loud, sudden, and frightening noise. They demonstrated that the conditioned fear response was stable over time and could be transferred to other inanimate objects with physical attributes similar to the white rat.

Although later investigators had variable results in replicating this study and criticized its methodology, it was historically important in developing the hypothesis that a phobia is a learned, conditioned anxiety or fear response and that the phobic object can be any neutral stimulus that has been present when a severe fear reaction is evoked. In this view, the phobia is a conditioned response to the sudden outbreak of anxiety rather than a defense against unconscious, intrapsychic conflict that was first manifested by anxiety.

This model has been further elaborated (Rachman & Costello, 1961) to include the following essential points: Phobias are initially neutral, learned responses that develop when they are associated with a fear-producing state of affairs. Those neutral stimuli that are of most relevance in the fear-producing situation and/or that make an impact on the person are most likely to develop phobic qualities than weak or irrelevant stimuli. Repetition of the association between the fear situation and the new phobic stimuli will strengthen the phobia, and associations between high-intensity fear situations and neutral stimuli are more likely to produce phobic reactions. Finally, generalization from the original phobic stimulus to stimuli of a similar nature will occur.

The model based on an operant-conditioning paradigm posits that phobias are induced and maintained by environmental factors that reinforce symptomatic behaviors and that can be identified by a systematic study of the child's total environment. Although we lack experimental data to support this hypothesis, it has face validity for many clinicians. In addition, similar concepts of etiology are implicit in many family therapy paradigms that conceptualize the child as the identified patient who is the symptom-bearer of a dysfunctional family and whose members unwittingly elicit and maintain patterns of pathological behavior in the child.

Other behaviorists have evoked social learning as a possible etiological factor in a phobia. Both direct verbal messages to a child that induce anxiety and significant adults modeling fear reactions in the child's presence have been posited as possible mechanisms of transmission of fear responses to previously neutral stimuli.

These theories have been criticized, however, on several counts (Shaffer, 1986). First, the classical conditioning model holds that a child develops a phobia after a single exposure to a frightening stimulus, such as a large dog. However, experimental evidence shows that single-trial learning of an anxiety response is not the rule, except when it occurs in response to a trauma of catastrophic proportions, such as a car accident. Moreover, classical conditioning and operant conditioning experiments usually show that fear responses extinguish unless constantly reinforced, while phobias in vivo stay the same or even intensify. Because of these contradictions, some behaviorists have posited etiological models that combine several of these mechanisms. Finally, even with modifications, learning theory does not satisfactorily explain why relatively few children develop phobias in a world in which children are almost universally exposed to anxiety-producing situations that could be readily paired with neutral stimuli.

TRAUMATIC ASPECTS

It is clinically common to see children develop fears and avoidance reactions after frightening experiences, such as being attacked or physically threatened by an animal or being in an accident. However, the vast majority of children with phobias have been exposed to an average, expectable environment of potentially or actually frightening experiences with which other children have coped without developing incapacitating fears and an avoidance response. In addition, children who suffer a severely traumatic experience often develop fears and avoidance responses within the broader framework of a post-traumatic stress reaction.

PSYCHOSOCIAL ASPECTS

Psychodynamic theory offers the one of the more powerful explanatory models for the development of a phobia. Stated in the most general terms, this model hypothesizes that a phobia is the result of an imbalance between the complex intrapsychic mechanisms that normally interact for the purpose of regulating aggressive and libidinal impulses and maintaining anxiety within normal and managable limits. Using more technical language, the phobia is seen as the product of an unsuccessful, neurotic resolution to intrapsychic conflict between internal impulses and feelings from the oedipal stage of psychic development and counterbalancing regulatory forces of the ego defenses, superego guilt and shame, and the demands and rules of the real world.

Freud (1909/1963) used the case history of "Little Hans" to clinically demonstrate the central role of both intensified oedipal conflicts and a specific combination of ego defenses in the genesis of a phobia. This work has been replicated many times over in the treatment of children and adults in psychotherapy and psychoanalysis, thus demonstrating a universal psychopathological mechanism for this disorder. In addition, this particular dynamic constellation is considered to be the underlying mechanism for the universal and normal fears of children in the oedipal stage of psychic development. Thus, classical psychodynamic theory views the phobic symptom as an extreme on the spectrum of sequelae of neurotic conflict and as a varient of normal psychological conflict.

Classical psychodynamic theory also has been criticized for not offering a satisfactory explanation to the question of why a universal psychological experience such as the Oedipus complex results in phobic symptoms in only a relatively small percentage of children. A modern psychodynamic model would answer this question by citing the fact that the phobia is a more severe form of very prevalent phenomena, the normal fears of early childhood. Moreover, modern psychodynamic theory utilizes a multivariate model of causation, which recognizes that preoedipal psychopathology, family dynamics, social learning, and biological predispositions are all additional factors that may contribute to the formation of a phobic disorder.

FAMILIAL ASPECTS

There is some anecdotal evidence that fearful families tend to have fearful children. In addition, we now have preliminary data from a family study in which Fyer et al. (1990) interviewed 49 first-degree relatives of 15 probands with simple phobia, contrasting them with 119 first-degree relative of 38 normal controls. This study showed that simple irrational fears that do not reach the severity of a *DSM-III-R* disorder do not appear to increase the familial risk for simple phobias but did demonstrate a greater prevalence of simple phobias in the families of simple phobic probands (31%) in contrast to the family of normal controls (11%). Moreover, 15% of the children of phobic probands suffered from simple phobias as opposed to 11% of controls. Of note is that 27% of daughters of probands showed simple phobias as opposed to 9% of the daughters of controls; this difference accounted for most of the variance between the two groups of children. This study supports the hypothesis that simple phobia is a familial disorder that does not transmit an increased risk for other types of anxiety disorder.

VULNERABILITY

The limited statistical data that exists indicates that daughters of phobic parents are at most risk for developing a simple phobia during childhood, while all children are highly vulnerable to developing at least one and often multiple fears during middle childhood.

Differential Diagnosis

Normal and developmentally appropriate fear reactions can be differentiated from phobias on the basis of whether the child consistently and persistently avoids the feared object or situation. In some cases, the child may have several persisting fears but reacts only to one of them in a phobic manner. In contrast, a child who has been relatively anxiety free will develop a single, pronounced phobia to a particular object or situation.

Posttraumatic stress reactions share with pho-

bias the diagnosic feature of an intense need to avoid fear-producing stimuli. However, in contrast to the phobic child's limited area of psychopathology, the clinical picture of posttraumatic stress reactions is of a more pervasive, incapacitating disorder following a readily recognizable traumatic event that would be distressing to any child of the same age group. PTSR additionally has more pervasive symptoms of anxiety and arousal, psychic numbing, and the reexperiencing of the traumatic event in dreams, fantasies, and flashbacks.

Obsessive-compulsive disorder in children can have symptomatology that closely resembles phobias. For example, compulsions about dirt and contamination or obsessive ruminations about hurting oneself with kitchen knives can be accompanied by anxiety responses to these stimuli and the intense wish to avoid them. However, the phobic child is usually anxiety free and comfortable when able to avoid phobic situations and objects totally, while the child with obsessive-compulsive disorder is driven to return to symptomatology despite discomfort and wish to avoid the thoughts or situation. In addition, the child with obsessive-compulsive disorder will present with a broader spectrum of fears, obsessions, and compulsions as opposed to the child with simple, single phobias.

Borderline and psychotic conditions can produce both phobic reactions and fear and avoidance responses to delusional beliefs that the child does not recognize as unrealistic or strange, such as a fear of clowns, balloons, or a particular television program with apparently neutral content. In general, the clinical picture of a more pervasive, severe disturbance with marked deficits in ego functioning is sufficient to establish the correct diagnosis.

Morbidity

EFFECTS ON CHILD'S FUNCTIONING AND DEVELOPMENT

With the exception of a small percentage of severe and incapacitating phobias, especially severe social phobias, the effects of simple phobias are few and relatively benign. This is because a stable, relatively mild phobia represents a neurotic compromise formation that binds and contains anxiety that might ordinarily interfere with functioning and the developmental process.

However, much depends on a combination of the nature of the child's phobia and environmental circumstances. Thus, a child with an animal phobia who lives in a protected urban environment with supportive parents may successfully avoid any contact with an animal and therefore function extremely well. The same child in a suburban neighborhood where household pets roam freely may be unable to play outside or visit friends, suffer from constant anticipatory anxiety, and become progressively more isolated, depressed, and frustrated. In extreme cases, sleep, schoolwork, social relationships, and family interactions may become progressively more compromised as anxiety spreads into all areas of the child's life.

As the child's functional capacity decreases, intrapsychic development may become compromised. For example, a phobic, housebound child who has the opportunity to play with young siblings only may be constantly tempted to behave in more infantile ways that will reinforce intrapsychic regression to more immature levels of object relationships, thinking, and adaptation. Thus a child whose oedipal conflicts generated a phobia may regress to controlling, dominating behaviors typical of fixations at the anal stage of development.

Children with social phobias are, as a group, more vulnerable to functional impairment because their fears are more likely to interfere with school performance and peer relationships, particularly in group activities.

IMPACT OF FAMILY/INTERPERSONAL/ SOCIAL ENVIRONMENT

The clinical picture and course of the phobia can be affected by external factors in several ways. First, the child's level of anxiety and psychosocial functioning partly depends on whether the family and environment can assist or impede attempts to avoid the phobic situation or object. Second, family members with emotional disorders, especially anxiety disorders, may reinforce a child's phobic anxiety by their own anxious, fearful, and phobic responses to the world. Third, less favorable socioeconomic circumstances may reinforce fears and phobic anxiety because the child lives in a generally less protected environment where there is a greater likelihood of encountering real danger and traumatic events that may trigger phobic responses.

COMORBIDITY

Multiple studies confirm a high degree of comorbidity among the different anxiety disorders of childhood and between anxiety disorders and depressive disorders (Bernstein & Borshardt, 1991). Given the widespread prevalence of both fears and phobias in the general population, it is possible to assume that many children with other anxiety disorders also will suffer from these symptoms. However, more specific patterns of comorbidity with phobias have not yet emerged from current epidemiological studies.

SEQUELAE AND PROGNOSIS

The general clinical course of the majority of untreated simple phobias is of onset in childhood and continuation of the symptoms through adolescence into adulthood with gradual improvement or even complete remission in some cases. Remissions may be due to the fact that some phobias, as is the case with childhood fears, may be transient developmental phenomena due to neurotic conflicts that can be resolved because of favorable environmental circumstances.

Currently available statistical data is sparse and contradictory, with recovery rates ranging from 20 to 100% of those phobics under 20 years of age (Bernstein & Borchardt, 1991). This wide disparity may be due to the fact that definitions of recovery may vary widely. Well-controlled outcome studies with treatment are lacking at this time.

Treatment

PSYCHOLOGICAL AND SOCIAL INTERVENTIONS

Individual psychotherapy has been a mainstay in the treatment of children with simple phobias for many years. Since the majority of children with mild phobias never present for treatment, clinicians tend to treat only the more severe and incapacitating phobic disorders.

Psychodynamically oriented psychotherapy and child psychoanalytic treatment aim at using a combination of play and verbal interventions to help phobic children gain insight into and control over their symptoms. It does this by gradually helping children to become aware of the unconscious neurotic conflicts that have generated phobic anxiety and avoidance patterns of feared objects and situations. In conjunction with this, the therapist helps the children to alter maladaptive ego defenses such as projection, externalization, reversal, and avoidance and to replace them with more adaptive mechanisms, such as intellectualizations, sublimations, displacements, and adaptive behavior patterns that lead to psychological mastery of the internal drives and to competency in the real world. In addition, the therapist provides emotional support and encouragement for the children to encounter and master the phobic situation in real life.

Many of the phobic children who are impaired severely enough to be referred for treatment also have significant preoedipal psychopathology that makes the clinical picture more complicated than those found in the early case reports of phobic children. For example, the famous report of the 3-year-long psychoanalysis of "Frankie" (Bornstein, 1949) describes a child with severe behavioral problems as well as several phobias whose initial problems were dramatically more severe than those of "Little Hans."

Although seasoned clinicians report good treatment outcomes using these methods, there are currently no controlled, well-designed studies of psychotherapy outcome for the treatment of phobic children. In addition, the anecdotal, single-case reports of treatment that do exist do not give a representative picture because they tend to describe unusual, complex, and severe cases that present particular or unusual therapeutic challenges and require special treatment techniques rather than describing the successful treatment of typical cases of varying severity.

Group treatment approaches sometimes have been used with adult patients suffering from agoraphobia as a way of providing group support and mutual reality testing during exposure and desensitization to phobic situations. We currently lack any information about the usefulness of this approach with children suffering from simple phobias.

Family treatment may be a useful approach with children whose phobic anxiety is being reinforced by a dysfunctional family system. In such an approach, the therapist attempts to understand what function the child's phobic anxiety avoidance might serve in maintaining the family's stability and emotional homeostasis. Therapeutic efforts are then aimed at blocking this reinforcement either through confrontation and interpretation or by altering the structure of the family in such a way as to remove the unconscious motives for this reinforcement by family members. For this therapeutic modality also, we currently lack any treatment outcome studies.

The most widely advocated cognitive/behavioral techniques for simple phobia all center around the "deconditioning," "desensitization," or extinction of the anxiety response to the phobic object or situation. Jones (1924) pioneered this approach by successfully using progressive, gradual exposure to phobic objects to decondition a 3-year-old boy who showed fear of white rats, rabbits, fur, and similar objects. This technique was later expanded by Wolpe (1958) into a "reciprocal-inhibition" or "relaxation" therapy. In this approach, the child was first taught to relax and to maintain a relaxed state while experiencing a graded series of in vitro or imagined exposures to the phobic object. The theoretical basis for this technique was Wolpe's hypothesis that a state of relaxation made it impossible to simultaneously remain anxious.

This approach has been further expanded to include combinations of in vitro and in vivo (live) exposures to the feared object, including sudden, prolonged, and overwhelming exposure to the phobic object in order to exhaust and extinguish the anxiety response by promoting massive discharge. This approach is not recommended for use with children.

More recently, cognitive/behavioral therapeutic techniques have been expanded to include a variety of relaxation techniques, contingent reinforcement, in vivo exposure to the phobic object, modeling, participant modeling, and cognitive restructuring techniques (Kendall, et al., 1991).

A large number of successful single-case treatment studies using these methods have been published. As a result, behaviorists have recommended these methods as the treatment of choice for simple phobias. However, the behavioral treatment literature must be read critically since many case reports seem to be describing the treatment of children with a variety of common fears rather than phobic disorders diagnosed according to *DSM-IV* criteria. Unlike the psychotherapy literature, many case reports seem to be written to validate treatment efficacy rather than to explore difficult and unusual clinical situations. In addition, like the psychotherapy literature, the behavioral treatment literature lacks well-designed research about treatment outcome with comparison groups of patients and controls. Finally, most single-case reports of behavioral treatment do not offer long-term follow-up or measure comorbidity, either before or after treatment.

EDUCATIONAL INTERVENTIONS

In general, educational interventions are not relevant in the treatment of phobias. There are two exceptions. First, an educational approach might be intially helpful as part of an integrated treatment program in order to help certain children understand that their phobic anxieties are unreasonable and excessive. However, this is usually done within the context of psychotherapy or cognitive/behavioral treatment and never as the only intervention. Second, some children who have been homebound or unable to learn as the result of severe phobic anxieties may need special tutoring to help their school performance to remain on grade level.

BIOLOGICAL INTERVENTIONS

Currently no evidence exists that biological treatments of any kind are effective in the treatment of children with simple or social phobias. In general, there are no indications that psychoactive drugs are at all effective in treating these disorders. However, some clinicians might empirically attempt to treat a child whose functioning is progressively worsening because of mounting anticipatory anxiety or sleep problems with careful, closely monitored, short-term administration of an anxiolytic drugs, such as the benzodiazapines or buspirone (Buspar) (Green, 1991).

MILIEU TREATMENT

There are currently no indications for the use of milieu treatment—outpatient, inpatient, or day treatment—for children with simple phobias.

Current Developments, Research, and Unanswered Questions

Researchers continue to search for biological, neuropsychological, and psychological markers that might aid in differentiating simple and social phobias from other anxiety disorders and in determining whether phobias in childhood are the precursors of adult phobias (Beidel, 1991).

Another important area of research is the investigation of possible relationships between phobias and panic disorder. Many important questions remain unanswered, including whether particular forms of childhood and adolescent phobias, such as agoraphobias or school phobias, are risk factors for later onset of panic disorders, or whether they are essentially independent disorders that may occur together because of unknown variables.

A third area of potentially fruitful research is the further study of variables that cause a particular child to develop a phobia rather than to remain simply fearful. Psychoanalytic theory points to a multivariate model of causes for the intensification of normal fears into a phobic disorder. On the other hand, Schaffer (1986) has suggested that the use of avoidance is the critical variable, one that might ultimately have a biological basis. Continued study of these potential models is sorely needed.

There is currently an increased interest in the role of psychotropic medication in treating adults with social phobias. Any positive clinical findings in this area eventually might prove to be useful in treating children with this disorder.

Well-designed treatment outcome studies of both psychodynamic and cognitive/behavioral modalities for phobic disorders as well as rest of the anxiety disorders are lacking; such research would add greatly to our knowledge base.

REFERENCES

Agras, S., Sylvester, L., & Oliveau, D. (1969). The epidemiology of common fears and phobia. *Comprehensive Psychiatry, 10,* 151–156.

American Psychiatric Association. (1969). *APA psychiatric glossary.* Washington, DC: Author.

American Psychiatric Association. (1987). *Diagnostic and statistical manual of mental disorders,* 3rd rev. ed. Washington, DC: Author.

American Psychiatric Association. (1994). *Diagnostic and statistical manual of mental disorders,* 4th ed. Washington, DC: Author.

Anderson, J., Williams, S., McGee, R., & Silva, P. (1987). DSM-III disorders in preadolescent children: Prevalence in a large sample from the general population. *Archives of General Psychiatry, 44,* 69–76.

Beidel, D. (1991). Social phobia and overanxious disorder in school-age children. *Journal of the American Academy of Child & Adolescent Psychiatry, 30* (4), 542–545.

Bell-Dolan, D., Last, C., & Strauss, C. (1990). Symptoms of anxiety disorders in normal children. *Journal of the American Academy of Child and Adolescent Psychiatry, 29,* 759–765.

Bernstein, G., & Borchardt, C. (1991). Anxiety disorders of childhood and adolescence: A critical review. *Journal of the American Academy of Child & Adolescent Psychiatry, 30* (4), 519–532.

Bornstein, B. (1949). The analysis of a phobic child: Some problems of theory and technique in child analysis. *Psychoanalytic Study of the Child, 3/4,* 181–226.

Bowlby, J. (1973). *Separation, anxiety and anger. Vol. 2: Separation.* New York: Basic Books.

Burke, K., Burke, J., Regier, D., & Rae, D. (1990). Age of onset of selected mental disorders in five community populations. *Archives of General Psychiatry, 47,* 511–518.

Costello, E. (1989). Child psychiatric disorders and their correlates: A primary care pediatric sample. *Journal of the American Academy of Child & Adolescent Psychiatry, 28,* 851–855.

Freud, A. (1936). *The ego and mechanisms of defense.* New York: International University Press.

Freud, S. (1963). The analysis of a phobia in a five-year-old boy. In J. Strachey (Ed. & Trans.), *The standard edition of the complete psychological works of sigmund freud* (Vol. 10). London: Hogarth Press. (Originally published in 1909.)

Fyer, A., Mannuzza, S., Gallops, S., Martin, L., Aaronsson, C., et al. (1990). Familial transmission of simple phobias and fears: A preliminary report. *Archives of General Psychiatry, 47,* 252–256.

Green, W. (1991). *Child and adolescent psychopharmacology.* Baltimore: Williams & Wilkins.

Jersild, A. T., Markey, F. U., & Jersild, C. L. (1933). Children's fears, dreams, wishes, daydreams, likes, dislikes, pleasant and unpleasant memories. *Child Development Monograph, 12.*

Jones, M. C. (1924). A laboratory study of fear: The case of Peter. *Journal of General Psychology, 31,* 308–316.

Kashani, J., & Orvaschel, H. (1990). A community study of anxiety in children and adolescents. *American Journal of Psychiatry, 147,* 313–318.

Kendall, P., et al. (1991). Treating anxiety disorders in children and adolescents. In P. C. Kendall (Ed.), *Child and adolescent therapy, cognitive-behavioral procedures.* New York: Guilford Press.

Lapouse, R., & Monk, M. A. (1959). Fears and worries in a representative sample of children. *American Journal of Orthopsychiatry, 29,* 803–818.

Marks, I. (1983). *Fears and phobias.* New York: Academic Press.

McGee, R., Feehan, M., Williams, S., Partridge, F., Silva, P., & Kelly, J. (1990). DSM-III disorders in a large sample of adolescents. *Journal of the American Academy of Child & Adolescent Psychiatry, 29,* 611–619.

Morris, R., & Kratochwill, T. (1983). *The practice of child therapy.* New York: Pergamon Press.

Rachman, S., & Costello, C. (1961). The etiology and treatment of children's phobias: A Review. *American Journal of Psychiatry, 118,* 97–105.

Schneier, F., Johnson, J., Hornig, C., Liebowitz, M., & Weissman, M. (1992). Social phobia: Comorbidity and morbidity in an epidemiologic sample. *Archives of General Psychiatry, 49,* 282–288.

Shaffer, D. (1986). Learning theories of anxiety. In R. Gittleman (Ed.), *Anxiety disorders of childhood.* New York: Guilford Press.

Watson, J. & Raynor, R. (1920), Conditioned emotional reactions. *Journal of Experimental Psychology, 3,* 1–14.

Weissman, M., & Merikangas, K. (1986). The epidemiology of anxiety and panic disorders: An update. *Journal of Clinical Psychiatry, 47* (Suppl. 6), 11–17.

Wolpe, J. (1958). Psychotherapy by reciprocal inhibition. Palo Alto, CA: Standford University Press.

44 / Panic Disorder in Children

John J. Stine

Background

HISTORY OF THE DISORDER

The diagnosis of panic disorder, with or without agoraphobia, was unheard of in the child and adolescent population until the last decade, when the first cases began to be reported in pediatric populations (Herskowitz, 1986; Van Winter & Stickler, 1984; Moreau & Weismann, 1992). More recently, a number of single-case reports and several pilot studies of patient populations have confirmed that panic disorder does indeed occur in children and is responsive to pharmacotherapy (Alessi & Magen, 1987; Biederman, 1987; Vitiello, Behar, Wolfson, & McLeer, 1990).

Increasing public awareness has made both case finding and the diagnosis of this disorder easier in adults; many adults are self-referred after having learned about this disorder through the popular media. However, the diagnosis is more difficult to make in children because they often are unable to describe verbally or even complain about their problem in an articulate, accurate manner. Correct diagnosis often depends on the clinician having a high index of suspicion for a disorder that, albeit very rare, can be a devastating problem for both child and family when it does occur.

Currently, children are diagnosed by using the criteria that apply to adults in the third revised edition or fourth edition of the *Diagnostic and Statistical Manual of Mental Disorders* (*DSM-III-R*, American Psychiatric Association [APA], 1987; *DSM-IV*, APA, 1994). The essential feature of this disorder is a history of at least 4 recurrent panic attacks within a 4-week period (*DSM-III-R*), or, alternately, at least 1 attack followed by at least 1 month of persistent fear of having another attack (*DSM-IV*).

The attacks themselves are of sudden onset and are unexpected rather than being triggered by a specific external stimulus. They must be accompanied by at least 4 different specific symptoms and also may be accompanied by agoraphobia. It is important to note that in contrast to the nonspecific nature of the panic attack, agoraphobia is a fear associated with a specific place or situation in which the patient is afraid of being trapped, embarrassed, or rendered helpless in the face of a panic attack. Characteristically, the agoraphobic patient will restrict contact with the feared situation, either using total avoidance or relying on the symbolic protection of a companion in order to endure the situation. Because of this, some clinicians have questioned whether at least some cases of school refusal or school phobia are actually panic disorders with an agoraphobic reaction to school.

COMPARATIVE NOSOLOGY

Descriptive Issues: Garland and Smith (1990) suggest that many cases that meet current diagnostic criteria for panic disorder have been previously incorrectly diagnosed as hyperventiliation syndrome, conversion syndrome, or irritable heart in pediatric practice. In addition, some children who suffer from depressive disorders and other anxiety disorders, especially separation anxiety disorder, may occasionally experience panic attacks that do not meet the full *DSM-IV* criteria for panic disorder.

Developmental Issues: Nelles and Barlow (1988) agree that many anxious children experience paniclike sensations such as dizziness, tachycardia, or dyspnea. However, they maintain but that the diagnosis of panic disorder depends not only on the presence of these symptoms of physiological activation but also on the presence of negative affect, a sense of uncontrollability, and a cognitive "catastrophic misinterpretation" of the somatic sensations. This misinterpretation typically results in thoughts of going crazy, losing control, or dying. They argue that there is only anecdotal evidence that children actually experience such thoughts during a "panic attack" and also question whether younger children have yet developed the cognitive capacity to experience such thoughts. Since there are case descriptions of children actually reporting such ideas, further research is necessary to clarify this issue and then to help us decide if the diagnostic criteria of panic disorder should be modified for children in order to take into account the developmental differences in cognitive functioning between child and adult patients.

EPIDEMIOLOGICAL DATA

Although there is growing awareness of the existance of panic disorder in middle childhood, its prevalence is estimated as rare, based on reports that the peak age for onset is between 15 and 20 years of age, the median age at onset is 24 years of age, and the peak hazard rate for males is 30 to 34 years of age and for females, 25 to 29 years of age (Burke, Burke, Regier, & Rae, 1990). Klein, Mannuzza, Chapman, and Fyer (1992) retrospectively studied the incidence of childhood panic attacks and panic disorder in 343 adult anxiety clinic patients and 560 of their relatives; only 1% of these subjects initially were judged to have experienced spontanious panic attacks in childhood. On closer examination of these subjects' narrative histories, the investigators concluded that only 3 (0.33%) provided clinically convincing descriptions of bona-fide, spontaneous panic attacks. A large proportion of adults with panic disorder, interestingly, typically report that their first attack occurred between 15 and 19 years of age, while 18% of adult patients report onset before 10 years of age (Von Korff, Eaton, & Keyl, 1985). However, in a study of 5,596, nonreferred adolescents, the lifetime weighted prevalence of panic disorder was found to be only 0.6% (Burke et al., 1990).

According to the data currently available, the prevalence of panic disorder in the general population of children and adolescents indeed appears to be rare, with girls being affected two to three times more frequently than boys. Since we lack well-controlled, well-designed epidemiological studies of large populations of children, however, we cannot conclusively state the actual frequency of panic disorder in children, especially because retrospective studies of psychiatric symptomatology may be quite unreliable. Moreover, some investigators argue that the childhood form of panic disorder may have a more heterogenous form of presentation that overlaps with psychosomatic symptoms, separation anxiety disorder, and school phobia (Abelson & Alessi, 1992) and is therefore harder to recognize and diagnose, especially in retrospective studies.

There have been a few reports, however, indicating that panic disorder may be more prevalent in patient populations than previously suspected. Alessi and Magen (1987) studied 136 child psychiatry inpatients and found that 5% had a diagnosis of panic disorder, while Last and Strauss (1989) reported a 9.6% prevalence in an adolescent psychiatry outpatient population.

Clinical Presentation and Diagnostic Assessment

OVERT SIGNS AND SYMPTOMS

Children with panic disorder usually report a specific, discrete onset of their first panic attack, which they characterize as extreme, unexpected anxiety not related to a specific anxiety-producing situation. In Vitiello et al.'s (1990) sample of 6 children, all described a pounding heart, weakness, trembling or shaking, and a fear of dying or going crazy. The majority of these children also experienced shortness of breath, feeling lightheaded or dizzy, chest tightness or pain, tingling of the fingers or face, and sensations of choking and sweating.

In fact, there is a strong statistical association between somatic complaints and the diagnosis of this form of anxiety disorder in children. Last (1991), for example, studied 158 anxiety disordered children who were clinic outpatients and found that 100% of children with panic disorder reported somatic complaints.

Although the initial panic attack is characteristically nonsituationally related, some children go on to develop a school avoidance or school phobia syndrome. At this point, it is unclear whether the problem should be classified as a separate disorder or as the secondary development of agoraphobic symptomatology. However, it is clear that some children do also develop the symptom of agoraphobia triggered off by situations other than school. Finally, some children may suffer from nocturnal panic attacks that awaken them from sleep and that may be confused with pavor nocturnus.

RELATIONSHIP TO OTHER DISORDERS

Anecdotal reports indicate a considerable overlap and comorbidity with other anxiety disorders, especially separation anxiety disorder and school refusal and school phobia. In all of these disorders, children may suffer from panic attacks that do not meet the full criteria for a panic disorder. There is a statistical association of mitral valve prolapse in adult populations with panic disorder; mitral valve prolapse occasionally is found along with this disorder in children.

PATTERNS OF PEER RELATIONSHIPS

Because of the rarity of this disorder, we are largely dependent on sparse anecdotal data and thus do not know if there are typical or distinctive patterns of peer relationships. In general, the age of onset, chronicity, and severity of the disorder are critical variables that might affect peer relationships. The child with later onset and largely situationally determined panic attacks would be most equipped to maintain normal friendships and peer activities. Unlike children with overanxious disorder or avoidant disorder, some children with panic disorder can be friendly, active, outgoing and socially successful. However, research indicates that some children with panic disorder may have the lifelong temperamental trait of "behavioral inhibition to the unfamiliar" and have developed either the personality traits of shyness and social withdrawal or another anxiety disorder prior to onset of panic disorder. In fact, the high rate of comorbidity with depressive and anxiety disorders make one prevailing pattern of relatedness unlikely. Finally, as Garland and Smith (1990) point out, some children with panic disorder may be treated by their families as if they were invalids suffering from a chronic physical illness; such children would be expected to suffer from a lack of social skills and a chronic avoidance of peer interactions that require confidence and assertion.

PSYCHODYNAMIC FORMULATION

Patterns of Defense: Children with a panic disorder, especially when it is accompanied by agoraphobia, often utilize defense mechanisms of denial, avoidance, and suppression. They will avoid discussing or even thinking about their symptoms, often with the conscious fear of precipitating a panic attack if they do so. Somatization and regression to a dependent, infantile relationship with parents is another typical pattern of defensive operation, especially for children whose parents consider them to be suffering from a chronic physical illness.

Because of the rarity of this disorder, we have limited data on which to base a psychodynamic formulation of the panic attacks themselves. However, two core intrapsychic conflicts seem to predominate. In the first instance, conflicts over separation and autonomy are central issues, and the child also suffers from a separation anxiety disorder. (These issues are discussed in detail in Chapter 39.) In the second, oedipal conflicts play a central role.

According to the psychodynamic model, the actual panic attack can be conceptualized as a compromise formation between the partial discharge of a forbidden wish, the defenses against this wish, and the unconscious punishment for the wish. For example, one 11-year-old boy suffered from severe panic attacks in crowded, hot closed spaces such as buses. Psychotherapy gradually revealed that he unconsciously linked his rapid heartbeat and labored breathing with a fantasy of strangling his mother, a severely alcoholic woman whose inability to nurture him filled him with rage. His panicky thoughts "I'm sick—I'm too weak to even go to school" served as denial in fantasy that he could perform such an act while the thought "God is angry with me today" represented the punishment.

Ego Functioning and Strengths: In general, the child with panic disorder maintains relatively intact ego functioning, with preservation of reality testing, secondary process thinking, and object constancy.

Self: Self-esteem in children with panic attacks may be increasingly impaired when the attacks become chronic. Such children may see themselves as chronically ill, "crazy," or mysteriously impaired by a disorder that they may not even be able to describe to others adequately. One 11-year-old boy, for example, described the typical onset of his nocturnal panic attacks in these words: "I begin to get really weird and freak out. . . . It's like my mind goes crazy and then I go crazy too. I'd never tell my friends because I don't want anyone to know that I'm so strange. Do we have to talk about this anymore?"

Superego: The latency-age child may unconsciously experience panic attacks as a punishment for forbidden sexual and aggressive impulses and fantasies. The fantasies of going crazy or being stricken by a mysterious illness that can be triggered off in a child's mind by these attacks may be then experienced as a concrete proof of badness that further intensifies feelings of shame and guilt. On the other hand, in those children with predominently oedipal conflicts, the fear of punishment or reactions of guilt to the partial breakthrough of forbidden impulses may be the immediate precipitant for the panic attack.

One 10-year-old boy, for example, experienced panic attacks regularly when alone with his mother while his father was away on prolonged business trips. As his psychotherapy progressed, it became clear that his labored breathing during these attacks was associated in his mind with fears that his father would be crushed to death in an automobile accident, leaving him alone to take care of his mother. As part of the treatment, his therapist slowly helped him to explore the multiple unconscious psychological meanings of his labored breathing: First, it became clear that the patient's terror that he would choke to death represented his fantasy of being punished for unconsciously wishing that his father would die. Second, the patient's dyspnea was unconsciously linked to his own breathing when he masturbated and represented a fantasied punishment for unconscious sexual feelings directed toward his mother.

COMPARISON WITH PRESENTATION OF SYNDROME IN OTHER STAGES OF LIFE

As indicated, children with panic attacks usually lack the cognitive capacity or fund of information required to understand what it is that they are experiencing. In contrast to adults, who may seek help from a mental health professional because they recognize that they are suffering from episodes of extreme anxiety, children may suffer with their symptoms in silence or complain of one of a multitude of somatic complaints, such as shortness of breath, palpitations, dizzy spells, or trembling spells, which can be easily misdiagnosed by the unwary clinician. Children with these problems usually are seen initially by pediatricians or general medical clinics and are only secondarily referred for evaluation by a child psychiatrist. Children also may present initially with a variety of other problems, such as school refusal, depression, or conduct disorders (Alessi, Robbins, & Dilsaver, 1987).

It should be noted that even with increased public awareness and education about panic disorder, a sizable number of adults still initially present to general practitioners, internists, and family practice Physicians with somatic symptoms. In addition, a sizable proportion of adults present with a combination of symptoms of agoraphobia and panic.

Etiology and Pathogenesis

BIOLOGICAL ASPECTS

Genetic Aspects: There are multiple reports (Biederman, 1987; Moreau, Weissman, & Warner, 1989; Van Winter & Stickler, 1984; Vitiello, Behar, Wolfson, & Delaney, 1987) of an increased family prevalence of panic disorder; multiple generations of the same family often are affected. Klein and Last (1989) cite Torgenson's (1988) review of genetic factors in the transmission of anxiety disorders and his conclusion that they play a definite role in the transmission of panic disorder. Others have proposed a single dominant gene mode of transmission with incomplete penetrance (Black & Robbins, 1990).

Neurochemical Aspects: A number of chemical challenges, such as intravenous infusion of sodium lactate or sodium bicarbonate or inhalation of 5% carbon dioxide–enriched air, can precipitate panic symptoms or a full-blown panic attack in adult patients with panic disorder. To date, however, no studies have been performed to replicate these findings in child or adolescent populations.

Neuropsychological Aspects: In a series of elegant and well-controlled studies, Jerome Kagan and his collaborators have investigated the role of "behavioral inhibition to the unfamiliar" as a risk factor for the later development of anxiety disorders in children. This phrase describes a combination of cautious, shy behavior with a vulnerability to excessive activation of the hypothalamic-pituitary adrenal axis, the sympathetic nervous system, and the reticular activating system (Kagan, Reznik, & Snidman, 1987). They have found specifically that children of adult probands with panic disorder and agoraphobia have an extremely high rate of behavioral inhibition (84.65%), a temperamental characteristic associated with elevated rates of anxiety disorders in childhood and possibly in adulthood (Rosenbaum et al., 1988). However, at this time, longitudinal data are not available to show whether behavioral inhibition is a biological marker that specifically predicts the later development of a panic disorder.

TRAUMATIC ASPECTS

Children who have been traumatized by catastrophic events or severe physical or sexual abuse may develop panic reactions, but usually as part of the symptom complex of a posttraumatic stress disorder. At this time we lack sufficient statistical data to validate the hypothesis of a link between less severe types of trauma and panic disorder.

PSYCHOSOCIAL ASPECTS

Some evidence does exists that there is an increased association between the onset of panic disorder and stressful life events that involve actual or symbolic separations from significant attachment figures, such as death and illness (Black & Robbins, 1990). In addition, there is a high rate of comorbidity and a strong familial association among panic disorder, separation anxiety disorder, and depressive disorders. These associations have led to the hypothesis that panic attacks and panic disorder and depression are extreme, symptomatic expressions of separation anxiety.

This hypothesis is compatible with a biological, ethologically based etiological model that views separation anxiety as an innate adaptive mechanism for enhancing survival. In this model, individual genetic variance drastically lowers the threshold for the mobilization of anxiety by symbolic or actual separation experiences, producing a spectrum of symptomatic expression that includes separation anxiety, panic, and depressive disorders.

This hypothesis is also compatible with a psychodynamic, ego-psychology model in which separation experiences trigger off severe intrapsychic conflicts that mobilize powerful and intolerable impulses and affects. In this model, the route of symptomatic expression would depend on multiple variables, including genetic, biological, and constitutional factors, ego strengths, and environmental influences. (Hartmann, 1952).

What is common to both models, however, is a lack of further specificity about the actual determinants of symptom choice or syndromic expression at this time.

FAMILIAL ASPECTS

As mentioned previously, there is strong evidence for an increased familial prevalence in this disorder. Several studies have found that first-degree relatives of probands with panic disorder have a 15 to 25% increased risk of developing this condition over their lifetime, with females being affected more than male relatives (Black & Robbins, 1990).

VULNERABILITY

In light of these findings, the child most vulnerable to the development of a panic disorder is a girl from a family with an increased prevalence of anxiety disorders and whose mother herself suffers from a combination of separation anxiety disorder, agoraphobia, and panic disorder. In addition, the girl would have preexisting separation anxiety disorder and an environment unstable enough to expose her to multiple real and symbolic separations from important attachment figures.

Differential Diagnosis

SOMATIC SYMPTOMS OF DISTRESS

Uncomplicated panic disorder may present in pediatric clinics as a "medical problem," such as idiopathic tachycardia, unexplained dyspnea, blurred vision, dizzy spells, paresthesias, or numbness of the extremities. These somatic symptoms of anxiety and panic can be misdiagnosed and incorrectly treated as one of a number of medical problems that include idiopathic bronchospasm, stress-induced asthma, temporal lobe epilepsy, pseudoseizures, conversion disorder, or hyperventilation episodes (Black & Robbins, 1990; Garland & Smith, 1990). Garland and Smith (1990) suggest that this pattern of presentation may occur in cases of panic disorder without coexisting psychopathology but that significant secondary psychosocial morbidity may occur when the child assumes the role of "sick patient" in the family system.

PANIC ATTACKS

There is a high rate of comorbidity with other anxiety disorders and with depressive disorders for both panic disorder and panic attacks that do not meet full *DSM-IV* criteria. The differential diagnosis is based on a full assessment of all symptomatology as well as a high index of suspicion for the coexistence of these disorders.

POSTTRAUMATIC STRESS DISORDER

Posttraumatic stress disorder sometimes can cause symptoms of extreme anxiety and panic, especially during flashback experiences and when the child is exposed to situations or objects associated with the original traumatic situation. However, in posttraumatic stress disorder, there is a history of severe, often catastrophic trauma, psychic numbing, pervasive anxiety, and severe interferences with functioning and development in many spheres of functioning.

Morbidity

EFFECTS ON CHILD'S FUNCTIONING/ DEVELOPMENT

The effect of multiple, uncontrolled panic attacks on social and psychological functioning can be devastating, especially when accompanied by clinically significant agoraphobic symptoms. When panic attacks are precipitated by specific types of

situations, such as school attendance, social functions, or sleep-overs, the typical pattern is of avoidance. School refusal can disrupt the educational process while social withdrawal can severely impair peer relationships and the development of social and or athletic skills. In cases where panic attacks occur more randomly, the child's general functioning can become impoverished by ever-increasing degrees of anticipatory anxiety.

IMPACT OF FAMILY/INTERPERSONAL/ SOCIAL ENVIRONMENT

Garland and Smith (1990) have described how children who present with primarily somatic symptoms of panic disorder may be misdiagnosed as suffering from a variety of obscure or vague medical problems. Such children rapidly can become induced into the role of chronically physically ill patients by dysfunctional families who handle anxiety and depression by denial, avoidance, and somatization.

COMORBIDITY

An extremely high rate (90–100%) of comorbidity with depressive disorder and separation anxiety disorders has been reported in the few existing systematic studies of panic disorder in children and adolescents (Alessi et al., 1987, Alessi & Magen, 1988; Black & Robbins, 1990; Moreau et al., 1989).

SEQUELAE

Herman, Stickler, and Lucas (1981, cited in Garland & Smith, 1990), reports that on long-term follow-up of children with "hyperventilation syndrome," at least half of them continued to suffer from anxiety symptoms and over one third developed depressive symptoms as adults. Additional sequelae may include dropping out of school, social withdrawal, and the development of passive-dependent, passive-aggressive, and narcissistic personality traits as the result of being regarded as too physically ill to meet the normal responsibilities and demands of everyday life (Pollack, Otto, Rosenbaum, & Sachs, 1992).

While we currently lack conclusive epidemeological data, the lifelong course of panic disorder seems to be chronic, with either continual or intermittent episodes of symptomatology. The most serious long-term sequelae to panic disorder in adult populations is an increased risk of death by suicide. Allgulander and Lavori (1991) found an almost 3-fold increase in suicide rate among 3,302 elderly patients with anxiety disorders. Many of these patients suffered with panic disorder either alone or in combination with phobias and generalized anxiety disorder.

There are some indications that panic disorder may increase the risk for alcoholism in adolescents, since there is a high incidence of alcoholism in populations of patients with anxiety disorders and an increased incidence of panic disorder and agoraphobia in adult alcoholics.

PROGNOSIS

We currently lack longitudinal studies of the course of panic disorder in childhood. However, adult patients with panic disorder show a wide range of comorbid pathology, including depression, agoraphobia, personality disorders, and substance abuse. In addition, adults with panic disorders with an onset before 18 years of age have a higher prevalence of alcoholism, suicidal ideation, and visits to psychiatric emergency rooms for psychiatric problems. In the absence of data to the contrary, it is logical to hypothesize that, without therapeutic intervention, children with panic disorder face a more disturbed adult life.

Treatment

PSYCHOLOGICAL AND SOCIAL TREATMENTS

Individual psychodynamic treatment and cognitive behavioral treatments all have been applied to children with panic disorder, but no systematic, well-controlled treatment outcome studies exist. In addition, because of the rarity of this condition, we lack reports of treatment of the pure form of the disorder; instead, existing case reports seem to describe children with multiple problems, including other anxiety disorders and affective disturbances. Psychodynamic treatment of the symptoms of panic often seem to take place in the context of psychoanalytic treatment of a multisymptomatic disturbance (Bornstein, 1949).

Cognitive/behavioral therapists use a wide variety of techniques in the treatment of panic disorder in adults, including relaxation techniques, systematic desensitization to phobic situations, cognitive restructuring, and systematic structured exposure to feared internal sensations of anxiety (Barlow, 1988). No systematic studies of the use of these techniques with children currently exist.

EDUCATIONAL TREATMENT

Although usually done as part of psychodynamic or cognitive/behavioral psychotherapy, many clinicians find it important to teach the patient about the clinical characteristics of the panic disorder. This is important in counteracting the patient's fears and fantasies that he or she is dying, has an unknown medical illness, is becoming psychotic, or the anxiety attack will never end. This intervention in itself can be immensely reassuring to the patient and often facilitates other therapeutic interventions.

BIOLOGICAL TREATMENT

Although systematic studies of pharmacotherapy of panic disorder in children currently are lacking, a few case reports document the efficacy of imipramine (Van Winter & Stickler, 1984), clonazepam (Biederman, 1987), and alprazolam (Ballenger, Carek, Steele, & Cornish-McTighe, 1989). Most clinicians use medication as part of an integrated treatment program that would include some combination of individual, cognitive/behavioral, and family interventions.

MILIEU TREATMENT

Because of its high rate of comorbidity with depressive and other anxiety disorders, one would expect that children on inpatient units and in day hospital programs would show a higher prevalence of panic disorder than children in other populations. Milieu treatment for such children may be useful both in managing their significantly greater degree of psychopathology and dysfunction as well as providing them with structure, protection, and emotional support while their disorders are being diagnosed correctly and treatment initiated.

Current Developments, Research, and Unanswered Questions

Research on panic disorder in children is at an early stage, and a host of important questions about this disorder remain unanswered.

One important issue is greater knowledge about the prevalence and epidemiology of this disorder as well as its longitudinal course, its relationship to the adult form of the disorder, and its sequelae. We already have good reason to believe that adults with panic disorder are at high risk for developing other types of emotional disorders that are serious and potentially dangerous, such as increased suicidality. More research on early identification and early, effective forms of treatment should have high priority.

Second, there is a disparity between the low prevalence of panic disorder in childhood and retrospective reports that a sizable number of adults experienced onset of the disorder before 18 years of age. This suggests that panic disorder in childhood might be more prevalent if different diagnostic criteria were in use. This issue needs to be studied in some depth, since early recognition and treatment might spare some children many years of needless suffering and perhaps prevent the development of serious sequelae.

Third, continued study of biological and behavioral markers for the development of this disorder might give invaluable insights into the neurobiology of this disorder and help to develop more effective treatment methods.

Finally, well-designed, placebo-controlled treatment outcome studies of biological and psychosocial techniques, alone and in combination, would be invaluable aids for the clinician.

REFERENCES

Abelson, J., & Alessi, N. (1992). Discussion of child panic revisited. *Journal of the American Academy of Child & Adolescent Psychiatry, 31,* 114–116.

Alessi, N. E., & Magen, J. (1988). Panic disorder in psychiatrically hospitalized children. *American Journal of Psychiatry, 145,* 1450–1452.

Alessi, N. E., Robbins, R. R., & Dilsaver, S. C. (1987). Panic and depressive disorders among psychiatrically hospitalized children. *Psychiatry Research, 20* (4), 275–283.

Allgulander, C., & Lavori, P. (1991). Excess morality among 3202 patients with pure anxiety neurosis. *Archives of General Psychiatry, 48,* 599–602.

American Psychiatric Association. (1987). *Diagnostic and statistical manual of mental disorders* (3rd ed., rev.). Washington, DC: Author.

American Psychiatric Association. (1994). *Diagnostic and statistical manual of mental disorders* (4th ed.). Washington, DC: Author.

Ballenger, J. C., Carek, D. J., Steele, J. J., & Cornish-McTighe D. (1989). Three cases of panic disorder with agoraphobia in children. *American Journal of Psychiatry, 146,* 922–924.

Barlow, D. H. (1988). *Anxiety and its disorders.* New York: Guilford Press.

Biederman, J. (1987). Clonazepam in the treatment of pre-pubertal children with panic-like symptoms. *Journal of Clinical Psychiatry, 48* (Suppl.) 38–41.

Black, B., & Robbins, D. (1990). Panic disorder in children and adolescents. *Journal of the American Academy of Child & Adolescent Psychiatry, 29,* 36–44.

Bornstein, B. (1949). The analysis of a phobic child: Some problems of theory and technique in child analysis. *Psychoanalytic Study of the Child, 3/4,* 181–226.

Burke, K., Burke, J., Regier, D., & Rae, D. (1990). Age of onset of selected mental disorders in five community populations. *Archives of General Psychiatry, 47,* 511–518.

Garland, E. J., & Smith, D. (1990). Panic disorder on a child psychiatry consultation service. *Journal of the American Academy of Child & Adolescent Psychiatry, 29,* 785–788.

Hartmann, H. (1952). The mutual influences in the development of the ego and the id. *Psychoanalytic Study of the Child, 7,* 9–30.

Herman, S., Stickler, G., & Lucas, A. (1981). Hyperventilation syndrome in children and adolescents. Long term follow-up. *Pediatrics, 67* (2), 183–187.

Herszowity, J. (1986). Neurological presentation of panic disorder in children and adolescents. *Developmental Medicine and Child Neurology, 28,* 617–623.

Kagan, J., Reznik, J., & Snidman, N. (1987). The physiology and psychology of behavioral inhibition in children. *Child Development, 58,* 1459–1473.

Klein, D., Mannuzza, S., Chapman, M., & Fyer, A. (1992). Child panic revisited. *Journal of the American Academy of Child & Adolescent Psychiatry, 31,* 112–114.

Klein, A., & Last, C. (1989). *Anxiety disorders in children.* Newbury Park, CA: Sage Publications.

Last, C. (1991). Somatic complaints in anxiety disordered children. *Journal of Anxiety Disorders, 5,* 125–138.

Last, C. G., & Strauss, C. C. (1989). Panic disorder in children and adolescents. *Journal of Anxiety Disorders, 3,* 87–95.

Moreau, D. L., & Weisman, M. M. (1992). Panic disorder in children and adolescents: A review. *American Journal of Psychiatry, 145,* (10), 1036–1314.

Moreau, D. L., Weissman, M., & Warner, V. (1989). Panic disorder in children at high risk for depression. *American Journal of Psychiatry, 146* (8), 1059–1060.

Nelles, W. B. & Barlow, D. H. (1988). Do children panic? *Clinical Psychology Review, 8,* 359–372.

Pollack, M. H., Otto, M. W., Rosenbaum, J. F., & Sachs, G. S. (1992). Personality disorders in patients with panic disorder. Association with childhood anxiety disorders, early trauma, comorbidity and chronicity. *Comprehensive Psychiatry, 33*(2), 78–83.

Rosenbaum, J., Beiderman, J., Gersten, M., Hirshfeld, D., Meminger, S., Herman, J., Kagan, J., Reznik, S., & Snidman, N. (1988). Behavioral inhibition in children of parents with panic disorder and agoraphobia. *Archives of General Psychiatry, 45,* 463–470.

Torgensen, S. (1988). Genetics. In C. G. Last & M. Hersen (Eds.), *Handbook of anxiety disorders.* New York: Pergamon Press.

Van Winter, J. T., Stickler, G. B. (1984). Panic attack syndrome. *Journal of Pediatrics, 105,* 661–665.

Vitiello, B., Behar, D., Wolfson, S., Delaney, M. A. (1987). Panic disorder in prepubertal children. (Letter to the editor.) *American Journal of Psychiatry, 144* (4), 525–526.

Vitiello, B., Behar, D., Wolfson, S., & McLeer, S. (1990). Diagnosis of panic disorder in prepubertal children. *Journal of the American Academy of Child and Adolescent Psychiatry, 29,* 782–784.

Von Korff, M. R., Eaton, W. W., Keyl, P. M. (1985). The epidemiology of panic attacks and disorder: Results from 3 community surveys. *American Journal of Epidemiology, 122,* 970–981.

Whitaker, A., Johnson, J., Shaffer, D., Kalikow, K., et al. (1990). Uncommon troubles in young people: Prevalence estimates of selected psychiatric disorders in a nonreferred adolescent population. *Archives of General Psychiatry, 47,* 487–496.

45 / Avoidant Disorder of Childhood

John J. Stine

Background

HISTORY OF THE DISORDER

Avoidant disorder of childhood is essentially a new diagnostic term for an old and familiar phenomena, the child who suffers from shyness and social discomfort. These personality problems have been described by authors and social commentators for many centuries. They are summarized vividly, for example, by Goethe in Faust's description of himself:

> I lack the easy social touch. . . .
> out in the world I never could fit in much.
> I fell so small in company
> I'll be embarrassed constantly. (Goethe, 1951)

The creation of a nosological term for this condition has the obvious advantage of focusing attention on a painful emotional disorder that can be approached therapeutically rather than dismissed as an immutable personality trait or, as in Faust's case, something that can be dissolved only via an alliance with Satan. The creation of a diagnostic category for this disorder in children focuses our attention on the need to devise methods for early recognition and treatment of a disorder that can otherwise result in a lifetime of silent suffering. In addition, Faust's need for an alliance with Satan in order to be able to venture out of his cloistered existence may prove a useful metaphor for understanding how some children with avoidant disorder may grow up to use alcohol inappropriately and to excess in an attempt to treat their own symptoms.

COMPARATIVE NOSOLOGY

Descriptive Issues: The hallmark of avoidant disorder of childhood is an excessive withdrawal from social interaction with unfamiliar people to the extent that there is significant functional impairment in social functioning. In order to distinguish avoidant disorder of childhood from schizoid personality disorder and pervasive developmental disorders, the child also must show a clear preference for social interactions and relationships with familiar people, such as parents, relatives, and close, familiar friends. Typically, such relationships are warm and emotionally rewarding. In order to distinguish ADC from acute stress reactions, the typical clinical picture must last for at least 6 months.

Developmental Issues: This disorder typically appears during early school years but may develop as early as 30 to 36 months, after stranger anxiety typical of the rapprochement stage normally recedes. However, the first precursors of this disorder may appear as early as infancy in the form of temperamental traits characteristic of the slow-to-warm-up child. These traits include normal activity levels, a tendency to withdraw from stimuli, low adaptability, a predominant negative mood, and low intensity levels of behavioral reactivity. (See Thomas & Chess, 1963.) More recently, Kagan, Beiderman, and other researchers have described a collection of traits called "behavioral inhibition to the unfamiliar," which they hypothesize is a precursor for the development of avoidant disorder as well as several other anxiety disorders.

EPIDEMIOLOGICAL DATA

Although we lack much research data about this disorder, avoidant disorder of childhood is thought to be relatively uncommon in the general population but more prevalent in girls. However, in a recent study of prevalence, expression, and developmental patterns of anxiety symptoms in 62 children randomly selected from the general population (Bell-Dolan, Last, & Strauss, 1990), 4.8% of the subjects were rated as "shrinking from others" to a clinically significant degree and at least 11% of children had subclinical symptoms of avoidant disorder. In this cohort, there was also a high prevalence of subclinical levels of symptoms of several other anxiety disorders, often in the same child.

In clinical settings, avoidant disorder usually presents with at least one other anxiety disorder, most frequently overanxious disorder or separation anxiety disorder. Last, Francis, and Strauss (1989) found that avoidant was found in 27.3% of children with overanxious disorder and about 5% of children with separation anxiety disorder.

The age of onset is usually under 13 years; the disorder tends to be seen in pure form more often. It is not clear whether this is because other, coexisting anxiety disorders tend to remit spontaneously in older children, whether there are two forms of the disorder, or if the finding is due to sampling errors. The clinical course is thought to be variable.

Clinical Presentation and Diagnostic Assessment

OVERT SIGNS/SYMPTOMS

Children with avoidant disorder are typically timid, shy, withdrawn, embarrassed, and anxious when in new situations or interacting with unfamiliar people. They show a typical, lifelong pattern of resisting being exposed to novel, unfamiliar situations, such as a new school, camp, play group, or social situation. On initial exposure, they have trouble with initiating or even accepting any kind of social interaction and will hang back, often appearing ill-at-ease or even frozen with anxiety and shame. At times, their social anxiety is so severe that they may be inarticulate or even electively mute. In less severe cases, such children will avoid social interactions but will adapt eventually, become progressively less anxious, and even wind up enjoying once-dreaded social situations once they have become more familiar.

RELATIONSHIP TO OTHER DISORDERS

In addition to the high rate of comorbidity with other anxiety disorders, there is some degree of overlap between the clinical picture of elective mutism and that of avoidant disorder of childhood especially extreme forms when a child is unable to talk because of overwhelming anxiety. It is possible that elective mutism is an extreme varient form of this disorder. Many children with avoidant disorder of childhood also may suffer from social phobias and are prone to depression because of their isolation and inability to function socially with peers. Finally, we have reason to believe that avoidant disorder of childhood may be a predisposing factor for the development of an avoidant personality disorder in later life, since patients with that disorder report a childhood onset of their pervasive social discomfort, timidity, isolation, and fears of criticism.

PATTERNS OF PEER RELATIONSHIPS

Because they are typically timid and unassertive, children with avoidant disorder tend to remain isolated or on the fringes of group interactions. They have difficulty in initiating and even maintaining friendships because of their social anxiety and fears of criticism, despite their longings for friendship and acceptance. In addition, they often are extremely uncomfortable in relationships with more social, assertive, and outgoing children who enjoy playing in groups, making new friends, and seeking new, novel situations and experiences. As a result, they tend to be either socially isolated or enjoy more exclusive relationships with a few children who may be equally shy and socially awkward. In the latter case, they may form emotionally warm, satisfying, and important friendships.

PATTERNS OF PLAY

Children with avoidant disorder of childhood usually do not develop age-appropriate social skills, particularly in group situations. As a result, they may not learn normal play skills and patterns, especially the skills required to participate in group games and popular sports such as baseball, soccer, or basketball. Play patterns that are usually learned within the peer group may be learned instead from older siblings, sometimes with disastrous results that reinforce children's social anxiety. One 7-year-old boy, for example, was referred for diagnostic evaluation because of an apparently increasing preference for playing with girls, feminine play patterns, and because of a mounting depression. Because of his severe avoidant disorder, he had played for years primarily with his older sister and had not learned the games, skills, and social interaction patterns necessary to relate to boys his own age. Once he started school, he became increasingly alienated from his male peers and could play only with several very gentle girls in his class. His apparent feminine "preferences," even though he had no wish to be a girl, were the occasion for much teasing and further rejection at the hands of his male classmates, leading to the development of a severe reactive depression.

In contrast to group activities, children with avoidant disorder may be very skilled and adept at activities and games that can be played alone or with another child. Many very intelligent children with this disorder become avid readers, skilled at activities on computers, or adept at solitary hobbies.

In individual, psychodynamically oriented play therapy, children with avoidant disorder may repetitively play out wish-fulfillment fantasies of successful social relationships within a group of peers. For example, one 8-year-old boy who was almost completely socially isolated would play repetitive fantasy games in which he was the admired, daring leader of an adventuresome group of children who eagerly followed him while dreading to become the target of his quick-witted sarcasm.

PSYCHODYNAMIC FORMULATION

Patterns of Defense: Children with avoidant disorder of childhood rely heavily on the defenses of avoidance. The turning of active impulses into passive ones, projection and reversal, regression to anal mechanisms of control, and wish-fulfillment fantasies of passive, masochistic surrender. Because of the early onset of this disorder, these unconscious defenses may be mobilized against forbidden impulses from every level of psychosexual development but will be especially prominent against exhibitionistic and phallic-oedipal strivings.

For example, one 6-year-old boy with severe avoidant disorder not only avoided social situations in reality, but equally so in his mental life by immersing himself in a fantasy world based on characters from the computer games that he played repetitively. In this world, he required no other people because every danger was conquered and his every whim was anticipated and immediately gratified by powerful, computer-controlled mechanical warriors who were totally devoted to his needs. When forced actually to interact with peers, he projected all of his aggression onto them, so that he experienced even younger children as overwhelmingly strong and dangerous. Too frightened to fight back, he would deal with peer aggression by retreat and surrender, telling himself that he eventually would be accepted if he allowed himself to be dominated.

Ego Functioning and Strengths: Many children with avoidant disorder function at a neurotic level of personality organization, with the major ego functions of reality testing, impulse control, affective modulation, secondary process thinking, and relationship to reality demands all intact. Like children with many other types of anxiety disorders, many can have excellent ego strengths, capacities, and talents while being seriously impaired in their social functioning.

Self: Children with avoidant disorder have achieved object constancy and have a clear boundary between self and object representations. However, self-esteem usually is severely impaired, and they are exquisitely sensitive to criticism, negative reactions, and rejection from others. As a result, they often react to the age-appropriate teasing and verbal and physical fighting of their peers with intense shame, anger, helpless rage, and withdrawal. In these situations, they tend to overpersonalize intergroup rivalry, competitiveness, and aggression, feel singled out and paralyzed, and then withdraw in frustration and rage.

Superego: The superego of children with avoidant disorder of childhood is usually quite severe and punitive: Guilt and shame are prominent problems for them. As a result, these children often are extremely critical of themselves for not being able to overcome their social inhibitions and become chronically depressed. One 7-year-old girl, for example, described herself as "I'm not popular . . . I'm kind of weird . . . a total loser." She frequently wished that she had never been born and entertained suicidal thoughts after unsuccessful social encounters.

COMPARISON WITH PRESENTATION OF SYNDROME IN OTHER STAGES OF LIFE

Avoidant disorder of childhood may appear to be less disturbing to patients and their family with increasing age because the children's pattern of social avoidance may become rationalized, accepted, and even partially ego syntonic. In other, more socially oriented families, however, the children's continued social isolation and anxiety remain a source of pain and concern.

Adults may present with a more severe and entrenched form of this psychopathology, the avoidant personality disorder. Here, patients suffer from more pervasive and incapacitating symptoms of social anxiety, fear of criticism, and timidity that have molded their life into rigid patterns of social constriction and withdrawal.

Etiology/Pathogenesis

BIOLOGICAL ASPECTS

At this point, we have little information about biological factors that might play an etiological role in avoidant disorder of childhood. We can speculate that the variously described temperamental traits of the "slow-to-warm-up child" (Thomas & Chess, 1963) or the "behavioral inhibition to the unfamiliar" (Kagan, Reznick, & Snidman, 1987) may be precursors to this disorder and that they have underlying genetic and neurochemical causes. However, further research is needed to provide confirmatory data for these hypotheses.

From an ethological point of view, it is possible to extend Bowlby's thesis about the phylogenetic survival value of separation anxiety to posit that both stranger anxiety and anxiety to the unfamiliar are parts of a separate, genetically regulated, neurobiological signaling system that functions to enhance infant survival in natural, primitive environments. Excessive anxiety reactions to unfamiliar stimuli may conceivably be caused by genetic variance and/or environmental stresses that further reinforce anxiety by means of classical or operant modes of conditioning as well as by social learning. If this hypothesis is correct, however, we would expect that excessive anxiety to strangers and to the "unfamiliar" in infancy would be a specific risk factor for the subsequent development of both avoidant disorder of childhood and avoidant personality disorder. However, current prospective research indicates only that behavioral inhibition is a nonspecific predictor of increased risk for multiple anxiety, overanxious, and phobic disorders (Biederman et al., 1990).

NEUROPSYCHOLOGICAL ASPECTS

According to the fourth edition of the *Diagnostic and Statistical Manual of Mental Disorders* (American Psychiatric Association, 1994), there is some evidence that specific developmental disorders of speech and language may be a predisposing factor for the development of avoidant disorder of childhood. This is supported by both the clinical observation of a frequent overlap between avoidant disorder of childhood and expressive and receptive language problems as well as Cantwell and Baker's finding (1989) of a 29% prevalence rate of avoidant disorder in a language-impaired population.

TRAUMATIC FACTORS

We currently lack any information about a possible etiological role for traumatic events in the development of avoidant disorder of childhood.

PSYCHOSOCIAL FACTORS

Empirically, psychodynamically oriented clinicians believe that the "temperamental" traits of shyness, social anxiety, and avoidance can be reinforced by defenses against excessive anxiety generated from intrapsychic conflicts over oedipal and preoedipal impulses. Furthermore, behavioral patterns of avoidance can be reinforced by unconscious identification with shy, anxious, and socially avoidant parents. In addition, researchers interested in emotional development and early social interactions in infancy have found that anxiety reactions to neutral stimuli can be triggered, shaped, and reinforced by early affective signaling between the infant and the mother (Stern, 1985).

FAMILIAL FACTORS

There is an increased prevalence of anxiety disorders in the mothers of children with avoidant disorder, but at this time we have no information as to whether mothers with a specific history of avoidant disorder of childhood have an increased risk of having a child with this disorder. In addition, because of the high rates of comorbidity of anxiety disorders in both adults and children, we are unable to determine whether excessive anxiety reactions to unfamiliar stimuli and people is a specific trait with a familial mode of transmission or a general characteristic of anxiety disorders.

VULNERABILITY

We currently lack confirmatory data about any specific risk factors for the development of avoidant disorder of childhood. The "behavioral inhibition" hypothesis, even though intuitively attractive, awaits further study and confirmation.

Differential Diagnosis

Avoidant disorder of childhood must be distinguished from the following other conditions: social reticence, social phobias, separation anxiety disorder, overanxious disorder, depressive disorders, adjustment disorder with withdrawal, elective mutism, avoidant personality disorder, and schizoid personality traits or disorder.

Socially reticent children who are slow to warm up but who can respond after a short time and do not show significant social impairment may represent a less extreme expression of the same underlying traits as exhibited in avoidant disorder of childhood.

In contrast to the child with avoidant disorder who show generalized social anxiety, the child with social phobia reacts with anxiety and avoidance to one or more specific situations in which he or she may be exposed to scrutiny. In addition, the child with avoidant disorder often will become slowly but progressively less anxious with continued exposure to an anxiety-producing situation, especially when given emotional support; in contrast, the child with a social phobia remains anxious with exposure and characteristically tries to escape as soon as possible. The differential diagnosis may be difficult when the socially phobic child's fear involve many social situations, such as a generalized fear of being asked questions or speaking in public. It may be clarified by the fact that the child with avoidant disorder shows a more pervasive and long-lasting trait of shyness while the child with social phobia functions well unless exposed to the specific fear-producing stimulus.

In separation anxiety disorder, anxiety is triggered to separation from important figures rather than by new situations or people. In contrast, children with avoidant disorder will not show anxiety about leaving parents or home unless they are encountering a novel or feared social situation.

In overanxious disorder, patients suffer from generalized anxiety and worry that is not confined to new situations or people.

Depressive disorders may result in a generalized withdrawal from social situations but also are distinguished by a pervasive depressed mood, anhedonia, and a loss of interest in social contact. In contrast, children with avoidant disorder long for social contacts and feel reactively depressed in social situations in which they are unsuccessful.

Adjustment disorder with withdrawal may appear similar to avoidant disorder but is usually preceded by a specific stressor, has a duration of less than 6 months, and lacks a premorbid history of social anxiety and withdrawal.

Descriptively, the child with elective mutism can show an extreme form of social avoidance coupled with a complete absence of verbal communication with adults and peers outside the family. There are occasional cases of children with elective mutism who seem to function well and relate well to peers except for a total lack of verbal interaction. However, more detailed examination of such patients often reveals both significant deficits in ego functioning and object relationships and considerable family psychopathology.

The avoidant personality disorder shows similar but even more pervasive and fixed pathology than the avoidant disorder of childhood. It is thought to be the sequela of avoidant disorder and by definition begins in early adulthood.

Schizoid personality traits or disorder may show similar patterns of social withdrawal and aloofness. In addition, however, the schizoid child has no interest in or desire for social relations, actively prefers solitary activities, and is completely indifferent to both the positive and negative opinions and reactions of other people. In contrast, the child with avoidant disorder actively yearns for personal relationships and friendships and is constantly worried and hypersensitive about the opinions and reactions of others.

Morbidity

EFFECTS ON CHILD'S FUNCTIONING AND DEVELOPMENT

Depending on the severity of the disorder, its effect on functioning and development can range from minimal to moderate impairment. Extremely anxious and socially avoidant children can grow up without friends and remain unable to acquire the social skills requisite to interact successfully with peers in later stages of development. Because of their natural intelligence and talents, they may be able to continue to be successful academically but remain severely socially handicapped for the rest of their lives.

IMPACT OF FAMILY, INTERPERSONAL, AND SOCIAL ENVIRONMENT

Family and interpersonal and social environment are important variables that may either reinforce or tend to alleviate the severity of the psychopathology. On the one hand, children with avoidant disorder who have a supportive, nonjudgmental family and a nurturant social environment may be helped either to adjust more comfortably to or even partially overcome their social anxiety. On the other hand, judgmental, insensitive, and aggressive parents, teachers, and friends who make a child with avoidant disorder feel humiliated will reinforce and solidify the psychopathology, often to a devastating degree.

COMORBIDITY

As mentioned earlier, avoidant disorder of childhood has a high rate of comorbidity with all of the anxiety disorders, especially overanxious disorder and separation anxiety disorder. It also may be seen with social phobias.

SEQUELAE

The most serious sequela to this disorder is the avoidant personality disorder, with severe impairment in social and occupational functioning. Such individuals suffer from intense social anxiety, have few or no close friends, lead constricted, timid, frightened lives, and avoid new, potentially stressful situations even to extent of turning down promotions and advancements in their careers.

PROGNOSIS

No information is currently available about general prognosis and predictors of favorable versus unfavorable outcomes.

Treatment

PSYCHOLOGICAL AND SOCIAL MODALITIES

Individual, family, and cognitive/behavioral therapies have all been reported to be useful treatment modalities by clinicians treating patients with avoidant disorder of childhood (McDermott, Werry, Petti, Combrinck-Graham, & Char, 1989). However, these reports are anecdotal, and well-controlled treatment outcome studies are lacking at this time.

Because children with avoidant disorder of childhood have high rates of comorbidity with other anxiety disorders, especially overanxious disorder and separation anxiety disorder, it is likely that treatment of this disorder will be only one part of the overall treatment goals for the patient.

Individual psychotherapists may use a combination of supportive and interpretative techniques to help the child understand the unconscious, dynamic origins of his or her social discomfort and hypersensitivity to negative signals from the environment. In addition, both children and adolescents usually require additional guidance, education, and support to help them find practical ways in which to overcome their isolation and to find a place for themselves in the wider community of their peers. Finally, some children with avoidant disorder may come from families that are themselves socially or culturally isolated, such as first-generation immigrants or parents who are struggling with chronic illness. Such children, especially those approaching adolescence, may need special help to deal with a developmentally heightened sense of shame about their origins and to deal with their ambivalence, loyalty conflicts, and guilty feelings about becoming more independent of their cultural milieu.

A variety of family therapy and parent counseling techniques can be useful in exploring and modifying family patterns that reinforce avoidant and anxious behaviors in a child. In some cases, parents who themselves are struggling with chronic social anxiety may need help in modifying their own patterns of social withdrawal so as to provide more effective role models for their children. In other cases, social anxiety and avoidance in a child may be reinforced by the attitudes and behaviors of families that are closely knit and overly dependent on each other or who regard a child's strivings for independence as potentially dangerous or rebellious. It is useful to remember that there is statistically an increased prevalence of anxiety disorders in the families of children with anxiety disorders. Because of this, it is likely that at least one other member of the child's family may need help with his or her own problems.

Group therapy approaches also may be very useful in selected cases, especially with children who need help in acquiring social skills that their families have not been able to teach them and who may benefit from the therapist's direction, support, and guidance. This type of therapy can be extremely useful for children whose parents are chronically isolated because of language barriers or because they suffer from incapacitating physical and mental illnesses.

Cognitive/behavioral therapists utilize various combinations of treatment techniques to treat children with avoidant disorders and other anxiety disorders. These techniques include training in deep muscle relaxation, cognitive restructuring, problem solving training, operant conditioning (also called contingent reinforcement), modeling procedures, and both in vitro and in vivo exposure. Many of these techniques seem to involve the systematic, organized application of time-honored parenting techniques and supportive advice-giving interventions.

To date, there is no information on well-controlled, well-designed treatment studies utilizing these techniques in child and adolescent populations, but case reports of therapeutic success with them indicate that further investigation is warranted, especially of the techniques of generalized imitation, participant modeling, and operant reinforcement (Kendall et al., 1991). The potential usefulness of these approaches is further hinted at by longitudinal research with young children with biological and behavioral markers for behavioral inhibition and shyness. Even though these markers have been shown statistically to predict increased risk for later development of anxiety disorders, including avoidant disorder, some children with these markers had a healthy outcome without any type of treatment. Perhaps this was the result of some parents making long-term systematic efforts to teach their more vulnerable children to cope, using home-spun variants of these cognitive/behavioral techniques.

EDUCATIONAL INTERVENTIONS

We lack any information about the usefulness of educational techniques in treating avoidant behavior of childhood. Empirically, however, it may be useful for the therapist to work with the child's teacher toward providing emotional support for the patient in anxiety-producing situations at school. In addition, behavioral interventions such as operant reinforcement of nonavoidant, assertive classroom behavior may be implemented by a cooperative teacher. Finally, special tutoring may be helpful for the child whose avoidant behaviors has led to educational gaps.

BIOLOGICAL TREATMENT

Pharmacotherapy also has been advocated (McDermott et al., 1989) as a treatment modality for avoidant disorder, although there are no systematic, controlled studies about its efficacy. Empirically, some clinicians may use low doses of diazepam (Valium) or another benzodiazepine for the short-term treatment of the anxiety that leads to social avoidance. The rationale for this approach is to provide the child with a period of time to learn to master a feared situation while his or her anxiety level has been lowered to normal limits. This approach may be combined with either psychotherapy and/or cognitive/behavioral techniques in the hope that they will act synergistically to modify the patient's response to social situations and help him or her to learn new coping techniques.

MILIEU TREATMENT

Milieu treatment has not been studied as a treatment modality. Empirically, it may be indicated when a child is functionally incapacitated by a combination of severe anxiety disorders and requires more structure and emotional support than can be provided by his or her usual environment.

Current Developments, Research, and Unanswered Questions

The information currently available about avoidant disorder of childhood is minimal, and further research is needed in every respect. Among the important unanswered questions about this disorder are, first, whether avoidant disorder is a truly valid diagnostic entity or only one symptomatic varient of a diffuse and pervasive anxiety diathesis. Second, are excessive stranger anxiety and "behavioral inhibition to the unfamiliar" valid risk factors for the later development of social anxiety and avoidance? Third, if they are valid predictors, are they valid predictors of a separate disorder whose existence can be validated statistically, or are they valid predictors of a personality and behavioral trait that can be found in a broad range of disorders, especially the anxiety disorders?

REFERENCES

Bell-Dolan, D., Last, C., & Strauss, C. (1990). Symptoms of anxiety disorders in normal children. *Journal of the American Academy of Child and Adolescent Psychiatry, 29,* 759–765.

Biederman, J., Rosenbaum, J., Hirshfeld, D., Faraone, S., Boldue, E., Gersten, M., Meminger, S., Kagan, J., Snidman, N., & Reznick, J. (1990). Psychiatric correlates of behavioral inhibition in young children of parents with and without psychiatric disorders. *Archives of General Psychiatry, 47,* 21–26.

Cantwell, D. P., & Baker, L. (1989). Stability and natural history of DSM-III childhood diagnoses. *Journal of the American Academy of Child and Adolescent Psychiatry, 28,* 691–700.

Goethe, J. W. (1951). *Faust* (L. Macneice, trans.). New York: Oxford University Press.

Kagan, J., Reznick, J., & Snidman, N. (1987). The physiology and psychology of behavioral inhibition in children. *Child Development, 58,* 1459–1473.

Kendall, P., Chansky, T., Friedman, M., Kim, R., Kortlandee, E., Sessa, F., & Siqueland, L. (1991) Treating anxiety disorders in children and adolescents. In P. C. Kendall, (Ed.), *Child and adolescent therapy.*

Cognitive-Behavioral Procedures. New York: Guilford Press.

Last, C., Francis, G., Strauss, C. C. (1989). Assessing fears in anxiety-disordered children with the Revised Fears Survey Schedule for Children. *Journal of Clinical Child Psychology, 18,* 137–141.

McDermott, J., Werry, J., Petti, T., Combrinck-Graham, L., & Char, W. (1989). Anxiety disorders of childhood or adolescence. In T. Karasu, (Ed.), *Treat-*

ments of psychiatric disorders: A Task Force report of the American Psychiatric Association. 1, 401–443.

Stern, D. (1985). *The interpersonal world of the infant: A view from psychoanalysis and developmental psychology.* New York: Basic Books.

Thomas, A., & Chess, S. (1963). *Behavioral individuality in early childhood.* New York: New York University Press.

46 / Overanxious Disorder of Childhood

John J. Stine

Background

HISTORY OF THE DISORDER

The earliest attention given to anxiety disorders in children appears in the 18th century, when European philosophers such as Locke and Rousseau advocated the treatment of irrational fears in children by gradual exposure (McDermott, Werry, Petti, Combrinck-Graham, & Char, 1990). The first modern approach to anxiety disorders began at the end of the 19th century, when Sigmund Freud (1895/1962a) invented the term *anxiety neurosis* to describe a syndrome in adults that he separated from the then widely utilized syndrome of neuresthenia. Except for the fact that he included phobias and anxiety attacks in this syndrome, Freud's diagnostic criteria were remarkably similar to current diagnostic criteria for both general anxiety disorder and overanxious disorder of childhood. (See Tables 46.1–46.4.)

Historically, although there had been long-standing recognition of the fact that children suffered from psychopathological states that included symptoms of tension and anxiety (Klein & Last, 1989), there was no systematic study of the childhood forms of these disorders until Freud (1909/1955) described the clinical picture and psychodynamic mechanisms of phobia in a child. His aim was to demonstrate the existence of the unconscious dynamics of the oedipal phase in a child in order to underscore the universality of the Oedipus conflict. In this work, Freud also began

to distinguish between anxiety neurosis and phobia, although some authors continued to use the term *anxiety neurosis* to include phobic symptoms, panic attacks, and other symptoms of anxiety.

Over the next 70 years, several different models were developed to conceptualize the clinical problem of anxiety in children. Some child psychiatrists continued to use the concept of anxiety in a generic, general way as a manifestation of neuropathological disorders usually found in adults but occasionally also affecting children. Others used it to describe a wide range of behavioral or subjective problems resulting from traumatic or stressful environmental events throughout the life course. Kanner (1948), for example, in one of the pioneering American textbooks of child psychiatry, utilized terms such as *anxiety, fears,* and *worries* without attempting to organize these problems into diagnostic categories or syndromes. He similarly proposed commonsense, empirically based therapeutic interventions. This trend of generalization and nonspecificity is also conveyed metaphorically by the title of once-important but now-defunct child psychiatry journal, *The Nervous Child.*

A similar trend is found in the literature of academic psychology and behaviorism, where anxiety in childhood was widely regarded as a learned, externally conditioned and reinforced habit rather than the manifestation of a clinical disorder or syndrome.

In contrast, psychoanalytically trained child

TABLE 46.1

Diagnostic Features of "Anxiety Neurosis" from Freud (1895/1962a)

1. Anxious expectation, hypochondriasis, and "moral anxiety" (literally "conscience anxiety" or guilt)

2. General irritability, often accompanied by sleeplessness and auditory hyperaesthesia

3. Anxiety attacks, alone or accompanied by fears about health and death and by disturbances in bodily functions that are signs of autonomic hyper-reactivity (sweating, palpitations, dyspnea, tremors and shivering, hunger, dizziness, diarrhea, nausea, vomiting, and paresthesias)

4. Panic attacks, pavor nocturnus

5. Nocturnal panic attacks (waking up at night "in a fright" with anxiety, dyspnea, and sweating)

6. Phobias of specific objects or agoraphobia

7. A spectrum of severity and complexity, ranging from "rudimentary" anxiety syndromes through simple or highly complicated admixtures of symptoms

TABLE 46.2

Diagnostic Features of Overanxious Disorder of Childhood from DSM-III-R (1987)

1. Excessive or unrealistic worry about future events

2. Excessive or unrealistic concern about the appropriateness of past behavior

3. Excessive or unrealistic concern about competence in one or more areas, e.g., academics, athletics, social

4. Somatic complaints, such as headaches or stomachaches, for which no physical basis can be established

5. Marked self-consciousness

6. Excessive need for reassurance about a variety of concerns

7. Marked feelings of tension or inability to relax

NOTE. From *Diagnostic and Statistical Manual of Mental Disorders*, 3rd ed., rev., p. 64. American Psychiatric Association, 1987. Washington, D.C.: Author. Copyright 1987 by the American Psychiatric Association. Reprinted with permission.

psychiatrists attempted to subsume a wide range of anxiety conditions affecting children under the diagnostic terms *anxiety hysteria* or *anxiety neurosis* (Fenechel, 1945). Their diagnostic criteria remained based largely on Freud's original descriptions of anxiety neurosis and phobia.

Since the publication of the third edition of the *Diagnostic and Statistical Manual of Mental Disorders* in 1980 (American Psychiatric Association [APA]), the entity of anxiety neurosis has been divided into a number of subcategories or types of anxiety disorder, including overanxious disorder of childhood. This change reflects both a desire for increasing specificity in diagnosis and treatment and a current resurgence of interest in studying possible biological causes for emotional disorders in both adults and children. However, there has been considerable controversy among child psychiatrists over the relative merits of this change.

Those with a commitment to epidemiology and empirical research have advanced the following arguments in support of this change: First, the division of childhood anxiety disorders into several categories facilitates empirical research and the development of phenomenological distinctions between clinical conditions. Second, many chil-

dren who present with anxiety disorders do not demonstrate the typical psychodynamics of a structured infantile neurosis derived from oedipal conflict. This is especially true of anxious children who show significant comorbidity with behavior or affective disorders and a history of illness that demonstrates considerable preoedipal pathology and etiological mechanisms. Therefore, replacing the term *neurosis* with *disorder* will facilitate objective research into etiology by removing the "presupposition" that these conditions are always due to neurotic conflict and may ultimately result in new treatment strategies.

On the other hand, many clinicians criticize these new disorders as artificially distinct because they often do not apply to the complexities of actual clinical pictures in "real-life situations." This position also seems to be supported by recent empirical studies that find both considerable diagnostic overlap and comorbidity between the different types of anxiety disorders described in the third revised edition of *DSM* (*DSM-III-R;* APA, 1987). Perhaps as a result of these criticisms, the most recent edition of the *Diagnostic and Statistical Manual of Mental Disorders* (4th ed.; *DSM-IV,* APA, 1994) has attempted to address the overlap in clinical features by including overanxious disorder of childhood within generalized anxiety disorder. Psychodynamically oriented clinicians and

TABLE 46.3

Diagnostic Features of Generalized Anxiety Disorder from DSM-III-R (1987)

A. Unrealistic or excessive anxiety and worry (apprehensive expectation) about two or more life circumstances . . . in children and adolescents; this may take the form of anxiety and worry about athletic, academic, and social performance.

B. At least 6 of the following 18 symptoms are often present when anxious . . .:

Motor tension
(1) trembling, twitching or feeling shaky
(2) muscle tension, aches, or soreness
(3) restlessness
(4) easy fatigability

Autonomic hyperactivity
(5) shortness of breath (dyspnea) . . .
(6) palpitations . . .
(7) sweating, or cold clammy hands
(8) dry mouth
(9) dizziness or lightheadedness
(10) nausea, diarrhea, or other abdominal distress
(11) flushes (hot flashes) or chills
(12) frequent urination
(13) trouble swallowing or "lump in throat"

Vigilance and scanning
(14) feeling keyed up and on edge
(15) exaggerated startle response
(16) difficulty concentrating or "mind going blank" because of anxiety
(17) trouble falling or staying asleep
(18) irritability

NOTE. From *Diagnostic and Statistical Manual of Mental Disorders*, 3rd ed., rev., pp. 252–253. American Psychiatric Association, 1994. Washington, D.C.: Author. Copyright 1987 by the American Psychiatric Association. Reprinted with permission.

TABLE 46.4

Diagnostic Criteria for Generalized Anxiety Disorder from DSM-IV (1994)

A. Excessive anxiety and worry (anxious apprehension), occurring more days than not for at least 6 months, about a number of events or activities (such as work or school performance).

B. The person finds it hard to control the worry.

C. The anxiety and worry are associated with three (or more) of the following six symptoms (with at least some symptoms present for more days than not for the past 6 months). Note: Only one item is required for diagnosis in children.

(1) restlessness . . .
(2) being easily fatigued
(3) difficulty in concentrating or mind going blank
(4) irritability
(5) muscle tension
(6) sleep disturbance . . .

D. The focus of the anxiety and worry is not confined to features of an Axis I disorder . . . and . . . do not occur exclusively during Posttraumatic Stress Disorder.

E. The . . . symptoms cause clinically significant distress or impairment in . . . functioning.

F. The disturbance is not due to direct physiological effects of a substance . . . or a general medical condition . . . and does not occur exclusively during a Mood Disorder, a Psychotic Disorder, a Pervasive Developmental Disorder.

NOTE. From *Diagnostic and Statistical Manual of Mental Disorders*, 4th ed., pp. 435–436, American Psychiatric Association, 1994. Washington, D.C.: Author. Copyright 1994 by the American Psychiatric Association. Reprinted with permission.

child psychoanalysts are additionally skeptical of a nosological approach that seems to minimize or even eliminate the central role of psychic conflict in the anxiety disorders.

Psychoanalytic developmental psychology provides one way to unify both the available epidemiological data and these seemingly incompatible theoretical positions by providing a framework for both a spectrum of etiological factors and a spectrum of psychopathology ranging from pure childhood neurosis to admixtures of preoedipal pathology that present with predominent symptoms of anxiety.

Although psychoanalytic theory initially focused on the centrality of sexuality, libidinal drive theory, and oedipal conflict in order to explain the etiology of anxiety neurosis, Freud was always very much aware of the contribution of multiple etiological factors. From the beginning of his study of anxiety (Freud, 1895/1962a), he postulated the existence of constitutional, specific, concurrent, and precipitating causal factors for anxiety neurosis. Over the course of his clinical career, he broadened this concept into a complemental etiological series for all psychic illness (Freud, 1917/1963).

Years of clinical experience and an increasing body of research support the applicability of Freud's hypothesis to the study of the anxiety in childhood. There is increasingly persuasive empirical evidence that biological, constitutional, familial, developmental, preoedipal, environmental, and traumatic factors, as well as oedipal conflicts, all can play complemental, important, and covarying roles in the etiology of overanxious disorder and in producing the wide spectrum of clinical pictures that may be brought together under this diagnostic heading.

In addition, psychoanalytically trained clinicians and theoreticians have been able to utilize a psychoanalytically informed approach to understand psychopathology that is not based primarily on classic oedipal psychodynamic mechanisms. For example, Anna Freud (1971) has pointed out that seemingly neurotic symptoms such as anxiety, fears, and worries may reflect either a structured, internalized infantile neurosis organized around the oedipal and castration complexes or a diffuse, unstable, and unorganized collection of neurotic-like symptomatology reflecting a developmental arrest on a preoedipal level of psychopathology. Similarly, Nagera (1963, 1964) has discussed how

the individual clinical picture is shaped by developmental interferences, developmental conflicts, and individual neurotic conflicts, all interacting with biological and environmental forces. Like Anna Freud, he emphasizes the importance of careful diagnostic evaluation to differentiate between true childhood neurosis and diffuse states of preoedipal pathology that superficially appear neurotic but are the result of developmental arrests and varying degrees of ego and superego pathology.

COMPARATIVE NOSOLOGY

For many years, children, like adults, were seen as simply having admixtures of symptoms of anxiety, phobias, and avoidant behaviors. Although Freud differentiated and described phobic condition in childhood (Freud, 1909/1955), he considered it to be a variant of a diffuse, underlying anxiety neurosis, differentiated only on the basis of choice of defense mechanisms in response to anxiety. Beginning with *DSM-III*, the anxiety disorders in childhood have been subdivided into three major categories: (1) overanxious disorder of childhood, (2) separation anxiety disorder, and (3) avoidant disorder. In addition, phobic disorders in children were to be diagnosed according to criteria developed for adults.

The separation of overanxious disorder of childhood from those disorders where anxiety is generated by more specific situations, objects, or fears was an important methodological advance in nosology because it provides a model for a more rigorous empirical study of anxiety disorders in children. However, as population studies have disclosed a significant degree of overlap and comorbidity between both the anxiety disorders and other emotional disorders of childhood, the statistical validity of these nosological categories has not been firmly established. In addition, many child psychiatrists argue that "anxiety neurosis" is still a clinically relevant and useful concept.

In *DSM-III-R* (APA, 1987), overanxious disorder of childhood was considered to be the most appropriate diagnostic term for pervasive anxiety states in child and adolescent populations, the volume specified that generalized anxiety disorder also be used as a Axis I diagnosis for children at the discretion of the clinician. More recently, *DSM-IV* (APA, 1994) includes overanxious disorder of childhood entirely under the rubric of generalized anxiety disorder (GAD). However, many researchers maintain that there is no empirical evidence that children with anxiety disorders actually do meet the diagnostic criteria for GAD. For example, Last (Klein & Last, 1989) reports that no cases of GAD could be found in a study of several hundred children and adolescents referred to an anxiety disorders clinic over a period of several years. Moreover, there is such overlap between these two diagnostic categories that some clinicians have hypothesized that they represent the childhood and adult forms of the same disorder. Unfortunately, the limited epidemiological data currently available does not clarify this issue.

In our present state of knowledge, we are unable to determine whether overanxious disorder and generalized anxiety disorder are different disorders with distinct underlying biological, familial, or psychodynamically determined causes or if they represent different modes of expression of the same underlying pervasive anxiety disorder. In overanxious disorder, there is more of a diagnostic focus on anxious ideation in the form of consciously experienced worries, while in generalized anxiety disorder, diagnostic criteria focus more on somatically experienced concommitants of anxiety, such as autonomic hyperreactivity. These differences in expression may depend on a complex mixture of factors, including relative ego strength, superego development, and family and cultural factors that shape the individual's characteristic patterns of experiencing and reacting to anxiety. However, the lack of any empirical evidence that GAD actually can be found in child populations leaves this issue essentially unresolved.

DEVELOPMENTAL ISSUES

Fears and anxieties are widely considered to be normal and universal phenomena in the developmental process. Stranger anxiety, separation fears, social shyness, fears of failure, and fears of the dark, animals, or bad dreams are all part of the everyday problems of childhood. From a developmental point of view, these symptoms occur frequently throughout childhood and tend to cluster at certain expectable points in the life cycle. One important view has been that they are the markers or epiphenomena of normative developmental crises, such as the development of attachment,

the transition to object permanence, the rapprochement crisis, and the height of the oedipal conflict. According to this model, symptomatic manifestations of these developmental crises may be prolonged or intensified by either chronic environmental stressors or acute traumatic events in a child's life.

A key question for the clinician is at what point is it appropriate to redefine these "normal symptoms" as an emotional disorder. The following four criteria may be useful:

1. Chronicity. Based on *DSM-IV* standards, for example, problems lasting for 6 or more months are somewhat arbitrarily considered to be chronic enough to constitute an emotional disorder.

2. Symptom intensity. Some researchers have assigned numerical ratings to the presence, probable presence, or absence of diagnostic indicators so that a numerical cut-off point can be used to define the presence or absence of an emotional disorder.

3. Interference with functioning. The existence of a group of symptoms is considered to be more likely evidence of emotional disorder if they seem to cause significant interference with age-appropriate social, cognitive, behavioral, and psychological functioning. Indeed, using rating instruments such as the Children's Global Assessment of Functioning Scale, epidemiological studies have shown a large difference in the prevalence of anxiety disorders based on whether impaired functioning is taken into account or not.

4. Interference with the process of psychological development. A methodical, careful assessment of the child's internal, psychological developmental progress is an invaluable supplement to assessment. This is particularly important in assessing the anxiety disorders, since an anxious, worried, conforming child may appear to be fitting in while quietly failing to develop age-appropriate object relationships, sublimations, defenses, and ego capacities. Conversely, the shy child with a mild avoidant disorder may appear to be much more impaired than is actually the case. Anna Freud's concept of developmental lines (1965) is valuable because its regular application also keeps the clinician alert for the more ominous occurrence of developmental regressions. For example, the pervasively anxious 9-year-old boy who now prefers playing games with much younger children and whose fantasy life is becoming increasingly concentrated on cartoon characters favored by 5-year-olds is in serious psychological difficulty, regard-

less of the manifest level of his functioning with adults or in school.

EPIDEMIOLOGICAL DATA

Prevalence of Anxiety Disorders: Based on current data, anxiety disorders are the most prevalent psychiatric conditions in the child and adolescent populations. Prevalence rates in a number of studies range between 8 to 9.5% when both *DSM-III-R* criteria and the presence of significant functional impairment were used as criteria (Anderson, 1987; Costello, 1989; Kashani & Orvashel, 1990; McGee et al., 1990).

Prevalence of Overanxious Disorder in the General Population: The 1-year prevalence of overanxious disorder ranges from 2.9 ± ½% in a study of 792 11-year-olds in the Dunedin longitudinal study of a representational cohort of New Zealand children (Anderson, 1987) to 4.1% in a study of 300 children drawn from a primary care pediatric sample of 7- to 11-year-olds in a medium-size U.S. city (Costello, 1989). This range is replicated in the majority of studies with the exception of a prevalence of 19.1% in a study of school-age children in upper New York State (Velez, Johnson, & Cohen, 1989). However, this may reflect the fact that Velez et al.'s cohort were diagnosed only on the basis of the presence or absence of symptoms, while the other studies used the additional criteria of significant functional impairment.

In one large nonreferred population of 5,596 adolescents, the lifetime prevalence of generalized anxiety disorder was found to be 3.7%; however, girls had a much higher prevalence (4.6%) than did boys (1.8%) (Whitaker et al., 1990). This is in general agreement with the Dunedin study of 953 adolescents age 15 from a general population (McGee et al., 1990), which found that overanxious disorder had a prevalence of 5.9 ± ½% with a 1.9:1 female-to-male ratio.

Prevalence of Overanxious Disorder in Clinical Populations: Last, Herson, Kazdin, Finkelstein, and Strauss (1987) found that of 91 children evaluated in an anxiety disorders clinic, 26% met the *DSM-III-R* criteria for overanxious disorder and 21% met criteria for both overanxious and separation anxiety disorders.

Male-Female Ratio: In general, sex ratio has been found to be approximately equal until adolescence, after which females predominate. The only exception was in the cohort of children studied by Cantwell and Baker (1989), which showed a proponderance of boys with the disorder. However, the fact that this population all suffered from coexisting speech and language disorders may have introduced confounding variables into the statistical analysis.

Age of Onset: The earliest reported age of onset has been at 4 years. Although the disorder can appear at any age, studies in clinical populations indicate that there is an increased onset with advancing age, especially in females after the beginning of adolescence.

Clinical Course: The limited data currently available indicates that overanxious disorder is a diagnostically unstable condition. The majority of cases disappear in about two years or seem to change into other types of anxiety disorder. An unknown minority run a chronic course.

Age of Presentation: Children with overanxious disorder have an older mean age at presentation to a clinic (13.4 years) than children with separation anxiety disorder (19.1 years) or children with both overanxious disorder and separation anxiety disorder (9.8 years) (Last et al., 1987).

Socioeconomic Status: Last et al. (1987) report that the majority (80%) of children with overanxious disorder come from families of middle or upper socioeconomic background while the majority of children with separation anxiety (75%) or separation anxiety plus overanxious disorder (61%) come from families of lower socioeconomic background.

Reliability and Validity of the Diagnosis: Continuing problems in establishing diagnostic reliability and validity confound attempts to distinguish overanxious disorder from other types of anxiety disorders. Although there is sufficiently good interrater reliability in a range of published studies to support the general utility of this diagnosis, cross-informant and test-retest reliability studies have yielded poor results (Werry, 1991). This lack of diagnostic stability over time is an important finding, reflecting the tendency for overanxious disorder to change into or emerge from other anxiety disorders.

In addition, there is significant overlap of *DSM-III-R* diagnostic criteria with other anxiety disorders. For example, items 1, 2, and 3 (excessive worries about past, future events, and general competence in school, athletics, and socially) clearly can be seen in social phobia and avoidant disorder. There is also a significant prevalence of the symptoms of overanxious disorder in the normal population (Bell-Dolan, Last, & Strauss, 1990). Because of these findings, some researchers have questioned the appropriateness of an exclusively biological-medical model for overanxious disorder. Beidel (1991), for example, suggests that it is a prodromal syndrome that precedes the onset of other anxiety disorders and remains after they have resolved. Many psychodynamically oriented clinicians similarly believe that overanxious disorder represents a predisposition to an anxiety diathesis that is shaped by changing developmental, environmental, and psychodynamic forces.

Clinical Presentation and Diagnostic Assessment

OVERT SIGNS AND SYMPTOMS

The essential clinical picture of this disorder is a child with generalized, excessive, and unrealistic anxieties and fearful, timid behaviors that have persisted for more than 6 months. This contrasts with other anxiety disorders in which signs and symptoms of distress are primarily related to specific types of situations (e.g., separations or phobic objects) or external stressors (e.g., recent acute stresses such as parental illness or divorce).

The patient's presenting problems can be placed in 3 subcategories: excessive and pervasive worries about every aspect of life, overconcern with competency and social acceptance, and psychophysiological expressions of anxiety. These categories can be expanded into 7 diagnostic criteria, 4 of which must be present frequently in order to establish the diagnosis by *DSM-III-R* criteria.

1. Excessive or unrealistic worry about future events. Parents often describe such children as tense and apprehensive about school exams, going into new situations, travel, and vacations. The children often describe themselves as nervous and unable to sleep the night before a test, a rou-tine visit to the pediatrician, or going off to summer camp. There is limited epidemiological evidence that this is a key criteria for the diagnosis. Bernstein and Borhardt (1991) indicate that 53 of 55 children and adolescents with overanxious disorder reported having unrealistic worries about future events.

2. Excessive or unrealistic worry about past behavior. Such children may dwell on minor imperfections or problems from the recent or distant past or worries about previous illnesses or family problems being harbingers of future disaster.

3. Excessive or unrealistic concern about competence in one or more areas, such as athletics, academics, and social situations. Such children can torment themselves with endless, self-critical thoughts about a less-than-perfect mark on a test, a dropped ball on the baseball field, or a minor slight from a friend that is part of the ordinary give-and-take of middle childhood.

4. Marked self-consciousness. Children with overanxious disorder are typically tense in public situations, worrying constantly about wearing the right clothes, being accepted by peers, not standing out as different, performing perfectly at school, not embarrassing themselves, or not being singled out for criticism. They often perceive themselves as disliked or criticized even when this is not the case.

5. Excessive need for reassurance. Younger children with overanxious disorder often need and sometimes are able to request constant reassurance that they are liked, loved, accepted, and will be protected from danger. They may barrage their parents with endless, anxious questions about the possible dangers that they anticipate or, alternatively, suffer in apprehensive silence and manifest their tension somatically.

6. Somatic complaints with no physical basis. Many children with OAD complain frequently about headaches, stomachaches, nausea, dizziness, and a multitude of nonspecific somatic symptoms. They frequently attribute their inability to sleep to these problems and are often subjected to multiple medical evaluations before their underlying anxiety is finally recognized. This is an important diagnostic factor that should alert the clinician to look deeper, since a large number of studies have demonstrated a significantly greater likelihood of psychiatric problems in groups of children with high frequencies of somatic complaints (Campo & Fritsch, 1996). Other children display more overt signs of anxiety, such as thumb-sucking, nail-biting, hair-twirling, and frequent anxiety dreams.

7. Marked feelings of tension and inability to relax.

Eliciting this symptom often depends on the interviewer's persistence, tact, and skill, since some children with overanxious disorder either do not have the proper "vocabulary" with which to describe their feelings or are used to covering up their distress because of shame, fear, or intense perfectionism. It is important for the interviewer to have a high rate of suspicion for unexpressed feelings of anxiety in children and not rely solely on parent or teacher reports. This clinical maxim is supported by epidemiological studies that show that there is a low level of agreement among parent, child, and teacher about the existence of a psychiatric disorder in the child and that mothers frequently underreport the presence of anxiety symptoms in their children (Costello, 1989).

In addition to these common manifestations, children with overanxious disorder can show a number of accessory signs and symptoms, including sleep disturbances, thumb-sucking, nail-biting, hair-twirling, enuresis, behavioral restlessness, inattention, daydreaming, social withdrawal, depressive mood, and general irritability. These can be alternatively seen as nonspecific signs of anxiety, neurotically determined symptoms, or learned, behaviorally reinforced manifestations of a disturbed and disturbing environment.

This clinical picture and the additional features described in the rest of this section are typical of cases of pure overanxious disorder. In patients who show significant comorbidity, the clinical picture will reflect the admixture of coexisting diagnostic entities manifested by the individual child.

RELATIONSHIP TO OTHER DISORDERS

Although about 50% of affected children show a pure form of overanxious disorder, there is growing evidence that children with this disorder show significant comorbidity with other disorders. In general, children presenting with any anxiety disorder have a greater than 50% chance of having a history or current clinical picture of multiple anxiety disorders (Last, Herson, Kazdin, Orvaschel, & Perrin, 1991). Last (1987b) found that, at least in a clinic population of 91 children and adolescents, children with overanxious disorder were more likely to show comorbidity with other anxiety disorders than children with separation anxiety disorder. She hypothesized that because of a younger age of onset, separation anxiety disor-

der may represent a risk factor or precursor to the later development of overanxious disorder.

In over 50% of cases, overanxious disorder is found to coexist with separation anxiety disorder, phobic disorders, major depression, mood disorders, and attention deficit disorder. Last (1987b) reported that more than half of a clinic population of children with overanxious disorder had at least one additional anxiety disorder. In this study, 26.9% had a coexisting simple phobia and 15.4% had coexisting panic disorder. In addition, 38.1% of these children had attention deficit plus separation anxiety disorder. In another study, 70% of adolescents with a primary of overanxious disorder suffered from separation anxiety disorder and 41% suffered from simple phobia (Strauss, 1988).

There is also a significant comorbidity with attention deficit disorder. Several studies of clinic populations show that between 15 and 35% of children diagnosed as having an anxiety disorder also met *DSM-III-R* criteria for attention deficit disorder (Anderson et al., 1987; Last, 1987b).

Finally, overanxious disorder has been found to have significant comorbidity with mood disorders. For example, 47% of a clinical population of adolescents with overanxious disorder also had major depression (Strauss, 1988). A retrospective study of 52 depressed children and adolescents seen at the Maudsley Hospital in the late 1960s and early 1970s found both a high prevalence of coexisting symptoms of anxiety and depression and that while 58% developed an affective disorder in adulthood, 31% of this same population *also* developed an anxiety disorder (Harrington, Fudge, Rutter, Pickles, & Hill, 1990). Last (1987b) reported that 42.3% of a clinic population of elementary-school-age children with overanxious disorder had a coexisting major depression.

PATTERNS OF PEER RELATIONSHIPS

Overanxious disorder can progressively interfere with normal peer relations, often causing social withdrawal, peer rejection, and failure to develop age-appropriate social skills. In comparison with normal controls, children with anxiety and depression become increasingly solitary, are less liked by their peers, and show decreasing self-esteem with advancing age (Anderson, Williams, McGee, & Silva, 1989).

While some children with overanxious disorder

do have a few close friendships that they are able to maintain over many years, they tend to be shy, submissive, inhibited, and passive children who have trouble socializing within large peer groups and in new social situations. When they do maintain friendships, they tend to gravitate toward other anxious, inhibited children and younger children, or they may become incorporated into the clique of a more assertive, controlling peer who enjoys dominating others. Occasionally such children can become the target for repetitive reenactments of sadomasochistic object relationships within the peer group. Unable to defend themselves or to establish other friendships, they may act out their frustration and chronic anger by teasing younger siblings or becoming passive-aggressively negativistic and irritable with their own families.

One 6-year-old boy, for example, was referred for chronic anxiety that disrupted his capacity to learn. Sweet, quiet, obedient, and eager to please, he did well behaviorally in school but at home was the bane of his parents' existence because of his chronic tantrums, negativism, infantile oppositionalism, and his tormenting of his 3-year-old sister with a never-ending barrage of teasingly sadistic threats. In psychotherapy, he gradually revealed how a smaller, younger, but more assertive and aggressive friend sadistically teased and bossed him around. Although literally the teacher's favorite child in her class, Bobby could not stand up to his friend because of his conviction that he and his entire family would get into serious trouble if he did. Instead, he would come home and displace his rage onto his family, whose gentle, supportive personalities made it difficult for them to set limits on his increasing misbehavior.

Boys with overanxious disorder often have increasing problems with peer relationships as they move into midlatency. Their pervasive anxieties make them avoid rough-and-tumble peer interactions and prevent them from acquiring athletic skills and the assertiveness necessary to function socially. As a result, they become less able to relate on an age-appropriate level and progressively feel different and alienated from their peers. Psychodynamically, this generates increased anxiety and further regressions. Many such boys develop progressively more inhibited and constricted personalities and unconsciously assume a passive, feminized, and latent homosexual stance because of an arrest in the negative oedipal phase of development. These maladaptive traits become increasingly ego syntonic in the 9- to 11-year age range, as defensive patterns consolidate and superego functioning becomes more integrated.

Girls with overanxious disorder often have less overt difficulties with peers because their shy, unassertive behavior may be more culturally acceptable. They too have great difficulties in asserting themselves in groups and tend to interact with a relatively small circle of friends. Because of their timidity and passivity, they are highly vulnerable to the normative intragroup fights and rivalries of midlatency-age girls. They easily can become the group scapegoat; alternatively, they may be protected and dominated by a more assertive peer with whom they enter into a thinly disguised, highly dependent, and often sadomasochistic relationship. With increasing severity of the disorder, girls too can become increasingly socially isolated. Their anxieties keep them from participating in social occasions, such as slumber parties or weekend trips. Instead, they often wind up taking a pseudomaternal but actually highly dependent role with younger children. For example, they may prefer to baby-sit, feed, and play with younger siblings, enacting with the younger child their own regressive wishes to be protected and nurtured.

PATTERNS OF PLAY

By midlatency, children with overanxious disorder generally play with peers in a constricted, inhibited, and timid manner. Boys often have great difficulty in engaging in the rough-and-tumble physical contact sports of the first stage of latency. Their anxiety about bodily injury and pervasive worries about disasters often make them so apprehensive about getting hurt that they cannot join in the adventurous, exploratory activities of their peers or develop the skills needed to participate in competitive, organized sports. This may reinforce their tendency to retreat into more passive play, such as an increasing reliance on fantasy play with action figures or computer and video games.

Boys with even higher levels of castration anxiety may retreat further from the latency heterosexual position and regress to an anal-sadistic libidinal position that is reflected in fantasy play that emphasizes themes of control, power struggles, and sadomasochistic struggle. By midlatency, many boys with overanxious disorder are able to use their high intelligence and perfectionistic tendencies to develop excellent skills at board games, hobbies involving collecting, mastery of computers, and other solitary play activities. In severe cases of overanxious disorder, children may entirely give up fantasy play because of the fears of breakthrough of their anxiety-laden and aggressive fantasies. Such children, unable to even entertain themselves, often retreat into endless hours of passive television viewing.

Girls with overanxious disorder in midlatency often appear to be much more socially appropriate in their play patterns. This is because fantasy play that enacts themes of dependency, nurturance, and protection from external danger is culturally more acceptable for girls. Like boys, girls with overanxious disorder tend to be timid and to avoid envolement with sports and activities that call for assertiveness or assuming leadership roles.

PSYCHODYNAMIC FORMULATION

Patterns of Defense: Children with a classical, pure form of overanxious disorder tend to use relatively "high-order" defense mechanisms such as displacement, suppression, avoidance, intellectualization, isolation, and rationization as defenses against exessive amounts of anxiety generated by intensified oedipal conflicts. In addition, they utilize the defense of projection of their inner sense of danger and anxiety onto the world, which they then experience as dangerous, frightening, and risk-filled. This is different from more pathological forms of projection in that fears are based in large degree on an exaggeration of realistic dangers rather than on the bizarre, unlikely sources of danger that the borderline or psychotic child may fear.

Other children with this disorder use regression to previous psychic fixation points as a defense against anxiety-producing, unacceptable oedipal wishes. As a result, they may behave in more obsessional or compulsive ways or become stubborn and obstinate when under stress.

Some children with overanxious disorder, especially when endowed with above-average intelligence, creative interests, and good imagination, will use immersion in fantasy as a defense. They can spend hours enjoying solitary fantasy play that repetitively reenacts the dynamic sources of their anxiety. This may assist them in their emotional functioning via a partial abreaction of their fears. However, there are several maladaptive aspects of this defense: first, because their fantasy play never successfully binds neurotic conflict but only holds it in partial check, the use of fantasy may spread and invade everyday life, resulting in excessive daydreaming in school. Second, excessive reliance on fantasy can reinforce the anxious child's tendency to withdraw socially and therefore fail to master age-appropriate social skills.

This process is often mirrored in the child's behavior in psychotherapy. Sarnoff (1989) has pointed out that such children often enthusiastically plunge into play therapy, producing voluminous amounts of highly symbolic, thematic material. However, as the therapy proceeds, it becomes clear that the patient has been using fantasy play primarily to discharge tension and actually is extremely resistant to discussing everyday problems and their connections to his or her fantasy life.

Ego Functioning and Strengths: Classically, children with overanxious disorder in general have been considered to have ego functioning in the neurotic range of personality organization. Although we lack empirical research data to support this view, it has face validity since it is precisely by the presence of intact ego functioning that overanxious disorder has been distinguished from more pathological sources of anxiety, such as borderline personality or pervasive developmental disorders. These children display many ego strengths, such as excellent reality testing, impulse control, a good capacity to modulate instincts and affects, good frustration tolerance, and an excellent capacity for secondary process thinking. They also often display hypermaturity and perfectionism that result from a combination of high intelligence, hypertrophied anal-sadistic defenses, and an overly demanding, punative superego. These traits can be considered strengths and assets but also can result in personality constriction and an increase in anxiety about failure and imperfection.

It is important to stress that this typical picture of a basically neurotic child may have been influenced by sampling bias, since it has been based largely on clinical experience in psychoanalytically oriented private practice or in outpatient clinics where more severe pathology is not treated. In fact, we are now learning that overanxious disorder often occurs comorbidity with other anxiety disorders as well as affective disorders and attention deficit disorders. More recent findings, although limited in scope, support the idea that comorbidity carries with it more impaired functioning.

By implication, such children may have more impaired ego functioning and more impaired cognitive capacities. Although they may appear superficially to suffer from neurotic symptomatology, a closer examination of their intrapsychic functioning may show a developmental arrest on the level of disjointed, diffuse, and unorganized neurotic symptoms in varying combinations with symptoms of other anxiety, conduct, and affective disorders. In addition, they will not show the hypermeticulous, perfectionistic trends that indicate that superego guilt is playing a role in neurotic conflict and compromise formation.

Self: In children with overanxious disorder, the "self-representation" and the capacity to maintain a firm boundary between self and object representations is intact. However, their self-esteem is typically low, and they regard themselves in a hypercritical, perfectionistic manner. Because they suffer from constant anxiety about being accepted and acceptable, their sense of self is highly dependent on the evaluation of others, and they are hypervigilant and hypersensitive to the slightest indication of slight and rejection. As a result, they often misinterpret the normally competitive, aggressive banter of their peer group as a devastating personal rejection that makes them withdraw still further.

Superego: In neurotic children with overanxious disorder, superego functioning is harsh, severe, and uncompromising; such children often suffer from intense unconscious guilt for their aggressive and sexual impulses. Consequently, their fantasies, dreams, and play activities will reflect neurotic compromise formations that embody forbidden oedipal wishes, symbolic punishments for these wishes, and defenses against the wishes. In addition, the children's guilt typically is projected and reversed, so that patients unconsciously experience others as disliking and disapproving of them. Simultaneously, the children's ego ideal is one of lofty and unattainable perfection; parents and authority figures are overidealized, and the children feel that they will never be able to measure up and be totally acceptable. Instead, self-worth becomes measured by relative success in meeting external, unrealistically high goals, such as very high school grades or scrupulously good manners. At the same time, high performance is often equated symbolically with expiation for guilt-laden, forbidden wishes. However, since external successes can ease unconscious guilt only temporarily, the children can never be satisfied but are driven relentlessly on to an endless succession of ultimately unsatisfying successes.

In children with significant comorbidity, superego functioning can be significantly impaired. Children with coexisting attention deficit disorder and conduct disorders may show deficient superego functioning, uneven superego functioning, or superego lacunae. Such children may have a conduct disorder because of a coexisting impulse disorder or superego deficit and not because they are acting out of guilt-charged unconscious wish to be punished.

COMPARISON WITH PRESENTATION OF SYNDROME IN OTHER STAGES OF LIFE

Older children report greater numbers of symptoms than younger children (MGee et al., 1990; Strauss, Lease, Last, & Francis, 1988). Strauss reports that 35% of children in 6- to 11-year-old group reported more than 5 symptoms while 66% of children and adolescents in 12- to 19-year-old group reported more than 5 symptoms and an increase in prevalence of worries about past behaviors (probably as result of superego consolidation). The general mode of presentation seems to be the same at all ages, although according to the diagnostic criteria of the generalized anxiety disorder of adulthood, there is more emphasis on somatic symptoms of anxiety.

Etiology and Pathogenesis

BIOLOGICAL ASPECTS

Genetic Aspects: Although epidemiological studies show that overanxious disorder and other anxiety disorders tend to have a higher familial prevalence, no clear evidence for genetic mechanisms of transmission have been found to date.

Neurochemical Aspects: Kagan, Reznick, and Snidman (1987) have demonstrated that young children with extreme degrees of "shy," "inhibited," or "introverted" temperamental characteristics not only preserve these traits over many years of growth but show statistically significant increased activation of those central nervous system physiological circuits that usually respond to novelty and challenge, namely the reticular activating system, hypothalamic-pituitary adrenal axis, and sympathetic nervous system. They have suggested that the threshold for activation in these systems is "tonically" lower for such children. Beiderman et al. (1990) have demonstrated that behaviorally inhibited children are at increased risk for developing overanxious disorder and multiple anxiety disorders, including separation anxiety, phobic, and avoidant disorders. This relationship held true for inhibited children who were the offspring of normal parents as well as the offspring of parents who were being treated for panic disorder and agoraphobia. This comparison is important, since Beiderman et al. also demonstrated that children of parents with anxiety disorders had significantly higher rates of anxiety disorders than children of a control population of normal adults. However, the presence or absence of behavioral inhibition in the child seems to be the critical predictive variable since rates of anxiety disorders were roughly identical in the two populations of children.

These findings imply that at least some children are predisposed to develop overanxious disorder because of altered functioning of neurophysiological circuits that mediate central nervous system reactions to external stress factors. However, these data also indicate that not all children with anxiety disorders were inhibited and that not all inhibited children developed anxiety disorders. This finding is in agreement with current findings from the study of the relationship between extreme temperament and diagnosis (Maziade, Caron, Cote, Boutin, & Thivierge, 1990), which indicates that while a large proportion of children in a psychiatric population were found to have difficult or extreme temperaments, a large proportion of children referred for a disorder did not show an extreme temperament and that some children with extreme temperamental profiles did not develop psychiatric disorder. Therefore, the available data support only the idea that behavioral inhibition is a possible risk factor for the later development of multiple anxiety disorders, including overanxious disorder.

NEUROPSYCHOLOGICAL ASPECTS

Shaffer et al. (1985) studied the relationship between the presence of psychiatric disorder at age 17 and the presence of neuropsychological abnormality at age 7 in a nonreferred population of 63 males and 27 females: neurological soft signs and IQ level were used as indicators of subtle neuropsychological dysfunction. The presence of 1 or more soft signs was found to be a statistically significant risk factor for the presence of psychiatric disorders characterized by anxiety and social withdrawal. Overanxious disorder of childhood was the most frequent diagnosis in this group of children. The prevalence of disorder increased with an increasing number of soft signs, with lower IQ, when the soft signs reflected problems in coordination (e.g., finger-to-nose movement, finger pursuit, and dysdiadochokinesia), and when the child also had demonstrated signs of early anxiety and withdrawal on examination at age 7. While those children with only signs of early anxiety had a risk factor odds ratio of 1.7 for developing an anxiety disorder, children with both 2 or more soft signs and early anxiety had a risk factor odds ratio of 24.9.

The authors speculated that the most parsimonious explanation for their findings was that some organic factor correlated with neuropsychological impairment may lead directly to anxious behavior. They referred to Lauretta Bender's hypothesis that neurodevelopmental delay can cause increased dependency needs that may lead to increased separation anxiety in the child; however, their data do not support this concept, since they report far more cases of overanxious disorder (12) than cases of separation anxiety disorder (1) in their patient population (Shaffer et al, 1985).

They also suggest that neurodevelopmental delay may heighten the child's dependency needs, heightening libidinal attachments to the parents and thereby intensifying neurotic conflict at every stage of psychosexual development. To this may be added the hypothesis that neurodevelopmental delay may cause increased difficulty in coping with environmental stressors, such as the acquisition of academic and athletic skills during middle childhood. These increased demands on ego functioning can lead to heightened anxiety, increased neurotic conflict, and severe challenges to the child's self-esteem, further disposing to the development of an anxiety disorder.

TRAUMATIC ASPECTS

Children with overanxious disorder often can have apparent onset of the disorder after a traumatic event. However, it is not clear whether this represents the actual beginning of the illness or merely an exacerbation of an underlying, milder form of the disorder.

PSYCHOSOCIAL ASPECTS

Psychosocial risk factors include recent stress in the child's life (Costello, 1989). In addition, chronic exposure to an anxious parent may induce chronic anxiety in a child through a variety of social learning mechanisms. For example, infant research has demonstrated how the affects of distress or anxiety can be produced in an infant via hearing other children cry, by nonlinguistically based signaling by the parent, or by repeated, subtle disruptions of early dyadic interactional patterns by a relatively unempathic or overly intrusive mother (Stern, 1985). Moreover, a child may unconsciously identify with a chronically anxious parent's coping style, fearful, inhibited patterns of behavior, or anxiety-filled belief systems about the world. These mechanisms provide us with a putative social-learning model for the transmission, induction, and maintenance of chronic anxiety in a child.

Chronic family conflict can become a source of anxiety for a child and skew intrapsychic development so that normal developmental conflicts cannot be resolved satisfactorily. As a result, successful resolution of the Oedipus complex is impeded, resulting in a state of chronic, neurotic anxiety.

In more severely disfunctional families, the child's earlier ego development may have been compromised, resulting in severe comorbidity with significant libidinal, ego, and superego fixations at differing stages of preoedipal development.

FAMILIAL ASPECTS

From a behavioral, psychoanalytic, or biological viewpoint, the construct that familial factors play an important etiological role in OAD has a high face validity. Epidemiological studies demonstrate a high degree of correlation between anxiety disorders in children and their relatives. For example, Last et al. (1987a) studied the lifetime prevalence of psychiatric illness in 56 mothers of children with separation anxiety disorder, overanxious disorder, or both, comparing them to 15 mothers of children with other psychiatric disorders. They demonstrated that mothers of children with overanxious disorder showed higher rates of generalized anxiety disorder (45.5 vs. 20%) and affective disorder (50 vs. 40%): Mothers of children with both overanxious and separation anxiety disorders showed even higher rates of psychiatric disorder. A more recent study (Last et al., 1991) of the lifetime prevalence rates of anxiety disorders in first-degree relatives of children with anxiety disorders showed that 50% of relatives of children with overanxious disorder suffered from at least one *DSM-III-R* anxiety disorder, 29.8% of relatives were given the diagnosis of overanxious disorder, 18.8% separation anxiety disorder, 11.5% panic disorder, and 3.8% generalized anxiety disorder. With the exception of generalized anxiety disorder, relatives of children with overanxious disorder, have the highest rate of prevalence rates of disorders compared to the relatives of probands with other anxiety disorders. In comparison with families of normal controls and children with attention deficit disorder, there was a high degree of aggregation of anxiety disorders within the families of children with anxiety disorders.

Workman (1980) contended that overanxious disorder is more common in firstborn or only children of small families in upper-socioeconomic groups in which there is a great emphasis on achievement. He speculated that such children are raised to feel that acceptance and self-esteem is based on a high level of conformity and achievement. More recent epidemiological studies, however, suggest that this disorder may be more evenly distributed between different socioeconomic groups but may have different forms of presentation depending partly on social and class differences.

Differential Diagnosis

Overanxious disorder of childhood must be distinguished from: normal, developmentally appropriate anxiety symptoms, adjustment disorder of childhood with anxiety symptoms, other anxiety disorders, medical conditions, borderline personality disorder, and depressive disorders.

Anxiety is a ubiquitous part of human existence. In addition, children suffer from a large number of anxiety symptoms as a part of normal development. Lapouse and Monk (1964), for example, found that the mothers of 43% of children between the ages of 6 and 12 years reported that their child experienced 7 or more fears or worries and that 41% reported separation anxiety in their children. More recently, Bell-Dolan, Last, and Strauss (1990) reported that between 10 and 30% of a randomly selected group of children between the ages of 5 and 18 years *who did not have a diagnosed anxiety disorder* nonetheless reported the presence of subclinical levels of each of the symptoms of overanxious disorder, with even higher prevalences of some symptoms in the 5- to 13-year-old group. The additional finding that the subclinical anxieties reported by these children tended to decrease at 12-month follow-up lends further support to the idea that many anxiety symptoms are a reflection of either the normal developmental process and/or of subclinical environmental stressors.

Differential diagnosis, then, depends not only on the presence or absence of anxiety symptoms as reported by child, parents, and teachers but the severity of both each symptoms and of the entire range of symptoms that exist. A second, equally important criteria is the degree with which the reported symptoms interfere *both with daily functioning* (in school, in the family, with peers and with sports, hobbies, activities) *and with normal developmental progression*. It is important not to overlook the fact that a "subclinically" anxious child who appears to be functioning well because of high intelligence, a compliant personality, and a favorable, highly supportive environment actually may be suffering from a phase-specific libidinal and ego developmental arrest. Such children may be considered as being in a pseudolatency and may become more manifestly impaired when they have to struggle with the demands of adolescence unequipped with necessary ego capacities and skills because of personality constriction and inhibition resulting from their overanxious disorder.

Adjustment disorder of childhood with anxiety symptoms may present with typical features of overanxious disorder of less than 6 months' duration and occurring after a significant psychologically traumatic event or severe psychosocial stressor, such as a severe accident, significant physical illness, or a death in the family.

In separation anxiety, avoidant disorder, school avoidance, or phobic conditions, the child's anxiety or excessive worries will be centered on a specific situation, object, or person. Theoretically, general anxiety disorder would be the preferred diagnosis when there is a predominance of somatic symptoms, such as hypervigilance, sympathetic discharge phenomena, and general irritability, but this has never been validated in child populations. It is important to keep in mind that overanxious disorder has a 50% comorbidity rate and that multiple anxiety disorders are frequently encountered in clinical practice.

Regarding medical conditions, thyrotoxicosis and hypersensitivity to medications such as adrenergic drugs for asthma should be ruled out.

Assuming that the validity of borderline personality disorder in childhood is accepted, it might present as a severe form of overanxious disorder. However, the presence of ego weaknesses, problems with object constancy, and the pathological defenses of splitting, denial, and projection serve as differentiating clinical characteristics.

There is a high degree of comorbidity between anxiety and depressive disorders. Because of this, some children with mood disorders may present initially with symptoms of anxiety. A complete diagnostic evaluation and a high index of suspicion for coexistence of these two types of disorder should clarify the diagnosis.

Morbidity

EFFECTS ON THE CHILD'S FUNCTIONING AND DEVELOPMENT

Overanxious disorder can moderately or severely impair a child's functioning and development. At one extreme is the neurotic child with good ego strengths and high intelligence who has the good fortune to live in a fundamentally supportive milieu. In such cases impairments in the spheres of social interaction, sports, or academic functioning may be real but may appear to be minimal because they are rationalized or denied by both the child and the family; for example, timidity and fearful avoidance of rough-and-tumble sports may be denied and rationalized away by claims of special interests or talents in quiet, solitary activities such as reading or model building.

At the other extreme is the anxious child with significant comorbidity and an insensitive, unsupportive milieu who may be severely impaired by crippling anxiety and depression in every sphere of daily activity. In such cases, a chaotic home, significant family psychopathology, and a deprived or even physically dangerous social environment may all intensify preexisting psychopathology and produce anxiety of crippling proportions.

SEQUELAE

At this time, we do not have sufficient epidemiological data to fully understand the sequelae of overanxious disorder of childhood. In general, the existing studies seem to indicate that this disorder, like all other anxiety disorders, has a lifelong course characterized by minor fluctuations in the intensity of symptomatology, in contrast to the affective disorders, which tend to show spontaneous remissions and episodic recurrences. This picture fits the developmentalist-psychoanalytic model of anxiety, especially the concept that severe anxiety in middle childhood may be the symptomatic manifestation of a structured neurosis that will have a lifelong course. From a biological and behavioral point of view, Gittleman (1984) has suggested that children with overanxious disorder may develop generalized anxiety disorder when they reach adulthood and that overanxious disorder may constitute a prodromal state or vulnerability factor for the development of other psychopathological conditions.

Cantwell and Baker (1989) found that although 75% of the children in their study of language-impaired children initially diagnosed with overanxious disorder still met criteria for a psychiatric diagnosis on follow-up, most of them had different diagnoses. Although implications drawn from this work are limited by the fact that all subjects had language impairment as an intervening variable, this study supports the concept that overanxious disorder may form a core of psychobiological vulnerability to the development of psychiatric disorder.

PROGNOSIS

It was generally believed that children with overanxious disorder have a relatively benign prognosis because of their intact ego functioning,

perfectionism, orientation toward achievement, and often high verbal and intellectual abilities (Workman, 1980). However, more recent information raises the possibility that this belief may be the result of sampling bias, since approximately 50% of this population have at least one other diagnosible *DSM-III-R* disorder (Werry, 1991) that may adversely affect outcome. For example, in Anderson's cohort (1987), parents reported an increase in anxiety-related problems in anxious-fearful children as they got older: more important, they reported an increase in aggressivity and a *marked* increase in anxiety in those children with three patterns of comorbidity (anxiety disorders plus conduct-oppositional disorders, anxiety disorders plus attention deficit disorder, and anxiety plus attention deficit disorder plus conduct-oppositional disorders).

Second, the signs and symptoms of overanxious disorder are relatively unstable and may be harder to identify as children get older, as symptoms become more ego-syntonic, and the child becomes more sophisticated at disguising signs of "imperfection" (Werry, 1991).

More recent studies suggest that impaired functioning is relatively common in some overanxious disorder children and is predictive of impaired functioning in adulthood. This may be particularly so with those children who show significant comorbidity, especially with conduct and affective disorders. It is certainly true of Cantwell and Baker's small sample (1989) of 8 children with overanxious disorder from a speech- and language-impaired population, only 2 (25%) of whom were entirely recovered on a 4-year follow-up. Of note is that only 2 of these children continued to show overanxious disorder as a diagnosis; the rest were diagnosed as having a mixture of attention deficit and behavioral disorders.

Treatment

To date, there are no controlled studies demonstrating the efficacy or superiority of any particular type of treatment for overanxious disorder. Choice of treatment modality therefore should be based on a careful, methodical evaluation of the individual child's clinical presentation, developmental and family history, degree of functional impairment, and pertinant etiological factors. Many experienced clinicians, despite their individual preferences for particular treatment modalities, often will simultaneously or successively combine several different approaches on an empirical basis. This approach is especially useful with those children who show significant comorbidity and a history of multiple etiological factors.

PSYCHOLOGICAL AND SOCIAL TREATMENT

Individual psychoanalytically oriented play therapy or child analysis traditionally has been the treatment of choice for the anxious child with good ego functioning and a good family support system. Treatment centers first on establishing a good therapeutic alliance with the child before interpretations are used to link the child's current behavior and problems with unconscious conflicts and fears. As with any other type of insight-oriented therapy, play therapy with children starts with the focus on how the children present themselves within the therapeutic situation as well as their problems in everyday life. The therapist begins by helping children indirectly to express their inner life through such media as fantasy play, drawings, and storytelling while carefully observing the nuances of the children's behavior, implied and unspoken attitudes and patterns of interaction in the therapeutic situation. The relative directness or indirectness with which the therapist interprets unconscious material and links it to everyday life depends in part on an individual child's capacity to tolerate direct confrontation; as a result, some therapists advocate interpretation that stays within the metaphor of the fantasy play that typical midlatency-age children bring to the therapy. While a more detailed discussion of the techniques of therapy is beyond the scope of this chapter, it should be stressed that individual therapy with children suffering from overanxious disorder requires that the therapist be especially careful to titrate the amounts of emotional support, explanations, and discussions of realistic problems that are optimal for each individual patient.

Individual therapy for children inevitably involves collateral work with parents. In some cases, however, the evaluation may disclose sufficient evidence that pathological family dynamics and interactions play a major role in the genesis and perpetuation of a child's problems. Then it becomes a question of clinical judgment as to when it is advisable either to refer a parent for individual treatment or to recommend family therapy as collateral or even the sole treatment modality.

The behavior therapy literature has an abundance of single-case reports of therapeutic success treating overanxious disorder using methods such as relaxation therapy, counterconditioning, systematic desensitization, in vivo exposure to feared situations, operant reinforcement, and participant modeling of strategies for coping with feared situations. More recently, the cognitive/behavioral technique of "cognitive restructuring" has been used to treat children with anxiety. In this procedure, the therapist first teaches children to identify conscious and preconscious thoughts and fantasies that reinforce anxiety and lead to subtle distortions and misinterpretations of reality. In the second step, children systematically are taught to replace these maladaptive thought processes with a positive frame of reference that focuses on coping strategies (Kendall et al., 1991).

Systematic and well-designed treatment studies of these techniques are still lacking. In addition, these techniques are so similar to common sense parenting techniques that it is easy to dismiss them as simplistic, naive, and pseudoscientific. However, they ultimately may prove to be quite useful, especially in cases where the clinician mistakenly assumes that the child's parents have had the capacity to already teach them to their anxious child. The fact is, however, that many children with anxiety disorders have parents who themselves are anxious and who have never acquired these coping techniques and life skills themselves. Therefore it may be very therapeutic for an anxious child to learn these techniques within the context of a positive, supportive relationship in which the power of a positive unconscious transference reinforces the child's unconscious identification with the therapist and his or her therapeutic messages.

Group therapy may be a helpful adjunctive therapy for children whose social skills have been severely impaired or underdeveloped as the result of social withdrawal.

EDUCATIONAL THERAPY

The child with overanxious disorder may have learning problems secondary to severe incapacitating anxiety that has blocked learning in the classroom. Tutoring may be indicated to help a child to begin to function on grade level in the classroom, but it should never be considered as a substitute for psychotherapy. In children who have severe academic problems, neuropsychological and psychological evaluation is indicated in order to rule out coexisting learning disabilities and/or attention deficit disorder.

BIOLOGICAL TREATMENT

Studies of the use of psychopharmacological agents in the treatment of children with overanxious disorder have been sparse, inconclusive, and limited to anecdotal reports or poorly designed open studies of small, diagnostically heterogenous populations. As a result, the use of these agents with overanxious disorder is largely based on a combination of caution, anecdotal evidence, practical experience, and a commonsense approach of extrapolating knowledge from basic research with animal models and clinical research with adult populations to the treatment of child populations.

Benzodiazepines, antihistamines, beta-adrenergic blockers, and buspirone have been used to treat both symptomatic anxiety and anxiety disorders in children (Coffey, 1990).

Although there have been few studies of benzodiazepine treatment of overanxious disorder, some clinicians use them empirically to treat the disorder, most commonly its acute exacerbations, associated sleep problems, and intermittent emotional crises precipitated by environmental stressors. In a recent review article, Coffey (1990) was able to cite only 5 studies demonstrating the efficacy of benzodiazipines in treating anxiety symptoms in children. The last one cited (Simeon & Ferguson, 1987) was an open study of alprazolam in 12 children ages 8 to 16 with overanxious disorder and avoidant disorder. Seven children showed at least moderate improvement with alprazolam, and there were no clinically adverse effects.

However, other studies indicate that some anxious children become more anxious in response to benzodiazapines. Pfefferbaum et al. (1987), for example, demonstrated modest efficacy of low-dosage alprazolam in successfully treating anticipatory and acute situational anxiety in 7 of 10 children undergoing stressful procedures for the treatment for cancer. At the same time, 3 of these children actually did worse on clinical measures of anxiety, a finding that underscores the principle

that these agents should be used cautiously because of the possibility of paradoxical exacerbations of anxiety. Amman and Werry (1982) found a mild increase in anxiety in some children with severe reading retardation who had been treated with diazepam, in contrast to placebo and methylphenidate.

Benzodiazapines commonly cause other adverse effects in some children, including sedation, cognitive and performance decrements, behavioral disinhibition, and benzodiazapine abuse. The latter may be an especially important problem for children who have significant comorbidity, especially with conduct disorders.

Even less is known about the efficacy of antihistamines, beta-blockers, and buspirone for children with overanxious disorder. These agents should therefore be used with caution and adequate documentation for the rationale in incorporating them into a therapeutic plan.

There seems to be general agreement that major tranquilizers have no place in the treatment of overanxious disorder because of the dangers of very serious side effects, such as increased cognitive impairment, oversedation, tardive dyskinesia, and movement disorders. However, in light of our increased knowledge about comorbidity, a cautious clinical trial of this type of agent might be considered appropriate for severely dysfunctional children with overanxious disorder plus multiple coexisting disorders who have failed to respond to adequate, documented trials of more usual forms of treatment. In such cases, it may be important to consider whether the patient is actually suffering from a borderline personality disorder that might respond symptomatically to low-dosage phenothiazine treatment as part of a comprehensive treatment plan. Extensive documentation is strongly recommended in such cases because of the controversy over whether borderline personality disorder should be diagnosed in children and whether low-dose phenothiazine treatment is useful for patients with this diagnosis. (See Gunderson, 1986, for a discussion of this issue with adult patients.)

MILIEU TREATMENT

Outpatient, inpatient, and day treatment usually are not appropriate for children with overanxious disorder unless there is severe comorbidity that cripples personality and social functioning or severe psychosocial problems that require a protective setting.

Current Developments, Research, and Unanswered Questions

As with all of the anxiety disorders, research is still at an early stage in all areas of inquiry, including longitudinal population studies, the further development of useful diagnostic criteria, and well-controlled treatment outcome studies.

Further research is needed to find possible biological markers for overanxious disorder that might aid in diagnosis and early case finding as well as longitudinal studies of the natural course of the disorder. More specifically, it is still unclear to what extent overanxious disorder is distinct or whether it is a basic substrate disorder from which other types of anxiety disorders may develop.

REFERENCES

American Psychiatric Association. (1980). *Diagnostic and statistical manual of mental disorders* (3rd ed.). Washington, DC: Author.

American Psychiatric Association. (1987). *Diagnostic and statistical manual of mental disorders* (3rd ed., rev.). Washington, DC: Author.

American Psychiatric Association. (1994). *Diagnostic and statistical manual of mental disorders* (4th ed.). Washington, DC: Author.

Aman, M. G., & Werry, J. (1982). Methylphenidate and diazepam in severe reading retardation. *Journal of the American Academy of Child & Adolescent Psychiatry, 21,* 31–37.

Anderson, J. (1987). DSM-III disorders in preadolescent children. *Archives of General Psychiatry, 44,* 69–76.

Anderson, J., Williams, S., McGee, R., & Silva, P. (1989). Cognitive and social correlates of DSM-III disorders in preadolescent children. *Journal of the American Academy of Child & Adolescent Psychiatry, 28,* 842–846.

Beidel, D. (1991). Social phobia and overanxious disorder in school-age children. *Journal of the American Academy of Child & Adolescent Psychiatry, 30,* 545–542.

Bell-Dolan, D., Last, C., & Strauss, C. (1990). Symptoms of anxiety disorders in normal children. *Journal of the American Academy of Child and Adolescent Psychiatry, 29,* 759–765.

Bernstein, G., & Borhardt, C. (1991). Anxiety disorders of childhood and adolescence: A critical review. *Journal of the American Academy of Child and Adolescent Psychiatry, 30,* 519–532.

Biederman, J., Rosenbaum, J., Hirshfeld, D., Faraone, S., Boldue, E., Gersten, M., Meminger, S., Kagan, J., Snidman, N., & Reznick, J. (1990). Psychiatric correlates of behavioral inhibition in young children of parents with and without psychiatric disorders. *Archives of General Psychiatry, 47,* 21–26.

Campo, J., & Fritsch, S. (1996). Somatization in children and adults. *Journal of the American Academy of Child and Adolescent Psychiatry, 33* (9), 1223–1235.

Cantwell, D. P., & Baker, L. (1989), Stability and natural history of DSM-III childhood diagnoses. *Journal of the American Academy of Child and Adolescent Psychiatry, 28,* 691–700.

Coffey, B. (1990). Anxiolytics for children and adolescents: Traditional and new drugs. *Journal of Child and Adolescent Psychopharmacology, 1,* 57–83.

Costello, E. (1989). Child psychiatric disorders and their corelates: A primary care pediatric sample. *Journal of the American Academy of Child and Adolescent Psychiatry, 28,* 851–855.

Fenichel, O. (1945). *The psychoanalytic theory of neurosis.* New York: W. W. Norton.

Freud, A. (1965). *Normality and pathology in childhood: Assessments of development.* New York: International Universities Press.

Freud, A. (1971). The infantile neurosis. *Psychoanalytic Study of the Child, 26,* 79–90.

Freud, S. (1955). Analysis of a phobia in a five year old boy. In J. Strachey (Ed.), *The standard edition of the complete psychological works of Sigmund Freud* (Vol. 10, pp. 3–149) (hereafter *Standard edition*). London: Hogarth Press. (Originally published 1909.)

Freud, S. (1962a). On the grounds for detaching a particular syndrome from neurasthenia under the description "anxiety neurosis." In *Standard edition* (Vol. 3, pp. 85–117). (Originally published 1895.)

Freud, S. (1962b). A reply to criticisms of my paper on anxiety neurosis. In *Standard edition* (Vol. 3, pp. 121–139). (Originally published 1895.)

Freud, S. (1963). Introductory lectures on psychoanalysis. In *Standard edition* (Vol. 16, pp. 339–357). (Originally published 1917.)

Gittelman, R. (1984). Anxiety disorders in children. In L. Gunspoon (Ed.), *Psychiatry update* (Vol. 3). Washington, DC: American Psychiatric Association.

Kanner, L. (1948). *Child psychiatry.* Springfield, IL: Charles C. Thomas.

Kashani, J., & Orvaschel, H. (1990). A community study of anxiety in children and adolescents. *American Journal of Psychiatry, 147,* 313–318.

Gunderson, J. (1986). Pharmacotherapy for patients

with borderline personality disorder. *Archives of General Psychiatry, 43,* 698–700.

Harrington, R., Fudge, H., Rutter, M., Pickles, A., & Hill, J. (1990). Adult outcomes of childhood and adolescent depression. 1. Psychiatric status. *Archives of General Psychiatry, 47,* 465–473.

Kagan, J., Reznick, J., & Snidman, N. (1987). The physiology and psychology of behavioral inhibition in children. *Child Development, 58,* 1459–1473.

Kendall, P., et al. (1991). Treating anxiety disorders in children and adolescents. In P. C. Kendall (Ed.). *Child and adolescent therapy, Cognitive-behavioral procedures.* New York: Guilford Press.

Klein, R., & Last, C. (1989). *Anxiety disorders in children.* Newburg Park, CA: Sage Publications.

Last, C. G., Herson, M., Kazdin, A., Finkelstein, R., & Strauss, C. G. (1987b). Comparison of DSM-III separation anxiety and overanxious disorders: Demographic characteristics and patterns of comorbidity. *Journal of the American Academy of Child and Adolescent Psychiatry, 26,* 527–531.

Lapouse, R., & Monk, M. A. (1964). Fears and worries in a representational sample of children. *American Journal of Orthopsychiatry, 29,* 803–818.

Last, C. G., Herson, M., Kazdin, A. E., Francis, G., & Grubb, H. J. (1987a). A Psychiatric illness in the mothers of anxious children. *American Journal of Psychiatry, 144,* 1580–1583.

Last, C. G., Herson, M., Kazdin, A., Orvaschel, H., & Perrin, S. (1991). Anxiety disorders in children and their families. *Archives of General Psychiatry, 48,* 928–934.

Maziade, M., Caron, C., Cote, R., Boutin, P., & Thivierge, J. (1990). Extreme temperament and diagnosis: A study in a psychiatric sample of consecutive children. *Archives of General Psychiatry, 47,* 477–484.

McDermott, J., Werry, J., Petti, T., Combrinck-Graham, L., & Char, W. (1989). Anxiety disorders of childhood or adolescence. In T. Karasu, (Ed.), *Treatments of psychiatric disorders: A Task Force report of the American Psychiatric Association, 1,* 401–443.

McGee, R., Feehan, M., Williams, S., Partridge, F., Silva, P. A., & Kelly, J. (1990). DSM-III disorders in a large sample of adolescents. *Journal of the American Academy of Child and Adolescent Psychiatry, 29,* 611–619.

Nagera, H. (1963). The developmental profile: Notes on some practical considerations regarding its use. *Psychoanalytic Study of the Child, 18,* 511–540.

Nagera, H. (1964). On arrest in development, fixation and regression. *Psychoanalytic Study of the Child, 19,* 222–239.

Pfefferbaum, B., Overall, J., Boren, H., Frankel, L., Sullivan, M., & Johnson, K. (1987). Alprazolam in the treatment of anticipatory and acute situational anxiety in children with cancer. *Journal of the American Academy of Child and Adolescent Psychiatry, 26,* 532–535.

Sarnoff, C. (1989). *Latency.* Northvale, NJ: Jason Aronson.

Shaffer, D., Schonfeld, I., O'Conner, P., Stokman, C., Trautman, P., Shafer, S., & Ng, S. (1985). Neurological soft signs: Their relationship to psychiatric disorder and intelligence in childhood and adolescence. *Archives of General Psychiatry, 42,* 342–351.

Simeon, J. G., & Ferguson, H. B. (1987). Alprayolam effects in children with anxiety disorders. *American Journal of Psychiatry, 32,* 570–574.

Stern, D. (1985). *The interpersonal world of the infant: A view from psychoanalysis and developmental psychology.* New York: Basic Books.

Strauss, C. C., Lease, C. A., Last, C. G., & Francis, G. (1988). Overanxious disorder: An examination of developmental differences. *Journal of Abnormal Child Psychology, 16,* 433–443.

Velez, C. N., Johnson, J., & Cohen, P. (1989). A longitudinal analysis of selected risk factors for childhood psychopathology. *Journal of the American Academy of Child and Adolescent Psychiatry, 28,* 861–864.

Werry, J. (1991). Overanxious disorder: A review of its taxonomic properties. *Journal of the American Academy of Child and Adolescent Psychiatry, 30,* 533–544.

Whitaker, A., Johnson, J., Shaffer, D., Kalikow, K., et al. (1990). Uncommon troubles in young people: Prevalence estimates of selected psychiatric disorders in a nonreferred adolescent population. *Archives of General Psychiatry, 47,* 487–496.

Workman, H. (1980). Anxiety disorders. In H. Kaplan, A. Freedman, & B. Sadock (Eds.), *Comprehensive textbook of psychiatry* (3rd ed.). Baltimore: Williams & Wilkins.

47 / Elimination Disorders: Encopresis and Constipation

Klaus Schreiber

The understanding, treatment, and service pattern regarding encopresis in children as a clinical syndrome has undergone considerable change during the past two decades. In the past, encopresis was considered primarily a psychiatric syndrome with emotional, familial, if not neurotic, causality and was readily referred to child psychiatrists for individual and/or family psychotherapy. More recently it has become a domain of behavioral pediatrics, to be evaluated with multiple laboratory studies and treated with a combined medical-behavioral approach. This change is also reflected in the published literature on the topic: Compared to the preceding decade, the *Index Medicus 1980–1991* shows a fourfold increase in the pediatric publications, while the psychiatric literature decreased by more than half, restricting itself to reports of those cases that behavioral pediatrics considers as resistant to its medical-behavioral treatment approach.

The term *encopresis* (from Greek *kopros,* meaning ordure) entered the psychiatric literature in 1925, when Pototzky mentioned it in a chapter on psychogenic causes of physical symptoms in children. Prior to this, it was referred to as "incontinentia alvi," and the first case reports are attributed to Fowler in 1882. Freud's hypothesis of intrapsychic conflicts due to traumatizing, harsh, and inconsistent toilet training became the central tenet in the understanding and treatment of encopresis during the first half of this century. The 1950s and 1960s showed interest in an experimental (Anthony, 1957) and epidemiological approach (Bellman, 1966) to the study of encopresis, laying the groundwork for a better definition of its clinical presentation as well as providing normative data on toilet training and achievement of continence. Following Bemporad's (Bemporad, Pfeifer, Gibbs, Cortner, & Bloom, 1971) conceptualization of encopresis as a symptom of a disturbed mother-child relationship in a dysfunctional family, a family and system orientation has become the focus of the psychiatric literature.

Definition

The fourth edition of the American Psychiatric Association's Diagnostic Statistic Manual (*DSM-IV,* 1994) defines functional encopresis as repeated involuntary (or, much more rarely, intentional) passage of feces into places not appropriate for that purpose. It specifies frequency (at least once a month for at least 6 months), age of onset (chronological and mental age of at least 4 years), and requires that a physical cause for fecal incontinence has to be ruled out. It separates primary from secondary encopresis by the absence or presence of a preceding period of fecal continence lasting at least 1 year. Relating encopresis to constipation, impaction, as well as retention with subsequent overflow, *DSM-IV* ascribes physiological as well as psychological reasons for the constipation and lists inconsistent toilet training and psychosocial stress as predisposing factors.

Epidemiology

In a study of 8,863 first-grade students in Stockholm, Bellman (1966) found that in the majority of the children, bowel control became established and stabilized during the child's fourth year. On an average, girls achieved bowel control six months earlier than boys. Prevalence of encopresis decreases from 1.5% during the early grade-school years (Bellman, 1966) to 1.0% at age 10 to 12 (Rutter, Tizard, & Whitmore, 1970), with a few chronic cases persisting into adolescence. In a follow-up study by Bellman (1966), none of the children reported soiling beyond their 16th birthday.

Encopresis is 3 to 4 times more frequent in boys than in girls. This is a consistent finding in total population studies (Bellman, 1966; Bosch, 1984; Rutter et al., 1970) and clinical studies

(Anthony, 1957; Levine, 1975; Olatawura, 1973). Since bladder control develops after bowel control, many studies (Bellman, 1966; Levine, 1975; Rutter et al., 1970; Stein & Susser, 1967) report association with enuresis as high as 30%.

Total population studies found an equal distribution of encopretic children among upper, middle, and lower socioeconomic groups (Bellman, 1966; Rutter et al., 1970; Stein & Susser, 1967) while psychiatrically referred children came from families of lower social class (Olatawura, 1973). Comparing encopretic children with normal controls, Stein and Susser (1967) found no differences with regard to family size, birth rank, or age of mother.

Development of Bowel Control

Achievement of bowel control is a complex interplay between maturation of anatomical structures, development of physiological functions, transmission of cultural norms and expectations, and repetitive experiences embedded in interpersonal relationships leading to a sense of mastery. Normal defecation requires synchronization of sensory and motor elements under the coordination of the autonomic and central nervous system. Stretch receptors are stimulated when a fecal bolus enters the rectum. Once a critical volume has been reached, the rectum contracts and simultaneously relaxes the internal anal sphincter via the rectosphincteric relaxation reflex. Synergistically, the external anal sphincter responds with a transient contraction to ensure continued continence for a brief time (Hatch, 1988). These reflexes are mediated by the hypogastric plexus (Younoszai & Tolaymat, 1989). In addition, rectal distension reaches conscious awareness through ascending sensory fibers and is experienced as a sensation of urgency that, children in particular find difficult to define (Hersov, 1985). Final passage of stool requires relaxation of the external anal sphincter and the puborectal sling of the levator ani as well as voluntary increase of intraabdominal pressure, both being mediated by facilitatory cortical pathways (Hatch, 1988).

Longitudinal studies (Largo & Stutzle, 1977a; Stein & Susser, 1967) show a high correlation of the developmental sequence from bowel control to daytime bladder and to eventual nighttime bladder control, and thus provide evidence that maturational processes determine readiness for bowel control. However, developmentalists such as Gesell, Ilg, and Ames (1974) caution that "voluntary defecation is not a simplified localized reaction but a total response" (p. 250). Brazelton (1962) pointed to a perceptible time lag between the capacity for reflex compliance and voluntary control as being similar to the delay from reflex standing at 5 months, to voluntary standing at 10 months. Trainability requires ability to sit and squat, readiness for verbal communication as well as interest in self-care (Gesell et al., 1974).

Following 413 healthy Swiss children from 6 months to 6 years of age, Largo and Stutzle (1977b) found that personal initiative of the child was positively correlated with early and secure achievement of bowel control, while early and frequent daily prompting by the parent accelerated bowel control only to a limited degree. Their study did not show any negative effect of early and intense potty training on the eventual achievement of bowel control or possible relapses in later years.

Clinical Presentation

Encopresis presents itself in a variety of contexts depending on the age and developmental status of the child, the duration and associated features of the problem, the parents' understanding and concern, and whether it is seen in a psychiatric or pediatric setting.

The majority of children with encopresis are seen and cared for by their primary pediatrician. When referred to tertiary care settings, they have reached grade-school age and account for 3% of cases of a behavioral pediatric (Levine, 1975), 6% of a child psychiatric (Olatawura, 1973), and 10 to 25% of a pediatric gastroenterology clinic population (Hatch, 1988).

In reporting on 76 cases, Anthony (1957) described encopresis as a syndrome "in which soiling acts as a nucleus around which there clusters a constellation of ancillary and related symptoms" (p. 157). He recognized three distinct prototypes of clinical presentation: "continous," "disconti-nous," and "retentive."

In the "continous" type, the child has never been continent, often is also enuretic, immature, and impulsive with little concern for the rights or feelings of others. The child's soiling frequently reflects the family's general messiness.

In the "discontinous" type, the child develops fecal soiling after a period of complete conti-nence. This symptom contrasts with the child's otherwise overcontrolled behavior and inhibited emotional life. While being ashamed of the soiling and trying to treat it like a secret, the child out-wardly appears casual in not recognizing defeca-tion cues. Stools are well formed and constipation is infrequent. In this child's compulsive, orderly family, he or she is the scapegoat for all the dirt that cannot be tolerated.

In the "retentive" type, the child represents a subgroup of the two previous types. Having en-dured severe toilet training, he or she has devel-oped stubborn, chronic constipation, which later leads to leakage.

The psychiatric literature describes encopretic children as passive (Bellman, 1966; Bemporad et al., 1971; Bosch, 1988; Shovelar, 1980). They have difficulty in handling aggression, either by being meek, dependent, and inhibited in the expres-sion of aggression (Bellman, 1966) or by being op-positional and demanding (Bemporad, Kresch, Asnes, & Wilson, 1978). Encopretic children usu-ally are socially withdrawn, particularly from peers. They show lowered self-esteem and a sense of worthlessness (Owens-Stively, 1987; Shovelar, 1980) as well as feelings of not being in control of positive life events (Landman, Rappaport, Fen-ton, & Levine, 1986). Moreover, they were con-flicted with regard to their masculinity (Bemporad et al., 1971; Shovelar 1980). Families of enco-pretic children are uniformly reported as dysfunc-tional with a separation/divorce rate of over 50% (Bemporad et al., 1971; Olatawura, 1973; Shov-elar, 1980). Precipitating events for secondary en-copresis are found frequently to be stressful life events, including separation or perceived threat of separation from the mother (Bellman, 1966; Bem-porad et al., 1971).

Behavioral pediatric literature questions the usefulness of distinguishing between primary and secondary encopresis, claiming that stool reten-tion is present in nearly all cases, at least intermit-

tently (Levine, 1982). Behavioral symptoms noted most frequently in encopretic children are low-ered self-esteem, social withdrawal, anxiety, de-pression, abdominal and extraabdominal somatic concerns, and externalized behavior disorders (Gabel, Hagedus, Wald, Chandra, & Chiponis, 1986; Levine, 1982). The symptoms are consid-ered to be moderate in degree and secondary to the experience of humiliation, fear of discovery, and peer ridicule (Levine, 1982). In Levine's study (1975), the number of disruptive life events connected with the onset of encopresis were con-siderably lower, as was the presence of parental separation and divorce rate; here it was 30% (Lev-ine, 1975).

Etiological Factors

Functional encopresis is the symptomatic expres-sion of a variety of etiological factors: physiologi-cal, behavioral, psychodynamic, family, and devel-opmental.

PHYSIOLOGICAL FACTORS

Active research by pediatric gastroenterologists during the past decade has contributed signifi-cantly to the understanding of alterations in the anal, rectal, and colonic physiology leading to con-stipation and encopresis. New diagnostic tools in-clude intestinal transit time determination, defe-cagraphy, surface perianal electromyography, and, most important, anorectal manometry, which allows for the measurement of pressure in the rec-tum and at the internal and external anal sphinc-ter during different phases of defecation. The growing body of research data shows an impres-sive association of delayed rectal transit time (You-noszai & Tolaymat, 1989), decreased awareness of rectal distension (Loening-Baucke, 1990), and in-crease of critical rectal volume with the clinical presentation of chronic functional constipation (Younoszai & Tolaymat, 1989). Paradox external anal sphincter contraction is found in a subgroup of children with encopresis (Wald, Chandra, Ga-bel, & Chiponis 1987). However, the latter re-searchers cannot confirm that the anorectal dys-function precedes the onset of soiling or is the consequence of chronic constipation in all studied children. Signs of neurological delay are reported frequently in studies of encopretic children: speech disturbance and dyslexia (Bellman, 1966), severe language disorder and primitive figure drawings (Bemporad et al., 1971), and specific learning disorder in arithmetic and spelling (Stern, Lowitz, Prince, Altshuler, & Stroh, 1988). However, in a comparative study, Bosch (1984) found language and other learning disorders at the same frequency in encopretic children as in normal controls.

BEHAVIORAL FACTORS

Behavioral pediatricians view encopresis as the end result of a continuum of bowel dysfunctions that invariably includes chronic constipation and the effects of a pain-retention cycle. Taking a developmental perspective, Rappaport and Levine (1986) described different patterns of bowel dysfunction related to the physiological and cognitive development of the child and the knowledge base of the parent. During infancy, constipation is extremely rare, and bowel dysfunctions usually are due to parental misperception of normal variation in frequency or apparent discomfort during bowel movements. With the beginning mastery of bodily functions, toddlers spend considerable time "trying to go to the bathroom" while in truth they might be trying not to have a bowel movement. Rappaport and Levine suggest this to be an expression of the pain-retention cycle. Food transition, anal fissures, occasional illnesses, and toilet training all can lead to discomfort during bowel movements and secondary mild constipation. This, in turn, can generate a self-perpetuating cycle of further pain and retention, since stool held in the rectum will harden by water reabsorption. Placing high priority on the avoidance of acute pain, children will avoid moving their bowels, leading to chronic retention with eventual leakage around it.

Onset of encopresis at the beginning of school is viewed as caused by fear of using the school bathroom or disruption of established bowel habits by a new and frenetic daily schedule that leads to new or exacerbation of previously established retentive tendencies.

While putting emphasis on developmental, physiological, and interactive factors, behavioral

pediatrics do not consider that psychological factors in both children and parents have any impact on the development of constipation and encopresis.

PSYCHODYNAMIC FACTORS

Psychoanalytic thinking had a major impact on the understanding of encopresis. This began with Sigmund Freud (1908/1958) referring to fecal soiling as a form of continued subsidiary pleasure seeking from defecation. Fenichel (1945) considered encopresis a conversion symptom expressing instinctual conflicts and being either the equivalent of anxiety, if it occurred infrequently, or as a substitute for masturbation, if it was habitual.

Delineating the developmental line of bladder and bowel control, Anna Freud (1963) attempted to integrate the effects of instinctual forces and superego demands on the mastery of bodily functions during successive stages: (1) complete freedom to wet and soil; (2) progression from oral to anal zone leading to intense cathexis of anal products with unfused libido and aggression; (3) accomplishment of bladder and bowel control through identification with mother while being dependent on a positive relationship with her; and (4) autonomous control of bladder and bowel function disconnected from object ties.

Utilizing this conceptualization, Shane (1967) reported the psychoanalytic treatment of an 8-year-old boy with primary encopresis due to pre-oedipal fixation, repeated separation trauma, and subsequent regression. During 3 years of treatment, Shane showed how step-by-step progression eventually allowed autonomous internalizing of bowel control after the oedipal conflict was resolved. Huschka (1942) focused on the history of coercive toilet training in his patients and claimed it to be a sufficient cause for encopresis. In his "experimental approach" to encopresis, Anthony (1957) agreed that coercive toilet training was the most consistent varible, at least in cases of discontinuous and retentive encopresis, but he cautioned against construing this as proof of a causal connection. Instead he viewed toilet training as a chronological event in the context of the total mother-child relationship. Referring to them as a "potting couple," Anthony focused on the mutual fine-tuning of signal reading and giving between mother and child with regard to the natural rhythms such as eating and elimination. He found maternal misreading of cues or inconsistent response to them as a major deviation. In addition, Anthony was impressed that the children's animistic thinking and narcissistic fantasies lead to an overvaluation of their feces as well as to fears of retaliation and physical damage.

FAMILY FACTORS

Reflecting the referral of more disturbed and treatment-resistant cases, child psychiatrists developed a more family-oriented multifactorial approach to encopresis. Bemporad et al. (1978) proposed the concept of chronic neurotic encopresis as a multifactorial psychiatric disorder in which encopresis is precipitated and maintained by physiological, personality, and family factors. Suffering from a dysfunctional developmental neuromusculature, these children may experience severe toilet training in an exaggerated manner. Living in families with nearly always absent fathers and domineering, emotionally blunted, and unempathic mothers, the patients are depressed, passive, and noncommunicative, and use soiling as the only successful although neurotic way to obtain favors from and to express anger at others.

Working with a group of preadolescent boys with severe and protracted encopresis, Shovelar (1980) was impressed with the chronicity and intensity of family disturbance as a major factor for the cause and maintenance of their symptoms. He noted that the absence of functional fathers allowed for the unchecked transmission of mothers' sense of worthlessness, inadequacy, and rejection onto the patients, leading to an arrest in the development of their ego functions. Denial of conflict and lack of conflict resolution, both in the marital and the parental relationship, contributed both to the maintenance of the symptom as well as to the poor response to treatment.

DEVELOPMENTAL FACTORS

Developmental psychopathology is a recently proposed scientific approach (Cicchetti, 1984; Sroufe & Rutter, 1984) to the understanding of etiology, future course, and treatment of childhood psychiatric disorders. It attempts to establish links between pathology and earlier and later behavior as well as to delineate processes underlying continuity and change in patterns of adaptation and maladaptation.

Failing to achieve bowel control in a socially expected time frame changes it from a developmental task into a manifestation of psychopathology. Just as parental understanding and response are critical for the future social-emotional development of the soiling child, the child's adaptation to his or her behavior is of equal importance to its future course. Noting that encopretic children in his clinical population were either oppositional and demanding or shy, anxious, and withdrawn, Bosch (1988) found that only the second group continued to be symptomatic into early adolescence. Following Bemporad's et al. (1978) suggestion, Bosch speculated that the developmental tasks of early adolescence toward increased autonomy from family and dependence on peers had a favorable impact on the active form of encopresis, while it did not affect at all or even negatively affected the passive form.

Assessment

A thorough pediatric evaluation including abdominal and rectal exam should help to exclude organic causes for encopresis, since a wide variety of clinical conditions can give rise to chronic constipation and encopresis, including structural (e.g., Hirschsprung's disease, anal fissures, anorectal malformations) and general diseases of the gastrointestinal tract (e.g., Crohn's disease, irritable bowel syndrome), endocrinologic or metabolic diseases (e.g., hypothyroidism, hypercalcemia), and neurological abnormalities (e.g., damage of the spinal cord, central nervous system disorders such as cerebral palsy). Barium enema and more elaborate physiological studies are indicated only if there is evidence of bowel-related disease.

A child psychiatric evaluation begins with a thorough history of fecal soiling in the context of developmental, psychological, and relationship factors as well as parental understanding, responses, and prior attempts at intervention. The interview with the child should focus on assessing the developmental level across different domains, perception of and fantasies about the symptom,

553

ability to recognize a sense of urgency, locus of control, and other signs of psychopathology as well as assets. In addition, family functioning, marital relationship, psychological makeup of parents and siblings, and peership and school environment need to be investigated in order to allow for a multimodal treatment plan.

Differential diagnostic consideration has to address the presence/absence of the following psychiatric disorders: developmental disorders (e.g., specific developmental disorders, language disorders, mental retardation), behavioral disorders (e.g., attention deficit hyperactivity disorder, oppositional disorder), or generalized reaction to stress.

Treatment

Clinical practice and published studies attest to a major shift in the treatment of constipation and encopresis in childhood from psychiatry to behavioral pediatrics, which reports a 60 to 80% success rate with a combination of education, medical management, and positive reinforcement (Levine, 1982).

Levine (Levine & Bakow, 1976) developed a treatment protocol that aims at vigorous bowel clean-out, prevention of reaccumulation of stool, and establishment of regular bowel habits. During the initial counseling with child and parents, encopresis is "demystified." With the help of simple drawings, bowel functions are explained in simple terms and encopresis is presented as just another physical problem, shared by many other children with nobody to be blamed. Treatment is presented in terms of mastery ("muscle training") with shared responsibilities for child and parents under the coaching of the pediatrician. While labeled as "education," this approach entails psychotherapeutic principles of working alliance, reframing, and clarification of roles.

The initial catharsis is accomplished with repeated high-normal saline enemas followed by Dulcolax suppositories for 3 to 7 days. This is followed by establishment of a regular toilet routine with positive reinforcement procedures and daily use of light mineral oil together with a high-fiber diet. This regimen must be maintained, with regular follow-up visits, for at least 6 months; at times, up to 2 years is considered necessary.

Treatment failure to what is now considered the "traditional" medical approach is ascribed to more severe and generalized behavior problems in the child of which encopresis is only one manifestation (Gabel, Chandra, & Shindledecker, 1988; Stark, Spirito, Lewis, & Hart, 1990), external locus of control (Rappaport & Levine, 1986), lack of motivation (Gabel et al., 1988), and poor family functioning (Stark et al., 1990). A variety of behavioral approaches have been advocated including rewards for clean pants (Taitz, Whales, Urwin, & Monar, 1986), hourly toilet sits and punishment in the form of time out for soiling (O'Brien, Ross, & Christophersen, 1986), as well as group treatment utilizing play with clay (Feldman, Villanueva, Lanne, & Devroede, 1993).

Identifying a subgroup of encopretic boys with expulsion dysfunction who were not responsive to medical treatment, Wald (Wald et al., 1987) reported a significant success rate with biofeedback training, which since then has become an important treatment modality by behavioral pediatricians (Benninga, Buller, & Taminiau, 1993; Loening-Baucke, 1995).

Sporadic case reports (e.g., Gavanski, 1971) claim usefulness of imipramine for the treatment of encopresis. Lacking systematic studies to evaluate its efficacy and given its cardiotoxic risk, it should be considered only for severe and treatment refractory cases.

The role of individual and family psychotherapy, for many decades the main form of treatment for children with encopresis, has been questioned by the growing behavioral pediatric literature (Landman & Rappaport, 1985; Stern, Prince, & Stroh, 1988) as well as by recent child psychiatric texts (Mikkelsen, 1991; Walsh & Menvielle, 1991). The American Psychiatric Association's publication *Treatments of Psychiatric Disorders* (1989) recognized that child psychiatrists will see only those children who have failed several attempts of medical/behavioral approaches. In this subgroup a thorough evaluation is essential in order to assess all factors in the child, family, and environment that are contributing to the presentation and maintenance of the symptom. More often than not, encopresis will be just one symptom of more serious psychopathology in the child and/or of the overall family system.

While individual psychotherapy with the child can address issues of autonomy vs. fear of abandonment, feelings of incompetence and lack of control, and inability to experience and express affect other than through soiling, it has to be embedded into a familial and social context. A major therapeutic goal of family therapy is to make family members aware of the pervasive and multiple familial sources of discontent beyond the symptom of soiling (Shovelar, 1980). This will reduce the pressure on the child by providing support for the entire family.

In addition to family intervention for the severely disturbed encopretic child and family, the recent child psychiatric literature (Bemporad & Hallowell, 1987) stresses the integration of medical, behavioral, and psychodynamic modalities into a multimodal approach.

Summary

Functional encopresis is a symptomatic manifestation of multifactorial origins. Growing evidence points to a physiological predisposition, to which developmental, familial, and psychological factors contribute in a wide variety of degrees. While the majority of children will respond to a combined medical/behavioral approach, 20% require more intensive child psychiatric intervention with additional individual and family therapy. Applying the concepts of developmental psychopathology to functional encopresis could lead to renewed interest of child psychiatry in this classical syndrome.

REFERENCES

American Psychiatric Association. (1989). *Treatment of psychiatric disorders* (Vol. 1, pp. 717–726). Washington, DC: Author.

American Psychiatric Association. (1994). *Diagnostic and statistical manual of mental disorders* (4th ed.). Washington, DC: Author.

Anthony, E. J. (1957). An experimental approach to the psychopathology of childhood: Encopresis. *British Journal of Medical Psychology, 30,* 156–175.

Bellman, M. (1966). Studies on encopresis. *Acta Paediatrica Scandinavica, 170* (Suppl.), 1–151.

Bemporad, J. R., Pfeifer, C. M., Gibbs, L., Cortner, R. H., & Bloom, W. (1971). Characteristics of encopretic patients and their families. *Journal of the American Academy of Child Psychiatry, 10,* 272–292.

Bemporad, J. R., Kresch, R. A., Asnes, R., & Wilson, A. (1978). Chronic neurotic encopresis as a paradigm of a multifactorial psychiatric disorder. *Journal of Nervous and Mental Disease, 166,* 472–479.

Bemporad, J. R., & Hallowell, E. (1987). Advances in the treatment of disorders of elimination. In J. D. Call, R. L. Cohen, S. Harrison, I. N. Berlin, & L. A. Stone (Eds.), *Basic Handbook of Child Psychiatry,* (Vol. 5, pp. 479–483). New York: Basic Books.

Benninga, M. A., Buller, H. A., & Taminiau, J. A. (1993). Biofeedback training in chronic constipation. *Archives of Disease in Childhood, 68,* 126–129.

Bosch, J. D. (1984). *Gedragsmodificatie van encopresis.* Lisse: Swets & Zeitlinger.

Bosch, J. D. (1988). Enkopresis als entwicklungsstoerung. *Zeitschrift für Kinder-Jugendpsychiatrie, 16,* 155–162.

Brazelton T. B. (1962). A child-oriented approach to toilet training. *Pediatrics, 29,* 121–128.

Cicchetti, D. (1984). The emergence of developmental Psychopathology. *Child Development, 55,* 1–7.

Feldman, P. C., Villanueva, S., Lanne, V., & Devroede, G. (1993). Use of play with clay to treat children with intractable encopresis. *Journal of Pediatrics, 122,* 483–488.

Fenichel, O. (1945). *The psychoanalytic theory of neurosis.* New York: W. W. Norton.

Fowler, G. B. (1882). Incontinence of faeces in children. *American Journal of Obstetrical Diseases in Women and Children, 15,* 984–988.

Freud, A. (1963). The concept of developmental lines. *Psychoanalytic Study of the Child, 18,* 245–265.

Freud, S. (1958). Character and anal erotism. In J. Strachey (Ed. and Trans.), *The standard edition of the complete psychological works of Sigmund Freud* (Vol. 12, 311–326). London: Hogarth Press, 1958. (Original work published 1908.)

Gabel, S., Hegedus, A. M., Wald, A., Chandra, R. & Chiponis, D. (1986). Prevalence of behavior problems and mental health utilization among encopretic children: Implications for behavioral pediatrics. *Journal of Developmental and Behavioral Pediatrics, 7,* 293–297.

Gabel, S., Chandra, R., & Shindledecker, R. (1988). Behavioral ratings and outcome of medical treatment for encopresis. *Journal of Developmental and Behavioral Pediatrics, 9,* 129–133.

Gesell, A., Ilg, F., & Ames, L. B. (1974). *Infant and child in the culture of today* (rev. ed.). New York: Harper & Rowe.

Gavanski, M. (1971). Treatment of non-retentive secondary encopresis with imipramine and psychotherapy. *Canadian Medical Association Journal, 104,* 46–48.

Hatch, T. F. (1988). Encopresis and constipation in children. *Pediatric Clinics of North America, 35,* 257–280.

Hersov, L. (1985). Faecal soiling. In M. Rutter & L. Hersov (Eds.), *Child and adolescent psychiatry: Modern approaches* (2nd ed., pp. 482–489). London: Blackwell Scientific Publications.

Huschka, A. (1942). The child's response to coercive

bowel training. *Psychosomatic Medicine, 4,* 301–308.

Landman, G. B., Rappaport, L., Fenton, T., & Levine, M. (1986). Locus of control and self-esteem in children with encopresis. *Journal of Developmental and Behavioral Pediatrics, 7,* 111–113.

Landman, G. B., & Rappaport, L. (1985). Pediatric management of severe treatment-resistant encopresis. *Journal of Developmental and Behavioral Pediatrics, 6,* 349–351.

Largo, R. H., & Stutzle, W. (1977a). Longitudinal study of bowel and bladder control by day and at night in the first six years of life. I: Epidemiology and interrelations between bowel and bladder control. *Developmental Medicine and Child Neurology, 19,* 598–606.

Largo, R. H., & Stutzle, W. (1977b). Longitudinal study of bowel and bladder control by day and at night in the first six years of life. II: The role of potty training and the child's initiative. *Developmental Medicine and Child Neurology, 19,* 607–613.

Levine, M. D. (1975). Children with encopresis: A descriptive analysis. *Pediatrics, 56,* 412–416.

Levine, M. D. (1982). Encopresis: Its potentiation, evaluation, and alleviation. *Pediatric Clinics of North America, 29,* 315–330.

Levine, M. D., & Bakow, H. (1976). Children with encopresis: A study of treatment outcome. *Pediatrics, 58,* 845–852.

Loening-Baucke, V. (1990). Modulation of abnormal defecation dynamics by biofeedback treatment in chronically constipated children with encopresis. *Journal of Pediatrics, 116,* 214–222.

Loening-Baucke, V. (1995). Biofeedback treatment for chronic constipation and encopresis in childhood: long-term outcome. *Pediatrics, 96,* 105–110.

Mikkelsen, E. J. (1991). Modern approaches to enuresis and encopresis. In M. Lewis (Ed.), *Child and adolescent psychiatry: A comprehensive textbook* (pp. 583–591). Baltimore: Williams & Wilkins.

O'Brien, S., Ross, L. V., & Christophersen, E. R. (1986). Primary encopresis: Evaluation and treatment. *Journal of Applied Behavior Analysis, 19,* 137–145.

Olatawura, M. O. (1973). Encopresis. *Acta Paediatrica Scandinavica, 62,* 358–364.

Owens-Stively, J. A. (1987). Self-esteem and compliance in encopretic children. *Child Psychiatry and Human Development, 18,* 13–21.

Pototzky, C. (1925). Psychogenese und Psychotherapie von Organsymptomen beim Kind. In O. Schwarz (Ed.), *Psychogenese und Psychotherapie Organischer Symptome* (pp. 385–424). Berlin: Springer.

Rappaport, L., & Levine, M. D. (1986). The prevention of constipation and encopresis: A developmental model and approach. *Pediatric Clinics of North America, 33,* 859–869.

Rutter, M., Tizard, J., & Whitmore, K. (Eds). (1970). *Education, Health and Behavior.* London: Longman.

Shane, M. (1967). Encopresis in a latency boy: A arrest along a developmental line. *Psychoanalytic Study of the Child, 22,* 296–313.

Shovelar, G. P. (1980). Commentary: Persistent encopresis in preadolescence. In G. P. Shovelar, R. M. Benson, & B. J. Blinder (Eds.), *Emotional disorders in children and adolescents* (pp. 187–191). New York: SP Medical and Scientific Books.

Sroufe, L. A., & Rutter, M. (1984). The domain of developmental psychopathology. *Child Development, 55,* 17–29.

Stark, L. J., Spirito, A., Lewis, A. V., & Hart, K. J. (1990). Encopresis: Behavioral parameters associated with children who fail medical management. *Child Psychiatry and Human Development, 20,* 169–179.

Stein, Z., & Susser, M. (1967). Social factors in the development of sphincter control. *Developmental Medicine and Child Neurology, 9,* 692–706.

Stern, H. P., Lowitz, G. H., Prince, M. T., Altshuler, L., & Stroh, S. E. (1988). The incidence of cognitive dysfunction in an encopretic population of children. *Neurotoxology, 9,* 351–358.

Stern, H. P., Prince, M. T., & Stroh, S. E. (1988). Encopresis responsive to non-psychiatric intervention. With remittance of familial psychopathology. *Clinical Pediatrics, 27,* 400–402.

Taitz, L. S., Whales, J. K. H., Urwin, O. M., & Molnar, D. (1986). Factors associated with outcome in management of defecation disorders, *Archives of Disease in Childhood, 61,* 472–477.

Wald, A., Chandra, R., Gabel, S., & Chiponis, D. (1987). Evaluation of biofeedback in childhood encopresis. *Journal of Pediatric Gastroenterology, 6,* 554–558.

Walsh, T., & Menvielle, E. (1991) Disorders of elimination. In J. M. Wiener (Ed.), *Textbook of child and adolescent psychiatry* (pp. 416–421). Washington: American Psychiatric Press.

Younoszai, M. K., & Tolaymat, N. (1989). Chronic functional constipation in infants and children. In E. Lebenthal (Ed.), *Textbook of gastroenterology and nutrion in infancy* (2nd ed., pp. 1311–1326). New York: Raven Press.

48 / Enuresis

Gregory K. Fritz and Randy M. Rockney

Enuresis is defined as the involuntary voiding of urine beyond the age when bladder control is usually attained. It is most appropriately viewed as a symptom, with multiple possible etiologies and treatments that span the boundaries of child psychiatry, pediatrics, and urology. The history of the symptom of enuresis, as summarized in Glickich's (1951) fascinating review, reveals a thread of punitive and desperate interventions that have been applied by frustrated adults for centuries to children who persistently wet. Currently our treatments have evolved beyond cautery of sacral nerves, penile ligation, inflated vaginal balloons to compress the bladder neck, and electric shocks to the genitalia. Nonetheless, family embarrassment, parental anger at what they see as "a willful child," and insensitive peers can together make life miserable for an enuretic child. Chronic anxiety, impaired self-esteem, and delayed developmental steps such as attending camp or sleeping at a friend's house may all be secondary problems that are more devastating to the child than the symptom of enuresis itself.

The reported prevalence of enuresis at different ages varies considerably due to inconsistencies in the definition of enuresis, differences in the method of data collection, and characteristics of the population sampled. Enuresis, the involuntary discharge of urine after the age when bladder control is usually attained, occurs in 12 to 25% of 4-year-old children, 7 to 10% of 8-year-old children, and 2 to 3% of 12-year-old children. It remains a problem even in late teenage years, where 1 to 3% may still be wetting the bed. Primary enuresis (bladder control never achieved) is twice as common as secondary enuresis (resumption of wetting after 3 to 6 months of dryness). The ratio of the incidence of enuresis in boys vs. girls is 2:1; enuresis is more common in lower socioeconomic groups and in institutionalized children. The spontaneous cure rate is 14 to 16% annually, as reported in Forsythe and Redmond's (1974) long-term study of 1,129 children. The spontaneous cure rate appears to change at around 4 years of age: 30% of the 2- to 4-year-olds who wet the bed may become dry in the next year compared with the fairly steady spontaneous cure rate of 14 to 16% in older children. This change in the spontaneous cure rate suggests that enuresis can be considered a clinical problem after the age of 4 or 5 years; before that time it is essentially a normal variant unless, as described later, specific causes are identified.

An overview of the development of urinary control in children is basic to understanding the symptom of enuresis. Urinary continence is obtained in three sequential steps: enlargement of the bladder capacity, voluntary control of the sphincter muscles, and voluntary control of the micturition reflex. In the first 2 years of life, voiding occurs in a reflex fashion: bladder distension results in detrusor contraction and sphincter relaxation via a spinal cord reflex arc. The sensation of bladder fullness develops in the second year, and the critical ability to control the sphincter muscles voluntarily occurs by 3 years of age. The final step is gaining the ability to inhibit the micturition reflex, after which urinary continence can be achieved. There is a consistent sequence of attainment of continence in children. Bowel control during sleep is attained first. This usually is followed by bowel control during wakefulness, bladder control during wakefulness, and last, bladder control at night. Girls typically achieve each of these milestones before boys.

Urodynamic studies of enuretic children most consistently reveal reduced functional bladder capacity (the volume that produces the sensation of needing to void), although anatomic bladder capacity, obtained under general anesthesia, is a function of body size. The formula "age in years + 2 = the functional bladder capacity in ounces" is a generally accepted approximation of an individual child's functional bladder capacity (Koff, 1983). Uninhibited bladder contractions, similar to the infantile pattern, are identified more commonly in urodynamic studies of enuretic than nonenuretic children. The relationship between these contractions and actual enuretic episodes, however, is as yet unclear.

Given that enuresis is most appropriately thought of as a symptom rather than a specific disorder, it is essential to conduct a thorough assessment of a child who presents with enuresis to determine whether any of a number of possible specific etiologies can be identified. A complete assessment may be the most important contribution a physician can make in that it relieves the child and parent of worry about a serious underlying problem if none exists and leads to proper intervention when an underlying problem is discovered. Shuffling a child and concerned parents between subspecialists, such as urologists, pediatricians, and child psychiatrists, to complete a thorough evaluation is traumatic and inefficient. The initial evaluation can be undertaken by any physician who has an interest in the problem and is willing to consider a broad range of possibilities as etiologically relevant. The following sections summarize the categories of etiologies.

Urologic Etiologies

Pathology of the urinary system may account for 2 to 4% of enuresis in children, depending on the speciality of the physician doing the evaluation. (Presumably the variation is due to patients with urologic problems consulting urologists rather than physician blindness or bias.) Several features obtained in the history will alert the clinician to the possibility of urological abnormality. These include a past history of uropathology in either the patient or other family members, dribbling or continuous wetting, significant daytime incontinence, an abnormal voiding pattern, or a history of urinary tract infections. Most commonly the urologic abnormalities identified include ectopic ureters that lead to continuous drainage, bladder dysfunction resulting from outflow obstruction in the urethra (e.g., caused by urethral valves or a prolapsed ureterocele), or neurologic impairment of the bladder and/or sphincter mechanism associated with myelomeningocele. A dysfunctional voiding pattern, if identified, may be associated with the Hinman-Allen syndrome (Allen, 1977;

Hinman & Brumann, 1973), also referred to as the nonneurogenic neurogenic bladder. Suspicion of any of these abnormalities is reason for further evaluation; however, renal ultrasound and voiding cystoureterogram followed by intravenous pyelogram or cystoscopic evaluation are not routinely recommended as part of the evaluation of every enuretic child because the tests are expensive, they can be traumatic to the child, and the yield is low if the indications just described are not present.

Medical Etiologies

Incontinence, polyuria, and polydipsia should make the clinician suspicious of diabetes mellitus or diabetes insipidus, either of which is an unusual but possible cause for secondary enuresis. Upper airway obstruction because of enlarged tonsils and adenoids may be etiologically related to the symptom of enuresis. Studies of the effect on enuresis show an improvement or complete cure of nocturnal enuresis in most patients after surgical removal of obstructing tonsils (Weider, Sateia, & West, 1991). Constipation also may be associated with enuresis, perhaps coming about through a similar neurologic or developmental mechanism, but presumably reducing bladder capacity because of the volume of stool in the abdomen.

Genetics

Genetics undoubtedly plays an etiologic role in enuresis. Bakwin (1973) showed that, compared to a 15% incidence of enuresis in children from nonenuretic families, 44% and 77% of children were enuretic when one or both parents, respectively, were enuretic. Approximately one third of fathers and one fifth of mothers of enuretic children were themselves enuretic as children. It is in fact unusual for a child with primary functional nocturnal enuresis not to have a close relative who was also enuretic. The developmental and perhaps even sleep aberrations of enuretics may be manifestations of the same genetic predisposition.

tion, although at this point a sleep disorder cannot be defined as a major etiologic factor in enuresis.

Developmental Delay

Pediatricians commonly accept the theory of developmental delay or immaturity in the attainment of central control of bladder function as the primary etiology of enuresis. Starfield (1972) found that the functional bladder capacity was less in enuretic children than in nonenuretic sibling controls, and urodynamic data on uninhibited bladder contractions tends to support the impression that enuresis is caused by an immature voiding pattern. Other reports of an increased incidence of physical characteristics suggest developmental immaturity, including lower average height and lower mean bone age, in enuretic than in nonenuretic children (Shaffer, 1985). Late sexual maturation has been associated with a higher prevalence of enuresis among adolescents, and there is a greater incidence of enuresis in children who were delayed in the attainment of motor and language milestones as well. Although the mechanism is not specified beyond these associations, developmental immaturity seems to be relevant in the etiology of primary enuresis for many children.

Sleep Disorders

Parents of enuretic children usually describe the child as very difficult to wake up (although parents rarely attempt to awaken nonenuretic children, who also sleep very soundly). Enuresis has been reported in association with specific sleep disorders, including narcolepsy and the sleep apnea syndrome. A series of studies reported from multiple sleep laboratories indicate a random pattern of wetting that occurs in all stages of sleep in proportion to the amount of time spent in each stage (Fritz & Armbrust, 1982). The question of how the arousal system may be dysfunctional in a subgroup of enuretic children needs further explora-

Psychosocial Factors

Enuresis has been considered a symptom of psychological disturbance, despite the lack of evidence beyond theoretical position statements and anecdotal reports from psychiatric treatment. At the same time, there is clear evidence that the rate of psychiatric disorders in enuretic children is higher than the rate found in nonenuretic groups (Shaffer, 1985). Most enuretic children show no symptoms of emotional or behavioral disturbance. Among those who do, it is frequently difficult to determine whether the relationship between the enuresis and the psychological problem has etiologic relevance or is either coincidental or occurring in response to the symptom of enuresis. The fact that psychological improvement has been noted to occur following successful treatment of enuresis suggests that at least in some cases, the psychological disturbance is in reaction to the symptom. Stress and/or anxiety at critical developmental periods may delay the attainment of dryness in a manner similar to the affect on other developmental milestones.

Although no prospective studies are available, both premature or coercive toilet training and overindulgent efforts have been examined in relation to enuresis. The symptom has been described as the child's efforts at retaliation against the parents or as symptomatic of an infantilized, overly dependent relationship on the caregiver. Enuresis also has been variously described in the psychiatric literature as a masturbatory equivalent, an expression of bisexuality, or the somatic expression of a defect in body image. Given the present state of our understanding, it is reasonable to conclude that for a small subgroup of enuretic children, the symptom has a psychological etiology. Those children are most frequently secondary enuretics who have experienced a stress, such as parental divorce, school trauma, hospitalization, or the like; their enuresis is a regressive symptom in response to the stress.

The other situation in which psychological factors can be seen to be etiologically central is in the rare instance where family disorganization or neglect has resulted in there never having been a reasonable effort made at toilet training. The child presents with primary enuresis and no other discernible etiologic factors evident beyond the negligent family history and associated psychosocial disturbance.

Diagnostic Assessment

Children can present with enuresis as a major or minor symptom of concern to a variety of physicians, including pediatricians, urologists, family practice physicians, and child psychiatrists. Reasons for presenting to one physician over another are variable and generally unsystematic; it also has been shown that as few as 38% of enuretic children had seen *any* physician about their symptom (Foxman, Valdez, & Brook, 1986). In every instance, sensitivity to the emotional consequences of the symptom of enuresis and thoroughness to avoid missing even its uncommon causes must be guiding principles of the evaluation. The assessment of enuresis begins with an extensive history, focusing on the symptom itself and involving both the patient in an individual interview and the parents privately as well. Optimally, a 2-week baseline record of the enuresis pattern is obtained prior to the initial evaluation visit. Not infrequently this baseline monitoring is associated with a dramatic improvement. It also serves as a standard against which the success of subsequent interventions can be gauged.

The initial history should explore every aspect of the urinary incontinence, and the genitourinary and neurologic systems reviews must be especially thorough. The frequency, time of day, course of the symptom, relationship of wetting to environmental changes, onset of the symptom, and concurrence of dribbling, dysuria, frequency, and urgency should be explored specifically. The child's reaction to the symptom and interest in working on it should be assessed (since without significant motivation, treatment is rarely successful). The family's response to the symptom, regarding who takes responsibility for it, how open and matter-of-fact they are about the symptom, the degree of

embarassment should all be assessed. Developmental history should be obtained in some detail to rule out the possibility of developmental delays in other areas as well as subtle neurologic symptoms. Symptoms of night waking, snoring, and upper airway obstruction are important, as are the sleeping arrangements for the child at home. The physician must be alert to the possibility of previous or ongoing inappropriate sexual contact. The history also should focus on the family history of enuresis. When the family history is discussed in the evaluation, it is not unusual for teenagers with enuresis to learn for the first time that one of their parents was enuretic until a similar age. Finally, the patient and the parents should be questioned about previous evaluations and attempts at therapy. Previous use of the conditioning alarm or medications may have been undertaken, but the thoroughness, dosage, and length of time the treatment was monitored should be assessed before concluding that the treatments have had a sufficient trial to be judged ineffective.

Every enuretic child needs a careful physical examination as part of the diagnostic evaluation. The genital focus of the symptom means that attention to issues of modesty, privacy, and the possible traumatic impact of the examination are especially important, but under no circumstances should treatment be started without an examination. The physical examination should emphasize the following: assessment of the patency of the nares and voice quality (for enlarged adenoids), examination of the nasal pharynx (for enlarged tonsils), palpation of the abdomen (for bladder distention, fecal impaction), examination of the genitalia (for abnormalities of the meatus, epispadias, phimosis, etc.), examination of the back (for a sacral dimple or other suggestion of a vertebral or spinal cord anomaly), and a thorough neurologic examination to rule out subtle dysfunction associated with the symptom.

Treatment

A thorough evaluation will identify a specific etiology or contributing disorder, implying a specific, definitive treatment, for perhaps *one third* of enuretic children. Most patients, however, will have no specific cause of the symptom diagnosed and will require "generic" treatment that is chosen on an individual basis depending on the child's and family's concerns, motivation, and intelligence. It is important to note that not all children with the symptom of enuresis require treatment. Many parents, after they are reassured that an underlying urological, medical, or psychological problem is not present, do not request treatment or are not willing to accept either the risks or inconveniences associated with treatment.

A number of commonsense approaches to enuresis have evolved over time and can be considered supportive but unproven interventions. They include the following:

1. Educate parents about the prevalence of enuresis (to reduce their guilt), the relatively high spontaneous cure rate (to encourage hope), and the unconscious nature of the symptom (to avoid a punitive response or the development of a control struggle).
2. Encourage the keeping of a journal or a dry bed chart by the child (as a sort of consciousness raising).
3. Reduce fluids prior to bedtime (to decrease the volume of urine produced during the night).
4. Awaken the child to void during the night (nightlifting, to preempt the symptom).

It should be noted that none of these approaches has empirical support for efficacy—one study even suggested that nightlifting actually was less successful than no treatment—but all entail no risk or expense and have proven to be useful in individual cases. It is not clear whether effective supportive intervention acts through a placebo effect, anxiety reduction, or simply filling the time until a spontaneous cure occurs.

Conditioning night awakening to the sensation of a full bladder is the most benign and successful of the generic treatments for enuresis. Decades of use of the night waking alarm have shown that approximately two thirds of the children who have a full course of treatment with professional supervision respond; the relapse rate is 20 to 40%, however. Portable transistorized alarms that the child wears on the body have replaced the old bell-and-pad type, but the principle is the same. The first drops of urine moisten the fabric separating two electrodes, thereby completing the circuit and setting off the alarm that the child is wearing. Gradually the child awakens earlier and

earlier in the course of the enuretic episode and the wet spot diminishes in size until the sensation of bladder fullness causes the child to awaken prior to wetting. Success is followed by overlearning and intermittent reinforcement in which the child uses the alarm every other day before discontinuing it. Few children awaken easily in the initial stages of conditioning treatment, and considerable parental investment is required. Lack of parental help to awaken the child to finish the voiding in the toilet is a major reason for failure of the conditioning treatment. If sleeping arrangements, family support, and reliability of the adults to monitor the situation are not adequate, undertaking conditioning treatment will lead only to frustration. Lack of success with the approach in the past or a relapse after previous success do not preclude successful treatment with a conditioning device subsequently. Throughout the behavioral treatment, monitoring the increasing success with a sticker chart and reinforcing positive change is critical to maintaining the child's investment in the process.

Over the last 20 years drug therapy for enuresis has involved imipramine primarily, with desmopressin (DDAVP) a recent addition. Imipramine has been used extensively for nocturnal enuresis despite the fact that the precise mechanism of action for enuresis is still poorly understood. Neither the anticholinergic effect nor the changes in sleep architecture (reduction in rapid eye movement sleep) has been shown to explain the effect of imipramine adequately. Imipramine is effective 40 to 60% of the time; the relapse rate is significant (up to 50%). The benefit of imipramine is seen more rapidly and at a lower dose than is common when the drug is used as an antidepressant. The usual dosage range is 1 to 2.5 milligrams (mg) per kilogram (kg) per day in a single dose at bedtime. When effective, the imipramine is continued 4 to 6 months. Recent reports of unexpected deaths due to cardiac arrhythmia in children taking imipramine or other tricyclic antidepressants suggest that a pretreatment electrocardiogram to determine an underlying rhythm disorder is indicated, with periodic monitoring thereafter. Children usually tolerate the imipramine at low dosage levels with minimal anticholinergic or cardiovascular side effects. Studies of serum levels of imipramine and its metabolite, desipramine, in relation to enuresis efficacy have been inconclusive, with individual variation being the most striking finding. At present, assessment of serum level is indicated only when there has been no effect despite a dose of 2.5 mg per kg per day. The most serious problem associated with imipramine is ingestion by the patient's younger siblings, often associated with serious or fatal consequences.

Desmopressin is a synthetic analog of the antidiuretic hormone vasopressin (ADH), and recently it has received increased use in the treatment of enuresis. There is some evidence that the normal diurnal variation in the ADH levels may be altered in some enuretic patients. Norgaard, Pederson, and Djurhuus (1985) demonstrated an absence of the normal nocturnal rise in ADH levels in enuretic children compared to controls. It is postulated that this results in increased urine output at night that exceeds the functional bladder capacity and results in a wet bed. Desmopressin is given intranasally at bedtime in doses of 10 to 40 micrograms (mcg) nightly (1 to 4 sprays nasally). Each spray is metered to instill 10 mcg. The initial recommended dose is 20 mcg, increased by 10 mcg weekly to a maximum of 40 mcg or reduced by 10 mcg weekly (if the higher dose is effective) to a minimum of 10 mcg. The drug's duration is 10 to 12 hours, and there is a compensatory polyuria the following day after the effect wears off. Although water intoxication is a potential problem, to date serious side effects with DDAVP have been reported in only 2 cases. Headache, abdominal discomfort, nausea, and nasal congestion have been relatively rare side effects. The success rates reported have ranged from 10 to 65%, with as many as 80% of patients relapsing after treatment (Thompson & Rey, 1995). DDAVP should be prescribed only for primary enuretics; we have found it most useful in older patients and those without a history of nasal congestion or sinusitis (which likely impair absorption).

Psychotherapy is indicated only when a specific psychological issue associated with the onset of the symptom (in secondary enuresis) is identified or a control struggle between parent and child is maintaining the symptom. Certainly enuresis itself does not constitute an indication for psychotherapy beyond the supportive counseling mentioned earlier. Typical disorders associated with enuresis that may be amenable to psychotherapy include a situational reaction with prolonged regressive symptomatology, a separation-individuation conflict between the parent and child in which the wet bed is the focus, and certain impulse disorders of adolescents.

Bladder training, in which daily stretching by retaining urine is intended to increase the functional bladder capacity, has been reported to be effective. The effort not to void despite considerable urgency is unpleasant for both the child and the family, making it a less desirable approach. Hypnotherapy has been reported to be successful in particular cases, but further research is needed regarding the application of this modality on a broad scale. The desperation many parents feel regarding the symptom of enuresis makes them vulnerable to exploitation by purveyors of high-priced, "guaranteed" treatments that are essentially variants of the conditioning treatment. The desperation also makes parents frequently ask about allergies and dietary contributions to enuresis, and education as to the insufficient evidence available at present is more useful than either desensitization or dietary manipulation.

REFERENCES

Allen, T. D. (1977). The non-neurogenic neurogenic bladder. *Journal of Urology, 117,* 232.

Bakwin, H. (1973). The genetics of enuresis. In I. Kolvin, S. MacKeith, & R. Meadow (Eds.), *Bladder control and enuresis* (pp. 73–77). London: Lavenhan Press.

Forsythe, W. I., & Redmond, A. (1974). Enuresis and spontaneous cure rate-study of 1129 enuretics. *Archives of Diseases of Children, 49,* 259.

Foxman, B., Valdez, R., & Brook, R. (1986). Childhood enuresis: Prevalence, perceived impact, and prescribed treatments. *Pediatrics, 77,* 482–487.

Fritz, G. K., & Armbrust, J. (1982). Enuresis and encopresis. *Psychiatric Clinics of North America, 5,* 283–296.

Glicklich, L. B. (1951). An historical account of enuresis. *Pediatrics, 8,* 859.

Hinman, F., & Baumann, F. W. (1973). Vesical and ureteral damage from voiding dysfunction in boys without neurologic or obstructive disease. *Journal of Urology, 109,* 727.

Koff, S. A. (1983). Estimating bladder capacity in children. *Urology, 21,* 248.

Norgaard, J. P., Pederson, E. B., & Djurhuus, J. C.

(1985). Diurnal antidiuretic hormone levels in enuretics. *Journal of Urology, 134,* 1029–1031.

Shaffer, D. (1985). Enuresis. In M. Rutter & L. Hersov (Eds.), *Child and adolescent psychiatry: Modern approaches* (pp. 465–481). London: Blackwell Scientific Publications.

Starfield, B. (1972). Enuresis: Its pathogenesis and management. *Clinical Pediatrics, 11,* 343.

Thompson, S., & Rey, J. M. (1995). Functional enuresis: Is desmopressin the answer? *Journal of the American Academy of Child and Adolescent Psychiatry, 34,* 266–271.

Weider, D. J., Sateia, M. J., & West, R. P. (1991). Nocturnal enuresis in children with upper airway obstruction. *Otolaryngology Head and Neck Surgery, 105,* 427–432.

49 / Somatoform Disorders, Factitious Disorders, and Malingering

Daniel T. Williams

Everyone at times experiences physical symptoms or abnormal body sensations that are not directly related to a physically based disease process. Sometimes these cause transient worry or discomfort that is not disabling and resolves without any specific treatment. However, some individuals become bogged down in extensive use of the body as a coping mechanism, either for expression of emotional distress and/or for personal gain. This may occur either acutely, in response to overwhelming life stresses, or chronically, when it may become integrated into one's basic personality style of coping and hence may become a way of life (Ford, 1983; Smith, 1990). There is a consensus in the literature on somatoform disorders, factitious disorders, and malingering that the propensity to chronic somatization often has its etiological roots in childhood (Williams & Hirsch, 1988). It is important that the well-trained child psychiatrist be sensitive and informed about the complexities of this group of disorders, so that appropriate evaluation and intervention at an early stage can minimize or prevent a progression toward chronic somatization.

Somatoform disorders, factitious disorders, and malingering are individually distinguished from each other by two key parameters: The question of conscious versus unconscious intentionality on the part of the patient with regard to symptom formation, and the question of whether the apparent goal of the symptom formation is readily recognizable in terms of evident external benefits from the symptoms.

Somatoform disorders are characterized by the presumption that the patient's psychologically based physical symptoms are unconscious in origin. Both factitious disorders and malingering involve conscious and purposeful symptom formation. In factitious disorders, the physical symptom is part of a psychiatric disorder that generates no apparent benefit to the patient. In malingering, which is not a psychiatric disorder, a readily recognizable benefit to the patient is evident, once all of the relevant circumstances of the case are known.

Somatoform Disorders

Somatoform disorders are characterized by physical symptoms suggesting physical disorder for which there are no demonstrable organic findings or known physiological mechanisms, and for which there is positive evidence, or a strong presumption, that the symptoms are linked to psychological factors or conflicts (American Psychiatric Association [APA], 1994). The symptom production in somatoform disorders is not under voluntary control, hence implying an unconscious mechanism in symptom formation. Conversion disorder is the subdivision of somatoform disorders most commonly encountered among children.

CONVERSION DISORDER

Conversion disorder is characterized by a loss or alteration of physical functioning that suggests physical disorder but that instead is apparently an expression of a psychological conflict or a need. After appropriate investigation, the disturbance cannot be explained by any physical disorder or known pathophysiological mechanism. Psychological factors may be judged to play a primary etiological role in a variety of ways. Thus, a temporal relationship may exist between the onset or worsening of the symptom and the presence of an environmental stimulus that activates a psychological conflict or a need. Alternatively, the symptom may be noted to free the patient from a noxious activity or encounter. Finally, the symptom may enable the patient to get help from others that might otherwise not be forthcoming. The most common conversion symptoms are those suggesting neurological disease, but virtually any known bodily disease may be mimicked unconsciously in a conversion disorder. Outlines of some of the common clinical features of conversion disorders follow (Nemiah, 1985; Williams & Hirsch, 1988).

Motor Disturbances: Conversion symptoms presenting as abnormal movements may take many forms, including seizures, coordination difficulties, and movement disorders. Conversion paralysis and weakness most often affect the extremities, either singularly or in combination. However, any body part may be affected, ranging from the vocal cords, leading to aphonia; to the trunk, leading, for example, to hysterical scoliosis (lateral curvature of the spine) or to camptocormia (forward flexion of the upper body on the hips).

Sensory Disturbances: Conversion disturbances of skin sensation may occur in any location and pattern but are found most often in the extremities. Disorders of motor function often are accompanied by diminished or totally absent sensation, often involving all modalities. As with motor disturbances of conversion etiology, the distribution of sensory disturbance follows a pattern determined by the patient's conception of the anatomic abnormality rather than the actual pattern of nerve innervations—hence, the frequently encountered postinjury pattern of glove and stocking anesthesia of the hands and feet and other clearly nonphysiological patterns of deficit that are commonly observed. The special organs of sense also may be affected, leading to impairment of hearing and vision to varying degrees. Sensory hallucinations sometimes are encountered, occasionally including auditory or visual components. Finally, pain may accompany other sensory and motor disturbances in many patients with conversion disorders.

Symptoms Simulating Physical Illness: The symptoms of conversion disorder may simulate physical disease so closely that diagnosis is difficult to establish. A common pattern here may involve an identification with the symptoms of the illness of a person with whom the patient has had a special relationship. A parent or close friend who has recently died, for example, may engender conversion symptoms in a vulnerable child as one manifestation of a pathological grief reaction.

Symptoms Complicating Physical Illness: Symptoms of bona fide physical illness may be protracted or complicated by secondary conversion symptoms. Thus, limb weakness or disuse that begins after an injury may be prolonged as a conversion symptom long after the initial physical injury has subsided. A patient with bona fide neurogenic seizures may develop secondary conversion seizures that can be difficult to differentiate from the neurogenic ones. Symptoms in this category often present challenging problems of differential diagnosis.

It is commonly assumed that conversion disorders are defined not only by the absence of demonstrable organic pathology at their onset but also by the failure of these symptoms to result in actual physical injury to the patient. Neither of these assumptions is necessarily true. Examples of secondary organic pathology resulting from conversion disorder include disuse atrophy of muscles from psychogenic paralysis of a limb and contractures from long-standing psychogenic dystonia (Fahn & Williams, 1988). Psychogenic seizures may on rare occasions result in serious self-injury. Iatrogenic problems may ensue from misguided medical and surgical interventions. One 10-year-old boy was spared from a scheduled exploratory laparotomy when psychiatric consultation led to the prompt resolution of what turned out in retrospect to be psychogenic abdominal pain.

Associated mental disorders often coexisting with conversion disorders in adults include dissociative disorders, major depressive disorder, and anxiety disorders on Axis I as well as histrionic, antisocial, and dependent personality disorders on Axis II of the fourth edition of the *Diagnostic and Statistical Manual of Mental Disorders* (*DSM-IV*) (APA, 1994; Williams, Ford, & Fahn, 1995). Psychiatric comorbidity of conversion disorders in children remains to be studied more systematically.

(SOMATOFORM) PAIN DISORDER

The characteristic feature of (somatoform) pain disorder is the complaint of pain in the absence of adequate physical findings to explain the pain in physiological terms and in the presence of positive evidence of the etiological role of psychological factors. (Somatoform) pain disorder will be considered here conjointly with conversion disorder, as the two appear to be closely linked (Grattan-Smith, Fairley, & Procopsis, 1988) and there is insufficient data regarding differences between the two among two children and adolescents to discuss them separately (Nemzer, 1991).

SOMATIZATION DISORDER

Somatization disorder (formerly called hysteria or Briquet's syndrome) most often has its onset in adolescence, with only rare documentation of prepubertal diagnosis (Livingston & Martin-Connici, 1985). The essential features include recurrent multisymptomatic complaints of several years duration beginning before the age of 30. Medical attention is sought repeatedly, but the symptoms are not found to be due to any physical disorder. Complaints of at least 4 pain symptoms—2 gastrointestinal symptoms, 1 sexual symptom, and 1 pseudoneurological symptom—must be elicited in order to establish the diagnosis according to *DSM-IV* criteria. Frequently associated psychiatric comorbidity includes major depressive disorder, panic disorder, and substance-related disorders on Axis I. Histrionic, borderline, and antisocial personality disorders are the most frequently associated Axis II diagnoses.

It has been estimated that approximately 1% of the adult female population has this disorder (Ford, 1983), while it is rarely diagnosed in males. There is a higher incidence of antisocial personality disorder among family members of those with somatization disorder than in the general population. The clinical course tends to be chronic but fluctuating, with extensive utilization of medical services over time and with rare incidence of spontaneous remission. As is noted later, a clinically important issue is the probability that untreated, protracted, or recurrent episodes of conversion disorder or somatoform pain disorder in childhood or adolescence may predispose to the subsequent development of somatization disorder.

In *DSM-IV* nosology, somatoform presentations that do not meet criteria for somatization disorder are classified as undifferentiated somatoform disorder if syndrome duration is 6 months or longer, or somatoform disorder not otherwise specified for presentations of shorter duration.

HYPOCHONDRIASIS

Hypochondriasis is characterized by an unrealistic interpretation of physical signs or sensations as abnormal, leading to preoccupation with the fear or belief of having a serious disease. A thorough physical evaluation does not support the diagnosis of any physical disorder that can account for the physical symptoms or sensations or for the individual's unrealistic interpretation of them. The unrealistic fear or belief of having a physical disease persists despite medical reassurance and has a duration of at least 6 months.

The disorder is equally common in males and females in adulthood, but epidemiologic data are not available regarding childhood. Common associated features include anxiety, depression, compulsive and narcissistic personality traits, and a history of many medical consultations. The age of onset is commonly in adolescence, though some cases are encountered during the school-age years. The course is often chronic with waxing and waning of symptoms. This disorder is seen more commonly in general pediatric and medical practice, yet such patients and their parents often resist a psychological interpretation of their symptoms and consequently often decline referral for psychiatric treatment.

A variation on the theme of hypochondriasis is body dysmorphic disorder, involving a preoccupation with an imagined defect in appearance. If a slight physical anomaly is present, the person's concern is markedly excessive. The preoccupation causes clinically significant distress or impairment in social, occupational, or other important areas of functioning.

From this description, it is clear that there is an overlap in phenomenology between somatization disorder and hypochondriasis. In addition to the quantitative distinction between the two having to do with symptom enumeration and duration, there is a qualitative difference in mode of presentation. Patients with somatization disorder tend to be more dramatic and extroverted in style, while those with hypochondriasis tend to be more obsessive and introverted. Similar questions rise with hypochondriasis as with somatization disorder regarding the possible role of early, extended experience with conversion symptoms in childhood as a predisposing factor to the development of hypochondriacal lifestyle.

Factitious Disorders

Factitious disorders are characterized by physical or psychological symptoms that are intentionally produced or feigned, hence being by definition under voluntary control (APA, 1994). The sense of voluntary control is subjective and can only be inferred by an outside observer, giving rise to ready diagnostic confusion with somatoform disorders. The judgment that symptoms are voluntarily produced is based on observations of behavior suggesting dissimulation or concealment, after excluding all other possible causes of the behavior. However, it should be noted that this behavior has a compulsive quality and hence is voluntary in the sense of being deliberate and purposeful, while implying a lack of full control that is an inherent feature of a compulsive behavior. Another essential feature is the psychological need to assume the sick role, as evidenced by the absence of external incentives for the behavior, such as economic gain, avoidance of onerous responsibilities, or attaining more comfortable circumstances via the sick role. This is important in distinguishing factitious disorders from malingering. An illustrative example of a factitious disorder would be a child with a spiking fever of unknown etiology who is admitted to the hospital and is subjected to numerous and sometimes painful diagnostic procedures who eventually is found, by unobtrusive observation, to be rubbing the thermometer against the bedsheets to generate an elevated temperature reading.

In its more chronic forms, factitious disorder may be associated with either physical symptoms (Munchausen's syndrome) or psychological symptoms (Ganser's syndrome, pseudopsychosis, or pseudodementia). These manifestations generally are associated with severe dependent, masochistic, or antisocial personality disorders. Here again, these chronic forms of maladaptation are thought to derive from uncorrected patterns of using factitious symptoms as expressions of distress that frequently date from childhood.

MUNCHAUSEN'S SYNDROME BY PROXY

This variant of factitious disorder was first reported by Meadow (1982). He reported on 19 children under 7 years of age, from 17 families, whose mothers consistently gave fraudulent clinical histories and fabricated signs that led to needless and harmful medical investigations, hospital admissions, and treatment over a period of time ranging from a few months to 4 years. Episodes of bleeding, neurological abnormality, rashes, fevers, and abnormal urine were commonly simulated. Often the mothers had previous nursing training, and some had a history of fabricating symptoms or signs relating to themselves. Two of the 19 children died. Meadow's study of these children and their families led to a list of warning signs to consider, together with recommendations for dealing with suspected acts. He noted the need to separate the mother and child in suspect circumstances to confirm the fabrication and emphasized the subsequent need to confront the families with the deception when it was confirmed. Of the 17 survivors in his series, 8 children were taken into protective care; the other 9 remained at home after arrangements were made for augmented supervision.

A follow-up study (Bools, Neale, & Meadow, 1993) evaluated 54 children who were studied a mean of 5.6 years after fabrications of illness had been identified. Thirty of the 54 children were living in families with their biological mothers and 24 were with other family members or in substitute families. Further fabrications were identified for 10 children who had been living with their mothers. Thirteen children residing with mother and 14 not residing with mother at follow-up had a range of disorders, including conduct and emotional disorders, difficulties in attention, and school nonattendance.

Malingering

Malingering is characterized by the voluntary production and presentation of false or grossly exaggerated physical or psychological symptoms. In contrast to factitious disorder, the symptoms in malingering are produced in pursuit of a goal that is readily recognizable with an understanding of the individual's circumstances rather than his or her individual psychology (Kellner, 1991; Yudofsky, 1985). Examples of such readily understandable goals include the avoidance of school or work, the securing of financing compensation, the evasion of punishment, or the acquisition of drugs. An example of parentally induced malingering in a school-age child would be parents encouraging their child, directly or indirectly, to persevere in reporting symptoms in the wake of an accident for purposes of enhancing financial claims.

As with somatoform disorders and factitious disorders, the clinician often cannot determine a patient's volitional intent with certainty, especially at the outset of the clinical assessment. The particular characteristic of the malingerer, namely that of deceiving and manipulating the physician into unwitting compliance with a goal of the malingerer's choosing, is particularly likely to elicit strong countertransference feelings on the part of the physician when this diagnosis is suspected. Because the confrontational presentation of such suspicion to a child or parent will irremediably sabotage any prospects of a therapeutic relationship and inevitably transform it into a hostile, adversarial one, it is particularly important to refrain from such confrontation until all other differential diagnostic possibilities have been adequately considered and explored. It is important to note that somatoform disorders may include "secondary gains," which may falsely lead to the presumption of malingering. In ambiguous cases it is therefore best to give the patient the benefit of the doubt, so as to preserve the clinician's therapeutic leverage with a view to symptom alleviation.

Differential Diagnosis

In addition to the complex and subtle discriminations required on the part of the clinician in distinguishing among the various somatizing disorders just outlined, the following two categories require special consideration.

UNDIAGNOSED PHYSICAL ILLNESS

Undiagnosed physical illness is probably the most common and certainly the most important source of differential diagnostic error in the diagnosis of the somatizing disorders. For example, of the 28 pediatric cases reviewed by Caplan (1972) with a diagnosis of "hysteria," a minimum of 13 were found on follow-up to have an organic illness related to the presenting symptom either by the time of discharge from the hospital or at follow-up from 4 to 11 years later. It should be emphasized that diagnosing a somatizing disorder requires more than simply the inability to find an organic basis for a given physical symptom on the initial medical evaluation. Many medical disorders, such as multiple sclerosis, lupus erythematosus, and dystonia musculorum deformans, may present with initially subtle, fluctuating, and insidiously progressive physical symptoms that frequently are misdiagnosed early in their course as "functional" or, more specifically, as somatizing disorders. Furthermore, it should be noted that patients with true medical disorders may develop secondary somatizing disorders as a reactive way of dealing with their anxiety about what they subliminally perceive to be an underlying physical derangement, about which they have difficulty communicating directly with those in their environment. The best defense against this common and sometimes treacherous source of diagnostic error is maintaining close contact between a consulting mental health practitioner and a coevaluating pediatrician or other examining physician, while keeping in mind the possibility during ongoing assessment and treatment that undiagnosed physical illness may exist.

PSYCHOLOGICAL FACTORS AFFECTING A MEDICAL CONDITION

The category of psychological factors affecting a medical condition is used in *DSM-IV* to describe not only disorders that have in the past been referred to as psychosomatic or psychophysiological but, more broadly, to delineate any physical condition in which psychological factors are judged to have a contributory role (Rubinstein, 1988). This judgment requires evidence that psychologically meaningful environmental stimuli are temporally related to the initiation or exacerbation of a physical condition. Furthermore, the physical condition must have either demonstrable organic pathology (e.g., ulcerative colitis) or a presumptively known pathophysiological process (e.g., migraine headache).

To illustrate the differential diagnostic complexity that may pertain, consider a child or adolescent with uncontrolled seizures who is referred by a neurologist for psychiatric consultation because of apparent emotional precipitant of at least some of the seizures. The referring and consulting clinicians must discern what proportion of the seizures represent uncontrolled epileptic seizures, a somatoform disorder, a factitious disorder, malingering, or psychologically precipitated epileptic seizures (psychological factors affecting a medical condition). Furthermore, they must consider whether some undiagnosed physical condition (e.g., central nervous system infection, tumor, or degenerative disease) may be contributory. They also must be aware that two or more of these conditions may coexist in the same patient. The result can be and often is a diagnostic challenge that taxes the resources of even the most seasoned neurologists and psychiatrists (Williams & Mostofsky, 1982; Williams, Pleak, & Hanesian, 1991; Williams, Spiegel, & Mostofsky, 1978; Williams et al., 1979).

HISTORY

Information supporting the impression that a given symptom is a manifestation of a somatizing disorder would include the following:

1. The historical data regarding the symptom are compatible with the primary diagnosis of a somatoform disorder.
2. There is a history of other symptoms (past or current) that clearly have the characteristics of a somatoform disorder, such as unexplained paralysis or anesthesia. Inquiry on such matters should apply not only to the patient but also to family members, who are a ready source of identification for the patient.
3. There is a history of other overt emotional or behavioral symptoms, such as anxiety, depression, obsessions, phobias, school avoidance, or separation anxiety disorder. As above, inquiry with regard to such symptoms in other family members is also of relevance.
4. There is a history of a recent death or other loss of a person important to the patient or some other major psychological stress temporally related to the onset of the presenting symptom or symptoms.
5. There is a history of a relative, friend, or acquaintance who has had a physical symptom similar to that which the patient now presents and the patient may have plausible reason to affiliate with this symptom by identification.
6. There is a history of recent or accumulated major stress or trauma, such as sexual seduction or abuse (Herman & Hirschman, 1981).

These historical features are suggestive but by no means exhaustive of the variety of life stresses and predisposing factors that should lead the clinician to consider the diagnosis of a somatoform disorder.

The clinician's tactical approach to the patient and family is of importance in establishing an appropriate rapport that is crucial for effective diagnostic assessment and treatment for all somatizing disorders. The patient with a somatoform disorder, for example, is by definition unaware of the relationship between environmental stress or intrapsychic conflict and the appearance of the presenting symptoms. In such a setting, a confrontational approach with the patient or parents during the initial assessment is clearly counterproductive. The patient or parents are likely to meet with denial or distortion any inquiries they perceive as seeking to establish such etiological connections in an accusatory tone. A preferable approach for all the somatizing disorders discussed in this chapter is to begin by explaining supportively to both the patient and parents that the referring physician sought a psychiatric consultation because of the possibility that psychological factors may be playing some role in the patient's presenting symptom, as they do in many commonly encountered medical problems. This opens the way for a collaborative dialogue in which the patient and parents will be helping the psychiatrist and co-treating physicians with two difficult tasks: first, understanding the genesis of the symptom and then, one hopes, enabling the patient to overcome it. If available medical information at the time of psychiatric referral is not conclusive regarding the presence or absence of physical disease, it is important to clarify that issue with the patient and family. It also should be explained that ongoing contact will be maintained with the primary referring physician, as physical and psychiatric assessments proceed concurrently.

Psychiatric assessment should yield a detailed picture of the patient's individual strengths and weaknesses, social relationships, school functioning, and pattern of family interaction. The process of exploring these areas often yields additional clues as to whether there exists a combination of intrinsic vulnerabilities in the patient and cumulative stressors in his or her environment that would predispose to the development of a somatizing disorder. Special attention should be paid to contingencies of behavioral reinforcement (e.g., increased parental attention and solicitude, avoidance of school) that may be contributing to the perpetuation of the symptom.

With the school-age child who is intrinsically less sophisticated about the distinctions between conscious and unconscious symptom formation, exploration of these matters often is best initiated with the parents separately from the child. Even with them, the tendency of parents to be protective of their child's integrity or to be defensive regarding their own possible contribution to the child's psychopathology requires a ginger and supportive approach by the child psychiatrist. Indeed, parental oversolicitude regarding physical illness is often a significant contributant to the child's tendency to somatize emotional distress. It is important to introduce this possible etiological contributant as the extension of a natural and well-intentioned parental instinct that may have inadvertently generated an untoward consequence by feeding into the child's own apprehension regarding physical vulnerability. Using this approach, parents feel supported and understood, which makes them more receptive to subsequent recommendations geared to therapeutic reorientation.

After the completion of physical and psychiatric evaluations, it is frequently helpful to have a joint meeting between the parents, the medical practitioner, and the child psychiatrist, particularly if the child has been hospitalized in a pediatric inpatient setting. Such a meeting serves to expedite clearing the air regarding the diagnosis and avoid misunderstandings on triangularizations between the parents, the child psychiatrist, and other physicians.

Only after this approach has been tried and failed should the child psychiatrist take a more confrontational stance. If clear evidence of dissimulation by the child or parent has been elicited, this needs to be presented to the parents, again, preferably initially separately from the child and preferably in a firm but supportive context, emphasizing not blame but the need to overcome a maladaptive coping strategy. Parental apprehension that a recommendation for psychiatric treatment means that their child is "crazy" or "bad" needs to be reality tested and refuted.

PHYSICAL EXAMINATION

Although physical examination is not generally the primary province of the psychiatrist in evaluating somatizing disorders, it is helpful for the child psychiatrist to be cognizant of some of the considerations that pertain in differentiating psychogenic from organically based sensory and motor deficits. Since space limitations preclude discussion of these here, the reader is referred to Weintraub (1977) and Williams and Hirsch (1988).

MENTAL STATUS EVALUATION

Children with somatoform disorders are generally alert, oriented, and in effective communication with the examiner. It is advisable for the clinician to make specific inquiry about feelings of depression and associated vegetative signs, although these are often not present. Thought content is generally not grossly abnormal, nor is there evidence of a primary process thought disorder or bizarre behavior. The most frequently described abnormality in the mental status of patients with conversion symptoms is *la belle indifference*. This refers to the patient's attitude toward the symptom, which suggests a relative lack of concern out of keeping with the significant nature of the impairment. This feature has limited diagnostic value, however, since it is also encountered in some seriously ill medical patients who are stoic about their conditions. Furthermore, it has been observed that many patients with conversion symptoms often experience diffuse anxiety and other painful affects concomitant with those symptoms, while remaining indifferent in regard to the conversion symptoms themselves. Finally, histrionic personality traits may or may not coexist with either a somatoform disorder or an organic illness.

If a documented psychosis is present, coexisting somatoform symptoms should be considered secondary to the underlying psychotic or schizophrenic process. However, in patients with recent onset of psychotic behavior associated with severe environmental stress, rapid decompensation, and other conversion symptoms or histrionic personality features, the diagnosis of historical psychosis should be considered (Spiegel & Fink, 1979). In such cases, differential diagnosis can be facilitated by using a standardized measure of hypnotic trance capacity. Patients with hysterical psychosis are generally highly hypnotizable, while those who are schizophrenic or otherwise psychotic generally have low to zero hypnotizability.

It should be emphasized that in all cases where an apparent somatizing disorder in a child is being evaluated, the securing of additional information from the parents and other potentially relevant informants is as important as interviewing the patient. This is obviously related to the patient's consciously or unconsciously withholding relevant historical and/or motivationally important information that others may be more willing or able to address. It is clearly important for the clinician to define this exploration in supportive terms, so that potentially helpful informants do not become alienated by what they perceive as an attempt to stigmatize or dismiss the patient's symptoms.

Characteristic behavioral features of patients with both factitious disorders and malingering include evasiveness, truculence, and manipulativeness. In the hospital setting a propensity for splitting may be observed, as manifested by playing on the sympathies of some staff members while angrily denigrating or threatening others. These features often become more pronounced as patients sense that their fabrications have been

recognized. In cases of malingering, the somatizing behavior tends to clear as soon as the recognizable goal is either attained or finally perceived by the patient to be clearly unattainable. With factitious disorders, by contrast, somatizing behavior tends to persist or recur independent of immediate consequences or irrefutable confrontation regarding the fabrications involved.

PSYCHOMETRIC EVALUATION

Formal psychometric testing can document learning disabilities or other intellectual limitations that may not have been recognized previously by parents, teachers, or the evaluating clinician. Delineation of such learning difficulties can be extremely helpful, both in understanding the evolution of the somatizing disorder in response to an unrecognized deficit and in formulating an appropriate treatment plan.

Projective tests, such as the Rorschach and the Thematic Apperception Test, may add observations that clarify or reinforce the clinician's own impressions, since they represent a standardized, structured form of clinical interview using a different format of eliciting clinical impressions. In comparison with patients having other "neurotic" syndromes, those with somatoform disorder tend to give test responses that are freer and more imaginative, accompanied by more labile affect and a tendency toward impulsiveness. In the case of factitious disorders, projective tests commonly have yielded profiles suggestive of borderline personality organization.

Some psychological tests, such as the Minnesota Multiphasic Personality Inventory, have "lie scales" that may support clinical suspicions in cases of factitious disorders and malingering. However, these scales also might implicate patients with somatoform disorders, who commonly make use of denial as a defense mechanism.

Etiology and Pathogenesis

The following sections briefly review some of the main contemporary conceptual formulations of the genesis of the somatizing disorders having relevance to the clinician working with school-age children. It should be noted that these formulations are not mutually exclusive but rather may be viewed as elucidating different possible contributants to the development of somatizing disorders in different individuals. In that sense, they are relevant to formulating plans for treatment intervention.

SOMATOFORM DISORDERS

Psychoanalytic Theory: Using conversion disorder as a paradigm of the somatoform disorders, a fixation is postulated in early psychosexual development at the level of the Oedipus complex (Adams, 1979). A failure to relinquish the incestuous tie to the loved parent leads to intrapsychic conflict over the sexual drive because it retains its forbidden incestuous quality. This drive is therefore repressed, and the energy associated with the drive is converted into a psychologically determined physical symptom. The symptom not only protects the patient from conscious awareness of the repressed drive but simultaneously often provides a psychologically significant symbolic expression of it.

In addition to this primary gain, often secondary gains of the symptom contribute to its retention. These include the attention, sympathy, and support often provided to an individual as a result of the conversion symptoms. The associated disability also may excuse the individual from onerous tasks and school responsibilities, thus gratifying dependency needs and reinforcing the perpetuation of the symptom.

Gratification of Dependency Needs: For some patients, gratification of dependency needs may be a primary rather than a secondary determinant of conversion symptoms (Nemiah, 1985). Experiences with psychiatric combat casualties of adults during the world wars disclosed many conversion disorders where the primary motivation of the symptoms appeared to be self-preservation rather than oedipal sexual drives. In these situations, the symptoms enabled the individual to escape a dangerous situation and to receive protection and support under the rubric of the patient role, which could not honorably be requested directly.

In school-age children, physical illness often is perceived unconsciously as an accessible route of escape from the onerous burdens of school and other competitive social situations about which

the youngster feels anxious or inadequate. When a child is faced with a conflict between unconscious dependency needs on the one hand and idealized demands of conscience to be persevering and productive on the other, conversion symptoms can provide a temporary albeit maladaptive escape hatch. Since the physical symptom is perceived by both the patient and others as an affliction over which he or she has no control, it brings relief of school and/or other social burdens and legitimizes the unconsciously coveted dependency status the youngster cannot honorably request directly.

Reaction to Environmental Stress: Another perspective on the phenomena of conversion disorder as a paradigm of somatoform disorders is offered by learning theory. From this perspective, behavior can be reinforced by reduction of the intensity of an inner painful psychological drive, whose reduction predictably follows the behavior. For example, a conversion symptom may result in a reduction of the painful drive of fear and anxiety, such as that associated with being at school. The relief obtained in this manner reinforces the conversion symptom that generated the relief and predisposes to a repetition of the same symptom each time the anxiety is experienced. In this manner, a pattern of behavior is reinforced repetitively and may eventually become chronic.

The Phenomenon of Dissociation: Both Janet and Freud used the term *dissociation* in describing hysteria to refer to the splitting off from consciousness of painful affects and associated ideas (Frankel, 1976). Insofar as our contemporary definition of somatoform disorders continues to emphasize that symptom reduction is not under voluntary control, there remains an intrinsic presumption that the phenomenon of dissociation plays a central role in these disorders. Thus, the curious phenomenon of a conversion paralysis that is mediated by the "voluntary" musculature, whose innervation is intact yet not under the conscious voluntary control of the patient, presents a conceptual paradox that is best understood in terms of the experience of dissociation.

Freud's early interest in the study of hysteria was integrally related to his interest in hypnosis, which is also characterized by the phenomenon of dissociation (Spiegel & Spiegel, 1978). Contemporary studies of the phenomenon of dissociation, as exemplified by the hypnotic trance state, thus provide a useful route of inquiry that can help us better understand the phenomenology of somatoform disorders. Thus, for example, the majority of the population has measurable capacity to experience dissociation under the controlled circumstances of a standardized measure of hypnotizability. Children are even more hypnotizable than adults. The standardized measure of hypnotizability itself demonstrates to the subject the ability of environmental cues and suggestions to alter subjective experience, including physical perceptions. This then becomes a heuristic paradigm, which the therapist can utilize to explain to the patient and family how cumulative environmental stresses can generate perceptual distortions that simulate the symptoms of physical illness (Williams, 1988, 1991).

NEUROPHYSIOLOGICAL PREDISPOSITION

Flor-Henry (1983) marshaled three lines of evidence to support the contention that a particular pattern of cerebral disorganization is fundamental to the most severe of the somatoform disorders, somatization disorder (hysteria). First, he undertook a historical reinterpretation of the case of Anna O., based on recently disclosed medical data that he felt supported the contention that a subacute limbic encephalitis is a more convincing explanation of her variegated symptomatology than the purely psychological theory advocated by Freud. He further cited a controlled neuropsychological investigation on 10 adult patients with the stable syndrome of "hysteria," who were matched for sex, handedness, and full-scale IQ with 10 normal controls, 10 psychotic depressives, and 10 schizophrenics. The findings were interpreted to suggest that dominant hemisphere dysfunction is fundamental to the syndrome of hysteria by engendering a defect in processing and integrating endogenous somatic signals. He further posited, citing genetic studies, that hysteria in the female is a syndrome equivalent to psychopathy in the male, insofar as psychopathic fathers tend to produce daughters with hysteria. Some support for this neurophysiological perspective as pertinent to childhood somatoform disorders is offered by Spierings et al. (1990); in a follow-up study of 84 children who were diagnosed as having conversion disorder, 51% had various slight to moderate electroencephalogram abnormalities.

The Role of Depression: Klerman (1982) noted that among adults, there appears to be a moderate overlap between the components of somatoform disorder and the clinical phenomenon of depression. Whether viewed from the vantage point of somatoform disorder or from that of depression, moderate percentages of patients with both disorders have manifestations of the other disorder.

A recent study has lent support for this association in children and adolescents. McCauley, Carlson, and Calderon (1991) obtained structured interview (Kiddie SADS) and Child Behavior Checklist data from depressed patients ($n = 100$) and nondepressed psychiatric controls ($n = 38$). Seventy percent of the children who met criteria for depression had significant somatic complaints, in contrast to 34% of controls. Findings revealed that frequency of somatic complaints increased with severity of depression.

McArdle and Madison (1989) studied a general population sample of 202 boys ages 6 to 11 years, using the Child Behavior Checklist. The most common type of symptomatic cluster was Symptomatic Complaints, subsumed under the larger category of Internalizing Behavior profiles. This is consonant with other studies that report that younger, preadolescent subjects are more likely to report somatic complaints than adolescents or adults (Carlson & Kashani, 1988; Ryan et al., 1987).

From a psychodynamic perspective, based on these studies, it might be hypothesized that school-age children who are by constitutional predisposition and/or prior life experience prone to internalization of stressful emotion may be at greater risk for both depression and somatization.

The Roots of Somatization Disorder: It seems plausible to suggest that untreated, protracted, or recurrent episodes of conversion disorder or somatoform pain disorder in childhood or adolescence would be likely predisposing factors for somatization disorder. Supporting this postulate are the observations that conversion disorders are more commonly diagnosed in children and adolescents than in adults, while the reverse is true for somatization disorder. Additional supportive evidence for this developmental transformation is presented by the work of Ernst, Routh, and Harper (1984). In a retrospective study of children with abdominal pain seen in a multispecialty medical clinic, those with organic findings were compared to those whose physical examinations were negative (the functional pain group). For children with functional abdominal pain (but not for the others), the number of symptoms of somatization disorder was significantly related to the chronicity of the child's condition. Thus, the longer the duration of functional pain, the greater the number of symptoms reported.

FACTITIOUS DISORDERS

In a developmental sense, it is possible that a child's early experience with conversion disorder that is inappropriately handled by parents or others may predispose not only to somatization disorder but also to factitious disorder, where the child has a more conscious and intentional secondary elaboration of symptoms. Some additional etiological considerations regarding factitious disorders are outlined next (Ford, 1983).

Family histories of patients with factitious disorder frequently yield reports of parental abuse, neglect, or abandonment. One or both parents usually are seen as rejecting figures who are unable to form close relationships. These observations have led to psychological models suggesting that patients with factitious disorder have been unable to achieve a necessary sense of acceptance by an early love object such as a parent, consequently leaving their dependency needs inadequately satisfied. The resulting personality of such persons is viewed as vulnerable to subsequent life events that produce persistent medical and hospital-seeking behavior.

These patients perceive the medical setting and hospital staff as a potential source of security and response to unmet dependency needs. An institutional dependency is created in which the hospital and staff become a surrogate home and family. However, by virtue of the pathological severity of the dependency needs, the resources of the hospital and staff are soon exhausted, leading to alienation and eventual rejection.

The inherent masochism of submitting to innumerable procedures is often interpreted as an attempt to relieve unconscious guilt. Alternative views of mutilating and self-destructive behavior have led to the idea that they can be equated with acts of suicide, representing aggression against the rejecting parents or family.

One young woman in our experience had 14 hospitalizations and 3 major surgical procedures between the ages of 10 and 19 (Fahn & Williams, 1988). The surgery, all retrospectively unwarranted, included placing a metal rod in her foot, placing a metal rod in her spinal column, and a craniotomy for laser thalamotomy. All of these procedures were based on a mistaken diagnosis of torsion dystonia, the symptoms of which only later were recognized to have been psychogenic in origin.

A history of work in the health profession is recorded in over 50% of recognized adult cases; numerous reports indicate patients have fathers or other relatives who are either physicians or other health-related practitioners, which may play a role in the problematic identity formation of youngsters with factitious disorder.

Treatment

Many different treatment approaches have been used with children and adolescents having somatizing disorders. As with most psychotherapeutic interventions (Frank et al., 1978), controlled studies are extremely difficult to implement and are simply not available for children with this group of disorders (Kellner, 1989, 1991). Those therapeutic approaches that eclectic clinical experience has found useful are considered here. Each of these treatment approaches has some potential value for some patients. Often different treatment approaches can be combined effectively in the management of a given patient. Consequently, it is advantageous for the clinician to be well informed about as many of these approaches as possible, to be able innovatively to structure a treatment plan that most effectively meets the unique needs of each patient.

REASSURANCE, PLACEBO, AND SUGGESTION

Variations on the theme of reassurance, placebo, and suggestion have been used throughout history, sometimes quite successfully, by religious healers, physicians, and others as a way of relieving the symptoms of the various somatizing disorders discussed here. Reassurance, placebo, and/or suggestion are used to foster symptom relinquishment without generating sophisticated grasp, by contemporary psychiatric standards, of the symptom's psychogenic determinants. Traditionally, this has involved the invocation of supernatural healing forces and/or the exorcism of nefarious illness-producing forces so as to restore the patient to health. Frequently, the use of prayer or an associated religious ceremony is involved, for which the patient and/or family makes some monetary or other contribution as part of a process of expiation of sin or appeasement of the deity. In a more secular context, the use of placebo can serve a comparable function in mobilizing the positive expectation and belief of the patient that relief of illness will be forthcoming thanks to the powerful forces of pharmacological intervention generated by the scientific revolution. It should be noted in passing that more recent studies have clarified the capacity of placebo to affect neurophysiological functioning by activating the release of endorphins within the central nervous system (Spiegel, 1988), so that dismissing this process as "merely suggestion" is unwarranted. The use of these nonspecific modalities, which pediatricians and other medical practitioners often employ prior to referral for psychiatric consultation, may be effective for the relief of acute conversion symptoms that arise in response to a short-term and self-limited environmental stress. When used supportively and sensitively in such a setting, this approach may be not only effective in symptom relief but also judicious in sparing the patient and family an expensive involvement in unnecessary psychotherapy.

Complications arise, however, when this treatment approach is used indiscriminately for all somatizing disorders, including those symptoms with complex, sustained intrapsychic determinants and/or in the presence of continuing, unmanageable environmental stress. In such situations, this approach is counterproductive. Here it will be either totally ineffective or of only short-term benefit, with prompt emergence of symptom recurrence or substitution. Furthermore, the patient and family lose confidence in the clinician who takes such an approach. This occurs because an attempt has been made to remove a symptom that has been serving a defensive function, albeit maladaptively, without an effort to alleviate the patient's underlying sources of distress.

INDIVIDUAL AND FAMILY THERAPIES

Individual and family therapies can be discussed here only briefly. Since a myriad of intermingling etiological factors may pertain, it behooves the clinician to address as many of the pertinent issues as possible in the course of history taking. Based on a thorough exploration of relevant factors in this context, a working hypothesis regarding the evolution of the somatizing disorder is likely to emerge. With this working hypothesis in mind, the clinician's next task is to explore possible ways to alleviate pathogenic environmental influences impinging on the patient and/or augment the patient's capacity for mastering ongoing sources of distress.

Alleviating environmental stress often involves working with the patient's immediate family and significant others, such as teachers. If marital conflict between the parents is apparently contributing to the youngster's somatization, for example, direct counseling of the parents should be considered regarding their marital adjustment and more appropriate ways of communicating with their child about it. Similarly, if a "valedictorian syndrome" exists whereby parents, teachers, and/or the patient him- or herself have generated excessive demands for academic achievement relative to the youngster's actual intellectual capacity, then direct, supportive counseling of both the patient and family as well as communication with teachers may be needed in order to alleviate this frequent contributant to somatization. As another example, if sexual abuse or seduction has occurred as a precipitating factor, clearly the protection of the patient from the perpetrator as well as supportive alleviation of associated feelings of guilt and/or violation are essential ingredients in the treatment plan.

Dealing with the apparent dynamics of intrapsychic conflict in youngsters with somatizing disorder requires tact and sensitivity. It is useful to view the somatizing symptom as a makeshift refuge to which the patient has intuitively and sometimes unconsciously retreated under duress. The clinician is challenged to formulate for the patient and family a safe and honorable route by which the symptom can be understood as a maladaptive defense encumbrance that can be relinquished with dignity in favor of a more effective coping method. There are many ways to do this, but the clinician commonly presents some version of a working hypothesis to the patient and the parents to aid the process of cognitive, emotional, and behavioral reorientation. The extent to which this process can be "worked through" with the patient and parents in terms of conscious understanding of the relevant dynamics is variable.

In the pursuit of the above-noted therapeutic goals, several specialized treatment approaches are often helpful in the context of individual and/or family therapy. Some of these are briefly noted.

Psychoanalysis: From the time of Freud's initial exploration of the dynamics of hysteria until recently, it was believed by many that psychoanalysis or intensive long-term dynamic psychotherapy were the specific treatments of choice for somatoform disorders (Anthony, 1975). It is now apparent that only a minority of the total number of patients with these disorders are candidates for such therapy, in part because of the combined demands of time, money, and intellectual investment, which most patients and families simply do not have. Equally important, however, is the variability in chronicity of symptoms and ego impairment among patients with somatizing disorders. Those with more severe impairment of developmental course will indeed often require a more protracted individual and family-oriented treatment format in order to achieve full symptom resolution. For many patients with more short-term symptomatology and greater resilience, however, other approaches often can enhance and expedite therapeutic intervention (Turgay, 1990).

In treating somatoform disorders, the psychoanalytic approach advocates uncovering the presumed neurotic conflict that led to the disorder and, as a result of this uncovering, helping the patient to reconvert (Anthony 1975). In the case of conversion symptoms, the decoding of the unconscious meaning of the symptom through interpretation is said to induce progressive alterations in the relationship with the therapist and change in the symptoms, until the work of reconstruction pieces together the historical development of the symptom, making use of dreams and fantasies as an adjunct.

Clearly, psychiatrists who work with children and adolescents having somatizing disorders must have a sophisticated grasp of the subtle and complex factors involved in the diverse intrapsychic, interpersonal, and environmental fields that impinge on these patients. It is not necessary, however, for each patient to attain a full level of insight in order to achieve effective and sustained symptom relief. Extended analytic work can certainly add new dimensions of self-understanding for those with the resources to use this approach. Yet for the many who for various reasons cannot or do not wish to do so, or do not need to do so, more supportive and directive methods of treatment are more appropriate.

Hypnosis: Freud's interest in developing the technique of psychoanalysis was heavily influenced by the limitations he observed both in his colleagues' and in his own use of hypnosis to treat hysteria (Freud, 1925/1955a). These limitations included the narrow use of abreaction and suggestion without benefit of the dynamic understanding of symptom formation that Freud was subsequently to develop. In later years Freud himself foresaw how public health needs would rekindle a need for hypnosis to enable more widespread therapeutic application of psychoanalytic insights in a more expeditious manner (Freud, 1919/1955b).

Further considerations regarding the use of hypnosis with children and adolescents having somatoform disorders are outlined elsewhere (Williams, 1988, 1991). Admonitions sometimes expressed against the use of hypnosis with such youngsters are based on the erroneous assumption that hypnosis necessarily involves the simplistic and heavy-handed use of direct suggestion that was the usual mode of Freud's contemporaries. Furthermore, there are some positive benefits to enabling a patient and family to learn that the patient's capacity for dissociation can be elicited under controlled therapeutic conditions. In this context, the patient and family can clearly understand the dissociation that is an essential ingredient in the symptom formation of somatoform disorders as a manageable psychological attribute that can be channeled, under therapeutic auspices, in the service of symptom alleviation. Teaching the patient a self-hypnosis exercise can help shift the youngster's and family's attention away from preoccupation with the sick role and toward the mastery experience of returning to normal functioning.

Behavior Modification: Therapeutic strategies geared to symptom alleviation in the somatizing disorders must deal with the "secondary gain" features of the symptoms. (In the case of malingering, these are equivalent to the primary gain features.) With children and adolescents especially, the long-range benefits of a therapeutic endeavor may be difficult for patients to appreciate if the immediate benefits of the symptom constitute a substantial deterrent to symptom relinquishment. It is therefore essential that any ongoing secondary gain features of a symptom be diminished or eliminated. Indeed, this is crucial if the symptom's removal is to be sustained.

A common source of secondary gain for children with somatizing disorders includes avoidance of the academic and social pressures associated with school attendance, while concomitantly garnering the hovering solicitude of worried and attentive parents. In such a scenario, a key task for the therapist before formulating behavioral suggestions would be clarifying the sources of maladaptation in the school, in the child, and in the family. Thus, for one child, a change from an inappropriate class placement because of an unrecognized learning disability may be a necessary behavioral intervention; for another, it might require addressing pathological patterns of family interaction. In general, however, a key goal therapeutically is to eliminate the school avoidance that the somatizing symptom has achieved, once the underlying sources of the problem have been understood and overcome. An obvious correlate of this would be counseling the parents to restrain previously evident lavish expressions of concern and anxious affection to the child, predicated on the presumption of a serious organic illness, and replacing these with an expression of confidence that the new diagnosis and treatment plan appear to presage a return to normality.

Feldman (1988) further illustrates a number of ways in which behavior modification strategies can be formulated with school-age children, taking into account the existing contingencies of reinforcement that impinge on the patient.

Physical Therapy: Although physical therapy does include some features of reassurance, placebo, and suggestion when used in treating patients with somatizing disorders, it does have noteworthy benefits in clinical practice, particularly for patients in whom motor deficits are involved. This is especially true if the somatizing symptom arises as a complication of an actual physical illness or injury. Obviously, to be most effective, such physical therapy should be combined with a psychological strategy that addresses pertinent psychodynamic issues and external contingencies of reinforcement that affect the symptoms. When this is done, however, physical therapy often provides a face-saving maneuver that the youngster can use as a supportive bridge to honorable resumption of normal functioning.

Medication: As implied earlier, medications frequently have been used as the key element in a placebo-based treatment approach to the somatizing disorders. When somatizing disorders arise in conjunction with associated psychiatric conditions for which medication is particularly indicated, medication has a specific role to play. One such condition is school refusal (or other variants of separation anxiety disorder), in which case antidepressant medications are often effective as a key component of the treatment plan (Koplewicz & Williams, 1988). As noted earlier, other conditions that may predispose to and/or accompany the somatizing disorders are depression and pathological grief reactions. In these instances, antidepressant medication also should be considered when initial psychotherapeutic efforts are ineffective. The merits of minor tranquilizers for the adjunctive treatment of associated generalized anxiety disorders should be noted as well. Finally, some clinicians specifically have advocated using the newer serotonergic antidepressants with hypochondriacal patients because of the frequent presence of obsessional and compulsive features, which have been found responsive to these medications.

In the absence of psychotic symptoms, there is no rational basis for using neuroleptic medications in the treatment of somatizing disorders. If there is clearly documented evidence that a youngster has schizophrenic disorder or other psychotic disorder upon which substrate somatizing symptoms may be superimposed secondarily, the psychotic disorder itself becomes the primary focus of therapeutic concern, with the somatizing symptoms being treated as secondary manifestation.

Supportive Reality Testing: Even the most experienced of clinicians will encounter some patients and families who defeat extensive supportive therapeutic endeavor geared toward symptom alleviation by their tenacious investment in the physical basis and sometimes in the incurability of the presenting symptoms. Clinical experience suggests that this occurs more commonly when a somatizing disorder has become chronic and has gone through repeated, failed psychotherapeutic interventions. In such cases, the somatizing disorder often appears to be interwoven with an associated personality disorder in the child and/or parent(s), variably involving dependent, histrionic, antisocial, masochistic, or borderline features. In such situations, the degree of family psychopathology is inherently greater, frequently constituting a substantial source of resistance to appropriate treatment. These circumstances are particularly common in patients with somatization disorder, hypochondriasis, factitious disorder, and malingering. In these circumstances, clinicians clearly must recognize an associated personality disorder in clinical assessment and treatment planning. Such patients or parents, initially unwilling to explore somatizing aspects of their illness, may be willing to address features of the child's anxiety, depression, or other dysphoric symptoms that can be the starting point for therapeutic work. Some patients and families will, however, be unengageable in treatment despite the most flexible and extended efforts. If parental mistreatment and/or unengageability in treatment is documented, court action and/or the involvement of child welfare services may be necessary.

Conclusion

Somatoform disorders, factitious disorders, and malingering present substantial challenges in both differential diagnosis and treatment to even the most experienced of child psychiatrists. Evidence available to date suggests that these are multidetermined sets of disorders that require the clinician to perform a sophisticated assessment of both the patient's psychological state and coexisting family and other environmental stresses. Of necessity, effective treatment requires that the clinician be able to integrate several therapeutic avenues of approach so as to meet most effectively the unique needs of each patient and family. Early intervention with children manifesting any of these disorders should be advocated strongly, as lack of treatment may generate, by neglect, a more chronic and intractable clinical course in later life.

REFERENCES

Adams, P. L. (1979). Psychoneuroses. In J. D. Noshpitz (Ed.), *Basic handbook of child psychiatry* (Vol. 2, pp. 194–234). New York: Basic Books.

American Psychiatric Association. (1994). *Diagnostic and statistical Manual of Mental Disorders* (4th ed.). Washington, DC: Author.

Anthony, E. J. (1975). Neurotic disorders in children. In A. M. Freedman, H. I. Kaplan, & B. J. Sadock (Eds.), *Comprehensive textbook of psychiatry* (Vol. 2, pp. 1736–1741). Baltimore: Williams & Wilkins.

Bools, C. N., Neale, B. A., & Meadow, S. R. (1993). Follow up of victims of fabricated illness (Munchausen Syndrome by proxy). *Archives of Disease in Childhood, 69,* 625–630.

Caplan, H. L. (1972). *A study of hysteria in childhood.* Unpublished master's of philosophy diss. University of London.

Carlson, G. A., & Kashani, J. H. (1988). Phenomenology of major depressive disorder from childhood through adulthood: An analysis of 3 studies. *American Journal of Psychiatry, 145,* 1222–1225.

Ernst, A. R., Routh, D. K., & Harper, D. C. (1984). Abdominal pain in children and symptoms of somatization disorder. *Journal of Pediatric Psychology, 9,* 77–96.

Fahn, S., & Williams, D. (1988). Psychogenic dystonia. In S. Fahn, C. Marsden, & D. Calne (Eds.), *Advances in neurology, Vol. 50: Dystonia 2* (pp. 431–454). New York: Reven Press.

Feldman, R. S. (1988). Behavior therapy. In C. Kestenbaum & D. Williams (Eds.), *Handbook of clinical assessment of children and adolescents* (Vol. 2, pp. 1111–1128). New York: New York University Press.

Flor-Henry, P. (1983). *Cerebral basis of psychopathology.* Boston: John Wright.

Ford, C. V. (1983). *The somatizing disorders: Illness as a way of life.* New York: Elsevier Biomedical.

Frank, J. D., Hoehn-Saric, R., Imber, S., Liberman, B., & Stone, A. (1978). *Effective ingredients of successful psychotherapy.* New York: Brunner/Mazel.

Frankel, F. H. (1976). *Hypnosis: Trance as a coping mechanism.* New York: Plenum Press.

Freud, S. (1955a). An autobiographical study. In J. Strachey (Ed.), *The standard edition of the complete psychological works of Sigmund Freud* (hereafter *Standard edition*) (Vol. 20, pp. 3–74). London: Hogarth Press. (Originally published 1925.)

Freud, S. (1955b). Lines of advance in psychoanalytic therapy. In *Standard edition psychological works of Sigmund Freud* (Vol. 17, pp. 159–168). (Originally published 1919.)

Grattan-Smith, P., Fairley, M., & Procopis, P. (1988). Clinical features of conversion disorder. *Archives of Diseases of Children, 63,* 408–414.

Herman, J., & Hirschman, L. (1981). Families at risk for father-daughter incest. *American Journal of Psychiatry, 138,* 967–970.

Kellner, R. (1989). Somatoform and factitious disorders. In American Psychiatric Association Task Force on Treatments of Psychiatric Disorders, *Treatments of psychiatric disorders* (Vol. 3, pp. 2119–2182). Washington, DC: American Psychiatric Association.

Kellner, R. (1991). *Psychosomatic symptoms and somatic syndromes.* Washington, DC: American Psychiatric Press.

Klerman, G. L. (1982). Hysteria and depression. In A. Roy (Ed.), *Hysteria* (pp. 211–228). New York: John Wiley & Sons.

Koplewicz, H. S., & Williams, D. T. (1988). Psychopharmacological treatment. In C. Kestenbaum and D. Williams (Eds.), *Handbook of clinical assessment of children and adolescents* (Vol. 2, pp. 1084–1110). New York: New York University Press.

Livingston, R., & Martin-Connici, C. (1985). Multiple somatic complaints and possible somatization disorder in prepubertal children. *Journal of the American Academy of Child Psychiatry, 24,* 603–607.

McArdle, J., & Madison, R. E. (1989). Child behavior profile types in a general population sample of boys 6 to 11 years old. *Journal of Abnormal Child Psychology, 17,* 597–607.

McCauley, E., Carlson, G., & Calderon, R. (1991). The role of somatic complaints in the diagnosis of depression in children and adolescents. *Journal of the American Academy of Child & Adolescent Psychiatry, 30,* 631–635.

Meadow, R. (1982). Munchausen syndrome by proxy. *Archives of Diseases of Children, 57,* 92–98.

Nemiah, J. C. (1985). Somatoform disorders. In H. I. Kaplan & B. J. Sadock (Eds.), *Comprehensive textbook of psychiatry* (4th ed., Vol. 2, pp. 924–941). Baltimore: Williams & Wilkins.

Nemzer, E. D. (1991). Somatoform disorders. In M. Lewis (Ed.), *Child & adolescent psychiatry: A comprehensive textbook* (pp. 697–706). Baltimore: Williams & Wilkins.

Rubinstein, B. (1988). Psychological factors influencing medical conditions. In C. Kestenbaum & D. Williams (Eds.), *Handbook of clinical assessment of children and adolescents* (Vol. 2, pp. 769–799). New York: New York University Press.

Ryan, N. D., Puig-Antich, J., Ambrosini, P., Rabinovich, H., Robinson, D., Nelson, B., Iyengar, S., & Twomey, J. (1987). The clinical picture of major depression in children and adolescents. *Archives of General Psychiatry, 44,* 854–861.

Sloane, R. B., Stapes, F. R., & Cristol, A. H. (1975). *Psychotherapy vs. Behavior Therapy.* Cambridge, MA: Harvard University Press.

Smith, G. R., Jr. (1990). *Somatization disorder in the medical setting.* Washington, DC: National Institute of Mental Health, U.S. Govt. Printing Office.

Spiegel, D. (1988). Hypnosis. In J. Talbot, R. Hales, & S. Yudofsky (Eds.), *The American Psychiatric Press textbook of psychiatry* (pp. 907–928). Washington, DC: American Psychiatric Press.

Spiegel, D., & Fink, R. (1979). Hysterical psychosis and hypnotizability. *American Journal of Psychiatry, 136,* 777–781.

Spiegel, H., & Spiegel, D. (1978). *Trance and treatment: Clinical uses of hypnosis.* New York: Basic Books.

Spierings, C., Poels, P. J., Sijben, N., et al. (1990). Conversion disorders in childhood; a retrospective follow-up study of 84 inpatients. *Developmental Medicine and Child Neurology, 32,* 865–871.

Turgay, A. (1990). Treatment outcome for children and adolescents with conversion disorder. *Canadian Journal of Psychiatry, 37,* 585–589.

Weintraub, M. I. (1977). Hysteria: A clinical guide to diagnosis. *Clinical Symposia* (Vol. 29, No. 6). Summit, NJ: CIBA.

Williams, D. T. (1988). Hypnosis. In C. Kestenbaum & D. Williams (Eds.), *Handbook of clinical assessment of children and adolescents* (Vol. 2, pp. 1129–1146). New York: New York University Press.

Williams, D. T. (1991). Hypnosis. In J. Wiener (Ed.), *Textbook of child and adolescent psychiatry* (pp. 627–636). Washington, DC: American Psychiatric Press.

Williams, D. T., Ford, B., & Fahn, S. (1995). Phenomenology and psychopathology related to psychogenic movement disorders. In W. J. Wiener and A. E. Lang (Eds.) *Behavioral neurology of movement disorders. Advances in Neurology* (Vol. 65, pp. 231–257). New York: Raven Press.

Williams, D. T., Gold, A. P., Shrout, P., Shaffer, D., & Adams, D. (1979). The impact of psychiatric intervention on patients with uncontrolled seizures. *Journal of Nervous and Mental Disease, 167,* 626–631.

Williams, D. T., & Hirsch, G. (1988). The somatizing disorders: Somatoform disorders, factitious disorders and malingering. In C. Kestenbaum & D. Williams (Eds.), *Handbook of clinical assessment of children and adolescents* (Vol. 2, pp. 743–768). New York: New York University Press.

Williams, D. T., & Mostofsky, D. I. (1982). Psychogenic seizures in children and adolescents. In T. Riley & A. Roy (Eds.). *Pseudoseizures* (pp. 169–184). Baltimore: Williams & Wilkins.

Williams, D. T., Pleak, R., & Hanesian, H. (1991). Neurological disorders. In M. Lewis (Ed.). *Child and adolescent psychiatry: A comprehensive textbook* (pp. 629–645). Baltimore: Williams & Wilkins.

Williams, D. T., Spiegel, H., & Mostofsky, D. I. (1978). Neurogenic and hysterical seizures in children and adolescents: Differential diagnostic and therapeutic considerations. *American Journal of Psychiatry, 135,* 82–86.

Yudofsky, S. (1985). Malingering. In H. I. Kaplan & B. J. Sadock (Eds.), *Comprehensive textbook of psychiatry* (4th ed., Vol. 2, pp. 1862–1864). Baltimore: Williams & Wilkins.

---

50 / The Psychology of Asthma in the School-Age Child

Mary D. Klinnert

The psychological adjustment of children with asthma has received much attention over the past half century, in part because asthma has been viewed as a psychosomatic disease, wherein people with asthma were believed to provide a fascinating prototype of the somatization of psychological conflicts (French & Alexander, 1941). When the allergic basis of most asthma was commonly recognized, much of the medical and psychological community rejected a psychological component to the disorder. Either studies reported minimal increased adjustment problems among people with asthma, or increases in problems were interpreted as a reaction to the stress of having a chronic illness. Nevertheless, there is mixed and somewhat confusing evidence that asthma has a psychological component, and asthma is still considered a psychosomatic disorder. At present many contradictions remain in the literature addressing psychological adjustment and functioning among children with asthma. The goals of this chapter are to review available information regarding the psychological adjustment of asthmatic school-age children, review evidence for psychological contributions to childhood asthma, examine some of the variables that have led to confusion regarding certain aspects of the literature, and attempt to integrate a variety of findings through the conceptual framework of developmental psychopathology, in an effort to bring an improved understanding of the developmental aspects of asthma and to generate hypotheses for further study of emotional development in children with asthma.

Psychological Adjustment in Asthmatic Children

Currently, the fact that children with asthma have more adjustment problems than healthy children is fairly well accepted. This conclusion was certainly less clear to some of the first investigators of this issue, although their data were similar in many ways to information derived from current research. The issue was first systematically addressed 25 years ago in several epidemiological studies. In a study on the Isle of Wight, Graham, Rutter, Yule, and Pless (1967) concluded that the amount of psychiatric disorder they found in asthmatic children was a "trivial and statistically insignificant" increase over that found in the rest of the children they studied (p. 81), and they questioned the classification of asthma as a psychosomatic disorder. In another epidemiological study in Australia, McNicol, Williams, Allan, and McAndrew (1973) reached similar conclusions. However, although these investigators did not find increased levels of emotional disturbance across the range of asthmatic children, they documented increased behavioral disturbances among children with severe, continuing asthma.

More recent studies have consistently found increased levels of behavior problems among asth-

Support for this project was provided by NIMH Grant No. R01MH44729 and the W.T. Grant Foundation. Special thanks are due to Elizabeth McQuaid, Ph.D., Leslie Gavin, Ph.D., Nona E. Bryant, B.A., Marianne Wamboldt, M.D., and Bruce Bender, Ph.D.

matic as compared to nonasthmatic children (Hamlett, Pellegrini, & Katz, 1992; Kashani, Konig, Shepperd, Wilfley, & Morris, 1988) or as compared to available normative samples (Bussing, Halfon, Benjamin, & Wells, 1995; Carson & Schauer, 1992; MacLean, Perrin, Gortmaker, & Pierre, 1992). On the Child Behavior Checklist (CBCL; Achenbach & Edelbrock, 1983), asthmatic children have been found to be elevated on the broad-band Internalizing scale but not on the Externalizing scale (Hamlett et al., 1992; MacLean et al., 1992), although in at least one study elevations on both scales were found (Kashani et al., 1988). High Internalizing scores are indicative of anxious, depressed, and overcontrolled behavior, whereas high Externalizing scores reflect acting-out, aggressive, undercontrolled behavior. In general, parents seem to view their asthmatic children as having more difficulties in the anxious and inhibited arena. It is of interest that the parent reports of their asthmatic children's problems tended to be consistently higher for the Internalizing scales; it is generally agreed that parent reports on their children are more accurate than the children's own report for Externalizing problems, but for young children it is not clear whether the child or the parent is more accurate in reporting Internalizing problems (Silverman & Eisen, 1992). Parents' reports of social competence among their asthmatic children have been somewhat mixed. MacLean et al. (1992) found that 6- to 11-year-old boys with asthma had poor social competence relative to norms, but Kashani et al. (1988) found no difference between asthmatic and control children on social competence or on self-concept. A recent study that utilized a parent-report measure, the Personal Adjustment and Role Skills Scale (PARS) III (Stein & Jessop, 1990), found no differences in social competence among asthmatic children, children with insulin-dependent diabetes mellitus, and healthy control children (Nassau & Drotar, 1995). Interestingly, these investigators also included a number of child and teacher informant measures, and none of these measures showed the asthmatic children to have increased problems with social competence. Asthmatic children's peer relationships, measured by self-report and peer-report, also have been found to be equivalent to their healthy classmates (Graetz & Shute, 1995).

The current consensus that there are higher levels of psychopathology in asthmatic than in healthy children is derived almost exclusively from parent reports of behavior problems. The several studies that obtain information about child functioning from informants other than the parents, either from teachers or directly from the child, are less consistent regarding increased levels of psychopathology in asthmatic children. For example, in their epidemiological study, Graham et al. (1967) obtained teacher reports, in addition to parent reports, about the children's behavior problems. The teachers did not report higher levels of behavior problems among the asthmatic children compared to other children, although the parents rated their asthmatic children somewhat higher on problems than other parents rated their children. Kashani et al. (1988) addressed the informant issue by including a structured child psychiatric interview, the Diagnostic Interview for Children and Adolescents (DICA; Herjanic & Reich, 1982), in their assessment of 7- to 16-year-old asthmatic children. The results of the child interviews contrasted with those of the parent questionnaire measures, which revealed more behavior problems among asthmatic children. The child interview measure revealed that neither number of symptoms nor number of diagnosed disorders were significantly increased among the asthmatic children when compared to a group of matched controls. The parent respondent version of this interview, the DICA-P, showed significantly more symptoms, mostly of the overanxious type, reported for the children with asthma than for the controls. However, even the parent report data did not reveal differences between the asthmatic children and the controls in terms of number or type of diagnoses.

A similar pattern of an increased number of parent-reported behavior problems that contrasts with clinician reports is emerging in a study of early school-age asthmatic children (Klinnert, McQuaid, Bryant, & Walker, 1994). These preliminary data are derived from a sample of 79 children between the ages of 6 and 7, with asthma at varying levels of severity, including children without asthma. Asthma diagnosis was confirmed by methacholine challenge, and severity level was established using medication level and symptom control criteria. Mothers completed the Child Behavior Checklist. The children were interviewed using the Semi-Structured Clinical Interview for

Children (SCIC; Achenbach & McConaughy, 1989). In this semistructured interview, a child clinician questions the child regarding various aspects of his or her life. The clinician then completes a checklist similar in structure to the CBCL. One portion of the checklist reflects the child's self-report of symptoms and is thus akin to child-respondent diagnostic interviews. A second portion is based on the clinician's observations of the child's behavior during the interview, including affect, attention, relational style, and so on. Scores are derived that reflect Self-Report and Observed symptoms, as well as broad-band Internalizing and Externalizing scales and a number of narrow-band scales. Preliminary data indicates that, using the CBCL, mothers of the asthmatic children reported higher overall behavior problem scores and more Internalizing problems compared to the reports made by the mothers of the healthy children. However, the results of the SCIC, completed by a clinician who was blind to asthma status, showed no significant differences between the group of asthmatic children and nonasthmatic controls.

There are a number of reasons why parents would report more adjustment problems among their asthmatic children than other informants would report. Next to the child, parents clearly have the most comprehensive vantage point for observing the child's behavior. This is true in terms of their having a longitudinal view, spending the most time with the child, observing the child in a broad array of contexts and, ideally, being the most likely or closest confidant of the child. Therefore, it can be argued that the parents' report of the child is the most accurate, even surpassing younger children's self-report. At the same time, in their privileged and emotionally invested position, parents are highly vulnerable to reporting bias. Reports could be influenced by the expectancy that asthmatic children will have greater difficulties adjusting, by their expectancy that asthma medications increase problems in their asthmatic children (Bender & Milgrom, 1992), by the additional child care burdens associated with having a child with asthma (Schulz, Dye, Jolicoeur, Cafferty, & Watson, 1994), or by increased stress or inadequate social support (MacLean et al., 1992; Wallander & Varni, 1989). Finally, the additional caretaking required by an asthmatic child might lead to increased conflict that is specific to the parent-child relationship and, while reflected in parental behavior ratings, may be circumscribed and therefore undetected by a teacher or an interviewing clinician.

Overall, the evidence for increased behavioral and emotional problems among asthmatic children as compared to healthy children is mixed. Reports vary, depending on whether the informant is a clinician, a teacher, or a parent. Parents see their asthmatic children as having increased emotional difficulties, while other observers do not report increased psychopathology among asthmatic children as a whole. Even in those studies that report increased numbers of symptoms in asthmatic as compared to other children, the numbers of symptoms are usually not sufficient to reach thresholds for diagnoses. Similarly, with the behavior problem checklists, only a subset of the children have problem levels in the clinical range. The rates of behavior problems tend to be midway between healthy and clinic-referred groups, leading Hamlett et al. (1992) to suggest that these children have "problems of adjustment or adaptation to the impact of a chronic illness on developmental tasks rather than frank psychopathology" (p. 34). While this statement may be true of school-age asthmatic children in general, it is important to keep in mind that asthmatic children are not a homogeneous group. They vary along several dimensions that are highly relevant to psychological adjustment. One significant source of individual differences among asthmatic children is the severity of asthma experienced. The quality of family functioning experienced by asthmatic children appears to have an important impact not only on their psychological adjustment but on their illness adjustment and the management of their asthma. Finally, the role of allergic factors in the children's asthma varies and has been found to be related to psychopathology. Each of these factors will be discussed in detail.

ASTHMA SEVERITY

Studies have found fairly consistently that children with severe asthma have more significant psychological difficulties than other asthmatic children. It is intuitively compelling that children with asthma classified in the severe range would be most likely to suffer psychologically. In their seminal study, Graham et al. (1967) looked at the psychological adjustment of the children in relation to the severity of their asthma. These investigators found a nonsignificant trend for the psychologically disturbed group to include a somewhat higher proportion of children severely affected by their asthma. Thus, the authors concluded that asthmatic children in general did not have an increase in adjustment problems, while the severely affected children did have more problems. McNicol et al. (1973) reported that behavioral disturbances occurred at a significant level only in the small group of children with severe and continuing asthma. In an attempt to clarify the relationship between severity of asthma and psychological problems, Norrish, Tooley, and Godfrey (1977) paid particular attention to the thorny issue of how asthma severity was measured. They broke asthma severity into two components: the medication level required for control of asthma symptoms and the extent to which the symptoms were controlled. With this approach, psychological problems were found to be unrelated to asthma severity as measured by medication levels required, but they were related to poor control of the asthma. These findings of a relationship between symptom control only and psychopathology speak to several central issues, and will be returned to later.

Since these early investigations, a number of studies have taken asthma severity into consideration in examining the psychological characteristics of asthmatic children. The findings appear mixed; some studies find severity level related to psychological impairment and some find little or no relationship. Perrin, MacLean, and Perrin (1989) used an objective composite measure of severity based on medication level, frequency of attacks, and days missed from school to look at a group of asthmatic children ages 5 to 16. In addition, mothers were asked to rate their children's asthma as mild, moderate, or severe. Mothers also rated their children's adjustment using the Health Resources Inventory, which focuses on social competence and resilience in meeting new tasks or challenges. Based on the mothers' severity ratings, the investigators found a U-shape curve; the children with lower adaptation scores were in the mild or severe asthma groups, while the children with moderate asthma appeared to be doing better. In contrast, the objective composite measure did not reveal differences in adaptation among the

three severity levels. However, when one component of the objective measure, medication level, was utilized to grade severity, the severely affected group had poorer adjustment than the mild and moderate groups. It is unclear whether low maternal ratings on these scales are comparable to other measures commonly used to assess psychopathology among asthmatic children, or whether they represent some other aspect of the children's functioning.

MacLean and colleagues (1992) utilized the Perrin et al. (1989) composite scale for assessing asthma severity and obtained maternal reports of the children's stressful life events and of behavior problems via the Child Behavior Checklist for asthmatic children ages 6 to 14. The children with severe asthma were found to have significantly poorer social competence than either mild or moderate asthmatic children and to receive significantly higher overall problem behavior scores than the children with moderate asthma. However, when negative life events and illness severity were entered into regression equations, asthma severity did not add to predictability of behavior problems over and above negative life events.

In the Klinnert et al. (1994) study previously described, the severity of the children's asthma was graded on the basis of a combination of medication level and symptom control. Although mothers of asthmatic children reported more behavior problems among their children than the mothers of the nonasthmatic controls reported, within the group of asthmatic children, mothers' reports of problem behavior were unrelated to asthma severity. In contrast, while the scores from the clinician-rated SCIC interviews were not different for the asthmatic and nonasthmatic children, within the asthmatic group increasing levels of asthma severity were related to more Observed problems. It is of interest that only the Observed scale, which reflects the ratings made on the basis of the child's observed behavior, were related to asthma severity; the scores on the Self-Report scale of the SCIC were unrelated to asthma severity. This is consistent with negative findings derived from interview data from young children, such as that reported by Kashani et al. (1988).

In contrast to this pattern of findings, Kashani et al. (1988) failed to find a relationship between asthma severity and psychological functioning. The authors examined both the parent report and the structured interview data in terms of the severity of the asthma experienced by the children. However, these investigators measured severity in terms of medication level only, following the procedure of Norrish and colleagues; both groups failed to find any relationship between asthma severity and psychological difficulties.

Finally, in a recent analysis of epidemiological data, Bussing et al. (1995) found that parents reported higher behavior problem scores, measured by the Behavior Problem Index (a shortened form of the CBCL), for asthmatic children than for healthy children or children with other chronic conditions. In examining the role of asthma severity in relation to behavior problems, these investigators utilized a dichotomous indicator, the presence or absence of bother or activity limitation. Using this split, the severe asthmatics were found to have much higher problem scores, while the scores of the mild asthmatics were indistinguishable from the comparison groups.

At first glance, these findings appear confusing, if not contradictory. However, on closer inspection, it is possible to see several patterns and even to be informed by the apparent contradictions. First, it appears that patterns of findings linking severity of asthma and psychological problems are related to the method and informant for assessing psychopathology. Parents are more likely than other adults to see and report difficulties in their children, and they often report more problems with increased asthma severity. When interviewed directly, children with severe asthma do not report more problems than those with milder asthma. However, on the basis of observations, clinicians blind to asthma status discriminate increased problematic behavior in severely affected children.

A second pattern is that the method by which asthma severity is measured has an important influence on the distribution of psychopathology found. The components of severity most frequently used are medication levels, poor control of symptoms, and measures of functioning such as school absence. Both Norrish et al. (1977) and Kashani et al. (1988) found no relationship between psychological difficulties and asthma severity indexed by medication level alone. However, Norrish et al. found significant relationships with psychopathology when asthma severity was defined as poor symptom control. This finding may

inform us regarding the process through which asthma and psychopathology interact.

One explanation for the relationship between severe asthma and psychopathology is that the relatively greater stress and adaptive challenges of severe asthma lead to greater emotional and behavior problems. While this may well be the developmental process for some children, if it were the most common pathway, more consistency in the relationship between asthma severity and psychological problems would be expected. Further, the specific component of asthma severity measured would *not* be expected to be systematically related to the presence and severity of psychopathology.

In general, children with high medication requirements that result in good control of symptoms very likely have quite different illness histories and social contexts than children with frequent, uncontrolled symptoms that at times escalate to critical levels. Several studies suggest that the latter group of children, those with poor symptom control, is more likely to have greater psychopathology. Several mechanisms might result in a correlation between poor symptom control and increased psychopathology. Children with greater psychopathology, whatever the determinants, may have more difficulty adhering to a regimen of medication and self-monitoring, and may be more likely to ignore or deny symptoms, all of which lead to out-of-control asthma. Thus, whatever the severity level of their asthma as measured by medication, poor control of symptoms will result in a higher grade of apparent asthma severity. Alternatively, there may be some emergent quality of symptom patterns that results from the combination of reactive airways and psychopathology that leads to unpredictable and difficult-to-control asthmatic symptoms, regardless of medication level. For example, an asthmatic child with a lifelong pattern of poor regulation of negative affect may reach a threshold whereby psychophysiological response patterns interact with the physiology of bronchial constriction in a qualitatively different way than that which occurs for the majority of asthmatic children with more adaptive affect regulation. In neither the hypothesized poor adherence explanation nor the emergent quality process would the psychopathology need to underlie, precede, or result from the asthma. It would simply be necessary that the asthmatic symptoms be present, having followed the natural course of asthma, and that psychopathology also would be present, as a result of its own developmental course. The two processes coexisting within the same individual could then have an emergent effect of asthma that is intractable and difficult to control.

The inclusion of functional status estimates as part of the measurement of asthma severity can be an additional confound when the focus of investigation is adaptive functioning. The inclusion of variables such as school absence in asthma severity ratings may be quite circular, leading to inflated estimates of relationships between severity and psychopathology, since school absence may be as much an indicator of how the asthma is managed by the family than of the severity of the asthma itself. In fact, when Graham et al. (1967) found a tendency to more psychopathology among the severely asthmatic children, severity was defined in terms of missed school and restricted activities. Similarly, being bothered by the asthma or experiencing limitations in activity was related to increased behavior problem scores in the Bussing et al. (1995) study. Klinnert et al. (1994) found that family functioning early in a child's life was not predictive of asthma severity by age 6 measured by medication level and symptom control but was predictive of functional status as measured by days of restricted activity and school absence. Similarly, earlier work by Stein and Jessop (1984) showed that psychological adjustment among chronically ill children, half of whom had respiratory conditions, was related to school absence, although it was not related to morbidity measures such as days in bed or hospitalizations.

In sum, the relationship between psychopathology and asthma has been shown most consistently among children with severe asthma. However, the manner in which asthma severity is measured is central to the issue. The relationship between psychological problems and specific components of asthma severity has the potential to illuminate critical aspects of asthma and its management. The few studies that have closely examined the relationship between asthma severity and psychopathology have used different measures of each of the severity components and of psychopathology. Further investigation is required to determine whether symptom control and functional impairment are the components of severity most

strongly related to psychological functioning. The interaction of these variables with psychopathology in the context of the children's families is discussed next.

FAMILY FACTORS

The effect of family factors on childhood asthma has been the subject of controversy at least since French and Alexander (1941) reported that a disturbed relationship between asthmatic children and their mothers played a role in the disease. This led to the therapeutic approach used in the 1960s of separating children with severe, intractable asthma from their parents as a means of reducing asthmatic symptoms. Purcell and colleagues (1969) demonstrated that emotionally triggered asthmatic children showed symptom alleviation during an experimental separation in which parents and siblings were removed from the home and the patient remained in his or her normal physical environment with a surrogate caregiver. The success of this intervention appeared to support the notion that for these children, symptoms were precipitated by exposure to some aspect of family functioning.

Investigators have attempted to understand this phenomena by examining aspects of the parent-asthmatic child dyad that may distinguish them from healthy children. Based on parent descriptions of their children and observations of mother-child interactions, Block, Jennings, Harvey, and Simpson (1964) reported increased interactional difficulties between mothers and their asthmatic children. Mrazek, Anderson, and Strunk (1985), who observed severely asthmatic preschoolers with their mothers, found that the asthmatic children were more likely to be oppositional, and the affective climate of the interactions with their mothers more negative, than healthy controls. In a study of school-age asthmatic children, Carson and Schauer (1992) also found more negativity in parent-child relationships when compared to control families, based on maternal report of greater stress within the mother-child dyad, including more parental rejection, overprotectiveness, and overindulgence. Many of those studies that document problems in the parent-child relationship imply that the interactional difficulties may have a causal effect on asthmatic symptoms in the children. However, these studies have not addressed the mechanism by which family dysfunction might have affected the asthma.

Several recent studies have examined the influence of critical parental affect on childhood asthma, suggesting that this might be the component of negative parent-child interactions that has the reported pernicious effect. Investigators have explored the effect of parental expressed emotion (specifically parental criticism and emotional overinvolvement measured during 5-minute speech samples) on asthma status in children. Hermanns, Florin, Dietrich, Rieger, and Hahlweg (1989) found that mothers of children with moderately severe asthma demonstrated more criticism of their child and had more negative verbal exchanges with their child than control mother-child dyads. In addition, they found that the amount of criticism was correlated with asthma severity (measured by frequency of attacks per year). In a similar study of father-child dyads, Schobinger, Florin, Zimmer, Lindemann, and Winter (1992) demonstrated more criticism of asthmatic children during 5-minute speech samples and more critical exchanges in the dyadic observational context. However, they did not replicate Hermanns et al.'s correlation of criticism with asthma severity.

The investigators in these studies implicating parental criticism, believe that such criticism functions as a chronic stressor for asthmatic children, affecting the severity and possibly the course of the disease through immunological mechanisms. However, there are other plausible explanations for these cross-sectionally derived data. Wamboldt, Wamboldt, Gavin, Roesler, and Brugman (1995) also found that parental criticism was prevalent among severely asthmatic adolescents. Higher rates of criticism were linked to greater improvement in asthma symptoms during hospitalization (and separation from parents). However, these authors point out that it is unclear whether symptoms remitted because the adolescents were removed from the chronic stressor of parental criticism, or whether the parents were critical in response to medical nonadherence by their teenagers, whose asthma improved during hospitalization under close staff scrutiny. Similarly, the classic Purcell (1969) study described earlier did not consider the effect of having a surrogate caregiver in the home who was a trained asthma manager and who may have been adminis-

tering treatment more effectively than the parent.

A variety of other family characteristics have been identified that may influence the course of asthma. For example, Di Blasio, Molinari, Peri, and Taverna (1990) found that on a communication task, asthmatic families displayed more chaos and had more difficulty making decisions than control families. In contrast, Hamlett et al. (1992) had families complete the Family Environment Scale (FES; Moos & Moos, 1986), and found that responses were not different between families with asthmatic children and controls. However, the family characteristics of Cohesion and Conflict were related to behavior problems, regardless of illness status.

In sum, a number of studies have reported that families of children with asthma display more negative characteristics than families of healthy children. Further, asthmatic children display more oppositionality with their parents, parents tend to be more critical, and interactions tend to be more negative and disorganized than those in control families. However, these relationships are demonstrated most clearly in families with severely asthmatic children. Perhaps most important, all of the studies are cross-sectional, which prevents us from understanding the direction of the effects. For example, interactional difficulties in the parent-child dyad may lead to worse asthma, or alternatively, having asthma may place stress on the parent-child relationship that leads to interaction problems. A third possibility might be that family dysfunction and disorganization may prevent families from carrying out an appropriate asthma management regimen, leading to worsening asthma status, chronic stress on the child, and more negativity in the parent-child dyad. In fact, some studies have demonstrated that high levels of family conflict and poor child behavioral adjustment were related to medical nonadherence in asthma (Christiannse, Lavigne, & Lerner, 1989) and, in the worst-case scenario, to death (Strunk, Mrazek, Wolfson Fuhrmann, & LaBrecque, 1985).

The psychopathological correlates of asthma severity and the findings regarding family factors and asthmatic children both lead in similar conceptual directions. Asthma treatment has progressed markedly in the past 20 years, and symptoms can be managed fairly well with current medical approaches and good adherence to medical recommendations (Weinstein, Faust, McKee,

& Padman, 1992). Thus, poor symptom control or high levels of functional impairment, such as school absence or restriction of activities, could result from either poor management by the family or physician or maladaptive motivation on the part of the patient or family. When poor symptom control or high functional impairment meets the needs of the patient or family and serves to maintain the symptoms, family dysfunction may be assumed. At the same time, children from dysfunctional families presumably would be at increased risk for psychopathology, whether they have asthma or not. Thus, increased psychopathology among severely asthmatic children may represent the intersection of two parallel developmental processes, the natural history of asthma and the development of psychopathology. This view is consistent with the findings of Steinhausen, Schindler, and Stephan (1983), who examined the relative strength of a number of predictors to psychopathology in children with asthma. A variety of family factors, such as family problems, parental disturbance, and marital problems, were among the strong predictors to child psychopathology. In contrast, severity of asthma (measured in terms of symptom frequency and severity) was the weakest of the predictors that were significant, contributing only a minuscule amount to the variance predicting child psychological difficulties. In other words, although a child with asthma who is reared in a dysfunctional family is at risk for psychopathology as well as poorer symptom control and greater functional impairment, the central processes leading to poor adaptation are probably much the same as those that lead to psychological problems among other children. Although known processes of developmental psychopathology may help to explain much of the correlation between psychological difficulties and asthma, there remains the possibility that the combination of asthma and psychopathology results in some emergent property that is manifested as severe, intractable, and difficult-to-control asthma.

NONALLERGIC ASTHMA

Several studies have demonstrated an inverse relationship between allergy and presence of psychopathology among people with asthma. This approach presupposes that there are at least two central mechanisms leading to wheezing symptoms: allergic processes and some unspecified

process by which emotional problems are related to wheezing. Since allergic involvement is sufficient to account for asthmatic symptoms, it is assumed that emotional disequilibrium leading to asthma symptoms will be more apparent in nonallergic children with asthma.

Block et al. (1964) developed an Allergy Potential Scale to measure allergic involvement and separated 7-year-old children with asthma into groups with high and low allergy scores. They obtained parents' descriptions of their children and observed the behavior of the children alone with an examiner as well as in interaction with their mothers. The results indicated significantly more psychopathology among nonallergic children and among their parents than among asthmatic children with allergies. Interestingly, while these investigators summarized their findings as representing increased psychopathology, they did not specify any particular disorder. Rather, they described the nonallergic group as children with predominantly negative affect and unpleasant interpersonal interactions. Other studies have found a similar inverse relationship between allergy and psychopathology among preschoolers with severe asthma (Mrazek and Strunk, 1984) and among asthmatic adults (Resh, 1970). In the Klinnert et al. (1994) study of early school-age children with asthma, allergic status is taken into account in investigating the children's psychological functioning. Early findings suggest that only nonallergic asthmatic children, who are severely affected by their asthma may have more problems. Observational ratings suggest that these children may show increased negative affect and poorer regulation of negative affect. In sum, nonallergic children with asthma, especially severe asthma, may not suffer from a substantially increased number of diagnosable psychiatric disorders, but some studies show more negative affect, increased interactional difficulties, and poorer affect regulation than other asthmatic children.

Other studies have tested the hypothesis of an inverse relationship between allergy and psychopathology and have failed to find support for this distinction. For example, Gauthier et al. (1978) studied mother-child interactions among mildly asthmatic toddlers and preschoolers, and found more behavior problems among the allergic than the nonallergic children. However, these children were very young compared to those studied by Block, and had very mild asthma. If there is a relationship between psychological factors and allergic status, it may exist for only a subset of asthmatic children, such as those with more severe asthma, and it almost certainly depends on how psychopathology is measured. Specifically, it may be necessary to focus on emotional qualities and the manner in which emotion is managed. Whether further support is found for greater emotional disregulation among nonallergic and/or severely asthmatic children or not, the characterization of the allergic status of these children is important to further understanding of the mechanism through which asthma and psychopathology may interact. For example, allergic children may be psychologically vulnerable because of associations between allergy and temperamental inhibition (Kagan, Snidman, Julia-Sellers, & Johnson, 1991), whereas nonallergic children with asthma may be characterized by particular patterns of autonomic nervous system functioning (Mrazek & Klinnert, 1991). In any case, it should be clear that children with asthma are not a homogeneous group. Investigative efforts to understand the psychological concomitants of childhood asthma must take into account the mechanisms involved in each child's asthma as well as the emotional functioning of the children.

Asthma as a Psychosomatic Disorder

A psychosomatic approach to asthma presupposes that psychological factors are intrinsically involved in the development of the disease, or in its exacerbations, or in both. Over the years, many studies have attempted to document the psychosomatic nature of asthma by examining emotional and physiological characteristics of people with asthma. The several ways of conceptualizing the effect of emotional state on asthmatic symptoms include generalized stress leading to increased asthmatic symptoms, emotional reactions triggering asthmatic episodes, and suppressed emotions having physiological sequelae related to the asthmatic condition or to symptom expression.

EMOTIONS AS TRIGGERS

States of emotional arousal consistently have been reported as precipitating episodes of wheez-

ing among some asthmatic children. The phenomenon is itself of interest, because it seems to indicate a fairly direct mechanism linking emotional arousal and asthmatic symptoms. In their classic study, Graham et al. (1967) defined "psychosomatic" as "the precipitation of attacks by events disturbing to the emotions" (p. 83). Although Graham et al. concluded their study by questioning whether asthma was a psychosomatic disorder, they did report that 35% of the parents interviewed indicated that some of their children's asthma attacks were brought on by emotion, most often by fear or anxiety, but also at times by anticipatory excitement or anger. A number of laboratory studies of both children and adults have demonstrated decreased lung functions in response to emotional stimulation.

Whether in an epidemiological study or a laboratory demonstration, emotional reactions typically trigger wheezing for only a subgroup of people with asthma. Some investigators have examined the characteristics of this emotionally triggered subgroup in order to better understand emotional contributions to asthma. Emotional triggers have been hypothesized to occur more frequently among nonallergic children with asthma and among asthmatic children with psychological problems or whose families are dysfunctional. Purcell (1963) found that reports of emotional upset as a trigger were predominant among a group of asthmatic children whose symptoms rapidly remitted on hospitalization, in contrast to steroid-dependent asthmatic children for whom allergic reactions were central. In fact, in the separation study previously discussed, Purcell and his colleagues (1969) used reports of emotional triggers to identify the group of children whose asthma remitted during the time that the children's families were out of the home. The implication was that asthmatic symptoms were triggered through a mechanism involving emotions, since by staying in the home, the children's exposure to allergens would have remained constant. Although these findings may have other explanations, this study provided modest support for the notion that emotional triggers may be associated with exposure to the family, presumably to stressful relationships or interactions of some sort. However, other studies have failed to find a link between emotional triggers and psychopathology or nonallergic asthma. Tal and Miklich (1976), who provided a laboratory demonstration of emotionally triggered decreases in the pulmonary functions of asthmatic children, stated that these were children with no psychopathology (although the method of ruling out "psychopathology" was not described). These investigators also found no relationship between the degree of response to the emotional triggers and the presence of allergy in these asthmatic subjects.

The triggering of asthmatic wheezing by emotional states often is equated with stress effects on asthma. There is much overlap between these phenomena, but there are differences as well. Reports of emotional precipitants for wheezing include negative affects such as anxiety, depression, and anger; positive affects such as excitement; and emotional behaviors such as laughing and crying. Stress is defined in terms of situations in which demands tax or exceed the adaptive capabilities of the individual (Cohen, Kessler, & Gordon, 1994). When such experiences are associated with affects (which is not always the case), the emotional experience is generally negative, for example, anxiety or depression. Such negative affects are believed to be signals indicating that the body is responding in a way that has been found to be related to illness. This process, on a chronic basis, is implicit in the report of Purcell and colleagues (1969) and more explicit in the Hermanns et al. (1989) study; in both, family interactions were seen as leading to stress. Stressful emotional precipitants or effects are thus to be distinguished from asthma triggered by excitement, which would appear to be wheezing associated with psychological and physiological arousal. These types of emotional triggers must be further distinguished from expressions of emotions such as laughing or crying, which involve mechanical stimulation of the airways, as well as hyperventilation, both of which can lead to wheezing. Creer (1993) has suggested that such processes generally underlie emotional triggers. However, Miklich, Chai, Purcell, Weiss, and Brady (1974) demonstrated that decreases in pulmonary function occurred both with emotional expressions that are mechanically associated with respiratory changes (laughing and crying) and with reported emotional states per se.

In sum, there seems to be consistent evidence that some children experience asthmatic symptoms triggered by emotions. However, the evidence is weak for an association between emotionally triggered asthma and psychological problems, perhaps in part because the precipitation of wheezing by emotional reactions is apparent in only a subgroup of asthmatic children, and such triggering may result from one of several different processes. There may be an increased likelihood of emotional triggering of wheezing whenever children's airways are in a highly reactive state, whether on a chronic basis or temporarily, for example, following a respiratory infection. Such an effect may occur through mechanisms such as generalized arousal, irrespective of psychological status. Alternatively, such susceptibility may be related not to psychopathology per se but rather to emotional dysregulation and related physiological correlates.

EMOTIONAL REPRESSION

Another approach to understanding the psychosomatic nature of asthma derives from a psychodynamic formulation wherein intrapersonal conflicts, presumably deriving from interpersonal experiences, are manifested physiologically. Traditional approaches have focused on the repression of emotion or the incapacity to experience affect, either of which may be related to somatization, or physiological expression, of emotions. Florin et al.'s (1993) report is an example of an effort to demonstrate physiological correlates of a style of emotion management. These authors reported on a series of studies investigating the hypothesis that asthmatic children show less facial expression of emotion than healthy children and that the lack of expressiveness is related to decreases in pulmonary function. Initial studies demonstrated an apparent deficit in facial expressions in response to stressful laboratory situations as well as changes in pulmonary function that suggested that the airways of asthmatic children were more reactive to stresses than were those of nonasthmatic children. However, the investigators could not replicate their initial findings and concluded that asthmatic children do not evidence a deficit in facial expression of emotion. Further investigations of asthmatic children's emotional expressivity in the context of interactions with their parents revealed that, rather than showing repression of emotion, there was some evidence for increased negativity within the interactions, on the part of both the children and the parents.

Despite these negative findings, psychophysiological correlates of emotion may reveal important aspects of the relationship between emotional functioning and asthma. However, searching for a pattern of emotional and physiological variables that is characteristic of all asthmatic children and distinguishes them from healthy controls probably is misguided. Some such relationships may hold for some asthmatic children, under some, as-yet undefined circumstances. The investigation of such processes, even if they occur for only some children and under limited circumstances, can yield significant information about mechanisms through which asthma and emotional functioning interact.

EMOTIONAL REGULATION AND PHYSIOLOGICAL CORRELATES

It is useful to examine the psychophysiology of asthma with a broader conceptual view of emotional processes and their regulation. Constraint of behavioral expressions of emotion is but one variation of the many ways of managing emotional stimulation. Lack of constraint, or poor control of emotional expressions, is another regulatory style that may relate to various aspects of asthma. The concept of emotion regulation has emerged over the past 10 years concomitant with a renewed appreciation of the functional and regulatory role of emotion (Campos, Campos, & Barrett, 1989). Emotional regulation encompasses the intrapersonal management of emotional state as well as the regulatory or disregulatory effects of interpersonal interactions (Garber & Dodge, 1991). Poor regulation is synonymous with poor adaptation, since it entails inappropriate and ineffective responses to environmental demands, in terms of subjective experience, physiological responses, and interpersonal exchanges. The development of children's ability to regulate emotions effectively can be tracked from birth onward and thus provides an underlying construct to follow through the behavioral transformations that occur with development. Finally, a central aspect of the construct involves the relationships among different emotional "response domains," behavioral-expressive, subjective-experiential, and neurophysiological-biochemical (Dodge, 1989). The investigation of the relationships among these emotional response domains among various sub-groups of asthmatic children (i.e., well vs. poorly adapted, well vs. poorly controlled, allergic vs. nonallergic) is now possible because of information available regarding emotional processes in healthy children.

There is increasing evidence that physiological patterns that characterize certain regulatory styles can be discriminated. Jemerin and Boyce (1990) reviewed evidence for physiological patterns in children that are related to developmentally stable emotional and behavioral styles. For example, they point to evidence that the temperamental characteristic of behavioral inhibition, or shyness, is associated with increased arousal as measured by heart rate, elevated salivary cortisol, and excretion of norepinephrine and its metabolites (Kagan, Resnick, & Snidman, 1988). They present evidence that vagal tone, derived from heart rate measures via respiratory sinus arrhythmia, may provide a window into the stress-reactivity of young children (Porges, 1990). There is evidence that such behavioral-physiological patterns result from genetic predispositions as well as from environmental experiences. These variables appear to represent individual differences among children that determine their susceptibility to external stressors or emotion-eliciting events. As such they may provide useful tools for the investigation of physiological and behavioral aspects of emotion regulation among children with asthma.

Childhood Asthma in the Context of Developmental Psychopathology

The studies just discussed demonstrate the complexity and contradictory nature of current findings addressing psychological aspects of asthma in school-age children. To summarize: Parents of asthmatic children report increased adjustment problems among their offspring. In contrast, other informants see significant problems only among severely asthmatic children, suggesting that the majority of children with asthma have a physical condition without apparent "psychosomatic" features. At the same time, children with severe asthma often have been reported to have serious difficulties, and there may be some qualitative differences between these children and those with milder forms of the illness. Family functioning appears to play a predominant role in the adjustment of asthmatic children, and it might be asked whether asthmatic children are any different from other children for whom family factors are central. Some studies have shown that asthmatic children show physiological differences from healthy children. While such findings often are fleeting and not replicated, sufficient data have continued to emerge over the years to suggest that physiological characteristics of asthmatic children may indeed have meaningful psychological correlates. How are we to understand the contradictions extant in each of these areas of inquiry?

To make sense of this body of research, it is essential to understand that asthma is an extremely complex, multifactorial condition. Even among asthmatic children who are fairly uniform in age, such as those of school age, there is wide variability among the conditions experienced by the affected individuals. The reactivity of the airways varies across asthmatic children as well as within individuals at different times and given different conditions. The role of allergic factors in the asthma of any individual is a central variable and, as described earlier, has been believed to be important for understanding whether and how psychological factors might interact with asthma. In addition, the autonomic nervous system is centrally involved in bronchial constriction (Mrazek & Klinnert, 1991). The predominance of one or the other process may vary within the same individual, so that one or the other mechanism may be predominant at different times (Lehrer, Isenberg, & Hochron, 1993). The manifestation of asthmatic symptoms varies within individuals over time, through the seasons of the year as well as from year to year. Other sources of variability arise from the manner in which the condition is managed by the family in concert with the physician, medications that are utilized for asthma management, and so on.

Because of the multivariate nature of asthma, it is not surprising that researchers have been unable to define psychological characteristics or abnormalities that might differentiate asthmatic from healthy individuals and have been unable to find consistent physiological markers that might provide a clear link between asthma and psycho-

logical factors. It seems highly unlikely that all or most asthmatic children would manage their emotional reactions in a similar manner, with similar physiological correlates. However, the fact that some children's asthmatic symptoms appear to be worsened by emotions suggests that asthma is a condition with the potential for a psychological component and that this potential will be actualized for some children under some conditions.

A more complex model of the parallel development in children of asthma and emotional functioning is needed that could predict the many different individual outcomes that are observed. Such a model must begin with the assumption that heterogeneity is the rule and that emotional functioning can be examined only in the context of the characteristics of an individual's asthma. It also must take into account organism-based predispositions, both in terms of genetic risk for asthma and biological predispositions for emotional functioning. A developmental approach is required in order to increase our understanding about onset and course of childhood asthma in parallel with emotional development as well as to clarify the possible ways in which emotional development might influence the course of asthma and the presence of asthma might influence emotional development.

The growing field of developmental psychopathology has been defined as "the study of the origins and course of individual patterns of behavioral maladaptation" (Sroufe & Rutter, 1984, p. 18). This developmental approach is particularly appropriate for multivariate phenomena with a variety of adaptational outcomes, only some of which fall into the psychopathological range. Genetic risk or predisposition is considered to provide the starting point for development. Emphasis is placed on processes that lead to specific types of adaptation at each developmental level. Early adaptive solutions are considered to lay the groundwork for and to influence the course of behavioral organization that occurs at subsequent stages. Thus, adaptation at any particular stage is viewed as the product of developmental history and current circumstances.

The developmental course of asthma, without regard to psychosocial contributions, has been described in epidemiological studies, some of which have been longitudinal (e.g., Jones et al., 1987). In contrast, when emotional development in asthmatic children has been addressed, it has been primarily through cross-sectional studies of adjustment problems or parent-child interaction patterns. A listing of the occurrence or nonoccurrence of such problems at different points in the lives of asthmatic children is limited in facilitating an understanding of the processes occurring within a child that underlie adjustment or lack thereof or in appreciating the continuity of development across time. As an alternative strategy, investigation of the development of the child's emotional regulatory capacities may make it possible to gain insight into those aspects of children's emotional lives that interact with asthma.

AN EXAMPLE: THE ONSET OF ASTHMA

The parallel development of asthma onset and course and emotional functioning and adjustment in children was investigated in a longitudinal, prospective study conducted by Mrazek et al. (1994). The children, who were followed from the prenatal period, were genetically at risk for asthma onset because their mothers had asthma. To track the developmental pathway for asthma, physiological and medical factors were assessed throughout. To track the emotional development of the children and possible contributions of psychological factors to asthma, parenting and infant emotional variables were followed closely. Among the parent variables assessed were family stress; maternal and paternal coping abilities, personality characteristics, and affective status; the quality of the marital relationship; and the quality of caretaking and stress modulation provided to the infant. Among the infant characteristics assessed were temperamental characteristics such as difficulty, emotional valence and equilibrium, rhythmicity, quality of attachment, and behavioral adjustment.

When the children were 3 years of age, the physiological and emotional variables were examined for their ability to predict to early asthma. The three variables that were significantly and independently related to asthma onset were the quality of parenting, assessed when the children were 3 weeks of age, immunoglobulin E (IgE) levels assessed at age 6 months, and the number of respiratory infections that occurred during the first year of life. We speculate that the quality of early parenting led to asthma onset due to inade-

quate efforts to regulate emotional states for young infants unable to do it themselves, which thereby exposed the infants to unmanageable stress. Conceptually, it is expected that, in general, infants with less adequate help with state regulation and stress buffering would have difficulty internalizing self-regulatory controls (Klinnert & Bingham, 1994). Indeed, the parenting risk variable that predicted to asthma onset at age 3 was consistently related to behavioral and emotional difficulties as the children developed. Thus, the quality of emotional regulation provided by mothers in early infancy may relate to children's subsequent functioning in both the asthma and emotional-behavioral domains. It is entirely possible that such an effect is specific to this early period and may not be generalizable to the effects of parenting on children's asthma in middle childhood. It is also important to point out that in this study, every child with asthma did not experience problematic parenting, every child with asthma did not develop behavioral difficulties, and many children who did not develop asthma did have adjustment problems. The parenting variable, hypothesized to increase the risk for asthma through stress effects and emotional disregulation, does not *cause* asthma, although the data suggest that it does put children at increased risk for asthma. The individual differences in stress susceptibility among children at risk for asthma is an area in need of further investigation.

Further examples of the interaction between the developmental courses of asthma and emotional adjustment have emerged from this longitudinal data set. Using a parent report measure, mothers of the children with asthma report higher levels of behavior problems than do the mothers of the healthy children. At least through age 4, the reports of increased behavior problems follow the onset of asthma rather than precede it. Thus, it appears that factors discussed earlier, such as increased burden, parent expectancy, or interactional difficulties, may account for the reports. However, maternal reports of behavior problems at age 4 precede and predict the maintenance of wheezing by age 6. This is true even after previous asthma status has been partialed out, to exclude problems that may have accompanied earlier wheezing (Klinnert, Nelson, Leung, & Mrazek, 1994). The other important predictor to active asthma at age 6 was skin test reactivity to allergens, demonstrating the independent and very significant contribution of this physical variable to maintenance of asthmatic symptoms. Finally, as discussed previously, the functional impairment of the asthmatic children at age 6 was related to parenting quality assessed early in life. This contrasted with the other components of severity, medication level and symptom control, which were not related to family factors. It is important to note that the actual number of children who developed asthma in this longitudinal study was small and that, despite a range of severity in the children's asthma, none of their asthma could be classified as severe. Nevertheless, these patterns illustrate the interactive influence of variables that can be traced within a developmental approach to both psychopathology and asthma.

Summary

This chapter represents an attempt to describe available information about the psychological functioning of school-age children with asthma. While there are parental reports of increased behavior problems among the group as a whole, these effects are fairly minimal and suggest that asthma is "not a psychopathological disorder," to paraphrase Graham et al. (1967). The exception is that portion of the children with severe asthma, for whom there appears to be a significantly greater risk of psychopathology. An analysis of the components of asthma severity suggests that psychological difficulties are most strongly related to poor symptom control and functional impairment. Since these are the components most likely to be related to inadequate management of the illness or to maladaptive motivational factors on the part of the child and the family, the correlation found between asthma severity and psychopathology may reflect the relationship between family dysfunction, poor asthma management behavior, and child psychopathology. Alternatively, the correlation between increased psychopathology and asthma severity may reflect a qualitative change in asthma symptoms that occurs when these factors coincide.

Psychosomatic aspects of asthma were examined in light of evidence that emotions or stressors function as precipitants for symptoms. While it is clear that this phenomenon exists, there is no strong evidence that emotional precipitation of wheezing is more frequent among children with psychological difficulties. However, this hypothesis has not been tested adequately. Further, efforts to define psychophysiological patterns among asthmatic children have not yielded a consistent picture. Current conceptualizations of emotional regulation and disregulation may provide a means of investigating more thoroughly the relationship between emotional functioning and the precipitation of symptoms through emotional arousal or stress exposure.

Finally, a developmental psychopathology approach was advocated to conceptually unify findings that, to date, often appear contradictory. Such an approach assumes a range of developmental outcomes, only a few of which might be considered pathological. This pattern precisely describes what is known of psychological adjustment among asthmatic children. An emphasis on developmental aspects of emotional functioning in asthmatic children would bring into investigative focus psychological risk factors for asthma onset and course. Such an approach would focus attention on developmental trajectories leading to individual psychopathology and family dysfunction as well as the mechanisms by which individual or family factors contribute to poor symptom control or asthma-related functional impairment. A longitudinal approach to the issues in question would provide information about the directionality of effects and may possibly lead us out of the inferential morass that results from a multitude of cross-sectional findings.

REFERENCES

Achenbach, T. M., & Edelbrock, C. S. (1983). *Manual of the Child Behavior Checklist and Revised Child Behavior Profiel.* Burlington: Department of Psychiatry, University of Vermont.

Achenbach, T. M., & McConaughy, S. H. (1989). *Semi-structured Clinical Interview for Children aged 6 to 11.* Burlington: Department of Psychiatry, University of Vermont.

Bender, B., & Milgrom, H. (1992). Theophylline-induced behavior change in children: An objective evaluation of parent's perceptions. *Journal of the American Medical Association, 267,* 2621–2624.

Block, J., Jennings, P. H., Harvey, E., & Simpson, E. (1964). Interaction between allergic potential and psychopathology in childhood asthma. *Psychosomatic Medicine, 26,* 307–320.

Bussing, R., Halfon, N., Benjamin, B., & Wells, K. B. (1995). Prevalence of behavior problems in US children with asthma. *Archives of Pediatric and Adolescent Medicine, 149,* 565–572.

Campos, J. J., Campos, R. G., & Barrett, K. C. (1989). Emergent themes in the study of emotional development and emotional regulation. *Developmental Psychology, 25,* 394–402.

Carson, D. K., & Schauer, R. W. (1992). Mothers of children with asthma: Perceptions of parenting stress and the mother-child relationship. *Psychological Reports, 71,* 1139–1148.

Christiannse, M. E., Lavigne, J. V., & Lerner, C. V. (1989). Psychosocial aspects of compliance in children and adolescents with asthma. *Developmental and Behavioral Pediatrics, 10,* 75–80.

Cohen, S., Kessler, R., & Gordon, L. G. (1994). Strategies for measuring stress in studies of psychiatric and physical disorders. In S. Cohen, R. C. Kessler, and L. G. Gordon (Eds.), *Measuring stress: A guide for health and social scientists* (pp. 3–26). Oxford: Oxford University Press.

Creer, T. (1993). Emotions and asthma. *Journal of Asthma, 30,* 1–3.

DiBlasio, P., Molinari, E. Peri, G., & Taverna, A. (1990). Family competence and childhood asthma: A preliminary study. *Family Systems Medicine, 8,* 145–149.

Dodge, K. A. (1989). Coordinating responses to aversive stimuli. *Developmental Psychology, 25,* 339–342.

Florin, I., Fiegenbaum, W., Hermanns, J., Winter, H., Schobinger, R., & Jenkins, M. (1993). Emotional expressiveness, psychophysiological reactivity and mother-child interaction with asthmatic children. In H. C. Traunc & J. W. Pennebaker (Eds.), *Emotion, inhibition, and health* (pp. 179–196). Seattle: Hogrefe & Huber.

French, T. M., & Alexander, F. (1941). Psychogenic factors in bronchial asthma. *Psychosomatic Medicine, 4,* 2.

Garber, J., & Dodge, K. A. (1991). *The development of emotion regulation and dysregulation.* Cambridge: Cambridge University Press.

Gauthier, Y., Fortin, C., Drapeu, P., Breton, J.-J., Gosselin, J., Quintal, L., Weisnagel, J., Tetreault, L., & Pinard, G. (1978). Follow-up study of 35 asthmatic pre-school children. *Journal of the American Academy of Child Psychiatry, 17,* 679–694.

Graetz, B., & Shute, R. (1995). Assessment of peer relationships in children with asthma. *Journal of Pediatric Psychology, 20,* 205–216.

Graham, P. J., Rutter, M., Yule, W., & Pless, I. B. (1967). Childhood asthma: A psychosomatic disorder? *British Journal of Preventative and Social Medicine, 21,* 78–85.

Hamlett, K. W., Pelligrini, D. S., & Katz, K. S. (1992). Childhood chronic illness as a family stressor. *Journal of Pediatric Psychology, 17,* 33–47.

Herjanic, B., & Reich, W. (1982). Development of a structured psychiatric interview for children: Agreement between child and parent on individual symptoms. *Journal of Abnormal Child Psychology, 10,* 307–324.

Hermanns, J., Florin, I., Dietrich, M., Rieger, C., & Hahlweg, K. (1989). Maternal criticism, mother-child interaction, and bronchial asthma. *Journal of Psychosomatic Research, 33,* 469–476.

Jemerin, J. M., & Boyce, W. T. (1990). Psychobiological differences in childhood stress response. II. Cardiovascular markers of vulnerability. *Developmental and Behavioral Pediatrics, 11,* 140–150.

Jones, D. T., Sears, M. R., Holdaway, M. D., Hewitt, C. J., Flannery, E. M., Herbison, G. P., & Silva, P. A. (1987). Childhood asthma in New Zealand. *British Journal of Disease of the Chest, 81,* 332–340.

Kagan, J., Snidman, N., Julia-Sellers, M., & Johnson, M. O. (1991). Temperament and allergic symptoms. *Psychosomatic Medicine, 53,* 332–340.

Kagan, J., Reznick, J. S., & Snidman, N. (1988). The physiology and psychology of behavioral inhibition in young children. *Child Development, 58,* 1459–1473.

Kashani, J. H., Konig, P., Shepperd, J. A., Wilfley, D., & Morris, D. A., (1988). Psychopathology and self-concept in asthmatic children. *Journal of Pediatric Psychology, 13,* 509–520.

Klinnert, M. D., & Bingham, R. D. (1994). The organizing effects of early relationships. *Psychiatry, 57,* 1–10.

Klinnert, M. D., McQuaid, E. L., Bryant, N. E., & Walker, D. A. (1994, May). *Psychopathology in asthmatic children.* Paper presented at the eighth biennial retreat of the psychobiology Research Group, Estes Park, Colorado.

Klinnert, M. D., Nelson, H. S., Leung, D. Y. M., & Mrazek, D. A. (1994). The relative contributions of allergy and psychological factors to childhood asthma. *Journal of Asthma and Clinical Immunology, 93,* 292.

Lehrer, P. M., Isenberg, S., & Hochron, S. M. (1993). Asthma and emotion: A review. *Journal of Asthma, 30,* 5–21.

MacLean, W. E. Perrin, J. M., Gortmaker, S., & Pierre, C. B. (1992). Psychological adjustment of children with asthma: Effects of illness severity and recent stressful life events. *Journal of Pediatric Psychology, 17,* 159–171.

McNicol, K. N., Williams, H. E., Allan,J., & McAndrew, I. (1973). Spectrum of asthma in children–III, Psychological and social components. *British Medical Journal, 4,* 16–20.

Miklich, D. R., Chai, H., Purcell, K., Weiss, J. H., & Brady, K. (1974). Naturalistic observation of emotions preceding low pulmonary flow rates. *Journal of Allergy and Clinical Immunology, 53,* 102.

Moos, R., & Moss, B. (1986). *Family Environment*

Scale manual (2nd ed.). Palo Alto, CA: Consulting Psychologists Press.

Mrazek, D., Anderson, I., & Strunk, R. (1985). Disturbed emotional development of severely asthmatic preschool children. In J. Stevenson (Ed.), *Recent research in developmental psychopathology (pp. 81–94). Journal of Child Psychology and Psychiatry Book Supplement No. 4.* Oxford: Pergamon Press.

Mrazek, D. A., & Klinnert, M. D. (1991). Asthma: Psychoneuroimmunological considerations. In R. Ader, D. L. Felten, and N. Cohen (Eds.), *Psychoneuroimmunology II* (pp. 1013–1035). Orlando, FL: Academic Press.

Mrazek, D. A., Klinnert, M. D., Mrazek, P., Rosenberg, D., Ikle, D., Brower, A., McCormick, D., Macey, T., Rubin, B., Larsen, G., & Jones, J. (1996). Prediction of early onset asthma in genetically at risk children. Manuscript under review.

Mrazek, D., Strunk, R. (1984). Psychological adjustment of severely asthmatic preschool children: Allergic considerations. *Psychosomatic Medicine, 46,* 85.

Nassau, J. H., & Drotar, D. (1995). Social competence in children with IDDM and asthma: Child, teacher, and parent reports of children's social adjustment, social performance, and social skills. *Journal of Pediatric Psychology, 20,* 187–204.

Norrish, M., Tooley, M., & Godfrey, S. (1977). Clinical, physiological, and psychological study of asthmatic children attending a hospital clinic. *Archives of Diseases in Childhood, 52,* 912–917.

Perrin, J. M., MacLean, W. E., & Perrin, E. C. (1989). Parental perceptions of health status and psychologic adjustment of children with asthma. *Pediatrics, 83,* 26–30.

Porges, S. W. (1991). Vagal tone: A mediator of affect. In J. A. Garber & K. A. Dodge (Eds.), *The development of affect regulation and dysregulation* (pp. 111–128). New York: Cambridge University Press.

Purcell, K. (1963). Distinctions between subgroups of asthmatic children: Children's perceptions of events associated with asthma. *Pediatrics, 31,* 486–494.

Purcell, K., Brady, K., Chai, H., Muse, J., Leizer, M., Gordon, N., & Means, J. (1969). The effect on asthma in children of experimental separation from the family. *Psychosomatic Medicine, 31,* 144–164.

Resh, M. (1970). Asthma of unknown origin as a psychological group. *Journal of Consulting and Clinical Psychology, 35,* 429.

Schobinger, R., Florin, I., Zimmer, C., Lindemann,

H., & Winter, H. (1992). Childhood asthma: Paternal critical attitude and father-child interaction. *Journal of Psychosomatic Research, 36,* 743–750.

Schulz, R. M., Dye, J., Jolicoeur, L., Cafferty, T., & Watson, J. (1994). Quality-of-life factors for parents of children with asthma. *Journal of Asthma, 31,* 209–219.

Silverman, W. K., & Eisen, A. R. (1992). Age differences in the reliability of parent and child reports of child anxious symptomology using a structured interview. *Journal of the American Academy of Child and Adolescent Psychiatry, 31,* 117–124.

Sroufe, L. A., & Rutter, M. (1984). The domain of developmental psychopathology. *Child Development, 55,* 17–29.

Stein, R. E. K., & Jessop, D. J. (1984). Relationship between health status and psychological adjustment among children with chronic conditions. *Pediatrics, 73,* 169–174.

Stein, R. E. K., & Jessop, D. J. (1990). *Manual for personal adjustment and role skills scale (PARS III).* PACTS Papers, Bronx, NY: Albert Einstein College of Medicine.

Steinhausen, H., Schindler, H., & Stephan, H. (1983). Correlates of psychopathology in sick children: An empirical model. *Journal of the American Academy of Child Psychiatry, 22,* 559–564.

Strunk, R. C., Mrazek, D. A., Wolfson Fuhrmann, G. S., & LaBrecque, J. F. (1985). Physiological and psychological characteristics associated with deaths from asthma in childhood: A case-controlled study. *Journal of the American Medical Association, 254,* 1193–1198.

Tal, A., & Miklich, D. R. (1976). Emotionally induced decreases in pulmonary flow rates in asthmatic children. *Psychosomatic Medicine, 38,* 190–200.

Wallander, J. L., & Varni, J. W. (1989). Social support and adjustment in chronically ill and handicapped children. *American Journal of Community Psychology, 17,* 185–201.

Wamboldt, F. S., Wamboldt, M. Z., Gavin, L. A., Roesler, T. A., & Brugman, S. M. (1995) Parental criticism and treatment outcome in adolescents hospitalized for severe, chronic asthma. *Journal of Psychosomatic Research, 39,* 995–1005.

Weinstein, A. G., Faust, D. S., McKee, L., & Padman, R. (1992). Outcome of short-term hospitalization for children with severe asthma. *Journal of Allergy and Clinical Immunology, 90,* 66–75.

51 / Gender Identity Disorders in Children

Susan Coates and Sabrina Wolfe

The fact that infants are identified at birth as either male or female has made it difficult to conceive that gender, though influenced by one's sex of assignment at birth, is not given but is a complex attribute of the self that is constructed over time and thus has its own psychological development. Accordingly, even when biologically given sex is completely unambiguous, gender is subject to disruption in very complex ways.

Childhood gender identity disorder (GID) is a rare syndrome in which the child shows a strong and persistent cross-gender identification and persistent discomfort with his or her biological sex. Typical is the case of Colin, a 3-year-old boy reported in detail in Coates, Friedman, and Wolfe (1991). Evaluation revealed that Colin's favorite activities at home included doll play, listening to stories with female heroines, putting on his mother's makeup and jewelry, and cross-dressing in his mother's clothes in front of a mirror. At school, Colin preferred girls as playmates and showed a strong aversion to rough-and-tumble play. He did not like who he was and although he knew he was a boy, he wanted to be a girl. Essentially similar cases have been repeatedly detailed in the literature (Coates & Zucker, 1988; Green, 1987; Stoller, 1968).

The diagnosis of childhood gender identity disorder first entered the psychiatric nomenclature with the third edition of the Diagnostic and Statistical Manual of Mental Disorders (*DSM-III;* American Psychiatric Association [APA], 1980). The syndrome is distinguished by its intensity, duration, and pervasiveness, and can be distinguished from both gender nonconformity and the expectable degree of cross-gender identification and behavior seen in young children. Boys are more often referred to gender identity centers than girls, with a ratio of reported cases of approximately 5:1 boys to girls (Zucker & Green, 1992). It is not clear whether this represents a true sex difference or rather a referral bias that reflects greater social tolerance of cross-gender behavior

in girls. Onset typically occurs in the preoedipal period, roughly between the ages of 2 and 4.

Diagnostic Criteria

Table 51.1 presents *DSM-IV* criteria for gender identity disorder of childhood.

History and Conceptual Issues

The relatively recent identification of gender identity disorder as a distinct syndrome of early childhood has been both spurred and complicated by interest in two adult conditions: transsexualism and homosexuality. Historically, the first clear descriptions of the childhood disorder were those retrospective accounts elicited from a subsample of adult homosexuals by sexual researchers such as Krafft-Ebing (1902/1965) and Moll (1907/1912) at the turn of the century in the context of attempts to resolve various etiological hypotheses with regard to the role of heredity and early experience in the genesis of adult homosexuality. With the subsequent widespread dissemination of psychoanalytic perspectives on development, however, and the concomitant focus on desire (and thus sexual orientation) and defense, the topic of gender identity as a separate issue became progressively obscured. This theoretical lacuna persisted despite the existence of occasional, clearly described case reports in the literature such as the watershed paper of Bloch (1978), who attempted to explain the dynamics of the syndrome as a defense against annihilation anxiety.

The contemporary era of research into the topic of gender identity began with the work of Money and his collaborators on hermaphroditic

TABLE 51.1

Criteria for Gender Identity Disorders of Childhood

A. A strong and persistent cross-gender identification (not merely a desire for any perceived cultural advantages of being the other sex).

In children, the disturbance is manifested by four (or more) of the following:

(1) repeatedly stated desire to be, or insistence that he or she is, the opposite sex

(2) in boys, preference for cross-dressing or simulating female attire; in girls, insistence on wearing only stereotypical masculine clothing

(3) strong and persistent preferences for cross-sex roles in make-believe play or persistent fantasies of being the opposite sex

(4) intense desire to participate in the stereotypical games and pastimes of the other sex

(5) strong preference for playmates of the other sex . . .

B. Persistent discomfort with his or her sex or sense of inappropriateness in the gender role of that sex.

In children, the disturbance is manifested by any of the following: in boys, assertion that his penis or testes are disgusting or will disappear or assertion that it would be better not to have a penis, or aversion toward rough-and-tumble play and rejection of male stereotypical toys, games, and activities; in girls, rejection of urinating in a sitting position, assertion that she has or will grow a penis, or assertion that she does not want to grow breasts or menstruate, or marked aversion toward normative feminine clothing . . .

C. The disturbance is not concurrent with a physical intersex condition . . .

NOTE. From *Diagnostic and Statistical Manual of Mental Disorders*, 4th ed. (pp. 537–538), American Psychiatric Association, 1994. Washington, DC: Author. Copyright 1994 by the American Psychiatric Association. Reprinted with permission.

children at Johns Hopkins University in the 1950s (Money, Hampson, & Hampson, 1955). Money was able to demonstrate that despite biological ambiguity, gender identity would prove stable at 2- and 5-year follow-ups, provided gender was unambiguously assigned at birth. This finding allowed the conceptualization of the reciprocal notions of gender identity and gender role, the outward behavioral manifestation of gender identity.

Further fueling research into the development of gender identity was the renewed interest in adult transsexualism that accompanied the initiation of sex-change surgery in the 1950s. (See, for example, Benjamin, 1966.) As adult transsexuals typically report intense gender dysphoria dating back to earliest childhood, it briefly seemed warranted to search for "pretranssexual children." Through further clinical and longitudinal studies, however, it has since emerged clearly that the childhood syndrome is a precursor to the adult disorder only in a small number of cases.

The pioneering systematic studies of children with extreme cross-gender identities were undertaken by Green and Money (1960) and Bakwin (1968). Green's (1987) follow-up study of his initial cohort of 44 "feminine" boys found that while overt cross-gender behavior appears to diminish during development, approximately 75 to 80% of

his sample were on a homosexual or bisexual course in adolescence in terms of sexual orientation. This finding coupled with the fact that adult homosexuals (Bell, Weinberg, & Hammersmith, 1981; Saghir & Robins, 1973) typically report childhood histories of "gender nonconformity" has unfortunately led some clinicians (Zuger, 1988) to conflate gender identity disorder with homosexuality and to reconceptualize gender identity disorder of childhood as a juvenile manifestation of adult homosexuality. Yet, empirically, the behaviors subsumed under "gender nonconformity" as reported by retrospective studies of adult homosexuals do not constitute behavior that would lead to the diagnosis of childhood gender identity disorder in the majority of cases. (See Coates and Wolfe, 1995, for a more detailed discussion of this issue.)

Closer scrutiny of the data indicates that only a very small percentage of adult homosexual men are likely to have had gender identity disorder as children. Meanwhile, in a recent major follow-up study of 45 boys with gender identity disorder, Zucker and Bradley (1995) reported that 50 to 60% of the boys appeared to be on a heterosexual course, while only 30 to 40% appeared to be on a homosexual course; however, fully 20% of the boys in the sample were extremely gender dysphoric and appeared to be on a transsexual course.

The important issue of level of psychological well-being irrespective of sexual orientation has yet to be assessed in follow-up studies.

Conceptually, sexual orientation, which involves the gender of the preferred object, can and should be distinguished from gender identity, which involves the felt relation of the self to one's own biologically given gender. We do not currently understand how either heterosexuality or homosexuality develops, nor do we understand the mediating mechanisms between gender identity and sexual orientation. Gender identity, sensuality, and sexuality have their beginnings in and then continue to evolve in the context of the child's early attachment relationships. All three are deeply rooted in a person's early object relationships. As a consequence, both well-functioning and derailed attachment relationships will exert their influence on each of these aspects of development.

Clinical Presentation and Differential Diagnosis

The syndrome of gender identity disorder is determined by its *pervasiveness, persistence, and duration of the cross-gender behavior.* Once established, it will evolve and develop as the child does, becoming progressively more autonomous from the forces that set it in motion as it inexorably becomes an internalized psychological structure. Despite its relative rarity, and the conceptual confusion originally attending its establishment as a diagnosis, childhood gender identity disorder has proved to be a robust syndrome that can be reliably discriminated upon a great variety of measures, including structured parent interviews regarding sex-typed activities, measurement of overt and covert sex-typed play in standardized situations, and projective tests (Zucker & Green, 1992). Parent interviews can independently and reliably detect the presence of the disorder.

Boys with GID typically will be described as repetitively engaging in cross-gender activities at home, as being preoccupied with the wish to be the opposite gender (often including reported statements indicating anatomical dysphoria, e.g.,

"I want my penis to go away"), as compulsively dressing up in girl's clothes and/or inventing girls clothes with towels, scarves, or any material that can be found, and repetitively play-acting female roles and preferring the company of females. In addition, they usually are reported as having a marked aversion to rough-and-tumble play with peers and as avoiding the company of male peers.

Parents' descriptions of girls with GID mirror the reports of parents of boys with GID. Girls with GID intensely dislike their own gender and want to be the opposite gender. They prefer playing with boys, tend to be athletic, and typically assert that they "hate playing dolls and Barbies." Girls with GID not only typically want to dress in pants, but many become enraged and/or panicked when told they must wear a dress for a special occasion. Many ask their parents to buy them male underwear and pajamas. They insist that their hair be cut short, and many adopt a gender-neutral nickname. Many want to wear trunks when bathing or to use the boys' bathroom when in public places. Because of the greater social tolerance for tomboyism, girls with GID, unlike boys, often have been able to dress in a way that disguises their gender, and not infrequently they become extremely distressed when parents clearly indicate to others that their child is a girl, for example, by referring to her with feminine pronouns or by insisting that she use the girls' bathroom or wear her bathing suit top. Although tomboys are typically athletic and prefer wearing pants and have numerous cross-gender interests, they do not show the extreme rigidity of cross-gender interests and preferences and do not have the intense dysphoria and dislike of being a girl that girls with GID have (Green, Williams, & Goodman, 1982).

Assessment

Once the clinician determines from parental reports that a child has a gender identity disorder, it is critical to obtain a careful developmental history and interview the child in order to begin to understand the function and meaning of the cross-gender symptoms both in terms of the child's intrapsychic organization and in terms of the family system. To this end, the developmental history should focus on eliciting information about the child's early temperament, the psychosocial milieu of the family during the child's first few years, with particular focus on intercurrent stress, and the parents' relationship at the time the child first begins expressing cross-gender fantasies.

It is important to note that most parents do not experience concern about the cross-gender behavior in the child until someone outside of the family, such as a teacher or family friend, expresses concern about it. All researchers of this disorder have identified inadvertent parental reinforcement, with Green (1974) going so far as to suggest that the failure to discourage cross-gender behavior is etiologically central. The consequence of these parental attitudes for assessment need to be noted. First, parents often describe a pattern of gradual onset, or they might say that the child has always been that way or else that they thought it was a stage that the child would grow out of. As for the lattermost statement, often the child's pediatrician or nursery school teacher will have told the mother that cross-gender preoccupations are just a stage that the child will outgrow. Many parents also note that the cross-gender behavior became very intensified after a significant trauma in the family or during a period of severe stress. But in numbers of families, it is not until the family has been in treatment for some period of time that they begin to recall that the cross-gender behavior first emerged on the heels of some severely stressing life event. Not infrequently, the stress had a cascading traumatic effect on one or both parents, on their ability to function cooperatively as a parenting unit, and on the child. In these latter cases the symptom picture often becomes consolidated in only a matter of weeks following the family stress but then is subsequently misremembered by the parents. In general, during periods of family crisis, the parents often are unaware of the distress in the child and instead see the cross-gender behavior as "cute" or as an expression of the child's "sensitivity and/or creativity."

Some facets of the presenting picture may be changed by the time an evaluation is sought. It is not uncommon for parents to report that the child's cross-gender behavior decreased following their decision to move ahead with an evaluation. Often enough the child begins to sense the parent's distress and attempts to comply by suppressing cross-gender preoccupations. This some-

times results in the child's denial in initial direct interview of the wish to be the other gender, but the wish will readily emerge indirectly when the child is asked questions such as what are good things and difficult things about being a boy and a girl. At the time of evaluation, typically a boy will say that there is "nothing good about being a boy" and "the bad thing is that you have to fight." while the good thing about being a girl is that "you can wear pretty dresses, don't have to fight, and can go to girl's birthday parties." When asked about favorite stories or movies, the favorite characters of such boys are heroines (not heroes) such as Cinderella, Snow White, the Little Mermaid, or Dorothy from the Wizard of Oz. In figure drawing they usually draw the female first, larger and more elaborately than the male figure. Although most children can identify their own and other's gender correctly by the time of referral, many believe that if you wear the clothes of the other gender you can *really* become the other gender, not just in fantasy. The latter belief becomes more diagnostically significant as the child becomes older. The direct expression of the wish to be the opposite gender usually emerges after the child has developed a trusting relationship with the diagnostician or therapist over the course of the first few sessions.

In play interviews, boys frequently spend the majority of their time compulsively playing with Barbie dolls, obsessively putting on and taking off her clothes with a repetitive, ritualized, and stereotypically elaborated fantasy. The fantasy often reveals a compulsive, driven quality, a lack of complex narrative, and the absence of joy. Most striking in the play of children with GID is its repetitiveness, restricted range of interests (Zucker, Doering, Bradley, & Finegan, 1982), and lack of joy in their play relative to their same-sex cohorts. These children lack the flexible and wide range of interests seen in gender-nonconforming boys.

In the course of repeated observations, the cross-gender play consistently reoccurs and its defensive uses become apparent. Most often it intensifies especially when concerns about aggression, bodily intactness, and separation emerge. For example, a boy who has drawn a picture of a boy during a therapy session may, when he is told that we will have to stop in 5 minutes, tear up the male picture and replace it with a drawing of an imposing, highly elaborated female and then begin in the last minute to comb Barbie's hair ritually. Or a boy, when he is asked what he does when he has angry feelings, might say, "I put on my ruby-red nail polish."

With girls, statements that it would be better to be a boy because boys get to do more things or because boys can wear pants only indicate that the child is a tomboy unless she also expresses significant distress about being a girl or states that she will grow up to be a boy. Not infrequently, girls with GID express discomfort with their anatomy directly in an interview.

Projective testing also proves to be a useful adjunct to the psychiatric interview. Cross-gender identifications, fantasy preoccupations involving loss and aggression, and, at times, annihilation fantasies often emerge in the projective records of children who in the face of parental and social disapproval have begun to deny their cross-gender feelings and fantasies. Projective testing also elicits information about the dynamic, and notably, defensive, significance of cross-gender fantasies for a particular child, information that even the most cooperative youngster could not provide in an interview. For example, a careful analysis of a child's sequence of responses on projective material can provide information about the content and associations that trigger cross-gender fantasies in him or her.

Differential Diagnosis

GENDER NONCONFORMITY

Children with GID can be readily distinguished from gender-nonconforming children who have specific cross-gender interests and identifications in the context of multiple interests and identifications that are flexibly pursued. Gender-nonconforming children do not dislike their sex or have a persistent wish to change it. Their range of interests potentially entails a significant degree of ego strength insofar as it reflects greater flexibility and a wider range of options in terms of self-experience.

CHILDHOOD TRANSVESTISM

In contrast to boys with GID who will wear externally visible female clothing to enact the fantasy of being a girl, childhood transvestism refers to boys who privately dress in female undergarments for the purposes of self-soothing and/or sexual arousal. Childhood transvestism typically emerges during the school-age years and typically occurs in boys who are otherwise unremarkably masculine. Childhood transvestism has been reported in girls only very rarely.

TRANSIENT CROSS-GENDER REACTIONS

At times children respond to a family or personal crisis by manifesting cross-gender behaviors and increased cross-gender interests. When this occurs in children whose gender identity has been reasonably well established, typically the behaviors diminish as the family stress decreases. If the behavior persists for more than 3 months (3 months is usually considered to be the outside limit of "transient" or "phase"-related behavior), then parents should receive help, as a more serious gender problem may be developing.

INTERSEX CONDITIONS

Where a true biologically based hermaphroditism or intersex condition exists, the child's sense of confusion and perturbation deserves attention and intervention, but this is not a GID. Research has shown that while intersex conditions can affect gender role behavior and contribute to gender dysphoria, they do not ordinarily result in a full-blown GID (Meyer-Bahlburg, 1991).

Associated Psychopathology

Research has shown consistently that boys with childhood gender identity disorder present with overall levels of psychopathology comparable to other clinic-referred children on general measures of psychopathology (Bates, Bentler, & Thompson, 1979; Bradley, Doering, Zucker, Finegan, & Gonda, 1980; Coates & Person, 1985). Moreover, approximately two thirds of boys meeting the criteria for childhood gender identity disorder also will meet the requirement for an independent *DSM-III* diagnosis of separation anxiety disorder (Coates & Person, 1985; Zucker, Bradley, & Sullivan, in press), 50% will have symptoms of depression and one third will suicidal ideation (Coates & Person, 1985). Recent research also has found that three quarters of a sample of boys with GID are insecurely attached when assessed with the Ainsworth Strange Situation paradigm (Goldberg, in press).

Far less is known about associated psychopathology in girls. Although girls with GID appear to have levels of underlying anxiety comparable to that of boys with GID, most often they manage their anxiety with counterphobic defenses—they act brave and even somewhat "macho" when afraid. Recently Zucker and Bradley (1995) found using the Childhood Behavior Check-list that a sample of girls with GID have levels of psychopathology comparable to that of boys with GID.

Also clinically central is the degree of self-dislike and self-reproach in the child. Often this can be seen in an extreme perfectionism that emerges as pervasive self-criticism about the adequacy of performance even on those tasks at which the child clearly excels. Given the fact that it is extremely rare for a gender identity disorder to emerge without collateral psychopathology, it is extremely important for the clinician to assess the child carefully for the presence of other psychopathology as well as to evaluate personality functioning, including self-esteem, impulse management, peer relations, and, perhaps most important, the attachment relationship with both the mother and the father.

Gender identity is a subdivision of self-concept and overall identity; as such, its assessment should be included in any comprehensive evaluation of a child presenting with significant emotional difficulties. Gender identity is evaluated most effectively in the context of an exploration of the self-concept and of overall identifications.

Predisposing Factors

ROLE OF BIOLOGY

The extremely low incidence of childhood gender identity disorder coupled with its onset during a specific developmental period and its symptomatic stability thereafter strongly suggests that multiple risk factors must be present simultaneously during a crucial maturational stage to produce the disorder. An understanding of those risk factors is indispensable for understanding the psychobiological and psychosocial factors involved.

To date, no sex-linked biological markers for the disorder, neither chromosomal nor hormonal, have been identified. Accordingly, in clinical assessment, no physical evaluation is called for or warranted unless a genital abnormality such as a hypospadias is present.

Evaluation of temperament is another matter. (See Coates & Wolfe, 1995.) There is now substantial evidence on the role of prenatal psychoneuro-endocrine influences on the development of both sexual and nonsexual behavior (Ehrhardt and Meyer-Bahlburg, 1981). Both human and animal research have shown that neonatal hormones can affect the structural organization of the brain and thus influence temperament even if they do not impact on gender identity or even on sexual orientation directly. Specifically, among boys with gender identity disorder, avoidance of rough-and-tumble play is characteristic. As the typical masculine predilection for such activities is known to be hormonally influenced, this finding suggests a temperamental predisposition for the disorder. Beyond the issue of temperament, animal models describing the relationship of prenatal and postnatal hormonal influences on sex-dimorphic behaviors in other species have been unproductive in generating sturdy hypotheses with regard to seemingly analogous human conditions in general (Byne & Parsons, 1993) and most particularly with regard to this disorder of childhood. This is hardly surprising given that gender identity is a meaning-making system that involves complex and multiple levels of cognitive and affective integrations, not a capacity that animals are known to have. Nor do any of the known intersex conditions regularly co-occur with the disorder. The syndrome of congenital adrenal hyperplasia, an autosomal recessive condition involving adrenal steroidogenesis that in girls results in excessive adrenal androgens prenatally and in masculinized external genitalia at birth, is accompanied by a full-blown childhood gender identity disorder only very rarely, although it does have an impact on gender role behavior (Ehrhardt & Baker, 1974) and gender dysphoria (Zucker, Bradley, & Hughes, 1987).

Notwithstanding the failure to find any significant biological markers, almost all researchers are agreed that an inborn constitutional predisposition is likely to lower the threshold for the impact of environmental factors. Descriptively, boys with GID appear to resemble Kagan's (1989) behaviorally inhibited type: They are shy in the face of novelty and slow to warm up, have a propensity for high arousal states, and may have a greater than average need for attachment. This view is consistent with Bradley's (1985) belief that the genetic diathesis in the development of gender identity disorder involves disturbances in the regulation of affect.

Although we know far less about the constitutional predisposition of girls with GID, they appear to be bold and highly invested in athletic activities. Recent research has found that they have higher activity levels than boys with GID, siblings, and normal controls and are rated as more extroverted than comparison controls (Zucker & Bradley, 1995).

For both boys and girls, temperamental styles will be taken up according to the parents' meaning-making systems, resulting often in attributions toward the child that can in turn shape the further unfolding of the temperamental givens. A majority of boys with GID have shy, inhibited temperaments, are avoidant of rough-and-tumble play, and exhibit special sensitivities to color and odor; some parents may see these traits as evidence of special sensitivity or giftedness and therefore evidence that their son is not like other boys.

In this context, a possible synergy between constitutional predisposition and early trauma to the child also should be noted. Although no empirical research on this issue exists, continuing clinical reassessment during the course of long-term treatment suggests that significant traumas to the child and family commonly occurred prior to the onset of the gender identity disorder. These traumas led to a shift in the child's behavior toward greater anxiousness, separation anxiety, and clinging although in many cases at the time of initial intake neither the trauma nor the shift in behavior was remembered by the parents. If present, early trauma to the child can affect temperament enduringly and so initiate or activate a constitutional predisposition (Kagan, 1989; see also Post, 1992).

Other aspects of these children suggestive of a constitutional diathesis have been described less consistently in the clinical literature. Pleak,

Meyer-Bahlburg, O'Brien, Bowen, and Morganstein (1989) have noted hyperactivity and poor impulse control in some cases; it may be that these cases represent a distinct subtype, but it may also be that socioeconomic factors play a role in shaping some of the collateral clinical features in some children.

ROLE OF DEVELOPMENT

Equally relevant to the understanding of the disorder is the cognitive developmental literature. Research has demonstrated that children typically begin to be able to classify peers and adults by gender reliably at age 2 and that this ability is accompanied by an increasing preference for the activities and company of the same gender (Fagot, Leinbach, & Hagan, 1986). However, research also has shown that children are relatively slow to develop either gender stability (the understanding that it is not possible to change one's gender) or gender constancy (the understanding that a change in one's activities or clothes does not change one's gender). There is thus a sensitive period in normal development, roughly between the ages of 2 and 4, when children can classify themselves and others by gender and begin to organize social information around this distinction but do not yet fully appreciate that gender is a fixed biologically given quality independent of clothes or activities. Except in a few cases, this period of cognitive immaturity is the time when a gender identity disorder becomes established. Zucker et al. (1993) have found that children referred for problems with gender identity have significantly more cognitive confusion about gender than either normal or clinical controls. Whether this is a predisposing risk factor or a consequence of the disorder is not yet known.

Certain variable features of the disorder, moreover, may reflect the specific level of cognitive development of the child at the time of onset. Anatomic dysphoria, for example, is a common but not universal feature. When present, it may reflect the contagion of the mother's feeling about the child's penis, but it often occurs after the child has first begun to understand conceptually that genitalia are an emblem of gender identity—and thus of the gender the child does not want to be.

The sensitive period in the cognitive development of the understanding of gender overlaps with another important developmental period, conceptualized by psychoanalysts as the rapprochement subphase of separation-individuation (Mahler, Pine, & Bergman, 1975). Recent research by Lyons-Ruth (1991) suggests that Mahler may have failed to differentiate clearly between normative and deviant development. Lyons-Ruth has shown that a rapprochement "crisis" is not universal but occurs in cases where the attachment bond to the primary caregiver is prone to disruption as a pattern of "disorganized attachment." Lyons-Ruth suggests that this phase might better be conceptualized as an attachment-individuation process in which the infant must "preserve emotional ties to preferred caregivers at all costs, while simultaneously attempting to find a place within these relationships for his or her own goals and initiatives" (p. 10). Given that gender identity disorder typically occurs during this period of increased relational vulnerability, there is a strong reason to suppose that it reflects similar issues intrapsychically, specifically conflict over attachment and autonomy, and in addition that it may originate out of a troubled mother-child attachment bond. The coexistence of a diagnosable separation anxiety disorder in over 60% of the children with gender identity disorder and insecure attachment in the Strange Situation in 73% of them strengthens this supposition.

ROLE OF FAMILY PSYCHOPATHOLOGY

The clinician should weigh the considerable etiological contribution of parental psychopathology and family dysfunction in the context of co-existing constitutional susceptibility to anxiety, derailments of the attachment system, and a sensitive developmental period. These two additional risk factors are almost always both present simultaneously, and they interact with one another and also with collateral trauma to the family, although the specific pattern will vary from case to case.

Research has revealed high levels of long-standing psychopathology in the parents of children with gender identity disorder, with anxiety, depression, hostility, substance abuse, and problems with impulse control being prominent (Bradley, 1985; Marantz & Coates, 1991; Mitchell, 1991; Wolfe, 1990). In general, in these families, long-standing parental psychopathology, most especially in the regulation of affect, gives rise to

and becomes embedded in attitudes and practices that operate to discourage stereotypically assertive masculine play and to reward stereotypically feminine play. In addition to individual psychopathology in the parents, family function also should be carefully assessed for: problems of generational boundaries, parental difficulties in setting limits of all kinds, serious unresolved marital difficulties, subtle conflicts organized around issues of gender that do not present in clinical intensity, and problems of unresolved mourning or trauma that affect the reliability of the parents' emotional accessibility to the child.

Significant trauma has been reported in 78% of the families where the information was elicited specifically (Coates, Friedman, & Wolfe, 1991). The clinician should be attuned to the possibility that these traumas will have had a cascading effect in the family. In many cases, furthermore, these traumas will echo and repeat traumas in previous generations. The stress to the mother from the trauma often leads to preoccupied inattention, emotional inaccessibility, and hostility to the child. This in turn will disrupt the mother-child attachment bond and foster separation anxiety and an insecure attachment in the child. Not uncommonly, the father may be distant from the mother-child bond and feel excluded from it, thus rendering him emotionally unavailable to the mother when she is most in need of him to help restabilize her. Nor will the father be able to take on the mother's caregiving role in relation to the child during the time that the mother is necessarily self-absorbed in her own attempts to repair herself. In addition, a withdrawn father will be unavailable to his son as a role model and a caregiver who will interfere with his son's developing cross-gender behaviors.

Within a significant proportion of families, the parents' pathology will be manifest, among other ways, in impairment in their management of aggression, resulting in episodes of uncontrolled rage at one another or at the child. In fathers this may result from substance abuse. In mothers this may reflect the severity of their depression. Lyons-Ruth (1992), in studying the behavior of depressed mothers, found that when symptoms of depression reach the clinical range, mothers become withdrawn from their children. As symptoms increase still further, the mothers' withdrawn behavior lessens and they become overtly hostile and intrusive. While this level of rage is often difficult to assess initially, clinicians must be on the alert for it, because by the time of the evaluation, the family has restabilized to some significant degree; moreover, such rages can occur in individuals with considerable ego strength who have a tendency to "lose it" with great intensity but who can reintegrate very rapidly and can otherwise appear very well integrated.

If individual parental pathology, family dysfunction, and trauma to one or both parents co-occur during a developmentally critical period in their constitutionally sensitive son's development, when both his sense of self and gender are still unstable, and where there is at least tolerance of cross-gender behavior within the home, the necessary multiplicity of risk factors will all be present.

Psychodynamics

All observers are agreed that, at least initially, the families of these children exhibit (TENT) inadvertent reinforcement of cross-gender behavior and that this is a necessary precondition for the particular behavioral pattern involved in gender identity disorder to become established. This observation has led some researchers to propose a straightforward social-learning theory for the disorder and others to attempt to treat it behaviorally. Extensive research into the social reinforcement hypothesis has yielded some positive results, but it has largely failed to provide a clear-cut discriminative portrait of parental behavior such as is called for by the etiological hypothesis. Moreover, the specific etiological hypothesis of selective maternal reinforcement for cross-gender behavior must operate across the conceptual chasm created by the fact that mothers of gender-identity-disordered boys spend less time, not more, with their sons than do mothers of controls (Green, 1974). Therefore we are led to suppose that it is the presence of other risk factors in the parents that makes their tolerance and/or encouragement of cross-gender behavior prepotent. It remains conceptually and empirically unclear, however, how this tolerance and/or encouragement intersects with and reflects the other risk factors in the

parents. The clinician should attempt to assess gender as a psychodynamically significant category both for the parents as individuals and for the functioning of the family system. No single pattern of concerns with regard to gender is to be expected, and contradictory combinations of idealization and devaluation with regard to both masculinity and femininity are rather the rule, but the very nature of the disorder coupled with the lack of felt concern by the parents suggests that the child's cross-gender identification has important reparative functions not only for the child but also for one or both parents.

The following dynamic formulation has proven heuristically useful in understanding and engaging the majority of boys referred to the St. Luke's/Roosevelt Childhood Gender Identity Center over the past decade. Gender identity disorder involves a fantasy solution to a derailed attachment system in a shy, anxious boy during a sensitive period of development. More specifically, it expresses an inner fantasy of becoming fused with an omnipotent maternal imago as a response to felt emotional abandonment by the actual mother. It mitigates separation anxiety by substituting an identification for a relationship. The internal self-identification as a girl then becomes indispensable for the further consolidation of ego structures especially in situations of internal anxiety or external stress. What is essential is that the implicated behaviors bind intense affiliative needs and anxiety and do so in a manner that allows the child to experience himself as existing independently and yet surviving. In essence, these boys first come to equate having Mommy with being like Mommy and then come to equate being a girl with being able to manage anxiety and aggression on their own. Interpersonal processes make their own contribution to the consolidation and perpetuation of the disorder. For example, some boys correctly assess that by the altruistic self-sacrifice of altering their gender, they have made a significant contribution to their mothers' emotional adaptation. Particularly in families where the mother has become depressed, the loss can be likened to what Andre Green (1986) describes as the "dead mother," a mother who is present but "not there," who is gone but cannot be mourned (see also Emde, 1980, 1983). If the cross-gender behavior revitalizes the "dead mother," this will in turn become a powerful reinforcer of the boy's cross-gender behavior. By identifying with her projections regarding gender, the boy becomes able to withdraw more successfully from her when she is emotionally inaccessible as a result of being either depressed and/or chronically anxious. Compliance and reparation thus are equally involved although they are not distinguished internally by the child.

Various other psychodynamic hypotheses have been suggested and described in individual cases, ranging from the existence of significant cross-gender identifications in the mother and/or father, to intense oedipal rivalry and/or rageful jealousy in the same-sex or opposite-sex parent, alleviated only if the child changes his or her gender. Any of these hypotheses may be directly relevant to the understanding of a specific case and will seem to explain why the child's disorder represents a "solution" for one or both parents that mitigates felt anxiety. Apparently no single psychodynamic formula will apply to the parent-child interaction in even a majority of the cases.

With regard to the very young child, clinicians must infer the dynamic reasons why changing gender represents a "solution" from observation in conjunction with etiological understanding of the particular case. What can be readily observed clinically both in younger and older children during the course of psychodynamically oriented treatment are the conditions in which the cross-gender behaviors are most readily elicited and/or become exacerbated. Most typically, though not invariably, these involve issues of aggression and separation. The phenomena themselves are quite striking in the clinical setting. In response to the challenge situation, such as a therapist announcing the end of a treatment session, or an impending vacation, or his or her mother's becoming depressed, the child will initiate some part of his or her cross-gender repertoire and engage in it repetitively and joylessly, as if it were essentially an empty comfort that nonetheless has become indispensable for modulating the level of anxiety. In the course of treatment, further, the child will begin to share some of his or her inner world, and the clinician comes to understand that feelings of abandonment, panic, psychic disintegration, annihilation, or self-hatred are being warded off by the cross-gender behaviors. Difficulties managing aggression are prominent in many cases, although where projection and dissociation are well estab-

lished as preferred defenses, these difficulties will be manifest in increased fearfulness (and thus in an exacerbation of the child's constitutional disposition).

No systematic research exists on the question of the more specific emergence and resolution of the oedipal stage in gender-disordered boys. Clinical experience suggests that oedipal phenomena are delayed and often emerge only after these children are well into therapy. So, too, castration anxiety often first emerges only well into treatment and then is superimposed on more fundamental unresolved anxieties stemming from the preoedipal period. The more specific supposition that the disorder is to be understood as a defensive exacerbation of the negative Oedipus complex has not proved itself in clinical work.

Because this already rare disorder occurs with even greater infrequency among girls, far less is know about the etiology, dynamics, and outcomes associated with girlhood gender identity disorder. Clinical experience indicates that, as with boys, the disorder is an enduring one once established, although there is reason to suppose that the degree of social ostracism girls experience during latency may not be quite so intense. Like boys, girls with GID tend to have sensitive, reactive temperaments, but unlike boys with GID, who tend to be behaviorally inhibited, girls with GID are often oppositional and aggressive. Then, too, the combination of predisposing familial factors that are most often found clinically in girls appears to be somewhat different; however, systematic information is currently lacking. Girls with GID perceive the female role as devalued and disidentify with their mothers while identifying with males whom they alternately perceive as aggressive and as nurturant. In general, girls with GID appear to equate changing their gender with their emotional, and sometimes even physical, survival. By the school-age years, girls with GID will manifest significant levels of psychopathology and behavioral disturbance.

COURSE

The consequences of this disorder for development during the latency-age period can be severe. Clinically, the children are anxiously attached to the mother. These are children in distress, whose range of activities, interests, and abilities has become constricted and whose adjustment in interpersonal situations is brittle. In short, childhood gender identity disorder is associated with significant inner suffering on the part of children, suffering that is being muted and masked, and ultimately perpetuated, by the cross-gender identity. The children's ability to utilize their innate creativity and special gifts, which are quite often very considerable, becomes progressively jeopardized by the rigid, stereotyped preoccupations and behaviors. And the overall level of social adjustment will steadily erode, despite maturational thrusts, in the face of peer rejection, which will in its own turn further add to the children's burden of feeling inwardly unacceptable. In both these respects the developmental pattern of children with gender identity disorder can be strongly contrasted with nondisordered children who have significant cross-gender interests (gender nonconformity) but are able to pursue them flexibly. Accordingly, gender identity disorder should be regarded as a severe disorder of childhood, one that requires and justifies significant efforts at intervention.

By the time of adolescence, most boys who have had childhood GID no longer exhibit cross-gender behavior; those who do to a very significant degree are often on a transsexual course. No systematic studies have followed the course of development from cross-gender behavior in early or late childhood to the development of an inner representation of gender identity in adulthood, nor have the mediating mechanisms between inner gender identity and sexual orientation, heterosexual or homosexual, been studied.

INTERVENTION STRATEGIES

Interventions with children with childhood gender identity disorder have been approached from a multiplicity of therapeutic perspectives, including behavior therapy, psychotherapy, child analysis, parent counseling, family therapy, group therapy, and eclectic combinations. As with many other childhood conditions, the research literature supporting the general effectiveness of interventions of any kind, let alone of a specific kind, is extremely weak, indeed virtually nonexistent. Most of what we have to say here addresses the specific needs of boys with GID. Much more needs to be learned about the specific etiology of

the syndrome in girls and about the clinical worthiness of different intervention strategies, before anything can be recommended with confidence regarding girls.

Following fast upon Green's original social learning theory and informed by the premise that collateral psychopathology in the child was the consequence of peer ostracism, behavioral interventions aimed at decreasing specific behaviors and increasing others have been tried (Rekers, 1977, 1985). While there is some evidence to suggest that such interventions have an impact on specific cross-gender symptoms and also on the child's overall sense of gender identity (Zucker, 1985), there remain important conceptual problems with such approaches, and clinical experience suggests strongly that the effect of these interventions in many cases is to drive the basic gender constellation underground rather than truly ameliorate it. Obviously, behavioral interventions aimed at altering the frequency of specific gender-typed behaviors do nothing directly to address collateral psychopathology in the child or family. Moreover, insofar as the etiological model and psychodynamic portrait presented here and elsewhere (Coates, 1992; Coates, Friedman, & Wolfe, 1991) applies to a given case, intervention aimed simply at eliminating the cross-gender behavior, which children experience as a solution, is likely to exacerbate their anxiety and may prove conflictual for the parents as well with further complications arising both during and after treatment. The legitimate and important aim of reducing peer ostracism might be better realized by helping children and parents become aware of the specific behaviors that lead to rejection, with a view to placing more control over these behaviors in the hands of the children.

In our view, it is crucial that treatment proceed on the basis of an understanding of how the cross-gender fantasies and behavior have come to constitute an important part of the self-system and, indeed, are most likely to be called upon in those situations that challenge the children's sense of autonomy. Accordingly, treatment needs to be flexibly directed to the adaptational issue that the children currently are having difficulty with, be it separation anxiety, depression, extreme compliance, or difficulties in managing aggression. Ideally this treatment is carried out in the context of repairing the attachment disturbance between the children and their parents. To these ends, we have found that treatment is most effective if children are seen in individual, psychodynamically oriented play therapy two times a week, while after the initial evaluation the parents are seen weekly, also by their child's therapist. Working with the parents signals to children that their primary caregivers are now being taken care of and that work is being done to help repair the derailed attachment system so that the caregivers will become more emotionally available to the children. Ideally, this treatment program also helps to provide the psychological space for the children to resume their own development. Treatment must be tailored to the specifics of each case; there are multiple pathways to the disorder, and the clinician must be sensitive to these different variations in planning specific treatment strategies.

The work with the children is focused on fostering the expression and management of basic conflicts and anxieties in representational thought and fantasy rather than in behavioral enactments, helping the children develop a flexible range of coping mechanisms and repairing the damaged sense of self. Therapeutic neutrality is best maintained by understanding the important intrapsychic purposes the cross-gender identity serves, not by adopting a posture of bland acceptance toward the behavior, and not be reinforcing it by providing props (such as dress-up clothes and wigs) and encouragement. Frankly encouraging cross-gender enactments can interfere with the therapeutic task of helping the children develop the capacity to represent and manage conflicts symbolically (as they are "stuck" in repetitive enactments).

Boys with GID can be treated successfully by either gender. If a female is the treating therapist, particularly in single-parent households where the mother is the primary caregiver, greater additional focus must be placed on helping the family to find appropriate male role models for the boy. If a male is the treating therapist, great care must be taken that fostering behavioral change, on the basis of the child's compliance and identification, does not become a substitute for addressing the child's underlying conflicts and anxiety.

Though comorbid symptomatology varies significantly, several dynamic issues almost invariably are significant for school-age youngsters with GID. These include anxiety about loss and separation, anxiety about aggression (much of which

may be projected), and a damaged sense of self. Over the course of the treatment the therapist helps the children to develop an observing ego vis-à-vis the cross-gender fantasies by connecting them to precipitating events and the resulting affects as they emerge during the therapy hour. In addition, as treatment progresses, it is often possible to begin to connect resurgences in the cross-gender fantasies to intercurrent family stresses with both the children and their parents. When this level of interpretation becomes possible, it often has a profound ameliorative effect for both the children and for the whole family system.

Although dynamic interpretation is the core of treatment, education also can play a useful role. The school-age boy with GID, for example, often benefits greatly from learning about his temperament and its special strengths, from being directly taught strategies for managing situations that are difficult for him, and from being helped to recognize ways of expressing his preferences, interests, and talents that do not involve sacrificing his gender. Such interventions can often serve to increase the boy's self-esteem, as many afflicted children have come to see something is wrong with them by virtue of their basic fearfulness and inhibition in new and/or aggressive situations. Notably, particularly once the boy's sense of security is better established, remarkable capacities for empathy and for creative expression are quite common and these can become a source of pride for the child. Then, too, the wish to be a girl, although not caused by it, often is compounded by the school-age boy's feeling temperamentally that he is different and not like other boys and as a result is comfortable playing only with the girls. It is essential to help him to learn how to find male peers with a similar temperament and/or interests.

Boys in the school-age years can be quite savage in their rejection of children with cross-gender behavior. Not infrequently, a boy with GID also must be helped to understand his peers' reactions to his cross-gender behaviors, as he often does not grasp what is causing him to be teased and scapegoated by classmates or to be suddenly rejected by a friend. Specifically helping children to become aware of behaviors that may cause rejection gives them greater control over their interpersonal environment.

The work with the parents has several different foci, and these will expectably shift back and forth during the course of treatment. Education about the development of gender identity in children, and gender identity disorder in particular, as well as the nature of the child's temperament, form the basis for maintaining a working alliance. Parents also often conflate their child's gender disorder with early manifestations of homosexuality; some seek treatment to "cure" what they regard as boyhood homosexuality, whereas others are loathe to bring a child for treatment for fear of interrupting what they see as a natural, biologically determined developmental process. We directly explain to parents that the mediating mechanisms between GID and adult homosexuality, between early experience and future sexual orientation in general, have not been identified, and that when evaluating and treating a child for GID, we are concerned with the child's immediate suffering, including separation anxiety, symptoms of depression, distress about his or her gender, and the ongoing consequences in terms of self-esteem, self-formation, and object relations.

In terms of the family system, several goals are essential: First is the establishment of an effective executive parenting subsystem within the marital contract. Part of this work involves establishing generational boundaries, helping parents to clarify their values and goals, and helping them to develop effective strategies for limit setting. An essential part of the work involves helping the parents become aware of the ways that they are consciously or subtly and inadvertently reinforcing the child's cross-gender behavior.

Parents often need to be educated about the role of temperament in both their child's difficulties and in parenting dilemmas that result from their child's anxious behaviors. Work with the mother needs to focus on helping her to differentiate normal assertive, rough-and-tumble play from aggression that is destructive. Mothers who have developed overprotective parenting styles in response to their sons' anxieties often need help in learning to incrementally "push" the children to confront and more adaptively manage situations that make them anxious. Fathers often need to be taught how to interact with their temperamentally sensitive sons in age-appropriate ways that will not escalate their sons' anxiety. Fathers who have withdrawn from their sons often need help in learning how to overcome their own reactions to the child's pushing them away.

Since part of gender socialization and the regulation of self-esteem occurs in the context of same-sex peers, parents need to help their child to develop friendships with temperamentally compatible members of their own gender. Also, they often need to directly help the children develop social skills at playing together with peers. Given the major role played by peers in socializing male gender (Fagot, 1993), this latter task is especially critical. It is essential that each week the child participate in at least two to three play dates and/or after-school groups for boys, although the clinician should expect that this goal will require much exploration, guidance, and problem-solving before it is achieved.

An essential part of treatment that rarely can be undertaken right at the beginning of therapeutic work is addressing individual psychopathology in the parents that is involved in the perpetuation of their child's disorder. Typically parents need to be helped with their child's problems before they are willing to begin to address their own psychopathology; nonetheless, clinicians need to be ever cognizant that the child's progress in treatment will be enhanced dramatically once the parents can be induced to engage their own psychopathology in their own psychotherapy. Most often this involves addressing chronic anxiety, depression, and unresolved mourning in the mother. Clinicians should remain on the alert for the possibility of significant and severe maternal trauma, often echoing trauma in the previous generation, even when this is initially unreported or even denied. If the mother's emotional problems go unaddressed, she will continue to be preoccupied, inattentive, rageful, and emotionally inaccessible to her child, which will in turn continue to fuel his separation anxiety, his anxious attachment to her, and his gender identity disorder. It is also essential that the father's difficulties with impulse regulation, management of anxiety, and problems with substance abuse be addressed. The former usually can be addressed effectively in intensive psychodynamic psychotherapy or psychoanalysis and the latter in a substance abuse program.

Often parents first become willing to explore the role their own psychodynamics play in perpetuating their children's problems when they find themselves unable to implement changes that are suggested in the parental guidance sessions. For example, it is not unusual to find parents continuing to reinforce the child's cross-gender fantasies, despite an intellectual understanding and recognition of the problems these are causing the child.

Often this situation provides an opportunity to explore their unresolved conflicts, which in many cases have become organized into the domain of gender.

Long-standing difficulties in the parents' relationship may have contributed to a mother becoming depressed, which in turn effects her capacity to be reliably and sensitively attuned to her child's needs. Fathers too, are unable to meet the child's needs because of their own unresolved emotional problems. Addressing both parents' needs is an essential part of therapeutic intervention for the child. Of particular note, we have found that when clinicians directly work to engage the fathers, they invariably become as involved in their treatment as their wives. Once fathers recognize that they will not be "blamed" for their son's problems, they often poignantly describe their own guilt over having been unable to establish a stronger relationship with their child and are eager for assistance in doing so.

The principle "less mother, more father" fails for several reasons. First, decreasing the mother's availability to her son often results in an increase in the child's separation anxiety, which may in turn result in an increase in the boy's reliance on cross-gender symptoms to maintain a connection to the mother in her absence. Second, the child's symptoms result from a derailed attachment relationship, whose outward appearance may be one of maternal overinvolvement but that, on closer inspection, often reveals a pattern of inconsistent and unpredictable attunement that is essentially being driven by the parent's own needs. Mothers therefore need active assistance in restoring a secure attachment relationship with their child. Finally, the principle of "less mother, more father" fails on conceptual grounds, as research has shown that mothers play a critical role in empowering and vitalizing the father-son relationship, not by fading into the background but by actively empowering and strengthening the father-child bond Atkins (1981, 1984).

Treatment must be conceived flexibly, and individualized for the particular child and family. Concurrent stresses on the child, on the parents, and on the family system must be addressed continually if progress is to be maintained.

The goal is not to eliminate cross-gender fantasies but to reduce the need for their compulsive use by reducing conflict and expanding the child's coping mechanisms. The ability to put oneself in the other's shoes, so to speak, is an important aspect of being able to empathize with the other gender. Put another way, the goal of treatment is to restore the derailed attachment system, repair the child's sense of self and ability to be a person in his or her own right as well as to restore the child's capacity for creativity. The focal disorder in gender, at once symptom, solution, and family system stabilizer, is not so much the direct target of treatment as it is the avenue and the occasion for addressing therapeutically the confluence of forces that, operating invisibly, together have brought it into being.

REFERENCES

American Psychiatric Association. (1980). *Diagnostic and statistical manual of mental disorders* (3rd ed.). Washington, DC: Author.

American Psychiatric Association. (1994). *Diagnostic and statistical manual of mental disorders* (4th ed.). Washington, DC: Author.

Atkins, R. N. (1981). Finding one's father: The mother's contribution to early father representation. *Journal of the American Academy of Psychoanalysis, 9,* 539–559.

Atkins, R. N. (1984). Transitive vitalization and its impact on father representation. *Contemporary Psychoanalysis, 20,* 663–675.

Bakwin, H. (1968). Deviant gender-role behavior in children: Relation to homosexuality. *Pediatrics, 41,* 620–629.

Bates, J. E., Bentler, P. M., & Thompson, S. K. (1979). Gender deviant boys compared with normal and clinical control boys. *Journal of Abnormal Child Psychology, 7,* 243–259.

Bell, A. P., Weinberg, M. S., & Hammersmith, S. K. (1981). *Sexual preference: Its development in men and women.* Bloomington: Indiana University Press.

Benjamin, H. (1966). *The transsexual phenomenon.* New York: Julian Press.

Bloch, D. (1978). Four children who insisted they belonged to the opposite sex. In D. Bloch, *"So the witch won't eat me": Fantasy and the child's fear of infanticide* (pp. 50–70). Boston: Houghton Mifflin.

Bradley, S. J. (1985). Gender disorders in childhood: A formulation. In B. W. Steiner (Ed.), *Gender dyspho-*

ria: Development, research, management (pp. 175–188). New York: Plenum Press.

Bradley, S. J., Doering, R. W., Zucker, K. J., Finegan, J. K., & Gonda, G. M. (1980). Assessment of the gender/disturbed child: A comparison to sibling and psychiatric controls. In J. Samson (Ed.), *Childhood and sexuality* (pp. 554–568). Montreal, Quebec: Editions Etudes Vivantes.

Byne, W., & Parsons, B. (1993). Human sexual orientation: The biological theories reappraised. *Archives of General Psychiatry, 50,* 228–239.

Coates, S. (1992). The etiology of boyhood gender identity disorder: An integrative model. In J. W. Barron, M. N. Eagle, & D. L. Wolitzky (Eds.), *Interface of psychoanalysis and psychology* (pp. 245–265). Washington, DC: American Psychological Association.

Coates, S., Friedman, R. C., & Wolfe, S. (1991). The etiology of boyhood gender identity disorder: A model for integrating psychodynamics, temperament and development. *Psychoanalytic Dialogues: A Journal of Relational Perspectives, 1,* 341–383.

Coates, S., & Person, E. S. (1985). Extreme boyhood femininity: Isolated finding or pervasive disorder? *Journal of the American Academy of Child Psychiatry, 24,* 702–709.

Coates, S., & Wolfe, S. (1995). Gender identity disorder in boys: The interface of constitution and early experience. *Psychoanalytic Inquiry, 15,* 6–38.

Coates, S., & Zucker, K. J. (1988). Assessment of gender identity disorders in children. In C. Kestenbaum & D. T. Williams (Eds.), *Handbook of clinical assessment of children and adolescents* (pp. 893–914). New York: New York University Press.

Ehrhardt, A. A., & Baker, S. W. (1974). Fetal androgens, human central nervous system differentiation, and behavior sex differences. In R. C. Friedman, R. M. Ricart, & R. L. Van de Wiele (Eds.), *Sex differences in behavior* (pp. 33–51). New York: John Wiley & Sons.

Ehrhardt, A. A., & Meyer-Bahlburg, H. F. L. (1981). Effects of prenatal sex hormones on gender-related behavior. *Science, 211,* 1312–1318.

Emde, R. N. (1980). Emotional availability: A reciprocal reward system for infants and parents with implications for prevention of psychosocial disorders. In P. M. Taylor (Ed.), *Parent-infant relationships* (pp. 87–115). Orlando, FL: Grune & Stratton.

Emde, R. N. (1983). The prerepresentational self and its affective core. *Psychoanalytic Study of the Child, 38,* 165–192.

Fagot, B. I. (1993, June). *Gender role development in early childhood: Environmental input, internal construction.* Paper presented at the International Academy of Sex Research, Pacific Grove, CA.

Fagot, B. I., Leinbach, M. D., & Hagan, R. (1986). Gender labeling and the adoption of sex-typed behaviors. *Developmental Psychology, 22,* 440–443.

Goldberg, S. (In press). Attachment and childhood behavior problems in normal, at risk, and clinical samples. In L. R. Atkinson & K. J. Zucker (Eds.), *Attach-*

ment and psychopathology. New York: Guilford Press.

Green, A. (1986). The dead mother. In A. Green, *On private madness* (pp. 142–173). Madison, CT: International Universities Press.

Green, R. (1974). *Sexual identity conflicts in children and adults.* Baltimore: Penguin Books.

Green, R. (1987). *The "sissy boy syndrome" and the development of homosexuality.* New Haven, CT: Yale University Press.

Green, R., & Money, J. (1960). Incongruous gender role: Non-genital manifestations in prepubertal boys. *Journal of Nervous and Mental Disorders, 131,* 160–168.

Green, R., Williams, K., & Goodman, M. (1982). Ninety-nine "tomboys" and "non-tomboys": Behavioral contrasts and demographic similarities. *Archives of Sexual Behavior, 11,* 247–266.

Kagan, J. (1989). *Unstable Ideas: Temperament, cognition and self.* Cambridge, MA: Harvard University Press.

Krafft-Ebing, R. (1965). *Psychopathia sexualis: A medico-forensic study* (H. Wedeck, Trans.). New York: G. P. Putnam's Sons. (Originally published 1902.)

Lyons-Ruth, K. (1991). Rapprochement or approchement: Mahler's theory reconsidered from the vantage point of recent research on early attachment relationships. *Psychoanalytic Psychology, 8* (1), 1–23.

Lyons-Ruth, K. (1992). Maternal depressive symptoms, disorganized infant-mother attachment relationships and hostile-aggressive behavior in the preschool classroom: A prospective longitudinal view from infancy to age five. In D. Ciccetti & S. L. Toth (Eds.), *Developmental perspectives on depression* (Vol. 4, pp. 131–170). Rochester Symposium on Developmental Psychopathology, Rochester, NY: University of Rochester Press.

Mahler, M., Pine, F., & Bergman, A. (1975). *The psychological birth of the human infant.* New York: Basic Books.

Marantz, S., & Coates, S. (1991). Mothers of boys with gender identity disorder: A comparison to normal controls. *Journal of the American Academy of Child and Adolescent Psychiatry, 30,* 136–143.

Meyer-Bahlburg, H. F. L. (1991). *Should the presence of intersexuality in a patient rule out the application of the diagnosis "gender identity disorder?"* Unpublished manuscript, DSM-IV Subcommittee on Gender Identity Disorders.

Mitchell, J. N. (1991). Maternal influences in gender identity disorder in boys: Searching for specificity. Unpublished doctoral dissertation, York University, Downsview, Canada.

Moll, A. (1912). *The sexual life of the child.* New York: Macmillan. (Originally published 1907.)

Money, J., Hampson, J. G., & Hampson, J. I. (1955). An examination of basis sexual concepts: The evidence of human hermaphroditism. *Bulletin of the Johns Hopkins Hospital, 97,* 301–319.

Pleak, R. R., Meyer-Bahlburg, H. F. L., O'Brien, J. D.,

Bowen, H. A. & Morganstein, A. (1989). Cross-gender behavior and psychopathology in boy psychiatric outpatients. *Journal of the American Academy of Child and Adolescent Psychiatry, 28*, 385–393.

Post, R. M. (1992). Transduction of psychosocial stress into the neurobiology of recurrent affective disorder. *American Journal of Psychiatry, 149* (8), 999–1010.

Rekers, G. A. (1977). Assessment and treatment of childhood gender problems. In B. B. Lahey & A. E. Kazdin (Eds.), *Advances in clinical child psychology* (Vol. 1, pp. 267–306). New York: Plenum Press.

Rekers, G. A. (1985). Gender identity problems. In P. A. Bornstein & A. E. Kazdin (Eds.), *Handbook of clinical behavior therapy with children* (pp. 658–659). Homewood, IL: Dorsey Press.

Saghir, M. T., & Robins, E. (1973). *Male and female homosexuality: A Comprehensive investigation.* Baltimore: Williams & Wilkins.

Stoller, R. J. (1968). *Sex and gender: Vol. 1. The development of masculinity and femininity.* New York: Science House.

Wolfe, S. (1990). *Psychopathology and psychodynamics of parents of boys with a gender identity disorder.* Unpublished doctoral dissertation, City University of New York, New York.

Zucker, K. J. (1985). Cross-gender-identified children. In B. W. Steiner (Ed.), *Gender dysphoria: Development, research, management* (pp. 75–174). New York: Plenum Press.

Zucker, K. J., Bradley, S. J., & Hughes, H. E. (1987). Gender dysphoria in a child with true hermaphroditism. *Canadian Journal of Psychiatry, 32*, 602–609.

Zucker, K. J., Bradley, S. J., & Sullivan, C. B. L. (In press). Traits of separation anxiety in boy with gender identity disorder. *Journal of the American Academy of Child and Adolescent Psychiatry, 35.*

Zucker, K. J., Bradley, S. J., Sullivan, C. B. L., Kuksis, M., Birkenfeld-Adams, A., & Mitchell, J. N. (1993). A gender identity interview for children. *Journal of Personality Assessment, 61*, 443–456.

Zucker, K. J. & Bradley, S. J. (1995). *Gender Identity Disorder and Psychosexual Problems in Children and Adolescents.* New York: Guilford Press.

Zucker, K. J., Doering, R. W., Bradley, S. J., & Finegan, J. K. (1982). Sex-typed play in gender disturbed children: A comparison to sibling and psychiatric controls. *Archives of Sexual Behavior, 11*, 309–321.

Zucker, K. J., & Green, R. (1992). Psychosexual disorders in children and adolescents. *Journal of Child Psychology and Psychiatry, 33*, (1), 107–151.

Zucker, K. J., & Green, R. (1993). Psychological and familial aspects of gender identity disorder. *Child and Adolescent Psychiatric Clinics of North America. 2* (3), 513–542.

Zuger, B. (1988). Is early effeminate behavior in boys early homosexuality? *Comprehensive Psychiatry, 29*, 509–519.

52 / Personality Disorders in Childhood and Adolescence: An Overview

Paulina F. Kernberg

Introduction

The existence of personality disorders in childhood and adolescence remains controversial. I have proposed elsewhere (Kernberg & Shapiro, 1990) that before we can talk about personality disorders in childhood, we have to consider whether children have a personality. Indeed, if we consider personality as the enduring patterns of perceiving, relating to, and thinking about the environment and the self, exhibited in a wide variety of important social contexts, or if we follow a psychoanalytic definition as Otto Fenichel (1945) has described, as the habitual modes of adjustment to

the external world, the id, and the superego, and the characteristic ways of combining these modes with one another, we can conclude that children do indeed have distinct personalities. Children show many individual differences that represent their individual synthesis of temperamental, constitutional, and genetic characteristics. They also have their own identity, which already is perceivable during school age, an age-appropriate sense of identity that describes a sense of self that is cohesive, intentional, relatively constant across situations in terms of gender, preferences, values, and that is also constant through time—past, present, and future—and with different persons. If children have individual differences, a wide variety of traits, and a sense of identity, it is also possible to see that because of genetic, constitutional, and environmental vicissitudes, these personality characteristics may be interfered with and result in personality disorders or personality trait disorders. (See Table 52.1.)

Indeed, the fourth edition of the *Diagnostic and Statistical Manual* (*DSM-IV;* American Psychiatric Association [APA], 1994) states that "personality disorder categories may be applied to children or adolescents in those relatively unusual instances in which the individual's particular maladaptive personality traits appear to be pervasive, persistent, and are unlikely to be limited to a particular developmental stage or an episode of an Axis I disorder" (p. 663). Moreover, "to diagnose a personality disorder in an individual under eighteen years, the features must have been present for at least one year" (p. 631). Even, in the case of antisocial personality disorder, "the essential feature of antisocial personality disorder is a pervasive pattern of disregard for, and violation of, the rights of others that begins in *childhood or early adolescence* and continues in adulthood" (p. 645, emphasis added). Moreover, certain children also present the associate features of disorders for antisocial personality such as lack of empathy, contemptuous attitudes for the feelings, rights, and suffering of others, inflated and arrogant self-

appraisal, superficial charm, and voluble and verbally facile communications intended to impress others who are unfamiliar with the topic. It is particularly important to consider this diagnosis for children who would meet all criteria given by the *DSM-IV* system short of age. Thus, from a descriptive perspective, if the child or adolescent meets adult criteria for a personality disorder or personality-disordered traits in a form that is consistently so across situations and across time for a minimum of 1 or more years, the child should be considered as suffering from a personality disorder. Thus, effective treatment and a realistic prognosis can be established. To pursue further this line of reasoning, I describe relevant constitutional, biological, and environmental studies related to the risk for personality disorders already present in childhood and adolescence. Next I consider the relationship between personality disorders in childhood and adulthood as well as the relationship between personality disorders and other child psychiatric syndromes. In the assessment of personality disorders, the role of defense mechanisms is referred to as one of the proposed axes in the *DSM-IV.* I include an in-depth look at narcissistic personality disorders in children, and end the chapter with general considerations of continuities and discontinuities in development and treatment.

TABLE 52.1

General Diagnostic Criteria for a Personality Disorder

A. An enduring pattern of inner experience and behavior that deviates markedly from the expectations of the individual's culture. This pattern is manifested in two (or more) of the following areas:
   (1) cognition (i.e., ways of perceiving and interpreting self, other people, and events)
   (2) affectively (i.e., the range, intensity, lability, and appropriateness of emotional response)
   (3) interpersonal functioning
   (4) impulse control

B. The enduring pattern is inflexible and pervasive across a broad range of personal and social situations.

C. The enduring pattern leads to clinically significant distress or impairment in social, occupational, or other important areas of functioning.

D. The pattern is stable and of long duration and its onset can be traced back at least to adolescence or early adulthood.

E. The enduring pattern is not better accounted for as a manifestation or consequence of another mental disorder.

F. The enduring pattern is not due to the direct physiological effects of a substance (e.g., a drug of abuse, a medication) or a general medical condition (e.g., head trauma).

Genetic and Constitutional Factors

One of the best-studied personality disorders is the borderline personality disorder. Torgersen (1994) examined the genetic aspects of this and schizotypal personality disorder. He indicates that, in general, the borderline personality disorder consists of two syndromes, an impulsive borderline and an empty borderline syndrome. Based on review of family, adoption, and twin studies, borderline personality disorder does not seem to be genetically transmitted. The comorbidity that exists between borderline personality disorder and depression, substance abuse, and antisocial personality may be artificial in that these very same comorbidities may be part of the diagnostic features of the disorder. In contrast, the genetic component of schizotypal personality, various authors have established most especially in such social features such as excessive social anxiety, odd behavior, odd speech, and inappropriate affects. The heritability of schizotypal personality disorder may be inflated in the case of false "schizotypals" among those patients with prodromal or residual symptoms of schizophrenia. Torgersen suggests that, in general, temperamental and constitutional factors account more heavily for personality whereas environmental factors play a more substantial role in personality disorders, especially cluster B personality disorders (antisocial personality, borderline personality, histrionic personality, and narcissistic personality).

Various authors have highlighted the increased incidence of childhood trauma, separation, sexual and physical abuse among children suffering from personality disorders (Herman, Perry, & Van Der Kolk, 1989; Ludolph et al., 1990; Shearer, Peters, Quaytman, & Ogden, 1990; Zanarini, Gunderson, Marino, Schwartz, & Frankenburg, 1989).

Andrulonis and his colleagues (1980), have described constitutional, biological factors, such as cognitive deficits, soft neurological signs, and episodic discontrol, which effect negatively the quality of exchanges with the environment, coping mechanisms, and the integration of identity.

Several positive findings in psychological testing seem to confirm the presence of constitutional organic factors as seen in the frequent association of personality disorders with learning disorders (Leichtman & Nathan, 1983). From another perspective, increasing evidence from prospective studies linking syndromes such as attention deficit hyperactivity disorder indicate that these children have progressive maladaptive, chronic patterns of interaction. In a five-year prospective study of a group of 91 subjects ages 10 to 18 with a control group matched for I.Q. and social class, hyperactive attention deficit disordered adolescents had 25% significant more delinquent behavior and were described as keeping their initial patterns of destructiveness, impulsivity, and immaturity (Weiss, Minde, Werry, & Douglas, 1971). Also relevant is the study by Satterfield, Hoppe, and Schell (1982) that reported on 110 adolescents, with an average age of 17.3 years at follow-up, with attention deficit disorder. Fifty percent of these adolescents had a felony arrest for burglary, grand theft, or assault with a weapon, compared to less than 10% of the controls; that is, these subjects had turned into severe conduct disorders. Moreover, in a 15-year follow-up of hyperactive youngsters, 23% had an antisocial personality disorder (Weiss & Hechtman, 1986). The implication from all these studies is that these children had, as children, personality disorder traits and, in the more severe conduct disorders, personality disorders.

Siever and Davis (1991) proposed a psychobiological look at the personality disorders in adults. Table 52.2 presents their summary of the existence of genetic and biological aspects of personality. These interrelationships need to be considered present since early childhood; it is unlikely that they appear for the first time in adulthood.

These authors suggest a possible relationship among personality disorders, defense and coping strategies, and characteristic traits that may coexist with the Axis I disorder. In other words, these factors are indeed in operation in childhood. Judith Rapoport (Rapoport & Ismond, 1990) has proposed some continuities between childhood disorders and adult personality disorders such as childhood pervasive developmental disorders continuing into adult schizotypal personality, the avoidant personality disorders leading to the adult form of the same name, childhood conduct disorders, and attention deficit disorders leading to adult borderline personality disorders, narcissistic personality disorders and/or antisocial personality

TABLE 52.2

Genetic and Biological Aspects of Personality

Dimension	Axis I Disorder	Axis II Disorder	Biological Indexes	Characteristic Traits	Defenses and Coping Strategies
Cognitive/ perceptual organization	Schizophrenia	Odd cluster (schizotypal personality disorder)	Eye movement dysfunction,[a] continuous performance task backward masking test,[a] plasma HVA,[a] CSF HVA,[a] evoked potential response, VBR	Disorganization, psychoticlike symptoms	Social isolation, detachment guardedness
Impulsivity/ aggression	Impulse Disorders	Dramatic cluster (borderline and antisocial personality disorders)	CSF 5-HIAA,[a] responses to serotonergic challenge, galvanic skin response,[a] continuous performance task	Readiness to action, irritability/ aggression	Externalization, dissociation, enactment, repression
Affective instability	Major Affective Disorders	Dramatic cluster (borderline and possibly histrionic personality disorders)	REM latency, responses to cholinergic challenges,[a] responses to catecholaminergic challenges[a]	Environmentally responsive, transient affective shifts	Exaggerated affectivity, "manipulativeness," "splitting"
Anxiety/ Inhibition	Anxiety Disorders	Anxious cluster (avoidant personality disorder)	Heart rate variability,[a] orienting responses, responses to lactate and yohimbine	Autonomic arousal, fearfulness, inhibition	Avoidant, compulsive, and dependent behaviors

[a]Preliminary data are available in patients with personality disorder.

NOTE. HVA = homovanillic acid; CSF = cerebrospinal fluid; VBR = ventricular brain ratio; 5-HIAA = 5-hydroxyindoleacetic acid; REM = rapid eye movement. From "A Psychobiological Perspective on the Personality Disorders," by L. J. Siever and K. Davis, *American Journal of Psychiatry, 148* (12), 1649.

disorders. The presence of personality disorders in adolescent patients who have completed suicide has been reported.

Frequently associated with Axis II personality disorders are eating disturbances, elective mutism, conduct disorders, oppositional defiant disorders, and attention deficit disorders. Axis I diagnoses such as phobias and separation-anxiety disorders can be associated with narcissistic personality disorders once the Axis I syndrome is addressed. It is important to reiterate that all these traits have to be chronic and seriously maladaptive to fulfill the criteria for personality disorders or disordered traits.

Specific Defense Mechanisms and Coping Styles in Relation to Personality Characteristics

From the perspective of defense mechanisms that can be defined operationally by defensive behaviors (Kernberg, 1994; Wallerstein, 1983), there is a convergent validity to the fact that certain personality disorders tend to use clusters of characteristic defenses—cluster B personality disorders (borderline personality, narcissistic personality, antisocial personality, and histrionic personality disorders). These defense mechanisms are splitting, projective identification, acting out, devaluation, omnipotence, and denial. These defensive behaviors can be evaluated through their particular forms of language, affect regulation, representation of self and others, and the capacity to observe self and others in the clinical interview setting (Selzer, Kernberg, Fibel, Cherbuliez, & Mortati, 1987).

Cluster C personality disorders, such as avoidant, dependent, obsessive, and compulsive personality disorders, tend to use intellectualization, isolation of affect, rationalization, and reaction formation,—that is, a cluster of neurotic defenses. Clinically, in children and adolescents, it is possible to see these patterns of defenses not only in personal interaction but through the quality of the play narratives.

Family Contributions

As for family contributions, Biederman, Munik, and Knee (1987) have reported that 64% of first-degree relatives of the children with attention deficit hyperactivity disorder presented a diagnosis of conduct disorder or oppositional disorder; significantly higher rates of antisocial personality disorder as well as other Axis I diagnoses, such as nonbipolar depressive disorder and anxious disorder, occurred in the relatives than in their control group.

As Hechtman (1989) has pointed out, in all of these factors not one predictor leads to a particular outcome; rather outcome depends on the incremental interaction of a variety of personality characteristics plus social and familial parameters. Indeed, the mental health of the family members, I.Q., and socioeconomic level are important factors for prediction in interplay with coexistent aggressive, conduct, or oppositional disorder. As proposed by Kernberg (1991), genetic and biological factors play a role in normal personality development in areas such as attention, memory, affect modulation, spatial orientation, and the quality of attachment. Indeed, Rutter and Hersov (1985) have described the importance of insecure attachment in the development of personality disorders.

It is now widely accepted that attachment patterns persist into adulthood and affect the working models of relatedness to self and others.

A developmental formulation for personality disorders can be based on Sandler and Rosenblatt's concept of the representational world (1962). In this context genetic, constitutional, and environmental factors impinge on the formation of self-representation, the representation of other important people in the individual's life, and the affective context of these self and object representational, or internal working schema. The same factors codetermine particular coping styles and/or defense mechanisms (Kernberg, 1994). Individual differences then predispose the person to acquire a personality style or a disordered personality style with the particular distortions of self and other internal representations and concomitant problems in the modulation of affects. The people resort to typical defense mechanisms and coping style clusters in moments of trauma and with regard to internal or external stressors. With chronic use of maladaptive patterns of coping and defensive styles, which further weaken the ego, the subject's personality becomes more rigid and maladaptive; in other words, a personality disorder is brought about.

Personality Assessment in Children and Adolescents

A number of personality assessment methodologies are available to the clinician. In Young, O'Brien, Gutterman, and Cohen's (1987) review of research on the clinical interview, one of six semistructured and structured interviews for children and adolescents included the assessment of borderline compulsive, histrionic, and schizotypal personality disorders for adolescents. Gunderson's Diagnostic Interview for Borderline Personality Disorders (McManus, 1984) and an adaptation of the Ronningtram, Gundersson Personality Disorder Diagnostic Interview for adolescents with narcissistic Personality Disorder (Kernberg, Hajal, & Normandin, in press) are equally useful for the corresponding personality disorders in adolescents.

Selzer, Kernberg, and their colleagues (1987) have developed an assessment interview for adolescents that assesses personality structure along six essential components: cognition, affects, self-representations, object representations, capacity to empathize with the interviewer, and capacity to observe the self (i.e., the observing ego). In this interview, patients not only talk about their personality characteristics but demonstrate their capacities to communicate and modulate affect, demonstrate defensive behaviors, as well as report on self-representations and object representations in a way that provides information about their personality structure.

Narcissistic Personality Disorders

Here we explore how the diagnostic criteria for narcissistic personality disorder (see Table 52.3), as outlined by the *DSM-IV* for adults, can exist in children and adolescents. Because these findings are less widely known, they are examined in more detail.

Additional developmental characteristics in children are related especially to play, patterns of peer interaction, patterns of academic performance, and gaze. Various implications are derived from the descriptive aspects of the narcissistic personality disorder in children's sense of self and patterns of interactions with family, friends and peers, and school performance. Because of their exaggerated sense of self-importance and, their lack of empathy with others, the level of their social interactions is very impaired. At best the children exploit other children and consider them as "employees" (Egan & Kernberg, 1984). Due to their sense of entitlement, these youngsters are prone to low frustration tolerance so that temper outbursts and rages are part of their everyday life. Moreover, because of their intense exploitativeness and sense of entitlement, they frequently are prone to manipulating others, lying, stealing, and other antisocial behaviors.

Since they require a constant sense of admiration to maintain their grandiosity, they have a paradoxical contrast between a self-centered and heightened sense of themselves on one hand, so that they appear haughty and arrogant, while at

TABLE 52.3

Diagnostic Criteria for 301.81 Narcissistic Personality Disorder

A pervasive pattern of grandiosity (in fantasy or behavior), need for admiration, and lack of empathy, beginning by early adulthood and present in a variety of contexts, as indicated by five (or more) of the following:

(1) has a grandiose sense of self-importance (e.g., exaggerates achievements and talents, expects to be recognized as superior without commensurate achievements)

(2) is preoccupied with fantasies of unlimited success, power, brilliance, beauty, or ideal love

(3) believes that he or she is "special" and unique and can only be understood by, or should associate with, other special or high-status people (or institutions)

(4) requires excessive admiration

(5) has a sense of entitlement, i.e., unreasonable expectations of especially favorable treatment or automatic compliance with his or her expectations

(6) is interpersonally exploitative, i.e., takes advantage of others to achieve his or her own ends

(7) lacks empathy: is unwilling to recognize or identify with the feelings and needs of others

(8) is often envious of others or believes that others are envious of him or her

(9) shows arrogant, haughty behaviors or attitudes

NOTE. From *Diagnostic and Statistical Manual of Mental Disorders*, (4th ed., p. 661), American Psychiatric Association, 1994, Washington, DC: Author. Copyright 1994 by the American Psychiatric Association. Reprinted with permission.

the same time they are extremely vulnerable and hypersensitive to criticism. Their sense of self-esteem, therefore, is in a precarious equilibrium. They cannot tolerate the frustration of having to accommodate to environmental constraints; their grandiosity is threatened. An example of this characteristic can be gleaned from their fluctuating levels of academic performance. These children feel entitled; they do not find it easy to have to apply themselves to master a new subject at school; either they get the best grades if they do not have to apply themselves or they get the worst grades at school due to their lack of effort. They develop a functional learning disability that has a different profile from the classical learning disabilities consisting of specific deficits in reading, writing, or in arithmetic.

Kernberg (1989) has outlined other clinical manifestations of narcissistic personality disorder in children. In order to elaborate these characteristics, it is important to contrast the pathological self-centeredness of these children with what is considered the normal narcissism of childhood. In normal narcissism, children's need for dependence and admiration is fulfilled by the age-appropriate attention that they receive. They are able to acknowledge nurturing with reciprocity and gratitude. In contrast, children with a narcissistic pathology deny their dependence, receive nurturance with a sense of entitlement, and do not reciprocate or experience any sense of gratitude.

In normal infantile narcissism, the tendency to be involved in exaggerated achievements and talents has to do with playful fantasies of being a superachiever or having extraordinary powers—children can play at being Superman. In the pathological narcissism of the narcissistic personality disorder, children have a strong belief that they have already achieved what they wish to be and there is nothing playful in this experience of the self (Egan and Kernberg, 1984). Normal children's dependency and demands on the environment correspond to realistic demands and can be fulfilled. In narcissistic personality disorder, the demands and coercion on the environment preclude any sense of gratification and appreciation. The envy that the children experience from the fact that they are not the center of all that is good and that there are others who have things that these children need impairs their capacity to receive and to be fulfilled. Because of their grandiosity, children with narcissistic personality disorder cannot admit that they do not have all outstanding traits or attributes.

ACADEMIC PERFORMANCE

Children with narcissistic personality disorder do not enjoy their learning experiences. While often they are good students, their learning is aimed at getting admiration from others rather than learning for the intrinsic value of knowledge or personal achievements.

IMPAIRED SOCIAL AND PEER INTERACTIONS

These children either do not have friends or lose friends more frequently than others. They are unable to empathize or appreciate the company of others unless the other child submits to their own grandiosity. It is not surprising that eventually these children are rejected by peers and friends.

In their peer interactions, these children are at a disadvantage because they cannot tolerate differences between themselves and others; because of their envy, they react with aloofness and haughtiness, which alienates peers. At best these children can be coercive and possessive. Reciprocity, which is normally expected in the school-age years, is practically nonexistent. In sum, peer relations and friendships are seriously impaired or at times absent.

GAZE AVERSION

The finding of gaze aversion in children with narcissistic personality disorder may have multiple determinants. The inability or refusal to have eye contact seems to be in the service of preserving the illusion that these patients are special, powerful, supergifted people, so any comparison with others is avoided to the extent that the patients literally do not look around. This characteristic also likely stems from the very early years, when these children did not receive the full emotional recognition of a parent who acknowledged their separateness and individuality; consequently, the children avoid the pain of not being fully acknowledged by their caregiver.

PLAY PATHOLOGY

Narcissistic children become bored easily with toys and, during their initial assessment, complain that there is nothing worthwhile in the playroom. This can be attributed to an inhibition of play. Several psychodynamic sources may account for this phenomena. First the children use devaluation to protect their inflated sense of self. Thus, it is not they who may have some problems in interacting and playing, but it is the toys that are not good. In addition, this boredom may disguise a sense of being threatened by the possibility of being defeated in structured games, defeat that may precipitate rages or temper tantrums. In the treatment process, narcissistic children defend against fantasies of sadistic and raw aggression where toys are dismantled, human dolls are dismembered, and massacres occur. This primitive aggression underlies a surface presentation of boredom.

616

SEPARATION ANXIETY

Another paradox in these youngsters occurs in the presence of separation anxiety. It is difficult to understand initially how children who show themselves as powerful, self-important, and entitled can feel so vulnerable that they cannot let go of their caregiver. They find it difficult to leave the house. They cannot go away for sleepovers or to sleep-away camp. Indeed, because their caregiver gives them the feedback necessary for the maintenance of their grandiose self, these children are extremely vulnerable to being alone. However, the separation anxiety is not a source of chief complaint; the grandiosity of these all-powerful children diverts the clinician's attention to aspects other than the sense of frailty these children experiences when confronted with separation or aloneness. Parents are indeed frequently apprehensive as to how their children will do without them. Their caregiver's presence serves as an auxiliary support to the grandiose self of these children that they take for granted. A example is of a 3½-year-old who would insist that his mother come into the room during treatment, but once the mother was in the room, he would not even look at or acknowledge her.

PREOCCUPATION WITH SELF-IMAGE

A variety of aspects concern the obsession with their mirror reflection of children with a narcissistic personality disorder. These children have a mirror addiction, spending a long time looking at themselves in a compulsive manner as if the mirror could give feedback to them as to who and what they are. However, the fact that their need to look at the mirror is never satisfied illustrates the missing human mirroring interaction with the caregiver. *Justin's Reflection* is the title of a videotape (Broussard, 1983) of a 4½-year-old boy who was considered at risk for a psychiatric disorder. At follow-up at age 17, he presented a narcissistic personality disorder. At 4½ Justin showed this fascination with his mirror image to the extent that he would spend long periods of time looking at himself, his gestures, his arms, while he excluded other people. The same preoccupation also can be seen in the investment in the body of narcissistic children, with frequent associated somatic complaints.

Kernberg, Hajal, and Normandin (in press) have applied through record reviews, the criteria of the Diagnostic Interview for Narcissism by Gunderson, Ronningstam, and Bodkin (1990) to an adolescent inpatient population ranging from ages 12 to 17. They found that there was a spectrum from moderate to high levels of narcissistic personality disorders even in the almost 50% of cases without a personality disorder in the discharged diagnoses. A greater degree of severity was found among the patients who did meet the criteria for narcissistic personality disorder. The category that accounted for the highest percentage of the variance was the quality of interpersonal relations (52.7%). The combination of grandiosity and reactiveness, a scale related to hypersensitivity, accounted for 87.6% of the variance. Moral and social adaptation category added to the variance so that 90.7% of adolescents could be predicted to have a narcissistic personality disorder, when their interpersonal relations, their grandiosity, and reactiveness scales and moral and social adaptation problems were combined.

PSYCHOLOGICAL TESTING

Projective psychological testing may contribute to an independent validation of this diagnosis. Abrams (1993) reported that in the child apperception test, heroes are at the same time ineffectual, wimpy, and overwhelmed. Father figures are seen mostly as immature, incompetent, boastful buffoons. Mother figures have contradictory aspects, from nurturing, to unprotective, to critical, immature, and self-centered. Peers are seen as undifferentiated or acting in parallel, compliant, or triumphant. Junior figures are not mentioned. This is an interesting aspect, for these youngsters already have intense problems of sibling rivalry bordering on sibling envy and outright sibling abuse. All cognitive functions seem to be intact. However, control of drives, mastery competence, and defensive functions are deficient, with the children resorting to less mature defenses. The world of object relations as described in the testing reflects little differentiation between people; they do not seem to be distinct individuals with clear identities but are instead shadowy, vague, and exaggerated, ineffectual, unprotecting, and unnurturing.

In a preliminary study, Bardenstein (1993) has reported on the Exner system characteristics in the Rorschach testing in children with narcissistic personality disorders. In the self-perception category, these children show reflection responses, a feature that is not common in nonpatient samples. The egocentricity index was remarkably high in 6 of 9 patients. They tend to be more hypervigilant, interpersonally guarded, and show ineffective, chaotic interpersonal skills. In terms of their style of thinking, they are more introversive—in other words, their thinking is less attuned to external reality. They also expect to have situations magically resolved by external agents. Anger with sadistic overtones, oppositionalism, and intolerance were also differential characteristics found in their Rorschach testing. Affects in general and anger specifically were felt to be uncontrollable. In addition to their hypervigilance, the subjects show very limited cooperative responses; this explains the lack of reciprocity seen clinically in their peer relationships.

CASE EXAMPLE

Matt: This case is abstracted from Egan and Kernberg (1984). Matt was 8 years old when he came for a diagnostic evaluation. He had severe social problems in nursery school and had problems that persisted during elementary school. His classmates avoided him and used him as a scapegoat. He in turn tended to be domineering and ordering others as if they were his slaves. He was an intelligent child functioning at the superior level but his grades and actual achievements were significantly below his potential, although there was no organic impairment. He did not participate in any sports and could not swim, ride a bicycle, skate, or throw a ball, as he was unable to confront himself with his need to put the slightest effort to learn these skills.

Matt was the older of two children. He physically tortured his younger brother, who was born after careful planning on the part of his parents, who did not want to inflict such a pain as having a younger sibling on their firstborn. Mother doted on her oldest child, attempting to fulfill her own ideals and ambitions through him. She was the dominant figure in the family, and Matt had identified with his mother's style in attempting to dominate his peers.

Mother's administrative and executive talents made her a prominent member in the community. This trait in regard to her son translated into her controlling Matt in his daily routine, in what he ate and how he dressed to such an extent that he had to develop narcissistic defenses to erect a grandiose self as a defense against the experience of being intruded upon and controlled by his mother. He considered himself a peer of his teachers and devalued his therapist to the point of insulting him at each session and setting tests for him aimed at making him look stupid.

In spite of Matt's serious difficulties in his daily life and his lack of friendships, he denied the existence of any problem and the importance of the therapist to him. He continually conveyed his sense of boredom and irritation at having to come to his sessions.

By age 8 Matt already had fulfilled the criteria of a personality diagnosis of narcissistic personality disorder with stability of his personality traits across time and across situations.

Matt's family dynamics and family structure illustrate some of the characteristics of the parents of these children. Mother was herself a narcissistic person who idealized her child and did not acknowledge his vulnerabilities. She only saw him as an agent for her own self-esteem. Father in turn was passive and seemed to be marginal in exerting his authority.

The parents illustrated Rinsley's description (1989) in that they facilitated a sense of individuation in terms of achievements but they did not facilitate a sense of separation as the child could not function as an autonomous person nor could he experience himself as such. In this connection adopted children, abusive children, overindulged or wealthy children, and children of divorce may be at risk for this psychopathology. In each of these special situations the child may be considered to be an extension of the parent's wishes and needs unable to separate and to function autonomously. If the child is there to replace the father, such as in the case of divorce, he fulfills the normal infantile wishes of competing against the same-sex parent; or if the parent wants to eradicate all traits of the former marital partner in his or her child, the child may need to develop a sense of grandiosity and entitlement to protect him- or herself from this experience of interference with an autonomous sense of self—although in many of these different circumstances, what happens is a prolongation of infantile narcissism, as in the case of the overindulged child or the physically handicapped child. The following dynamic family constellations, in different combinations, may trigger this syndrome:

- A dependent, insecure mother who wants her own child to increase her sense of self-esteem by behaving like a perfect little boy.
- A father who seems to be unable to establish his

authority and appears extremely indulgent and unable to set consistent limits.

- A mother's overinvolvement and intrusiveness, which does not allow the child to develop a sense of his or her own body and his or her own separate self. (Here the infantile narcissistic gratification of being the center of mother's attention becomes distorted because mother is experienced as an invader triggering aggressive impulses that interfere with separateness.)
- Parents who are unable to assume their roles as parents by failing to establish generational boundaries leave the child emotionally neglected regarding his or her needs to overcome and grow out of infantile omnipotence.
- Parents who do not provide feedback to their child and who do not convey a sense of emotional availability induce in the child the need to be his or her own ideal parent to compensate for the frustrating external caregiver.

ASSOCIATION WITH AXIS I *DSM-IV* DISORDERS

Depressive disorders, anxiety disorders, especially separation anxiety and phobias, anorexia nervosa, and disruptive disorders are frequent comorbid conditions in children and adolescents who are hospitalized—that is, in the more severe forms of pathological narcissism or narcissistic personality disorder. It is important to consider this Axis II diagnosis (*DSM-IV*) in conjunction with other Axis II diagnoses, such as borderline and antisocial personality disorders. Narcissistic personality disorders in which the antisocial behavior is marked particularly worsens the prognosis.

TREATMENT APPROACHES

The aim of treatment is to transform the patient's pathological narcissism into a normal infantile narcissism in the case of a child or normal narcissism, in the case of an adolescent. This implies that the various maladaptive ways of self-esteem regulation should be addressed so that sources of gratification and self-reward promote rather than interfere with emotional development. A first consideration has to do with a need for the therapist to have both a psychodynamic background as well as a developmental understanding of the factors entering into this pathology so that specific focused interventions can address the developmental level of the patient and the specific personality pathology.

Individual Therapy: Insight oriented psychoanalytic treatment is recommended with sessions twice to four times a week at a minimum. One important goal is the resolution of the grandiosity and self-centeredness. What Kohut (1971, 1972) described as the grandiose self is the personality structure that accounts for 7 of the 9 criteria described in the *DSM-IV*, (APA, 1994), namely a grandiose sense of importance, preoccupation with fantasies of unlimited success, feeling unique, entitled, exploitative, arrogant, and haughty. The goal here is to help patients see the disadvantages of their "solution," to enable them to begin to accept their realistic assets, and to accept that they have not reached some of their idealized versions of themselves so that there will be self-ideals that they will try to strive toward. They also will learn to accept that others have qualities the patients can emulate without appropriating and assuming that they have all those qualities. The pathological regulation of self-esteem maintains the grandiosity, hence these individuals require constant excessive admiration and lack empathy with others.

In the relationship with the therapist, these personality traits unfold and need to be clarified so that patients can confront themselves with these maladaptive solutions while they learn to acquire alternative ways of dealing with their needs for positive self-esteem and self-regard.

The next goal is to change the immature defense mechanisms that maintain this pathology so that higher-level coping mechanisms be achieved. In order to protect their grandiosity, these patients resort to splitting, denial, idealization, omnipotent control, projective identification, and most characteristically devaluation. All these mechanisms of defense (O. Kernberg, 1975) weaken the ego's capacities and therefore the individual's effective adaptation to others and to their surroundings. What is characteristic of these immature primitive defense mechanisms is that they are expressed interpersonally, hence the impaired interactions with others that these patients induce. Work with these personality traits requires tact and empathy as the patients have a vulnerable self-esteem; many patients may drop out of treatment, become intensely depressed, or act out if they are confronted with their patterns without tact or an appropriate sense of timing.

Third, the patients' characterological depression needs to be understood in terms of their progressive realization that they have had an illusion of self-sufficiency, achievement, and relationships caused by their grandiosity; at the same time they need to explore how this has been self-deceiving and maladaptive.

In terms of their separation anxiety, working on the resolution of the grandiose self and on the use of more mature coping mechanisms is beneficial. Target medications during this transition period may be helpful.

Another goal is to work actively on age-appropriate peer relationships. The capacity to have and to maintain friendships is a most important factor in self-esteem regulation. For this purpose, the therapist needs to facilitate patients' empathy and tolerance for relationships from dyadic or one-to-one relations to triadic or more complex relationships so that they can tolerate not being the exclusive center of attention and become more aware of the presence of reciprocal exchanges with others.

Narcissistic Transferences: The therapist must work tactfully on making the children realize the disadvantages of their grandiose self. To achieve this goal, various paradigms in the relationship that unfolds with the therapist may need to be pointed out—patients' tendency to feel that they are twins of the therapist; how they eliminate differences with the therapist that can make them feel envious; how they either need the therapist to admire them unconditionally, not to threaten their vulnerable self-esteem, or need to see the therapist as admirable and all-powerful, in order to bask in his or her shadow; or, at times, their need to devalue the therapist while thinking they can be a better therapist to themselves. These paradigms of what Kohut (1971, 1972) has described as narcissistic transferences in adults can be seen in children as well. When these distorted forms of relating are worked through with the children so that they can see not only the advantages but more important the disadvantages of this illusory ways of relating, the children can slowly give up these immature forms of interactions or immature defenses or coping styles and reassume development.

Countertransference: Therapist effectiveness may be threatened by the fact that these patients tend to provoke the therapist toward a rejecting behavior or to induce the therapist to withdraw due to the intense emotions, including devaluation, aggression, and envy that patients reenact in the therapeutic relationship. Moreover, the therapist may submit to patients' grandiosity and omnipotent control by trying to appease them rather than to work directly with these problematic interactions.

Group therapy: Group therapy is psychodynamic in its theoretical framework. Work with the interpersonal difficulties as they now emerge not only between the group therapist and the patient but between peers in the small group may be quite effective in some youngsters who have extreme impairment both in their perception of others and in their social skills in friendships and peer interactions.

Family therapy: Family therapy can be useful, because the family tends to maintain the pathological interactions that patients employ; the use of primitive defense mechanisms, such as devaluations, idealizations, and appeasement, tend to occur and the family withdraws or submits to the patients. Thus the object relational theoretical framework is applied to specific family therapy techniques (Berkowitz, Shapiro, Zinner, & Shapiro, 1974).

Histrionic Personality Disorder

CASE EXAMPLE

Tina: Six-year-old Tina already showed some characteristics of histrionic personality disorder. She was extremely envious of her younger brother and was chronically dissatisfied and demanding of her parents since his birth. She was haughty and so eager to be the center of attention that at school nobody wanted to be next to her. During the evaluation she behaved in a theatrical manner, coming in with a scarf that was dragging on the floor. She was constantly demanding to be the center of attention, and she had exaggerated facial and emotional expressions. She was extremely seductive toward her father, kissing him on the mouth frequently, while she complained of aches and pains to obtain a nurturing response from her mother.

Treatment of Personality Disorders

Most personality disorders can benefit from individual psychodynamic psychotherapy or child psychoanalysis aimed to work on the impulsivity, and the identity problems and to resolve patterns of maladaptive interaction with their underlying conflicts, so that more adaptive and higher-level defenses may replace the more maladaptive and/or primitive ones.

Although this particular approach has been described for adults, a similar psychodynamic expressive psychotherapy for adolescents has similar outcomes. Usually long-term psychotherapy occurs two to four times a week. Therapists must be specially trained to be able to contain the stormy course of treatment and not to be driven into pathological role interactions. Gunderson (1994) has described a course of this treatment for adults, which is applicable to adolescents as well. In terms of social function from several interpersonal relations to more stable friendships, from a position of distrust toward the therapist toward a dependent, collaborative and warm relationship. This type of successful outcome requires patients who can establish a therapeutic alliance and therapists of particular skill and training.

For younger children, a supportive, expressive approach is indicated, as described by Kernberg (1983). The psychoanalytic oriented psychotherapy should be conducted optimally two to three times a week for a minimum of 1 to 3 years. Play materials should be simple and include opportunity for use. These children have difficulties in symbolic play, and their capacity to play needs to be encouraged and modeled. Objectives of this type of therapy focus on identity, on superego functions, and on social skills as these children present themselves first with the therapist and then in relation to others. The treatment also includes family therapy and counseling to liberate the child from the interfamilial interactions that maintain the pathology.

Medication may be indicated for comorbid target syndromes; for example, a low dose of neuroleptics can help in reducing the tendency to severe regression in some of these children, or methylphenidate helps children with attention deficit disorders. Medication enables some children to integrate and utilize the psychotherapeutic experience better.

Prognosis of personality disorders can be significantly improved, provided intervention occurs for children and their immediate environment, the family, and provided long-term treatment is offered (Fonagy & Target, 1994).

REFERENCES

Abrams, D. M. (1993). Pathological narcissism in an eight year old boy: An example of Bellak's TAT and CAT diagnostic system. *Psychoanalytic Psychology, 10*(4), 573–591.

American Psychiatric Association. (1994). *Diagnostic and statistical manual of mental disorders* (4th ed.) Washington, DC: Author.

Andrulonis, P. A., Glueck, B. C., Stroebel, C. F., Vogel, N. G., Shapiro, A. L., & Aldridge, D. M. (1980). Organic brain dysfunction and the borderline syndrome. *Psychiatric Clinics of North America, 4,* 47–66.

Berkowitz, D. A., Shapiro, R. L., Zinner, J., & Shapiro, E. R. (1974). Family contributions to narcissistic disturbances in adolescents. *International Review of Psychonalysis, 1,* 353–362.

Bardenstein, K. (1993). *Psychological testing in the exner system of Rorschach interpretation in narcissistic personality disorders.* Paper presented at the annual meeting of the American Psychological Association Annual Conference, Chicago.

Biederman, J., Munik, K., & Knee, D. (1987). Conduct and oppositional disorders in clinically referred children with attention deficit disorder: A controlled family study. *Journal of the American Academy of Child and Adolescent Psychiatry, 26,* 724–727.

Broussard, E. (1983). *Justin's reflection* [Videotape]. Pittsburgh: University of Pittsburgh Graduate School of Public Health, Department of Health Services Administration. Infant-Family Resource Program.

Egan, J., & Kernberg, P. F. (1984). Pathological narcissism in childhood. *Journal of the American Psychoanalytic Association, 32*(1), 39–62.

Fonagy, P., & Target M. (1994). The efficacy of psychoanalysis for children with disruptive disorders. *Journal of the American Academy of Child and Adolescent Psychiatry, 33*(1), 45–55.

Fenichel, O. (1945). *The psychoanalytic theory of neurosis.* New York: W. W. Norton.

Gunderson, J. G. (1994). Building structure for the borderline construct. *Acta Psychiatrica Scandinavica, 89* (Suppl.), 12–18.

Gunderson J., Ronningstam, E., & Bodkin, A. (1990). The diagnostic interview for narcissistic patients. *Archives of General Psychiatry, 47,* 676–680.

Hechtman, L. (1989). Attention deficit hyperactivity disorder in adolescence and adulthood: An updated follow-up. *Psychiatric Annals, 19*(11), 597–603.

Herman, J. L., Perry, J. C., & Van Der Kolk, B. A. (1989). Childhood trauma in borderline personality disorder. *American Journal of Psychiatry, 146,* 490–495.

Kernberg, O. F. (1975). Normal and pathological narcissism. In *Borderline conditions and pathological narcissism* (pp. 315–343). New York: Jason Aronson.

Kernberg, P. F. (1983). Issues in the psychotherapy of borderline conditions in children. In K. S. Robson (Ed.), *The borderline child* (pp. 223–234). New York: McGraw-Hill.

Kernberg, P. F. (1989). Narcissistic personality disorder in childhood. *Psychiatric Clinics of North America, 12*(3), 671–693.

Kernberg, P. F. (1991). Personality disorders. In J. M. Wiener (Ed.), *Textbook of child and adolescent psychiatry* (pp. 515–533). Washington, DC: American Psychiatric Press.

Kernberg, P. F. (1994). Mechanisms of defense: Development and research perspectives. *Bulletin of the Menninger Clinic, 58*(1), 55–87.

Kernberg, P. F., Hajal, F., & Normandin, L. (In press). Narcissistic personality disorders in adolescent inpatients: Descriptive characteristics and treatment issues. In E. Ronningstam (Ed.), *Disorders of narcissism: Theoretical, empirical, and clinical implications.* Washington, DC: American Psychiatric Press.

Kernberg, P. F., & Shapiro, T. (1990). Resolved: Borderline personality exists in children under twelve. Debate Forum Series Editor Lenore C. Terr, M.D. *American Academy of Child and Adolescent Psychiatry, 29*(3), 478–483.

Kestenbaum, C. J. (1983). The borderline child at risk for major psychiatric disorder in adult life: Seven case reports with follow-up. In K. S. Robson (Ed.), *The borderline child: Approaches to etiology, diagnosis and treatment* (pp. 50–81). New York: McGraw-Hill.

Kohut, H. (1971). *The analysis of the self.* New York: International Universities Press.

Kohut, H. (1972). Thoughts of narcissism and narcissistic rage. *Psychoanalytic Study of the Child, 27,* 360–400.

Kohut, H. (1980). Diagnosis and treatment of borderline and narcissistic children and adolescents. *Bulletin of the Menninger Clinic, 442,*(2), 147–170.

Leichtman, M., & Nathan, S. (1983). A clinical approach to the psychological testing of borderline children. In K. S. Robson (Ed.), *The borderline child: Approaches to etiology, diagnosis and treatment* (pp. 121–170). New York: McGraw-Hill.

Ludolph, P. S., Westen, D., Misle, B., Jackson, A., Wixom, J., & Wiss, F. C. (1990). The borderline diagnosis in adolescents: Symptoms and developmental history. *American Journal of Psychiatry 147,* 470–476.

McManus, M. (1984). Assessment of borderline symptomology in hospitalized adolescents. *Journal of the American Academy of Child and Adolescent Psychiatry, 23*(6), 685–694.

Petti, T. A., & Law, M. (1982). Borderline psychotic behaviors in hospitalized children: Approaches to assessment and treatment. *Journal of the American Academy of Child and Adolescent Psychiatry, 21,* 197–202.

Rapoport, J. L., & Ismond, D. R. (1990). *DSM-III-R training guide for diagnosis of childhood disorders.* New York: Brunner/Mazel.

Rinsley, D. (1989). Notes on the developmental pathogenesis of narcissistic personality disorder. *Psychiatric Clinics of North America, 12,* 695–707.

Rutter, M., & Hersov, L. (1985). Psychopathology and development: Links between childhood and adult life. In M. Rutter and L. Hersov (Eds.), *Child and adolescent psychiatry: Modern approaches* (pp. 720–739). Oxford: Blackwell Scientific Publications.

Sandler, J., & Rosenblatt, B. (1962). The concept of the representational world. *Psychoanalytic Study of the Child, 17,* 128–145.

Satterfield, J., Hoppe, C., & Schell, A. (1982). A perspective study of delinquency in 110 adolescent boys with attention deficit disorder and 88 normal adolescent boys. *American Journal of Psychiatry, 139,* 797–798.

Siever, L. J., & Davis, K. (1991). A psychobiological perspective on the personality disorders. *American Journal of Psychiatry, 148*(12), 1647–1658.

Selzer, M. A., Kernberg, P. F., Fibel, B., Cherbuliez, T., & Mortati, S. G. (1987). The Personality Assessment Interview: Preliminary report. *Psychiatry, 50*(2), 142–153.

Shearer, L. S., Peters, C. P., Quaytman, M. S., & Ogden, R. L. (1990). Frequency and correlates of childhood sexual and physical abuse histories in adult female borderline inpatients. *American Journal of Psychiatry, 147,* 214–216.

Torgersen, S. (1994). Genetics in borderline conditions. *Acta Psychiatrica Scandinavia, 89* (Suppl. 379), 19–25.

Wallerstein, R. (1983). Defenses, defensive mechanisms, and the structure of the mind. *Journal of the American Psychoanalytic Association, 31*(Suppl.), 201–225.

Weiss, G., Minde, K., Werry, J., & Douglas, V. (1971).

A five year follow-up study of 91 hyperactive school children. *Archives of General Psychiatry, 24*(2), 409–414.

Weiss, G., & Hechtman, L. (1986). *Hyperactive children grown up.* New York: Guilford Press.

Young, J. G., O'Brien, J. D., Gutterman, E. M., & Cohen, P. (1987). Research on the clinical interview.

Journal of the American Academy of Child and Adolescent Psychiatry, 26(5), 613–620.

Zanarini, M. C., Gunderson, J. G., Marino, M. F., Schwartz, E. O., & Frankenburg, F. R. (1989). Childhood experiences of borderline patients. *Comprehensive Psychiatry, 30*, 18–25.

53 / Childhood Schizophrenia

Mae S. Sokol

Childhood-onset schizophrenia is among the most severe psychiatric disorders. In many ways, it is more devastating to children and their families than most physical illnesses. Psychotic symptoms impair not only the ability to interact with others appropriately but impede normal development, sometimes irreversibly. While the importance of understanding these symptoms is evident, little is known thus far. Much of the early literature on psychotic children is ambiguous due to diagnostic confusion and frequent changes in nomenclature, as well as methodological flaws. Further, until recently all functional psychotic disorders in childhood were referred to as "childhood schizophrenia." In this chapter the term *childhood schizophrenia* refers to schizophrenia as defined in the fourth edition of the *Diagnostic and Statistical Manual of Mental Disorders* (DSM-IV; American Psychiatric Association [APA], 1994) in children under 12 years old. Pubertal status will not be specified as its role has not been clearly delineated in the literature.

Background

HISTORY

Throughout history, psychosis in children has inspired great interest and controversy despite the relative lack of objective data and effective cures. Nineteenth-century literature focused on the importance of nature vs. nurture in pathogenesis. Several reports described "insanity in children" as rare and focused on parents' accountability and children's diathesis for such disorders (Brierre de Boismont, 1857).

Kraepelin proposed the term *dementia praecox* in the late 19th century, and in 1906 De Sanctis called childhood-onset psychotic disorders *dementia praecoxissima*. Bleuler noted in 1911 that approximately 5% of cases had their onset in childhood. In 1919 Kraeplin put this figure at 3.5%.

The emphasis in the 1930s was on attempts to describe the exact nature of childhood schizophrenia. Potter (1933) presented a set of diagnostic criteria for childhood schizophrenia and stressed its distinctiveness from the adult form and other childhood psychoses. Despite his careful attempt, however, the term *childhood schizophrenia* continued to be used to encompass all childhood psychoses.

Study of psychotic children intensified in the 1940s. The nature of schizophrenic children's language, including their "tendency to disassociate sign from function," was described by Despert (1947, p. 685). She also disputed the concept of similar reality testing in adult schizophrenics and normal children. Kanner's historic paper, "Autistic Disturbances of Affective Contact" (1943), described the syndrome of infantile autism, which he viewed as distinct in various ways from other psychoses. This investigation led to the recognition that childhood psychoses were a heterogenous group of disorders. During the same period, Bender (1947) studied a large group of autistic and psychotic children with a broad and inclusive diagnosis of "childhood schizophrenia." She described the disorder as a "diffuse encephalopathy" and highlighted neurological as well as cognitive aspects of childhood psychosis.

The relationship between autism and other psychotic disorders in children has been controversial since the 1940s. By the 1970s, several studies in various cultures highlighted characteristics differentiating various psychoses in children. On descriptive grounds these disorders are segregable. In particular, age of onset has a bimodal distribution. The early-onset group includes children who display significant symptoms by age 3 years or less, usually within the first year of life. This group includes youngsters with autism and pervasive developmental disorder. Children in the late-onset group exhibit psychotic symptoms after age 7, with a clinical picture similar to that seen in adult-onset schizophrenia. Only a very small number of children develop psychotic features between ages 3 to 6 years. This fact led to the widely held view that early- and late-onset psychoses are distinct disorders, and that autism and childhood schizophrenia are unrelated. However, it was not until the advent of the ninth revision of the *Manual of the International Statistical Classification of Diseases* (*ICD-9;* World Health Organization, 1977) and the third edition of the *DSM* (APA, 1980) that infantile autism and schizophrenia were classified as distinct entities. *DSM-III* also marked the reacceptance of identical criteria for diagnosing schizophrenia in children and adults. This trend has continued in *DSM-IV* (Werry, 1990).

Mahler (1952) argued against "the contention of certain psychiatrists and psychoanalysts, that schizophrenia does not occur before puberty" (p. 294). She described "symbiotic infantile psychosis . . . in which the early mother-infant relationship is marked, but does not progress to the stage of object-libidinal cathexis of the mother. The mental representation of the mother remains, or is regressively fused with—that is to say, is not separated from the self. It participates in the delusion of omnipotence of the child patient" (p. 292).

Childhood schizophrenia has been studied far less than infantile autism. The standardization of definitions and increase in empirical measures, however, have led to improved research in this area. The recent increase in biological studies reflects emphasis on physiological over psychological aspects of psychotic disorders.

DEFINITIONS

A number of problems make it difficult to clearly define psychosis in childhood, and schizophrenia in particular. These disorders are rare and their careful description in the literature, even rarer. Many cardinal symptoms are difficult to differentiate from normal developmental variations, particularly in the very young child.

Children as young as 3 years old can manifest psychotic symptoms and have been diagnosed with schizophrenia. Psychotic symptoms, however, can be difficult to differentiate from age-appropriate fantasies, such as imaginary friends and belief in magic or monsters; logical conceptualization of reality and ability to abstract are achieved only in adolescence. Developmental disorders such as mental retardation or language difficulties also complicate assessment.

Clinical evaluation remains the fundamental diagnostic tool, with laboratory tests and imaging techniques mainly useful in diagnosing organic psychoses. The diagnosis of schizophrenia, and psychosis in general, should be made cautiously. It is important, however, to recognize the presence of these conditions so that appropriate treatment can be provided. Evidence exists that prognosis improves when neuroleptic treatment is instituted promptly during the first episode of adult schizophrenia (Loebel et al., 1992).

The *DSM-III, DSM-III-R,* and *DSM-IV* omit the term *childhood schizophrenia:* all volumes specify the same criteria for the diagnosis of schizophrenia in all age groups. While pragmatic, this approach can obfuscate the differentiation of the adult- and childhood-onset forms. Besides symptomatology, the possibility of differences in prognosis, pathogenesis, and natural course need to be taken into account. Psychotic symptoms, deterioration in adaptive functioning, no identifiable organic cause or marked affective symptoms, and duration of at least 6 months are the essential features. *DSM-IV* diagnostic criteria for schizophrenia are listed in Table 53.1.

A specific factor in making the diagnosis in children is the failure to achieve expected level of social development. Unlike adults, children do not need to have deterioration in functioning. Children with autistic disorder should receive an additional diagnosis of schizophrenia only when

624

TABLE 53.1

Diagnostic Criteria for Schizophrenia

A. *Characteristics symptoms:* Two (or more) of the following, each present for a significant portion of time during a 1-month period (or less if successfully treated):
  (1) delusions
  (2) hallucinations
  (3) disorganized speech (e.g., frequent derailment or incoherence)
  (4) grossly disorganized or catatonic behavior
  (5) negative symptoms, i.e., affective flattening, alogia, or avolition
  Note: Only one Criterion A symptom is required if delusions are bizarre or hallucinations consist of a voice keeping up a running commentary on the person's behavior or thoughts, or two or more voices conversing with each other.

B. *Social/occupational dysfunction:* For a significant portion of the time since onset of the disturbance, one or more major areas of functioning such as work, interpersonal relations, or self-care are markedly below the level achieved prior to the onset (or when the onset is in childhood or adolescence, failure to achieve expected level of interpersonal, academic, or occupational achievement).

C. *Duration:* Continuous signs of the disturbance persist for at least 6 months. This 6-month period must include at least 1 month of symptoms (or less if successfully treated) that meet Criterion A (i.e., active-phase symptoms) and may include periods of prodromal or residual symptoms. During these prodromal or residual periods, the signs of the disturbance may be manifested by only negative symptoms or two or more symptoms listed in Criterion A present in an attenuated form (e.g., odd beliefs, unusual perceptual experiences).

D. *Schizoaffective and Mood Disorder exclusion:* Schizoaffective Disorder and Mood Disorder With Psychotic Features have been ruled out because either (1) no Major Depressive, Manic, or Mixed Episodes have occurred concurrently with the active-phase symptoms; or (2) if mood episodes have occurred during active-phase symptoms, their total duration has been brief relative to the duration of the active and residual periods.

E. *Substance/general medical condition exclusion:* The disturbance is not due to the direct physiological effects of a substance (e.g., a drug or abuse, a medication) or a general medical condition.

F. *Relationship to a Pervasive Developmental Disorder:* If there is a history of Autistic Disorder or another Pervasive Developmental Disorder, the additional diagnosis of Schizophrenia is made only if prominent delusions or hallucinations are also present for at least a month (or less if successfully treated).

Classification of longitudinal course (can be applied only after at least 1 year has elapsed since the initial onset of active-phase symptoms):

Episode with Interepisode Residual Symptoms (episodes are defined by the reemergence of prominent psychotic symptoms); *also specify if:* With Prominent Negative Symptoms
Episodic With No Interepisode Residual Symptoms

Continuous (prominent psychotic symptoms are present throughout the period of observation; *also specify if:* With Prominent Negative Symptoms

Single Episode In Partial Remission; also specify if: With Prominent Negative Symptoms
Single Episode In Full Remission
Other or Unspecified Pattern

NOTE. From *Diagnostic and Statistical Manual of Mental Disorders*, 4th ed. American Psychiatric Association, 1994. Washington, DC: Author, pp. 285–286. Copyright 1994 by the American Psychiatric Association. Reprinted with permission.

prominent hallucinations and delusions are also present.

EPIDEMIOLOGY

There is little conclusive information about the epidemiology of psychosis in childhood. Evidence does indicate that childhood schizophrenia is rare and about 1/50th as prevalent as in adults, in whom the incidence is approximately 1%. The basic literature on demographic characteristics of schizophrenic youngsters consists of 11 studies employing fairly strict diagnostic criteria, 6 of which are retrospective chart reviews on 4- to 15-

year-olds. Schizophrenia can occur in children as young as 3 years (Russell, Bott, & Sammons, 1989).

Most of these studies show about 1.5 to 2 times as many males as females with childhood schizophrenia, although one report had 4.33 males per female. In adults the sexes are about equally affected. Schizophrenic children are more likely to be from the lower socioeconomic classes, although symptoms do not vary across social or economic spectra. Intelligence level is slightly lower than in the general population. Onset is generally insidious with gradual deterioration in functioning. As in adults, males appear to have younger age of onset.

Although most psychotic children do not have psychotic parents, there is strong evidence that children of parents with schizophrenia and major affective disorders are at increased risk to develop these respective illnesses. Offspring of schizophrenic parents are particularly at risk to develop the disorder when the following are present: developmental delay, perinatal problems, nonfocal neurological signs, cognitive limitations (especially when verbal IQ scores are lower than performance scores), attentional or conduct problems, loose associations or concrete thinking (Kestenbaum & Kron, 1986). The estimated prevalences of schizophrenia and autism in children are respectively 3 and 4 to 5 children in every 10,000.

Clinical Presentation and Diagnostic Assessment

SIGNS AND SYMPTOMS

Except for developmental differences, schizophrenic symptomatology is basically quite similar in children, adolescents, and adults. This is corroborated by the pertinent literature, and therefore the same diagnostic criteria are employed by *DSM-IV* in all age groups. (See Table 55.1.) Hallucinations, formal thought disorders, and poor reality testing often are present in children, whereas flat affect, delusions, poverty of thinking, and catatonia are rarer. Except in the most severe cases, children's ability to relate to others remains intact. Undifferentiated schizophrenia appears to be most common, although the paranoid type was more frequent in one study (Eggers, 1978).

Subtyping of schizophrenia in adults is based largely on the relative presence of positive and negative symptoms. This rubric is useful in children as well. Positive symptoms, including hallucinations, delusions, formal thought disorders, and bizarre behavior, are more frequent in children with superior cognitive abilities. Negative symptoms include deficits such as social withdrawal, emotional blunting, and paucity of thought and speech. They have been demonstrated to be associated with brain damage in children. Adults with predominant negative symptoms are more likely to have poor psychosocial functioning, impaired cognitive abilities, chronicity, and organicity.

Positive and negative symptoms can be measured in schizophrenic youngsters with the Scale for the Assessment of Negative Symptoms (Andreason, 1982) and the Schedule for Assessment of Positive Symptoms (Andreason, 1984).

Auditory hallucinations are the most frequently reported symptoms in childhood schizophrenia. In most studies, they are consistently reported in about 80% of cases. Children report command, persecutory, running commentary, or conversing voices. Visual, somatic, olfactory, and gustatory hallucinations are less common.

A hallucination can be defined as "an apparent perception of an external object when no such object is present" (Hinsie & Campbell, 1989, p. 314). This definition is not fully satisfactory because it does not discriminate parahallucinatory phenomena, which can be normal at all ages, especially in childhood. Rothstein (1981, p. 633) espouses "careful consideration of the phenomenology of the child's experience and his developmental capacities [which] must lead to the firm conclusion that the child is perceiving something that is not there and that he is not in a sleep or presleep state, and that he is unable to reflect upon its lack of external objectivity." Rather than having absolute clarity about the nature of the phenomenon, understanding the meaning of the child's experience and its impact on his or her level of functioning often can be more clinically germane. There appears to be a spectrum of hallucinatory phenomena, with imaginary companions and eidetic imagery at one end, and clear-cut hallucinations at the other (Pilowsky, 1986). Eidetic imagery consists of vivid visual images that are not confused with reality. Common in normal preschool children, its incidence decreases with age. Normal children, especially lonely ones, experience imaginary companions, which they can distinguish from real friends. Other normal physiological phenomena on this spectrum include hypnopompic and hypnagogic hallucinations. These occur, respectively, while awakening and falling asleep.

Developmental considerations are necessary in assessing hallucinations and other psychotic symptoms in children. Children must attain the cognitive ability to distinguish between internal and external reality before an experience can be described as an actual hallucination. Children of average intelligence should be able to make this distinction by age 3 years (Despert, 1947). Limited vocabulary, variable attention span and memory, and changes in affect or consciousness may be factors obfuscating the evaluation of hallucinations. Situational anxieties and the wish to be oppositional or compliant with the interviewer may be additional factors. Young children may not spontaneously report that what they saw or heard was in a dream or daydream. Age-appropriate egocentricity may account for young children assuming it is understood that the imaginary phenomena they describe are not real. Children may deliberately withhold information about hallucinatory phenomena because they fear being labeled "crazy" or being hospitalized. They may not wish to discuss "bad thoughts," especially when violent or sexual themes are involved. On the other hand, normal and psychotic children alike may consciously use the concept of hallucinations to manipulate their environment. Children who say "The voices told me to hit my brother" or who respond to bad news with "My voices say fuck you" may be examples of this.

Direct observation of the child hallucinating is the most reliable; but this is rare, and does not mitigate a difficult phenomenological distinction. Clinicians usually must rely on reports from the child and family. Spontaneous reports are generally more reliable than material obtained on questioning, as children can be highly suggestible. Children often take on a "trained patient" quality when they have been interviewed numerous times and know the answers expected of them. Consid-

eration of the child's ego functions, developmental stage, and cultural background are also essential.

Criteria for distinguishing hallucinations from parahallucinatory phenomena include the following (Pilowsky, 1986):

1. *Vividness* of the perception can be determined by asking if the child sees objects or persons like in "real life," in the movies, or "make believe" as when one's eyes are closed. For auditory hallucinations, ask if the voice is heard the same way the examiner's voice is heard.
2. *Credence:* Does the child believe the object is actually present? Can it be touched? Does the child act on or follow commands? What affective response is displayed?
3. *Origin:* Perceptions from ego-alien sources are more likely to be hallucinatory phenomena than those experienced as emanating from the child's subjective experience. Voices that seem to come from outside the child's head and make ego-dystonic statements are more likely to be hallucinations.
4. *Volitional Quality:* Children are unlikely to be able to control perceptions voluntarily when actually hallucinating. If the perception's presence or content can be manipulated, it is more likely to constitute eidetic imagery. Can the voices or images be made to appear or disappear? Can they be made nicer or scarier?

Making children feel comfortable is essential, as hallucinatory phenomena can be frightening and hard to talk about. Children's discomfort level in discussing this material is important to note. Discomfort often bespeaks an acute symptom with recent onset. Relative disconcern is suggestive of more chronic process or a hysterical symptom. When asked what kind of people hear voices or see things that are not there, typical responses from children include "crazy people" or "people in the cartoons who do that get locked up in mental hospitals." With this in mind, the interviewer must be as concerned with children's motives for sharing such information as with the content of the material.

Delusions are much rarer in children than hallucinations, and are usually encountered only in such serious disorders as schizophrenia and major affective disorder. Developmental issues can cause the assessment of delusions in this age group to be particularly difficult. About 50% of schizophrenic youngsters have delusions, whether persecutory, somatic, grandiose, or religious delusions and ideas of reference. There is a trend for delusions to be present in lower-functioning children with more hallucinations.

Systematized, persistent, and abstract delusions are more likely to be present in older, more developmentally advanced children, usually of at least 12 years of age. A 10-year-old schizophrenic boy with severe identity disturbance complained of "a girl growing up inside me every time I eat ladyfingers." Another 11-year-old hoarded paper clips and silver foil to fulfill her mission from God: to build a spaceship to save the aliens. She slept under a table covered with silver foil, which she said was to protect her from radiation.

Formal thought disorders are disturbances in the manner in which thoughts are communicated. Loosening of associations, illogical thinking, neologisms, and poverty of content of speech are some examples of these difficulties in conceptual or abstract thinking. Few studies have been conducted on the phenomenology or pathogenesis of thought disorders in children, although there is evidence of frontotemporal involvement.

Assessment of formal thought disorders in children can be particularly problematic due to cognitive and developmental concerns. It is therefore important to be cognizant of developmental norms to differentiate immature speech from thought disorders. Loose associations and illogical thinking are normally present in children under 7 years of age. The Kiddie Formal Thought Disorder Rating Scale and the Kiddie Formal Thought Disorder Story Game are useful instruments designed to address these concerns (Caplan & Tanguay, 1991). The Thought Disorder Index, a reliable and valid instrument for thought disorder assessment in adults, has also proven helpful in children (Arboleda & Holzman, 1985).

Children with schizotypal personality disorder or schizophrenia or at risk for schizophrenia frequently present with formal thought disorders. Loosening of associations and illogical thinking are often observed in childhood schizophrenia, usually in the later phases of the illness. Incoherence and poverty of content of speech, while very common in adult schizophrenia, are rarely seen in the childhood disorder. Schizophrenic children and adults produce less speech and have more incoherent speech than normal individuals (Caplan, Guthrie, & Foy, 1992). Developmental delays in the schizophrenic children probably account for

their having additional discourse deficits not found in adults. Caplan et al. (1992) postulate that the presence or absence of loosening of associations might be as clinically significant in childhood schizophrenia as positive and negative symptoms in adults. Neuroleptics can effectively alleviate loose associations as well as other positive symptoms in all age groups.

Communication with thought-disordered children can be very difficult. An 11-year-old psychotic girl was told that her psychiatrist would not be able to meet at their next usual time because he would attend a seminar. She replied, "A seminar? What's that? You must be going to a cemetery. Why do you want to visit the dead? I'm in the live living flesh here. This news deadens me. The news is all about war and fighting anyway. War in the world and war on the ward."

A schizophrenic 11-year-old girl was admitted to the hospital because of school refusal and chronic complaints of abdominal pain, which increased after suspected sexual activity with an older cousin. She presented with a significant increase in loosening of associations and poverty of content of speech. When asked why she was in the hospital, she wrote, "I mate a nice boy." After several weeks of neuroleptic treatment, she began to talk about fears of pregnancy and losing closeness to her parents.

A bright 12-year-old schizophrenic boy treated with haloperidol believed his computed tomography scan to be curative. He repeatedly said:

> "Doc, I'll tell you the news,
> I got the haldog blues.
> They're gonna zap it with a cat,
> That CAT scan's where it's at."

As in adults, a wide variety of symptoms occur in association with schizophrenia in children. Affective symptoms are common and were present in over half the cases across several studies. There may be an affective component to the illness, or children may be appropriately sad about their illness. Unmodulated and intense affective states often are present in psychotic children. Aggressive behavior often results and maladaptively protects against feelings of isolation.

Schizophrenic children's behavior and grooming may appear bizarre. Ritualistic or stereotypic movements are frequent as well as alterations in psychomotor activity. Thinking tends to be concrete, although cognitive immaturity can make assessment particularly difficult in this age group. Depersonalization, derealization, and hypochondriasis may occur. There is usually no disturbance of the sensorium, although confusion may occur in the acute phase of the illness. Certain physical characteristics, including hypotonia, brachycephaly, decreased muscle power and mass, and prominent nasal bridge and lordosis appear to occur more frequently in schizophrenic youngsters (Cantor, 1988).

The illness is usually chronic with insidious onset. Parents may develop concerns about their child's behavior or development even before the end of the second year of life. Premorbid functioning is more frequently impaired than in adolescent-onset schizophrenia. As in adults, males appear to have an earlier age of onset. Most patients display skewed development in cognitive, motor, sensory, and social functioning (Werry & McClellan, 1992).

PATTERNS OF PEER RELATIONSHIPS

Psychotic children typically have poor peer relationships. The psychotic process impedes progression along the developmental line of egocentricity to companionship described by Anna Freud (1965). This interferes with development from dependency to emotional self-reliance and mature object relations (Freud, 1965). Depending on severity of disturbance and developmental level, these children are preoccupied by their symptoms and have a narcissistic, selfish view of others. Peers are ignored, seen only as rivals for the caregiver's attention, or related to like toys. Also, normal children tend to be very sensitive to the strangeness of psychotic children and generally will shun them.

PATTERNS OF PLAY

Psychosis impedes the ability to play, just as it adversely affects any interaction with the world. Psychotic children's overwhelming involvement with themselves hinders the normal developmental process in which transitional objects and eventually toys are cathected with object and narcissistic libido.

The play of psychotic children is characteristic in several respects. Their play is repetitive and more difficult to interrupt than that of normal children. These youngsters are less in touch with reality and tend to use toys in an idiosyncratic, less symbolic way. One schizophrenic 9-year-old insisted on being a bowling pin for Halloween. Psychotic children may hit themselves with dolls in stereotypic or ritualistic manner, rather than as representations of transference figures such as parents and siblings. When symbolic play is possible, these children often exhibit extraordinary imagination, frequently displaying themes of annihilation, separation, loss, and omnipotence.

PSYCHODYNAMIC FORMULATION

Psychodynamic understanding of psychotic youngsters' subjective experience is essential no matter which theoretical treatment approach is employed. The meaning of these symptoms may provide one of the clearest views into primary process thinking. In fact, often it is easier for children to tell adults about psychotic perceptions than certain real ones. For example, a 7-year-old boy whose only symptom was visual hallucinations of "a scary man's face" under hypnosis admitted being sexually abused repeatedly by "a scary neighbor." Psychosis in children leads to an internal world of disorganization, fragmentation, and confusion, which can be frightening. This internal world not only manifests in the form of clinical symptoms but hinders the normal unfolding of development. Psychotic children also can serve as barometers of emotional fluctuations in family and group dynamics.

Hallucinations, from either an interpersonal or object relations viewpoint, are expressions of internalized objects, usually parental representations distorted by instinctual wishes. From a structural viewpoint, hallucinations can be seen as originating from any of the three psychic structures. As superego functions, hallucinations involve an externalized conscience that belittles the patient or warns him or her of punishment for unacceptable behavior. Usually these are auditory hallucinations representing the internalizations of punitive parental objects. Hallucinations serve ego functions when they reflect attempts at mastery or gaining satisfaction in more or less adaptive ways. Examples are voices giving advice or teaching schoolwork. Such hallucinations represent the idealized parental relationship. Id functions are served when projections of unacceptable impulses are involved. Commands to do bad things, such as to hurt others or oneself, can be seen as expressions of aggressive libidinal impulses.

From a psychoanalytic viewpoint, object relations development can be seen as the construction of "bipolar units (object- and self-image) linked by affect as a reflection of the original infant-mother relationship and its development from diadic to triangular and multiple internal and external interpersonal relationships" (Kernberg, 1980, p. 604). These bipolar units determine the development of superego, ego, and id. In psychosis, there is distortion in the development of these bipolar units in the context of the affective connection between the self- and object image. This leads to the subjective experience of intense, unstable affects that cannot be modulated as well as to disorganization and fragmentation. Infiltration of the representational world into subjective experience of external reality follows.

Along the lines of this theory, Kernberg postulates that very primitive defense mechanisms are used to deal with anxieties arising from psychotic conflicts. These anxieties are different from those of neurotics. They involve affects attached to psychotic ambivalence about contradictory self- and object images existing simultaneously. These children fear loss of identity, loss of ego boundaries, and total annihilation. This is eloquently described in the novel *Jordi*, a story about a psychotic boy (Rubin, 1960, p. 126): "His sobbing tore out of him in spasms ... He felt himself drowning in anguish. Through his tears he suddenly saw the tattered paper. . . . The form and color it kaleidoscoped. He pictured it ... sharp, dull with jagged holes and hating him. He stopped. He hit his jaw with his closed fist. . . . His face was very swollen, but the monster had gone."

Muscular rigidity, stereotyped behavior, or wearing multiple layers of clothing may sometimes be a psychotic child's way of expressing fear of body disintegration. Deanimation—the perception of persons as inanimate—can be an attempt at protection from dangerous projections. Other psychotic defense mechanisms employed include psychotic denial (a struggle to disavow the existence of an unpleasant reality), projection (psychological dissimilation), and introjection (psychological assimilation).

It should be noted that the quality of object relations can deteriorate along different axes. A patient thus can have psychotic object relations (with shallow relationships and poor boundaries) and still maintain normal moral functioning. Patients who display psychotic as well as antisocial object relations are generally more difficult to treat than moral psychotic ones. The difficulty in understanding object relations in children is compounded because of the dearth of knowledge about normal moral development and its interplay with the psychotic process.

In a sense, psychotic symptoms may be regarded as extreme expressions of strong emotions. Just as normal individuals may say "I wish you were dead" in a moment of rage, psychotic children may hear voices telling them to kill a parent. Such children may talk about anger at the parent when the psychotic process resolves. The content of hallucinations may even have prognostic value in medical illness. Blank and Perry (1984) report that delirious adult burn patients whose psychotic perceptions involved reexperiencing the traumatic event have a higher mortality rate and more severe psychiatric symptoms upon resolution of the physical injury than those who avoid the trauma in their psychotic perceptions. The authors suggest that certain psychotic phenomena may protect against overwhelming emotions and need not necessarily be corrected in these cases.

Etiology

Schizophrenia is rare before puberty. The elements that increase or decrease the risk to develop the clinical syndrome have not been elucidated. A variety of etiological models have been proposed. Most describe schizophrenia as a diathesis-stress disorder. That is, the clinical condition manifests when genetic predisposition is aggravated by psychosocial or physical stressors.

NEUROLOGICAL ASPECTS

No specific biological cause of psychosis has been identified, although much evidence exists that pathophysiological processes are involved. (For review, see Caplan & Tanguay 1991.) Gestational and perinatal insults may be involved. (For review, see Beitchman, 1985.) Electrophysiological abnormalities may indicate neurological dysfunction in behaviorally disturbed children in general and in schizophrenics in particular, although the results are nonspecific and inconclusive. In adults, electroencephalographic (EEG) studies yielded no significant findings in schizophrenia. However, computer-analyzed electroencephalograms (CEEG) of adult schizophrenics were characterized by desynchronized fast activity with some slow waves and decreased alpha activity (Itil, 1979). Studies of cognitive event-related brain potentials on EEG suggest attentional and information-processing anomalies in children at risk for schizophrenia. (For review, see Campbell, Spencer, Kowalik, & Erlenmeyer-Kimling, 1991.)

Computed tomography (CT) of the brain has been studied in schizophrenic adults for more than a decade (Gershon & Rieder, 1992). It appears that some patients have enlarged lateral cerebral ventricles, signifying loss of brain tissue or absence of development. Magnetic resonance imaging (MRI) and autopsy studies confirm this. MRI and positron emission tomography (PET) in adult schizophrenics reveal functional abnormalities suggesting localization of psychotic processes in the limbic system, especially the hippocampus (Tamminga et al., 1992). The only known study of CT scans in children shows significantly enlarged ventricles in 5- to 15-year-old psychiatric patients with a range of diagnoses including schizophrenia, many of whom have neurological abnormalities (Reiss, Feinstein & Weinberger et al., 1983). CT scans of schizophrenic adolescents and young adults display no difference from normal controls (Benes et al., 1982).

The few neurotransmitter studies have equivocal results. Neuropsychological studies show deficits in attention and information processing. Pathogenesis of schizophrenia also may possibly be related to autoimmune mechanisms. Increased B lymphocytes expressing the CD5 (Leu-1) surface antigen are found in certain autoimmune conditions and in a subgroup of adult schizophrenics (McAllister et al., 1989).

Gestational and perinatal insults may be involved in the etiology of childhood schizophrenia (Cantor, 1988; Green, Padron-Gayol, Hardesty, & Bassiri, 1992). One study has shown adolescent-onset schizophrenics to have more minor congenital anomalies than adult-onset subjects (Green, Satz, Soper, & Kharabi, 1987). In adult schizophrenic studies, a variety of such factors have been suggested, including pregnancy complications (Cantor-Graae, McNeil, Torrey, et al., 1994; Mednick, Machon, Huttunen, & Bonett, 1988) and perinatal trauma (Cantor-Graae, McNeil, Rickler, et al., 1994).

The most convincing evidence of a biological basis for schizophrenia comes from genetic studies. Genetic involvement in adult-onset schizophrenia is supported by twin, adoption, and segregation studies (Lombroso, Pauls, & Leckman, 1994). A report of genetic linkage for schizophrenia in adults (Sherrington et al., 1988) has not been replicated (Kennedy et al., 1988). A specific chromosomal region responsible for the adult-onset disorder also has been reported but not duplicated. It has been proposed that pandysmaturation, a neurointegrative defect in infants, may be the manifestation of a genotype that predisposes to schizophrenia (Fish, Marcus, Hans, Auerbach, & Perdue, 1992).

While there is much evidence that many childhood-onset mental illnesses have a hereditary basis, no specific genetic defect has yet been identified for any psychiatric disorder in children (Lombroso, Pauls, & Leckman, 1994). Studies in childhood-onset schizophrenia do suggest a genetic basis to the disorder and a genetic association with the adult disorder (Hanson & Gottesman, 1976; Kolvin, Ounsted, Richardson, & Garside, 1971). Schizophrenics whose illness began before age 15 had a concordance rate of 71% in monozygotic twins and only 17% in dizygotic twins. When cotwins who developed schizophrenia at a later age were included, there was a concordance rate of 88% for monozygotic twins and only 23% for dizygotic twins.

These concordance rates are higher than usually seen in twins with adult-onset schizophrenia (Gottesman, McGuffin, & Farmer, 1987). However, this may reflect the greater severity usually seen in the earlier-onset disorder, since more seriously ill adult twins appear to have a higher concordance rate.

There is an increased prevalence of schizophrenia in parents and siblings of schizophrenic children compared to the general population. About 10% of schizophrenic children have a schizophrenic parent (Green et al., 1992; Kolvin, 1971).

These rates appear comparably elevated in the relatives of adult onset schizophrenics.

Studies suggest that environmental factors either trigger the development of schizophrenia or lead to an unexpressed genotype. This is best substantiated by the fact that monozygotic twin studies so far have never shown 100% concordance for psychiatric conditions. The relative contributions of genetic and environmental factors for age of onset in schizophrenia remain unclear. It is hoped that future research will indicate which predispositions and insults determine when illness onset will occur (Asarnow, Sherman, & Strandburg, 1986).

PSYCHOSOCIAL ASPECTS

Schizophrenic children have no particular premorbid presentation or personality type. However, certain characteristics are common in these children. Psychotic children have difficulty forming well-integrated and stable internalizations, possibly because of inborn ego defects, inimical relationships with parent figures, or traumatic events during early psychosexual development (Rothstein, 1981). Hallucinations and delusions thus can be seen as maladaptive attempts to maintain or defend against relationships with important external objects. Increased cortical arousal due to emotional stress may contribute to these symptoms.

Studies have shown that various learning and attentional problems as well as neuromotor and neurosensory deficits are more prevalent among schizophrenic children and those at risk for the disorder. Common characteristics include shyness, withdrawn behavior, relational difficulties, magical thinking, impulsive aggression, and academic and behavioral problems. Evidence exists that certain stressful life circumstances, including deprivation or abuse by parent figures, sensory deprivation, or prolonged isolation, can be factors in the development of psychotic symptoms in children. Other factors that predispose to the development of psychotic symptoms include low intelligence, familial religious beliefs, and stressful events leading to hypercathexis of a particular sensory mode. Normal adults have been reported to have illusions and brief pseudohallucinations in posttraumatic stress disorder (Horowitz, 1987). After the traumatic loss of a family member, nor-

mal children may have visual or auditory hallucinations of these important love objects (Terr, 1985; Yates & Bannard, 1988).

The pathogenetic role of familial and interpersonal dynamics in schizophrenia merits further investigation. It must be noted that no simple correlation exists between environmental factors and the age of illness onset. Various studies, mostly in adults, have focused on the etiological contribution of certain patterns of communication: inconsistencies or high levels of affective expression (Goldstein & Doane, 1982; Jackson, Smith, & McGorry, 1990). Children with schizophrenic family members are at increased risk for the disorder (Kolvin, Ounsted, Richardson, & Garside, 1971). Cultural factors may be salient as well (Jenkins & Karno, 1992), although schizophrenia's prevalence does not appear to vary among diverse societies.

Symptomatology in schizophrenic children is remarkably similar across socioeconomic spectra. The families of schizophrenic children, however, are more frequently of lower socioeconomic status. It is unclear whether this indicates environmental etiology or downward drift due to parental psychopathology. Children whose only psychotic symptoms are hallucinations have more psychotic relatives, frequently with affective symptoms (Burke, DelBeccaro, McCauley, & Clark, 1985). This may reflect genetic predisposition, learned behavior, or identification.

In studying children of psychotic parents, E. James Anthony (1971) concluded that outcome was best predicted not so much by severity or nature of the psychotic parent's illness but rather the normal coparent's type of psychopathology and involvement with the child. Prognosis is decreased, however, if the parent's psychosis involves the child. An example of such an "involving psychosis" is a paranoid schizophrenic father who believed since his daughter's birth that all his troubles were due to her propensity to grow up to become a prostitute. He was, however, concerned about the effects of self-fulfilling prophecies, so in the child's presence he and his wife would shout about whether she was a "w-h-o-r-e," thinking that the girl would not understand if they spelled. Greater identification and involvement with a psychotic parent plus an adaptable, passive personality style increase the risk for psychosis in childhood. A sort of *folie à deux* may develop.

TABLE 53.2

Comparison of Schizophrenia and Autistic Disorder

Characteristic	Schizophrenia	Autistic Disorder
Age of onset	Rarely before age 5	Usually before age 3
Prevalence (cases per 100,000 individuals)	14–35	20–50
Male:female ratio	1.5–2:1	4–5:1
Intellectual functioning	Low average IQ	75% in mentally retarded range
Hallucinations and delusions	Yes	No
Clinical course	Progressive deterioration from a relatively normal level of functioning	More delayed and deviant functioning from the onset of illness

NOTE. From M. S. Sokol, "Schizophrenia in Children and Adolescents," in D. X. Parmelee (Ed.), *Mosby's Neurology Psychiatry Access Series: Child and Adolescent Psychiatry*, 1996. St. Louis: Mosby-Year Book, p. 161.

Differential Diagnosis

Childhood schizophrenia must be differentiated from a wide variety of mental disorders. As mentioned, until recently, all functional psychotic disorders in childhood were referred to as "childhood schizophrenia." This practice is now discouraged, and other classifications are possible in *DSM-IV*, including pervasive developmental disorders, psychotic disorders not elsewhere classified, mood disorders with psychotic features, and organic mental disorders.

PERVASIVE DEVELOPMENTAL DISORDERS

Past controversy as to whether infantile autism is the earliest manifestation of childhood schizophrenia or a distinct disorder had been resolved by the studies of Rutter (1967) and Kolvin (1971), leading to the *ICD-9* and *DSM-IV* classifications of autism and schizophrenia as distinct entities.

Childhood schizophrenia is about 70% as prevalent as autism. While it is extremely rare for schizophrenia to begin before adolescence, pervasive developmental disorders as defined by *DSM-IV* are usually first diagnosed in infancy and childhood. Autistic disorder is characterized by a specific constellation of behaviors: qualitative impairment in communication and social interaction, and restricted repertoire of activities and interests. Autistic children are more likely to be disinterested in people and lack imaginative play. They have more gaze avoidance, echolalia, and stereotypic movements. Intellectual functioning is generally better in schizophrenic children, who have IQs usually in the low-average range. Only about 25% of autistic children have IQs above the retarded range. Schizophrenic children are of lower socioeconomic status on average. Psychopathology, especially schizophrenia, is more common in the parents of schizophrenics. Perinatal complications and electroencephalographic abnormalities are more frequent in autistic children. In the rare case of autistic disorder in which schizophrenic symptoms develop, the additional diagnosis of schizophrenia is made, according to *DSM-IV*. (See Table 53.2.) However, the diagnosis of schizophrenia supersedes pervasive developmental disorder not otherwise specified.

MAJOR AFFECTIVE DISORDERS

The differential diagnosis with mood disorders is particularly important because of treatment and outcome considerations. It is important to remember, as Kraepelin (1971) noted in 1919, that the diagnosis can be made only by observations over time. The differential can be particularly difficult because mood disturbance often accompanies schizophrenia. Depressed children also have psychotic symptoms, especially hallucinations (Burke et al., 1985; Chambers, Puig-Antich, Tabrizi, & Davies, 1982). Hallucinations and delusions are generally bizarre in schizophrenia, while they tend to be mood-congruent in affective disorders. A family history of schizophrenia or affective illness is a good indicator that a similar illness is more likely in the offspring. Manic disorders are probably underdiagnosed in children (Bowring & Kovacs, 1992). Irritability, distractibility, loosening of associations, and other psychotic features that arise with manic disorders make them difficult to distinguish from schizophrenia.

If a prominent mood disturbance is present for a considerable time during the active phase of a psychotic illness, schizoaffective disorder or mood disorder with psychotic features must be considered. Schizoaffective disorder is diagnosed if hallucinations or delusions occur without prominent mood symptoms for at least 2 weeks. If these symptoms occur only during mood disturbance, the diagnosis is mood disorder with psychotic features.

ORGANIC MENTAL DISORDERS

Schizophrenia is diagnosed only when organic mental disorders have been clearly ruled out. Symptoms resembling schizophrenia or any of the functional psychiatric disorders can occur in children with physical illness or organic factors. In particular, organic delusional syndromes can present in a manner similar to schizophrenia. Abuse of psychotomimetic agents, such as lysergic acid diethylamide (LSD), phencyclidine (PCP), cocaine, or marijuana, can produce episodes indistinguishable from schizophrenia. History and clinical course are necessary to make the differential. Psychosis can be an adverse effect of prescribed medications, such as psychostimulants or corticosteroids. An interictal schizophreniclike picture can occur in association with seizure disorder, especially when there is left temporal lobe involvement (Caplan, Shields, Mori, & Yudovin, 1991). Other neurological disorders, such as brain tumors and metabolic or infectious diseases, including acquired immune deficiency syndrome, warrant consideration in the differential.

Formal thought disorders manifest differently in the organic and functional psychoses. Often there is a positive correlation between severity of thought disorder and global cognitive impairment when the etiology is organic. Extreme incoherence is most often organic in origin. Formal thought disorders are usually constant in organic disease but tend to modulate in the functional variety.

PERSONALITY DISORDERS

Schizotypal, schizoid, borderline, and paranoid personality disorders may present with transient, mild psychotic symptoms. Children with schizotypal personality disorder have peculiarities of behavior, thought, and speech less severe than in schizophrenia. Diagnostic criteria are the same as for schizotypal adults, except that bizarre fantasies or preoccupations can be part of the diagnostic criteria in children.

OTHER DISORDERS

Schizophreniform disorder, brief reactive psychosis, and psychotic disorder not otherwise specified present similarly to schizophrenia, but do not fulfill *DSM-IV* criteria. The duration of illness is under 6 months in schizophreniform disorder. Brief reactive psychosis is diagnosed when psychotic symptoms occur for several hours to 1 month's duration in response to a precipitating traumatic event. There also must be return to premorbid level of functioning. It must be noted, however, that onset of psychosis in schizophrenic children may be in response to stress. Psychotic disorder not otherwise specified, or atypical psychosis, is a category for psychiatric disorders for which there is not enough information to make a specific diagnosis or for those not meeting criteria for other nonorganic psychotic disorders.

Children with obsessive-compulsive disorder sometimes have ideas difficult to differentiate from delusions. Conduct disorder and sociopathic behavior may be early manifestations of what formerly was called pseudopsychopathic schizophrenia. Symptoms of dissociative disorders, such as multiple personality disorder, can be confused with the delusions, hallucinations, and illogical thought processes of schizophrenia.

Developmental disorders can be confused with psychosis because they affect cognitive functioning and language. Retarded, blind, deaf, and other developmentally disabled children often lack stimulation and exhibit behaviors and symptoms that can be confused with psychosis. Components of formal thought disorder are present in the speech of normal children before age 7. Retarded children therefore can display formal thought disorder because of their low mental age. Developmental expressive language disorder involves deficits in the social use of language, which is frequently misdiagnosed as thought disorder. The concept of psychosis is particularly problematic to apply to children, because they normally do not master the full adult concept of reality until adolescence (Piaget, 1954). It is normal for children to regress under stress to the magical thinking of the preschool preoperational stage.

Hallucinations can occur in otherwise normal children in response to traumatic events, sensory deprivation, or a shamanistic altered state. In the latter case, ingestion of psychotomimetic agents should be ruled out.

Prognosis

Data are lacking on the natural course and treatment outcome of childhood-onset schizophrenia. From the few available studies, prognosis appears more guarded and medication response poorer than in the adolescent- or adult-onset form. The best predictors of positive outcome are good premorbid psychosocial functioning, acute onset after the age of 10 years, and well-differentiated symptomatology.

Course of illness in adults is usually one of increasing deterioration after acute psychotic cycles, followed by a recuperation phase, leading to remission or a residual state lasting months to years. Characteristically, there are multiple cycles with increasing deterioration of psychosocial functioning after each cycle. Approximately 10 years after onset, positive symptoms subside, leaving a residual state with poor psychosocial functioning and predominant negative symptoms.

Treatment

No definitive interventions have been established for the severe impairments caused by childhood schizophrenia. Individualization of treatment is necessary to meet specific children's needs, depending on the phase of the illness and the strengths and weaknesses of patients and their families. Individualizing treatment is particularly important in this age group, as the goal of treatment is not only to decrease symptoms but to enhance development, which may need to occur within a certain time frame. A multimodal approach by a multidisciplinary team is essential. Complete psychiatric, psychological, neurological, pediatric, psychoeducational, and familial assessments should be performed prior to treatment. While it is preferable for children to remain at home, short-term psychiatric hospitalization is often necessary for comprehensive evaluation and initial treatment as well as to protect those dangerous to themselves or others. Many children also require follow-up residential treatment or long-term hospitalization (Green et al., 1992).

PHARMACOTHERAPY

Medication is an essential part of treatment for schizophrenic children, but it only serves as a useful adjunct to a comprehensive treatment plan. Neuroleptics are currently the drugs of choice, although no particular agent has proven superior. Factors in drug choice include side-effect profile, administration route, cost, patients' response history, and physicians' familiarity with medication. Efficacy of antipsychotics in schizophrenic adults suggests their usefulness in children, although clinical wisdom holds that youngsters respond less well to these agents. A recent study by Spencer, Kafantaris, Padron-Gayol, Rosenberg, and Campbell (1992) suggests haloperidol is effective in treating schizophrenic youngsters. In an ongoing, double-blind, crossover trial of haloperidol and placebo, 16 hospitalized subjects ages 5.5 to 11.75 years, with a mean age of 8.86 years, responded better to haloperidol than placebo, with optimal doses of 0.5 to 3.0 milligrams per day, or 0.02 to 0.12 milligrams per kilogram per day. All 16 subjects continued to benefit from haloperidol after completion of the study.

In an open clinical trial, administration of various neuroleptics to 35 schizophrenic children, ages 5.7 to 11.11 years, in an open clinical study, yielded the following results (Green, et al., 1992). Twenty-one children showed modest to moderate improvement and 7 improved minimally. Six patients had no positive response and 1 dropped out of the study. In no case was total symptom remission achieved.

Once the decision has been made to institute

neuroleptic treatment, informed consent is obtained from the parents and, if possible, from the child. A thorough physical examination should be done and baseline symptoms noted, to prevent confusion with adverse medication effects. Pretreatment laboratory evaluation should be done as clinically indicated, including complete blood count, electrolytes, thyroid function tests, electroencephalogram, and electrocardiogram. Careful monitoring is needed throughout the medication trial because of concerns about adverse effects: hypotension, akathisia, extrapyramidal effects, cognitive impairment, and especially tardive dyskinesia. In children, the prevalence of neuroleptic-induced dyskinesias ranges from 8 to 51% (Campbell, Grega, Green, & Bennett, 1983; Gualtieri et al., 1986). The clinical and medicolegal problem may have been overstated, however, as benign withdrawal dyskinesia appears to be the most common form, occurring in about one third of children after neuroleptic withdrawal. The Abnormal Involuntary Movement Scale (AIMS; Guy, 1976), for example, can be completed and videotaped before and during treatment to monitor dyskinesias.

Another adverse effect of antipsychotic treatment is neuroleptic malignant syndrome. Its presentation and treatment is quite similar in all age groups, except that a single exposure to neuroleptics can cause the syndrome in youngsters (Steingard, Kahn, Gonzalez, & Herzog, 1992). Unlike adults, neither gender is more affected, and concomitant lithium salt treatment appears not to be etiologically significant in children.

Neuroleptics are not only efficacious in the acute psychotic state but also prevent relapse. Especially when medication is prescribed for children following the first psychotic episode, a drug-free trial is recommended after about 3 to 6 months of treatment. This allows for a baseline evaluation. Many children will not relapse after this and can remain off medication (Werry, McClellan, & Chard, 1991). The timing of drug holidays needs to be considered carefully. In one extreme example, a psychotic boy's mother abandoned him at the hospital when the doctor insisted on a drug holiday from antipsychotic medication. Medication should be used judiciously in children to enhance development and render youngsters available to profit from other treatment modalities. Optimal dose is typically lower in this age group, even though children may metabolize neuroleptics more rapidly than adults and adolescents (Meyers, Tune, & Coyle, 1980).

Clozapine, a dibenzodiazepine, was recently approved for use in the United States. An atypical neuroleptic, its antipsychotic effect apparently involves serotonin receptor blockade rather than dopamine antagonism. This theoretically precludes tardive dyskinesia, ostensibly an antidopaminergic effect. Adverse effects of concern with clozapine include agranulocytosis and seizures. In children, weight gain and enuresis are common. Clozapine appears to be effective in approximately 30 to 50% of treatment-resistant schizophrenic adults (Safferman, Lieberman, Kane, Szymanski, & Kinon, 1991). In its initial stages, the first controlled clozapine trial in young adolescents with childhood onset schizophrenia has yielded positive results (Gordon et al., n. d.). Five subjects with poor response to haloperidol underwent a 6-week open clozapine trial with a mean daily dose in the sixth week of 412 to 475 milligrams. Significant decrease in positive and negative symptoms occurred in each case. Other novel investigational antipsychotic agents, such as risperidone, are now being studied in adults.

Other psychotic disorders may require different pharmacological interventions. Tricyclic antidepressants, fluoxetine, or lithium salts may be indicated for psychotic depression. In schizoaffective disorder, the therapeutic agent is determined by the predominant symptomatology, and medications are changed or added only when the value of a particular agent has been demonstrated clearly. In youngsters with a history of psychosis, psychostimulants are relatively contraindicated because they tend to exacerbate psychotic symptoms. Obviously, not every psychotic symptom warrants psychopharmacological intervention. Voices saying "eat your dinner" or "clean your room" should not be of particular concern. Brief reactive psychotic symptoms often resolve quickly and spontaneously. Medication trials in such cases would only cloud the picture.

PSYCHOLOGICAL AND SOCIAL INTERVENTIONS

Although there are no known objective studies of the efficacy of psychotherapy in schizophrenic children, a few basic principles can be stated.

When individual psychotherapy is undertaken, a delicate balance must be struck between encouraging the expression of unconscious material so that it can be interpreted and suppressing this material to strengthen ego functioning and awareness of reality. As described by Kernberg, "The treatment of these children implies the task of deciphering the components of self and object, as they are fragmented, bizarre, projected, or introjected in the most unexpected combinations, and of exploring primitive fantasies [which] . . . are gradually replaced by ego functions such as imagining, remembering [and] thinking" (1980, pp. 614–616).

Psychotic children have not achieved Margaret Mahler's (1952) object constancy, normally attained between 5 and 36 months of age in the separation-individuation stage of development. In therapy, these children are in need of what she termed a "corrective symbiotic experience." Erik Erikson and Anna Freud each observed that the therapist can be the psychotic patient's bridge to reality. As a transference object, a real object, and an auxiliary ego, the therapist can help the patient establish a sense of him- or herself in relation to the real world. The therapist also must serve as the coordinator of the treatment team, which includes a variety of psychiatric professional, school personnel, the pediatrician, and family.

The choice of psychotherapeutic technique should depend on the needs of the patient and family. Many clinicians believe supportive therapy to be most valuable, especially when active psychosis is present. Behavior modification can help to decrease maladaptive behaviors and increase children's availability for educational and other interventions. The usefulness of psychoanalytically oriented therapy has not been demonstrated objectively, but its principles are certainly germane to formulating assessment and treatment strategies.

An essential element of the treatment team is the child's family. It is not psychotic behavior per se but the burden of that psychotic behavior on the family is what brings children to clinical attention and psychiatric hospitalization. The goal of work with families should be to enhance intrafamilial communication and involvement, increase the family's understanding of the patient and illness, and decrease feelings of guilt and stigmatization. Recent studies have focused on expressed emotion (Goldstein, 1989). Schizophrenic children apparently have higher relapse rates in families in which emotions are highly expressed, especially when criticism or overprotectiveness are directed at the patient. It must be remembered, however, that any illness has intrapsychic and environmental ramifications for the patient that are often hard to differentiate from etiological factors.

Parent counseling and family therapy are important therapeutic modalities. Parent support groups, such as NAMI-CAN (National Alliance for the Mentally Ill Children and Adolescents Network) (Padilla, 1992), are useful for self-help and networking. The shift toward community-based treatment for emotional disorders has led to a growing recognition of the importance of supportive services for families.

It should be noted that even nowadays, the families of psychotic children have been given a series of mixed messages. They are constantly barraged by treatment fads and false hopes. The concept of the schizophrenogenic mother is also still present. It is the clinician's job to help families sort out this confusing information.

Special education is a necessary component of the treatment plan. Academic as well as social, adaptive, and vocational skills need to be taught. Music therapy and communicative body movement can help these children increase nonverbal communication, define body image, and develop self-concept.

Individualized curricula, specialized teachers, high staff-to-student ratio, and self-contained classrooms often are required. Day hospital or residential treatment is often advisable, where educational and psychiatric interventions can be combined. Social work services can help to coordinate the various treatment modalities as well as to maintain the patient in treatment.

Future Directions

While childhood schizophrenia is rare, its investigation will have important implications for understanding schizophrenia in all age groups. Lack of adequate research is due to the limited number of affected subjects and hesitancy to expose youngsters to potentially harmful psychoactive agents or procedures (CT scan, PET scan, etc.). The advent of safer and improved techniques, such as MRI and medications with fewer adverse effects, may aid in reversing this trend. Research is needed on all aspects of the disorder, especially prospective longitudinal and at-risk studies to improve treatment and elucidate etiology and natural course.

Knowledge of the genetics of childhood-onset schizophrenia is extremely limited, although there is evidence of genetic etiology in adults. Future studies need to address genetic penetrance and its relation to environmental events. Premorbid characteristics of children who develop childhood- and adult-onset schizophrenia need to be compared. Is it the magnitude or the nature of the insult that leads to schizophrenia at a particular age in a predisposed individual?

As the disorder's neurobiological basis becomes more compelling, psychosocial aspects need to remain in focus. The relative merits of various psychotherapeutic interventions warrant objective study. Negative symptoms may prove particularly interesting to look at systematically in children,

because the secondary negative symptoms seen in adults from chronicity and long-term neuroleptic treatment would be minimized. Especially given the disorder's rarity, developmentally appropriate diagnostic criteria and standardization of methodology are indicated. Pooling of data across studies also would be desirable. It is paradoxical that less is known about this disorder than autism, despite schizophrenia's major impact on health in the general population and the large number of reports over the years on the broadly defined category of "childhood schizophrenia."

Although childhood-onset schizophrenia is ostensibly on a phenomenological continuum with adult-onset schizophrenia, certain differences may elucidate protective factors in childhood. Studying the uniqueness of childhood-onset schizophrenia will aid in understanding schizophrenia's pathogenesis, which should have important implications for treatment: strategies to delay illness onset and provide more specific interventions once clinical manifestations do occur.

REFERENCES

American Psychiatric Association. (1980). *Diagnostic and statistical manual of mental disorders* (3rd ed.). Washington, DC: Author.

American Psychiatric Association. (1987). *Diagnostic and statistical manual of mental disorders* (3rd ed., rev.). Washington, DC: Author.

American Psychiatric Association. (1994). *Diagnostic and statistical manual of mental disorders* (4th ed.). Washington, DC: Author.

Andreason, N. C. (1982). Negative symptoms in schizophrenia. *Archives of General Psychiatry, 39,* 784–788.

Andreason, N. C. (1984). Scale for the assessment of positive symptoms (SAPS). Iowa City: University of Iowa Press.

Anthony, E. J. (1971). A clinical and experimental study of high risk children and their schizophrenic parents. In A. R. Kaplan (Ed.), *Genetic factors in schizophrenia* (pp. 380–406). Springfield, IL: Charles C. Thomas.

Arboleda, C., & Holzman, P. S. (1985). Thought disorder in children at risk for psychosis. *Archives of General Psychiatry, 42,* 1004–1013.

Asarnow, R., Sherman, I., & Strandburg, T. (1986). The search for the psychobiological substrate of childhood onset schizophrenia. *Journal of the American Academy of Child Psychiatry, 25,* 601–604.

Beitchman, J. H. (1985). Childhood schizophrenia: A review and comparison with adult-onset schizophrenia. *Psychiatric Clinics of North America, 8,* 793–814.

Bender, L. (1947). Childhood schizophrenia: Clinical study of one hundred schizophrenic children. *American Journal of Orthopsychiatry, 17,* 40–56.

Benes, F., Sunderland, P., Jones, B. D., LeMay, M., Cohen, B., & Lipinski, J. (1982). Normal ventricles in young schizophrenics. *British Journal of Psychiatry, 141,* 90–93.

Blank, K., & Perry, S. (1984). Relationship of psychological processes during delirium to outcome. *American Journal of Psychiatry, 141,* 843–847.

Bleuler, E. (1950). *Dementia praecox or the group of schizophrenics* (J. Zinkin, Trans.). New York: International Universities Press. (Original work published in German in 1911.)

Bowring, M. A., & Kovacs, M. (1992). Difficulties in diagnosing manic disorder among children and adolescents. *Journal of the American Academy of Child and Adolescent Psychiatry, 31*(4), 611–614.

Brierre de Boismont, M. (1857). On the insanity of early life. *Journal of Psychological Medicine and Mental Pathology, 10,* 622–638.

Burke, P., DelBeccarro, M., McCauley, E., & Clark, C. (1985). Hallucinations in children. *Journal of the American Academy of Child Psychiatry, 24*(1), 71–75.

Campbell, M., Grega, D. M., Green, W. H., & Bennett, W. (1983). Neuroleptic-induced dyskinesias in children. *Clinical Neuropsychopharmacology, 6,* 207–222.

Campbell, M., Spencer, E. K., Kowalik, S. C., & Erlenmeyer-Kimling, L. (1991). Schizophrenic and psychotic disorders. In J. M. Weiner (Ed.), *Textbook of child and adolescent psychiatry* (pp. 223–239). Washington, DC: APPI.

Cantor, S. (1988). *Childhood schizophrenia.* New York: Guilford Press.

Cantor, S., Evans, J., Pearce, J., & Pezzot-Pearce, T. (1982). Childhood schizophrenia: Present but not accounted for. *American Journal of Psychiatry, 139,* 758–762.

Cantor-Graae, E., McNeil, T. F., Torrey, E. F., Quinn, P. Q., Bowler, A., Sjöström, K., & Rawlings, R. (1994). Link between pregnancy complications and minor physical anomalies in monozygotic twins discordant for schizophrenia. *American Journal of Psychiatry, 151,* 1188–1193.

Cantor-Graae, E., McNeil, T. F., Rickler, K. C., Sjöström, K., Rawlings, R., Higgins, E. S., & Hyde, T. M. (1994). Are neurological abnormalities in well discordant monozygotic co-twins of schizophrenia the result of perinatal trauma? *American Journal of Psychiatry, 151,* 1194–1199.

Caplan, R., Guthrie, D., & Foy, J. G. (1992). Communication deficits and formal thought disorder in schizophrenic children. *Journal of the American Academy of Child & Adolescent Psychiatry, 31*(1), 151–159.

Caplan, R., Shields, W. D., Mori, L., & Yudovin, S. (1991). Middle childhood onset of interictal psychosis. *Journal of the American Academy of Child and Adolescent Psychiatry, 30*(6), 893–896.

Caplan, R., & Tanguay, P. E. (1991). Development of psychotic thinking in children. In M. Lewis (Ed.), *Child & adolescent psychiatry* (pp. 310–317). Baltimore: Williams & Wilkins.

Cantor, S., & Kestenbaum, C. (1986). Psychotherapy with schizophrenic children. *Journal of the American Academy of Child Psychiatry, 25*(5), 623–630.

Chambers, W., Puig-Antich, J., Tabrizi, M., & Davies, M. (1982). Psychotic symptoms in prepubertal major depressive disorder. *Archives of General Psychiatry, 39*(8), 921–927.

Despert, J. L. (1947). The early recognition of childhood schizophrenia. *Medical Clinics of North American Pediatrics, 31*(3), 680–687.

De Sanctis, S. (1969). On some varieties of dementia praecox (M. L. Osborn, Trans.). In J. G. Howells (Ed.), *Modern perspectives in international child psychiatry* (pp. 590–609). Edinburgh: Oliver and Boyd. (Reprinted from *Rivista sperimentale di freniatria, 32,* 141–165, 1906.)

Eggers, C. (1978). Course and prognosis of childhood schizophrenia. *Journal of Autism and Childhood Schizophrenia, 8*(1), 21–36.

Erlenmeyer-Kimling, L., & Cornblatt, B. (1987). High-risk research schizophrenia: A summary of what has been learned. *Journal of Psychiatric Research, 21,* 401–411.

Fish, B., Marcus, J., Hans, S. L., Auerbach, J. G., & Perdue, S. (1992). Infants at risk for schizophrenia:

Sequelae of a genetic neurointegrative defect. *Archives of General Psychiatry, 49,* 221–235.

Freud, A. (1965). *Normality & pathology in children.* New York: International Universities Press.

Gershon, E. S., & Rieder, R. O. (1992). Major disorders of mind & brain. *Scientific American, 267*(3), 127–133.

Goldstein, M. J. (1989). Psychosocial treatment of schizophrenia. In S. C. Schulz & C. A. Tamminga (Eds.), *Schizophrenia: Scientific progress* (pp. 318–324). New York: Oxford University Press.

Goldstein, M. J., & Doane, J. A. (1982). Family factors in the onset, course and treatment of schizophrenic spectrum disorders. *Journal of Nervous and Mental Disease, 170,* 692–700.

Gordon, C. T., Casanova, M., Zametkin, A., Zahn, T., Hong, W., & Rapoport, J. L. (n. d.). Childhood onset schizophrenia: Neurobiologic characterization and pharmacologic response. NIMH Studies in Progress. Unpublished manuscript.

Gottesman I. I., McGuffin, P., & Farmer, A. E. (1987). Clinical genetics as clues to the "real" genetics of schizophrenia: A decade of modest gains while playing for time. *Schizophrenia Bulletin, 13*(1), 23–47.

Green, M. F., Satz, P., Soper, H. V., & Kharabi, F. (1987). Relationship between physical anomalies and age at onset of schizophrenia. *American Journal of Psychiatry, 144*(5), 666–667.

Green, W. H., Padron-Gayol, M., Hardesty, A. S., & Bassiri, M. (1992). Schizophrenia with childhood onset: A phenomenological study of 38 cases. *Journal of the American Academy of Child and Adolescent Psychiatry, 31*(5), 968–976.

Gualtieri, C. T., Schroeder, S. R., Hicks, R. E., & Quade, D. (1986). Tardive dyskinesia in young mentally retarded individuals. *Archives of General Psychiatry, 43,* 335–340.

Guy, W. (Ed.). (1976). *ECDEV assessment manual for psychopharmacology.* Publication ADM 76–338. Washington, DC: U.S. Department of Health, Education & Welfare.

Hanson, D. R., & Gottesman, I. I. (1976). The genetics, if any, of infantile autism and childhood schizophrenia. *Journal of Autism and Childhood Schizophrenia, 6,* 209–234.

Hinsie, L. E., & Campbell, R. J. (1989). *Psychiatric dictionary.* New York: Oxford University Press.

Horowitz, M. (1987). Stress-response syndromes: Past-traumatic and adjustment disorders. In R. Michels & J. Cavenar (Eds.), *Psychiatry* (Vol. 1, pp. 1–16). Philadelphia: J. B. Lippincott.

Itil, T. M. (1979). Computer analyzed EEG findings in adult schizophrenics, psychotic children, and "high-risk" children for schizophrenia. In J. Obiols, C. Ballus, & A. Gonzalez-Monclus (Eds.), *Biological psychiatry today* (pp. 1295–1305). Amsterdam: Elsevier.

Jackson, H. J., Smith, N., & McGorry, P. (1990). Relationship between expressed emotion and family burden in psychotic disorders: An exploratory study. *Acta Psychiatrica Scandinavica, 82*(3), 243–249.

Jenkins, J. H., & Karno, M. (1992). The meaning of expressed emotion: Theoretical issues raised by cross-cultural research. *American Journal of Psychiatry,* *149,* 9–10.

Kallman, F. J., & Roth, B. (1956). Genetic aspects of pre-adolescent schizophrenia. *American Journal of Psychiatry, 112,* 599–606.

Kanner, L. (1943). Autistic disturbances of affective contact. *Nervous Child, 2,* 217–250.

Kay, S. R., & Lindenmayer, J. P. (1987). Outcome predictors in acute schizophrenia: Prospective significance of background and clinical dimensions. *Journal of Nervous Mental Disorders, 175,* 152–160.

Kennedy J., Giuffra L., Moises, H., Cavalli-Sforza, L., Pakstis, A., Kidd, J., Castiglione, C., Sjogren, B., Wetterberg, L., & Kidd, K. (1988). Evidence against linkage of schizophrenia to markers on chromosome 5 in a northern Swedish pedigree. *Nature, 336,* 167–169.

Kernberg, P. F. (1980). Childhood psychosis: A psychoanalytic perspective. In S. I. Greenspan & G. H. Pollock (Eds.), *The course of life: Psychoanalytic contributions toward understanding personality development* (Vol. 1, pp. 603–617). Adelphi, MD: U.S. Dept. of Health & Human Services.

Kestenbaum, C. J., & Kron, L. (1986). Children at risk for psychotic disorders in adult life. In C. J. Kestenbaum & D. T. Williams (Eds.), *Handbook for clinical assessment of children and adolescents* (pp. 650–672). New York: NYU Press.

Kolvin, I. (1971). Studies in childhood psychoses. I. Diagnostic criteria and classification. *British Journal of Psychiatry, 118,* 381–384.

Kolvin, I., Ounsted, C., Richardson, L. M., & Garside, R. F. (1971). Studies in the childhood psychoses: III. The family and social background in childhood psychoses. *British Journal of Psychiatry, 118,* 396–402.

Kraepelin, E. (1971). *Dementia praecox and paraphrenia.* (R.M. Barclay, Trans.) Huntington, NY: Robert E. Krieger Publishing. (Original work published in German in 1919.)

Loebel, A. D., Lieberman, J. A., Alvir, J. M. J., Mayerhoff, D. I., Geisler, S. H., & Szymanski, S. R. (1992). Duration of psychosis and outcome in first-episode schizophrenia. *American Journal of Psychiatry, 149,* 1183–1188.

Lombroso, P. J., Pauls, D. L., & Leckman, J. F. (1994). Genetic mechanisms in childhood psychiatric disorders. *Journal of the American Academy of Child and Adolescent Psychiatry, 33,* 921–938.

Mahler, M. S. (1952). On child psychosis and schizophrenia: Autistic and symbiotic infantile psychoses. *Psychoanalytic Study of the Child, 7,* 286–305.

Makita, K. (1966). The age of onset of childhood schizophrenia. *Folia Psychiatrica Neurologica Japanica, 20,* 111–121.

McAllister, C. G., Rapoport, P. D., Pickar, D., Podruchny, T. A., Christison, G., Alphs, L. D., & Paul, S. M. (1989). Increased numbers of CD5+ B lymphocytes in schizophrenic patients. *Archives of General Psychiatry, 46,* 890–894.

Mednick, S. A., Machon, R. A., Huttunen, M. O., & Bonett, D. (1988). Adult schizophrenia following prenatal exposure to an influenza epidemic. *Archives of General Psychiatry, 45,* 189–192.

Meyers, B., Tune, L. E., & Coyle, J. T. (1980). Clinical response and serum neuroleptic levels in childhood schizophrenia. *American Journal of Psychiatry, 137,* 483–484.

Padilla, R. V. (1992). The National Alliance for the Mentally Ill-Children and Adolescents Network (NAMI-CAN): Moving mountains in the mental health arena. *Journal of Child and Adolescent Psychopharmacology, 2(2),* 145–147.

Pauls, D. L. (1990). Genetic influences on child psychiatric conditions. In M. Lewis (Ed.), *Child and adolescent psychiatry: A comprehensive textbook* (pp. 351–363). Baltimore: Williams & Wilkins.

Piaget, J. (1954). *The construction of reality in the child.* New York: Basic Books.

Pilowsky, D. (1986). Problems in determining the presence of hallucinations in children. In D. Pilowsky & W. Chambers (Eds.), *Hallucinations in children* (pp. 1–16). Washington, DC: American Psychiatric Press.

Potter, H. W. (1933). Schizophrenia in children. *American Journal of Psychiatry, 12,* 1253–1270.

Reiss, I. D., Feinstein, C., Weinberger, D. R., King, R., Wyatt, R., & Brallier, D. (1983). Ventricular enlargement in child psychiatric patients: A controlled study with planimetric measurements. *American Journal of Psychiatry, 140,* 453–456.

Rothstein, A. (1981). Hallucinatory phenomena in childhood. A critique of the literature. *Journal of the American Academy of Child Psychiatry, 20,* 623–635.

Rubin, T. I. (1960). *Jordi.* New York: Macmillan.

Russell, A. T., Bott, L., & Sammons, C. (1989). The phenomenology of schizophrenia occurring in childhood. *Journal of the American Academy of Child and Adolescent Psychiatry, 28(3),* 399–407.

Rutter, M. (1967). Psychotic disorders in early childhood. In A. Coppens & A. Walk (Eds.), *Recent developments in schizophrenia, British Journal of Psychiatry Special Publication No. 1* (pp. 133–158). Ashford, England: Royal Medico-psychological Association, Headley Bros.

Safferman, A., Lieberman, J. A., Kane, J. A., Szymanski, S., & Kinon, B. (1991). Update on the clinical efficacy and side effects of clozapine. *Schizophrenia Bulletin, 17(2),* 247–261.

Sherrington, R., Brynjolfsson, J., Petursson, H., Potter, M., Dudleston, K., Barraclough, B., Wasmuth, J., Dobbs, M., & Gurling, H. (1988). Localization of a susceptibility locus for schizophrenia on chromosome 5. *Nature, 336,* 164–167.

Spencer, E. K., Kafantaris, V., Padron-Gayol, M. V., Rosenberg, C., & Campbell, M. (1992). Haloperidol treatment of schizophrenic children. *Scientific Proceedings of the 145th Annual Meeting of the American Psychiatric Association* (pp. 142–143). Washington, DC: American Psychiatric Association.

Steingard, R., Khan, A., Gonzalez, A., & Herzog, D. B. (1992). Neuroleptic malignant syndrome: Review of experience with children and adolescents. *Journal of Child and Adolescent Psychopharmacology, 2*(3), 183–198.

Tamminga, C. A., Gunvant, K. T., Buchanan, R., Kirkpatrick, B., Alphs, L. D., Chase T. N., & Carpenter, W. T. (1992). Limbic system abnormalities identified in schizophrenia using positron emission tomography with fluorodeoxyglucose and neocortical alterations with deficit syndrome. *Archives of General Psychiatry, 49*, 522–530.

Terr, L. C. (1985). Remembered images of trauma. *Psychoanalytic Study of the Child, 40*, 493–533.

Volkmar, F. R. (1991). Childhood schizophrenia. In M. Lewis (Ed.), *Child and adolescent psychiatry: A comprehensive textbook* (pp. 621–628). Baltimore: Williams & Wilkins.

Volkmar, F. R., Cohen, D. J., Hoshino, Y., Rende, R., & Paul, R. (1988). Phenomenology and classification of the childhood psychoses. *Psychological Medicine, 18*, 191–201.

Werry, J. S. (1990). Schizophrenia in childhood [cassette recording]. Fifteenth annual review in child and adolescent psychiatry. Chicago: American Academy of Child and Adolescent Psychiatry.

Werry, J. S., McClellan, J. N., & Chard, L. (1991). Childhood and adolescent schizophrenic, bipolar, and schizoaffective disorders: A clinical outcome study. *Journal of American Academy of Child and Adolescent Psychiatry, 30*, 457–465.

Werry, J. S., & McClellan, J. M. (1992). Predicting outcome in child and adolescent (early onset) schizophrenia and bipolar disorder. *Journal of the American Academy of Child Psychiatry, 31*(1), 47–150.

World Health Organization. (1977). *Manual of the international statistical classification of diseases, injuries and causes of death* (9th rev.). Geneva: Author.

Yates, T., & Bannard, J. R. (1988). The "haunted" child: Grief, hallucinations and family dynamics. *Journal of the American Academy of Child and Adolescent Psychiatry, 27*, 573–581.

54 / Schizoid Spectrum Disorders

Jules R. Bemporad

Historical Overview

In the early years of this century, both Kraepelin and Bleuler described individuals who were seclusive, unable to make friends, emotionally distant, and possibly predisposed to dementia praecox. Bleuler coined the term *schizoid* to describe such individuals whose difficulties appeared to extend back into early childhood. Since these pioneer efforts, the existence of a schizoid personality type has been established by numerous authors, some of whom have noted a possible genetic relationship to schizophrenia. Currently, schizoid individuals are described as socially and emotionally detached from others, with an early onset of a lifelong pattern of social isolation, lack of friendship, and indifference to the attitudes and feelings of others. Occasionally such individuals may pursue solitary and idiosyncratic interests (Gunderson, 1988). The diagnosis schizotypal personality disorder refers to an individual who, in addition to

schizoid characteristics, demonstrates oddities or eccentricities in speech and appearance, paranoid suspiciousness, and somatic concerns. Such individuals appear more disturbed than schizoid personalities and have great difficulty keeping jobs, relating to others, or adapting to social mores (Gunderson, 1988).

A different line of investigation based on the actual clinical study of children themselves added to the literature of schizoid disorders of early life just as these forms of personality disorders were being defined for adults. In 1943 Kanner reported the syndrome of infantile autism, consisting of an inability or unwillingness to relate to other people in a normal manner; peculiar, noncommunicative use of language; a desire for sameness; and fascination for specific, idiosyncratically chosen objects. One year later the Austrian psychiatrist Hans Asperger described a syndrome similar to that reported by Kanner, which he named *autistic psychopathy* (using the latter word to denote an abnormality of the personality) (Wing, 1981). The children described by Asperger were characterized by abnormalities of gaze, poverty of expression and gesture, uneven intelligence (with expertise in some areas and learning difficulties in others), impaired social adaptation with lack of empathy, solitariness, obstinate nonconformity, and an underdeveloped emotional life (i.e., lack of interest in humor or sexuality, callousness toward others). Asperger's syndrome appears quite similar to autism but possibly less severe in that many of these children were able to function independently as adults.

Relationship to Other Disorders

These early efforts were among the first to delineate syndromes of severe psychopathology in childhood that mirrored the serious decompensation of adults. In the ensuing years, children have been described who manifest some of the symptoms of autism or Asperger's syndrome but incompletely or in attenuated forms. These children have been labeled as suffering from "benign psychosis" (Mahler, Ross, & DeFries, 1949), as "atypical children," or as borderline disorders. Within the larger configuration of borderline disorders, some authors have described patients who resemble childhood forms of adult schizoid personality. For example, Pine (1974), in a discussion of the concept "borderline" as applied to children, describes 6 different clinical types, which he believes could be subsumed under this diagnostic umbrella. One of these represents a schizoid personality of childhood, which Pine defines as evidencing a constriction of affective life, emotional distance in human relationships, and a preoccupation with an "often rich and at least in part peculiar" (p. 360) fantasy life. Pine presents two illustrative case vignettes: one of a 9-year-old boy who appeared bland, spoke in a monotone, but revealed his preoccupation with a rich and strange fantasy life on testing, and another of a 7-year-old girl who preferred being alone to playing with other children and had created a fantasied imaginary companion who was more of an object than a person. Pine comments that while demonstrating emotional distance from others and preoccupation with peculiar thoughts, both children functioned sufficiently well to remain in school. These children apparently were able to deal simultaneously with reality demands and their own idiosyncratic thought processes. Pine believes that, for these children, the elaborate fantasizing works so well as a defensive structure against inner drives and external relationships that they do not experience panic or anxiety but are able to form a stable character structure albeit at the price of eccentricity and isolation.

Wolff (1969) also described schizoid personality in childhood as one type of disorder among children more generally diagnosed as borderline. She presented findings on 12 children (11 boys and 1 girl), most of whom had been referred for problems in school, particularly in their relationships to their teachers and peers. Some of the children were very shy and quiet while others talked freely about their often-eccentric ideas. Several children displayed precocious areas of knowledge. All felt themselves to be different from other children. Wolff quotes one child, who had constructed a number of radio and television sets, and who had compiled lists of electronic suppliers in Edinburgh and who corresponded with them, as follows: "I'm an odd person, different from most people. I have different tastes. I like being by myself. It is my nature. I'm more fond of things than people. I see a lot of people with each other and I can't fit in. They have interests like fishing and pop records and I'm a square. I don't mind; it's other people who object" (p. 161). This boy excelled in mathematics while doing poorly in all of his other subjects. At age 5, he invented an imaginary island populated by peculiar inhabitants. At age 13, he was still preoccupied with his fantasied island but had learned to keep his thoughts about it to himself for fear of ridicule.

Wolff also describes these children as rigidly stubborn, insisting on getting their own way and refusing to conform to ordinary social demands. Other characteristics included temper outbursts when frustrated and a mixture of concrete and metaphorical thinking. The parents of these children reported personality problems in them since preschool years. Some parents were puzzled by their children's behavior, particularly noting the lack of emotional relatedness. Wolff found that one parent or grandparent of the sample often exhibited the same disturbance. Nine parents were classified as schizoid but only one had been psychiatrically ill with a brief delusional disorder following childbirth. While socially peculiar, these adults managed to function in their everyday life. Aside from this strong family history of schizoid disorders, these children differed from those with borderline disorders in that they lacked the physical and psychological abuse frequently found in the histories of the latter group (Bemporad, Hanson, Smith, & Cicchetti, 1982; Bentivegna, Ward, & Bentivegna, 1985).

Clinical Presentation and Differential Diagnosis

Robinson and Vitale (1954) have supplied excellent clinical descriptions of schizoid children in an article entitled "Children with Circumscribed Interest Patterns." One child described, called Tom by the authors, presented a typical history of an unremarkable infancy and early childhood only to show disturbance when first entering school at age 5. At that time Tom remained by himself, preferring to read chemistry books, at which he excelled, to socializing with other children. He also was unable to tolerate any frustration. Throughout his childhood, Tom was strongly encouraged by his parents to join in activities with other children, efforts he resisted strongly. When forced out of the house to play with neighborhood children, Tom would sit by himself and read, ignoring his peers. Eventually he was routinely teased by his schoolmates, and his psychological problems, particularly his extreme fear of reciting in front of his class, were noted by his teachers. When admitted to a psychiatric inpatient unit because of his unusual behavior at age 12, Tom left his distraught parents with no show of emotion. On the unit, Tom continued to shun others and sat apart most of the day, absorbed in reading encyclopedias. He often took walks alone on the grounds, learning the names of various plants and shrubs. By his third week of hospitalization, the other children began teasing Tom incessantly and playing practical jokes on him. At one such confrontation, Tom frightened his peers by responding with extreme anger and screaming at the other children that he would not be "kicked around." After this outburst, he was left alone.

Robinson and Vitale (1954) describe Tom as having amassed an amazing fund of information, chiefly of scientific or mathematical subjects. He continued to show little emotion or facial expression and answered comments briefly and directly to the point. Another child, called John by the authors, also provides a good description of a schizoid child. John was referred for inpatient treatment at age 9 because of his constant quarreling with his younger brother. His mother stated that she had to be away from John because she was unable to persuade or force him to cease his quarrels with his brother, which were disturbing to the younger boy. The mother also was concerned about John's carelessness about his appearance and belongings. When the mother tried to correct his behavior, John would retaliate by damaging articles in the house or his mother's clothing. John's history revealed that he had never wanted to play with other children, preferring his books, even as a small child. John also was teased by his peers when he attempted to join in their activities; however, he also demonstrated a need to order other children around. Gradually he had developed an interest in art and in spaceships, stating he wished to become an astronomer. On evaluation, he told his interviewer that he had given a four-hour lecture on astronomy to the eighth-grade class of his school. John was pedantic in his speech and actually seemed uncomfortable engaging in routine conversation. He seemed acutely aware that other children disliked him, which he stated was because of his interest in astronomy and his disinterest in outdoor sports. The staff reported that John resisted any attempt to engage in regular group activities; however, he was discovered giving lectures on the planets to younger children. This child demonstrates the not-uncommon association of a narcissistic component with an obliviousness to the needs of others in schizoid children. Therefore, an important feature of schizoid children is their lack of friends and the rigid, over-intellectualized nature of their play behavior.

Robinson and Vitale (1954) have commented on the similarity of these children to Kanner's description of autistic youngsters. However, these children "with circumscribed interests" are reported to have been normal babies, having been able to react to their mother with appropriate emotion. They also present less interpersonal withdrawal and less of the obsessive need for sameness than encountered with autistic children. Also absent in these children is the neologistic or meaning-restricted language found in autistic individuals. Robinson and Vitale also consider the appropriateness of the diagnosing these individuals childhood schizophrenics. They argue against this inclusion, noting that the children they describe manage to retain the ability to relate emotionally to others, although in limited ways, since if the interviewer is willing to discuss an area of interest to the child, the latter will engage in an animated conversation. These children also lack the disorder of thought processes and rituals or compulsions manifested by schizophrenics. Usually these children are referred for treatment when their social disabilities and lopsided intellectual abilities and interests are noticed in school. The parents of these children are noted to be somewhat aloof, as originally mentioned by Kanner in his description of the parents of his sample of autistic children. Many of the parents were successful in their careers and had strong intellectual interests. They often welcomed and encouraged their children's particular scholarly pursuits initially and became concerned about their children only at the insistence of others. Usually the parents seemed to be more distressed by the child's lack of academic achievement in some subjects than by the child's emotional or social difficulties. The authors conclude that they are describing a uniform, demarcated group of children who show similarities to, but are less pathologic than, schizophrenia and autism. The primary symptoms are social isolation, emotional constriction, obstinacy, intolerance of frustration, and an obsession with idiosyncratic interests. Pine's emphasis on the fantasy life of schizoid children is most appropriate since these youngsters often reveal highly detailed, intricate, but frankly bizzare fantasies that are one of their major preoccupations. Imaginary worlds filled with robots or intergalactic space wars are not uncommon themes. Yet these singular fantasies are repeated endlessly, with the children refusing to consider other imaginary topics. In this sense, while there may be a richness of detail, there is a poverty in the variation or scope of their imaginary productions.

Others have noted that schizoid children present with some, albeit attenuated, features similar to autistic children, such as low emotionality, preference for isolation, and bizarre ideation. Wolff and Barlow (1979) compared groups of high-functioning autistic children, schizoid children, and normal controls (matched for sex, age, and nonverbal intelligence) on a variety of structured tests for intelligence, linguistic ability, and emotionality. They found that the schizoid children generally tested in an intermediate range between the poorer performance of autistic children and the superior performance of controls.

This study, as well as clinical data, suggests that there exists a spectrum of schizoid psychopathology with shy but essentially normal children at the healthier end and autistic children at the most disturbed opposite end. In between, in order of increasing severity may be placed (1) schizoid personality as described; (2) schizotypal personality that demonstrates in addition odd mannerisms and a peculiar appearance, paranoid ideation, and unusual perceptual experiences, and (3) Asperger's syndrome, with almost total isolation, impairment of language, gaze avoidance, and lack of emotional responsiveness. Although each disorder may appear on a conceptual continuum of severity, this continuity does not necessarily imply that an individual patient will progress along this line during his or her life history. Rather each disorder appears to represent a specific degree of impairment that remains stable throughout development. Therefore, shy children seem to become shy adults, and, conversely, autistic children grow into autistic adults (Eisenberg, 1957).

Clinical Course, Etiology, and Treatment Attempts

Wolff and Chick (1980) followed up 22 male adults (mean age: 22 years 2 months; range: 17 to 28 years) who had been diagnosed as schizoid in childhood and found that 18 were "definitely schizoid" as adults, an additional 2 were "equivocally" schizoid, and 1 more had some schizoid features. None of these individuals was married, although 5 had girlfriends. Ten of the follow-up subjects admitted to suicidal ideation and, of these, 5 had made suicide attempts.

Half of the former schizoid children demonstrated some psychiatric symptoms at the time of follow-up. Two could be diagnosed as schizophrenic. Nine reported "mystical" experiences. Most were employed, with a wide variety of occupations, from successful engineers and academics to unskilled manual workers. Several were active on committees or in organizations while avoiding more intimate contact with others. This study strongly suggests that schizoid personality is a stable condition that persists from childhood to adult life.

The possible cause of schizoid personality, whether in children or adults, is unknown. Some genetic etiology is suggested by the high rate of schizoid traits found in parents or grandparents of schizoid children (Robinson & Vitale, 1954; Wolff, 1969); however, the exact nature of the inherited defect (and its possible relationship to predisposing factors in the more benign or malignant spectrum disorders) remains to be clarified. One finding that eventually may lead to some understanding of the basic deficit in schizoid-spectrum disorders is the higher autonomic activity found in extremely shy children (Kagan, Reznick, & Snidman, 1988). This biological characteristic can be documented in children as young as 21 months and predicts greater sympathetic reactivity at 7½ years of age. It could be hypothesized that this greater inner reactivity, experienced as anxiety, to novel or social situations would discourage socialization and preferentially lead to solitary pursuits and interests. However, it is unclear whether this reactivity is a primary disorder of autonomic responsiveness or a secondary reaction to a more basic cognitive disorder that inhibits the integration of or adaptation to novel or social stimuli. In either case, this work demonstrates an innate difference between shy children and controls in response to socialization that also may be found in schizoid, schizotypal, or autistic children.

Treatment for disorders of the schizoid spectrum is limited, at best. Any therapeutic approach must take into account the severity of symptoms, which vary greatly from one individual to another. Often the best that can be accomplished is to help the individual adjust to his or her basic defect and to find a somewhat satisfying lifestyle despite limitations. Some schizoid children are so aloof that it is impossible for them to form any sort of therapeutic alliance. As noted by Robinson and Vitale (1954), these children are more difficult to engage after the first few interviews when they have finished reciting their repertoire of knowledge, having nothing left to talk about and finding the therapist of little interest. While the therapist may promote a continuation of motivation by sharing the particular pursuits of the child, such as discussing astronomy or biology, he or she may find that the child has derived very little from this ongoing relationship beyond intellectual interchange and persists in having no feeling of camaraderie or closeness toward the therapist.

Family therapy may be helpful in teaching parents how to cope more effectively with an isolated and stubborn child. Parents can learn to respect the child's oddities while still insisting on conventional behavior in certain areas. They also may find that they can reach the child more through reasoning than by demonstrations of affection or punishment. Group therapy, which, it is hoped, would help children learn to interact with peers in a more appropriate fashion, is too often perceived as frightening and overwhelming. Drug treatment has not been evaluated in controlled studies but, based on Kagan, Reznick, and Snidman's report (1988), anxiolytics may be beneficial in some instances.

Adolescence appears to be a time that is particularly difficult for schizoid individuals. Wolff and Chick's follow-up study (1980) revealed that, by early adult life, almost half the sample of schizoid children had thought seriously of suicide, and almost one quarter had attempted to take their own lives. At this developmental stage, schizoid individuals may become truly aware of how different they are from their peers, just when they are expected to separate psychologically from their families of origin to join the society of these peers. Sexual or romantic longings may intrude upon the prior self-sufficient isolation without the individuals having any idea of how to fulfill these desires.

This author saw one such individual who at age 18 presented with confusion and depression. The youngster stated that he did not know how to act with others and felt different from his peers. He remembered that no one had ever really understood him or shared his interest for math and science. He desired to have a girlfriend but did not know how to talk to girls. He also believed that he must be very ugly for others to shun him as much as they did. While he was listing his complaints, it became clear that this young man had never attempted to meet others on their terms: He refused or was unable to make small talk, he ridiculed the interests of his peers as elementary and stupid, and he could not understand that his superior and condescending attitude toward his classmates would offend them and prevent their befriending him.

History revealed that this youngster had been socially awkward and isolated since childhood. School records indicated that while brilliant in mathematics and physics, he showed little interest in other subjects. His teachers noted that he was indifferent and, on occasion, actually cruel to other children, who responded in kind. He seemed content with his isolation until his midteens when he decided he wanted a girlfriend, becoming increasingly depressed over his failure to initiate social contacts with male or female age mates. Therapy consisted of a rather painstaking education in social behavior and conventions as well as exploration of avenues for socialization around areas of interest (science clubs, joint projects with peers, etc.). This young man lacked the ability to empathize fully with others or to respond intuitively in social situations but could appreciate the need to learn appropriate behavior based on a rational, deliberate basis. Eventually, some gains were achieved although he remained basically an odd person who had to "think" how to react rather than trust his spontaneous actions.

Conclusions

In summary, schizoid disorders exist on a continuum of severity, demonstrating certain diagnostic characteristics such as social isolation, obstinacy, peculiar interests, deficiencies of empathic relatedness, and unevenness of developmental abilities. These disorders usually first appear in early childhood, and the symptoms are noted most frequently as the child attempts to adjust to the social demands of a school setting. The etiology of these disorders is unknown, although a high rate of schizoid traits has been noted in first-degree relatives. Finally, these disturbances, which are first observed in childhood, persist throughout life, somewhat modified by respective social requirements through the life cycle.

REFERENCES

Bemporad, J. R., Hanson, G., Smith, G., & Chetti, D. (1982). Borderline syndrome in childhood: Criteria for diagnosis. *American Journal of Psychiatry, 139,* 596–602.

Bentivegna, S. W., Ward, L. B., & Bentivegna, B. S. (1985). Study of a diagnostic profile of the borderline syndrome in children. *Child Psychiatry and Human Development, 15,* 198–205.

Eisenberg, L. (1957). The course of childhood schizophrenia. *Archives of Neurology and Psychiatry, 78,* 69–83.

Gunderson, J. G. (1988). Personality disorders. In A. M. Nicholi, Jr. (Ed.), *The new Harvard guide to psychiatry* (pp. 327–357). Cambridge; MA: Harvard University Press.

Kagan, J., Reznick, J. S., & Snidman, N. (1988). Biological basis of childhood shyness. *Science, 240,* 167–171.

Kanner, L. (1943). Autistic disturbance of affective contact. *Nervous Children, 2,* 217–250.

Mahler, M. S., Ross, J. R., & De Fries, Z. (1949). Clinical studies in benign and malignant cases of childhood psychoses. *American Journal of Orthopsychiatry, 19,* 293–305.

Pine, F. (1974). On the concept "borderline" in children: A critical essay. *Psychoanalytic Study of the Child, 29,* 341–368.

Robinson, J. F., & Vitale, L. J. (1954). Children with circumscribed interest patterns. *American Journal of Orthopsychiatry, 24,* 755–766.

Wing, L. (1981). Asperger's syndrome: A clinical account. *Psychological Medicine, 11,* 115–129.

Wolff, S. (1969). *Children under stress.* London: Penguin Press.

Wolff, S., & Barlow, A. (1979). Schizoid personality in childhood: A comparative study of schizoid, autistic and normal children. *Journal of Child Psychology and Psychiatry, 20,* 29–46.

Wolff, S., & Chick, J. (1980). Schizoid personality in childhood: A controlled follow up study. *Psychological Medicine, 10,* 85–100.

55 / Borderline Disorders of Childhood

Jules R. Bemporad,
Graeme Hanson, and Donna Lofgren

History of the Borderline Concept

A rich clinical literature concerning borderline conditions of childhood has existed for at least four decades. Although the earliest retrospective description of a borderline child may be Freud's case history of the Wolfman in 1918 (Anthony, 1983), the main impetus for the delineation of the diagnosis of borderline child conditions began in the 1940s and 1950s. At that time a number of psychodynamic and psychoanalytic clinicians began to identify groups of children who exhibited severe disturbances in ego development but who did not meet criteria for a diagnosis of psychosis (Beres, 1956; Geleerd, 1949, 1958; Mahler, Ross, & DeFries, 1948; Weil, 1953, 1956).

Borderline children were described as employing a variety of neuroticlike defenses but also exhibited precipitous psychoticlike lapses in their functioning. When stressed by either internal or external stimuli, these children tended to decompensate to psychotic levels of functioning characterized by significant losses of reality testing, severe and unmanageable affective and behavioral storms, experiences of overwhelming anxiety, and lack of ability to maintain organized or soothing contact with significant others. This decompensation could be reversed dramatically and rapidly by the reintroduction of adequate external structure and the removal of stress. This reversibility appeared quite different from the clinical behavior of psychotic children who exhibit no such striking functional sensitivity to environmental shifts in amount of support or stress.

Borderline children also were viewed as exhibiting uneven developmental achievements and high degree of impairment in (or markedly fluctuating strengths and deficiencies in) drive regulation, frustration tolerance, object relations, and ability to engage in age-appropriate autonomous functions (e.g., learning, the formation of satis-fying peer relationships, etc.). As in the adult borderline literature, these early reports did not use the diagnostic label of borderline. Rather, most early studies referred to these children as suffering from mild or "benign" (e.g., Mahler et al., 1948) forms of childhood psychosis or schizophrenia.

Over the years, different authors focused their attention on various aspects of the symptom picture, metapsychological formulations, and on approaches to treatment. Geleerd (1945, 1958) reported on the low frustration tolerance and poor impulse control of such children, describing their frequent temper tantrums resulting from the escalation of terrifying fantasies against which the children are defenseless. Geleerd believed that the helplessness of the borderline child and his or her continued reliance on the protection of another person to maintain inner calmness were core features of the disorder. Weil (1953, 1956) commented on the borderline child's failure to acquire latency functions on time, lacking age appropriate ego consolidation that would result in the normal ability to control and integrate inner life and relationships to others in the context of greater reality testing. Anna Freud (1956/1969) assessed borderline children within a framework of overall psychological development, concluding that in this condition there exists a qualitative and not just quantitative distinction from normal or neurotic children. She described the borderline child as manifesting deeper levels of regression and more massive developmental arrests, a greater withdrawal of interest from the external world and the subsequent centering on the self or the body, together with a range of deficits in cognition and reality testing.

Ekstein and Wallerstein (1954, 1956) were the first to use the label *borderline* to describe these children, basing this term on their being on the "border" of neurotic and psychotic personality organizations. They describe the borderline child as rapidly fluctuating from normal functioning to psychotic decompensation when threatened by a lack of emotional connection with another individual or by the emergence of frightening fantasies from within. The recovery from this "micropsychotic" episode may occur just as quickly when the child feels reassured or secure. This fluidity of transformation from normal to psychotic functioning and back to normal again has been mentioned repeatedly in papers on the difficulties encountered in the treatment of borderline children (Rosenfeld & Sprince, 1963, 1965; Smith, Bemporad, & Hanson, 1982) and in their psychometric assessment (Engel, 1963).

These early contributions helped to delineate various aspects of the borderline child syndrome, with different authors presenting their own experiences in the assessment and treatment of a few cases. From this literature, a stable clinical picture gradually began to emerge that could be used to identify such children in clinical situations. But rigorous or systematic attempts at enumerating diagnostic criteria were still lacking. As the syndrome of borderline disorders of childhood was coalescing into a recognizable clinical entity, a similar descriptive development was occurring in the study of adult borderline disorders. Originally, both adults and children labeled borderline were conceptualized as exhibiting neurotic symptoms that masked a psychotic core (Hoch & Polatin, 1949). The syndrome of borderline personality disorder in adults has since evolved to include individuals with an array of chronic symptoms, only some of which may apply to children who continue to be diagnosed according to the older meaning of the term. The fact that the same term has different connotations when applied to individuals of different ages has created understandable confusion in the literature, particularly when diagnostic criteria intended for adults have been used to identify children.

Despite the differences in symptomatology, there is a good deal of overlap in the clinical presentation of borderline adults and children. A study by Greenman, Gunderson, Cane, and Saltzman (1986), which retrospectively diagnosed hospitalized children by criteria for adult borderline disorder, found that two thirds of these patients also were diagnosed as having borderline disorder based on child-centered diagnostic criteria. These results ultimately may affirm the finding that both adults and children diagnosed as borderline present disturbances in most, if not all, significant areas of everyday functioning. Whether children termed *borderline* conform to a different disorder than similarly labeled adults or whether both are part of the same disease whose manifestation may be modified by developmental characteristics, the term *borderline* has been retained to describe children because it has appeared repeatedly in prior works and the creation of a new label might add to the confusion.

Finally, as there is no separate diagnostic listing for borderline disorders of children in the fourth edition of the *Diagnostic and Statistical Manual of Mental Disorders* (*DSM-IV;* American Psychiatric Association, 1994), appropriate patients may be assigned diagnoses from those adult personality disorder categories that best approximate their clinical picture. As will be discussed, a substantial number of these children also may meet criteria for conduct disorder or attention deficit disorder.

The Development of Objective Criteria

In the past decade more objective criteria have been developed in an attempt to standardize the diagnosis of borderline children. In the early 1980s, Bemporad, Smith, Hanson, and Cicchetti (1982; Bemporad, Bemporad, Hanson, & Smith, 1981) proposed 5 criteria for the diagnosis of borderline children based on a review of the literature and their clinical experience with a group of children who had eluded appropriate placement in existing diagnostic categories. The 5 characteristic areas of disturbance are: (1) fluctuation of functioning between neurotic and psychoticlike states secondary to environmental reassurance or threat; (2) difficulty managing overwhelming anxiety; (3) excessive fluidity of thought and poor differentiation between fantasy and reality; (4) difficulty establishing relationships with others except for relationships aimed at need fulfillment and excessive reliance on others to maintain internal stability; and (5) deficiency of control, including difficulties managing anger, delaying gratification, and repressing primary process material. In addition, it was noted that social awkwardness, uneven development, a high frequency of nonspecific neurologic symptoms, and histories of physical and sexual abuse were prevalent in the borderline child group. Bemporad et al. (1982) stressed that no one symptom was pathognomonic of the borderline child diagnosis but that the whole spectrum of symptoms had to be considered. While individual children might have had more or less marked difficulties in specific areas of functioning, all borderline children in the authors' original group exhibited difficulties in each of the 5 identified areas of disturbance.

In 1983 Vela, Gottlieb, and Gottlieb proposed a diagnostic schema based on descriptions of borderline children in 7 seminal clinical papers. The diagnostic criteria independently derived by these investigators were found to constitute a significant overlap with the criteria previously identified by Bemporad et al. (1981, 1982). This provided converging evidence that borderline children are an identifiable group. In 1985 Bentivegna, Ward, and Bentivegna demonstrated that use of the criteria previously established by Bemporad and his colleagues reliably discriminated borderline children from two other control groups of psychiatrically disturbed children. It was also found that the criteria clustered together statistically and were predictive of each other.

Recently Petti and Vela (1990) reviewed the literature in this area and suggested that borderline children may be subclassified into at least two categories. One group may lie within the borderline personality disorder spectrum while another category of these children may fit more within a schizotypal/autistic/schizophrenic spectrum. Continuing clinical experience and research with different subgroups of "borderline" children may result in greater specificity of child diagnoses (and treatments) in the future.

In summary, the borderline child may be conceptualized as one who has failed in most of the developmental tasks of middle childhood and is still functioning as a much younger individual. This failure or retardation of development cuts across a variety of psychological functions and affects many crucial areas of everyday behavior.

Clinical Presentation

The syndrome of borderline disorder, as described in this chapter, is most applicable to latency-age children. The diagnostic criteria for this condition are difficult to apply to the younger child who, due to his or her immaturity, may exhibit behavior that at younger ages may be within the broad range of normal but that would be identified as clearly aberrant during latency. Similarly, the borderline adolescent presents with difficulties more germane to the particular developmental tasks of that phase of life (Masterson, 1972). The following description pertains to middle childhood, when the disorder usually is first manifested or at least identifiable with some degree of confidence.

The clinical picture presented by borderline children is best identified in terms of a combination of difficulties and deviations across a wide range of personality and ego functions. It is the overall picture that is important; no single symptom or problem area is diagnostic. In assessing these cases, it is important to compare them with relatively well-functioning latency children. Children in the latency period demonstrate increasing mastery of both their internal and external worlds. More specifically, the latency-age child shows increasing success in a number of areas:

1. Impulse control and modulation of affect
2. The development of successful interpersonal relationships, especially with peers outside the nuclear family
3. The internalization and stabilization of superego functions, with a more consistent moral sense
4. The stabilization of obsessive-compulsive defenses as important mechanisms to deal with anxieties
5. The organization and control of fantasy life
6. The capacity for work in school and for learning
7. The development of successful sublimations, such as hobbies and collections

As will be seen in the following text, borderline children fail in most of these areas. In fact, borderline children show little developmental change through the latency years, and at the end of latency they are still struggling with basic issues more typical of preschool children. One of the most telling disturbances of borderline children is their inability to utilize play as a means of asserting mastery over fantasies or diverting everyday strivings into an imaginary realm for symbolic gratification. For these children, free play elicits a progression of ever more frightening fantasies that arouse such anxiety that play must be discontinued. Another abnormal feature of borderline children's play behavior is the loss of a protective displacement whereby the children understand that the play activity is not real and is just make-believe, even though highly personal wishes or thoughts may be expressed via the content of play. For borderline children, the play activity becomes real and spills over into their own behavior so they become part of the fantasied play, often with terrifying consequences. Therefore, borderline children are unable to use play as a means of sublimation or of displacement from the real to the imagined.

Borderline children demonstrate difficulties in almost all areas of psychic functioning. When the complex array of dysfunctions is evaluated, a consistent pattern emerges that may be differentiated from the other well-defined psychiatric childhood conditions. Often the extent of the problem is not apparent at initial interview and may become manifest in the course of ongoing treatment or extensive evaluation. The signs and symptoms to be described may not be observed in a routine or structured interview. In fact, many of these children function quite well in a one-to-one contact with a trusted adult. Only after the clinician has become familiar with the child and has obtained detailed information about his or her overall functioning in a variety of settings can the diagnosis be made with any certainty.

Areas of Psychopathology

FLUCTUATIONS OF FUNCTIONING

One of the most frequently observed characteristics of the borderline child is rapid shifting in levels of psychological functioning from healthy, age-appropriate ego organization to psychoticlike states with intrusions of bizarre thinking, grossly inappropriate behavior, and extreme anxiety. This psychological disintegration occurs rapidly, often followed by equally rapid reintegration to a healthier level of functioning. Ekstein and Wallerstein (1954) observed that this fluctuation in ego state seemed to occur when an empathetic connection with another person was interrupted. Once a feeling of being understood by the other person is reestablished, the child is then able to function at a higher level. It is often very difficult to identify the precipitant to such deteriorations. These fluctuations are one of the major differences between these children and healthy children or children with more clearly defined disorders, such as affective, behavioral, or anxiety disorders. These other children may display extreme anxiety or behavioral discontrol, but their thought process remains relatively age-appropriate and reality-based. At the other extreme, psychotic children or children with pervasive developmental disorder rarely show periods of healthy, age-appropriate overall functioning, and evidence of pathology remains relatively consistent or deterioration of functioning appears relatively unrelated to actual external events.

The blow-ups of the borderline child tend to involve others or even provoke others into an engagement. For example, an 11-year-old borderline boy reacted to the head nurse's paying attention to another child by suddenly running around the ward muttering to himself and bumping into the corridor walls. Then, in full view of a ward counselor, he picked up another child's toy and smashed it, forcing the counselor to give him attention. When he had been attended to and calmed by the staff, he again became reasonable and was able to relate in a more age-appropriate fashion.

NATURE AND EXTENT OF ANXIETY

Another area of difficulty for the borderline child is the presence of constantly varying degrees of anxiety and an inability to modulate or contain even small amounts of anxiety. These children do not seem capable of responding to signal anxiety with adequate defensive maneuvers or activities, so that anxiety from a conflictual situation rapidly mounts to panic and terror. Some borderline children will call on trusted adults to give them reassurance. Others simply escape physically from conflict situations. They will stay away from any object or experience that might arouse their anxiety, a fact that only adds to their behavioral peculiarity. Many such children, however, decompensate in the face of anxiety-provoking situations and experience states of panic.

The anxiety of the borderline child appears to be more global and overwhelming and to derive from a different magnitude of the threat to the self than that experienced by other psychiatrically disturbed children. Neurotic children may experience anxiety over an urge to disobey some socially or parentally imposed restriction that they are aware may result in punishment or loss of esteem. In healthier children the source of the anxiety usually comes from higher-level concerns—for example, a threat of loss of love, bodily injury, guilt, or even separation and loss. In contrast, the borderline child's anxiety appears to derive from a fear of psychological annihilation, bodily mutilation, or catastrophic destruction or loss of self through fusion with another. This fact is seen especially clearly on projective tests during psychological testing (e.g., Engel, 1963). It would appear that these fears of destruction are too easily aroused in borderline children when they are stressed by frustration, interpersonal difficulties, or other conflicts. However, at more secure and peaceful times, such apprehensions appear absent. It is also important to note that the fears of borderline children typically are not elaborated into forms of the more gross distortions of schizophrenic defenses, despite similarities in the nature of the causative anxiety.

THOUGHT CONTENT AND PROCESS

Borderline children demonstrate an excessive fluidity of thought and, as mentioned, do not use signal anxiety to initiate modulation or control of their thoughts when frightening or anxiety-provoking fantasies or themes begin to be elaborated. Unlike healthy latency-age children, who can use fantasy creatively to solve problems or to deal with hurts, losses, or frustrations, borderline children associate quickly to dangerous, frightening, and primitive ideas. Although reality testing is in general intact, borderline children appear to have some fluidity in the area of reality testing and for brief periods appear to have transient breakdowns in reality testing (Engel, 1963). In a way, they scare themselves with their own fantasies.

Their fantasies usually involve themes of bodily destruction, death, or psychological discontrol and appear prompted either by an external stress such as rejection by a needed other or by a neutral stimulus that has taken on a particularly threatening significance, such as the sight of a broken toy, a penknife, or a toy gun. As mentioned earlier, these intrusions of frightening themes may be clearly observed in unstructured play situations when the children's inner life is activated by the play materials and they begin to introduce fantasy into their play. In play therapy, the associations turn to frightening, overt, sexual, or aggressive fantasies that are acted out in play with increasing anxiety and physical activity until the use of displacement dissipates and the children themselves become part of the play they are describing.

Carl: An 8-year-old inpatient, Carl, entered the play room with his new male therapist and began to play building the Eiffel Tower with Lego blocks. He was quite organized and directed in his play at the beginning of the session and actively and quite carefully built the tower. However, as the tower got higher and higher, the boy became increasingly excited. He then had two small dolls, a male and a female, climb to the top of the tower. They began to kiss on top of the tower; then he said they were having intercourse on top of the tower. At this point he was quite agitated and excited and was clearly becoming overstimulated by his fantasy. He then said they were having anal intercourse, that the female doll was pregnant and the male doll was pregnant. Carl took a pencil and tried to jab it at his own rear. At this point he was clearly physically very agitated as well as very excited. He then took clay and merged the two dolls together on top of the tower as one big ball. Then they fell down and the tower fell down, and he threw them into the sink with water, all the time becoming even more physically agitated and overwhelmed. He then ran over to the therapist, stomped on the therapist's foot, hit him in the crotch, and ran out of the room, back to the children's ward. When the therapist recovered his composure and returned to the unit, he found Carl there talking very appropriately and calmly to his male counselor, with whom he had a very close attachment. In this play sequence one can see both the deterioration and regression of the themes in the play and the increasing excitement, agitation, and loss of control by this borderline child. He had great difficulty keeping psychological boundaries clear and, without adequate supportive structure from the therapist, the stimulating fantasies clearly overwhelmed him. This would not have happened in a healthier latency-age child who has developed a wide range of mechanisms to maintain creativity, enjoyment, and self-control in relatively unstructured play situations.

RELATIONSHIP TO FRIENDS, PEERS, AND ADULTS

Borderline children have serious difficulties in the area of object relationships. As can be inferred from the description of their fluctuations in functioning, their impulse control problems, and their high level of anxiety, they are difficult children for peers to relate to. They are so intensely involved in their own internal preoccupations, so needy of attention, and so unreliable and inconsistent that most peers become frustrated with them. The intensity and volatility of their emotions are threatening to the average latency-age child, who prides himself or herself on being organized and in control.

We have observed a variety of disturbed modes of relating in our sample of borderline children. Often children form a close, need-fulfilling relationship with one adult who is sought out as a source of security and protection against anxiety, while relationships with others are fraught with fear and hostility. Other children appear to be able to substitute one person for another, with little regard for who the other person is as long as personal needs are fulfilled. Whatever the quality or depth of attachment, borderline children get along better with adults than with peers, who will not take pains to gratify needs and who will not tolerate the peculiarities of their behavior. Classroom teachers frequently report that such children attempt to climb on their laps during class or ask for some sort of tangible show of emotional support. Borderline children usually do not grasp the nuances of social behavior and misinterpret group situations, causing them embarrassment and anxiety. Often they are perceived as odd by their peers, who eventually avoid them or make them the butt of jokes.

The sharp contrast between the borderline child's behavior in a group of peers and his or her behavior in a one-to-one situation with a benevolent adult may lead to conflicting reports being brought to the attention of the clinician. Similarly, if the clinician is supportive and the diagnostic interview is relatively structured and nonthreatening, the child may evidence little pathology, presenting a markedly different clinical picture from that provided by his or her history. Later on during the course of therapy, when free play is introduced or nonsupportive interpretations are ventured, the extent of psychopathology may rapidly become manifest.

Many of these children have multiple perceptual motor difficulties and visual motor difficulties that interfere with their overall coordination, making them clumsy and awkward. In particular, many of these children are not successful at team activities and sports. Combined with their difficulty compromising their immediate needs to the needs of other individuals, this contributes to their being very poor group members, particularly in the school playground and in most other unstructured peer situations.

DEFICIENCY OF CONTROL

The clinical parameter of deficiency of control refers to areas that borderline children find so difficult to master in an age-appropriate manner, such as containing anxiety, managing anger, delaying gratification, and repressing very primitive fantasies. These difficulties represent a failure on many levels to contain negative affects and thoughts that too readily spill over into hyperactivity, impulsive acts, panic, and temper tantrums. Borderline children are deficient in the ability to modulate and sublimate drives that are activated by stimuli in the environment and/or fantasies from within. This is all in great contrast to the late latency-age child, who takes great pride in being in control, producing highly integrated behavior, and in mastering both his or her internal and external worlds. For instance, a 10-year-old borderline boy used puppets to play out a scene of a bad child being punished. As the play continued, the punishment became more and more severe, with increasing agitation on the child's part. He appeared panic-stricken, had to stop suddenly, and ran from the room. Some of these children are particularly sensitive to environmental tension, becoming barometers of familial stress and responding with inappropriate hyperactivity or tantrums, which results in their being scapegoated by family members.

ASSOCIATED SYMPTOMS

In addition to the areas of pathology just outlined, some borderline children exhibit additional symptoms that are not easily categorized under one area of functioning. Among these symptoms may be listed poor social awareness, lack of concern for bodily safety or personal grooming, and an inconsistent ability to adapt to new situations. In our experience many of these children, in addition to their visual/motor integration problems, also show soft neurological signs, which add to their overall awkwardness. These children display a general unevenness in development, which may be seen in a mixture of age-appropriate and infantile ways of relating to people, an unevenness in the level of defenses ranging again from age-appropriate defense mechanisms at times and to very infantile, primitive defenses at other times. These children present a conglomeration of advanced, normal, and grossly delayed behavior all at the same time, with fluctuations between high and low levels of functioning in almost all areas.

A subgroup of children present with a slightly different picture. These children do not display the rapid, unpredictable fluctuations in functioning, and their problems in interpersonal relationships are characterized more by withdrawal and isolation and a lack of involvement rather than by inconsistent, close, demanding, tumultuous relationships of the more typical borderline child. This group, which has a more isolated, schizoid quality recently have been described by Petti and Vela (1990), who consider them diagnostically to be a separate group, more in the schizoid personality disorder spectrum and distinct from borderline personality disorder. (See Chapter 54.) They do, however, share some of the other characteristics of borderline personality disorder in children, including problems with object relations, primitive fantasies, preoccupations with primitive concerns of annihilation and destruction, and poor use of sublimations.

Clara: A 10-year-old girl named Clara, who is bright, articulate, superficially quite competent in school, was preoccupied with the ancient dynasties of Egypt and all of their burial rituals. She also has severe conflicts over her sexual identity and dressed, talked, and behaved like a boy, so successfully that she fooled most people who came in contact with her superficially. Her fantasy life was filled with preoccupations of life and death and power and weakness. When her pet guinea pig died, she developed a prolonged burial ritual in the backyard of her house based on her notions of burial procedures in pharaonic Egypt. She did this all in an isolated fashion involving no friends or peers. In fact, her peer rela-

tionships were limited and superficial. There was little change, even after several years of intensive therapy. Although very intelligent by IQ testing and relatively successful at school, she appeared to gain no satisfaction from her schoolwork.

Clinical Course

Another way that the validity of the diagnosis of borderline disorders of childhood is being investigated involves the study of such children over time. Etemad and Szurek (1973) followed a group of 84 severely impaired children for 5 to 23 years. Approximately one third of these children originally had been identified as borderline; it was reported that 41% of the whole group had required hospitalization by the time of follow-up. Diagnoses at follow-up were not determined. Wergeland (1979) followed 29 borderline psychotic children for 4 to 19 years. Approximately one third of the subjects were borderline or psychotic at the time of follow-up. Aarkrog (1981) followed a group of 50 borderline adolescents who were further subdivided according to a Danish classification system including infantile borderline psychosis (with 4 subtypes), pseudoneurotic, and pseudopsychopathic borderline states. At the time of follow-up, 70% of the adolescents still were considered to be borderline. These studies suffer from use of nonstandardized defining criteria, inconsistencies as to whether diagnoses were determined at follow-up, and possible selection biases. In essence, they fail to provide conclusive evidence of the validity of the child borderline diagnosis.

One of the best small clinical follow-up studies is by Kestenbaum (1983). She retrospectively identified 7 borderline children using Vela's criteria (Vela et al., 1983) and she reported extremely varied outcome for this group. After 14 to 30 years, each of the 7 was found to have a different diagnosis, ranging from anxiety neurosis to paranoid schizophrenia. This study suggests that there is no specific predictive validity for the child borderline diagnosis.

A recent prospective study of borderline children was conducted by Lofgren, Bemporad, King, Lindem, and O'Driscoll (1991). In that study a group of 19 young adults were available who had originally been diagnosed by Bemporad and his colleagues (1981, 1982) approximately 10 to 15 years earlier, when the subjects were between 6 and 10 years of age. In spite of the high level of affective dysregulation in this group (both as children and at the time of follow-up), and in spite of the prevalence of psychoticlike symptoms when they were children, none of these young adults met criteria for Axis I mood or schizophrenic disorders at follow-up. In contrast, 16 of the 19 subjects had Axis II diagnoses. However, no specific connection between the childhood borderline diagnosis and the adult borderline personality diagnosis was found. Rather the childhood borderline diagnosis seemed to be a precursor to the development of a wide array of severe personality disorders. In that sense the childhood borderline diagnosis may be the child version of borderline personality organization in adults, if the latter entity is understood as encompassing a wide range of personality types. These findings also provide support for the idea of a kind of continuity of pathology over time. Children who were neither neurotic nor psychotic as children remained in that broad midrange category as young adults. This study documents the continuity of a severe childhood personality disorder well into adult life.

Etiology

The cause of borderline disorders of childhood is unknown. Authors who have reported on series of such cases have noted that in addition to the symptoms of the disorder, these children also present with a variety of neurological deficits (Bemporad et al., 1982; Bentivegna et al., 1985; Kernberg, 1983). Neuropsychological testing of borderline children suggests difficulties in organization of stimuli, problems with attention, language disorders, and hyperactivity. These organic liabilities could be understood as contributing to problems of social cognition, of maintaining affects, and of controlling impulses that form part of the overall clinical picture.

Familial disturbances also have been reported frequently in the history of borderline children. Bemporad et al. (1982) found a high presence of psychological abuse, which took the form of in-

volving the patient in bizarre parental activities—such as force feeding until the child vomited, being given LSD as an infant, and being treated by the mother as a witch who could cast spells on others. The households were characterized by strange beliefs, constant arguing, violence, and inappropriate sexual behaviors and sexual and physical abuse. It may be speculated that children, particularly those who are neurologically compromised, who grow up in chaotic, harmful, and/or unstructured households may be more vulnerable to the development of multiple deficiencies and symptoms within the range of the borderline child disorder. Therefore, this disorder may be best understood as resulting from a combination of etiological factors including mild or severe organic deficits, a chaotic family experience, and a lack of age-appropriate socialization experiences.

Treatment Considerations

The first descriptions of borderline children were written by clinicians who had attempted to engage these patients in traditional psychoanalytically oriented psychotherapy. The major focus of these early contributions was to alert other practitioners of the need to modify usual therapeutic techniques considering the particular vulnerabilities concerning regression in this diagnostic group.

Clinicians such as Ekstein and Wallerstein (1956) advised that therapists should never confront cognitive distortions of the borderline children but rather should stay as close as possible to the child's own (distorted) perceptions while making interpretations or other interventions. These clinicians noted the extraordinary sensitivity of these children to breaks in the connection to their therapists and believed that if the therapist could "stay with" the child as much as possible during psychotic episodes, the frequency of these episodes eventually would lessen and the child would move to higher developmental levels, thereby becoming more amenable to traditional psychodynamic interventions where insight could become a realizable therapeutic goal.

Other clinicians understand the needs of these children in treatment differently. They believe that rather than having a goal of insight or of making the unconscious conscious, as in more traditional analytic treatment, and rather than remaining with the child in regression, the therapist's task is to help the child to shore up and build defenses and to impart a sense to the child that the containment of anxiety is an achievable and worthwhile goal. Others explicate the role of the therapist as serving as an "auxiliary ego" to the borderline child. The importance of examining distortions, helping the child to deal with real-life difficulties, and identifying boundaries between reality and fantasy are considered crucial aspects of therapeutic work (Chethik, 1986; Gilpin, 1976; Lewis & Brown, 1979; Petti & Vela, 1990; Rosenfeld & Sprince, 1965). Some therapists may even feel it necessary to be more directly confrontational and to provide whatever structure and containment necessary to curtail all acting out and maladaptive or psychotic behavior (Petti & Vela, 1990).

Smith et al. (1982) conceptualized the treatment of borderline children as divisible into three stages: allaying anxiety and making an alliance, promoting ego development, and internalization. During the first of these stages, it is recommended that the therapist refrain from making interpretations, curtail play or other activities that arouse threatening themes, and diminish anxiety through empathic understanding and emotional support. The second focuses on helping the child to develop adequate latency-age functions through joint exploration of possible distortions of reality-finding measures to channel aggression and control impulses, initiating constructive activities to enhance self-esteem, and mutually discussing appropriate social modes of relating to others. This stage is usually prolonged, with frequent setbacks. The final stage of internalization often is more ideal than actualized, for with each step toward healthier functioning, the child simultaneously grows older and faces new developmental and environmental demands. Nevertheless, it is hoped that children can internalize the experience of mutuality and trust from the therapeutic setting so as to build a more secure foundation upon which to attempt mastery of subsequent psychological challenges. In addition, these researchers supported the use of family therapy, medication, and environmental support in addition to psychotherapy. A recurrent theme in discussions of the treatment of borderline children is that this group of patients requires an ego-supportive rather than a regressive treatment approach, at least in the beginning of treatment and perhaps for a long time thereafter.

Pharmacotherapy of the borderline child aims at the reduction of specific target symptoms, which may vary greatly from child to child. Medication may prove useful in preventing decompensation secondary to environmental crises and in creating a more tranquil state of mind so that normal developmental progress is not impeded by the upsurge of overwhelming affects. The crippling anxiety and panic of these children may be ameliorated by the judicious and intermittent use of major tranquilizers, such as thioridazine. Petti (1983) has advocated the use of antidepressants such as imipramine when depression is a pronounced component of the clinical picture. Many borderline children also demonstrate symptoms of attention deficit disorder; this aspect of their presentation can be treated with stimulants, such as methylphenidate or dextroamphetamine. While medication can be of great help in treatment, its prolonged or maintenance use is not advocated (Petti, 1983), nor is medication recommended in the absence of psychotherapeutic treatment.

Many borderline children present with massive problems in so many crucial areas of functioning that a special environment is needed to protect them from an upsurge of anxiety from within and, not uncommonly, overstimulation by peers from without. Other borderline children come from home environments that are so chaotic and destructive that treatment would prove ineffective if they remained with their families, which are actively abusive or provoke decompensations. As a result, hospitalization or day treatment frequently are required to provide a secure setting for the mastery of latency skills. Finally, the families of borderline children require attention if they are to provide an adequate environment for growth. Usually these families show areas of gross pathological functioning, which should be addressed because these disturbances enhance and promote the child's disturbances, reenforcing irrational fears, magical thinking, and bizarre modes of relating. The series of borderline children followed by Lofgren et al. (1991) received extensive individual psychotherapy, long-term hospitalization, and a variety of pharmacological interventions, yet the only childhood factor that predicted adequate adjustment for these children by young adulthood was the creation of a stable family environment. This finding strongly underlines the need for family therapy in the treatment of borderline children.

Conclusion

The validity of the diagnosis of borderline disorder in children has yet to be established. Currently it is uncertain whether these children are a truly homogenous group, if they consist of a variety of similar yet distinct disorders, or if there is little coherence to the syndrome and they are simply a mixture of severely impaired individuals who do not fit readily into other diagnostic categories. Without the recognition of a pathognomic sign or symptom, diagnosis has had to rely on the presence of a constellation of diverse pathological manifestations. The clinical descriptions of these individuals by various authors are strikingly similar and were so, even before there was any attempt at encompassing their pathology by a diagnostic label. However, large-scale studies with standardized criteria are infrequent, as are investigations of the course of the illness or its response to various treatments. Knowledge of borderline children remains at the stage of clinical description. Future work may offer a more thorough understanding of the causes of this condition, its diagnostic boundaries, and its eventual outcome.

REFERENCES

Aarkrog, T. (1981). The borderline concept in childhood, adolescence and adulthood. *Acta Psychiatrica Scandinavica* (Suppl.), 293.

American Psychiatric Association. (1994). *Diagnostic and statistical manual of mental disorders* (4th ed.). Washington, DC: Author.

Anthony, E. J. (1983). The borderline child in an overall perspective. In K. S. Robson (Ed.), *The borderline child* (pp. 11–29). New York: McGraw-Hill.

Bemporad, J. R., Hanson, G., & Smith, H. F. (1981). The diagnosis and treatment of borderline syndromes of childhood. In S. Arieti (Ed.), *American handbook of psychiatry* (Vol. 7, pp. 227–252). New York: Basic Book.

Bemporad, J. R., Smith, H. F., Hanson, G., & Cicchetti, D. (1982). Borderline syndromes in childhood: Criteria for diagnosis. *American Journal of Psychiatry, 139*(5), 596–602.

Bentivegna, S. W., Ward, L. B., & Bentivegna, N. P. (1985). A study of a diagnostic profile of the borderline syndrome in childhood and trends in treatment outcome. *Child Psychiatry and Human Development, 15* (3), 198–205.

Beres, D. (1956). Ego deviations and the concept of schizophrenia. *Psychoanalytic Study of the Child, 11,* 164–235.

Chethik, M. (1986). Levels of borderline functioning in children etiological and treatment considerations. *American Journal of Orthopsychiatry, 56,* 109–119.

Ekstein, R., & Wallerstein, J. (1954). Observations on the psychology of borderline and psychotic children. *Psychoanalytic Study of the Child, 9,* 344–369.

Ekstein, R., & Wallerstein, J. (1956). Observations on the psychotherapy of borderline and psychotic children. *Psychoanalytic Study of the Child, 9,* 344–369.

Engel, M. (1963). Psychological testing of borderline psychotic children. *Archives of General Psychiatry, 8,* 426–434.

Etemad, J. G., & Szurek, S. A. (1973). A modified follow-up study of a group of psychotic children. In S. A. Szurek & I. N. Berlin (Eds.), *Clinical studies in childhood psychoses* (pp. 348–371). New York: Brunner/Mazel.

Freud, A. (1969). The assessment of borderline cases. In *The writings of Anna Freud* (Vol. 5, pp. 301–314). New York: International Universities Press. (Originally published 1956).

Frijling-Schreuder, E. C. M. (1970). Borderline states in children. In *Psychoanalytic Study of the Child, 24,* 307–327.

Geleerd, E. R. (1945). Observations on temper tantrums in children. *American Journal of Orthopsychiatry, 15,* 238–246.

Geleerd, E. R. (1949). Contributions to the problems of psychoses in childhood. *Psychoanalytic Study of the Child, 2,* 279–295.

Geleerd, E. (1958). Borderline states in childhood and adolescence. *Psychoanalytic Study of the Child, 13,* 279–295.

Gilpin, D. C. (1976). Psychotherapy of borderline psychotic children. *American Journal of Psychotherapy, 30,* 483–496.

Gilpin, D. C. (1981). The true fluid borderline child in psychotherapy. In E. J. Anthony & D. C. Gilpin (Eds.), *Three further faces of childhood* (pp. 257–267). New York: Spectrum Publications.

Gottlieb, E. H., & Gottlieb, H. P. (1983). Borderline syndromes in childhood: A critical review. In K. S. Robson (Ed.), *The borderline child* (pp. 31–48). New York: McGraw-Hill.

Greenman, D. A., Gunderson, J. G., Cane, M., & Saltzman, P. R. (1986). An examination of the borderline diagnosis in children. *American Journal of Psychiatry, 143,* 998–1003.

Hoch, P., & Polatin, P. (1949). Psychoneurotic forms of schizophrenia. *Psychiatry Quarterly, 23,* 248–276.

Kernberg, P. (1983). Borderline conditions: Childhood and adolescent aspects. In K. S. Robson (Ed.), *The borderline child* (pp. 101–119). New York: McGraw-Hill.

Kestenbaum, C. (1983). The borderline child at risk for major psychiatric disorder in adult life. In K. S. Robson (Ed.), *The borderline child* (pp. 49–81). New York: McGraw-Hill.

Lewis, M., & Brown, T. E. (1980). Child care in the residential treatment of the borderline child. *Child Care Quarterly 9,* 41–50.

Lofgren, D. P., Bemporad, J., King, J., Lindem, K., & O'Driscoll, G. (1991). A prospective study of so-called borderline children. *American Journal of Psychiatry, 148,* 1541–1547.

Mahler, M., Ross, J., & DeFries, Z. (1948). Clinical studies in benign and malignant cases of childhood psychosis. *American Journal of Orthopsychiatry, 19,* 295–305.

Masterson, J. F. (1972) *Treatment of the borderline adolescent: A developmental approach.* New York: John Wiley & Sons.

Petti, T. A. (1983). Psychopharmacologic treatment of borderline children. In K. S. Robson (Ed.), *The bor-*

derline child (pp. 235–256). New York: McGraw-Hill.

Petti, T. A., & Vela, R. M. (1990). Borderline disorders of childhood. *Journal of the American Academy of Child & Adolescent Psychiatry, 29,* 327–337.

Rosenfeld, S. K., & Sprince, M. P. (1963). An attempt to formulate the meaning of the concept "borderline." *Psychoanalytic Study of the Child, 18,* 603–635.

Rosenfeld, S. K., & Sprince, M. P. (1965). Some thoughts on the technical handling of borderline children. *Psychoanalytic Study of the Child, 20,* 495–516.

Smith, H. F., Bemporad, J. R., & Hanson, G. (1982). Aspects of the treatment of borderline children. *American Journal of Psychotherapy, 36,* 181–199.

Vela, R., Gottlieb, H., & Gottlieb, E. (1983). Borderline syndrome in childhood: A critical review. In R. S. Robson (Ed.), *The borderline child* (pp. 31–48). New York: McGraw Hill.

Weil, A. (1953). Certain severe disturbances of ego development in children. *Psychoanalytic Study of the Child, 8,* 271–287.

Weil, A. (1956). Some evidence of deviational development in infancy and childhood. *Psychoanalytic Study of the Child, 11,* 292–299.

Wergeland, H. (1979). A follow-up study of 29 borderline psychotic children 5 to 20 years after discharge. *Acta Psychiatrica Scandinavica 60,* 465–476.

56 / **Tourette's Disorder and Atypical Tic Disorders**

Gail E. Solomon

Tics are the most common form of movement disorder in children. A wide spectrum of such abnormal movements vary from transient tics of childhood to Tourette's disorder (Golden, 1987; Kurlan, 1989; Kurlan, Behr, Medved, & Como, 1988). Tics are defined as involuntary, sudden, random, repetitive, rapid, purposeless stereotyped movements or vocalizations (Solomon, 1991). At least 5% of all children have a single transient tic, usually lasting from a few weeks to several months, which then disappears.

The simple motor tic involves a limited group of muscles usually beginning in the face, head, or neck. Commonly an eye blink, a shoulder shrug, or a head jerk is the first manifestation. The simple tic also can be a vocal tic, such as barking, throat clearing, or snorting.

Complex tics are coordinated pattern movements, such as eye deviation, facial grimacing, touching, smelling, or obscene gestures (copropraxia). Complex vocal tics include utterances, words such as "no," phrases "go there," sentences, echolalia, or coprolalia. Most vocal tics tend to occur at phrase junctions during speech, appearing as a hesitation in speech.

Many patients with tic disorders describe uncomfortable sensations preceding or provoking the motor and vocal tics. Having the tic provides relief. Forty percent of patients with Tourette's disorder report the sensory phenomenon, described as a tickle, a temperature change, an irritation, or mental pressure (Kurlan, Lichter, & Hewitt, 1989). Tics can be suppressed for a few seconds to minutes but then are relieved by initiation of the tics. Patients tend to mask symptoms by converting them into movements that look as if they are voluntary. Tics often are increased by emotional stress and excitement and are usually only minimal during sleep.

The tics vary in severity and frequency over time. Children may suppress these tics in school or while at the physician's office visit even though there may be a marked increase of the tics at home.

The fourth edition of the *Diagnostic and Statistical Manual of Mental Disorders*, (DSM-IV, American Psychiatric Association [APA], 1994) classifies the tics. Transient tic disorder (TTD) of childhood begins during childhood or adolescence. It must last at least 2 weeks but not more than 1 year. Tics can disappear and recur during periods of stress. They are three times more common in boys than girls and can be either motor or less often vocal.

Chronic tic disorders are subdivided on the basis of whether there are only motor phenomenon, only vocal tics, or a combination of motor and vocal tics. Only motor tics or only vocal tics are designated chronic motor tic (CMT) or chronic vocal tic (CVT) disorder. If both chronic motor and vocal tics are present, the diagnosis is Tourette's disorder. The *DSM-IV* defines chronic motor tics as tics involving several muscle groups at one time. Vocal tics can be either simple or complex. The tics must be present at least 1 year for the diagnosis of chronic tic disorder. The age of onset of tics is between 2 and 15 years.

It is impossible to know whether children presenting with a tic will develop a chronic tic disorder or not. The natural history must be followed. Tics wax and wane whether they are transient tic disorders or chronic tics. They exacerbate and remit at different times and, as mentioned, must be present for at least 1 year to establish the chronic diagnosis.

Differential Diagnosis

When a child presents with a movement that suggests a tic disorder, the differential diagnosis must include other movement disorders. Among the most common to be distinguished in childhood

are: chorea—dancing, nonrepetitive movements; myoclonus—brief contractions of muscle; athetosis—slow or writhing movements of the fingers, toes, and face; dystonia—slow twisting movements; hemiballismus—large, coarse limb movements; tremors; and seizure disorders.

Tourette's Disorder

In 1885 Gilles de la Tourette cited the cardinal clinical manifestations that are still the hallmarks of the disorder named after him.

1. The affliction is hereditary, beginning in young people, and is characterized by motor incoordination in the form of brisk muscular jerks.
2. This incoordination can be accompanied by the emission of inarticulated or articulated sounds. The vocalization can be echolalia.
3. Obscenities (coprolalia) are among the expressions that the patient can utter.
4. The physical and mental state of these subjects is totally intact.

Tourette's disorder consists of multiple involuntary motor tics and one or more vocal tics. Tics begin before the age of 21, usually between the ages of 2 and 15, with the peak at age 7. Commonly the tics begin in the head, face, and neck. Vocal tics first begin with clicks, grunts, barks, sniffs, throat clearing, and coughs. Later more complex vocalizations can occur. Coprolalia, the complex uttering of obscenities, occurs in one third of the cases. Coprolalia usually occurs in late childhood or early adolescence. Although coprolalia is an outstanding feature of Tourette's disorder, it is not necessary for the diagnosis. Echolalia is not seen frequently. Palilalia and echokinesis, imitation of another's movements, are not essential. Dementia is not part of the disorder.

Often 5 or 10 years intervene between the onset and the correct diagnosis. The original diagnosis is often "nervousness" or "psychiatric problem." In Golden's series, parents, relatives, or friends had made the appropriate diagnosis in up to 85% of the cases based on information in the lay press, rather than physicians (Golden & Hood, 1982).

In interviewing children and adolescents with

Tourette's disorder, the patients often describe the frustrations and social disasters they experience with their peers. They also may explain some of their strategies in dealing with the disorder, as the following children did.

An 11-year-old boy who had Tourette's diagnosed at age 6 years talked about hating school because "when I'm writing a report my hands start to tic . . . my fingers do stuff." On request, he began to write in the office. When tics emerged he hit his fingers five times counting "1, 2, 3, 4, 5." When asked why, he said, "It slows the tics."

An 8-year-old boy was ostracized by his peers and their parents and not invited to parties because of his tics and coprolalia, all unprovoked and embarrassing to the child.

A 10-year-old girl with simple barking and yelping vocal tics and eye blinks would try to convert the moves into socially acceptable coughs.

The natural history of Tourette's disorder involves many exacerbations and remissions of both the motor and vocal tics (Erenberg, Cruse, & Rothner, 1987). During adolescence the patients may experience spontaneous remission or marked decrease in all symptoms. Complete remission is expected to occur in 24 to 61% of cases, improvement in 26 to 68%, and no change or worsening of the tics in 3 to 24% (Shapiro, Shapiro, Young, & Feinberg, 1988). In Shapiro's experience of over 22 years, 8% of Tourette's disorder patients have complete and permanent remissions when followed for 7 to 19 years during puberty and during adolescence. Remission in adults is unlikely. The natural history is very variable and not predictable for the individual (Shapiro et al., 1988). There are no reliable prognostic tools, and no specific diagnostic laboratory tests differentiate tics from other movement disorders.

Studies of patients with Tourette's have shown no specific associated electroencephalogram (EEG) abnormalities in patients with pure Tourette's disorder (Krumholz et al., 1983). A higher incidence, of about 35 to 50% of patients who have attention deficit disorder with hyperactivity (ADHD) show abnormal EEGs. Patients on neuroleptic medications also have a higher incidence of EEG abnormalities. Earlier studies showed that up to 50% of patients with Tourette's disorder had EEG abnormalities (Sweet et al., 1973), however, many of those patients were on medication or had ADHD.

Computed tomography (CT), magnetic resonance imaging (MRI), and positron emission tomography (PET) studies have shown no specific diagnostic abnormality in the tic disorders. However, recent quantitative MRI imaging studies suggest that subtle structural abnormalities in the caudate nucleus may play a role in the pathophysiology of TD (Hyde et al., 1995). Positron emission tomography scans in 10 patients with TD using 18-F-dopa suggest normal striatal metabolism of exogenous levodopa and normal density of D2 receptors. The authors conclude that TD dose not arise from a primary dysfunction of dopaminergic terminals (Turjanski et al., 1994). Using [18-F] fluorodeoxyglucose PET, regional metabolic rates for glucose in 16 drug-free TD patients were compared to 16 age and sex-matched controls. The TD patients had decreased metabolic rates in paralimbic and ventral prefrontal cortices as well as subcortical regions including ventral striatum and in the midbrain. The findings were more marked in the left hemisphere. The TD patients had concomitant bilateral increased metabolic activity in supplementary motor, lateral premotor, and Rolandic cortices. The findings suggest an altered relationship among limbic lobes, striatum, and cortical regions involved in initiating movements (Braun et al., 1993).

In recent years the most significant advances in research have included the documentation of underlying genetic factors. Gilles de la Tourette stated that the disorder was hereditary. Now, with sophisticated genetic studies, his clinical impression has been validated. There is a high association of Tourette's with obsessive-compulsive disorder, and about 50% of Tourette patients have attention deficit disorder with hyperactivity.

GENETICS OF TOURETTE'S DISORDER

Tourette's disorder affects about 100,000 people in the United States with a 3:1 male-to-female sex ratio (Golden, 1987). Although there are many sporadic cases of Tourette's, 30 to 50% are familial. Segregation analyses have shown that TD is transmitted as an autosomal dominant gene disorder; classical linkage analysis should be able to identify susceptible loci (Brett, Curtis, Robertson, & Gurling, 1995). In 1991 investigators reported a highly significant association between TD and a restriction fragment length polymorphism (RFLP) of the dopamine D2 receptor gene (DRD2) locus. The A1 allele was present in 45% of the TD patients compared with 25% of controls. The authors proposed that the A1 allele of the DRD2 gene acts as a modifying gene (Comings et al., 1991). While other groups of investigators tried to replicate this finding, their data do not support the hypothesis that the DRD2 locus acts as a modifying gene in the expression of TD in TD probands (Brett et al., 1995; Curtis, Robertson, Gurling, Gerlernter, Pauls, Leckman, Kidd, & Kurlan, 1994; Nothen et al., 1994).

Recent genetic studies suggest a sex-specific expression of TD behaviors but not a sex-associated difference in their transmission. Maternal transmission of TD showed a trend toward greater motor tic complexity and more frequent noninterfering rituals. Paternal transmission was characterized by increased vocal tics, earlier onset of vocal tics, and more prominent attention deficit hyperactivity disorder (ADHD) symptoms (Lichter, Jackson, & Schacter, 1995).

Other familial studies support the contention that bilineal transmission (from maternal and paternal sides) and homozygosity are common in TD. The frequency of both parents being affected was higher in families in which the probands' symptoms were most severe. The authors postulate that these genetic phenomena might play a role in determining the severity of the TD and also may explain difficulties in localizing the gene defect by linkage analysis (Kurlan, Eapen, Stern, McDermott, & Robertson, 1994).

Genetic studies have identified families with probands who have multiple chronic motor tics and others with Tourette's (Pauls et al., 1984).

The rate of obsessive-compulsive disorder (OCD) among first-degree relatives is significantly higher in the Tourette's population than estimates for the general population. Some forms of OCD may represent an alternative expression of the factor that is responsible for Tourette's and chronic motor tic disorder (Pauls et al., 1986).

Genetic studies have identified families with probands who have multiple chronic motor tics and others with Tourette's disorder (Pauls et al., 1984). The rate of obsessive-compulsive disorder (OCD) among first-degree relatives ... and chronic motor tic disorder (Pauls et al., 1986).

In an attempt to evaluate the relationship between TD and chronic tics, investigators examined whether they share similar neuropsychological and psychiatric correlates using standardized testing and clinical observations. Thirty-two children with TD and 39 children with chronic tics were examined under standardized testing. The children with TD and those with chronic tics were similar to each other and differed from controls in psychiatric comorbidity, school problems, and neuropsychological and psychosocial impairments. The patients with TD also had higher rates of obsessive-compulsive disorder, oppositional defiant disorder, and simple phobia than did the patients with chronic tic disorder. The authors postulate that TD and chronic tic disorders are part of the same disease entity, with TD being a more severe form of tic disorder (Spencer, Biederman, Harding, Wilens, & Faraone, 1995).

In a study of 43 same-sex twins, of which 30 pairs were monozygotic, at least one of whom had Tourette's, the concordance rate for Tourette's was 53%. Thirteen dizygotic pairs showed a concordance rate of 8%. If all of the tic disorders were considered, the concordance rate was 77% for monozygotic and 23% for dizygotic twins. Failure of complete concordance in monozygotic twins was felt to be the effect of nongenetic factors controlling onset and progression (Price et al., 1985).

Tourette's disorder is more frequent in Caucasians than in blacks and Hispanics (Singer & Walkup, 1991). Isolated case reports associate the disorder with chromosome abnormalities. Whether these are coincidental or represent some pattern is not established. There have been 3 cases with trisomy and 1 with deletion of the terminal portion of the short arm of chromosome 9 (Taylor et al., 1991). A partial trisomy 16p was reported in a 14-year-old male with autistic disorder and complex motor and vocal tics diagnosed as TD (Hebebrand et al., 1994).

NEUROCHEMISTRY, ANATOMY, AND PATHOPHYSIOLOGY

A dopamine hypothesis has been postulated for many of the symptoms of Tourette's disorder. Haloperidol, a dopamine receptor blocker, was first used successfully to suppress tics in Tourette's patients in 1961. It was postulated that overactivity of dopaminergic neurotransmitters might cause tics. The highly specific response of postsynaptic DA-D-2 receptors to haloperidol suggests that hyperactivity and supersensitivity of dopaminergic systems is responsible for some of the symptoms (Shapiro et al., 1988; Singer & Walkup, 1991).

Another point in support of the dopamine blocking action causing Tourette's is that cocaine can exacerbate tic symptoms in an otherwise controlled Tourette's patient (Mesulam, 1986). Cocaine inhibits the reuptake of norepinephrine and dopamine. Tricyclic antidepressants, which inhibit reuptake of norepinephrine but not dopamine, do not exacerbate the tics; this fact also supports the dopamine hypothesis.

Devinsky (1983) postulates that because some of the tics are similar to those seen in patients who had encephalitis lethargica, periaqueductal gray matter and midbrain tegmentum may be damaged.

Many Tourette's patients also have lower levels of homovanillic acid (HVA) in spinal fluid, which returns to normal after haloperidol treatment (Singer & Walkup, 1991). This observation supports the theory of postsynaptic receptor hypersensitivity. When dopamine production is decreased, the HVA level decreases.

Drugs can affect many transmitter systems and have significant compensatory feedback. Although the dopamine system is the most studied, other systems may be involved. The evidence that there is supersensitivity of the dopamine receptors is indirect and inferential and is not proven.

The dopamine hypothesis is postulated to explain many other illnesses that are different from Tourette's. For example, it has been used in trying to explain the etiology of schizophrenia, bipolar disorder, tardive dyskinesia, and other hyperkinetic conditions that have many features different from the Tourette's disorder.

Other theories have implicated other neurotransmitter systems. Hydroxyindolacetic acid (HIAA), the major metabolite of serotonin, is also decreased in Tourette's disorder. The clinical significance of this finding is uncertain (Singer & Walkup, 1991).

An initial report of a beneficial response to naltrexone in a few patients suggests that pharmacological manipulation of the endogenous opioid system can influence Tourette's symptoms (Kurlan et al., 1991).

Based on clinical observations of children with Sydenham's chorea, Tourette's disorder, and/or obsessive-compulsive disorder, investigators have hypothesized that infection with group A beta hemolytic streptococci may trigger autoimmune responses that cause or exacerbate some cases of childhood-onset tic disorders. If this hypothesis is correct, then immunological treatments should lead to decreased symptoms in some cases. Four small series of patients were followed for more than 1 year and demonstrated symptom exacerbations correlated with increased antibody titers. The proposed mechanism is that antineuronal antibody-mediated CNS dysfunction may be localized on the basal ganglia and its associated pathways. In some patients with Sydenham's chorea, during an acute attack, MRI with gadolinium shows enhancement in the basal ganglia. So far no similar examinations have been reported in OCD or TD.

Investigators at the National Institute of Mental Health in Bethesda are conducting an ongoing study of penicillin prophylaxis trials in TD and OCD patients to determine whether antineuronal antibody related neuropsychiatric exacerbations can be prevented. Four children with abrupt severe onset or worsening of OCD or tics were reported in an open treatment study. The patients were all boys between the ages of 10 and 14 years. One had OCD; one had TD; and two had both OCD and TD. Two had evidence of recent group A beta hemolytic strep infections, and the others had histories of recent viral infections. Two were treated with plasmapheresis, one with intravenous immumoglobulin, and one with immunosupressive doses of prednisone. All had clinically significant responses after treatment. However, it must be remembered that the course of Tourette's disorder and obsessive-compulsive disorder is one of waxing and waning. Investigators speculate that there may be a syndrome of antineuronal antibody mediated neuropsychiatric dysfunction; this could explain a subgroup of children with OCD, tics, or TD, because not all the children have such episodic courses with abrupt onset with increased antibodies. An autosomal dominant mode of inheritance has been proposed for this disorder; however, the specific gene defect has not been found. The investigators postulate that a small subgroup of the children may have an inherited susceptibility to an exaggerated immune responsivity. However, the authors ask an appropriate question: Given the high background rate of antibodies to group A beta hemolytic strep infections in the population, why do more children not exhibit neuropsychiatric dysfunction? Further investigation is needed to try to verify these observations and answer the questions posed by this interesting observation (Allen, Leonard, & Swedo, 1995; Swedo, Leonard, & Kiessling, 1994).

Attention Deficit Disorder

As mentioned, 35 to 50% of children with Tourette's disorder also have attention deficit hyperactivity disorder (ADHD), which is characterized by inattention, impulsivity, hyperactivity, short attention span, and inability to focus. The child may have "soft" neurologic signs and associated learning disabilities. A child with ADHD has particular problems in group situations in school and difficulties with peers. The diagnosis of ADHD is based finding 8 of 14 specific behavior symptoms according to the *DSM-IV*.

The incidence of ADHD is 6 to 9 times higher in boys than in girls. ADHD symptoms usually precede motor and phonic tics by 2 to 3 years. The incidence of ADHD is higher in more severe Tourette's cases, where 70% are so affected; 50% of moderately affected Tourette's children and 30% of those mildly affected also have ADHD (Comings & Comings, 1984). Often the symptoms of ADHD are more difficult to treat than the tics. Stimulant medications are effective in ADHD, but they may exacerbate tics (Denckla, Bemporad, & Mackay, 1976; Erenberg, Cruse, & Rothner, 1985; Lowe et al., 1982; Mitchell & Matthews, 1980).

Children with Tourette's disorder have a higher incidence of learning disabilities, particularly in grapho-motor, visual-motor skills, and organizational skills (Matthews, 1988). Shapiro found 83% of Tourette's subjects had "marked organicity," suggesting neurological abnormality with testing by the Bender test and a 14-month lag in visual-motor copying skills (Shapiro et al., 1988).

Obsessive-Compulsive Disorder

Obsessive-compulsive disorder (OCD) is characterized by symptoms of recurrent stereotyped behavior and/or thoughts that intrude into the patient's consciousness or actions and are experienced as senseless and cause significant distress and impairment of functioning. Common symptoms include repetitive hand washing, frequent counting, and checking rituals. Obsessive symptoms include fears or images of being harmed or of being contaminated or poisoned. Obsessive-compulsive symptoms are seen not only in patients with Tourette's disorder but in other psychiatric disorders as well.

Other Behavior and Associated Problems

In addition to the ADHD and OCD, children with Tourette's disorder have an increased incidence of other behavior problems, such as conduct disorders, depression, discipline problems, phobias, and stuttering.

Disturbed sleep patterns have been reported in 12 to 44% of patients with Tourette's. There are reports of somnambulism, night terrors, nightmares, restlessness, and difficulty falling asleep. Polygraphic sleep studies show a decreased amount of rapid-eye-movement sleep. Tourette's has been postulated to be a disorder of arousal, with impaired transition from Stage 3 and 4 slow-wave sleep to lighter states. A disorder of arousal is postulated because of an increased incidence of somnambulism, night terrors, enuresis, and persistence of high-voltage rhythmic generalized slow-wave electroencephalogram activity in Tourette's disorder (Glaze, Frost, & Jancovic, 1983; Singer & Walkup, 1991).

In a study of 20 newly diagnosed patients with TD ages 10 to 36 years, outpatient four-channel cassette electroencephalogram (EEG) sleep recordings were performed. TD patients had reduced sleep, decreased sleep efficiency, increased awakenings, and decreased slow wave sleep. The patients had increased nocturnal awakenings and movements, especially those who had tics during sleep. In the TD patients with associated ADHD, sleep fragmentation and loss of slow wave sleep was most marked. In TD patients with OCD, sleep latency was increased, REM sleep was reduced, and REM sleep latency was decreased.

Findings were in accord with previous reports that indicate that TD with ADHD may be associated with a disorder of arousal and alertness and TD with OCD may be associated with abnormalities in REM sleep (Drake, Hietter, Bogner, & Andrews, 1992).

Atypical Tic Syndromes

Other tic syndromes that do not fit the criteria for transient tic disorder or chronic motor or chronic vocal tics or Tourette's disorder do have some of their features. For example, adults rather than children who begin to have multiple tics and vocalizations that wax and wane for more than 1 year often are said to have "Tourettism" (Dickman, Fleiman, Perl, 1990; Sacks, 1982). It was first described following the epidemic of encephalitis lethargica in 1920. "Tourettism" also has been reported with acute and chronic neurologic disorders including toxic and metabolic encephalopathies, head trauma, strokes, cerebral tumors, multiple sclerosis, syphilis, and Huntington's, Alzheimer's, or Creutzfeldt-Jakob disease (Singer & Walkup, 1991). A 6-year-old girl with no family history of Tourette's developed a Tourette-like syndrome a few weeks after herpes encephalitis (Northam & Singer, 1991).

Motor and vocal tics also have appeared in patients who are withdrawn from chronic treatment with neuroleptic drugs. Tardive Tourettism is similar to tardive dyskinesias (Singer, 1981).

Treatment

The decision to treat Tourette's disorder with medication has to be based on the severity of the specific symptoms as perceived by the individual patient, the family, and the physician (Solomon, 1991). There is a definite risk-benefit ratio that must be assessed closely before any treatment is instituted. A single simple tic does not need any intervention, for most will resolve within weeks or months. If more tics develop and evolve into chronic tic disorder, then medication may be indicated (Cohen, Bruun, & Leckman, 1988).

Medication can suppress the tics in 80 to 85% of patients with chronic motor or vocal tic disorder or Tourette's disorder, but side effects often occur. About 50% of treated patients will have moderate to severe side effects of drug therapy. There is no supporting evidence that therapy modifies the eventual prognosis.

The physician usually should not begin medication at the first visit. Rather he or she should use the first few weeks or months to get a baseline in order to determine if there are other difficulties in addition to the tics, such as attentional problems at school, low frustration tolerance, impulsivity, and/or obsessive-compulsive symptoms. Perhaps precipitants that aggravate tics could be improved with changes in the environment or in a behavior modification plan. The physician should use this time to explain the disorder to the child and the family and educate the school.

When the diagnosis is explained to parents and children, sometimes they are relieved that the symptoms have a medical basis rather than a psychological etiology. Others reject the diagnosis, particularly when the symptoms wax and wane. Eventually, when the symptoms are more persistent, the diagnosis is apparent. In caring for patients, the physician must educate patient, family, and teachers. Encouraging the child's strengths and interests helps in building self-esteem. Associated psychological factors involved in symptoms of ADHD and OCD should be evaluated. When indicated, neuropsychological testing and academic evaluations clarify and lead to appropriate management. Often academic and educational problems can be managed by tutoring and school placement in appropriate classes. Specific help in educational situations include using a typewriter rather than a pen or pencil for students with poor handwriting, a tape recorder instead of making an oral presentation, and working in small groups. Using untimed tests also may be of benefit (Shapiro et al., 1988). If, despite understanding and modification of the home and school program, the tics are interfering with function, then medication, which is palliative, not curative, should be considered.

A general principle of treatment of Tourette's disorder and chronic tics is that the smallest possible amount of medication is used to see the patient's tolerance and sensitivity. The dose is gradually titrated with attention to side effects as well as positive effects. Raising the medication slowly and cautiously usually will result in fewer side effects. The process takes many weeks. Once the medication is found to produce improvement, it still may be necessary to change the dosage in the future and to try to taper it periodically to see if it is still necessary.

The major drug used for treatment is haloperidol (Haldol) (Shapiro et al., 1988). In the 1960s it was noted that this dopaminergic blocking agent, in much lower doses than are used for psychosis, can stop or diminish tics in patients with chronic tic syndrome. Haloperidol, a butyrophenone, is begun in low doses, usually .25 to .5 milligrams (mg) per day. After 5-day intervals the dose usually is increased by 0.25- to .5-mg increments, with the total daily dose divided into two or three equal portions. The therapeutic end-point is different for each patient, depending on the balance between the suppression of tics and side effects, such as sedation. A child with Tourette's usually is maintained on 2 to 2.5 mg per day of haloperidol. If there is no response at 6 mg per day, it is unlikely that haloperidol will be helpful for that individual. Some patients improve initially and then develop tolerance and may not respond at higher dosages.

Major side effects are the same as for all dopaminergic receptive blockers, and children must be monitored closely. Lethargy, depression, dysphoria, cognitive problems, and declining school performance are adverse effects. A common side effect is acute dystonia. In less than 10% of children there can be extrapyramidal side effects such as torticollis or oculogyric crisis as an idiosyncratic reaction. Parkinsonian symptoms and akathisia are unusual. Acute dystonic reactions respond to diphenhydramine (benadryl) or benztropine mesylate (Cogentin). Extrapyramidal reactions respond to treatment with anticholinergic drugs, such as 0.5 to 2 mg per day of benztropine mesylate. Since the extrapyramidal reaction incidence is low in children, the anticholinergic drug usually is prescribed only as an adjunctive medication if symptoms occur.

Tardive dyskinesia is rare. Orobuccolingual dyskinesia with choreiform movements of the extremities can occur. In children who get dyskinesias, usually limb and choreiform movements are more prominent than the orobuccolingual movements seen in older women with dyskinesias. In these Tourette's patients, it is difficult to distinguish tics from extrapyramidal side effects. If the neuroleptic is discontinued soon after the new symptoms occur, dyskinesias usually disappear within weeks or months, but discontinuation often also unmasks a tic disorder. Patients with emergent syndrome dyskinesias develop choreiform movements of the extremities. Withdrawal emergence syndrome, which is usually transient, occurs when a stable dose of medication is reduced. It is best to avoid this by reducing the drug very slowly.

Pimozide (Orap) is now available to treat patients with Tourette's disorder (Shapiro, Shapiro, Fulop, 1987). Pimozide is a diphenyl-butylpiperidine derivative and a postsynaptic blocker of DRD_2 receptors. It is highly selective and has no effect on central norepinephrine receptors. This selective feature supposedly is why it has fewer side reactions than haloperidol. It is as effective as haloperidol for treating tic disorder but it is less sedative. The starting dose in children is .3 mg per kilogram; for example, 1 mg at bedtime usually increasing by 1 mg every 5 to 7 days until symptoms decrease by at least 70%. The average dose of Pimozide is about 8 mg. Extrapyramidal reactions do occur in 10 to 15% of patients and will respond to anticholinergic drugs. Unlike haloperidol, pimozide has a potential cardiac side effect—it can prolong the QT interval of the electrocardiogram (ECG). Pimozide is contraindicated in patients who have prolonged QT interval or patients with cardiac arrhythmias. Baseline ECG must be obtained and periodically monitored. If the QT interval is prolonged more than 25% above the baseline or more than 0.47s in children, pimozide should be discontinued. Fluphenazine (Prolixin) a potent phenothiazine, is another neuroleptic medication used for treatment of Tourette's disorder (Singer, Gammon, & Quaskey, 1985–86). Patients who are intolerant to haloperidol have benefited from fluphenazine, which is used only in patients who do not respond to other medicines. The starting dose of fluphenazine is 1 mg per day with eventual doses of up to 5 mg per day. In a trial of 21 patients, 76% showed a favorable response with fewer side effects than with haloperidol; there was less sedation. On average, the dose range is usually 2 to 4 mg pimozide to 1 mg haloperidol to 1.5 mg fluphenazine. Haloperidol, pimozide, and fluphenazine all can have the potential extrapyramidal side effects of emergent dyskinesias.

Risperidone (Risperdal), a neuroleptic with serotonin and dopamine blocking properties, was effective in reducing tic frequency and intensity in a small group of children and adolescents with chronic tic disorders. The trial included 7 children, and there was a statistically significant reduction in tic scores ranging from 18 to 66%. The most common side effect was weight gain, which ranged from 8 to 14 pounds over the 11-week open-label trial. Further studies are needed to see if this is a consistent response to risperidone in children with TD. (Lombroso et al., 1995).

Clonidine (Catapres) is an alpha-adrenergic agonist that works in the central nervous system and reduces noradrenergic activity. It has been helpful in 25 to 50% of children in some studies (Cohen, Detlor, Young, & Shaywitz, 1980; Leckman, et al., 1985). However, one study found clonidine to be no more effective than placebo (Goetz et al., 1986). Clonidine has been found to be effective in some children with ADHD, particularly when there are behavioral and conduct problems. Since clonidine does not have the potential side effect of tardive dyskinesia, it is sometimes used particularly in children who have attention deficit disorder and tics. The most frequent side effect is sedation. It should be titrated slowly. Clonidine's primary use is as an antihypertensive medication, and hypotension and dizziness are potential side effects, particularly at higher doses. Clonidine is not as potent for controlling tics as the neuroleptic agents but has less potential side effects. Clonidine, which is available in .1 mg tablets, is begun at .05 mg per day and increased by .05 mg per day every 5 to 7 days. The usual dose, .25 mgs per day, is achieved in about 6 weeks. Dosages as high as .3 to .5 mg per day may be tolerated, with a benefit seen within 3 months of starting. There is a possibility that the drug can precipitate diabetes mellitus. Patients must be closely followed, particularly if there is a family history of diabetes mellitus. If the patient is not benefited or has adverse effects, clonidine should be tapered over a minimum of 1 week rather than acutely stopped.

Guanfacine (Tenex) is an alpha 2-adrenergic agonist that may have beneficial effects on attention, without the hypotensive or sedative effects of clonidine. An open-label study of guanfacine (average dose of 1.5 mg/day) in 10 children with TD plus ADHD ages 8 to 16 years showed a significant decrease in the severity of the motor and phonic tics. The most common side effects are transient sedation and headaches. Guanfacine may provide a safe alternative for children with ADHD and tics (Chappell et al., 1995).

Although monotherapy is preferred, the combination of a neuroleptic and clonidine may be helpful when one medication alone is only partially effective. If one drug in high doses is controlling the symptoms but producing adverse side effects, a combination of lower doses of the neuroleptic and clonidine may achieve better results.

Clonazepam (Klonopin), a benzodiazepine, has been reported to be helpful in some patients (Truong, Bressman, Shale, & Fahn, 1988). Therapy is usually started with .5 mg a day and is increased by .5 mg a day each week until there is a clinical response or adverse effects. Generally it is not believed effective alone; it can be an adjuvant agent when monotherapy does not give the desired response. For example, 7 children and adolescents with a tic disorder and concomitant ADHD were treated successfully for their ADHD symptoms with clonidine; however, the patients experienced persistent tics. The addition of clonazepam resulted in decrease in tic frequency and severity without affecting the coexisting ADHD symptoms. The authors suggest that clonazepam may be a useful adjunctive pharmacological intervention in treating tics in children with comorbid ADHD (Steingard, Goldberg, Lee, & DeMaso, 1994).

There are anecdotal cases where addition of calcium channel blockers such as verapamil (Calan, Isoptin) or nifedipine (Procardia, Adalat) produced a response in refractory Tourette's disorder (Alessi, Walden, & Hsieh, 1988).

Stimulant medications, such as methylphenidate (Ritalin), pemoline (Cylert), and dextroamphetamine, which are indicated for ADHD, can exacerbate tics in some patients (Denckla et al., 1976; Erenberg et al., 1985; Mitchell & Matthews, 1980). Some patients who were started on psychostimulants developed tics. Generally the tics resolved, but in some cases tics remained, despite cessation of the stimulant. It is possible that the stimulants unmasked Tourette's disorder in these children. Some patients with Tourette's have benefited from stimulant medication, and their tics do not exacerbate (Erenberg et al., 1985). If a patient has tics or a strong family history of tics, stimulants should be avoided. However, in individual cases where ADHD is interfering with functioning and other medications and behavior modification are not effective, stimulants may be considered.

Tricyclic antidepressants do not precipitate tics. For example, imipramine (Tofranil) and desipramine can help some patients with ADHD symptoms (Pliezka, 1987; Singer, Brown, Quaskey, Rosenberg, Mellits, & Denckla, 1995; Spencer, Biederman, Kerman, Steingard, & Wilens, 1993). These tricyclic medications do not aggravate tics. However, carbamazepine (Tegretol), an anticonvulsant with similar structure to tricyclics, has been reported rarely to produce tics (Neglia, Glaze, & Zion, 1984). Three children with epilepsy developed facial motor tics after initiation of carbamazepine for complex partial seizures. All three had carbamazepine blood levels in the therapeutic range and no signs of clinical intoxication. After 2 of the children developed tics, carbamazepine was continued at the same or higher dose and tics abated and stopped spontaneously in 6 months or less. In the third child, the tics ceased after carbamazepine was discontinued. These idiosyncratic reactions may be transient and do not always necessitate discontinuation of the carbamazepine (Robertson, Garofalo, Silverstein, & Komarynski, 1993).

If an associated obsessive-compulsive disorder has to be treated, clomipramine (Anafranil), a tricyclic antidepressant, appears to be the most effective agent. The heterocyclic antidepressant fluoxetine (Prozac) is also useful in patients with both Tourette's and OCD; usually it does not increase tics (Kurlan, 1989). In 11 children with Tourette's syndrome and associated OCD treated for 4 months, fluoxetine (Prozac) therapy was associated with a trend toward some improvement in tic severity, attentional abilities and social functioning (Kurlan, Como, Deely, McDermott, & McDermott, 1993). However, a case of tics associated with fluoxetine treatment has been reported in a depressed adolescent. Following 8 months of fluoxetine therapy, the patient developed numerous tics, which subsided 6 months after discontinuation of the fluoxetine (Eisenhauer & Jermain, 1993).

Although Tourette's disorder is a medical con-

dition, some patients do have a coexisting behavior problem that requires psychotherapeutic intervention and counseling for them and their family. The problems of growing up with any chronic illness are in the category of "coping" rather than psychopathology (Shapiro et al., 1988). In the management of certain patients, psychotherapeutic intervention, family therapy, and group therapy with similar affected children may be helpful. Another aspect of therapy includes working with the parents about what to expect. Some parents tend to be overindulgent and tolerate all behavior over and above the tics because this is a medical condition. They also can feel hostile toward the child, who now dominates all family activities. The parents should be helped to realize that the child has an illness and to accept the illness and behavior realistically. The parents should expect the child to do as well in school as his or her intelligence and capabilities permit. The effect of the medications should be carefully monitored to avoid sedation, but medications often help the child in eliminating the tics and performing better. All children should be informed about their disorder and, as they get older, they should take increased responsibility for monitoring their own medication (Shapiro et al., 1988).

Medical management and drug therapy are the mainstay of treatment with Tourette's disorder. However, behavioral therapy, including massed negative practice, contingency management, relaxation training, self-monitoring, and habit reversal, may reduce the frequency of some Tourette's tics (Cohen et al., 1988). Behavior techniques can be an adjunct to drug therapy in patients who do not respond enough or who have to take low doses because of adverse medication side effects. For massed negative practice, the patient is instructed to perform the tics voluntarily until he or she tires, theoretically developing reactive inhibition to the tics. Contingency management is positive reinforcement by rewarding the patient with praise, money, or other rewards for not performing the tic. Relaxation training uses deep breathing, verbalization, or other means to relax the muscles involved in the tics. Self-monitoring consists of counting and documenting the number of tics to try to lead to self-control. Habit reversal is performing compensatory motor actions in inhibitory muscles that might inhibit the tics.

A comprehensive but individualized treatment approach is imperative in Tourette's disorder to ensure optimal benefit in each patient.

Summary

In summary, a wide spectrum of tic disorders are common in children, ranging from the transient tic disorder (TTD), to Tourette's disorder with both chronic motor and vocal tics. Genetic factors have been implicated, especially in Tourette's disorder and chronic motor tic disorder. There is a genetic association between Tourette's disorder, chronic motor tic disorders, and obsessive-compulsive disorder.

Pharmacological therapy is used when the tics interfere with function. Major drugs include haloperidol and pimozide. Less often clonidine is used when ADHD is a major problem in association with tics. Stimulant medications may aggravate tics.

In the original description, Gilles de la Tourette said that the syndrome is a lifelong disorder (1885). Recent studies have found, however, that up to 73% of patients report that tics decreased markedly or had almost disappeared as they entered the end of adolescence or early adulthood. Exacerbations may arise later in adulthood, and there may be continuing associated behavioral difficulties (Cohen et al., 1988; Erenberg et al., 1987; Shapiro et al., 1988).

The outcome and adjustment of patients with Tourette's disorder is not related merely to the severity of the tics. Associated ADHD, OCD, and adjustment problems may influence outcome more than the tics themselves. In addition to early diagnosis and treatment, a better understanding of the disorder is essential. One of the main ways to help these children and adolescents is through better education enabling child, parents, teachers, the general public, and physicians to understand the disorder. An excellent resource for the community is the Tourette Synd Association, which provides important facts and excellent educational information for patients, families, and professionals. (Contact the association at 42-40 Bell Boulevard, Bayside, NY 11361-9596, 718-224-2999.)

REFERENCES

Allen, A. J., Leonard, H. L., & Swedo, S. E. (1995). Case study: A new infection-triggered, autoimmune subtype of pediatric OCD and Tourette's syndrome. *Journal of the American Academy of Child & Adolescent Psychiatry, 34* (3), 307–311.

Alessi, N. E., Walden, M. E., & Hsieh, P. S. (1988). Nifedipine augments haloperidol in the treatment of Tourette syndrome. *Pediatric Neurology, 4,* 191.

American Psychiatric Association. (1994). *Diagnostic and statistical manual of mental disorders* (4th ed.). (Washington, DC: Author).

Braun, A. R., Stoetter, B., Randolph, C., Hsiao, J. R., Vladar, K., Gernert, J., Carson, R. E., Herscovitch, P., & Chase, T. N. (1993). The functional neuroanatomy of Tourette's syndrome: An FDG-PET study. I. Regional changes in cerebral glucose metabolism differentiating patients and controls. *Neuropsychopharmacology, 9* (4), 277–291.

Brett, P. M., Curtis, D., Robertson, M. M., & Gurling, H. M. (1995). The genetic susceptibility to Gilles de la Tourette syndrome in a large multiple affected British kindred: Linkage analysis excludes a role for the genes coding for dopamine Da, D2, D3, D4, D5 receptors, dopamine beta hydroxylase, tyrosinase, and tyrosine hydroxylase. *Biological Psychiatry, 37,* (8), 1533–1540.

Chappell, P. B., Riddle, M. A., Scahill, L., Lynch, K. A., Schultz, R., Arnsten, A., Leckman, J. F., & Cohen, D. J. (1995). Guanfacine treatment of comorbid attention-deficit hyperactivity disorder and Tourette's syndrome: preliminary clinical experience. *Journal of the American Academy of Child and Adolescent Psychiatry, 34* (9), 1140–1146.

Cohen, D. J., Detlor, J., Young, G. J., & Shaywitz, B. A. (1980). Clonidine ameliorates Gilles de la Tourette syndrome. *Archives of General Psychiatry, 37,* 1350–1357.

Cohen, D. J., Bruun, R. D., Leckman, J. F. (Eds). (1988). *Tourette's syndrome and tic disorders: Clinical understanding and treatment.* New York: John Wiley & Sons.

Comings, D. E., & Comings, B. G. (1984). Tourette's syndrome and attention-deficit disorder with hyperactivity: Are they genetically related? *Journal of the American Academy of Child Psychiatry, 23,* 138–146.

Comings, D. E., Comings, B. C., Muhleman, D., Dietz, G., Shahbahrami, B., Tast, D., Knell, E., Kocsis, P., Baumgarten, R., Kovacs, B. W., Levy, D. L., Smith, M., Borison, R. L., Evans, D. D., Klein, D. N., MacMurray, J., Tosk, J. M., Sverd, J., Gysin, R., & Flanagan, S. D. (1991). The dopamine D_2 receptor locus as a modifying gene in neuropsychiatric disorders. *Journal of the American Medical Association, 266*, 1793–1800.

Denckla, M. B., Bemporad, J. R., & Mackay, M. C. (1976). Tics following methylphenidate administration. *Journal of the American Medical Association, 235*, 1349–1351.

Devinsky O. (1983). Neuroanatomy of Gilles de la Tourette's syndrome. Possible midbrain involvement. *Archives of Neurology, 40*, 508–514.

Dickman, M. S., Fleiman, M., & Perl, E. (1990). Late adult onset Tourette's-like syndrome. *Neurology, 40* (Suppl. 1), 222.

Drake, M. E., Jr., Hietter, S. A., Bogner, J. E., & Andrews, J. M. (1992). Cassette EEG sleep recordings in Gilles de la Tourette syndrome. *Clinical Electroencephalography, 23* (3), 142–146.

Eisenhauer, G., & Jermain, D. M. (1993). Fluoxetine and tics in an adolescent. *Annals of Pharmacotherapy, 27* (6), 725–726.

Erenberg, G. (1988). Pharmacologic therapy of tics in childhood. *Pediatric Annals, 17*, 395–404.

Erenberg, G., Cruse, R. P., & Rothner, A. D. (1985). Gilles de la Tourette's syndrome: Effects of stimulant drugs. *Neurology, 35*, 1346–1348.

Erenberg, G., Cruse, R. P., & Rothner, A. D. (1987). The natural history of Tourette syndrome: A follow-up study. *Annals of Neurology, 122*, 383–385.

Gelernter, J., Pauls, D. L., Leckman, J., Kidd, K. K., Kurlan, R. (1994). D2 dopamine receptor alleles do not influence severity of Tourette's syndrome. Results from four large kindreds [see comments]. *Archives of Neurology, 51*, (4), 397–400.

Gilles de la Tourette, G. (1885). Etude sur une affection nerveuse characterisee par de l'incoordination motrice accompagnee de echolalie et coprolalie. *Archives Neurologigue* (French), *9*, 19–42, 158–200.

Glaze, D., Frost, J. D., Jr., & Jancovic, J. (1983). Sleep in Gilles de la Tourette syndrome: Disorder of arousal. *Neurology, 33*, 586–592.

Goetz, C. G., Tanner, C. M., Wilson, R. S., Carroll, S., Como, P. G., & Shannon, K. M. (1986). Clonidine and Gilles de la Tourette's syndrome: A double-blind study using objectives rating method. *Annals of Neurology, 21*, 307–310.

Golden, G. S. (1987). Tic disorders in childhood. *Pediatric Review, 8*, 229–234.

Golden, G. S. (1990). Tourette syndrome: Recent advances. In John B. Bodensteiner (Ed.), *Pediatric neurology. Neurologic Clinics* (Vol. 8, No. 3, 705–714). Philadelphia: W. B. Saunders.

Golden, G. S., & Hood, O. J. (1982). Tics and tremors. *Pediatric Clinics of North America, 29*, 95–103.

Hebebrand, J., Martin. M., Korner, J., Roitzheim, B., deBraganca, K., Werner, W., & Remschmidt, H. (1994). Partial trisomy 16p in an adolescent with autistic disorder and Tourette's syndrome. *American Journal of Medical Genetics, 54* (3), 268–270.

Hyde, T. M., Stacey, M. E., Coppola, R., Handel, S. F., Rickler, K. C., & Weinberger, D. R. (1995). Cerebral morphometric abnormalities in Tourette's syndrome: A quantitative MRI study of monozygotic twins. *Neurology, 45* (6), 1176–1182.

Krumholz, A., Singer, H. S., Niedermeyer, E., Burnite, R., & Harris, K. (1983). Electrophysiological studies in Tourette's syndrome. *Annals of Neurology, 14*, 638–641.

Kurlan, R. (1989). Tourette's syndrome: Current concepts. *Neurology, 39*, 1635–1630.

Kurlan, R., Behr, J., Medved, L., & Como, P. (1988). Transient tic disorder and the spectrum of Tourette's syndrome. *Archives of Neurology, 45*, 1200–1201.

Kurlan, R., Como, P. G., Deely, C., McDermott, M., & McDermott, M. P. (1993). A pilot controlled study of fluoxetine for obsessive-compulsive symptoms in children with Tourette's syndrome. *Clinical Neuropharmacology, 16* (2), 167–172.

Kurlan, R., Eapen, V., Stern, J., McDermott, M. P., & Robertson, M. M. (1994). Bilineal transmission of Tourette's syndrome families. *Neurology, 44* (12), 2336–2342.

Kurlan, R., Lichter, D., & Hewitt, D. (1989). Sensory tics in Tourette's syndrome. *Neurology, 39*, 731–734.

Kurlan, R., Mujamdar, L., Deeley, C., Mudholkar, G. S., Plumb, S., & Como, P. G. (1991). A controlled trial of propoxyphene and naltrexone in patients with Tourette's syndrome. *Annals of Neurology, 30*, 19–23.

Leckman, J. F., Detlor, J., Harcherik, D. F., Ort, S., Shaywitz, B. A., & Cohen, D. J. (1985). Short- and long-term treatment of Tourette's syndrome with clonidine. A clinical perspective. *Neurology, 35*, 343–351.

Lichter, D. G., Jackson, L. A., & Schachter, M. (1995). Clinical evidence of genomic imprinting in Tourette's syndrome. *Neurology, 45* (5), 924–928.

Lombroso, P. J., Scahill, L., King, R. A., Lynch, K. A., Chappell, P. B., Peterson, B. S., McDougle, C. J., & Leckman, J. F. (1995). Risperidone treatment of children and adolescents with chronic tic disorders: A preliminary report. *Journal of the American Academy of Child and Adolescent Psychiatry, 34* (9), 1147–1152.

Lowe, T. L., Cohen, D. J., Detlor, J., Kremenitzer, M. W., & Shaywitz, B. A. (1982). Stimulant medications precipitate Tourette's syndrome. *Journal of the American Medical Association, 247*, 1729–1731.

Matthews, W. S. (1988). Attention deficits and learning disabilities in children with Tourette's syndrome. *Pediatric Annals, 17*, 410–416.

Mesulam, M. (1986). Cocaine and Tourette's syndrome. *New England Journal of Medicine, 315*, 398.

Mitchell, E., & Matthews, K. L. (1980). Gilles de la Tourette's disorder associated with pemoline. *American Journal of Psychiatry, 137*, 1618–1619.

Neglia, J. P., Glaze, D. G., & Zion, E. (1984). Tics and

vocalizations in children treated with carbamazepine. *Pediatrics, 73,* 841–844.

Northam, R. S., & Singer, H. S. (1991). Postencephalitic acquired Tourette-like Syndrome in a child. *Neurology, 41,* 592–593.

Nothen, M. M., Hebebrand, J., Knapp, M., Hebebrand, K., Camps, A., von Gontard, A., Wettke-Schafer, R., Lisch, S., Cichon, S., Poustka, F., et al. (1994). Association analysis of the dopamine D2 receptor gene in Tourette's syndrome using the haplotype relative risk method. *American Journal of Medical Genetics, 54* (3), 249–252.

Pauls, D. L., Kruger, S. D., Leckman, J. F., Cohen, D. J., & Kidd, K. K. (1984). The risk of Tourette's syndrome and chronic multiple tics among relatives of Tourette's syndrome patients obtained by direct interviews. *Journal of the American Academy of Child Psychiatry, 23,* 134–137.

Pauls, D. L., & Leckman, J. F. (1986). The inheritance of Gilles de la Tourette's syndrome and associated behaviors. Evidence for autosomal dominant transmission. *New England Journal of Medicine, 315,* 993–997.

Pauls, D. L., Towbin, K. E., Leckman, J. F., Zahner, G. E., & Cohen, D. J. (1986). Gilles de la Tourette's syndrome and obsessive-compulsive disorder. Evidence supporting a genetic relationship. *Archives of General Psychiatry, 43,* 1180–1182.

Pliszka, S. R. (1987). Tricyclic antidepressants in the treatment of children with attention-deficit disorder. *Journal of the American Academy of Childhood and Adolescent Psychiatry, 26,* 127–132.

Price, R. A., Kidd, K. K., Cohen, D. J., Pauls, D. L., & Leckman, J. F. (1985). A twin study of Tourette syndrome. *Archives of General Psychiatry, 42,* 815–820.

Robertson, P. L., Garofalo, E. A., Silverstein, F. S., & Komarynski, M. A. (1993). Carbamazepine-induced tics. *Epilepsia, 34* (5), 965–968.

Sacks, O. (1982). Acquired Tourettism in adult life. *Gilles de la Tourette syndrome.* In A. J. Freidhoff & T. N. Chase (Eds.), *Advances in Neurology, 35,* 89–92. New York: Raven Press.

Shapiro, A. K., Shapiro, E., & Fulop, G. (1987). Pimozide treatment of tic and Tourette disorders. *Pediatrics, 79,* 1032–1039.

Shapiro, A. K., Shapiro, E. S., Young, J. G., & Feinberg, T. E. (1988). *Gilles de la Tourette syndrome* (2nd ed.). New York: Raven Press.

Singer, H. S., Brown, J., Quaskey, S., Rosenberg, L. A., Mellits, E. D., & Denckla, M. D. (1995). The treatment of attention-deficit hyperactivity disorder in Tourette's syndrome: A double-blind placebo-controlled study with clonidine and desipramine. *Pediatrics, 95* (1), 74–81.

Singer, H. S., Gammon, K., & Quaskey, S. (1985–86).

Haloperidol, fluphenazine and clonidine in Tourette syndrome. Controversies in treatment. *Pediatric Neuroscience, 12,* 71–74.

Singer, H. S., & Walkup, J. T. (1991). Tourette syndrome and other tic disorders. Diagnosis, pathophysiology and treatment. *Medicine, 70* (11), 15–32.

Singer, W. D. (1981). Transient Gilles de la Tourette syndrome after chronic neuroleptic withdrawal. *Developmental Medicine and Child Neurology, 23,* 518–521.

Solomon, G. E. (1991). From tics to Tourette syndrome. In N. Amir, I. Rapin, I. Branski, & D. Branski (Eds.), *Pediatric neurology: Behavior and cognition of the child with brain dysfunction* (Vol. 1, pp. 95–109). Basel: Karger.

Spencer, T., Biederman, J., Harding, M., Wilens, T., & Faraone, S. (1995). The relationship between tic disorders and Tourette's syndrome revisited. *Journal of the American Academy of Child and Adolescent Psychiatry, 34* (9), 1133–1139.

Spencer, T., Biederman, J., Kerman, K., Steingard, R., & Wilens, T. (1993). Desipramine treatment of children with attention-deficit hyperactivity disorder and tic disorders of Tourette's syndrome. *Journal of the American Academy of Child and Adolescent Psychiatry 32* (2), 354–360.

Steingard, R. J., Goldberg, M., Lee, D., & DeMaso, D. R. (1994). Adjunctive clonazepam treatment of tic symptoms in children with comorbid tic disorders and ADHD. *Journal of the American Academy of Child and Adolescent Psychiatry, 33* (3), 394–399.

Swedo, S. E., Leonard, H. I., & Kiessling, L. S. (1994). Speculations on antineuronal antibody-mediated neuropsychiatric disorders in children. *Pediatrics, 93,* 323–326.

Sweet, R. D., Solomon, G. E., Wayne, H., Shapiro, E., & Shapiro, A. K. (1973). Neurological feature of Gilles de la Tourette's syndrome. *Journal of Neurology, Neurosurgery and Psychiatry, 36,* 1–19.

Taylor, L. D., Krizman, D. B., Jankovic, J., Hayani, A., Steuber, P. C., Greenberg, F., Fenwick, R. G., & Caskey, C. T. (1991). 9p monosomy in a patient with Gilles de la Tourette's syndrome. *Neurology, 41,* 1513–1515.

Truong, D. D., Bressman, S., Shale, H., & Fahn, S. (1988). Clonazepam, clonidine and haloperidol in treatment of multifocal disorders (Tourette syndrome). *Southern Medical Journal, 81,* 1103–1105.

Turjanski, N., Sawle, G. V., Playford, E. D., Weeks, R., Lammerstma, A. A., Lees, A. J., & Brooks, D. J. (1994). PET studies of the presynaptic and postsynaptic dopaminergic system in Tourette's syndrome. *Journal of Neurology, Neurosurgery and Psychiatry, 57,* 688–692.

NAME INDEX

Name Index

SUBJECT INDEX